FOR REFERENCE

Do Not Take From This Room

DEC '88

Contemporary
Literary Criticism

Guide to Gale Literary Criticism Series

When you need to review criticism of literary works, these are the Gale series to use:

If the author's death date is:	You should turn to:
After Dec. 31, 1959 (or author is still living)	**CONTEMPORARY LITERARY CRITICISM** for example: Jorge Luis Borges, Anthony Burgess, William Faulkner, Mary Gordon, Ernest Hemingway, Iris Murdoch
1900 through 1959	**TWENTIETH-CENTURY LITERARY CRITICISM** for example: Willa Cather, F. Scott Fitzgerald, Henry James, Mark Twain, Virginia Woolf
1800 through 1899	**NINETEENTH-CENTURY LITERATURE CRITICISM** for example: Fedor Dostoevski, Nathaniel Hawthorne, George Sand, William Wordsworth
1400 through 1799	**LITERATURE CRITICISM FROM 1400 TO 1800** **(excluding Shakespeare)** for example: Anne Bradstreet, Daniel Defoe, Alexander Pope, François Rabelais, Jonathan Swift, Phillis Wheatley **SHAKESPEAREAN CRITICISM** Shakespeare's plays and poetry
Antiquity through 1399	**CLASSICAL AND MEDIEVAL LITERATURE CRITICISM** for example: Dante, Homer, Plato, Sophocles, Vergil, the Beowulf Poet

---

Gale also publishes related criticism series:

CHILDREN'S LITERATURE REVIEW

This series covers authors of all eras who write for the preschool through high school audience.

SHORT STORY CRITICISM

This series covers the major short fiction writers of all nationalities and periods of literary history.

ISSN 0091-3421

Volume 51

Contemporary Literary Criticism

Excerpts from Criticism of the
Works of Today's Novelists, Poets,
Playwrights, Short Story Writers, Scriptwriters,
and Other Creative Writers

Daniel G. Marowski
Roger Matuz
EDITORS

Sean R. Pollock
Thomas J. Votteler
Robyn V. Young
ASSOCIATE EDITORS

Gale Research Inc.
Book Tower
Detroit, Michigan 48226

REF
PN
771
C59
Y51

STAFF

Daniel G. Marowski, Roger Matuz, *Editors*

Sean R. Pollock, Thomas J. Votteler, Robyn V. Young, *Associate Editors*

David Segal, Anne Sharp, Jane C. Thacker, *Senior Assistant Editors*

Cathy Beranek, Kent Graham, Bridget Travers, *Assistant Editors*

Debra A. Wells, *Contributing Assistant Editor*

Jeanne A. Gough, *Production & Permissions Manager*
Lizbeth A. Purdy, *Production Supervisor*
Christine A. Galbraith, Suzanne Powers, Kristine E. Tipton,
Lee Ann Welsh, *Editorial Assistants*
Linda M. Pugliese, *Manuscript Coordinator*
Maureen A. Puhl, *Senior Manuscript Assistant*
Donna Craft, Jennifer E. Gale, *Manuscript Assistants*

Victoria B. Cariappa, *Research Supervisor*
Maureen R. Richards, *Research Coordinator*
Mary D. Wise, *Senior Research Assistant*
Joyce E. Doyle, Kevin B. Hillstrom, Karen D. Kaus, Eric Priehs,
Filomena Sgambati, Laura B. Standley, *Research Assistants*

Janice M. Mach, *Text Permissions Supervisor*
Kathy Grell, *Text Permissions Coordinator*
Mabel E. Gurney, *Research Permissions Coordinator*
Josephine M. Keene, *Senior Permissions Assistant*
H. Diane Cooper, Anita Lorraine Ransom,
Kimberly F. Smilay, *Permissions Assistants*
Melissa A. Brantley, Denise M. Singleton, Sharon D. Valentine,
Lisa M. Wimmer, *Permissions Clerks*

Patricia A. Seefelt, *Picture Permissions Supervisor*
Margaret A. Chamberlain, *Picture Permissions Coordinator*
Pamela A. Hayes, Lillian Tyus, *Permissions Clerks*

Mary Beth Trimper, *Production Manager*
Anthony J. Scolaro, *Production Assistant*

Arthur Chartow, *Art Director*
Linda A. Davis, *Production Assistant*

Laura Bryant, *Production Supervisor*
Louise Gagné, *Internal Production Associate*

Since this page cannot legibly accommodate all the copyright notices,
the Appendix constitutes an extension of the copyright notice.

Copyright © 1989 by Gale Research Inc.

Library of Congress Catalog Card Number 76-38938
ISBN 0-8103-4425-4
ISSN 0091-3421

Printed in the United States of America

Contents

Preface

Literary criticism is, by definition, "the art of evaluating or analyzing with knowledge and propriety works of literature." The complexity and variety of the themes and forms of contemporary literature make the function of the critic especially important to today's reader. It is the critic who assists the reader in identifying significant new writers, recognizing trends in critical methods, mastering new terminology, and monitoring scholarly and popular sources of critical opinion.

Until the publication of the first volume of *Contemporary Literary Criticism (CLC)* in 1973, there existed no ongoing digest of current literary opinion. *CLC,* therefore, has fulfilled an essential need.

Scope of the Work

CLC presents significant passages from published criticism of works by today's creative writers. Each volume of *CLC* includes excerpted criticism on about thirty-five authors who are now living or who died after December 31, 1959. Nearly 2,000 authors have been included since the series began publication. The majority of authors covered by *CLC* are living writers who continue to publish; therefore, criticism on an author frequently appears in more than one volume. There is, of course, no duplication of reprinted criticism.

Authors are selected for inclusion for a variety of reasons, among them the publication of a critically acclaimed new work, the reception of a major literary award, or the dramatization of a literary work as a film or television screenplay. For example, the present volume includes Tom Wolfe, a proponent of New Journalism whose first novel, *The Bonfire of the Vanities,* received much attention in literary circles; Horton Foote, who won Academy Awards for his screenplays for the films *To Kill a Mockingbird* and *Tender Mercies;* and Nadine Gordimer, whose recent novel, *A Sport of Nature,* depicts a future South Africa after the overthrow of the country's apartheid system. Perhaps most importantly, authors who appear frequently on the syllabuses of high school and college literature classes are heavily represented in *CLC;* Sylvia Plath and Yevgeny Yevtushenko are examples of writers of this stature in the present volume. Attention is also given to several other groups of writers—authors of considerable public interest—about whose work criticism is often difficult to locate. These are the contributors to the well-loved but nonscholarly genres of mystery and science fiction, as well as literary and social critics whose insights are considered valuable and informative. Foreign writers and authors who represent particular ethnic groups in the United States are also featured in each volume.

Format of the Book

Altogether there are about 600 individual excerpts in each volume—with approximately seventeen excerpts per author—taken from hundreds of literary reviews, general magazines, scholarly journals, and monographs. Contemporary criticism is loosely defined as that which is relevant to the evaluation of the author under discussion; this includes criticism written at the beginning of an author's career as well as current commentary. Emphasis has been placed on expanding the sources for criticism by including an increasing number of scholarly and specialized periodicals. Students, teachers, librarians, and researchers frequently find that the generous excerpts and supplementary material provided by the editors supply them with vital information needed to write a term paper, analyze a poem, or lead a book discussion group. However, complete bibliographical citations facilitate the location of the original source and provide all of the information necessary for a term paper footnote or bibliography.

A *CLC* author entry consists of the following elements:

- **The author heading** cites the author's full name, followed by birth date, and death date when applicable. The portion of the name outside parentheses denotes the form under which the author has most commonly published. If an author has written consistently under a pseudonym, the pseudonym will be listed in the author heading and the real name given on the first line of the biographical and critical introduction. Also located at the beginning of the introduction to the author entry are any important name variations under which an author has written. Uncertainty as to a birth or death date is indicated by question marks.

• A **portrait** of the author is included when available.

• A brief **biographical and critical introduction** to the author and his or her work precedes the excerpted criticism. However, *CLC* is not intended to be a definitive biographical source. Therefore, *cross-references* have been included to direct the reader to these useful sources published by Gale Research: *Contemporary Authors*, which includes detailed biographical and bibliographical sketches on more than 90,000 authors; *Children's Literature Review*, which presents excerpted criticism on the works of authors of children's books; *Something about the Author*, which contains heavily illustrated biographical sketches of writers and illustrators who create books for children and young adults; *Dictionary of Literary Biography*, which provides original evaluations and detailed biographies of authors important to literary history; *Contemporary Authors Autobiography Series*, which offers autobiographical essays by prominent writers; and *Something about the Author Autobiography Series*, which presents autobiographical essays by authors of interest to young readers. Previous volumes of *CLC* in which the author has been featured are also listed in the introduction.

• The **excerpted criticism** represents various kinds of critical writing—a particular essay may be descriptive, interpretive, textual, appreciative, comparative, or generic. It may range in form from the brief review to the scholarly monograph. Essays are selected by the editors to reflect the spectrum of opinion about a specific work or about an author's literary career in general. The excerpts are presented chronologically, adding a useful perspective to the entry. All titles by the author featured in the entry are printed in boldface type, which enables the reader to easily identify the works being discussed. Publication information (such as publisher names and book prices) and parenthetical numerical references (such as footnotes or page and line references to specific editions of a work) have been deleted at the editor's discretion to provide smoother reading of the text.

• A complete **bibliographical citation** designed to help the user find the original essay or book follows each excerpt.

Other Features

• A list of **Authors Forthcoming in *CLC*** previews the authors to be researched for future volumes.

• An **Appendix** lists the sources from which material in the volume has been reprinted. It does not, however, list every book or periodical consulted during the preparation of the volume.

• A **Cumulative Author Index** lists all the authors who have appeared in *CLC, Twentieth-Century Literary Criticism, Nineteenth-Century Literature Criticism, Literature Criticism from 1400 to 1800*, and *Classical and Medieval Literature Criticism*, with cross-references to these Gale series: *Short Story Criticism, Children's Literature Review, Authors in the News, Contemporary Authors, Contemporary Authors Autobiography Series, Contemporary Authors Bibliographical Series, Dictionary of Literary Biography, Something about the Author, Something about the Author Autobiography Series*, and *Yesterday's Authors of Books for Children*. Readers will welcome this cumulated author index as a useful tool for locating an author within the various series. The index, which lists birth and death dates when available, will be particularly valuable for those authors who are identified with a certain period but whose death date causes them to be placed in another, or for those authors whose careers span two periods. For example, Ernest Hemingway is found in *CLC*, yet a writer often associated with him, F. Scott Fitzgerald, is found in *Twentieth-Century Literary Criticism*.

• A **Cumulative Nationality Index** alphabetically lists all authors featured in *CLC* by nationality, followed by numbers corresponding to the volumes in which they appear.

• A **Title Index** alphabetically lists all titles reviewed in the current volume of *CLC*. Titles are followed by the corresponding page numbers where they may be located in the series. In cases where the same title is used by different authors, the authors' surnames are given in parentheses after the title, e.g., *Collected Poems* (Berryman), *Collected Poems* (Eliot). For foreign titles, a cross-reference is given to the translated English title. Titles of novels, novellas, dramas, films, record albums, and poetry, short story, and essay collections are printed in italics, while all individual poems, short stories, essays, and songs are printed in roman type within quotation marks; when published separately (e.g., T.S. Eliot's poem *The Waste Land*), the title will also be printed in italics.

• In response to numerous suggestions from librarians, Gale has also produced a **special paperbound edition** of the *CLC* title index. This annual cumulation, which alphabetically lists all titles reviewed in the series, is available to all customers and will be published with the first volume of *CLC* issued in each calendar year. Additional copies of the index are available upon request. Librarians and patrons will welcome this separate index: it saves shelf space, is easily disposable upon receipt of the following year's cumulation, and is more portable and thus easier to use than was previously possible.

Acknowledgments

No work of this scope can be accomplished without the cooperation of many people. The editors especially wish to thank the copyright holders of the excerpted essays included in this volume, the permissions managers of many book and magazine publishing companies for assisting us in securing reprint rights, and the photographers and other individuals who provided portraits of the authors. We are grateful to the staffs of the Detroit Public Library, the Library of Congress, the University of Detroit Library, the University of Michigan Library, and the Wayne State University Library for making their resources available to us. We also wish to thank Anthony Bogucki for his assistance with copyright research.

Suggestions Are Welcome

The editors welcome the comments and suggestions of readers to expand the coverage and enhance the usefulness of the series.

Authors Forthcoming in *CLC*

To Be Included in Volume 52

Peter Ackroyd (English novelist, biographer, and critic)—An acclaimed biographer of such esteemed writers as T.S. Eliot and Ezra Pound, Ackroyd has also elicited significant praise for his novels focusing upon prominent literary figures. Among the works to be covered in his entry are *The Last Testament of Oscar Wilde, Hawksmoor,* and *Chatterton.*

Conrad Aiken (American poet, novelist, short story writer, critic, dramatist, memoirist, and autobiographer)—A major figure in twentieth-century American literature who was awarded the Pulitzer Prize in Poetry in 1930, Aiken employed formal stylistic techniques and an often somber tone in his verse to examine themes related to such topics as spirituality, philosophy, psychology, and science.

Woody Allen (American dramatist, short story writer, scriptwriter, and director)—Best known for his work as a comedian, actor, and filmmaker, Allen is also a noted author of fiction and drama. Criticism in his entry will focus upon the short story collections *Getting Even, Without Feathers,* and *Side Effects* and such plays as *Don't Drink the Water* and *Play It Again, Sam.*

Clive Barker (English short story writer, novelist, dramatist, and scriptwriter)—Considered one of the most promising horror writers to have emerged in the mid-1980s, Barker often focuses upon ordinary characters who are forced to confront senseless brutality, decadent obsessions, or supernatural terrors. Such short fiction collections as *Clive Barker's Books of Blood* and the novels *The Damnation Game* and *Weaveworld* have gained a wide following for Barker among aficionados of horror literature.

Gregory Benford (American novelist and short story writer)—Benford has written several works of speculative science fiction in which he contrasts the negative and positive aspects of such phenomena as alien contact and technological advancement.

Maryse Condé (Guadeloupean-born French novelist, short story writer, and dramatist)—Condé's novels often portray the lives of contemporary Caribbean and African women. Included in her entry will be criticism of *Moi, Tituba, sorcière, Noire de Salem,* a fictionalized biography of Tituba, a Barbadian slave who was tried for witchcraft in colonial Massachusetts.

William Faulkner (American novelist, short story writer, poet, and scriptwriter)—A seminal figure in modern literature, Faulkner was best known for novels and short stories set in his fictional locale of Yoknapatawpha County. Criticism in this volume will focus upon *Absalom, Absalom!,* one of Faulkner's most frequently analyzed works.

Christopher Hope (South African novelist, poet, short story writer, and dramatist)—In his novels *A Separate Development* and *Kruger's Alp,* Hope employs black humor, surrealism, allegory, and satire to explore the implications of racial discrimination in South Africa under the apartheid system.

Gloria Naylor (American novelist and short story writer)—Recognized as the author of *The Women of Brewster Place,* for which she received the American Book Award for best first novel, Naylor often examines the experiences of black American women in her fiction. Criticism in Naylor's entry will focus upon her novels *Linden Hills* and *Mama Day.*

Erika Ritter (Canadian dramatist, essayist, and short story writer)—Ritter's plays follow the plight of intelligent contemporary women who attempt to balance love and careers in the wake of the feminist movement. Ritter's entry will also include criticism of her collection of satirical essays, *Urban Scrawls.*

Edward Albee (American dramatist and scriptwriter)—Acclaimed for such plays as *The Zoo Story, The American Dream,* and *Who's Afraid of Virginia Woolf?,* Albee was considered one of the most prominent avant-garde American dramatists of the 1960s. In his recent work, *Marriage Play,* Albee examines the complex motivations underlying a middle-aged couple's determination to endure their marriage despite dissatisfaction and conflict.

Paul Celan (Rumanian-born Austrian poet, translator, and essayist)—Recognized as among the most important poets to emerge in Europe after World War II, Celan frequently drew from his experiences as an inmate of Nazi labor camps to create lyrical poetry rich in dreamlike imagery.

William Demby (American novelist)—Best known for his earliest novels, *Beetlecreek* and *The Catacombs,* Demby is praised for universalizing black concerns by focusing on characters who examine their ethnic heritage in relation to such issues as love, personal growth, and artistic freedom.

Nuruddin Farah (Somalian novelist and dramatist)—In such novels as *From a Crooked Rib, Sweet and Sour Milk,* and *Maps,* Farah explores the effects of colonization, independence, and civil war upon twentieth-century Somalian society.

Robert Harling (American dramatist)—Harling's first play, *Steel Magnolias,* which is being adapted into a major motion picture, is a dark comedy that examines the humor and sadness of everyday life in a small Southern town.

William Kennedy (American novelist, scriptwriter, short story writer, and critic)—Kennedy is best known for his novel *Ironweed,* for which he received a National Book Critics Circle Award as well as the Pulitzer Prize in fiction. In his recent novel, *Quinn's Book,* Kennedy extends his series of works set in Albany, New York, combining history and magic realism to depict a young man's quest for freedom and love during the nineteenth century.

Louis MacNeice (Irish-born English poet, critic, translator, dramatist, scriptwriter, and novelist)—A member of the "Oxford Group" of poets of the 1930s that included W. H. Auden, C. Day Lewis, and Stephen Spender, MacNeice is known for verse in which he examined social concerns and the vagaries of the human condition.

Bharati Mukherjee (Indian-born novelist, short story writer, and nonfiction writer)—Mukherjee's writings largely reflect her personal experiences as an exile and immigrant while investigating clashes between native Indian culture and Western society. Works to be covered in Mukherjee's entry include the novels *The Tiger's Daughter* and *Wife* and the short fiction collections *Darkness* and *The Middle Man and Other Stories.*

Pierre Reverdy (French poet, novelist, critic, and editor)—An important figure in the development of literary cubism and surrealism, Reverdy founded the influential magazine *Nord-Sud,* which provided a forum for such innovative writers as Guillaume Apollinaire, Louis Aragon, André Breton, and Max Jacob. In his own verse, Reverdy employed sharp visual imagery and fragmentary language, blended philosophical and mystical elements, and endeavored to reveal what he termed "the sublime simplicity of true reality."

Anatoli Rybakov (Russian novelist)—Rybakov attracted a wide readership in the Soviet Union with his novel *Heavy Sand,* an epic portrait of two Russian-Jewish families before and during World War II. His recent novel, *Children of the Arabat,* examines events leading to the purges initiated by Communist leader Joseph Stalin in the late 1940s and 1950s and their effect upon the collective Soviet conscience.

(Albert) Chinua(lumogu) Achebe

1930-

Nigerian novelist, short story writer, poet, essayist, editor, and author of children's books.

Achebe is widely regarded as one of the most important figures in contemporary African literature. His novels, which chronicle the colonization and independence of Nigeria, are among the first works in English to present an intimate and authentic rendering of African culture. Achebe's major concerns, according to Abiola Irele, involve "the social and psychological conflicts created by the incursion of the white man and his culture into the hitherto self-contained world of African society, and the disarray in the African consciousness that has followed." Critics regard Achebe's fusion of folklore, proverbs, and idioms from his native Ibo tribe with Western political ideologies and Christian doctrines as the most distinctive feature of his writing. Bernth Lindfors observed: "Achebe's proverbs can serve as keys to an understanding of his novels because he uses them not merely to add touches of local color but to sound and reiterate themes, to sharpen characterization, to clarify conflict, and to focus on the values of the society he is portraying."

Achebe's first novel, *Things Fall Apart* (1958), is considered a classic of contemporary African fiction for its realistic and anthropologically informative portrait of Ibo tribal society before colonization. Set in the village of Umuofia in the late 1880s, when English missionaries and bureaucrats first appeared in the region, this book traces the conflict between tribal and Western customs through Okonkwo, a proud village leader, whose refusal to adapt to European influence leads him to murder and suicide. Arthur Ravenscroft noted: "*Things Fall Apart* is impressive for the wide range of what it so pithily covers, for the African flavour of scene and language, but above all for the way in which Achebe makes that language the instrument for analyzing tragic experience and profound human issues of very much more than local Nigerian significance." *No Longer at Ease* (1960), set in the Nigerian city of Lagos during the late 1950s, details the failure of Obi Okonkwo, the grandson of Okonkwo from *Things Fall Apart,* to successfully combine his traditional Ibo upbringing with his English education and affluent lifestyle. While *No Longer at Ease* was less universally praised than *Things Fall Apart,* some critics defended its stylistic weaknesses as a deliberate attempt to demonstrate the consequences of one culture's dilution by another.

In his third novel, *Arrow of God* (1964), Achebe returns to Umuofia to describe life in the village during the 1920s. This book centers on Ezeulu, the spiritual leader of the region, who sends his son Oduche to a missionary school to discover Western secrets. Upon his return, Oduche attempts to destroy a sacred python, setting in motion a chain of events in which Ezeulu is stripped of his position as high priest and imprisoned by the English. Critics noted a change of thematic direction in Achebe's next novel, *A Man of the People* (1966). By focusing upon the tribulations of a teacher who joins a political organization endeavoring to remove a corrupt bureaucrat from office, Achebe condemns the widespread graft and abuse of power among Nigeria's leadership following its independence from

© Lutfi Özkök

Great Britain. Adrian A. Roscoe commented: "Achebe's first three novels showed the author as teacher. . . . From instructing his society to lashing it with satire; from portraying with a touching nostalgia the beauty of a vanishing world to savagely pillorying what is succeeding it—*A Man of the People* indeed marks a new departure."

Anthills of the Savannah (1987), Achebe's first novel in two decades, garnered widespread acclaim as his most accomplished work of fiction. In this book, according to Nadine Gordimer, "22 years of harsh experience, intellectual growth, self-criticism, deepening understanding and mustered discipline of skill open wide a subject to which Mr. Achebe is now magnificently equal." Set in Kangan, an imaginary West African nation, *Anthills of the Savannah* revolves around three childhood friends who become leaders in their country's government. Ikem is the editor-in-chief of the state-owned newspaper; Sam is a military leader who becomes President of Kangan; and Chris serves as Sam's Minister of Information. Their friendship ends tragically when Sam fails in his attempt to be elected President-for-Life and begins to ruthlessly suppress his opposition. Ikem is murdered by Sam's secret police after publishing several articles denouncing the government; Sam's corpse is later discovered in a shallow grave on the palace grounds following a military coup; and Chris is killed in a street riot. In *Anthills of the Savannah*, Achebe examines the ways in which individual responsibility and power are often exploited to the detriment of an entire society. He also emphasizes the roles of women and the urban working class while retaining the use of Ibo proverbs and legends to enhance his themes. Ben Okri stated: "All those who have inundated Achebe with critical analysis, and who spoke of him as the grandfather of African literature before he was 36, have [*Anthills of the Savannah*] to wrestle with for some time to come. Chinua Achebe has found new creative fire."

Achebe is also the author of *Morning Yet on Creation Day* (1975), a collection of literary and political essays, as well as several volumes of poetry and short stories that delineate the social and political turmoil within Nigeria. Among his verse and short fiction compilations, *Christmas in Biafra and Other Poems* (1973) is highly regarded for its ironic depiction of the Nigerian civil war, while *Girls at War and Other Stories* (1973) reflects Achebe's disillusionment with war and nationalism.

(See also *CLC*, Vols. 1, 3, 5, 7, 11, 26; *Contemporary Authors*, Vols. 1-4, rev. ed.; *Contemporary Authors New Revision Series*, Vol. 6; and *Something about the Author*, Vols. 38, 40.)

PRAFULLA C. KAR

[*The essay from which this excerpt is taken was originally delivered as a speech at the Post-Graduate Department of English and the Centre for Commonwealth Literature and Research, the University of Mysore, in September, 1981.*]

The concept of the Vanishing African is similar to the concept of the "Vanishing American" which Leslie Fiedler discusses in great detail in his mythopoetic approach to American history and culture. Fiedler tries to salvage the pre-lapsarian image of the American Adam from the labyrinth of history in order to create a sustaining myth surrounding a changing culture. The image of the vestigial American in his Edenic state of exclusiveness is systematically corroded through centuries of "progress" and "enlightenment" in the wake of scientific and technological advance. The enigmatic nature of Crèvecoeur's "new man" continues to haunt the memory of the modern American writer who is searching for his ancient roots in the debris of history. The idea of the loss of the self is almost a recurrent idea in all literature, particularly in the literature of the twentieth century. To the African writer of today this idea has a deeper psychological and emotional significance. Africa has been going through quick changes through certain accidents in history, and in the midst of social, economic and political turmoil the image of the traditional African will necessarily change. It is gradually losing its distinct shape and colour and tends to become amorphous. The contemporary African writer is deeply, and perhaps obsessively, concerned with the changing image of the African as he struggles desperately to cope with a fast changing society. Chinua Achebe is perhaps the most sensitive writer in Africa today who tries to capture the sense of this mutation in the African character during the colonial period and after. But Achebe's vision of change occurring in Africa is more philosophical than historical. Although he deals in great detail with the impact of colonialism on the African character, he is more concerned with a broad, comprehensive and dynamic idea of history as a transforming process. In this regard he may be compared with Faulkner whose depiction of the decay of the old South is governed by a phil-

osophical conception of culture in transformation. Faulkner is inclined to believe that the Civil War only quickened the process of change from an agrarian society to an industrial one, but it did not start the process; the process was a part of the subtle linear movement of history from one stage to another. There was something inexorably deterministic about the way the American south was slowly dying, a process which suggests that a new order was in the offing. Similarly, Achebe seems to believe that the British administration and the Western missionaries in Africa acted as mere catalysts in accelerating transformation of old Africa, a process which was under way before the Westerners arrived. . . . Achebe is more concerned with broad philosophical questions concerning the nature of change when a culture tries to shed its superfluities and transform itself than with specific changes occurring as a result of Africa's colonial experience. He seems to believe that the African in his primitive, agrarian and blissful state taking pride in his religion, numerous gods, folklore, magic and rituals no longer exists now; it is transformed into a myth and an archetype which are slowly passing into the ancestral memory of the race. This transformation of reality into myth is a part of the general shift of culture . . . Achebe's evocation of the image of the archetypal African has both elements of pathos and celebration, and as a creative writer he is impulsively attracted to its power. That is why, the past in its haunting quality of magic and power, remains in his consciousness as a seminal force to be invoked as a talisman. Achebe, [in his essay **"The Role of the Writer in a New Nation"**] asks a vital question concerning the responsibility of the African writer in a changing milieu:

> . . . how does a writer re-create this past? When I think of this I always think of light and glass. When white light hits glass one of two things can happen. Either you have an image which is faithful if somewhat unexciting or you have a glorious spectrum which though beautiful is really a distortion. Light from the past passes through a kind of glass to reach us. We can either look for the accurate though somewhat unexciting image or we can look for the glorious technicolor.

This is a very pertinent question, involving the integrity of a writer. Achebe, as is made clear above, prefers the "unexciting image" to the "distorted" "technicolor."

In his delineation of the African past, Achebe tries to re-create the sense of it by evoking its magic and rituals. In the past, the African lived in a world where the social life, religious life and aesthetic life were integrated as one indivisible unit. The individuals were a part of the group and believed in a general code of conduct derived from the group. This aspect of life in Africa has been exaggerated in much of the African writing now, and there is a tendency to be sentimental about the African past. Achebe is opposed to this tendency, and, therefore, he tries to give an accurate, though unexciting, image of the archetypal African in his native surrounding before his encounter with an alien culture. In *Things fall Apart* and *Arrow of God,* the novels dealing with the pre-colonial Africa, he examines the nature of the traditional African without trying to idealise it. He makes this point clear in the essay . . . from which the above passage is quoted. He remarks:

> The credibility of the world he is attempting to re-create will be called to question and he will defeat his own purpose if he is suspected of glossing over the inconvenient facts. We cannot pretend that our past was one long, technicolor idyll. We have to admit that like other people's pasts ours had its good as well as its bad sides.

This is an important statement, and in the context of the background of *Things fall Apart* and *Arrow of God,* it gives us another dimension to the nature of reality represented in the two novels.... Before the English missionaries and the government came to be entrenched on the African soil, the traditional society was already giving out slow symptoms of change. The idea of closely knit, harmonious, integrated social order was being wrecked from within, by a centrifugal impulse challenging the very idea of order.... [In *Things Fall Apart*] Okonkwo is caught in the midst of this subterranean change trying to affect the structure of reality already established as a unifying frame of reference. He is like Faulkner's Quentin Compson in *The Sound and The Fury*. Quentin's problems stem from his inability to stop the flow of time. He had the vision of the south as an unspoiled Eden almost in an abstract, Puritanical sense, a vision that became increasingly difficult to sustain because of the quick changes in the South. He commits suicide as the ''last romantic'' of the aristocratic South. The death of Quentin symbolises the death of the old South. Similarly, Okonkwo's tragedy springs from his refusal to compromise with the change that is slowly coming over Africa.... The title of the novel taken from Yeats's ''Second Coming'' suggests an apocalyptic and ironic vision. In ''Second Coming'' Yeats is celebrating the second coming of Christ in the form of an animal ''slouching towards Bethlehem to be born'', an idea of a disruptive order taking over the already existing one. Achebe must have chosen this title to present a similar view of change occurring in Africa. The dominance of the centripetal over the centrifugal, Achebe seems to suggest, represents an inevitable movement of history, and when Okonkwo refuses to accept the Christian missionaries and the British administration, he, in a way, obstructs the flow of history and, in the process, is swallowed. His tragedy, like Quentin Compson's, stems from his refusal to ''grow'', to lose his ''innocence'' in the ''rite of passage.''

In Okonkwo's death Achebe symbolises the death of traditional Africa. But again, like Faulkner's vision of the South, Achebe's has a curious mixture of irony and ambivalence. Achebe could never have saved Okonkwo from death, since his death could be seen as the logical conclusion of a chain of events having the inevitability of a Greek tragedy. Okonkwo has the inadequacies of a primitive man, is like a caterpillar who refuses to become a butterfly. He believes that his physical strength can win everything for him; his stress on emotional, not intellectual, life limits him as an individual. His instinct for the group, ironically, hinders his growth as an individual.... When Okonkwo kills the messenger of the British administration he invites troubles for himself, not by his act of revenge but, by trying to check the natural flow of events. This makes him a tragic character who becomes a victim of both an error of judgment an an unknown deterministic force operating from outside.

Okonkwo's friend Obierika, who is like Horatio to Hamlet, acts as a foil, a counterforce to the former's conception of reality. His conception of change sweeping through the entire Africa is based on a broad, philosophical awareness, a conception which could be taken as Achebe's own.... [Obierika suggests] that it is impossible to drive out the white man from Africa, and even if he is physically removed, he will leave behind him a symbolic trait, a kind of scar that can never be wiped out.... That they have ''fallen apart'' and will never act ''like one'' implies that the society has already passed from the *Gemeinschaft* to the *Gesselschaft* stage by an imperceptible movement of history. An act of suicide, Obierika says, is a

kind of sacrilege and they must make sacrifices to ''cleanse the desecrated land.'' So, Okonkwo's death by suicide is taken not as a triumph over forces of disintegration but a vile act to be purged off.

In *Arrow of God* the transition has already passed and the new culture is solidly entrenched on the African soil. The kind of African which Okonkwo represents is already a part of ancient history. The facade of traditional culture is still present in the setting of *Arrow of God,* but its inner force and vitality is lost. The characters in this novel are more open in their attitudes to the changing scene, and some of them even try to reap benefits from the new reality. Ezeulu, the Chief Priest of Umuaro is very different from Okonkwo in character, attitude and response to the changing cultural scene. He seems to have accepted the fact of the inevitability of change and tries to modify his traditional vision of reality to suit the needs of change. He wields considerable power in the community by his position as the Chief Priest, but Achebe makes it clear in the novel that within the apparent stability and cohesiveness in the community, there exist disruptive elements which threaten that stability from within. Nwaka, Ezeulu's opponent in the novel represents such a force. He not only questions Ezeulu's special prerogatives as the Chief Priest, but also the very existence of the god that Ezeulu has forced them to accept. He is a man of self-interest begotten by an individualistic and competitive society. The structure of reality presented by Achebe in this novel demonstrates that the culture is at the beginning of transformation, not by the impact of any external force, but more importantly, by a subtle inner mechanism from within, which is accelerated by the coming of Christian missionaries and Western administration. Ezeulu seems to recognise this change, and his deliberate delaying of the harvest to take revenge on a recalcitrant community can be seen as precipitating the movement to its logical step of liquidation of the community. He even tries to benefit from the new order and sends one of his sons to the Christian missionaries to be a convert, a step which represents Ezeulu's somewhat eclectic approach to reality and makes him a little advanced over Okonkwo. He compares the world to a Mask-dancing in which one has to turn round and round to have the full view of the dance:

> I want one of my sons to join these people and be my eye there. If there is nothing in it you will come back. If there is something there you will bring home my share. The world is like a Mask dancing. If you want to see it well you do not stand in one place. My spirit tells me that those who do not befriend the white man today will be saying had we known tomorrow.

This is a significant point and expresses Ezeulu's intuitive understanding of the dynamics of cultural change, and it suggests that he has moved a long way from where Okonkwo had stood. But, ironically, Ezeulu is defeated by the same forces he seems to be friendly with. His defeat can be taken as the defeat of a man who is not properly formed in intellect, is not properly balanced.

Ezeulu is the link between Okonkwo on the one hand and Obi Okonkwo and Chief Nanga on the other. In Obi Okonkwo and Chief Nanga, the protagonists of *No Longer at Ease* and *Man of the People* respectively, the image of the African is pushed to its farthest limits. In these characters there is no vestige of the traditional African. They even do not seem to understand the roles played by their ancestors in the evolution of their culture. They are beneficiaries of a changed system, but they too are defeated at the end. Their defeat can be explained in terms of their divided status, which means they have left their native culture without being able to grasp another. They suffer the fate of intermediaries, dangling between two cultures. Obi Okonkwo, essentially a good man, educated in England and having illusions of doing good to his country after his return from England, is caught in a terrible maelstorm of change sweeping through his country and is pushed into an extreme situation in which he is unable to decide his fate and finally commits an act which he cannot accept himself in his own code of morality. (pp. 149-57)

But Chief Nanga is a much different man. He is shrewd, Machiavellian and extremely opportunistic. In him the image of the African has reached the extreme limits. He is more or less like Jason Compson of Faulkner's novel, a character who adopts a new code of values and tries to benefit from it. . . . Chief Nanga succeeds for a time, but by the same logic of history he too is defeated. Achebe seems to sing the dirge over the death of the African character in the fall of Nanga when a military coup takes over the country and a seeming peace is restored. Achebe is intensely nostalgic about the African past and is deeply sad at the loss of the African character, but like a philosopher of history he accepts the change with detachment and mute resignation. The change that has come over the entire country after independence is the logical result of the subtle process in the mechanism of culture trying to adapt itself to the psychology of change. . . . The epigraph which he attaches to *No Longer at Ease* suggests his broad, philosophical and almost tragic sense of loss which is irreparable. The lines are taken from Eliot's poem "The Journey of the Magi." They are as follows:

> We returned to our places, these Kingdoms,
> But no longer at ease here, in the old dispensation,
> With alien people clutching their gods.
> I should be glad of another death.

The vision here is ironic and tragic. Like Ulysses dissatisfied with his own country after his return from adventures, Obi Okonkwo, the grandson of the protagonist of *Things fall Apart* may be thinking of fresh territories, but he has forfeited his rights for adventure since he is now a mixed man combining two diametrically opposed cultures but without having any clear conception of either. Achebe's own dilemma and the dilemma of the African writer is implicit in this epigraph. (pp. 157-58)

Prafulla C. Kar, "The Image of the Vanishing African in Chinua Achebe's Novels," in The Colonial and the Neo-Colonial Encounters in Commonwealth Literature, *edited by H. H. Anniah Gowda, Prasaranga, University of Mysore, 1983, pp. 149-59.*

EUGENE P. A. SCHLEH

Immediately following World War II political movements started or developed all over Africa, which led to the independence surge of the late 1950s and the 1960s. Concurrent to these movements was a continental-wide cultural assertion which both complemented and supported political activities. Like the political, the cultural practitioners adapted new structures and methods from the relatively brief, but impressive era of European control. Ballet, oil painting, symphony music began to be produced by African artists. Reaching by far the largest African and foreign audiences was a rapidly growing body of literary figures, especially those using the borrowed form of the novel. These men and women not only entertained, but presented revisionist history, a new Africa, to hundreds of

thousands of readers. Among the very first, and the most influential to date was the Nigerian, Chinua Achebe. (p. 125)

Achebe's style and use of language have already received considerable attention from literary scholars. For me, as a historian, however, and for my students over the years, the major import of Achebe's work has been what he has had to say about Africa and why. Achebe has repeatedly addressed the subjects of the role of the writer and of the traditional culture and social system of the Igbo, using the latter as a case study for Africa in general. In his novels the two themes blend. Just as he sees the traditional Igbo artist as "using his art to control his environment" so he sees the artist in the new medium of the written word using his art for a needed, useful purpose. Thus Achebe has consistently spoken out against vague concepts of "universality" of literature or "art for art's sake." In the early stages of his writing Achebe wrote as a historical revisionist, intent on awakening in his readers, Igbo and alien alike, the knowledge that, contrary to popular Western opinion, the Ibgo indeed have a history, a culture, and a well-functioning, if not perfect, society. (p. 126)

Over the years, Achebe has seen the artist as responsible for correcting politically charged visions. As political independence came to Nigeria (1960) and new social-political problems became apparent, he revised his views on the primary roles of artists. "The first stage, the writer as teacher-historian, the rediscovery of Africa's past was necessary but it went on too long. 'So while the African intellectual was busily displaying the past culture of Africa, the troubled peoples of Africa were already creating new revolutionary cultures which took into account their present conditions.' The artists . . . must now catch up with 'the people who make culture.'" The change involved becoming more of a social critic and then becoming a social reformer, actively working to renovate society. This active role is much more intense than the first stage, and Achebe attributed to this change in tone and pressure the reason he ceased to write novels and turned to the more succinct expressions of essays and poetry.

The novels thus belong to earlier stages and, according to Achebe, to the period when he was very much the historian and social observer. This is true of *Things Fall Apart* which is perhaps more of an active instrument pushing toward a new image of Africa than even Achebe has perceived. . . . Even today this novel is increasingly used in African schools and continues to spread its influence throughout the world. The artist may have been called on to new tasks, but the art created still fulfills its original function.

Achebe's first novel is set in Igboland during the latter part of the nineteenth century, the time of the coming of the Europeans and of European political control. Much of *Things Fall Apart* is set against the background of the everyday details of Igbo village life. What emerges is a well-ordered society in which individual achievement is honored, hard work is expected, close ties are maintained to ancestors and spirits, government is a form of participatory democracy and the "world" is small-scale, in this case the related villages around Umuofia. The main character is Okonkwo, a man driven to succeed by the memory of his lackadaisical father. By sheer effort Okonkwo has risen to be one of the most respected men in Umuofia and he aims at achieving the highest honors, acquirable titles, available. Okonkwo is imperfect. His temper is uncontrollable and causes him to violate village rules; his fear of failure or of being thought weak makes him do more than is expected of him, most notable personally killing a youth who has lived with his family as a hostage after a local war. Finally an accidental killing requires Okonkwo to leave Umuofia for a seven year exile at his mother's village. During his absence Europeans arrive, missionaries, traders, and government officers. The colonial era begins and Igbo society undergoes change. Upon his return Okonkwo tries to reverse the changes. He fails and in a fit of anger kills a government messenger, and finally hangs himself, suicide being intolerable to Igbo society. The dual tragedy theme often ascribed to the novel has been fulfilled, the individual is destroyed and the culture taken over by another. But Achebe has fulfilled a much greater goal. He has demonstrated to the reader that Igbo society existed, functioned relatively smoothly, and provided for the needs of most members. He certainly has made it clear that the Igbo were not in need of rescuing from savagery by Europeans. He has not, as others have, gone overboard by describing some idyllic, romantic, perfect pre-European world. Just as Okonkwo the individual has flaws, so too does Igbo society. The reader may choose which imperfections are most distrubing: the killing of twin babies, the role of women, the existence of osu, a despised class of outcasts based on a distant religious role. These flaws assist the European takeover, as when *osu,* having least to lose in the existing system, become among the most receptive to the missionaries' new message. But others "defect" also, particularly Nwoye, Okonkwo's first son. The existence of imperfections is not denied; existence of the culture is established so vividly that a reader must forever henceforth think of the partitioning of Africa as the takeover by one people and culture of another people and culture. A simple lesson? Yes! But one of major import for the intellectual and political history of the world.

No Longer At Ease moves in time to the 1950s and continues the family history begun in *Things Fall Apart.* Obi Okonkwo is the son of Nwoye, now a retired church functionary, grandson of Okonkwo. He returns from university in Great Britain and takes a civil service job in the government. This is the time when Great Britain was trying to hasten the Africanization of government personnel in preparation for eventual independence. Obi falls in love with a British-educated nurse, Clara, and foresees a comfortable, properous life. Yet Obi is doomed. . . . Obi's finances become impossible. He is also psychologically crushed by traditional forces when his parents refuse to consider his marriage to Clara because, although they too are good Christians, her family are *osu.*

No Longer At Ease was one of the first of what has become a sizeable number of novels about what is commonly classified as the man caught between cultures. Obi is a product of Western education and values, yet he must also live in a world where traditional values are strong. Like all of Achebe's lead characters, Obi has flaws. Initially he scorns those who take bribes, even blaming the act on the lack of education of Africans. Ultimately he succumbs himself. He hesitates too long in choosing between Clara and his family's objection to an *osu,* with the end result that Clara goes off to a dangerous abortion and is lost forever to Obi. In the end, Obi finds that his world too has fallen apart. He faces imprisonment for bribery with aloofness: he becomes a rather distant observer of his own fate rather than a participant.

Achebe, however, is not just writing a formula novel about a character caught between two worlds, although, at the time, he was in fact helping to create the formula. He is demonstrating the novelist moving between roles from observer-historian to social critic. *No Longer At Ease* shows the reader

much about urban life in the 1950s. It also makes clear that the European failed in trying to pass on his tastes and his values, without adaptation to the African as, ultimately, would become clear about his forms of government. But Achebe would not be true to himself if he placed all blame in one direction—and he never does. The Igbo, too, have erred in their choices and judgments of European culture—most clearly in the characters' consistent assessment that people go to the city for one reason only—money. In this they may not have changed so completely when one considers the achievement-oriented basis of traditional Igbo society. But some, at least, can be faulted for the totality of their change, for their quest for the material while failing to observe the best of either traditional or Western values.

After his second novel Achebe seemed ready, thematically, to move on to the role of social reformer. In his writing itself, Achebe had already demonstrated through his use of the English language a point one could make about virtually all Western culture exported to Africa. Not that all was to be cast out now that the colonial era was ended. That would be foolish. All, however, must be assessed and modified when needed to suit.

In his third novel, however, Achebe seemed to drop back in his role as well as in time. He continued his job as revisionist historian while also pursuing the development of his uses of English. *Arrow of God* is set in the 1920s at a time when the British were trying to devise an administrative system which would fit the decentralized Igbo. It is conceded to be the most difficult novel for Achebe's foreign readers to understand, for it is so rich with the unique details of Igbo village life, social, political, and religious, that the Westerner may find himself confounded. Achebe very seldom "explains"; rather he narrates and leaves it to his alien reader to eventually understand things in context—or, failing that, to turn to other clarifying sources. (pp. 127-31)

Ezeulu is the chief priest of Ulu, a god created by a grouping of six villages to bind them together at a troubled time in the past. Ulu has precedence over other village gods and, as his voice, Ezeulu has a primary role in the community. But two forces are working against Ezeulu; jealousy of factions in the community and the continuing encroachment of the Europeans. Ezeulu's village of Umaro goes to war with the neighboring village of Okperi over some land, despite Ezeulu's counsel that their claim to the land is weak and the war unjust. After the Europeans intervene to stop the war, they conduct a hearing at which Ezeulu testifies that the land is Okperi's. This impresses the District Officer, Winterbottom, who later remembers and selects the priest to be a warrant chief. This position was created by the Europeans as a way of coping with the decentralized Igbo political system. There were no chiefs or kings for the British to co-opt and use as agents in their system of Indirect Rule, so among the Igbo they set out to create chiefs. Ezeulu turns down the offered position and in a series of mutual misunderstandings is imprisoned. This means the priest is unavailable to announce the beginning of each new month and without this important religious act, the clan cannot begin the harvest. To avoid starvation many people send sons to the missionaries for the Christians' blessing and then gather the crops in the sons' names. A pragmatic solution to a complex problem, but it marks a further change in the people's culture. Torn by questions of faith and personal family tragedy, Ezeulu breaks down mentally and lives out his days unaware of reality. Igbo society continues to change, to adapt to the Europeans in order to survive.

In his fourth novel [*A Man of the People*] Achebe came to grips with the current conditions of his country in the mid 1960s, only slightly disguising reality with fictitious geographic names. The time is several years after independence, African politicians rule, but matters are still falling apart. Corruption has become the ruling ethos and is personified by the title character, Chief the Honourable M. N. Nanga, M. P., Minister of Culture. The country is viewed by the first-person narrator of the novel, Odili Samalu, a young, university educated teacher at a private secondary school.

Odili stands against Nanga in an upcoming election and in the context of the campaign, Achebe tells his readers much of African politics, including the determination of the politicians who came to power at the time of independence to stay in office and the scale and ubiquitousness of the corruption ruining the country. Yet the common people play the game with as much vigor as the politicians. . . . (pp. 131-32)

There is no real hope of defeating Nanga at the ballot box, but then there is little chance to solve the country's problems through the formal political process. They had grown too large and the world was quickly learning that systems and structures developed over generations in a European society oftentimes did not fit radically different colonial societies.

While Odili is unconscious and hospitalized from political violence the only apparent "solution" occurs. The military stage a coup and wipe the slate clean. *A Man of the People* was published the month of the first Nigerian coup and reviewers hailed Achebe more as a prophet than as a mere insightful observer. This prophetic designation was all too soon enhanced. While planning a hurried marriage, Odili thinks "a coup might be followed by a counter coup and then where would we be?" Six months later Nigeria had her second coup.

Coups were followed by riots, secession, civil war, reconstruction. Events moved quickly and Achebe became an active participant. He laid aside novels—we can only hope not forever, for in them Achebe has provided us with something of great value. In a format conducive to relaxed reading Achebe has offered many truths. He has told the world of a society, representative of many on the continent, which flourished, was subjugated by alien invaders, adapted, survived and continues to evolve. This is basic history. It needs to be told and studied, it can be learned from. Achebe cannot guarantee the learning, but in a marvelous manner he has taken on the telling and reached a world audience. He has added a new role to his full and productive life. He has become for many "The Voice of Africa." (pp. 132-33)

Eugene P. A. Schleh, "Chinua Achebe: Voice of Africa," in Essays in Arts and Sciences, *Vol. XII, No. 2, May, 1983, pp. 125-34.*

REED WAY DASENBROCK

Achebe's first novel, *Things Fall Apart* (1958), is customarily praised as the classic novel of the moment of colonialization, in this case the takeover of the land of the Ibos by the British. But it is just as emphatically the classic novel of de-colonialization, for it is as much about the moment in which it was written as about the moment in which it was set. Essential to an understanding of the novel is an understanding of the colonialist vision of the past and the future as taught by the British to such bright colonials as the young Chinua Achebe. Colonialism in a sense deprived Africans of both their past and their

future. They were assured that they had no past worth bothering about, only a past of brutish savagery. Europe was the continent with the glorious, rich past, and the history they studied in school was the history of Europe and the European presence in Africa, just as the literature they studied was European. This denial of an autonomous, valued African past was one with a denial of an autonomous, valued African future. For Africa's future was already given: it was to outgrow its savage past and approximate the condition of Europe as closely as possible. And when today we speak of developed and underdeveloped countries, we are of course subscribing to the same sense of history, the same narrative vision.

In this context, a historical novel like *Things Fall Apart* has a decidedly political point to make. Published after Ghanaian independence (1957) and two years before Nigerian independence, it gives the lie to that European presentation of the African past as a way to suggest alternatives to the European vision of the African future. When the novel begins, we have no hint that the British are about to arrive; instead, we are given a portrait of the structure and values of a traditional Ibo village from an insider's perspective. . . . And as the novel continues, Ibo customs and words are depicted and used without any explanation or glossing. To explain or gloss would be to admit that glossing is needed, that one is depicting the unfamiliar. Instead, for the narrator of the novel and for the implied audience, everything is familiar. And the effect of this on those to whom it is not familiar is that we too are brought into a circle of intimacy. By the middle of the novel, we feel completely comfortable with the world of the novel even if it had been utterly foreign to us before. Achebe thus successfully familiarizes and domesticates the traditional Ibo life he depicts, doing so not by assuming that his audience needs information about his subject but by assuming their acquaintance with it. This strategy of defusing any problems of communicability by pretending that they cannot exist has its counterpart in the novel's style. Achebe employs an Ibo style of narration in that his prose is studded with traditional proverbs, so that we feel that we are being told this story as its protagonists would have told it. And this insider's perpective presents this society as self-sufficient, coherent, satisfying and participatory. Thus, by the middle of the novel, the reader has vicariously lived in a traditional Ibo community, has seen that it worked, and has even to a certain extent adopted its norms.

This sets the stage for the impact of the second half of the novel, in which things fall apart. The British begin to take control. First, missionaries arrive, and they are followed by soldiers and government officials. In Achebe's analysis it is no accident that the missionaries come first, for they prepare the way for the others by destroying the cultural and spiritual unity of the community. The villagers they convert, convinced that European ways are superior, are therefore not prepared to oppose European domination. This creates a division within a community that has no titular head and depends instead on a wide base of consensus in making decisions. And this proves a fatal hindrance to the plans of those, like the protagonist Okonkwo, who would oppose the whites with force. Achebe's honesty as a novelist and historian is shown in the fact that he does present the missionaries as gaining a foothold because their values offer an improvement over some real moral lapses in the traditional Ibo culture. Not everyone was included in the Ibo community: there were outcasts, and twins were abominated and left out in the forest to die. It should therefore occasion no surprise that the first converts to Christianity are outcasts and parents of twins. But we have adopted enough of the perspective of men such as Okonkwo that we still feel with him that Christianity represents an alien and intrusive incursion into the community. Okonkwo's suspicions, moreover, prove to be prescient, for Christianity, when it is strong enough, brings white political domination to the village in its wake. By the end of the novel, British domination is complete, and Okonkwo has hanged himself in despair over his fellow Ibos' refusal to oppose the British with what would have been futile force.

In the very last paragraph of the novel, the narrative perspective shifts to that of the British District Commissioner who is in charge when Okonkwo's body is found. This shift signals the collapse of the traditional viewpoint that has authorized the story so far. And the District Commissioner regards this tragic episode simply as material to be included in a book he hopes to write, titled, as the very last words of the novel inform us, *The Pacification of the Primitive Tribes of the Lower Niger*. This shift comes as a shock, and that shock reveals the magnitude of Achebe's achievement. The inadequacy of that colonial officer's perspective is palpable to any reader. These were no tribes in need of pacification; they were a dignified, culturally rich, politically self-sufficient society in no need of British rule.

Of course, this returns us to the moment in which Achebe is writing, specifically the moment of de-colonialization. Achebe re-creates a past of which his people can be proud and shows that they have their own indigenous cultural and political traditions. "We did rule ourselves very well in our own way, and we can do so again": so *Things Fall Apart* suggests. They need not accept a colonialist vision of the past in which they were barbarous savages; neither do they need to accept a colonialist vision of the future in which they will cast off any remaining remnants of savage customs and mimic the Europeans as carefully as they can. Instead, they have models in their own past on which they can build, political models as well as cultural and religious ones. And the fact that Ibos were not ruled hierarchically by all-powerful chiefs, that in fact the British themselves later imposed such a system on the naturally participatory and democratic Ibos, is a major theme of Achebe's later novel *Arrow of God* (1964). Things fell apart with the coming of the British; with their leaving, perhaps Africans can put things back together by returning to their own ways and traditions.

There can be no doubt that this political point needed to be made in the late 1950s. And it has a formal or aesthetic dimension as well. Achebe's novels mark the beginning of major African writing in English insofar as their valorization of African ways and modes of narration opens up a space in which one can be authentically African in English. Yet one can grant that *Things Fall Apart* is an undoubted masterpiece without thinking that its strategy of valorizing the African past against everything that has happened since "things fell apart" offers a coherent and viable model for how to put things back together again. Achebe's novel is best considered as a corrective, but his vision has been taken instead as a complete and wholly adequate vision of history, with disastrous results. The subsequent history of Achebe's own Nigeria provides all the illustration one needs, for the community of Ibo speakers Achebe prized and depicted later found itself in mortal conflict with other communities of ethnically, religiously and linguistically diverse Nigeria. They tried to form their own independent nation of Biafra and were crushed with genocidal intensity.

This is not to suggest that the warring factions in the Nigerian/Biafran civil war were all reading *Things Fall Apart* and trying to implement its political vision. Art rarely has such a direct effect on the world. But I would argue for a tragic resemblance between the political vision of the book and that of the politicians and generals. Achebe's work is the best articulation of a nostalgic vision of the African past that implicitly calls for a return to that past. If the past was so pure and wonderful because the community was so intact and strong, and if the present colonialism has created is so debased, why don't we make our past our future and reconstitute the community of the past? Similar visions of the past and of the future as a return to the past have motivated many movements, states, and dictators in contemporary Africa. The results have always been disastrous, as the history of Uganda, Zaire and many other states in addition to Nigeria reveals. To be fair to Achebe, by the time *Arrow of God* and his fourth (and apparently last) novel, *A Man of the People* (1966), appeared, he had become aware that things had not gone well in independent Nigeria. But neither novel moves beyond the nostalgic vision of the past offered in *Things Fall Apart*. *Arrow of God* implicitly blames the British for creating authoritarian structures in Nigeria, and *A Man of the People* denounces the corruption of independent Nigeria without suggesting a solution to it. The Biafran tragedy must have brought home to Achebe the inadequacy of his nostalgic political and aesthetic strategy of reconstruction, but he has yet to replace it with anything more adequate. (pp. 313-17)

> *Reed Way Dasenbrock, "Creating a Past: Achebe, Naipaul, Soyinka, Farah," in* Salmagundi, *Nos. 68 & 69, Fall, 1985 & Winter, 1986, pp. 312-32.*

BEN OKRI

Chinua Achebe's new novel, [*Anthills of the Savannah*], his first for 18 years, is one of the most eagerly awaited in African literature. It is set in the imaginary West African country of Kangan, a place with alarmingly contemporary parallels, where the military have taken over from the politicians. The Head of State who promised to return power to the people has failed to get the referendum passed that would make him president for life.

The region of the country responsible for the failure of the referendum is Abazon. It suffers a drought; the Head of State is asked to visit and help with the problem. At first he says he will, but the novel opens with his change of mind: he has not forgotten his slight. The only member of his Executive Council who dares to question his refusal is Chris Oriko, Minister for Information.

A delegation from Abazon turns up outside the presidential palace, and matters subtly take a different turn. The Head of State sends a bland message and then attempts to manipulate public opinion by giving instructions to Ikem Osodi, editor of the state-owned *National Gazette*, to make the event look favourable.

The Head of State, Chris, and Ikem have all been at school together. Now they are a generation in power. But as the Head of State is overtaken by the intoxication of his new role, Chris becomes disillusioned. He discovers, gradually, that to remain disaffectedly within a circle of power is a trap: power demands continual declaration of support. . . .

[Chris is subsequently] declared a wanted man. He goes underground and hides with his working-class supporters, discovering for the first time the appalling conditions in which they live. In most West African countries repression ends with a *coup*. In this case, however, the Head of State simply vanishes. A cycle of tyranny has ended, but this does not necessarily mean change for the better. The novel closes with the suggestion that power should reside not within an élite but within the awakened spirit of the people.

Achebe's novel contains many surprises. He describes the working class and the condition of women in Africa more fully than ever before. He writes more openly and robustly about sex. The language is freer and Achebe takes greater risks than before. Sometimes his control wavers and the writing suffers from conflicting fictional traditions. But humour and irony help make it his most complex and his wisest book to date. . . .

Achebe's command of the traditional African world remains, though he now sees its increasing powerlessness in the face of State control. . . .

[*Anthills of the Savannah*] is a study of how power corrupts itself and by doing so begins to die. It is also about dissent, and love. 'Writers don't give prescriptions,' one of his characters notes. 'Writers give headaches.' All those who have inundated Achebe with critical analysis, and who spoke of him as the grandfather of African literature before he was 36, have this novel to wrestle with for some time to come. Chinua Achebe has found new creative fire.

> Ben Okri, *"Vicious Circle," in* The Observer, *September 20, 1987, p. 28.*

BERNARD LEVIN

In 1960 I was sent to Nigeria to report on the ceremonies and celebrations of Independence and the handover of power to the new state.

The local newspaper's front-page account of the proceedings was surmounted by an enormous headline reading ''Yaplika wake for sileep no mo!'', and I was thus introduced to two symbolic themes, one provided by that extraordinary language called Pidgin, the other, tucked away in the corner of the history to be unfolded over the years, consisting of Nigeria's succession of coups, assassinations, power-struggles, massacres and ultimately civil war, duly followed by a decline into stupendous corruption, which the most recent coup may or may not have affected.

Anyone who thinks that the foregoing is the work of a prejudiced European incapable of understanding Africa should shut up and read this amazing book [*Anthills of the Savannah*], a good deal of which is written in Pidgin and all of which is more savage in its depiction of what Nigeria has become (or at the very least *had* become) than anything the most red-necked honky could produce. Achebe is one of the most distinguished artists to emerge from the West African cultural renaissance of the post-war world; his first novel, *Things Fall Apart,* set the tone he has sounded ever since, in his constant warning that the struggle between black and white, tribe and tribe, power and corruption are far more complex than those engaged in the struggles are willing to recognise.

The detached approach does not denote detached feeling (he was active on Biafra's side in the civil war), and his distinctive voice has also been heard in essays and short stories, though this is his first novel since 1966.

Let us start with Pidgin. The word is probably a mutation of *business,* devised not by the educated settlers but by the indigenous peoples who needed a means of communication with white rulers who couldn't or wouldn't learn the local tongues; today it has a force and freshness that make Yiddish the only comparison. . . .

Now for the politics. In the first 25 pages, Achebe strips away every rag of dignity and decency from the brutal thug who rules ''Kangan'' after a military coup, and then does the same to the horrible crew of sycophants who surround His Excellency, jostling for his smiles and shopping their rivals. . . .

A tiny handful of men and women hold out: Chris Oriko, the Commissioner for Information, Ikem Osodi, editor of the National Gazette (who I guess is at least partly autobiographical), the student leader Emmanuel Obote, Beatrice Okoh, the lover of Chris. When the storm breaks, each of these rises to the occasion, and as in all such stories, whether history or fiction, the exhilaration of being both right and in mortal danger comes through; there is a comradeship on the sinking vessel that the torpedo can never know.

But this author is not content to tell a plain tale of villainy and courage; he goes deeper. African legends wander in and out of the book, their central figures making parallels with those in the story; African proverbs—''The goat owned in common dies of hunger'' (which might be black Africa's epitaph)—add salt to the tragic comedy; pessimism and cynicism contend for mastery, and hope, almost incredibly, walks off with the prize.

Two immense speeches stand out from the book, symbolising the best in the old Africa and the new. One is by a tribal elder, who speaks in metaphor and ambiguity of the injustice his people are suffering; the other is by Ikem (this *must* be autobiographical), addressing the students at the University with an equally subtle, but modern, irony. In the end, death settles the score, not only for Chris and Ikem (significantly, Emmanuel and Beatrice survive, to represent youth and continuity, those hopes of the future) but also for His Excellency. ''What must a people do'' asks Beatrice when it is all over, ''to appease an embittered history?'' She gets no answer to her question, but we can guess at Achebe's: Be patient; Africa is older than any of us.

The form of the novel takes some getting used to: the voice changes without warning, between Chris, Ikem, Beatrice and the author, but since all these are on the same side, it is a fruitful device, enabling us to see the shades of difference in the pattern. But at the beginning of Chapter 11 the author drops the mask and speaks plainly in the first person, torn in two by disillusion and faith. . . . Mr. Achebe would do well to buy a large false beard, against the possibility that the next Nigerian coup will be another military one.

> Bernard Levin, *"What Must a People Do?" in* The Sunday Times, *London, September 20, 1987, p. 56.*

MARGARET BUSBY

No one has done more than Chinua Achebe to bring African writing in English to the attention of the world, while in the process charting the socio-political development of contemporary Nigeria. . . .

Now, over 20 years since his last novel, [*A Man of the People*], comes Achebe's most complex, enigmatic and impressive work yet. Reading *Anthills of the Savannah* is like watching a master carver skilfully chiselling away from every angle at a solid block of wood: at first there is simply fascination at the sureness with which he works, according to a plan apparent to himself. But the point of all this activity gradually begins to emerge— until at last it is possible to step back and admire the image created. True, there are occasional slips, lines one night wish less awkward, but the overall effect is undeniably powerful.

The book tackles the power relations in an imaginary West African state where a military coup has brought to prominence a Sandhurst-trained officer ill prepared for political leadership. Before long 'His Excellency' transforms his initial insecurity into paranoid despotism, suspecting even well-meaning allies of disloyalty. This becomes the fate of his two boyhood friends, Chris Oriko, Commissioner for Information, and Ikem Osodi, poet and editor of a national newspaper, who in different ways both refuse to play safe by compromising. Through them come many of this novel's resonant and challenging statements, as much comments on the real world as on the fictional state of Kangan: 'It is the failure of our rulers to re-establish vital inner links with the poor and dispossessed of this country, with the bruised heart that throbs painfully at the core of the nation's being.' And: 'To blame all these things on imperialism and international capitalism . . . is like going out to arrest the village blacksmith every time a man hacks his fellow to death.'

But the inescapable observation governing the novel is that 'in the absurd raffle-draw that apportioned the destinies of post colonial African societies two people starting off even as identical twins in the morning might easily find themselves in the evening one as President shitting on the heads of the people and the other a nightman carrying the people's shit in buckets on his head.' And the person who understands this best— Beatrice Okoh, interacting crucially with the three main male characters—is ultimately the survivor. . . .

The blurb promises a drama of love and friendship, betrayal and death, and *Anthills* does indeed gather thriller-like pace as each of the main protagonists is poised for an accidental fall. Leisured lyricism, however, is never far away, and one of the appeals of Achebe's style has always been his mesmeric ability to combine traditional proverbs and concepts effectively with sophisticated Western allusions. There are episodes, too, of characteristic humour, as where the fugitive Chris has to pretend to be 'small man' in order to reassure a vigilant soldier.

Achebe offers no remedics for disenchantment; after all, as Ikem maintains, 'Writers don't give prescriptions. They give headaches.' Yet hope remains that something lasting will survive in the barren landscape. . . .

Margaret Busby, "Bitter Fruit," in New Statesman, *Vol. 114, No. 2948, September 25, 1987, p. 34.*

EILEEN BATTERSBY

[*Anthills of the Savannah* is an] extremely political novel, . . . its value lying more in what Achebe is saying than in how he says it. Yet it is hard to accept the didactic message when it is conveyed through such unconvincing stereotypes telling their own stories. Sam is a parody of every scared megalomaniac history has ever produced, while Ikem and Chris are largely interchangeable—both are clever, brash, opinionated and very exasperated. Chris's lover Beatrice, beautiful and brilliant (whom

Achebe unnecessarily hampers with a First in English from London University), provides a central consciousness, but inspires some of the weakest writing: 'Chris saw the quiet, demure damsel whose still waters nonetheless could conceal deep overpowering eddies of passion.'

It's a novel of rhetoric: 'What must a people do to appease an embittered history?' It's also a novel of inspired moments—a traffic jam, confrontations with stupid policemen, a memorable scene in which an old man takes the stage and tells Kangan's story from the peasant viewpoint. Achebe is at his best when his characters are speaking Pidgin, or are quoting proverbs: 'A man who answers every summons by the town crier will not plant yams in his field.' The richness of traditional African folklore and native speech are contrasted with the sterile politicking inherited from outsiders who ruled, influenced, then left.

Anthills of the Savannah does not approach the brilliance of *Things Fall Apart* or the comic artlessness of *A Man of the People*. It is not a great novel. Its awkward phrasing, often jagged dialogue, stylistic unevenness and unexceptional multiperspective narrative are too glaring for that. But its truth and realism make it an important statement about the nature of power. During an address to the local student union, Ikem declares: 'Story-tellers are a threat . . . they threaten all champions of control'. Later, he adds: 'Writers don't give prescriptions . . . writers give headaches.' Chinua Achebe is expressing his own political sentiments, his fears and anger—these are the elements which make this, his first novel after an 18-year silence, worth reading.

Eileen Battersby, " 'Story-tellers Are a Threat'," in The Listener, *Vol. 118, No. 3033, October 15, 1987, p. 29.*

NADINE GORDIMER

Set an African writer to judge an African writer? But I need no special knowledge of a writer's people, country or continent; my criterion is to receive from any writer the revelation of what his or her sensibility, alone, succeeds in conveying as a transformation of a specific reality. How this revelation is to be measured depends on the skill of the writer and not the knowledge of the reader. To say: yes, it is exactly like that! is to recognize homebodies in a Polaroid print. To be moved to cry: *now I know!* is to recognize the achievement against which every writer makes his height mark on the wall of world literature.

"In such a regime, I say, you died a good death if your life had inspired someone to come forward and shoot your murderer in the chest—without asking to be paid." That was the final sentence of Chinua Achebe's previous novel, *A Man of the People*, published 22 years ago. Mr. Achebe's new book, *Anthills of the Savannah*, is set, according to the author, in a backward West African state called Kangan under that same rubric. Kangan is an imaginary country, and it is many countries, not only the Nigeria from which Mr. Achebe has been in and out of exile during that period, and not only those countries in the Southern Hemisphere. It is the country of a—the?—condition in which, as Mr. Achebe puts it, "the rich man . . . holds the yam and the knife." But this novel is not a repetition coming from the bottom of an old barrel. It is a work in which 22 years of harsh experience, intellectual growth, self-criticism, deepening understanding and mustered discipline of skill open wide a subject to which Mr. Achebe is now magnificently equal. The work's flaws simply point up its abundance. (p. 1)

Mr. Achebe is a novelist who makes you laugh—and then catch your breath in horror. He has found the mode for his subject. Humor is not associated with horror; therefore, he uses the clash to startle one into response. For he understands the danger of comic-opera events. Easy to laugh at Idi Amin's medals or (as I have done) at the capitalist West's obeisance to Jean-Bedel Bokassa, exemplified by his portrait hung as a sign of prestigious royal patronage in the most elegant hotel in Nice. The discovery of what these men were doing stopped the laugh in the throat. In the person of Sam, President of Kangan, Mr. Achebe sagely illustrates that those whom the gods would make mad with power to destroy us they first disguise to us as absurd.

Mr. Achebe is a moralist and idealist, but he rarely allows himself to put a word in; these positions are perfectly integrated in his characters. . . .

Mr. Achebe always has been a master of idiom as characterization, even as entertainment; but idiom is the root language of a people's ethics and values, and now he has mastered the immensely difficult art of using idiom at this deepest level. Beyond cant, this is the wisdom of the people. He knows how to glean it even from their cupidities and contradictions, constantly turning around the situations of daily life in his narrative, so that the downtrodden taxi driver who battles in ridiculous belligerence with Ikem in a traffic jam reveals a different code when Ikem is on the run from Sam's charges of treason. For—still deeper—there is an idiomatic code of behavior, too, that when cracked gives some troubling messages. The taxi driver blames the "wahala" of the traffic incident on the fact that Ikem doesn't travel around in a chauffeur-driven car that befits his position and demands a clear path, and Ikem marvels at "an insistence by the oppressed that his oppression be performed in style! What half-way measure could hope to cure that?"

Ikem is a writer, one in whose utterance the people's struggle will stand reincarnated, and yet he does not see revolution as the cure. . . . Kangan, dealing with the problems of the second stage of liberation, after Westminister-granted freedom, has had no revolution; but one wonders how Ikem could see South Africa, for example, getting rid of white domination without one. The ethos of this book is individual responsibility, and, whatever one's experience of the individual's limited effectiveness in the struggle for justice may have been, this ethos is presented with overwhelming conviction. It reaches a magnificent climax in Ikem's speech to students after he has been dismissed as editor—witness, reincarnator of the downtrodden's struggle. Novelists often tell their readers that this or that character is a poet or wit or orator; seldom are they able to produce, lacking these qualities themselves, other than lame evidence. But Mr. Achebe's creations fulfill all that he claims for them—Beatrice in her reflections and growth, Chris in the manner of meeting his death, Ikem in his passion, appalling honesty and command of the word.

There is a world in these individuals. Chinua Achebe takes full responsibility for it, as himself the individual with the chalked-ringed eye, a writer who has no illusions but is not disillusioned, loves the people without necessity for self-hatred and is gloriously gifted with the magic of an ebullient, generous, great talent.

There is only one comment left to make after turning the final page of *Anthills of the Savannah. Now I know!* (p. 26)

Nadine Gordimer, "A Tyranny of Clowns," in The New York Times Book Review, *February 21, 1988, pp. 1, 26.*

NEAL ASCHERSON

In this decade of African catastrophe, it is hard to reconstruct the optimism and certainties of the emergent African political class thirty years ago, and of their liberal-minded European sympathizers. Independence seemed the happy-ever-after conclusion, even to those territories—the Portuguese domains, Rhodesia-Zimbabwe—that were destined to fight long, bitter wars before they could claim to "govern themselves." Instead, so often although not everywhere, independence set off a degenerative process: freedom became corruption, while democracy collapsed into autocracy, "life-presidencies," and finally military dictatorship; the country people faced starvation brought by crop failure and mismanagement while the town people withered in colossal, spreading slums where the AIDS pandemic is beginning to reap its harvest.

Who or what is to blame? For a time, it was fashionable to blame "neo-colonialist exploitation," real and ruthless enough indeed. Later, in a Europe still clinging to the tatters of fond hopes, there emerged a wry defense of corruption as no more than the modern form of traditional African clientship relations, something "natural" and not to be judged by European standards of public life. Patronizing and even racist, this explanation too was less than a half-truth.

In [*Anthills of the Savannah*], . . . Chinua Achebe says, with implacable honesty, that Africa itself is to blame, and that there is no safety in excuses that place the fault in the colonial past or in the commercial and political manipulations of the First World. The first postcolonial leaders, for all their European educations and sophistication, utterly failed to meet their responsibility. And by the time that they began to understand the scale of their failure, their own brief period of hegemony was beginning to fall apart as power passed into the hands of more limited and infinitely more ferocious men, usually military. During the years of open political contest, the first "independence" generation recklessly allowed the distinction between power and force to be blurred, until those whose trade was force began in increasing numbers to drive their tanks across that line.

The "Kangan" of *Anthills of the Savannah* is more or less Achebe's own Nigeria. That country is today governed by General Babangida, among the least oppressive and most enlightened of Africa's military rulers. But as I write, the newspapers report that there is little popular enthusiasm for the slow return to civilian rule that he intends. Civilian politicians have discredited themselves. A diplomat in Lagos is quoted as saying: "Who could stand over Babangida's murdered body and proclaim liberty? Answer: nobody!"

At the beginning of the novel, the reader meets four members of Kangan's elite, "the cream of our society and the hope of the black race." Chris Oriko is Commissioner for Information, Ikem Osodi is a poet and the restless, rebellious editor of the *National Gazette*. Beatrice Okoh, lover of Chris, is a strong and independent young woman, an intellectual with a first-class English degree from London who is a senior civil servant. The fourth character is Sam, otherwise "His Excellency," the new military ruler of Kangan. Sam, Chris, and Ikem were all at school together at "Lord Lugard College," one of those little black Etons peculiar to the old British Empire. His schoolmates, in fact, helped Sam into power, considering him to be a slightly slow-witted but basically decent fellow who would clear up the mess left behind by the corrupt civilian government that preceded him.

As the novel opens, they are discovering how wrong they were. Sam—"not very bright, but not wicked," in Ikem's original estimate—is turning himself into a "Great African Leader." He is no longer Sam but "H. E." His cabinet (the novel's first pages describe a cabinet meeting with murderous satire) is already reduced to a pack of nervous toadies, jostling to throw doubts on each others' loyalty. At some moments, H. E. luxuriates in his own sense of achievement. . . . But he can banish only for a few minutes his gnawing humiliation over the recent referendum to make him President for Life; he has failed to gain the necessary majority, and failed because the people of the distant, dry savannah province of Abazon boycotted the poll. He has punished them by denying them water during a disastrous drought. Now a delegation from Abazon has had the impudence to arrive unlicensed in the capital to petition him for aid. Who put them up to it? H. E. suspects a plot, possibly by those classmates who still secretly think they are much better than he is. Trouble is brewing in Kangan.

After this introduction, the novel slows and broadens out as Achebe explores more deeply the character and meditations of Chris, reluctant to abandon what remains of his influence over the political scene, of Beatrice as she treads warily along the fringe of H. E.'s set of cronies, and of Ikem. It is Ikem whose shift from meditation to action provides the theme of the book. But all three of them share something "Russian," both in their thoughts and in their relation to the social and political setting; their fears are the fears of Herzen's "superfluous" people, and their sense of privilege, guilt, and impotence constantly reminded me of the novels of Turgenev. . . .

In [*Anthills of the Savannah*], Achebe's characters are obsessed with the problem of "the people"; they act in their name, and yet are painfully aware that they have lost contact with them. In a very Russian way, they debate the nature of "the people," at times confident that the humility and good nature of the masses will save the nation from its leaders, at others fearing that the goodness has been turned to evil and cruelty, which any revolution would release as a tide of dark savagery. (p. 3)

Language at once unites and divides the poor and the powerful. Chris, Ikem, and their British-educated friends talk sophisticated London English among themselves. But at intimate moments—loving, teasing, trying to express something special to their country—they resort to the vivid West African version of pidgin English which is the nation's real lingua franca. Much of the novel's dialogue is in pidgin, as when the two drivers try to thank Ikem for defending the cause of the poor. . . .

H. E. orders Chris to fire Ikem from the *National Gazette*, on the grounds that he is suspected by the "State Research Council" (security police) of having organized the delegation of protest from Abazon. Chris refuses, but Ikem is removed anyway. He addresses an incandescent student rally at the university, as the Abazon leaders are arrested; incautiously, he answers a question about a rumor that H. E. will put his own head on the coinage with a jest that the ruler is "inciting the people to take his head off." Next day, the tamed *National Gazette* leads with the headline: "EX-EDITOR ADVOCATES

REGICIDE!" Within hours, Ikem is dead, murdered by security police after a raid on his house. Chris manages to gather a few foreign correspondents in order to tell them the truth, then goes into hiding. A few days later, in ragged disguise, he boards a bus heading for the North and the arid, rebellious province of Abazon.

A bus! Chris Oriko has not ridden a bus since before he left for Britain as a student. The people he meets in the office, at cocktail parties, at any gathering of the elite have no idea what it means to travel on a bus. This becomes Chris's own pilgrimage to the people, a liberation from the "Mercedes class" registered by Achebe in one of those curious, spreading, raft-like sentences he uses—much as Tolstoy used them—to describe a change in the heart. . . .

But this is also the journey of Chris Oriko to his own death. On the borders of Abazon, the bus is stopped by a drunken mob celebrating news on the radio from the capital: there has been another *coup d'état* and Sam, "His Excellency," has been kidnapped. His chief of staff proclaims with unconvincing outrage that the abductors will be found, but it is "H. E." who is soon found in a shallow grave. Chris never learns this. Attempting to save a young girl in the crowd from a police sergeant bent on rape, he is shot dead.

In their very different ways, the three boys from Lord Lugard College have all expiated the sin that two of them recognized but one did not: that "failure to re-establish vital inner links with the poor and dispossessed." The three murders, senseless as they are, represent the departure of a generation that compromised its own enlightenment for the sake of power—even the power of bold opposition enjoyed by Ikem Osodi. They are succeeded by altogether cruder and less inhibited men: the inner, African danger that they all underestimated. (p. 4)

It is the courage of this complex novel to cast Africans, even in this wretched decade, always as subjects and never as the objects of external forces. It is a tale about responsibility, and the ways in which men who should know better betray and evade that responsibility. Women, in Achebe's novel, do not betray. Not only the figure of Beatrice Okoh but the main female characters here show a "priestess-like" strength and calm. They endure, angrily enough, the "Desdemona complex" that tempts their men to make fools of themselves with white women; they are the bearers of traditional morals and perceptions to which they coax their erratic, ambitious men to return. They pick up the pieces after male disasters. They are left to mourn.

And yet this is neither a solemn work nor an entirely pessimistic one. It has wonderful satiric moments and resounds with big African laughter. Legend and tradition have their places here, as characters recount old myths of creation or new parables about the abuses of power. The question of how deep and lasting are the wounds to the "heart of the people" is left open. But Achebe emphasizes that the strength of the human race is its unpredictability: "man's stubborn antibody called surprise. Man will surprise by his capacity for nobility as well as for villainy."

All that can be done is to understand what cannot be done, that all total solutions fail and that therefore "we may accept a limitation on our actions but never, under no circumstances, must we accept restriction on our thinking."

That is the conclusion of a young student leader, at a gathering to mourn Ikem and to give a name (Amaechina: may-the-path-never-close) to his fatherless baby. Ikem himself, with Chinua Achebe perhaps speaking through him, has already found his way to the humility of liberalism. "Experience and intelligence," he says, "warn us that man's progress in freedom will be piecemeal, slow and undramatic. Revolution may be necessary for taking a society out of an intractable stretch of quagmire but it does not confer freedom, and may indeed hinder it." (pp. 4, 6)

Neal Ascherson, "Betrayal," in The New York Review of Books, *Vol. XXXV, No. 3, March 3, 1988, pp. 3-4, 6.*

Philip (Dean) Appleman

1926-

American poet, novelist, nonfiction writer, and editor.

Considered a technically accomplished writer whose works combine political and social commentary with personal experience, Appleman examines themes related to such diverse topics as history, ecology, evolution, individual identity, war, and romantic love. Although occasionally faulted for not fully developing his disparate concerns, Appleman has elicited praise for his strong characterizations and concise, evocatively detailed descriptions. In *Summer Love and Surf* (1968), Appleman employs various stylistic devices to create lyrical poems that celebrate a husband's love for his wife. *Open Doorways* (1976) looks nostalgically to the past while emphasizing Appleman's interest in contemporary political and social issues, particularly the causes and consequences of war. Stanley Plumly commented: "[Appleman's] thoughtfulness, his care and concern . . . , amount to a moral obligation to witness and withstand the daily bad news of the world. His headlines, his reports back define what he sees as an ongoing crisis in citizenship." In *Darwin's Ark* (1984), Appleman draws upon his knowledge of the writings of English naturalist Charles Darwin to explore the processes of creation, evolution, and extinction. Using simple, precise diction and an informal tone, Appleman blends apocalyptic images and elements of humanist philosophy to construct what Daniela Gioseffi described as "an elixir for the anxiety of nuclear end, full of lyric wit and insight."

Appleman's first novel, *In the Twelfth Year of the War* (1970), focuses upon a crew of marauding sailors who travel the world's seaports in search of fortune and pleasure aboard a retired warship that is preserved as a commercial freighter. Cloaking incisive social and political observations in farce, satire, irony, and black humor, Appleman depicts through symbolism and allegory the classic struggle between good and evil. His second novel, *Shame the Devil* (1981), portrays the adventures of two New York swindlers who journey to Indiana and discover an isolated community of Norse descendants whose Viking customs have been undisturbed by modern society. By interweaving history and geography and alluding to Norse and Persian legends, Greek mythology, astrological mysteries, and runic inscriptions, Appleman endeavors to establish parallels between ancient and modern civilizations. In addition to his poetry and novels, Appleman has published *The Silent Explosion* (1965), a nonfiction study concerning overpopulation, and has edited several volumes of critical essays, including *1859: Entering an Age of Crisis* (1959) and *Darwin* (1970). He is also the founding editor of the scholarly journal *Victorian Studies*.

(See also *Contemporary Authors*, Vols. 13-16, rev. ed. and *Contemporary Authors New Revision Series*, Vol. 6.)

Courtesy of Philip Appleman

THE VIRGINIA QUARTERLY REVIEW

The wide range of this poet's experience would seem to promise a poetic vision possessing both acuity and richness. But too often [in *Summer Love and Surf*] Appleman fails to confer upon the poem the intensity necessary to fulfill the experience suggested at the heart of the poem. Appleman is usually at his best in the poems which speak of his love for his wife. They are poems drawing on the traditions of love poetry and yet creating uniquely the ambience of this couple's small world. And so, to judge Appleman in terms of his best work is to see him as a poet with unusual grace and control.

A review of "Summer Love and Surf," in The Virginia Quarterly Review, *Vol. 45, No. 3, Summer, 1969, p. 96.*

THOMAS LASK

The ship Betsy Ross, whose voyage around the globe makes up the odyssey of this beautifully written first novel [*In the Twelfth Year of the War*], is a relic of the war. Originally a Liberty ship designed neither for looks nor comfort, she has somehow evaded both the mothball and the blowtorch and more by perseverance than by innate ability lives up to her schedule as a hauler of freight. She carries in her capacious hold only stuff not perishable: marble, sisal, hemp and, when she is lucky, cases of brandy. She creaks her way from port to port; anywhere, in fact, where her home office thinks there is a dollar to be made. Her crew too are relics, gutted husks of humanity, working through biological tropisms away from pain toward the fulfillment of bodily needs. They drink, they whore, they fall into animal forgetfulness. And in between they do only as much work as allows them to lurch from one state to another. They are marine existentialists, men for the moment. For them 5,000 years of culture fall away in a moment. They emerge from the ship when in port as from a cave, and with spear and club seek women, intoxicating beverages, physical pleasure. It is not a case of sitting in judgment on their existence. No one has the formula for the good life, and Mr. Appleman, a poet and teacher, is not so arrogant as to suggest one. But his crew, in spite of its abilities, is as near to primitive man as one can come and still be counted part of today's world.

This is not true, of course, of every soul on board. It is one of the author's more conspicuous qualities that he can create and manipulate symbols unobtrusively. They are there as part of the fabric of the book, making their narrative contribution to the story, yet available for contemplation outside their narrative function. The symbols, in short, are there, not inserted.

Three of the characters form a triptych against the backdrop of ship and crew. One is Kravitz, a seaman from Detroit, who is all evil, the Claggart of the Betsy Ross. In another age, say that of Melville or the Elizabethans, Kravitz would be all Evil, part of the motiveless malignity that strives for mastery in the universe. But Mr. Appleman is as much a child of the time as the rest of us, product of an age that sees our lives determined by economic, psychological and recently by behavioral forces beyond our control. So he has invented for Kravitz a brutal father, a weak mother and an indifferent environment. But I think he would have had in this character a figure of almost classical stature had he allowed him to surface unencumbered from the underworld, a Satan who owed allegiance to no force but his own dark divinity.

Next to him is Red, the typical man in the middle, all of whose resolution goes into staying free of entanglements. His impulses are decent but his actions compromise them. He knows what is just, but he will do nothing to maintain the balance of justice. A man can go through life with such a position, but only at the constant erosion of his decency. With each compromise, something of his manhood is lost.

And finally there is the author's most complicated creation, Benjamin Burr, former miner, barber, poet manqué, prober of the universe, asker of impossible questions. Burr is also the bosun of the Betsy Ross, the foreman who tries to keep everything shipshape, to see that the work gets done, who tries to make the ship better than it is. He battles reality for a Platonic ideal and alienates every man in the crew. With the captain a drunken nonentity, the mate a frenzied bundle of hateful ineffectiveness, the contest comes down to Burr the dreamer and Kravitz the evildoer.

All this makes the book sound portentous, which is unfair to the author. For though he is always serious, he is never grim. The writing is leavened by parodies and literary extravaganzas; many of the incidents rise to desperate farce; in fact the combination of nautical exactness and wayward characters puts this reader in mind of one of the great books of ships and the sea: Marcus Goodrich's *Delilah.*

As the Betsy Ross completes what later proves to be her last voyage home, she stops at a small nondescript port in the Caribbean, at an island that could easily have been Cuba before the Castro revolution. A Trujillo-like tyranny weighs on the island. For decent people, the town is a sinkhole of oppression,

corruption and greed. The attitude of the American crew, that of tolerant superiority to an inferior civilization, brings into play a whole host of ironies. For while the crew gambols and plays, a revolution is in the making. But the Betsy Ross contributes nothing to the new freedom. The rebels board the ship to confiscate the stores, but there are no stores. The crew has already managed to steal everything in sight.

Mr. Appleman has managed to avoid all the snares of a first novel. It is a contained, shaped and molded work and it is as auspicious as the fictional signs can be.

Thomas Lask, "The Long, Long Voyage Home," in The New York Times, *November 30, 1970, p. 37.*

ROBERT PHILLIPS

[Philip Appleman is not well known], though other poets have known and admired his work for years. His latest collection, *Open Doorways,* demonstrates real growth and an admirable dedication to craft. The title is significant: the book reveals an openness to experience, to travel, to history. A predominant theme is nostalgia or regret—a longing for a time before cement covered everything, for sounds of train whistles moaning in the dark. Yet the tone is not soft. Appleman's language is as tough as many of his subjects which, in **"Alive,"** includes a painful plea for mercy killings of the likes of his Uncle Jimmie, who became "whittled down like a dry stick, but living: the heart, in its maze of tubes, pumps on." Appleman's accomplished new collection is a big book, as poetry books go—88 pages. And it is diverse—poems on love, war, ecology, identity. I hope it brings him the greater recognition he has earned.

Robert Phillips, in a review of "Open Doorways," in Commonweal, *Vol. CIII, No. 25, December 13, 1976, p. 792.*

STANLEY PLUMLY

Philip Appleman, contemplator as much as craftsman, is a rationalist. That is, he has a passion for perspective, balance, and the tricky terms of comprehensibility. In [*Open Doorways*], he would, and usually does, negotiate the tough compromise between intuition and information. His is the art of premeditation, of planning—of anticipating, as opposed to discovering, the next move. He is preoccupied with the surfaces, the incoming data, with the meanings of all the sums of all the details he can reasonably order and charge with significance—even when that significance comes out as a question, "What has gone wrong / with our lives?" When the considering voice in his poems is surrounded by circumstance and reporting directly from the evidence, Appleman's results are impressive.... But when the voice begins to lose sight of itself and its individual circumstance, when it begins to sound glibly generalized or socially self-conscious, when subject matter begins to replace the attention paid to specific objects, the poems take on a public, easing-into-profundity posture.

> When crisp catalpa leaves
> come tumbling down the frosty morning air
> like tarpaulins for tulips,
> it's spring again in little college towns,
> October nipping at our brave beginnings . . .

The simile here has the poetic tone and studied economy of the fifties; and "nipping" is what Jack Frost does. The title of the poem is **"October Spring."** It concludes by telling us that "we are clinging to / our thinning years because brown leaves / are clumsy promises.'' This is poetry at one remove from itself, a poetry of propriety. Appleman's strength is in the middle range and middlewest of experience—fixed, sure centers of common sense. His thoughtfulness, his care and concern in poems as various as **"New Year's Resolution,"** **"Afterward,"** and **"In Two Degrees Cold,"** amount to a moral obligation to witness and withstand the daily bad news of the world. His headlines, his reports back define what he sees as an ongoing crisis in citizenship, from **"Fighting the Bureaucracy"** to **"Winding Down the War."** "In a cold month I fold / my *Times* with care,'' the poet tells us . . . "Headlines / hack at my heart.'' What is too often missing, however, whether the poems mark an achievement or an approximation, is an intensity, a severe and irreducible inner music. Forms and degrees of intensity are the most personal and individual qualities of any poem. When Appleman is able to internalize the event, change its life, and his, in a process of give and take, he compels such intensity. **"Waiting for the Fire"** is genuinely moving precisely because of the depth at which it registers—

> Not just the temples, lifting
> lotuses out of the tangled trees,
> not the moon on cool canals,
> the profound smell of the paddies,
> evening fires in open doorways,
> fish and rice the perfect end of wisdom;
> but the small bones, the grace, the voices like
> clay bells in the wind, all wasted.

The poem winds down, and up, to such a point that "no matter where you stand / the path of light comes to you.'' The music of these good lines is obviously inherent to the action, the emotion. Yet in so many of the poems in *Open Doorways,* from **"Memo to the 21st Century,"** the first, to **"Scrapbook,"** the last, the music has the feel of public utterance, pubic sanction ("That is how it was in Indiana.''), as if the mind had formed a committee and voted compromise. To repeat, the music of a poem, the measure of its intensity, is its most intimate sense of itself. War and rumors of war are Appleman's *subjects:* they intensify his passion as they enlarge his reason. A man of his multiple talents should leave his civic conscience to prose.

*Stanley Plumly, in a review of ''Open Doorways,''
in* The American Poetry Review, *Vol. 6, No. 4, July-
August, 1977, p. 42.*

JAY PARINI

Philip Appleman's new book, *Open Doorways,* has virtues—the poems are clear-eyed, musical, and well-crafted. And a poet deserves to be judged by his best poems. **"Love Poem,"** in spite of its title, is terse and evocative. . . . Nevertheless, some of the phrases lack freshness: "The thrill of cool / skin'' and "sing-song of / her breath''. Further, one tires of hearts going *thump.* The problem I think, is that Appleman does not stand close enough to his language; he has not made it an extension of his body, an active limb. A good poet invents a new tongue, inhabits a separate country of the imagination with its own idioms, laws, and boundaries. Philip Appleman has appropriated too many worn-out poetical stances and second-hand phrases. (p. 296)

One looks for simplicity and finds it in Appleman; but simplicity has no value unless the poet makes something difficult *appear* simple. Frost instantly comes to mind, for in a poem like **"Dust of Snow"** he can take our breath away with language gathering to itself a wide range of difficult emotions on a point of fire. He achieves what Emerson called *correspondence,* a

condition wherein the inner axis of subjective experience lines up with the outer axis of the world. This coincidental vision makes for great poetry. By contrast, Appleman's poems skitter over the surface of experience, which lies beneath them like a cold pond. He never breaks the crust; the shock of reality is missing. One feels the grating edges, where language and experience do not align themselves. And while there is no mistaking the technical competence of this poet, who has a marvelous ear, the language itself never measures up to the sound it makes.

When he does make a desperate effort to shock us with reality, the result is tragic, as in **"On a Morning Full of Sun."** The speaker in the poem is a soldier in Viet Nam, overcome by the sight of burning huts:

> I stagger up the sand,
> press my M-16
> to the skull of a peasant girl,
> and watch the bone
> go chipping off and dancing
> through the flat blue keening
> air.

"Stagger'' seems pretentious, swollen with meaning. How should we react to Appleman's message? Is there a message? If the soldier is so overwhelmed by battle that he does not know what he is doing, must we forgive him? The self-consciousness of "stagger'' contradicts the symbolic potential of "flat blue keening / air.'' In any case, why give "air'' a line to itself? Poets rarely make good poems from such inflated subject matter because the emotional overcharge already present before the poet goes to work has to be defused. How do you begin to write about Dachau, Hiroshima, or Viet Nam? And though we certainly need poems to explain why we insist on butchering fellow human beings on a regular basis, we do not need Appleman's poem very badly. (p. 297)

Jay Parini, ''The Small Valleys of Our Living,'' in
Poetry, *Vol. CXXX, No. 5, August, 1977, pp. 293-303.*

DAVID QUAMMEN

In his blurb for *Shame the Devil,* John Gardner heartily recommends Philip Appleman's novel "to anyone who has ever liked any two of the following: the Hardy Boys, the King James Bible, *The Hobbit,* or *Fritz the Cat.*" Perhaps he has reasons, but judging from my experience, the King James alone is insufficient; and I suspect that Mr. Gardner may be doing some injustice to Fritz.

Shame the Devil is a cartoon without comedy, a satire without bite, a riddle that doesn't provoke much curiosity. The best that can be said of Philip Appleman's novel is that it doesn't take itself seriously, but that doesn't leave much incentive to take it at all. The setting is small-town Indiana and the premise is that two New York con men, Frank and Julian, have stumbled upon an insular community of closet Vikings, men and women descended with undiluted blood from Norse raiders who somehow hove to in the Hoosier state a millennium ago. Frank and Julian arrive just in time for the community's midsummer fair, get into various kinds of trouble, explore a few caves and treasure chambers, solve a few puzzles, fondle a few women. Mr. Appleman decorates this framework with considerable Norse and Persian legendry, astrological mumbo jumbo, runic inscriptions, clumsily expository dialogue that strains to pass as snappy patter and a proliferation of bad baseball metaphors. To his credit, the author maintains a tone of jaunty self-mockery throughout, but tone is not enough to make a feeble performance entertaining.

Shame the Devil reads like a novel written very quickly and without much authorial conviction about the value of the enterprise. Some gifted writers can toss off delightful baubles on those terms. But Philip Appleman is evidently not one of them. Late in the story Julian says: "We've stepped right into a B-movie thriller. Worse than that, even. Into the third verse of some god-awful country music." Worse than that, even. (pp. 13, 26)

David Quammen, "Four Novels," in The New York Times Book Review, *August 9, 1981, pp. 12-13, 26-7.*

DAVID WINN

Philip Appleman has a wonderful idea for a novel. Two academic shills from New York, who make their living counterfeiting doctoral dissertations for Ed.D. candidates, journey to the Midwest in search of lost Viking treasure. What they find in Ash Garden (read Asgard), Indiana, is a mythic and ancient landscape underlying a prosaic and modern one.

Unfortunately, *Shame the Devil* unravels so quickly and so untidily that neither landscape compels belief in the mystic or genuine recognition of the day-to-day. This "wonderful idea" rides the text so hard that the book fails to hang together. What ought to come out of such an original juxtaposition of history and geography is humor and a sense of the unexpected. What the reader gets instead is a kind of "TV movie" view of a small town in some sort of vague but violent political turmoil.

The source of the turmoil is never explained but its effect upon the two shills, Frank and Uncle Julian, is to drive them into hiding in a cave beneath the town where the more obvious aspects of Ash Garden's Precolumbian Norse past are supposed to reside.

One begins to long for the days of American fiction when caves were simply places where treasure was found or people got lost. This cave, however, *stands for something* in the manner of Walker Percy or John Gardner.

Perhaps it would be safest to say that the cave is a kind of repository. But since it is impossible to connect the cave and what it contains to what is going on in the town above, reading the book is a cheat, rather like going through a box of Crackerjacks to find no prize.

There is a kind of hypocrisy at work here and its victim is the reader. The attempt to work in a mythic significance and attach it to the everyday world is so labored and misleading that one searches the prolix and redundant narrative, the blinkered characters and the clumsy shorthand insistence of a basted plot for something overlooked or too subtle to notice at first.

There is no denying Appleman's wealth of invention. In addition to the Norse Pantheon and berserker seafaring legends, there are references to Greek and Mithraic oracular mysteries, the divine cycles of Mazda and Parsi bull worship. These come courtesy of Uncle Julian, a sort of Doctor Zarkoff for the university educated; whose purpose, nevertheless, seems to be that of a running gloss just in case some of us don't catch on.

Uncle Julian is also a compulsive eater of junk food and he consumes innumerable Paydays, Baby Ruths and Hersheys-with-almonds while expounding on the probability of Roman legions bringing vulgar forms of Mithraic worship to Northern Europe. In the meantime his nephew Frank fights off inimical villagers, makes love to a sort of vestal teenager and talks out of the side of his mouth constantly about how confused and suspicious of everyone's motives he is. Since Frank is more or less the focus of the narrative, the book's one compensation may be that the reader does not feel quite so alone.

In fact all the characters conduct themselves with equal incoherence. They are not people so much as they are representatives of either the modern or the ancient realm. If they are of the modern they are unknowing and blighted; if they are of the ancient they seem whole and redeemed. It's as though Travis McGee and Meyer were turned loose among the Medievalists at an Ivy League school.

The problem is, limited as John D. MacDonald's characters are as *literati*, they work as characters in popular fiction because Meyer *does* know the ins and outs of small town economics and fortune making, and McGee is something of a thug, although an attractive and eloquent one. Frank and his Uncle Julian are intellectual pretenses and Appleman appears to know little about life in a small American town.

Some credit ought to be given to American writers of pop-schlock fiction. At least their descriptions of the toxic, industrial, commercial and suburban scenery of this country have the ring of truth.

Whitley Strieber's *The Wolfen* and *The Hunger* come to mind. Not so much as books about werewolf covens and vampires in New York. Rather, as the clever plays they are on the urban dweller's fear of mugging and the pervasive, free floating anxiety about the consequences of anonymous sexual encounters.

Stephen King, whose prose is certainly no *more* graceless than Appleman's, has, in his novel *Carrie,* written with some real effect about the basic experience of high school: getting your hash settled and surviving to take your revenge. . . .

Certainly, most of what Appleman has to say about the covert spread and survival of a suppressed culture is interesting. And no defense of Strieber or King as stylists is intended here. But Appleman, for all his erudition, cannot do what they can do: describe the commonplace circumstances of American life and connect them to its frightening, invisible resonance.

David Winn, in a review of "Shame the Devil," in The American Book Review, *Vol. 3, No. 6, September-October, 1981, p. 15.*

B. WALLENSTEIN

Appleman, the author of three previous collections of poetry and two novels, has [produced in *Darwin's Ark*] a beautiful and perhaps necessary book for our time. His unifying theme is nothing less than the beginnings of the human race and the danger of its extinction seen through the Darwinian lens. However, the many apocalyptic images—and even the direct statements—enlarge the poetry's vision beyond Darwin, who is regarded as both scientist and humanist. This is a poetry of current consciousness: awareness and celebration of life's fragility in the nuclear age. Each of the book's four parts has marvelous epigraphs from Darwin and others. Generally, the poems themselves are carefully structured with lengthy stanzas; but Appleman is not writing deeply sonorous lines or elaborate metaphors, nor is the imagination unbridled or wildly inventive. Rather, the verbal technique is clear and unassuming, with precise, intelligent diction that is informal, at times casual, almost prosy. Nonetheless, amid the meditative, inquiring, warning tones there are expressions of joy and ascending spirit. Least successful, for this reviewer, are the short, light verse poems, **"Darwin's Bestiary"** and the **"Phobias."** But in the longer, richer poems involving history, geology and the poet's protest, we hear a thinking man reading and revering another man from another time, and all that he loved. The book is also a prayer that all such feelings and recognitions may continue.

> *B. Wallenstein, in a review of "Darwin's Ark," in* Choice, *Vol. 22, No. 7, March, 1985, p. 984.*

BETTE CHAMBERS

This beautiful book [*Darwin's Ark*], which can be read in a trice and savored for a lifetime, is a collection of poems, written by a noted Darwin scholar and stunningly illustrated by [Rudy Pozzatti], a colleague in fine arts, both at Indiana University.

Appleman confirms the prescience of William Wordsworth, who said, "The remotest discoveries of the chemist, the botanist, or mineralogist will be as proper objects of the poet's art as any upon which it can be employed."

Here we have several poems touching upon evolutionary scenes where we are unaccustomed to finding them. In **"After the Faith Healings,"** a child dies in the hills of rural Tennessee of an easily treatable disorder, victim of the cruel triumph of blind faith over "satanic" science, crying out his last breath in vain for the evil pills which can readily save him.

Some of these poems are hauntingly disturbing, others uproariously funny. In **"Darwin's Ark,"** from which the book takes its title, taken literally from the biblical account and spoken in the modern idiom, we ride out the Great Flood with Noah, his family, and his incredible menagerie, all part of a nightmare Darwin has one night when his early theological training hilariously crosses synapses with his later scientific views.

Scenes from the animal world, familiar to us, change when seen through Appleman's evolutionary lens. First, lions feast at a fresh kill, followed by lesser predators—the hyenas, then the jackals and buzzards. Suddenly, we are transported to the nighttime streets of a crime-ridden city, where thieves strip a "Rabbit" (a Volkswagen), leaving assorted cheaper parts to lesser thugs to pick clean until only the frame is left for an arson's torch. Thus does man, the ultimate predator, go a progress through the guts of a rabbit.

In **"Mr. Extinction, Meet Ms. Survival,"** we have a universal biography in verse, written as though it were dedicated, as it may have been, to all of us who labor to improve the conditions of life and who are tired unto death with the unrelenting litany of oil spills, dented fenders, half-soles, lapsed subscriptions, subcommittees, late trains, who one day snap....

In **"The Voyage Home,"** the majestic final work of this collection, the author meets the Great Biologist aboard a ship. At the same age that Darwin set sail on the *Beagle*, Appleman

read Darwin's words for the first time aboard a merchant ship. Summarizing the life-affirming philosophy of humanism, the author concludes with a phrase of Darwin's:

> . . . Darwin
> will soon be home, his five-year
> voyage on this little brig
> all over; but when will I
> be home, when will I arrive
> at that special creation: a decent animal?
> The land is failing the horizons, and
> we only know to take the wheel
> and test the ancient strength of human struggle,
> remembering that we ourselves, the wonder
> and glory of the universe, bear
> in our lordly bones the indelible stamp
> of our lowly origins.

> *Bette Chambers, in a review of "Darwin's Ark," in* The Humanist, *Vol. 45, No. 2, March-April, 1985, p. 37.*

DANIELA GIOSEFFI

Aesthetically designed as an antidote to apocalypse, Philip Appleman's fourth and best collection of poetry [*Darwin's Ark*] is an elixir for the anxiety of nuclear end, full of lyric wit and insight. Appleman begins with a powerful poem, **"The Skeleton of Dreams,"** in which he quotes the master of evolution, Darwin on whose works he is an expert. "When a species has vanished from the face of the earth, the same form never reappears." He goes on in his own Yeatsian-Midwestern American style, ". . . so after our million years / of inventing a thumb and a cortex, / and after the long pain of writing our clumsy epic, / we know we are mortal as mammoths, / we know the last lines of our poem; / And somewhere in curving space / beyond our constellations, / nebulae burn in their universal law; / nothing out there ever knew / that on one sky-blue planet / we dreamed that terrible dream. / Blazing along through black nothing / to nowhere at all, Mastodons of heaven / the stars do not need our small ruin." The poet, who has edited definitive editions of Darwin and Malthus for Norton, traverses all of Earth from her muddy fields out into her galaxy, with verse anyone can appreciate and find solace in. Wittily, he warns, telling of **"The Booby and the Noddy,"** who are two birds "so relaxed . . . that survival on this planet seemed none of their concern." Extinct, they appear in a Darwinian bestiary full of the charm and survival wisdom of the rabbit, ant, elephant, or cockroach. Appleman's epic journey takes him "slouching toward Tokyo" to the death of Hiroshima, with terrible irony, where at last he asks, "When will I / arrive at that special creation: a decent animal?" Appleman's ark brings us full circle back to our own private conscience with all the gentle wisdom of a Darwinian sensibility. Poets like this one offer hope that we might yet, in some inch of evolutionary time—see the light and save the planet and all her species from extinction.

> *Daniela Gioseffi, in a review of "Darwin's Ark," in* The Small Press Review, *Vol. 18, No. 4, April, 1986, p. 7.*

John (Simmons) Barth

1930-

American novelist, short story writer, and essayist.

Barth is an eminent practitioner and theoretician of postmodernist fiction, a movement in which literary works are often interpreted as studies of how fiction is created and how reader and text interact. Barth's approach to writing derives from his belief that the narrative possibilities of the traditional novel have been exhausted. In "The Literature of Exhaustion," an essay first published in the *Atlantic Monthly* in 1967, he describes the contemporary experimental writer, who "confronts an intellectual dead end and employs it against itself to accomplish new human work." Rather than attempt to convey the experience of reality, Barth investigates authorial imagination in "novels which imitate the form of the Novel, by an author who imitates the role of the Author." Recurring features of Barth's work include black humor, bawdy wordplay, vivid imagery, labyrinthine plots, blurring of past and present, and the often farcical use of mythical and historical characters. Throughout his fiction, Barth is primarily concerned with the question of whether individuals can transcend the innate absurdity of human existence.

While an undergraduate at Johns Hopkins University, Barth studied such classic Oriental tales as *The Legend of Story* and *The Arabian Nights,* which influenced his interest in literature as well as his later writing. Barth's subsequent career as an English professor also plays an important role in his fiction; many of his books are set in universities and contain allusions to works of literature. Although Barth's early novels were not commercially successful, they garnered him an elite readership of scholars and college students. His first two novels, *The Floating Opera* (1956) and *The End of the Road* (1958), realistically explore comic and tragic dimensions of philosophical questions related to nihilism. *The Floating Opera* is the story of Todd Andrew, a lawyer and bachelor who concludes that since no action has inherent worth, he will commit suicide. He fails, however, and later realizes that if there is no ultimate reason to continue living, there is also no final justification to end one's life. The ribald humor and philosophical digressions of this novel prompted comparisons to Laurence Sterne's *Tristram Shandy*. In *The End of the Road,* protagonist Jacob Horner literally becomes immobilized by what Barth terms "cosmopsis, the cosmic view," a condition that results in indecision when one is faced with an overabundance of "desirable choices." After being ordered by a psychiatrist to take a teaching job at a small college, Horner becomes entangled in conflict with Joe Morgan, a fellow instructor and his compulsive opposite, with whom he competes for mental and sexual dominance over Joe's wife, Rennie. When Rennie becomes pregnant, Horner abandons his indecision and impulsively arranges for her illegal abortion, from which she dies. As the novel concludes, Horner reverts to his paralyzed condition. Jerry Bryant observed: "What [Barth] shows in *The End of the Road* is the profound difficulty of getting along after we have lost our confidence in the objective absolute, and our tendency to find relief either in the abandonment of all guides or the substitution of objective values with other kinds of values just as absolute."

© Jerry Bauer

Barth's next novel, *The Sot-Weed Factor* (1960), evidences his growing preference for fantasy, history, myth, and self-reflexive narrative. *The Sot-Weed Factor* is a pastiche in which Barth parodies the Gothic and picaresque traditions by blending history, fiction, and legend to relate the passage from innocence to depravity of Ebenezer Cooke, Poet Laureate of the colony of Maryland during the seventeenth century. A complex, epic work with several subplots, *The Sot-Weed Factor* secured Barth's reputation among literary critics and scholars and elicited favorable comparisons to such works as Henry Fielding's *Tom Jones,* Voltaire's *Candide,* and Miguel de Cervantes's *Don Quixote*. Leslie Fiedler deemed *The Sot-Weed Factor* "closer to the 'Great American Novel' than any other book of the last decade," and Richard Kostelanetz praised it as "one of the greatest works of fiction of our time."

Barth achieved widespread critical and commercial success with *Giles Goat-Boy; or, The Revised New Syllabus* (1966), a mythical and allegorical novel reflecting his attempt to write what he termed a "souped-up Bible" or "comic Old Testament." In this intricate work, Barth posits a modern university divided into two opposed campuses as a metaphor for the cold war situation of the 1950s and early 1960s. Barth frames his story with several self-reflexive narratives in which he addresses political, religious, literary, and philosophical issues while detailing the life and teachings of George Giles, a messiah figure possibly born of a computer and a human mother who will bring a redeemed consciousness to the world in the form of a Revised New Syllabus. Although Giles becomes Grand Tutor of the University and discovers the essential oneness of all existence, he is ultimately renounced. Richard Poirier commented: ''More than merely playing literary tricks and games [in *Giles Goat-Boy,* Barth] is really questioning the stability of what we take to be natural and obvious in the political, physical, and sexual organizations of life. The implication is that the human imagination, out of which all of these have issued, is impossibly entangled in its own creations.''

Barth's preoccupation with mythology continues throughout his next two works, *Lost in the Funhouse: Fiction for Print, Tape, Live Voice* (1968) and *Chimera* (1972). These volumes of short fiction are often considered among his most experimental works. A montage of fourteen pieces, *Lost in the Funhouse* evinces Barth's search for alternatives to conventional writing through his use of diverse styles and his exploration of the creative process. The stories in this volume portray characters who experience intellectual and spiritual disorientation in a seemingly arbitrary world. In *Chimera,* for which he received a National Book Award, Barth creates three interlinked novellas depicting mythic heroes in the process of philosophical reorientation, and he reinterprets Arabic, Greek, and Roman legends to demonstrate how myth permeates everyday life. *LETTERS* (1979) recapitulates Barth's literary career by juxtaposing letters exchanged between himself and characters from his previous works. This novel represents Barth's attempt to write sequels for each of his books, to resurrect the epistolary novel, and to rewrite American history through allusions to literary, local, and national politics. Benjamin DeMott noted: ''Time and again in *LETTERS* [Barth] invites his reader to ponder the present status of the idea of the real and the unreal, present thinking about the arbitrariness of signs, present critiques of naive realisms, scientific and otherwise. Time and again his narrative becomes an instrument for renewing comprehension of the universal human enclosure in fictions novelists never made—the truth, that is, 'that our concepts, categories, and classifications are ours, not the World's.' ''

In *Sabbatical: A Romance* (1982), Barth returns to conventional realistic narrative while adding a metafictional twist by depicting two characters who are in the process of writing the book as the reader peruses it. During a cruise on Chesapeake Bay, protagonists Fenwick Turner, a former officer for the United States Central Intelligence Agency, and Susan Seckler, an English professor, debate the correct way to tell the story of their journey and the question of whether or not to bring a child into a world threatened by nuclear destruction. *The Tidewater Tales* (1987), like *Sabbatical,* features two narrator-protagonists who sail Chesapeake Bay while discussing literary theory, procreation, sailing, and the CIA. Ominous events in the world of the novel provoke the characters to retell such stories as *The Odyssey, Don Quixote, The Arabian Nights,* and *The Adventures of Huckleberry Finn.* John W. Aldridge called *The Tidewater Tales* ''the richest, most ebullient and technically daring of any [novel Barth] has hitherto written.'' Barth has also published *The Friday Book; or, Book-Titles Should Be Straightforward and Subtitles Avoided: Essays and Other Nonfiction* (1984), a collection of writings on his own work and literary theory.

(See also *CLC,* Vols. 1, 2, 3, 5, 7, 9, 10, 14, 27; *Contemporary Authors,* Vols. 1-4, rev. ed.; *Contemporary Authors New Re-* *vision Series,* Vols. 5, 23; *Contemporary Authors Bibliographical Series,* Vol. 1; and *Dictionary of Literary Biography,* Vol. 2.)

JAC THARPE

Barth is the completely intellectual comedian. He makes comedy of all things through the simple method of observing inconsistency, limitation, relativity, and paradox. Things are somewhere between the ridiculous and the hilarious; exactly where depends on the value generally assigned to these same things in the everyday world. They must eventually fall into places determined by their ultimate valuelessness and uselessness. The universe itself is included among the things about which the judgment is made, whether the universe is an entity by itself with its conglomerate of laws and probabilities or is merely a conglomerate of separate existences such as people and things. (p. 111)

One who is determined to avoid moralism has to be careful about what he takes seriously. If he has concluded that nothing has intrinsic value and has also decided to laugh because of that realization, he must avoid taking anything seriously. No man is more a victim of the paradox paradigm than the man who sees the paradigm. One of Barth's reactions to the situation is to include himself in his fiction. If he writes of the whole universe, he can think of himself as a powerful linguistic magician in that universe, who is a part of the comedy. If he creates universes, he may as well be a creator, a deity. He can possibly then write fictions about created universes in which the creator appears, as he does in no other universe we know. In this self-enclosed situation, finite but unbounded, the creator of the paradox is the incarnation of the paradox. Barth as-ifs Barth.

Yet a major difficulty exists. A self-contained universe makes neither more nor less sense than an infinite universe with or without a deity. The last paradox is never resolved, and the last truth is never revealed. In effect, finally, one returns to his starting point. Here, from some point of view, he merely writes. In Barth's case, the writing is of what is.

Barth writes a combination of the human comedy and the divine comedy, well aware of Balzac's use of the first term and Dante's use of the second. The result of the combination is a description of the human condition with no regard to the divine. The myths have lost their value. One can at best do no more than compose his own set of myths. Comedy, then, is an attempt to escape to freedom from realizations, intellectualization, and awareness. To that point, Barth has gone; and under the circumstances, the act of creating comedy is making an ethic of a metaphysics. If one concludes that freedom lies only in a deliberately comic view of things, he will simply indulge in comedy. Comedy will *be* his activity.

Barth's genius lies in his awareness of magnificent ironies and his ability to dramatize paradox. He is able even to suggest that, since the universe operates consistently on paradox, the universe may to that extent and in that respect actually be rational instead of absurd. The right approach to such a universe would be an appreciation of its paradoxes; which amounts to developing a transcendentalist view, cosmophily instead of cosmopsis, with all the ironies implied in the tortured misuse of "transcendentalism." The result is *farce splendide*. Outdo the universe with laughter and enthusiasm, realizing that in fact the universe seems out to get you and, with despair and death as methods, will get you. But you can laugh hilariously, and even genuinely, while you are being garroted.

Barth reveals, throughout his work, that he has found it difficult to come to such a conclusion as cosmophily suggests. What he has finally done is say that, since human life exists, its very existence, with all the mysteries and mistakes, is all the significance there is. This realization is all that we know, if not all we need to know or wish we knew, though the awareness does not mean that resignation is good. But the dark of the mystery is impenetrable and will remain so. What is so very absurd among all the absurdities is that the mystery should be such that the yearning and anguished human mind should both find the mystery impenetrable and conclude that it must remain so, since the mind cannot conclude that a power—deity or demon—exists that will provide significance. (pp. 113-15)

Barth recognizes that he engages in an impossible enterprise when he tries to analyze such matters as human motives, activities, character, and mind. Answers do not exist. Nothing in the realm of human thought provides an answer to a practical question—as Ebenezer [the protagonist of *The Sot-Weed Factor*] discovers when he needs to wipe himself—neither philosophy, nor the sciences, nor literature. When the questions are put to the universe, man has done his job—and done it hopelessly, because the universe will supply no answers.

Barth writes in and of a world in which people must face all the big problems for which no explanation exists. His solution to this problem is to create a body of art that uses the technique of language to metaphorize—to put the ultimate reality off where it will bother nobody. Since we cannot find out what reality is, we shall simply create one to serve. Ordinarily, the result of this process was either myth or ideology. In Barth's case, it is to create a world of fiction, not a fictional world. (pp. 115-16)

Unfortunately, the artist of words in a universe that uses language and the printed word is bounded by his medium or his media. The most one can do is use a technique and also comment on the technique. One could engage in that process wherein the artist uses the technique subtly and leaves it to the chance perception of others; but at the point that Barth has reached, a part of being the artist is that one should also gloss his own content. Language, finally a limited vehicle at its best, must yield all it contains and express all potential.

Presumably, it is because Barth finds language ultimately deficient for the artist's purposes that he tries to develop such multimedia as those mentioned in the preface to *Lost in the Funhouse*. He must try to escape the bounds of language. But Barth eventually finds silence at the heart of language. The discovery reveals a secret—and that is pleasant—but the truth itself is very unpleasant.

Ultimately, Barth says nothing—positively. There is nothing positive to say. No truth to tell. All one can do is tell the story. By implication, one says a very great deal, of course, about all that need not be said. But it is all negative. A statement of the human condition is an outline of black upon gray. But an infinite number of words in an infinite number of combinations is required to make that statement. The Book of the Decaying and Dead, if it is to be accurate, ought to record the formation and dissolution of every cell. In a wry version of the idea, Barth writes then the library of Babel that Borges describes.

The knowledge that Barth's characters acquire is a terrifying awareness of the heart of darkness. **"Night-Sea Journey"** dramatizes the floundering swim through that bounded flux in one elaborate metaphor that symbolically includes all the basic metaphors of metaphysics—what Stephen Pepper called "world hypotheses." One of the main horrors in Barth's funhouse is the realization that Sphincter's law is a riddle, no matter how much one knows of both riddle and law. Proctoscopy recapitulates hagiography. What is becomes a symbol for what might be. (pp. 116-17)

Jac Tharpe, in his John Barth: The Comic Sublimity of Paradox, *Southern Illinois University Press, 1974, 133 p.*

JEROME KLINKOWITZ

"In a sense, I am Jacob Horner," proclaims the narrator of John Barth's second novel, *The End of the Road* (1958). Sentenced to a self-consciously absurdist therapy of teaching college English, Barth's narrator reminds us of the dispensation under which Barth himself felt he must write. It was 1958—an era which, as Barth saw it, had rejected the Cartesian definition of ego so central to traditional novelistic design. A hero could no longer speak with confidence and coherence and so define himself, since under contemporary philosophical pressure the old *cogito, ergo sum* had become a farcically painful lie.

The End of the Road and Barth's first novel, *The Floating Opera* (1956), were written in the same burst of creative energy during the mid-fifties, when the promise of commercial publication drove Barth to a frenzy of literary production he has not since matched. That first work was not to have been a novel at all, but "a philosophical minstrel show," as Barth described it, not wanting to write a novel yet hoping to make it "a work of literature" nevertheless. Both books turned out to be rather conventional novels in the then-popular style of André Malraux, Albert Camus, and other such reflective writers. Each was heavily philosophical, and the first brushed so closely with absolute nihilism that its original publishers insisted on a different, more humanistically acceptable, ending. (Barth's preferred text is found in the revised and restored edition published by Doubleday in 1967.) But these initial works won Barth the beginnings of a substantial following: not among the reading public (less than 5,000 copies of the two books are estimated to have been sold), but with John Barth's colleagues in the profession of English. A knowledge of literary and philosophical tradition complemented by the experience of teaching were the qualifications of Barth's ideal reader.

Barth's eloquent justification of his technique appeared in his article **"The Literature of Exhaustion,"** published in the *Atlantic* in 1967. A sequel, called **"The Literature of Replenishment,"** for the same magazine's January 1980 issue added further commentary pertinent to his works of the intervening years (*Lost in the Funhouse: Fiction for Print, Tape, Live Voice*, 1967; *Chimera*, 1972; and *Letters: A Novel*, 1979). Barth explained that any educated writer in this day and age was faced with "the used-upness of certain forms or exhaustion of certain possibilities" and that this is "by no means necessarily a cause for despair."

In *The Sot-Weed Factor* and *Giles Goat-Boy,* Barth employed various eighteenth-century conventions to make twentieth-century artistic statements. In the former, the secret journal of a character named Henry Burlingame is framed within the narrative adventures of the poet, Ebenezer Cooke; and all the familiar Fieldingesque techniques, so tedious in the hands of anyone but their inventor, are interesting and entertaining because they must be read, not as the product of a third-rate contemporary, but as the studied parody by a brilliant scholar of Fielding's art. In similar manner *Giles Goat-Boy* takes what it can from Swift, substituting an allegory of mid-twentieth-century academic politics as a comment on the state of the world. As technique, the transpositions from Fielding and Swift are flawless; but as Robert Garis and others have complained, they are only technique, offering no new perspective at all and telling readers nothing they do not already know. *Lost in the Funhouse* and *Chimera* are more deliberate investigations of narrative itself, including a cutout Moebius strip, a series of quotations successively swallowed up by the necessary punctuation marks, a story which narrates its own inception and dissolution, and various retellings of ancient myths. *Letters* functions as a coda to Barth's entire literary career so far, for its seven epistolary authors who exchange correspondence among themselves are either characters from the previous six books or John Barth himself and some of his newly created characters.

This seven-book canon, no small achievement for a writer born in 1931, would be the perfect index of a literary age except for one fact, which its author keeps repeating in his influential essays: he does not sympathize with the spirit of his times. **"The Literature of Exhaustion"** opens with a playfully sarcastic dismissal of a style of work then being produced by a young writer-publisher outside the conservative academic community, Dick Higgins of Something Else Press. To illustrate this style, Barth includes a good sample (but not all properly attributed to their best practitioners) of literary, theatrical, musical, and artistic work unlike his and his academic colleagues' own, including the assemblage novels of Robert Filliou, the Happenings of Allen Kaprow, the music of John Cage, and the pop art of Robert Rauschenberg. All were whimsically degraded as lacking seriousness, discipline, and achievement of stable form, as if these were the prime requisites of artistic success—which Barth indeed believed they were. "The New York Correspondence School of Literature," as he collectively referred to them, was capable of producing interesting ideas for beer-drinking conversation, but was incapable of producing great art.

What Barth overlooked, and what he overlooked more deliberately in his sequel essay in 1980 [**"The Literature of Replenishment"**], was that the steady effacement of represented action from works of art in all disciplines—whether literary, dramatic, musical, or graphic—established the esthetic of the twentieth century. This esthetic is traced most easily in the work of artists Barth dismisses as impertinent to his own "high art." (pp. 409-10)

[In **"The Literature of Replenishment"**], Barth recalled that his first essay was conceived and written on a university campus beseiged by the challenging forces of demonstrating students and tear-gassing police. It appears that he himself was quite uncomfortable in these circumstances, which others saw as genuinely revolutionary in terms of both curricular and esthetic change. The key to Barth's personal esthetic is in that original essay written during the hectic days of the sixties, where he states his admiration for writers atypical of those times—that is, for writers who replace the representation of one action (an Aristotelian mimesis of behavior within the social world) with another: the act of writing a novel. Each of his examples, which include conventionally modernist works by Nabokov, Beckett,

and Borges, is similar to his own works, in that each is essentially a mimesis of literature. "Novels which imitate the form of the Novel, by an author who imitates the role of the Author" are the books which Barth appreciates and writes himself.

Literary works which suspend the suspension of disbelief, which in anti-Aristotelian fashion include the art of writing by the author and the act of reading by the reader as integral parts of their esthetic, are excluded from Barth's pantheon. He prefers fictions which represent, fictions whose events are metaphors for something else, not something in themselves. For Barth, fiction should forever be an imitation of an action, and not an action in itself. (pp. 410-11)

Jerome Klinkowitz, "John Barth Reconsidered," in Partisan Review, Vol. XLIX, No. 3, 1982, pp. 407-11.

MALCOLM BRADBURY

Pynchon's massive enterprise has its parallels in other American novels—most notably in the work of William Gaddis, whose *The Recognitions* (1955) was a remarkable exploration of fiction and forgery, and whose second novel *JR* (1976) is an encyclopedic novel about modern money, with a cybernetic theme. But other potent versions of the postmodernist impulse existed, especially in the novel of self-conscious fictionality, the novel that exposed the novelist as artificer and sought to explicate the form's inherent *as if*. Of the writers who have exemplified this nominalist tendency and chosen to introduce the reader into the workshop of composition, John Barth, a novelist who has long insisted on his dissent from mimetic realism ('What the hell, reality is a nice place to visit but you wouldn't want to live there, and literature never did, very long,' he once said), is central. His earlier novels, *The Floating Opera* (1956) and *The End of the Road* (1958), are comedies of existential absurdity. The first treats a suicidal hero from the point when he decides, the world being meaningless, to commit suicide, to that at which he decides, the world being meaningless, to stay alive ('There is, then, no "reason" for living (or suicide)'); the second introduces a first-person but personless hero ('In a sense, I am Jacob Horner,' he begins), a weatherless man without feeling or sense of purpose who, after being given 'mythotherapy', goes to teach grammar in a college, and finds his problems summed up in the contrast between 'descriptive' and 'prescriptive' grammar. Drawn into adultery with a colleague's wife, which ends in a bungled abortion and her death, he reverts to weatherlessness, and the black comedy ends as he is directed to the railroad terminal, an apt place for an ending to occur. These books express the feeling that there is no significant text in the world, and they thus lead the way to Barth's fiction of the Sixties, which went on joyously to celebrate textuality and intertextuality. *The Sotweed Factor* is a marvellous exercise in pastiche, a pseudo-history of Barth's local domain of Maryland, where most of his fiction is set, telling the mock-story of its founding poet Ebenezer Cooke through the romping mannerisms of the novelists of the eighteenth century. *Giles Goat-Boy* comes closer to Pynchon's themes; it is a parody myth for modern times, set on the campus of the modern cosmos, a global semi-allegory about competing computers with alternative political programmes, and about life's other generic divisions: mind and body, human and animal, male and female. Appropriately divided into 'reels' and 'tapes', it takes cybernetic form, calling up structures of traditional myth to introduce the fractures and intertextual allusions that the ethically weakened modern writer, conscious of writing his writing, feels compelled to introduce into his story.

Barth's 'literature of exhaustion' was evolving; his fictions showed signs of spiralling round themselves, turning into re-writings of prior rewritings, generating intertextual allusions not just to the works of other authors but to the author's own. Story arrests, tales within tales, techniques for asserting and withdrawing stylistic authenticity, enquiries into the history of narrative, form the method, with at the centre a bewildered author. *Lost in the Funhouse* is founded on the Möbius strip, and is a mixed group of items for print, tape, and live voice, open to multiple re-fashioning. The book attempts a radical redisposition of the materials of authorship; of the author himself, presented as lost in the funhouse of his own creations, fragmenting, subdividing, losing order and seriality, moving through various textual and verbal systems to find himself as a speaker. The three novellas of *Chimera* (1972) then return to narrative's origins, in that founding story of stories, *The 1001* (or *Arabian*) *Nights*, and the Greek myths of Perseus and Bellerophon. The opening tale, the **"Dunyazadiad"**, updates the story of the most successful of all story-tellers, Scheherazade, who, by endlessly generating plots, counterplots, and narrative suspense, saved her own life. Barth himself appears in the story as a genie, only to confess his own lostness: 'I've quit reading and writing; I've lost track of who I am; my name's just a bundle of letters; so's the whole body of literature: strings of letters and empty spaces, like a code I've lost the key to.' The chimera of *Chimera* is the elusive reality at the heart of fiction—that which justifies its bewildering array of devices, multiplication of narrators, tales-within-tales, its ciphers, hieroglyphs, letters and alphabets, mazes and labyrinths, writings and rewritings, its approaches, suspenses, deferrals, and consummations. Indeed Barth uses the analogy between foreplay, deferral, and consummation in sexuality and in fiction to spiral towards the narrative heart, to discover that 'the key to the treasure is the treasure', the being of the story the meaning of the story; fictional being is being, discourse about realities a reality.

Chimera postulates many more stories than it tells, including a failed or blocked book called *Numbers* and another called *Letters*. In 1979 appeared a novel called *Letters,* written by but also to an author, John Barth. Functioning according to a complex alphabetical code, it sought over 772 pages to put together, through epistolary means, the central characters of all Barth's previous books and stories. Breaking down the discreteness of the fictions Barth had already written, it took the form of a self-disfiguring momument, while revealing that there was a monument there to disfigure, the existence of his own writings. But it also reached back through the stock of the Anglo-American tradition of the novel as such, introducing a new muse, Germaine Pitt, Lady Amherst, a visitor from the literary circles of Britain. The path is towards realism, though Lady Amherst disappoints by declaring: 'I am *not* the Great Tradition! I am *not* the ageing Muse of the Realistic Novel!'; as might many a contemporary British writer. Since then, Barth has offered us *Sabbatical* (1982), another work of exposed piping and service-ducts, narrative Beaubourg, equipped with footnotes and *two* assumed authors, one male and one female. A story of sea-voyaging and sea-mysteries, again set off Maryland, it goes back to the sea-story origins of narrative—origins that have been particularly important for the development of American fiction. *Sabbatical* is Barth's attempt at a modern version of the American romance novel, drawing on its twin traditions of terror and sentimentality. Twins are everywhere, even down

to the twin authors, representing in their marriage the generative source of creativity. (pp. 179-82)

Malcolm Bradbury, "Postmoderns and Others: The 1960s and 1970s," in his The Modern American Novel, Oxford University Press, Oxford, 1983, pp. 156-86.

STEVEN M. BELL

Self-consciousness in prose fiction—metafiction—was not invented yesterday. John Barth, one of its champions in America, himself readily concedes its unoriginality, albeit hyperbolically and with tongue-in-cheek, as is his nature. "Self-conscious, vertiginously arch, fashionably solipsistic, unoriginal—in fact a convention of twentieth-century literature. Another story about a writer writing a story!" What such playful exaggeration does effectively point out is that, while the self-consciousness of much of today's prose fiction does not itself break new ground in the field of literature, in the history of man (which is nothing if not a history of consciousness), self-consciousness, specifically linguistic (and literary) self-consciousness, has never been so prevalent as in the present century: it has engulfed not only literature, but also history, philosophy, and the social or human sciences. (p. 84)

In what follows I discuss Barth's *Lost in the Funhouse* (1968) in the context of this general, twentieth-century heightening of linguistic self-consciousness. As I read it, *Lost in the Funhouse*—Barth's fifth book and only collection of "short stories" to date—affirms "play" as a solution to existential anguish and doubt (a very Nietzschian notion), and posits writing (and indirectly reading) as a possible escape from madness. It seems unwittingly, and so all the more significantly, to embody Derrida's "program" for "the end of the book and the beginning of writing." Seen in this light, *Lost in the Funhouse* reflects the notion of language/written discourse as the play of infinite substitutions within the closure of finite possibilities, and it foregrounds the artist's never-ending search for new and better ways to speak the unspeakable, to write what has already been written, but has somehow never been gotten quite right. I would suggest, furthermore, that the assumptions underlying the trajectory Barth follows through the *Lost in the Funhouse* pieces undercuts his **"The Literature of Exhaustion"** essay of 1967, their theoretical counterpart. That is the stories as collected *already* embody and in essence anticipate the theoretical formulations only recently recorded by Barth in his 1980 re-writing of the "exhaustion" essay, **"The Literature of Replenishment"**; it is in the latter that Barth essays the idea of literature as a series of almost repetitions or substitutions, of "virtually infinite" play within a "doubtless finite" system, in Barth's own words, and of the movement of literature—at all levels and in all senses, by allegorical analogy—as thus circuitous, or rather spiral-like. This play, and this spiral-like movement, function not only at the level of the individual book—*Lost in the Funhouse* in this case—but also at the level of Barth's oeuvre to date, and in turn for the whole of Western literature; as such, the play in *Lost in the Funhouse* is as a metaphor or microcosm of the Barthian oeuvre, and ultimately of the history of Western literature itself. (p. 85)

There are of course innumerable ways to categorize or group the various stories. One which deserves some attention is found in the . . . **"Author's Note."** In it Barth explains that not all of the stories were composed "expressly for print," and he proceeds to elaborate on their different, "ideal media of presentation." These prefatory remarks are clearly, if taken seriously, attempts at radical innovation of the narrative medium and of narrative technique; but as Barth suggests, anticipating his critics, they easily come off as pretentious. It is in fact difficult to decide to what degree Barth wants to be taken seriously in the matter, for the **"Author's Note"** and the **"Seven Additional Author's Notes"** represent a virtuoso performance in violating the expectations a particular text induces in its readers, by constantly mocking itself, and frustrating any possibility of proceeding solemnly. The voice that speaks in the "Note" is just one more of the roles Barth is playing, one more of the masks he dons. Toward the end of his exposition of the different ideal media of presentation, Barth, through exaggeration ad absurdum, pulls the rug out from under himself, parodies himself, and puts everything he has just said in doubt: "'Title' makes somewhat separate but equally valid senses in several media: print, monophonic recorded authorial voice, stereophonic ditto in dialogue with itself, live authorial voice, live ditto in dialogue with monophonic ditto aforementioned, and live ditto interlocutory with stereophonic et cetera, my own preference; it's been 'done' in all six." After ending the first "Note" with "on with the story," the hyperbole and the undercutting continue: we promptly turn the page and find **"Seven Additional Author's Notes"**; only to feel deceived still again upon reading that "the 'Note' means in good faith exactly what it says."

There is indeed a certain movement or progression perceived as one moves through the pieces in *Lost in the Funhouse,* and there are indications that it is in some respects circular. But more important, *Lost in the Funhouse* does not come full circle, and it certainly does not represent a closure. Being a collection of autonomous units, and not exclusively (as in the novel) a "whole" which corresponds directly to the covers of a book, *Lost in the Funhouse* exemplifies well Maurice Blanchot's contention that the "work" of a particular writer can never correspond to a single book. Only the author's death, Blanchot insists, can put an end to the serious and truly dedicated writer's work, to a work that continues from one book to the next, and ends due to circumstances generally beyond the writer's control; it is never finished. The "book" as Blanchot would have it, and as *Lost in the Funhouse* demonstrates, fixes or freezes illusorily what is in actuality a continuous and never-ending process.

If we look to certain formal and technical considerations—what Barth at one point calls the "vehicle" of a particular fiction—the various compositions in *Lost in the Funhouse* can be loosely but meaningfully categorized into three groups: allegories, self-referential fictions, and myths rewritten. Allegory predominates toward the beginning of the collection ("**Night-Sea Journey**," "**Petition**," "**Lost in the Funhouse**"), self-reference or involution in the middle ("**Autobiography**," "**Title**," "**Life-Story**"), and mythical elements in the book's final third ("**Echo**," "**Glossolalia**," "**Menelaiad**," "**Anonymiad**"). These three formal devices are not of course mutually exclusive; all of them are present to some degree in most of the stories, and although the term "formal device" or "vehicle" is not very precise, the generalization is helpful and by and large valid. Such a grouping of the stories leads to insights not only into *Lost in the Funhouse* and its place in Barth's corpus of literary production, but also is significant as an indirect indication of Barth's ideas about literature and fiction in the broader sense—a central concern in all of his work.

The image of the spiral is again called to mind with regard to the arrangement of the pieces: the concluding stories reject in part the purely self-referential mode predominant in the center pieces; at the same time the allegorical elements—present in most of the stories but especially the opening ones—regain some importance, though mythical ones are the central motif and "vehicle" of the final stories. John Stark sees the spiral image as representative of the diachronic trajectory of Barth's entire oeuvre, but does not comment upon its usefulness with regard to *Lost in the Funhouse.* Its spiralling is just one of the ways in which the **"Frame Tale"**'s Möbius strip is emblematic of the work as a whole: *Lost in the Funhouse,* like the Möbius strip, is not just a circle, but rather a circle with a twist; the book does not circle back upon and close itself so much as it is open-ended, or rather open at both ends. From this point of view, if the book could be said to "close" at all, it would be only (paradoxically) at its center, an artificially static moment (as the present is so fleeting as to be practically nonexistent) in an essentially dynamic process. The movement from allegory, through self-referentiality, to myth which is perceived in *Lost in the Funhouse*—undoubtedly a protracted process for Barth—is frozen, made static, recorded for posterity, and documented with the publication of the collection, which then marks a definable moment in the evolution of the whole of Barth's work as it stands (in progress, never finished) at present. The important role of allegorical patterning in *Giles Goat-Boy* (1966), the last Barth novel published before *Lost in the Funhouse,* is picked up right where it left off in the opening stories. Likewise, the rewriting of myth, the predominant mode of the final stories, is continued in *Chimera* (1972), Barth's next book, while hardly missing a beat. The self-referential pieces then, in this arrangement, are at the center of the "funhouse" in more ways than just the literal, physical one might suggest: they are clearly the collection's most distinctive feature, the ones which most clearly differentiate it from Barth's other texts. The center of *Lost in the Funhouse,* in this view, is a pivot, a "twist" in the spiral which is the linear development of the tales, and in that of Barth's entire oeuvre "in progress," for the former are but a moment in and a metaphor for the latter.

The initial use of allegory seeks out and traces parallels between life and literature, in hopes of finding a role or place for literature in life. The subsequent self-referential pieces correspond most closely to Barth's "exhaustion" essay. "**Title**," the most obvious instance of this, is really a rewriting, a fictionalization of that essay. These central stories mark a vacillation, a certain recognition of and resignation to the supposed exhaustion, and the most truly static moment in the linear, spiralling progression of the book. The rewriting of the myths signals a new direction, a new beginning, an at-least-temporary solution to the crisis, and a leaving behind of pure self-referentiality and self-consciousness, which the voice in "**Title**" comes to "abhor." Most significantly, for my purposes, the turn to myth marks an implicit recognition in Barth of the possibilities for infinite "play," infinite, almost repetitions or substitutions, within a finite system.

The image of the labyrinth, central in the writings of Jorge Luis Borges, is not surprisingly an appropriate metaphor for the path John Barth has followed in his literary labors: he is constantly testing new possible solutions to the maze, retaining what he has found useful, and moving on in new directions. The self-referential pieces at the center of *Lost in the Funhouse,* as Robert Scholes points out, are at times painfully and paralyzingly involuted, but they are in fact only a turn in the spiral, a pivot and a moving on, both in the context of the *Funhouse* collection and the Barthian oeuvre in progress. In spite of the charges of narcissism leveled against him, Barth's artistic trajectory remains one of the most dynamic and refreshing in literature today. Barth is programmatic in his writing, and extremely conscious of his power to shape literary history, wherein lies the greater part of his energy and vitality. What Barth's most outspoken detractors do see however, which his loyal admirers tend to pass over, is the need to question the deeper implications of the artistic self-consciousness so present in all of his work.

One possible explanation for the new predominance of self-consciousness, in Barth's prose fiction and in the humanistic disciplines in general, is the very polemic notion that we are approaching the end of a significant period of Western culture, the "civilization of the book," whose origins are found in the inception of phonetic writing, and which explodes with the coming of the printing press to Renaissance Europe. The "Author's Note" to *Lost in the Funhouse,* with its pretentions of moving beyond the medium of print into the electronic media, some of the more recently developed "extensions of man," echoes unmistakably Marshall McLuhan's thought. (pp. 86-8)

Another possible explanation for the self-conscious artistry in *Lost in the Funhouse,* the one set forth in this essay, is as an affirmation of the Derridean notion of the "play" of written discourse as an exit from and possible solution to existential doubt. We cannot "know," so why not play? Play, for Derrida, is language itself: "Sign will always lead to sign, one substituting the other (playfully, since 'sign' is 'under erasure') as signifier and signified in turn. Indeed, the notion of play is important here. Knowledge is not a systematic tracking down of a truth that is hidden but may be found. It is rather the field 'of free play, that is to say, a field of infinite substitutions in the closure of a finite ensemble'." Such a conceptualization of language repeats several of the implications I have drawn from *Lost in the Funhouse:* for Barth not only language, but analogously the whole of literature can be depicted as the play of infinite formal and technical substitutions in the closure of a finite (theoretically exhaustible) set of possibilities. "One should, if it's worthwhile, repeat the tale. I'll repeat the tale," Barth's narrator in **"Echo"** says, and Barth proceeds to undertake a recasting of Western myth, the very foundation of Western literature.

Following this Derridean train of thought, what Blanchot says about the writer in a generalized sense applies simultaneously to *Lost in the Funhouse* as an individual work, to Barth's entire oeuvre, and to the whole of our literature: "The writer never knows if the work is done. What he has finished in one book, he begins again or destroys in another. . . . the work—the work of art, the literary work—is neither finished nor unfinished: it is. . . . The writer who experiences this void simply believes that the work is unfinished, and he believes that with a little more effort and the luck of some favorable moments, he—and only he—will be able to finish it. And so he sets back to work. But what he wants to finish by himself, remains something interminable, it ties him to an illusory labor." This notion of the whole of literature as a single, unfinished book constantly being written upon is one we also find in Borges, and it is diverting to speculate that it came to Barth through the Argentine master. *Lost in the Funhouse,* just as the whole of Barth's literary production, is like an open book. It is always pushing forward, and yet constantly circling back, not only upon itself, but upon the entire Barthian oeuvre, and the whole of Western literature. It would seem, then, that it is not so much through his experiments with the recorded media that

Barth transcends the printed book, as he may have hoped at one time, but rather a movement away from the closedness and supposed unity of the book in favor of a new concept of literature as "writing" that represents Barth's accomplishment in the *Funhouse.* (p. 89)

> Steven M. Bell, "Literature, Self-Consciousness, and Writing: The Example of Barth's 'Lost in the Funhouse'," in The International Fiction Review, Vol. 11, No. 2, Summer, 1984, pp. 84-9.

DAVID MORRELL

In addition to three forewords and two chunky epigraphs ("Prefatory notes and other introductory material should be avoided wherever possible," Barth drolly remarks), there are 37 pieces about writing, philosophy, and esthetic theory collected [in *The Friday Book*]. Some are not so much essays as introductions to readings or remarks made by Barth while he served on literary panels. These are by definition short and undeveloped, though nonetheless fascinating. Many others, however, are essays—long, elaborate, fully developed, and even more fascinating. With one exception (a 1982 autobiographical **"Some Reasons Why I Tell the Stories I Tell the Way I Tell Them . . ."**), the sections are arranged in the order of their composition, starting in 1960. Each has a headnote, often lengthy, that explains the circumstances under which it was written.

Several pieces have been published before—Barth's much discussed, often misunderstood, hence controversial views on the state of modern fiction, **"The Literature of Exhaustion"** (1967), and what he describes as its corrective companion, **"The Literature of Replenishment"** (1980). A 1964 afterword to the Signet edition of Smollett's *Roderick Random* is included, as is a 1973 Penn State *Festschrift* essay on that frame tale of frame tales, *The Ocean of Story.* There are items from *The New York Times Book Review, The Boston Globe, The Washington Post,* and *Esquire,* not to mention less available sources. Devotees of Barth will be pleased to have these diverse items brought together and to rid their bookshelves of long-since wrinkled, yellowed clippings. Those coming new to Barth will have the pleasure of first acquaintance.

But even Barth's fans will encounter the unfamiliar, for many of these Friday-pieces have never been in print until now. Of these, an essay about Barth's most recent novel, *Sabbatical,* is a special pleasure. Another, **"The Self in Fiction,"** has a dizzyingly-compact two-page backward summary of the history of literature. Yet another, the last and among the most enjoyable, proposes an ingenious, biological (might as well say fertile) explanation for Scheherazade's narrative (sexual?) strategy in saving her life by telling stories to her king for a thousand and one nights. Why that particular number? Barth asks. And what about those three children that she suddenly mentions at the end of the cycle?

These Friday-pieces have the qualities suggested by the metaphoric title of one of them, **"Algebra and Fire."** Skill and knowledge, technique and information—they are the algebra. And the fire is passion—for ideas, for literature, for words.

Whether discussing modernism, postmodernism, semiotics, Homer, Cervantes, Borges, blue crabs or osprey nests, Barth demonstrates an enthusiasm for the life of the mind, a joy in thinking (and in expressing those thoughts) that becomes contagious. Indeed, if you've ever wondered what modernism, postmodernism and semiotics mean, you've found the right place to learn. A reader leaves *The Friday Book* feeling intellectually fuller, verbally more adept, mentally stimulated, with algebra and fire of his own.

> David Morrell, "Algebra and Fire," in Book World—
> The Washington Post, *November 18, 1984, p. 9.*

EDWARD M. WHITE

Fiction writing, John Barth told the 1973 graduating class of Western Maryland College, is "the fine art of turning one's worst experiences into money." As this collection [*The Friday Book*] makes clear, if the fiction writer is as excellent and highly reputed as Barth, he need not stop with his worst experiences. . . . This first nonfiction collection by the most eminent American academic fiction writer must have cleaned out his file drawers of all but his most recent shopping list.

But while the redundancies and uneven quality of the collection must be the despair of every reader, the general level of literary intelligence and personal wit (particularly in the extensive headnotes to the various pieces) is so high that we skip selections at our peril. The assumption behind such a book is both self-indulgent and correct: Almost anything Barth felt seriously enough to write about is important in itself as a historical record of the developing opinions of an important literary intellectual. . . .

Every now and again little unsuspected gems appear in odd places, often as marvelous quotations. Toward the end of the book, in a piece responding to some reviewer's attacks on his last novel, we come across Randell Jarrell's "wonderful definition of the novel—a prose narrative fiction of a certain length that has something wrong with it." At least three different essays give us one of the earliest extant literary fragments, an Egyptian papyrus from about 2000 BC, in which a scribe named Khakheperresenb complains that there is nothing, at such a late date, left to be said: "Would I had phrases that are not known, utterances that are strange, in new language that has not been used, free from repetition, not an utterance which men of old have spoken."

Several themes appear time and again, not always as mere repetitions. The most important of these is represented by Barth's patron saint, Scheherazade, the model of the endlessly fertile storyteller. Using his recurrent academic metaphors, Barth points out that she must indeed publish or perish, at least until the king grants her marriage-tenure (which, the final essay points out, is "the best guarantee of further good production"). Such Oriental tales provide patterns of storytelling, particularly of entwined narrative technique, that have continued to stir the novelist's imagination. Barth is also much taken with God as a fellow novelist, a creator of universes; our reality, he argues, is God's fiction, and not a wholly successful one. What he calls "capital-R Reality" thus turns out to be "a shared fantasy."

The most substantial essay in the book is a thoughtful and creative piece from 1980 entitled **"The Literature of Replenishment."** In it, he defines his "modernist" predecessors and his "post-modernist" contemporaries (including himself) in original ways that help us understand the literature of our century. Other fine pieces emerge from the author's academic experiences at the State University of New York, Buffalo and at Johns Hopkins. Indeed, the individual pieces stand alone quite well, suited to their different purposes. But it seems as if neither the author nor the editors at Putnam's ever imagined

a reader moving through the book sequentially. How else can we explain the same sentences, paragraphs and sources appearing over and over in different essays?

Barth calls the collection *The Friday Book* after the day he reserves for nonfiction in his workshop. The collection shows the powerful analytical thinking of those Fridays, the warm human being behind the monumental fictions and (in passing) the responsible academic career that seems to have gone hand in hand with strong, creative production. Though this is no book, it is a collection of admirable essays by an admirable writer.

> Edward M. White, in a review of "The Friday Book:
> Essays and Other Nonfiction," in Los Angeles Times
> Book Review, *November 18, 1984, p. 3.*

WALTER KENDRICK

[*The Friday Book; or, Book-Titles Should Be Straightforward and Subtitles Avoided: Essays and Other Nonfiction*] is John Barth's first volume of nonfiction. The subtitle is a typical Barthian joke; so are the two short essays, **"The Title of This Book"** and **"The Subtitle of This Book."** . . .

[But most] of these "Friday-pieces" [in *The Friday Book*] are straightforward. . . . The joking, mercifully, is done with by page xx. On the pages with Arabic numbers, Mr. Barth refrains from essaying about essaying or lecturing about lectures. Instead, he takes on those rare things in the Barthian universe, subjects distinct from their own narration. The range of those subjects is broad, including, at their best, a brief autobiography in **"Some Reasons Why I Tell the Stories I Tell the Way I Tell Them Rather Than Some Other Sort of Stories Some Other Way"** . . . and a pair of crankily complementary studies of postmodernism, **"The Literature of Exhaustion"** (1967) and **"The Literature of Replenishment"** (1980). With the exception of **"Some Reasons,"** written recently but placed first, the pieces are ordered chronologically and introduced by new headnotes, so that the reader can follow the course of Mr. Barth's peeves and preoccupations from 1960 till almost the present moment.

He changed his mind about postmodernism, the movement to which he is usually said to belong. In 1967, having just finished the very long novel *Giles Goat-Boy* and plagued by the tear gas-scented turmoil of the State University of New York at Buffalo, where he then taught, Mr. Barth was inclined to gripe about the mood of would-be apocalypse he saw all around him. Such tricky avant-gardisms as unbound, unpaginated novels or novels devoted entirely to the description of objects on a table seemed to him cop-outs rather than steps forward, lazily dodging tradition while claiming to transcend it. He was irked by facile pronouncements that the novel, or the printed word, or Western culture as a whole, was at the point of death. He found the needed corrective in Jorge Luis Borges, whose elegant short fictions Mr. Barth had recently discovered. Borges knew quite well all the paradoxes and dead ends that writing leads to—he did not, however, throw up his hands in easy despair, but rather speculated profoundly on those very problems, absorbed the lessons tradition had to teach him and enriched Western literature with his own work.

This, Mr. Barth felt in 1967, was a task too serious and strenuous for the spoiled-brat young writers then in vogue. Slapping their wrists, he was embarrassed to find his essay reprinted and misread as "one more Death of the Novel or Swan-Song of Literature piece.'' Thirteen years later, in a calmer place (John Hopkins) and time (the relative somnolence of the Carter Administration), he took a new look at postmodernism and produced an essay with, he admits, ''a more tenured, middle-aged air about it.'' Having noted the rise of genuinely enriching postmodernists like Italo Calvino and Gabriel Garcia Márquez, Mr. Barth had grown optimistic enough to propose a synthesis of past and present in an ''ideal postmodernist author'' who ''neither merely repudiates nor merely imitates either his twentieth-century modernist parents or his nineteenth-century premodernist grandparents.'' This author had not yet arrived, but when he came he would bring us replenishment rather than exhaustion.

In the meantime, of course, Mr. Barth himself was far from idle, turning out the experimental short pieces of *Lost in the Funhouse* (1968), the three linked tales of *Chimera* (1972), and the monumental epistolary novel *LETTERS* (1979). Though he does not claim the distinction, these books show Mr. Barth working toward his own goal for the ideal postmodernist, endeavoring to fuse the forms of the past with the awareness of the present. They also show that he had read his Borges well, perhaps too well: especially in *LETTERS,* he strains to accomplish in hundreds of pages what Borges had already done in half a dozen. *LETTERS,* on which Mr. Barth labored for seven years, was a flop with critics and public alike; some of the most amusing moments in *The Friday Book*—in particular **''Speaking of LETTERS''** and **''Revenge''**—were spawned by his unease before the novel's publication and his indignation afterward. His latest novel, *Sabbatical: A Romance* (1982), fared better; but at least one reviewer panned it, inspiring the entertainingly testy **''Prose and Poetry of It All, or, Dippy Verses.''** Mr. Barth should try testiness more often. He has a flair for it.

Mr. Barth's still-debatable standing in the literary tradition will be determined by his fiction, not the slight and sometimes scrappy pieces that make up *The Friday Book.* They portray him in a wide variety of moods, from the rather inflated rhapsody brought on by his beloved Chesapeake Bay to the painstakingly analytical approach he takes to his favorite book of all time, *The Arabian Nights.* They reveal little about his private life, but they have a consistent tone of warm personal enthusiasm that is often beguiling. They are not, as the title of *The Friday Book* concedes, the products of his closest attention or deepest engagement. Their value—not great, but not negligible—resides in the light they cast on the work to which Mr. Barth devotes the other four-fifths of his week.

Walter Kendrick, ''His Peeves and Enthusiasms,'' in The New York Times Book Review, *November 18, 1984, p. 16.*

JEROME KLINKOWITZ

Sabbatical is aptly titled. Supposedly about a vacation retreat during which its man-and-wife narrators, after seven years of a second marriage, will take stock and determine future directions, the novel is in fact a reconstitution of Barth's technique in the wake of his first seven novels. As fiction in an age of criticism, it is productively self-conscious, with none of the awkward posing which marked *Giles Goat-Boy* and the works which followed. Its narrative situation comfortably accommodates talk about fiction writing without turning into self-reflexivity: co-narrator Fenn Turner had tried to be a novelist twenty years before, enrolling himself in the old-fashioned

practices of authorship complete to a year holed up in Europe on a shoestring budget with nothing to do but write. But with nothing to do, nothing has resulted beyond metafiction of the most ill-considered type: ''It was supposed to be about the politics of political journalism,'' Fenn recalls, ''but it had taken an autobiographical turn and was more and more about a frustrated writer and a marriage strained by its first reciprocal adulteries.'' ''The story, bogged down in self-concern, of a story bogged down in self-concern'' is a deliberate parody of the Moebius strip style of fiction which obsessed Barth in his *Lost in the Funhouse* exercises. For *Sabbatical,* however, these memories have a more salutary effect, and his unfinished novel remains ''the story of the story that taught me I couldn't write stories''—in the conventional sense, that is—and therefore it becomes a valid part of the new style of novel being composed before our eyes.

Fenn the failed novelist had become a CIA man, deciding to live a story because he feels he can't write one; but this very life of fiction offers the key to Barth's *Sabbatical.* As Fenn and his young wife, Susan, complete their half-year's cruise through the Caribbean and return to home port in Maryland, they shape their experiences into a story—a necessarily artificial act with its principles of composition and exclusion. By doing so, they recall adventures and fill each other in with their own memories, in the process treating the reader to a fully natural workshop session on narratology. Susan tells the story of her sister's torture and rape; Fenn fills in scenes from his first marriage; the happy circumstances of their meeting are recalled as well, so by novel's end the reader knows everything needed to appreciate their lives. They debate the contrary virtues of realism and fantasy, seeing the need for each. Myths and dreams are introduced for their structural services, and several of Barth's own stories and favorite notions (including the sperm-swim of **''Night-Sea Journey''** and the notion that ''the key to the treasure is the treasure'') are entertained.

What is being created, however, is their own narrative as their lives revolve about it, and in this case the key to the story is the story. As Fenn admires in Cervantes, the road is more comfortable than the inn. And as Susan, a scholar of nineteenth-century American literature and a descendent of Edgar Allan Poe (as Fenn is of Francis Scott Key) can explain, a compellingly interesting story such as *The Narrative of Arthur Gordon Pym* derives its effect from the fact that although the tale itself ends with the character's disappearance into the texture of narrative itself, its very telling testifies to his survival in its transmission. This life of fiction is what Susan and Fenn eventually find for themselves, amid the shambles of abortion, family dissolution, and vexing career decisions. As with *Pym,* ''It is not that the end of the voyage interrupts the writing, but that the interruption of the writing ends the voyage''—and in an endless repetition of the tale, their writing never ends, since they ''begin it at the end and end at the beginning.'' In this formulation, there is no imitation of imitation of reality. The fiction is most clearly and productively itself, making John Barth once more a timely representative of his literary age. (pp. 15-17)

Jerome Klinkowitz, ''John Barth: Fiction in an Age of Criticism,'' in his Literary Subversions: New American Fiction and the Practice of Criticism, *Southern Illinois University Press, 1985, pp. 3-17.*

JOHN W. ALDRIDGE

A remarkable fact about John Barth is his capacity to change, even reverse his creative direction, and this new novel, *The Tidewater Tales,* is a brilliant case in point. (p. 1)

[In] *Sabbatical,* his most recent novel before the present one, something truly remarkable happened. It seemed that Barth in that book had reversed his former advance into neutralizing relativism, which came to a dead-end in *Letters,* and returned to a certain Barthian variety of more or less conventional realism. At least he seemed to have decided which, out of all the possible realities, was the one with which he wished to deal. The result was that the action of the novel develops along a clear narrative line and establishes without ambiguity the situation and character of the two narrator-protagonists, a couple named Fenwick Turner and Susan Seckler who are voyaging aboard their sailboat from Chesapeake Bay to the Caribbean and back. Along the way they become involved in certain nefarious CIA machinations and other sinister and wondrous events. While to be sure the story does contain elements indicating that the familiar temporizing mind of John Barth is still hard at work, they are effectively subordinated to the strong realistic thrust of the narrative and so provide the book with an agreeable controlled complexity instead of burying it beneath the old fog-bank of endless equivocation.

The Tidewater Tales both does and does not mark Barth's further progress toward the clarity of narrative daylight. In fact, taken in terms of its characters and central situation, it so closely resembles *Sabbatical* that it can be considered, if not quite a sequel to that novel, at least a companion volume. Once again the story is told by twin narrator-protagonists, this time Peter and Katherine Sagamore, who are very much like the Secklers and who are also sailing, although their radius is limited to the waterways of the Chesapeake Bay. They too are involved in a marginal way in CIA activities, and they even have a friend, one Frank Talbott, who once wrote a novel about his and his wife's sailing experiences in the Caribbean, a novel that is actually *Sabbatical* with the Talbotts renamed [Fenwick Turner and Susan Seckler]. In that novel Mrs. Seckler has an abortion. In *The Tidewater Tales* Mrs. Talbott has had an abortion but by the end has become happily pregnant, even as Katherine Sagamore, who has had a miscarriage, is also throughout the novel happily pregnant with twins. Her husband, Peter, furthermore, will use the experiences they are having in *The Tidewater Tales* as the materials of a novel to be called, of course, *The Tidewater Tales.*

Peter is a writer of minimalist short stories and has adhered so religiously to the principle that less is more that he is on the verge of creative self-strangulation. But by making use of the massively abundant materials provided by the voyage, he will presumably enjoy replenished vitality as well as a new belief in the principle that much more is, after all, much, much better.

If the sheer bulk of this novel is any indication, Barth seems now to share this belief and to have undergone a similar liberation—in his case, from his former obsession with self-cancelling versions. In his performance here he reminds one of Saul Bellow who, after being strait-jacketed by formal restraints in his first two novels, burst out in *The Adventures of Augie March* into a loose and baggy picaresque saga, an extravagant sprawl of language, and a huge cast of wildly eccentric characters. Barth seems similarly larky and euphoric, gleefully at play in the fields of his own fiction, sporting outrageously with his medium, clearly loving himself as the cre-

ator of all this abundance, and adoring his characters as much as they adore one another.

And in truth, while this is not Barth's most intellectually complex novel, it is without question the richest, most ebullient and technically daring of any he has hitherto written. It is crowded with grand virtuosic effects that seem to have nothing to do with the action except to interrupt it, yet are offered simply because they are such fun.

There are odd excursions into dreams, some of which are uncannily prophetic of the future action. There are encounters with strange exotic people like the beautiful Greek couple who may very well be contemporary incarnations of Odysseus and Nausicaa or like Captain Donald Quicksoat, a contemporary Don Quixote whose adventures, as imagined by Peter Sagamore, occur in the centuries following the end of Cervantes' novel. Scheherazade comes to life to explain why she told her stories for exactly a 1,001 nights and not 62 or 94. The Sagamores carry on conversations with their as yet unborn twins who, as the novel proceeds, grow into fetal characters known by innumerable cutesy names like Fore and Aft, Spit and Image, Toil and Trouble, Fish and Chips and Blam and Blooey. It is all a delightful romp through fantasy, myth, fiction and fact, and it is also a hugely joyous celebration of life.

It would seem on the evidence of this remarkable novel that Barth has finally found his way out of the funhouse and back into the world. Or perhaps he has learned to adjust its mirrors so that they no longer give back endless images or versions of his baffled self but instead reflect the reality he once disdained in all its diversity and richness. (p. 14)

*John W. Aldridge, "John Barth Sets a New Course,"
in* Book World—The Washington Post, *June 7, 1987,
pp. 1, 14.*

RICHARD LEHAN

In *The Tidewater Tales,* the two main characters are named Peter and Katherine Sherritt Sagamore—the latter 8-1/2 months pregnant—who spend the last two weeks of her term cruising Chesapeake Bay in their sailboat "Story," telling stories to—and being told stories by—the people they meet.

Their major preoccupations involve the sea, sex and stories, and the tales we hear are mostly about seamen and semen, navigation and narration, textuality and sexuality. Matters nautical and narrative become entwined, giving Barth's narrators the chance to retell the stories of Odysseus, Don Quixote, Scheherazade, Huck Finn and many more. This aspect of the novel is dominated by Barth's interest in narrative theory and literary criticism, which is the base from which he has long been writing his novels. Barth is an expert at reading not only the lines of our major classical texts but of reading the "spaces" as well, by which I mean the stories in these stories that never get told, or the stories that have the potentiality for being retold or told differently. What he does with the Odysseus story here is truly wondrous.

Given the nature of such pure literariness, we have narrative worlds within worlds in *The Tidewater Tales:* Chesapeake Bay supplies the modern equivalent of the Aegean Sea, holds also Cervantes' Cave of Montesinos, is subject to "Tempest" tempests and contains modern swimmers who find their equivalent in a three-act drama involving the story of sperm and ovum swimming toward fertilization. This is a world of doubling. Peter and Katherine meet Theodoros and Diana Dmetrikakis, who give us a radically revised version of the Odysseus story; meet a modern Don Quixote who finds a modern Lady Belerma and her daughter; and meet also Fenwick Turner and Susan Seckler, who (renamed) come sailing into the action from *Sabbatical.*

All the major characters are doubles who in turn double themselves in a novel about doubling, ending with Katherine giving birth to (you guessed it!) twins. . . .

The Tidewater Tales is 624 pages, 364,000 words by my calculation, 1.8 miles long from start to finish. In a novel almost two miles long, Barth's literary self-consciousness is sometimes too much. Less would have been More. The novel becomes a giant literary game, the emphasis upon intertextuality or the relationship of one story to another. The idea of reality simply becomes another form of representation; fictionality is totalized as we imagine ourselves into being and become the fictions that we imagine.

The narrative functions on two levels—a foreground and a background—the former made up of the people Peter and Kate meet on their sea journey, the latter the classical stories their lives replicate. Since this narrative is replete with Adam and Eve, it must include evil, which is embodied by the workings of the CIA and KGB. Here what is "real" is equally problematic, especially when we encounter double and triple agents, in a world where the capacity for fictionalizing is as inexhaustible as that of Barth's narrators, albeit less redemptive because we are being told the wrong kind of stories. (Much of the action here, as in *Sabbatical* is based on newspaper accounts of the J. A. Paisley and Philip Agee stories.)

Another element of narrative evil is supplied by Willy Sherritt (Kate's brother) and Porter "Poonie" Baldwin Jr. (her former husband). Willy and Poonie—like the WESCAC computer in *Giles Goat-Boy* and the rapists in *Sabbatical*—embody the Doomsday aspect of modern life and technology: Their mentality is inseparable from the whole urban, industrial, bureaucratic process run amok. They are literally rapists and defilers, and what they warp sexually finds its equivalent in their willingness to make a buck by dumping toxic waste into Chesapeake Bay.

The CIA-toxic-waste aspect of Barth's plot has a very different quality from the story about stories. It is less literary, less absorbed into the novel and seems to set the limits to what Barth's imagination is able to accommodate. Even as a form of representation, this element of plot is more lumpish, more intractable, less absorbed by the fictionality upon which this novel so self-consciously insists. The story of Willy and Poonie never gets much beyond cliche, and they meet a most melodramatic end at the novel's close when their helicopter is blown out of the sky in a storm. Whatever literary suggestion may underpin this ending, nature seems to cleanse itself—which seems at variance with the idea that art (that is, fiction) supposedly holds this function.

Barth has now written the same novel twice, and many of his earlier novels and stories anticipated, worked, and reworked much of this material. This raises the question of where Barth goes from here. There is no one writing today who has the resources of his imagination or the depth of understanding about the nature of narrative. His novels are too complex to become predictable, too full of surprises not to interest. But how many times can he rewrite the same story, recast the same tale? Barth can always write the theory of narrative that he has, in effect, been writing in his fiction. He could also turn more seriously

to the Willy-Poonie plot of his stories—that is, to the way that evil comes into being and how we best cope with it. Here he would be changing narrative modes, moving from Homer, Cervantes and Twain to Melville, Dostoevski and Conrad and such postmodern equivalents as Nabokov and Pynchon. In the Willy-Poonie plot, a sense of fictionality meets head on with a sense of reality, which, in *The Tidewater Tales,* is confronted by the storm rather than Barth. Such "reality"—no matter how defined—is too complex, too much with us today, to be blown away so easily.

Richard Lehan, in a review of "The Tidewater Tales: A Novel," in Los Angeles Times Book Review, *June 28, 1987, p. 10.*

WILLIAM PRITCHARD

Five years ago Mr. Barth published *Sabbatical,* a relatively short (366 pages) cruise of a novel in which a married couple sail up the waters of Chesapeake Bay while various stories get told about them and their friends and enemies, making up the narrative of which they are part. The new book [*The Tidewater Tales*] is much longer, almost as long as *Letters,* and swallows up *Sabbatical,* inasmuch as the main couple from that book, Fenwick Turner and Susan Seckler, turn up in the middle of *The Tidewater Tales* under their "real" names, Franklin Key Talbott and Leah Allen Silver Talbott. Frank has written a novel, *Reprise,* exposing the C.I.A. (of which he was a member), in which novel he and his wife figure under the names given them in *Sabbatical.* Now they meet up with the central couple of *The Tidewater Tales*—a writer, Peter Sagamore, and his wife, an oral historian named Katherine Shorter Sherritt. Both are on the edge of turning 40, and Katherine is on the edge of delivering twins. The present action of the book takes place in the two-week interval from June 15 to June 29, 1980, in which the book gestates and is born (so are the twins), an interval bounded at beginning and end by two storms, Blam and Blooey, that had already shown up in *Sabbatical.*

As a man and a writer, Peter Sagamore shows some of his creator's inclinations, and I suspect (though it's none of my business) that the relationship between Peter and his wife has a few analogues in Mr. Barth's "real life." But in an extremely clever stroke of reversal, Peter is made a professor of "the Art of Everdiminishing Fiction." Having begun his career with a "fine fat novel," he followed it with a leaner one, then two slim novellas, then a "landmark story" titled "Part of a Shorter Work," then even briefer fictions. . . .

Katherine, on the other hand, although her maiden name is Shorter, deplores Peter's minimalism. Carrying two embryos rather than one, she shows her maximalist tendencies by the fact that Whitman is her favorite poet—"*I contain multitudes*"—unlike her husband, whose "pet poet is Emily Dickinson: *zero at the bone.*" Since Peter is blocked as a writer and his wife's pregnancy has not come to term, the "well-coupled couple" and not only Jack Sprat-wise" decide to sail on a voyage "without itinerary timetable or destination," to take "a cruise through the Ocean of Story" (their boat is, of course, named Story) while sharing stories (Katherine's last name is Sherritt) with each other and with their "postmodern children." After all, sex and stories, like life and art, feature "teller and listener changing positions and coming together till they're unanimous." In the words of the book's introductory directive, the endeavor is to "navigate the tale itself to an ending more rich and strange than everyday realism ordinarily permits.'' The allusion to *The Tempest* is wholly intended.

As the previous quotations suggest, this is lively stuff, and Mr. Barth has never been more engaging, nor more engaged in his narrative complications, than in the first 150 or so pages of *The Tidewater Tales*. For all its high jinks, there is an easy intimacy to the writing, an attractive tone taken toward both the reader and the lovers (who, we are convinced, really *are* in love) that is infectious. One of the book's major plots, involving the C.I.A. and its various moves on the local scene (already developed in *Sabbatical*), is enliveningly complicated here, especially as it involves other people and events in the pre-1980 life of Peter and Katherine.

But since, unlike his hero, Mr. Barth is a professor of the art of ever-expanding fiction, his narrative swells to include stories about Homer's *Odyssey,* about Don Quixote, Scheherazade and other mythical characters and stories. I much enjoyed the Odyssey sequence, but enjoyed much less the Don Quixote and Scheherazade ones that eventually followed it—sometimes More may be Less. Katherine's unborn twins are regularly addressed by various dualities: I laughed at Pride and Prejudice, Salt and Pepper, Sturm und Drang, Pins and Needles, Phylogeny and Ontogeny, but then—it may have been at Hoot 'n' Nanny or Chick 'n' Little—I stopped laughing. Many pages are taken up with something fished from a canister in the waters and read by the Sagamores; titled *"SEX EDUCATION: Play,"* it is characterized by Katherine as ''the queerest mix of sophomoric and serious she's seen in a while.'' I thought it pretty unmixed sophomoric.

But Mr. Barth gives ample food to please or displease everyone's taste, and there is no use regretting that he will write no more novels like his early, memorable and short one, *The End of the Road.* Anything he produces now is calculated to tease readers into a state where they are uncertain whether it's brilliant artistry they are in the presence of, or insufferable, inflated self-indulgence, a thousand and one ways of behaving—in the infamous words of a reviewer of *Chimera*—like a narrative chauvinist pig (Mr. Barth claims to relish the phrase). He said once about his stories from *Lost in the Funhouse* that he was striving for ''passionate virtuosity'': however expert they might be, ''If these pieces aren't also *moving*, then the experiment is unsuccessful, and their author is lost in the funhouse indeed.'' It seems to me that what is moving about *The Tidewater Tales* is its frequent and frequently incidental richness as a love story—marital, filial, domestic—and also its love of a place, of a country, even as place and country are scarred by human depredations. Whether the novel's ending—or its various coves and shallows sailed into along the way—give us something more rich and strange than a funhouse may be left to the reader who starts and finishes *The Tidewater Tales.*

William Pritchard, ''Between Blam and Blooey,'' in The New York Times Book Review, *June 28, 1987, p. 7.*

SVEN BIRKERTS

The Tidewater Tales, a shipboard divertissement, follows in the wake of Barth's *Sabbatical: A Romance* (1982), which likewise took place on the deck of a cruising sailboat. ''My books,'' writes the author, ''tend to come in pairs; my sentences in twin members.'' He relates the fact to his own biological circumstances, to his having been born an opposite-sex twin. Within the pairing, however, thematic opposition often prevails. Where the husband and wife in *Sabbatical* agonize over whether or not to bring children into this ''powder-keg'' world, and ultimately decide not to, Katherine and Peter Sagamore, the protagonists of the new novel, are in a very different situation. As the narrative begins, Katherine—or ''K,'' or ''Kate,'' or ''Katydid''—is eight-and-a-half months pregnant with, you guessed it, twins.

''SET ME A TASK!'' demands Peter Sagamore of his wife. The two are ensconced in the luxury guest house belonging to Katherine's parents, the more than moderately well-to-do Sherritts. There Katherine plans to await her full term, while Peter, a writer, hopes to come to terms with the increasingly diminishing returns of his minimalist aesthetic. Over the years he has pruned down his once-amplitudinous fiction until the merest bones remain. These, too, he has whittled. Of his latest work only the title still stands. When Peter finds himself deleting that as well, he knows that he has come to a crisis. His capitalized cry is one of artistic desperation.

Katherine is afflicted with her own uncertainties. She has fears about bringing children into the world. Her well-meaning parents are smothering her with their solicitude; she has to keep reminding them that she is almost 40. She therefore harkens to Peter's call, countering with a command of her own: that he take her sailing. Before long, they are aboard their own vessel, the *Story,* leaving the family cove for the open waters of the Chesapeake. Their plan is to sail, swim, rest, reconnoiter their lives, and indulge their mutual love of storytelling (Katherine happens to be the founder of the American Society for the Preservation of Storytelling). So great is their delight in the first day's sailing and telling, however, that they risk a change of plans. Trusting in their shortwave radio and the propinquity of the Sherritt family's sophisticated yacht, they decide to extend their jaunt for as long as they can, perhaps right up to the onset of labor.

Barth's opening chapters commence an engaging periplus. We are given lively and witty introductory sketches, not just of Peter and Katherine, but also of the patrician senior Sherritts and their two sons—the ne'er-do-well entrepreneur Willy and the winningly pubertal ''Chip.'' In the course of their first day's sailing we are also told just how Peter, the boat-builder's son from Dorchester, came to be the one-night lover and then, years later, husband of the beautiful and accomplished Katherine. Barth weaves these establishing accounts together with the sense-active descriptions of the *Story's* progress over the waters. As we read we feel ourselves moving among the coves, rivers, and estuaries of the Chesapeake. In time, through the skillful counterpointing of anecdote and present-tense depiction of surroundings, these labyrinthine waterways become the topographic equivalent of the stories that keep emerging.

Tales within tales within tales. In several of the essays in *The Friday Book,* Barth rhapsodizes about the complexity of pattern in the ancient story cycles, remarking in particular the interplay between the frame narrative and the subsidiary tellings imbedded within it: ''It was never Scheherazade's stories that seduced and beguiled me, but their teller and the extraordinary circumstances of their telling.'' If there is a central weakness in *The Tidewater Tales,* it's that Barth has nothing like the threat of a vizier's dagger to tense up his frame. The kicks and quivers of the forthcoming twins are nothing to the stroke of a blade. The hard work of seducing and beguiling therefore has to fall to the stories themselves.

Fortunately Barth has command over the full narrative lexicon. Short, long, realistic, fantastic: he spins out legends of every description. In the course of the book we are treated to personal histories (the romance between Peter and Katherine, Katherine's first marriage to the boozy pervert "Poon" Baldwin, Peter's journey from the docks of Dorchester to literary and academic success); intrigue (an impossibly involved account of CIA and KGB double-dealing with regard to the prospective sale of a certain Bayside property to the Soviet Embassy); farce (the Sagamores find floating canisters containing installments of a preposterous play for eggs and sperm); and, finally, epics. Or, to be precise, epical retellings of epics. These are the mainstay of the novel. . . . (p. 36)

[Barth later includes two] variations on the familiar, first when Peter and Katherine encounter a garrulous old mariner named Donald Quicksoat (his boat: the *Rocinante IV*), and then when they hook up with the Talbotts, who tell how the original enchantress, Scheherazade, magically appeared in their lives. We are given proof positive, should we need it, that the old tunes can still be made to dance. Still, it is a fine line that Barth elects to tread. For one thing, these airings of the incredible strain forcibly against the otherwise scrupulously rendered here and now. For another, the novel is severely hobbled by its lack of a governing structure. Barth's sly self-critique—he has Peter muse about writing a novel "in which next to nothing happens beyond an interminably pregnant couple's swapping stories"—cannot disarm the reader's own critical impulse. The book's success has nothing to do with its design: the whole lives only through the vitality of its parts.

On the surface, these parts have about as much in common as the objects in a scavenger's bag. A play for sperm and eggs? A CIA-KGB thriller? An apocryphal eipsode from the life of Don Quixote de la Mancha? But Barth's art is such that a subtle thematic tension emerges from beneath the surface jumble. We find an insistent to-and-fro starting up between the cyclic and the linear. Repetitive patterning yields to the eruptive breakthrough, then reasserts itself. On the one hand: tides, menses, the nightly appeasement of the vizier, Penelope's weaving and unravelling. On the other: the issue of twins, the sailing forth out of time by Odysseus and Nausicaa, the end of Scheherazade's inventions after the 1001st night—I cite but a few of myriad instances. They function, much like the meta-metaphors of telling and sailing, to hold the heteroclite pieces of Barth's collage together.

The contesting forces don't finally discharge themselves in any dramatic fashion. The babes (cleverly, then irritatingly, addressed with in utero monikers like "Tweedles Dum and Dee" and "Toil and Trouble") are born; the off-stage villains (Willy and "Poon") reap their reward; and Peter passes through the needle's eye of his artistic crisis and starts to write. He closes the circle with his last-sentence decision to pen: "THE TIDEWATER TALES: A NOVEL." But for all its sprawl and diffuseness, the book is decidedly uplifting. The means so overwhelm the ends that we give up questioning necessity. We accept the gifts in the spirit in which they are offered. (p. 37)

Sven Birkerts, "The Modern Mariner," in The New Republic, *Vol. 197, Nos. 6 & 7, August 10 & 17, 1987, pp. 35-7.*

Jacques (Martin) Barzun
1907-

French-born American historian, critic, nonfiction writer, essayist, and editor.

An eminent cultural historian and critic, Barzun has inspired respect and controversy for his ideas on a wide range of topics relating to art, science, philosophy, education, and history. Informed by the tenets of pragmatism and pluralism expounded by William James, Barzun argues against absolute and fixed systems of belief that purport to explain and define particular facets of nature and human conduct. Instead, Barzun promotes intellectual analyses that offer varied and evolving approaches to understanding existence and intellect. Albert Guerard stated: "All human truths are tentative, hypothetical, experimental. This is the well known philosophical attitude of Bacon, Voltaire and William James. And this, Jacques Barzun contends, is culture." While Barzun was lauded as a progressive humanist for much of his career, critics note that his later works generally espouse more conservative views, including attacks on contemporary trends in such disciplines as history, art, education, and science. In honor of his achievements, Barzun was awarded the Gold Medal for Belles Lettres and Criticism by the American Academy and Institute of Arts and Letters in 1987.

Born and raised in France, where his father was a respected writer, Barzun was exposed to the burgeoning artistic milieu of Paris during the World War I era. Attracted to the political and intellectual environment of the United States, he enrolled at Columbia University in the early 1920s. While working on his doctorate in 1929, Barzun began a long and distinguished career as a professor at Columbia, during which he became recognized as an exceptional educator. With Lionel Trilling and several other colleagues, Barzun helped revise and expand the school's Humanities curriculum. He became Dean of Graduate Faculties in 1955, and in 1958 he assumed the newly created position of Dean of Faculties and Provost, which he held until 1967. Barzun expresses his philosophy of education in such works as *The Teacher in America* (1945; published in Great Britain as *We Who Teach*) and *The American University: How It Runs, Where It Is Going* (1968). In general, Barzun disapproves of progressive trends in education that de-emphasize the traditional relationship between student and teacher.

Barzun's early works evince his belief in the necessity of questioning theories that have become accepted as truths and of promoting a society in which such analysis is encouraged. In his first two books, *The French Race: Theories of Its Origins and Their Social and Political Implications Prior to the Revolution* (1932) and *Race: A Study in Modern Superstition* (1937), Barzun argues that the modern concept of race evolved from unsubstantiated claims made by several nineteenth-century scientists interested in advancing nationalism and has no biological foundation. He contends that these notions have exerted a wrongful and dangerous influence on the course of science, history, and politics. In his next work, *Of Human Freedom* (1939), Barzun addresses the concept of freedom and advocates a society in which theories that propose absolute truths can be challenged and tested. R. L. Duffus commented: "Dr. Barzun seeks an art which is interpreted but not terrorized by criticisms; a science which is experimental and elastic, never attempting

Courtesy of Columbia University

to 'solidify one result, one happy thought, into a universal rule'; an education that teaches how rather than what. . . . Freedom, democracy, equality, are, in short, ways of doing things rather than objects in themselves. They are ways of growth, experience, satisfaction." *Darwin, Marx, Wagner: Critique of a Heritage* (1941) focuses upon three influential nineteenth-century figures whom Barzun believes have exerted too great an influence on twentieth-century thought. Barzun faults Charles Darwin's theory of evolution, Karl Marx's views on history, and Richard Wagner's aesthetics for being overly mechanistic and deterministic and for applying rigid and limiting principles to inquiry and exposition within their respective fields.

Several of Barzun's later works admonish contemporary trends in American culture and scholarship. In *The House of Intellect* (1959), Barzun claims that American intellectuals are undermining their social purpose of exploring and disseminating significant ideas. In particular, Barzun indicts artists who stress creativity and personal expression while forsaking order, scientists who promote untested multidisciplinary theories, and philanthropists who reward lavish group efforts rather than modest individual achievements. Daniel J. Boorstin noted: "We cannot be beyond hope if one of us, in a position of Mr. Barzun's dignity and power, can still be so ruthless, so honest and so precise in attack. This book—the most important critique of American culture in many years—is itself one of the most encouraging symptoms of recent American thought.'' Barzun examines specific disciplines in three later works. *Science: The Glorious Entertainment* (1964) expounds upon the dangers of scientism and technology; *The Use and Abuse of Art* (1974) laments the passing of artistic ideals associated with the Renaissance and attacks avant-garde art forms; and *Clio and the Doctors: Psycho-History, Quanto-History, and History* (1974) disparages such contemporary approaches to understanding history as psychoanalysis and forming generalizations from computer-generated statistical data.

Barzun is also a renowned critic of music and the social and artistic ideals associated with Romanticism. His work *Romanticism and the Modern Ego* (1943; revised and expanded as *Classic, Romantic, and Modern,* 1961) is considered an insightful exploration of the Romantic sensibility as well as an elucidation of the tenets which inform Barzun's aesthetics. Victor Lange noted: ''The chief romantic premise, [Barzun] insists, was the desire to create a new society, different from its immediate forerunner. As against the classical faith in stability within known and defined limits, the romantic is dedicated to the acceptance and exploration of an open universe.'' Barzun contends that twentieth-century wars and ideologies have destroyed the romantic purpose and have led to widespread confusion in the arts. Barzun's acclaimed books of music criticism include *Berlioz and the Romantic Century* (1950) and *Music in American Life* (1956). Among his other works are *On Writing, Editing, and Publishing: Essays Explicative and Honoratory* (1971), which contains essays on a variety of topics related to writing; *A Stroll with William James* (1983), a widely acclaimed study that blends biography with analysis and explanation of James's philosophy while also illuminating Barzun's own views; and *A Word or Two Before You Go . . .* (1986), in which Barzun reflects on the use and misuse of language.

(See also *Contemporary Authors*, Vols. 61-64 and *Contemporary Authors New Revision Series*, Vol. 22.)

E. L. WOODWARD

Mr. Barzun has written an interesting book [*Race: A Study in Modern Superstition*] to show that the common concept of ''race'' has no scientific foundation. The thesis is, of course, not a new one; Mr. Barzun sets it out in short chapters, full of snap and point, supported by a great deal of knowledge, though too much of it is of the card-index type. Mr. Barzun concentrates upon the history of race-doctrines in France, partly because he wants to show that the pedantic and brutal use of these doctrines in [Nazi Germany] is merely the application of fallacies taken from elsewhere. The sum of his argument is that ''race'' is an out-of-date hypothesis which does not fit the facts; that the expression of this hypothesis in terms of ''blood''. . . is nonsense, and that the sooner we can get rid of the absurd superstition of ''race,'' the better for our science, our history, and our politics.

Taken in the large, the advice is sound, and those who try to think clearly about the differences between various political and social groups of mankind will read Mr. Barzun's book with profit to themselves. At the same time Mr. Barzun would be more convincing if he were a little more careful to avoid making some of the mistakes which he denounces in others. . . .

It is easy to show that historians and anthropologists have made hasty generalisations, but is not Mr. Barzun himself a little rash in concluding, from his conversations with Frenchmen, that race-beliefs are ''quasi-universal'' in France; in other words, that most Frenchmen hold these beliefs? Has Mr. Barzun spoken to a majority of Frenchmen? Is he quite sure that he has understood what Frenchmen mean when they talk of *la France,* or *les française;* or does he realise, for example, the distinction between *les allemands* and *les boches*? A good many of Mr. Barzun's citations are as superficial as those of his opponents. . . .

This lack of precise thinking and clear definition affects the whole structure of the book. There is also a certain confusion of purpose. If Mr. Barzun is writing for the public he is too allusive; his text includes lists of names which will mean little to any reader outside France, and not very much to the ordinary Frenchman. One of these lists contains 31 names, without any reference to the date, works, or importance of the people concerned. If, on the other hand, the book is intended for the learned, the treatment of technical questions is far too sketchy. One does not need to be a physical anthropologist to notice that Mr. Barzun's criticism of anthropological methods is not altogether fair. (p. 280)

Nevertheless Mr. Barzun's shrewd and sceptical judgements are worth reading. He may try to prove, or to disprove, too much. If he is dealing with the loose employment of the term ''race'' by historians, publicists, and men of letters, he ought to take more trouble about analysing the words used in different languages for race, and the distinction, which is not uniform in English, French and German, between race, nationality, and people. It is also necessary to remember that these words— race is not the only word—are used to denote, provisionally, a number of observed facts and relationships of a very complicated kind, and that many writers who use the terms are fully aware that there are not pure ''races,'' that there is no such thing as fixity of race, and that ''national characteristics'' are known to change in the course of time. All these considerations must be taken into account; one does not solve a problem by showing that on explanation of it is unsatisfactory. At the same time it is well to be reminded that the provisional conclusions of the learned can be translated too easily into popular myths, and that when we are, rightly, indignant about the stupid and cruel exploitation of the myth of race in Nazi Germany, we must be on our guard against falling into errors no less vulgar, and, in their ultimate implication, hardly less dangerous. (pp. 280, 282)

E. L. Woodward, ''The Myth of Blood,'' in The Spectator, *Vol. 160, No. 5721, February 18, 1938, pp. 280, 282.*

BRIAN HOWARD

''I am not a Jew, I am just an ordinary Briton of Aryan stock.'' This remark was once made, according to Mr. Barzun [in *Race: A Study in Modern Superstition*], by Sir John Simon, and it is a magnificent example of what may come to be called Racism. In point of anthropological fact, of course, there is no such thing as an ''ordinary Briton,'' and no such thing as ''Aryan stock.'' Most educated people to-day are aware, as an unforeseen result of Nazi propaganda, that there is something suspect about the words ''Aryan race,'' and many of these realise that ''Aryan'' is only permissible as a purely linguistic term. But the majority of such people still believe in ''Races'' as entities.

How long it will take to persuade them that the comparatively parvenu word "Race" has lost its meaning from the scientific standpoint, is a matter for conjecture, and when one considers the sociological effects of Racism, for intensely gloomy conjecture. (pp. 300, 302)

[Barzun's style in **Race**] is clear and pungent, except when overstuffed with proper names. It is difficult, however, to see how he could have avoided this: his book is an attack on racist-thinking, and its interest consists in the vast amount of evidence, chiefly among French historians and scientists, that he has managed to compile. . . . [Racism] is proto-Fascism, based on mysticism on the one hand, and pseudo-biology on the other. Count Arthur de Gobineau published his fateful *Essai sur l'inégalité des races humaines* in 1853, and Mr. Barzun has adduced a formidable array of celebrities in support of his theory that it was Gobineau's influence, more than that of any other one thinker, which transformed the nationalism of the nineteenth century into the xenophobia of the twentieth. He stresses the point that Gobineau was very arbitrarily interpreted, and is, indeed, inclined to overpraise him as a man and an intellect. Nevertheless, this chapter will be of value to the student, and does advance his claim that what Tacitus sowed, Gobineau reaped, and marketed. It was he who is largely responsible for the appearance of the great racial bogyman, the dolicocephalic Aryan-Nordic hero, whose mission it is to administer the globe. Mr. Bazun successfully demonstrates that, while Gobineau himself saw no hope of this being realised, believing in inevitable degeneration for a "semitised" and "nigritised" Europe, the political programme of Maurras and the *Action Française* is simply the development of the same ideas. At the time, Gobineau influenced Taine, Renan and Sorel in France; Carlyle, J. R. Green and Kingsley in England, and Wagner, Nietzsche and Schopenhauer in Germany. The infection spread so rapidly and so insidiously, not only among philosophers and historians, but also among scientists, that it is almost with surprise that one is reminded of the lonely protests of such men as Virchow and John Stuart Mill. The author quotes the latter, and I agree with him that "in that calm statement is condensed the nature and danger of the error."

> Of all the vulgar modes of escaping from the consideration of the effect of social and moral influences on the human mind, the most vulgar is that of attributing the diversities of conduct and character to inherent natural differences.

In Germany, of course, Gobineau received an increasingly warm welcome, and it is an ironic thought that the dream-world of Hitler and Rosenberg is directly traceable to a peevish French diplomat.

From the ethnological point of view, it is to be regretted that Mr. Barzun has rather fought shy of genetics, the principal enemy of the Race concept. From the historical, it is a pity that he did not deal more fully with Houston Stewart Chamberlain, Wagner's son-in-law, whose vulgarisation of Gobineau earned him subsidies, and immense letters, from the Kaiser. Chamberlain is the point at which Racism (in his case, the Nordic myth) first becomes seriously grotesque, and seriously dangerous. Sadly enough, there is room here for only one more of the author's specimens of Racism in recent years. It concerns an eminent Frenchman, Dr. Edgar Bérillon, who had governmental authority to lecture all through France during the war. His findings are recorded in the reports of the Society of Medicine of Paris, and of the French Association for the Advancement of Science:

His discovery is that the German race suffers from Polychesia (excessive defoecation) and bromidrosis (body odour).

In concluding, I should like to draw the author's attention to one sentence of his own:

> English historians should have known better, but they did not refrain from chorusing the same opinions compounded of race-fictions and national hatreds.

Should have known better? Why, Mr. Barzun? (p. 302)

> *Brian Howard, "The Great Psychosis," in* The New Statesman & Nation, *Vol. XV, No. 365, February 19, 1938, pp. 300, 302.*

R. L. DUFFUS

Freedom is so alluring a word that even dictators have to call their wars of conquest wars of liberation. Modern man is fascinated by the word even when he seems to reject the reality. It is inseparable from the idea of democracy and equally so from the idea of equality, considered in terms of human rights. But it is not a simple conception, as one finds in reading this penetrating and sometimes difficult analysis by Dr. Barzun [*Of Human Freedom*]. It may be easier to go over the top for freedom, and it is certainly easier to shout for it at public meetings, than it is to define it. . . .

Readers who like to work out their trips on road maps before stepping on the starter might wish in this case to turn to Page 264 of the book, at which point the author summarizes what he has been trying to reason out. For him "democratic conduct is primarily cultural and only indirectly political" and its philosopher is William James. For James the truth was what worked. There could be no absolute truth—not even an absolute democracy or an absolute freedom. Following this clue Dr. Barzun seeks an art which is interpreted but not terrorized by criticisms; a science which is experimental and elastic, never attempting to "solidify one result, one happy thought, into a universal rule"; an education that teaches how rather than what; a realization that if we are to avoid such "absolutes" as have brought war to Europe we must give up the notion of perfection, in government or anywhere else. Freedom, democracy, equality, are, in short, ways of doing things rather than objects in themselves. They are ways of growth, experience, satisfaction.

For our dismayed generation this line of thought is fruitful. It has a bearing on topics which may be discussed in this morning's newspaper, such as how American neutrality is to be preserved; to what extent we are called upon to meet the general danger by preserving domestic "harmony"; what Russia is likely to do next and what the Russian revolution really has signified, and whether moral strength has any military significance. Dr. Barzun does not discuss these particular points. He could hardly have done so without finishing his book at ten last night and going to press at five this morning. But he will help readers who are trying to think things through. He will be of especial help to those who not long ago believed democracies to be "decadent" or "inefficient" or who thought (and how long ago that was!) that they must make the dreadful choice between Rome and Berlin on the one hand and Moscow on the other hand.

The belief that there is no final answer to the world's specific problems, that it is in the nature of the problems and of life itself that they shall not be finally solved, and that the key to conduct here and now is in the avoidance of tawdry pretenses of solution is somehow a comforting one. If we get rid of "absolute truth" we get rid of much horrifying nonsense, for, as Dr. Barzun says, "if we believe in absolute truth, how can we help murdering one another as heretics?" Enough murder has been committed since he wrote the words to add something to their pointedness. We cannot, in the light of his reasoning, find refuge either in revolution or in counter-revolution. He devotes considerable space, indeed, to an effort to prove that revolution is, as Robespierre said, itself a system. And it is systems from which he is trying to free himself. (p. 1)

The reader may guess that this is a provocative and often baffling book. The tough-minded will get much mental exercise out of it. It will probably have its effects on other writers and thinkers and it may be one of the symptoms of the turning of the intellectual tide away from pure emotionalism and action for action's sake into more rational channels. At least this is a possibility if we are not drowned in the backwash of Europe's passions. (p. 17)

> *R. L. Duffus, "The Nature of Human Freedom," in*
> The New York Times Book Review, *September 17, 1939, pp. 1, 17.*

ALBERT GUERARD

When we defend "democracy," we mean liberty. When the authoritarians sneer at democracy as feeble and chaotic, they mean liberty. Jacques Barzun's book [*Of Human Freedom*] is an apologia for a "liberal" culture. If we have to fight—even if only on the intellectual plane—it is expedient to know what we are fighting for.

A defense of liberty might be Fourth of July claptrap. It might be the old-fashioned anarchism of Herbert Spencer, which Albert Jay Nock, a brilliant and amiable critic, still dishes out in tempting mid-Victorian essays. It might be linked with the "eternal verities," the virtues of the party machines and the holiness of profiteering. Jacques Barzun's apologia is none of these familiar things. It is a cogent inquiry into the nature and implications of liberty. The argument could be summed up in the great words that William James borrowed (unconsciously?) from Proudhon: "Damn the Absolute!"

For faith in any absolute, religious, political, social, racial, implies dogmatism, and dogmatism is incompatible with tolerance. We cannot condone essential evil, spiritual murder, the destruction of fundamental values. And we cannot admit that an absolute be subordinated in any way to mere relative considerations. If race, for instance, be our faith, everything else must yield. . . . And all dogmatism implies theocracy: what could an absolute truth be, if not the thought and will of God? The inevitable result of totalitarianism.

At this we shudder, virtuously, and reassert our desire for freedom, limited only by the freedom of others. But the defense of freedom implies relativism, pluralism, pragmatism. . . . All human truths are tentative, hypothetical, experimental. This is the well known philosophical attitude of Bacon, Voltaire and William James. And this, Jacques Barzun contends, is culture. For, if culture is incompatible with anarchy, it is even more radically opposed to tyranny. Culture is liberation. No dogmatist is free; nor can he tolerate that any one should be free.

The experimental attitude is essentially scientific: science seeks to establish verifiable relations between ascertained facts. But Barzun warns us to be on our guard against pseudo-science: dogmatism camouflaged with impressive and cryptic formulae.

A loose statement does not become scientific because it is translated into obscure and pedantic terms, or thickly veiled under a complicated equation.

In the sciences which deal with matter, the demand for experimental verification cannot long be suppressed. . . . In the social sciences, experimentation is in many cases impossible. The remedy to dogmatism has to be sought in history, which broadens enormously the basis of observation and makes the comparative method practicable. Like Ernest Renan and William James, Jacques Barzun, a historian, believes in the historical approach. So do I: with qualifications. In the purely physical sciences, history is irrelevant. It can be shown that water is H_2O without referring to Boyle and Lavoisier. . . .

What history can do for us is to show how recent, how limited, how precarious, are some of our alleged "eternal verities." History is the great teacher of relativism: it registers the birth and the toppling down of every absolute. . . .

For Jacques Barzun, the last citadel of human freedom is Art. The artist inevitably is limited by tradition: no poet can evolve a totally new idiom. But he is also an experimenter. . . . Art shrugs away the obligation of conforming to the statistics of Fechner or Birkhoff, to the rules of Julius-Caesar Scaliger, to the morality of Jeremy Collier, to the economics of Granville Hicks, to the anthropology of Gobineau and Houston Stewart Chamberlain. It insists on seeking and experimenting forever. This is the essence of freedom. . . . [So] long as science and art endure, freedom shall not disappear from the world.

In his defense of democracy as Freedom, Jacques Barzun is realistic and honest enough to reject the hoary Vox Populi fallacy. Vox Populi can never formulate any definite proposition. It can only shout vague applause, grunt ambiguous dissent, or remain sullenly silent. The initiative invariably belongs to the conscious few. Every regime is at bottom an oligarchy— would it were an aristocracy! This conception, in agreement with the democracy of Jefferson, is not opposed to the democracy of Lincoln. The leadership of the few (pioneers of thought, apostles, propagandists, party leaders, lobbyists pressure groups) is not anti-democratic, so long as there are many freely organized minorities; so long as these minorities remain open to free converts; so long as their aim is to propose, but not to compel. The one danger is enforced unanimity, hundred-per-centism, one hundred and twenty million minds with but a single thought. Democracy is pluralism.

Such is the line of argument of this extraordinarily substantial little book. Readable and epigrammatic like a column, it is packed with serious thought. The range of topics is amazing; it might seem like a treatise "Of All Things Knowable, and a Few Others Beside." But the purpose is plain, the reasoning straight and the conclusion unequivocal:

> In the name of peace and pragmatism let us face with open eyes a pluralistic world in which there are no universal churches, no single remedy for all diseases, no one way to teach or write or sing, no magic diet that will make every one healthy and happy, no world poets and no chosen races cut to one pattern or virtue, but only the wretched and wonderfully diversified human race which can live and build and leave cultural traces of its passage in a world that was apparently not fashioned for the purpose.

> *Albert Guerard, "In Defense of Liberal Culture," in* New York Herald Tribune Books, *October 15, 1939, p. 2.*

IRWIN EDMAN

Mr. Barzun has a lively, learned, and catalytic mind. This he uses, as he uses intellectual history, as an instrument for contemporary understanding and criticism. He is not simply a historian; he is obviously greatly concerned with the incidence of past ideas in present consequences. He is not a dazed admirer of grandiose nations—quite the contrary. He is never dazed by, and always skeptical of, the pompously systematic. (p. 618)

[In *Darwin, Marx, Wagner: Critique of a Heritage*, Mr. Barzun examines] three nineteenth-century figures. These three are, in his erudite and documented judgment, central as symptoms and as symbols, and decisive as influences in the patterns of both actions and ideas in our own day. Darwin, Marx, and Wagner are important, not because they were original or because any single work of theirs was a masterpiece. In Mr. Barzun's handling, all three men turn out to be strikingly derivative and suspiciously second-rate. Not one of the three is a "hero" of the author's. His reasons for spending such loving care upon figures for whom he loses no love are those of a critic and a historian. The point is that, implicitly or explicitly, each of these three men has been the "hero" of a cult, and has, directly or indirectly, shaped the pattern of much that passes for "scientific ideas" in the last three-quarters of a century. Mr. Barzun clearly thinks it is high time that the isms which these three men propagated—though they did not originate them—be reexamined.

It should be stressed at once, especially because at first sight Wagner seems to fall oddly into this trio, that Darwin, Marx, and Wagner are, for Professor Barzun, three facets of the same tendency, three variations on a common and dangerous nineteenth-century theme, the worst consequences of which are with us still. They are responsible, in considerable measure, for our heritage of confusions, fanaticisms, and despairs. It is a tribute to the author's cogent marshaling of unassailable materials that by the end of the book one wonders why no one earlier discerned with such revealing clarity the common atmosphere which these men breathed, the identic idols which, for all their differences, they worshiped.

The unity of which this trinity are the expressions is Science, with a capital S, and Science as System, as Necessity, as Truth, with the implication of a fatal necessity and an unmanageable progress. "Science" revealed to Marx the "laws" of history which determine the process out of which the classless society was to emerge. . . .

In Darwin "history was a sieve that worked. Man was the residue." In Marx the sieve was history too; "the proletarian Utopia was the residue." Similarly in Wagner, but here the residue was "the artwork of the future," Wagner's own grandiose term for his own work.

These conclusions—they occur in pages 351 to 355 of a four-hundred-page work—are the distinctive contribution of the book, an ordering not into a system but into a clear point of view of biography, history, methodological analysis, and aesthetic criticism. To these conclusions are added certain consequences. These three men invented slogans which are in our mouths, and their slogans had many sources and one character: that character was, in an age of materialism and machinery, the predominant faith in mechanical law and in a fatal burgeoning of history in terms of these mechanical laws.

Much of the book consists of highly entertaining and edged pictures of these three teachers and their doctrines, their personal histories and the sources of many of their alleged originalities in thought. These provocative sketches do not add, and are not intended to add, cubits to the stature of any of the three men. But the book, like *Of Human Freedom*, is in a high sense a tract for the times. The conception of Progress in the fatal and external terms of "mechanical law" has led, as Professor Barzun sees it, to many grave distortions. It has distracted us from the really fruitful business of specific inquiry into the diversity of processes natural and human. It has clamped down on the minds of men reasons for despair that flow from the fatal necessities of science, allegedly discovered, but really self-imposed. It has generated dogmatisms of race and nationalism and waves of a future dialectically guaranteed. It has substituted system for inquiry in science, pseudo-science for flexible understanding in society, and elaborate contraptions and devices for genuine and organically living art. And we are paying for these things in brutality in world politics, enthroned obscurantism in science, and pastiche deceptions in art.

The elevation of scientific system, moreover, has blinded us to the insights provided by the great romantics, because we have been taught by alleged realists to ignore their awareness of the interior realities of feeling and of thought. One of the most interesting and original themes of this book is that of the close affinity between the celebration of all diversities of experience in the romantic poets, painters, and musicians, and the pragmatic emphasis on the many kinds of things current, and the many kinds of dealings with them necessary, in the world.

In the interest of making Mr. Barzun's theme briefly clear, I have been compelled to omit much: the happy and encyclopaedic range of illustration, the shrewd analysis of the Marxian theory of surplus value, the engaging malice of the epigrams, the obvious passion for human individuality and for human freedom, the contempt for fake "culture," and the fresh, non-idolatrous critiques of the three non-heroes. There are pictures, too, of the author's own heroes, too long, he thinks, obscured: Lamarck, Samuel Butler, and Berlioz, among others. Those who think these choices for admiration are reactionary or obscurantist show themselves particularly in need of this book. Those who have mouthed slogans as science, dialectic as discovery, and artifice as art need it even more. (p. 619)

Irwin Edman, "The Trinity of Materialism," in The Nation, *New York, Vol. 152, No. 21, May 24, 1941, pp. 618-19.*

MORTON WHITE

[*The essay excerpted below originally appeared in a slightly different form in* Partisan Review, *September-October, 1941.*]

Professor Jacques Barzun's purpose in *Darwin, Marx, Wagner: Critique of a Heritage* is to give "a critical account of mechanistic materialism in science, art, and social science" from the days of its great apostles down to ours. (p. 186)

[Darwin, Marx and Wagner], he claims, separated man and his soul, all of them believed that "things were the only reality—indestructible matter in motion", and all of them helped people think that "feeling, beauty, and moral values were . . . illusions for which the world of fact gave no warrant". This is the thesis of the book, but it is far from the only kind of utterance that appears in it. Presumably in support of this thesis, Mr. Barzun brings out material of all varieties: biographical data, facts concerning the readers of the terrible trio, pronunciamentos in biology, references to the development of economic theory, detailed esthetic analyses, materials from the history of music, opinions on the method of science, its significance for our lives, values, problems, etc., etc. Reviewing the book becomes quite difficult under these circumstances. For this reason I shall treat some of the many, far-flung statements separately.

Nothing is more shocking than Mr. Barzun's utter lack of conscience about using the phrase "mechanical materialism" precisely. We learn that a mechanical materialist is someone who separates man and his soul, someone who thinks that nothing exists but concrete material objects, someone who doesn't think that beauty, feelings, and moral values exist, someone who thinks that the world is cold and that man's will is powerless. If one tries to get further than this, one is at a loss, except, perhaps, for learning that a mechanical materialist is someone who *reduces* all observable phenomena to matter. That a writer working with criteria as vague as these could ever be in a position to declare anyone a mechanical materialist is incredible. And yet Mr. Barzun damns three tremendous figures, using his unclear definition and depending, not on detailed textual evidence, but on impressions of how cold and alien the world felt after putting down a book or leaving an opera by one of them.

Where the criteria used are a little less lyrical, Mr. Barzun's statements cease to be unclear and become obviously false. For instance, where do Darwin and Marx (I don't know about Wagner) deny the *existence* of beauty, feelings, and moral values? And consider that supposedly accurate phrase "reduction to matter". What Mr. Barzun means by it is hardly fathomable in these pages. But perhaps we take him too literally; perhaps he does not mean that Darwin, Marx, and Wagner *say* explicitly what he attributes to them, but that they seem to imply it or suggest it in some way. His interpretation of Wagner's leitmotif is typical of this kind of analysis. The leitmotif represents, and when an artist, especially a composer, uses representative devices, he is concerned with the *materials* represented. Therefore we have evidence of Wagner's *materialism*. Because Darwin thought that random variations appear and that useful ones are preserved and inherited, and because he thought that human beings were subject to this process of natural selection, he was, in Mr. Barzun's eyes, a mechanical materialist. And because Marx believed that there were uniformities in history, and that there were limitations upon the action of single individuals, he too was a mechanical materialist. Leaving aside the analysis of Wagner's leitmotif, one can only come to the conclusion that to seek regularities in human behavior, in short, to use scientific method, is to be a mechanical materialist. Apparently Mr. Barzun finds it impossible to believe both that there are biological and social laws and that man's will is not powerless. That Darwin believed men consciously sought goals is indicated by the fact that the whole theory of natural selection is modeled after the *willed* activity of breeding. And that Marx thought men were not powerless is indicated by the fact that he held out the possibility of barbarism if they did not use their power to produce a better world. (pp. 186-88)

The history of ideas is an important, fascinating, and far-reaching subject. Workers in it must be capable of understanding ideas in many fields and also able to correlate them with various cultural, non-intellectual phenomena. It is with this in mind, I suppose, that Mr. Barzun spends so much time on the personalities of Darwin, Marx, and Wagner, and their disciples. If Mr. Barzun were interested only in recording facts about these men, this might be understandable. But since the essay is critical, and tries to cast doubt upon the truth or beauty of what they created, it becomes important to ask whether the slander is at all relevant. What significance, even if they were true, would the attacks on the personalities of Darwin, Marx, and Wagner have? It is one thing to be told that Darwin was not a thinker, that Marx was prurient, and that Wagner was an ingrate, but given the information one pauses between deprecatory remarks to ask what connection they have with the major point of the book. And one asks this question under the guiding influence of the author. For nothing, he keeps insisting, is so terrible as the genetic fallacy.

There is one other theme that deserves examination. It involves the reverse of the genetic fallacy, perhaps best called "the fallacy of consequences". Pragmatists and instrumentalists have succeeded in convincing many people that theories are to be tested by observing their consequences. Unfortunately, many of the converts understand by "consequences" the reactions of the people who read the book in which the theory is presented. This fallacy is not the fallacy of origins, but is equally vicious. The formula is simple. Prove a man has been read and quoted favorably by a fascist, and he becomes a fascist. Prove that someone who read Darwin urged the destruction of all social reforms, and refute the theory of natural selection. The tendency appears throughout Mr. Barzun's book, and is one of the many things in it which are irrelevant to its thesis.

The book is not very good. Perhaps Mr. Barzun puts his own finger on the reason when, in explanation of the alleged failure of Darwin, Marx, and Wagner, he says: "The explanation is that none of our three men was content to stay within his specialty. Darwin made sallies into psychology and social science; Marx was a philosopher, historian, sociologist, and would-be scientist in economics; Wagner was an artist-philosopher who took the Cosmos for his province". But consider Mr. Barzun, who makes more than sallies into philosophy, history, economics, sociology, and art. (pp. 192-93)

*Morton White, "Darwin, Marx, and Materialism,"
in his* Pragmatism and the American Mind: Essays
and Reviews in Philosophy and Intellectual History,
Oxford University Press, 1973, pp. 186-93.

DANIEL J. BOORSTIN

In an age flooded by books giving us the answer to the weaknesses of American culture, written by people who have never even begun to define the question, it is a relief to have Jacques Barzun's brilliant and modest book [*The House of Intellect*]. We cannot be beyond hope if one of us, in a position of Mr. Barzun's dignity and power, can still be so ruthless, so honest and so precise in attack. This book—the most important critique of American culture in many years—is itself one of the most encouraging symptoms of recent American thought.

According to Mr. Barzun, the Jeremiahs of our age have been framing the wrong indictment of the wrong people for the wrong crimes. The death of the intellect—so widely and vaguely decried by American intellectuals—is a case not of murder, but of suicide. The motives, the opportunities and the weapons of self-destruction, as Mr. Barzun explains, have been provided by the whole community. But the crime is being committed by the intellectuals themselves. And not only in America.

The House of Intellect as Mr. Barzun describes it comprises three groups of subjects:

The persons who consciously and methodically employ the mind; the forms and habits governing the activities in which the mind is so employed; and the conditions under which these people and activities exist.

He calls it a house "because it is an establishment, requiring appurtenances and prescribing conventions." Intellect presupposes literacy, rules and traditions. It cannot do everything: for example, it is not necessary to art, and it should not dominate government. But it can do much, and its master virtues are "concentration, continuity, articulate precision and self-awareness." He thus carefully distinguishes "intellect" from intelligence, which is widely distributed in the animal world and serves an infinity of purposes.

In our age [according to Barzun], the great enemies of intellect are three: art, science and philanthropy. . . . Art has become the idealization of the unintelligible, the justification of the amateurish, the anarchic and the incompetent—under the banner of "creativity." The fantasy of the schoolboy, the blundering of the Sunday-painter, the wackiness of the arty, all draw energies into aimless self-expression.

Scientists have joined the war against intellect. They assume either "that science is radically unlike any other intellectual pursuit—in method, language, and type of mind" or "that the scientist's work is essentially akin to that of the poet. It relies on inspiration and a God-given power to handle symbols creatively." In either case they are "shrinking from the common ground of intellect"—from the belief in communication, language, discipline, and work.

Philanthropy has become an evil spirit, no less destructive because its evil is unintended. By philanthropy, Mr. Barzun means "the liberal doctrine of free and equal opportunity as applied to things of the mind"—"impartiality" between strong and weak minds and between strong and weak institutions. It is the spirit which encourages teachers to aim at "helping" rather than "instructing"; which encourages foundations to "projectism." The anti-intellectualism of the foundations is expressed in their insistence that projects be novel and collective and promise to cure the ills of mankind, and in their reluctance to support superlative individual minds or the prosaic work of established institutions.

Mr. Barzun laments the spread of pedantry (affectation, pretense, and pomposity) from the classroom to the kitchen, the office, and the White House. . . .

This book is the work of a courageous and unbiased radical. But Mr. Barzun is not a revolutionary. On the contrary, he complains that we do not do enough for existing institutions. . . .

Mr. Barzun's book is valuable precisely because it is a diatribe against our supposed virtues: the proliferating "creativity" of would-be artists, the "interdisciplinary" application of scientific methods, the expanding foundation support of vast and novel projects, the "enlivening" of magazines, newspapers and advertising, and the extension of academic vocabulary to boards of directors. He leads us toward national humility, for other nations, lacking our New World bounty and our peculiar liberal institutions, may be partly compensated by their freedom from the peculiar corruptions in our House of Intellect.

> *Daniel J. Boorstin, "Eggheads Are Their Own Worst Enemies," in* The New York Times Book Review, *April 26, 1959, p. 5.*

THE TIMES LITERARY SUPPLEMENT

One of the most sacred articles in the faith of Western democracy is that education in Communist countries must necessarily be degrading and inferior to our own. Marxist indoctrination must lead to double-think and muddled administration; ruthless specialization in science and engineering must produce stunted intelligence; and the evil influence of men such as Zdanov and Lysenko must paralyse discovery. Conversely we accept as axiomatic that progress and the good life depend on an education which is based on intellectual freedom and a healthy development of the child's personality. At school this means that children should be able within limits to study what they like best and that they should not be crammed with facts but learn how to handle concepts; while at the university students should be capable of learning on their own, and dons should be mainly free to research on whatever subject, useful or useless, they like. Will historians in centuries to come judge that this happy faith was justified? Or will they note that in fact it weakened the West because, when applied in countries which were also dedicated to equality of opportunity, majority rule and to voluntary (and haphazard) philanthropy, it corroded the core of what it was designed to strengthen?

Such is the background to Professor Barzun's philippic on education [*The House of Intellect*]. In only a few years Mr. Barzun has won renown as a brilliant Dean of the Graduate School of Columbia University, and American education is his target. But readers of his work will know that, although born a Frenchman, he has transferred his heart to the United States; and this is not the book of a fastidious European soured by American culture. It is an indictment of all Western education and the diagnosis of an intellectual disease. (p. 489)

Mr. Barzun begins by defining intellect as "tradition of explicitness and energy, of inquiry and debate, of public secular tests and social accountability" satisfying in us "the need for orderly and perspicuous expression which may lead to common belief and concerted action." As such it is something which is peculiarly Western and rarely to be found in Eastern philosophy or religions which do not express themselves in logical and universally coherent forms. Logic, coherence and clarity in argument; argument which proceeds to conclusions, conclusions which recommend us to act upon them; intellectual analysis which can be refuted only by another more convincing intellectual analysis; this is the tradition of thought for which centuries the West has upheld. It is a tradition which has always had enemies, but to-day its enemies are curious. Mr. Barzun identifies them as Art, Science, Philanthropy—and democratic educational ideals.

Mr. Barzun begins with the well known theme that is the background to any examination of Western culture. Other-directed man, to use Mr. Riesman's famous category, does not want to believe in the existence of superior intellects who should be directing society. He looks to the public opinion poll to tell him what to do, and if he is to be given ideas they must be "human," unchallenging and palatable. Nothing must be done to awaken his envy of the intellect, nothing must be set before him which frightens, surprises or makes him suspect that he is ignorant. . . . The flattery of the common man is paralleled by the invariably deflating and derisory manner in which newspapers refer to intellectuals and artists and make it clear that they are cutting them down to size. Mr. Barzun makes it clear that he is not, however, referring merely to the mass media and retailing the old horror story of mass culture. His polemic differs by claiming that all media, even the highbrow, have now become infected.

Nor is this odd because by now, he argues, the intelligentsia themselves spread the contagion. To disagree and contradict in conversation is considered intolerant and bad manners. When, if ever, do we say: "I disliked that man but we had a fine conversation"? Fear of being thought dogmatic or of being slapped down leads to the apologetic, "I am only thinking aloud." "I feel," has replaced "I think." And this desire to promote a cosy community has produced a relatively new activity in the lives of the intelligentsia—pseudo-work, *e.g.*, the informal committee, the exchange of ideas, international conferences, dictating reports and drafting schedules. Fraternity has us in its grip, and the intelligentsia are particularly frightened lest anyone should suspect them of aspiring to leadership or power. Power and ambition are evils: liberty and self-abnegation are good. Literary criticism, sociology and relativism in morality are all called in to justify the contention that men are not heroic or conceivably the captains of their souls. Today it is solemnly argued that Don Juan is simply a dilettante carried away by his desire to get on with the girls.

But the real enemy of the intellect to-day is education; and with this paradox Mr. Barzun warms to his work. When schooling became education and pupils children, the rot set in. Competition, discipline, driving facts, methods and subject-matter into the heads of pupils, have practically disappeared. Adjustment, development of personality, learning as one lives, "look and learn," communication have taken their place. Teachers are taught the theory of education yet are unable to teach: how should the unlearned instruct the ignorant? The object of education nowadays is to make children happy and fit in with their peers. Children must be helped not taught, and in fact American education is inspired by a fierce anti-intellectual spirit. For fear of creating an élite, the clever are held back and the idle are never rebuked. The pupils say what they are to be taught. Group-projects replace learning: children are told to write what they know of Greek life, manners and customs and not to bother with dates or names; or eleven-year-olds cut out cardboard microscopes but never learn to focus one. Every school claims that students are taught to think for themselves: but as they know no facts they have nothing to hang their thoughts upon. Nor is college better. Much of undergraduate teaching is done by "instructors," who are in fact Ph.D. students of many years' standing whose wives supplement their inadequate incomes. And how are they to instruct their pupils? They have often never written more than a page of prose in their life; as Ph.D. students they learn a deplorable jargon, the official academic language of America, and transmit this to their bemused charges. . . . The universities lie to-day under a fog of pseudo-scientific jargon which affects every discipline. Methodology killed the cat, and Mr. Barzun's devastating quotations from critics such as John Crowe Ransome or grammarians such as Fries or the tribe of sociologists will convince anyone who can be convinced that mere information is unlikely ever to bring the cat back to life.

If the hatred of the artist for ratiocination has been erected into a cliché that "free creativity" alone is valuable; and if scientism obscures in a mist of verbiage the very virtues of precision and logic implicit in the natural sciences, philanthropy, for so long the prop of education which was starved by the State, has now become a menace. Foundations will support most willingly "new projects." New projects must be costly and preferably promise social benefits. They woo the best brains from the hard but far more important task of teaching. At these projects these brains are put to work in teams. Teams may discover new facts but they never make original hypotheses: that is to say they rarely invent. The first cousin of the project is the conference. . . . Worse still is the "matching grant" whereby a Foundation offers a bribe to a university to set up a research unit if the university will itself subscribe to the cost: the parasite soon sucks blood from its host.

In his polemic Mr. Barzun often compares the happier state of affairs that exists in [England], where intellectual standards are preserved by a national system of examinations and by respect for those who win the blue ribands of academic success such as scholarships or fellowships. But he warns us that, once egalitarian principles prevail, the status of the intellect will decline and we shall follow America. (pp. 489-90)

The American intelligentsia are gravely perturbed about their schools, and the fact that Mr. Barzun's book is a best seller in America makes one hope that, as always when Americans decide to tackle a problem which in its magnitude seems insoluble, they astonish the world by doing so. On the other hand this is not a problem which can be solved by technical knowhow and the lavish use of resources. The roots of the disease lie deep in American culture—and often in those parts of it which we ought to admire, such as faith in individualism, freedom, lack of snobbery, and delight in experiment. Can we, however, afford to be complacent in this country? It is true that here the intelligent child has a better chance than in America. But it is also clear that the real battle lies in the secondary modern schools—do we show many signs of being able to fight this battle any more effectively than America? The working-class children, whatever their talents, leave school as soon as they can; when many, especially girls, are soured by out-of-date school regulations that bear increasingly less relation to the life of the community; when teachers are underpaid and the provision of science and mathematics teachers is left to the chances of the labour market; when the status of education is forever falling in the eyes of the majority of the voters, we can be sure that Mr. Barzun speaks to our condition. (p. 490)

> *"What Is to Be Done?" in* The Times Literary Supplement, *No. 3000, August 28, 1959, pp. 489-90.*

DAN JACOBSON

As a chamber of horrors, [*The House of Intellect*] is entertaining and instructive. However, it purports to be much more than this. *The House of Intellect* tries to establish itself as a coherent theoretical structure; and the harder it tries the more does it arouse one's misgivings.

Intellect is defined by Mr. Barzun (rather inelegantly) as

> the capitalised and communal form of live intelligence; it is intelligence stored up and made into habits of discipline, signs and symbols of meaning, chains of reasoning and spurs to emotion—a shorthand and a wireless by which the mind can skip connectives, recognise ability, and communicate truth. . . . Intellect is community property and can be handed down . . . [it] is an institution; it stands up as it were by itself, apart from the possessors of intelligence.

Elsewhere Mr. Barzun refers to 'the tradition of explicitness and energy, of inquiry and debate, of public, secular tests and social accountability.' It is this tradition which Mr. Barzun believes to be in a state of decay, and there is no one who studies the examples of confusion offered in the book who will fail to give his agreement. But when he writes that the major enemies of Intellect are Art, Science and Philanthropy, one's agreement comes to an end; and nothing Mr. Barzun writes subsequently can restore it.

Why Art? Well, says Mr. Barzun, 'art has put a premium on qualities of perception which are indeed of the mind, but which ultimately wage war against Intellect.' In our art, we prefer 'what is ambiguous, what titillates through irony, what touches only the sensibility, what plunges the imagination into a sea of symbols, echoes and myths, from which insights may be brought to the surface, but no arguable views.' Why Science? About science Mr. Barzun speaks more cautiously: he points out that 'through the increasing fantasy of its concepts and symbols, through its diverging technical tongues, science has also receded from the common world'; and he castigates would-be scientists who try to render their subjects esoteric by special terminology and the use of numbers. But generally, Mr. Barzun, who is lavish in the space he devotes to Art and Philanthropy, is inclined to veer rather rapidly away from any prolonged discussion of Science. And lastly, why Philanthropy? Here Mr. Barzun speaks of the 'liberal doctrine of free and equal opportunity as applied to the things of the mind'—a doctrine which must lead to the corruption of judgment and hence to the corruption of the products of intellect.

In fact, what Mr. Barzun does is to enumerate a number of attitudes and expectations which are either undesirable in themselves or undesirable in their extension outside certain limited fields: some of these attitudes and expectations he identifies with Art, some with Philanthropy and a few, uneasily, with Science. Then he reaches for his revolver and goes bang! and again bang! and bang! once more, bringing down a sacred cow every time. But it is much too easy: no wonder the beasts fall down dead, leaking cotton-wool and sawdust from every bullet-hole, when it is Mr. Barzun who stuffed their bodies beforehand, and manœuvred them, glass eyes and all, into their positions right in front of his gun. And no wonder, too, when we look at them lying there, that we are moved to deny that these are our cows at all or ever have been.

But they have been, they are, Mr. Barzun insists: look at your schools, look at your magazines, look at your intellectual conferences, look at your learned journals, the way you talk to one another, the way you conduct your political debates. All right, we look at them, and see evidence of intellectual confusion everywhere. But arguing as Mr. Barzun does, we could reasonably and legitimately remark that Politics is the enemy of Intellect, History is the enemy of Intellect, Education is the enemy of Intellect, Intellection is the enemy of Intellect. . . . Any human activity is the enemy of Intellect, and of itself, once it is exercised without a delicate and continuous awareness of its proper limits. Without such an awareness, one is not conducting politics, or studying history, or furthering science, or creating and enjoying art, but merely indulging oneself to the top of one's own particular bent. And self-indulgence is self-indulgence, and folly is folly, and there is no need to decorate them by giving them the names of better things.

I do realise that in its way Mr. Barzun's book is an attempt at just the kind of delimitation called for above; but the way does not seem to me to be a helpful one. I realise, too, that if we care for the tradition Mr. Barzun has tried to define, it is difficult to know where to begin its restoration, in the face of the fragmentation and dispersion of the intellectual community. The moral of Mr. Barzun's book, however, seems to be that we should certainly not begin by shaking our sticks at large abstractions, by drawing up lists of vague culpabilities. Such lists always include too much, always exclude too much. Rather let us accept that we are fragmented and dispersed, and for the moment can do no more, and can do no better, than to watch ourselves and others; to watch particularly those who assure us that we could be brought together again, if only we would close our eyes for a moment and *listen* to them. (pp. 308, 310)

Dan Jacobson, "Shots in the Dark," in The Spectator, *Vol. 203, No. 6845, September 4, 1959, pp. 308, 310.*

VICTOR LANGE

[*Classic, Romantic and Modern*], which first appeared some twenty years ago under the title: *Romanticism and the Modern Ego* and is now reissued with a new concluding chapter, is not merely a defense of the romantic sensibility but a magnificent philippic against the perverters of those immensely influential beginnings of the modern intellectual temper. In 1943 the book offered, first of all, a long-needed attempt at terminological housecleaning: it exposed the various platitudinous uses of the term "romantic" and defined the context within which romanticism must be seen. As one of our ablest cultural historians, Mr. Barzun sought to provide the sober perspectives of historical judgment that would enable us to salvage from an onrushing wave of intellectual confusion, whatever strength there lay in the beginnings of our "modern" experience. . . .

In his specific account of the historical topography of Romanticism, Mr. Barzun properly deplores and corrects the perversion which the political views of Rousseau and Burke have suffered from the hands of their exaggerators and false disciples, their views of individualism and tyranny, and the inevitable ambiguity in romantic political thinking of the terms liberal and conservative. The chief romantic premise, he insists, was the desire to create a new society, different from its immediate forerunner. As against the classical faith in stability within known and defined limits, the romantic is dedicated to the acceptance and exploration of an open universe: reason, nature and feeling may be terms common to both attitudes, but through the romantic revolution Mr. Barzun rightly shows them to have been reappraised in the light of new biological insights. Romantic art and romantic life are the two areas in which the fresh sense of the concrete, the particular and the energetic is demonstrated in some detail: the romantic life, Mr. Barzun argues, was robust and productive, largely because the romanticists were stimulated, pressed onward, justified by extraordinary events and by the challenges of political, social and aesthetic issues that transcended their personal selves. . . .

After a brief period of cultural effervescence in the ten years before the First World War—the era of socialism, internationalism and futurism—twenty subsequent years of disillusionment, self-distrust and futile promises of new realisms have destroyed the heritage of romanticism in violence and confusion.

From this harsh but passionate condemnation of the contemporary failure of nerve and imagination, Mr. Barzun does not detract one iota in his concluding **"Epilogue: Romanticism in 1960."** Whatever hope there may have been in the stirring of the individual and social conscience immediately after the Second World War, its cruel effect has been to ensure "the elimination not alone of Romanticist art and its sequels, but of all high art of the last five centuries." Mr. Barzun here echoes the chief thesis of his book *The Energies of Art* (1956) in which he described the "abolitionist" character of our present art, the intention no longer merely to shelve the past but to erase it, and by doing this to reproduce in man a wholly new consciousness. The divorce of the "act" of creating from mind and all remembered ideas has resulted in an aesthetics of annihilation. With its dislike and distrust of ideas, the substitution of sensation for strong emotion, and the taking refuge from aesthetic understanding in the intricacies of technique, modern art has deprived itself of all possible effectiveness. The single achievement of Cubism "the most productive, the purest and strongest of all the movements of this century" has been altogether forgotten or denied. There remains only the melancholy certainty that the philosophy of absolute denial which Mr. Barzun recognizes in our contemporary culture will produce a void in which the true impulses of the tradition described so brilliantly and urgently in this essay, may be remembered; for

> alternately dominant and submerged, romanticism seems to be a permanent trait of Western man. It expresses and exalts his energetic, creative, expansive tendencies by recognizing that, although he is but a feeble creature lost in the universe, he has unpredictable powers that develop under stress of desire and risk.

Victor Lange, "Romanticism and the Modern Ego," in The New Republic, *Vol. 145, No. 25, December 18, 1961, p. 26.*

FRANK KERMODE

Jacques Barzun's **Romanticism and the Modern Ego** came out in 1943, and attracted little attention [in Great Britain]. . . . Now it has come out in a revised edition [**Classic, Romantic, and Modern**], and it should be widely read. It won't have the impact it could have had earlier, because some of its battles are won, and also because it remains in many ways a book of the war years. Barzun has written a new preface and a new conclusion, and he has made a great many changes in the text, but there doesn't seem to be any change of mind on the central issues, though of course there are alterations of emphasis.

I notice, for instance, that Barzun has grown more tender to T. S. Eliot, omitting a page or more which attacked [his essay "Tradition and Individual Talent"], and also a whole section—his original conclusion—deriding 'Mr Eliot's candlelight search for the European mind', on the ground that what is so painfully sought is in fact all about us, 'the ideas floating in the air, in the very chaos itself, which is so uncomfortable but so European . . . This *is* tradition, this *is* history.' The 'sampling of modern usage' of the word 'romantic' is reprinted unchanged; it should have been expanded to cover the past 20 years, and the whole book might have taken more account of the profound changes that have recently affected the historical concept of Romanticism. (p. 258)

[Barzun's] book isn't in the Johns Hopkins tradition of history of ideas, being much more topical and concerned with cleansing a situation not merely semantic but also political; but he has a polemical vigour to compensate for his failure to produce definitive descriptions and differentiations. It is, nevertheless, disappointing that the new epilogue says little about recent historiographical positions, concentrating on the destructive qualities of post-war romanticism. Barzun thinks that having destroyed the classical forms (a beneficent act) the Romanticist tradition is now destroying art itself, by treating the past as exhausted and encouraging anti-art—action painting and *mu-*

sique concrète. For this nihilism is, unlike fascism, a true descendant of Romanticism, and the new mechanical vulgarization of the classics aids rather than prevents the work of destruction. He concludes that a new consciousness and a new realism (in his view true Romantic is Realist writ large) are due to be born.

This apocalyptic conclusion (expressed with Barzun's usual urbane vigour) is really the basis for another book. To reconcile it fully with the original text is a task not here attempted. Still, that older book is worth the attention of anybody who has missed it up to now. It argues against the bogus modern neoclassicisms; against the view that the Romantics destroyed civility, produced an art of escape, were the fathers of modern chaos. Some passages are closely argued, for example the defence of Rousseau against Babbittry, but the virtue of the book lies rather in its energetic ranging over many literatures and many fields of study, not only in the historical Romantic period. There is a brisk assault on the shibboleths of classicism, notably on the myth of 'classical balance', and a splendid defence of Romantic energy and seriousness, which perhaps even now we tend to dismiss with Arnoldian formulas. This is a book not perhaps improved by the author's revisions, but still in its present form a lively and important contribution to the study of Romantic and modern thought. (pp. 258-59)

Frank Kermode, "Europe by Candlelight," in New Statesman, *Vol. LXIV, No, 1642, August 31, 1962, pp. 258-59.*

MARTIN DUBERMAN

[*The essay excerpted below originally appeared in* The Atlantic Monthly, *November, 1968.*]

[In **The American University**] Barzun begins his discussion of the college population by adopting the Olympian view: they are, after all, young men, and that means "turbulence is to be expected, heightened nowadays by the presence of girls. . . ." In other words, a certain amount of inherent anger adheres to the condition of being young (it *is* a "condition," in Barzun's view), and anger must find its outlet. The nature of the outlet is almost a matter of indifference: if "the people of the town" do not provide a convenient target, well then, it might just as well be politics.

Still in the Olympian vein, Barzun further suggests—it is as close as he ever comes to implicating society—that "perhaps our lack of proper ceremonies for initiation into the tribe leaves the young to devise their own proof of manhood." Barzun loves dismissing the young with this kind of casual irony. Its elegant offhandedness is a useful device for keeping a proper distance between the generations. It is also useful—though of this Barzun seems unaware—for expressing the savagery which he likes to think is confined to the student population. Barzun claims the undergraduates would themselves welcome rites of initiation, for what they really want, he insists, is more, not less, discipline. When they speak of the impersonality of the university, they mean, it seems, "the looseness of its grip upon them.". . . In Barzun's phrasing, they are looking for "order," for "intellectual habits"; they sense that this is the balance they need, for like all youngsters they are in a "fever and frenzy," "their mind is monopolized by their inner life."

To meet this "rage for order," Barzun [posits] . . . a properly antiseptic university, a place of "respite and meditation" whose "proper work," in Barzun's phrase, is "in the catacombs under the strife-torn crossroads." He fills this subterranean cemetery with properly lifeless figures; they are "somewhat hushed," they give pause, as at Chartres, to the "spiritual grandeur of their surroundings." Yet just as one begins to feel, in the rush of Christian imagery, that Barzun has spent so many years surrounded by campus Gothic as to have lost all sense of distinction between the university and the church, he stoutly declares that *his* catacombs will not be peopled by early Christians. He dislikes that breed; it was marked by the same distasteful qualities he associates with today's young radicals: "indifference to clothes and cleanliness, a distrust and neglect of reasoning . . . a freedom in sexuality, which is really a lowering of its intensity and value . . . and—most symptomatic—a free field given to the growth of hair."

Barzun also . . . [proposes] that "emotion" has no place on campus, and that since student rebels tend to be emotional, it can be safely assumed they are also unreliable. (pp. 315-16)

Barzun is also huffy at . . . "nonsense" currently being peddled about teaching, especially the idea that teacher and student should explore together, each learning from the other. This view, he asserts, has done "immense harm to both parties. The teacher has relaxed his efforts while the student has unleashed his conceit." And of what does that "conceit" consist? Barzun is quick to tell us: the conviction that they (the students) have something to contribute. "Only rarely," he declares, with a hauteur appropriate to the century from which most of his ideas spring, does a teacher "hear from a student a fact he does not know or a thought that is original and true . . . to make believe that their knowledge and his are equal is an abdication and a lie."

And so we are back, as always in Barzun's schema, to the confinement of his starting assumption: students are children and, usually, fools. His contempt for undergraduates is pervasive. They are, very simply, not to be trusted; "student reliability is at a low ebb," he warns, and especially among radical students, who have but one purpose: to destroy. The evidence Barzun marshals to justify his contempt is so exasperatingly trivial (as well as suspect in its accuracy) that it demeans its compiler far more than the students. The undergraduates, he asserts, cheat a lot on exams and papers; they obtain pocket money by stealing books from the college bookstore; they keep library books out as long as they like and let fines go unpaid; they deny their roommates "the slightest considerateness"; students of both sexes live "pig-style" in their dormitories; their conversations "usually cannot follow a logical pattern," and so on.

The first thing to be said about these accusations is that Barzun has seized upon the occasional practices of a few undergraduates in order to damn a whole generation. The second is that even if these qualities did characterize a whole generation, they hardly seem heinous when compared with the sins of the fathers—when compared, that is, with racism at home and imperialism abroad.

The distressing consequence of this obsession with the peccadillos of the young is an avoidance of those genuinely important problems to which the young are calling attention. Mandarins like Barzun . . . are so preoccupied with manners that they forget matter. They are so certain of the rightness of their own patterns of thought and action and so eager to denounce all deviations by the young from those patterns that they blind themselves (and others) to the serious questions this new generation has raised—questions about the nature of ed-

ucation, the proper functions of a university, the very quality of American life. (pp. 317-18)

> *Martin Duberman, "On Misunderstanding Student Rebels," in his* The Uncompleted Past, *Random House, 1969, pp. 309-31.*

PAUL WILKINSON

Professor Barzun's new volume [*The American University: How It Runs, Where It Is Going*] belongs to a select company of great books on the university. It will be welcomed by all who care for the idea of the university as *studium generale* and who are thinking their way through the full implications of the impact of contemporary industrial society on the university as a social institution. The author, who has a distinguished experience as a professor of history and as Dean of Faculties at Columbia, develops an impressive range of axioms of academic prudence and a 'minimum programme' to bring some order into what he has termed 'the House of Intellect'. (p. 47)

Professor Barzun conceives of the purpose of the university as the preservation of 'the unity of knowledge, the desire and power to teach, and the authority and skill to pass judgement on what claims to be knowledge . . .' Implicitly the essential work of the university can only be carried out by members qualified to discriminate between 'what fits and what does not fit the purpose of higher education'. Clearly this conception of the university implies that both *socii* and *discipuli* constitute an elite, not in the sense of power but in terms of academic excellence. Further, Barzun endorses Newman's view that 'excellence implies a centre' and implies not only that *studia generalia* as a whole comprise an educational elite, but also that the *socii* form an elite within an elite. He argues that teachers and students do not start from a position of parity either in knowledge or capacity to contribute to the academic purpose of university. As Barzun conceives it the university is not to be confused with a *microcosmographia,* a miniature political and social order, or a 'democratic institution', in which some form of popular majority rule might be appropriate. He defines it as an academic institution in which teaching scholars and academic administrators (responsible to their disciplines and their trustees as well as their students), must take full responsibility for the educational direction, teaching, and administration of the university.

In terms of Professor Barzun's rigorous redefinition the main function of the student is to learn, while it is the main task of the *socii* to impart knowledge. Necessarily, however, the teacher must be constantly engaged in extending his own knowledge, and it is in the single-minded pursuit of this extension, Barzun argues, that too many scholars have been diverted from their primary work of teaching into a fight for promotion in the academic mandarinate. Driven by the injunction 'publish or perish', pressed to accept overloading with government-science research contracts, or hustled into premature production of a Ph.D. demanded by the structure of the profession, the scholar has neglected his teaching and has left his students too often with inadequately challenging intellectual discipline and lack of personal supervision.

Although Professor Barzun's own experience leads him to acute awareness of the dilemmas of the academic administrators, they are by no means exonerated in his analysis. They must take a good deal of responsibility for having allowed the university to become what the author calls a 'residual institution'. By this he means the university has been treated as a last resort for the performance of an incredible variety of quasi-governmental and social welfare functions that are entirely incompatible with its academic purpose, and which have drained their finances, energies, and manpower to the point of near bankruptcy. What business have the universities providing for psychiatric care for the young delinquent, slum clearance programmes for cities, military training and spying for Pentagon and C.I.A. and vocational instruction and promotion of commercial profit for manufacturers?

It is still not too late to ask these questions about the projected 'multiversities' in America. It is certainly not too late to ask them in Europe. Universities should be regarded as but one form of higher education, and if they are diverted from their central purpose they risk wreck. Heaven forbid we should all reach the stage when universities become, as Barzun acidly remarks, like medieval guilds, expected to provide every social service with the possible exception of masses for the dead!

Surely this book is also right to insist that the *discipuli* are not wholly innocent victims of the modern university. Many student militants responsible for inciting the abusive violence of 'campus demos' and proudly promoting the fashionable 'pig-style living' are well aware that their demands involve the destruction of the university as *studium generale*. To demand constant excitement, the constant drama of 'revolutionary experience' involves replacing the university by some form of 'stimulation palace'. Asking for continual 'relevance' (as if this were a commodity and not a connection originated in the mind) amounts, as Barzun argues, to a demand for a current affairs magazine produced by Ph.D.s. Others expect to be provided with a wardrobe of values, a 'new religion' to 'end the perplexities of life'. Some militants envisage turning the university into an experimental commune for utopianism, black power, or free love, or for use as a base for organising a popular revolutionary movement. None of these aims is compatible with the academic function of a university.

From practically every quarter the idea of the university is under attack. Professor Barzun's carefully thought out redefinition of the university's aims, and of their institutional implications, provides a brilliant defence. (pp. 47-8)

Paul Wilkinson, "Redefinition and Defence: Jacques Barzun on the American University," in Contemporary Review, *Vol. 216, No. 1248, January, 1970, pp. 47-8.*

HILTON KRAMER

"The cultural critic," wrote the late Theodor Adorno,

> is not happy with civilization, to which alone he owes his discontent. He speaks as if he represented either unadulterated nature or a higher historical stage. Yet he is necessarily of the same essence as that to which he fancies himself superior.

It is useful, if not indeed imperative, to bear this observation in mind in approaching [*The Use and Abuse of Art*], Jacques Barzun's new jeremiad on the cultural sins of our present civilization. . . .

It was avowedly as a mission in "cultural criticism" that he undertook last year "to assess the worth and the uses of art" in the A. W. Mellon Lectures at the National Gallery of Art in Washington. The result was anything but the display of sweetness and light one had long associated with this stalwart of liberal culture.

Prompted by his conviction that "we do art no honor and no justice when we represent it as invariably humane, heroic and disinterested in its intentions, exclusively good in its effects, and thus not subject to reproach or accountability," Prof. Barzun went on to prove beyond doubt that under the exacerbated pressures of our culture a spokesman for humanistic values and intellectual *mesure* could be as vehemently nea-saying and as sweeping in his anathemas as the most ardent votary of contemporary nihilism.

If this were not irony enough, the very circumstances of these lectures provided still another. Under its present director, the National Gallery is engaged in an energetic attempt to bring representative examples of modern art, including the most recent movements, into the museum's collections for the first time. Like other institutions of its kind, it is also busily at work disseminating information about art to the widest possible public. From all of this Prof. Barzun recoils in an agony of horrified distaste. The spirit animating those recent movements represents, for him, nothing but destruction. The expanded public interest in art—"unexampled in the history of our civilization," as he acknowledges—gives him no pleasure. The aim of these lectures is quite simply "to sing a Requiem for high art," and the singer seems scarcely to notice his surroundings.

Instead he seizes on the easiest targets. "A few years ago, for instance," he writes, "a painter in New York exhibited works done in human excrement; another exhibited molded plastic genitalia around a coffin in which he himself lay naked. A third cut off pieces of his own flesh and photographed them." And so on. Not exactly a comprehensive survey of what the contemporary art scene offers for our delectation. . . .

At least he understands, as many complacent camp followers of such cultural atrocities do not, that "art is power" and therefore holds within its grasp the means of destroying as well as creating something infinitely precious.

The trouble is, alas, that he brings such a parochial and intolerant taste to bear on these questions that he cannot really distinguish a genuine danger from an esthetic disturbance—or even, at times, from an esthetic achievement. A writer who blandly condemns the art of Picasso and Giacometti for representing "a dismemberment and defamation of man" is not to be trusted as an arbiter of artistic values. The unfortunate truth is, Prof. Barzun cannot forgive modern art for having, as he says, "abandoned imitation, representation, naturalism," and he therefore reserves his deepest contempt for those who have led the way toward symbolism and abstraction.

But it isn't even one or another of the hateful modern styles that is the real villain of Prof. Barzun's historical scenario. What really elicits his wrath is what he calls "the confusion of styles" that prevails at the present moment—"this coexistence, this pluralism that marks our age in the history of art"—and the "babel of arguments" that follows in the wake of this pluralism. What he yearns for is unanimity of taste and homogeneity of purpose, and he seems not to notice the extent to which this yearning places him at odds with the democratic ethos—at odds, indeed, with the bourgeois values he is so concerned to protect from artistic subversion.

"The cultural critic," Adorno observed, "can hardly avoid the imputation that he has the culture which culture lacks." But the culture that Prof. Barzun offers us as an alternative to our current mixture of misery and splendor is not only feeble but a little frightening. Toward the end of *The Use and Abuse of Art,* when we find him looking forward to a new, post-modern, "communal" culture—"Art will undergo a return to the medieval pattern; a literature of low intensity, paired possibly with a monumental architecture, in which the figurative arts will find an organic place"—we can only despair at what the liberal ideal of culture has come to. For Prof. Barzun's despairing treatise is a grim example of liberalism turning into reaction. In its refusal of variety, complexity and conflict in the cultural arena, it is sometimes more alarming than the genuine horrors it indicts.

> *Hilton Kramer, in a review of "The Use and Abuse of Art," in* The New York Times Book Review, *June 23, 1974, p. 2.*

RICHARD SENNETT

In their own way intellectuals are as fashion-conscious as the editors of Vogue. Every year sees the appearance of some new "discipline"—hermeneutics, ekistics, cognitive dramaturgics—each claiming it has synthesized knowledge previously scattered among various fields, each setting itself up as an imperial Court of Higher Meaning. In the flux of these various fashions, good scholars become skeptics on principle. But there are times when this skepticism turns into blindness; one fashion can show itself to be a serious way of looking at the world, and the scholar who is inclined to do things pretty much as he always has finds the ground cut from under him.

Many historians think this is what has happened to their field in the last 15 years. Psychiatrists, for one, have laid claim to the past. Psychiatric work is built on unraveling the life-history of a living person, and psychiatrists reasoned that their expertise might equally well be applied to the life-histories of the dead. Thus there came into being the field of psycho-history. . . . Around the same time, the application of the computer to historical records began to threaten the historians' claim to interpreting the more impersonal aspects of past society. Instead of writing a city history, for instance, using scattered individual memoirs, government documents and other "literary" sources, the computer historians could study census and other demographic records on every single person in the city.

At first, ordinary historians were inclined to snoot at both psycho-history and quanto-history as interesting oddities at best, but now they look at them as threats: they seem to make the ordinary historian a man with a subject but without a discipline. Jacques Barzun's new book, *Clio and the Doctors,* represents the feelings of a good many older historians toward these innovations that simply didn't go away as fashions usually do.

Barzun, like many older historians, is not opposed to these new tools per se; rather, he thinks that those who understand how to use them do not understand how to stop using them. (p. 27)

Barzun, no less than the new men themselves, is obsessed by the tools of psycho-and quanto-history. Like many older historians, he takes the new practitioners at their word and grants that they do have special expertise; instead of challenging their chain of proof, he proceeds to argue that history is proof-proof. History, he tells us, has an "integrity" of its own and the reason it is untouchable is that it embodies Culture, Humane Values and, yes, Man's Spirit.

Many old conceptual friends are to be found in *Clio and the Doctors:* C. P. Snow's two cultures; the quantifiers as Jacob Burckhardt's "terrible simplifiers"; the psychoanalysts as re-ductionists. Because Barzun has a sharp eye, he does find many delicious examples of stupidity among both psychoanalysts and statisticians. But a disturbing sleight-of-hand is going on in his defense of the "integrity" of history. Barzun metamorphoses the intellectual vulgarity and simplicity of some of his opponents into social vulgarity. The real sin of the quanto-historian holding a batch of computer tables in his hand is that he is talking too loud at the Dean's Tea; the historian who resists this boor and his "data" has more refined tastes. It is a pleasing formula; in being out-of-date, one shows oneself to be something of an aristocrat. To achieve this sleight-of-hand Barzun is not even-handed. He deals mostly with one work of quantitative history, and in discussing psycho-history he totally ignores European historians such as Philippe Ariès or Michel Foucault, who are nuanced and subtle writers.

There is something odd about Barzun's distaste for these new methods. He is undoubtedly one of the great music historians of modern times, and his greatness lies precisely in the fact that he jumped conventional lines of inquiry. In his writings on Berlioz, Wagner and other 19th-century musicians he went far beyond recounting the factual circumstances—when Berlioz wrote this or that, what he ate on New Year's day, 1831—which limited so much earlier musicological history. Barzun showed how developments in other fields influenced the people who made music, he showed how the experiences of a musician's youth could influence the work of his mature years. In *Clio and the Doctors* Barzun seems to have forgotten his own youth and its achievements.

If this is a sad book for this man to have written, it is nonetheless an interesting revelation of a state of mind. The historian as aristocrat is shown to be very much like his enemies: the Freudian wandering through Dante's hell, the computer scientist mad with his latest print-out. Both the old and the young in this quarrel concentrate on the foreground: what is historical material, what is a datum. Neither focus on themselves, on the interpretive work they do with these data. There is a general lack of what Alvin Gouldner calls "reflexivity," the capacity of a writer to stand back and study his own process of making connections. Therefore this quarrel between generations of historians, like so many quarrels, turns out to be no argument at all; the fathers' vice—a certain anti-intellectuality, a certain unreflectiveness in the writing of history—has been passed down intact, if disguised, to the sons. The new age of intuition is very much the child of the old. (pp. 27-8)

> *Richard Sennett, in a review of "Clio and the Doctors," in* The New York Times Book Review, *October 20, 1974, pp. 27 8.*

JOHN FISHER

Many art critics are reading [*The Use and Abuse of Art*] with that special sense of outrage usually reserved for the most philistine purveyors of commentary on art and culture. Admittedly, Barzun attacks recent developments and movements in painting, sculpture, and all the arts with the zeal of a hatchet-wielding Carry Nation breaking up a turn-of-the-century Kansas saloon. Yet the indignant reaction of moderns may suggest just a hint of their own misgivings. Jacques Barzun is not, as Hilton Kramer has written [see excerpt above], a grim example of a liberal metamorphosized into a reactionary. Barzun's affection for the nineteenth century and his harshness toward his own century is spelled out in all of his works. Thirty years ago he was defending his alleged leniency toward the nineteenth century by suggesting that a judgment is not necessarily a condemnation. "Far from condemning it," he wrote, "I think the present period so much less fortunate than the nineteenth century that it needs all our sympathy." The intervening years have only enhanced his disaffection for the present, and even his sympathy is obscured in this work.

In *The Use and Abuse of Art* the modern age is looked at apocalyptically, the end of the grand era which began with the Renaissance. This book is a Requiem for high art. The post-Renaissance period is over, and his expressed sorrow for its demise is not nostalgia but anguish, for with it went not only sweetness and light, romanticism and illusion, but humane instincts and human rationality, and, one senses, all the good things that five wonderful centuries could provide.

The Use and Abuse of Art is a series of six lectures, the 1973 Mellon Lectures in the Fine Arts at the National Gallery in Washington. The fact that they are published largely as delivered indicates something of the skill of the author, who lectures with the patient scholarly care of a writer and writes with the lively wit and passion of a lecturer. This is an eminently readable book, and few readers will be left unaffected by its clearly expressed theses concerning the arts today. It is not easy to accept them, but even more difficult to ignore them.

Barzun is not an aesthetician by trade, but many of the perennial theoretical problems of aesthetics are raised here with a pungency and a sense of importance missing in most volumes of aesthetics. (p. 239)

The work is in part a ruthless attack on contemporary art. It is easy enough to criticize Barzun for hunting and picking the examples which justify his suspicion that modern art is not only not worth our time, but a serious corrupter of values. On the other hand, if his nineteenth-century, Nietzschean vision is accepted, that the role of art is to "enhance life," that is to deepen, enrich, ennoble, and refine it, then his judgment is, on the whole, not so farfetched. Most of contemporary painting, not just carefully selected examples of it, is not "in love with life." His bone-deep distrust of art that condemns rather than affirms life makes sense if we understand his initial commitment. It is true that the hero has disappeared, that much of what appears today shows (not merely hints at) the superfluity of man and, as Barzun sees it, his "fear of being caught in a belief." If art is to restore and heal, one can only deplore an era in which the proposed cure serves sedulously only to keep the wound open.

Indeed, the picture is even more desperate than his carefully chosen instances maintain. It is not only in the crude and the vulgar, the genital and scatological works to which he alludes and discreetly does not identify, but the elaborate, sophisticated works of Rauschenberg and Rosenquist and Johns and Pollack and de Kooning which he does not mention that the assault on Barzun's notion of art is mounted. The pivotal notion of the book is the Nietzschean hypothetical, the big IF. *If* art is what he sees the nineteenth century making it to be (and it may, of course, well be) then cultured people (and the National Gallery) must resist not only the painters of today, but the critics who, Mailer-like, accept anything, including graffiti on subway cars, or leaning a broom against a museum wall, as the prodigious new high art, the new Renaissance.

Now that is something that the reader will have to settle for himself. Barzun's admiration for the true Renaissance and his appreciation of the past century are beautifully portrayed in this work, and his suspicion of the widespread democratization

of taste and standards ("Art is of all subjects the last on which one should defer to the judgment of the crowd, even a crowd waving paint brushes"), may be one which more people should share. At worst his concern suffers only from bitter exaggeration. But only a fool would call little Leonard's finger painting as good as a Leonardo canvas. Only a fool would belittle the art of the last five hundred years because of its historical links with something called the Renaissance, which fools cannot understand. Barzun understands the past with a clarity that few men possess. What will puzzle many readers is his grasp of the present, for in spite of wistful remarks like "It would be a new and perhaps a fruitful position to say on some appropriate occasion: 'It is because I understand this work of art that I dislike it,'" one wonders how much he has tried to sort out the serious and the sane in recent art from the silly and the sick, of which there is indeed, far too much. (pp. 239-40)

> *John Fisher, in a review of "The Use and Abuse of Art," in* The Journal of Aesthetics and Art Criticism, *Vol. XXXIII, No. 2, Winter, 1974, pp. 239-40.*

BURTON BENDOW

[In *The Use and Abuse of Art*] Jacques Barzun calls attention to one of the great casualties of the age. He examines the present condition of the arts, sees no help for it and, since something more than a curt announcement is required, tries to account for it. He is one of the few men to be aware of the gravity of the case and the only one, as far as I know, to attempt a diagnosis.

The trouble began, according to him, when the art of the 19th century usurped prerogatives that did not belong to it. It stole the thunder of a dying God and took on the airs of a full-blown religion. Worse, it turned militant and fought holy wars on two fronts. There was, first, the art that spoke as the conscience of a godless world and denounced iniquities and cried out for reform. Then there was the art that renounced the wicked world and even gave up trying to represent it and resolved to reform itself. The enemy here was the bogus official art that aped the successes of the past and had the support of the academies and the philistines.

Barzun goes on to tell where these two crusades led. They were both defeated—the just society is not here yet and the billboards are still with us—and the defeat only provoked a more intense enmity. Revolutionary art became an assault on our sensibilities, a weapon to jolt us out of our bourgeois complacency. Realists who professed to be leading us to utopia rubbed our noses in squalor. Preachers of peace exposed the horrors of war. Champions of the poor and oppressed took pimps and pushers as their heroes. Liberators of the sexual impulse contrived the most frigid perversions. The result was an art that grew more and more narrow in scope, and more and more violent in its efforts to be shocking. And an audience that grew more and more numb and bored, and either demanded stronger shocks and madder outrages or could bear no more and melted away.

As for the art of the *avant-garde,* it turned on itself and shook off the bad habits of the past with the convulsive starts of a man who gives up smoking. Cults and sects, credos and manifestoes, succeeded one another with bewildering rapidity, each one repudiating the practices of its immediate predecessor and laying claim to a more unfettered spontaneity. Every form of art struggled to erase every trace of resemblance to its former self. . . . The end was suicide—disposable art, the empty canvas labeled white-on-white, the mobile that destroys itself, the sonata that consists of three minutes of silence.

No audience and no art, not a soul in the theatre—and yet the show did not fold! It carried on by cutting costs, by performing with the least possible expenditure of energy and even with tongue in cheek, abandoning all pretensions to high purpose or profound meaning and traveling light, aiming at no more than titillation. Art is no longer serious. (pp. 344, 346)

This is a much abbreviated and distorted summary of the text. Barzun's full argument is much more convincing, for he has room to explain things more fully, trace the course of events more accurately, furnish hundreds of illustrations and make any number of shrewd comments. He points out, for example, the repetitive character of the whole enterprise. When the work of one generation of artists suffers an eclipse—owing to war, censorship, or some other disaster that interrupts the continuity of cultural life—the next generation returns to the charge in ignorance of what the earlier one did and does the same thing, often with less skill and fervor. . . .

Barzun would like to wash his hands of this hopeless case but, to his credit, he cannot. Any egregious symptom—say, an exhibit of twelve empty television screens oscillating in a darkened room—provokes him to denounce modern art *in toto*. He calls it a "destroyer," a "lethal influence" that attacks the vitals of our spiritual life and leads us to "a dance of death." In the last few pages he wishes away not only the art but the age that produced it as well, and foresees a new art created by the men of a new society in the dim future, so that from this imaginary vantage point he may have the satisfaction of looking back on ruins. This vehemence suggests that he, too, was once swept up in the crusade and is now, more than most of us who were never there, disenchanted.

Sure enough, when offering his credentials in the opening lecture, he tells how he grew up "in Paris, and not merely in the atmosphere of the new art of the century but in the very midst of its creation . . . surrounded by the young poets, painters, musicians, and sculptors who made Cubism, concrete poetry, atonality, and the rest." It is this kind of art that first captivated him and that still preoccupies him in its decline. I must add at once that he is not engaged in repudiating his juvenile enthusiasms. He has long since outgrown them and speaks with the authority of long experience. His illusions were shattered, or his efforts to say so were encouraged, at a later date.

He glosses over this painful experience when he claims, "my exposure to the arts of the Cubist decade made me see clearly how un-modern, un-contemporary a large part of our artistic output is now." It was the decade after World War II that exposed everyone to disenchantment and to a very virulent strain of it. (p. 346)

At Columbia University where Barzun was established as the leading cultural historian, scholars were busy saving the radical cause by ridding it of all compromising associations—of Marxist materialism and later accretions of dogma, of visionary utopianism, above all, of the revolutionary nihilism that aims only at destruction. . . . I have in mind the revisionists of the Left, whose views were more or less expressed by Lionel Trilling in *The Liberal Imagination*. These men left their mark on those whom they taught, but not on later generations— witness the student riots of the late 1960s. And this short-lived resurgence of barricade storming can only have confirmed their suspicions of revolutionary ardor and aggravated their sense of the futility of human endeavor.

Starting from very different premises, Barzun shares this distrust of ideology, this distaste for ill-considered passion. That is what makes him so impatient with the arts. He scolds them as if they were young agitators rushing about with half-baked ideas in their heads and bombs in their pockets. He longs for the happy days before they got religion and took to fulminating, the days when they served the purposes of life, when Samuel Johnson could say, "the end of writing is to enable the readers better to enjoy life, or better to endure it." Then, when the arts do lose their animus and become mere diversions, Barzun takes them to task for being trivial and meaningless and complains of "the vacuum of belief."

Or, as a third alternative, he reproves them for not having "had a new idea in fifty years," for continuing to attack the same enemy in the same way. Unfortunately the enemy, except for ominous technological advances, is still the same and is far more tiresome—still out for power and plunder while bleating the praises of free enterprise, still indifferent to things of the spirit unless they can be packaged and sold. No wonder the arts repeat themselves. And they are not as repetitious as Barzun makes out. He mentions only those works that suit his gloomy picture of the current trend and ignores everything else. *Sanctuary* may serve as an illustration of the shock tactics he deplores. But Faulkner's later novels are too Faulknerian, too much a part of the writer himself and his view of life as pain, too original to be cited as horrid examples.

Barzun would have put his case better had he avoided blanket anathemas and distinguished between those artists who take up arms for some cause and those in whom belligerence is mere self-assertion or conventional gesture. He might have taken a position above the battle, seen more clearly what all the shouting was about, and written history. As it is, his account of how the arts achieved their present insignificance has the heat and sharpness and salutary emphasis of a good polemic. (pp. 346-47)

Burton Bendow, "Present Condition of the Arts," in The Nation, *Vol. 220, No. 11, March 22, 1975, pp. 344, 346-47.*

PAUL F. CRANEFIELD

In *Clio and the Doctors,* Barzun offers various criticisms of "psychohistory" and "Quantohistory"—the latter, one gathers from *The New York Times,* being but a division of cliometrics. Readers of *Clio and the Doctors* may well give thanks that it was written before Barzun came across the term cliometrics, for that chance has spared them several pages of urbane indignation.

Having unburdened himself of a variety of sound and unsound objections to psycho-and quanto-history, Barzun dwells at some length on the nature of the real thing, telling us what history is and what it should be. We can, perhaps, best begin by examining what history should be since that will enable us more readily to judge the nature of the heresies. The great historian must be a worldly man, knowledgeable about men and affairs and thus preferably "acquainted with public life and over forty years old". To this he must add imagination, the judicial temper and "the power of solitary industry among books and papers". Finally, he must be a gifted writer capable of visual and verbal imagination, able, with "sagacity and style, art in composition and skill in exposition" to give form to the facts, the hard facts to which he gives his ultimate loyalty. His method is "the old familiar search for documents and the play of imagination and judgment upon them''. He uses evidence of a kind accessible to any intelligent and literate person rather than ''translating'' into (or out of) the language of numbers or of symptomatography.

The nature of his evidence and the manner of exposition employed by him mean that the results of his studies can be not only understood but also evaluated by the average literate critic. History thus has its being ''within the realm of common sense; its judgments, attitudes and language are those of common sense''. Common sense is ''defined'' by Barzun in one of the finest passages in this book:

> The common-sense habit of thought starts from a total absence of cant. It is a clear vision in common things, and it is marked by a composure akin to the judicial temper; a detachment from ready-made doctrines, which does not prevent the holding of strong convictions; an ability to see through shams, including advanced intellectual ones; a repugnance for sentimentality and other forms of emotional cowardice, and an untaught knowledge of how the world goes . . .

Just as the great historian must have this sort of common sense so can the reading of history free the reader from credulity, and from a susceptibility to accepting, without examining them, conventional ideas, whether those ideas are engendered by tradition or by novelty-hunting. This is not to say that history leads to certainty nor that reading it is a moral and intellectual panacea. Indeed it is the ability to tolerate uncertainty that distinguishes history from psycho-and quanto-history. History is for the tough-minded; the ''tender-minded in search of fixity must consequently turn for satisfaction to special studies done according to method.'' Although Barzun does not expand on this point, it strikes me as a telling one, for the psycho-historian and quanto-historian who claim to be courageous innovators are not infrequently touchingly reactionary in their belief that their methods yield ''truth'' whereas traditional history merely spins novelistic fantasy. (p. 157)

Only true history can tolerate complexity, uncertainty and the mysteries of human behavior.

If the reader correctly concludes . . . that I sympathize with many of Barzun's positions, he should not also conclude that I do not find much in this book to occasion great dismay. For one thing, Barzun often seems almost willful in his misunderstanding of the arguments of ''heretical'' historians. (p. 158)

And what are we to make of the claim that history and history alone provides a ''spectacle of continuity in chaos, of attainment in the heart of disorder, or purpose in the world'' when Barzun follows that claim by saying of such continuity ''science denies it, art only invents it''? Are we to conclude that, for Barzun, among the fragmentary world views that replaced the religious synthesis, only history can command the respect of a serious intellect? Does the Newtonian synthesis deny continuity? Is *War and Peace* mere invention? Or is it that the greatest merits of each are to be found in the fact that they to some degree attain the dignity of history? I am, on the contrary, inclined to search this statement for traces of cant, sentimentality or advanced intellectual sham just as I would search any other claim to superior insight into the relative merits of various kinds of human endeavor. I do not claim to have found those traces but the statement is one of many in the book that suggests that Barzun's view of the nature of history leads him to share with Melville's Ishmael the feeling that he alone survives to tell the tale. Nor am I particularly happy with Barzun's mildly patronizing view of ''special studies'' that ''take up questions

that are of small scope, or obscure, or moot, or time-consuming, or requiring uncommon knowledge to pursue''. Such studies are, it seems, acceptable if they are useful to the ''great'' historians. Although Barzun's criteria for the validity and usefulness of such special studies are sensible and persuasive, his attitude towards them evokes more than a little uneasiness when viewed in the light of his concept of ''great historians'' who must avoid the ''mole-role''

The ultimate question this book raises in my mind is whether anyone can now or ever again will be able to write the sort of history Barzun admires? I myself have never attempted more than a few ''special studies''; those of my friends whose historical scholarship far exceeds my own in breadth and depth are in some instances over forty years old, have a good command of form, never psychologize and seldom count or measure. But they are, I fear, largely unacquainted with public life and the management of affairs and might well, to Barzun, be mere makers of special studies, witless players of the mole-role. I agree that much psycho-history and quanto-history is, to use a word Barzun does not use, piffle; pretentious piffle that may serve to advance academic careers but is on the wrong side of the war against cant, sentimentality and advanced intellectual shams. I would, nevertheless, feel better about *Clio and the Doctors* if Barzun had offered us some really persuasive evidence that the sort of history of which he approves can be and is being written today. (pp. 158-59)

Paul F. Cranefield, in a review of "Clio and the Doctors: Psycho-History, Quanto-History, and History," in American Notes & Queries, *Vol. XIII, No. 10, June, 1975, pp. 157-59.*

JOHN W. BICKNELL

''It is not overconfident to prophesy that in any new vale which the muses may elect for their abode, Clio will again be found among them, *virgo intacta*.'' So ends this slim volume [*Clio and the Doctors: Psycho-History, Quanto-History, & History*], a revised and expanded version of a long article first published by Professor Barzun in the *American Historical Review* in February 1972. The medical metaphor of his title is indicative of his theme: he portrays the virgin, history, as being tinkered with by the doctors of psycho-history and the doctors of statistics in ways which threaten her hymen and may well violate her womb. Among the many threats to history common to these doctors Barzun sees the absorption in methodology, the construction of models, and philosophies of history (for example, Toynbee or Marxism) as especially dangerous, for, he claims, they impose a construct upon historical materials that essentially distorts and oversimplifies the complex, unpredictable, and ultimately irrecoverable past. The virtue of ''history,'' on the other hand, is that it has no method save that of being ''rational and resourceful, imaginative and conscientious''; it possesses the saving grace ''of calculated common sense.'' It is rational and resourceful in its interpretations and discovery of data; it is imaginative in that it is narrative and concrete in its presentation (not obfuscated by jargon or abstraction) and conscientious in its refusal to appear omniscient or dogmatic when there are grounds for neither. . . . Lest anyone should think Barzun is waging war on interdisciplinary studies, he asserts categorically that ''history was interdisciplinary from the outset; its contents were mixed before the disciplines were invented''. No, the historian is presumably hospitable to information or suggestion from any source that may illuminate the events he is engaged with; what he presumably refuses to do is to use theory as reductive or as a source of an impossible certainty about the way human affairs are conducted. The trouble with psycho- or quanto-historians is that they are essentially nonhistorical; they are concerned with "diagnosis, typology, and technical analysis"; the one imports a new terminology into history and thinks it is doing something new; the other attempts to reduce history to graphs and/or paradigmatic abstractions. They produce studies or diagrams or structural patterns, but not histories.

Naturally, in shooting down the enemies of history, Barzun is able to trot out some horrendous examples. Anyone can. As a literary historian I could point to several fatuous adventures by psychoanalysts into the field of literary criticism, such as the famous (or infamous) theory that King Lear chose to stay a month at each of his daughters' houses because this expressed Shakespeare's private anxieties at the time of his mother's menstrual period, or that Lear is outraged at the reduction of his entourage because his knights are faeces symbols. A bad application of a method, however, does not necessarily invalidate the method or the approach. In fact, I would argue that the examples Barzun uses are bad not so much because they are bad history, but because they are bad examples of psychologizing. Not long ago Harry Schlochower pointed out in *Imago* (the periodical he edits) that the trouble with much psychoanalytic criticism is that it violates its own clinical methods; it tends in examining works of literature to ignore the manifest content of the work in favor of the latent content, thus reversing analytic practice with patients, in which it is only a careful examination of the manifest that can lead effectively to the diagnosis of the latent.

The same point might be made about Barzun's objections to some of the sociological statisticians. He complains that they often generalize from insufficient data or uncritically examined statistics. All very well, but what it comes to is not so much that they are bad historians, but rather that they are bad sociologists or statisticians. (pp. 341-43)

Barzun's second major objection is that the scientific precision claimed or aimed at by the psycho-quanto complex is untenable because in both fields there is no orthodoxy or agreed school that can be relied on: shall the psycho-historian be a Freudian or a Jungian or a Sullivanian, or the quanto-historian be a structural anthropologist, a Parsonian, a Weberian, or a Mertonian? A good question, but on the same page he admits that historians too have been of different schools, an admission that somehow makes Clio into a multi-faced muse rather than an integral virgin. Thus a kind of unexamined assumption runs through his essay, that the historian has some magical immunity from the diseases that infect the new disciplines, that historians (especially if they are not Buckles or Spenglers or Toynbees) are a race apart untouched by the forces of prejudice, political preference, moral stance, or even by unconscious forces. He seems to have forgotten such cautionary epigrams as, "History is a fable agreed on" or "History is a bag of tricks the living play on the dead," and has neglected the ways in which even the great historians of the past and present evoke, willy-nilly, not only a vision of the past but a vision informed by their individual judgments of the past shaped by the world in which they live. (p. 343)

Moreover, the fact that historians, psycho-historians and quanto-historians are tendentious is not of itself deplorable. One may disagree with a Marxist historian, but the fact remains that the Marxist historians, because of their bias (or whatever you wish to call it), have introduced materials about the working class

or economic forces that other historians have neglected; the story of American history can no longer be written in the old way because liberal and leftist historians have demonstrated the distortions created by omitting serious considerations of American Blacks and American Indians, not to mention American women. . . . Neither Barzun nor anyone else is going to stop scholars from erecting theories, constructing models, employing computers, or imposing patterns on historical data; nor can he stop scholars (including historians) from describing the past within a perspective or a methodology shaped by their discipline or world-view. The phenomenon is inevitable; the conclusion is to take insight wherever we can find it and to pillory nonsense and shoddy scholarship relentlessly.

Barzun might reply that this is what he is really doing, for, indeed, in his conclusion he speaks of the value of special studies and admits that useful studies may be "inspired and carried out" by what he calls the "methodists." He even lays down rules for their utility, rules with which no one would really quarrel. They are the rules or principles of humanized scholarship and are at work in all the great scholars in whatever field and are equally violated by hordes of alleged scholars in every field. The trouble is, as I have remarked above, that the polemical force of his essay overwhelms this sensible conclusion; we carry with us the image of the virgin muse, Clio, under assault by the wicked doctors. History is the discipline that carries human values, whereas the doctors dehumanize; history gives us "the imaginative grasp of the real" while the doctors give us formulae, jargon, abstractions, and pseudo-analogies; history is formative while the doctors are what—deformative? Now no such passionate reader of history as I am is going to kick Clio down the back stairs, but Barzun seems to have drawn the battle lines incorrectly; the antagonism is not between history and the encroaching disciplines, but between the values he assigns to history exclusively and their opposites in any discipline (including history) whatever. (pp. 344-45)

Finally, I must be a little naughty about Barzun's assertion of Clio's virginity. Having quoted Barzun earlier to the effect that history was always interdisciplinary, we might remark that Clio must therefore never have been a virgin—not that she had been raped—but instead was an eager and fecund mother from the beginning. I have no quarrel with virginity, but one thing virgins don't do is have children. I would be pleased, too, if Barzun would consult his handbook of mythology; if he did he would find that Clio was not a virgin, that, according to one legend, she had a son by Magnes. That son was Linus, a musician, the inventor of rhythm and melody and the teacher of Orpheus. One story has it that he was murdered by Apollo, who, as in the case of Marsyas, destroyed all rivals; another that Linus was destroyed by the Dorian Heracles. Just what Barzun would make of this I don't know, but I find it amusing to discover that the creator of the arts of music, of which Barzun has written so beautifully in his studies of Wagner and Berlioz, was the son of the muse he claims to be *virgo intacta*. And he might meditate on who it was who murdered Linus—either the jealous God or brute force; in fact, we might all meditate those alternatives when we try to identify the enemies of promise. (p. 345)

John W. Bicknell, "Minnows among the Tritons," in The Journal of General Education, *published by The Pennsylvania State University Press, University Park, PA, Vol. XXVI, No. 4, Winter, 1975, pp. 341-45.*

ROBERT COLES

America never had—and may never enjoy again—another pair like William and Henry James. The brothers' combined genius appeared, out of nowhere it seemed, in the last third of the 19th century as evidence of a young nation's cultural distinction and a reminder to Europe (where Henry lived for so long and to which William frequently traveled) that the forbidding forests of the New World had indeed been tamed. . . .

[Jacques Barzun] believes their contribution was a collective one, a statement both powerful and tactful: the mind as the repository of a life's secrets to be fathomed through suggestive stories or literate essays rather than the mind as an excuse for ambitious, overwrought conceptual performances, if not hanky panky. The use of "stroll" in [*A Stroll with William James*] is no mere conceit or selling device; the author wants to make an immediate statement about the nature of his literary involvement with a particular historical personality—an enjoyable, active encounter.

Mr. Barzun gives plenty of biographical details, but his primary interest is in William James's work rather than the events in his life. The point of the exercise is an engagement of two congenial human beings—thus the presence of generous quotes from *The Principles of Psychology, Talks to Teachers on Psychology: And to Students on Some of Life's Ideals, The Varieties of Religious Experience, A Pluralistic Universe* and the posthumous *Essays in Radical Empiricism,* as well as from letters and anecdotal remarks. This manner of exposition . . . is an edifying act of affection toward a man who loved frank and animated intellectual exchanges and mocked pedantry. As Mr. Barzun keeps emphasizing, James had no interest in lording his ideas over friends, colleagues, students. He was openminded and kindly; he invited criticism—even, to the consternation of some, pursued it. He had an innate generosity of spirit, an inclination to share his ideas with others, and so his writing naturally favors a response like the conversation through quotation that Mr. Barzun has sought with him. . . .

"A person's character is known by the concepts he keeps," Mr. Barzun observes and then reminds us that James declared himself "never able to forget" what he called "the difference between all possible abstractionists and all livers in the light of the world's concrete fullness." On the same page Mr. Barzun insists that "history is the realm in which the particular is the center of interest." He pointedly adds: "Generalities help to organize and relate, but reification—making agents or forces out of generalities—is the unforgivable fault." (This is Alfred North Whitehead's "fallacy of misplaced concreteness.")

There is some marvelous polemic in this book. James energizes Mr. Barzun, although their dialectic is not quite Hegel's. (p. 7)

James shunned reductionist thinking. He was comfortable—eerily so, many felt—with life's confusions, contradictions, inconsistencies, ironies, ambiguities. In a marvelously compact, knowing summary, Mr. Barzun has his spiritual kinsman regarding the human mind as "a stream running after some half sensed goal, yet capable of attention, forming objects like an artist and concepts like a geometrician, while the whole organism, acting like a sounding-board, generates the emotions that reason is meant to serve." Such a view is, of course, inadequate for many of us who find behaviorist or psychoanalytic imagery (often called "scientific") more appealing.

But James was no stranger either to experimental psychology or Freud's theoretical writing. He had studied in Germany, and he devoted 200 pages of his *Principles of Psychology* to a discussion of the work of Helmholtz, Fechner and Wundt. He was a physician, keenly interested in neurology and physiology. Moreover, in 1909 he was at Clark University in Massachusetts to welcome Freud and Jung and wish them well—though he quickly noticed the stubborn ideological assertiveness of those two fellow physicians, a willingness to be (he put it) "obsessed with a fixed idea." The contrast with his own relaxed, self-critical point of view is instructive: "We should not treat our classification with too much respect." For such, however, there is a price: There have been few self-declared Jamesians.

On that score, Mr. Barzun is very loyal; he refuses to turn his hero into yet another doctrinal disciplinarian insistent on the letter of a given series of laws. He reminds us that James possessed an artistic temperament; he studied painting with William Morris Hunt, and John La Farge was a fellow student. Mr. Barzun also notes that James was an adventurer of sorts who boldly interrupted his studies at Harvard Medical School to accompany Louis Agassiz on an expedition to the Amazon. James's strong interest in religious matters, in the so-called psychical, was abiding. He was an eager but tolerant observer, wary of absolutes, always willing to take a metaphysical chance, though no one's fool. In pragmatism, with its emphasis on the practical consequences of any interpretive foray, he offered a way of looking rather than a tidy bundle of rules. His passion was experience: the rendering of its complex texture. (pp. 7, 15)

In many respects he anticipated the second half of the 20th century; relativism and urgent existentialism are more than implicit in his thinking. However, he was also an old-fashioned Yankee stoic, skeptical but always yearning for a faith he knew he would never really have. In this book he emerges as a friend to a distinguished contemporary historian—Jacques Barzun's intellectual guide and moral example. Somewhere in the universe the ardent, robust walker William James must be quietly delighted at receiving this eloquent and wise testimonial from a longtime traveling companion. (p. 15)

> Robert Coles, "A Passionate Commitment to Experience," in The New York Times Book Review, May 29, 1983, pp. 7, 15.

JOHN J. McDERMOTT

Writing about William James's classic work on *The Varieties of Religious Experience,* Jacques Barzun laments to his readers that he can only "sample the feast." In reviewing *A Stroll with William James,* I am in a similar position, for seldom has a major creative thinker received such a rich, detailed, and correct evocation of the main facets of his thought. Barzun is a premier intellectual historian and an exemplary man of letters and culture. William James is his mentor in matters intellectual, philosophical, and even personal, so far as that latter term involves the religious question. Barzun's book is not another in the now steady stream of monographs on the thought of William James, many of which are characterized either by a desire to show where James allegedly went wrong on this or that isolated point or by an effort to explain what James really meant but never quite said himself.

To the contrary, *A Stroll with William James* is written in the grand style: wide ranging, adulatory, critical in a helpful way, and, above all, driven by a passion to share the majesty of James's thought with readers of every persuasion. Furthermore, Barzun is not only a careful student of James's writings but knows as well the writings of the father, Henry Sr., and of the brother, Henry Jr., both powerful and creative figures of the time. Barzun is also profoundly informed by the intellectual and cultural ambience of the world of William James, which he brilliantly limns in the opening pages of his chapter on "The Reign of William and Henry." So telling is his grasp of this context, that if someone were to ask me what it was like to live reflectively in the European-New England world from 1870 until 1910, I would reply, "Read Barzun on William James."

Barzun's "Stroll' is actually a voyage through the evolving thought of William James, with contextual asides that award novelty and originality to the now classic positions taken in the *Principles of Psychology,* the "Will to Believe," *The Varieties of Religious Experience, Pragmatism,* and *Essays in Radical Empiricism.* Many other works of James's are cited throughout, and the reader soon grows confident that Barzun is familiar with the complete body of James's writings. In a book of this kind, it is appropriate that Barzun avoid scholarly philosophical tangles, although his use of the secondary literature on James is idiosyncratic, and it is to be lamented that he makes only passing use of the Harvard Critical Edition of *The Works of William James,* the introductions and text of which would have assisted and supported him in most of his positions.

Barzun does not hesitate to take sides on a controversial issue, and it is refreshing to read someone whose interpretation is willing to acknowledge and absorb the resulting conflict. Despite his many strident opinions, Barzun is faithful to the spirit of James and twice cites James's proscription: "What has been concluded that we should conclude about it?" Central to Barzun's approach is the key line in James's thought, written but a year before his death, found in *A Pluralistic Universe* (1909): "Let me repeat once more that a man's vision is the great fact about him." More than any other commentator by far, Barzun has remained faithful to that vision.

The William James who emerges in the pages of this book has two facets. First, I believe that Barzun is sentimental and hagiographic about James's personal character. James was genial but self-centered and abysmally ignorant of massive social inequities. . . . Quite simply, James, like most of us, is a complex person, and his failings should have been acknowledged more completely by Barzun.

Barzun, following the suggestion of James's student the late Horace Kallen, states that to understand James, we must realize that he was a "gentleman" and then cites Andrew Lang to the effect that "no gentleman ever consciously misrepresents the ideas of an opponent." In that respect, James certainly was a gentleman. Unfortunately, a gentleman, more often than not, has no clue about how it is with the masses. The paradox here is that although James did not understand the social forces that dominated the "public," individuals understand James. Actually, James makes more sense, to more people, for more reasons, and with less academic trapping than any other American thinker. Barzun acknowledges this strength by reference to James's intelligible lecture style; I would add James's uncanny insight into the unusual and the personally precious experience of the uncommon.

On the second facet of his presentation, James's thought, Barzun is to be commended. Even more than in Ralph Barton Perry's too often ignored book *In the Spirit of William James,* Barzun captures the philosophical vision that animated James. Both James's technical and the popular writings are detailed

and analyzed, and Barzun, with his lucid and informative prose, is able to cull from James's most sophisticated philosophical positions cultural and intellectual ramifications that are as fresh to present inquiry as they were when first written. Although James was a philosophical maverick, who opposed most classical doctrines, Barzun's rendition of James's thought serves to assign it a permanent place in the "philosophia perennis," no matter the point of view from which that tradition is assessed. (pp. 126-29)

Following James, if objects are mock-ups, whereas relations are real and affectively experienced, then to propose a truth is to await its consequences, that is, how the emergence of future relations sustains the claim. Lamentably, Barzun does not make the necessary extrapolation from the radically empirical metaphysics of James, for he does not sufficiently explore the full implications of this new doctrine of relations. Nonetheless, contrary to most commentators on James, including Bertrand Russell and G. E. Moore, Barzun does understand that pragmatism is not a vulgar manipulation of the truth for personal and self-aggrandizing ends. Barzun correctly sees that James's pragmatism follows from his empirical description of the person as an interest-oriented organism whose evaluation of the world is as much dependent on outcomes as it is on description. Barzun's educated understanding of modern science is helpful on this issue, for he is not seduced by any classical coherence or correspondence theory concerning how the world "is" rather than how it "works." Responding rather to James, and therefore ignoring the jejeune assumptions that govern most contemporary teaching of science, Barzun boldly acknowledges the anthropomorphic character of scientific inquiry, including its covert and patently pragmatic methodology.

Jacques Barzun also is not taken in by the never-ending spate of silly and uninformed critiques of James's doctrine of "The Will to Believe." He knows too much of Nietzsche's thought to be so misled and recognizes, furthermore, that neither the conservative nor the radical thinker is pleased with James's position. Moreover, Barzun, from what he tells us throughout this book, also knows too much of how life is actually lived to be unaware that James is prescient in his diagnosis of belief, especially overbelief. James's position is clear. Given that we are trapped in a repetitive and defined environment, the human task is to project possibilities beyond our present ken. As James writes in his crisis "Diary," we have no guarantee for these beliefs, and they may, indeed, prove to be counter-factual. The text of 30 April 1870 reads: "My belief, to be sure, can't be optimistic." Despite this disclaimer, however, James concludes the entry with the remark that life shall be built in "doing and suffering and creating." James, then, affords us the opportunity of having one foot firmly planted and the other foot springing for the stars. This paradox is central to James, and it is to Barzun's credit that he both understands and accepts it.

Jacques Barzun's book on William James is superb, the best commentary ever written on James. To be sure, there are blemishes. In addition to glorifying James the man, Barzun also badly misinterprets the thought of Josiah Royce and John Dewey—a common failing in followers of James, but Barzun should know better. Also, Barzun occasionally vents some spleen on contemporary issues, especially in footnotes. I find him mostly accurate, but the posture is olympian as though, for example, the proletarians rather than the gentlemen are at fault for the collapse of the American public schools. This is vintage James but bad history, and it mars Barzun's otherwise excellent performance. (pp. 129-30)

John J. McDermott, in a review of "A Stroll with William James," in The New England Quarterly, *Vol. LVII, No.1, March, 1984, pp. 126-31.*

MARTIN LEBOWITZ

One of the country's greatest teachers (until his retirement from Columbia in 1975), Jacques Barzun is our most notable critic of the cultural climate of the industrial revolution. His bête noir is mechanical materialism, the governing concept of a "block universe" or monistic deterministic system that reduces experience, both physical and mental, to the "fortuitous concourse of atoms" or of electromagnetic phenomena. He calls this scientism or the tyranny of science because it nullifies the palpable diversity of possible points of view, the inconsistencies of science, and the empirical reality of emotion, spirit, and the teleological function of consciousness. He is also hostile to the monism of idealistic metaphysics because that, too, is a form of determinism, an absolute view of reality. Thus William James is his cultural hero. The radical empiricism of James allows objectivity, utility, and scope to *all* varieties of experience or existence, while his pragmatism—an antidote to the arbitrary rule of conceptual or theoretical thinking—provides a human test of knowledge and our intuitions: does it work? and indeed how does it work for us? (p. 545)

[In *A Stroll with William James*] Barzun ascribes to the period between 1890 and 1914 a sort of cultural renaissance tragically cut short by World War I; he views this period as the Reign of William and Henry James, since both are remarkable not only for their magnificent prose but for reinstating the point of view as a precondition of experience and indeed of moral or esthetic existence. The egalitarian implications of this attitude are obvious. Thus the two brothers contributed to the "permissive" or "enlightened" cultural and esthetic climate of this century, as well as to its "estheticism" as such—and hedonism. (The present reviewer has pointed out that Henry's novels are in fact Hegelian in their perception of consciousness as a specious approximation to something ineffable or unknowable—thereby recalling William.)

The moral necessity of a perspective or point of view means, in Barzun's terms, a restoration of that concreteness of immediacy—the matrix of factuality, the greater the better—upon which our opinions, if they are to be profitable and useful, must of course be based. Barzun, like James, belongs indeed to a tradition comprising the British empiricists, notably Berkeley (who advocated the creative view of mind), and including William Blake and Nietzsche, for both of whom experience in its concrete magnitude and scope implies vitalism, relativism, "functionalism"—the mythopoeic role of man in and of himself. (Barzun confesses his own belief in polytheism.) This "tradition" might be said to culminate in the work of men like Vaihinger, Poincaré, and Duhem—epistemological philosophers whose conventionalism paved the way for the profound liberation of imaginative theorizing that marks recent physics, for example. In all this Barzun is a deeply respectful admirer of technology and technique but not of the scientific attitude so far as it limits or indeed defines the magnitude of human nature.

Technically speaking, the problem that engages Barzun lies in the fact that once cognition or discrimination commences—perception, conceptualization, and the practical or theoretical organization of experience—antinomies or self-contradictions appear necessarily to ensue. (pp. 546-47)

This is Barzun's best book since *Darwin, Marx and Wagner* (1941), containing as it does the central constructive thesis upon which its author's profound reputation is based. It is, in itself, an education in the liberal arts. (p. 549)

Martin Lebowitz, "The Reign of James," in The Virginia Quarterly Review, *Vol. 60, No. 3, Summer, 1984, pp. 545-49.*

Richard (Carl) Bausch

1945-

American novelist, short story writer, and songwriter.

Bausch's novels and short stories portray the lives of ordinary people and focus upon such topics as family, love, marriage, fear, and loss. Contending that the primary responsibility of fiction is to convey emotion and encourage personal expression, Bausch employs simple, direct language and a straightforward narrative style that stresses characterization and plot. Although many critics consider his works to be independent of literary schools and traditions, Bausch's Southern Catholic sensibility and his emphasis upon spiritual crises and the tenuous nature of human relationships have elicited comparisons to the writing of Flannery O'Connor. Thomas Cahill predicted: "[In] the second and third decades of the twenty-first century, all of Bausch . . . will be in print, and names like Updike, Roth, Bellow will have faded from view."

In his first novel, *Real Presence* (1980), Bausch examines the efforts of an aging priest to overcome a crisis of faith. Set in rural West Virginia and narrated in a terse, austere tone, this work centers upon Monsignor Vincent Shepherd, whose preoccupation with his own mortality has caused him to neglect his convictions and has impaired his ability to lead his congregation. He is challenged in his state of spiritual ennui by the plight of a homeless family that has moved into the parish rectory, and he experiences rebirth through the humility and grace of their pregnant mother. *Take Me Back* (1981) portrays the lives of an unhappily married couple residing in an apartment outside Washington, D.C. Alternately narrated by the husband, the wife, and her illegitimate twelve-year-old son, this novel presents a grim examination of despair, apathy, and self-imposed helplessness through the family's attempts to cope with their situation.

Bausch's third novel, *The Last Good Time* (1984), is a simultaneously disturbing and humorous story of two elderly men whose long-established ways of life are disrupted by the appearance of a young prostitute in search of the man by whom she became pregnant. While one of the old men dies during the course of the narrative, the other becomes infatuated with the prostitute and, inspired by a newfound vitality and joy, resolves to care for her and her child. The pieces collected in *Spirits and Other Stories* (1987) depict problems of everyday life through the experiences of a variety of characters. Emphasizing such thematic concerns as the survival of marital and familial relations, the role and effect of fate in daily existence, humanity's ability to endure loss and disappointment, and society's attempts to confront temptation and vice, Bausch balances potentially negative situations with elements of affirmation and hope. Sharon Dirlam stated: "If there is a message in [*Spirits*], maybe it's that things don't quite work out as they might; life is sadder and more complicated than it ought to be, and yet the struggle continues and is somehow worth it."

(See also *Contemporary Authors,* Vol. 101.)

© Jerry Bauer

DORIS GRUMBACH

[With *Real Presence*], Richard Bausch has written a book distinguished by its distance from the customary first novel subjects. No childhood nostalgia, no celebration of boyhood or young manhood anguish here; instead, he has written a perfectly wrought imaginative experience that comes to life at once, and stays alive throughout the entire extent of its telling.

Bausch's theme is not especially unusual. Graham Greene has explored it a number of times: the crisis of faith that comes to a committed, religious man through contact with unlovable humanity.

Monsignor Vincent Shepherd, the priest in *Real Presence,* is aging, discouraged, tired and sick. He has had a serious heart attack and is assigned to a country parish in rural Virginia, a parish previously served by a beloved priest. Monsignor Shepherd, in contrast to his predecessor, is withdrawn and bitter: he is expecting death, but his visitors do not include that august personage. Instead a grapes of wrath family arrive, Duck Bexley, his wife and their five children. Elizabeth Bexley is expecting her sixth child. They have come to the area to find work. There is none, and so the family becomes the responsibility of the priest, camping in the rectory, invading every corner of his existence and his consciousness and straining the virtue of charity he has sworn to practice.

Bexley is a Korean war veteran, an ex-convict, and now mortally ill with lupus: "Life had gotten away from him." His wife is a strong, loving accepting woman who is not easy on the priest, and will not allow him to retreat from them. The children are, well, children of such an uncertain existence, secretive, distrustful, pilfering, noisy. Bausch is concerned with discovering if Monsignor Shepherd can survive the onslaught of this unwashed, demanding family, if he can learn to accept and love the unlovable, if his Christianity will disintegrate before this severe test. Long before we reach the end and the answer, we have accepted as perfectly believable the person of the priest and the real and terrible presence of the family, as well as the situation, and the place. All this is a tribute to Bausch's skill with words, with characters, with the uncomfortableness of the human condition.

> *Doris Grumbach, "A Fanfare for Five First Novels," in* Book World—The Washington Post, *June 15, 1980, p. 4.*

THOMAS M. GANNON

Set in rural western Virginia, *Real Presence* is a story of three people—the defeated, angry, and doomed Duck Bexley, his pregnant wife Elizabeth, mother of five children already and the "real presence" of the title, and Monsignor Vincent Shepherd, an aged, ill and withdrawn priest for whom Elizabeth becomes a transforming sacrament. The author's principal task in the novel is to communicate the experience of this transformation to his readers. He does not fully succeed.

Bausch writes convincingly of Duck and Elizabeth. Permanently unnerved by his experiences in the Korean war, terminally ill with lupus, and choked with inarticulate rage at the cramped, unyielding circumstances of his life, Duck is out of work and palpably desperate. When he imposes his otherwise homeless family on Monsignor Shepherd's grudging hospitality, his own long journey toward tragedy enters its final stages. No more articulate than her husband, but far less bitter with her lot, Elizabeth loves Duck loyally, to death and beyond. Her devotion to him and her children is uncomplicated and uncomplaining, and could touch even a near-recluse like the monsignor.

Bausch's major problem, however, is to render the eventual upheaval in Monsignor Shepherd's character believable. Here the author stumbles. Early in the novel, the monsignor is letting the clock run out on his life, waiting for death in a tiny country parish, his primary companion a television set. Paralyzed by worry about his uncertain health, he is remarkably alone, and prefers to remain so. Nevertheless, though, he does not want the Bexleys in his life, he is so devoid of personal force that even they, perpetual victims themselves, succeed in overriding his will.

In this portrayal of Monsignor Shepherd's paralysis and ineffectuality lie the roots of the novel's most obvious flaw, the implausibility of its ending. Duck has died, and Elizabeth is in labor with her sixth child. For the first time, the monsignor reveals that he contemplates leaving the priesthood. Then, a few hours later, after Elizabeth gives birth, he declares that he is ready to take responsibility for both Elizabeth, who is 30 years his junior, and the six children. This is entirely too ambitious a program for an elderly bachelor who barely has the strength to read his breviary. The abrupt disregard for the emotional and physical limitations the author has previously imposed on this character is a serious defect in Bausch's oth-

erwise careful effort to write simply and sensitively about the power of love's example to transform pain, suffering and isolation into occasions for rebirth and redemption. (pp. 77-8)

> *Thomas M. Gannon, in a review of "Real Presence," in* America, *Vol. 143, No. 4, August 23, 1980, pp. 77-8.*

THE CRITIC

Shades of Flannery O'Connor's "Displaced Person" may be evoked for some readers by this excellently crafted first novel [*Real Presence*].... Duck Bexley, a decorated Korean War veteran, his pregnant wife and brood of unruly children thrust their impoverished, surly selves into the life of the temporary pastor of a small rural community in Virginia. The priest, Vincent, is recovering from a massive coronary and spiritual ennui. Bexley is a loser, sore at his past and furious with his hopeless present. Reluctantly, Vincent gives them shelter in his parish hall and they soon invade the rectory. The wife, Elizabeth, is long-suffering humanity itself. Bexley's past catches up with him and he begins to think of killing and robbing the local rich lady—who is semi-crazy and eggs him on. But Bexley fails at this would-be killing even while getting himself trapped by circumstances which make it appear that he did in fact commit murder. The kids steal Vincent's silver chalice; Elizabeth delivers her baby; Bexley is killed. Author Bausch brings it all to a fiercely tragic end but one in which Vincent is able to glimpse, finally, the "true presence" of God in man. The dialogue is terse, angry, and largely humorless. The comparison to O'Connor is not an idle one. Bausch has not yet reached her range and depth or bitterly ironic humor—but he's definitely on the way.

> *A review of "Real Presence," in* The Critic, *Chicago, Vol. 39, No. 3, September, 1980, p. 8.*

SCOTT SPENCER

Real Presence by Richard Bausch is the story of a dying, ornery, emotionally frozen priest who hopes to sneak through his remaining years in a small Virginia parish. But his parish and his life are invaded by an inarticulate, threatening, poverty-stricken family.... Clearly this is a story of redemption, of chaos informing order and giving it resonance, but unfortunately the theme announces itself early and there are few surprises along the way.

Mr. Bausch is a formal writer whose austere tone often works to good effect. But there is also a certain tyranny in Mr. Bausch's control: the prose stiff-arms the characters and keeps them in place. This is a carefully observed book, but the fact remains that Monsignor Shepherd's spiritual predicament is immediately familiar to us and Mr. Bausch spends far too much time explaining and describing it. And the priest's eventual salvation, while moving and even satisfying, is a foregone conclusion. It isn't pleasant to say this about a book written by a manifestly talented, scrupulous and hard-working novelist, but *Real Presence* is too long, perhaps by half. (p. 38)

> *Scott Spencer, "Three Finished First Novels," in* The New York Times Book Review, *September 7, 1980, pp. 13, 38.*

MAYO MOHS

Something is wrong with the crucifix. Hanging in the tiny church in a Virginia country town, it distresses the new pastor. The wooden corpus, Monsignor Vincent Shepherd, [protagonist of *Real Presence*], observes, has "square, unsuffering eyes" that symbolize to the priest so much that is wrong with his church and his world. The sense of crucifixion is gone. Instead, he reflects, "it was as if Christ had never really suffered and died, but had only had the Last Supper, with twelve smiling men of social commitment and three folk guitarists, and then knocked the stone away from the tomb."

But something is wrong with the priest too. Shepherd has suffered a heart attack, and he is preoccupied with his own mortality. He clings to time as if to fend off eternity, but does little with it. He sits for hours in front of the rectory television set, resentful of parishioners who disturb him with their problems, unmindful that their private griefs are real wounds.

Into this desiccated shell of a man blows an outlandish wind of salvation, a rickety truck full of outcasts who make the Joads seem like landed gentry. . . .

This is Flannery O'Connor country, where souls are gnarled and agony seems the only common measure of humanity. Even the corpulent landlord, Mr. Wick, who first comes into focus as a Dickensian villain, on closer inspection becomes merely a grownup, terrified boy forever humiliated by a sadistic father.

The doctrine of the Real Presence, in Christian theology, is the belief that Jesus Christ is truly present, body and blood, in the bread and wine of the Eucharist: the living symbol of God among men. For Bausch's troubled priest, it becomes a metaphor for the world beyond the sanctuary, where the Real Presence must be sought among the lowliest of people and the darkest of hearts.

Bausch suggests that the Monsignor's conversion may have to be a journey away from the priesthood to the fatherhood of the forlorn Bexley family. It is a measure of this fine first novel's catholicity—with a lower-case *c*—that the choice seems almost irrelevant. In or out of the collar, this Shepherd seems at last to have found his calling.

Mayo Mohs, "Body of Christ," in Time, New York, Vol. 116, No. 12, September 22, 1980, p. E4.

RICHARD P. BRICKNER

Richard Bausch's exceptionally well received first novel, *Real Presence,* was published only last year. One must speculate that *Take Me Back* was written too rapidly after *Real Presence* or too long before it. Whether written too quickly or too early, *Take Me Back* is not ripe, even though it offers pages of uncanny skillfulness in dialogue and atmosphere, and made me want it to overcome its self-provided obstacles. As it happens, the book is mostly of interest because of the way in which it handles despair, and because of the questions it prompts about despair and about fiction.

The novel takes place in contemporary Point Royal, Va., in an apartment complex, a nearby trailer court and environs. The summer air is polluted; the air conditioners are blowing fuses. In *Take Me Back,* all air is poor, all air conditioners, in effect, are busted. Gordon Brinhart, a halfhearted insurance salesman, is married to Katherine, a retired rock guitarist. Katherine has an illegitimate son by the drummer of her former group. The boy, Alex, is exclusively interested in baseball. Katherine thinks

this interest unhealthy—"he's a zombie about it now." Alex is subdued enough so that he could fairly be called a zombie about everything. But it's summer, and he's 11 years old. Why not baseball? Give him a break.

The problem is Katherine's, not Alex's; and Katherine is the book's chief character problem, its focal zombie. In a novel whose greatest strength is its accurate depiction of behavior, Katherine is only a spottily authentic creation. She is miserable—critically but vaguely miserable. Katherine has an "it." "It was worse this time: it had never been this bad. . . . There was a game, a secret game she played when it was bad. It involved two people: Katherine, and the Other. The Other was the frightened one, the one afraid to close her eyes, who had no love or feeling or hope." Readers may recognize Katherine's personality, but I do not see how they will be able to empathize with her condition. The author's external rendering of Katherine's character and condition has the disadvantages and limitations of that approach but in this case none of the advantages.

Brinhart has taken to drinking too much. He has also begun taking an interest in Shirley, a young lady from the trailer court who has an infant son and lives with an elderly man who is neither her husband, nor the father of her child, nor her father. Katherine thinks Brinhart is sleeping with Shirley. She's wrong, but not for long.

Also living in the trailer court is a family with a 13-year-old daughter, Amy, who has cancer. With a combination of dirty and high-flown language, she befriends Alex, and engages him in a few brief episodes of peripheral sex. Her bluntness comes close to being touching. She's not going to have time for much further experience, and she behaves in her aggressive, peculiar, ungainly way because she knows she is dying. Unlike the stagnating adults in the novel, Amy is going somewhere, even if it is to her death. And there is nothing she can do about it.

Amy tries to be old, Katherine and Brinhart try to be children. They behave with a tedious unwillingness to cope, a rebellious, sulky passivity. They bicker and smoke and drink to excess. While their behavior (if not, in Katherine's case, her motivation) is believable, it provokes the same kind of impatience we feel with friends who remain hobbled by misery when, without resorting to extreme measures, they could kick free of it.

In fact, both Brinhart and Katherine do resort to extreme measures, but they are none the grander, or the worse, for having done so. They stew for pages, then throw fits, make messes that are more embarrassing than sympathetic and more irritating than upsetting. Although they have no enemies but themselves and their own parents' continued indifference, their misbehavior is of the kind likely to make a reader wish that a doctor or a cop would intervene. Katherine and Brinhart "need help."

Take Me Back lacks the coerciveness or vitality of tragedy. It has no evident conviction beyond the glum one that life stinks. The book, by its smallness of vision, frees us to resist its argument. Its hurried balancing of scales at the end is sentimental, like a tardy and insincere apology.

Fiction dealing with failure of will, avoidable helplessness, life as stifling, must be much more imaginative, or peculiar, or furious, or witty—or brief—in order to sustain itself. It must have more originality and courage of bias, if it lacks a more subtly balanced perspective. *Take Me Back* is depressing, but not depressing enough.

Richard P. Brickner, "Troubled Lives," in The New
York Times Book Review, *April 26, 1981, p. 14.*

BRUCE COOK

Richard Bausch, out of the Iowa Workshop a few years and
the author of an earlier novel that everybody liked titled **Real
Presence,** has written [**Take Me Back**], a book about the way
we live now—and you know that has to be pretty grim stuff.
Today, given half a chance, people seem to make messes of
their lives. And Gordon Brinhart and his wife Katherine, the
couple of **Take Me Back,** seem more adept at it than most.

For Katherine, the damage was done years before. Back in the
'60s, in that eye blink between adolescence and young womanhood, she gave her soul to rock and roll (as the song has it).
She was a guitar player, and a good one, a girl who led a group
up and down the East Coast and into New England. Accepting
the hazards of the road—the hard-traveling, the crazy life, even
an unwanted pregnancy—she kept right at it because all she
ever wanted to do, really, was play the guitar. But suddenly,
we're told, it all turned sour for her. Maybe it was the fact
that the baby's father, the group's drummer, took off for parts
unknown as soon as he heard she was pregnant; maybe it was
just that it was so hard to keep a good band together with him
gone. Or maybe it was this male groupie named Brinhart just
out of the Army and Vietnam, who kept showing up at gig
after gig, asking her to marry him. In the end, she gives in.
They collect the baby from the parents where she had parked
him, and they head south to Brinhart's home in Virginia, just
outside Washington, and there they get married.

And now, as the novel begins, that's where they are still. The
boy Alex is 12 years old, a distant, miserable kid. Katherine
has not touched a guitar since the moment she agreed to marry.
And Gordon Brinhart? He's selling insurance, drinking too
much, and spending idle moments ogling the juicy 17-year-
old morsel who lives in the trailer park behind their garden
apartment. The Brinharts, in other words, are already halfway
to perdition.

Things get a lot worse. Telling the story skillfully from the
alternating points of view of the three members of the family,
Bausch has us suffer through the whole ordeal right along with
them. Gordon goes off on a drinking jag, misses work, loses
his job, and winds up in bed with the 17-year-old. Katherine,
naturally hurt, sends him away, and spends the next few days
assuring her son and herself they really don't need Gordon
anyway—and then she winds up attempting suicide. Alex sees
and hears most of this and occupies himself trying to make
sense of it—that is, when he's not busy with the new neighbor
girl who, as it turns out, has leukemia.

Now, there's no way to put a pretty face on a story like that—
and no, **Take Me Back** isn't pretty. It is, however, as well
written as any novel I have read in a while. The characters,
all of them, are very well realized. When you come to the end
of the book you know them about as well as the people next
door—hell, they might *be* the people next door! That's it, you
see: Richard Bausch has captured something essential in the
quality of American life today in these pages. Even in details
and individual scenes he adds brilliantly to this picture. For
example, the trip that Katherine makes to the local discount
store when she is losing control completely is absolutely realistic in its details yet slightly surrealistic in its effect. Anyone
who reads the scene will be unable to visit one of the stores
again and be able to ignore the boorish sales clerks and the

constant badgering to buy-buy-buy. Bausch makes the reader
see and hear better what is happening around him.

Bruce Cook, "The Day the Music Died," in Book
World—The Washington Post, *May 3, 1981, p. 5.*

NANCY FORBES

[**The Last Good Time** is a] fine, tactful novel about two old
men, whose long-fixed ways get shaken up and newly inspired
by the advent of a young hooker. In the odd-couple friendship
between the two men as they slowly move through their pared-
down lives, steadily approaching the decrepit and grotesque,
The Last Good Time might pass for a milder, more naturalistic
Waiting for Godot. But in Mr. Bausch's novel, the men have
more depth; they are capable of love, memory and even real
conversation. Unlike Samuel Beckett, Mr. Bausch finds the
human condition most activated not in solipsism but in communication.

Edward Cakes has been living along for over 30 years, ever
since the deaths of his son and wife. He held the same job all
his life, as a violinist in the city symphony orchestra. Edward
is a modest, genteel man. His marriage was moderately unhappy; his passivity as a father helped shape his monstrously
selfish son; and as a musician he was competent without being
outstanding. Once he lost his family, Cakes easily withdrew,
eventually moving into a one-room apartment on the outskirts
of the unidentified city where the novel takes place. He spends
hazy hours in the neighborhood library or in his chair by the
window. His only gesture toward others has been to befriend
his upstairs neighbor, Arthur Hagood.

Arthur's life has been very different. Raised as a Jew in the
Middle West, he cultivated his sense of humor and indulged
his raging lust whenever he could, meanwhile teaching English
in high school and raising a family. Now, lying in his hospital
bed, Arthur dwells on the memory of his last good time—his
last affair, when he was 75. ("She was uglier than hell, Edward, but a lovely woman all the same.")

When Mary Virginia Bellini, age 24, comes to Edward's room,
she is looking for the upstairs tenant, the man who got her
pregnant. She is tough, knowing and secretive, and Edward
falls in love. As Arthur begins to die ("I must be dying . . .
my daughter sends me a plant"), Edward is stirred into living
again. Mary is as compelling as a young, taciturn tramp can
be, and when they make love Edward is revived. Although she
hurts and humiliates him, she also provides him with a "good
time."

Mr. Bausch's narrative style respects the way old people can
experience time. He's unable to render how time gets jumbled,
fades, lurches forward and fades again as Edward's and Arthur's physical powers slip. But it is the life of the spirit, equally
unpredictable, with its unaccountable shifts from despair to joy
to peace, that especially grips Mr. Bausch. Beneath its vernacular comedy, this book contains a submerged allegory of
Christian redemption. In places the allegory is intrusive, as in
the naming of the characters (Mary Virginia, Arthur Hagood)
or the forcing of certain coincidences in the plot. Moreover,
the symbolism is the least original aspect of a highly original
novel.

For the most part, however, the novel's effectiveness is undisturbed by the symbolic machinery—for example, in the final, redemptive scene, in which Edward visits Ida Warren, the
irritating, talkative old woman upstairs ("We'll listen to music.

I have the complete everything, you know,'' she says). Like the novel itself, this scene is satisfyingly elusive. *The Last Good Time* has a way of being superlatively funny and disturbing by turns, but the experience that emerges most strongly is that of spending an interesting time getting to know the sort of people whose lives we take for granted. It is a rewarding entertainment.

Nancy Forbes, "Redeemed by Love at 75," in The New York Times Book Review, *December 23, 1984, p. 25.*

MADISON SMARTT BELL

[*Spirits,* a] thoughtful, honest collection of short fiction by the well-regarded novelist Richard Bausch, is a carefully organized group of stories about the hazards of ordinary living. Most of them have a slight Southern accent, but none are regionally fixed; they have to do with quite average American experience, the affairs of people with relatively modest ambitions and problems and dreams. Whatever is striking in their circumstances comes from the common run of luck, sometimes good, more often bad.

Vexed relationships of different kinds are central to almost all the stories. In some the problem seems fairly minor: for instance, a young girl's fierce jealousy of her sister's fiancé, rendered with subtle irony in **"The Wife's Tale."** More often, the bonds among the characters are complicated by sudden death or some other sort of catastrophe. **"What Feels Like the World"** is a minutely observed story of an overweight child's determined but hopeless effort to pass a fitness test; it is seen through the eyes of her grandfather, who has been her guardian since her mother's death in a car crash. In this, as in several of the stories, the violent accident forms the background, while up front the survivors toil to construct new emotional lives beyond pain they can only partially share.

In **"Wise Men at Their End,"** the accident itself becomes the basis for a new connection. When elderly, cranky Theodore Weathers breaks his leg falling down the stairs, he finds himself, all through his hospitalization, stuck with Alice Karnes, a chance acquaintance he never wanted to meet in the first place. When he goes home she still attends him; though they don't yet wholly like each other, "they looked like a couple long married, still in the habit of love."

Five of the nine stories are more directly involved with marriage, usually marriages that are collapsing or in serious danger of doing so. **"Ancient History"** is another story whose premise is supplied by an accident—the fatal heart attack of the husband and father. However, the crux of the issue turns out to be 18-year-old Charles's growing realization that the dead man was probably about to leave him and his mother. Rage at the anticipated desertion of his wife goads the narrator of **"Contrition"** through a sequence of events that ends with his attacking a policeman; "he knows, even while it's all happening to him, that this is the one truest mistake of his life and that he'll never outlive it."

In other stories, that insight turns into a kind of prescience. The narrator of **"Police Dreams"** is not really aware that his wife is about to leave him for no good reason (and later intrigue to take their children from him), but he is tormented by a recurring dream in which unknown thrill-killers destroy his whole family. **"All the Way in Flagstaff, Arizona"** presents the ruined marriage of an alcoholic who unwittingly frightens

his children when drunk, though his drinking is only a refuge from the memory of his father, a much more purposeful torturer who never drank at all. Talking to a psychiatrist, he identifies what might serve as this collection's thesis: "the ancient story: the man who, in the act of trying to avoid some evil in himself, embraces it, creates it."

This fatalism, though pervasive, is not common to every story. **"Spirits,"** the longest and most complex of the group, takes a rather different approach to marital upheaval and is chiefly about a marriage that in the end survives. Its narrator, a young academic, has the leisure to contemplate the examples of an older colleague whose marriage has foundered on mutual indifference, and of the landlady of the motel where he stays, whose estranged husband resurfaces as a confessed serial child-murderer. Between these two extremes of self-destruction, he and his wife are able to steer a middle course, arriving at a reasonably peaceful conclusion.

Still, on the whole this book is more concerned with trouble than tranquillity, and it is best at showing how the lives of plain good people can go badly wrong. Mr. Bausch—whose three novels include *The Last Good Time*—handles his subjects with thorough precision, writing with no superfluous stylistic flash.

Madison Smartt Bell, "Everyday Hazards," in The New York Times Book Review, *June 14, 1987, p. 16.*

MICHAEL DORRIS

Richard Bausch is a master of the short story. In nine distinctive, unforgettable and marvelously crafted tales, he brings to life characters and situations as vivid and compelling as any in contemporary literature. *Spirits and Other Stories* is a collection that ranks with those of Bobbie Ann Mason and Jayne Ann Phillips in its range, its risks and its raw power, but Bausch's literary voice is reminiscent of no one else's; he is an original.

To read this book is to attend, hungry, the most fabulous buffet in town. You load your plate time and again, and everything you sample is terrific. Even when you're full, the memory of surprising tastes draws you back to the table.

There isn't a weak story here, though some pieces are more ambitious than others. In the long, seven-part **"Spirits,"** which ends the book, the narrator, a passive young college instructor, is inexorably drawn into the psychological intrigues of an illustrious colleague and his wife. Their reality both parallels and supersedes his own, and only through an act of conscious disillusionment is he able to extricate himself and return to his own, less-charged, existence. Tension builds line upon line in this deceptively quiet unfolding, as if the grace and pacing of Peter Taylor's "The Old Forest" has been wedded to the understated profundity of Philip Roth's *The Ghost Writer*. Like the protagonist, the reader is imprisoned in an imagined world where none of the familiar rules apply.

Many of Bausch's stories deal with the reflection upon a dramatic event—a death, a divorce, a loss—just past. In **"Ancient History,"** a young man grapples with the altered roles within a family constellation following the collapse of his father. Accompanying his mother for a Christmas visit to her sister-in-law, Aunt Lois, he must relinquish the very innocence and naiveté that have previously been the traits with which he was most identified and in which he took most pride. The situation, with high potential for sentimentality, is redeemed by the author's unerring skill. The characters are so fresh, particularly the unflinching Aunt Lois, that you forget any writer ever dealt before with coming of age. The writing suggests more than it states, leaving the reader with ideas that spring from the story but are by no means tied to it.

"Police Dreams" chronicles the confusion of a marriage in which the husband was "smack-dab in the middle of happily ever after" and the wife was, unguessed by him, frustrated and unhappy. When she announces her intention never to return, he is incredulous—"Jean, we didn't even have an argument . . . I mean, what is this about?"—but we the readers can sympathize with both characters, with the unfairness of disappointment.

The remarkable opening story, **"All the Way in Flagstaff, Arizona,"** again recounts the deterioration of a nuclear family, this time because of the narrator's alcoholism, the nagging result of his own physical abuse as a child. The past intrudes upon and spoils the present, a theme that recurs in different ways in **"The Man Who Knew Belle Starr"** and **"Contrition."**

But in the world of *Spirits,* life is not all loss, love is not all unrequited, as demonstrated by **"Wise Men at Their End."** Here a difficult octogenerian, Theodore Weathers, finds himself at odds with his well-intentioned, widowed daughter-in-law, Judy. . . .

When Judy attempts a kind of match-making and brings her elderly friend Alice Karnes to visit, Theodore is at first irritated and then, almost against his will, intrigued. Immediately, however, he suffers a fall that requires painful hospitalization and it is there, in traction, that their odd, affecting, cranky and totally believable courtship takes place. Disaffection is constantly and earnestly proclaimed, but the story concludes with Alice and Theodore sitting together on his front porch, looking "like a couple long married, still in the habit of love."

Finally, in perhaps the most striking piece of all, Bausch gives us a portrait of human bonding that seems somehow an antidote and a hope for all the losses endured by other characters. **"What Feels Like the World"** is the story of the protective, hopeless devotion of a man for his grand-daughter, in his custody since the loss of her parents. He wants to spare her every injury, every hurt, but she is a realistic, pragmatic child determined not to run from any challenge. "When she looks at him . . . he sees something scarily unchildlike in her expression, some perplexity that she seems to pull down into herself."

At the end he has no choice but to come to the school gymnastic program where her humiliation at being the only child in the class who cannot perform a simple handspring seems assured. He despairs that there is nothing he can do to help her, to lift the burdens that will come to her in life, but he shows up.

> She stands in the doorway, her cheeks flushed, her legs looking too heavy in the tights. She's rocking back and forth on the balls of her feet, getting ready. It grows quiet. Her arms swing slightly, back and forth, and now, just for a moment, she's looking at the crowd, her face hiding whatever she's feeling. It's as if she were merely curious as to who is out there, but he knows she's looking for him, searching the crowd for her grandfather, who stands on his toes, unseen against the far wall, stands there thinking his heart might break, lifting his hand to wave.

That passage, beautiful, restrained, moral and wise, is emblematic of the writing and the vision that makes *Spirits and*

Other Stories a cause of celebration. Richard Bausch, who lives in suburban Washington, has created an enduring work of art.

Michael Dorris, "The Drama of Ordinary Life," in Book World—The Washington Post, *June 28, 1987, p. 6.*

SHARON DIRLAM

Spirits is called a collection of short stories, but it is more a collection of characters captured and considered at the moment fate twists their lives around.

The nine stories follow no discernible rules of plot or narrative; some have little sense of a beginning or satisfying denouement. The writer seems simply to arrive at the place where these people exist, to perceive them, and to give a penetrating account of their situations. Each one seems completely real.

The tensions of the characters are those of bewilderment and often their inability to cope with what life throws at them. Their motivations, one and all, are braided of that common thread of life: to do well, to be happy or at least contented, to survive. . . .

The first story in the collection begins with a postscript. A man is sitting in a churchyard in Arizona, remembering a picnic with his wife and five children, a fifth of Jim Beam hidden in the trunk of the car, a series of promises, all unkept. We never know how the man, Walter, got to Arizona, except that the time is after the end of life as he knew it.

An earlier memory, from childhood, haunts him as well, when his father "became a sort of dark gibbet that Walter danced beneath, held by the wrist within the small circumference, the range, of a singing swung belt." In the churchyard, Walter continues to wrestle with his demons. Everything has changed, but nothing is resolved. . . .

If there is a message in Bausch's collection, maybe it's that things don't quite work out as they might; life is sadder and more complicated than it ought to be, and yet the struggle continues and is somehow worth it. Bausch combines a poet's sense of rhythm with a philosopher's quest for truth, but he is first of all a most original storyteller.

Sharon Dirlam, in a review of "Spirits and Other Stories," in Los Angeles Times Book Review, *July 12, 1987, p. 7.*

THOMAS CAHILL

It is easy not to like these stories [in *Spirits*], to try to get away from them as quickly as possible. That is why, as I have read from one to another, I have tasted a sort of metallic panic, almost a despair. It is my deep, perverse suspicion that, when I am an old man, in the second and third decades of the twenty-first century, all of Bausch—this book, his three novels, anything he may write—will be in print, and names like Updike, Roth, Bellow will have faded from view. But how to capture Bausch for the reader? For though his fiction is indeed contemporary, it is in no way "of the moment." He rides no current, catches no wave.

First of all, there is his style. It seems almost not to be there. One word follows another plainly, ploddingly. They seem the inevitable words, serviceable, and nothing more. "About a month before Jean left him," begins the third story, "Casey dreamed he was sitting in the old Maverick with her and the two boys, Rodney and Michael.'' That's how all the sentences go, almost algebraically. No flash, no fireworks, nothing to admire—except, of course, the supreme artifice that so conceals itself. Sometimes the dialogue has a quiet crack to it. ''I'll tell you,'' says one minor character. ''It's a terrific misfortune to have to be raised by a human being.'' But the remark is so much in context, such a part of seamless whole, that the reader is well into the next paragraph before he realizes he's been hit, is bleeding from the abdomen.

Then there are Bausch's characters. They are the plainest people. They must usually ask themselves if they have enough change for two sundaes at K-Mart. Since they are not good consumers, they do not allow us even that *frisson* of product recognition that has become such a staple of contemporary fiction. And they are so inadequate to their situations. They lead impossible, unsatisfactory lives. ''What's happened to you? How could you wind up like this—how could you let it happen?'' asks a sister of her brother in **''Contrition.''** These are questions that could be put to all Bausch's characters.

In the first story (**''All the Way in Flagstaff, Arizona''**), a vagrant whose life has been ruined by drink stands shaking with the D.T.'s in a strange town that has no meaning for him, and recalls his beloved, lost family. In the second story (**''Wise Men at Their End''**), a gruff, graceless man must summon up his meager personal resources to meet his impending disintegration. In the third story (**''Police Dreams''**), a devoted husband and father who is completely in the dark about why his wife left him experiences recurrent nightmares in which he and his family are stalked by murderers. How could anyone take a steady diet of such people? Except that they are all nonentities, their sadnesses are like the griefs of ancient tragedy. *Sunt lacrymae rerum et mentem mortalia tangunt* rises from Bausch's pages like incense.

But if his almost monosyllabic style fails to stir us to superlatives and his casts of characters set our teeth on edge, Bausch's plots are things to wonder at, for they draw us like magnets to a pole. It is virtually impossible not to finish a Bausch novel at one sitting, and of these stories it can be said that while you are in the midst of one you will not be able to answer a ringing telephone.

How does he do it? I don't know. All I can say is that he imagines so *completely*. You feel, reading these stories, that Bausch has imagined everything about these characters—the way they cried and held their bodies as infants, the way they hurt and admired themselves as adolescents, their secret yearnings, their middle-aged bowel movements, all their years and idiosyncracies, far beyond anything he sets on the page. (''I've had three husbands in my life and they all had things about them that you couldn't say was too normal,'' says the landlady in **''Spirits,''** the title story. ''Who doesn't? Who's normal in private?'') He sees his characters so organically, so inter-relatedly that everything has meaning, nothing is an accident. And yet this vision is so whole that no element ever clanks like a symbol in a surrealist painting. Rather, like the weather in *Lear* (and there is much weather in Bausch), you need not advert to the symbols. They are not stuck in; they are integral as a chordal progression in Josquin Desprez.

The only twentieth-century American writer to whom he may be valuably compared is Flannery O'Connor. Both are Georgians, Catholics, both think of life as a spiritual crisis. But Bausch is hopping with sex, *all* kinds of sex, all of it salvific—and a turn-on to the reader. Bausch's characters never illustrate a thesis. And though their lives are truly sad, God is never fierce with them—no fiercer, at least, than is absolutely necessary. At the end of *Real Presence*, Bausch's first novel, a man reaches into a fish tank to prod a lackadaisical fish. ''Let's see. . . . If it's alive, and I irritate it enough, it'll move,'' says he. Bausch's God prods and irritates, but seldom traumatizes his creatures. (In one of these stories, **''The Man Who Knew Belle Starr,''** Bausch deliberately provokes comparison with O'Connor's ''A Good Man Is Hard to Find.'' In Bausch's story, as in O'Connor's, a person's whole psyche is rearranged when a gun is pointed at him and he knows he will be killed in minutes. But Bausch's message is not O'Connor's; in fact, he gives us no message, but leaves us to finish the story.)

I feel sure that Bausch's experience of sex led him, as it does all men who grow up, to his experience of fatherhood—and this fatherhood is the matrix of his stories. His constant theme is how much people really care for one another—beneath the monosyllabic surfaces and the apparent indifference—without their ever saying so, often without their knowing so themselves. Thus, his characters are usually husband-wife, parent-child, though they are sometimes strangers who (perhaps only momentarily) act these roles toward one another. In this caring lies the Real Presence—our meaning, the Father in our lives. In our not recognizing it lies our real tragedy. (pp. 568-69)

Thomas Cahill, ''Fireworks Hidden & Deep,'' in Commonweal, *Vol. CXIV, No. 17, October 9, 1987, pp. 568-69.*

Anita Brookner

1928-

English novelist, nonfiction writer, critic, and translator.

Brookner is best known for her novels about lonely, sensitive women who are often betrayed by their unrealistic notions of love and marriage. The typical Brookner heroine is intelligent and affluent yet dissatisfied with her life and emotionally incapable of change. Sheila Hale observed: "Although [Brookner] knows exactly how it feels to be this woman, she doesn't always like her. . . . Nor does Anita Brookner pity the inevitable loneliness of her creation." While some critics fault the lack of thematic variety in her works, many regard Brookner's elegant prose and detailed descriptions of place, her use of literary devices common to eighteenth- and nineteenth-century French literature, and her confessional tone as features that elevate her fiction above the romance genre.

Brookner's first novel, *A Start in Life* (1981; published in the United States as *The Debut*), depicts the efforts of Ruth Weiss, a literature professor who specializes in the works of Honoré de Balzac, to free herself from her restrictive, elderly parents. Influenced by the romantic escapades of Balzac's heroines, Ruth journeys to Paris, where she believes she will find happiness and love, but fails in her search. The novel ends with Ruth returning to her empty existence at her parents' home. Critics noted several parallels between this book and Balzac's novel *Eugénie Grandet,* in which the eponymous heroine is condemned to a similar fate. *Providence* (1982), Brookner's second novel, also features a female scholar whose distorted notions of romance render her emotionally defeated. In this book, the protagonist falls in love with a colleague who fails to reciprocate her feelings. *Look at Me* (1983) portrays Frances Hilton, a timid librarian for a medical institute, who is befriended by the hypocritical wife of an associate. When Frances's promising love affair with another employee of the institute is undermined by her female companion, she withdraws from society and begins to write fiction. Mary Cantwell commented: "It would be an error to see *Look at Me* simply as a novel about a self-conscious young Englishwoman who becomes a writer. . . . Instead, it is a horror story about monsters and their victims told in exceptionally elegant prose."

Brookner gained widespread critical acclaim in England and the United States with her fourth novel, *Hotel du Lac* (1984), for which she received the Booker-McConnell Prize for fiction. While *Hotel du Lac* examines many of the same themes as Brookner's previous novels, critics single out the heroine's self-determination as the book's most distinctive feature. This work probes the psyche of Edith Hope, a writer of popular romance novels, who vacations at an off-season Swiss resort hotel to escape both her impending marriage and a recent affair. Unlike Brookner's other heroines, who often subject themselves to emotional flagellation and social isolation, Edith comes to realize that the men in her life do not necessarily satisfy her definition of true love and learns not to compromise her ideals for conventional notions of romance. In comparing her to Brookner's earlier protagonists, Anne Tyler declared that Edith "is more philosophical from the outset, more self-reliant, more conscious that a solitary life is not . . . an unmitigated tragedy." *Hotel du Lac* was adapted for British television in 1985.

Photograph by Mark Gerson

In her next novel, *Family and Friends* (1985), Brookner focuses upon the lives of several major characters. Her portrait of the Dorns, a Jewish-European family, addresses such topics as parent-child relationships and the conflict between old-world traditions and contemporary values. Set in London between the two World Wars, this work revolves around the attempts of Sofka, the strong-willed Dorn family matriarch, to dominate the lives of her four adult children. Her favorites, Frederick and Betty, rebel against their mother's adherence to familial duty, while her other children, Alfred and Mimi, remain loyal to Sofka and her traditional values at the cost of their independence. Although Brookner garnered praise for technical virtuosity and her use of photographs as a device to examine the Dorns's past, *Family and Friends* drew mixed reviews. Michiko Kakutani stated: "[Brookner] seems so intent on proving her thesis that the virtuous are 'born to lose' (and that the wicked are born to win) that she reduces all human relationships to a blind Darwinian struggle, devoid of chance and magic and love." Jane Gardam, however, asserted that the book "is not only a statement of life's sorrows. It sets down with great control and precision the importance of the freedom of the spirit."

In her next two novels, Brookner again portrays the tribulations of distressed women. *A Misalliance* (1986) relates the story of Blanche Vernon, who attempts to restore order in her life after her husband leaves her for his secretary. Discovering that her friends have begun socializing with her husband's lover, a vibrant and free-spirited young woman, Blanche becomes obsessed with a wayward mother and her mute daughter until she discovers the motivation within herself to control her own life. *A Friend from England* (1987) is a tale of self-deception and envy centering on Rachel, a bitter, insecure young woman, who keeps company with Heather, the spoiled daughter of a former employee of Rachel's family. Viewing herself as emotionally independent, Rachel attempts to mold Heather's life into an existence similar to her own. When Heather decides to marry an Italian beneath her social class, Rachel tries unsuccessfully to thwart her plans, realizing that this union will reveal her own life to be a lie. In her review of *A Friend from England*, Kathy Stephen commented: "Although Anita Brookner has not blazed wildly innovative imaginative trails in her novels, she has gone deeper and deeper . . . into the question of how and why some people connect and others never do."

Brookner is also a renowned scholar of eighteenth- and nineteenth-century French art and has published nonfiction works on such painters as Jean-Baptiste Greuze and Jacques-Louis David. In addition, Brookner has translated critical studies of the artists Maurice Utrillo and Paul Gauguin.

(See also *CLC*, Vols. 32, 34; *Contemporary Authors*, Vols. 114, 120; and *Dictionary of Literary Biography Yearbook: 1987*.)

JANE GARDAM

Anita Brookner has chosen as an epigraph for her new novel [*Family and Friends*] a passage from Goethe which says that the acceptance of conventions leads to neighbourliness, decency and good taste but kills our appreciation of nature and our powers of expression. Fortunately this monumentally unexciting text is not an adequate comment on the book.

For while *Family and Friends* does examine a group of people in the grip of a seductive tribal code—particularly in the grip of a seductive and tribal mother—it has other themes moving about and through it in fascinating intersecting circles—big themes like the conflict between classicism and romanticism, reason and emotion, the bounds of duty and the burden of 'charm'—or however one is to translate what Anita Brookner calls 'the wild card' which some people are dealt at birth. This card, she says, causes 'singularity' and 'the ludic impulse' (i.e. the need to give oneself a good time?) and results in alienation from loved-ones and general infantilism and inadequacy.

She also examines various kinds and degrees of love, the hazards of being in thrall to sentiment, which she sees as 'a lingering illness' and discusses the age-old fate of the virtuous woman—the folded hands and downcast eyes, the waiting to be loved, which results in 'the good being unhappy ever after.'

None of these is an entirely new theme in Anita Brookner but clearly *Family and Friends*, from its first sentence, is very different from her other books. She is concerned for a start not with a single and solitary heroine but with a large group. She is examining the group over a long period of years and using for the first time a clear authorial voice. . . . In her earlier books Anita Brookner has been saying '*Look at me*' in fact and now is saying 'Look at them.' 'Here is Sofka' she says, 'Here is

Alfred.' 'Here are the girls whose hair I know to have been red.' For this is an old family wedding photograph she is holding up and we are being invited to examine it as she analyses each of the guests, the men and the women, in turn.

For the first time in this book the men are of equal importance and properly alive . . . and clearly-defined, not leading shadowy romantic and usually caddish lives at other addresses. They have their own destinies and functions other than abandoning their women to an introverted and usually bookish fate. There is nobody bookish in this book—again for the first time—and there are no villains.

The women are different too and there is more than one heroine. Certainly they suffer as much—more—than the earlier ones— very much more than the tiresome one in *Hotel du Lac*—but they do not suffer for lack of love. One girl, the 'ludic' sister Betty, suffers from being if anything too successful with men, finding herself as a result stuck beside a swimming-pool in Hollywood, too proud to go home, gazing at the colour of the water because it reminds her of a childhood hair-ribbon. Mimi, the virtuous daughter, suffers dreadfully but not through loss of a man so much as through the fantasy that she ever had a man to lose. . . .

Her mother, Sofka, is also without a man and a lonely figure but is not a woman to yearn for a partner. Her husband has been unfaithful ('so sensible' she says) and is now dead, releasing her for her destiny of 'triumphant mothering', delicious flirtation with an elder son and her subtle demands of general filial loyalty. When poor Mimi strums the keys and refuses an offer of marriage from an old family retainer, Sofka suddenly rages: '"Daughter" she cries, in a loud voice that startles them both, as does the archaic use of the word, "I do not want to die and leave you alone".' And Mimi marries.

But if all this is Anita Brookner using a clearer voice—a rather startling voice, like Sofka's—there is much in *Family and Friends* that is very familiar. The usual Brookner sadness is there—the queer dark nimbus that hangs about the characters, the sense in them of some distant European family disintegration which has brought them all a generation or so ago to England, to the dark London houses over-full of foreign furniture which we have seen before. Occasionally a character puts on a sort of cloak of Englishness—Frederick, the easygoing 'ludic' son in this book, is said to have the qualities of an English aristocrat. He can work without seeming to try. And his brother Alfred strives after Dickensian food on Sundays and searches for a country house with dogs on the lawn. But there is in the stifling family closeness, the separateness from English social life, the thick walls of the prosperous London houses and apartments, with their cigar-coloured walls and thick brown carpets, a sense of a separate world. The gloom is very heavy. (p. 26)

This makes for as bleak a book as any Anita Brookner has yet written—perhaps bleaker. Yet there are moments of haunting, almost heart-breaking beauty in it. Paris in the early morning and 'the globe-shaped lights and the ineffable blue Parisian evening'. A white dress flickering into trees in an English summer twilight. Alfred standing all night at the foot of his mother's deathbed. '"I never meant to leave you" he says and now knows it to be true.'

Family and Friends is not only a statement of life's sorrows. It sets down with great control and precision the importance of the freedom of the spirit; what in the 19th century romantic novel, in which Anita Brookner has always been interested, might have been called the freedom of the heart. (pp. 26-7)

Jane Gardam, "The Freedom of the Spirit," in Books and Bookmen, *No. 359, September, 1985, pp. 26-7.*

DERWENT MAY

Anita Brookner's new book is certainly a novel—but is it a story? Stories imply event, drama, change. But *Family and Friends* is more like some strange kind of painting, with a group of figures who take on different appearances as you tilt it or rotate it, but are always held in exactly the same pattern, and only give the faintest impression of movement of their own.

There seems no doubt that this is Miss Brookner's intention, and not just a failure on her part. To begin with, the whole book is written in the present tense—and not some sort of terse, dramatic present tense ('I go. I come back!'), but a dreamy, languorous tense that seems to eliminate time. . . .

Sofka is the mother; Frederick and Alfred, Mimi and Betty are her children. But when and where do they live? Well, they live in England, and the Second World War takes place during their lives, and occupies a few sentences of the book. But what country does the émigrée Sofka come from, what is made in the factory that her late husband owned and ran, who are these family and friends that drift richly through the eternally repeated summer days? Those are questions which Miss Brookner gracefully but pointedly declines to answer. She is interested here in emotions and moods, elements in her personages to which incidental, temporal fact is really of no consequence, for the mood and the emotion always suffuse such fact so completely that it loses its character anyway. Consequently another feature of her language here is that it is nearly always analytical and general. . . .

Miss Brookner acknowledged that she has drawn in this book on her own family of her parents' and grandparents' generation. She felt 'the exhilaration of disposing of these characters whom I had always seen as immensely powerful'; and she laughed as she wrote the last sentence of the book, in which a little girl of Miss Brookner's own generation called Victoria appears. Might it be that in freezing her characters practically into immobility in *Family and Friends,* she was driven mainly by the urge to strip that power from her elders? If so, she has succeeded. The mastery, the artistry, the elegance are now hers all right. But for us, to be frank, the result is a little boring.

Derwent May, "Still Life with Elders," in The Listener, *Vol. 114, No. 2925, September 5, 1985, p. 26.*

MICHIKO KAKUTANI

In the British writer Anita Brookner's four previous novels, a recognizable vision of society, of the interactions between men and women, has been elegantly mapped out. It's a vision of the world as a dangerous, predatory place, peopled by two sorts of individuals—sophisticates and innocents. And while Miss Brookner always sides with her naifs—in each case, a Pym-like spinster, diligent, correct and impeccably earnest—she also makes it clear that she regards them as losers in society's hypocritical games. It's the carelsss, tempestuous people who get ahead and who win the love of others—not her discreet little heroines, who seem doomed by their own good intentions. . . .

Now, with her latest novel, *Family and Friends,* Miss Brookner seems to be making a bid to open out her canvas: Her subject is not one waif-like woman, but an entire family; her focus, not simply the consequences of romantic love, but also the effects of the enduring, changing bonds between parents and their children, sisters and their brothers. Writing in careful, angled prose, Miss Brookner conjures up the vanished world that a distinguished European family inhabited in London: a world of chauffeurs and gardeners, tea parties and wedding feasts full of "things in aspic, things in baskets of spun sugar"; and she delineates, for us, too, the heavy sense of familial duty and social obligation that obtained in that unliberated age.

The story of this family unfolds as though one were studying the faded pages of an old photo album. We see sepia images of them, decade by decade, caught in ritualized poses; the pretty children slowly maturing into the hectic flush of adolescence, and from there, into the more blunted space of young adulthood and middle age. A curtain of doom hangs gently over their heads, for their fates, seen in retrospect anyway, seem to have been arranged long ago. . . .

Using her delicate sense of gesture and detail to give the reader a sense of these characters' daily lives, Miss Brookner swiftly sketches in the changes that will overtake the family. The war, of course, brings its own dislocations, as do assorted moves, marriages and deaths. It is the changes wrought on each of the children's personalities by time and will, however, that concern her most—how, by rebelling or acquiescing to [the mother's] master blueprint, each determines his or her own life. . . .

Miss Brookner puts a little spin on these tales, foiling some of the reader's more obvious expectations, and her storytelling abilities are so assured, so graceful, that we're drawn, eagerly, along. At the same time, however, we're apt to chafe at her italicized applications of Freudian logic—for instance, practically every male character's exchange with a woman is defined in terms of his relationship with his mother—and at her unremittingly cynical view of society. When she writes that Alfred's character "will be a burden to him rather than an asset. But that is the way with good characters," she seems so intent on proving her thesis that the virtuous are "born to lose" (and that the wicked are born to win) that she reduces all human relationships to a blind Darwinian struggle, devoid of chance and magic and love. It's a pretty bitter way to look at the world, and in *Family and Friends,* Miss Brookner leaves neither her characters nor her readers a way out.

Michiko Kakutani, "Family Bonds," in The New York Times, *October 12, 1985, p. 18.*

ADRIANNE BLUE

There is a certain kind of woman—articulate, feminist, the kind of woman I admire—who defends the Brookner mystique. At dinner parties, on the telephone, she has been telling me, 'Oh, Anita Brookner, she writes the same book over and over and I know she is not a feminist, but I always read it. Because she writes about the sort of people I know.' Not so. What Brookner is cooking up is Mills & Boon for bluestockings.

Brookner writes about the meek inheriting the earth, after a fashion. She turns the 'Reader, I married him' notion around, but not quite on its head. Her heroines, as passive as Jean Rhys's, as unemphatic as Barbara Pym's, are—up to a point—their own women. They throw aside a marriage proposal here, hang onto a neglectful married lover there; they quietly, narrowly, prevail. Men, those rough boys of whom we are fond in spite of the mud pies in their brains, do indeed prefer shallow blonde to deep, decent mouse. But they hanker most for respectability. . . .

In *A Misalliance,* once again, a Brookner heroine detests champagne—or, rather, fears it. The best realised scene in this short novel is the description of the migraine Blanche gets after sipping champagne at the Dorchester. She is there tippling on behalf of a self-centred, young woman who is rather like the woman Blanche's husband Bertie has gone off with. Add to that misalliance Blanche's longtime admirer, a maidenly male civil servant, and the estate agent husband who repeatedly drops in. The novel shows how Blanche comes to terms with the hole Bertie's absence has made in the fabric of her life.

The migraine works exquisitely as a scene and as a symbol of this depressed heroine's woes, and as a device for allowing more characters into her empty life, thereby supplying the mild suspense that precedes the bittersweet ending, which is very clever.

The beginning, though, fails. For 30 pages Blanche ruminates about characters who don't yet exist for us. Then Blanche complains to her sister-in-law that people think Bertie left because she is frigid, and there is no way to refute them. 'You could sleep with their husbands,' says Barbara. I laughed out loud. But there is not much of this sort of thing. No doubt I am a more vulgar reader than Brookner has in mind.

Adrianne Blue, "Floral Print," in New Statesman, Vol. 112, No. 2891, August 22, 1986, p. 26.

JOHN BAYLEY

Anita Brookner has much in common with Barbara Pym. They can both be formidable—battle-axes under the banter. Male readers, who like to wonder fondly at the sharpness of nice women, enjoy this severity. Love is the big reality to them both, though its objects and stratagems are inevitably comic. Pym seems to write as naturally as Miss Bates talks (and Miss Bates is Jane Austen's most significant and most original heroine), but the Brookner style gets in the way when we begin the novel. It is the product of care and scholarship, seminars and concentration, and at first one fans it away rather pettishly, like the smoke of an exotic cigarette. But soon, as with all really good novels, it becomes its own proper and revealing medium. Blanche Vernon, in *A Misalliance,* is as much a Brookner heroine as Prudence or Wilmet, or Caro in *An Academic Question,* are Pym heroines. It used to be a specification of the separate reality of the Brookner world that the heroine's obsession—timid and honourable as it might be—deprived the other characters of ordinary credibility. That has changed. The Brookner heroine has learned to make her acquaintance as real as herself, if she has learnt nothing else. Blanche has a 'timorous decency, disguised as brusqueness'. Like a Pym heroine, with whom below the surface she has a kind of secret relationship, she desires to be of service, and for that reason is usually overlooked or victimised by pushier types, even by her nice husband, 'who would have valued her much more if she had been sought after by other men, if she had been vain rather than bookish'. The Brookner heroine is more stylised, more stereotyped, more compulsive even, than the Pym one, but she can grow on the reader just as much. She values the ridiculous more discreetly, but with just as much relish, and she is the perfect foil to and observation post on Sloane Rangers, stripe-

shirted worldly ones, and other London fauna, with whom she strives without entire conviction to keep up. (p. 20)

Blanche's husband, head of a highly prosperous firm of estate agents, abandons her for his secretary, and it is the consequences of this effectively commonplace situation that the novel explores. The Brookner method is both literary and painterly, with a strong Continental streak—Constant, Fromentin, that sort of thing. Her most moving moments—and they really are moving—go right back to Racine. All her heroines give the impression that they could recite the famous lines of his forsaken queen. . . . And they would recite them with the same stoicism and the same reserve. The underpinning of the novel depends on the ancient formula of 'mousy woman makes good and wins in her own way', with the added irony that Blanche's rival, the detestable secretary who carried off her spouse, is actually known as 'Mousie'. The banal simplicity of the plot is a perfect foil for the meticulous sympathy with which its true innerness is dissected, its meaning for a woman who found only in her vanished husband 'intimations of her own validity': 'without him that validity disappeared. This was no way, she knew, for a self-respecting modern woman to feel.' Nonetheless, she feels it, and the novelist makes us feel it too—very intensely. It is her best novel so far: *Hotel du Lac,* the Booker Prize-winner, was the weakest.

As in all Brookner novels, there is a good deal of emphasis, not really needed, on the metaphysics and the meaning, underpinned by analogies and examples from the world of painting and art. *Providence,* a touching and highly successful novel, hardly required its extended twinning with a reading of *Adolphe.* Here the forsaken Blanche makes visits to the National Gallery a part of her pattern of loneliness: she makes the discovery that art has specialised in adulatory tributes to her actual or putative rivals—tough, hard-faced gods and goddesses of what she has come to see as London's pagan world. Her eye is constantly meeting 'the knowing and impervious smiles of those nymphs, who, she now began to see, had more of an equivalence in ordinary life, as it is lived by certain women, than she had ever suspected'. A more specific analogy is with the Tiepolo allegory of Venus and Time, which is related to a louche young mother with a child, with whom Blanche in her loneliness takes up. She is one who thrives on 'close shaves, ill-gotten gains, flights to freedom, escapes of all sorts. Truly weightless, like the characters in mythology. And, like them, unscrupulous.'

All this art is well enough in its way, though it lacks the generic point and fantasy of Anthony Powell's excursions into the fine arts in *A Dance to the Music of Time.* Far from being pretentious, or a form of showing-off, it reveals a touching lack of self-confidence. She no more needs it than Pym needs the comedies and rituals of a churchy setting. Art, or the Church, lends the reassurance of familiarity to situations which remain, where fiction is concerned, essentially modest. But both novelists are masters of the trade, and nothing shows this more than their handling of plot. . . . Brookner's air of stasis has an infinite economy about it, particularly where characters are concerned. It is as if she had absolutely to brace herself for the introduction of a new one. This whets the appetite, and the new one is always fascinating. Patrick, the family friend, a high-ranking civil servant who repairs harpsichords and who lives for moments of social tension—'Patrick sat, his patrician features minimally relaxed, enjoying the spectacle'—is a masterpiece. He belongs to that not uncommon category of people today who 'want to be reprehensible'.

In an early Pym novel a character assumes an enigmatic smile when a question about her 'past' comes up, and the novelist herself not infrequently comments on people's need, where romance is concerned, to have both a past and a future. Both she and Brookner give the impression of having their 'secret', and, however vulgar this may sound, it does unquestionably add to our sense of their work, and to our pleasure in it. Contact with a personality is one of the most obvious joys of novel-reading, but how very seldom is such a contact provocative and absorbing, or even interesting. In our shameless age the novelist is usually all too accessible: the pleasures of specu-lation seem beside the point. This is where the gentility of Pym and Brookner is a priceless though always slightly mysterious asset, for on the face of it both are almost brutally honest about themselves and their situation. (pp. 20, 22)

Ladies don't cry for help. The nearest they come to it could be in writing wonderfully accomplished humorous novels, in which a cry can be heard, a cry on behalf of their characters, and only by implication for themselves. Novels like these are also a way of dealing with dreams, fantasies and obsessions, with things that might have happened but didn't, with custodial disappointments, with the long perspectives in life as fiction, and fiction as life, that link us to our losses. One of the strangest things about these novels—and about Jane Austen's—is that they raise the question of what it means to be a 'born novelist'. So many writers are simply and definitively nasty by nature, and their art is a secretion of their condition, a secretion that makes a pearl. Both Brookner and Pym can be imagined as living miles away from the novel, busily cooking, sewing, being sharp but kind, making marmalade, raising happy fam-ilies. And yet they are also dedicated souls who from the age of sixteen or so wanted above all things to write. Could their secret be that they write in the full knowledge of what it means to be happy and fulfilled, in ways in which art by its nature brings no fulfillment? They are anti-Flauberts, embodying in their art, like the scrofulous beggar in *Madame Bovary*, another world, a world of sunshine and green leaves. But enough of the 'romantic touches', at which Pym would smile. In the throes of an unhappy love affair during the war she noted in her diary: 'Patience and Courage still—and struggle on.' And then added that if she ever had any children, 'I think I must call them Patience and Courage. Twins—rather dreary stolid little girls.' (p. 22)

John Bayley, "Ladies," in London Review of Books, *Vol. 8, No. 15, September 4, 1986, pp. 20, 22.*

MICHIKO KAKUTANI

At first, Anita Brookner's latest heroine, Blanche Vernon, would seem to have nothing whatsoever in common with her famous namesake in *A Streetcar Named Desire*: she has none of Blanche DuBois's ravaged sensuality, none of her dark se-crets to conceal. Rather, Miss Brookner's Blanche—one of those terribly proper women who have led careful, decorous lives—is a woman routinely commended and condemned for her "docility," her "seriousness" and her "goodness."

What the two Blanches share is an emotional neediness and a capacity for victimization—both look to men for salvation; both stand as symbols of vanished, anachronistic cultures, and both are attracted to the very harsh, vulgar reality that threatens to destroy them.

Certainly *The Misalliance* [published in England as *A Misal-liance*] neither aspires to—nor comes close to achieving—the

tragic stature of *Streetcar*. Like Miss Brookner's earlier works, it's a small, immaculately orchestrated novel, set down in precise, unforgiving prose. It, too, offers another variation on the author's favorite theme: the race, in life, between the tor-toises and the hares—the plodding innocents and the careless sophisticates, the earnest do-gooders and the unscrupulous users. As in *Look at Me,* the heroine—a decided tortoise, if there ever was one—is mesmerized by the hectic world of the hares, and her attempts to observe and even enter into their games will very nearly destroy her. This time, however, the experi-ence will also jar her into self-awareness, and in doing so, will hold out the promise of starting over.

The interplay between innocence and sophistication, of course, has long been a favorite topic of novelists—from Choderlos de Laclos, the author of *Les Liaisons Dangereuses,* who used it to examine the cynicism of the aristocracy in the declining years of the ancien régime, to Henry James, who used it to look at the relationship between America and Europe. Though her novel reverberates with echoes of such books, Miss Brook-ner's aims, again, are considerably more modest: she simply wants to use the dichotomy as an explanation for the fact that some women are more successful than others in the departments of sex and romance. . . .

Much of this will be overly familiar to readers of Miss Brook-ner's five previous novels. In fact, much of *The Misalliance* finds Blanche blurring into a pretty, if undistinguished, amal-gam of such previous Brookner heroines as Frances in *Look at Me,* Kitty in *Providence* and Edith in *Hotel du Lac.* What is different about Blanche is supplied by this volume's startling—and expertly rendered   conclusion. It points to a new and altogether welcome turn in Miss Brookner's career, away from the bitterness of her last novel (*Family and Friends*), toward something just a little brighter: the promise of new life, and redemption.

Michiko Kakutani, in a review of "The Misalliance,"
in The New York Times, *March 25, 1987, p. C23.*

FERNANDA EBERSTADT

The Misalliance is about Blanche, a woman whose husband, Bertie, has recently left her for his secretary. Worse, their former friends, finding Blanche increasingly eccentric, have switched their allegiance to Bertie's more lively and approach-able young girlfriend, who bears the incongruous nickname Mousie. Reduced to days of wandering around the National Gallery and doing volunteer work at the local hospital, Blanche becomes obsessed by the lives of two strangers: a 3-year-old who won't talk and her delinquent mother, Sally, a young beauty whose furious hedonism, propensity for getting into scrapes and rather steely insistence that others extricate her embody, in Blanche's mind, the "pagan" principle of life. In the end, tainted and finally disgusted by Sally's rapacious ex-ploits, Blanche finds the strength to cut free and to seize for herself a little of life's sweetness.

The novel displays in spades Ms. Brookner's characteristic strengths and failings. As always, the prose is crisp, tart and unerring in its sense of the just word. . . . Ms. Brookner is superb, too, at conveying the taste or feel of such essential fictional commodities as a dish of Dover sole, a bottle of Sauternes, a city street, the inside of an apartment. It is a pleasure and a stimulation, moreover, to enter the mental world of a contemporary novelist whose work encompasses the dialogues of Plato, the Brandenburg Concertos, Marcus Aurelius, Hercules and the Italian collection of the National Gallery.

In these and other respects, Anita Brookner seems quite an old-fashioned novelist. But the appearance is partly deceptive. If the traditional novel takes society for its subject, the prototypical subject of the modern novel is alienation. Few writers have come close to Ms. Brookner in the depiction of female loneliness, particularly in its more gradual, unspectacular and mundane effects. Despite her heroine's bland and muted life, *The Misalliance,* like all Ms. Brookner's fiction, exercises an almost inexplicable grip on the reader—a tribute to her formidable gifts as a psychologist of the wounded woman's heart.

The weakness of *The Misalliance* is twofold. As a narrator, Ms. Brookner has a compulsion to explain to the reader, over and over, what her characters are like; her fiction is in general virtually devoid of those gestures, conversations and minutely discriminated acts of self-revelation that the novel is best designed to convey. An all-too-typical passage from *The Misalliance* runs: "Mousie needed to function from a position of emotional dominance.... Bertie, used to the calm, unemotional woman whom Blanche had become, had been enchanted by the petulance, the self-assurance, and the shamelessness of Mousie. He took all these qualities as evidence of passion, in which he was mistaken, although it was an easy mistake to make, and he was not alone in making it."

Concomitantly, and in contrast to the achingly vivid reality of Ms. Brookner's heroines, her Berties and Mousies and Sallys, those supposedly robust and pleasure-loving deities who stride out to conquer the world, are patently unconvincing types whom she makes scant efforts to realize. Like her heroines, she sometimes seems to get her ideas about other people from books and not from life.

But if her "pagans" disappoint, her thin-blooded heroines—"doomed to serve, to be faithful, to be honourable, and to be excluded"—are a fictional achievement of high magnitude. Moreover, *The Misalliance*—like *Hotel du Lac* and *Family and Friends*—has in the end a rather salutary and peculiarly welcome message, namely, that keeping up appearances in hard times is a virtue in itself, that kindness, self-restraint, good housekeeping and a certain cheerful worldliness may after all save the day. To this message, delivered with a lucid and refined intelligence and an invigorating asperity of tone, one can respond only with gratitude and pleasure.

Fernanda Eberstadt, "Good Works and Bad Lovers," in The New York Times Book Review, *March 29, 1987, p. 10.*

PETER PARKER

It comes as something of a surprise to find a character in a novel by Anita Brookner winning the pools. However, by page 62 [of *A Friend from England*] we are back in familiar—perhaps too familiar—territory: 'I long ago decided to live my life on the surface, avoiding entanglements, confrontations, situations that cannot be quickly resolved, friendships that lead to passion.' The speaker is Rachel, a single woman, apparently not without a bleak self-sufficiency, who narrates the story of her involvement with the pools-winning Livingstone family. (p. 26)

The Livingstones are described at exhaustive and exhausting length. It is difficult to summon up even Rachel's mild, comfortably supine interest in the lives of these people, particularly

when dealt with in so dilatory a fashion, and when characterisation is shaky or contradictory. For instance, Rachel casts an expert's eye over the Livingstones' style in furnishings . . . , but does not know a Knole settee when she sees one. Where is the wit, the assurance, the control of *Look at Me*? A comparison of the opening chapters of these two novels, both of which treat of the entanglement of a single woman in the lives of a couple, points up the alarming ennervation of *A Friend from England.*

Things liven up a little with Rachel's sceptical account of Heather's wedding, but at some cost. The shock when Heather's gilded husband is 'unmasked' lies less in the revelation itself than in the crudity with which it is presented. Indeed, so unconvincing is it that I imagined that the scene had been set up to expose Rachel's naivety and would later be shown to be a misunderstanding. Alas, no. It would be unfair to say much more about this, since it constitutes plot, except to note that Barbara Pym, with whom to her apparent chagrin Brookner is frequently compared, handled a similar scene with a great deal more subtlety back in 1958.

There is a certain amount of satisfaction to be gained when Rachel finally summons up courage to confront Heather, but one feels that her manners are not quite bad enough. The reasons for Rachel putting up with this intolerable family, one which anyone sensible would have jettisoned at the first opportunity, are insufficiently realised. One simply does not believe that someone as intelligent as Rachel would not have cut and run a good deal earlier. Except, of course, that this is the scheme of the novel and that it is necessary for Rachel to follow the story to its conclusion in order to become undeceived about herself.

Since the deservedly popular *Hôtel du Lac,* which displayed a nice ironic wit and a genuine toughness, similar indeed to Pym, Brookner's novels have become more and more melancholy (a favoured Brookner state) and less and less funny. The problem here is not unlike that of *Family and Friends* where one was unsure whether it was the characters or the author who had become effete. Heroines who once were sharp are now just sour; stories that once were piercingly sad have become merely depressing; narratives that were spry have become enfeebled. Brookner's admirers praise her delicacy, but this novel is delicate in the sense that an invalid is delicate. Indeed, one is tempted to be *indelicate* enough to suggest that Brookner should rally herself and cast around for a new theme. This particular seam and its diligent investigator appear to be equally exhausted. (pp. 26-7)

Peter Parker, "Melancholy Stylist," in Books, *No. 5, August, 1987, pp. 26-7.*

HEATHER NEILL

Like Blanche, the heroine of Anita Brookner's last novel, *Misalliance,* Rachel, the narrator of her latest [*A Friend from England*], has chosen to live life on the surface. She avoids emotional commitments and entanglements with an almost pathological fervour, having suffered once (an episode referred to only briefly in her climactic outburst of uncharacteristic anger) and has since determined on a life of self-sufficiency. *A Friend from England* shows, by chronicling her relationship with the suburban Livingstones, how Rachel has deceived herself. Ironically, it is dull, complacent, spoilt Heather, the daughter of the family, who turns Rachel's certainties on their head and she is left to contemplate a life which seems lonely and empty rather than liberated. She has failed to pass—and can no longer discount—what she now sees as society's test: she has no man of her own and no children.

As often, then, this Brookner heroine is a woman on her own. Loneliness is certainly a theme and Rachel sees herself, distastefully, as likely to be pitied. Yet she is sure she has life under control. There is her work (she has a third share in a bookshop), she has 'friends' (never introduced) and passionless affairs which are obliquely hinted at. When all else fails, she walks the streets of nighttime London for hours at a time. Her friendship with the Livingstones—whose very name suggests stolid, unimaginative security—provides her, an orphan, with a window on to a way of life that might have been: cosy, conventional and virtuous. (p. 18)

Anita Brookner writes with perfect control. She has an unrivalled eye for the details of appearance and behaviour, pinning down with ruthless accuracy the minutiae of style in dress, interior decoration and eating habits. Often she writes like someone describing a painting or a photograph (a technique used to good effect in *Family and Friends*), but this time we are too closely focused on Rachel and her internalised brooding on a woman's lot. It is as if the frame is frozen and Rachel takes us by the lapels to make us consider what we see in the suburban drawing room, the hospital ward of the little unloved flat she refers to as her bunker and all that these scenes signify. Rachel is observant, if sometimes mistaken, but she becomes repetitive, reminding us too often of the sweet, melancholy rituals of the Livingstones, of her—ultimately doubted—assumption of Heather's underlying shrewdness, of the anxiety engendered by family closeness, of Heather and Michael's perpetual childishness, of her own fear of drowning. The latter is mentioned matter-of-factly, Rachel apparently making no connection between it and her fear of passion. The final scenes in watery Venice, where she goes on a last, abortive errand of kindness for Oscar and Dorrie—to bring Heather back, represent a particular torture for her. The 'shock of truth' could not have a more chilling backdrop.

The Livingstones are memorably drawn, a picture of simplicity and innocence, and Rachel's ironic certainty, culminating in the dreadful, angry exposure of her real life to Heather, is painfully real. For the rest, Heather is a passive foil, Michael and Marco barely present and the surrounding Livingstone family of aunts and cousins reduced to a sketchy comic chorus. Only Michael's slimy father, 'Colonel' Sandberg (dreadfully unreliable as a foundation, sand) insinuates his way satisfactorily among the minor characters. This is something of a disappointment: Ms Brookner has produced some fine exotic cameos in earlier books.

Other Brookner trademarks *are* here, though. She is always brilliant at showing her purposeless heroine painstakingly filling unfillable time. She can take her reader into an environment, conjuring the feel of a place, paying particular attention to light and heat, colour and texture. And there is irony. The ultimate irony here is that Rachel, who does not scruple to judge others, who is so sure she understands herself, time and again unwittingly reveals the gap between the truth and her perception of it. The brave feminist is really a sad Brookner heroine after all and the light of reason just another name for fear. (p. 19)

> *Heather Neill, "The Shock of Truth," in* The Listener, *Vol. 118, No. 3025, August 20, 1987, pp. 18-19.*

KATHY STEPHEN

A long, sustained battle has raged throughout Anita Brookner's fiction between the forces of reason, balance, morality, and the brute strengths of passion, selfishness and impulse. The carnal forces often triumphed but they did so at the price of seeming to be second best. The classically lonely Anita Brookner heroine was left with at least the satisfaction that she had not behaved in a shoddy manner.

But in her seventh novel in seven years, *A Friend from England,* Miss Brookner takes away even this comfort from her high-minded heroine. There is an air of some decision about this book: the war between a circumscribed version of goodness and powerful insensitive action has effectively been won by the side from which the heroine feels herself to be excluded, and she is burdened with the bleak realisation that she has, all along, been wrong, having misapprehended the strategy and what was at stake.

Those who have been wishing that Anita Brookner would change . . . may feel some satisfaction that, in this novel, she is trying to. But the essential Anita Brookner heroine—in this case Rachel Kennedy, aged 32—remains a character of fascinating but infuriating opaqueness.

A Friend from England is emerging into the light of the amazing, even comically unlikely, revelation that Anita Brookner, unbeknownst even to herself, was involved in the world of espionage as a courier of information, according to the banned confessions of an exiled spymaster. It is dangerous to compare art and life, but this unexpected turn-up—too dramatic in itself to have occurred within the pages of a Brookner novel—somehow provides an odd insight into this small dissatisfaction with Miss Brookner's finely wrought work: that she is telling the truth, but only part of it. The exposure of a secret that Miss Brookner did not know herself seems to comment upon the lives of her heroines, who have yet to reveal what may be a secret (certainly not the same one as the author's) at the bottom of their lives.

In most of her previous novels, Anita Brookner has walked round and round the dilemma of the type of woman—moral, intellectual, independent—who cannot get and keep a man. She seems to be insisting that there is nothing more to disclose about these women; it is all within the state of things. That anyone can marry is a truism which, of couse, Anita Brookner knows. Her heroines are perfectionists and they want to make the perfect match, even if they feel others should be content with a more common lot.

The author's fifth and sixth novels were partial exceptions to the Anita Brookner rule. *Family and Friends* provided glimpses of a fulfilled family life for at least some of the participants; *A Misalliance* had the astonishing conclusion of what appeared to be a happy ending when the husband came home to his prim wife, after a foray to the other side of the Brookner divide.

These books offered some respite from the impossible struggle. *A Friend from England* does not. (pp. 27-8)

What increasingly marks Anita Brookner out as an especially fine novelist, despite impasses in her characters, is the marriage in her work between beauty of expression and infinite emotional pain, mitigated by irony. The prose rings so very true; her sentences have an effortless design. Comparisons to Jane Austen are not accurate, but there is the same containment of feeling beneath an exquisite surface.

Miss Brookner displays modern life as an experience of un-resolved moral dissonance: along with everything else she has to contend with, Rachel Kennedy must *envy* those who live irresponsibly; at the same time she refuses to allow herself to be like them. Except for glimpses into the marriage of the elder Livingstones, of a gentler and more romantic generation, there is apparently no possibility for sexual and moral impulses to find a home together.

Anita Brookner's typical vision of life is particularly acted out within the character of Heather Livingstone, the young woman who passes through an essential phase of decision in the course of the novel. On first meeting, Heather is silent, dutiful, in-nocent. . . . By the end of the book, she has shifted allegiances and made the ruthless moves necessary to survive. She has changed; Rachel has not, except to realise she should have done; and Rachel, the 'friend from England', cannot persuade Heather that she should have behaved more responsibly.

Although Anita Brookner has not blazed wildly innovative imaginative trails in her novels, she has gone deeper and deeper, as on a spiral staircase, into the question of how and why some people connect and others never do. Yet there are aspects of this question she has refused to consider. Loneliness may be an insoluble universal mystery, but perhaps in future books Anita Brookner will be forced to reveal more about her her-oines—that they may be unconscious couriers of classified information, carrying the secrets of their own fraught condi-tions within themselves. (pp. 27-8)

> *Kathy Stephen, "No Respite from the Struggle," in*
> The Spectator, *Vol. 259, No. 8302, August 22, 1987,*
> *pp. 27-8.*

CAROL ANSHAW

In the string of novels she has written these past several years (most notably *Providence, Hotel du Lac, Look at Me*), Brookner has done the same sort of PR for depression that Joan Didion did for ennui—making a pathology seem simply the most in-telligent response to the circumstances at hand. In Brookner's world, these circumstances usually occur in London and sur-round a certain kind of single woman—a sensibly shod, car-diganed gal, on her way back to her flat, carrying a small piece of sole for her dinner, her gaze fixed on a specific point in the middle distance, just beyond the weekend.

For loneliness is the dread enemy of the Brookner protagonist, and it's a loneliness precisely defined. It's Not Having a Hus-band. Husbands are for other women, the bold ones who seize men and whisk them away and bear their babies and bake their scones and live happily ever after, a state Brookner seems to believe in quite ingenuously—for these Other Women. Her protagonists, however, are usually relegated to another sus-pended state, with their noses forever pressed against the win-dows of their "fulfilled" sisters. Brookner draws her line with heavy marker—between those who live life and those who can only hang around the edges and observe it: The damaged and undamaged.

A place for everyone and everyone in her place. It's a tidy world with squared-off corners and characters that can be in-troduced with a single sentence and counted on to spend the next 200 pages corroborating that first impression. Having cre-ated this universe, Brookner steps back as its astronomer, look-ing from a great, dispassionate distance on an earth where the meek inherit nothing but the crumbs of the bold, and where

the bold make rather trivial use of their loaf. And where every-one behaves with enormous civility around this unfair division of spoils.

This is decidedly not a feminist vision, and it would seem almost comically loony (all these blissed-out wives and hollow-eyed career women) if Brookner weren't such an excellent writer—lucid, logical, seductive, gently taking you around by the elbow to see things from her point of view, holding you there a little longer than is comfortable. It takes a couple of days to spring back. But of course you do. And it's an inter-esting test for the feminist to read Brookner, an opportunity to stand one's careworn set of truths against the elegantly pre-sented lie. . . .

I think Brookner herself might be getting a glimpse of the lie, or at least getting tired of assembling all this restraint and good behavior and tidy emotion around her truth. At any rate, there's a promisingly weird restlessness in the underneath of her new novel, *A Friend from England.* At the start, much is the same. Rachel, the protagonist-narrator, is 32, part owner of a small bookshop. She knows she's one of the damaged, and so ar-ranges a limited, manageable life for herself. . . .

Rachel does have a sex life. It is, however, so dark and furtive and lived among the creatures of the night that Brookner has extreme difficulty bringing herself to describe it. "I rushed to the bedroom again," Rachel tells us, "opened my wardrobe, instinctively chose a plain but flattering sweater and skirt, made up my face, prepared to go out. It is something I have to do from time to time. I have my own techniques for dealing with such sieges and fugues as lie in wait for me. . . . I force the note, I go out, seek companions, bear them home. . . ." And that's that. If you think you're going to find out more about those sieges and fugues, forget it and switch to Jackie Collins.

Rachel's pale spot of sunshine in this vampirish existence is her friendship with her old accountant Oscar Livingstone and his wife, Dorrie. . . . Although she presents them as relentlessly dull, Rachel claims to be drawn to Oscar and Dorrie, to their devotion to one another, their impeccable subscription to con-vention, their warmth and stability. . . .

Oscar and Dorrie enjoy Rachel in a passive way—they are at home to her when she calls—and innocently see her as a friend/chaperone for their daughter Heather, a bovine, affectless girl in her late twenties, who has been set up with her own little boutique but is tacitly expected to be about her real business—snagging a husband. Her parents feel that in some vague way, Rachel will be able to help Heather in this pursuit. They don't understand that Rachel is beyond husbands, that she inhabits the farthest reaches of Brookner Territory, a terrible place of holding oneself together through cynical pragmatism, a bleak plain where days are seqences of motions to be gone through briskly and in their proper order, where vacations are the means to gather up conversational anecdotes for the coming year, where sexual connection is a way to get rid of those sieges and fugues as though they were so much tartar buildup. . . .

Brookner strips Rachel down, exposing her layer by layer, from hard to embittered to creepily parasitic to deranged. This time it is not a cruel and unjust world that's the problem; it is the distortion in the protagonist's perception of that world. What an interesting breakthrough for Brookner, wrestling some of the blame away from those dreary fates and laying it at the feet of her "passive victim" protagonist. Maybe she was be-ginning to feel dead air gathering around her stories—so many cautious variations on a theme—and thought she'd open a vent, let in a breeze to rustle all that caution around a bit. . . .

Until recently, [Brookner] wrote her novels during holidays from teaching at London's Courtauld Institute of Art, each book done during a summer, which may account for their neat, tucked-in quality. Real life—and the best fiction—is more rumpled up, and in this new book, Brookner seems to be stretching to accommodate that, moving away from the small, safe, "accomplished" set piece into a riskier artistic venture. Unfortunately, the book is not a great success. Too much is left over of the novel of manners—stationary side characters and well-made plot are suddenly crashed into by roiling neurosis and Freudian imagery. It's like Blanche DuBois coming to visit the Pallisers.

Brookner has quit teaching and plans to devote more time to her fiction. This may change the sort of book she writes, expand her ambitions. *A Friend from England* is not her best work, but it may be a bridge to something better. And in the meantime, it's not so awful reading about Rachel's boring obsession with the Livingstones. At least the woman *has* an obsession. At least she's not another of those doomed souls sitting forever at the kitchen table, watching the candles gutter out and the dinner go to ruin in the oven while Mr. Right is off, casually getting engaged to someone else.

> Carol Anshaw, "A Gloom of One's Own," in VLS, No. 64, April, 1988, p. 11.

(Sir) Noël (Pierce) Coward

1899-1973

English dramatist, scriptwriter, songwriter, short story writer, novelist, autobiographer, poet, actor, director, and editor.

Coward's reputation as one of the most popular dramatists of the twentieth century derives primarily from his plays *Hay Fever, Private Lives, Blithe Spirit,* and other sophisticated comedies of manners he authored prior to the end of World War II. Originally written to showcase the talents of a group of performers with whom he associated, these plays established Coward as a gifted and versatile actor, writer, director, and composer. Rejecting the epigrammatic dialogue of most early twentieth-century drama, Coward used a clipped, naturalistic style that captured the rhythms of everyday speech to detail the follies, pretensions, and unconventional love affairs of vain, affluent hedonists whose glib behavior reflects the spirit of the post-World War I generation. Douglas Dunn maintained: "Coward's quarrelling couples, their high-pitched silliness, their vindictive affections, their inability to be civil even in love, are among the most amusing spectacles in the English theatre." Although critics sometimes faulted Coward for flat characterizations, deliberate superficiality, and a penchant for licentiousness and frivolity, most praised his diverse theatrical talents and his ability to create witty repartee.

Coward first appeared on London's professional stage at the age of twelve and began composing songs and writing plays before he was twenty years old. Many critics have attributed his mastery of dramatic structure and of such disparate theatrical forms as melodrama, the musical revue, comedy, and psychological and social drama to his early interest in stagecraft. Coward's first significant work for the theater was *The Vortex* (1924), a realistic problem play about a young man's drug addiction and his obsession with his mother. Like much of Coward's early work, this play was popular with British youth for its cynical approach to generational conflicts. *Fallen Angels* (1925), the first of several lighthearted sexual farces that established Coward's international reputation as a dramatist and performer, addresses the humorous complications that result when two married women encounter their former lover. *Hay Fever* (1925), regarded as Coward's most enduring comedy of the 1920s, was inspired by a weekend he spent at the home of actress Laurette Taylor. This play revolves around the Blisses, an obnoxious family of eccentrics, who invite four acquaintances to their home and then alternately insult and seduce their guests until they flee the house. Jack Kroll noted of the play's 1985 revival: "With his astonishing craftsmanship Coward turns the bower of Bliss into a castle of emotional vampires chomping away on their terrified victims. But every bite is a laugh in this timeless comedy of ill manners." Other noteworthy theatrical works Coward completed during the 1920s include a romantic melodrama, *The Queen Was in the Parlour* (1926); the comedies *"This Was a Man"* (1926), *The Marquise* (1927), and *Home Chat* (1927); and the musical revues *This Year of Grace!* (1928) and *Bitter-Sweet: An Operette* (1929).

Coward's popularity reached its apex during the 1930s and early 1940s. *Private Lives: An Intimate Comedy* (1930), considered one of the finest light comedies of the twentieth century, was a resounding critical and commercial success in both Great

The Granger Collection, New York

Britain and the United States. This play examines the potential destructiveness of romantic relationships in its story of Amanda and Elyot, a divorced couple who renew their acquaintance when both arrive at the same hotel to honeymoon with their new spouses. Recalling the more radiant moments of their tumultuous marriage, Amanda and Elyot decide to elope in Paris but promptly return to their habitual quarreling. *Private Lives* has been compared by several recent critics to the later works of Edward Albee and Harold Pinter for its darkly satirical portrayal of love and marriage. *Cavalcade* (1931) is one of several serious dramas in which Coward extols his nationalistic beliefs despite his cynicism toward conventional moral values. Spanning British history from 1899 to 1930, this play combines music and drama to document the hardships of two families, the upper-class Marryots and the lower-class Bridges. *Words and Music* (1932; produced in the United States as *Set to Music*) is a musical revue for which Coward composed one of his most popular songs, "Mad Dogs and Englishmen." His next significant achievement, *Design for Living* (1933), relates the story of Gilda, a sprightly young sophisticate who falls in love with two artistic men, Leo and Otto, but who opts for a marriage of convenience with a stodgy, dependable art dealer. At the play's conclusion, which some reviewers deemed offensive during its initial run, Gilda forsakes her unsatisfying domestic life for Leo and Otto, and the three collapse in laughter on a sofa as her husband leaves, suggesting, among other possibilities, a future *ménage à trois. To-Night at 8:30* (1936) consists of nine one-act dramas in which Coward utilizes various styles to satirize such subjects as marriage, adultery, etiquette, and theatrical life.

The most popular work of Coward's career was *Blithe Spirit: An Improbable Farce* (1941). In this comedy of manners, the household of Charles and Ruth Condomine disintegrates into chaos when Charles's spiteful first wife, Elvira, is inadvertently summoned from the grave. Attempting to reclaim her husband, Elvira accidentally kills Ruth, and Charles finally decides to exorcise the ghosts of his nagging spouses. *Present Laughter* (1943) offers a comic portrait of an immodest matinee idol whose growing disenchantment with fame and superficial love relationships leads him to rejoin his wife, from whom he had been separated. Douglas Watt commented of *Present Laughter*'s 1982 revival that "one can only marvel at Coward's knack for spinning so slight a story to such engaging lengths . . . and at the work's waspish strength as well as its good humor." *This Happy Breed* (1943) and *Peace in Our Time* (1947), which Coward wrote during World War II, celebrate British nationalism and ideals.

Coward's dramas of the 1950s and 1960s failed to elicit the critical attention and praise of his earlier work. Due in part to a lack of public interest in comedies of manners following World War II, Coward employed a more topical, broadly satirical humor in his later plays. In such full-length works as *Island Fling* (1951; produced in Great Britain as *South Sea Bubble*) and *Nude with Violin* (1956), he bitterly attacks political liberalism, intellectualism, and the modern art movement. Coward's other plays of the 1950s include *Ace of Clubs* (1950), *Relative Values: A Light Comedy* (1951), and *After the Ball* (1954), an adaptation of Oscar Wilde's comedy *Lady Windermere's Fan*. The most celebrated drama of Coward's later career is *Waiting in the Wings* (1960), a sentimental comedy set in a home for retired actresses. According to John Lahr, Coward uses the nursing home "to show off the gallantry of the performers' charm while exploring their fear of losing it. The notion of stars being forgotten . . . touched something deep in Coward." Although largely inactive as a dramatist during the 1960s, Coward regained some of his former stature as an entertainer through his nightclub performances of songs, revues, and sketches.

In addition to his dramas, Coward also created works in several other genres. *In Which We Serve* (1943), a film for which Coward is credited as scriptwriter, producer, actor, and, with David Lean, co-director, pays tribute to the British Royal Navy. Music and lyrics from Coward's career have been collected in *The Noël Coward Song Book* (1953) and *The Lyrics of Noël Coward* (1965). Coward also authored a best-selling novel, *Pomp and Circumstance* (1960), as well as several acclaimed short story collections, including *To Step Aside* (1939), *Star Quality* (1951), *Pretty Polly Barlow and Other Stories* (1964), and *Bon Voyage and Other Stories* (1967). Compared by some to the work of Evelyn Waugh, Coward's fiction, like his drama, displays a mocking wit and focuses on the idle rich. John Rees Moore remarked that Coward's "range in fiction is surprising. He can write . . . of ship cruises with a sardonic eye on the rich and spoiled but also with a sympathy that comes from close identification, on the servants' eye view of their 'betters,' on the humorous perils of fame and fortune, and on the emptiness of mere worldly success." Coward's short fiction has been gathered in *The Collected Stories of Noël Coward* (1983)

and *The Collected Short Stories, Volume 2* (1985). Coward chronicled events from his personal and professional life in *Middle East Diary* (1944), *The Noël Coward Diaries* (1982), and *Autobiography* (1986). The latter book combines two previously published volumes, *Present Indicative: An Autobiography* (1937) and *Future Indefinite* (1954), with *Past Conditional*, an incomplete work written by Coward in 1965.

(See also *CLC*, Vols. 1, 9, 29; *Contemporary Authors*, Vols. 17-18, Vols. 41-44, rev. ed. [obituary]; *Contemporary Authors Permanent Series*, Vol. 2; and *Dictionary of Literary Biography*, Vol. 10.)

DOUGLAS WATT

How welcome Noel Coward is on a summer night, . . . with his *Present Laughter,* a revival of which opened last evening. . . .

The fun, perversely, is centered around [a strongly heterosexual actor] . . . playing a role steeped in the homosexual sensibility. Garry Essendine, the arrogant romantic comedy star who imagines he would make a magnificent Peer Gynt, is still adored by the wife from whom he is separated and is sought after by countless women. Yet he is such a model of self-centered bitchiness that it is hard to imagine his ever entering the same bedroom with any of his putative conquests. Much of the play's basic humor lies in this contradiction, and one can easily imagine Coward's joy in playing the role he created onstage as well as on paper. . . .

[One] can only marvel at Coward's knack for spinning so slight a story to such engaging lengths (this is a three-act play) and at the work's waspish strength as well as its good humor. For Coward, we must never forget, believed firmly in the homely virtues, and husband and wife are rejoined in a happy and amusing ending.

*Douglas Watt, in a review of "Present Laughter,"
in* Daily News, *New York, July 16, 1982.*

CLIVE BARNES

Do plays themselves actually change, or is it only taste—our perception of plays at a certain time and place. Last night . . . they revived Noel Coward's *Present Laughter* . . . , and I thought, on virtually every count, it was smashing.

This is a most civilized play. Coward used the English language with a deftness that had not been heard since Oscar Wilde. He can dazzle with the commonplace.

He can make strange English place names, such as Uckfield or Stoke Poges, extravagantly funny. With climactic timing he can bring the house down with a line like "What a day for Cunard!" Genius.

Yet I think I did not always think so. I first saw *Present Laughter* in its 1947 revival, with Coward himself playing the egocentric, idolized actor-hero, Garry Essendine.

It seemed minor Coward in London at the time. In 1946 it had seemed minor Coward in New York. Even Coward thought the evening "gruesome," and wrote in his soon to be published diaries that, apart from Clifton Webb, "the cast was tatty and fifth-rate."

The cast is not tatty and fifth-rate at this new revival—yet I think its success runs deeper even than the production. Simply because Coward's talent to amuse was so urbane and well-publicized, simply because he wrote what critics called "thin plays," and he staunchly refused to write what he called "fat plays for fat critics," even when praised he was usually patronized.

Now nearly 10 years after his death his talent can be seen as a divine gift for comedy. Such productions as this help Coward come into his own.

Present Laughter was the nearest Coward came to writing a French farce. With its fantastic characters, its oscillating bedroom door and its gentle emphasis on sex as the action's mainspring, it could indeed be almost an Anglicization of Feydeau. But it is a little bit more.

Essendine is an obsessive self-portrait of the artist as a middle-aged queen. For reasons of then current custom, the actor has been conveniently decked out as a heterosexual, but that was presumably more out of convenience and necessity than conviction.

The character, an actor and the kingpin of his complex circle, is seen in the hectic midst of his intriguing life. As he prepared to tour Africa and open a later London season, his life, affectionately supervised by an ex-wife and an implacable secretary, whirls around in dotty, but flamboyant, anguish. He is plagued by people, circumstances and his sense of self. But he keeps his sense of humor waving like a flag . . . in a shipwreck. . . .

What a really lovely evening in the theater—basking in the sunshine of laughter, enjoying the dappled shadows of wit, and revelling in the sweet pungency of the deadly commonplace.

Who but Coward would think of sending matches to boy scouts or direct us to find compulsive humor in a line as apparently flat as: "Happy? There is something so *awfully* sad about happiness?" Genius—unalloyed.

> Clive Barnes, "Great Scott in Smashing 'Laughter'," in New York Post, *July 16, 1982.*

JOHN LAHR

Noël Coward never believed he had just a talent to amuse. A man who spent a lifetime merchandising his de-luxe persona, Coward liked to make a distinction between accomplishment and vanity: 'I am bursting with pride, which is why I have absolutely no vanity.' A performer's job is to be sensational; and in his songs, plays and public performances, Coward lived up to the responsibility of making a proper spectacle of himself. His peers had difficulty in fathoming this phenomenon. T. E. Lawrence thought Coward had 'a hasty kind of genius'. Sean O'Casey spat spiders at the mention of his name: 'Mr. Coward hasn't yet even shaken a baby-rattle of life in the face of one watching audience.' J. B. Priestley, as late as 1964, taxed him mischievously: 'What is all this nonsense about being called the Master?' Shaw, who prophesied success for the fledgling playwright in 1921, warned him 'never to fall into a breach of essential good manners'. He didn't.

A star is his own greatest invention. Coward's plays and songs were primarily vehicles to launch his elegant persona on the world. In his clipped, bright, confident style, Coward irresistibly combined reserve and high camp. He became the merry-andrew of moderation, warning mothers to keep their daughters off the stage, confiding, in *Present Laughter* (1942), that sex was 'vastly overrated' and sardonically pleading: 'don't let's be beastly to the Germans'. Coward was a performer who wrote: not a writer who happened to perform. He wrote his svelte, wan good looks into the role of Nicky Lancaster in *The Vortex* (1924): 'He is extremely well-dressed,' explain the stage directions. 'He is tall and pale, with thin nervous hands'. The play made Coward a sensation both as an actor and as a playwright. Coward was his own hero; and the parts he created for himself were, in general, slices of his legendary life. (pp. 1-2)

Like all great entertainers, Coward knew how to exploit his moment. In the thirties Cyril Connolly was complaining that his plays were 'written in the most topical and perishable way imaginable, the cream in them turns sour overnight.' The American critic Alexander Woollcott dubbed Coward 'Destiny's Tot', but he was England's solid-gold jazz-baby who later turned into an international glamour-puss. Coward swung with the times and suavely teased them. 'I am never out of opium dens, cocaine dens, and other evil places. My mind is a mass of corruption,' he told the *Evening Standard* in 1925. Every new-fangled idiom found its way into his dialogue, even if he didn't always fully grasp its meaning: 'You're psychoanalytic neurotics the both of you', complains one of the characters in *Fallen Angles* (1925). *The Vortex* exploited the clash between Victorian and modern mores, the old and the young idea. *Fallen Angels* and *Easy Virtue* (1925) mined the mother-lode of sex, scandal and pseudo-sophistication. *Cavalcade* (1931) and *This Happy Breed* (1942) spoke directly to the political chauvinism of the day. All these plays had great commercial success and the last two were considered serious patriotic statements about England and her fighting spirit. But Coward was not a thinker (at the mere suggestion O'Casey exclaimed 'Mother o'God!'). His genius was for style. When his plays aspired to seriousness, the result was always slick (O'Casey compares the sketchy characters in *Cavalcade* to 'a tiny monogram on a huge bed-spread'); and when he wrote himself into the role of ardent heterosexual lover (*Still Life,* which he himself called the 'most mature' of the one-act plays in *Tonight at 8:30*) or ordinary working-class bloke (*This Happy Breed*), the characterisation is wooden. The master of the comic throw-away becomes too loquacious when he gets serious, and his fine words ring false. Only when Coward is frivolous does he become in any sense profound.

Frivolity, as Coward embodied it, was an act of freedom, of disenchantment. He had been among the first popular entertainers to give a shape to his generation's sense of absence. His frivolity celebrates a metaphysical stalemate, calling it quits with meanings and certainties. 'We none of us ever mean *anything,*' says Sorel Bliss amid the put-ons at the Bliss house-party in *Hay Fever* (1925). The homosexual sense of the capriciousness of life is matched by a capricious style. 'I think very few people are completely normal really, deep down in their private lives. It all depends on a combination of circumstances. If all the various cosmic thingummys fuse at the same moment . . .': thus Amanda in *Private Lives* (1930). This high-camp style, of which Coward was the theatrical master, worked as a kind of sympathetic magic to dispel both self-hatred and public scorn. 'Has it ever struck you that flippancy might cover a very real embarrassment?' someone asks, again in *Private Lives.* The most gossamer of his good plays, *Private Lives* is adamant on the subject of frivolity. (pp. 2-4)

In *Design for Living* (1932), the laughter of the *ménage à trois* reunited at the finale ('they groan and weep with laughter; their laughter is still echoing down the walls as the curtain falls') is frivolity's refusal to suffer. Even as she leaves her third husband, aptly named Ernest, Gilda, like Elyot Chase, insists that she is not serious. The battle in Coward's best comedies is not between licence and control but between gravity and high spirits. At least three times in *Private Lives* people shout at Elyot (Coward's role) to be serious. 'I fail to see what humour there is in incessant trivial flippancy', says Victor, sounding like one of Coward's critics. . . . Elyot, Coward's spokesman, lives in the world of appearances, the world of the moment, and he celebrates it: 'Let's be superficial and pity the poor Philosophers. Let's blow trumpets and squeakers, and enjoy the party as much as we can, like very small, quite idiotic school-children. Let's savour the delight of the moment . . .'

Coward's best work follows, more or less, this recipe for chaos. His reputation as a playwright rests on *Hay Fever, Private Lives, Design for Living, Present Laughter, Blithe Spirit* (1941) and the brilliant cameo *Hands Across the Sea* (1936). In all these comedies of bad manners, the characters are grown-up adolescents. There is no family life to speak of, no children, no commitment except to pleasure. The characters do no real work; and money, in a time of world depression, hunger marches and war, is taken for granted. Monsters of vanity and selfishness, they appeal to the audience because their frivolity has a kind of stoic dignity. Written fast and in full, confident flow (*Hay Fever*—five days; *Private Lives*—four days; *Present Laughter* and *Blithe Spirit*—six days), Coward's best work has the aggressive edge of his high spirits (even his bookplates show him winking). (pp. 4-5)

In *Present Laughter,* Garry Essendine (a successful actor and another Coward star turn) is trapped in his performance. 'I'm always acting—watching myself go by—that's what's so horrible—I see myself all the time, eating, drinking, loving, suffering—sometimes I think I'm going mad.' Essendine is another of Coward's irresistible heterosexual postures: 'Everyone worships me, it's nauseating'. Garry is fantastically successful—and success can be the most effective mask of all. The jokes in the play belie concerns of a different nature. Although elsewhere Coward sang about following his secret heart and being mad about the boy, he didn't push it on stage. His plays tread cautiously around their deeper meanings. The comedies hurry the audience past issues which the dialogue tries tentatively to raise.

Only in *Semi-Monde* (unpublished, 1929) does Coward find a successful metaphor for the sexual complications that lie behind his posturing. *Semi-Monde* is easily the most visually daring of his comedies, and the most intellectually startling. Set in a swank Paris hotel lobby and bar over the years 1924-1926, with dozens of lovers continually making their predatory exits and entrances, *Semi-Monde* is made up of sexually mischievous *tableaux vivants* and gets much nearer the homosexual knuckle than Coward's public image allowed. . . . In this play, where everyone is on the make, there is no need for Coward's statements about role-playing, the transience of relationships, the need to be light-hearted—his usual comic hobby-horses—because here the game is shown in action. 'I'm going to be awfully true to you', says Tanis to her husband Owen on their honeymoon in 1924. 'I've got a tremendous ideal about it'. But by the third act (1926) she is having an affair with a successful writer, Jerome Kennedy. Owen is smitten by Kennedy's daughter, Norma. It is to the writer, as usual, that Coward allows a few closing moments of articulate disgust: 'We're all silly animals', he says, when the affair is finally

out in the open, 'gratifying our beastly desires, covering them with a veneer of decency and good behaviour. Lies . . . lies . . . complete rottenness . . .' But Jerome, like the others, can't and won't change. 'There's nothing to be done, you know—nothing at all.' The only thing left is to put on a good show. (pp. 5-7)

Coward has an immense reputation for wit, but unlike the rest of the high-camp brotherhood, Wilde, Firbank and Orton, he rarely essays epigrams, or sports directly with ideas in his plays. 'To me', he maintained, 'the essence of good comedy writing is that perfectly ordinary phrases such as "Just fancy!" should, by virtue of their context, achieve greater laughs than the most literate epigrams. Some of the biggest laughs in *Hay Fever* occur on such lines as "Go on", "No there isn't, is there?" and "This haddock's disgusting". There are many other glittering examples of my sophistication in the same vein . . .' Such famous Cowardisms as 'Very flat, Norfolk', 'Don't quibble, Sybil', 'Certain women should be struck regularly like gongs' have the delightful silliness of an agile mind which was never as bold on stage as it was in life. 'Dear 338171,' Coward wrote to the shy T. E. Lawrence in the RAF. 'May I call you 338?' Nor are Coward's theatrical put-downs ('AMANDA: Heaven preserve me from nice women. SYBIL: Your reputation will do that') as bitchy as some of the real-life improvisations like 'Keir Dullea, gone tomorrow'. (pp. 7-8)

In his memorial to Coward, Kenneth Tynan remarked that Coward 'took the fat off English comic dialogue'. Tynan tried to float the notion that the elliptical patter characteristic of Harold Pinter's plays originated in Noël Coward's. In support, he quoted a line out of context from *Shadow Play* (1935): 'Small talk, a lot of small talk, with other thoughts going on behind.' But Coward's characters live nervily on the surface of life, and say pretty much what they mean. The reticence in the comedies comes not from the characters holding back, but from the author. He defends his artifice to the end. 'Equally bigoted,' he wrote in his diatribe against the New Wave, 'is the assumption that reasonably educated people who behave with restraint are necessarily "clipped", "arid", "bloodless" and "unreal".'

Tynan called Coward 'a virtuoso of linguistic nuance'. But it is a disservice to the splendid energy Coward gave to his half-century to put him so elegantly on the literary shelf. His triumph was noisier and, thankfully, more vulgar. He ventilated life with his persona. And it is the frivolity in his plays which has proved timeless. The reason is simple. Frivolity acknowledges the futility of life while adding flavour to it. (pp. 8-9)

> *John Lahr, in his* Coward the Playwright, *Methuen, 1982, 179 p.*

DOUGLAS WATT

It takes one full act to warm up, but once it does there's still some fun to be found in Noel Coward's giddy comedy *Design for Living*. . . .

The revival is neither ideally cast nor directed. But then, how could it be? For this utterly scandalous, yet strangely sexless, comedy was created by the author expressly as a vehicle for himself and the Lunts. And who could ever possibly top, or come close to, that combination?

Nevertheless, as the production loosens its joints and gathers momentum, we develop an irrational fondness for Gilda, and Otto and Leo, both of whom Gilda adores and is adored by in turn, while her two lovers adore each other, as well.

No wonder the play caused a commotion when it first appeared, at a time when the mere mention of the term "free love" raised eyebrows. And yet it circles about its implied permutations with complete discretion, depending on the author's flair for chitchat to keep it going.

It can't match the earlier (by two years) *Private Lives* in craftsmanship or wit. In fact, the late George Jean Nathan, in a particularly devastating mood, allegedly traced every Coward jest back to its alleged burlesque or vaudeville source in one of his columns. But the childish goings on (not far removed, after all, from the tone of countless film comedies of the period) can become surprisingly pointed now and then, as when Leo, suddenly a success as a playwright, stoutly defends his pleasure in being lionized rather than pretending to abhor the roar of the crowd. His lack of cant was one of Coward's more attractive qualities.

The play covers a lot of ground: from Otto's modest painting studio in Paris to Leo's handsome London flat 18 months later, to the New York Penthouse in which Gilda, an interior decorator, is living with her stuffy husband Ernest two years later when Otto and Leo, returned from a freighter cruise to far-off places (apologizing thusly for their resplendent appearance in top hat and tails), bob up to rescue her. At long last, a ménage à trois seems to have been arrived at as Ernest storms out and the loving trio collapses in each other's arms on the sofa.

I have remarked on Coward's speech as, for example, in a line such as Leo's to Gilda, going, "If, in my dotage, I become boring, you won't scruple to tell me, will you?" Without feeling it necessary to dwell on such matters as homoerotic sensibilities at work, along with what would appear to be a flagrant disregard for propriety, I suggest that Coward was nothing if not entirely proper in his treatment of these specimens, and that these midcareer plays would be merely quaint were it not for his word play.

Douglas Watt, "'Design for Living' Still Fun," in Daily News, New York, *June 21, 1984.*

CLIVE BARNES

With a glance of wit, a dazzle of merriment, and a finesse of style, Noel Coward's *Design for Living* finally returned to Broadway last night. . . .

Two men. One woman. Remember how in *Private Lives* Amanda and Elyot couldn't live with one another, but couldn't live without one another? Well, this is an extension of that concept into another space. All three cannot live without each other, and the equation is difficult to settle.

Otto is a painter. Leo is a playwright. Gilda is . . . well . . . an interior decorator, but, mostly, Gilda. Otto loves Leo and Gilda. Leo loves Otto and Gilda. And Gilda loves Otto and Leo.

The potentials for bisexuality in this situation are never stressed, if present. . . . After all this was 1933, and even with all the play's tact, it took it until 1939 to make it to London.

Nowadays it is one of the most admired plays in the Coward canon, it has had two major revivals in London in recent years, and is popular in the American resident theater. Now New York can see what it has been missing.

It is an exquisitely constructed comedy of manners. The comings and goings are perfectly timetabled. In the first act Gilda leaves Otto for Leo. In the second act Otto wins her back, but she leaves both of them, and Otto and Leo go off together.

In the last act Otto and Leo return to take back Gilda from the dull art dealer she has somehow married on the way, and all ends disreputably happy. It is, as Coward puts it in the play, "one long convulsive sequence of ups and downs." Very elegant convulsions.

This hymn to hedonism contains some of Coward's most polished writing. There are masses of crypto-epigrams, pseudo-aphorisms, and the like. There are memorable phrases such as someone "stamping on qualms like killing beetles."

But, as ever, where Coward shows the staying power of greatness is in his ability to invest the most ordinary phrase with, in its own context, a gurgling humor. Consider: "I'm always dreadfully undecided about mustard." Does that sound funny? Wait till you hear it in the play.

There are many reasons now to suspect that the best of Coward's comedies will live as long as our theater. But what made him such a successful, and superior, boulevard writer in his own day was his manner of taking the audience into his confidence, and setting up a dramatic feeling of them against us—them being the outside world, and us being his favored characters, his cherished audience, and himself.

Seeing a Noel Coward always makes one feel sophisticated even if one isn't—that talent to amuse was also a calculation to flatter. But he was such a good playwright that art won out over contrivance.

Clive Barnes, "'Design' Alive & Well," in New York Post, *June 21, 1984.*

FRANK RICH

Noel Coward's *Design for Living,* an uninhibited account of a pansexual love triangle, was considered somewhat shocking stuff when it first opened in New York in 1933. To see the comedy now in its first Broadway revival is to realize that Coward's capacity to provoke, like his talent to amuse, has not at all faded with time. *Design for Living* isn't one of this writer's best plays, but it's an astringent, shapely piece that unabashedly celebrates money, success and emotional greed. . . . [The play is] a pleasant, elegant diversion about uncommonly unpleasant people. . . .

Design for Living tells of an indolent interior decorator, Gilda, who bounces back and forth between two best friends—Leo, a Coward-like playwright, and Otto, a fast-rising painter. Whatever the explicit and implicit sexual geometry of this ménage à trois, it's not mined in this version—and even if it were, who in 1984 would be titillated? What really seems startling about *Design for Living* now is that lust, love and other emotional imperatives are almost beside the point. Coward isn't merely attacking the easy target of conventional morality; he's mocking feeling itself.

And so, even as we chuckle at the blithe wisecracks, the most inflammatory credos tumble about the Art Deco landscape. As independent-minded a woman as Gilda may be, she champions "the survival of the fittest" and declares, "I don't like women at all." Leo announces that the idea of living "for art alone" is "as much bunk as a cocktail party at the Ritz"; he loves being "successful and sought after." The characters disdain the idea of marriage because it brings children—but wouldn't mind having a wedding in order to receive "expensive presents" and stage "a 'do' at Claridge's."

It's this selfish brand of behavior that is Coward's self-protective design for living—and that dictates the highly stylized design of his play. His lovers often talk in theatrical jargon: they forever note their own bad entrances and timing as if they were drama critics. All three acts of *Design for Living* contain stagey variations on the same classic bedroom-farce premise—an unexpected entrance by a cuckolded lover—and none of the betrayals really hurt. If living well is the characters' best revenge, so is play acting: as long as everyone retains his "veneer" and pretends to be happy, introspection and heartbreak can be banished. Life can remain, in Leo's words, "a pleasure trip"—"a cheap excursion.". . .

[The] fact that we feel so little about the people in *Design for Living* helps make the point. The iciness of Coward's ménage lingers as long as his best lines.

> Frank Rich, "'Design for Living'," in The New York Times, *June 21, 1984, p. C15.*

EDWIN WILSON

[*Design for Living*] concerns a sophisticated menage a trois: Otto, a successful playwright, Leo, a successful painter, and Gilda, the woman who loves both of them and whom they love in return. . . .

Coward wrote *Design for Living* for himself and the acting team of Alfred Lunt and Lynn Fontanne. From the original production there was a much-reproduced photo of the three performers in the final tableau, their bodies entwined, laughing their heads off. In the final scene, Gilda's husband Ernest denounces them for their "disgusting, three-sided, erotic hotch-potch;" they in turn scoff at Ernest's conventionality and he leaves. Coward wrote that the characters were laughing at Ernest; "it was certainly cruel, and in the worst possible taste." Coward insisted, however, that they were laughing at themselves."

The fact is, though, that much of the laughter in the play is cruel. The three principals see themselves as above everyone else. "We are different," insists Otto, "our lives are diametrically opposed to ordinary social conventions." *Design for Living* argues that talented people have the right to flaunt their success. Unfortunately Coward has his characters do so at the expense of bumbling boors. One target of their ridicule is a maid who cannot answer the phone correctly.

Even so, Coward does have the talent to amuse. Many of his lines still sparkle half a century later. . . .

> Edwin Wilson, "On Theater: Rambling Rabe, Classic Coward," in The Wall Street Journal, *June 26, 1984.*

ARCHIE K. LOSS

Private Lives is an enduring work for the stage not only because it is representative of sophisticated comedy of its period, but also because it looks ahead to future developments in the theatre. It is in fact Noël Coward's most modern work—theatre of the absurd thirty years ahead of its time. In the spirit of Borges's Hawthorne, our reading of him influenced by Kafka, we now see—after Beckett, Albee, and Pinter—Coward, in this play at least, as a comedian of the absurd.

Very early in the work it is made clear that what *Private Lives* is about is not divorce and remarriage . . . but rather about love and hate, emotions which the principal characters feel toward one another in nearly equal measure. Like Alice and the Captain in Strindberg's *Dance of Death,* Amanda and Elyot are wedded eternally by their mutual attraction and repulsion: "Selfishness, cruelty, hatred, possessiveness, petty jealousy," as Amanda puts it. "All those qualities came out in us just because we loved each other." These qualities re-established, and Amanda and Elyot together again by the end of the first act, the real subject of the play begins: language and theatrical situation.

The frequent criticism that nothing happens after Act One of *Private Lives* misses the point. The point is that in the sort of relationship Amanda and Elyot have—one based on conflicting emotions—nothing ever can happen; they are bound to repeat themselves, playing out their scene again and again with different words and different props but always with the same result. In the long second act, in which (until the very end) only Amanda and Elyot appear, that point is made abundantly clear. Here, in the very heart of the comedy, they find ways to act out their feelings of love and hate in language and gesture which virtually become ends in themselves:

AMANDA: How long will it last, this ludicrous, overbearing
           love of ours?
ELYOT: Who knows?
AMANDA: Shall we always want to bicker and fight?
ELYOT: No, that desire will fade, along with our passion.
AMANDA: Oh dear, shall we like that?
ELYOT: It all depends on how well we've played.

As the subject matter of the dialogue skips from recollections of their past relationship to recollections of past relationships with others (including their recently rejected spouses, Sibyl and Victor), the verbal ploys and rhetorical tricks increase. The list includes deliberate malapropism, [mixed metaphor, and paradox]. . . . There are also simple puns, as when Amanda says of the Hungarians, "Very wistful. It's all those pretzels I shouldn't wonder," and Elyot replies, "And Poostza; I always felt the Poostza was far too big, Danube or no Danube," and litotes, as in Amanda's eloquently deflating, "I must see those dear flamingoes." (pp. 299-301)

Structurally the second act also depends upon a verbal device, set up toward the end of Act One, when Amanda and Elyot agree that their reconciliation can last only if they find some means to keep from bickering:

AMANDA: . . . the moment we notice we're bickering, either
        of us, we must promise on our honour to stop dead.
        We'll invent some phrase or catchword, which when
        either of us says it, automatically cuts off all con-
        versation for at least five minutes.

With Elyot's qualifier that they agree on two minutes, "with an option of renewal," they settle on the name Solomon Isaacs, shortened to "Sollocks."

In Act Two, in Paris, the word comes to have the effect of an incantation, as the lovers build up to their final quarrel. Whenever they threaten to explode, it stops them and, at the same time, it slows down the pace of the scene. Twice it works as intended before a third time when it fails, but between these moments, as part of the slowly building emotion, various scenes occur—situations which divert the lovers from their differences and enhance the theatricality of the act as a whole. (p. 301)

Role-playing has a special significance in *Private Lives* from the beginning of the play to the end, but particularly in the second act, as Amanda and Elyot try out various attitudes toward one another only to end in the same inevitable conflict. As a final touch to this theme—a suggestion at least of its universal applicability to the human species—Victor and Sibyl, in the final act of the play, change from indignant spouses to quasi-lovers, showing the same outrageous behavior to which we have become accustomed in Amanda and Elyot. As the act concludes, we realize not only that Victor and Sibyl are attracted to each other, but also that their attraction has the same degree of repulsion built into it as that of the principals. When, at the end of play, Amanda and Elyot tiptoe out, leaving Sibyl and Victor in violent argument in the flat, we also know that their function has been to serve as doubles for the major characters, reflecting in this final scene the major theme of the play.

That theme is less flippant than it might appear at first glance, for humorous as the ending of the play may seem, there are serious touches throughout. These touches suggest an underlying pessimism which, while not strong enough to make Coward's comedy black, nevertheless gives that comedy a mordant quality, a cutting edge, which keeps it from being merely trivial. (pp. 302-03)

[While] outwardly *Private Lives* conforms to the conventions of its genre, inwardly—at the level which the title suggests is most appropriate for an understanding of the action—it goes beyond these conventions to establish a tone uniquely Coward's. At the same time, this tone—of serious flippancy and flippant seriousness—anticipates forms of drama which have become familiar in the past twenty-five to thirty years.

The pattern of attraction and repulsion which we see in *Private Lives*—one couple's self-destructiveness mirrored in another's—also characterizes at least two other major plays of the modern theatre, *Waiting for Godot* and *Who's Afraid of Virginia Woolf.*

Like Amanda and Elyot, Vladimir and Estragon [in *Waiting for Godot*] seem to have been together for a long time and promise to remain so till the end of their lives. Their dialogue has the same mixture of seriousness and flippancy, of mordant wit and sheer ludicrousness, as much of the dialogue in *Private Lives.* Their relationship is mirrored in that of another couple—Pozzo and Lucky—as Amanda's and Elyot's is mirrored ultimately in that of Sibyl and Victor. The play in which they have their life emphasizes, like *Private Lives,* language, from Lucky's speech in Act I, which suggests the failure of language, to the puns and other verbal ploys which, in Didi's and Gogo's speeches, abound. The play also emphasizes theatrical situations, the pair of tramps moving from scene to scene like two old vaudevillians. Finally, in terms of structure, both plays are as far as one can imagine from the standard of the *pièce bien faite.* Rather than building to a turning point or climax, both end more or less where they begin. Vladimir's "Well? Shall we go?" and Estragon's "Yes, let's go," followed by the famous last direction line, *"They do not move,"* is the equivalent in Beckett's play of Coward's lovers viewing themselves in Sibyl and Victor and going smilingly out of the door, *"with their suitcases,"* as the curtain falls.

There are obvious differences between *Waiting for Godot* and *Private Lives*—differences of tone and dramatic development, of philosophical vision and even of aesthetic intent—yet in their comic effects (given the additional difference of the social level of their principals) and in their essentially static structure—movement in each play coming in language and theatrical

contrivance, not in large incidents or plot—they are notably alike as plays of the modern theatre.

More notably alike, however, are *Private Lives* and *Who's Afraid of Virginia Woolf.* (pp. 303-04)

George and Martha, like Amanda and Elyot, have a fundamentally destructive relationship. They have not found it necessary to conjure up a divorce and remarriage to force themselves, through separation and the pretense of new relationships, to recognize their mutual dependence. They have, however, created their own fantasy of a son who has never existed over whose affection they vie while in fact seeking the affection of each other. Like Amanda and Elyot, they come to realize their mutual dependence in part because of the example of another couple—in Albee's play Nick and Honey—who come to visit and who in some ways are worse off than George and Martha themselves. By the end of each play there is a point of recognition when the principals realize that, in spite of all their flaws, all their destructiveness, they are bonded together indissolubly against a world which expects them to come apart. Each play, to make its point, depends upon a repetitive structure as well as upon verbal games and theatrical situations. "Get the Host," "Get the Guest," "Hump the Hostess"—these games of Albee's play have become synonymous with a whole attitude toward life, and the silly rhyme of "Who's Afraid of Virginia Woolf" has the same effect of incantation as the "Sollocks" of Coward's comedy. Finally, the amount of time devoted in Albee's play to what words and concepts *mean*—from the "bunch," or "gangle," or is it "gaggle," of geese in Act II, to the meaning of history itself, as George expounds it—compares with the fascination of Amanda and Elyot for certain words and rhetorical ploys. Coward's play lacks the naturalistic detail and the sheer weight of Albee's, but in structure and intent *Private Lives* and *Virginia Woolf* are remarkably similar. (pp. 304-05)

No single play of Pinter's bears comparison with *Private Lives* in the way *Godot* or *Virginia Woolf* does, but like all of Coward's best comedies (a list which would also include *Hay Fever, Design for Living,* and *Blithe Spirit*), Pinter's plays typically focus on a small group of closely related characters in whose lives minor events acquire major significance. Pinter's humor, like Coward's, depends much upon verbal play, and the structure of his dramas, like Coward's, is repetitive. The concept of character of each playwright also tends to be static. In short, there are as many points of relationship between Pinter's work and Coward's (social level and certain aspects of philosophical and aesthetic intent again aside) as between Coward's work and that of the dramatists already cited.

What makes Coward's best work modern is not so much its pessimism about human nature—it is difficult to feel pessimistic after any Coward play—as the sense it conveys, comic but serious, that action is futile and that we are all creatures of chance. Like the great masterpieces of modern literature in other genres, Coward's best work is anti-heroic and anti-romantic; to Coward, the heroic sentiment was "big romantic stuff," and, like Amanda and Elyot, he was not having any of it. (p. 306)

Archie K. Loss, "Waiting for Amanda: Noël Coward as Comedian of the Absurd," in Journal of Modern Literature, *Vol. 11, No. 2, July, 1984, pp. 299-306.*

JOHN REES MOORE

Of Noël Coward's many talents—as playwright, film writer, composer, actor, and entertainer—the least known is his skill as a short story writer. Yet his range in fiction is surprising. He can write of "Aunt Tittie" with affection and pathos, of ship cruises with a sardonic eye on the rich and spoiled but also with a sympathy that comes from close identification, on the servants' eye view of their "betters," on the humorous perils of fame and fortune, and on the emptiness of mere worldly success. He seldom attempts anything that would stretch his powers, being content to observe foibles and illusions with an amused and easy-going detachment.

A striking feature of [*The Collected Stories of Noël Coward*] . . . is the length of many of the stories. Several are forty to fifty pages, and two, "**Pretty Polly**" and "**Bon Voyage,**" are almost seventy pages. Such leisure is seldom permitted to the short story writer today. Robert Phillips remarks in his preface that the story writers Coward most admired were Maupassant, Maugham, Mansfield, O. Henry, and Saki. Obviously Coward preferred stories with a firm structure and an element of narrative surprise. The psychological element in the stories is by no means missing, but the characters are eccentric in a theatrically effective way rather than in the inward and more nuanced way of what we think of as "modernist" fiction.

As we might expect, Coward is good at dialogue and confrontation scenes. He uses irony to "destroy" a character like Mrs. Radcliffe in "**The Kindness of Mrs. Radcliffe.**" The poor woman is shown as impervious to her own hatefulness: in a series of scenes she meddles cruelly in the lives of others, all the while persuading herself that she is a model of long-suffering Christian charity. The one good deed she does during the long day of the story, giving a half crown to a beggar woman, is inspired by her desire to make an impression on a lady sitting across from her whom she assumes to be rich and noble. At the end of the day she is still able to reassure herself of her own superior kindness as she prepares to say her prayers. Coward makes this moral snob reveal herself by her own thoughts, and his language is generally convincing. He is equally successful with a very different personality in "**Me and the Girls.**" Here a rather seedy character from the show biz world is in the hospital dying. Each day he gives us fragments from his life and up-to-date accounts of his condition and treatment in the hospital. A picture emerges of a man of considerable resourcefulness, courage, and honesty who has nevertheless never quite had the talent or luck to "make" it. Coward understands this man very well. Toward the end the man is forced to skip a couple of days. The device of keeping a kind of diary plus memoir is not strictly realistic, but the interest of the story never flags.

Coward's range is considerable, both in tone and content. But he is chatty rather than concise, tolerant rather than passionate. If the stories now seem old-fashioned in their directness and refusal to be glum or vulgar, that shows how times have changed, for the themes are as timely as ever—sexual confusion, discomfort about class distinctions, the fear of failure, and the longing for romance. What very likely shocked some at the time now seems old hat; Coward is decently reticent about physical details which many contemporary writers would feel required to dwell on in all their gory specificity. Coward is a thoroughly competent professional—he gives you honest weight for your money. Perhaps his talent as a writer came too easily for him to be forced to the heights or the depths. Or perhaps his view of life precluded any attempt to be grand or deeply rebellious. At any rate he is not pretentious. (pp. 409-10)

John Rees Moore, in a review of "The Collected Stories of Noël Coward," in Studies in Short Fiction, *Vol. 21, No. 4, Fall, 1984, pp. 409-10.*

VALERIE SHAW

It is to the 1960s that most of the stories in [*The Collected Short Stories, Volume 2*] belong, the exceptions being "**The Wooden Madonna**" (1939) and "**Theatre Party**", a hitherto unpublished story of the 1920s in which the male lead wears a 'faultless coat with a suspicion of velvet at the collar' and an equally irreproachable white silk scarf. No more than a 'light sketch', "**Theatre Party**" displays a concern for appearances that pervades all of the stories: dress and make-up, along with food and drink, feature prominently, as might be expected from an accomplished comedian of manners. But Coward's prose is far less witty, far less 'easy' and 'flexible', than his dramas and songs are, and sometimes it becomes embarrassingly sentimental. . . .

In general, the nastier Coward means his characters' behaviour to appear, the more zest seems to go into their creation, though they all remain types, like the 'sob-sister journalist' in "**Penny Dreadful**", the snob, Lady Bland, in "**Bon Voyage**", and the materialistic "**Pretty Polly Barlow**" in the cynical story of that title. But despite the sharpness of some of their satiric humour, these stories have a melancholy cast; there is a preoccupation with death, not only as a convenient plot device for getting rid of disagreeable characters, but as an implacable fact that brings 'abrupt intolerable tragedy', as it does in '**Bon Voyage**'', making all the eating, drinking, and looking in mirrors that Coward's people so enjoy seem absurd and rather pitiful.

Valerie Shaw, in a review of "The Collected Short Stories, Vol. 2," in British Book News, *August, 1985, p. 498.*

CLIVE BARNES

Hay Fever—am I being dim? I have never really understood the title—is not among Coward's best plays, although it is a stately vehicle for actors. . . .

Nowadays the play enjoys a special distinction as the work that really reclaimed Coward's reputation as a major 20th-century playwright when he himself, in 1964, staged a spectacularly brilliant version for Britain's National Theatre. . . .

Since then, *Hay Fever* has assumed the patina of a classic—but it remains a thin patina, and a minor classic.

The idea is intriguing. The play—it is said by Coward and legend to have been written in three days—was inspired by the playwright's weekend visit to the household of an eccentric but great American actress, Laurette Taylor.

If it was anything like the occasion enshrined in *Hay Fever* with the Bliss family, it must have been some weekend.

Unfortunately the idea, thus intrigued, never amounts to anything, other than an exercise of style. We meet a frightful—although, to us, highly amusing—family at the beginning, and they are just as frightful and just as amusing at the end. . . .

This disastrous family has each—without informing one another—invited an unsuspecting and essentially unsuitable guest to weekend in their country house in Surrey.

They then contrive to insult their guests—when they are not flirting with them, and sometimes even then—from the moment of the Saturday arrival until the four guests, after tipping the unobliging but jovial maid, flee back to town, leaving the family still squabbling over the Sunday breakfast.

The comedy of bad manners was a style curiously popular between the wars, but Coward invests it with a particular grace.

To be sure he actually used the play's ending to far more telling effect in the infinitely superior *Private Lives,* and even the insults to the out-crowd are more subtly conveyed in *Design for Living.* Yet in the right staging, with the right performers, *Hay Fever* can still be light, luminous, and charming.

Coward is expert at finding the truth beneath the ordinary; phrases slip away across the actors' tongues, yet so often it is what is not being said that is more important than what is. Coward was a master of what we would now call a sub-text.

Clive Barnes, *"For Rosemary Harris—Love & Gesundheit!" in* New York Post, *December 13, 1985.*

FRANK RICH

In the unlikely event that you stop laughing and start thinking at the sparkling new Broadway revival of *Hay Fever,* you may notice that Noël Coward's comedy has skin-deep characters, little plot, no emotional weight or redeeming social value and very few lines that sound funny out of context. All of which goes to show that some plays defy the laws of theatrical gravity. In this now 60-year-old jape, Coward demonstrates that pure fluff also rises: *Hay Fever* is a classic spun out of the thinnest and most dizzying of air. . . .

[The play's protagonist, Judith Bliss, is] an actress who purports to be retired from the theater but who still glides through life as if every small event were a cue for a big scene. Coward's comedy describes a weekend at the Bliss country home during which Judith, her novelist husband, David and her grown children, Sorel and Simon, each receives a separately invited guest. By Sunday morning, the visitors are fleeing the Bliss manse en masse, driven away by a family whose rudeness, bad manners and self-absorption know no bounds. "You haven't one sincere or genuine feeling among the lot of you," says one scandalized reveler, the fading vamp Myra Arundel. The Blisses' response is clear enough: "If people don't like it," says Simon, "they must lump it."

This egotistical attitude reflects the playwright's own. For Coward, the best defense against the humdrum bourgeois world was to defy conventional manners and follow his own wittily inverted, highly theatrical rules of behavior—to live as if all existence were artifice, a game, a play. *Hay Fever* is surely a major document in the history of the sensibility now known as camp. The Blisses are never so blissful as when they are striking extravagantly Bohemian poses that leave their beleaguered, terribly straight houseguests completely on the outside of their various in-jokes.

Frank Rich, *" 'Hay Fever,' Noël Coward Comedy,"* in The New York Times, *December 13, 1985, p. C3.*

HOWARD KISSEL

Judith Bliss, the character most often centerstage in Noel Coward's *Hay Fever,* is an actress who has specialized in mediocre well-made plays, having developed a range of poses that express indignation, surprise, sorrow, etc., in as obvious a way as possible. Her husband confesses he writes "very bad novels." From the titles of his books we suspect he is a practitioner of literary arts comparable to his wife's. (As he puts it, he likes to see things the way they are before he proceeds to seeing them the way he wants to.)

In the second act of the play they make it clear that they understand what is the matter with their "art" by applying it on a grand scale to annoy a houseful of tiresome weekend guests. While it might be stretching things, one could make a case that the reason *Hay Fever* has survived 60 years and is still an extremely funny play is that—just as much as *Oh, Dad, Poor Dad*—it is a statement on the conventions of its period, a declaration of awareness on Coward's part of what was phony about the "well-made play" mentality that still dominated the London stage. One of the guests, in fact, comments on the Blisses—"The house is a complete featherbed of false emotions."

But the guest doesn't realize the Blisses know what they are doing. In their self-consciousness and wit the characters in Coward's plays are aiming for an honesty the world around them did not necessarily understand. That world was still bound to the conventions of its Victorian forebears. Coward's people are "modern" in their recognition of the falseness of predictable emotions—they may not have genuine emotional lives but they will not suffer emotional or social cliches.

Howard Kissel, *in a review of "Hay Fever," in* Women's Wear Daily, *December 16, 1985.*

JACK KROLL

In his diary for 1968 Noel Coward wrote, "Good old *Hay Fever* certainly has been a loyal friend. Written and conceived in exactly three days at that little cottage in Dockenfield in 1922! What a profitable weekend *that* was." Twelve years after his death, *Hay Fever*—dashed off when Coward was only 22—is still producing profit. Coward's ability to turn out plays (he wrote more than 50 in all) with such debonaire speed has reinforced his reputation for superficiality. But the much-revived *Hay Fever* isn't superficial, it's *about* superficiality, which Coward clearly sees as one of the more profound human qualities.

The delightfully appalling Bliss family (based on the household of the celebrated American actress Laurette Taylor and her English playwright husband, J. Hartley Manners) is, as one aghast observer puts it, "artificial to the point of lunacy." Actress mother, novelist father, spoiled daughter and inane son have invited guests to a weekend at their country house. . . . These feckless wretches—a witless flapper, a veteran vamp, a flibberty diplomat and a goony youth—are seized upon by their hosts and seduced, traduced and finally reduced to emotional marmalade.

With his astonishing craftsmanship Coward turns the bower of Bliss into a castle of emotional vampires chomping away on their terrified victims. But every bite is a laugh in this timeless comedy of ill manners. The play sparkles with classic scenes, such as the parlor game in which everyone must act out adverbs and the tea party in which the hosts slurp voraciously, as if refueling for another assault on their bewildered and ignored guests.

Jack Kroll, *"Serving Up the Guests," in* Newsweek, *Vol. CVI, No. 26, December 23, 1985, p. 77.*

HUMPHREY CARPENTER

[Formal] autobiography was not a genre that brought out even the second best in Coward, as [*Autobiography,* a] bulky reissue of his two published autobiographies, together with a new fragment, shows at considerable length.

Present Indicative, the first section of the memoirs, covering boyhood to the early years of success, was first published in 1937. Cyril Connolly greeted it with a scathing review in which he judged it a "shallow" and "carefully incomplete" picture of an "essentially unhappy" man, someone who had achieved public success at the expense of virtually all human feeling. In this review, Connolly also dismissed Coward's plays as merely topical and perishable. Time has proved Connolly wrong about the plays, for that very brittle and perishable quality makes them an attractive memento of a brittle and perishable age. But *Present Indicative* has no such endearing characteristics. It is a rather bored and stodgy recitation of the externals of Coward's early years; and one cannot feel that Connolly was much mistaken about the man.

Perhaps "essentially unhappy" is not quite right. Certainly Coward suffered, at various junctures, from nervous breakdowns that are not altogether explained by overwork in the theatre. But though the autobiographies remain totally silent about his homosexuality, one does not get the impression that there was really very much to hide. He does not seem to have suffered from deep unhappiness; rather, his life was pervaded by a kind of bored restlessness. Even his songs—his most accomplished work—are infused with world-weariness, and seem to be perpetually stifling a yawn. . . .

Present Indicative and *Future Indefinite,* the two previously published parts of the autobiography, demonstrate that Coward was perpetually sailing away on some sort of cruise, tour, or expedition, very often for convalescent purposes. Of course, he was escaping from himself; but he is far too complacent to admit that, and instead he churns out a weary travelogue. One longs for fewer cruises and more cruising.

The newly published section of the memoirs, *Past Conditional,* was begun towards the end of Coward's life, and was supposed to cover the years of his greatest success, the 1930s. He abandoned it after forty pages, presumably when he realized it was going to be just as dull as *Future Indefinite.* . . .

In the *Future Indefinite* section, which covers the Second World War, such jokes as enliven the travelogue are mostly against Coward, and he seems unaware of it. There is an unintentionally hilarious account of a visit to Sibelius, who had obviously never heard of Coward and resented the intrusion, while Coward for his part seemed to think he was meeting the composer of "Brigg Fair" and "On Hearing the First Cuckoo." But Sibelius observed the rules of hospitality, and Coward afterwards wrote a note of apology, since the composer "had at least received me with courtesy and given me a biscuit". Just as unintentionally funny is Coward's visit, on the outbreak of war, to Winston Churchill. Coward asks how he can best be of service to his country. Churchill, who perhaps had other things more urgently on his mind, advised: "Get into a warship and see some action! Go and sing to them while the guns are firing—that's your job!" Coward chose to take this as an insult. "With, I think, commendable restraint, I bit back the retort that if the morale of the Royal Navy was at such a low ebb that the troops were unable to go into action without my singing **'Mad Dogs and Englishmen'** to them, we were in trouble from the outset."

Humphrey Carpenter, "Perpetually Sailing Away," in The Times Literary Supplement, *No. 4336, May 9, 1986, p. 507.*

PETER CONRAD

The 40 pages of *Past Conditional,* never before published, are [in *Autobiography*] a sliver between the two reissued volumes [*Present Indicative* and *Future Indefinite*]. The new section doesn't do Coward much credit, for his response to the crises of the 1930s was brittle and silly. He brushed off the ogres who were ravaging Europe as absurd or (even worse) ugly. Hitler he believed to have been disqualified for public office by his bulbous hips, stumpy girlish legs and ludicrous moustache: 'even during the gloomiest days of the war I was unable to look at him on a cinema screen without giggling.' His apocalyptic harangues were merely bad acting.

Mussolini was at least a hunk, possessing 'a certain masculine virility'; if Fascism was judged as a beauty contest, 'compared with the Führer [the Duce] was Adonis.' Yet he, too, reduces Coward to helpless tittering, and when at a rally in Rome Mussolini swaggers forth with the face of a ripe plum to execute some routines worthy of a clockwork doll, Coward is overcome by a *fou rire* and has to quit the arena pretending to be the victim of a coughing fit. . . .

The chronicle of applause and parties, hotel suites and ocean liners, neon and caviar, soon turns shrill and fatuous. His favourite adjective, which has acquired more militant meanings since his day, campily eroticises his every experience: 'We were a gay little troop' he notes confidentially of the entourage with which he toured Australian Army camps in 1940, and for a moment his mission sounds like 'Privates on Parade.'

Nevertheless, an octave below the posturing and affectation, there's a human truth in the autobiography. Coward's secret is his ambition, which secured his release from the chintzy purlieus of Teddington (where his Aunt Hilda, famous for her coloratura, was known as 'The Twickenham Nightingale') and ensured that the fantasies of the stage-struck child came promptly and precociously true. He records the fanaticism of his drive to succeed, in 'prophetic orgies' of daydreaming with the Lunts; he also admits its psychological cost, in recurrent 'nervous disorders, fevers and despairs.' . . .

The refrain of the autobiography is the ego's crowing insistence 'Look at me now!' It's not surprising that Coward mocks Hitler and Mussolini for being plump and dwarfish, physically miscast as 'world-conquering demagogues and leaders of men'; his power, as he sees it, upstages theirs, just as his height of 5ft 11½in entitles him to patronise them. For all its mannered, manicured langour, Coward's career is in its own exemplary way a triumph of the irresistible will.

Peter Conrad, "Beyond the Titters," in The Observer, *May 18, 1986, p. 25.*

ROBERT F. KIERNAN

[Camp frivolity] was for Coward the ultimate mask. It implied a stoical dignity that abjured the solemnity of stoicism. It was a declaration of freedom from metaphysics and morality. His best songs and plays are about frivolity, and his most lasting work has been his most insistently shallow. "Don't Let's Be Beastly to the Germans," he cooed to wartime London. "Why Must the Show Go On?" he demanded in his cabaret performance in New York. *The Vortex* is about the terrible spector of frivolity no longer possible; *Design for Living,* about frivolity on the ropes; *Hay Fever, Easy Virtue,* and *Private Lives,* about frivolity triumphant. The greatest of Coward's plays, *Private Lives,* is the most articulate on the subject of frivolity, both its masks and its moments of honesty.

Frivolity implied mettle to Coward when it was edged with insouciance. There is an element of fortitude in his characters skipping away from their messes in plays like *Design for Living, Blithe Spirit, Hay Fever,* and *Private Lives.* Only in a superficial impression of the plays are the characters irresponsible children. The inescapable ménage à trois, whether astral or earthly, is cause for neither rebellion nor prostration in their mode of behavior, but for a Chaplinesque pirouette. Coward always admired such masquers. His personal writings overflow with praise for those who "behave perfectly" or "gaily" in difficult circumstances. "Vivien [Leigh], with deep sadness in her heart and, for one fleeting moment, tears in her eyes, behaved gaily and charmingly and never for one instant allowed her private unhappiness to spill over," he rhapsodized in his diary. "There is always hope for people with that amount of courage and consideration for others."

Frivolity was even a kind of aesthetic for Coward. Not for him the Victorian equation of amplitude and seriousness, of facticity and probity, of solemnity and depth. His comic plots are famous for their minimal development and capricious denouements. What could be more insouciant than the singing of "Même les Anges" that concludes *Fallen Angels* or the stage laughter that concludes *Design for Living*? His characters have little mooring in economic realities; less, in behavioral orthodoxy; and they confront their fates with a candor not of this world. Such mysteriously great comic lines as "The haddock's disgusting" and "Very flat, Norfolk" are not intellectually witty but gamesome and blithe—brilliant throwaways that make the cleverness of Wilde seem labored. "Coward took the fat off English comic dialogue," Kenneth Tynan once observed. It is equally true to say that The Master put dramaturgy itself on a diet, and that the result was comedy as elegantly and stylishly trim as he was himself.

Coward's melodramas are esteemed less than his comedies, of course, and rightly so. Many of these long-unstaged plays are comparable to the most durable works of Maugham or Lonsdale, but even the best of them pay tribute to orthodoxies of conduct that the comedies pare away, disclosing trivialities that enchant us. Coward was so much the master of trivialities that in other modes and other moods he seems not quite himself, not quite "The Master."

Frivolity was ultimately style for Coward, not just *a* style, but *style*—the dashing extravagance that puts impudent fate in its place and that says, "I am what I choose to be." To style's efficacy as his professional trademark, the fabulous dressing gowns stand silent witness today in museums. To its timeless appeal as an aesthetic, his comedies stand living witness on the stage. To its winged spirit in his person, countless anecdotes and numerous tributes are memorial. (pp. 157-59)

> *Robert F. Kiernan, in his* Noel Coward, *Ungar, 1986, 183 p.*

CLIVE BARNES

Hail to thee, *Blithe Spirit!* Bard thou never wert. Shelley got it almost right, even though he bought the wrong vowel—using bird for bard. But then he was writing about a skylark, and not Noel Coward's minor classic, which last night underwent a starry, but not very skylarky, revival. . . .

It is a difficult play to stage—for by now it is a classic, though scarcely of Bardic proportions. It is not even a very important play in Coward's own canon. . . .

The play is fragile—its humors are not iron-cast in character, as are those in *Design for Living, Private Lives* or *Hay Fever.*

The modestly diverting story has a writer, Charles Condomine, researching occult science for a novel about a medium, and inadvertently materializing the spirit of his dead first wife, Elvira, to the acute discomfort of himself and his living second wife, Ruth.

However, nearly all the jokes hinge on the same vaudeville routine, in which one person imagines that remarks are intended for him or her when they are in fact directed at another, unheard, person.

Thus, laugh after laugh must be squeezed from the confusion of Ruth overhearing Charles talking to the invisible Elvira. It's funny the first two or three times, but the jape wears out its welcome. . . .

What keeps this "improbable farce" (Coward's own phrase for it) afloat is Coward's wit and dialog. The people are not people but puppets—they are not meant to feel anything. There is no subtext, no satire, no brave pain beneath the laughter, no sociological dust under the fancy carpet.

> *Clive Barnes, " 'Blithe Spirit' Misses Mark," in* New York Post, *April 1, 1987.*

JACK KROLL

Noel Coward wrote *Blithe Spirit* in five days in 1941, commenting that he would always be grateful for the "psychic gift" that enabled him to perform his feat. He was referring, of course, to the play's plot, which concerns Charles Condomine, a chap "hagridden" by his two wives—the late Elvira, whose ghost returns to hagride Charles again, and Ruth, who after being liquidated by the spiteful spook also returns as a second specter to bedevil the poor fellow in a phantasmal *ménage à trois.*

In *Blithe Spirit* Coward retained his fabled "talent to amuse," but a streak of gentility softens the brittle genius of *Private Lives* and *Design for Living.* Still, Coward's beautiful bitcheries are enough in evidence to remind us that he was a precursor of playwrights like Harold Pinter and Joe Orton. Orton in fact brought the bitch out of the closet with his scathing, perverse black wit.

> *Jack Kroll, "A Blond Ghost in a Lacy Lilac Negligee," in* Newsweek, *Vol. CIX, No. 15, April 13, 1987, p. 79.*

Philip Dacey

1939-

American poet and editor.

An author of witty, affirmative verse, Dacey combines traditional poetic forms with such elements as wordplay, irony, surreal imagery, and unusual syntax to convey the significance and value of commonplace events. According to Vernon Young, Dacey "more frequently writes poems on the connotations of phenomena than he does on the phenomena themselves." Dacey's early publications include the pamphlets *The Beast with Two Backs* (1969), *Fish, Sweet Giraffe, the Lion Snake and Owl* (1970), and *Four Nudes* (1971), but he first attracted significant critical attention with his initial full-length collection of verse, *How I Escaped from the Labyrinth and Other Poems* (1977). In this work, Dacey attempts to discover beauty and joy in all phases of human experience, applauding the necessity for humanity to retain the violent and carnal instincts associated with animals as well as such civilized ideals as love and art. While some critics faulted Dacey for using inconsistent poetic voices, Ronald Wallace called *How I Escaped from the Labyrinth* "an accomplished first book, pulsing with love and affirmation, acceptance and celebration. Dacey's voice is healing and compassionate; his style is limpid and lucent."

In his next collection, *The Boy under the Bed* (1981), Dacey combines confessional poetry and personal narrative to describe, among other subjects, his growth from childhood to middle age and from innocence to experience. Barry Wallenstein asserted: "[In *The Boy under the Bed*] we have a true voice that sings in various tones. . . . The full lines sing off the page while remaining firmly in touch with natural speech rhythms. Adventurous imagination informs the whole." In *Gerard Manley Hopkins Meets Walt Whitman in Heaven and Other Poems* (1982), Dacey employs a humorous documentary approach to approximate the styles and ideologies of several poets while blending fact and fiction to produce letters, transcripts of imaginary conversations, and lost entries from Hopkins's personal journal. One critic commented: "[In] Dacey's hands each character has a way of revealing an aspect of Hopkins' shadowy personality that we have always sensed but never defined. Dacey's portrait is memorable and a joy to read."

In *Fives* (1984), Dacey establishes the importance of the number five in biology and other physical sciences prior to exploring the numeral's metaphysical connotations. Composed of five sections, each containing five poems of five lines in length, this volume was described by Brown Miller as "a gentle, relaxed excursion into metaphoric seeing and knowing." In *The Man with Red Suspenders* (1986), Dacey investigates the importance of sexual attitudes in human relationships. According to Dabney Stuart, this collection reflects Dacey's belief that human beings "are defined in their most private meditations and their most apparently political acts by their sexuality." Dacey has also edited several anthologies of verse and served as editor of the journal *Crazy Horse* from 1971 to 1976.

(See also *Contemporary Authors*, Vols. 37-40, rev. ed. and *Contemporary Authors New Revision Series*, Vol. 14.)

Photograph by W. Patrick Hinely. Courtesy of Philip Dacey.

DABNEY STUART

These sixteen poems by Philip Dacey [collected in *Fish, Sweet Giraffe, the Lion Snake and Owl*], being accomplished poems, don't *need* anything, least of all a favorable note which runs the risk of overpraising them tonally, but they do deserve readers, and are not likely to get many if only because of the simple but staggering problems that attend the distribution of a small chapbook. And readers will, I think, miss a good deal if they miss these poems.

They are about animals, largely, perceived and imagined simultaneously. Most of them are quietly resonant with their own exactitude and modesty, and they achieve what much poetry seeks: the illusion of their own disappearance in the sources out of which they emerge and toward which they tend. There is no fanfare, only an occasional self-consciousness, and, to quote from **"Rise and Fall,"** "a continuing, precisely / right rhythm." They give some clue, in the only way we have of approaching a sense of it, to what Adam's vision might have been. (p. 89)

The shape of some of the poems, in the spirit of Christopher Smart, allows an aphoristic control of what might not be understood so much as absorbed by a whole person, part of whose wholeness is verbal: from **"The Five Senses: A Bestiary"**:

> the ears a pair of birds
> they want to lift the head off
> and fly it back to heaven . . .

[Such a passage suggests] a central quality of Mr. Dacey's work, that a poem is a *way* of understanding, different from other ways, perhaps, in its inclusiveness, and that there is a possibility of the word touching the thing and opening us to its many dimensions.

This can involve extending one's self into an animal, which is different from forcing our terms on one. . . . Or it can involve *seeing* from a perspective both our own and not our own. "Fish at the hole / cut wide in ice" look up at snow falling:

> Slowly their mouths
> open and shut,
>
> breathing nothing
> translatable about
> this whiteness broken
> so beautifully in air.

All this is about birth, I think, the birth of perception. . . . (pp. 89-90)

> Dabney Stuart, *"Awaking to Find It True," in* Shenandoah, *Vol. XXII, No. 2, Winter, 1971, pp. 89-91.*

RONALD WALLACE

In an interview in *Crazy Horse*, the fine magazine that Philip Dacey used to edit, David Wagoner distinguished three voices in contemporary poetry: "the Searching and Questioning Voices, the Warning and Accusing Voices, and the Healing and Celebrating Voices." Philip Dacey's long overdue first book [*How I Escaped from the Labyrinth and Other Poems*] is a beautiful example of the healing and celebrating voice.

Dacey's poems are characterized by love, elegance, grace, wit, delicacy, gentleness, quiet, and affirmation. Even in the potentially violent and painful poems that make up the middle two sections of the book, Dacey manages to find beauty and joy. In **"The Amputee"** for example, the speaker conjures up a new hand more powerful than the one he's lost, and "With that new hand, / I will make signs / In the air. Even I / Shall not understand them." And in **"The Stricken Child"** the reader ends up "Witnessing how / Death and beauty / Flash there / Along thin tracks." For Dacey, wounds, both physical and psychological, are real and painful, but they also "sing." "The sweetness of this violence / will never cloy. / It is an air / a wound sings" (**"After A Fifteenth-Century Miniature Showing King Mark Stabbing Tristram in the Presence of Ysolt"**).

If the two middle sections focus on death and pain, the first and last sections focus on love and generation. The first section, **"Smile A Beast-Smile,"** is a series of animal poems in which Dacey speaks eloquently for the beauty of beastliness, the lovely dumbness of the animal world. Rather than humanizing the animals, Dacey depicts them in all their alien strangeness, investing them with an inhuman grace and mystery. And yet the poems are "romantic" in the best sense of the word, for Dacey sees in nature an innocence akin to Christliness (**"The Animals' Christmas"**) and an honesty that human beings might well emulate. Two poems in the section are, in fact, phrased as lessons, one in snarling, and one in copulation, in an effort to restore a necessary beastliness to our lives.

The final section balances the first. If the first evokes beastliness, the last evokes godliness in a series of poems about women and love and the power of art and the imagination. **"Instructions Toward a Nude"** and **"A Surrealistic Photograph by Manuel Alvarez Bravo (1938),"** for example, combine awe and sensuality in a beautiful depiction of the female body. **"Porno Love"** manages to transform even a pornographic picture into a gesture of love and trust. (p. 93)

How I Escaped from the Labyrinth is an accomplished first book, pulsing with love and affirmation, acceptance and celebration. Dacey's voice is healing and compassionate; his style is limpid and lucent. In these days of the agonized complaint, the glib joke, and the knotty intellectualism, Dacey is refreshing and necessary. (p. 94)

> Ronald Wallace, *"An Air a Wound Sings," in* The Chowder Review, *No. 9, 1977, pp. 93-4.*

PETER STITT

The first half of Philip Dacey's title, *How I Escaped from the Labyrinth,* is promising—it leads us to expect a book detailing one man's quest for self-knowledge, or freedom, or something else equally absorbing. But the rest of the title, *and Other Poems,* undercuts this promise entirely, throwing us back into the realm of the loose collection of individual lyrics. The title poem itself gives a good indication of the relatively scattered nature of the book; I quote it in its entirety, beginning with the title:

> **"How I Escaped from
> The Labyrinth"**
>
> It was easy.
> I kept losing my way.

Trivial, clever, thoughtless, perhaps even irresponsible. It may be that my sense of humor is deficient and that this is a very funny poem; I don't think so, but I could be wrong. Certainly Dacey is trying to be funny in these lines from a poem called **"The Recovery"**:

> For years
> I had put my head on the block
> for the executioner, me.
> It was a serious business
> I failed at it in the neck of time;
> don't axe me why.

Dacey's epigraph ("It is only when people begin to laugh that sanity returns."—Robert Moses) is, I guess, meant to prepare us for such knee-slapping humor. But the tone of the poem is badly mixed, at best, or utterly trivial, at worst. Dacey is not facing up to the implications of his theme, his title, nor even of his chosen epigraph.

More surprising and disturbing is the careless writing that one finds here. Surely Dacey nods when, in **"Porno Love,"** he writes: "I've been exposing my genitals / in poems for a long time now, / at least when they're good." I presume that the last line is intended as literary criticism, with "they" referring to "poems," but it could be taken in a reductive, confessional sense, leading us to wonder about Dacey's genitals when they are bad. Perhaps this is lazy, rather than stupid, writing—but laziness is not a good excuse either. (pp. 103-04)

Dacey also has trouble with pronouns and prepositions. In **"Form Rejection Letter"** he writes: "It requires delicate handling, at this end. / If we had offered it to you . . ." The second "it" obviously refers to something different from what the first "it" refers to; but what might that be? The poem contains no antecedent for the pronoun, and the idea is so vague that a reader cannot easily supply one for himself. I could go on like this for another page or two, but will limit myself to one more instance. In **"The Fish of His Woman,"** Dacey compares fish to imagined, night-time sheep, saying they are good "for counting / on sleepless nights." I wish he meant "count on" in the sense of "depend upon," but he doesn't. He means "during" rather than "on."

Perhaps the most distressing thing about this book, for the persistent reader, is its tone. I believe in the virtue and necessity of tonal consistency; a poet who adopts too many voices is a poet with no voice of his or her own. But that tone or voice should also be lively, imaginative, captivating. The voice in this book is so consistently gray that a real effort of the will is required to stay with it. And yet there are good poems here, especially towards the end, but they are hard to spot in the haze that surrounds them. I would recommend especially **"A Surrealistic Photograph by Manuel Alvarez Bravo"** and **"Edward Weston in Mexico City."** Dacey's quiet, investigative voice is just right for the subtle artistic analysis and character portrayal in these poems. He is a poet who is best taken in small doses—a good magazine poet who is, unfortunately, not impressive in book form. (pp. 104-05)

> *Peter Stitt, "The Necessary Poem," in* The Ohio Review, *Vol. XIX, No. 2, Spring-Summer, 1978, pp. 101-12.*

DAVE SMITH

Dacey's *How I Escaped From the Labyrinth* contains poems selected from a decade of writing and suggests he is something of an anachronism among contemporaries. His "labyrinth" is the solipsism of the Romantic self. He likes wit, irony, pun and finds his authority more in Wintersian reason than in feeling. His is a poetry of statement. . . . Dacey's subjects are animals, sex, the process of art, and various instructions on how to do things. These, however, are intrinsically less important than the angle of vision they afford the poet, restrained observation and satire coupled with a minimum of personality and whatever generalizing light of emotion it might shed. But Dacey, nonetheless, is a contemporary poet and cannot entirely avoid the poem-as-ritual which sacramentalizes the world. Though his passion be more checked than obvious, it appears in a strong current of violence ("Such a charming stabbing!''). And this, in turn, is balanced by the gentle surprise, a balance that gives his poems substance, integrity, and beauty. (pp. 278-79)

> *Dave Smith, in a review of "How I Escaped from the Labyrinth," in* Western Humanities Review, *Vol. XXXII, No. 3, Summer, 1978, pp. 278-79.*

ROBERT PHILLIPS

When Philip Dacey's first book, *How I Escaped from the Labyrinth,* was published in 1977, it was apparent that he was a poet of considerable talent. That book contains, among other beauties, a 150-line poem which became my favorite of all contemporary poems on the unicorn. Not all Dacey's poems were long. In fact, one was one line long. Called **"Thumb,"** it went,

> The odd, friendless boy raised by four aunts.

There were far more hits than misses in the collection. The misses occurred when Dacey seemed to be struggling to assimilate a voice not entirely his own. But in *The Boy Under the Bed,* Dacey's hefty (100 pages) second volume, there are no such misses. He has progressed from a poet in transition to one fully arrived. Whether he is writing in traditional or free verse forms—and there are plenty of examples of both— Dacey's poems are as individual as fingerprints.

The book is carefully arranged. It begins with a section called **"apple-doors,"** about beginnings and entrances and permissions and mysteries. There is a very real poem on the disappearance of animals from a rural clearing which closes with an invocation to the animals themselves; and a very surreal poem on rural school-bus drivers and their young charges, "who have waited all night, / alone, at the ends of driveways, / their little lunches tight in their hands."

The second grouping, **"Spanish Artifacts,"** follows the poet from Cordoba to Alea to Alicante. They reveal Dacey's antennae always out to experience. They recreate the poetical from the quotidian. He likes getting caught in a rainstorm, because the water brings nature's colors out. A child's plastic ballpoint pen bends sunlight into a tiny rainbow, alerting Dacey to the fact that prisms wait in disguise where you least expect them—like the material of all art.

"Nipples Rise to Spirit" is a third grouping, and these follow the poet-protagonist's growth from childhood to early middle age, innocence to adultery. Among these is **"Caroline Naked: A Husband to His Wife,"** and **"One of the Boys,"** which carry all the suburban freight and guilt of a good John Cheever short story. There is also a fine **"Hortatory"** to a refrigerator, written with the affection and wit of a Christopher Smart praising his cat. I like Dacey's ability to praise the commonplace and homely, the trustworthiness of wood, a worn spot in a carpet, a circular kitchen table. As psychologically penetrating and honest as his poems of monogamy and adultery appear to be, I prefer these simple celebrations of the trappings of life, rather than those of life's entrapments.

A brief final section, **"The Presence of Presence,"** strives toward a redefinition of Dacey's faith and his pursuit of perfection of the life and the art, and the necessity for trust's renewal. It is a strong conclusion to a wise and unassuming book. (pp. 426-27)

> *Robert Phillips, in a review of "The Boy under the Bed," in* The Hudson Review, *Vol. XXXIV, No. 3, Autumn, 1981, pp. 426-27.*

CHOICE

Some of the poems in Philip Dacey's *The Boy Under the Bed* echo the workshop poem, the confessional poem, and the urbane poem of the 1950s, but Dacey does not imitate; he betters many of his masters and makes these poems his own with his distinctive voice and manner. . . . By far the best poems are the personal narratives and monologues. They are never self-indulgent confessions but familiar experiences heightened and transformed by the poet's subtle imagination. Dacey's voice is characterized by his intelligent play of wit, word, sound, and form. These new poems are marked by a balance of irony and self-irony, of the artificial and the natural.

> *A review of "The Boy under the Bed," in* Choice, *Vol. 19, No. 2, October, 1981, p. 236.*

VERNON YOUNG

From the evidence of his earlier volume [*How I Escaped from the Labyrinth and Other Poems*], if I recall, added to several poems in [*The Boy under the Bed*], Philip Dacey may justifiably be called a poet of genera. He more frequently writes poems on the connotations of phenomena than he does on the phenomena themselves, taken as actual. Turn to the first in this collection, **"The Door Prohibited,"** which has as its text a sign on a library door: *Do not open this door as part of the morning opening procedure.* That is all Dacey needed to take off into a suave theme-and-variations in which, among other merriments, he exhibits his mischievous ear for the solemnities of liturgical verse. (p. 164)

The image as a state of mind, beyond that the image as a state of being: this can be the supreme elegance of a poet's work. One of Dacey's subtlest accomplishments in that form (not facetious) is **"Where We Were,"** a poem Michael Ryan might worry over because, if I mistake not, its subject is that "perfect connection," the absence of which Ryan was lamenting. Characteristically, the forest in this poem is on no map; it's a figment. For Dacey, reality is not conditioned by place and person, save in respect to his own. He names his children in many poems and makes veiled, if ardent, allusions to his wife, but in the so-called **"Spanish Artifacts,"** named for the towns where they were ostensibly conceived, there is no touch of Spain and the bored bargirl could be bored anywhere. Why he bothered to locate these verses in a geography of no character is mystifying, unless he was archly trying to insist that characterization is in the mind alone.

Clearly he is a Platonist of sorts, dedicated to ideal extensions and largely indifferent to the carnal basis which for most of us defines the earth on which we lucklessly exist. I can think of no other contemporary poet who believes that almost everything is for the best in this best of possible worlds. Dacey writes as if he believed so. My question is: how much of a gap is there between the convention he has adapted for his eulogies and the actuality he has lived? All the mid-section poems in this book accept without reservation the principal dimensions and events of his world: the backward look at a chummy childhood; Dad and Mother, wife and kiddies and supermarket abundance: the whole calamity. To be sure, he translates them into *spirit,* if you will; but the supports of his solipsism he never questions. I hope my incredulity sounds authentic. Faced by the hype of American society today, by the fall of the city, the apotheosis of the third-rate, the intolerable alternatives, the hypochondria and the self-programming of the average American creature—and by the corresponding resistance to it all which I usually encounter in the nation's poetry—I am frankly astounded to find a poet unshaken, whose conception of the Good Life is exactly what, *au fond,* the advertising fraternity, with considerable absence of art, implies it should be! (pp. 165-66)

[In **"The Presence of Presence,"** the final group of poems in *The Boy under the Bed*], Dacey has extended metaphor into parable (cf. **"The Blizzard"** and **"The Runner"**). He incarnates death and his brother, sleep; narrates phylogeny; smiles at reason. That these poems attempt to redefine religious experience is confirmed by the jacket synopsis: they could well lead to a commitment far from the concerns he has carefully nourished up to now. I do not assume that transcendence is a superior condition for writing poems, and by the final lines of **"Putting Your Body to Sleep,"** which closes the book, I am made somewhat nervous.

And Head. You pride yourself on your wakefulness. That is good.
But in the dark there is someone I want you to meet.

Personally, I am too much in the world to encourage revelations from the dark. Even so, I shouldn't care to dismiss so fine a poet without a hearing. So let the dark be lightened—if there is a light.

A last word. Dacey has thought to sanction his verse in this instance with that all-too-familiar quotation from W. H. Auden, "We must love one another or die," electing to ignore the fact that Auden himself rejected the line from his *Collected Poems* on the grounds that it was false: as he explained, we shall die whether we love one another or not. (pp. 167-68)

> *Vernon Young, "An Irishman and Three Americans," in* Parnassus: Poetry in Review, *Vol. 9, No. 2, 1981, pp. 155-68.*

BARRY WALLENSTEIN

[Philip Dacey] succeeds in what Alan Lau calls "recreation of experience," but goes a step further—the creation of experience. In *The Boy Under the Bed,* his second volume of poems, we have a true voice that sings in various tones and whose songs pretend not to be songs at all. The full lines sing off the page while remaining firmly in touch with natural speech rhythms. Adventurous imagination informs the whole. . . .

In **"Levitation,"** the first poem of the book's last section, **"The Presence of Presence,"** Dacey works off a headnote by Judson Jerome: "A child watching a magician perform levitation misses the point if he simply accepts miracles and thinks the lady is actually floating through the air." The poem begins:

> Wrong. She is floating.
> And because she is floating
> I can float, too.
> And do.
> Even now I am writing this poem
> with both feet off the ground.

This is very much the mood or spirit of the whole collection. Images turn surreal rapidly. This poem ends with his falling in love with the "faith" of the magician's assistant and, of course, with the lady herself. He embraces her and "she whispers, / You have nothing to rely on. / Go higher, / higher." Dacey has the rare ability to separate himself from himself in his poetry.

If I were to pick a quarrel with the book (and I'd be forcing it), I'd note that some surreal fantasies seem a little flip: "One man rounds third base, pumping hard, / and is never seen again." This idea, already worn thin by Rod Serling and company, appears three times in different masks in one poem, but this is an atypical example.

Another device that works when Dacey applies it to his inventive imagination and lyricism is his daring syntax. In **"The Runner,"** the device works to make the subject of these lines other than merely the information:

> How strange, he thought, that I should think myself
> in training to meet death. That I prepare
> my body for him. He thought that. As he ran.

However serious this becomes, the poet is, here and generally, playing with language and with himself, and with the ideas he started with. This interesting mind at work captivates and energizes the reader's mind.

Barry Wallenstein, in a review of "The Boy under the Bed," in The American Book Review, *Vol. 4, No. 6, September-October, 1982, p. 17.*

JOSEPH A. LIPARI

But for Dacey's intelligence and skill, this audacious and fine biographical sequence of poems on Hopkins' life from 1868 to his death in 1889 [*Gerard Manley Hopkins Meets Walt Whitman in Heaven and Other Poems*] could easily have been a disaster. The approach is pseudo-documentary, including transcriptions of imaginary conversations, apocryphal letters, and "lost" entries from Hopkins' journals. Dacey's approximations of Hopkins' inimitable wordplay are remarkable. . . . These moving poetic "documents" capture some essential truths about a great writer.

Joseph A. Lipari, in a review of "Gerard Manley Hopkins Meets Walt Whitman in Heaven and Other Poems," in Library Journal, *Vol. 108, No. 2, January 15, 1983, p. 134.*

THE VIRGINIA QUARTERLY REVIEW

A poem-by-poem, imagined account of Hopkins' daily life, both while alive and in heaven, [*Gerard Manley Hopkins Meets Walt Whitman in Heaven and Other Poems*] is chock-full of humor and an abiding love for its subject matter. Dacey has given us, as it were, concise and pithy snatches from the poet's conversations, journals, letters, and musings. . . . [In] Dacey's hands each character has a way of revealing an aspect of Hopkins' shadowy personality that we have always sensed but never defined. Dacey's portrait is memorable and a joy to read.

A review of "Gerard Manley Hopkins Meets Walt Whitman in Heaven and Other Poems," in The Virginia Quarterly Review, *Vol. 59, No. 3, Summer, 1983, p. 99.*

CHOICE

Philip Dacey's *Gerard Manley Hopkins Meets Walt Whitman in Heaven and Other Poems* is a remarkable tour de force—primarily a collection of monologues and dialogues emulating the voice, style, and manner of Hopkins, Whitman, and others also. (Is there, though, an occasional lapse as Hopkins's voice and linguistic wit seep into Whitman's lines?) Though a blend of fact and fiction, as the author carefully tells us, the poems illuminate Hopkins's inner mind and turmoil and his sexuality in a way more intimate and convincing than possible in biography. Most remarkable of all, Dacey manages to retain the integrity of his own poetic voice while adopting the role of his characters. The reader is subtly aware of illusion and of the poet-actor behind the cassock, or the skin—in the tradition of the best dramatic monologues.

A review of "Gerard Manley Hopkins Meets Walt Whitman in Heaven and Other Poems," in Choice, *Vol. 21, No. 2, October, 1983, p. 274.*

BROWN MILLER

[*Fives*] is a gentle, relaxed excursion into metaphoric seeing and knowing. Dacey's work never fails to amaze me, and in this book we find him at his best, playful yet full of deeply felt significance. *Fives* is made up of five groups of five poems each, a structure suggested by the biological fact that the number five crops up repeatedly in the formations of plants and animals. Dacey, without a bit of awkwardness or excessive weight, moves us right into the metaphysical realm.

Brown Miller, "Best Poetry of 1984," in San Francisco Review of Books, *January-February, 1985, p. 23.*

MARTIN J. HUDACS

Fives is an anthology of previously published poems of Philip Dacey. . . .

The title is significant in theme and organization. The preface notes the importance of the number five in physical and metaphysical matters. The book itself is divided into five sections, each section with five poems, each poem with five stanzas, each stanza with—well you get the picture.

Dacey shows a wit and interesting perspective on life's common problems in some of these poems.

"Not Correcting His Name Misspelled On The Mailing Label," for example, hits home with word play that cleverly shows how mangled our names can get on mailing labels yet still capture some trait of our personality.

Dacey is best when he looks at the commonplace and lets his imagination develop a new perspective. His imagery is clever, his word play delightful as shown in **"Arriving Late For A Movie"** and **"Staying Thin."**

Dacey's **"Lines"** is an emblematic poem on a woman's shape and its metamorphosis through life. It starts with a shapely representation then moves to a pregnant representation in the "marriage" stanza then to a solid block stanza at the poem's conclusion.

It is in these types of poems that I like Dacey best. Occasionally his poems get carried away with the image. In such poems he loses the thread of universality, or the common experience that appears to be his forte. . . .

[Yet *Fives*] is largely a collection of enjoyable and witty poems.

Martin J. Hudacs, in a review of "Fives," in Best Sellers, *Vol. 44, No. 11, February, 1985, p. 432.*

DABNEY STUART

Philip Dacey's work has always centered on sexuality. This broad subject sometimes includes sex, too (see, for instance, the Coda poem in his *Gerard Manley Hopkins Meets Walt Whitman in Heaven*, 1982), but never reductively, as Big Mama patting the bed and explaining that trouble in a marriage is invariably "right here." Nor does he take a cynical position such as John Barth's in "Lost in the Funhouse," where all human activity is "prelude and interlude" to/between making it. Dacey assumes that since men and women are sexual creatures to begin with, all aspects of their relationships are sexual, too, and that they are defined in their most private meditations and their most apparently political acts by their sexuality. (They are also spiritual beings, which I will come to later.)

In short, for his new volume [*The Man with Red Suspenders*] as well as the three that have preceded it, journalistic stereotypes don't apply. The subject is too subtle, pervasive, and complex.

One would expect, then, for it to turn up in unexpected ways and places. A man shops at the supermarket (**"The Shopping List"**) and finds, after some confusion about vegetables and cheese, "women on display." He checks his list, discovering "every item refers to women. / My mother is on the list, / and my sister. Others." In **"The No"** a condom salesman has "the sense of what / confines just so, that you can live in, / a way to breathe without the need to breathe." In **"A Used Car Lot at Night"** the cars, which "under the sun . . . were hard, flawed," become changed, "flow together like water." The many colors of the triangular flags strung across the lot "become a single color / dreaming desire." (p. 46)

Dacey is a poet with extraordinary powers of connection, and he rarely forgets, even in awe, what the uses of things are. **"The Shopping List"** turns toward dream; the speaker finds no checkout area, but, instead, "a vast plain."

> People walk there,
> as if forever,
> shopping for nothing,
> their grocery carts
> full of everything
> they need, empty.

The poem concerns, finally, sexual need in a domestic context (we go to the grocery store to buy sustenance) and becomes, at least, unsettling in its implications about the speaker's mistaken understanding. In like manner, **"The No"** never veers away from one basic purpose of a condom, the denial of life; the salesman is "the salesman of the means / of going out of business." It is a mark of Dacey's talent for mordant understatement that the salesman "smiles to turn / aside a question about price." . . .

The poems whose contexts are more explicitly sexual—those about marriage, family, lovers, and desire *per se*—rehearse similar themes with equal force. Along with **"The Other Woman," "Owning a Wife,"** and **"The Dacey Players. . . ."** I would recommend a particularly effective poem spoken by a woman, **"The Nightgown,"** which combines skillful word-play, the use of an item central to a relationship to reveal the people involved, and precisely appropriate metaphor. Two other poems, **"Not Going to See a Movie about a Nuclear Holocaust's Aftermath,"** and **"Bourgeois Poem,"** placed near the end of the book's second section, suggest that political experience is at bottom sexual. (p. 47)

[Much] of Dacey's work in this book (as well as his others) incorporates . . . spiritual agency as a given in the world he creates. It is this, more than a deftness with metaphor, that makes effective his joining of usually disparate circumstances and categories. Orthodox religion isn't the concern here; it is a matter of the active life of spirit in material and corporeal forms. Dacey makes this dramatically vital by understanding that spirit wishes to be free of those forms as well as being simultaneously curious about and in love with them.

This surfaces most obviously in *The Man with Red Suspenders* in **"The Swan."** Knowing Yeats's famous vision of Zeus's rape of Leda gives a historical richness to reading Dacey's poem, but even without its predecessor it is a magnificent performance. The speaker is the consciousness of the swan which has to evacuate its swan body to allow Zeus to enter to enact the rape. The swan watches "off to the side . . . in some indefinable / space where I'd become pure soul, as if / I'd died." Bodiless, a spectator, the swan is nonetheless attracted to Leda, too, "a woman . . . brimming with herself," and after he reenters his body, he touches, "with the tip of one wing, her hair." Needless to say, the swan is changed forever by a god's having inhabited his body. Whereas Yeats asked questions about this change, Dacey has his speaker turn to prayer.

> I lived between two dreams, of being-here
> and not-being here. I said a swan-prayer
> as I lay down my long neck beside her.

The prayer, as the rest of the poem, focuses the spiritual center of the vision: "I am no swan if I am only / swan." **"Placating the Gods,"** and seven of the poems (not consecutive) in the volume's third section (**"Hopkins to Whitman"** is the first of these, and **"Sailing"** their radiating locus) complicate the articulation of **"The Swan."**

The doubleness of many of Dacey's poems, I think, isn't a traditional mind-body split, or the objectification of a particular schizophrenia. What he presents is rather the spirit seeking its procreation, a task made difficult by its necessary bodies. Spirit is sexless, but mates nonetheless (**"Sailing"**). It is confused by the sexuality of its incarnations. I apologize for the abstruse sound of such considerations, but Dacey's poetry doesn't, a source of its central joy and perplexity. To find such accessible complexity is rare in our period of emphasis on the flat voice, the reduced fiction, and, at the other extreme, the Baroque convolutions of self-reflexive Narcissism.

Dacey's work, in fact, illustrates what is probably true anytime: substantial poetry proceeds, whatever its degree of conscious intention, from an integral view of all aspects of human being. This, happily, includes humor, and the distance and wisdom it affords. Dacey's wit and playfulness are abundant. (p. 48)

Nobody I know of holds up better. (p. 49)

Dabney Stuart, "Sex and Violence," in Tar River Poetry, *Vol. 26, No. 2, Spring, 1987, pp. 46-53.*

Stanley (Lawrence) Elkin

1930-

American novelist, short story writer, scriptwriter, and editor.

Considered one of the most entertaining stylists in contemporary American fiction, Elkin has been variously described as a black humorist, a Jewish-American author, and a metafictionist. He rejects these designations, however, favoring universal rather than exclusively literary or ethnic themes. Often preoccupied with disease and death, Elkin's novels typically feature rootless male protagonists who seek through obsessive interest in elusive goals to compensate for the absence of their families, overcome their feelings of powerlessness, and assert their individuality. Through extensive use of metaphor, Elkin transforms grotesque situations and the drab vulgarity of popular consumer culture into comic affirmations of human existence. His rapid-fire, rhetorical style is characterized by wordplay, dense imagery, Jewish idioms, and a blend of formal and colloquial language reminiscent of a sales pitch. Although some critics fault Elkin's novels for their episodic, seemingly plotless structure, most praise the poetic vigor and comic ingenuity of his prose. Thomas LeClair observed: "Sentence for sentence, nobody in America writes better than Stanley Elkin. For him, the novel is primarily a place for language, energized and figurative language, to happen."

Elkin's first novel, *Boswell: A Modern Comedy* (1964), is a picaresque narrative centering on the comic efforts of an ordinary man, James Boswell, to aggrandize and immortalize himself by becoming the founder of a club for famous individuals. Like many of Elkin's protagonists, Boswell is an orphan and loner obsessed with mortality who searches for a surrogate family. Ironically, Boswell achieves his goal but rejects the club, since joining the establishment would signify the death of his ego and individuality. *Criers and Kibitzers, Kibitzers and Criers* (1966) is a collection of Elkin's short stories that combines humor and tragedy to portray individuals in various dualistic relationships. In Elkin's second novel, *A Bad Man* (1967) entrepreneur Leo Feldman, dissatisfied with traditional family life and influenced by his deceased father's advice to sell all his possessions in preparation for disaster, arranges to be sent to prison to test his fortitude. In this increasingly surreal environment, Feldman encounters a tyrannical warden who makes him a scapegoat and has him sentenced to death by a kangaroo court for violating petty rules. Raymond M. Olderman noted that *A Bad Man* removes "the last toehold on reality—the formal distinctions between good and evil. . . . [The novel] is a demonstration of what is fabulous about the actual world we live in."

The narrator of Elkin's next novel, *The Dick Gibson Show* (1971), is a bachelor in search of an ideal job, which he finds as a radio talk-show host. As his anonymous callers relate their unusual problems and obsessions, they come to represent for Gibson the family that he lacks. Critics generally praised Elkin's knowledge of the radio industry and his humorous rendering of a wide range of voices. *Searches and Seizures* (1973; published in Great Britain as *Eligible Men: Three Short Novels*) collects two long stories, "The Bailbondsman" and "The Condominium," and a previously published novella, *The Making of Ashenden* (1972). The protagonists of these narratives are

Photograph by Roberto Celli. Courtesy of Stanley Elkin.

archetypal Elkin orphans and bachelors who pursue ideals of truth, order, and meaning only to reach unexpected personal conclusions. Elkin achieved substantial critical and popular recognition for *The Franchiser* (1976), a novel that many critics considered among his best works. This book depicts the transcontinental travels of Ben Flesh, a buyer of franchises who takes credit for standardizing the commercial landscape of the United States. Another of Elkin's orphaned bachelors, Flesh is adopted as an adult into the Finsberg family, whose eighteen children are afflicted with rare diseases. When the Finsberg children begin to die, Flesh is able to come to terms with his own multiple sclerosis.

The Living End (1979), which Elkin described as a "triptych" of interrelated stories, combines realism and fantasy to dispel common assumptions regarding heaven and hell. In "The State of the Art," Elkin depicts God as a temperamental artist who destroys the world because He was misunderstood. Henry Robbins remarked: "Half farce, half morality play, *The Living End* puts God himself on trial, the Lord faced off against the damned who in their countless number equal Everyman. Quite possibly only Stanley Elkin possesses the exact blend of irreverence and care, of hard-core realism and fabulous invention, to have pulled this off." *George Mills* (1982), for which Elkin won a National Book Critics Circle Award, spans a thousand-year period to chronicle the descent of a line of individuals named George Mills, each of whom is obsessed with his inability to rise above the working class. This picaresque novel combines the tragic experience of the contemporary George Mills, an American furniture mover, with chapters on his forefathers, including the first George Mills, a crusader in eleventh-century Poland. Joel Conarroe commented: "A master of comic effects, Elkin is also our laureate of lamentation. Among the dominant motifs in [*George Mills*] . . . are pain, isolation, missed opportunities, and the fear of death."

Stanley Elkin's The Magic Kingdom (1985) is one of Elkin's more conventionally plotted novels. This work describes a trip to Disney World arranged for seven terminally ill British children by Eddy Bale, whose own son's premature death from an incurable disease leads him to believe that "there is a reason for everything." Conceiving of the trip as a reward for the children's persistence, Bale later acknowledges the futility of the idea and reflects that despite his best efforts, the children "died in pain." Describing the novel as "[part] sick joke, part lyrical meditation on the nature of disease," Max Apple noted: "Mr. Elkin strips away the sentimentality and replaces it with an honest look at the grotesque possibilities we all carry around and prefer not to see, not even in fiction." *The Rabbi of Lud* (1987) details the domestic problems of a rabbi who presides over the funerals of strangers in a town of the dead.

(See also *CLC*, Vols. 4, 6, 9, 14, 27; *Contemporary Authors*, Vols. 9-12, rev. ed.; *Contemporary Authors New Revision Series*, Vol. 8; *Dictionary of Literary Biography*, Vols. 2, 28; and *Dictionary of Literary Biography Yearbook: 1980*.)

WILLIAM GASS

Stanley Elkin puts his imagination to work by placing it like a seed within the soil of some vocation. *Vocation:* that is no trade school word for him. (p. 29)

In *Boswell,* Elkin's first novel, the occupation was that of a celebrity seeker, but it may be a merchant's, as it is in *A Bad Man,* or a bailbondsman's, as it is in the brilliant story of that name. Again, a gloomy grocer may be his concern, or a debt collector, the disc jockey of *The Dick Gibson Show,* or a franchiser like Ben Flesh—jobs which are often seedy or suspect in some way. Elkin does not wonder what it would be like if he were a professional bully, or an elderly ragman, though new to the nation, a peddler trundling a cart down the street and crying, "regs, all cloze." He does not say: what if I were running my own radio show—and then write. His fictions are not daydreams; there is no idleness in them, no reveries. They are not acts of ordinary empathy either, in which the novelist listens in on some way of life and then plays what he hears on his linotype. Instead, Elkin allows the activity itself to create his central characters, to find its being in some gainly or ungainly body, and then he encourages that body to verbalize a voice.

Voice: for Elkin, that's no choir boys' word. Just as in Beckett, the *logos* is life. There is not a line in *The Franchiser* that doesn't issue from one. And what is this occupation it speaks for but acts and their names, agents and their frailties, the texture of their environments? . . . things, words, sensations, signs—all one. And the mouth must work while reading him,

must taste the intricate interlace of sound; wallow, as I now am, in the wine of the word. One is compelled to quote:

> He loved the shop, the smells of the naphthas and benzenes, the ammonias, all the alkalis and fats, all the solvents and gritty lavas, the silken detergents and ultimate soaps, like the smells, he decided, of flesh itself, of release. . . . And hanging in the air, too—where would they go?—dirt, the thin, exiguous human clays, divots, ash and soils, dust devils of being.
>
> 'Irving, add water, we'll make a man.'

And this is precisely how Elkin makes a man—out of the elements he lives in, the body he is confined to, the world he works in, the language he knows.

From time to time the voice [in *The Franchiser*] halts, fills its trunk, and sprays us with speech. How long has it been, how far back must we go, to encounter such speeches, such rich wild oratory? If I were to hazard a guess, I would say we should find it again in *The Alchemist,* in *Volpone,* in *Every Man in His Humor,* and if that seems an extreme claim, simply compare Jonson's characteristic rodomontade (as wonderful as the word which is supposed to condemn it) with the speech which begins: "How crowded is the universe. . . . How stuffed to bursting with its cargo of crap." And goes on: "A button you could be, a pocket in pants, a figure on print." And on: "I am talking of the long shot of existence, the odds no gambler in the world would take, that you would ever come to life as a person, a boy called Ben Flesh." . . . Until it ends:

> 'So! Still! Against all the odds in the universe you made happy landings! What do you think? Ain't that delightful? Wait, there's more. You have not only your existence but your edge, your advantage and privilege. You do, Ben, you do. *No?* Everybody does. They give congressmen the frank. Golden-agers go cheap to the movies. . . . Benny, Benny, we got so much edge we could cut diamonds!'

Central to the theme and movement of the book, this harangue is one of fiction's finest moments.

The Franchiser is engaged, then, in the naming of names, the names of places and people, of course, but above all the names of things: commercial enterprises of all kinds, name brands, house brands, brandless brands, labels, logos, zits. Elkin composes a song from the clutter of the country, a chant out of that "cargo of crap" which comprises our culture, the signs, poles, boxes, wires, the stores along the roads and highways, our motorcars. He writes with the stock in trade and with the salesman's slang. About the tissues, rags, and wipers, which are appropriate to every fixture and furnishing—bowl, screen, or clock face, asshole or cheery cheek—he knows, and taps out the call sign, grasping the peculiar argot of every agency, the specific slant of every occupation, the angle, the outlook— the edge.

There is, in Elkin, only the "rich topsoil of city asphalt"; there are no lisping winds or drooling streams. He dances to a wholly urban oo-la-la. He cannot see the forest for the picnic tables, the cookout pits, the trash containers with their loose heaps of bottles, Dixie Cups, and paper plates; and on those plates he spots the catsup smears, the mustard marks, the crumbs from cookies and potato chips, and he understands at once whether they were reconstituted, ruffled, extra hearty, or Mexicanized. Nature is a Kodacolor picture wall in one of Ben Flesh's Travel Inns. It is where you go to get wool for fine suits, wood for boardwalks, food for fast foods, electric warmth for blankets, power for power tools. (pp. 29-30)

Elkin is not concerned with High Culture. . . . He knows it not. The city, itself, is his Smithsonian, and there is real lust in his love for it, not merely the usual honor and respect. He has been happily captured by this vast dump of dreck the city has become, and the country has become as it has become a city. . . . Elkin has an embracing passion for it. He celebrates it as no one has or has been able (if we except only Augie March), and although he knows motels, as habitable space, are like the shaven cunt of a packaged whore; still he hums his hymns, although he knows how many streets are ugly, foul smelling and dangerous, as full of *e coli* as a lower intestine; he warbles away, even though he knows money is society's perfumed, silver plattered shit, nevertheless he goes on loving the prime rate; he knows fame is a faded billboard now for rent, and yet he goes on touching the famous as if they were kings who could cure; he knows, and yet he goes on loving the menace and the waste, the tacky, cheap, lovelorn, gim-cracky life our modern lot has all too often come to; he loves it exactly as the saint loves the leper—*despite* and *because*—not in blindness or through any failure of taste, but because it is all so deeply and dearly human to him; because, as Rilke put it, it is good just to be here—*Siehe, ich lebe!*—since existence itself is outrageously chancy and strange and stable and ordinary (it is like that flameless combustion of gabardine and pee); and all of it—our whole cornpone commercial culture—becomes so transformed by Elkin's attention, his love and his writing, so altered beyond any emblem, that even an enemy of crud such as I esteem myself to be—grim and unforgiving—am won over, and I walk through the dime store in a daze of delight.

Here then we have no namby-pamby style. The rollcall rolls on: wrist watches and lamps, you name it and Elkin will name it; the rhetoric rises like a threatening wind, and the effect is like that on those who like storms: exhilarating, and a little scary. . . . There is no fear of excess . . . because Elkin over-subscribes to everything. Centers will not hold him in spite of his academic training, his professorial position. He goes to extremes simply to have his picture taken standing at an edge. His language carries him away (there is a pile-up of images at every corner like a crash of cars); his characters get carried away; his words first explore, then explode, the world.

He is not content with nice precise observations, in which, for instance, a policeman's long holster looks like a weapon, "its pistol some bent brute at a waterhole, the trigger like a visible genital" (wonderful and radical enough), but the uniform itself becomes a weapon, and then the parts of this new mechanism are beautifully described. . . . (pp. 30-31)

[Elkin] is not satisfied with the simply sensuous (Ben Flesh standing in his tux, "his formal pants and jacket glowing like a black comb, his patent-leather shoes vaulted smooth and tensionless as perfect architecture," as though he "might be standing in the skin of a ripe bright black apple"). It does not matter that apples are every other color, or that eggplants come close to patent black in their most bruised moods, just try eggplants instead of apple and feel the effect of the change.

Not satisfied, never content, Elkin presses beyond his mountains of apparently realistic detail, with their dangerous slides of wit; he passes safely through the misleading forests of simple fun, the satiric gibes, the siren-like lists; he pushes on into the nuclei of his various vocations (the dance studio, for instance,

one of Ben Flesh's failing franchises), pushes, presses, until they are more than metaphors, more than merely the nice idea that "work for rent" has been set up on signs. He searches inside of whatever one of them possesses his imagination at the moment to find the form—the spreading itch—of the image itself: its finality, its limits, its outer edge; for then that occupation, because it is the wholehearted consequence of a thought which has put on a pair of pants and found a passion which they conceal like an excited penis; this work, with all its learning and its lingo, dreams itself back over the whole world of the fiction like a cloud, settles over us all like a communal hallucination; whereupon we realize that Elkin is a visionary writer; he is Brueghel or he is Bosch. . . . (p. 31)

Vision, I said. For Elkin, it is no visionary's word, no politician's promise, preacher's ploy. It is the unerring instinct of the verbal eye.

Ben's name knows the worst: the flesh fails, and Ben is stricken with a scribbler's sickness; he is MS'd up, to put it as poorly as possible; nevertheless (our author notes), though as illnesses go, MS is truly big league, while sitting down (as authors do) it is an invisible disease. In-visible. Our language, in Elkin's hands, opens like a paper flower. The symptoms of this sickness are drawn inside out with an unfailing artistry of line. Once again, they circumscribe a vision. It involves the unity of hell and heaven—this vision—even a nervous interplay; it is a vision of value, to complete the Vs, of how life is nurtured by decay; it is a victory for the material, for the carnal spirit, because even as Ben weakens, as both his flesh and his Fotomat fold, and the hyper-real world of the novel completes its business and makes its final sale, its hero is having an ecstasy attack; and because love is finally Ben Flesh's *forte*, he retains his edge to the end.

To turn to account . . . to disable disabilities by finding their use . . . to celebrate circumstance . . . to turn on a light in the heart of darkness . . . well, all flesh is grass, as the prophet said, but the word of the Elkin shall franchise it forever. (p. 32)

Willam Gass, "Stanley Elkin's 'The Franchiser'," in The New Republic, *Vol. 182, No. 3416, June 28, 1980, pp. 29-32.*

JOHN DITSKY

In seven volumes of fiction published since the mid-Sixties, Stanley Elkin has made clear claim, by reason of the quality inherent in his work, to consideration as a major contemporary American writer. Yet though his books have inspired a following of devoted readers—both in and outside of the academic community—Elkin can be said to have largely missed out on the recognition due him. I should like to make a gesture towards righting that wrong by attempting a necessarily brief survey of Elkin's fictional works, and by making some general observations about his style and themes. For Elkin seems to be some sort of spiritual descendant of Nathanael West in the ways in which he attaches out-loud, falling-on-the-floor humor to reflections on the human state as a steady downward plunge to death, he is nevertheless very much his own man in the manner in which he explores and develops that tradition.

Indeed, the very first words of Elkins' first published novel, *Boswell* (1964), seem designed to establish a keynote for the book as a whole, if not an entire career—picking up as they seem to from the ending of the film *Body and Soul:* "Everybody dies, everybody. Sure . . ." People don't believe in death, Boswell claims, but Boswell does; as much a convert to death as Larry in O'Neill's *Iceman*, he seems to think that life acquires its form and definition from the fact of death, much as Wallace Stevens would say it acquired beauty. The notion that we all face death alone, and that we can cope with this situation only by a kind of manic fortitude, is developed by Boswell over the first few pages of the novel—pages that can be said to meander somewhat, while Boswell (surely named for Johnson's biographer, though Elkin leaves the allusion implicit throughout the book) reflects on what the succession of odd adventures which constitute his life has taught him. Yet Elkin believes committedly in the necessity for living an examined life. In a summation he made for me of an article he once published on the nature of plot, he defines the term in terms intrinsic to his notion of the rigor, the discipline, of his craft: "Plot is the willingness of a character to pay close and absolute attention to the situation in which he finds himself."

But not until the appearance in the novel of the "amazing" Dr. Leon Herlitz does Elkin really hit his stride—and establish his peculiar strengths. Herlitz has been a mover and shaker, a man who has influenced the course of history for well over half a century; among his other accomplishments are the facts that "he put Freud into psychiatry in the last century," made staff appointments which "account for the effective participation of the German army in the First World War," "talked Lindbergh into flying the Atlantic" and "counseled the French Existentialists." Remarkable as he is from such a fanciful description, Herlitz really comes alive when Elkin lets us hear his *voice*—and only then does *Boswell* truly come alive as well. Here is Herlitz talking about a character, Schmerler, whom he killed:

> Who knew Schmerler? I told him a million times, 'Schmerler, you're an enigma, Schmerler.' It was a shame he didn't make himself understood better. He could have been the biggest name in the Zionist Movement. But no, *he* had to insist upon making the Jewish Homeland in Northern Ireland. He used to argue with Weizmann night and day. 'Weizmann,' he says, 'your Jew isn't basically a desert-oriented guy,' That was Schmerler for you. If you say you don't know him, there's your clue. He was always correct in principle, in theory. Mao used to call him 'The On-Paper Tiger.'"

This is a sampling of Herlitz's speech merely, and hardly establishes the man's significance to the plot (Herlitz predicts the course of people's lives, as casually as the Puerto Rican God in Bruce Jay Friedman's *Steambath*). What it does most clearly do, however, is to establish for us a sense of Elkin's splendid *ear*.

That ear for the true cadences of American speech, particularly *funny*, American speech, and particularly *Jewish-American* speech (itself almost always funny even when dealing with the most moving, the most pathetic, of situations), is for me Elkin's greatest gift as a writer, the one which finally enables the other gifts to express themselves in a particularly concentrated manner. As a Beckett character talks to fill the omnipresent sense of Void, so Elkin's characters talk as if to combat the imminence of the true implications of their own existential plights. Elkin is a funny writer, then; to my mind the funniest writer alive. At Jewish-American speech, especially, I think he beats the other masters of the game: Bellow, Malamud, Richler, Roth. But he is far from being simply funny, funny-for-its-own-sake.

To Elkin, humor is the natural result of what he has already told us he thinks plot is. He has commented on humor in a letter to me:

> When I first started publishing, critics called me "a black humorist," switched over to a "bleak absurdist" in subsequent books, and now I find that I am called a "humorist." I decline all of these labels, and though there is comedy in my work, I think most of it obtains through the powerlessness of the characters, powerlessness being not only the central condition of most of our lives but the great joke of all comedy. I'm referring to my characters' use of irony and verbal aggression, which is the way they make Lucky Jim faces behind the backs of the folks who don't like them very much. I agree that humor must emerge from personality and situation. Otherwise it doesn't work and is reduced to riddle or pun or joke, the parlor car stories of the opportune. (I believe that humorists per se are mere opportunists.)

I am glad to have Elkins' direct statement on this subject, if only because a less direct route—deducing the credo from the works themselves—would risk having the critic make repeated suggestions that the reader look here and there—and laugh. Laugh he would, but perhaps at the cost of missing Elkin's connection of humor and character, and his drawing attention to the way in which "irony and verbal aggression"—perhaps the essences of Jewish humor—become means of disguising and coping with "powerlessness."

Boswell is largely a figure of helplessness, despite Herlitz's casual designation of him as a future "strong man." Condemned by Herlitz to a life of having things happen to him, he recites his Popeye's-spinach-line before testing his enormous physical strength ("Because my heart is pure."), yet remains very much the Prufrock on the sidelines of life, obsessed with other people's lives, but still feeling "a sort of shame . . . in not being one of the Trinity . . ." Because of his fixation on others' lives, he is even only "really at ease in a movie" during the cartoons, because "There *is* no Bugs Bunny. There *is* no Mickey Mouse." (Boswell's manager—ironically, if Elkin thought of it, for a man who feels he ought to be "one of the Trinity"—is named "Bogolub," arguably formed of Slavic roots for "God" and "Pigeon.") Yet in time Boswell confesses that, "on the make for the great," their company has taught him little after all.

> . . . He means, perhaps, that everybody's happiness and unhappiness total up to the same thing finally— that the bill, when it is presented, is always the same. Perhaps. I see that no one ever really gets away with anything, that we all owe a death, but surely it is senseless to argue that some of us do not get more for our death than others. . . .

Boswell demands his history, his succession of meaningful events, but in time concludes that he himself has not, cannot have, changed: "Boswell is Boswell is Boswell. His truth is that the personality is simply another name for habit and that what we view as a fresh decision is only rededication, a new way to get old things; that the evolving self is an illusion, fate just some final consequence. . . ." In a moment of temporary happiness, Boswell again thinks of death, and suddenly imagines his whole life running out like a movie reel. Marriage to a Principessa, which entitles him to pal around with the famous and great; diversion (hilarious stuff!!) through hokey "Holiday-of-the-Month" tours; direction of a quasi-Johnsonian "Club"; none of this satisfies Boswell, or gives him a sense of purpose. Life leads nowhere except, inexorably, into death; we are "settled by our past," and greatness gives us no comfort. The novel ends in bursts of comedy, absurd bits of action and patter that remind the reader of another master of the Jewish cadence, Groucho Marx.

Perhaps *Boswell* tells us too much; perhaps Elkin ought to have relied upon speech even more. At any rate, his 1965 collection of short stories (some of which made their first appearances as long before as 1959) *Criers and Kibitzers, Kibitzers and Criers* can be said to provide even better examples of the Elkin pattern than does *Boswell,* if only because of the concentration of effect, the clarity of impression, characteristic of the short story form. *Boswell* was a strong man, and many of Elkin's characters are from fringe occupations, full of the arcane speech of their trades. But many of them are, in fact or in effect, salesmen, as if Elkin accepted the Arthur Miller notion that the salesman is the archetypal American. The story collection is full of *podlers,* people on the make, and of those who try to accommodate themselves to a corrupt culture by means of speech. The central character of the title story, Greenspahn, owns a store, and has just lost his son. He is surrounded by small-time thieves who try to steal from him, and by colleagues whose luncheon habits betray their inadequacies:

> . . . The criers and kibitzers. The criers, earnest, complaining with a peculiar vigor about their businesses, their gas mileage, their health; their despair articulate, dependably lamenting their lives, vaguely mourning conditions, their sorrow something they could expect no one to understand. The kibitzers, deaf to grief, winking confidentially at the others, their voices high-pitched in kidding or lowered in conspiracy to tell of triumphs, of men they knew downtown. . . .

One notes here Elkin's mastery of the small catalog of pertinent details, the absolute assurance of content and rhythms with which he builds his effects. Greenspahn's lingering sorrow over his son's death becomes somehow one with his despair over the characters who inhabit this typical deli lunchtime scene— one would love to quote great chunks of the dialogue by means of which Greenspahn keeps despair at bay—and yet at the end the two merge: Greenspahn sees in a dream his son stealing from the till, and knows the dream for truth. (pp. 1-4)

In *A Bad Man* (1967), Stanley Elkin finally hits his novelistic stride—never to surrender it. The novel opens with a visit to "Enden" by Leo Feldman, under arrest, the owner of a department store; Feldman is en route to prison, and is not being treated extremely well. By this time, Stanley Elkin has learned to mix his business and pleasure—rhetoric and dialogue—to the point at which Feldman can pray, "Troublemaker, . . . keep me alive." Feldman has been guilty of more than shady business dealings; he has even dealt with his own son in the sale and purchase of stars, making a little on the side. But then, that is his heritage: his own father had dragged young Feldman with him on his peddler's rounds, taking it as part of his Jew's fate that he should adopt, and then exploit, the stereotype created for him. . . . Dragging about his "Inventory" as though it were his special curse, Feldman's father treated life as a stock-reduction sale, parodying Bible and *Walden* in trying to reduce himself to—and get rid of—the "unsalable thing": himself. When the old man dies, his son sells his body to the hospital.

With this as his heritage, it is no wonder that Feldman, guilty of doing questionable "favors" for others (as his father had specialized in disposing of the second-rate), ends up in a prison where the warden takes a special dislike to him; for among the criminals there, Feldman stands out as a "bad man." Feldman is given a uniform that parodies his business suit, for in the warden's eyes a bad man is a clown and should look the part. But in Feldman's eyes, goodness equals loss of liberty, and happiness equals darkness. The prison is simply itself a parody of the life he has always known: "The place was not surreal; it was a place of vicious, plodding *sequiturs . . .*" At the head of the system, equated with the system itself by reason of his capacity to arbitrarily set its rules, stands the warden, by reason of his office symbolic of virtue.

Feldman plays with the notions of "virtue" and "virtu," and much seems to hinge on the notion that being true to oneself constitutes a state superior to one obtained through adherence to abstract moral systems, such as that of the warden—whom Feldman finally recognizes as being a bad man too. Thus the warden identifies himself with Christianity—his surname is Fisher—and with civilization, and Feldman, the Jew, with merchandise. Feldman is in jail because he overextended his notion of commerce into personal matters, and now he is to suffer for his interventions. ("Cell" and "sell" are at one point punrelated.) The warden preaches a parable on the need for flexibility, insists that life is ordinary, and attacks the sense of exceptional self. But Feldman, holding on to a sense of self, comes at the end to feel—as he is being beaten by his fellow prisoners—that he is innocent after all.

A Bad Man, with its final trial scene, repeats Elkin's pet device of the wildly dramatic crisis scene. Here, too, are the verisimilitudinal trappings of a specialized state of existence, along with an imaginative, last-judgment cosmic imminence. There is, then, a tension between surface realism and an improbably heightened consciousness of metaphysical stakes—something akin, of course, to what Elkin says about plot. Bridging the two is his luxuriant language, language capable of such poetic excesses as this one: "Unambushable he was, seeing slush at spirit's source, reflex and hollow hope in all the duncy dances of the driven. He was helpless, however. . . ." If Elkin's work often suggests the anguished laughter of a book like *Miss Lonelyhearts,* there is also something Celtic about his way with words—for all their ostensible Jewishness. (pp. 5-6)

In 1976's *The Franchiser,* Elkin his upon the brilliant notion of coming to grips with the inhabitants of the world in which the word is sold en masse: the dealers in product franchises whose efforts guarantee the impossibility of distinguishing the outskirts of one American city from those of another. The novel begins with a traveler in this "packed masonry of states," quite uncertain which of them he is in. Ben Flesh, the franchiser (or buyer of franchises), has M.S. (in remission), has problems with his ability to *feel,* and thus becomes an appropriate protagonist in a book which constantly confronts the presences of illness and death. Yet the book is also a "road" novel which delights in the sound of American place names as much as do *Lolita* and *Mobile,* and it abounds in rich catalogs of nouns, common and proper both—places, products, names of brands, etc. In the elegance with which its author uses language, finally, *The Franchiser* is clearly in a league with the works of Joyce, Updike, Burgess, and Nabokov.

Given a bequest of "the prime rate" and a foster family of "godcousins"—all of them multiple-birth siblings with showbusiness names—[the protagonist Ben] Flesh sets out to "buy" "men's names," as if to borrow an identity ("Me and my trademarks"). The godcousins are all peculiar as well; one of them, for instance, constantly delivers herself of insights, her inventiveness peaking during sexual climax. The novel's voyage of self-discovery includes this flight of Flesh's fancy:

> "... We owe everything ... to dress, garb, caparison, wardrobe. We are what they wore. Millinery made us. Raiment did, weeds. Vestments, trousseau, togs, layettes.... Breechclouts and sou-westers. Spatter-dashes. Greaves and ruffs. Unmentionables and Sunday-go-to-meeting. Irving, Irving, call the pelisse!"

The novel in its cocky verve even contains a lateral allusion to *The Dick Gibson Show*.

Yet there is also, again, that focusing on death throughout [*The Franchiser*].... But there is balance; Ben Flesh obeys the Elkin dictum that he interest us by paying attention to the situation "in which he finds himself." At the end, facing the imminence of his own doom, he can still find cause for a crazy joy:

> ... Within weeks he would be strapped to a wheelchair. And ah, he thought, euphorically, ecstatically, this privileged man who could have been a vegetable or mineral instead of an animal, and a lower animal instead of a higher, who could have been a pencil or a dot on a die, who could have been a stitch in a glove or change in someone's pocket, or a lost dollar nobody found, who could have been stillborn or less sentient than sand, or the chemical flash of someone else's fear, ahh. *Ahh!*

There is at the end, then, a kind of affirmation coming out of Ben Flesh's manic odyssey.

Stanley Elkin's characters' contemplations of their situations have always been informed by the inevitable facts of their own deaths and those of others, giving his fiction an eschatological emphasis uncommon in contemporary letters. In *The Living End* (1979), Elkin moves beyond the point of death in an assault on received notions of theological order. That a lonely author of the universe should find confirmed by the behavior of his creatures the notion that his ways are not our ways, nor ours his, seems the suggestion of this short volume described on its cover as a "triptych." The allusion to paintings in panels of three, particularly altar panels, is fitting. The book is as crowded with scenes from the far side of the grave as something by Bosch or Grünewald. Ellerbee, another of Elkin's well-meaning liberals in a time of neighborhood decline (a subject on which Elkin waxes most lyrical), accompanies an "eschatological angel" to Heaven after being killed in a holdup. However, Ellerbee has himself transgressed God's inscrutable law, and is no sooner feeling happy to be there when St. Peter tells him "Go to Hell"—a place described as "the ultimate inner city." Ellerbee nervily "prays" to God ("Lord God of Ambush and Unconditional Surrender ... Power Play God of Judo Leverage. Grand Guignol, Martial Artist—"), and learns that his transgressions include thinking Heaven looked like a theme park. In the second panel of the triptych, God comes to hell as if to Mahagonny, and deals with questions and objections like some Chairman of the Board. The focus is on a new character called Ladlehaus, who lies in his grave but can communicate with the nearby living. We are told:

> "[God] asks nothing of us beloved. Not our lives, not our hearts. He would not know what to do with such gifts. He would be embarrassed by them. He does not write Thank You notes. He is not gracious. He is not polite or conventional. He has no thought for the thought that counts."

What God *is*, is someone who will "Smash us" if we aren't good, because those are the rules.

In the third panel, Jesus and Mary appear, the former reminding us that "I raised the dead.... I ran them up like flags on poles. I gave the blind 20/20 and lepers the complexions of debutantes. Miracle was my métier." Amid scenes of Hell that are horrific enough to suit the Medieval mind, God gives his explanation: the world is as it is because it makes a better narrative this way; God never found his "audience"; and so, on the book's last word, God annihilates *"everything."* (pp. 9-11)

> *John Ditsky, " 'Death Grotesque as Life': The Fiction of Stanley Elkin," in* The Hollins Critic, *Vol. XIX, No. 3, June, 1982, pp. 1-11.*

CHARLES MOLESWORTH

In at least three of his novels—*Boswell, The Living End,* and *The Dick Gibson Show*—Stanley Elkin does not become fully self-reflexive, and by ostensibly *not* writing about writing, he may be said to elude the category "metafictionist." Likewise, he has also been frequently quoted as rejecting the label of "black humorist." Yet his work is avidly read and praised by many critics who champion those contemporary fiction writers that are often identified by either of these labels, or both. If Elkin is like, and yet unlike, Barthelme, Sukenick, and Federman, how can we best place him in the available spectrum of styles and postures? The improvisatory nature and feel of Elkin's work might cue us to accept all spectrums in less structured ways, to hear the chorus as instead a babble, and take each writer and even each novel as it presents itself. While that is more or less what many general readers do, critics and academics often read novels, in one of their guises at least, as ways of problem solving. If a novel sets out to address a problem, whether of epistemology, sociology, psychology, or whatever, we have to have some prior knowledge of what the problem is and how it's developed historically. I propose to see the three novels I mentioned above as attempts to solve, fictionally, a set of problems, problems that have often been addressed by metafictionists and black humorists. Of course, if the novels are addressed under the guise of delight or entertainment, they may seem obvious, and any problem itself treated merely as a *donnée* for the tale's otherwise formless energies. Elkin's work can easily be read as sheer entertainment, and its apparent formlessness invites such a response. On the other hand, the novels can be more in the grip of the problems they address, with such apparent playfulness, than they are willing to acknowledge. My reading inclines to the latter probability.

Before spelling out this set of problems, let me say that I think Alan Wilde has the case essentially right when he defines Elkin's work by the term "Midfiction." Midfiction, in Wilde's view, uses parable to enable the author to suspend his irony between the poles of mimetic realism and the free-play of metafiction's self-reflexivity. Parable "intends to render more fluid and existential our sense of the world's meaning and ... our connection with it." By using ambiguity, indirection, and open rather than closed forms, parables defy univocal interpretations or fixed contents, though they can exploit some or many of the features of traditional, mimetic realism. Elkin often employs the surface textures of realism, such as colloquial dialogue, standard exposition of spatial and temporal "scenes," consistent characterology, and so forth. Where he mostly clearly deviates from realistic canons is in his characters' implausible obsessions, the use of fairly frequent empirical impossibilities, and, rather than a constant welter of juxtaposition, an almost endless string of additional details or occurrences to the point of madcap exhaustiveness or an epistemological exhaustion. We're told a great deal about Boswell and Gibson, yet both characters are more reflectors of the experiences of others than they are deeply complex subjects in their own right. Also, and this contributes to the feeling of a parable (though it is not a characteristic singled out by Wilde), Elkin's language is frequently playful and spotted with puns and one liners, but his style has a high percentage of sentences that are "merely" expository in a straight-forward, prosaic way. The comparison many critics have made between Elkin and the patter of the stand-up comedian is apt, and I often expect Elkin to say, "Now seriously, folks," though if he did say this, we couldn't tell if he meant it straight or not.

Now, for the set of problems both faced by and embodied in the three novels: can characters' actions be seen as governed by deterministic models of free-will; can a story tell its whole secret by attending only to surfaces; and, finally, can a novel render justice, not to the complexity, but simply to the *expanse* of American life in the last half of the twentieth century? These admittedly general formulations will cover a great many writers' problems, obviously, but I suggest that Elkins is virtually unique in the way his works interlock these three problems. (pp. 93-5)

Perhaps the "passed on or handed down" model most apt for Elkin's first novel, *Boswell,* is Flaubert's *Bouvard and Pécuchet*. With only one main character instead of the two clerks in the earlier novel, Elkin sets out to reveal a series of false or empty possibilities of meaning. Boswell's life is landmarked by a group of would-be heroes, a set of not-quite Dr. Johnsons who could supply Boswell's sycophancy with the focus it needs. From Penner the selfish ascetic, to Sandusky the broken-down strong man, to Messerman the rabbi with no congregation, to Lano the masochistic revolutionary general, Boswell learns how humdrum, how ordinary are the great and famous. Or rather, he doesn't quite learn this lesson in Flaubertian nullity until the end of the book. Then, having formed a club of Great Men, Boswell discovers "a new knowledge that it was not enough, that nothing was ever enough," and ends by shouting *"Down with The Club!"* Where Flaubert's clerks discovered only the endless pieties of the half-enlightened bourgeoisie, Boswell finds the insatiable desires of post-industrial man afloat in a world of means without ends. *Boswell* is a book obsessed with values, especially the value of learning how to live the good life, but it's also a book with no values to center its vision, and in this it most resembles its Flaubertian model.

The book's picaresque structure is ironically at odds with its obsessional characters and even its sense of character as destiny. "Oh, what a thing it is to be settled by our past—to be no better, finally, than our toilet training, than domestic arrangements we don't even understand at the time." This lament against Freudian determinism can be read as a mockery of such explanatory schemes, but the novel offers it as at least as plausible as any other scheme. This particular passage occurs in a long sequence in which Boswell "practices" for death, trying through a series of madcap scenes to acclimate himself to the mortality he announces as inevitable (and inevitably repressed) in the very first paragraph of the book. (The themes of death's inevitability and the nature of greatness are never successfully mediated in the novel, in my opinion, and this more than anything gives the book its open form.)

The novel also uses its picaresque structure in an attempt to capture a fullness of material reality and incorporate its obsession with surfaces. One formulation of the concern with surfaces occurs as a parenthetical paragraph, but its offhandedness is, I would suggest, a clue to its very centrality in the novel. There are also similar reflections and formulations on the same theme scattered throughout the book, and the lack of inner reality in the novel is dialectically related to this theme. But here is the passage:

> (I have just thought of something. Perhaps cause and effect are somehow mixed up here. Perhaps we pick our leaders as we pick our actors—for their looks; perhaps the great are destined by nothing so much as their physical well-being; perhaps the world *is* all appearance. Is this the meaning of life? I may have stumbled onto something. I shall have to think about it.)

If the world is to be known through appearances, then such principles of organization as subordination or hierarchy or classification must be revalued (and even discarded, perhaps). Furthermore, the emphasis on surface and appearance opens the door to inclusiveness, as principles of exclusion or selectivity become harder to justify. There is in *Boswell* a very brief interlude where the main character quite casually begins to photograph, at their request, a family in the park. Boswell imagines the family's domestic life as a "demolishment of empty space, an ethic of filled drawers, closets, rooms, houses, devoted as misers to some desperate notion of accumulation." In photographing them, Boswell (and Elkin) sees them as perfectly normal; it's the narrative unimportance of the incident that makes the people so typical, so representative of the general object-world of the book. "Their substantial laughter, their little private gestures of affection seemed hollow but tremendously brave." They are the irreplaceable but unimportant cogs in the wheels of the world's consumption, the lubricant for all the dominant market-oriented motives of modern production.

By demolishing empty space through the accumulation of objects, the people in Elkin's America seem to achieve their basic values, and this throws them into the maelstrom of inclusiveness, another source of the novelist's concern. Time after time we are given lists of things, occurrences, qualities, or even formulations of ideas or feelings, lists whose repetitiveness eventually feels like a desperate attempt to master the expanse or fullness of material life in America. I say expanse or fullness rather than plenitude, because this characteristic hardly seems a genuine cultural value or accomplishment, yet neither does it come into direct or explicit satirical focus. We might eventually feel Elkin attacks this acquisitiveness or materialism, but one could argue just as convincingly that he accepts it for what it is, a stable and inescapable aspect of life in post-industrial twentieth-century America. And it is not only things but people that fill and overfill our lives. . . . (pp. 97-9)

Indeed the climactic moment in *Boswell* occurs when the seeker realizes that it's not enough to "collect" great men or to conquer death, that the gathering of world leaders engaged in conversation finally isn't sufficient. What is really needed is a total fullness, a total incorporation of all reality, far beyond the select or élite (or artistic) refinement of reality as it might be filtered down to and through a single consciousness.

> It was no longer enough simply to live forever. It was no longer enough to be just one single man. I wanted to be everyone in this room and all the people in the crowds outside and all the people everywhere

who had ever lived. What did it mean to be just
Boswell, to have only Boswell's experience? . . .

The art of selecting great men to teach us things has been
replaced by the hunger to assume all of reality. The nineteenth-
century myth of the great man has been replaced by the late
twentieth-century myth of the universal common man.

Shortly after his marriage, Boswell is described by allusions
to Hawthorne's "Wakefield" and Eliot's "Prufrock," both
exemplars of the anti-heroic, men defeated by their own ordinariness and limited horizons. Though he is clearly in this
tradition of the modern anti-hero, Boswell has little real angst,
and very few demons, and his author's tone towards him is
neither satirical nor acerbic nor even melancholic. There is
irony, to be sure, in this anti-heroicism, but only because we
still expect some saving grace or transforming power to define
the central character in the books we spend time reading. But
for Elkin such an absence of heroism, or its ironic inversion,
is merely par for the course in a world where the only measure
of achievement is accumulation and the only test of reality is
surfaces. Of course Elkin "knows" accumulation and surfaces
can hardly ground any ethics that looks to be transcendent. But
transcendence is not what obsessions are about. Knowing or
desiring something obsessively is its own reward.

> There are only two kinds of intelligences, the ob-
> sessive and the perspectual. All dirty old men come
> from the former and all happy men from the latter,
> but I wouldn't trade places. In this life frustration is
> the Promethean symbol of effort.

Notice, the Promethean *symbol* of effort, not the actual attainment of a Promethean status or essence, is what justifies the
frustration endemic in all obsessive efforts. (pp. 100-01)

[In ***The Dick Gibson Show***] Dick Gibson's struggle with what
he calls his apprenticeship is an effort to master all the knowledge of radio, and through this all knowledge altogether. Even
as he becomes "not just the voice of radio but radio itself,"
Gibson's fascination with voice is also a fascination with narrative, with the penchant for ordinary men and women to tell
their stories obsessively. What Gibson discovers in and through
these narratives is that people are surrounded by, drenched in,
constituted out of the welter of clichés they have imbibed and
recycled and appropriated since their first moments of consciousness.

> . . . his apprenticeship was truly finished, the last of
> all the bases in the myth had been rounded, his was
> a special life, even a great life—a life, that is, touched
> and changed by cliché, by corn and archetype and
> the oldest principles of drama.

The "oldest principles of drama" might well include those
elements and characteristics that God requires in ***The Living
End*** which are necessary for a simple, single reason: *"Because
it makes a better story is why."* The better stories are the ones
that are built on corn, cliché, and archetypes, because they
deal with the surfaces of things, they include all experience,
and because they let us know all the stories are the same (and
hence determined) while still deeply satisfying for each of us
(desperate to believe in our individual freedoms.) (pp. 101-02)

Dick Gibson hears many stories throughout [***The Dick Gibson
Show***] and most of them are marked by banality and cliché. It
might be interesting to contrast this novel with Bakhtin's notion
of the dialogic, in which the genre of the novel is defined as
a compendium of voices whose forms are determined in significant ways by their expectations of being heard and re-

sponded to. To my ear, Elkin's characters' stories are not
genuinely dialogic, resembling as they do the patter of the
stand-up comedian. Or, to be more precise, their dialogic openness to response is very narrow, since they do little beyond
pause over various puns and gag-lines and are always rushing
on to some usually pointless or predictable conclusion. (p. 103)

Perhaps the most revealing passage in the book concerns Gibson's view of his family and their character-playing shenanigans. (In fact, Dick Gibson's puzzlement at his father's meanings can be read as an allegory of the reader facing an Elkin
novel.) This incessant role-playing is frankly labelled a way
of dealing with surfaces in order to avoid the inner feelings
and states of mind that ordinarily are expected to be shared
and tested among family members. The harsh truth behind the
passage is how real it is despite its theatricalizing exaggera-
tions. Notice, too, how the word "everything" occurs to convey the expanse of human situations and behaviour, as if the
family, like the novelist himself, felt compelled to include all
their experience even if it has been transformed into a kind of
indifference and superficiality:

> They were zany, and Dick remembered why his fam-
> ily's characters oppressed him so. It wasn't simply
> that they worked so hard to show off. Rather it was
> that their divertissements were a delaying action that
> held him off. In a while they would drop their roles
> and behave normally. Their masquerades were re-
> served for homecomings like this one, or leavetak-
> ings, or their first visit to a patient in the hospital,
> say. It was their way of concealing feeling, thrusting
> it away from them until all the emotional elements
> in a situation had disappeared. . . . He recalled the
> story Miriam had told about her father, how she'd
> had to shield him. Why, *his* family was like that and
> he hadn't even known it. Why couldn't folks take
> it? Why did they insist upon the quotidian? What was
> so bad about bad news? Surely the point of life was
> the possibility it always held out for the exceptional.
> The range of the strange, he thought.

The strange and the ordinary truth merge into the theatrical,
the stylization of communication acting as a way of deadening
its import and the feelings that animate it.

In ***The Living End*** this same way of dealing with surfaces and
including "everything" takes the form of all the clichés about
Heaven and Hell being true: the pearly gates, the heavenly
choir, the sulphurous stench, the sadistic multiplication of punishment and abasement. It is all as if Elkin wanted to see the
afterlife as designed by some Popular Culture, Incorporated,
a public relations triumph as everyone's hopes and fears are
"perfectly" realized. God himself is both a free, spontaneous
actor and a deterministic force, the "Microfiche God, Lord of
the Punched Cards," who is nevertheless capable of being
"mildly bemused as He had been briefly surprised." God destroys *"everything"* (that final word of the book italicized in
its manic inclusiveness), essentially because he has never found
his audience. Without the theatrical "fix" of cheers, applause,
and the adoration of fans, there's nothing left for God to do
but deny the very expanse he is credited with creating. (One
thinks of Woody Allen's one-liner from "Love and Death":
"God is an under-achiever.") "Everything" becomes one of
the book's key words, like "nothing" in *King Lear,* and "everything" means every thing that is conventional, even the
conventional focus of consciousness, which is the individual
self, both the source of, and a challenge to, such a totalizing
notion.

Athwart this conventionality are the zany turns and reversals that Elkin uses to make the story fresh. Joseph doesn't accept Jesus as the Messiah, Mary mothers another child, God accidentally kills someone in a moment of pique and Jesus has to redeem him. But such reversals are not articulated towards some coherent satirical aim, leaving aside the rather obvious point that the subject of the book is the received piety of totally empty forms of belief and worship. The novel, it seems to me, is best read as an allegory of the novelist's perplexity in the face of those insoluble problems I have mentioned. With the climactic line of the theodicy, *"Because it makes a better story is why,"* Elkin comes closest to announcing his poetics, closest to making the book self-reflexive, a story about the hunger for narrative interest. But the destructiveness of the deity might then be read allegorically as the fundamental smashing of the problems, an apocalyptic refusal to continue with either the interpretive manipulations of parable or the presumptive maintenance of meaning involved in realism. (pp. 103-06)

To determine what level of realism Elkin's novels retain, or to ask *why* Elkin avoids operating in either a clearly realistic or metafictional or black humor style, is to ask very difficult questions. My brief answer would be something like this: Elkin is both baffled and stoic in the face of the expanse of material reality as well as the persistence and virtual inseparability of clichés and mythic patterns. This stoic bafflement leads him away from black humor or satire in the traditional sense, and also provides no ground for a transcendent spiritual or historical vision. As Thomas Le Clair rightly points out, "Elkin's heroes ... develop their obsessions from natural authorities, common deeds, or the promises of a popular culture rather than from some social psychological or religious ideology." Elkin's work might be read as the perfect fictional complement to the notion of our age as one marked by "the end of ideology"— but of course we now see how such a notion was itself sodden with ideological thought. In short, Elkin needs realism to anchor his stoicism, but he "violates" realistic canons because he is baffled by the very excessiveness of the banal in American life. No formal structure, no shapely closure can contain "everything," and the aestheticism implicit in formalist finesse or lyrical expressiveness will not answer to the overwhelming presence of surface meanings. Elkin's response is but one variation in what I would call the post-Joycean novel, that myriad attempt to redeem the commonplace without resort to patently transcendent means.

To give a longer answer to these questions would require more space than is available here. But I would suggest that Marshall Brown's superb article, "The Logic of Realism: A Hegelian Approach," *PMLA*, 96, 2 (March, 1981), is a good place to begin. Of the three conceptions of reality—"the reality of universal types, the reality of individuation, and the reality of patterned regularity"—that Brown adduces as the bases for various theories of realism, Elkin grants credence to each, but withholds assent from any. The reality of patterned regularity, relying on the predictability of "natural and causal forces," might seem the least important to Elkin. But as we've seen, the "originality" of his characters' obsessions only serves to make them part of the general pattern of behavior, since all people have some obsession. This dominant fact in Elkin's characterology folds back into the other two bases of realism, since we recognize in a person like Boswell or Gibson both the type of modern man and a fully detailed, finely "surfaced" individual.

What Brown's essay also allows us to see is how Hegel's triad of Contingency, Relative Necessity, and Absolute Necessity can illumine Elkin's project. Though many of his characters are known by their obsessions, and hence would seem defined by Absolute Necessity people who are fully determined from within, not subject to definition by others—these characters nevertheless are often existing in a world of contingency, and thus reject any "form of grounding or causation" and refuse to be parts of a system. This is an elaborate way of saying that Elkin refuses to choose between free-will and determinism as an exclusive or even dominant explanation of his characters' behavior. For Elkin, Absolute Necessity only springs from an unbreakable attachment to some reductive object or ineradicable fear that motivates the obsession. And conversely, his characters' apparent contingency, the madcap inventiveness of the plot and the picaresque and open structure, nevertheless reflect an inescapable sameness and limitation in people's lives and desires, bound as they are by "cliché, by corn, and archetype."

At the end of his essay Brown offers a quick historical sketch of "pre- and postrealistic styles," explaining that "loose but repetitive organization" is what marks postrealism, and we see how "Texture replaces shape as the unifying force." I have argued implicitly that Elkin's texture—the feel of his characters' obsessiveness, the lists, the madcap atmosphere, and so forth—clearly unifies his work more than any shapeliness of plot or clear teleological narrative development. But I also want to argue that Elkin's apparently loose and carefree texture, his prestidigitatious distance from severe meanings or "serious" characters is not an escape from ideology and is not sheer entertainment. Elkin has views and he has problems. Like so many of his characters, Elkin lives in large part out of obsessions, locked in a pattern that is "justified" only by the judicious use of "taste—the soul's harmless appetite." But is it harmless because everyone shares it, or because it comes to nothing in the face of larger forces? The same two questions are what we should finally ask of any novelist's vision, as well as of his or her style. (pp. 108-09)

Charles Molesworth, "Stanley Elkin and 'Everything': The Problem of Surfaces and Fullness in the Novels," in Delta, *France, No. 20, February, 1985, pp. 93-110.*

CHRISTOPHER LEHMANN-HAUPT

Once again, Stanley Elkin has come up with an idea for a novel that only he would dare to attempt. [In *Stanley Elkin's The Magic Kingdom*], Eddy Bale, an Englishman who has just lost his 12-year-old son, Liam, to a congenital disease, decides that he and his wife have gone about things all wrong in their desperate struggle to prolong the child's life.

As he tells Queen Elizabeth, when his cause takes him to Buckingham Palace, "We never rewarded him for his death." Warming to his theme, he declares,

> We should have hijacked the sweet shoppe and turned him loose at the fair. . . . We should have sent him to sleep past his bedtime. We should have burned him out on his life, Dynast. We should have bored him to death.

As a memorial to Liam, Eddy now proposes to pick half a dozen or so terminally sick children and give them the vacation of their lives and their deaths, a dream holiday in Disney World—not as a memorial to Liam, mind you, but as "bonus pay for hazardous duty" to "deal reality the blows of fantasy." Done, says the Queen, and writes out a check for 50 quid.

And as usual, Stanley Elkin has embellished his idea with brilliant comic invention. . . .

And as always, Mr. Elkin plays the crazy music of his prose—takes off at the hint of a theme on his soaring funky riffs and jazzy blue notes. "They died in pain," Eddy reflects about the sick children, "language torn from their throats, or, what little language they had left, turned into an almost gangster argot, barbaric as the skirls and screaks of bayed prey." . . .
Yet there seems to me a difference to *The Magic Kingdom*. . . . Never before in his longer fiction has Mr. Elkin paid such conventional attention to pure plot. For a change, his story isn't just a platform for his gags and shtick but instead an architecture that frames and contains what he builds. For once (except in his short stories and novella), his plot inspires comic ideas that return the favor and inspire the plot. And his prose is a sound backed up by orchestra and chorus.

The result is not only among Mr. Elkin's best works of fiction to date—a remarkable turnabout from his last book, the turgid, word-impacted *George Mills*—but a comedy that cuts so many ways that it leaves us bleeding with laughter. It plays on the vulnerability of children, or at least the painful susceptibility that parents feel for their offspring. It plays on the nightmare underlying the theme-park of amusement, on the idea that hell may be whatever deprives us of a concept of hell. It plays on doctors, on undertakers, on airlines.

It plays on the art of death and death as an art. . . .

In Mr. Elkin's gifted hands, the show business of death is remarkably healthy.

> *Christopher Lehmann-Haupt, in a review of "The Magic Kingdom," in* The New York Times, *March 18, 1985, p. C16.*

MAX APPLE

In *The Magic Kingdom,* the wild language that has always been Mr. Elkin's meets the least likely subject of rich playful prose, a group of dying children. Suffering and death usually wear the mourning clothes of language, but not in this novel.

> Noah Cloth, confined to hospitals at a time in his life when other boys his age were in school, could not read well or do his maths. His history was weak, his geography, most of his subjects. Only in art had he done well, and now he'd lost his ability to draw. Nine times he'd been operated on for bone tumors: in his right wrist, along his left and right femurs, on both elbows, once at the base of his skull, and once for little garnetlike tumors around a necklace of collarbone.

The narrative concerns the trip Noah and his companions are taking from England to Disney World for their dream holiday. When we read of such journeys in the newspapers, we see the sweetness in the gesture of such arranged happiness. We see the sentimental kindness of granting a last wish. We see everything except the dying children as they are. Mr. Elkin strips away the sentimentality and replaces it with an honest look at the grotesque possibilities we all carry around and prefer not to see, not even in fiction.

The seven children in *The Magic Kingdom* are traveling, but they have lost the one passport that matters—they cannot be admitted to the province of health and longevity, but everything else is theirs, including this well-intentioned journey to Disney World.

Even fiction, that familiar opener of eyes, rarely opens our eyes to the interior terrors. We are accustomed to metaphors of disease and decay. Mr. Elkin presents the real thing; not metaphors, kids. Novelists may X-ray the soul and the psyche, but we leave the body to technicians.

Not Stanley Elkin. His magic kingdom is the domain of "fallen pediatric angels," the province of children defined by their diseases, children who have slipped through not only the safety net, so cozy to politicians, but children who have defied the trickiness of evolution. They are the owners of blasted genes, they are hopeless, doomed beings, and on their way to Disney World in a hysterical farce that sounds like Shakespeare reading aloud from *The National Enquirer*.

These children on a Disney World holiday are nothing like the adult sufferers to whom we are accustomed. This is the magic kingdom, not the magic mountain, nothing as pastoral as tuberculosis for this crew; no philosophical discussions, just a pretty good shot at living out the week. And the work is aptly titled. It is not Disney's magic kingdom but Stanley Elkin's. Disney's mechanical and electrical shenanigans, his puppets and animals, are no match for the fireworks of Mr. Elkin's imagination.

In this novel, as in no other, the lyrical merges with the clinical, the romantic motif of the journey couples with the vocabulary of the hospital ward. People are the incarnations of their diseases and the names of their drugs and chemical medicines rings out as harmoniously as the names of Homeric gods in the *Odyssey*. Mr. Elkin is weaving the tapestry of disease, the language and the technique of having your last good time. In this tapestry, pharmacology replaces mythology. . . .

As in traditional literary journeys, [Elkin's] young children have a leader. And what a leader, Eddy Bale, the entrepreneur of the hopeless, the father of "Our Liam," the boy whose suffering and death captured the heart of England. . . .

Liam died of incurable bodily disease; in the course of his son's lingering, Eddy contracted the sentimental disease that is the satiric target of this novel. In the years of fund raising and publicity Eddy Bale has become a believer in the key tenet of sentimental affliction, the doctrine of "there is a reason for everything."

Because dying children are No. 1 on virtually everyone's pathos list, because dying kids, above all, make you believe there is a reason for everything, Eddy Bale's scheme reaches high places. He calls on the Royal Family, is admitted to their "rec room." The prince who greets him wears a T-shirt that says "*Buckingham Palace*" in embossed Gothic." Eddy meets the Queen, she "takes a checkbook and gold pen from her purse. The checks are imprinted with her image and look rather like pound notes. Bale notices that they've already been signed."

The pilgrims, under the royal aegis, begin their resonant journey with two nurses, a doctor and a nanny. The children carry allegorical names, "Tony Word," "Lydia Conscience," "Noah Cloth;" the nurses are "Cottle" and "Bible," the nanny is a "Carp." But far more intimate to their beings than their own names are the names and insignias of their afflictions. . . .

We are accustomed to using the language of health even when we speak of those in the kingdom of disease. We use active images, we "battle" illness, we "conquer" adversity. Mr. Elkin strips away this false language of valor and health. He creates a crazy quilt, words connect wildly, as desperate as the characters who wish to connect to the healthy world.

But there is also a quiet language in this work. A language that draws on James Joyce. And in a way Eddy Bale, leading the dying children, is Mr. Elkin's version of Leopold Bloom, yet another mock Ulysses, this one even more hopeless than Joyce's.

These doomed children, the barely living, first glimpse Disney world in a rich prose that echoes the end of Joyce's story "The Dead." (p. 34)

The resonance of "The Dead" is not only a literary suggestion, it is the melancholy truth that we prefer not to hear. Mr. Moorhead, the pediatrician, understands it. "He had to revise all his old theories. Disease, not health, was at the core of things." . . .

If not for the hyperbolic comic voice, we could hardly bear the pathos of these young sufferers. When the comic lets down its guard even for a half sentence, the effect is devastating.

> Tony is now two years beyond his last remission but freckles have begun to reappear around his jawline and his renal functions are in an early stage of failure.

That mixture, the emerging freckles combined with the emerging renal failure is the sad sweet music of this prose, as pervasive as the snow upon the living and the dead.

For Eddy Bale, Mr. Elkin's Ulysses, the passage to Disney World includes no exotic temptations, no one-eyed giants, no offers of beauty or eternal life. Eddy is a fool, he has lost his son to nature, his wife to the corner tobacconist. The Queen asks for her money back, even the children disappoint him by acting like normal children. Yet the farcical plot of *The Magic Kingdom* moves Eddy to the bed as surely as the adventures of the *Odyssey* moved Ulysses to Penelope. Eddy Bale encounters his Penelope but there are none of the glories of stony Ithaca, not even the brown solemnity of Bloom's Dublin.

Eddy Bale's Penelope has been weaving the poison web of herself. Instead of Molly Bloom's "Yes," she becomes a chorus of "Now." Her other suitors are her own hands, her offsprings are stillbirths. She and Eddy are as hopeless as the group they shepherd, yet the fun goes on.

The comic vision of this work is both hysterical and profound. Part sick joke, part lyrical meditation on the nature of disease, the journey to this magic kingdom earns its place among the dark voyages that fiction must chronicle. (p. 35)

> *Max Apple, "Having Their Last Good Time," in* The New York Times Book Review, *March 24, 1985, pp. 34-5.*

LEE LESCAZE

"My life is hard," a dying 12-year-old remarks early in *Stanley Elkin's The Magic Kingdom.* Then he doesn't mind dying? "Yes. Yes I do," the boy says.

Life is precious even in the bleakest circumstances. So what can you do for dying children? If you're Mr. Elkin, angered by kids' suffering and armed against the horseman Death with a lance of wit, you write a novel in which you fly seven of them, short-timers all, to "the Magic Kingdom" of Disney World.

This may seem an unlikely plot, certain to tumble into bad taste or worse. But *Stanley Elkin's The Magic Kingdom* . . . is packed with moments of beauty in the ugliest surroundings,

aching love-of-life in human beings with excellent reasons to curse it, and bravery everywhere.

As the book's title suggests, this magic kingdom is more the world of Stanley Elkin than of Walt Disney. The story is swept along on the currents of Mr. Elkin's dark wit, from his sketch of a fictitious, tightfisted Queen Elizabeth II, who helps finance the tour, to the children's betrayal by a lounge-act version of Mickey Mouse.

The "dream holiday" to Disney World is the wild plan of protagonist Eddy Bale, a desperate idea that comes to him after the death of his 12-year-old son.

"Oh, I think we were mad," Eddy tells the queen, of the four-year, several-continent search for a treatment to beat his son's disease. The treatments were a series of tortures and left Eddy with a question: "Wouldn't we have been better off to have given him a cram course in debauchery? Whatever it took?" . . .

So Eddy takes seven of England's dying children into the heart of Walt Disney fantasy, as a sort of reward, or as he puts it, "bonus pay for hazardous duty."

As may be clear already, Mr. Elkin is a master builder of language. His words dazzle, his sentences tempt you to read aloud. For example, he describes the children waking up,

> the sluggish ways of the dying, their awful morning catarrhs and constipations, the wheezed wind of their snarled, tangled breathing, their stalled blood and aches and pains like an actual traffic in their bones . . . stomachs floating a slick film of morning sickness, the torpid hangover of their medications. . . .

These children are weak from disease, but never pathetic. They are more courageous than the adults and often wiser. Still, they know too much of pathology, too little of the world outside hospitals. . . .

While death is the primary obsession of *The Magic Kingdom,* sex gives it a run for the money. Sex has its own morphology here—onanistic, homosexual, pubescent, voyeuristic. There's not much garden-variety baby-making in the landscape of this fable, yet, in the end, Mr. Elkin's riposte to the blows of disease and death is procreation. A child dies, have another.

It's in ending the fable, in trying to haul back into order all the manic spirits he's loosed along the way, that *The Magic Kingdom* runs into trouble, exiting the stage less elegantly than it enters.

Still, few can balance between the gasp and the laugh as skillfully as Mr. Elkin does, digging his grim jokes from unpleasant soil, mixing characters such as a mad doctor with a fixation on Holocaust victims and a nanny who's seen the movie *Mary Poppins* 17 times.

And, of course, there are the children, including the remarkable Charles Mudd-Gaddis, prematurely aged by progeria; dreaming the dreams of aged men although he's only eight years old. All of them struck down for no good reason. Eddy Bale, whose sufferings have made him foolish, says over and over that there is a reason for everything.

Mr. Elkin knows better.

> *Lee Lescaze, "Voyage to the End at Disney World," in* The Wall Street Journal, *April 12, 1985, p. 26.*

STEPHEN KOCH

Stanley Elkin's The Magic Kingdom is a rich but macabre business, a novel—a *comic* novel—about the death of children. And it manages to slide this almost unendurably poignant subject along the whole razor's edge between realism and fantasy without once seeming to draw blood. Elkin's literary specialty always has been the American surreal, by which rather academic-sounding phrase I suppose I mean that Elkin writes novels in which dream characters park dream cars in real parking lots; in which we see dream dances, dream deaths in real American rec-rooms; in which literally real people—the present queen of England is a favorite—caper improbably in a magic kingdom of Elkin's creation. He is a fantasist of the here and now.

To this enterprise, Elkin brings an ear that is exceptionally sensitive to the music of our vast and—to so many—baffling language; a somewhat self-absorbed esthetic virtuosity; a wide vulgar streak; and a rather professorial, though happily usable, erudition. (His work is filled with persiflages of Joyce, Woolf, and other classroom greats of the high modern). . . .

The central figures in *Stanley Elkin's The Magic Kingdom* are seven British children, each suffering from some horrific terminal disease. Galvanized by the death of his own small son, a character named Eddy Bale (as in baleful) arranges to cicerone this sad group of kids on a—what is the phrase?—"dream trip" to Disney World in Florida.

Now, it must be admitted that the deaths of seven sweet boys and girls may strike some, even many, as an unpromising subject for a comic novel. Well, to begin with, granting a fair number of real laughs in spite of it all, Elkin's mode is tragicomedy. Second, while I cannot recommend reading this novel while in any kind of hypochondriacal mood, the diseases in it don't *feel* particularly real. Elkin's dying bairns are only real-*ish:* their very names—Tony Word, Lydia Conscience—quickly betray them as ciphers—allegorical ciphers?—populating Elkin's Disney World Within. The magic kingdom in question is the imagination, and it is Stanley Elkin's very own, which is why he puts his own name—as did the mighty Walt before him—over the gates. In this novel, Elkin carries us to someplace like what Eliot called "death's dream kingdom," but in fact it's dream, not death, that actually rules there.

So our true subject is sickness and dying in Elkin's imagination. The subject has not been frivolously chosen; many years ago, Elkin himself was discovered to suffer from multiple sclerosis, an incurable deteriorative disease. Elkin has the inside dope, all right, yet he seems to have found all his characters within. There is, for example, Benny Maxine, a nervy little cockney who each night dreams about high rolling in Monte Carlo, and who in his sleep mutters one of the novel's many poignant lines: *"If you can't afford to lose, don't gamble."* There is a male nurse named Colin Bible; there is little Janet Order, whom the hole in her heart has turned, from tip to toe, a cyanotic blue. Speaking of the American surreal, even Disney World is appropriated as Elkin's own kind of playground, though his remark that the park is steadily visited by real dying kids on "dream trips"—a "reverse Lourdes," as he calls it—has the ring of truth.

This appropriation of the mass-market magic kingdom for his own private one provides a theme long familiar in Elkin; the nefarious infiltration of mass culture into the private identity. At the murky end of this novel, we see a rough vision of a crude, carnival Mickey Mouse as *angelo della morte*. Another theme is childhood itself, since, healthy or moribund, childhood is the storyteller's age, and an ideal ground on which a grown-up can ponder the ultimate frustrations of life's first perfect promises. Then another theme—I suppose the most important—is Elkin's fine, furious, intensely ironic, late-modern meditation on that link between love and death that has for so long played so large a role in major lit. Eros. Thanatos. All that.

Truth to tell, *Stanley Elkin's The Magic Kingdom* strikes this reader as rather more, push come to shove, about Eros than Thanatos. It is more about ecstasy than extinction. . . .

Like Disney's own adorable dwarves, these seven little people seem to bask in the erotic glow of some notably resurrectable Snow White. . . . There is more obsession with life in Elkin's kingdom than with the end. Elkin obviously viewed his imagination as an essentially redemptive instrument and his "magic"—all irony and language—is an effort to rise above the Mickey Mouse maxim of the Real, repeated in a dreary, moribund, squelching rhythm through the book: "Everything"—even, presumably, the ultimate outrage—"has a reasonable explanation."

Stephen Koch, "The Dark Side of Mickey Mouse,"
in Book World—The Washington Post, *April 14, 1985, p. 9.*

JOHN SEABROOK

There's so little life in *The Magic Kingdom* and so much disgust. Disease and death are not new themes for Elkin, but with *The Magic Kingdom* disease takes a new place in his fiction. In *The Franchiser* Ben Flesh's multiple sclerosis is the plot complication, the challenge to which the novel's wit, energy and compassion are the response. The life-affirming ending is dramatic and thoroughly earned. What little vitality *The Magic Kingdom* possesses seems mechanical in comparison. Even the language, the exotic diction and rhythm that are Elkin's signature, can't quicken this morbid kingdom for long. There's some comedy in the book's early scenes, which take place in England, but the humor quickly turns antic and then mirthless. It's as if "all the body's punch lines," which were to be vehicles of Elkin's irony, overwhelmed his comic resources and became his subject. Disease itself is his inhuman hero.

A few sentences from the novel help illustrate what I mean. One of the healthy characters, a doctor named Moorhead, is thinking about his career. He remembers his early days as a physician, when "he was smitten by an ideal of health and life, some full-moon notion of the hale and hearty." Then he happened to see some photographs of the survivors of the Nazi death camps, and the obscenity of those living corpses forced a change in his vocation:

> He had to revise all his old theories. Disease, not health, was at the core of things; his idea of pith and gist and soul obsolete for him now, revised downward to flaw, nubbin, rift; incipient sickness the seed which sent forth its contaged shoots raging through the poisoned circuits of being.

That passage makes a pretty astute précis of *The Magic Kingdom*; unfortunately the novel suffers from the condition it describes. Pith becomes flaw; instead of soul there is rift. There's absence at the heart of the novel, where there ought to be significance. By absence I don't mean pessimism. Of course it's possible for a novelist to represent successfully a negative vision of life. Had such a vision been Elkin's intention, he could have made Moorhead his central character. That's been his method in the past, to develop one character—Dick Gibson, Ben Flesh, Ellerbee—within and around whom the novel coheres. *The Magic Kingdom* has no central intelligence. Nor does it mingle dynamically opposed points of view. It's like an allegory without the substratum of meaning. It neither affirms nor denies life. It exploits, rather than represents, the horror of physical corruption. (pp. 681-82)

Why Elkin chose to make his dramatis personae English isn't clear, except that he delights in British argot, words like "cagmag" and "codswallop," and needs an excuse for his characters to speak it. Elkin's ear is amazing. His own voice, however, is distinctly American in rhythm and idiom, and the trans-Atlantic hybrid is more disorienting than enriching. The narrative voice has more personality than the people whose story it narrates. Instead of establishing the characters it upstages them.

Why Elkin chose to set most of the novel in Disney World is more obvious: "because something of what they did here was always a *little* slanted toward death." The spook-house rides, the monuments to the past—Main Street, U.S.A.; Liberty Square; Frontierland. Geriatrics come to Florida to die. Tomorrowland is a kind of hereafter.

> And how about those Seven Dwarfs? Yeah, how about them? Sneezy, Dopey, Grumpy, Happy, Sleepy, Bashful, and Doc. Cholers and pathologies. Wasn't there an analogue to be discovered between the dwarfs and these wise-guy kids?

Plenty of analogues, but they're too heavy-handed to be entertaining and too random to have much point. Each is an episode: the kids go to the Haunted Mansion, where little old Mudd-Gaddis panics; they visit the Epcot Center to examine a future they won't live to experience; they watch the Disney characters parade past, a kingdom as cartoonish as their own. The tortoise-paced narrative creeps along. It halts periodically for long digressions into the sexual lives of the adults. Colin Bible thinks about his homosexuality; Nedra Carp remembers her incestuous longing for her half-brother; Mary Cottle masturbates. Gradually sex comes to preoccupy the children, too. Rena, cystic fibrosis, falls in love with Benny, Gaucher's disease. Her desire stimulates the "great dollops of black congestion" that clot her chest. She asks Benny to hold her. She dies wallowing in a puddle of mucus, killed by "the squalls, blasts, and aerodynamics of passion, all the high winds and gale-force bluster of love."

It's not exactly tender, this climactic scene, but it's about as upbeat as *The Magic Kingdom* gets. Love is Elkin's *deus ex machina,* his surprise which wrenches the novel away from despair. Or tries to. But it's hard to feel anything by this point, hope or pity or irony, so numbing is the catalogue of sick jokes. I only felt relief that the freak show was finally over. (p. 682)

> *John Seabrook, "Freaks," in* The Nation, *New York, Vol. 240, No. 21, June 1, 1985, pp. 681-82.*

ROBERT COHEN

"I was no prodigy," Stanley Elkin warns in his introduction to [*Early Elkin*], the odd assortment—three stories, one critique-cum-story, one memoir—that make up the 1950's wing of "my little awful Elkin museum." But he would have us

take this book to heart, regardless, as a sort of pep talk on the virtues of resolve, patience and desire in the making of a writer. Indeed, in the long story, "**The Party**," it is difficult to see the wit or edgy tough-mindedness that would later distinguish such bravura performances as *The Dick Gibson Show* and *The Franchiser.* Instead we find ethnic sentimentality, clumsy flashbacks, portentous phrasings. Yet, even amid failures of technique and imagination, the Elkin sensibility struggles to its feet. . . . In my opinion, the only wholly successful piece—aside from the wise, funny memoir, "**Where I Read What I Read**"—is "**Fifty Dollars**," and it strikes me as an untypical effort, more somber and mannered than the mature work. Mr. Elkin, it appears, really *wasn't* a prodigy. But he was very good, and he got much, much better, and nothing he writes—or has written—should escape our notice.

> *Robert Cohen, in a review of "Early Elkin," in* The New York Times Book Review, *May 18, 1986, p. 24.*

RHODA KOENIG

Elkin's novel [*The Rabbi of Lud*] is the story of Jerry Goldkorn, a "pickup rabbi, God's little Hebrew stringer in New Jersey," who presides over the congregation of Lud—"not one of Judaism's plummier posts. It's hardly the Wailing Wall. Hell, it's hardly Passaic." What distinguishes the Luddites from the usual crowd is that they are all dead—Lud consists of a small shopping street and two vast cemeteries, whose inhabitants the rabbi inters with the usual uninformed oratory. It is the best, however, that he can expect. (pp. 88, 90)

I liked Shelley, his lubricious wife, who wants him to wear his tallith in bed ("It's the fringes, Jerry. They do something to me"), and his rebellious daughter. . . . But Elkin gives them hardly anything to do, except for two extravagantly insane sections that relate to nothing else in the novel: Jerry goes to Alaska and is saved from a plane crash by supernatural intervention, and his daughter meets the Virgin Mary in a graveyard. Both of these episodes are bizarre without being interesting; the novel, which begins with its roots in solid earth, suddenly takes off into space, flashing colored lights and making weird noises. (p. 90)

> *Rhoda Koenig, in a review of "The Rabbi of Lud," in* New York *Magazine, Vol. 20, No. 40, October 12, 1987, pp. 88, 90.*

CHRISTOPHER LEHMANN-HAUPT

Lud lies in the New Jersey flats, a town where Colonial Jews once chose to bury their dead and their ancestors have been following suit ever since. "The cemetery came first," writes Stanley Elkin in his new novel, *The Rabbi of Lud,* "and was out here on its own for a good many years like, oh, say, the Valley of the Kings in Egypt, but then somebody had the bright idea of bringing all death's service-related industries together under one roof," so Lud is a town of the dead, "funerary, sepulchral, thanatopsical."

The rabbi of Lud is Jerry Goldkorn, from Chicago. He had such a poor aptitude for Hebrew that his bar mitzvah haphtara, already the shortest of the year, had to be written out for him phonetically. . . .

Rabbi Goldkorn is happy enough with his calling, even if Lud is "theologically speaking . . . the sticks—ultima Thule God—

and I'm talking in my rabbi mode here—forsaken.'' He loves his wife, Shelley, who is turned on by his phylacteries. . . .

The only drawback to his life is that his daughter, Connie, can't bear living in Lud.

> I hate it here, Mama. I don't have any friends my own age. They're afraid to come. The place stinks of dead people. Anyway, it isn't as if he was a *regular* rabbi. All he does is bury people.

As always in his fiction, Stanley Elkin makes of his plot a stage to mount inspired gags, and on which to play his funky, bluesy language, whose comic effects depend on incongruous juxtapositions of the trivial and the grandiose, of the technical and the idiomatic, of Yiddish and the American vernacular.

When his wife and daughter demand that he take them away from Lud, he recalls the last time he left home, a time when he accepted a position as rabbi of the Alaska pipeline, traveled north, and discovered the principle and practice of the potlatch, the ceremonial festival at which gifts are bestowed on the guests and property is destroyed by its owner in a show of wealth which the guests later try to surpass. . . .

When Rabbi Goldkorn's unhappy experience in Alaska prompts him to resist leaving Lud, Connie decides to embarrass him by going to the local courthouse and swearing out a deposition in which she describes her experiences in Lud's graveyards with the "Holy Mother," who came to her on snowy days, taught her to harrow "the poor lost souls of the Jewish dead," learned Hebrew from her by reading gravestones, and introduced her to St. Myra Weiss, "the patron saint of kids whose dads get transferred and have to relocate in a different city."

Such gigs and gags can be hilarious. But as always in Mr. Elkin's fiction, the question remains. Do they advance the plot, or does the plot advance them? The answer in this latest book appears to be the latter. Anything for a laugh. Still, one must take into account Mr. Elkin's essentially static view of life. His heroes are always obsessed and go to comic extremes in the service of their obsessions. . . .

But they never seem to get anywhere. They go round and round making jokes and trailing clouds of gloriously goofy language. Yet they always seem to end where they started, Dick Gibson still disk-jockeying in *The Dick Gibson Show*, Jerry Goldkorn still stuck in Lud.

This is hard on a novelist, and Mr. Elkin acknowledged as much in an interview several years ago when he observed of his work, "What I like best about it, I suppose, are the sentences. What I like least about it is my guess that probably no one is ever moved by it."

Well, it's hard to be moved by characters who are stuck. But one has to love the sentences. The stuckness of the characters and the eloquence of their language come together at the end of *The Rabbi of Lud*. Rabbi Goldkorn is eulogizing a dead woman he has loved, but he keeps sliding off the subject and confessing his own shortcomings. "What was I up to," he wonders, "the offshore yeshiva butcher with the tiny haphtarah passage? What was I up to with my spilt-milk penitentials and public-domain regrets and all my deplored, gnashed teeth, learned-my-lessons?"

So he tries to change the mood by reciting some special blessings he'd learned in yeshiva.

> I offered the broches you say when you see a rainbow, when you eat ripe fruit, when you hear good news,

when you laugh out loud, when you buy new clothes, when you kiss a woman, when you repair an appliance, when you touch a giant, when you smell sweet wood.

With these words, *The Rabbi of Lud* ends. Like Mr. Elkin himself, Rabbi Goldkorn is stuck and running on. But the unresolved chords have a not unpleasant bittersweetness to them. They fade in a minor key, but they suggest what is unusual, even memorable, about Stanley Elkin's music.

> *Christopher Lehmann-Haupt, in a review of "The Rabbi of Lud," in* The New York Times, *October 29, 1987, p. C29.*

WILLIAM PRITCHARD

In *The Rabbi of Lud,* Jerry Goldkorn, married to Shelley and the father of Connie, addresses us loudly and at length, speaking passionately, humorously and hopelessly of his lordship (his Lud-ship, one might say) over the sizable stretch of New Jersey flats—with Ridgewood only 12 miles away—that is the burial ground of his dead congregation (they never congregated when alive). Some centuries previous, their ancestors, led by the "founding Jew," crossed the Hudson and discovered Lud—"the vast, once and future compound of departed Jews to come."

As the presider over their last rites, Jerry Goldkorn is apologetic for not sounding like the real thing, being instead only "just this pickup rabbi, God's little Hebrew stringer in New Jersey." Yet even though "our Christian friends" have all the good music (whereas the Jews have only "Bei Mir Bist Du Schön"), there is something compelling about being responsible for burial operations at Lud, one of "those perfectly logical closed systems outside connection." As the rabbi puts it—and in Mr. Elkin's liveliest kind of idiomatic confidence—"No school board, no health department, no tax collector, no department of streets. We're this company town. (There's no company.) We're this ghost town. (No ghosts either, but lots of potential.)"

In the novel's first third, our rabbi mainly does his thing, sounding off (while continually deprecating or justifying his rabbilike tone) in what aspires to be an entertaining line of talk—as, for example, how "that Lord-of-Kit-and-Kaboodle" who "set Eve up" and was "never any equal opportunity Creator" anyway, "disdains women": "He doesn't like the way they smell . . . that's why He gave them periods in the first place and relented only after He invented hot flashes and then gave them those intead." . . .

Most surely this is snappy writing, but the jokes—good or not so good considering where one stands—are not unknown to the stand-up, hard-working young comic doing his TV Evening at the Improv. And in the "perfectly logical closed systems outside connection" developed in the novel's early chapters, it feels as if such snappiness might well go on endlessly. There is no other act in town—at least in North Jersey.

Which is not to say that other characters don't appear on stage for their routines, some of them funny and expert. There are Jerry's employers, the funeral directors Tober and Shull, who have been known to threaten the rabbi with what may happen if the real estate business falls off: "If this cemetery goes belly up you could finish your career in some condo on the Palisades! You could be The Bingo Rabbi, the Theater Party Rabbi." Tober especially needs to husband his resources, since his son

Edward has been blind since birth—and only in Mr. Elkin's world could mere blindness not be a sufficient cross for a character to bear.

Edward has been born not only blind but without "a labyrinthine sense," so that—equipped with perfect pitch, a great sense of smell and a good heart—he yet lacks any sense of direction: "He could not tell left from right, up from down, or even in from out. There he was, a loose cannon on the deck, apparently without the gift of gravity, unfixed as an astronaut. Thrown into a pool, or fallen into the sea, he would as likely swim to the bottom as to the top." This is brilliant, ruthless writing, and it continues as Mr. Elkin warms to the exhilarating and nasty task of delineating Edward's errant instincts and movements: "He forced both feet into the same pants leg, blew his ear in his handkerchief and wore his hat rakishly on his shoulder." . . .

One of the few bits of plot interest in **The Rabbi of Lud** attaches to the hero's daughter, Connie, who quite understandably finds something oppressive about living in this company town with no company ("Daddy, our back yard is a *cemetery!*") and yearns to leave Lud. This propels the rabbi into remembering the time, 10 years previously, when he departed for a year to be the Chief Rabbi of the Alaska Pipeline, caring for the spiritual needs of Jewish construction workers in Anchorage and environs.

The second third of the novel consists of this flashback, an elaborate tall tale without, in my judgment, much point. The concluding section, in which we return to the rabbi's present trials at Lud, is also its weakest, though containing a nice insert on how a young woman got to be "St. Myra Weiss"—"the patron saint of kids whose dads get transferred and have to relocate in a different city." But there is also some intolerable dialogue involving Mrs. Goldkorn's presumably comic use of the diminutive: "'Later-le.' 'Later-le's too late. Right-e-le now.' 'Leave-e-le-now?' 'Talk-e-le-now, ask-e-le questions afterward.'" The novel ends happily, with the rabbi reciting "some special blessings I'd learned in yeshiva" ("broches you say when you see a rainbow, when you eat ripe fruit, when you hear good news"). Blessings such as these, regarded unironically by both the rabbi and his author, strike a surprisingly sweet, if not saccharine, note untypical of Mr. Elkin's usual tone.

Reading **The Rabbi of Lud** with recent novels by Saul Bellow and Philip Roth in mind, one is aware of how little connection, by comparison, the "perfectly logical closed systems" of Mr. Elkin's operation have with contemporary life, politics, culture. Just as one of his characters lacks the labyrinthine sense, so the writer's relative lack of interest in moving deftly in these various directions makes for an oddly airless fictional world. Yet within his relatively narrow range of reference and concerns, Mr. Elkin has in the past performed memorably, while leaving us with the sense of something more than a man performing. In stories from **Criers and Kibitzers, Kibitzers and Criers** (1966), such as "**I Look Out for Ed Wolfe**," "**In the Alley**" and ["**Criers and Kibitzers, Kibitzers and Criers**"]; or in the three linked parts of **The Living End** (1979), in which are detailed the sufferings of God-cursed Ellerbee, Mr. Elkin managed to be both very funny and truly disturbing. But these were short fictions that knew when to stop when their point was made. As a novelist, his tendency is to run on (as novelists often do) and the effect is dilution, not concentration. So the new book as a whole is less amusing and pointed than some of its individual parts.

William Pritchard, "Thank God for Rashes and Toothaches," in The New York Times Book Review, *November 8, 1987, p. 12.*

MAURICE CHARNEY

Stanley Elkin defines himself "as a writer who happens to be Jewish, happens to be American, and happens to be a writer." This is charmingly disingenuous, if not actually a way of thumbing one's nose at all critical affiliations. Elkin has emphatically separated himself from the ghetto of Jewish-American (and Jewish-Canadian) writers, all comic and all black humorists: Roth, Richler, Heller, Bruce Jay Friedman, and others. Yet there is a catch to his separation: "I don't identify myself with Jewish writers. However, you know, I resent it if I see an anthology with Jewish writers, and I'm not included." Similarly, he is repelled by the term "black humor," which he claims was invented by *Time* magazine, but his resistance has definite limits: "I resent the term 'Black Humor' tremendously. I hate that term. I don't know what it means. Yet if there is an anthology of Black Humorists I resent it if I'm not included in the anthology." It is obvious that Elkin is cultivating paradox. The two issues, Elkin's Jewishness and Elkin's black humor, are intertwined, because to be a Jewish writer almost necessarily implies that you will work by means of an ironic self-consciousness that is essentially comic. Insofar as the Jewish writer makes claims upon us for his Jewishness, he also casts himself in the role of the alienated observer of a scene to which he only partly belongs. He looks at American or Canadian life from the outside, with comic detachment and ironic indulgence. From this perspective everything is absurd and grotesque almost by definition.

In *Bright Book of Life,* Alfred Kazin shows contemporary Jewish writers one way to resolve the dilemma of their relation to their own Jewish background. The concept of "constructed folklore" applies with special force to Elkin's Jewish black humor:

> Jewishness as the novelist's material (which can be quite different from the individual material of Jews writing fiction) is constructed folklore. It is usually comic, or at least humorous; the characters are always ready to tell a joke on themselves. With their bizarre names, their accents, *their* language, they are jokes on themselves. And so they become "Jewish" material, which expresses not the predicament of the individual who knows himself to be an exception, but a piece of the folk, of "Jewishness" as a style of life and a point of view.

If Jewishness is a style of life and a point of view, we don't need to insist on historical, liturgical, or ritualistic detail, or authenticate the materials the writer of fiction is drawing from his own "Jewish" experience. In Kazin's telling phrase, the folklore is not natural and spontaneous but artful and constructed. It is a fiction of Jewishness—the quality of being Jewish in America, the sense of a Jewish character with a gamut of defined traits, a special language and syntax that is neither Yiddish nor Standard English—rather than an accurate report on Jewish life. And the charm of "constructed folklore" is that the characters don't have to have Jewish names or be specifically identified as Jews. (pp. 178-79)

In the broader definition of Jewish black humor as "constructed folklore," Elkin's latest novel, *George Mills* (1982), an historical extravaganza of the unheroic ordinary man, is very Jewish in feeling even though most of the characters are clearly not Jewish. The one thoroughly Jewish character, Moses Magaziner (later in the guise of the merchant, Guzo Sanbanna), the unlikely British Ambassador to the Court of Mahmad II, is really a grotesque parody of a Jew, including an absurdly Yiddish, Bronx peddler's accent. We don't really need Magaziner to authenticate the Jewishness of the novel. In fact, his presence is rather jarring and intrusive.

Elkin's Jews tend to be grotesquely clownish figures, as if the need to declare one's Jewish identity were in itself an act of alienation from American middle-class values. Even among other Jews, the Jew who insists on his Jewishness tends to be a bizarre, comic-strip character, more a caricature than a rounded human being. There is a curious passage in the tragicomic story, **"The Condominium,"** in which Preminger, the *schlemiel*-like hero, feels with acute anxiety his separateness from the tightly organized Jewish community of his friends and neighbors in the apartment complex. He feels tentative, uncertain, disestablished, a stand-in for his father:

> "I've lived provisionally here," he said. "Like someone under military government, martial law, an occupied life. This isn't going as I meant it to. I'm a stranger—that's something of what I'm driving at. My life is a little like being in a foreign country. There's displaced person in me. I feel—listen—I feel— *Jewish*. I mean even here, among Jews, where everyone's Jewish, I feel Jewish."

To feel Jewish even among Jews is one of the crisis signs of Preminger's nervous breakdown that eventually leads him to jump off his balcony.

Elkin's first published novel, *Boswell: A Modern Comedy* (1964), in which the hero, like Johnson's Boswell, lives by proxy in the lives of acknowledged celebrities, curiously anticipates the chameleon-like comic passivity of Woody Allen's movie, *Zelig*. In this novel the Nobel Prize-winning anthropologist, Morty Perlmutter (who will reappear later in **"Perlmutter at the East Pole,"** a story in *Criers and Kibitzers, Kibitzers and Criers*) defines the Jewish God for Boswell in hippy terms:

> "Now, though I was a Communist in those days I believed in God. The God I believed in was a Jewish-Brahmin-Zen Buddhist mystic who wore a *yarmulke* and squatted in a room filled with art treasures, telling his beads. You prayed to this God and he turned a deaf ear. He was supposed to, you understand. Acceptance of fucking suffering was what he taught. He bled in four colors over the art treasures and posed crazy riddles. He answered all questions with questions. Revelation was when he said, 'The meaning of life is as follows,' and he'd pick his nose with his little finger. Profound? Bullcrap, my young friends who still believe in such a God, a tongue-tied God who is not so much indifferent as bewildered by life."

The God who picks his nose, answers questions with questions, and is bewildered by life is Elkin's grotesque, Old Testament Jehovah, who still maintains an authority he cannot himself understand. The leering, insatiable Perlmutter, all-wise and all-foolish, ritual clown and shaman, trickster and seer, is himself like the obscene and terrifying gods in Bellow's novel, *Henderson the Rain King*.

Religious awe and reverence are linked in Elkin's mind with vaudeville. . . . In *The Franchiser* (1976), a panegyric of American business, Ben Flesh's godfather is a theatrical costumer for the great Broadway musicals. The mythical capital in the novel derives from profits made in the theater, and Ben con-

ceives his franchises as stage sets for the American dream. Although Ben Flesh is only partially Jewish in origin, his turgid and tawdry dreams of America have the peculiar grandiosity of a first-generation immigrant. He is so archetypically and histrionically American that, by the very magnitude of his effort to belong, he is immediately alienated. Beginning with the hundreds of used color television sets that Ben buys as distressed merchandise for his franchise motel, the Travel Inn in Ringgold, Georgia, everything that Ben touches is overwrought and unreal. This endows *The Franchiser* with a peculiarly hallucinatory and theatrical quality.

Although Elkin resists being categorized as a Jewish-American writer, the experience of his novels and stories is peculiarly Jewish. He is, willy nilly, a Jewish black humorist, if not by conscious design then by an inevitable expression of point of view. In other words, aside from the sardonic, mocking, unstable, and treacherous world of his fictions, there is no alternative reality, and we see the existential absurdity of modern man in Elkin as essentially a "Jewish" condition. Suffering is never heroic but always trivialized; tragedy is rendered in its black comedy equivalent. Since we see the fictions through the author's consciousness, specific points of Jewish doctrine, ritual, speech, and identity hardly matter. . . . Yet Elkin creates a world that is convincingly Jewish, just as Faulkner's Yoknapatawpha County is convincingly southern. It is Jewish in its spontaneous assumptions, its feeling that triumph is inexplicably mixed with catastrophe, its manic urge for the small man, through cunning, slyness, and whimsy, to conquer the world. Its protagonists speak with prophetic fervor tinged with neurotic insufficiency. The large effects always fall short and the leading characters always turn out to be con men and vaudevillians. The pervasive irony undercuts pretension in favor of flights of fancy, arrant self-aggrandizement, and blatant wish fulfillment.

One large division in Elkin's world is that between criers and kibitzers, as in the title story of his first collection of short fiction, *Criers and Kibitzers, Kibitzers and Criers* (1965). All of reality seems to be divided between criers and kibitzers, as if there were no place for any other type of Jew. (pp. 180-82)

The criers are the *kvetchers* and *schreiers,* the professional complainers who take pleasure from telling you how bad it is and how much worse it could have been. This is not masochism at all, but a kind of *Schadenfreude* and gallows humor because the *kvetchers* compete with each other in negative hyperboles of disaster. One *schreier*'s troubles are intended to top the *tsuris* that has just been related, so that the atmosphere is always that of a contest to see who is the biggest and most thoroughly cast-down victim of God's injustice. . . .

The kibitzers are in symbiotic relation to the criers; one could not exist without the other. A kibitzer is an ironic commentator, a non-participant, who typically observes card games, checkers, and chess and offers free and unsought advice about the card you should have played or the piece you ought to have moved. The kibitzer is always very knowing about why you lost. In his own eyes, the kibitzer is always a being of superior intelligence and discernment, but cold and detached. He is the archetypal artist/observer, always ready with a comment and a wry joke (or, in the noun form, a kibitz). (p. 183)

Elkin loves freaks and misfits. Virtually all the characters in *Criers and Kibitzers, Kibitzers and Criers* are maladapted in one way or another; that is the source of both their vitality and their humor. Elkin has expressed great disdain for his short stories, some of which he has never bothered to collect in volume form. It is as if the long novel is a much better medium for hyperbole and extravagance. Thus in **The Franchiser,** which may be Elkin's black humor masterpiece—it is certainly his most eloquent fiction—all eighteen twins and triplets of the Finsberg clan are freaks, genetically damaged, "Human lemons, Detroit could recall them":

> LaVerne's organs lined the side of her body, her liver and lungs and kidneys outside her rib cage. Ethel's heart was in her right breast. Cole had a tendency to suffer from the same disorders as plants and had a premonition that he would be killed by Dutch elm blight.

All the twins and triplets suddenly start dying one after the other from their bizarre inheritance. By cultivating such outrageously surrealistic detail, Elkin cuts off our human responses and prefers instead to disorient us with a curious mixture of tragic and comic materials. As audience, we are not allowed to follow through with our warm and sticky human responses. Both the crying and the kibitzing take the form of a stage performance, preferably the sort of heavily costumed musical on which the Finsberg fortune was made in **The Franchiser.** Life may resemble *Oklahoma,* but the converse of this comforting proposition is emphatically untrue.

The archetypal Jewish character in Elkin is the salesman. It is not surprising that the author's own father was a salesman, whom he remembers with affection and comic adulation:

> He sold costume jewelry, and I went with him once on one of his trips through the Midwest. . . . I was with him in small Indiana towns were he would take the jewelry out of the telescopes, which are salesmen's cases, and actually put the earrings on his ears, the bracelets around his wrists, and the necklaces about his throat. This wasn't drag, but the prose passionate and stage business of his spiel. The man believed in costume jewelry, in rhinestones and beads, and sang junk jewelry's meteorological condition—its Fall line and Spring.

This is not *Death of a Salesman,* but more like *The Salesman Unbound* and *Paradise Regained.* The frantic, obsessive, and manic tone is entirely in keeping with Elkin's fiction, and Elkin admits that his father is the model for Feldman's father in his second novel, **A Bad Man** (1967), and even more so of Feldman himself, the ironic "bad man" of the title, society's scapegoat Jew, who is imprisoned and eventually martyred. It is hard to know what Elkin means when he says: "There is little autobiography in my work." He obviously means this in the literal sense that his characters are distanced from his life, but still they are very close. Elkin's father seems also to be the model for Ben Flesh, the super salesman and spieler in **The Franchiser,** despite Elkin's disclaimers that Ben Flesh is not even fully Jewish. What difference could that detail make? He is the Word made Flesh.

In **A Bad Man,** Feldman is a very comfortable department store owner and commercial tycoon before he becomes a convict, but his father is the archetype of the Jewish peddler, a parody of the Yankee peddler and his covered wagon—a romantic image also echoed in Miller's *Death of a Salesman.* His selling is a dionysiac frenzy of wild excess that has little to do with commercial activity. Feldman's father is more like a revivalist preacher than a business man. His language is hyperbolical and apocalyptic. Selling is an end in itself. . . . (pp. 184-86)

What finally lands Feldman in jail in **A Bad Man** are the clandestine activities of his department store basement, where Feldman the confidence man sells advice: drugs, abortions, paramilitary equipment. Selling is power: "It hadn't ever been profit that had driven him, but the idea of the sale itself, his way of bearing down on the world." In this formulation the salesman is the existentialist hero, and selling is a way of confronting reality. Thus Feldman's father seeks out the difficulties of selling sleazy merchandise and "neo-junk" because only this kind of salesmanship will testify to his art: "'Sell seconds,' he'd say, 'irregulars. Sell damaged and smoke-stained and fire-torn things. Sell the marred and impaired, the defective and soiled." As the elder Feldman scrutinizes ladies' underwear, the young Feldman gets a lesson he will never forget about the ethics and rhetoric of merchandising:

> He would pick up a pair of ladies' panties from the lingerie counter. "Look, look at the craftsmanship," he'd say distastefully, plunging his big hand inside and splaying his fingers in the silky seat, "the crotchmanship." He'd snap the elastic. "No sag, no give," he'd say to the startled salesgirl. "Give me give, the second-rate. Schlock, give me. They're doing some wonderful things in Japan."
>
> "*Because,*" he'd say, explaining, "where's the contest in sound merchandise? You sell a sound piece of merchandise, what's the big deal?"

The salesman is the artist of the beautiful, the Platonic idea of the kibitzer, who, through his spiel, wants to bear down on the world. To sell schlock is a way of asserting your power and declaring your freedom from the material world. (pp. 186-87)

If selling is a form of superiority, like kibitzing, it is also a vehicle for acting out scenarios with all of their grand rhetoric and perfect timing. The salesman is a performer, and selling is a proof that you are alive. (p. 187)

For a contemporary Jewish novelist, Elkin is surprisingly short on fictional families. His novels and stories are dominated by lonely, powerful, obsessed, brooding males always seeking masculine goals that elude their grasp. Jewish macho is not primarily sexual, but it seeks power, money, status, and recognition by the world. Women play a minor role in Elkin. They are alternatively either nurturant or sex objects, but they never really impinge on the male world. Elkin's males are often unmarried or widowed—Boswell, Dick Gibson, Flesh, the Bailbondsman—and, because of their constant travel, they have no fixed abode (or they live, by preference, in hotel rooms). They seem to incarnate the Wandering Jew, who is also cunning, resourceful, and fully able to thrive without women or family. Wives, when they exist, like Mrs. Feldman in **A Bad Man** or Mrs. Ellerbee in **The Living End,** are usually colorlesss and overweight housewives who are bent on the destruction of their mates. In **"The Condominium,"** both the son and his recently deceased father suffer from an infuriatingly prissy and legalistic relation (orchestrated by long letters) with their seductive neighbor, Evelyn. The men wait for erotic trysts that will never occur.

Sex in Elkin tends to be an unsatisfactory product of lust, with a strongly voyeuristic element. It is tawdry, quick, and furtive. The women inspire a prurience they cannot possibly satisfy; Elkin confesses that he is "incapable of writing about a love affair." This is a strange admission for a novelist to make. Like Alexander Portnoy, impotent in Israel in Roth's *Portnoy's Complaint,* Elkin's Jewish heroes seem to need the degradation of the sex object that Freud speaks of in his essay, "The Most

Prevalent Form of Degradation in Erotic Life.'' The classic Jewish mother type, like Mrs. Portnoy, raises fears of incest that are too powerful to overcome. (pp. 187-88)

Is there a distinctive style for Jewish black humor? Writers on Jewish themes have strongly emphasized the central voice of the *schlemiel*. The downtrodden *schlemiel*, a victim of awkwardness and bad luck (*schlimazel*), establishes a perspective from which we see the world. He is the little man with grandiose visions, who is able, through ironic and defensive humor, to transcend his metaphysical condition. Elkin's *schlemiel* protagonists tend to be eloquent buffoons and tricksters who tease the most arcane reality to yield up its secrets.

Elkin avoids the heavily Yiddishized diction and syntax of *Portnoy's Complaint;* the Yiddish of Moses Magaziner in *George Mills* is self-consciously vaudeville Yiddish, a ridiculous parody of the immigrant Jew. There are relatively few Yiddish expressions in Elkin, yet his voice and tone seem distinctively Jewish—literary Jewish in the sense of "constructed folklore"—in three ways: his style is grotesque, exhibitionistic, and obsessive. Since style expresses a unique and personal organization of experience, these three characteristics—there are obviously many more—define Elkin's special way of coming to grips with the world, his assumptions, his metaphysics, and his own idiosyncratic rhetoric. Why are these characteristics especially Jewish? I think the grotesque, the exhibitionistic, and the obsessive are all part of the defensive persona of the Jewish humorist, clown, or stand-up comedian. They all represent stylistic ways of depersonalizing a hostile reality and making it more detached and dream-like. We are removed from the sphere of everyday reality and the harsh vulnerabilities of simple moral judgments. Everything is cloaked in self-conscious irony.

All black humor is grotesque, so we begin with the most general quality. The vision is deliberately distorted, blurred in some perspectives and super-clarified in others, so that certain details we had not noticed (or could not possibly have noticed) are brought into prominence. A dream-like if not actually hallucinatory feeling is created in the spectator. In *The Franchiser,* Ben Flesh throws a final, apocalyptic party for his failing Fred Astaire franchise. His wild and ranting oration is grotesque in most of the black-humor senses of the term, because Ben takes his advertising clichés literally, and he justifies and rationalizes the American Dream with crazy fervor. The tone is hysterically inappropriate for a bankrupt enterprise and for a party in which the guests have been dragooned off the streets. They are a ragged and joyless crew.

A woman in her mid-fifties dancing with a golden-ager is carrying her shopping-bag on the dance floor [and drops a bottle of ketchup]. . . . This is a typical Elkin grotesque because it mixes so easily the sleazy and the grandiose, the tawdry details of the ketchup and the high-flown conceit of the dance writing itself out on the floor in the ketchup alphabet. Ben focuses on things rather than people—the flesh rather than the spirit—the people only the bearers of the symbolic paraphernalia of civilization. Ben is the prophet exhorting the masses and also at the time selling dance lessons in a defunct studio. Elkin specializes in grand soliloquies which don't involve any conversation. There is a total lack of communication between Ben and the dancers. He is speaking for his own edification and amusement.

Like Elkin's use of the grotesque, he employs the exhibitionistic style for purposes of bravado and display. His enormous

catalogues are a kind of Whitmanizing, but utterly unheroic and deflationary. What is most flamboyantly displayed is the flotsam and jetsam of ordinary life, dreck, crap, detritus, rejects, discards. As Philip Stevick notes in his essay, "Prolegomena to the Study of Fictional *Dreck,*" "the junk of current fiction represents a new way of giving fictional specificity to a meaningless quality of life," which is balanced against "a sense of wit and play that makes that meaningless quality bearable and often very funny." In Elkin's Jewish context the fictional dreck defies the rational order and middle-class purpose and trimness of American life. (pp. 189-91)

Elkin's vision is so firmly anchored in the material world that it seems much more surreal than real, by the familiar optical illusion by which intense concentration on a material object causes that object to disappear as such and to disintegrate into new and startling combinations of its qualities. Everything is in excess, overflowing, a cornucopia, as if the characters are trying to stay alive by their ability to see and name the physical world. It is a kind of word magic, what Maurice Samuel has called "the humor of verbal retrieval, the word triumphant over the situation." . . . (p. 191)

Elkin's obsessiveness has been much noted both by himself (in interview) and by critics. He says flatly that "fiction is about obsession," and that "most of the characters I write about are obsessed by death." This is undoubtedly true, but it is too large a generalization to do justice to the obsessiveness of Elkin's characters. At their best, they are wonderfully energized, concentrated, self-directed on some single idea or vision. They illustrate, with great appropriateness, Bergson's theories of comedy: his ideas of professional deformation, mechanization, and comic inelasticity. Elkin's characters possess a form of manic monomania, which expresses itself in a highly obsessive language of jargon, shoptalk, and professional acting-out.

Elkin singles out **"The Bailbondsman"** as his favorite story and its protagonist, Alexander Main, as his most representative character. Without elaborating on the autobiographical assumptions, Elkin says: "I admire him for his rhetoric. I, myself, am closer to Main than any other character." Why should this be so? Main has a mad obsession with his job. Outside of being a bailbondsman in the world of courts and prisons, Main has no other identity, and he has inflamed dreams in the style of *Raiders of the Lost Ark* of pyramid thieves and mummy despoilers for whom he offers bail in unimaginable sums. He is Alexander Main, the Phoenician, the Ba'albondsman. Elkin has always been fascinated by obsessive excess and has felt only boredom for well-rounded and versatile human beings. The Bailbondsman has a Dickensian fervor and eccentricity, like some legal fiction dropped out of *Bleak House.* . . . The bailbondsman has the salesman's obsessive self-love for his stock, and is in fact a kind of salesman. He is a freedom merchant. He is in love with legal paper and the power this gives him to control human destiny. Like many of Elkin's protagonists, he is a spieler and charlatan as well as a man of the highest probity. He feels a mad and unpredictable compassion for human suffering and weakness in all of its sordid manifestations.

In his avalanche of metaphors and figurative language, Alexander Main is also intensely literal. He is talking about the physical contract itself that constitutes the bail bond:

> No, I'm talking the *look* of the instrument, texture, watermark, the silk flourish of the bright ribbon, the legend perfected centuries . . . , the beautiful for-

mulas simple as pie, old-fashioned quid pro quo like a recipe in the family generations. My conditions classic and my terms terminal. Listen, I haven't much law . . . but am as at home in replevin, debenture and gage as someone on his own toilet seat with the door closed and the house empty. I have mainpernor, bottomry, caution and hypothecation the way others might have a second language. I have always lived by *casus foederis;* do the same and we'll never tangle assholes.

The language here is both effortless and endless, and it comfortably mixes technical jargon with street slang. Elkin is wonderfully cozy with his puns, wordplay, and self-conscious verbalizing. This is the kind of tumescent rhetoric that has no relation at all to real life. It creates its own obsessively believable world.

I began by trying to define Stanley Elkin, against his own vociferous objections, as a Jewish black humorist. Yet I must conclude that if Elkin is indeed a Jewish black humorist, he is unlike any other Jewish black humorist of our era. He certainly avoids any sentimental identifications with Jewish char-

acters, and most of his protagonists are not specifically Jewish at all. I have invoked Kazin's concept of "constructed folklore" to explain Elkin's Jewishness, as if it were not a matter of conscious intent and as if there were no need to inject Jewishness into one's fictions. In other words, Elkin's imaginative evocation is Jewish even if it is not neatly labeled in the Jewish Ghetto Exhibit. From a stylistic perspective, Elkin writes with an extravagance, a mingling of the trivial and the grandiose, and ironic undercutting of all pretension and mindless optimism that does not need Yiddish diction to make it feel Jewish. (pp. 192-94)

No one can accuse Stanley Elkin of being bland. In the aggressive incisiveness of his Jewish black humor, he seems to be saying not that the world is a good place to live in, but that the only true man is the wise fool, and that comic acceptance and exaltation can come only through suffering. (p. 195)

Maurice Charney, "Stanley Elkin and Jewish Black Humor," in Jewish Wry: Essays on Jewish Humor, *edited by Sarah Blacher Cohen, Indiana University Press, 1987, pp. 178-95.*

Kenneth (Flexner) Fearing

1902-1961

(Also wrote with Donald Friede and H. Bedford James under joint pseudonym of Donald F. Bedford) American poet and novelist.

Best known for the psychological suspense novel *The Big Clock,* Fearing wrote poetry and fiction in which he attacked the sterile, dehumanized conditions of modern urban society. Fearing's verse depicts the plight of the common individual in times of economic depression and technological advancement, expressing through Marxist tenets his desire for a rebirth and celebration of humanism. His novels feature the concise style of "hard-boiled" detective fiction originated by Raymond Chandler and Dashiell Hammett while using multiple first-person narrators and offering critiques of twentieth-century civilization.

Fearing began his literary career as a poet. His first collection of verse, *Angel Arms* (1929), contains representations of people whose individualism is stifled by the mechanisms of society. In this volume, as in such later works as *Poems* (1935), *Dead Reckoning* (1938), *Afternoon of a Pawnbroker and Other Poems* (1943), and *Stranger at Coney Island and Other Poems* (1948), Fearing utilized repetition, satire, cataloguing, parallel structure, long, cadenced lines, rhetorical questions, and ironic employment of the clichés and jargon of advertising, radio, films, and tabloids to depict the fate of the urban working-class citizen in a callous modern world. Critics frequently compared Fearing's verse to that of Walt Whitman and Carl Sandburg for its democratic perspective, celebration of the common person, and reproduction of colloquial American speech. In a review of *New and Selected Poems* (1956), Judson Jerome commented: "As a bard, as a cataloguer of our times, as one who demonstrates, documents, the *feeling* of conformity and spiritual deadness, [Fearing] is a remarkable and individual poet."

In his first novel, *The Hospital* (1939), Fearing exposes the corruptions of a large medical facility, using the institution as a metaphor for society in general. The title character of *Clark Gifford's Body* (1942) leads a revolution in a mythical future nation by raiding a radio station. Although Gifford is captured during the attack and later executed, the rebellion succeeds. Critics lauded the novel as a convincing portrait of what could happen in the United States after World War II. *The Big Clock* (1946), which has twice been adapted for film, most recently as *No Way Out,* is widely considered a classic of thriller fiction. In this novel, publishing magnate Earl Janoth kills his mistress after an argument and is seen leaving the premises by an unidentified passerby. Janoth assigns George Stroud, editor of his *Crimeways* magazine, to capture and dispose of the witness. What Stroud immediately realizes, however, is that the unknown witness is Stroud himself. Throughout the story, Fearing alludes to The Big Clock, a symbol not only for the predicament of Stroud, for whom time must run out, but for the mortality of all humankind. In *Loneliest Girl in the World* (1951), Fearing warns against the dangers that increasingly sophisticated machines pose to humanity. *The Generous Heart* (1954) and *The Crozart Story* (1960) respectively portray duplicitous activities of a charitable organization and the public relations profession.

(See also *Contemporary Authors,* Vols. 93-96 and *Dictionary of Literary Biography,* Vol. 9.)

EDA LOU WALTON

Kenneth Fearing is a poet of the city who has no sentimental longings after meadow or barn. He has gone to school to both Sandburg and John Weaver. From the former he caught the trick of repetitive parallelism as basis for free-verse rhythm and from the latter, something of the "American" language. His lyrics and dramatic studies [in *Angel Arms*] are of street characters. His desire is to indicate the intensity and poetry which these very dulled minds may be capable of. Although "none of their faces are cooked enough" (which is, I think, a perfect phrase), these characters are capable of their own worship of a flashing jazz beauty. They know their own yearnings and contemplate life and death as breakfast with coffee, and as no breakfast with coffee. The volume is alive and democratic in outlook.

Eda Lou Walton, "Dollar Poetry," in The Nation, *New York, Vol. CXXIX, No. 3339, July 3, 1929, p. 22.*

EDWARD DAHLBERG

The evolution of the author of *Angel Arms* is amazing, and his place in American Literature is not as easy to define as a glance at [*Poems*] would immediately suggest. So close to America, he is actually more in the tradition of the French Symbolists. There is very much in his life, temperament and talents that recall Tristan Corbière. His fantastic patterns of slang and speech, "reasoned derangement of all the senses," his gargoylish diableries, are those of a Tristan Corbière, torn out of context and place, but a Corbière with Marxian insights.

Angel Arms was a slender but gifted volume of lean ironies, acid portraits of Woolworth shopgirls and New Yorkese cadences of doggerel lives. In his *Poems,* Kenneth Fearing has succeeded in inditing the sleazy cinema dreams, the five and dime loves and frustrations, the mystery pulp heroism and furnished-room microcosm of the pulverized petty bourgeois. And this he has done with a novelist's technic; for besides being poems they are, in effect, short novels, with all the day-to-day thickness of incident, smell, dust, walls of the French nouvelles.

The poems have also the narrative development of the novel: at the beginning, there are close-ups of the bought-magistrates, the disincarnated radio voice, the swivel-chair magnates, heard in private monologue and seen in "unrehearsed acts." The theme unscrolls and the "bargain heroes" stalk across the screen: the Will Hays, the Gene Tunneys, the Al Capones—and "the ectoplasm" of the "profitable smile hovers inescapably everywhere about us."

The poet interweaves comments done with a news reel eye, but with inexorable, Marxist interpretations: "All winter she came there begging for milk. So we had the shacks along the river destroyed by police." "The child was nursed on Government bonds. Cut its teeth on a hand grenade. Grew fat on shrapnel . . . Laughed at the bayonet through its heart." Here is the entire cycle of life and death today; and here are lines from a deeply imagined poem which make a perfect slogan.

Kenneth Fearing's irony is very special, unique in the history of American poetry. Were it not freighted with pity and a gnarled, pulsating tenderness it would be a leer. But here is one of the most perfect examples of satire in literature in its truest light, that is, in its most tragic hue. It is as if Satire had ironically disrobed herself.

His names, symbols, Beatrice Fairfax, Jesse James, Aimee Semple McPherson, selected with uniform intention, are, to make use of the poet's own words, Rialto Equations. Thus, the apostrophe to Beatrice Fairfax becomes clear: she is a reversed dantean Beatrice in a Paramount moving picture *Vita Nuova*. And this is as near to Rimbaud's hell as any mortal would care to approach. Behind these equations, these "reasoned derangements," is satire turned up side down, that is, horror and revulsion. Underneath the "death-ray smile," anguish and torture. The reader must reverse every ironic comment and title to uncover the true intention.

The poet's outlook, which in *Angel Arms* was like an elliptical recollection of the laughing gas of rodents in a dismembered dream, becomes something very positive in the *Poems*. Here the intuitions and picture are an accusation and a foreshadowing

of the doom of the whole capitalistic society: "Maggots and darkness will attend the alibi." And as the poems in their chronological progression become more incisive and attain Marxian lucidity the ironic comments rise and expand into an affirmative Communist statement. (pp. 11-12)

Kenneth Fearing is a poet for workers; his poems are deeply incarnadined in evictions, strikes, hunger; but his appeal is not restricted to his class. His poetry, for those who are still wavering, is one more piece of documented evidence of the horrible mutilation of human dreams and nobleness under capitalism. In very truth, such a fecund talent of poetic insight belongs especially to us. (pp. 13-14)

Edward Dahlberg, in an introduction to Poems *by Kenneth Fearing, Dynamo, 1935, pp. 11-14.*

KENNETH BURKE

Despite superficial differences, E. E. Cummings' *No thanks* and Kenneth Fearing's *Poems* have important ingredients in common. Both poets have an exceptional gift for the satirically picturesque. Both specialize in rhetorical devices that keep their pages vivacious almost to the extent of the feverish. Both are practised at suggesting the subjective through the objective. And both seem driven by attitudes for which there is no completely adequate remedy in the realm of the practical (with Cummings, a sense of isolation—with Fearing, an obsession with death). . . .

Fearing's clearly formed philosophy of history gives his work much better coördination and direction as satire. Cummings the antinomian symbolizes refusal as the little boy that won't play. Fearing, the poet as politician, can offer a take-it-or-leave-it basis of collaboration, a platform, a communist set of values that makes for an unambiguous alignment of forces and a definite indication of purpose. He has a frame of reference by which to locate his satire. Whereas Cummings as satirist is driven by his historical amorphousness into *personal moods* as the last court of appeal, Fearing can attack with the big guns of a *social framework*. He can pronounce moral judgments; and remembering Juvenal or Swift we realize what an advantage this is, for any invective, implicit or explicit, is strongest when the inveigher is appealing to a rigorous code of likes and dislikes. Whereas both poets are alive to the discordant clutter about us, Cummings tends to be jumpy, shifty, look-for-me-here-and-you'll-find-me-there. (After reading him for an hour or so, I show the tetanic symptoms of a cocaine addict.) Fearing is better able to take on something of the heavy oratorical swell, which he manages by an exceptional fusion of ecclesiastic intonations (the lamentation) and contemporary cant (slang, business English, the imagery of pulp fiction, syndicated editorials and advertising).

An inverted Whitman, Fearing scans the country with a statistical eye; but where Whitman sought to pile up a dithyrambic catalogue of *glories,* Fearing gives us a satirically seasoned catalogue of *burdens.* Whitman, the humanitarian, could look upon a national real-estate boom and see there a mystical reaching out of hands. Fearing conversely would remark upon the "profitable smile," the "purpose that lay beneath the merchant's warmth." This method leads at times to the mechanical device of indictments held together by a slightly varied refrain, but for the most part the poet is as ingenious as he is sincere. (p. 198)

Through the volume, Fearing's discerning hatred of all that the "fetishism of commodities" has done for us, as regards the somewhat prospering as well as the destitute, is brilliantly conveyed, along with a quality of reverie, of fears and yearnings that delve far deeper than the contemporary. (p. 199)

Kenneth Burke, "Two Kinds of Against," in The New Republic, *Vol. LXXXIII, No. 1073, June 26, 1935, pp. 198-99.*

EDA LOU WALTON

Kenneth Fearing's second book [*Poems*] is not very different from his first, **Angel Arms**. Both books spring from the same impulse. Perhaps, in his second volume, the poet is more definitely critical of what he sees, more revolutionary in his attack. But that is all. Nor does [Edward] Dahlberg's confused and emotional introduction [see excerpt above] help the reader of Fearing's poems. Actually, the reader does not need help. One phrase of Mr. Dahlberg's is, however, very apt. He speaks of Fearing's "news-reel eye." Fearing's poems are, indeed, like flashes from the news-reel interwoven, as the novelist says, with comments by the observer. And Fearing's talent is that of pointing typical catch phrases from our American culture:

> She said did you get it, and he said did you get it,
>   at the clinic, at the pawnshop, on the bread line, in jail,
> shoes and a roof and the rent and cigarette and bread and
>   a shirt and coffee and sleep—

These lines represent, also, the typical form of Fearing's poems— a form based entirely on parallelism of line and phrase. There are a good many special references made in some of these poems. And one wonders how long these will be moving. They are references to our capitalist world, scathing references to, for example, the Guggenheim fund, to certain capitalists, to specific radio programs, to Roosevelt, to Hearst. It is always questionable, whether a hundred years from now, readers would find vitality in such local references. But poetry of today is, of course, important to us. And more important is the conviction Fearing holds that this world must undergo a terrific change, that our whole culture epitomizes vacuity.

Kenneth Fearing has wit, too—not so clownish a wit as Mr. Cummings, but more biting and more critical. He can take slogans and show how funny they are and how pathetically necessary. He can give, in a few lines, the feeling of life's meaninglessness and still be humorous. . . . Actually for all of his proletarian feeling, Mr. Fearing is doing . . . all the authentic American poet can do today: he is showing us the world as it is now, not as it will be after any revolution. And if this isn't a very pleasant picture, it is so incongruous a one, so cheap, that the reader will feel moved to change it.

But what a relief it is when Mr. Fearing plunges suddenly into such lines as these beginning **"Denouement,"** the single finest poem in his book. Here Fearing's technique is the same, his rhythms the same, but his references are to the old, completely emotionalized symbols which man has so long understood:

> Sky, be blue, and more than blue; wind, be flesh and blood;
>   flesh and blood, be deathless;
> walls, streets, be home;
> desire of millions, become more real than warmth and
> breath and strength and bread;
> clock, point to the decisive hour and, hour without name,
> when stacked and waiting murder fades, dissolves,
> stay forever as the world grows new;

Truth, be known, be kept forever, let the letters, letters
souvenirs, documents, snapshots, bills be found at
last, be torn away from a world of lies, be kept as
final evidence, transformed forever into more than
truth

Not a single phrase here lacks its fringe of emotional connotation. And such lines, I think, are better than those where the "news-reel eye" takes in the typical slogans, the realistic references of our world. They are better because they have the appeal of true poetry wherein every phrase hits immediately its mark, stirs the feelings as well as the minds of the readers. This very poem comes to a fine end in a complete call to arms.

Eda Lou Walton, "Fearing, Poet of a Transformed World," in New York Herald Tribune Books, *July 7, 1935, p. 5.*

PHILIP BLAIR RICE

A poet's vision of evil may take various forms. Satire, of the usual sort, is the mildest of them; however stern the satiric poet may be in his primary intent, an irrepressible sympathy with human nature and a sense of the universality of folly cause him to wear the mask, at least, of geniality. Then there is the philosophical poet's attempt to explore and fix the laws of evil; his desire to extract the essence of the bad and the good may lead him to do a certain violence to the mixed quality of human character and action, and to set an Inferno in unrelieved blacks against the whites of a Paradiso. There is, finally, the nightmare vision of horror, chaotic and meaningless, which springs from overwrought nerves.

Kenneth Fearing's poems [in *Poems*] have something in common with each of these types. In the first place, they are intended as social satire, and more specifically as an indictment of capitalist civilization. The cruelty and hypocrisy of the present order are driven home by ironic juxtapositions: "It is Infant Welfare Week, milk prices up, child clinics closed, relief curtailed"; and "All winter she came there, begging for milk. So we had the shacks along the river destroyed by police." Sometimes the irony overreaches itself by crossing the borders of the fanciful. . . .

Against the background of a bourgeois hell are flashed revelations of a future proletarian heaven. That these seem to be conjured out of a hat, and are not made to emerge inevitably from their context, is caused in part by the general atmosphere of the poems, which is that of the nightmare vision. This atmosphere is created very skilfully, with a craft which draws upon the French Décadents and Surréalists and the advanced movie. The repetitious, hypnotic rhythms punctured by shocks of surprise, the rapid shifts of perspective, the cinematographic fadings and fusions of characters, all contribute to the effect of a grotesque and convulsing dream, tense with "stacked and waiting murder" and permeated by "a touch of vomit gas in the evening air." The horrors are cumulative. . . . (p. 138)

The result is very pungent stuff, and, with regard to its "literary" qualities, some of the most capable verse written so far by the revolutionary group. But these poems are primarily designed, I gather, not as a kind of macabre entertainment— for the sufferings of people today are hardly a fit subject for that—but as a social weapon. Although it is close enough to current realities to be often very telling, the social criticism tends to be submerged in caricature and melodrama. From a proletariat bled until it is dazed, and from a ruling class so demoniacal, the promised land seems very remote. Like a cross-section of events in a newsreel, Fearing's picture of the contemporary world is pieced together out of "shots" chosen for their sensational quality, and it conveys no sense of direction. (That Fearing's Metrotone News gives us scenes ignored by Hearst's is highly commendable, but does not affect this particular criticism.) Consequently it is much less effective as commentary than the work of such poets as Hart Crane and Day Lewis, who bind the future to certain elements of the present and the past in a continuity of purpose and aspiration. (pp. 138, 140)

Philip Blair Rice, "Fearing's Metrotone News," in The Nation, *New York, Vol. CXLI, No. 3656, July 31, 1935, pp. 138, 140.*

T. C. WILSON

In form and in substance, *Dead Reckoning* represents less a new phase of Kenneth Fearing's talent than a continuation and development of his earlier work. The subject-matter, in a broad sense, is the same as that of his *Poems,* published in 1935: "war and the threat of war, unemployment, the systematic poisoning of whole sections of society, the mounting delirium, in short, that is the night-and-day background of any life anywhere in the modern world." The quotation is taken from a review of Fearing's, as summing up very exactly the material he is himself concerned with. In a large number of his new poems, however, he is less interested in presenting the externals of present-day life than he is in articulating the feelings and states-of-mind which they give rise to. Class-oppression, organized brutality and betrayals, increasing armaments—these and similar manifestations of contemporary society are not ignored by Fearing, but they are often most forcibly present in his work when they are implicit rather than directly stated. We are shown not war and unemployment so much as their *effects* on men's lives and sensibilities.

To put it another way, one might say that Fearing now gets "inside" his subjects to a fuller degree, extracting their inherent human values, and that the new dimension he thereby attains gives his work an added depth and tonal richness. His range is still not wide, but the material is more deeply felt and fully realized. . . . Fearing achieves his effects in the whole poem, and isolated lines or passages give an inadequate idea of his qualities. But if the reader will compare such poems as "Memo" and "Tomorrow" with "Portrait" and "The Program" which are written in the author's more familiar satirical style, he will see what I mean. The last-named poems may seem the more impressive on a first reading for their qualities of feeling and style are more immediately apparent. But they do not retain their initial effectiveness, whereas the subtler pieces—and here I would select for special praise, "Debris," "If Money," "Q & A," "Bulletin," "Flophouse," "American Rhapsody (5)," "Pantomime," and especially "Memo" and "Tomorrow"—are more powerful and moving on each reading. The depth of feeling and tonal richness of which I have spoken are much greater; consequently, there is more to apprehend and appreciate.

This greater depth and richness have resulted also in greater intensity. Yet it would be idle to deny that the prevailing temper of the book is something less than cheerful. (pp. 26-7)

Technically, Fearing is at once surer of himself than formerly and less dependent on certain stylistic devices which he tended to over-work. I refer particularly to his use of the jargon and clichés taken over from the tabloids, the movies, the comic strips, advertising, etc. Although he adapted this jargon to his own purposes and often with brilliant results, there was some danger that his very virtuosity in this respect might come to seem sufficient in itself. It is thus encouraging to note that, without relinquishing his highly-charged colloquial idiom, he now relies less often on these rather mechanical tricks of style. The best of his new poems prove that he does not need to.

Two other aspects of his style deserve more attention than I can give them here. One is his ability to revitalize stock images and symbols so that they become once more fresh and living things. The other is his ability to pass from the flat, hard idiom of urban life to the conventionally tender in the same poem, and to do this unobtrusively, almost effortlessly, without violence to the feeling or the language.

It is true that Fearing has serious limitations. Intellectually and emotionally he has still to reach maturity. The profounder, ever-perplexing questions, *sub specie aeternitatis*, that have occupied such men as Rilke, Eliot and Yeats, have awakened little interest in him. At times he even seems unaware of their existence. But within his limitations he is an authentic poet. He has wit and sympathy and understanding; his best work possesses remarkable vigor and speed as well as sensitivity of rhythm and phrasing. As much can be said of very few poets writing today. (pp. 28-9)

T. C. Wilson, "The Real Thing," in Poetry, *Vol. LIV, No. 1, April, 1939, pp. 26-9.*

RUTH LECHLITNER

When Kenneth Fearing's *Poems* appeared in 1935 most evaluators of the writing of our younger American poets placed him—and I think rightly—just about at the top of the list. None saw more clearly than Fearing the tragic and terrifying implications in the contemporary American scene. None observed more keenly, "with hatred and pity exactly matched," the ironic meanings behind breadline, billboard, night court, stock market, money lender, the "majesty" of the statesman at the microphone, the "trembling limbs of ancient millionaires." No one since Cummings had so vitalized and individualized his form, nor integrated more successfully the pace and idiom of modern American speech. On all counts it seems to me that Fearing's "American Rhapsodies" will stand among the best poems written during the last two decades.

In *Dead Reckoning* Fearing continues to see what is alive and real, and what is dead or dying; and to record what he sees in terms that are simple, vital and recognizable to a contemporary. Like ideographs in a running telegraphic framework his poems flash the news of our time. But the real poems (as they should) take form under the surface comment; there haste and despair ache along the tense nerve channels, anger and terror graph the fever-chart drama. Hence his modern symbols—radio, ticker tape, "movie," tabloid—resemble shades called up out of Hades in comparison to the awful reality, the naked imminence of doom just beneath the ordinary thing, the every-day street— waiting around the corner, behind the door. . . . Perhaps the most important thing Fearing does for poetry is to combine the popular appeal of the myth and fairy-tale ideology with symbols from life today. If poetry is to be brought back to the people this is one valid way of doing it. Fearing has taken his cue from one of the things he satirizes—advertising. He uses in his poems those capitalized signboard warnings that are reminders, as John Peale Bishop points out in his discussion of the Federal Poets . . . , "of all those dictates which seek to impress by the enormity of their print, while they admonish us that only by so doing what they say can we escape the feeling of fear."

But a real danger to Fearing himself, as poet, lies in the tendency, clearly marked in these later poems, to grow inward, to draw his pattern of reference too closely around a single theme. The poem **"Requiem"** embodies that theme—and in this respect almost every poem in the book is a requiem—that we meet to say farewell to a civilization already dead of its long malady, but which nevertheless goes on with the illusion of life, the fake symbols of reality. Robinson Jeffers came to that conclusion some time back, fled to his stone tower and wrote finis to his growth as a poet. Is Fearing to give ear to the lovely but fatal Lorelei of the rocks? Like Auden, he cries the doom of a class. But unlike Auden, he seems to be suffering, temporarily at least, the malady of the introvert.

Ruth Lechlitner, "Ideographs of Our Time," in New York Herald Tribune Books, *April 2, 1939, p. 25.*

BABETTE DEUTSCH

[Fearing] is a man who, if he does not share Whitman's faith in the divine average, or his mystic feeling for the cosmos, has made a powerful answer to Walt's demand for a poet who must "flood himself with the immediate age," is aggressively intent on "delivering America . . . from the thin, moribund, and watery but appallingly extensive nuisance of conventional poetry," above all, is convinced that "what American humanity is most in danger of is an overwhelming prosperity, 'business' worldliness, materialism." It is particularly this fear and hatred of the business man's ideal, expressed in repeated angry satires on the success story, that set Fearing's work apart from that of contemporaries no less aware of their time and inclined to be as unconventional in their response to it. (p. 201)

[*Dead Reckoning,* like *Poems*] (*Angel Arms* I have not read), is a violent attack on violence, an outcry against the clamorous voices of the high-pressure salesman, the insurance agent, the public-relations counselor, the radio announcer advertising wars, whiskeys, crises, and cosmetics with the same smooth-tongued glibness. The authentic noises of the day are caught in the slogans and clichés that crowd the lines. They blare out again in the obtrusive ugliness of the capitals that shout from a dozen pages: HOW DO WE KNOW YOU'RE THE PERSON THAT YOU SAY—CAST, IN THE ORDER OF DISAPPEAR-ANCE—THE TWENTIETH CENTURY COMES BUT ONCE—ARREST THAT MAN. The sense of panic which much of Fearing's verse voices pervades throughout this book. It shows a kind of nervous energy typical of his time and place. The poems have some kinship with the savage grotesqueness that a few Americans have learned from their French confrères, but they are essentially native, closer to Sandburg than to any other writer, but more febrile and turbulent, and by the same token expressive of a younger, more disillusioned generation.

There is a minimum of music here, and what there is of it is jazz and "blues." Poems in the elegiac key of **"Lullaby"** are more frequent than in the earlier volume, but for the most part this slim book is made up of feverish notations on current horrors. Nor does Fearing permit himself the vulgar optimism of those poets who fly from the headlines in the morning newspaper to the altar of Marx and the arms of Stalin.

Indeed, the timeliness of these verses is at once their virtue and their flaw. They are so immediately of the moment . . .

that it is hard to believe that they will last, and certain that they will become as obscure in their references as a good deal of Villon. Their power derives from the same source. The pity and the terror of this age have more eloquent spokesmen but none more vehement. (pp. 201-02)

Babette Deutsch, "Flooded with the Immediate Age," in The Nation, *New York, Vol. 149, No. 8, August 19, 1939, pp. 201-02.*

ROSE C. FELD

Kenneth Fearing, poet, twice recipient of a Guggenheim Fellowship, once worked in a hospital. What his job was his publishers do not say, but *The Hospital,* his first novel, clearly indicates that he is at home in this world of the sick. . . . *The Hospital* tells the story of one day in a large city institution and the characters are the people who contribute to its life.

Mr. Fearing's technique is a singularly effective one. The book is not long—less than 300 pages—but he divides it into fifty chapters and each chapter adds to the pattern through the bit contributed by the individual telling of his participation in the scene. Through the interplay of thought and action between the various characters, the story gathers shape, detail and momentum.

The main plot in the novel is the story of Helen, Steve and Freya. Steve is a ship's radio operator out of a job in spite of the fact that a short time before he was hailed as a hero in disaster at sea. Freya is his wife, selfish, ambitious and faithless to him; Helen, the girl he loves. On the day the events in the lives of the characters in the book are unified, Freya is at the hospital undergoing an operation for a lump in her breast which may or may not be malignant; Helen has come to the clinic to find out whether the various tests she had previously taken show that she has tuberculosis. In the delineation of the two young women Fearing makes it clear that in the event that Freya's tumor turns out to be cancerous, she will stick to Steve, for nothing else will be left her, and that if Helen finds out that she has tuberculosis she will break off their affair.

Following the hopes and the fears of these two in the course of the day, Fearing has opportunity to tell in a few brilliant vignettes the life stories of those who make up the network of hospital routine. In one room, Dr. Gavin, one-time brilliant surgeon, now old, is mercifully eased out of life by a friend with a hypodermic; in his office, Dr. Kane, fashionable diagnostician, commits suicide because of participation in a financial scheme . . . ; in the operating room, Dr. Cavanaugh, Freya's surgeon, is caught in a panic of terror remembering his recent record of surgical failures; in the clinic, Dr. Clayborn, Helen's physician, son-in-law of Dr. Kane, is entangled in family complications. Downstairs, those who serve the hospital express their failures and rebellions.

The dramatic moment in the book comes when Pop Jarnecke, the watchman, runs amok in a drunken frenzy and pulls the switches in the generator room, shutting off power in elevators, electric fans and, what is more critical, the light thrown on the operating table. It is precisely the moment that Dr. Cavanaugh is performing the operation on Freya after getting the laboratory report that the specimen taken from her is cancerous.

Exciting and dramatic as is the story, it is Fearing's treatment which calls for highest praise. He has the poet's gift of expression and condensation and, within the compass of a few pages, creates the pattern of a life. While his sympathies are broad enough to take in all human weakness, he is particularly concerned with those whose lives, metaphorically speaking, are spent in the world's basement. For them he has tenderness and for those who keep them there a stinging bitterness. The end of the book is not happy, but it is a realistic tying up of human threads.

> *Rose C. Feld, "City Hospital," in* The New York Times Book Review, *September 3, 1939, p. 6.*

OTIS FERGUSON

[*The Hospital*] is more interesting as an accurate-sounding cross-section of a big New York institution than as fiction. Possibly it falls down because of that supreme irritant to the reader, the device of having a hundred things happen in a half-hour of time, carrying each a few minutes along, dropping it for another. The constant start-stop of the method gives a curious effect of slow motion in spite of the way you are jerked around. The characters (all of whom unfortunately speak in the first person) don't get a chance to matter individually; and in spite of the death, the double suicide, the operation, separation, accident and new-lease-on-life which occupy the foreground, it is mostly a setting without action. A good setting, though; and well understood. . . .

There is some good lean writing in the book, and something like a staccato prose poem in the sections leading up to the last delirium of Dr. Gavin. The people are likely, too—but they don't stay with you long, being swallowed up in numbers. The hospital itself remains longer. That the hospital is finally an empty shell results from the fact that the novel both tries to include too much life and fails to get enough in.

> *Otis Ferguson, in a review of "The Hospital," in* The New Republic, *Vol. LXXXX, No. 1294, September 20, 1939, p. 195.*

F. W. DUPEE

Kenneth Fearing has almost succeeded Ogden Nash as the poet-laureate of *The New Yorker*, and one is apt to forget that he is also a candidate for more serious honors in poetry. His success in journalism is no accident and no disgrace. To be a good *New Yorker* poet one must command a number of definite skills, such as a sense of timing, an ear for the fine points of the cliché, and an ability to project emotion with a perfectly "dead pan." All these talents Fearing shares with his fellow humorists of *The New Yorker*. Where he differs from them and approaches a poet like Eliot is in his conviction that the age is horrible—not merely perplexing or vulgar or ludicrous or dull. Its horrors, to be sure, he apprehends mainly through the lushness of its slogans and the foolish self-importance of its routines—that is to say, through the medium of its clichés. And the irony that arises from contemplating the rhetoric of our time in conjunction with the realities, is almost the whole matter of his poetry, its subject and its form.

In short, Fearing seems to represent a compromise between the urbane satire of Mencken and Nash and the more sulphurous humors of the puritan imagination. For surely he is a puritan, in the best sense, in his tendency to convert the minutiae of life into phantasmagoria which loom big and sinister and obscure. He cannot travesty a musical "forum" without magnifying into something diabolic the crudeness and clownishness of the performers; and to make fun of the mass worship of movie stars is for Fearing to imply a parallel with the cult of the Virgin. This sort of thing has no place in the Mencken tradition; nor is it, on the other hand, entirely a product of recent social radicalism. Fearing is possibly the best poet who has come under the wing of the American Left; yet he is hardly the "social poet" that he used to be called. A doctrinaire nihilism is restricted and generalized, but Fearing's is comprehensive and personal. And he came through the communist movement relatively undamaged as a poet, because he was conditioned to reject its programmatic side while absorbing its negations.

Yet he did owe a great deal to that post-war rebellion in letters, of which the communist phase was only the last phase. It afforded him a community of protestant feeling which reinforced his own irony; and his art was able to profit by the common stock of symbols. His first two books, *Angel Arms* and *Poems,* are without any question fine vigorous achievements, in an idiom which seemed to embody the actual pulse of his angers and anxieties. In his more recent work [as exhibited in *Collected Poems of Kenneth Fearing*] he lacks direction and becomes locked up in his irony. And the more his feeling is stifled or diffused, the more inflexible becomes his technique of reiterations and symmetrical arrangements. Similarly, the influence on his work of other poets seems to become more external, so that some poem he has read, say Eliot's "Difficulties of a Statesman," will show its face again and again in his pages like a family ghost. This seems to be Fearing's moment—and possibly it is only a moment—for introducing *The Waste Land* to Park Avenue.

> *F. W. Dupee, "Sinister Banalities," in* The New Republic, *Vol. 103, No. 18, October 28, 1940, p. 597.*

LOUIS UNTERMEYER

[In *Collected Poems of Kenneth Fearing,* the author] says: "The idea underlying my poetry, as well as anything I write, is that it must be exciting." He knows what he is doing; he has succeeded; his poetry excites. Moreover, if it sometimes startles by mere novelty, it often surprises by "a fine excess." Its fault is a self-imposed restriction of tone. Fearing has purposely discarded "the entire bag of conventions and codes usually associated with poetry." While this is commendable (if possible) it forces upon the poet a limitation even more severe than the traditional demands; worse, it makes for a prescribed attitude and a continued flatness. To save his work from monotony, Fearing ranges widely for his material. . . . The idiom which Fearing uses is savagely appropriate: it is the glaring script of neon lights, the language of locked hotel rooms and casual death, the brusque statement of headlines, the jargon of culture clubs, advertising patter, and the slang of the streets (with a nod to Carl Sandburg), trade lingo, chatter of penthouses and hospitals, dialectics in the boiler-room, patois of mortgages and the movies. (p. 384)

If this poetry does not achieve emphasis as poetry, it gains tension by its very pitch and tempo. Fearing is at his worst in his mystical moments; he loses himself and his reader in a blur of mumbled implications and vague, unfinished gestures. He is at his best in his characters and caricatures: in the etching of **"Minnie and Mrs. Hoyne,"** in the **"Portrait of a Cog,"** in the maladjusted terrors of **"The Doctor Will See You Now,"** in the unhappy doomed suspense of **"American Rhapsody (4)"** and in that relentless composite of the successful man (**"Portrait: 2"**) whose soul is "soothed by Walter Lippmann and sustained by Haig & Haig.'' The varied elements are brought to a fitting climax in **"Readings, Forecasts, Personal Guidance,"** a poem which combines vision and hard anguish. It is this blend of pathetic insight and quiet tragedy which is characteristic of a poet who, even when he fails, never flinches. (pp. 384-85)

> *Louis Untermeyer, in a review of "Collected Poems of Kenneth Fearing," in* The Yale Review, *n.s. Vol. XXX, No. 2, December, 1940, pp. 384-85.*

WELDON KEES

Contemporary civilization has been anything but reserved in providing its satirical writers with abundant horrors; and Fearing, who [in *Collected Poems of Kenneth Fearing*] gathers up-to-the-minute horrors with all the eager thoroughness of a bibliophile cackling over pagination errors, has as much cause to be grateful to civilization's provision as have Mr. Céline, Mr. Faulkner, and Mr. Henry Miller. With more anger than hate he probes the choicest exhibits: "the daughters, living but mad," Hitler and Jack the Ripper, "dreamworld Dora and hallucination Harold," the "gutters, scrapeheaps, breadlines, jails.". . . It is a civilization of gunmen and dope addicts, madmen and the dead, "realistically" presented and remarkably like the tabloids. Fearing's horrors are rigorously prevented from assuming the tortured shapes of those neo-surrealistic hobgoblins that, popping out at us from certain poems in increasing numbers, seldom say Boo with sufficient clarity or conviction.

The world of Fearing is nothing if not metropolitan. He is as involved in, and fascinated by, metropolitan existence (with its "touch of vomit-gas in the evening air") as Frost with his New England landscape, decorated with commonplaces, and Jeffers with his prop boulders and gulls. There is no relief or escape from the city, from the "profitable smile invisible above the skyscrapers," "the loud suburban heroes," "the lunch-hour boredom," "the street that sleeps and screams" where "only desire and profit are real." The occasional references to "cool valleys," "fresh green hills," and "scented air from the fields" seem almost exotic and unreal. West of New Jersey there is scarcely any world—Butte and Detroit and "the empty barns of the west" are only names, faint in the smoke of Manhattan Island. Held by this life in a futile ambivalence that has persisted for fifteen years, Fearing's mood appears to have changed little from the "fly-specked Monday evening" of *Angel Arms* to the "champagne for supper, murder for breakfast" of the most recent poems, although the tone has become increasingly harsh. In the ticker-tape, the radio, the tabloid, the pulp magazine and the advertisement he has found an objective correlative that has never deserted him.

"The idea underlying my poetry, as well as anything I write, is that it must be exciting; otherwise it is valueless," Fearing has written. "To this end it seemed to me necessary to discard the entire bag of conventions and codes usually associated with poetry and to create instead more exacting forms which, in all cases, are based on the material being written about. Besides being exciting, I think that poetry necessarily must be understandable. Everything in this volume has been written with the intention that its meaning should disclose itself at ordinary reading tempo." Elsewhere Fearing has very conveniently supplied critics and readers with the names of those who have influenced his work: Maurice Ravel, George Grosz, Walt Whitman, and Carl Sandburg.

Far from discarding "the entire bag of conventions and codes usually associated with poetry," he has rather taken over and extended techniques of the anti-poetic common to both Whitman and Sandburg, supplementing them with more raucous tricks not unknown to the soap-boxer, the radio orator, and the side-show barker. Principal among these are the device of repetition, esteemed also by the writer of advertising copy; and the device of listing and cataloguing. (pp. 264-66)

Although [Fearing's] vision of life in general, once limited largely to the vision of a *New Masses* cartoon, has broadened little, it is a tribute to his very real gifts (supplemented by a temperament chary of uplift) that within such limits he has written a number of the best poems deriving from a source that is at once narrow, born of immediacy, and stifling, and one that has fathered few poets of his sharp awareness. He is a genuine "natural," a figure rare enough at any time to be appealing. Even at the last, when his sour wit shows signs of having curdled, and when his repetitions and lists, forceful and effective in limited amounts, become tiresome and mechanical, degenerating into a facile and overwrought shrillness, there are still more than a few poems that are exactly what their author wished them to be; they are valuable and exciting. (pp. 269-70)

> *Weldon Kees, "Fearing's Collected Poems," in* Poetry, *Vol. LVII, No. IV, January, 1941, pp. 264-70.*

WILL CUPPY

If you want to be thoroughly entertained by hellish doings in an art colony and left with incipient nervous prostration by a dubious conclusion, read [*Dagger of the Mind*]. After hurried consultations with fellow fans, our own critical powers having cracked under Mr. Fearing's highly unconventional approach, we are sticking to the theory that *Dagger of the Mind* is a mystery must because of its mood, manner and miscellaneous, whatever one may think of the last chapter, where the author has what amounts to a literary fit. (Or does he? That's the whole problem.) Personally, we didn't mind the controversial solution. What we crave is a grand build-up, and this Mr. Fearing provides with a generous display of narrative art, a whole menagerie of writers, musicians, painters, sculptors and loafers, most of them victims of the author's lethal satire, a touch of the screwball and two lovely killings by skewer and butcher knife.

Take it any way you like, the story is a novelty in the mystery field and the total effect is most impressive. Does it matter if some of the old guard are miffed at a slight dearth of actual detectivism? . . . The theme, if we may lapse into classical jargon, is "Somebody ought to kill that guy!"

> *Will Cuppy, in a review of "Dagger of the Mind," in* New York Herald Tribune Books, *February 2, 1941, p. 13.*

ISAAC ANDERSON

The average person who is not a student of history is likely to have only a confused impression of events of the past, even of the comparatively recent past. The picture in his mind is made up of fragments—newspaper reports, word-of-mouth accounts of persons who took part in those events, and rumors whose source can seldom be traced. All this is colored by one's own opinions and prejudices. Such a picture is what Kenneth Fearing seems to have attempted in [*Clark Gifford's Body,* the] story of a civil war some time in the future and in an unidentified country. The events of the war are described by different persons, and they are not presented in chronological order. Indeed, Mr. Fearing appears to have made a special effort to be as unchronological as possible.

The central figure is Clark Gifford, leading spirit of an underground organization which calls itself the Committee for Action. This organization is dissatisfied with the coalition government which has been set up five years previously and more particularly with that government's conduct of a war with a foreign power or powers. This war has been going on for years and no decisive end is in sight. It may even be the war in which we are now engaged, but that is left to the reader's imagination.

The first step in Gifford's revolt against the provisional government is the capture of a number of radio stations in various parts of the country. Gifford himself leads the attack on Station WLEX at Bonnfield. It is a surprise attack and entirely successful, but only for a short time. Soon Station WLEX is recaptured, as are most of the other stations taken by his men. Gifford is captured, tried and executed along with several of his lieutenants. But this does not end the revolt. It goes on with renewed strength, and it is still dominated by the brave spirit of its dead leader. Some of the men who have previously opposed Gifford now join the crusade which he started. Others, who have supported him secretly and for their own selfish ends because they hope to profit from the confusion which his revolt must inevitably bring about, are now on the other side.

In the end—it is actually the first chapter in the book—Gifford's cause appears to have triumphed. At all events, the country is at peace. And yet, there are indications that all is not well. The people are too complacent. They have forgotten too much. Many of them look upon Clark Gifford as we now look upon John Brown—as a wild-eyed fanatic who started something that he could not finish.

This is an oddly disturbing novel, and it is difficult to say whether the general effect of it is or is not heightened by the curiously episodic manner in which it is told—a manner which begins by being annoying and ends by having a fascination all its own.

> *Isaac Anderson, "Future Civil War," in* The New York Times Book Review, *June 28, 1942, p. 22.*

L. BELL

All the events in [*Clark Gifford's Body*] . . . , says Kenneth Fearing, "are inventions, loosely shaped again into one of history's much repeated patterns." The action takes place in a "mythical country, of no particular time," and it is unfurled in a series of staccato chapters—straight narrative, news bulletins, radio broadcasts, letters, magazine excerpts—which illuminate the actual climax of the story in perspective. They date from thirty years before the attack on Radio Station WLEX, which is Chapter 29, to thirty years after the attack, which is Chapter 1. As an experiment in discontinuity, the novel is of considerable interest, but most readers will keep hoping that Mr. Fearing will stop hopping. It is difficult to discover a fixed point for observation. The attack on the radio station, however dramatic in itself, has only an abstract importance, for it is not quite clear whether the forces involved are ultimately good or evil in what they accomplish. Or is anything accomplished. . . .

Clark Gifford's Body is a poet's transcript of plot into symbolism. The content of that symbolism is doubtless crystal clear to him, however inaccessible it may be to the cursorial eye.

> *L. Bell, in a review of "Clark Gifford's Body," in* New York Herald Tribune Books, *July 5, 1942, p. 8.*

KERKER QUINN

Kenneth Fearing is the boy who scooped the depression by publishing a book of depression poems (*Angel Arms*) in 1929. It was six years before he had another book ready, but the *Poems* of 1935 showed a beautifully ripened technique which put him head and shoulders above the by-then-numerous social protesters. He had developed a "style" of his own: long-lined free verse with jazzy rhythms and pool-ball vocabulary, ironic distortion of prevalent "literature" (films, radio, billboards, sports columns, advice to the lovelorn), and a kind of playback-machine method of letting city dwellers hear what they had been saying to each other and to themselves.

In his three books of poetry since 1935 Mr. Fearing has been trying to retain that patented style without permitting us to complain that he has added to his song repertory but not extended its scope. In neither *Dead Reckoning* (1938) nor *The Agency* (1940)—despite the superb poems in both—did he succeed; he was playing the same things over, but a little louder, with more brass. *Afternoon of a Pawnbroker,* however, makes us listen by means of modulation.

We listen more attentively, too, because we are no longer so concerned over whether the world is coming to an end that every sound is distorted. We can think once more of the shape of things to come. And Mr. Fearing is a good man to heed. He has no proposals for world currency, basic English or zones of safety. His is the simple lesson of telling us to examine ourselves and pointing out some things that need examining. He has watched society slice off one monster head and then fail to notice that a dozen others grow out, Hydra-like, where it had been. He chides us for our confidence in statistics (whether they solve or reveal anything or not), in the miracles of "commonsense analysis," in the longevity of the status quo (as permanent as rivers and sky), in the value of constantly and hopefully searching (for what?), in the cathartic properties of confession (as if we stopped being social ostriches by frankly confessing that we are). In general, what Fearing has to say is as timely as it was in 1935, and it has greater penetration.

The somewhat more solemn voice, then, is right. And the best of the twenty-one new poems are the most restrained, the most deliberate—at times suggesting Kafka's prose, as in the excellent **"Confession Overheard in a Subway."** The failures are the exceptions in the volume; the unimaginative piece about a juke box, the bogus-melodramatic **"Public Life,"** the outdated **"Beware."** Occasionally we are annoyed when we see from the opening lines what a wonderful opportunity the chosen situation gives Mr. Fearing (as in **"Travelogue in a Shooting Gallery"**) and then proceed to concoct a better poem on the subject than he actually manages to give us. But his brand of folksong is still exceedingly fresh and will remain so at least until the American folk stop deserving the taunts he feels compelled to make.

> *Kerker Quinn, "Fresh Brand of Folk Song," in* New York Herald Tribune Weekly Book Review, *October 10, 1943, p. 25.*

WILLIAM POSTER

Of all modern poets Fearing has been, perhaps, the one most sympathetic to those elements of the world which strike us as fundamentally unpoetic.... He was at once both a member and spectator of his own vivid and eclectic environment—an environment of Bohemians and gamblers, drunks and poets, dreamers of revolution and perfect poker-hands.

His earliest book, *Angel Arms,* found him most deeply concerned with the discord between his sensitivity to this world and his inheritance of a poetic tradition. Later, he is more assured of his poetic mission. The discord becomes the basis for intense collisions between poetic sensibility and the world in which it resides. In his second volume [*Poems*] may be found poems of explosive power, ironic fragmentations of metropolitan existence and lyric memorials of daily chaos.

But successful as this exploitation of the immediate undoubtedly was, it entailed definite sacrifices. The form was slight and often watered down into prosiness. The irony was without clear values and tended to be blanketing rather than discriminatory. The negation of intellectual tradition tended to foster sentimentality and the advertisement of seemingly latent, but actually nonexistent, profundities.

These faults persist. In [*Afternoon of a Pawnbroker*], the title-poem describes a pawnbroker, who is visited by Gabriel and Adam and holds various legendary pledged articles. The events themselves are pointless (though a seeming point is advertised) except as they occasion the rather easy humor of the humdrum suddenly electrified by apparitions too big for it.... In **"The Joys of Being a Business Man,"** the irony of realistic statement collapses into journalistic flatness accompanied by the fixed grimace of habitual mockery. Among the best poems in the volume are **"Art Review,"** a clever fantasy on mustache-artists and privy-wall murals, a poem on Representative Dies—a perfect runway for Fearing's take-off—and a poem called **"Certified Life,"** a mildly ironic discourse with exceedingly apt illustrations on the theme that we all have "a patent on life," be it love, chess or knowledge.

A considerable change has taken place since Fearing's last volume. His original excitement, the kind of auto-intoxication that produced the unexpected image or the startling juxtaposition, has cooled somewhat and there is little to replace it. With maturity has come a clearer focus and a greater control of his material, but there is a perceptible lack of the imaginative extravagance and casual marksmanship so well adapted to this genre. In all, though, Fearing still succeeds in obtaining a considerable exchange-value from his special brand of direct commerce between the poetic and the unadorned commonplace. (pp. 628-29)

> William Poster, "Poetry of the Immediate," in The New Republic, *Vol. 109, No. 1509, November 1, 1943, pp. 628-29.*

DELMORE SCHWARTZ

By now no one interested in modern poetry can be unaware of what new poems by Kenneth Fearing will probably be like. In reading *Afternoon of a Pawnbroker,* one feels that Fearing is always genuine and interesting—but that it is becoming more and more difficult to tell his poems apart. If this seems a severe remark, consider such lines as "The instrument cannot be played, not correctly"; "The telephone is gone, the phone that rang and rang and never did connect with any other phone"; "And it never happens, when the doorbell rings, that you find a troupe of hours is standing on your stoop." These lines (and there are more) are from three different poems, but there is no reason, given Fearing's one theme and his method, why they should not be in the same poem and even the same stanza. It is almost as if Fearing were using carbon copies of old poems.

Fearing's theme, here as before, is the anguish of metropolitan life. His use of shouting slang and his ironic use of the idioms of the press and radio constitute a style which he did not invent (its inventor may be T. S. Eliot, in *Sweeney Agonistes*), but which he has made his own by extending it in detail, using New York and the depression, instead of Eliot's London and Eliot's Puritan sense of life. But there is a narrow limit to such variety. If tone, emotion and versification remain the same, the effect intended by the poet, the excitement, leaves us merely enervated. The monotony of the drum was present in Fearing's verse from the start, and it was appropriate; but this third volume in the same limited style gives an old admirer of Fearing's verse the impression of an orchestra of drums, beating out a dead march without end.

> Delmore Schwartz, in a review of "Afternoon of a Pawnbroker and Other Poems," in The New York Times Book Review, *November 7, 1943, p. 34.*

RUTH STEPHAN

There has been no one in recent years as dramatic, direct, picturesque and entertaining in commenting on American city life as Kenneth Fearing. With the publication of [*Afternoon of a Pawnbroker*] the reader is more aware of this than of the fact that he began his writing career as the most vivid exponent of socialism in poetry. The satirical explosions that characterized his early work are subsiding. He is neither as sharp nor as flashing as he was. It is not that he is less a poet, for he may be closer to the nature of poetry than ever before, but that the impelling force of his poetry has changed.

When Fearing's *Collected Poems* was published several years ago he appended his own definition of poetry: "The idea underlying my poetry . . . is that it must be exciting; otherwise it is valueless. To this end it seemed to me necessary to discard the entire bag of conventions and codes usually associated with poetry and to create instead more exacting forms which, in all cases, are based on the material being written about. Besides being exciting, I think that poetry necessarily must be understandable." This apparently simple statement precipitates a great many more questions than it answers. What does it mean by new exacting forms? It is true he dispensed with certain verse forms which had been popular, but others, notably Gertrude Stein and E. E. Cummings, had done this before him. If he had waved his hand in the air and insisted it was a poem, he would have had a juster claim, for he kept the essentials of the code of poetry which are words and imagination. After all, the form is only the casing of a poem and always can be devised to suit the intention of the poet.

Then, what kind of excitement? Understandable to whom? (pp. 163-64)

What Fearing probably means is that he wants his poetry to have the instantaneous widespread effect of a newspaper headline. He wants as many people as possible to react with immediate horror or delight; consequently he has dramatized the most ordinary sights and happenings of every day living. What, then, is added to make it poetry and not mere reporting? Principally, it is Fearing's imaginative viewpoint. He has the double vision of the poet who sees the object we all see and sees at the same time its universal shadow. He observes in the continuous performance of a movie that the cycle of life and history may be likewise repetitious; in a juke box, the humble estate of being a man:

> Its resourceful mind, filled with thoughts that range
> from love to grief, from the gutter to the stars, from
> pole to pole,
> Can seize its thoughts between fingers of steel,
> Begin at the start and follow them through in an
> orderly fashion to the very end.
> Can you do that?

With such a vision it is possible to use a particle of dust, or anything, as the subject, for it is the perception and communication which are important.

Fearing's power as a poet lies in these flashes of perspicacity and in his ability to transfer his perception into words. His weakness is that his perception is apt to be one-sided. Where is the evidence of nobility in the average man's day or year or life? It is not apparent on the surface Fearing portrays, yet anyone who is familiar with human beings knows it is there. He may have omitted such a significant, and necessary, trait because he has not completely overcome the singleness of outlook of the socially conscious group of writers and artists, of whom he was originally a part, who used their art as a means of pointing out the ills of society and of urging society to purge itself of those ills. Political poetry can be admirable and moving, but it is limited in its sphere and temporal in its communication.

There is no need for Fearing to be either, and he himself seems to be realizing this. Instead of poems in startling phrases about pickets, poison gas, fingers combing the city's refuse and spendthrift magnates, he is writing in a chimerical vein about live people haunting the dead, seers discussing the fate of the world and, vaguely, about business men and suburbanites. Happily he has retained his carnival humor. If he is not always as clear as he was in his previous books, it may be because his vision is changing and he is not certain himself of what he sees. (pp. 164-65)

> *Ruth Stephan, "Fearing and the Art of Communication," in* Poetry, *Vol. LXIII, No. III, December, 1943, pp. 163-65.*

C. V. TERRY

Mr. Fearing's short and continuously entertaining novel [*The Big Clock*] may be classified as a whodunit in reverse—plus a certain social comment that may be taken painlessly, along with the whirligig action. New York's Huckster Alley is the scene: this time, however, the hucksters inhabit a heaven all their own, high above the teeming Radio City pavements. Here, they are engaged in the processing of their own peculiar (and more than slightly terrifying) product, the magazines of Earl Janoth's enormously profitable chain. . . .

If Earl Janoth has a prototype, the reader's guess is as good as the reviewer's. We will only add that Janoth is a one man Gallup poll in himself—that he is a maker of opinion in his own right, and a mighty maker of ulcers among his janizaries—that his murder of his blond mistress, and his scramble to cover his tracks are rich in high-powered melodrama.

Most of the story is told through the mind of George Stroud, an important editor in the magazine chain. George is a wry, too-wise young man who has worked up to the swivel chair at Crimeways via the newspaper-advertising route. Now, he is determined to fight this dog-eat-dog routine until he has established some measure of security for his wife and daughter in their still-shaky suburban haven. Unfortunately, George is not above a bit of extra-marital sinning—strictly by way of relaxation when the heat is on at the office. How was he to know that ice-blond Pauline . . . was the boss' true solace? Or that the boss would be lurking at her apartment door when George dropped her discreetly at the corner, after a week-end in Albany?

But the gimmick is Mr. Fearing's own patent, and we refuse to more than mention its *modus operandi*. When Janoth staggers out of Pauline's apartment a half-hour later (after a tautly written murder scene) he knows he is in the clear if only he can pin down that dimly glimpsed escort who dropped Pauline at the corner, and put him where he'll never talk again. Naturally, he must move faster than the police. With the clues at his disposal, and the undercover organization provided by his magazines, it should be a simple matter—particularly if he puts George Stroud in charge of the manhunt.

From that point on, the tick of Mr. Fearing's big clock is remorseless as doom itself. The texture of his plot is stretched tight as a drum—and he maintains the tautness artfully until the final page. Several chapters tell the story on the bias, as it were, as he holds his prism up to others—a dangerous device in a tightly plotted novel, but one that pays dividends here.

In these quick-paced vignettes, we meet more than one member of Janoth's harried staff—grim reminders, all of them, of the wages of sin and razzle-dazzle journalism. We meet Janoth himself, after he's smashed his lady's skull with a brandy decanter—and Mr. Fearing has made his twisted tycoon a thing of pathos as well as a Daliesque buffoon. There is even time to explore the psyche of a slap-happy artist—who makes a specialty of abstract canvases and quite normal love children, who all but gives the show away until she takes a yen for George. . . . But, as we said above, it's Mr. Fearing's gimmick.

> *C. V. Terry, "High-Powered Whodunit in Reverse," in* The New York Times Book Review, *September 22, 1946, p. 6.*

HOWARD HAYCRAFT

Ever since Kenneth Fearing's intellectual thriller *The Dagger of the Mind,* some five years ago, discriminating fanciers of the murder novel have been hoping for a return engagement. *The Big Clock* is both a reward for patience and a disappointment. . . .

Telling the story in rapidly shifting sequences through the minds of the several participants, Mr. Fearing uses all his wit and undeniable literary skill to create a mood of mounting tension and excitement seldom surpassed in this type of writing.

Then, with the climax, comes the jolt. It is difficult to make clear the nature of Mr. Fearing's failure without betraying the reviewer's code—even though the novel is not a "mystery" in the conventional sense. First, he resolves the immediate predicament by a dubious *deus ex machina* device. This is structurally weak, but not fatal. What is much more serious, he rests his ultimate conclusion on an assumption so amazingly disregardful of the stated facts that credibility is all but destroyed and enough plot ends are left to choke a reasonably conscientious pulp editor.

It would seem axiomatic that an author who essays the novel of plot undertakes the obligation to make factual sense to his readers if nothing else. This Mr. Fearing has failed to do in his headlong dénouement, and an otherwise brilliant and exciting tale suffers in consequence.

The pseudo-philosophical passages about Life which give the novel its title would not be missed by one reader. Apart from these, Mr. Fearing's prose is lean, vernacular, and effective.

> *Howard Haycraft, "With Clay Hands," in The Saturday Review of Literature, Vol. XXIX, No. 41, October 12, 1946, p. 50.*

DIANA TRILLING

For some reason the wonderful central idea of Kenneth Fearing's *The Big Clock* calls to mind an otherwise unmemorable novel, *The Chinese Room,* which could boast a character who experimented on his own mind by writing himself anonymous letters. In Mr. Fearing's anti-detective story—since we always know whodunit, Mr. Fearing's book can scarcely be called a mystery—the basic notion is even more beguiling. Here a young man is appointed to supervise a hunt for himself, though he knows that to discover himself means death. Unfortunately, the resolution of this dilemma is not equal to its invention: the conclusion of Mr. Fearing's novel is as fortuitous as the arrival of the marines in an old movie thriller. But we cannot have everything, even in books whose only purpose is entertainment, and despite the letdown of its ending, *The Big Clock* is one of the pleasantest suspense stories to appear in a long time. And this is not a matter only of its central device. There is also its light-fingered but telling satire of the intellectual high jinks that go on high in the offices of *Crimeways,* where the hero is employed. Of the several novelists who have had their fun with a certain fabulous magazine empire, Mr. Fearing is the most intelligent and economical.

> *Diana Trilling, in a review of "The Big Clock," in The Nation, New York, Vol. 163, No. 17, October 26, 1946, p. 479.*

LEE E. CANNON

On several occasions Voltaire referred to Deity as "the big clock-maker." That might serve to explain any philosophical implications of Mr. Fearing's [*The Big Clock*], and they are of the slightest. The author, who is one of our minor poets, uses in this narrative the same American vernacular of advertising, radio and the newspaper which appears in much of his poetry and which is likely to irritate anyone who prefers standard English. The plot of his novel is the old one of pursuer and pursued, but the narrator has changed the formula by making the two identical. The pursuer, then, by the force of circumstances, has to try to identify himself and, since he is an amateur detective and journalist, working for a large syndicate, he is able to employ the help of numerous other members of the organization and at the same time keep all the strings in his own hand. He is no Sherlock Holmes, however, and he makes several mistakes that enable his pursuers to come panting hot on his trail. The reader is kept informed of the development of events by a series of mental recapitulations flowing through the thought currents of various characters. Just in the nick of time, the long arm of coincidence, like the god's from the

basket, reaches in and saves the pursuer from having to put the finger on himself or seize himself by his own coat-tail. The suspense is not so tense that it cannot be borne with equanimity. It would not have been too great a calamity if pursuer had caught pursued. The author may now take his tongue from his cheek.

> *Lee E. Cannon, "Tick, but No Tock," in The Christian Century, Vol. LXIV, No. 1, January 1, 1947, p. 17.*

IDWAL JONES

In a little while it will be a hundred years since the wondering James Marshall at Sutter's Mill held in his palm some flakes of gold, and for a brief moment became the most significant figure on the planet. In the rush that followed, when he and Sutter were trampled out, history was changed. That event was, in the economic as well as the picaresque sense, continent-tipping. Seen now in the retrospect, as we see the Civil War, wholly and in the round, it manifests a pattern so verging on abstract beauty that it has become the classic of spontaneous migration. Also, one must say, it is a thrice-told tale, and one familiar to satiety. When fiction writers rehearse it, they deal with the same materials, and their novels are as alike as so many reports of the same forest fire. No conflagration of epochal size can be adequately described. There can be no personal response to it. We would want to know what one being thought of it and felt, watching the blaze from a keyhole in his forest hut—in short, as a simple, personal experience.

Such accounts of the Argonaut period we have come across, but they are in unaffected memoirs, not in the formula novel. . . . With the anniversary at our heels, we shall be seeing many such goldrush novels as *John Barry,* by [Kenneth Fearing, Donald Friede, and H. Bedford James], who have pooled their labor under the pseudonym, Donald F. Bedford. They have been indefatigable in research. They have put within the covers of their tale more history than it would seem possible to pack into that compass, and the tale racks along at thumping speed.

But withal, the tale has a carpentered air, like a briskly done serial. The list of *dramatis personae,* obligingly put in the front, has seventy names, all out of the directory of San Francisco and New Orleans, only a handful of them fictitious. And all these persons appear in the chain of briefly told events, with the hero in the thick of them. He arrives, does Barry, in 1846, when 20 years old. It is Barry with the first wave of Donner party rescuers, and Barry, still more heroically, with the second wave. It is Barry discovering gold with Marshall, and Barry as partner with that apostate Mormon, Sam Brannan.

The episodes are more like notes to be expanded later, the dialogue is in today's speech, the sequence like a chain of montage shots, and the hero is so much where things happen that he is like Rollo among the Argonauts. If no sense of immediacy lifts from his tale, the writers do know their history texts.

> *Idwal Jones, "Forty-Niner, Sandpapered," in The New York Times Book Review, October 19, 1947, p. 24.*

SELDEN RODMAN

With [*Stranger at Coney Island*], his sixth book of poems, one feels justified in saying that Kenneth Fearing has sought and found his permanent level in the range of modern verse, and that it lies somewhere between Auden and Ogden Nash. With something of the former's surrealist imagination and a good deal of the latter's urban ability to pillory suburban mediocrity, Fearing does not, of course, derive his style from either. His style (it is a very good one, and by this time wholly his own) originated in Walt Whitman's long and casual line. But in that origin, or in the uses Fearing has made of it, there is occasion for regret. For the Fearing of 1948, more suave, more skillful, and certainly more sophisticated politically, is not the Fearing of *Poems* (1935), angry, naive, and brashly Marxist, but capable, at least occasionally, of rising to the level of Whitman at his most inspired.

Yet Fearing is a curiously typical man of his generation, almost a caricature of him, who, seeing the light (of disillusionment with leftist faith) stepped backward into the negative cynicism of the Lost Generation rather than forward into any reappraisal of democracy, socialism or the human spirit.

No one, of course, can say whether a reversal to a position of affirmation would have made Fearing a better poet, or even as good a one as he is today. Negative as they are, the poems in *Stranger at Coney Island* are inimitable. Only in two poems, **"This Day"** and **"Long Journey,"** is there the tiniest hint of a more personal statement, of some answer to the questions that keep plaguing one. Why is Fearing so very limited in the range of his poetic feelings? Is he never simply happy to be alive, or in love, or just enjoying something? It is not that these poems shouldn't be written, or that anyone writes them better than Kenneth Fearing, but that one expects, or at least hopes, after six volumes of it, for more.

Selden Rodman, "New Verses by Fearing," in The New York Times Book Review, *October 24, 1948, p. 18.*

PETER VIERECK

Free verse (prosaic, irregular, formless verse) is still being written, though it has become as yawn-provoking and arthritic a form of modernism as a glamorous rally of the Prohibitionist Party or the Townsendites. One of its most gifted and intelligent practitioners today is Kenneth Fearing. His school would perhaps repudiate the label "free verse" (a question of definition)—such arguments go back to the 1920's—in which case let's compromise by calling it half slave and half free.

Fearing is good at the game in [*Stranger at Coney Island and Other Poems*], but is the game worth the candle? The reason irregularity can be so attractive in poetry is its contrast with a background of some recurrent beat, scansion, and (often) rhyme-scheme. When the regular background does not exist at all, then the irregular foreground falls flat for lack of contrast and esthetic tension. This is why even the best free verse and formless verse gets forgotten so quickly (poor Amy Lowell); it simply does not sing its way into our memory. The challenge, to use a Toynbee metaphor, of rigorous form, is what helps evoke the beautiful response. Or, to use a Frostian metaphor, Fearing's verse is like playing tennis without a net.

More brilliant than beautiful, *Stranger at Coney Island* is best at scathing our big-city banalities. No stranger to corny island, the author spots a cliché at every *cliché d'oeil*. The café night life of city slickers trying to be men-about-town gets duly unmasked—is it worth the bother?—for its pitiful secret loneliness. Fearing's O. Henry mood of breezy, yet compassionate,

knowingness is typified by a title like **"4 A.M."** and a final punch-line like: "The booth where last night's love affair began, the spot where last year's homicide occurred, are empty now, and still." These enormously long, unrhymed, irregularly accented lines are so sentimentally earnest and yet so incongruously and unintentionally reminiscent of Ogden Nash's light verse. The sentiment and earnestness don't come off because the flabby, sprawling formlessness prevents the needed trilogy of concentration, condensation, and intensity. The slapstick social satire does come off. If this were all Fearing aimed at, his success would be unquestioned. But he is too sincere a poet to be satisfied with cleverness; judging by his themes and his earlier books, he is aiming higher.

When I asked the girl at the book counter for "the new Fearing book," she replied: "Heavy stuff. Wonderfully intellectual!" Perhaps the *mot juste* for this book is: a Heavy Stuff version of Ogden Nash. The trouble is that some of us lowbrows and highbrows like our Ogden Nash straight. Or else our Longhair Stuff straight. *Aut Caesar aut nihil*. (pp. 30-1)

Peter Viereck, "Heavy-Stuff Version of Ogden Nash," in The Saturday Review of Literature, *Vol. 31, No. 47, November 20, 1948, pp. 30-1.*

M. L. ROSENTHAL

The familiar rhythm of a typical Fearing poem, that rhythm which is a cross between a compulsion neurosis and a kindly psychoanalyst's parting words, anxious and sardonic and soothing all at once, never palls on us. The reason is, perhaps, that it is a perfect device for nagging at the universe. Most poets seem to find modern life—that is, the actual "secret" life of individuals which determines how really joyous or miserable they are—intolerably subject to mechanized "forces" prevailing in a deathly atmosphere of hypocrisy and humiliation. [In *Stranger at Coney Island* and other works] Fearing more directly than almost any other serious poet now writing, communicates this reaction which speaks for the muffled sensibilities of millions. Irony has been his weapon and his shield from the start, though in the past more often combined with anger or bitterness.

Within the limits of a style which seems to forbid the immediate lyrical expression of personality . . . he has explored the possibilities of irony pretty thoroughly. The ominous note is always present, the suggestion that there is more than meets the eye, even when the poet kids some symbolic charlatan. . . . It is, ultimately, the note of negative criticism, a poet's method of refusing to allow himself to be drawn into the maelstrom of impersonal, commercialized pseudo-life.

New developments are the possibly religious implications of [**"Stranger at Coney Island"**], the skillful handling of parallel lines of thought—realistic, artificial and mystical—in the gentle yet powerful **"Long Journey,"** the diabolically accurate indictment of a civilization in **"Museum,"** and the almost hysterical **"M.D."** and **"Mrs. Fanchier at the Movies."** These poems, especially the last one, project a little farther than before that nightmare of the complete loss of individual differentiation which has always been suggested in Fearing's poems of time and death, as well as in the close-ups of an unreal world "where there is no score, in any game, less than a million magic bells and a billion electric lights"; where every one, whether he knows it or not, is a "castaway," and where, in place of the old-fashioned relationships of actual human beings, we have "many new and kindly companions" on the radio and screen to whose voices we have no way of replying and who make it terribly difficult to remember "what it really was I at one time felt so deeply for." It is hard to see how Fearing can push much farther in this direction without going full circle or trying new forms.

> M. L. Rosenthal, "Irony vs. the World," in New York Herald Tribune Weekly Book Review, March 13, 1949, p. 15.

WILLIAM ABRAHAMS

The poems in *Stranger at Coney Island* display the same qualities and defects of much of [Fearing's] more recent works: that is to say, they are a kind of sophisticated entertainment. Here once again is the Fearing subject: an urban, machinal society in which even the forms of belief have been lost, where the jukebox is like a "beating human heart," only the radio "knows what we feel, knows what we are, really knows what we merely think we know," and "the spark of life is very low, if it burns at all." Yet it is strange that this vision of life, so terrifying in its implications, should almost never seriously move us. The single response these poems elicit is a melancholy pleased assent. We are entertained by them; the neuroses they describe are so comfortable, so familiar, so harmless. . . . What Mr. Fearing has done, I think, is to adopt certain of the materials of *The Waste Land* and make them immediately, factitiously effective, much as advertising artists have utilized for their own purposes the austere discoveries of Braque, say, or Mondrian.

But for all their effectiveness, none of these new poems is equal to the **"Dirge"** which appeared in Mr. Fearing's *Poems* of 1935:

And wow he died as wow he lived
  going whop to the office and blooie home to sleep and
  biff got married and bam had children and oof got fired,
zowie did he live and zowie did he die

With who the hell are you at the corner of his casket
  and where the hell we going on the right hand
  silver knob, and who the hell cares walking second
  from the end with an American Beauty wreath
  from why the hell not.

The brilliant staccato surface and rowdy satire have been replaced by a kind of "poetic" croon, an elegiac sentimentality; the minute particulars, which were at once the justification and device of Mr. Fearing's irony, are here dissolved in a stream of innocuous generality.

You must remember the fateful beginning, fully to understand
  the end,
(Though of course there can be no real end);
To grasp the motives, fully, it is vital to remember the stamp
  of the mind,
Vital to know even the twist of the mind . . .

As a promise for the poem not written, or as a poetic program, this is admirable, but the poem itself lies inert on the page. Regretfully one looks back to Mr. Fearing's earlier work, where what was promised was performed. (pp. 118-19)

> William Abrahams, "Program of Entertainment," in Poetry, Vol. LXXIV, No. 2, May, 1949, pp. 118-20.

JOHN BROOKS

For readability, humor, sound characterization and firm but understated dramatic significance *Loneliest Girl in the World* is a story worthy to stand beside Mr. Fearing's justly famous *The Big Clock.*

The lonely one is Ellen Vaughn, daughter of the late Adrian Vaughn of Vaughn Electronics. Vaughn Senior and his eldest son Oliver have both been killed in a presumably accidental fall from the ledge of their penthouse on top of the Envoy Hotel. Under the terms of her father's will Ellen owns the penthouse and all that is in it. What makes her an object of interest to several sinister operatives in the sound-recording business is her possession of "Mikki," the crowning invention of her father's career—a "sound library" containing in wire recordings what would require fifty years to play off a record of Adrian Vaughn's somewhat musty business and personal life. Every recording in the library is indexed and can be selected in a few seconds by means of a dial system allowing for ten billion entries.

On this ingenious framework Mr. Fearing has unusual talents to exercise. As Ellen, chiefly through the agency of the weird and inscrutable Mikki, gradually comes upon the many unsuspected skeletons in her father's closet, she and her two brothers emerge as deft and memorable portraits of the children of a strong and dominating man. Ellen herself is a passive, wavering shadow, just the way her father had hoped to keep her. . . .

Charles, harebrained and irresponsible, is the overpowered and resentful son, unconsciously cruel and potentially dangerous. The late Oliver, whom the reader meets only through the recordings of his voice, was the son who dared come to grips with his father, to his cost. . . .

Mr. Fearing is also a poet, and a certain stark poetry illuminates the best scenes in this book—a scene, for example, in which Ellen is discovered "talking" to Mikki by Storch, the Vaughns' butler. Since he knows his business, Mr. Fearing keeps his mind on people rather than symbols, story rather than significance; but every good story has a point, and Mr. Fearing's Mikki, for anyone who cares to think about the matter, is not only a symbol but a pretty scary one.

> John Brooks, "The Scary Machine," in The New York Times Book Review, July 29, 1951, p. 4.

HARVEY BREIT

The only masterpiece *Loneliest Girl in the World* may conjure up is Fearing's earlier *The Big Clock,* or possibly those wonderful Graham Greene champions in the genre of psychological suspense. Fearing, in the thirties, was one of the most inventive of the young poets. In his new novel he reveals an easy mastery over language, and in the business of creating atmosphere and expectancy, a mastery possibly too sure-fire.

For just about one half of his book Fearing holds the reader. He has developed an absorbing situation. An attractive, shy, rich girl (who almost *is* the loneliest girl in the world) comes into possession of a fabulous "thinking" machine and a roomful of recordings, one of which—or some of which—appears to hold a powerful and valuable secret. It was time that a smart author fastened on to cybernetics, and Fearing fastens on with convincing adeptness. But the author succumbs to the temptations of the genre: the easy solution, the intoxicatingly gay resolution—and the jig is really up. How can an author who introduces the idea of cybernetics and uses it as an intrinsic part of his novel ignore it totally in his resolutions? Does facility, an engaging style, excuse such shoddiness? The poet Fearing knows better. Does the reader of a novel of suspense derive more pleasure than the operator of a crossword puzzle? I suspect it is the same *kind* of pleasure, at any rate, the source of which is the minimal engagement of our complex total selves. (pp. 82-3)

> *Harvey Breit, in a review of "Loneliest Girl in the World," in* The Atlantic Bookshelf, *a section of* The Atlantic Monthly, *Vol. 188, No. 2, August, 1951, pp. 82-3.*

MILTON CRANE

The novels of Kenneth Fearing continue to find ever more ingenious ways of shocking and delighting the hardened reader of thrillers. In *Dagger of the Mind* he explored the lurking horror beneath the surface of an artists' colony; in *The Big Clock*—perhaps his most perfectly sustained nightmare—he took to pieces a glossy news magazine and its Caligari-like director; and in *The Loneliest Girl in the World* he fabricated a superb puzzle out of a gigantic recording apparatus.

The Generous Heart, like Fearing's earlier novels, takes an institution for its setting. Campaign Consultants (itself a horrid but too plausible invention) is a high pressure, fund raising organization whose professional services are eagerly sought by a new, buccaneering charity-on-the-make: The Generous Heart (motto: "The Generous Heart Grows Rich in Giving").

Jay Ravoc, the head of Campaign Consultants, finds himself and his fiancee the targets of a deadly campaign to terrorize him into signing a contract to promote The Generous Heart. The rest is a characteristic Fearing cyclone of psychological and physical violence, culminating in a studiously contrived scene of horror that would have staggered "Monk" Lewis.

Here again are all the best Fearing ingredients: The skilfully economical construction of plot, the gradual awakening of suspicion between friends and lovers, the shift in narrator from chapter to chapter, the trick that Fearing may have learned from William Faulkner and that he has so effectively domesticated for his own purposes.

His characters (even the psychopaths) are not puppets but men and women, in whose problems one can take more than a passing interest without ever being diverted from the plot— the be-all and the end-all, as Fearing so well knows, of the novel of suspense.

> *Milton Crane, "Fearing's New Delight for the Hardened Thriller Fan," in* Chicago Sunday Tribune Magazine of Books, *April 11, 1954, p. 5.*

JOHN BROOKS

Suppose two professional fund raisers—members of a generally respected and respectable firm—were to see another of their partners, something of a no-good, commit a hit-and-run killing in Central Park one night? The witnesses, both decent fellows, know they should report the crime to the police. On the other hand, in the already queasy business of collecting charity for profit, such adverse publicity would permanently ruin the firm. What to do?

Jay Ravoc, one of the two thus sorely tried in [*The Generous Heart*], Kenneth Fearing's newest suspense parable of metropolitan American life, happens conveniently to be leaving town the next day. His escape is only temporary. While he is in Atlantic City, many things happen. It develops that Stanley Thornhill, the partner in the "death car," is privately in league with some particularly unsavory crooks who are engaged in milking an old-line charitable organization, The Generous Heart. Heretofore, Stanley "had always seemed a little too responsible, . . . yet there were other moments when he really lit up with all kinds of fancy lights." From here on, Ravoc understands his partner's strange illuminations all too well. . . .

It is interesting to see the way Mr. Fearing . . . always seems to be intent on writing a straight suspense story, a pure entertainment, only to find a certain moral force creeping in, willy-nilly. *The Generous Heart* is his most unpleasant, even at times flesh-crawling, story. Its subject-matter is made up largely of a folderful of tabloid clippings, all painfully familiar to city dwellers: hit-and-run accidents, leaps from windows, murder in the park, sudden insanity. It ends a little trickily and patly, mystery fashion, and it contains one or two romantic love sequences that clash seriously with its dominant mood of horror. Yet for all this oddly ill-assorted horror and flummery, it is finally a bitter indictment of hypocrisy.

Mr. Fearing's method is to take some corner of big-city life that casts a symbolic shadow, and weave around it a story of violence and intrigue. The professional fund-raising business, being paradoxical at its core, is right up his alley. *The Generous Heart* is fiendishly readable, not so much because of its dense plot as because of the fact that the author, in spite of himself, cannot help caring about his characters and the state of the society they inhabit. One can only feel a little exasperated at the unpretentiousness which causes so gifted a writer to confine himself to the suspense-story formula.

> *John Brooks, "Without Charity," in* The New York Times Book Review, *April 11, 1954, p. 4.*

M. L. ROSENTHAL

I don't think a poet can be much more American, in the psychological if not the Fourth-of-July sense, than Kenneth Fearing. He talks the lingo straight, simple, and sardonic and knows the native panic at being lost in the shuffle which has created it. . . .

One would expect his work to be popular as the plays of Odets and Miller have been popular, if anyone ever opened a book of poems voluntarily. He too writes of the success-dream and the shock of meeting oneself face to face with it. "What does it mean," he asks in **"Twentieth-Century Blues"** [from *New and Selected Poems*], "when the get-away money burns in dollars big as moons, but where is there to go that's just exactly right?" And he is like Hemingway and Fitzgerald in expressing the great national nostalgia for irrecoverable moments of passion ("You will remember the kisses, real or imagined") and of communication. . . .

The range of his humor is that of a great mimic and clown. The reverse *morbidezza* of **"Thirteen O'Clock,"** in which ghosts tremble at the grisly thought of living creatures, is pure comedy. The affectations of critics are amiably crucified in **"Art Review."** . . .

But clowns do not *look* gay, and by well-founded tradition do not feel so either. Some of Fearing's most hilarious effects are at the same time painful views of the human condition. **"Love, 20c the First Quarter Mile"** is a dramatic monologue which, though weak with laughter, gives a picture of genuine anguish. The absurd, sub-articulate dialogue of **"How Do I Feel"** exposes the uneradicable residue of distrust between person and person, as **"Yes, the Agency Can Handle That,"** does the apparently irreversible bargain-packaging of literature for the market. The latter poem, like many of Fearing's, hardens into dismayed realization of waste and pointlessness, of lost possibilities unsalvagable by the most savage yearning for their return.

This realization is Fearing's firing-line. Here he takes his stand as a serious poet. It is the romantic realization that loss is implicit in life, that even in fulfillment the present instant is already becoming the past and losing its reality except in skeptical memory. It is the terrible hunch that there is nothing to the reality anyway, a hunch stated in all its naked desolation in the early **"Green Light"** and fought, but never quite to a standstill, in poem after poem. It is interesting that Fearing's most ringing poem of "social" affirmation in the Thirties—his **"Denouement"**—begins with a demand for an end to this fear of meaninglessness:

> Sky, be blue, and more than blue; wind, be flesh and blood;
> flesh and blood, be deathless . . .

"Denouement" closes in a crescendo of political imagery, but the real issue is stated in its second section:

> You, whose ways were yours alone, you, the one like no one
> else, what have you done with the hour you swore to
> remember, where is the hour, the day, the achievement that
> would never die?

The Depression poems of protest, and those which cried out so desperately against the coming of war and the rise of Hitler and Mussolini, were never merely tendentious. Their wit was too original, and they were always true to a deeper concern for the individual's fate amidst the soul-swamping impersonality of the new orders of destiny: "nothing left to chance, no hysteria and above all, no sentiment." As for the victims (almost everyone), their choice is not usually presented as activistically as in **"Denouement."** Generally they are seen as helpless, anxious, passive. . . .

In Fearing's writing, the "enemy" gradually becomes the Mob, official and unofficial, that thrives on the regimentation of individual thought and feeling through ever-greater control of the avenues of communication. Its triumph, he says, is being brought about by "the revolution that calls itself the Investigation." Fearing's cocky introductory essay, **"Reading, Writing, and the Rackets,"** defines this revolution, commenting pointedly on its heavy employment of the "True Confession Story" as the literary form best calculated to stifle free expression and on the parallel rise of the Investigators and of television in recent years. Ultimately, we are dealing with a racket, non-political and amoral, which cherishes secrecy and destroys genuine communication because there are money and power in so doing. The Mob operates in the same way everywhere, the same types in all countries employing the Investigation and the mechanical media of information for the same ends; the system proliferates, is perhaps too pervasive for individuals to handle. (p. 64)

The most recent of the poems printed here, the four **"Family Album"** poems, deal directly with the wrecking of integrity, intellect and morale by the mob—"God's public relations." In this sequence the Investigation has triumphed, and its early

true-confessors are now looked upon as "the pioneers" and "martyrs" of the new order, who "lived with dangers they alone could see" and "freed that raw, mid-century chaos of little empires from the pestilence of false thought." Like so much else in this book, these poems, with their mock-nostalgia, are very sad and very funny. Fearing is an original, a canny Quixote and—more to the point—a kind of melancholy Jacques of the age, whose writing has often a topical surface that belies its depths of wry compassion and its stylistic purity. Edward Dahlberg once compared him with Corbière, and the comparison was apt. But there are also American comparisons: He is one of the harder-bitten sons of Walt Whitman, a more mordant Masters or Sandburg, a poetic Lardner of wider scope. Let us hope that tough humorous voice of his will continue to be heard for a long time to come; we shall never have another quite like it again. (pp. 64-5)

> *M. L. Rosenthal, "Don Kenneth and the Racket,"*
> *in* The Nation, *New York, Vol. 184, No. 3, January*
> *19, 1957, pp. 64-5.*

DUDLEY FITTS

More years than one cares to count have passed since *Angel Arms* marked the emergence of a vivid and alertly satirical young American poet whose experiments with the common language in free but masterfully contrived verse forms made a promise of brilliant achievement. These early poems of Mr. Fearing's were extraordinarily moving. One found in them what one was always just missing in Sandburg and the few serious poets who approached Sandburg in the American and proletarian commitment: a compassion without mawkishness, an irony without self-congratulation, a certainty of direction and a wit that dared to be funny.

It was a minor art, deriving much of its force from the fact that it never pretended to be anything else; but it was a minor art of the kind that has its own inevitability, that seems destined from the beginning to outlast many more spectacular monuments. *New and Selected Poems*—there are relatively few "new" ones in the collection, and one or two remembered triumphs have unhappily not been "selected"—provides a timely occasion for reappraisal and for the reassertion of one's early convictions.

The promise has been largely fulfilled. One notes that what was valid a quarter of a century ago is still valid: the force is real, the voice clear, the *anima* as true and persuasive in the recent poems as in the first. If there has been a dampening in the pure sardonic *élan* that made certain poems memorable—**"Cultural Notes,"** for example, or that **"Dirge"** for the common man. . . .—there has also been a compensating reinforcement of drive, a spareness, a concentration of language for the delivery of most telling blows.

For it is a fighting poetry, thank God, a poetry of angry conviction, few manners and no winsome graces. It is stubborn in its Old Guard attitude, stubborn in its technique; so unfashionable, indeed, in its resistance to the prevalent obsession with metrical vacuity, that a well-bred young neo-classicist might regard it as almost theatrically conservative. And here, of course, is precisely the place where we came in.

Yet the promise promised more, or seemed to. One turns the pages now with a certain regret, a sense of having somehow been cheated—but of what? . . .

Possibly the answer is to be deduced from Mr. Fearing's prefatory essay, which he calls "**Reading, Writing, and the Rackets**"—an extended onslaught upon Loyalty Hearings inhibiting investigations, the applauded patriot tongues of paid informers and reformed liars. Here his aims are angelical, but his arms are not: a scolding, splitting prose unparagraphed in the manner of the late Arthur Brisbane's editorials, an unhappy private performance that supplies two red herrings for every one that it manages to can. *Hic jacet* something; was it perhaps the material for the definitive poems that should have been written instead? One can only wait and see. Mr. Fearing, at this point in his career, shows no signs of weariness.

> *Dudley Fitts, "Out of Love, Anger, and Conviction," in* The New York Times Book Review, *February 17, 1957, p. 4.*

JUDSON JEROME

[Kenneth Fearing] is still plugging away at seedy America with a murder on every other page. His poetry is much the same as always, although, in what I take to be his latest poems, with more indirection and obscurity. In [*New and Selected Poems*] he provides a long invective of an introduction ["**Reading, Writing, and the Rackets**"], all about the Investigation and the public-relations phoniness of much of the mass literature of our times, wrought to comply with the social lie. What he says is all stimulating enough but repeated and repeated obsessively, proving nothing so much as that the '30's are not dead—or that they are.

Poets should avoid prose as they should I.Q. tests. So long as they break their writing up into short lines, no one, in good taste, examines their ideas very strenuously. Yeats can see spectres, Pound and Eliot and Cummings can get away with the most outrageous distortions of modern experience, provided they attend the decorum of a semblance of form. But in prose, nonsense is nonsense. And a second-rate social analyst is a second-rate social analyst. Nothing Fearing has to say about conformity, suppression of individuality, spiritual deadness in our brave new world, is very original, or, in his prose, much worth reading.

There is a shade of difference, however, between his prose and his prosy poetry—and the shade is significant. As a bard, as a cataloguer of our times, as one who demonstrates, documents, the *feeling* of conformity and spiritual deadness, he is a remarkable and individual poet. His verse is coarse-grained, formless, overstated, illuminated by almost no metaphor, but although I disapprove of what he is doing in the name of poetry, I go on reading—and am really touched by the evocative detail, the hard humor, and, above all, the pervading compassion he feels even for those he hates. . . . (pp. 139-40)

> *Judson Jerome, "Ten Poets: Rare to Overdone," in* The Antioch Review, *Vol. XVII, No. 1, March, 1957, pp. 135-44.*

STANLEY KUNITZ

[*The essay excerpted below was originally published in* The Saturday Review, *June 29, 1957.*]

The voice of Kenneth Fearing is an unmistakable one. No contemporary poet has more effectively dedicated his career to the representation of what T. S. Eliot, in his essay on Baudelaire, described as "the sordid life of a great metropolis."

It cannot be said flatly that Fearing either loves or hates New York, but he is not seduced by it, he does not habitually celebrate it, and he never forgets, in the role of the quizzical pedestrian, those bleak images of the city's meanness and indifference and violence that crowded his eyes in the Depression years when his art matured.

In *New and Selected Poems*, . . . which affords a welcome opportunity to review the work of some thirty years, we cannot fail to note the constancy of his vision. The same cards, however reshuffled, keep turning up; we are in a world threatened by newspaper headlines and sudden death; a world of cops and gangsters, the hunters and the hunted; of stuffed shirts and frightened little men; of cigar stores and drugstores and seedy barrooms and pinball arcades; of doubts and guilts and inquisitions. Such material would seem to posit a poet of rage and revolution, but Fearing does not characteristically climb to that level of intensity. His tone, for the most part, remains ironic. If he is a revolutionary poet, out of the proletarian tradition of the thirties, and the best survivor of that tradition, he is one without a revolution to propose. One of his favorite disguises is that of the investigator, the private eye, whose professional pride constrains him, almost against his will, to crack the case.

Fearing's poems are always asking questions. . . . The structures are incremental, largely based on repetitions, with little impulse towards the grandeur of resolution. (pp. 210-11)

Though a handful of Fearing's poems evince a degree of optimism about man's destiny, he is usually too aware of the malady of our time to deceive himself with easy formulas for salvation. At times indeed he seems to settle a bit too comfortably, with a shrug of his shoulders, into the resignation of spiritual fatigue. "I am tired of following invisible lives down intangible avenues to fathomless ends."

Somewhat paradoxically, this realist speaks to us of the unreality of modern existence. His poems are populated by cliff-dwellers who own neither gods nor heroes, and who have lost finally their faith in themselves. It is by no means an accident that Fearing so frequently introduces sorcerers, wizards, astrologers, and other apostles of the degraded miracle into the world of his invention.

Fearing's ear for speech rhythms is remarkably keen, and he handles the vernacular without any trace of self-consciousness. His long cadenced line derives from Whitman, but he has made it very much his own, tinctured with an acidulous wit and sensitive to varying pressures. He aims at a poetry that is at once exciting and understandable. . . . I am not inclined to quarrel with the virtues of excitement and readability, but I wonder, as I look back at Fearing's career, with a good deal of admiration for his gifts and accomplishment, whether his development has not been restricted by the stubborn limitations of his esthetics. His art of brilliant surfaces and quick contemporaneity seemed more daring once, as a poetic configuration, than it does today, though the best poems keep their early lustre. (pp. 211-12)

> *Stanley Kunitz, "Private Eye," in his* A Kind of Order, a Kind of Folly, *Little, Brown and Company, 1975, pp. 210-12.*

LEONARD NATHAN

In [*New and Selected Poems*], as in all Fearing's books, individual poems are usually well put together and sometimes moving. Poems as widely separated in time as **"Green Light"** (late twenties) to **"Sherlock Spends a Day in the Country"** (early fifties) have the special force and rightness that the poet's approach attains at its best.

But reading Fearing's poems in a group is another matter. After a while, the impression is that you have read the same poem over and over until discriminations blur and curiosity is put to sleep. While it is far from fatal for a single style to dominate the whole career of a poet, that style must have sufficient breadth and suppleness to forestall its becoming a ready-at-hand appliance for every occasion. Fearing's style, for all its apparent freedom from traditional limitations, is clogged with mannerisms and archly stylized habits: you are forever confronted by the momentous rhetorical question, the cosmically significant repetition, the meaningfully twisted popular slogan, the prophetic line (with appropriate Old Testament echoes). . . . And there is no suggestion from poem to poem of a fresh approach to a fresh experience. A deadening consistency is the result.

But habits of technique that lead to monotony do not, I think, get at the source of the trouble. That source is found rather in Fearing's relationship to his subject matter, the individual's Fate in the modern city. Fearing's poems are almost always commentaries on the meretriciousness of that Fate. The individual, under the pressure of bad authority (advertising, business, mass communications, etc.) to conform, banks an infinite and hopeless frustration which finally is corrupted or wiped out in the moral bankruptcy of the society. Fearing's almost inevitable response to these conditions is heavy irony in which he suspends fragmented and random impressions of squalor, violence, and suffering. The subject matter and the response to it are certainly fit bases for poetry. And yet the impressions of which Fearing's "vision" mainly consists are vague and abstract (and sometimes merely hackneyed), and the irony in which they are suspended cannot seem to resolve them, or make more than superficial sense of them. Particular impressions and ideas are apt to be so generalized that the poet's response to them is generalized to the point where depth and subtlety of discrimination are lost. . . . The irony sometimes seems dated and callow, despite its honesty and technically accomplished presentation. It is as if Fearing's habitual irony only permitted him to see things by the gross or in generalities (as conventional as the "finny tribes" of earlier mannerists). Often, the consequence is too insufficient a discrimination to see a world behind the old stereotypes. For thirty years Fearing has fought the dragons of commercialism and conformity; the effects of the struggle on his poetry have not been altogether good. But there are those poems like **"Five A.M.,"** **"Continuous Performance,"** and **"The Face in the Bar Room Mirror"** that transcend the struggle and comment on it with the ominous and witty power Fearing can achieve at his best. Such poems help make up for deficits elsewhere. (pp. 327-28)

> *Leonard Nathan, in a review of "New and Selected Poems," in* Poetry, *Vol. XC, No. 5, August, 1957, pp. 327-28.*

ROBERT C. HEALEY

When Steve Crozart, one of the more flamboyant practitioners of the fine art of public relations, was reported killed in an ocean plane crash, some of his fellow wolves in the Madison Avenue image factories went into action. Lee Hoyt, for one, decided to capitalize immediately on the Crozart legend, even

if it meant fabricating posthumous materials. But Crozart, ever the astute operator, had worked out his own ingenious plans for his death and its sequel. The battle for the Crozart name that rages in the plush offices and cocktail lounges is the subject of Kenneth Fearing's biting new novel [*The Crozart Story*].

By now novels about the struggle for power in high places usually follow a familiar pattern. What gives *The Crozart Story* a certain freshness and distinction is its sardonic cynicism, its self-incriminating narration by the principal characters and its generally convincing air of X-raying the machinery of communications. The publicity didoes of Congressional investigating committees also come under Fearing's mordant scrutiny. The whole is realistically buttressed with exhibits of pertinent scripts, announcements, newspaper clippings, etc.

Essentially a serious examination of the inside of the communications industry, *The Crozart Story* is also a mystery which relies on pure melodrama for its final pages. There are no fine and upright individuals in this ruthless world, only unscrupulous operators who are prepared to manipulate the public and each other with equal relish. The men who specialize in images themselves will probably groan at this persuasive variation of the popular image that the novelists have created for them.

> *Robert C. Healey, "Old War with a New Tactic," in* New York Herald Tribune Book Review, *September 4, 1960, p. 7.*

RICHARD ELMAN

When it was first published in 1946, *The Big Clock* was an intellectual's crime novel; it had social significance. The murderer—and later self-murdering victim of his own unpremeditated rages—was a stewardly, self-pitying bully who resembled the late Henry Luce.

Much of the action of the novel also took place in the offices of a publishing conglomerate very much like Time Inc. With prophetic accuracy, Kenneth Fearing depicted the Earl Janoth Enterprises as the publishers of *Personalities* (fictive forerunner to Time's *People* magazine), as well as *Sexes* and the newsmag *Newsways*. All were staffed with hacks, intellectuals *manqués* and the other callow disaffected types whom we now recognize and refer to as "the media."

Like Raymond Chandler, Fearing started out as a poet. He was an original at giving the impression of improvisation—the metropolitan beat. He had, moreover, an artist's quick distrust of commerce, and he polarized the argument of *Clock* between the money-grubbing hacks employed by Janoth Enterprises, and the genuine artist-painter Louise Paterson.

Fearing's protagonist and chief narrator, George Stroud, is also one of the Janoth boys, although he is redeemed by his open cynicism. This misogynistic philanderer is endowed with a certain Chandleresque, epigrammatic charm: "She was tall, ice-blonde, and splendid," he says of the soon-to-be-murdered Pauline Delos, Janoth's mistress, with whom he will commence an affair: "The eye saw nothing but innocence, to the instincts she was undiluted sex, the brain said here was a perfect hell."

That Pauline's last name may remind us of Grecian love is not coincidental; she brings Janoth to his murderous ecstasy of jealousy for her affairs with women, as well as men, and he bashes her skull with a decanter, I suppose, because no amphorae were available in her 40s Manhattan flat. To save his own skin, Janoth, with his homosexual chum, Hagen, will have their employee Stroud combing the city for somebody who was with Pauline that night (Stroud, of course, though they still don't know that) to be their fall guy.

So *The Big Clock* contains all the elements of a cautionary pop fable about instinct versus property. An angry book, it uses its considerable slickness and knowing metropolitan details to depict the sellout of the radical intellectuals of Fearing's time:

> *Newsways, Crimeways, Personalities* . . . overrunning with frustrated ex-artists, scientists, farmers, writers, explorers, poets, lawyers, doctors, musicians, all of whom spent their lives conforming . . . to a sort of overgrown aimless haphazard stenciling. . . why should I pay more tribute to this fatal machine? It would be easier and simpler to get squashed stripping its gears than to be crushed helping it along. . . .

Such broad characterization may seem a little too recognizable to us in the 1980s, but it also seems all-too-generally true about those who take jobs at *Time* and *Newsweek* seriously; and the characterization is central to the plot of *The Big Clock* because once George Stroud recognizes his own worth, and ceases to be a company man, he is able to extricate himself from the complications of the murderous Janoth machine. In other words, in the novel's value system, owning anything . . . must be based on love. . . .

Rereading *The Big Clock,* so many years later, reminded me of how all popular forms inevitably parody their subjects, even when they are engaged in serious criticism.

> Richard Elman, *"Durable Time Piece," in* The Nation, *New York, Vol. 231, No. 8, September 20, 1980, p. 256.*

ROBERT M. RYLEY

Kenneth Fearing's *The Big Clock* is so consummate a thriller that only aficionados of the genre take it seriously. . . .

More than novels lacking action and suspense, to be sure, thrillers are likely to be potboilers. But the notion that action and suspense are necessarily incompatible with artistic merit is a peculiarly modern form of intellectual snobbery. As a matter of fact, *The Big Clock* ought to satisfy just about anybody's requirements for seriousness in fiction. I will discuss the novel's many excellences under three heads: originality and vividness of characterization, sophistication of literary technique, and significance of theme. (p. 354)

[Fearing's protagonist, George Stroud], shares a number of characteristics with the tough-guy heroes of Hammett and Chandler. The hardbitten intonations of a Marlowe or a Continental Op can be heard, for example, in this account by Stroud of a chance meeting with Pauline Delos:

> I picked up my drink and went to her table. Why not?
>
> I said of course she didn't remember me, and she said of course she did.
>
> I said could I buy her a drink. I could.
>
> She was blonde as hell, wearing a lot of black.

As well as a style, Stroud shares with the tough-guy heroes a metaphysical despair, a conviction that human suffering is ines-

capable and meaningless. The big clock that gives the novel its title is his metaphor for the blind mechanism of the universe and for the human institutions—society, corporations—that reflect its inexorable and crushing power. Like the tough-guy heroes, Stroud gives his loyalties to individuals rather than to abstractions, and like them he accepts without self-pity the ordeals of pain and endurance that his loyalties demand.

But Stroud is both less admirable and more likable than the conventional tough-guy heroes. He is less admirable because, unlike them, he willingly participates in the corruption and hypocrisy he disdains. He wants bourgeois success: a higher salary and a bigger house in a more exclusive section of the suburbs. He works at a job he dislikes, with colleagues he regards for the most part as pompous fools, to produce a magazine he knows exerts an unwarranted and baleful influence on the public. He betrays his most important personal loyalty, that to his wife. The affair with Pauline Delos is only the most recent in a long series of infidelities, and we know it won't be the last. The conventional tough-guy hero, judged by his own standards, is very nearly a saint. Judged by anybody's standards, Stroud is, in Julian Symons's phrase, "morally null."

But it was Cardinal Cushing, I think, who said that while saints may be all right in heaven, they're hell on earth. For all his virtues, the tough-guy hero doesn't exactly inspire affection. It's not only that he's almost always right about everything, or that, as one critic points out, he discovers guilt everywhere but in himself. It's also that the bleakness of his vision reflects the bleakness of his soul. To protect himself against the disappointments that his radical pessimism tells him are inevitable, he smothers his own capacity for joy. The range of emotion in tough-guy mystery novels is extraordinarily limited, for all loss and disappointment and sin are absorbed into the uniform drabness that constitutes the tough guy's world.

Stroud is different. In spite of his tough-guy *Weltanschaung* and along with his tough-guy capacity to endure pain, he has the vitality, the *joie de vivre*, the charm of an aristocratic amateur sleuth in a traditional British mystery. "Normally," his wife says of him, "he wrapped himself in clouds of confetti, but anyone who knew him at all understood exactly what he meant and just where he could be found." The confetti is playfulness and whimsicality, exemplified by the funny and imaginative (and, it may be added, significant) stories he tells his daughter, and by his delight in harmless eccentrics like Gil the tavern-keeper, who stores an enormous pile of junk behind his bar and defies his customers to name something he doesn't have. Stroud's interests are wide and varied. He is moved by the beauty of a landscape, reads poetry, theorizes about the aesthetics of film and radio, knows boxing, and collects antiques and modern paintings—the latter a passion that nearly results in his exposure. If this exuberant versatility makes his metaphysical pessimism almost paradoxical, it also makes poignant his weaknesses and failures. Loss has meaning in *The Big Clock* because there is more than tough-guy seediness to lose.

If Stroud is an unconventional hero—part tough guy, part Cheeveresque suburbanite, part intellectual and dilletante—Janoth is an unconventional villain. . . . Janoth has at least three personalities. . . . Here is Stroud's initial description of him (one that also suggests, of course, Stroud's intelligence and sensitivity):

> There was one thing I always saw, or thought I saw, in Janoth's big, pink, disorderly face, permanently fixed in a faint smile he had forgotten about long

ago, his straight and innocent stare that didn't, any more, see the person in front of him at all. He wasn't adjusting himself to the big clock. He didn't even know there was a big clock. The large, gray, convoluted muscle in the back of that childlike gaze was digesting something unknown to the ordinary world. That muscle with its long tendons had nearly fastened itself about a conclusion, a conclusion startlingly different from the hearty expression once forged upon the outward face, and left there, abandoned. Some day that conclusion would be reached, the muscle would strike. Probably it had, before. Surely it would, again.

> He said how nice Georgette [Stroud's wife] was looking, which was true, how she always reminded him of carnivals and Hallowe'en, the wildest baseball ever pitched in history, and there was as usual a real and extraordinary warmth in the voice, as though this were another, still a third personality.

The passage about Janoth's mysterious inner life prepares us for the outburst of violence that will later destroy Pauline Delos. What Stroud senses in Janoth but cannot define is a proneness to waves of despair, to the feeling that "everything in the world was ashes." In many ways innocent, lacking Stroud's cynicism—"He didn't even know there was a big clock"—he is an uncertain judge of men. Contrast Stroud's accurate assessment of Janoth with Janoth's underestimation of Stroud.

> He was [Janoth says of Stroud] what I had always classified as one of those hyper-perceptive people, not good at action but fine at pure logic and theory. He was the sort who could solve a bridge-hand at a glance, down to the last play, but in a simple business deal he would be helpless. The cold fighter's and gambler's nerve that Steve [Hagen] had was completely lacking in him, and he would consider it something foreign or inhuman, if indeed he understood it at all.

It is true that Stroud finds Hagen's toughness inhuman, but Janoth's certainty that Stroud can't match it comes at a time when he is single-handedly opposing the entire Janoth organization.

More serious than Janoth's misjudgments of others is his inability to understand himself. He naïvely imagines that his own feelings of despair are unique, and he is astonished as well as homicidally enraged when Delos accuses him of having a homoerotic relationship with his best friend, the bachelor Hagen. Everything Janoth does after the murder—obliterating his fingerprints, stealing out of the apartment, taking a taxi two blocks away from the building and getting out two blocks away from his destination—shows that he wants to conceal his guilt. But in his conversation with Hagen, he seems really to believe that he intends to turn himself in to the police. Unable to contemplate the baseness of his own motives, he needs to be told that his escape will serve the interests of his employees and the public. This isn't so much hypocrisy as self-hypnosis, and it isn't entirely unattractive because it implies at least some respect for the idea of altruism if not for the reality. A measure of Fearing's departure from the conventions of popular fiction is that almost the only character in the novel to have ideals is the murderer.

The Big Clock also differs from run-of-the-mill thrillers in the subtlety of its narrative technique. Fearing tells the story by means of multiple narrators, a device that he uses in all his novels, not always happily. Sometimes there are too many narrators (*The Hospital, Clark Gifford's Body*); sometimes

(*Loneliest Girl in the World, The Generous Heart*) chapters narrated by minor characters turn into self-contained short stories. *The Big Clock,* on the other hand, effects a perfect marriage of plot and points of view. Fearing insures that Stroud will be the focus of the reader's interest and concern by having him narrate eleven of the novel's nineteen chapters and by delaying the first shift in point of view until almost a fourth of the way into the book. By this time the direction of the plot is so clearly established that, without distracting the reader from Stroud's story, Fearing can use each of the six other narrators for a variety of subordinate purposes. For instance, Stroud tries to misdirect the search for himself by assigning people jobs for which they are temperamentally unsuited. To stake out Gil's shabby Third Avenue bar he sends Edward Orlin, a humorless literary intellectual with an interest in Henry James. Orlin himself tells the story of an afternoon at Gil's in a chapter that not only furthers the plot as Orlin gathers information that may help to identify the missing witness, but also produces social comedy as Gil's tackiness registers on Orlin's effete sensibility. A variation on this device occurs in a later chapter narrated by the painter Louise Patterson. Through her irreverent eyes the reader sees the stuffed shirt sent by Stroud to interview her. Respectability's judgment on the disreputable in one chapter is balanced by Bohemia's judgment on respectability in the other.

The latter chapter also contains one of the most dramatic moments in the novel when Patterson, brought to the Janoth Building to identify the missing witness, meets Stroud and realizes that the leader of the hunt is also the quarry. Since the plot requires that she conceal her knowledge, having the confrontation narrated from her point of view serves to clarify her motives more fully than might otherwise have been possible. But there are additional advantages. Other narrators have noticed that Stroud looks haggard and drawn—Fearing's way of emphasizing the pressure he is under, while at the same time preserving his silent stoicism in the chapters he narrates himself. Patterson the artist, however, is more sensitive to the signs of strain than anyone else in the novel:

> His eyes were like craters, and I saw that their sockets were hard and drawn and icy cold, in spite of the easy smile he showed. I knew this, and at the same time I knew no one else in the room was capable of knowing it. . . .

Perhaps the most important advantage of the use of a slightly hostile narrator in this chapter is that the reader is distanced from the protagonist at a moment of intense crisis. This has a strangely unsettling effect, like that of being denied communication with a friend while watching him undergo a painful ordeal.

The climax of *The Big Clock* parodies almost too cleverly the nick-of-time escapes of conventional thrillers. . . . It must be conceded that the coincidence by which Janoth is deposed at the very moment when a posse closes in on Stroud is made especially outrageous by Fearing's unwillingness to let the reader know beforehand that a crucial executive meeting is in progress. I write "unwillingness" rather than "failure" because the absence of preparation for the meeting is clearly deliberate, an intentional effort to force the reader to share the ignorance of Stroud and his colleagues. In this connection it is instructive to compare Fearing's use of multiple narrators with that in nineteenth-century mystery novels such as Wilkie Collins's *The Woman in White* or *The Moonstone*. Each of Collins's narrators writes all that he knows, and what he knows completes the jigsaw puzzle of the plot, so that those who survive can read and understand the whole. Fearing's narratives, however, are interior monologues and are therefore inaccessible to the other characters. Furthermore, the most important narrator doesn't tell all he knows. That Stroud has had an affair with a woman named Elizabeth Stoltz is made known in the chapter narrated by his wife; that he used to get drunk and pass out at Gil's is made known in the chapter narrated by Orlin. Stroud reveals just enough about his arrangement with the manager of a residential hotel to indicate that he's been using the hotel for his sexual liaisons, but not enough to indicate how or when the arrangement began, or how often he's taken advantage of it. Such indirectly conveyed and incomplete information suggests a side of his character that's vaguely disquieting, not so much because it's sordid as because it's impenetrable. Even when the various narrators tell all they know, uncertainty remains. Since none of them has taken part in the conspiracy to unseat Janoth, neither they nor the reader can know how it happened. This isn't careless exposition. It's twentieth-century epistemological scepticism.

Still, since the reader is privy to more information than anyone else, he's expected to make connections and draw inferences on his own. He's expected, in fact, to tie up the loose "plot ends.". . . There are three of them: Stroud's handkerchief, with his laundry mark, left behind in a bar he had been to with Delos; pictures of people known to have been acquainted with the victim, including one of Stroud, that the police are showing to the staff of the hotel where Stroud and Delos spent the night; and a taxi driver, tracked down by Stroud, who remembers driving Janoth on the night of the murder from the neighborhood of Delos's apartment to the neighborhood of Hagen's. Though much is made of these pieces of evidence when they are introduced, they seem to lead nowhere because, at the end of the book, Stroud is still unsuspected as the missing witness and Janoth, who has killed himself, is still protected by an airtight alibi. The reader has to infer, however, that by means of Stroud's photograph the police will expose his affair with Delos and thus destroy his marriage; that the handkerchief will place him with Delos shortly before the murder and thus make him a suspect; but that the taxi driver will explode Janoth's alibi and thus save Stroud from being punished for a crime he didn't commit. And to help the careful reader make the proper connections, after the climax Fearing has Stroud tell his daughter a story about a little girl who "started to pick at a loose thread in her handkerchief"—significant detail—and who ended up as "just a heap of yarn lying on the floor." The moral of the story, Stroud explains, is "not to pull out any loose threads. Not too far." In the final scene of the novel, still giddy with relief at his miraculous escape, Stroud is on his way to meet his wife for a night on the town. He knows that the big clock will "get around to me again. Inevitably. Soon." But he refuses to make conscious his knowledge of the evidence that will trap him. . . . [He] refuses "to pull out any loose threads. Not too far." (pp. 354-58)

Robert M. Ryley, "More than a Thriller: 'The Big Clock'," in The Armchair Detective, *Vol. 16, No. 4, Winter, 1983, pp. 354-59.*

DAVID ROSENTHAL

[Fifty years ago, Kenneth Fearing] was recognized as a major writer. Nowadays, scarcely anyone knows his name, and those who do usually associate it with his murder mystery, ***The Big Clock***. Yet Fearing's work—edgy, syncopated, alive to the pathos of inarticulateness, the sound of American speech, and the media static that keeps us from knowing what we think or feel—has lost neither its jagged music nor its emotional wallop. His writing is no more dated than Hart Crane's, and his 1930s cocktail of impending holocaust, canned dreams, and dire straits is as apt today as it was then.

Fearing's first book of poetry (*Angel Arms*) was published in 1929. Despite some derivative pieces, he had already developed his own volatile voice in poems like **"Green Light,"** in which the language of consumerism mingles with dread and longing. . . .

Fearing's great decade was the '30s; the doom and entropy of the period suited him to a T. Though political, his poems are generally free from mere topicality, sloganeering, and phony optimism. For Fearing, social reality is part of a vision at once alienated and jauntily hard-nosed. . . .

Fearing's tonal variety—his ability to encompass so many linguistic levels—paralleled and drew upon his varied work experience. He held jobs as a salesman, mill hand, clerk, and free-lance writer and editor. His writing assignments were not always literary, which surely fed his obsession with the language of advertising. . . .

Many other modernists contrasted colloquial and literary language for ironic effect, but unlike most of them, Fearing didn't look down his nose at anyone. However he might snarl, he was no snob. In his fiction as well as his poetry, he introduces an enormous variety of characters with robust sympathy. His finest novel, ***The Hospital***, gives a multilayered view of one sweltering day. We meet, among others, Helen, who believes she has tuberculosis; her lover Steve, a sailor; an aging doctor who's lost his shirt on the stock market and kills himself with an overdose of morphine; a receptionist dreaming of a union that'll win her a living wage; a dockworker blinded by acid in a mafia turf battle; the women in the laundry room—a whole tangle of lives in a life-and-death institution. . . .

Somber, cocky, haunted by death and penury, Fearing's work is as powerful as when it was first written. Like such modern Mediterranean writers as Yehuda Amichai, Cesare Pavese, and Joan Vinyoli, he knew how to be straightforward without sacrificing subtlety.

David Rosenthal, in a review of "Collected Poems of Kenneth Fearing" and "The Hospital," in VLS, *No. 53, March, 1987, p. 4.*

Penelope Fitzgerald
1916-

English novelist and biographer.

In her novels, Fitzgerald combines a humanistic approach and a compressed, witty narrative style to reveal the strength and nobility of her characters as they cope with life in contemporary society. Her works often revolve around a small group of people who are brought together by a common interest or shared environment. Anne Duchêne observed that Fitzgerald's fiction "has a natural authority, is very funny, warm, and gently ironic, and full of tenderness towards human beings and their bravery in living."

Fitzgerald's first novel, *The Golden Child* (1977), is a mystery of deception set in an art museum in which a prized exhibit is discovered to be a forgery and a well-known explorer is murdered. Her next novel, *The Bookshop* (1978), which earned Fitzgerald significant critical attention in England, concerns the resiliency of the human spirit. This work takes place in a deteriorating Suffolk village where Florence Green attempts to make a success of her recently opened bookstore. Her efforts are opposed and eventually defeated by Violet Gamart, a society matron who wants the building for her own vague purposes. In *Offshore* (1979), for which she received the Booker McConnell Prize for fiction, Fitzgerald relies on her reminiscences of life on a houseboat to recreate the camaraderie among boat-dwellers on the Thames River during the 1960s. Critics noted her restrained, poetic prose and her sharply defined characters, and Digby Durrant praised *Offshore* as "deft, ironic, original and enjoyable."

Fitzgerald's next novel, *Human Voices* (1980), is loosely based on her experiences as a programming assistant for the British Broadcasting Corporation. Set in 1940, the year Nazi Germany began its air offensive against England, this book examines the importance of truth in both public communications and personal relationships. Fitzgerald was widely commended for her stylistic control and her insights into human character. Penelope Lively commented: "[Fitzgerald] achieves a remarkable range of comment about how people behave, told in a voice that is both idiosyncratic and memorable." *At Freddie's* (1982) details the efforts of a drama school proprietress to keep her business financially solvent. *Innocence* (1986) is generally considered Fitzgerald's most ambitious novel. Set in Florence, Italy, this work chronicles the lives of the Ridolfis, a decaying aristocratic family, and the Rossis, a working-class family of Communist sympathizers. Through the courtship and marriage of Chiara Ridolfi and Salvatore Rossi, Fitzgerald examines various levels of human innocence as well as ways in which individuals can become trapped by their family histories. C. K. Stead praised *Innocence* as "a work of strange, muted power and intelligence."

Fitzgerald has also published several literary biographies, among them *The Knox Brothers* (1977), which includes an examination of the career of her father, Edmund George Valpy Knox, a respected essayist and humorist who edited *Punch* magazine from 1932 to 1949.

(See also *CLC*, Vol. 19; *Contemporary Authors*, Vols. 85-88; and *Dictionary of Literary Biography*, Vol. 14.)

© Tara Heinemann 1986

ANNE DUCHÊNE

Taking a lovable old eccentric as the protagonist of a story must always threaten to make its centre soft. Taking as protagonist a lovable old eccentric who is also the female head of a run-down but still bravely flamboyant juvenile dramatic school would seem to compound the risk, by embracing all the dead or deadening ends of theatrical narcissism—which threaten to make the edges of the story a bit soggy too. Penelope Fitzgerald has taken on both challenges in [*At Freddie's*], and generously failed to overcome them.

Her central figure, Freddie, once worked with Lilian Bayliss, from whom she learned "the craft of idealism, that is to say, how to defeat materialism by getting people to work for almost nothing", and such habits as waiting on a Word for guidance. . . . [The] story covers the months in 1963 when Freddie, who has never set her sights for her pupils lower than Shakespeare, *Peter Pan* and pantomime, has to acknowledge television commercials.

In itself, this might have made a caustically funny little story; but the author's own generosity disperses it. Much of the interest devolves upon the new teachers among Freddie's staff, and a few of their pupils. The teachers are Irish: Hannah, aged twenty, at large in London with nothing but her goodness of heart to guide her, and wholly in thrall to the lure of "everything theatrical, which can persist in the most hard-headed, opening the way to poetry and disaster"; and Pierce ("from Castlehen, a short way out of Derry"), older and more sedately—indeed, almost sedately—serene. . . . Pierce can "only be himself, and that not very successfully". Cue, here, for a little love-interest, admirably charted and poignantly doomed.

Their pupils, meanwhile, the child-actors . . . , represent a concatenation of immature egotism: "all they wanted was to be noticed, and to be seen not to care whether they were noticed or not". One of the two singled out is genuinely gifted; the other, a Dickensianly knowing little boy, is only "a success". Sadly, the reader may often find difficulty, and a certain amount of tedium, in remembering which is which; until the end, when one takes part in a production of *King John* and the other is still rehearsing it.

About *King John*, the author is justly funny. . . .

About the whole matter of theatrical illusion, though, Fitzgerald is always exuberantly exact. Freddie, for instance,

> believed that the theatre should never be exposed to the air, or taken outdoors, or brought to the people. The theatre was there for audiences to come to. . . . They were creators in their own right, each performance coming to life, if it ever did, between the actors and the audience, and after that lost for eternity. The extravagance of that loss was its charm.

It is a pity to hit this nerve, and then to waste it; but somehow the obligations of fleshing out a novel seem here to have run counter to the author's will to celebrate an idea. Instead of concentrating, she has dissipated; even her commas sometimes proclaim her reliance on the tiresomely weakening *faux-naif*. One does not want to see a writer of such ease and exuberance retreat into the cosy, confidential mugginess of much of her writing here. Penelope Fitzgerald began to write, or anyway to be published, fairly late in life: all the more reason for her to centre down, hard, on what she is able to say, rather than to waste time in trying to make herself agreeable to us.

> *Anne Duchêne, "All for Loss," in* The Times Literary Supplement, *No. 4122, April 2, 1982, p. 370.*

JUDY ASTOR

Occasionally, one picks up a book and knows by the bottom of page one that nothing but pleasure lies ahead—all one has to do is surrender and enjoy it. Muriel Spark's *The Girls of Slender Means* came into that category. And so does Penelope Fitzgerald's *At Freddie's.*

They occupy much the same novelistic territory. Like Muriel Spark, Penelope Fitzgerald knows exactly what she's doing. In three lines and a snatch of dialogue she can nail a character, in a paragraph conjure up a place and an atmosphere—a Lyons tea-shop, backstage at the theatre or the streets of Covent Garden. . . .

Funny, yes; but there is affection along with the beadiness. Freddie, the vast ageless institution who bullies, flatters and manipulates to keep her crumbling stage-school—the Temple, better known as 'Freddie's'—out of the hands of the bailiffs, is a monster, but a sacred monster. As she flattens the opposition, whether it's a casting director who wants to get rid of

one of her pupils, her own accountant who is trying to keep her solvent, or the Committee of the National Theatre who misguidedly recommend setting up a rival stage school, the reader can only cheer.

More impressive still, one's sympathies are firmly engaged by the children, Freddie's pupils. They are most of them brattish and precocious, as avid for attention as they are incapable of telling the truth. . . .

But Mrs Fitzgerald never quite lets high comedy turn into farce, or character into caricature. Freddie's children are real children, distorted by the pressures of an adult world—their only playground the streets of Covent Garden. There's not a wasted word or a detail that doesn't tell, and it's so deftly done that one is hardly aware of the artistry because one is enjoying the jokes too much. (p. 23)

> *Judy Astor, "Children in Trouble," in* The Listener, *Vol. 107, No. 2755, April 8, 1982, pp. 23-4.*

PENELOPE LIVELY

The pleasures of Penelope Fitzgerald's novels are stylistic; there are few who can match her when it comes to the nailing of a character in a few words, the turn of phrase that brings a person or a place smoking off the page, the wry comment that sums up a situation. *At Freddie's,* like *Human Voices* and *Offshore,* does not bother much with plot but offers instead a string of elegantly contrived episodes involving a group of people caught up in an institution: in *Offshore* the institution was the eccentric society of Thames barges; *Human Voices* beautifully satirised the wartime BBC; *At Freddie's* is concerned with the oddities and humanities of a stage school. Freddie herself, the proprietress, is "one of those few people . . . whom society has mysteriously decided to support at all costs." . . . Such narrative as the novel has is concerned with her attempts to save the school from closing down; since it has apparently always existed on a financial brink, one assumes that this kind of thing has happened before. One knows also that Freddie will survive. We have after all been told that.

And so, the framework established, the author can get down to some graceful and good-natured comedy. She is particularly good on the wizened youth of theatrical children, corrupted by their trade until they can barely distinguish between fact and fantasy—Dickensian children, and rightly given Dickensian centrality in the novel. Two of them—a prematurely worldly lad called Mattie, and the younger, and genuinely talented, Jonathan—are involved in a production of *King John* which gives Mrs Fitzgerald the opportunity for a lot of wry fun; on the problems of producing the play at all . . . and then with the engaging lunacies of a presentation in Edwardian dress in which Shakespeare's court is a lavish billiard room at Sandringham and the red-hot pincers are ingeniously battery-powered, fading from red to black. The attitudinising Mattie meets his match in a ham old actor called Boney ("No emotion can be so pure as the hatred you feel for a child"); and Hannah, the young teacher at the school whose half-hearted love affair with a colleague is the other central strand in the plot, gets a glimpse of the world of the real stage. At the end of the book we leave Jonathan, jumping off a wall over and over again, alone, in rehearsal for his role. This last is a moving moment; Mattie, it is hinted, is heading for commercial success, but it is Jonathan who has the lonely gift of artistic dedication. The ambivalences of the theatre are suggested here and there throughout the book: that strange mix of seriousness and vulgarity, of art and artifice, of the sublime and the meretricious. Indeed, they are personified by Freddie herself in whose complex character integrity and guile comfortably coexist. I did once or twice have the feeling that beyond the surface skills (and they are considerable) of *At Freddie's* a more serious book was lurking: that, given a more vigorous narrative intention and without the affectionately treated but ultimately inessential romantic sub-plot it might have become quite another book.

That being said, *At Freddie's* is full of treats. Penelope Fitzgerald is a thoroughly English writer; her talent has all those English qualities of understatement and irony and lightness of touch—qualities which can be mistaken for an underlying failure of purpose. This is to misinterpret: at their most powerful they are lethal (Kingsley Amis, Evelyn Waugh, Anthony Powell); *At Freddie's* is not forceful in that way because it does not set out to be. Its strength is to use this kind of deft—and deceptively laconic—manner to create fiction that is wonderfully entertaining and in which style and content achieve a perfect harmony. (p. 88)

Penelope Lively, "Backwards & Forwards," in Encounter, Vol. LVIII, No. 6 & Vol. LIX, No. 1, June-July, 1982, pp. 86-91.

ROXANA ROBINSON

What's to be said about a well-meaning book like [*At Freddie's*]? We approach with respect the British novelist Penelope Fitzgerald's first work to appear in America; she won the prestigious Booker Prize for an earlier novel, *Offshore*. And *At Freddie's* is a hard book to dislike; it isn't a glitzy bid for easy sales, or an etiolated highbrow puzzle. It is well mannered, well written and instantly forgettable. Freddie is a subtle and powerful old woman, legendary in the London theatrical world. The Temple, her school for child actors, is famous, her stinginess fabled, her methods baffling. Hannah and Pierce are her ill-paid instructors, Mattie and Jonathan her precocious young students. Pierce loves Hannah, who loves Boney, an actor; Mattie yearns for Jonathan's genius; Freddie's aims are unrevealed. Pierce pursues Hannah, Mattie pursues Jonathan, investors pursue Freddie. Nothing is resolved. Often the dialogue and narrative achieve a serpentine intricacy, both exhausting and obscure. . . . And though we are told repeatedly that Freddie is fascinating, she appears merely to be a shabby old woman with boiled blue eyes, a musty smell and plans too complicated to reveal, for which last we may feel grateful.

Roxana Robinson, in a review of "At Freddie's," in The New York Times Book Review, September 8, 1985, p. 24.

C. K. STEAD

Penelope Fitzgerald's *Innocence* is set in Florence, the principal characters are Italian, and I kept asking myself: how is it done? She knows quite a lot about Italian society: but more important, she has somehow got inside her Italian characters, so that when a young Englishwoman appears on the scene she really seems a foreigner and not, as one might expect, the focus of the novel's consciousness. Imagination is part of the mystery; the other part is pace. This novel seems to impose its own slow pace on the reader. Probably that means one has a sense that nothing we are told is insignificant. It has, not opacity, but density. It is a book that never seems to settle back, as so

much currently admired fiction does, into a conventional exercise, fiction as a pastiche of itself.

The time is 1955. Centre-stage are a young doctor, Salvatore Rossi, and a young woman just out of school, Chiara Ridolfi. They fall quite violently in love, and marry. There is some deft movement back and forward in time, giving us their respective backgrounds. Chiara is heir to a house of faded nobility. Salvatore is the son of a village Communist. He has resolved when young to have nothing to do with politics. Nevertheless he is enraged to find himself helplessly in love with the Ridolfi scion—and Fitzgerald clearly enjoys doing characters whose impatience borders on passion and whose passion compels anti-social behaviour. Chiara's English schoolfriend, a young woman known as Barney, is another character in that mould. Compulsive and overbearing, she falls in love with Chiara's taciturn cousin, Cesare, who runs the family winery—and tells him so, offering to marry him. It looks as if the novel is heading for a parallel pairing: but disconcertingly Cesare doesn't respond, except to indicate that he knows Barney loves him. By one hint only (and Fitzgerald requires us to read attentively) it is signalled that Cesare, though sympathetic to Barney, is in love with Chiara. This in turn explains his otherwise inexplicable behaviour at the dramatic climax.

But there is an older story than the one we are being told. In the late 16th century the Count Ridolfi was a midget. He married a midget and they produced a midget daughter. To save the child from a sense of inadequacy they employed only midgets. She was to be protected from the world of full-sized people. They acquired for her a midget companion, whom she loved—but then at some point in childhood the companion put on what is called these days a 'growth spurt'. What should be done about it? The midget daughter, believing her companion's size to be a misfortune, suggested she should be blinded so she would not see what 'ordinary' people looked like, and cut off at the knees so that her deformity would not be excessive.

We are told this in the opening pages. But what happened? It is not until late in the novel that one of the Ridolfi houses is more or less requisitioned by the Italian Tourist Board. For a tourist brochure a version of the 16th-century story more palatable than the real one is invented, telling how the companion child escaped over the wall. Thanks to that, and the fact that a Communist novelist wants to make a film about how a 'child of the people' was mutilated by corrupt aristocrats, we acquire—obliquely—an answer to the question which those opening pages has left us with.

Are the Ridolfi in fact cruel mutilators of the people? They are represented as vague, well-intentioned and inconsequential. Chiara's Aunt Mad runs an asylum for homeless old women and orphaned babies, her idea being that the old women will enjoy looking after the babies. They do, but won't later give them up, hiding them in cupboards and washing baskets. Even those ancient dwarf Ridolfis were absent-mindedly thinking of their daughter's happiness, and she of her companion's 'misfortune', when they agreed to the removal of her eyes and lower legs. The 'innocence' of the title belongs as much to the Ridolfi as to 'the people'. In both it is a quality to be feared. Fitzgerald's view of the world is witty and arcane. But do the two parts of the story—the 16th century and 20th—join? The link is made with the subtlest of strokes.

What is it that especially fascinates Fitzgerald in her two central characters? It is partly just their human uniqueness: but there is an 'idea' there as well, and I think it is that these Italians are not free (are less free, even, than Britons) of their past. Though Salvatore has in effect renounced the family politics he is still 'a child of the people'. And though Chiara's family is in hopeless decline, she cannot help being a Ridolfi. They fall in love as individuals: but they bring with them into marriage their respective histories. In a state of paranoia as the climax of the story approaches, Salvatore is thinking about Chiara: 'But he would hardly have thought it possible that at nineteen—even though she loved him, which of course gave her an unfair advantage—she would have known how to cut down a grown man.' Cut down. The phrase occurs so casually it would be easy not to notice it: but it is surely not there by accident—and it makes the link between the old story and the modern one. Is the explosive Salvatore another victim of the Ridolfi 'innocence'? Or of his own? Or need there be no victim at all? The novel ends one way, but goes so close to ending another; it seems to offer two opposite answers to its own implied questions. It is a work of strange, muted power and intelligence. (p. 21)

C. K. Stead, "Chiara Ridolfi," in London Review of Books, *Vol. 8, No. 17, October 9, 1986, pp. 21-2.*

PAUL STUEWE

Innocence should please those who have been converted to [Fitzgerald's] subtle brand of humanistic fiction. Unlike many contemporary writers, Fitzgerald approaches her characters with a healthy respect for their essential integrity: she assumes that actions have their origins in experience and a coherent view of the world; she refuses to set up flawed personalities simply for the malicious pleasure of knocking them down. However, in addition to this basic compassion (which in lesser hands might tend to the maudlin), Fitzgerald possesses an incisive intelligence that delights in generating fresh insights into familiar fictional situations. Thus, in this highly recommended book, the central love affair between a virginal convent-school girl and a dedicated young doctor steers an unpredictable—but always believable—course between emotional attraction and the effects of their disparate backgrounds. Along the way she treats us to a portrait of Italian society that provides a vivid context for a touching personal drama.

Paul Stuewe, in a review of "Innocence," in Quill and Quire, *Vol. 53, No. 2, February, 1987, p. 21.*

JOHN GROSS

[Penelope Fitzgerald] is an attractive writer, with a fine sense of irony and an unostentatious sense of style, and *Innocence* shows her in full command of her powers.

The main story is fairly slight. Chiara and Salvatore meet at a concert, and after a series of comic misunderstandings, brought about by their failure to understand themselves, they get married. Their marriage isn't the hoped-for idyll, but it isn't bad either; and though Aunt Mad, in what is meant as a philanthropic gesture, inadvertently unleashes a crisis, the predominant mood of the closing pages could reasonably be called Chekhovian—a mixture of the sad, the hopeful and the absurd. . . .

A particularly fine piece of comedy is the scene where Salvatore nerves himself to tell his mistress that their affair is at an end, and she infuriates him with her unexpected sympathy and solicitude. But there are many other entertaining moments, and some excellent secondary characters. Chiara's hefty, slangy

English school friend Lavinia Barnes—Barney—is hit off to perfection, and so, as far as I can judge, are most of the Italians. Certainly the Italian landscapes and interiors are very solidly set before us.

There is also an allegorical element in the book, turning mainly on a Ridolfi family legend handed down from the 16th century. This seems to me less successful, and since it looms largest in the opening pages, it makes for a slow start.

Potential readers shouldn't let this put them off, however. In the story proper the theme of innocence, which extends to Giancarlo and Maddalena and indeed many of the other characters, is treated with a subtlety that goes far beyond cut-and-dried allegorical patterns. No one in the book is wholly innocent, and innocence itself is shown to have its undoubted drawbacks. Still, it is the relative innocence of the characters that enables Mrs. Fitzgerald to see through their follies and take an affectionate or lenient view of them at the same time. The result is as satisfying as it is entertaining.

John Gross, in a review of "Innocence," in The New York Times, *April 28, 1987, p. C17.*

ELIZABETH WARD

"Happiness destroys the aesthetic sense," remarks the narrator of *Innocence,* apropos of love. Equally, the happiness of intellectual delight, which is what one is accorded in this novel, may temporarily destroy the critical sense; *Innocence* is as civilized and intoxicating as a shot of aged brandy, leaving the reader with the same unanalyzable sensation of having briefly tasted perfection. . . .

A satirist of morals and manners, Fitzgerald has frequently been compared with Waugh, Pym, Spark or Powell in the effort to define her particular blend of detachment, sympathy and amusement in the face of absurd or pitiable human behavior. Like them, she is at her driest on the intemperate activity of love, the old conflict between sense and sensibility, impulses and appearances, though her recognition of the disabling pain of wanting "what . . . you can't have" is perhaps more generous.

In fact, the spirit of *Innocence,* which is set in Florence and takes both Italy and Italians as satirical subjects, might be more accurately described as Giuseppe di Lampedusa à la Dame Rose Macaulay. A Macaulay-like moral intelligence and compassion is brought to bear on a Florentine scene as plangently sensuous and nonsensical as anything in Lampedusa's Sicily, all moldering villas, eccentric families and fruitless politics. Devotees of either should find the combination irresistible.

Innocence is the contemporary story of the Ridolfis of Florence, a family of antique lineage and reduced circumstances, headed by the old Count, Giancarlo, and his sister Maddalena, both as decrepit as their villa, the half-abandoned Ricordanza. But the Count's daughter, Chiara, a beautiful, guileless child of 18, possesses life abounding. She falls violently in love with poor, brilliant, thirtyish Dr. Salvatore Rossi, a neurologist from the South, who is seeking to avoid both the machinations of women and the imperatives of his past, particularly of his father's devotion to Antonio Gramsci. . . .

The bare story-line concerns Chiara's and Salvatore's mutual and inevitable pursuit and seduction, their wedding and their tempestuous early married life. But the novel is so much richer than its plot, fleshed out with utterly memorable characters.

Besides their importunate families, the lovers each have a confidant or mentor, who moderates their salient qualities: hotheaded Salvatore is advised by his practical colleague, Dr. Gentilini; artless Chiara calls upon her equally practical, plain-speaking English friend, Barney, for assistance. Barney herself, a figure of pure, hilarious energy, causes quite a flutter in the Ridolfi hen-house, appalling Salvatore, disconcerting the old Count and inspiring a speechless admiration in Cesare, Chiara's farmer-cousin, who is and remains reticent to the point of catalepsy. A series of opposites is subtly established, in which the creatures of impulse and abandon, like Salvatore and Chiara, are ranged against the disciples of reason and stability, like Cesare and Gentilini. . . .

What all this adds up to—though not nearly as schematically as I have suggested—is a moral fable, for Penelope Fitzgerald is at bottom interested in nothing less than the origins of suffering and the possibility of human happiness. She knows, like Salvatore, that the mental pain of unfulfilled desire, in the broadest sense, "is as genuine as pain with a recognisable physical origin." But she also knows, like the legendary midget Ridolfi, "that [pain] was worth suffering to a certain extent if it led to something more appropriate or more beautiful." Images of amputation, of flood-prevention, of plant cultivation, of the philosophy of Rousseau reconsidered, are scattered all through the novel, reinforcing the central debate about human behavior: how may nature be contained, and to what moral end? When all is done, something approximating a final word is permitted to, of all people, Cesare, "trained to . . . tedium" and half-dead with self-denial. Restless Salvatore is distraught again over some misunderstanding with his bride and threatens to shoot himself. He throws up his hands. "What's to become of us? We can't go on like this." 'Yes, we can go on like this,' said Cesare. 'We can go on exactly like this for the rest of our lives.'"

Yet, for all its moral authority, *Innocence* is not cerebral. Penelope Fitzgerald's wit is exhilarating; her gift for advancing her plot by means of anecdotal digressions guarantees entertainment as well as depth; and she has a true sensualist's feeling for the textures and colors and smells of Italy.

Elizabeth Ward, "Love in Florence," in Book World—The Washington Post, *July 12, 1987, p. 4.*

Horton Foote

1916-

American dramatist, scriptwriter, and novelist.

A respected writer and adapter whose best-known works include the screenplays for the films *To Kill a Mockingbird* and *Tender Mercies,* Foote typically focuses on the experiences of characters living within rural Southern milieus. His dramas are distinguished by emotional and narrative restraint and generally emphasize character development while examining themes related to social and individual change. Commonly incorporating autobiographical elements into his works, Foote portrays the family institution as a potential source of personal stability while depicting his protagonists' endeavors to thrive amid the turbulence of small-town life. Although some critics fault Foote for unoriginal thematic concerns and antiquated dramatic techniques, many applaud his deliberate avoidance of melodrama and recognize intelligence, compassion, and humor in his writing.

Foote was born in Wharton, Texas, a small town resembling the fictional settings of many of his dramas. Following graduation from Wharton High School, Foote pursued an acting career, studying in California and New York before being cast in several Broadway productions between 1939 and 1942. While working as an actor, his first play, *Texas Town* (1942), was produced in New York City. During the next three years, while Foote managed a production company in Washington, D.C., several of his subsequent works were staged, including *Out of My House* (1942) and *Only the Heart* (1944). These plays, like his first piece, are concerned with the difficulties of life in small Texas towns during the early 1900s. In *The Chase* (1952), a Western drama that examines the effects of an escaped convict's vengeful return to his hometown, Foote focuses particularly on a sheriff who is committed to recapturing the escapee.

While remaining active in the theater throughout the 1950s, Foote garnered a reputation as a prolific writer of well-regarded television dramas for such shows as "Kraft Playhouse" and "Playhouse 90." These scripts include versions of his own stage plays, including *Only the Heart, The Traveling Lady* (1954), and *The Dancers* (1963), and adaptations of works by other Southern writers. In *The Trip to Bountiful* (1953)—which Foote originally wrote for television, later adapted for Broadway, and eventually reworked into an acclaimed screenplay—an elderly woman escapes the cramped Houston apartment that she shares with her contentious daughter-in-law and unsupportive son and journeys to her hometown, hoping to relive her peaceful and fulfilling past. Arriving in Bountiful, she discovers the town deserted and her childhood home overgrown with weeds. Disillusioned, the woman nevertheless enjoys several blissful reveries before being retrieved by her son and his wife. Described by Richard A. Blake as "an odyssey of the human spirit," *The Trip to Bountiful* reveals the elusiveness of the past while reflecting on relationships between such subjects as time, memory, death, and rebirth.

During the 1960s, Foote established himself as a successful Hollywood scriptwriter. Although his initial motion picture drama, *Storm Fear* (1956), gained little popular or critical attention, his second, *To Kill a Mockingbird* (1962), was en-

Jack Manning/NYT Pictures

thusiastically received, and Foote won an Academy Award for best screenplay. Based on Harper Lee's Pulitzer Prize-winning novel, this work documents the maturation of a ten-year-old boy and his younger sister in Maycomb, Alabama, during the 1930s. In the culminating courtroom scene, the children's father defends a local black man who is falsely accused of rape by several townspeople. The bigoted jury is unconvinced of the man's innocence, however, and the children witness the unjust consequences of prejudice and hate while also experiencing, through the actions of their father, the value of courage and integrity. In *Baby, the Rain Must Fall* (1964), which Foote adapted from his stage and television drama *The Traveling Lady,* an ex-convict and his loyal wife are betrayed by citizens of a Texas town who will not allow them to lead conventional lives. Foote's subsequent screenplays include *Hurry Sundown* (1967), an adaptation of K. B. Glidden's novel written in collaboration with Thomas Ryan that examines racial problems in the South; *The Stalking Moon* (1968); and *Tomorrow* (1972), a critically admired reworking of his own theater piece based on William Faulkner's short story.

Following several projects unaffiliated with the motion picture industry, notably two plays for public television—*The Displaced Person* (1977), based on a story by Flannery O'Connor, and *Barn Burning* (1980), another adaptation from Faulkner—Foote returned to writing film scripts. *Tender Mercies* (1983), considered by many critics Foote's finest achievement, focuses on a country music singer's recovery from alcoholism through his devotion to a dignified young widow and her son. An understated, subtle work that celebrates humanity's potential for redemption, this piece derives dramatic action, according to David Sterritt, from "the thrill of watching characters grow, personalities deepen, relationships ripen and mature. It's the pleasure of rediscovering the dramatic richness of decency, honesty, [and] compassion." *Tender Mercies* earned Foote a second Academy Award for best screenplay.

During the 1980s, Foote began producing his nine-piece dramatic cycle, *The Orphan's Home*. Based on Foote's ancestral history, these works, which include *1918* (1985), *On Valentine's Day* (1986), *Lily Dale* (1986), and *The Widow Claire* (1986), chronicle several generations of the Robedaux family, exploring the ability of kindred relationships to endure social, political, and personal crises in the fictional town of Harrison, Texas. *1918* and *On Valentine's Day* were adapted for film, while Foote reworked material from *The Orphan's Home* for the television miniseries "Story of a Marriage" (1987). In addition, Foote has published *Harrison, Texas* (1956), a selection of his television plays, and written the dramas *The Road to the Graveyard* (1985) and *Blind Date* (1986), which focus on the outmoded sexual conventions of two rural Texas communities.

(See also *Contemporary Authors*, Vols. 73-76 and *Dictionary of Literary Biography*, Vol. 26.)

BROOKS ATKINSON

[*Texas Town*] is the drama of a young man who tries desperately to leave a small town in Texas and find some work—any work—to do. But that is only the thread of a narrative that runs through an engrossing portrait of small-town life. It is set in a drug store where old and young people naturally congregate for gossip and relaxation. Although Mr. Foote has no particular ax to grind, his play gives a real and languid impression of a town changing in its relation to the world—the old stock drifting down the economic and social scale, the young people at loose ends in an organization that does not employ them.

If *Texas Town* does not derive from Mr. Foote's personal experiences and observations, he is remarkably inventive. For none of the parts is stock theatre, except perhaps the part he plays himself without much talent and with no originality. And it is impossible not to believe absolutely in the reality of his characters. The melancholy doctor who drinks in the back room, the hearty judge and his cronies, the bored wife who is looking for excitement, the chattering girls, the bumptious boys, the sharp edges of bad feeling that cut through the neighborhood leisure, the quick impulses of emotion, the sense of drifting without purpose or direction—these are truths of small-town life that Mr. Foote has not invented.

> *Brooks Atkinson, in a review of "Texas Town," in* The New York Times, *April 30, 1941, p. 21.*

BROOKS ATKINSON

In case any one asks Horton Foote, "How's your last act?" he can reply, "Stunning." Mr. Foote is the young man who

disturbed the calm of last Spring with an interesting play entitled *Texas Town*. Since then he has been in Texas long enough to gather the material for a sort of successor, *Out of My House*. . . . The new play, written in four parts, is loosely-contrived, and sometimes seems to be a footless variety show. But after he has portrayed the decadence of "certain levels," as the program calls them, of a Southern cotton town, Mr. Foote pulls himself together in a vibrant and glowing last act that is compact and bitterly realistic and also remarkably well played. Although *Texas Town* was a better play than *Out of My House*, none of *Texas Town* was so good as this last act.

On the whole, Mr. Foote seems to be saying that things are pretty bad in Texas. Since he is representing four different phases of life in a Southern cotton town without bothering to relate them dramatically, a Northerner is a little vague about the culprits. Apparently Mr. Foote believes that pride, family and snobbishness are either the causes or signs of decay, for he devotes two overwrought acts to showing aristocrats on the way out. These acts are so shrill in the acting that it is hard to judge the writing of them, although this department suspects that the aristocrats are not Mr. Foote's best stock in trade.

But in the last act he brings his theme into focus in a sharp scene between the members of a middle-class family that is on its last economic legs. One brother is trying to re-establish the family by a servile attitude toward the influential people of the town. The other brother thinks that the disgrace of servility is more odious than the disgrace of poverty. Even in this act Mr. Foote does not identify his villains. He calls them "they." "They" are liars, cheats and thieves, and apparently an evil brood altogether. But whoever "they" are, both brothers have it out at last in some caustic and wounding plain-speaking.

> *Brooks Atkinson, "Those Southern Blues," in* The New York Times, *January 8, 1942, p. 28.*

LEWIS NICHOLS

Mr. Foote can always be counted upon to have some ideas in his plays, and that also is true of his *Only the Heart*. . . .

Mr. Foote is writing again of money, which playwrights other than he have found to be a curse, and a lack of love, which is a curse, too. His leading character is Mamie Borden, who manages to get rid of her family in devious ways. For marrying for position rather than liking, she drives her husband to arms across the tracks and she prevents her sister from making a happy marriage also. Her daughter grows up, and the mother being what she is, she marries her off to position and the whole thing repeats itself, with another husband crossing the tracks. At the end Mamie Borden is wealthy, but she is all alone.

Only the Heart is not a great play, probably it is not even a good play as they would reckon those things uptown. Its somberness is unrelieved and there are script attitudes which lie lurking for unwary actors. But Mr. Foote is in earnest and he is sincere in stating a case.

> *Lewis Nichols, "Mamie Borden," in* The New York Times, *December 7, 1942, p. 22.*

LEWIS NICHOLS

[*Only the Heart*, a] drama about money as the root of all evil—in 1921 in Texas, at least—is not a Broadway play in the usual sense of that word. It might get by elsewhere as an exercise, but on Forty-fifth Street it is talky, old-fashioned and dull.

Mr. Foote's chief character is a woman who amassed some wealth during the last war and who grew interested in wealth and allowed her husband to look elsewhere for happiness. She persuades her daughter to marry the young man the woman thinks will be best for her, not the one she wants. The girl finally decides, after much talk and little action, that the second generation had better get away to Houston before another marriage collapses, and her young husband shows enough energy at the end to follow her. The woman is left with her telephone and an announcement that an oil well has come in and she is rich, even richer.

The author has scraped the bones of this plot rather than padding them. His Mamie Borden is not clearly drawn; she is mean, but not sufficiently mean to arouse contempt or horror, and an audience is likely to care nothing much about her either way. She lacks the forthright approach of Lizzie B., who disposed of people with forty whacks. The daughter is colorless and the son-in-law, and the action is sleepy.

> *Lewis Nichols, "Pistol Packin' Mama," in* The New York Times, *April 5, 1944, p. 17.*

BROOKS ATKINSON

Horton Foote has written a Western with an ethical point, *The Chase.* . . . After three acts and nine scenes, a ruminative theatregoer is likely to wonder whether the Western without the ethic or the ethic without the Western might not be an improvement. For *The Chase* is neither one thing nor the other. . . . Apart from some well-written small scenes, which are also well-acted, Mr. Foote's drama does not make much impression on the theatre.

As a native Texan who has not lost his fondness for home, Mr. Foote contributed a savory and tenderly-written essay about his home-town to the world's most cultivated newspaper last Sunday. At least one reader hoped that *The Chase* would bring a town to life just as vividly. In a sense it does. Sheriff Hawes is the focal point of many things that are going on in town. The sheriff, his wife, his deputies, the citizens who drop in for a visit and even criminals and ne'er-do-wells on the outskirts are interesting people. Mr. Foote's character sketches are honest and have literary flavor. . . .

His story may be equally authentic, but it gives an impression of being imposed on the characters by the author. A killer has broken out of jail, and is loose in the town again. Although he intends to kill the sheriff, the sheriff is sworn to capture him and return him to jail alive. At the crucial moment the sheriff loses his nerve and kills the escaped prisoner. Mr. Foote intends this to be a highly dramatic point. But by the middle of the third act there is not much drama left in his play.

> *Brooks Atkinson, in a review of "The Chase," in* The New York Times, *April 16, 1952, p. 30.*

BROOKS ATKINSON

[*The Trip to Bountiful*] by Horton Foote is a narrative that supplies [an actress] . . . with honest material but does not take much of the burden off her shoulders. All it has to say is that Mrs. Watts is a lonely woman who has to live with a daughter-in-law who hates her and a son who does not dare take her side.

Life being intolerable for every member of the family in their small Houston apartment, Mrs. Watts dreams of escaping back to Bountiful where she was born and once lived a fruitful and peaceful life. She does run away. She catches a bus for the next town to Bountiful. She finds friendly people on the bus and along the way. And she does have a few blissful moments in the weed-grown dooryard of her old home before her son and daughter-in-law come to fetch her back to Houston. . . .

That does not make a very substantial play for a whole evening. Nor does Mr. Foote make things any better by underwriting. He is a scrupulous author who does not want easy victories, and that is to his credit morally. But he might also do a little more for the theatre by going to Bountiful himself as a writer, providing his play with more substance and varying his literary style. He writes *The Trip to Bountiful* as though it were a point of honor with him never to let go. The story is thin, and the dialogue is all in one tone of deliberate flatness.

> *Brooks Atkinson, in a review of "The Trip to Bountiful," in* The New York Times, *November 4, 1953, p. 30.*

BROOKS ATKINSON

The Traveling Lady is a series of minor characterizations arranged around a major one. It is strung together loosely. It substitutes local color for drama. And . . . it has trouble in saying anything. Mr. Foote makes a moral point of never making a statement except in extremis. He is the most tight-lipped playwright in the business. The basal metabolism of *The Traveling Lady* is low.

But that does not conclude the subject. For there are some very genuine and very poignant scenes in his play, the result, no doubt, of the decency and humanity of the characters. Even the bum has his points. His impulses are decent enough, but he lacks strength and goes to pieces in the crises. Slim Murray, the man of a family that takes in Georgette and her daughter, is a likable young man with the instincts of a gentleman; and his sister, Clara Breedlove, is a wise and compassionate lady in the best tradition of a small town.

This department is not much interested in the bucolic characters that Mr. Foote introduces for comic effects. They are too glib and facile to count for much in a serious play. Mr. Foote, who is loyal to his small-town background, could probably write them with his eyes closed and perhaps does.

But the major characters are admirable people with some depth of feeling and understanding. In a theatre that is largely populated by decadent people who don't understand anything, it is a pleasure to watch Mr. Foote's characters behave like normal human beings. When they do manage to say something— as, for instance, in the final scene—they are wonderfully honest. The emotional scenes of *The Traveling Lady* are worth the languors that stretch in between.

> *Brooks Atkinson, "Texas Drama," in* The New York Times, *October 28, 1954, p. 45.*

WILLIAM J. SMITH

Mr. Foote enters upon the literary scene with a flourish, publishing a first novel, *The Chase,* and a collection of eight television plays, *Harrison, Texas,* on the same day. Previously Mr. Foote has been best known as the author of several ill-fated tries at Broadway (*The Chase, The Traveling Lady, The*

Trip to Bountiful) and as a television dramatist for the Goodyear-Philco Playhouse and the Gulf Playhouse. The present novel is an adaptation of the earlier Broadway work, and the collected television plays include the short original version of *The Trip to Bountiful*. Since *The Chase* is a natural for the movies, Mr. Foote would seem to be making the most of his material. Similarly, he has made the most of his locale. The plays and the novel are all set in a Texas town which Mr. Foote says resembles his native Wharton.

Life and other literary periodicals have hailed Mr. Foote's TV work as that presaging the development of the television-inspired artist. Certainly his work would seem to be a cut above run-of-the-mill TV drama. Mr. Foote says his themes are "acceptance of life" and "preparation for death," and indeed these themes are tenderly and honestly explored in the examples he gives us of his work. These playlets, incidentally, have the additional lagniappe of treating the economic facts of life in a somewhat more realistic vein than TV usually offers. But, all in all, it is a little difficult to see why Mr. Foote was hailed as the Paddy Chayefsky of his time. Perhaps it is merely that the quiet, matter-of-fact dialogue of his domestic dramas needs something in the way of visual appeal to fill out the skeleton. It is hard, at least, to imagine the book having much appeal to other than students of the drama.

The novel is an entirely different matter. The play from which it was adapted (if such, indeed, was the succession) was generally condemned as a bad combination of Wild West action and stodgy philosophizing. As a novel, *The Chase* succeeds in being a first-rate thriller with most of its philosophizing implicit or non-existent. The situation involves the return of a vicious escaped convict to his home town and the impact of his venture on the lives of the townspeople during one eventful night. Action centers around the sheriff, who has sickened under the pressure of his work and knows only that he does not want to kill or be killed. The characterizations are excellent, the action is fast and suspenseful and the ramifications of the plot neatly interlocked.

The novel attains a level beyond that of the mere thriller—psychological melodrama, perhaps, describes it better. Unfortunately, the author attempts to give the book further stature by adding a lengthy epilogue tracing the subsequent fate of his characters. This does not come off as an effect, probably in part because Mr. Foote's purely narrative style is exceedingly flat and burgeons with clichés.... (pp. 626-27)

With a style like this it is a wonder that Mr. Foote's story gets off the ground at all. The fact remains that it does and provides an excellent and provocative evening's entertainment. (p. 627)

> *William J. Smith, "From Screen to Book to Screen,"* in The Commonweal, *Vol. LXIII, No. 24, March 16, 1956, pp. 626-27.*

DAVID STERRITT

The excitement of *Tender Mercies* lies below the surface. It's not the quick change of fast action, the flashy performances or the eye-zapping cuts.

Rather, it's something much more rare—the thrill of watching characters grow, personalities deepen, relationships ripen and mature. It's the pleasure of rediscovering the dramatic richness of decency, honesty, compassion and a few other qualities that have become rare visitors to the silver screen. It feels good to have them back again....

[The story centers on] Mack Sledge, a country singer with a broken career and a drinking problem. Down and out in rural Texas, he puts up at a roadside motel, and eventually marries the young widow who runs the place. By slow degrees, he puts his life back together by devoting himself to his new wife and stepson.

Problems from the past keep dogging him as old entanglements creep into his new situation. They bring confusion and disappointment. But the movie's whole thrust is on Mack's progress from dissoluteness to dignity, and on the people who help him make the trip. It's a moving and life-affirming story—riveting to watch, refreshingly humane in its attitude and tastefully handled.... (p. 36)

Tender Mercies is a daring picture, tossing decades of Hollywood convention cheerfully out the window. Faced with temptation, the former drunk stays off the bottle! Widowed early, the young mother keeps her home together and raises a fine son! That carload of beefy youths isn't a gang looking for trouble, but a country-music band hoping for a glimpse of their hero! Surprises galore, most of them heartily underscoring the good in people.

As written by Horton Foote, and directed by Australian film maker Bruce Beresford, ... *Tender Mercies* combines delicacy of detail with great strength of structure. Though the story and performances thrive on subtlety, the underpinnings of the film are as firm and palpable as human nature itself. Capitalizing on this, Foote and Beresford make masterful use of understatement, letting the emotions of the story speak for themselves through quietly framed shots that deftly sidestep sentimentality.

Their style culminates in a brilliant scene late in the film, as Mack struggles to work through an unexpected tragedy. "I don't trust happiness. I never have and I never will," he tells his wife with breaking voice, bowed by the weight of his trouble. Yet there's a profound irony to the moment, since happiness is all around him—in his family, his home, his work, his future. He even knows it, in a dim sort of way, and he's bound to know it better as time and experience roll on. It's a deeply stirring moment, and all the more so for the gentleness with which it's conveyed.

Tender Mercies has flaws, like all movies. There's a bit of syrupy music on the soundtrack, especially at the end, which is also marred by a few cute close-ups that overstate their case. A couple of scenes also slip into melodrama, pushing their moods just a little too far. Most of the way though, *Tender Mercies* builds a marvelous flow of suspense and surprise precisely by refusing to "pay off" on situations that would plunge toward sensationalism in any conventional picture. (pp. 36-7)

Horton Foote came to the *Tender Mercies* project from a long career of stage, television and movie work. A veteran playwright and TV dramatist, he turned to films in 1963, when he won an Oscar for *To Kill a Mockingbird,* based on Harper Lee's fine novel. His other Hollywood credits include *Baby the Rain Must Fall* and *Hurry Sundown* as well as *Tomorrow.*... (p. 37)

The idea for *Tender Mercies* came from watching a nephew try to make it in the country-music business, in a band that was helped along by an older musician. "This older man had been through it all," Foote told me over lunch the other day, speaking in the faint Southern accent that's a legacy from his Texas upbringing. "As I thought about a story line, I got very interested in that type of character."

Another key element, the hero's victory over drinking, also came from Foote's own observations. "I've spent my life in the theater," he recalls, "and I've known performers who have struggled with this problem. It's a shattering thing to see a wonderful artist ruined by such a thing—and yet some have the humility and grace to fight it off and come back. That's what I had in mind."

Asked about the movie's gentle approach, Foote says he looked for the best way to treat this subject matter. "I wanted to show a man coming out of something," he says, adding that a melodramatic slant would have undermined his intent: "That's been done so many times, and I didn't know what purpose it would serve."

Then too, a certain restraint is part and parcel of the Foote style. "It's just how I write," he says. "I've been told often that it's not commercial, but that's how I do it, and I'm stuck with it. When I try the other way, I get into trouble. I'm not against jazzing things up, I just don't know anything about it! Some of those quiet long-shots in *Tender Mercies* even make *me* nervous. But if that's your talent, that's your talent...."

One of the pinions of *Tender Mercies* is the hero's wife, a strong and sturdy woman whose touchingly honest conversations with her little boy are some of the film's most exquisitely written scenes. How did her character come about?

"There's a kind of woman who crops up in my plays, and in a lot of American literature," Foote replies. "She's not intellectual, but kind of intuitive. I go to the South a lot, and I'm struck by these women who have very little in possessions but have great dignity, even though they've married young and often have to raise children alone.... I write them from a sense of affection and admiration. I don't find them sentimental. They can be very confident, though they've certainly been given more than their share of difficult problems to work out."

The title of *Tender Mercies* from the Book of Psalms, also relates to the character of Rosa Lee.... "I looked for something that would express the expectations that kind of person has," Foote explains. "It's all she asks for—certain moments of gentleness or respite. She has a sense of appreciation for what she has; it's nothing to do with grandness or largeness, but just thanks for a nice day or some such thing. Mack must learn to evaluate and appreciate this quality in her."

Though it's his newest child, *Tender Mercies* isn't the only thing on Foote's mind these days. He is also working on a cycle of nine plays called *The Orphans Home,* which grew out of his "meditating and thinking about the South," and has roots in the story of his own father's life. One portion, *1918*— about the "moral and spiritual journey of an orphan at the age of 12"—may be made into a film. (pp. 37-8)

It's a huge project, reflecting Foote's continuing love of the stage. He comments, "The Broadway arena doesn't have much room now" for serious playwrights like himself—or peers like David Mamet and Sam Shepard—but he finds a lot of energy and ferment in other parts of the theater world. By contrast, he sees little good on the TV scene and has written little for that medium in recent years.

So expertly is *Tender Mercies* put together, it's hard to believe it marks the first time Foote has written directly for the screen. If moviegoers are fortunate, it won't be the last. "I guess I finally, deeply, inside myself do feel," he says, "that in spite of all the chaos around us, there's an awful lot to celebrate in

human beings." It's a philosophy that Hollywood, and the rest of the entertainment industry, could profit by. (p. 38)

David Sterritt, *"Let's Hear it for the Human Being,"* in The Saturday Evening Post, *Vol. 255, No. 7, October, 1983, pp. 36-8.*

VINCENT CANBY

Much like its small-town Texas characters, Horton Foote's *1918* . . . is a movie of such tight-lipped self-control—and such distrust of fancified melodramatic conceits—that it's not easy at first to get to know it.

The movie . . . seems standoffish until one finds its rhythm. At that point, what seems to be a conventional if diffident film reveals itself to be a moving, idealized reverie about a time and place and people who, being so resolutely ordinary, become particular.

The setting is the fictional town of Harrison, Texas. . . .

The time is the hot, early autumn of 1918 when the citizens of Harrison are doing their patriotic best to protect the home front from the Kaiser's fiendish hordes, approximately 5,000 miles to the northeast.

Every afternoon, a half-dozen of Harrison's male misfits, fellows whom even Uncle Sam doesn't want, drill on the courthouse lawn. The ladies of Harrison come to the second-floor, one-room headquarters of the Red Cross to roll bandages and gossip. Horace Robedaux, the young owner of Harrison's main drycleaning establishment, has just committed his entire fortune—$4,000—in the latest Liberty Bond drive. Having a wife, Elizabeth, and a three-year-old daughter, Horace has not felt free to sign up.

Brother, Elizabeth's 17-year-old brother, has flunked out of Texas A&M and is a major worry to his parents. He lazes around Harrison, gambles away money he doesn't have, dreams of enlisting but spends most of his time at the Harrison movie theater, watching things like *Johanna Enlists,* with Mary Pickford, and perhaps *The Hun Within* and *Lafayette, We Come.*

However, life in Harrison is far less serene that it initially seems. Present but unseen, and striking with an awful, sudden randomness that tests Harrison's uniformly Christian faith, is the great influenza epidemic of 1918, which, in a few months, carried off 20 million people around the world, including 500,000 in this country. In *1918,* it's like a medieval plague, one that breeds not in the squalor of ancient, overcrowded cities but in a well-ordered, American cleanliness that is supposed to be next to Godliness.

Yet, *1918* is not about the great influenza epidemic. It plays a fateful role in the lives of Horace and Elizabeth Robedaux, their family and friends, but in *1918* it lacks the mystical importance it possesses in Katherine Anne Porter's *Pale Horse, Pale Rider.* Mr. Foote's characters—those who survive—absorb the effects of this remarkable phenomenon and resolutely get on with life.

One of the things that makes *1918* special is that, I suspect, it's exactly the sort of film that Mr. Foote visualized when he was writing it. It's very much a writer's movie. By this I don't mean that it's self-consciously "literary," which it isn't, but one that, for better or worse, pays no attention to the demands for pacing and narrative emphasis that any commercially oriented Hollywood producer would have insisted on. The very flatness of its dramatic line is its dramatic point. . . .

Mr. Foote adapted *1918* from a play, one of a cycle of nine examining life in a small Texas town over a period of four or five generations. I've no idea where *1918* comes in the cycle, titled *The Orphans' Home,* but the fact that there are works surrounding it must contribute to the feeling that the film really doesn't have a beginning or an end. It's all middle, like the central chapters of a mini-series that began earlier and will go on after one leaves the theater.

That it works so well can be credited to the clarity and discipline of the writing and to the quality of the performances and of the physical production. The settings not only look right but sound right. *1918* manages to hear that special kind of hollow noise that footsteps make on the floors of houses without basements—a genuinely rural sound.

> Vincent Canby, "Texas, Vintage '1918,' Directed by Ken Harrison," in The New York Times, April 26, 1985, p. C8.

VINCENT CANBY

[*1918*] is a leisurely, almost halcyon film about love, death and the resurrection of the spirit in a small Texas town in the months just before and just after the end of the World War I. . . . [The] film's true auteur is certainly Mr. Foote, the winner of Oscars for his screenplays for *To Kill a Mockingbird* and *Tender Mercies.*

1918 is nothing if not a writer's film, which is what gives it its particular resonance. This is evident from the unashamedly sweet opening credits, in which we see tinted postcards of the period and hear on the soundtrack . . . "Keep the Home Fires Burning," through the rest of the film, which takes on the unhurried pace of the lives it's depicting.

1918 doesn't rush from one melodramatic incident to another. It doesn't fret about keeping the audience's attention by artificial means—it trusts the instinct that tells the writer, "If this interests me, it should interest other people." Not everybody, perhaps, but to attempt to please everybody is to court the kind of madness that, in Hollywood, passes for sanity.

Mr. Foote's screenplay, adapted from one of a cycle of nine plays he's writing about Texas life, collectively titled *The Orphans' Home,* unfolds as something recollected at a distance, in tranquillity, which has the effect of smoothing out the spaces between the highs and lows.

It's a chronicle about two families, the Vaughns and their daughter, Elizabeth Robedaux, their son-in-law, Horace, and grandchildren, and how they deal with the uncertainty of the far-off war and, closer to home, with the great influenza epidemic of 1918, which sweeps as mercilessly through Harrison, Texas, the film's fictional town, as it does through the rest of the world. (p. 17)

> Vincent Canby, "It's That Time of Year When Unusual Movies Blossom," in The New York Times, April 28, 1985, pp. 17-18.

FRANK RICH

At the end of **The Road to the Graveyard** . . . , a small-town Texas family sits in its homey parlor, each member lost in silent contemplation. The year is 1939, and the air is warm and still. The only sound is that of distant waltz music drifting in from a party of Mexican laborers enjoying a night off.

The music is sweet, as is the reposeful final tableau. But the effect of **The Road to the Graveyard** is something else. While Mr. Foote may have simulated a vintage *Saturday Evening Post* cover, there is an unbearable turbulence beneath that tranquil surface. The only peace in this play is indeed the discordant peace of the graveyard. A family is dying, and so is a social order soon to be upended by World War II.

These themes are not new to Mr. Foote, who has been writing about a changing Texas for decades, most recently in the films **Tender Mercies** and *1918*. This work . . . may be among the finest distillations of his concerns. In roughly a half-hour, he surveys the tragic ruins of a household—even as he looks back, with more anger than nostalgia, at a world whose idyllic glow belies all manner of unacknowledged neuroses and sexual and economic injustices.

All of this is accomplished with a subtlety that suggests a collaboration between Faulkner and Chekhov. Not much happens in **The Road to the Graveyard**. A middle-aged spinster, India, goes about the daily business of nursing her elderly, failing parents. India's brother, Sonny, who has spent 18 years working as a menial at the local "picture show," contemplates getting married. A neighbor drops by for tea and gossip.

But pain keeps seeping through. . . . India seems grotesquely disfigured by sexual repression and by the dread fear of her parents' and brother's imminent desertions. Sonny, a mild-mannered and overgrown mamma's boy, politely excuses himself to tend to the violently nervous stomach where his unexpressed bitterness resides. The nearly senile matriarch, though often dreamily plucking imaginary "bunny rabbits" out of the air, can still inflict guilt on her adult children and on the husband who failed to buy cheap land before Texas was carved up by speculators. The prattling neighbor is revealed to be an insomniac who spends most nights driving her car aimlessly on empty roads. . . .

[The] initially airy atmosphere [of **The Road to the Graveyard** thickens] into a suffocating, magnetic field of anxiety.

> Frank Rich, "In Marathon '85, 'Road to the Graveyard'," in The New York Times, May 27, 1985, p. 11.

JOHN SIMON

I had high hopes for *1918,* written by Horton Foote, the scenarist of, among other films, the wonderful **Tender Mercies**. This movie, however, is a well-intentioned but unmitigated bore, as only something based on a group of plays about one's own nice, dull family by a nice, sentimentalizing playwright can be. . . . [In] **Tender Mercies** Foote had to create his characters and story; here he had a ready-made one that neither Marcel Duchamp nor even the cat would have dragged in—only a tenderhearted, nostalgically reminiscing scion.

We are in the small Texas town of Harrison, where the local yokels drill clownishly in front of the town hall on the unlikely chance of fighting in France, where their betters are already beginning to fall. Horace has a tailoring and dry-cleaning establishment, but because of his wife, Lizzie, and their baby girl, he won't enlist, his rich, gung-ho father-in-law's urgings to the contrary. Lizzie's younger brother, Brother (*sic*), is, on the contrary, spoiling to go off to war. A college dropout at

17, he spends most of his time at the nickelodeon devouring jingoistic war films when not incurring gambling debts or impregnating the odd girl. He is also a great purveyor of war news and local gossip, which, in these days of the Spanish-flu epidemic, comes down to who has just sickened or died.

1918 is one part gently bittersweet family conflicts; one part war hysteria as seen through the distancing and miniaturizing end of the telescope; one part involuntary parody, as messengers keep coming to announce the death of yet another person we neither know nor care about; and several parts sweet affirmation of life. For Lizzie, who lost her baby to the flu when both Horace and she came down with it, is happily pregnant again, and both the war and the epidemic are over, and so, best news of all, is the film, after 91 interminable-seeming minutes. For *1918* is, first of all, evasive, showing little or nothing of the horrors of actual illness, but without finding a stirringly poetic equivalent for it, as Katherine Anne Porter did in her novella *Pale Horse, Pale Rider.* . . .

[There] is nothing new about this film—not a single revelation that makes these people worth recording at length, no epiphany of any sort. It may still be possible to get away with a slice of life, but you have to be extremely careful where you slice it: There is precious little ordinary life—whether of the 1985 or 1918 variety—that hasn't already been sliced to the bone. (p. 49)

> *John Simon, "Deadly Amnesia, Deadlier Recall,"*
> *in* National Review, *New York, Vol. XXXVII, June*
> *14, 1985, pp. 48-50.*

STANLEY KAUFFMANN

I wish Horton Foote would leave the past alone. Not his personal past, about which he might write well, but his own past writings. *Tender Mercies* (1983), a new piece of his about contemporary Texas, was one of the best American screenplays in years. The film's success apparently encouraged Foote to rummage in his trunk of manuscripts. *1918,* released last year, was made from a Foote play written several years before *Tender Mercies*; it managed to be simultaneously flaccid and overactive. Now Foote has dug up *The Trip to Bountiful,* which was written for TV in 1953 and was then produced on Broadway the same year.

The trouble is not, of course, simply that this material is old but that it is stamped with Foote's chief occupation for decades before *Tender Mercies:* merchant of pathos, Southern style. He flourished in the 1950s during the so-called Golden Age of TV, which seemed even then the Age of Golden Syrup. The main impulse of that age was anti-Hollywood: the small screen was used to celebrate the Unbeautiful People, in contrast to the perfection-worship of Hollywood. So we got on TV the pathetic types from big cities (*Marty, Queen of the Stardust Ballroom*) and we also got, among other small-town confections, Foote's Texan wistfulness. These TV plays, which seemed the predominant types, were carpentered as traps for tears. The very title of *The Trip to Bountiful* suggests that it's a sight for moist eyes. The new 1950s realism, which in fact reduced realism to facile pathos, is almost cartooned in Foote's title.

The protagonist is a gentle, aging widow living, not very happily, with her son and daughter-in-law (and you know what *they're* like) in a crowded Houston apartment. The old woman wants to see her hometown, Bountiful, before she dies; she has tried to go several times but has been thwarted. Finally

she steals away—with some small change (so help me) in a knotted handkerchief and an uncashable pension check—and boards a bus. When she gets there (if you're following the allegory implied in the title), the town no longer exists. The last inhabitant died a few weeks earlier. She waits on the front porch of her dilapidated former home for her son and daughter-in-law to come and fetch her. Oscar Wilde said of *The Old Curiosity Shop* that the reader who did not laugh at the death of Little Nell must have a heart of stone. I confess I didn't actually laugh at *The Trip to Bountiful,* but I smiled a lot, so perhaps Wilde would give me a passing grade. (p. 24)

As for Foote, he doesn't seem to have comprehended the phenomenon in his career. A writer in his 60s, pretty firmly confined by tendrils of wisteria and honeysuckle, broke loose to write *Tender Mercies*. But then, instead of forging ahead from that breakout, he decided to go back and root around in material that he had progressed from. I've read that he's busy with one more rummaging in his past work. I hope there's still time for him to put the best Foote forward. (p. 25)

> *Stanley Kauffmann, "A Carpenter, An Architect,"*
> *in* The New Republic, *Vol. 194, No. 13, March 31,*
> *1986, pp. 24-5.*

RICHARD CORLISS

Welcome to regional-theater cinema, where locale is a crucial character, the pace is measured in eye drops, and everyone on both sides of the camera aspires to the ordinary. As playwright (*The Trip to Bountiful*) and screenwriter (*Tender Mercies*), Horton Foote has backpacked over this terrain for two generations. *On Valentine's Day,* the prequel (though not the equal) of last year's *1918,* marks one more stroll through Foote's family plot. Again we find the Vaughn and Robedaux families forcing smiles and small talk as the Great War rages 5,000 miles from their southeastern Texas town. Again we see Horace Robedaux pledging love to his gentle bride Lizzie and declaring his independence from her father's wealth. Drama is tamped down by propriety until it explodes, like a defective firecracker, into the DTs, psychosis and suicide. (p. 104)

The mood is so lulling that the intrusion of climactic plot devices involving an alcoholic friend and a cooty cousin seems not only extraneous but downright rude. There goes the neighborhood, and the movie. Instead of a valentine to his ghosts, Foote finally delivers a tardy, clumsy Easter present: *Horton Hatches an Egg.* (pp. 104-05)

> *Richard Corliss, in a review of "On Valentine's Day,"*
> *in* Time, *New York, Vol. 127, No. 15, April 14, 1986,*
> *pp. 104-05.*

RICHARD A. BLAKE

The Trip to Bountiful is the adventure of an elderly woman, Carrie Watts, as she schemes to visit her hometown, Bountiful, Tex., once more before she dies. She lives under an uneasy truce with her son and his wife. Money is a problem because of his recent illness; peace is even more of a problem because his wife is a soured prom queen whose life consists of visits to the beauty parlor and the drugstore to drink Coca-Cola with her friends. Mother Watts is forced to live with them, and her fussiness, hymn-singing and forgetfulness become a constant irritant. The apartment is cramped and cluttered, and while the claustrophobia created by the tight camera positions does not exactly generate sympathy for the younger Watts, it does make their impatience understandable. As Mother Watts natters on, we join them in yearning for a moment's peace, which we know will never come as long as Mother Watts has breath in her body.

Not only does the journey home cover the Texas Gulf Coast landscape; it is an odyssey of the human spirit as well. Mother Watts tries to return to the land of her girlhood and to relive her past, even the painful parts of it, but in fact the past no longer exists except as a bundle of memories. The friends are dead, the houses dilapidated and even the town itself has ceased to exist. The fields, long overplanted, are now barren, but with the constant turning of the seasons they may one day return to life. Life renews itself with the coming generations, just as Mother Watts hopes to leave her barren life behind to be born again in Jesus.

Horton Foote's screenplay lacks the laconic vigor of *Tender Mercies,* which he also wrote. It is rather a prolonged monologue for [Mother Watts], whose principal audience is Thelma, a gentle young woman she meets in the bus station. Through their travel hours together, Mother Watts reveals hidden corners of her past; she never loved her husband but was kept from marrying the man she really loved. The device is cinematically and dramatically weak, but it is an acting tour de force.... The film as a whole, however, ... remains curiously flat. The reflections on time and memory, death and rebirth, are disembodied from the script, the photography and the music, as though these were ideas that Mr. Foote wanted to discuss but never quite found the proper vehicle for seeing the project through. (p. 385)

Richard A. Blake, "Two Fables," in America, *Vol. 154, No. 18, May 10, 1986, pp. 385, 392.*

JOHN SIMON

For many years now, Foote has been tirelessly churning out a continuous chronicle of his Texas family and their fellow smalltowners. Written for stage, screen, and TV, these works could, laid end to end, out-distance Lanford Wilson's Talley plays ten times over, and may rival in length the family novels of a Galsworthy, Romains, or Martin du Gard. Foote writes with intelligence, sensitivity, humor, and compassion, yet all this isn't quite enough when you consider how puny many of these characters are, how similar these works must of necessity be, and to what extent a host of southern writers—some of them geniuses—have already covered this or like terrain.

Paradoxically, however, one must also admire the mileage—or, given the microscopic view, the yardage or footage—Foote is able to get out of his simple ingredients; in [*Blind Date*], from a fluttery, exaggeratedly feminine aunt trying to get some young man to date her visiting niece, a bookish, frumpish, shrewish girl. The henpecked uncle sympathizes with the niece, who will have none of the boring young undertaker-to-be doing his proper best at a game his heart is not in. What makes these intrinsically mundane characters interesting is that they must struggle with—or against—a set of antiquated conventions, and that Foote understands the sadness of their victories and the joke of their defeats. (pp. 95-6)

John Simon, "Marginalia," in New York *Magazine, Vol. 19, No. 21, May 26, 1986, pp. 95-6.*

CHILTON WILLIAMSON, JR.

All [of Horton Foote's films] are, or seem to be, based on a cycle of stage plays he has been tirelessly turning out over the years, plays that form a family chronicle of his small-town Texas kinfolk and their friends and fellow townspeople. Most recently we have had *The Trip to Bountiful* ... and, just now, *On Valentine's Day,* a prequel to *1918.* ... Now, Foote is the sort of writer who observes provincial life minutely and affectionately without *deliberately* glossing over its lowly tragedies and spiritual attrition. This is the Gothic South (you wonder how the two or three sane people in town manage to minister to the assorted loonies who beset them without losing their own sanity) and you can't help feeling that Foote is an epigone. From O'Connor to McCullers, from Faulkner to Capote, from Williams to Welty, this territory has been plowed to smithereens: Not one lump of lovable craziness, ferocious eccentricity, or comic despair has been left unturned.

Too bad, because Foote has radar in his eyes and ears, and a good sense of destiny even if not of economy. But he lets his characters take him in: He believes their stories too readily, makes as many excuses for them as they do for themselves, and admits of no villains: The mother and daughter-in-law of *The Trip to Bountiful* who drive each other crazy are both really good underneath; the jilting madman and jilted drunkard of *On Valentine's Day* are victims of circumstance, fundamentally sweet, and Foote relishes their tiny preposterousnesses to the point of pointless iteration. The final effect is neither funny nor sad, just ludicrous.

The conclusion is not that happy families have no histories (these families, in any case, are not happy), but that the happy historian cannot make them worth attending to. Accepting the weird without an underlying sense of evil, substituting forgiveness for every grain of moral indignation, trivializes life into a banal serenity. Even a man's suicide ends up looking grotesque, almost humorous, as it is absorbed into a great, flattening benignity. (pp. 59-60)

Chilton Williamson, Jr., in a review of "The Trip to Bountiful" and "On Valentine's Day," in National Review, *New York, Vol. XXXVIII, No. 10, June 6, 1986, pp. 58-60.*

FRANK RICH

Horace Robedaux [in *Lily Dale*] is a typical specimen of polite young Texas manhood, circa 1909.... [He] has pink cheeks, glistening eyes, pomaded hair and a toothy, ingratiating grin that spreads reflexively whenever he isn't earnestly answering whichever "ma'am" or "sir" has addressed him last. Although Horace is a lapsed Episcopalian, there's the sweetness of the choirboy in his kindly, modest demeanor. His tightly buttoned dark suit is soiled, and his existence is the solitary, straitened one of a clerk in a provincial dry-goods store, but somewhere, somehow, there is faith.

When a turn-of-the-century innocent like Horace travels to a bruising big city, the stage is set for a Dreiserian American tragedy. In *Lily Dale,* such indeed seems the fate that inexorably awaits Mr. Foote's hero. Horace journeys a long distance by train to Houston to visit and possibly settle with the long-widowed mother, Corella, and the teen-age sister, Lily Dale, whom he hasn't seen in a year. But Corella is remarried now, to a strapping, surly railroad laborer named Mr. Davenport, and her new husband will neither let Horace stay in his home nor help him find work. Mom must defer to Mr. Davenport's commands, and her daughter is scarcely more hospitable. A self-absorbed flirt, Lily Dale gets along just fine with her step-daddy and wants no part of her brother's fond memories of the father who died a drunk so many faint years ago. Yet even banishment can't dampen Horace's good nature: As he's ordered to leave the same night he arrives, he pauses to hand out carefully chosen presents, no doubt above his means, that his stepfather and sister then reject just as callously as they've rejected him.

To understand the source of Horace's amazing resilience—and, as the story develops, the nature of a mysterious "fever" that causes him to faint and extends his Houston stay after all—one needn't necessarily see *Lily Dale*. Anyone familiar with the Foote canon will recognize this hero's symptoms, their cause and their cure. Like the much older Carrie Watts, the heroine who runs away to find her childhood's ghost town in Mr. Foote's *Trip to Bountiful*, Horace is searching for the spiritual sustenance of home and will endure any hardship to get it. While home for Horace was once the town of Harrison—the place where his mother and father first lived, the proximate setting of the film *Tender Mercies* and most everything else Mr. Foote has written over 40 years—his father's death has relocated that home to an almost tangible state of mind. Horace won't leave Houston until Corella and Lily Dale return there with him—not by train, but by joining him in a communion with the past.

Lily Dale is one of nine autobiographical plays Mr. Foote has written about the Robedaux family of Harrison under the umbrella title *The Orphans' Home*. (Two of the others, *1918* and *On Valentine's Day*, have been adapted into recent films; another, *The Widow Claire*, will be produced Off Broadway next month.) Though it's hard to judge from the generally inadequate production at hand *Lily Dale* seems a relatively slight but by no means empty chapter in the saga. The heart of the play . . . is preceded by a wan first act. Until then, and sometimes after, . . . perfunctory staging and some modest acting call attention to the creaky theatrical conventions (bald exposition, symmetrically matched scenes) that Mr. Foote preserves unabashedly from the 1940's New York theater in which he began his dramatist's career.

When Horace collapses in the parlor with his "fever," however, we do see a writer of far more diaphanous means at work. If Horace's mother diagnoses her son's illness as malaria and her husband assumes it to be a faked ailment for purposes of free-loading, the audience may suspect that Horace is suffering an unacknowledged and, for 1909 Texans, undefinable nervous breakdown. The young man's sudden mad fits—involuntary screams of hatred and sobs of dreamy longing that subside as unexpectedly as they begin—are all the more rending for everyone's inability to recognize or cope with their import. The genteel working-class milieu of *Lily Dale*—in which "good manners" and "hard work" are the displaced rural characters' only protection against the sinful new mercantile ways of the big city—gives no quarter to peeks into the void.

As Mr. Foote uncovers the discrepancies between what little the characters articulate and what they actually feel, *Lily Dale* finds its modern, psychologically subterranean drama.

> Frank Rich, "Horton Foote's 'Lily Dale'," in The New York Times, November 21, 1986.

ALLAN WALLACH

It would be wonderful to see all the installments in Horton Foote's nine-play cycle, *The Orphan's Home*, on successive nights and watch members of a Texas family grow and change over the years. Meanwhile, *Lily Dale* provides a generous sampling of the penetrating insights into character and the sepia-toned nostalgia we've come to associate with Foote.

Foote is looking back in these nine plays at his own family between 1902 and 1928 . . . , and though the circumstances are special, timeless chords are sounded. Warm-natured *Lily Dale* kindles feelings that embrace us all. . . .

Despite the title, *Lily Dale* is more about Horace (who figures in the films *On Valentine's Day* and *1918*, based on plays in the cycle) than Lily. It is he who is seen in two framing train rides that indicate his transformation. It is he who keeps reaching back to the family's past, who keeps alive the memory of the father who died a drunken failure, who struggles to recall the song, "Lily Dale," the father used to sing to Horace and Lily. The very different Lily, living for the present and eager to curry favor with her stepfather, claims to reject the past.

The play takes place in 1909 when Horace visits Lily and their remarried mother, Corella Davenport, in their Houston home. Horace, a good-hearted boy who clerks in a dry-goods store near Harrison, Texas—which represents Foote's hometown of Wharton—encounters an unexpectedly chilly reception.

Mrs. Davenport's second husband, Pete, a gruff railroad-yard worker who scorns the educated Robedaux clan, has cut short a trip to Atlanta. Though he dotes on Lily, he is so hostile to his stepson that he scarcely acknowledges his presence. The fearful Mrs. Davenport tries to send Horace packing immediately, but before he can leave he becomes seriously ill and is forced to remain on the Davenport couch.

A great deal occurs during his two-week recuperation period. Lily's ambitious boyfriend, Will Kidder, not only overcomes Pete's initial hostility but also gets marriage-shy Lily to accept his proposal. Foote, however, is interested primarily in the shifting emotional currents. The most significant shift occurs during a wrenching scene in which Lily discloses her long-suppressed feelings to Horace. . . .

As in other period plays and films, Foote fills *Lily Dale* with touches that lovingly evoke a period. Lily plays (badly) self-composed rags—all with the identical tune—and a "classical piece" on an upright piano. She, Horace and their mother listen on a Victrola to a scratchy record of the Irish tenor John McCormack. These touches make the play seem like a fondly regarded family album, but it's one whose pages keep revealing people of unexpected complexity.

> Allan Wallach, "Molly Ringwald in Foote's 'Lily Dale'," in Newsday, November 21, 1986.

EDITH OLIVER

The events of *The Widow Claire* take place during one evening and night in Harrison, Texas, in 1911. Horace is back in his home town after a disastrous visit to his mother, sister, and stepfather in Houston two years earlier. He plans to return to Houston to go to business college, but he now lives in a men-only boarding house. As the show opens, he is getting ready for a date with a local widow named Claire. His fellow-boarders—poker players—are much amused; they tease him about her and her reputation, and warn him of constant intrusion by her two children, a small boy and a girl. And they are right: the children are natural tryst-busters, and Horace and Claire are barely able to kiss chastely or dance without one or the other of the kids clamoring to be sung to or told a story. The boy, whose hobby seems to be troublemaking, foments a middle-of-the-night fight between peaceable Horace and a tougher suitor of Claire's. At the end, Horace is as defeated in his first try at courtship as he was, in *Lily Dale,* in his attempt to rescue his mother from her miserable marriage to a dockworker and his sister from her bewildering family life. Horace, still hurt by the first defeat and by the death of his father some years before, remains "the quality" cut adrift in a world of cheap boarding houses and all-night card games. But this time he is able to maintain his decorum and natural courtesy, and his kindness as well. He is never ruffled by the children, even at their most pesky, and is never impatient with them. He doesn't wince (though we do) when the widow asks him again and again which of two other suitors she should choose.

As was true in *Lily Dale,* theatricality is at a minimum. The script is a matter of details, in the hands of a craftsman who evokes a time and place. (p.78)

Edith Oliver, "Thwarted Love," in The New Yorker, *Vol. LXII, No. 45, December 29, 1986, pp. 77-9.*

JOHN SIMON

While most of our younger playwrights . . . write as if there were no tomorrow, Horton Foote writes as if there had been no yesterday. *The Widow Claire,* the latest installment in his nine-play cycle about the Robedaux family, *The Orphan's Home*—whose hero, Horace Robedaux, is clearly Foote's grandfather—may be the most shopworn, contrived, and soporific of the four that have thus far left their drawer for the stage or the screen. This long night's journey into day has Horace, 21, on a last date with Claire, 28, the merry widow of the pseudonymous Texas burg, Harrison; tomorrow, he leaves for six weeks of business school in Houston. Claire has two small, infuriating children who evidently never sleep but pester their mother's gentlemen callers in a fiendish variety of ways all night through. These callers include Ned (an offstage character), an elderly but well-to-do Galveston tradesman, whom Claire doesn't care for but who offers marriage and security; Val, an impecunious, violent ne'er-do-well, who beats her and would marry her for her real estate and who has a strong sexual hold over her; and, of course, Horace, whom she is drawn to as purely as he to her, but who is too young, too poor, and without obvious prospects. They dance together, kiss chastely, exchange life stories, and yearn for each other tacitly and helplessly.

There is also a lot of local color, embodied in some boozing, gambling, whoring layabouts and their rowdy stories, counterpointing Horace's and Claire's tales of poverty and shabby gentility. But there is nothing here that hasn't been heard from dozens of southern and southwestern writers, high and low, from Faulkner to Reynolds Price, from Tennessee Williams to Robert Benton. Foote is more likable, less sensational than many, but at a great gain in tedium. The filial piety may well surpass—at least in cumulative length—what has been written about the Tyrones, Talleys, and Jeromes; but the Robedaux' chief specialty, alas, is their déjà vu.

Take the pathetic efforts at humor: In his sleep, a drunken loafer invokes a 50-cent whore over and over again, while his fellows speculate about her identity; Claire's kids, whenever their mother and Horace start getting close, promptly interrupt them in trying and trite ways. And the pathetic efforts at pathos: Horace, who hasn't a penny and will be in Houston, tries to

pay a friend to take Claire to an upcoming dance she longs to go to, or gets himself beaten to a pulp while attempting to defend Claire from Val as she stands unhelpingly by. It is bad enough to pile Ossa on Pelion, but *The Widow Claire,* for 90-odd repetitious minutes, piles corn pones on hominy grits. (p. 50)

John Simon, "Milking Honey," in New York Mag-azine, *Vol. 20, No. 1, January 5, 1987, pp. 49-50.*

DON MERRILL

"Story of a Marriage" is the kind of thoughtfully written, capably performed drama old-timers are thinking of when they wax nostalgic about the Golden Age of television. . . . [It] is the work of Horton Foote, one of the Golden Age's brilliant playwrights who, with his contemporaries—Paddy Chayefsky, Tad Mosel, J. P. Miller, Gore Vidal and many others—went on to win recognition for their work on stage and in movies. . . .

Much of Foote's work is based on his own roots, and the several plays that make up this miniseries concern his parents and their life in a Texas town in the few years during and after the First World War. His deliberate pacing, something one seldom sees on standard television, serves to provide depth and believability to the characters, so that we understand and care about them. The themes range from parental disapproval of a marriage and small-town gossip to alcoholism and madness. People love, overcome obstacles or are overcome by them, are alternately happy and sad, and eventually they die. It is the simple drama of life, more moving and powerful as Foote tells it than the glitter and forced excitement of the heavy-breathing miniseries we see on the commercial networks during ratings sweeps. Indeed, the most daring dialogue—or action—in the series is about a young woman who died in premature childbirth on her wedding day. (She had corseted herself too tightly, to conceal her condition.)

The central figures are Elizabeth Vaughn, member of a rich, respected family, and Horace Robedaux, a young salesman and storekeeper. When her parents express strong disapproval of Horace, the young people elope. Their love, Elizabeth's strength and Horace's nobility make up the central theme of their own story and those of their friends and relatives. . . .

Without revealing too much of the plot, it can be said that one of the highlights is an early moment when Elizabeth and Horace are on the porch of her home while her father fumes inside the house. It is a credible, touching love scene during which the two engage in awkward conversation that makes us understand how deeply they care for one another. It is remarkable writing, beautifully acted—which description applies to their performance not just in that scene, but throughout the series.

Although you may find the going slow at first, we urge you to stay with "**Story of a Marriage.**" You will find that leisurely pace has only piqued your interest and your curiosity about what these (mostly good) people will do next.

Don Merrill, in a review of "Story of a Marriage," in TV Guide®, *Vol. 35, No. 14, April 4, 1987, p. 1.*

JOHN LEONARD

We are surrounded in "**Story of a Marriage**" by death. Children die, and women in childbirth, and young men gone to war, and what seems to be half the population of the small town of Harrison, Texas, during the influenza epidemic of

1918. There are also suicides and public hangings. We are always at the cemetery, often to place flowers on tombstones attached to the wrong burial plots. And when people aren't dying, they go mad from shell shock or alcohol or heartbreak, and in their madness they speak to the dead, especially to the ghosts of their mothers, as if time itself were a delirium.

And yet "**Story of a Marriage**" is not the least bit southern Gothic. It doesn't smack its lips and howl or smell. Death just happens to be its weather. The real story is adult love, risked and endured and transcendent. For five and a half careful hours, the playwright Horton Foote remembers his own parents. I very much like his memories.

We know Horton Foote, of course, from television's so-called golden age of the fifties, and from a dozen plays on and off Broadway, and from such movies as *Tender Mercies* and *The Trip to Bountiful.* That is, we know not to expect much trickiness, any icon-smashing or lyric excess. He's so quiet we have to slow down to hear him, and then what he says is not so much surprising as confirming: We knew that, didn't we? In fact, his characters often have a hard time finding the language appropriate to their feelings. The result is a freeze-frame of the emotions instead of a purge.

This matters. "**Story of a Marriage**" is absorbing and intelligent television, but it doesn't scare us, and it is oddly weightless, innocent of history and philosophy. Elizabeth Vaughn, a young music teacher, will fall in love with Horace Robedaux, a young clothing salesman; her wealthy parents will object; the young couple will elope; after estrangement will come reconciliation—rather like *The Waltons* without tooth decay.

In other words, "**Story of a Marriage**" isn't *Scenes From a Marriage,* with which Ingmar Bergman scared us in six episodes for Swedish television in 1973. Its bones are small. In Harrison, family *is* history, and marriage *is* philosophy. That this works so well—in my living room, anyway—suggests that we aren't grown up enough yet to contemplate disintegration. When we look at ourselves on TV, we want to see something warm; the set is supposed to be user-friendly, even when it's trying hard to tell the truth. We insist on sentiment as a sort of glue, especially after death.

There is no evil in Harrison, just the climate of dying and gusts of madness that aren't anybody's fault. Ronald Reagan might have lived here, if he were a better actor. I wanted something more from all this sincerity than a facile, if stoic, affirmation of family values against the claims of history and conscience. All accounts are too neatly paid in full, and therefore no one is accountable.

But I still believe every syllable of Horton Foote, and envy him. He doesn't know how to lie. . . . (p. 87)

"**Story of a Marriage**" is the only American mini-series this winter or spring that we can watch without feeling ashamed of ourselves. (p. 88)

John Leonard, "Places in the Heart," in New York Magazine, *Vol. 20, No. 14, April 6, 1987, pp. 87-8.*

George (Palmer) Garrett (Jr.)

1929-

American novelist, poet, short story writer, editor, dramatist, critic, translator, and scriptwriter.

A respected writer who is noted for his efforts in several literary genres, Garrett combines imagination and personal experience to create works characterized by diverse styles, settings, and subjects. Informed by an understated Christian sensibility, Garrett's writings frequently make use of biblical allusions to examine such themes as humanity's capacity for violence and cruelty, continuities between past and present, aging and loss of innocence, and relationships between individuals and society. Garrett's use of satire and dark humor and his interest in Southern milieus, the processes of history, and the significance of family tradition have evoked comparisons to the works of William Faulkner and Flannery O'Connor. W. R. Robinson observed: "[For] insight into man as a finite creature in time and this world, and into proper valuing and affirmation of a human life and art, there is no clearer or saner vision than that provided by the fiction of George Garrett."

Garrett's literary career began in 1951, when several of his poems were published in Princeton University's *Nassau Literary Magazine*. In these and subsequent pieces collected in such volumes of verse as *The Reverend Ghost* (1957), *The Sleeping Gypsy and Other Poems* (1959), *Abraham's Knife* (1961), *For a Bitter Season: New and Selected Poems* (1967), and *The Collected Poems of George Garrett* (1984), Garrett employs a variety of linguistic styles and poetic forms while analyzing a broad range of themes and concerns. Garrett's topical poems, for example, in which he uses devices and conceits drawn from Elizabethan and Jacobean literature, are marked by satiric social criticism. Commonly focusing on contemporary events and celebrities, these works endeavor to explore and define modern society while presenting an affirmative outlook that derives from Garrett's moral and religious foundations. His pieces focusing on childhood and innocence also stem from Christian viewpoints, as they examine the birth of religious ideas and the purity of youth. Family and tradition likewise serve as fundamental elements in Garrett's poetic vision by providing constancy and certitude in an otherwise chaotic world. In other poems, Garrett deals with such topics as aging, love, and literature.

While highly regarded for his poetry, Garrett is probably best known for his fiction, in which he blends authentic regional dialects, vivid characterizations, and various fictional devices. His first novel, *The Finished Man* (1959), is set in contemporary Florida and concerns events surrounding a hotly contested senatorial election campaign between a popular incumbent, an ambitious young lawyer, and his father, a retired judge. Utilizing precise imagery, Garrett reveals the corruption, illusions, and self-serving motivations behind much modern political maneuvering. In his next novel, *Which Ones Are the Enemy?* (1961), Garrett applies his experiences in the armed forces to explore the consequences of an uninvolved life. Set in and around a United States military base in Trieste, Italy, during the early 1950s, this book examines the protagonist's avoidance of love and caring due to his fear of vulnerability. *Do, Lord, Remember Me* (1965) manipulates various points of

Photograph by Pryde Brom. Courtesy of George Garrett.

view to detail the demise of an itinerant evangelist who is incapable of reconciling his divine powers with his self-destructive nature and carnal desires. In his next two novels, *Death of the Fox* (1971) and *The Succession: A Novel of Elizabeth and James* (1983), Garrett uses multiple perspectives to create vast historical fictions which venture, according to Garrett, "into the imaginary past." In *Death of the Fox*, Garrett recreates the final two days in the life of Sir Walter Raleigh through the interior monologues of several characters while providing detailed evocations of life in England during the Renaissance. *The Succession*, which Maureen Quilligan described as "a subtle, complex meditation on the poetry of time," features a nonlinear narrative and such disparate characters as an actor, a Scots reiver, a persecuted priest, and King James. Using heavily cadenced, formal prose intended to echo Elizabethan diction, Garrett explores the complex relationships between past, present, and future. In *Poison Pen* (1986), Garrett implements metafictional devices to present an irreverent portrait of contemporary American society. Constructed of a series of venomous letters addressed to actual people and signed with various pseudonyms, this novel purports to be the handiwork of a single fictional character who functions as Garrett's alter ego. Featuring scatological humor and profanity, these letters comment on a conglomeration of popular topics and concerns.

In his short fiction, which is collected in several volumes, including *King of the Mountain* (1958), *In the Briar Patch* (1961), *Cold Ground Was My Bed Last Night* (1964), *The Magic Striptease* (1973), and *An Evening Performance: New and Selected Short Stories* (1985), Garrett examines many of the themes of his novels and poems by using a similar assortment of techniques and subjects. These pieces focus particularly on the consequences of war, humanity's potential for violence, and the frustration that results from society's demands upon individuals. Garrett has also written the plays *Garden Spot, U.S.A.* (1962), *Sir Slob and the Princess: A Play for Children* (1962), and *Enchanted Ground* (1982), as well as several screenplays, including *The Young Lovers* (1964) and *The Playground* (1965). In addition, he has served as an editor for numerous literary publications, including *Transatlantic Review* and the *Hollins Critic*, and has received many awards, grants, and fellowships for his work.

(See also *CLC*, Vols. 3, 11; *Contemporary Authors*, Vols. 1-4, rev. ed.; *Contemporary Authors New Revision Series*, Vol. 1; *Contemporary Authors Autobiography Series*, Vol. 5; *Dictionary of Literary Biography*, Vols. 2, 5; and *Dictionary of Literary Biography Yearbook: 1983*.)

JAMES STERN

This first book by George Garrett [*King of the Mountain*] begins in innocence, with a boy's whimper, and ends in evil, with a bang. Long before the bang comes you will know that the author is out of the top of the literary drawer.

Mr. Garrett is aware, as was the young Hemingway, of the attraction of the first person singular and the second plural ("Ask me why I pick that time and I'll tell you"), of the sense of immediacy and intimacy the confidential technique can produce, of the power it has, like the sudden use of Christian names, to engage your full attention. But Mr. Garrett is no mere charmer. In some twenty stories he says more, and more forcefully, than is commonly said in as many full-length novels. Every page of *King of the Mountain* rings true, and the author has some profound and terrible tales to tell.

The subjects of the stories can be roughly divided between father-son relationships and war, or rather the effects of war upon its survivors. Some stories are likely to make the middle-aged feel old. "Our generation," says the narrator of **"The Seacoast of Bohemia,"** which is Greenwich Village, "had come to life after the war." For Mr. Garrett, who comes from Florida, there have been two wars: the American Civil War and Hitler's war. For those to whom memories of the Kaiser's war are still very much alive, it may come as something of a shock to learn that Garrett himself is an Occupation veteran who will be 30 next year.

His is the generation that was conceived in the Depression, "that anxious time" when, in the center of Florida, the scene of ["**King of the Mountain**"], a child learned the meaning of bitterness by having to watch as a mob beat his father into a cripple for publicly criticizing the Ku Klux Klan. This story has something of the chilling violence, the authority and the power of the work of Robert Penn Warren and James Baldwin. That no Negro figures prominently in its pages, that no one is

likely to guess the awful irony of its dénouement, only enhances the story's stature as a work of art. . . .

For most people, I think, it's the bang with which this book ends that will remain longest in the memory. These are Occupation stories appearing collectively under the title: "What's the Purpose of the Bayonet?" "The Art of Courtly Love" is about a D. P., a German refugee war-widow in Austria whom the American narrator is determined to seduce. Which he does. Only to discover that the woman has an Austrian lover. How the American then behaves makes reading only a few degrees less appalling than the behavior of Americans to Americans and Austrians to Austrians in the seven blood-and-terror pages that follow.

As indictments of war, of the military system, these three short tales talk very loud. Courage of a high order, moreover, was required to write them, for if you write in the first person, and as truly as Mr. Garrett, you are likely to be associated with your "I." But this author is out to fool no one. As the American lover says: "You can fool yourself quicker in a dozen ways than it takes to tell about it." And he knows that what he has said is a cliché.

James Stern, *"With a Whimper and a Bang," in* The New York Times Book Review, *March 2, 1958, p. 4.*

GENE BARO

Variety of subject and versatility of treatment mark [*King of the Mountain*]. Not all of these pieces succeed, to be sure, but some of them are genuinely impressive, moving. The writing is always deft and readable.

Mr. Garrett is a poet, and one of his modes is to exercise his poet's imagination in stories that are rather abstract and symbolic; but such stories as **"The Witness,"** **"The Accursed Huntsman,"** and **"How the Last War Ended"** seem in essence much more than clever experiments, interesting tricks played with reality. These stories lack the sense of an engagement with living experience.

Then too, Mr. Garrett commands a "naturalistic" manner. Here the surface of experience is adroitly, even brilliantly, rendered. A sharp eye for detail, an ear tuned to the rhythms of living speech, a sense of the ironies at the heart of human suffering give rough strength and plausibility to some stories that center upon wartime circumstances or army life. But this group partakes of a curious obviousness; in substance, we have been told these stories before, often with even more vigor and punch.

Yet Mr. Garrett is a short story writer of considerable promise. This is seen in work that moves delicately between extremes, that blends the imaginative and the prosaic and gives us a fresh insight into our familiar world. There are a number of these pieces. Indeed, in such stories as **"The Rivals,"** where an adolescent boy comes into consciousness of his true relationship with his father; **"A Hard Row to Hoe,"** where the pride of two classes and generations of Southern men is revealed; and in ["**King of the Mountain**"], where we are shown a demagogue on the "right" side, through the eyes of his son, Mr. Garrett brings his talents up to their pitch of achievement.

Gene Baro, *"A Poet's First Short Story Collection," in* New York Herald Tribune Book Review, *April 6, 1958, p. 3.*

BABETTE DEUTSCH

[*The Sleeping Gypsy and Other Poems*] by George Garrett, who has a collection of masterly short stories to his credit as well, will give the reader the pleasures that he has provided hitherto. He is one of those poets, rare in our time, who can communicate his own delight in this outrageous world. His "still life" is never still. And he has a gift for the unhabitual metaphor that quickens whatever he touches. Occasionally one is troubled by an angular cadence or the obtrusion of a pet word, but there is variety and control in his metres and his vocabulary. His interest is not limited to the lovely or the noble. The grotesque, the homely, the disproportionate continue to engage him. He has met head on the furies that assail the flesh and those that harry the soul. A savage honesty, a finely ironic wit are among his weapons. This is a book to read and reread.

> Babette Deutsch, "Sundry Aspects of One Poet's Delight," in New York Herald Tribune Book Review, *August 3, 1958, p. 4.*

HARVEY SHAPIRO

George Garrett is a young American poet already laden with honors: he is this year's Rome Fellow of the American Academy of Arts and Letters and recipient of a Sewanee Review fellowship. The poems in *The Sleeping Gypsy,* his second book, have a pleasantly extemporized quality and are musically phrased. But some are marred by fuzziness, as if the impulse behind them were insufficiently strong. For example, searching for a simile to describe "all things classic, balanced and austere in grace," Mr. Garrett likens them to "Tallchief in Swan Lake, a white thing floating like the feather of a careless angel, dropped." I suppose that angel has to be careless or he would not have dropped his feather, but the word "careless" works against the poet's intention. And the arrangement of the second line emphasizes the word "dropped"—not fair to Miss Tallchief, and again not to Mr. Garrett's purpose.

> Harvey Shapiro, "The Many Voices of the Poet," in The New York Times Book Review, *September 28, 1958, p. 40.*

DONALD HALL

George Garrett, I think, is not a poet; pompous words, but I intend to gloss them. Perhaps *he* is a prose writer; for he has published a well-reviewed book of short stories. Yet these [pieces in *The Reverend Ghost*] are not the poems that we would expect, naïvely, to be the by-products of a talent for fiction. They look like poetry; they are lyrical and learned in intention; they resemble overmuch the poetry that has appeared in the quarterlies since the war. In one of Auden's essays or reviews, he speaks of his ability to judge a book of poems by taking a peek at pages at the beginning, middle and end. (Does he judge the Yale Younger Poets by this method?) The method has its points for the weary reader, but it can fail when the poet is someone like Auden—a good poet who writes many inferior poems. For a truly consistent poet like Garrett the method works—though to ascertain consistency you have to violate the method! There is in Garrett a lack of distinction in the choice of the individual word, the line and its rhythm, and the poem and its shape. From the first page to the last, we hear a toneless, insistent voice in the ear "which will not stop / For breath or logic till its victim drop." The sound of the poems is random, and the words invoke alternatives. If we look for a parallel

elsewhere in literature, we think of translation. The approved contemporary idea-for-a-poem walks around in a haphazard selection of second-hand clothes. As in most translation, the diction belongs to other men, and is just out of date enough to be reactionary. The word "praise," which only a hacker will henceforth use in a poem, occurs more than once. Yeats invented it, Auden used it well, but then four-hundred lesser talents trampled around on it, and it is as dead and despicable as rhyming "fire" with "desire." (pp. 86-7)

Garrett's poems are careful in the way they are put together as "ideas," yet the feeling of translation is the feeling of haste or at least inadequacy, a reckless carefulness. . . . In Garrett's poems the ideas never engender the emotions appropriate to them, for the reason that the texture is unworked. A feeling of haste implies a feeling of complacency: the idea-for-a-poem narcissistic over its own excellence. Let me pick a single whole poem, again, to illustrate; and I think that I am picking one of the best:

OF NATURAL RETICENCE

> The Sorcerer's apprentice
>   was alarmed at what appeared
>   to be the outcome of impudence.
>   You should be humble
>   in magic as in love.
>
> On the other hand I know
>   there's a certain arrogance
>   in fables, an element
>   of necessary pride:
>   Cinderella at the dance.
>
> These facts are well hidden
>   from the cursory, this paradox
>   kept secret from the crowd until
>   the true prince arrives,
>   the sleeping beauty wakes.

Is this poem really "Of Natural Reticence?" What is it of? I feel that it is of wanting to write a poem, or of the Richard Wilbur who took lessons from Marianne Moore. The art of Wilbur and Moore is lacking; the last line falters down the page in its sad approximateness. Poetry exists where the tributaries of art (the best that has been written, the Muse, the sense of perfect symmetry and beauty) and truth (the Meaning of Life, what must be said, the Answer) meet to make the Mississippi. . . . Garrett lacks the art; he does not love his words enough to drive them into poems. (pp. 87-8)

> Donald Hall, "Poets of Today," in The Western Review, *Vol. 23, No. 1, Autumn, 1958, pp. 83-9.*

EDWARD ABBEY

Besides being an able poet, George Garrett is a storyteller of malleable gifts. His *The Finished Man,* a first novel, is a jostling tale of disgruntled Southern politics. Mike Royle, his hero, is a young man with Southern roots and a modern conscience, who, as campaign aide to politically battle-scarred Florida senator Allen Parker, discovers a few truths about himself.

The stumping speeches of Senator Parker and his opponent John Batten have a gramophone fidelity:

> "Where, O where, is Little Boy Blue?" Allen Parker demanded, "Where is this child who wants to look after the sheep? I'll tell you where he is. He's under

the haystack of Privilege, of Special Interest, of Big Business, fast asleep.''

And, if Mike Royle is the Stephen Dedalus of this book, the old artificer of it is Judge Joseph Royle, his father. As a ''cracker'' who becomes the dark horse of the campaign, running against Parker and Batten, knowing the futility of it, Royle runs on the adrenalin of faith, yet aware of the corruption of the fix. His death before election leaves the possibility alive that good might have triumphed—had not the tower of strength tumbled before the tower of Babel.

The plot is not the most important thing about this book. The characters and their illusions are. Definition is by image. When Mike Royle's heart ''sagged in its net of veins like a rock in a sling,'' no precise thesaurus word is necessary. And Jojo Royle, his wastrel brother, is seen as a ''cookie man waiting his turn in the oven,'' a blurred picture which captures the essence of an unfinished man.

The ''finished man'' then is Mike Royle, who, after Senator Parker concedes the election, ''takes his stand'' in Dixie.

> ''Are you really going to defend that nigger when he stands trial?'' asks the Senator.
>
> ''If he wants me.''
>
> ''A lot of people are going to misunderstand that. You'll make yourself a lot of enemies.''

Which hearkens back to Yeats' ''A Dialogue of Self and Soul'':

> The unfinished man and his pain
> Brought face to face with his own clumsiness;
> The finished man among his enemies. . . .

An almost flawless novel (the publisher could have helped by supplying better proofreaders), *The Finished Man* augers well of books to come by Mr. Garrett. (pp. 379-80)

> *Edward Abbey, in a review of ''The Finished Man,'' in* New Mexico Quarterly, *Vol. XXIX, No. 3, Autumn, 1959, pp. 379-80.*

MARTIN PRICE

George Garrett's *The Finished Man* is about the imperfect world of politics, that border land between high aspiration and low cunning. The fastidious shrink from its compromises, its calculation, its histrionic self-exploitation; others enjoy the tactical surrender of principle, the illusionist's sense of risk and power, the frankness of open ambition. Judge Royle is a man who has come up from poverty, fought his way into political office, and married well. He is a man of just and violent feeling, directness and courage; he has been disenchanted in the way his wife has been sold to him by a distinguished but selfish family, but he has sacrificed his wife and children to his own drive. Jojo, his elder son, has drifted away into a nocturnal voice on a disk-jockey program, as jealously free of commitment as his father has been dedicated to it. The Royles cannot accept the cost of politics: Mrs. Royle and her daughter at the close are leaving for Europe and the comforts of a gracious past.

Mike Royle attaches himself to Senator Parker in a fight for reelection. Parker has created an image of himself which he has come to believe. As success begins to slip away he is ready to adopt any device for holding it. He introduces Vivian Blanch as a campaign adviser; she is an unhappy woman, incapable of simplicity or love, who has made herself a kind of priestess

of the unreal. The novel is concerned with Parker's campaign, which opens with a shrewd double-crossing of his opponent and is met with similar maneuvers, the worst of which involves the sacrifice of Judge Royle's life in a futile diversionary candidacy.

The dominant note of the book is its insistence upon a double view of man; he is, in Frost's words, a ''diminished thing,'' and what to make of him is Mike Royle's problem. (pp. 126-27)

Garrett might have done better to dramatize [his]. . . perceptions rather than give them so many voices. The action is complex and lively; but it always wants to be discussed, like a drama school play, after the performance. Mike Royle's coming to awareness is not, after all, very interesting in itself, if only because he seems to exist for the sake of the observations he can make. To have built those observations into the pattern of action and image would have made for a far more stylized book but one with stronger coherence and perhaps subtler characterization. For in this version the characters tend to take positions, and they soon flatten into spokesmen or rather obvious symbols. Mike Royle, like many counterparts in recent novels, is so enmeshed in the action as to discern its import only slowly and painfully; yet he is sufficiently detached to expatiate in terms of high generality, laced with vivid colloquialism. Since he has neither a strongly defined personality (such as Bellow and Nabokov have lately presented) nor a subtle and original mind (such as C. P. Snow can suggest), he becomes a latter-day Man of Sensibility. And when he strikes a somewhat febrile and ironic note, he does not count the words. But Mike Royle is scarcely the worst of his kind, and the book has much in it to demand strong praise. There are several fine dramatic scenes, a few memorable characters, and altogether a richness of conception that can afford to be wasteful. There have been better first novels, but this is the kind that promises an interesting, and perhaps important, career. (p. 127)

> *Martin Price, in a review of ''The Finished Man,'' in* The Yale Review, *Vol. XLIX, No. 1, Autumn, 1959, pp. 126-27.*

FRANK H. LYELL

George Garrett's first novel will disappoint those who admire the fresh style and substance of *The Sleeping Gypsy and Other Poems* (1958) and the noteworthy short stories in *King of the Mountain* (1957). *The Finished Man* treats an anything-but-fresh subject: the backstage hullabaloo of a Southern Senatorial race, the on-stage mud-slinging, and the clash between appearance and reality in the candidates' private lives. The plot is designed to illustrate the willingness of rival candidates to turn an important campaign into a superficial battle of personalities, and the widespread conception of office-seeking as a game or ''grandiose hobby,'' satisfying principally to the ego and allowing full scope for ''the cult of the gesture, preferably the absurd gesture.''

Mr. Garrett's main characters are unsympathetic, especially the central one, Mike Royle, a detached, passionless lawyer, who ''like many a Southerner loved and hated his own history just as he loved and hated himself.'' The novel lacks intensity because Mike shows no special urge to resolve his loves and hates and decide exactly where he stands intellectually, politically, and emotionally. ''The perennial spectator, uncommitted,'' he divorces his wife and returns home to Oakland, Fla., to work for Senator Allen Parker's re-election.

Parker, an aging, moderately liberal New Dealer, has decided not to retire because he has discovered that all his old enemies are grooming John Batten, his former protégé, for the race. Young Batten will be hard to beat, but the lure of a "real, rowdy, rousing campaign" is irresistible. Mike's father, Judge Royle, tops this *bella figura* when *he* is coaxed out of retirement to become the third candidate.

The Royles are an embittered lot, each one stuck in the "furious, invincible rigidity" of his chosen form of isolation. The judge, twice defeated as candidate for Governor, has been a distinguished county magistrate and private lawyer; but simple, unselfish, personal affection is beyond him. (He avoids "the stink of man, the foulest thing in creation" by raising pigs.) A neglected, aristocratic wife and unmarried daughter, Mary Ann, also inhabit the loveless home from which Mike has escaped.

Much is told of the Royles in sporadic flashbacks, but not until the disease of politics kills the old campaigning judge does Mr. Garrett tell enough about the family's past to explain their estranged attitudes. Indeed, too much is told too late for many episodes in the novel to be clear—let alone as affecting and dramatic as they might be.

The early events of the campaign seem plausible enough. When Election Day nears, however, Mr. Garrett uses all the clichés of racial strife and sexual promiscuity among the candidates to whip up a melodramatic climax which results in Parker's defeat. Within the melee uncommitted Mike has finally taken a few significant steps toward self-knowledge. He still seems more the "unfinished man, face to face with his own clumsiness" than a "finished man among his enemies."

> Frank H. Lyell, "Dogfight at the Hustings," in The New York Times Book Review, *October 11, 1959, p. 34.*

ROBERT C. HEALEY

George Garrett is an extremely gifted, prolific and perplexing young writer.... The perplexing element that crops up in his work is a seeming disparity between manner and matter, between the cool intelligence and sensibility of a careful craftsman and materials that are essentially gritty and unyielding.

Which Ones Are the Enemy? his second novel, is an excellent example of his talent. Johnny Riche, who tells his own first-person story with a jaunty mixture of pride and bravado, is a real anti-hero, by his own admission a confirmed heel and operator with no scruples or visible means of moral support. He is comfortably at home in the regular army and can soldier with the best of them when he wants to, but most of the time he is making a first-hand study of army courts-martial and prisons. The fact that he has picked up a Distinguished Service Cross and Purple Heart in Korea comes out almost in passing.

Fresh from an army stockade in Germany, Johnny is assigned to an artillery battalion with the American occupation forces in Trieste during the early '50s. It is an oddball outfit of misfits, the description of which Garrett has lifted bodily from one of the stories in his first collection, *King of the Mountain.* He had been behaving unusually well until an Italian B-girl who is openly contemptuous of privates and privates' pay wounds his pride and self-respect. No one, especially a woman, can treat Johnny Riche so lightly, and he recklessly puts in his bid on the spot. The girl, who has had her own share of misadventures with Germans and Americans, is quite agreeable to being set

up in a cosy little apartment as his exclusive property. Since this requires major financing, Johnny is forced to scout around for some easy money. With typical efficiency he organizes a black market operation in drugs stolen from the local army hospital.

At first their relationship is businesslike and matter of fact. After all, they are both in a sense professionals. But somewhat to their horror they find they are beginning to violate their own credo of noncommitment and to care deeply for each other. It is the ultimate tribute to Garrett's skill that he has been able to make this shift convincing and moving, so much so that the eventual collapse of this strangely touching idyl has the deceptive ring of authentic tragedy. It is a virtuoso performance, in which he proves in bravura style how something tender and fragile can blossom out of a romance between two such unlikely lovers.

His manner and matter are more surely mated in the thirteen stories of *In the Briar Patch.* Here his keen sensibility goes to work on everyday life in the small-town South, particularly in his native Florida. He is at his best in conveying the clear-eyed, uncluttered perceptions of children—the boy who becomes aware of his latent capacity for sadism, the boy who learns something about responsibility from the death of a chum. Jojo, the small boy who sets out to tame his own secret lion, is a particular delight. The boy in the title story is the terribly sage commentator on the amatory troubles of the family's Negro maid. Stories revolving around adults are most effective when they are purely character studies, least successful when they attempt to externalise complicated emotional states.

This is an unsentimentalized rural South seen cleanly and sharply. Negroes, white trash, aristocrats and plain everyday folk all receive equally unvarnished treatment. The only melodrama is that of character and the unsuspected depths in people, and except for the senseless killing in **"The Victim"** there is no fuzziness of intention. Character is pinpointed or emotional atmosphere established in sure, quick strokes. George Garrett's talent speaks out directly and unmistakably in these two volumes.

> Robert C. Healey, "An Extremely Gifted Young Writer," in Lively Arts and Book Review, *May 21, 1961, p. 27.*

THOMAS E. COONEY

George Garrett's new novel [*Which Ones Are the Enemy?*] is picaresque, but it departs from tradition by telling the story of a rogue who settles down to practice one grand fraud within unities of time, place and action—and in the process discovers that he is evolving from Don Juan to Romeo.

Mr. Garrett's picaroon is Pvt. John Riche, a professional artilleryman attached, after the Korean war, to Trieste United States Troops (ironically labeled TRUST). Riche is also an experienced diverter of United States supplies into the black market and a convinced cynic about everything except what he calls "soldiering"—which to him is any actual military operation in field or garrison, including inspection, guard duty, maneuvers and combat. Unfortunately for Riche, there is much to Army life that is not soldiering—for instance, the problem of financing a mistress on a private's pay. This is the genesis of his great fraud. It is also the spark for the peculiar *hubris* that topples this prince of Bilkos.

In a first-person narrative, in which he sounds a little like Huck Finn and a lot like Holden Caulfield, he describes his cold-blooded plan to conquer a Trieste night-club "hostess" who has scorned him as a nonentity: he will buy the girl on her own terms, seduce her into caring for him—which she stipulates she will never do—and then leave her. But for Riche and his Angela, familiarity breeds pity, and pity drifts into love.

By the time he knows that he wants to live happily ever after, the black market scheme he has launched to finance his ménage is too big and dangerous for him to quit. The story, which has had a dreaming, reminiscent quality up to this point, suddenly moves into a fast, solid climax of action and a bitterly graceful resolution of feeling.

Although this novel is chiefly notable for its fine projection of the autobiography of a born loser in his own engaging idiom, it also offers a startling picture of the peacetime military underworld of G. I. gangsters and black-market operators. This Army is different from Irwin Shaw's and Norman Mailer's, and it is even different from the one that James Jones knew before Pearl Harbor.

Thomas E. Cooney, "Military Underworld," in The New York Times Book Review, *June 25, 1961, p. 24.*

BABETTE DEUTSCH

These pages [in *Abraham's Knife and Other Poems*] belong less to song than to speech, but speech so honest, so intimate, so tersely meaningful, as to give it the indubitable quality of poetry. . . . One of the pleasures afforded by George Garrett's new volume is that it is the work of a man going his own gait and speaking in an individual voice. And if he is intensely conscious of the plight that he shares with his fellows, he is clean of self-pity, and quick to acknowledge the joys, as well as the big and little jokes, that relieve our anxiety, our ennui, our griefs.

The volume has three sections. The first of these is subtitled "Roman Poems." Dealing with the ancient city as it came to be known to an American who first saw the Old World in the European theater of war, the poems recreate Rome's unique character, which periodically unites the glories and shames of antiquity with life here and now. This section of the book is introduced by the four last lines, in the original, from Quasimodo's *"Umo Del Mio Tempo,"* which Garrett has himself translated in full. "Children, forget the bloody clouds / that mushroom from the earth. Forget / your fathers. Their tombs are ashes. / Their hearts belong to the wind and the dark birds." The poems that follow are more concrete, more colloquial, more complex, but not less sobering than this apostrophe. "Satires and Occasions," the second part of the book, bears an epigraph from Catullus: *"O saeclum insapiens et infacetum"* which, for those who do not read *Winnie Ille Pu,* may be rendered: "O coarse and ignorant generation!" and happens to conclude a lyric about a girl. Not all the poems that Garrett gathers here bear out Catullus's scornful lament, but if some of the finest are the gentlest, there are also a few sharp pieces that he might have saluted. The final section, which includes ["Abraham's Knife"], gives more than one Old Testament tale a fresh, pregnant interpretation. In his latest book George Garrett confesses skepticism, discouragement. He also, however tacitly, sets questions. And he finds the words and imagery of a poet for a courageous, compassionate understanding. (pp. 6-7)

Babette Deutsch, in a review of "Abraham's Knife and Other Poems," in Books, *July 30, 1961, pp. 6-7.*

WILLIAM DICKEY

[Garrett's language in *Abraham's Knife and Other Poems*] is relaxed, conversational, not intended to astonish: "It fits his hand like a glove," "The early myths / sing in my mind like a choir." Many of the poems are occasional, though the occasions vary, and few are as colloquial as this, from "Politician:" "'My word's good as far as the Savannah River,' / he said. 'After that you're in the hands / of Herman Talmadge.'"

The usual danger for this kind of poetry is that it should become prosy and flat, and infrequently Garrett's does: "They fall naturally into poses / mostly seen in advertisements / in magazines like the *New Yorker,* / dedicated to the cause of The Good Life." But his real problem arises when he tries to force an unnatural violence on his essentially non-violent verse, as in "The Mower:"

> A week of rain has made my lawn run wild:
> a prophet's beard, a mob with swarming blades,
> except where, here and there, like a bad child,
> a lone tongue flutters pure derision.
>
> Well, then, it's time for cutting, it appears.
> Time to meet force with force, to roll
> a keen and leveling weight on ragged sneers,
> to snip off foolish tongues and shut them up.
>
> So I sweat behind a lawn mower knowing
> prophet's head will haunt me and these slaves
> will own my acres and, in spite of mowing,
> green tongues will bronx the air above my grave.

What Garrett does in the second stanza is what he does well: the tone relaxed and direct, the colloquial force of the fourth line. But "bronx" is not easily forgivable; it is an arbitrary insistence on liveliness that can only end in a mechanical dance of death. There are too many such insistences in these poems, and I hope Garrett decides to get rid of them. They divert attention from his real strengths, the direct anger of "Solitaire," the serious conversation of "The Window" or the controlled language of affection in "For My Sons." . . . (p. 127)

William Dickey, "Revelations and Homilies," in Poetry, *Vol. XCIX, No. 2, November, 1961, pp. 124-29.*

J. A. BRYANT, JR.

The rough spots that characterize even the best of the stories in [*In the Briar Patch*] testify to [Garrett's] ability to let a story discover itself; for if Garrett's stories are sometimes not quite finished, they are also never finished off. The title story, "In the Briar Patch," wanders somewhere along the road that stretches between Br'er Rabbit's "Please, Br'er Fox, don' throw me in de briar patch" and Hamlet's "rather bear those ills we have / Than fly to others that we know not of." It takes shape in the consciousness of a small boy, whose naïveté has preserved for him the independence of his elders' self-made mantraps and who can thus appreciate both the principle that Br'er Rabbit acts upon in the tar-baby tale and something of Hamlet's apprehensiveness about trying his luck in a strange world. This enables him to understand the plight of a young Negro soldier named Leroy whom his father has caught intimidating the household maid and turned over to the police. Leroy, it turns out, has been using the device of A. W. O. L. to move freely between the Army and the world of colored folk, two briar patches that he knows well; and he earns the little boy's admiration when he uses the rabbit's stratagem to persuade the civil authorities to turn him back to the military. Yet from his own protected position, the boy also has the insight to sympathize with his frustrated parent, who senses Leroy's victory and happiness but has long since lost the capacity to comprehend either.

Garrett's portrayal of the wisdom of innocence appears again and again in these stories: in a young girl, who, without instruction, acts out the timeless pastoral of love-making by trading buttermilk for kisses; in the simple-minded mountaineer who learns the knack of getting gifts from the sophisticated people who give him rides; in a young boy who in ignorance, innocence and wonder shelters and feeds a runaway lion. This last story, called simply **"Lion,"** is symbolic of what Garrett seems to be doing in much of his work. One of the mottos that he places at the beginning of his collection, a passage from the Bible, says the same thing: "Let brotherly love continue. Be not forgetful to entertain strangers: for thereby others have entertained angels unawares." To Garrett the incident, the man, the lion, all are strangers and all are to be entertained, not because they are angels or even because they may turn out to be; but simply because brotherly love needs to continue. In short, Garrett's humility before the object and his respect for it seem to be the important reasons for his writing. He loves the lion because it is there, not because it can ever conceivably prove useful. He tames nothing. He protects and feeds everything. That is why his stories, even the roughest of them, seem to have an additional capacity for growth, and why the best of them are unmistakably alive. (pp. 120-21)

J. A. Bryant, Jr., in a review of "In the Briar Patch,"
in The Sewanee Review, *Vol. LXXI, No. 1, Winter,*
1963, pp. 120-21.

JAMES B. MERIWETHER

Garrett's reputation as a poet depends at present upon his three books of verse, *The Reverend Ghost, The Sleeping Gypsy,* and *Abraham's Knife.* In his introduction to *The Reverend Ghost* (1957), John Hall Wheelock called attention to the qualities which have continued to characterize Garrett's work: the "bare but often strangely musical" verbal effects; the driving concern for inner truth, the essence of things; the splendid variety of talent and interest displayed in lyrics, character studies, meditative essays upon other poets, descriptions of the American landscape, and a whole spectrum of humor. Wheelock also noted the "curiously abstract quality" of some of the poems, product, he thought, of the poet's "struggle to pierce through appearance to the truth."

Wheelock's high praise was repeated and elaborated upon by many reviewers of the second and third volumes—Babette Deutsch, among them, should be singled out for two especially perceptive reviews [see excerpts above]—in 1958 and 1961. His later poems have been marked by a continued experimentation with metre and verbal texture, a recent interest in translations see especially those from the Italian of Salvatore Quasimodo), and steadily increasing control. So far he has published no long poems, but within the limits of shorter forms his range is remarkable, his power impressive. Although as a man and as a poet Garrett is too independent and forceful (the young Faulkner is an appropriate comparison) to be in line to receive the benefits which our literary world bestows upon those who play literary politics, his verse is steadily if slowly achieving the wider recognition which his fellow poets like John Crowe Ransom and Richard Wilbur have for several years predicted for him.

Although he has by no means lost interest in poetry in the past few years, or ceased to grow as a poet, Garrett has devoted increasing attention to fiction. His first novel, *The Finished Man,* he completed in December 1958 in Rome, where he was enjoying a year of writing on the American Academy's Prix de Rome and a *Sewanee Review* fellowship. Earlier in 1958 had appeared his first collection of stories, *King of the Mountain.* A second novel, *Which Ones Are the Enemy?,* and another book of stories, *In the Briar Patch,* were published in 1961 within a month of each other. A third novel is now under way. Though lack of space makes impossible any discussion of the individual works of fiction here, I must express in passing my admiration for that beautiful and moving army novel, set in occupied Trieste, *Which Ones Are the Enemy?,* and my respect for *The Finished Man,* in some ways a more ambitious book but for me a less successful one. Among the stories I have a special fondness for the army section of *King of the Mountain,* **"What's the Purpose of the Bayonet?"** and for many—perhaps all—of the stories of *In the Briar Patch.* There are enough stories, published and unpublished, to make another collection no less distinguished than the first two. What a commentary upon the present state of the market for books of stories it is, that this third collection has not yet been published, and that the second appeared under the imprint of a university press. (It must be added, though, that the University of Texas Press made beautiful books, designed and decorated by Jo Alys Downs, of *The Sleeping Gypsy* and *In the Briar Patch,* in striking contrast to the poor appearance of Garrett's books from commercial publishers.)

Brief mention too must be made of the other elements in Garrett's career as a professional writer. Two years with the Alley Theatre in Houston (1960-1962), the first on a Ford Foundation grant, the second teaching at Rice, produced a children's play, *Sir Slob and the Princess* (opened March 25, 1961 and since published) and a two-act comedy, **"Garden Spot U.S.A."** (opened April 25, 1962). In July 1963 he flew to Hollywood to be on location for the shooting of his first screenplay, **"The Young Lovers,"** that rarity in the present movie world, an entire script done without collaborators, by a writer new to Hollywood. And no examination of Garrett's literary accomplishment is complete without mention of his critical writing, which has produced two of the best articles ever written on Faulkner (on the verse and the early criticism), and a brilliant study of Joyce Cary's mature poems, to cite only three examples. In criticism Garrett displays the same independence of judgment and familiarity with a wide range (both chronologically and geographically speaking) of literary models that he has shown in his poetry and fiction. That is to say, he has written some of the most distinguished short critical pieces of his generation.

The variety of media in which he has worked does not conceal certain constants in Garrett's writings. There is his restless urge to experiment, which is balanced both by his desire to communicate (his poems are often demanding but are not "difficult" in any conventional sense) and the need to polish and perfect which is evident in the gradual evolution of some of his poems through several different published versions and many manuscript drafts. There is his interest in the visual arts, manifest from the early *Nassau Lit* contributions to his recent article on Joyce Cary.

Although Garrett has traveled and lived widely in America and abroad, I am tempted to single out his Southern background for mention in some detail for its importance throughout the whole range of his work, particularly in his fiction. In 1957, in his first published critical article, his important and groundbreaking study of Faulkner's poetry, Garrett quoted with approval a statement Faulkner had recently made concerning the difference between the aims of verse and prose: "The poet deals in something universal, while the novelist deals in his own traditions." That distinction makes a useful taking-off point for a consideration of Garrett's use of the materials of his native region. His verse, like Faulkner's, on the whole owes little to Southern models or traditions, although his range is wider than Faulkner's and he does things with his poems that Faulkner did not permit himself to do. "Faulkner's concept of the use of poetry is . . . in a sense an inhibiting one for the poet," Garrett wrote; marked by restraint and formal diction, Faulkner's poetry "would tend to avoid the light, the occasional, and, to a degree, the colloquial." Garrett's verse, on the other hand, is often light in touch, and frequently colloquial in idiom. Those who have heard him read it are aware how closely tied to the spoken word are the humor, the dialogue, and the frequent changes of pace in the written words of his poetry. But aside from the matter of diction, the poetry shows few signs of the strength and vitality of the influence of Garrett's Southern background, which is of such importance in his other work.

The first novel, *The Finished Man,* and the play, "**Garden Spot U.S.A.,**" both set in Florida, and many of the short stories have strongly realized Southern settings, with Southern language, scenes, humor, and a Southern emphasis upon character (often magnified to the mythical, or twisted to the grotesque). A lecture Garrett gave in Richmond in 1959, but never published, reveals clearly his conception of the tradition in which he works as a writer born and brought up in a Southeastern state in the second quarter of the twentieth century. Illustrating his lecture with some quotations from his recently published *The Finished Man,* along with a rousing delivery of that fine old burlesque sermon "The Harp of a Thousand Strings," Garrett emphasized the diversity of a tradition that included in his own time writers as contrasting as Faulkner and Welty, Williams and Wolfe, Porter and O'Connor. But in spite of this diversity, he stressed, certain constant factors have existed which are still significant in the work of most authors who write from a Southern background or point of view.

First of these he put the sense of place—"You can hardly find a Southern writer who does not love the land he writes of," he said. The land "sings lyrically in their work," even today; "even the cities and suburbia and the new industry cannot efface that almost instinctive affection for the land—for there is too much of it and it is too strong. It triumphs over our best intentions."

After the sense of place comes tradition—"With the love of the land goes an awareness of its history." And closely connected to these is the strong sense of family, which Garrett suggested may have a connection with the development of the grotesque as a mode in Southern writing. "If we live in families extending through threads of cousins and uncles and aunts, then we must come to terms with *characters* and eccentricity. A big family has a place for this, just as, curiously, our small towns do, a place for the winners and the losers, the proud and the misbegotten."

The family sense, too, may have played a part in the development of Southern literary humor. "We have to have a sense of humor to tolerate some of our relatives and some of our fictional characters and humor is and has been from the start a vital part of our literature," he told his Richmond audience. "It may be subtle and cosmopolitan, as, for example, the humor of your own James Branch Cabell; it may be feminine, beautiful and gossipy like that of Eudora Welty. . . . This humor may be the humor of the grotesque—deriving maybe from the tall tale. . . . The range of humor is enormous—and like all jokes some of it is for one audience and some for another."

In the end it is the language that is the all-important basis of what is Southern in literature. (pp. 27-31)

By 1961 Garrett's work either as a poet or as a short story writer would by itself have placed him, at the age of thirty-two, high among the important literary figures of his own generation. Taken together, and added to his accomplishments as a novelist, critic and playwright, this body of work constitutes an achievement which is, so far as I am able to judge, unique in this country, in this time, for a writer under forty. I have not seen the screenplay but his other work, in every field, is solid, professional, and distinguished by originality, high seriousness, a first rate talent, a first rate mind, and a sense of humor. The great importance of the diversity of the fields in which he has worked so capably can hardly be overemphasized. For, though he has worked in so many media, he gives no impression of uncertainty, of diffusion of interests. Rather, one feels that here is an extraordinarily disciplined young writer—young in the sense that he is still learning and growing—who is taking advantage of every professional opportunity to perfect his craftsmanship in any field within his wide range of interests. Without venturing to predict that this powerful, restless artist will eventually concentrate upon any one of these fields, I feel sure that the concentration and strength which now characterize individual poems and stories will ultimately mark the work as a whole. He has certainly prepared himself to do work of singular excellence in the novel, and perhaps that will be where his most enduring contribution will be made. But his work to date leaves no sense of incompleteness or lack of fulfillment. If George Garrett never writes another word he will have already left his mark upon the literature of his generation. (p. 32)

*James B. Meriwether, "George Palmer Garrett, Jr.,"
in* The Princeton University Library Chronicle, *Vol. XXV, No. 1, Autumn, 1963, pp. 26-32.*

THOMAS WHEELER

Mr. Garrett, a poet and a novelist as well as a short-story writer and prize winner, has a swift and telling talent that brings enormous happenings within the scope of his varied characters [in *Cold Ground Was My Bed Last Night*]. He gathers brilliant insights in surprising places: he summons up the faculty and the Army, the small town and the city with evocative voices admirably adapted to each region. The hungry thrust of his roots into different places suggests how deep he might go—if the era itself were not transient, or if he were cantankerous enough to look one way.

His dirt farmers and unsteady matrons can both live vividly because he has the sure skill of transforming characters. His gifts are especially strong in the expert title story, where a small-town Florida sheriff, his cocky deputy and a vagrant prisoner move toward their new selves under a subtle spell of interaction. An emancipated Southerner, Mr. Garrett suggests thunder when the gentry comes north and the talented let their talents decay. In the fine story **"Man Without a Fig Leaf,"** one bright youth nurses the synthetic beauties of an office receptionist; another (a dry poet from the South who has gone in and out of jobs and asylums) seeks a city in the snow as God's only glory. But character is always more important than trouble, as in the allegory of the cruel world, **"The Wounded Soldier,"** freshened beyond the routine by its final human ironies.

Within his characters, Mr. Garrett often plumbs the crucial myths that make their lives important, which may be the real depth that he will develop. Character, now his constant, takes him a long way into men rather than into man.

> *Thomas Wheeler, "Moments of Reality," in* The New York Times Book Review, *June 14, 1964, p. 4.*

PAUL LEVINE

Mr. Garrett's triumph [in *Cold Ground Was My Bed Last Night*] is not that he glorifies the commonplace but that he tries to understand it. Most of these stories deal with institutional life—the army or the academy—and the protagonists are invariably the non-commissioned officers of society—sergeants, sheriffs and professors—who "stand between the world and [the uninitiated]... all too familiar with their vices and stifled virtues... the steadfast preserver[s] of those secrets and their illusions." In **"The Old Army Game"** a draftee learns that "soldiering" means hating, not loafing, while in **"Texarcana Was a Crazy Town"** a discharged sergeant discovers that the civilian world is more brutal than the army. The long title piece [**"Cold Ground Was My Bed Last Night"**] is one of the few modern stories to make complex sense of sudden violence. Mr. Garrett writes in a low-keyed style that makes his incidents seem more ordinary and his stories more extraordinary.

> *Paul Levine, in a review of "Cold Ground Was My Bed Last Night," in* The Hudson Review, *Vol. XVII, No. 3, Autumn, 1964, p. 474.*

PAUL WEST

[Garrett's method in *Do, Lord, Remember Me*] is tellingly indirect. He sets the characters soliloquizing in turn, almost as if he's unpicking a part-song or a round: the voices don't overlap or clash, but their respectively imperfect, cranky versions of the story do, coinciding and colliding in the mind. This choric type of narration is a vexingly difficult thing to do: if it isn't just about perfect it merely confuses the reader and becomes an expense of wit in a waste of sameness. In a word: fog.

There is no fog in this novel. Mr. Garrett has planned, arranged and interlocked until everything that happens—a sudden new perspective, a switch in style or speed or chapter-length—comes pat off the page, assimilable and timely. This is pretty much the method that Andrei Bely called "symphonic," and Mr. Garrett beautifully controls it. The prose has a magniloquent rawness never otiose or fancy, and the basic story is shrewdly chosen.

Into a sleazy town in the South come Big Red, a hot gospelier, and his troupe: Miami, his shop-soiled beauty of a mistress; Cartwright, avaricious and priapically obsessed; and Moses the Jew, numb with the guilt of having accidentally machine-gunned

a cellarful of children during the war. Red, who has been everywhere—Bringing the Good News to Everybody—is a boldly conceived maelstrom of a character: imperious as a god, golden-tongued, a genuine healer, but also self-destructive and daft with hubris. It will take little to destroy him just as, in the past, it has taken little to inspire him to charismatic intensity. The little arrives in the form of Judith, a traumatized hummingbird of a woman, whom he once helped. She gradually, in her wordy way, shoves him to the brink while the troupe's uneasy serviceable loyalties disintegrate.

Here and there Mr. Garrett gives Judith some polysyllabic mouthfuls which conflict with her predominant way of raving, and I'm not sure that the occasional interventions by an impersonal narrator are really necessary: meant to enlighten, they seem merely knowing. But these are minor blemishes in a radiant, vibrant novel of sultry vividness and almost irresistible vernacular flow. And if, as I think, the ghost of Faulkner stalks in these pages, he is at least talking uncommonly well.

> *Paul West, "Southern Cross," in* Book Week—The Sunday Herald Tribune, *September 19, 1965, p. 24.*

THE VIRGINIA QUARTERLY REVIEW

Sex and religion have long been associated as dual themes in literature; faith healers and evangelists in particular have often been represented as sinners rather than saints, with their tent revival meetings a mere incitement to intimately described revelry in adjacent woods once the services inside have been concluded. Mr. Garrett, while accepting the basic outlines, has dignified his material [in *Do, Lord, Remember Me*] and given it some importance through a discerning study of his principals, their motivations, and personalities, a field quite rich enough when consideration is given to their respective backgrounds: an ex-convict turned preacher, a gifted female with few morals and a warmly responsive Body Beautiful, and a feeble-minded nymphomaniac whose wonder at the phoenix-like attributes of the male organ leads her into endless experiments of a more or less gratifying nature. Such lubricious elements of contemporary story-making are handled by the author with commendable delicacy and gravity, but serious readers will applaud his superior intelligence and writing skill. Mr. Garrett renews faith in his literary finesse with each successive book.

> *A review of "Do, Lord, Remember Me," in* The Virginia Quarterly Review, *Vol. 42, No. 1, Winter, 1966, p. viii.*

THE VIRGINIA QUARTERLY REVIEW

[*For a Bitter Season: New and Selected Poems*] presents almost too much variety for an individual to handle and, after repeated readings, a richness that comes as a constant surprise. The best ones, finally, are the long meditations, **"Salome," "Rugby Road," "Crows at Paestum"**—but this is unfair to the briefer protests, the cries of a man tortured by passion, God, and self and willing to mock all three. At times Garrett is trying to reject a kind of secular sainthood or innocent hope with a wisecrack, and in those poems his spare diction may produce lines that are simply flat. But in his most frothy topical poems he demonstrates he can do anything he wants with sounds and rhythms.

> *A review of "For a Bitter Season," in* The Virginia Quarterly Review, *Vol. 44, No. 3, Summer, 1968, p. cv.*

LAURENCE LIEBERMAN

A virtuoso of many talents, George Garrett vivifies the interior life of a gallery of offbeat characters in his dramatic monologues [in *For a Bitter Season*]. In **"Ventriloquist's Dummy,"** one of the slower-paced short pieces, nearly every line contains firecrackery images, flashing and spitting a trail of sparks. . . . But in longer poems like **"Salome,"** his style varies from a memorable and distinctive language ("my mouth, my lips, / a red yawn, a taut shriek, my tongue / fluttered like a dead leaf . . .") to the language of journalistic blandness; from a scissoring just out-of-balance rhythm to rhythms that all seem to run one way, all at the same speed, and often—for my ear—too fast for the pace of his thought. I get the impression that the slack passages were composed with haste by a fast typist at one sitting. At such times, I'd like to confine Garrett to a locked cell with a scratchy old-fashioned quill pen.

His vivid characterization and talent for satire, strengths evidently acquired in the development of his fiction, carry over best into two story-telling poems, **"Excursion"** and **"Egyptian Gold."** Garrett is most brilliant when he sets himself to many tasks at once. Since his style is usually clean and fluent, a complex poem can carry much thematic baggage, and perform on many levels, without growing prolix or heavy-handed. He has mastered, in these poems, the art of oddly opposed juxtapositions: the clash of contrary personalities, divergent societies, and historically irreconcilable ideas. All are geared to a common scale by the poet's comprehensive wit.

> *Laurence Lieberman, in a review of "For a Bitter Season," in* Poetry, *Vol. CXII, No. 5, August, 1968, p. 340.*

J. R. FRAKES

For years, I have felt an ever more anguished indifference toward historical novels. Well, I have finally found the "right novel" and the "right author." Now, I *do* care what happened to Sir Walter Ralegh when James took over from Elizabeth. And I care because George Garrett, a solid poet, short-story writer, and novelist, has *made* me care, because he has made "a work of fiction, of the imagination, planted and rooted in fact." The truths, triumphantly, are in the fiction. To check the details of [*Death of the Fox*] against the "factual" accounts Garrett so honorably provides in his preface would be to subject a perfect martini to the grim analysis of a chemical engineer. Life is here, and concern and conviction and a peculiar kind of beauty that lights up an age and a culture hitherto hidden.

The Fox is, of course, Sir Walter Ralegh, and the death (in 1618) that around which this boiling book centers like a beneficent hurricane. The research that must have gone into this work is muscle-aching to reflect upon, but the reading is sustaining and enriching. Quarrel if you will with Garrett's version of the delicate slidings of oily ambition, the convolutions of double and triple agents; grumble at his perpetuation of Ralegh legends; grouse at his refusal to exploit poetic license in clarifying Ralegh's Guiana expedition and subsequent return to almost-sure execution in England; fret at the nougaty details of architecture, costumes, interiors, landscapes, tastes, oaths, farts; squirm at the deep-deep-purple patches; wince at the obviously topical descriptions of My Lai-type massacres in Ireland and the absurdity of the concept that any man fights for a "cause." Do all that, and then see how petty your quibbles become, how all that cargo of topography, that thread-by-button detail of dress, that quoting of Coke and Harrington and

Bacon, that suspect reference to the "restless young"—how all the poetic reveries, often over-lush, become clangingly congruous, delineated with flavor, style, drama.

What would in feebler hands become grave-robbing becomes here revivification. From the chapters narrated by the Elizabethan-Jacobean soldier, courtier, and sailor, I learned—the word is "experienced"—more about that whirling era than I ever got from volumes of "authentic" history. The feel, man, the feel! And that, as you must have guessed, is the key to Ralegh himself—feeling, shadings of paradox and perversity, eros and agape, love and lust, ruthless ego-drive and inexplicable self-sacrifice. And with Ralegh and his fellow-courtiers, Garrett illuminates the entire smarmy world of royalty and commoners, jewels and gutter-garbage, politic church and sharkfight state. All very rich, thick-textured, uncheating, nourishing. If his glittering subject, Ralegh, had style, George Garrett has even more—many styles, many perspectives, many talents. *Death of the Fox* is a lovesong to England, a threnody to mutability, a work of committed art, informed with a rare fusion of guts and spirit.

> *J. R. Frakes, "Just like a Perfect Martini," in* Book World—Chicago Tribune, *October 24, 1971, p. 19.*

THE VIRGINIA QUARTERLY REVIEW

Garrett's novel about the life and death of Sir Walter Ralegh [*Death of the Fox*] ought to delight a great variety of readers, and it deserves high praise any way you look at it, since the book contains wit, charm, some enormously moving episodes, and much skillful, evocative prose. *Death of the Fox* fits no familiar form, as it refuses to be a costume novel, nor does it indulge in the usual fantasies of historical fiction. Garrett mainly interests us in the irony of life and the multiplicity of a human character—as we try to understand what brought Ralegh into and out of existence. Garrett probably would agree with Goethe that it is dangerous to define a person, for a single conception at one moment cannot sum up a living man who is always becoming. When we define someone our active relation to him dies, for his has died for us in spirit if not in body. Reading this impressive book creates some such living experience that goes beyond simple understanding, as we discover Ralegh always in process. Through the eyes of the old Ralegh about to be executed for treason we see his memories, his London, his England, his antagonist King James, his friends, wife, executioner; through other eyes we see him, in a fascinating variety of consciousnesses, mirroring the bold and careless soldier, sailor, courtier, husband, legal debater, gambler with life, conquistador, lover, prisoner, doting father, proud and humble Christian—all the paradoxes of the inner and outer man are presented. An astonishingly rich character emerges from the story, growing in our consciousness from a series of types into a profounder archetype: a superbly human creature, a genuine hero and maker of myths that we live by. The book's narrative strategy allows Garrett to evoke the man in a stream of time by use of reveries of telescoped events, told in magnificent, long, rapid sentences, curiously broken up yet continuous—suggesting the baroque prose of the early seventeenth century, without its obscurity or tedium. The sense of place comes alive too as Ralegh walks through the Tower of London, rows up the river to Westminster while the Thames watermen doff their caps in honor, as he entertains in the upper room of the Gate House, and finally when he delivers his oration from the scaffold in the Old Palace Yard. The moving dramas of the book occur in these places. In substance this book becomes a wonderful thing in itself, a processional novel, touching all the sacred places of Elizabethan England and imaginatively evoking the minds of its greatest people. It renders Ralegh in his complexity of time and place so intensely that he lives in our time.

A review of "Death of the Fox," in The Virginia Quarterly Review, Vol. 48, No. 2, Spring, 1972, p. xlviii.

MARTIN LEVIN

Three long stories [in *The Magic Striptease*]. The title piece ["**The Magic Striptease**"], "a comic strip fable," is about a protean prankster who can change his shape at will, and uses his gift to fulfill his misanthropy. When Jacob Quirk finally eschews malice for an evangelical guise, he is committed to the booby hatch and his last metamorphosis. George Garrett's irony is alloyed with lead. "**Noise of Strangers**" is about a rotten Southern sheriff who pins a bum rap on a very nice guitar playing vagrant. Meanwhile, a trigger happy assistant cop goes scot free. You were expecting maybe justice? "**The Satyr Shall Cry**" is an ambitious tale of Southern discomfort in the Erskine Caldwell tradition. Throw a lubricious revivalist and a nude girl bank teller into a blazing tent filled with venomous snakes—and you can expect more than flesh wounds. For a short story, it has more stock characters than a full-sized novel.

Martin Levin, in a review of "The Magic Striptease," in The New York Times Book Review, December 16, 1973, p. 18.

DAVID TILLINGHAST

[*The Magic Striptease*], three novellas under one cover, is so outlandish and mischievous that the reader really questions its intention, but again the imagination of the author fascinates—especially in the book's first novella ["**The Magic Striptease**"], about a man named Jacob Quirk, who can change himself into another person, and not simply another flesh and blood human being, but a character in fiction. Ridiculous, extravagant, and successful, *The Magic Striptease* fulfills the basic requirement of all good fiction: the reader wonders what in the world is going to happen next—and keeps flipping the pages. (pp. 22-3)

David Tillinghast, "George Garrett," in The South Carolina Review, Vol. 9, No. 1, November, 1976, pp. 21-4.

MAUREEN QUILLIGAN

In *The Succession,* George Garrett's historical "Novel of Elizabeth and James," chronological sequence is elided in favor of a subtle, complex meditation on the poetry of time. Mr. Garrett's inclination is not surprising, for he is the author of six books of poetry, as well as much fiction and drama. The book's title refers, then, not only to the historical transfer of political power from one Renaissance monarch (Elizabeth I of England) to another (James I of England and Scotland) but to the succession of time itself. The novel is a choral reflection on how our memories and imaginations shape time and history into polyphonic music.

In choosing not to follow a straightforward chronological sequence, Mr. Garrett offers his reader even more responsibility than he did in his earlier Renaissance novel, *Death of the Fox.*

In that brilliant, sensuously detailed and politically acute work, Sir Walter Raleigh's life was the peg on which Mr. Garrett hung a narrative that, like some rich damask cloak, folded back on itself. *The Succession* repeats these techniques (in its chorus of many voices an disruptions of chronology) without a focus on any one central figure. It is more purely antiphonal and more complex than *Death of the Fox.*

As Mr. Garrett explains in a prefatory note, the book began as a meditation on the letters between the old Queen Elizabeth and the young King James, her godson and the child of her great rival, Mary, Queen of Scots. But, he tells us, other voices broke into his story to tell their own versions of this history. We eavesdrop on their conversations, read their private letters. An outlawed Catholic priest writes unfinished, unsent letters to his parents and former teachers, asking forgiveness, confessing his fear of the torture he will eventually die of. His letters are part of a packet of evidence obtained by an unnamed governmental authority connected to Elizabeth's court. . . .

The most wonderful and ambitious of these voices—because it is so reminiscent of the great Elizabethan stage—is the man Mr. Garrett calls the Player. He is a poet whose words "run like hounds finding and following one scent after another. More (it seems) for the joy of running, for the sake of barking and belling, than for anything else." Like Scheherazade, he tells a long, perhaps untrue, tale of his life to postpone danger, to put off the moment when a spy for some unnamed parties will bribe him for the papers he wrote years earlier while he himself was spying on the Earl of Essex, Elizabeth's most famous rebel.

Also in Mr. Garrett's chorus are the musings of the Messenger, who first brings news of James's birth to England and threads his way through the entire story, riding down the map of Scotland and England, journeying into the even more personal territory of his memories of being turned spy by the inexorable politics of his time. If there is a spine to *The Succession,* it is the Messenger's minutely rendered travelogue, as if the map of the two separate countries could only be joined together by the devious twistings of espionage. The Messenger's ruminations, however, will not serve the narrative function served by the dramatic figure of Raleigh in *Death of the Fox*. In *The Succession,* that function becomes the responsibility of the readers. We, like the characters in the story, are asked to assemble a coherent narrative from disparate pieces of testimony.

Thus when we finally come to the letters between the two major figures, Elizabeth and James, we read them as Elizabeth's brilliant, devious and powerful secretary, Robert Cecil, a spymaster himself, reads them, searching for the patterns of power in this succession. . . .

When Cecil, exhausted, puts away all the letters—among them some of his own secret correspondence with James—the statesman recognizes the folly of his reading, "As if he himself studying these papers, even his own letters, like a scholar from another era, had not long since committed himself." The phrase "scholar from another era" might be taken as anachronistic coyness on Mr. Garrett's part. I think rather that it is a Brechtian reminder of the intricate and intellectually dazzling artifice that underlies this novel. Mr. Garrett could be the "poet from another era," for it is he who re-creates history into poetry. . . .

With intelligence and sympathy, he takes us into the minds of both the shrewd, aging Queen and the younger, impatient King. Becoming privy to the thoughts and feelings of the great is usually the reason we read historical novels. But Mr. Garrett allows us to eavesdrop on clowns as well as kings.

After all his complicated play with time, Mr. Garrett ends with a "Christmastide" and a drunken plowman "fearful of nothing, not past or future," who reels in frozen silence and wishes his Queen a good night. Only a poet and scholar who knows and loves the Renaissance as well as George Garrett obviously does would attempt such a lovely Shakespearean ending. *The Succession* could simply be categorized as a historical novel, but it is also a major achievement in fiction.

> *Maureen Quilligan, "A Time of Spies," in* The New York Times Book Review, *December 25, 1983, p. 6.*

FRED PFEIL

It is true that historical events enable *The Succession*—the riven factionalisms and power plays of the last thirty-five or so years of Elizabeth's reign, culminating in the difficult, delicate uncertainties of the Succession itself. It is also true that the novel's sixteen separate dechronologized sections, ranging from eight to nearly one-hundred pages apiece, are nominally centered around a multitude of presiding consciousnesses or narrative perspectives, from lowly actor (and double agent) to persecuted Catholic priest, from Scots reivers sitting around a fire on a wet night in the borderlands, telling stories to pass the time, to King James himself, fretting and chafing in the wings. And yet the novel, with occasional and quite brief exceptions, remains stalwartly detached from any truly interiorized, individuated evocation of character, and for the most part avoids any direct scenic renditions of dramatic events. The adventures of the Priest come to us through the letters and documents found on his person when captured; the Queen's Secretary peruses and meditates on the correspondence which has passed between Elizabeth and James; even the novel's most vividly realized character, Essex, and his doomed rebellion, the most dramatic and compelling action in the book, come to us obliquely, through a set of astonishingly novelistic notes taken by the Player in his capacity as double agent, confiscated and perused by yet a third agent of another group of nobles (and perhaps James himself) eager to cover their tracks.

Finally, though, what most effectively subverts any sense of classically totalizable dramatic action in *The Succession* is the uniformly performative action of Garrett's style itself, which effectively transforms every "referent" it touches, whether meditation, document, or dramatic action itself, into something like yet another delicate figuration in a uniformly two-dimensional tapestry or set of tableaux. It is not just that all voices sound alike, that every utterance and scrap of writing is as fulsomely turned out and richly worded as every other; the problem is the extent to which each situation and every character is merely a subordinated pretext for the release of yet more of the same gorgeous decorative prose. Nowhere is this more clear than in those five sections of the novel devoted to the passage on horseback of a secret messenger from Edinburgh to London, to inform his master, the Queen's Secretary Cecil the elder, of James' birth; with each successive section, the point and urgency of the journey itself, as well as the individual character of the Messenger, are more and more attenuated, smothered by the ravening exigencies of Garrett's performative prose:

> If only he still had his little Scots mare and time to spend. Then he would linger long enough to relieve

some Yorkshiremen of their prosperity. But he must be gone. First through sandy country to the village of Bawtry. A poor place with a few shabby half-timbered houses set close to a little pond. Lying low and swampy next to River Idle. Then farewell to Yorkshire and welcome to Nottingham. Road running through flat red-clay fields. To Scrooby (a mere hamlet only) with its large moated manor house for the Archbishop of York.

Admittedly, such a passage represents *The Succession* at its antiquarian-guidebook worst. But in its verbless, heavily-cadenced flow and faintly formal echoes of Elizabethan diction it does legitimately suggest something of the degree to which the novel's dramatic and historical referents are enveloped and overcome by the sheer static blanketing weight of a style which is itself, one comes to realize, the novel's main attraction, a kind of sumptuous, exhaustively-researched, culinary pastiche. (pp. 137-38)

> *Fred Pfeil, "Fred Pfeil on Jay Cantor and George Garrett," in* fiction international, *No. 2, 1984, pp. 135-41.*

LINDA W. WAGNER

A prose poem in its subtle changes from speaker to speaker, [*The Succession: A Novel of Elizabeth and James*] is filled not so much with action as with the absence of action. All attention is focused throughout on "the succession," on who, indeed, will inherit Elizabeth's throne. Circumstances—and the earliest set of numbered episodes, dating to James's birth in 1566—point to King James of Scotland, but the novel reveals that outcome only near its end. The reader's interest turns instead to the way the panorama of historic acts is arranged and, of even more interest, conveyed: what seems to be an historical novel becomes, finally, a surfiction passing as historical novel. Garrett has, deftly, unobtrusively, made his book into a commentary upon the genre, and he has done it chiefly by shifting points of view so as to keep "fact" subjective rather than objective.

Like Faulkner's *As I Lay Dying*—with which *The Succession* shares many qualities in addition to narrative method—this novel works through named sections: Messenger, Player, Courtier, Priest, Secretary. The seemingly insignificant figures in the Historic pageant are given leading roles, telling the already familiar "story" from their respective vantage points so that it often bears scant resemblance to the "known" version, telling more about themselves as narrators than about the "event" being described.

Once Garrett has his cast of disparate speakers assembled, he uses them to tell Elizabeth's story as well as their own, and that of the intriguing, divisive court. From the Courtier, we hear the Leicester and Elizabeth romance; from the Player, the execution of Essex; from the Priest, the execution of Mary, Queen of Scots, and her son's almost casual response to that death, an event replayed from different vantage points throughout the book; from the Messenger, the crucial role of Sir William Cecil (and Sir Robert Cecil, perhaps the most visible character in the novel, appears as "Secretary" throughout, keping our attention on the 1603 panorama). To achieve the chronological movement of the story, which runs from 1558, Elizabeth's accession, to 1603, James's accession, Garrett aligns each character with key dates through the period: the Messenger speaks from 1566 as he carries the news of James's birth to London; the Priest, from 1587, the date of Mary's execution;

and perhaps most interesting of all, the Courtier, from 1626, recalling the events of 1603, the actual focus of the book. The effect is an intricate tapestry that draws the reader into the novel as a sleuth and fact-finder, rather than as a passive receptor of information.

The obviously "lead" characters—Elizabeth and James—appear in cameo segments and through letters; but both their appearances and their writings influence the tone and pace of the novel proper. Garrett opens *The Succession* with Elizabeth, aged and discomfited, waiting to die yet feisty with the impatience of the put-upon: "all news of this world is stale," "my only miracle, it seems to me, is to have lived as long and to have become so old. . . ." The passages create the incremental rhythms characteristic of the musing mind. . . . The heart of the whole saga, its incriminatory baseness revealed again and again, occurs early in Elizabeth's opening monologue, her description of false tongues:

> Their tongues are not to be trusted. Not now or then or ever after, world without end. Tongues which rest heavy and meaty in the mouth. Swimming fatly in the broth of sweet lies and the savory tastes of flattery. Tongues as fat and still as fish in a creel. And yet those same heavy, lazy tongues are quick enough, when called upon, with their flourishes of wit. . . .

For all its deliberate pace, its subliminal impassioned movement, Garrett's novel is primarily an exposé of cruelty and manipulation, like his earlier novel on Sir Walter Raleigh, *Death of the Fox*. It seems appropriate that fictions about the Age of Shakespeare should compel the reader to search for truth among sequences of self-justifying monologues.

I particularly admire the way the author controls the tempo of the book. Near the center of the text—once we have begun to become involved with Elizabeth and her arduous life—Garrett mimicks *The Odyssey* and stops short for a session of storytelling by a group of marvelously hearty Scotch reivers. Sly, Blind Jock, and Red Tom tell three tales that embroider the events of James's court, and help to show (by 1602, when this segment occurs) the mythic dimensions of James and Elizabeth as rulers, and the age-old skepticism, even hatred, of women in power. The contrast between the characters' own "voices" as they occur in the novel and the legends about them is one of Garrett's most effective ways of creating a multi-dimensional view of the period. While the ostensible plot comes to a stop, we are gaining much insight into the emotional center of the Scots culture, and into the novel's identity as metafiction. (pp. 446-48)

Peopled with narrators, each speaking an appropriately Elizabethan language, *The Succession* parades Garrett's versatility as well as it does the history of Elizabeth and James's barbed relationship. A popular success as well as a novelists' novel, this anatomy of the Renaissance mentality is a book for all seasons. (p. 448)

> Linda W. Wagner, "A Sense of the Past: Three Historical Novels," in Michigan Quarterly Review, *Vol. XXIII, No. 3, Summer, 1984, pp. 446-51.*

BOOK WORLD—THE WASHINGTON POST

The versatile George Garrett is equally adept at writing poems, novels, short stories, biography and plays. . . . [*The Collected Poems of George Garrett*] displays his remarkable gift for words to advantage. Moving from World War II to the present, from Rome to Cheyenne, from darkness to light, from early to late love, the poems display a strong and authentic American voice not always visible in Garrett's marvelous historical novels of Tudor England, *The Death of the Fox* and *The Succession*. They are always a pleasure to read. . . .

> *A review of "The Collected Poems of George Garrett," in Book World—The Washington Post, August 5, 1984, p. 12.*

JONATHAN HOLDEN

[*The Collected Poems of George Garrett*] is not, like most such summations, simply the reprinting of earlier collections arranged chronologically. Rather, it is organized thematically, in three large sections; and within each of these sections the cunningly orchestrated thematic and tonal clusterings of related poems is beautiful. This book is made to be browsed over in much the same way that good oil paintings—paintings scaled not for the museum but for a domestic area—are made to be lived with: to be observed, often peripherally, to be returned to moodily at moments when the daily hubbub recedes and the painting, like a family face, beckons us over and we discover richness which, even though the painting has been part of the living-room landscape for years, we had never noticed before.

If I were to characterize Garrett's voice, I would say that in its decorum it's classically southern, with a tinge of romance, of courtliness undercut by a learned, tough-minded, metaphysical wit reminiscent of Ransom and, further back, the English metaphysicals. Add to this voice a wild strain—the incantatory, obsessive, ecstatic echoes of a Roethke—and we have something like Garrett's poetic voice, a voice which, though rich with echoes, is singular and unmistakable. (p. 161)

> *Jonathan Holden, "In the Field," in Western Humanities Review, Vol. XXXIX, No. 2, Summer, 1985, pp. 155-64.*

JOSEPHINE JACOBSEN

The dangers for a short-story writer inherent in being also a poet and novelist are very real, and one of the major victories of this splendid collection [*An Evening Performance: New and Selected Short Stories*] is that those dangers have been avoided; there is no "poetic prose"—although there is plenty of poetry in the stories—as there are none of the lulls and detours which the novel can afford.

Of his stories, Garrett says, "I stand by them one and all with a full awareness that many of them are less than they might be, and none, not one, is as good as it ought to be. . . . Meantime, this is what I have and who I am."

What he has and who he is is a gift for all of us. These are stories never taped down and finished off with a stitch. They are open-ended: these people lived before the story began, and most of them will continue their complex and often desperate lives after its final word. One of Garrett's special triumphs is that, while he opts for the traditional action of moving human beings from here to there, showing their changes in the process, he also forces the reader to imagine something beyond the printed conclusion. Certainly that is a characteristic of the finest kind of short story.

Army life looms large in the book and is responsible for a number of Garrett's funniest (he is very, very funny when he chooses), most vivid and most appalling stories. One of the themes of the book—perhaps its central theme—is the grimness of self-discovery, its unforeseeable, irrevocable quality. Just as pride, loyalty, courage, and that battered word, compassion, are seen as the touchstones of what is most valuable and essential in human nature, so cruelty, treachery and brutality are seen as the interior enemy—the unrecognized but ever-present possibility that any human may inflict or suffer shame. Here cruelty in a variety of forms is seen to be contagious as any plague; applied to the helpless, it can kindle its replica in the most unlikely spot.

In these stories, there is always a double level: the one on which we like to, and tend to believe we do, live, and the one below it, secret until brought suddenly into consciousness. "I was sick of walking about the fine avenues and boulevards of this world where you walk with your head up, strut if you want to like a god, and meanwhile all the time there's an invisible world breeding and thriving. In back rooms, in hidden corners, behind blank smiles." This, from a series of four short pieces grouped under the title **"What's the Purpose of the Bayonet?"**

Garrett is fascinated by the fringe figures who have in their oddity or loneliness something of the mythical: the circus-woman, grifter, lion-tamer, clown, prisoner, hobo, or, as we unctuously express it, "the physically disadvantaged." . . .

Though the writing is perfectly straightforward, every story carries with it what Garrett refers to as "the old sad weight of complexity." A nurse who witnesses the onslaught of a violent crime and refuses to become involved, loses her capacity for sympathy, first with herself and then with her patients. Full of contempt for them, she addresses herself furiously to becoming a popular and valued nurse. "She felt a sense of exhilaration . . . she saw herself wielding a knife she had not owned before."

It would be all wrong to give the impression that the overall impact of the book is grimness. On the contrary, humor is not only everywhere present, but a number of the stories, including some of the most sobering, are hilarious. A number are concerned also with the nature of justice and its virtual impossibility as humanly applied. In the section headed **"In The Briar Patch,"** the epigram from Isaiah reads in part: "We look for judgment but there is none. . . . But if the achievement of justice is dubious, the search remains vital. It is when the spirit of resistance to cruelty, to smugness, to injustice dies that all is over; resistance is all."

"That's how real resistance goes on," Garrett writes, "and its strength is directly proportionate to the number of people who can let themselves be taken to pieces, piece by piece, without quitting too quickly. It is an ugly business and there are few if any wreaths for them."

Wisely, the book closes with a long story, **"Noise of Strangers,"** which it is no exaggeration to refer to as a contemporary classic. To describe it would be to injure it, but it deals, brilliantly, with the possibility of justice, and its chances. The story moves easily, rich in detail, superb in characterization, to a conclusion that the reader is not likely to forget. In it Garrett's strengths are at their height: atmosphere, characterization, dialogue, scope. Read three or four times, it increases its force. It is very sad, and very funny, and has the kind of gritty pathos which makes it a small masterpiece. Alone, it would be, as we say, worth the price of admission.

Josephine Jacobsen, "Stories from a Lifetime," in Book World—The Washington Post, *September 15, 1985, p. 5.*

GREG JOHNSON

The stories collected [in *An Evening Performance*] describe the conflicts of adolescence, romantic and domestic turmoil, life in small Southern towns, academic life and wartime experiences, and they range in manner from the naturalistic to the near-farcical. Never less than workmanlike, solidly traditional in form, Mr. Garrett's stories frequently sound the theme of human cruelty. "Human beings are the foulest things in all creation," says a character in **"Wounded Soldier,"** while the boy-narrator of **"The Last of the Spanish Blood"** is made to confront his own potential for evil and violence. **"What's the Purpose of the Bayonet?,"** a powerful story of wartime, ends by indicting "the whole inhuman race." This abiding misanthropy does, however, allow for the saving grace of humor. **"Bread From Stones,"** an amusing tale of a feckless gigolo, also forms a tiny critique of the American dream. Perhaps the best story in the volume, **"Texarkana Was a Crazy Town,"** tells of a likable former soldier who finds "real life" much more fearsome an wondrous than anything he had encountered in the military. With few exceptions, the stories seem defiantly "unfashionable" in style. In our age of pared-down realism, Mr. Garrett's flaws as a writer—a fondness for elaborate similes, an occasional straining after poetic effects and a general prolixity—are particularly noticeable. Especially in the earlier pieces, the reader often must cut through a wilderness of verbiage to get to the heart of the story. As a whole, however, this volume displays a fitful but genuine power and shows Mr. Garrett as a master of this distinctive form.

Greg Johnson, in a review of "An Evening Performance," in The New York Times Book Review, *October 6, 1985, p. 28.*

MADISON BELL

On one of its several faces, *Poison Pen* purports to be a literary biography/bibliography of [John] Towne (an eminently unworthy subject for any such project) produced by Lee Holmes, a fifth-rate academic who has to fulfill a book contract he'd much prefer to default on. So there are many layers of supposed authorship, from parodic publishing correspondence relating to Holmes's compilation of Towne's papers to the work of the prolix characters invented by Towne himself in his numerous unfinished novels. All these fragments are pieced together into a cross-section of ersatz literary history worthy of Nabokov, with the further complication that the whole scheme is deliberately undercut by George Garrett, who has interleaved the document with authorial intrusions, labeled as such.

John Towne emerges from this patchwork portraiture as an exceptionally sleazy picaro. He is an academic charlatan of the lowest order, designer of courses like "A Phenomenon of Recent Culture: 'Camp'" and "Cowboys an Indians: Growth and Development of an Indigenous Form." His scholarly career chiefly consists of filing libelous memos and artlessly seducing faculty and students alike. He's an unsuccessful novelist, author of *Live Now and Pay Later, Goldwyn Boy,* and two incomplete manuscripts whose scraps form most of the text of *Poison Pen: The Realms of Gold* and *Life With Kim Novak Is Hell* (the latter composed without revision under the influence of 10 successive doses of the amphetamine Desbutal). His vita further includes stints as a screenwriter (with credits such as

Mondo Teeny Boppo); as Doctor Wisdom, advice columnist for a porno magazine; and as a black evangelist, the Reverend Radio P. King.

As a character, Towne is pure parody; as a correspondent, he is something else again. His finest moments come in the letters he writes, beginning as Doctor Wisdom and proceeding through a variety of other fictive personalities. Just before deserting his desk at the porno mag, Towne indulges his worst nature by answering his last batch of mail in an unusually candid way, e.g., "Dear Mrs. Longsuffering . . . You imagine yourself being stripped and beaten and 'lewdly treated' by Nazi Stormtroopers, because in your heart you think that's what you deserve. And you are so right!" A taste of this sort of thing proves addictive; Towne splits his personality into a few dozen alter egos who write letters to a wide variety of public figures. . . .

Slapstick in their inception, the letters to politicians veer toward a truth of our times: American political life has become a traffic in illusions. That's a commonplace, but its consequences are somehow ignored. . . .

Towne sees politicians as indistinguishable from other celebrities who participate in the culture of the image. Some of his most acid comments are addressed to starlets—for instance, a letter ostensibly by Idabell Brunk, who's recently had a mastectomy, and has just found her husband and son quarreling over possession of a *Playboy* spread of Ursula Andress. Idabell takes Ms. Andress on a tour of the vicissitudes of aging, summed up by the remark that "the only changes you will ever notice will be changes for the worse." Further underscoring the absurdity of our cult of the body is a letter to Hugh Hefner from a spastic, who must throw all his weight at the keyboard to type a single character, and who is having some understandable difficulties practicing "the Playboy Philosophy."

Most Americans, while not physically handicapped, are not particularly celebrated either. . . .

The many personae Towne uses for his letters seem to agree on one thing: celebrities are not robbed of their souls; they sell them, and so they deserve whatever happens to them—up to a point, that is. As Garrett himself observes (in a personal and private concluding letter addressed to Christie Brinkley), Americans have a fine old tradition of killing their political leaders, but it's comparatively recently that we've begun to kill our celebrities too.

> What has happened, Christie, in my lifetime is that Politicians and Celebrities have become at last one and the same thing. From which, it could be argued, we now have the right not to take any Politicians, living or dead, seriously. And, by the same token, we can now water the roots of the Trees of Liberty with the blood of Celebrities.

The conclusion of *Poison Pen* comes a long way from the comic antics of John Towne; that last notion isn't terrifically funny any more, but as Garrett points out, there's "a high level of crazy hostility out there," and no wonder. If politicians and celebrities sell themselves as participants in an infinite number of fantasy lives, what happens when the divided image fails to conform to the dream? Disillusionment may well make assassination seem like a modest and reasonable proposal, as it apparently has in a number of prominent cases. It is almost enough to make one think that our public life ought to be less involved with imagery and more involved with truth, but Towne, in his parting shot, has covered this alternative too:

> If, for some utterly whimsical and unanticipated reason, *honesty* were to become a factor in American Life, it is obvious that the immediate result would be chaos and anarchy. The People, instantly deprived of their leaders in every known field of endeavor, would be a swirling mass of bleating helpless sheep. And there would be no wolves left to profit from this condition.

With his two rich and extraordinary Elizabethan novels, *Death of the Fox* and *The Succession*, Garrett established himself as a formal innovator of considerable importance; *Poison Pen*, seemingly ripped from the underbelly of his long and various career, is among other things a parody of experimental forms. In both the historical books, as in *Poison Pen*, the connection of political machination to skilled manipulation of the image is clearly delineated, but the historical novels also manage to pierce that screen of illusions and arrive at a durable sense of truth. The skewed world of *Poison Pen* can be balanced with the more agreeable vision of Garrett's other work, like a counterweight, in the form of a hanged man, screaming and wriggling all the way.

Madison Bell, "Mail Chauvinism," in The Village Voice, *Vol. XXXI, No. 30, July 29, 1986, p. 42.*

HARVEY PEKAR

[In *Poison Pen*, George Garrett] seems to be trying to make up for lost time, as if he'd been suppressing some things for 30 years and wanted to let them out. This is his satirical hoot at contemporary America. . . .

Mr. Garrett quickly establishes that he is going to write informally, using vernacular and profanity, that he's going to be irreverent and that he wants to present himself as lecherous. His book, he tells us, is going to be composed mainly of a series of poison pen letters, signed with various phony names but actually written by a fictitious man, John Towne, a character in Mr. Garrett's unfinished novel, *Life With Kim Novak Is Hell*. Towne seems to be the author's alter ego, although Mr. Garrett winkingly assures us that he considers the adulterous pornographer and failed academic Towne a low-life crank, and warns that their opinions should not be confused. Some of Towne's letters are contained in the manuscript of a novel *he'd* been working on, called *The Realms of Gold*, about a man named R. C. Alger, who himself has a book in progress, *America the* Beautiful?: *From Pioneers to Pansies*," and also writes poison pen letters. Thus Mr. Garrett creates characters as did Andrei Bely in *Petersburg* and Flann O'Brien in *At Swim-Two-Birds*.

Many of the letters in *Poison Pen* were supposedly written in the 1960's and early 70's. In them Mr. Garrett tries mightily to be funny. Sometimes he succeeds, sometimes he doesn't; even when he does, the humor is often trivial and coy.

Another reason for the failure of certain Garrett letters is that he views technical facility as an end in itself, getting so involved in exhibitionistic writing that some of his characters express themselves inappropriately. A man described as a lower-class rural Southern black criminal writes things like "*soupçon* of real hope," "an almost Pavlovian reflex" and "Faulknerian heart of darkness."

There is among the early letters one really funny one, written to a real-life editor who, according to *Poison Pen,* suckered Mr. Garrett into sending some of his work and then used the idea, without the author's knowledge, as the basis of his own novel. Here Mr. Garrett, who signs this letter himself, abandons artificiality and writes with true malice.

Also excellent are some 1980's dirty-old-man letters to Brooke Shields, Cristina Ferrare and Cheryl Tiegs. These are more conversational, less studied than the early ones. However, Mr. Garrett's last letter, to his supposed heartthrob Christie Brinkley, is pathetic. He carps about The Media, liberalism, the phoniness of Modern Life, and the Literary Establishment—that is, critics who ignore him or don't praise him enough. Does he think he's a genius living in an attic? He is a well-respected writer with a prestigious academic position—he's Henry Hoyns Professor of Creative Writing at the University of Virginia. Self-pity is a wonderful thing; I don't know where I'd be without it, but there are limits.

Mr. Garrett also makes slighting cracks about avant-garde writers to whom, ironically, he may owe something. They employed the absurdism, references to pop culture, irreverence, scatology and loose construction found in *Poison Pen* long before he did.

However, he's added to his repertoire of techniques with this work, and some of the writing in it is admirable. I hope it's a beginning, not an anomaly, for him. I recommend it especially to Christie Brinkley and members of her immediate family.

Harvey Pekar, "From the Desk of a Dirty Old Man,"
in The New York Times Book Review, *October 5,*
1986, p. 25.

Nadine Gordimer

1923-

South African novelist, short story writer, critic, and editor.

Gordimer has earned international acclaim as a writer who explores the effects of South Africa's apartheid system on both ruling whites and oppressed blacks. Although the political conditions in her country are essential to the themes of her work, Gordimer focuses primarily upon the complex human tensions that are generated by apartheid. Lauded for her authentic portrayals of black African culture, Gordimer is also praised for using precise detail to evoke both the physical landscape of South Africa and the human predicaments of a racially polarized society. While some critics claim that Gordimer's detached narrative voice lacks emotional immediacy, many regard her fiction as compelling and powerful.

Gordimer's early work focuses upon the intrusion of external reality into the comfortable existence of South Africa's middle-class white society. Her first novel, *The Lying Days* (1953), is a largely autobiographical portrait of a sheltered Afrikaner woman who gains political consciousness through her affair with a social worker. This book generated positive reviews, particularly for Gordimer's vivid evocation of place. *A World of Strangers* (1958), her second novel, is set in Johannesburg and relates a British writer's attempts to unite his white intellectual companions with several black Africans whom he has recently befriended. This work contrasts the superficial lifestyles of the white characters with the warmth and honesty of the black community. Most critics deemed *A World of Strangers* less successful than *The Lying Days,* claiming that Gordimer relied on didacticism to advance her thematic intentions. *A World of Strangers* was banned by the South African government. Gordimer explained in an interview: "[There] was still at that time this fruitless attempt to discourage the idea that there could be absolutely equal human contact. . . . There was a close friendship in the novel that showed up the cruelty and idiocy of apartheid and the dangers of daily life for blacks."

Many critics have noted a connection between Gordimer's thematic direction during the late 1960s and the deterioration of race relations and escalation of violence in her country. Unlike her first two novels, which ended with hope for South Africa's future, Gordimer's subsequent fiction displays a growing sense of pessimism. The novella *The Late Bourgeois World* (1966), for instance, which was banned in her homeland for twelve years, reconstructs events leading to the suicide of a white political activist who had betrayed his compatriots in exchange for clemency. This work evidences Gordimer's belief that whites as well as blacks are victims of apartheid. *A Guest of Honour* (1970), for which Gordimer received the James Tait Black Memorial Prize, is regarded by many critics as her finest work. This novel tells of Colonel James Bray's ill-fated return to a newly-independent African nation from which he had been exiled for supporting black revolutionaries. Bray's discovery of corruption, greed, and self-interest among the country's leaders causes him to disavow his idealistic political beliefs and condemn the new government, resulting in his assassination. *The Conservationist* (1974), which was awarded the Booker McConnell Prize for fiction, focuses upon a wealthy white landowner's struggle to come to terms with his guilt and

© Jerry Bauer

sense of displacement as he grows increasingly threatened by the presence of poor black squatters on his estate. *Burger's Daughter* (1979), which was banned briefly, details the efforts of Rosa Burger, the daughter of a martyred leader of the South African Communist party, to pursue an apolitical existence. *July's People* (1981) confirms Gordimer's cynical social stance. Set in the aftermath of a future revolution, this work centers upon a liberal white family forced to depend on the providence of a black man who was previously their servant. Through this reversal of roles, the novel reveals deep-rooted feelings of prejudice and racial supremacy in even the most open-minded individuals. Anne Tyler commented: "*July's People* demonstrates with breathtaking clarity the tensions and complex interdependencies between whites and blacks in South Africa. It is so flawlessly written that every one of its events seems chillingly, ominously possible."

Several critics contend that *A Sport of Nature* (1987) best represents Gordimer's belief that South Africa's existing social order will eventually be destroyed. This novel's title refers to a botanical phenomenon in which a plant suddenly deviates from its parent stock. The mutated offspring is personified by the book's heroine, Hillela, who is a proponent of political and social change in South Africa. Raised in middle-class surroundings, Hillela leaves her home at age seventeen and travels throughout Africa, the United States, and Europe, often as the mistress of an influential man. Hillela's liberal world view is formed through her romantic liaisons, and by the novel's end, she has played a significant role in South Africa's revolution. *A Sport of Nature* generated mixed reviews. Paul Gray commented that feminists "may not be happy with a character whose identity and importance depend so thoroughly on the men she sleeps with." Diane Johnson, however, contended: "This final fantasy of a political eventuality so desirable and unlikely must doubtless be reassuring to the South African reader. For others, it calls into question the generic assumptions of the book, the rules by which we must try to understand it."

In addition to the reputation she has garnered for her novels, Gordimer is considered an accomplished short fiction writer. Her stories often employ thematic concerns similar to those of her novels, portraying individuals who struggle to avoid, confront, or change the conditions under which they live. Gordimer's early short stories were originally published in such American periodicals as the *Atlantic*, the *New Yorker*, and the *Yale Review* and were subsequently collected in her first major volume, *The Soft Voice of the Serpent and Other Stories* (1952). Several of the works included in *Six Feet of the Country* (1956) and *Friday's Footprint and Other Stories* (1960) display the influence of such nineteenth-century French authors as Guy de Maupassant, Honoré de Balzac, and Gustave Flaubert in their objectivity, realism, and satiric edge. *Not for Publication and Other Stories* (1965) and *Livingstone's Companions* (1971) depict ordinary people defying apartheid in their daily lives. The pieces in *A Soldier's Embrace* (1980) offer an ironic historical overview of South African society. In *Something Out There* (1981), Gordimer examines the temperament of individuals who unwittingly support the mechanisms of racial separatism. In her review of *A Soldier's Embrace*, Edith Milton summarized Gordimer's literary achievements: "Gordimer is no reformer; she looks beyond political and social outrage to the sad contradiction of the human spirit, which delivers to those in power an even worse sentence of pain than they themselves can pass upon their victims."

(See also *CLC*, Vols. 3, 5, 7, 10, 18, 33; *Contemporary Authors*, Vols. 5-8, rev. ed.; and *Contemporary Authors New Revision Series*, Vol. 3.)

PAUL GRAY

[How can the sweeping, unresolved saga that is South Africa's recent history] be captured in fiction? In her eight previous novels, Nadine Gordimer has offered some excellent answers. She has fused her native land's agonies and contradictions into intense portraits of ordinary lives: that of a reactionary but troubled landowner (*The Conservationist*), for example, or of a white housewife caught up in the melee of a successful black revolution (*July's People*). *A Sport of Nature* is no less detailed and gripping than its predecessors, but its reach is more ambitious; a panoramic view not only of what has already taken place in South Africa but of what the future, inevitably or at least imaginatively, will become.

Gordimer's heroine appears, at first glimpse, an unlikely focus for any story with epic intentions. Hillela Capran comes onstage as an aimless teenager with a penchant for trouble. Effectively orphaned by the breakup of her parents' marriage,

the girl proves to be too much for either of her mother's sisters, Aunt Olga and Aunt Pauline, to control. Nothing seems to register with the child, not Olga's antique collecting and social climbing, not Pauline's furious campaigning for black civil rights and social progress. When Pauline discovers Hillela in bed with her son Sasha, the welcome at the last possible adoptive home wears out. Before long, Hillela quits school and is on her own, drifting somewhere in Johannesburg. Eventually she takes up with an antigovernment journalist and then, during the summer of 1963, flees the country with him after the cottage they share has been ransacked by police. She is some months shy of her 20th birthday.

The reporter ditches Hillela in Dar es Salaam, which has become an important port of call for exiled members of the African National Congress. She has neither ambition nor money, no currency at all except her formidable good looks. The expatriate conspirators, white and black, who gather each afternoon to plot and gossip on Tamarisk Beach are distracted by the dark-eyed, full-breasted young woman in the skimpy yellow bathing suit. She is wooed by men who want not only to possess but to politicize her as well. After hearing Hillela admit that she does not understand anything that she has not directly experienced, a high-ranking ANC offical says, "Someone needs to take you in hand, my girl. You are not a fully conscious being." . . .

Gordimer takes risks with Hillela. Feminists may not be happy with a character whose identity and importance depend so thoroughly on the men she sleeps with. Early in the novel the author starts dropping hints that Hillela will someday be famous, and that of course is what happens. The former beach girl becomes the wife and then the widow of an important black revolutionary, assassinated by South African security forces. She later marries another black, who becomes President of his (unnamed) liberated country. She hobnobs with Indira Gandhi and Bishop Desmond Tutu. She and her husband are honored guests at the ceremony marking the accession of black rule in South Africa.

But Hillela is more than just another woman who has turned sexual attractiveness to her own advantages. Gordimer writes that her heroine "has never been one to make mistakes when following her instincts," and this judgment is confirmed throughout the novel. Hillela's behavior, even at its loosest and least conventional, does not seem calculated but rather a natural response to the proper, perhaps even the moral, demands of shifting situations. Looking back on his time with her, a friend from the early days says, "She was innocent." Later, marked by personal tragedy and the rough-and-tumble life she has led in the "territory of exile," she seems oddly innocent still.

A Sport of Nature will surely provoke controversy. Its denunciations of South African politics are ferocious, its portraits of whites often scathing. The argument implied throughout the book can be caricatured: all South Africa needs is love. But Gordimer is saying much more than that. Her novel is both richly detailed and visionary, a brilliant reflection of a world that exists and an affirmation of faith in one that could be born.

> Paul Gray, *"Life in the Territory of Exile,"* in Time, New York, Vol. 129, No. 14, April 6, 1987, p. 76.

PATRICIA CRAIG

[*A Sport of Nature*] is a forward-looking, not an inward-looking, novel. Hillela is kept at a certain distance from the reader, and indeed disappears altogether from time to time. "Where", we are asked, "was the seventeen-year-old on the Day of the Covenant . . . when bombs exploded in a post office, the Resettlement Board headquarters and the Bantu Affairs Commissioner's offices?" No one can say for sure, not even Hillela herself. When she fades out of the picture, historical events crowd in—Congress of Democrats, Sabotage Act. A device is used (though not consistently) in relating Hillela's story, to gain a quasi-documentary effect: it is as if the biographer of a distinguished woman were building up the framework of her life, relying on the recollections of others, acknowledging gaps and resorting to speculation. "Some people claim to remember that particular young woman with her black baby", we are told; perhaps confusing Hillela with someone quite different. The baby, though; she's part of the story, the daughter of a black South African revolutionary, an ANC man, whom Hillela has married (after a liaison with a diplomat) only to lose to assassins, government agents.

The story goes on: more lovers, in different settings—Eastern Europe, England, America. Here is Hillela as a fund-raiser for the African National Congress, a platform speaker, relief worker dispensing soup to refugees. Repetition is the technique Gordimer adopts to fix a pungent image of Hillela, at successive stages, in the reader's mind. The safety-pin marks her time on the beach; soup powder denotes her "aid and research" activities in stricken parts of Africa. The author doesn't minimize the part played by uncalculating eroticism in Hillela's odyssey (uncalculating, and therefore unimpeachable, on a par with the absence of ill-will in her abandonment of benefactors). In this respect, as in others, she is simply following her nose. Over and above this sexual quality, however, is a more durable ideal of comradeship, symbolized by the handclasp between Hillela and her first husband after he's taken her into his confidence over political matters.

Mutability, you could say, is her dominant trait. Her conduct of her life shows a considerable advance on the decent, limited liberalism of her Aunt Pauline's home. Insufficient egalitarianism is something the author is adept at detecting, and condemning. A recurrent concern of her novels is the way in which personal relations are complicated, or distorted by political realities, of which the most striking is the reality of apartheid. There is also the dilemma confronting those (white) who devote their lives to people who have no time for them (black)—and the need to understand that there is more to this issue than a simple matter of ingratitude. At a crucial moment in *Burger's Daughter*, for example, a black boy who once shared Rosa Burger's enlightened South African home disclaims her and her family and all their efforts on behalf of the black population: "Killed in prison. It's nothing. I know plenty blacks like Burger. It's nothing, it's us, we must be used to it. . .".

Burger's Daughter, which opens with the schoolgirl Rosa outside a prison waiting to visit her mother, and ends with Rosa herself as a political detainee, is in many ways a stronger and more implacable work than *A Sport of Nature* (impressive though the latter is). The difference is one of tone—hopeful, now, instead of disabused. The new book imagines, in its triumphal ending, a black African state in the place of South Africa, with Hillela and her second husband, a revolutionary general and reinstated president, standing for the wished-for integration within it. (It's a sunnier eventuality, too, than the black uprising postulated in *July's People*, with white South Africans not showing at all well in the altered conditions.) Hillela, the "sport of nature"—defined as something that "departs from the parent

stock or type"—with her independence of spirit and her indifference to the past, represents a new departure, an access for social justice.

Patricia Craig, "The Wayward Girl's New Departure," in The Times Literary Supplement, *No. 4385, April 17, 1987, p. 411.*

MERLE RUBIN

[Gordimer's] extraordinary gifts were evident from the start: a precise ear for spoken language that lent great authenticity to her dialogue; a sensitivity to the rhythms and texture of the written word that gave her prose the power of poetry; a keen eye that made her a tireless observer; an even keener sense of social satire based upon her ability to see through appearances to the heart of the matter, and a strong feeling of moral purpose, composed in equal parts of her indignation at the sheer injustice of South Africa's entrenched racial oppression and of her commitment to speak the truth as she saw it.

Yet, as Gordimer's reputation has steadily and deservedly risen, there have been signs of falling off in her most recent work. The possibility that success is "spoiling" her is, frankly, unimaginable. It is possible, however, that success has isolated her—not so much from the realities of political life as from the kind of truly critical response an artist needs to gauge the effect and effectiveness of her work. It is also possible that the weaknesses afflicting her ninth and latest novel, *A Sport of Nature*, as well as some of the stories in her last collection, *Something Out There* (1984), are reflections of her deepening pessimism about the future of her country and a growing disillusionment, not only with liberalism, which she dismissed decades ago, but with all kinds of human endeavor from rationalism to radicalism.

Because Gordimer is a voice worth listening to, it is important, before going on to evaluate her latest novel, before giving vent to one's own reactions, first to take account of what this book has to tell us. Gordimer begins with a definition of the book's title, taken from the Oxford English Dictionary. The Latin term, we are told, is *lusus naturae;* the meaning has to do with change. A sport of nature is a "spontaneous mutation" exhibiting "abnormal variation from the parent stock" and productive of new varieties.

The heroine of this novel is just such a "mutation." She is the product of a "typical" South African Jewish family, given the name "Hillela" in memory of a Zionist grandfather, and brought up in the comfort of white bourgeois surroundings in the years following World War II. Yet, from the outset, she is something of an oddity: Her real mother, Ruthie, ran off with a Portuguese dancer from Mozambique when Hillela was still a baby, leaving Hillela's nominal father free to attach himself to a lower-class restaurant hostess in then-Rhodesia. (p. 2)

Throughout her experience, [Hillela] remains the same: cunning, seductive, adaptable, unreflective. She does not bother to distinguish between a sincere revolutionary and one of Pretoria's spies. She does not feel the suffering of black South Africans until the black man she marries is gunned down in the kitchen before her very eyes. She becomes, nonetheless, an able advocate for revolutionary African causes. . . . Her being white and Jewish is never held against her. Nor does she experience any problems because she is a woman. . . . She triumphs, becomes first lady of an independent African state, and is an honored guest, along with her husband, at the inauguration of the new, black-run state of South Africa.

What are we to make of Hillela's story, even if we are willing to accept its improbabilities? It can hardly be called a celebration of revolutionary opportunism, yet neither is it a scathing, Dostoevskian denunciation of the same. Gordimer's attitude toward Hillela—and the other characters—is detached, distant, sometimes bitterly ironic. Yet, she also takes a grim satisfaction in the story she has chosen to tell—the satisfaction of someone proud to have swallowed a harsh, unpalatable potion in the belief that it is the strong medicine required. Gordimer would have us confront a bitter reality. The justice of a case does not ensure its triumph. But within this cloud, a silver lining—of sorts. Although morality may be of no avail, the mysterious, blind forces of nature and mutability will have their way, and a "liberated" South Africa is part of this wave of the future. Thus, change itself is the hero of this novel. Yet it is a change based not on choice but on chance. As a "spontaneous mutation," Hillela may pass for a "free spirit," but she does not exercise the kind of freedom associated with the ability to make moral choices. . . .

Not only Hillela, but all the characters are portrayed from a distance, with a superficiality that may be deliberate but that certainly makes them less than involving. They seem to have no interiors. Perhaps they are meant to be viewed as "types," but, if so, they lack the mythic dimensions of archetypes: Instead of seeming larger than life, they seem smaller: not types, but putative specimens, glimpsed from afar with little sense of their reality. Hillela disappears, turns up in news items, reports, gossip, photographs taken in the company of the dubious political "celebrities" of our time. What she feels or thinks, we do not know. We constantly hear the refrain "Trust her," meaning not that she is implicitly trustworthy but rather that she may be trusted to do all right for herself. . . .

In casting Hillela as unheroic heroine of the struggle for freedom, Gordimer pays homage to the ironies of living in a "media age" where image prevails over substance. But, I think, this is needlessly trendy. From a novelist of Gordimer's stature, readers may well expect more in the way of substance and critical perspective.

Sadly, this novel is as weak in purely literary terms as it is lacking in positive political wisdom. Not only is the characterization thin, but the prose is convoluted, dense—even rough at times, lacking Gordimer's trademark diamond-hard brilliance and sculpted clarity. Perhaps, after all, it is South Africa that has finally done her in this time. In trying to confront the harsh reality of the present and to outrun in fiction the dangers that lie ahead for her country and its benighted peoples, she has simply fallen victim to the hugeness of her task. (p. 9)

> Merle Rubin, in a review of "A Sport of Nature," in Los Angeles Times Book Review, *April 19, 1987, pp. 2, 9.*

MAUREEN HOWARD

A Sport of Nature opens with a girl called Kim discarding her name. On a train coming home from Rhodesia to South Africa, "she threw Kim up to the rack with her school panama and took on Hillela." This is the first stir within the chrysalis of the seemingly ordinary child who will become an African legend, a mythic figure of Nadine Gordimer's Promised Land. The names are carefully chosen. Kim is Ms. Gordimer's witty

reference to Kipling's famous tale of colonial life. Her family has also called the child Hillela, a name she has never used, a name meant to honor her great grandfather, a Zionist, who came steerage to Cape Town fleeing the Cossacks in a forgotten pogrom, but the girl Hillela, with no mind for history, simply wants to be different. The change of name is a beautifully observed adolescent gesture, but it is also the first move in a powerful novel of awakening, emergence, and, in so far as fiction can make it possible, a call for a new order. (p. 1)

Hillela, as we might presume from the title, comes into the world "a departure from the parent stock or type . . . a spontaneous mutation." . . . [She] is a girl without guilt or remorse, without the old responses that should tie her to her culture, for in some way her family cannot perceive, it is not Hillela's culture. Only once in this novel does she say "My fault," confessing that she made love with Sasha, her first cousin, but then—"'When they found us,' She gasped, laughing. 'It was like the three bears. Who's been sleeping in *my* bed?'" Turned out of the house by [her aunt] Pauline . . . , Hillela takes to the world, a curious and lively place, with healthy self-interest.

It is now, as she disappears from the small domestic novel, that we are drawn into a larger game by a narrative voice, wise, often amused, but driven to record history, public and private. We are to have a guide: the journey is long and Hillela is an original—we cannot recognize her type. She falls in with one man or another, one set or another, passing from the psychiatrist who finds her engaging the minute he sets eyes on her selling *The World Atlas and Encyclopedia of Modern Knowledge;* passing on to a debonair ambassador, to a tricky journalist with an Irish passport. We see her as a creature of circumstance, but Hillela is never a victim, never used. "A natural mistress," says the ambassador's wife. "She's a-moral," says Pauline, covering herself with a fitting liberal disclaimer, "I mean in the sense of the morality of this country." . . .

Ms. Gordimer has always written well about sex—the idle attraction to young girls of Mehring in *The Conservationist;* the disaffection of husband and wife in *July's People;* Rosa Burger's love affair that in part sets her free in *Burger's Daughter.* Here the sexual dimension is thematically central. Hillela is sexually gifted, endowed, and because she can detect the moral constriction and the flimflam standard of the society she's grown up in, she trusts the sexual encounter as her proving ground. "Use what you have to love with, you know? You don't have to try to reach him, help him, teach him—you can't lie, or spy or kill, so what could ever be wrong about it? . . . Those others on the beach; they have no home . . . because they are brave and believe in the other kinds of love, justice, fellow man—and inside each other, making love is the only place we can make, here, that's not just a place to stay."

It is an attitude both advanced and limited, generous and ruthless. Something is missing in this beautiful, unclassified specimen and that is what the rest of *A Sport of Nature* is about. How, in fact, this imperfect woman gains her heroic stature, confronting the world with this daring but merely personal view. Through the exiles on the beach Hillela begins to comprehend, almost as an adaptation, not only the South Africa she rejects but the possibilities of other worlds. Incest, betrayal, even ecstasy have not set their mark on her. "Nothing really terrible's happened to me," Hillela says, and close upon that insight comes her attention to political matters. Here Ms. Gordimer unites sexual energy and political energy in the responsive but undeveloped Hillela. Reading *A Sport of Nature,* what comes to mind is George Eliot's view of the novel as "a set of experiments in life." (p. 20)

Though there are excesses of pure accumulation, a triple-decker effect that may encourage some readers to go at *A Sport of Nature* with blockbuster inattention, Ms. Gordimer is technically nimble, her grand design intricate and satisfying. We are always kept informed about that family back in South Africa, of Sasha, most particularly, first cousin, first love, who takes a more traditional route to the heroic, dedicated to the overthrow of the State. Given all the political import, let it be known that Nadine Gordimer has not lost her satiric powers: the chapter titles are flip—"Time Out for a Love Story," "The Diplomatic Bag" and "Trust Her!" Olga and Pauline with their staked-out positions are comic relief. The Afrikaner politicians in their "three piece American suits and Italian silk ties" are sharply seen, for in the end, Hillela's story is not meant to read as tragedy. (pp. 20, 22)

The last 200 pages of *A Sport of Nature* are a risk, a fine writer's challenge to the romantic conclusion. We have had the sorrowful burial and the prefiguration of that drama. . . . After the great sacrifice, we are left with Hillela Kgomani. Will her life become epilogue? We have not been led to expect that, though she is human now—subject to heartbreak like the rest of us. She accepts the political lineage of her husband's name, lecturing (in America), doing good works, photographed with Yasir Arafat, but the long denial of the roles she has been assigned—girl of good family, mistress, revolutionary groupie—has not prepared her to become a keeper of the flame. In a last flutter against the weblike shreds of the past, the new mutant embraces her destiny. Of Hillela, who accumulates commentary, it is said, she "moves on." But now her moves are by choice, with direction: determined by neither circumstance nor sex.

We leave behind the safe berth: really, how could Hillela marry well, live in a brownstone? Plotting in this novel becomes epic. We've known all along that our heroine has somehow attained, beyond her public role, a symbolic stature. *A Sport of Nature* concludes in clearly stated counterpoint. Hillela marries yet another black leader—pragmatic, powerful, humane. The happy ending is dreamlike but in no way is this escapist literature: fantasy runs, note against note, with Sasha's imprisonment and trial in South Africa and the bloody fall of that regime, imagined here and imaginable in all its horror to the reader.

But the final frame is operatic—the clock has been set forward, apartheid abolished, a general amnesty declared in South Africa. We are to witness along with Hillela the declaration of the new order, representatives of East and West, the media of course, in attendance. Kim/Hillela, now called Chiemeka—as the president's wife renamed yet again, stately in her native dress, has come home. But in Puccini, in Verdi, such triumphal scenes occur before the tragic fall from grandeur and grace. We can surmise that Ms. Gordimer's spectacular ending, her dream Africa, her play into the future is designed to make the present bearable. What we actually witness is the great moment in which the novelist settles all scores and differences, assembles, at her will, the disparate nations of a free world. . . . We close the book, rise from our orchestra seats knowing the painful story of South Africa is still with us and more's to come.

For many years Nadine Gordimer has been troubled by the difficulty of writing about her country, her own place—troubled by the difficulty and necessity: history, politics, and "back there," as she calls the old frame of moral judgments and

solutions—all large matters for the frail structure of modern fiction, usually so self-conscious and often so dependent on the little stories of our lives. "The ideal achievement, from the point of view of literature," she has written, "occurs when a man's experience and his talent are equal to each other." In *A Sport of Nature* she has drawn up the perfect equation: it is only an act of the imagination but a grand one. She has built the ark. (p. 22)

Maureen Howard, "The Rise of Hillela, The Fall of South Africa," in The New York Times Book Review, *May 3, 1987, pp. 1, 20, 22.*

JENNIFER KRAUSS

There has been a rather narcissistic focus in recent years, by both the white South African literati (Nadine Gordimer included) and the foreign press, on the importance of white involvement in the emancipation of the oppressed black majority in South Africa. Such paternalistic posturing has glossed over the complexities of the internal reality there and downplayed the role of black South Africans in the achievement of their own independence. Now, as if in response to her own previous work and to the work of others, Gordimer has written [*A Sport of Nature*], a mock history of South Africa's liberation from apartheid—which here happens virtually overnight, on page 337—as if it were the story of the rise of one self-absorbed white woman to greatness.

In preceding novels Gordimer has charted the evolution of the white liberal consciousness in South Africa to its hypothetical end. Her heroines have either made peace with their limited ability to effect change (Rosa Burger in *Burger's Daughter* . . .) or they've run away (Maureen Smales in *July's People*). Gordimer's new novel begins where these works leave off. "It will take another kind of being to stay on, here," one character declares somberly, "a new white person. Not us. The chance is a wild chance—like falling in love." *A Sport of Nature* glorifies this "new white person," a person for whom *everything* is "a wild chance," a person whose political purpose is dependent on whom she happens to be sleeping with at the time, a person who becomes very famous by doing very little.

This is a book about the fiction that surrounds fame, or, more accurately, the often undeserved fame of fiction; it is about political naïveté, about looking at the world through rose-colored glasses. And it is Gordimer's most deeply cynical novel.

But Gordimer's tone is so deceptively manipulative that even her publicist has been taken in. Appropriately, and ironically, the book's own dust jacket is inflationary, boasting that *A Sport of Nature* is Gordimer's "largest, most reverberant work." In some sense this is true: it transcends the bounds of her past novels not only in place (its heroine's travels span the globe) but in time (it begins in the South Africa of the 1960s and ends in an imaginary future free from racial strife). Attempting to snag the would-be reader with such teasers as, "Is she an innocent, grasping for survival, or a seeker after power . . .?" publicity for the book moves her work, as Gordimer moves her heroine, into the realm of popular, blockbuster, Book-of-the-Month Club fiction.

In a way, *A Sport of Nature* fits quite comfortably into this milieu. It lacks the lyricism and emotional concentration of much of Gordimer's earlier work. But Gordimer may well have the last laugh: for the very preposterousness of her heroine's celebrity is the point here. The narrative mode is pseudo-documentary: Gordimer's historian/narrator tries to piece together—from letters, recorded interviews, newspaper clippings, photographs, reference book citations, and hearsay—the motivating factors of a life that is essentially motiveless. (pp. 33-4)

Rosa Burger, who makes a brief cameo appearance toward the beginning of *A Sport of Nature,* haunts this novel as the political and historical consciousness, however ineffectual, that Hillela doesn't have. Rosa will forever be "Burger's daughter," defined by her father's unfulfilled hopes for South African unity. Hillela takes her parents where she finds them. She is "like a daughter" to relatives and lovers and passing ideologies alike. Amoral, irreligious, apolitical, Hillela is without convictions or ambitions. She exists in a vacuum. . . .

Still the narrator portrays Hillela as deserving of idolatry, mentioning her in the same breath with Christ and Shakespeare. The weightiness of the tone is broadly comedic: "Christa Zeederburg, urged to reminisce at the end of her life, never forgot the safety pin [that held together the waistband of Hillela's jeans]." And after almost 200 pages of commentary on Hillela's individuality and monumental importance, Gordimer's narrator lets slip: "It is easy . . . to confuse Hillela with someone else."

Hillela begins her "brilliant career" with a series of meaningless odd jobs and sexual exploits, which the narrator feels compelled to inflate (in less than compelling fashion) into a sprawling, picaresque odyssey. When the apartment of the subversive journalist with whom she has been living is ransacked . . . , they both flee South Africa to Tamarisk Beach in East Africa, where he eventually abandons her. It is only through his actions, then, and her single-minded devotion to him, that she becomes a political refugee.

The "moment" toward which the narrator insists Hillela's life is "always moving"—the moment of black majority rule in South Africa—is arrived at in a similarly random way. When, having been spirited away from a curio shop where she worked as a clerk, Hillela is employed as a governess and social secretary in an ambassador's household (becoming the ambassador's mistress in the bargain), she goes wherever the ambassador and his family are posted; and when she collides with and marries Whaila Kgomani, a black South African revolutionary with the ANC, she exhibits the same passivity. . . . (p. 34)

Like the "revolutionary woman" of Sheila Fugard's 1985 novel of the same name, Hillela is, if anything, anti-revolutionary. She is not a "navigator of the world's courses"—this is left to men—but a highly impressionable sexual object. "If things had turned out differently," a friend suggests, "she was the type to have become a terrorist, a hijacker."

But when Whaila, a key figure in the planning of armed infiltration, is assassinated, the narrator seizes on what she (or he) believes to be a turning point in Hillela's life: the realization that Whaila's death "belongs to tragedy, not grief." "A tragedy," someone had once explained to Hillela, "is when a human being is destroyed engaging himself with events greater than personal relationships. . . . A tragic death results from the struggle between good and evil. And it has results that outlast grief. Grief is a rot, it belongs with the dead, but tragedy is a sign that that struggle must go on." Activism 101. Yet despite this impassioned politics, the real struggle for Hillela—which takes her to London, Eastern Europe, and the United States—is still "the struggle in bed."

Eventually she marries Reuel, a black general in the process of launching his second coup to return the unnamed West African country of his birth to civilian rule. As a result, Hillela is "taken" everywhere. . . . (pp. 34-5)

Yet, operating on the theory that information about Hillela's life has been lost or suppressed, the narrator seems to feel that any impression that Hillela has played a subordinate role is erroneous:

> It has never been clear what her position with the African National Congress was, beyond that of Whaila Kgomani's widow, at that period. And the uncertainty of future political alliances between countries makes it always wiser for references other than "she played her role in active support of her husband's determination to restore peace, prosperity, and justice to his country" to be excluded from data available at the General's Ministry of Information and Public Relations.

The truth of the matter is that there is no information to the contrary. Even some of Hillela's own statements about the momentous occasions in her life are apocryphal.

When Reuel finally retakes his country—although the "official story" is one of liberation, of democracy and prosperity—he establishes a one-party state. . . . Hillela, the supposed savior of oppressed peoples, becomes involved in preserving and decorating the imperial palace. The hollowness of this liberation is a mirror of Hillela's own hollowness.

Then suddenly, after a quick summary of what happened to all the supporting players in Hillela's life story during the intervening years, the novel jumps to the proclamation ceremony for "the new African state that used to be South Africa," a ceremony that Reuel (as chairman of the Organization of African Unity) and Hillela attend. As might be expected, the narrator focuses all attention on Hillela—even though she has no connection with this fairy tale transformation of the South African state. . . . This moment toward which Hillela's life has always been moving has significance for her only in terms of her martyred husband, not in terms of those it will emancipate in the present. (p. 35)

Hillela has no guilt, no doubts; she does not feel compelled to address the human mass because South Africa is not her country; nor, ultimately, is this story (in any real sense) her life. She has not developed, she has merely existed, unburdened by the past and hopelessly complacent about the future. She takes at face value—and if the promotional material is any indication, so will many readers—the fiction that while yesterday South Africa was awash in blood, tomorrow all might be magically healed.

Like the encyclopedias that Hillela peddles at one point in her "career," Gordimer's narrative is a "fraudulent offer of encapsulated knowledge," a fictional history that ends in the best of all possible worlds. Political reform in South Africa is a series of quick fixes, Gordimer intimates, and the cycle is bound to continue. Hillela's daughter by Whaila, named after Nelson Mandela's wife and referred to as "the namesake" (although Hillela knows hardly anything about Mandela), becomes a model, and the description of her worldview seems a perfect summing up of the cynicism the new novel both castigates and imitates: "An international model does not hamper her image with national politics; to the rich people who buy the clothes she displays or the luxuries her face and body promote, she is a symbol of Africa, anyway. . . ." Hillela is happy to have merely "reproduced herself." Nevertheless, the white mother and her black daughter become an "icon of liberation and reconciliation between the Third World and the Western World." A far cry (although equally bleak) from *Burger's Daughter,* which ends, as it began, at the prison door, with Rosa in jail like her father. (p. 36)

Jennifer Krauss, "Activism 101," in The New Republic, *Vol. 196, No. 20, May 18, 1987, pp. 33-6.*

DIANE JOHNSON

One comes to Nadine Gordimer's new novel, *A Sport of Nature,* conscious of a certain critical division about it. On the one hand it is called by Maureen Howard in *The New York Times Book Review* "the perfect equation" between talent and experience, a grand act of the imagination [see excerpt above]. On the other hand, to Jennifer Krauss in *The New Republic* it is a "deeply cynical novel" in the realm of "popular, blockbuster, Book-of-the-Month Club fiction" [see excerpt above]. . . . Indeed the tone of the novel is elusive, the narrative method susceptible to either interpretation.

To this reader, it seems to boil down to how much credit Gordimer has built up for the vigor and courage of her anti-apartheid politics over the years, and the beauty and power of much of her other recent writing, for this book seems compounded of mythic and modernist elements too resistant quite to work as a novel. It may be that an American reader, owing to the different rhythms of his history, has certain disadvantages. Since there is no defense on apartheid, it can seem that something obvious is being advanced with great righteousness here. In another Gordimer novel, *Burger's Daughter,* someone says, "Yes, it's strange to live in a country where there are still heroes." What that's like is something hard for an American to remember. The South African world, in its turmoil, in the accelerating pace of its changes, has, perhaps, a greater need for saints' legends and inspirational fairy tales, while the disaffected American can no longer believe in them.

Gone is the spare, meditated manner of *July's People*; here Gordimer returns to certain themes and episodes found in her earliest, seemingly autobiographical, and often somewhat tendentious works, fitting them almost at random into a romantic political newsreel. No doubt there are moments in history when the idea of art for art's sake is offensive; that old debate has ever only arisen in those moments of calm between wars. Liking it or not, Gordimer was born into interesting times, and has reported and judged them. Twenty-five years ago, in *The Late Bourgeois World* and *A Guest of Honour,* Gordimer captured the secret meetings, the clandestine intrigues, the secret dreams of the politically forward-thinking. She has pointed out that the voice of a "politically devout" life is always addressing "the human mass." Her early work was reminiscent of old Marxist novels reset (quotations from Fanon and so on—the sort of novels the heroine in Doris Lessing's *The Golden Notebook* doesn't want to write).

But in her finest work—her superb short stories, for instance—Gordimer's polemics are only implicit, and her ability vividly to present people caught in the moral dilemmas and actual peril of a foundering society is consummate and, we are bound to feel, so correct that what it lacks in charm and humor—there are no jokes in Gordimer, anywhere—is more than made up for by her powerful descriptive language, her passion, an impressive ability to put herself not only in the mind but in the body of anybody, male or female, black or white, and a sort

of supercharged landscape that simultaneously operates as the beautiful natural world and the arid metaphoric country of the blighted South African soul. Even if Gordimer were not a wonderful writer, the setting and subject of her stories are themselves so interesting and exotic that we would be drawn to her work. South African sins are not (we tell ourselves) ours, and the heroism of people under oppression, or caught in forbidden interracial love, is so much more stirring than marital discontent on Central Park West.

In this new book, with the world catching up to, or on to, the events that Gordimer has been explicitly predicting for thirty years, one senses a rush to the dais. Narrative founders under the double burden of prediction and justification, and under the weight of reality, and under the weight of a prophet's hard-earned crown. A friend once remarked, speaking of his admiration for Gordimer's novels, that they were so good he didn't actually bother to read them. One senses, embedded in this apparent paradox, an elusive but eternal literary fact. But what is it? Perhaps it is that readers in some way wish a writer to affirm his humanity by making a mistake, if it is a small one. One felt, say in *July's People,* or *The Conservationist,* with something like the perfect combination of narrative interest, rich, accomplished language, high moral seriousness, round characters, and so on, that there were no mistakes. There is, at least, something urgent and appealing in this riskier, less successful work. (p. 8)

The possibility of satire occurs to the reader. But one is told by South African friends that there are details, keys, allusions to real events and people, known to other South Africans, that are obscure, naturally, to the average American reader, for whom Hillela's romantic story seems more to be a dream sequence than grounded in quotidian political reality. In all, her story has many of the common features of the lives of mythic heroes—uncertainty of parentage, incest (here modified in that she only sleeps with her cousin), orphan or foundling status. Or Hillela is like Cinderella, the despised daughter, who rises to palaces and presidencies through her alliances with a series of princes—though the sexy, charming, energetic, handsome black princes of this narrative, it must be admitted, with their glossy bodies and their wit, do not seem much like the real African dignitaries we meet on the MacNeil/Lehrer show. Or Hillela is the inspiring Woman of those political narratives of the Thirties, the perfect political adjunct and sexual handmaiden. It seems unlikely that Gordimer did not have these antecedents in mind.

As in Gordimer's other work, we often feel a certain malice toward white people, especially those of her own camp—English speakers, bourgeois liberals, radicals, Jewish intellectuals. The Afrikaners are either beyond the pale or, in their benightedness, due a certain sympathy. One always feels her empathy and affection for blacks. As for Hillela, there are often in the works of good writers one or two characters to whom the author seems more tender than the reader can be, and this partiality may bring out in the reader a certain irritation, like that one feels for the favorite but unattractive child of a friend, who never notices its faults. One thinks, say, of certain Salinger characters, or of the potent Irish giant O'Shaugnessy in Norman Mailer's *Advertisements for Myself*—most writers have an idealized self somewhere. Hillela, in fact, seems a lot like Gordimer's own description of herself when young: "a bolter, . . . I seem able to discipline myself, but from a very early age have been unable to be disciplined by other people." In describing other characters, Gordimer usually writes with a kind of objectivity amounting almost to distaste; we like Bam and Maureen, in *July's People,* better than she may. We may like Hillela less than she does. Or are we meant to?

The language can be powerful, or parodic, as here, in an insignificant episode where a schoolboy is embarrassed to get an erection:

> His distress caused his flesh to rise. The other boys, and some of the girls, almost forgot the danger of shrieking with laughter. They pelted uprooted lily pads on the poor blind thing Hillela saw standing firm under baggy school underpants.

That "poor blind thing" is reminiscent of nothing so much as Lawrence at his most miscalculated. But, elsewhere, Gordimer gives us an Africa clearer than any other writer has done:

> The black labourers who did not see her in their inward gaze of weariness, their self-image of religion and race, suddenly unrolled mats towards the East and bowed their heads to the ground. Their seamed heels were raised, naked, as they kneeled, their feet tense. The draped fishnets enlaced the sunset like the leads of stained-glass windows.

But Hillela herself, because always reported on from a distance, with almost none of her thoughts or feelings revealed, is remote and therefore not sympathetic or "real." This is obviously for a writer of Gordimer's technical skill a matter of deliberate strategy. It seems possible that the author is trying, as Krauss points out, to have it both ways by imitating, while castigating, romantic delusion, but one is reminded of those school-day admonitions against the fallacy of imitative form.

The tone of the political interpolations is angrily authentic:

> The laws made of skin and hair fill the statute books in Pretoria; their gaudy savagery paints the bodies of Afrikaner diplomats under three-piece American suits and Italian silk ties. The stinking fetish made of contrasting bits of skin and hair, the scalping of millions of lives, dangles on the cross in place of Christ. Skin

and hair. It has mattered more than anything else in the world.

This is not, however, an unfamiliar exhortation, or one we need to be convinced of. . . .

The work ends with an image of black power and potency: "Cannons ejaculate from the Castle." Blacks have evicted the white regime in South Africa. All is orderly and gracious: A new flag "flares wide in the wind, is smoothed taut by the fist of the wind, the flag of Whaila's country."

> There is a sense that the liberation army is protecting the police from the crowd; for many years these black policemen took part in the raids upon these people's homes. . . . Every now and then they cannot avoid meeting a certain gaze from eyes in the crowd that once burned with tear gas.

This vision is in such obvious contrast to real black policemen being burned to death or dismembered by their angry confreres in South Africa that one can only wonder if the author, borne along by revolutionary hopes, really intends us to believe it, or whether she is mocking the future.

Amid much singing and dancing, a harmonious assemblage of "diplomats, white and black, white churchmen and individuals or representatives of organizations who actively supported the liberation struggle sit among black dignitaries." Hillela is of course there, on the podium. Various white members of her family have stayed and accepted positions in the new government. . . . This final fantasy of a political eventuality so desirable and unlikely must doubtless be reassuring to the South African reader. For others, it calls into question the generic assumptions of the book, the rules by which we must try to understand it. Is the author mocking, predicting, or merely wishing? (p. 9)

Diane Johnson, "Living Legends," in The New York Review of Books, *Vol. XXXIV, No. 12, July 16, 1987, pp. 8-9.*

Katherine Govier

1948-

Canadian novelist, short story writer, and journalist.

In her fiction, Govier portrays women in the process of self-discovery. For example, the troubled heroine of her first novel, *Random Descent* (1979), attempts to develop a stronger sense of personal identity by reconstructing her family history. *Going through the Motions* (1983), Govier's next novel, concerns a disaffected former ballerina who struggles to recover her dignity and establish a more respectable lifestyle after becoming an exotic dancer. David Myers observed that Govier is most interested in "the inner life of a serious-minded woman who must bare herself for a living—someone like a novelist, for that matter." The characters in Govier's short story collection *Fables of Brunswick Avenue* (1985), like those in her novels, are emotionally confused and unable to maintain satisfying relationships. One of these stories, "Going to Europe," concerns the tenuous friendship between two women—a prominent motif in Govier's work—and introduces historian Suzanne Vail, the central character of Govier's third novel, *Between Men* (1987). This work offers a historical view of relationships between the sexes through Vail's discoveries concerning sexual politics and the development of Western Canadian society during her investigation of a notorious crime of passion that occurred in Calgary, Alberta, in 1899.

(See also *Contemporary Authors,* Vol. 101 and *Contemporary Authors New Revision Series,* Vol. 18.)

Photograph by Christina Hartling. Courtesy of Katherine Govier.

ANNE GILMORE

The family-chronicle novel is an ever popular, although seldom well-executed, literary genre. Its major difficulty is that the final tying together of the story's many threads must be both intellectually and emotionally satisfying to the reader. Unfortunately, this is not the case in *Random Descent.*

Still, it is an exceptionally well-written family saga, spanning 150 years, five generations and two countries. In rich, yet unpretentious prose, Govier weaves a believable story of two families' merging, the Olivers and the Beechams, and follows the growth of the family tree from its roots in the indomitable, magically mysterious Submitta Bapett to her great-great-great-granddaughter, Jennifer Beecham, a not so gay divorcee in search of her past and her future.

Along the way, we meet rogues and ne'er-do-wells, dreamers and pragmatists. Govier draws her characters well, with an economy of words and an awareness of both the frailty and strength in the human condition. Her portraits of Edouard Beaupré, the village giant, and the physically and emotionally scarred Constance Beecham are notable for both their skill and insight....

But the story's ending is a letdown. The dialogue becomes stilted and ridiculous metaphors appear—the families' gradual migration westward is symbolically represented by a parade of Vancouver ducks stopping six lanes of traffic to cross a bridge.

> *Anne Gilmore, in a review of "Random Descent,"
> in* Quill and Quire, *Vol. 45, No. 2, February, 1979,
> p. 40.*

BARBARA AMIEL

Katherine Govier's *Random Descent* cleaves to the Canadian experience and gives it to us in much detail and undeniably fluent writing. This is the story of a fairly unremarkable Canadian family traced back four generations. As a historical or sociological piece of Canadiana the book is vastly superior in quality of prose and detail to any textbook. As a work of fiction it all seems rather pointless except perhaps as therapy or practice for the author. (p. 47)

> *Barbara Amiel, "Out of the Desk Drawer and into
> the Fire," in* Maclean's Magazine, *Vol. 92, No. 18,
> April 30, 1979, pp. 46-7.*

PHIL LANTHIER

[In *Random Descent*], Katherine Govier takes more than her title from Sylvia Plath's poem "Black Rook in Rainy Weather."

There's a whole attitude towards fictional material available in the poem which Govier has used to tune this promising first novel. Observing a rook arranging its feathers in the rain, Plath declares that she can expect no miracle "to set the sight on fire," that revelations will come simply as a fall of leaves "without ceremony or portent." Whatever miracles may occur will be "spasmodic truths" patched together in a content "of sorts." The poem expresses a readiness, however, to accept any revelations which might suddenly and inexplicably appear at one's elbow. . . .

Govier's **Random Descent** is characterized by an admirable restraint of method and manner. Though there are moments of scandal, violence, disfigurement and suicide, these do not sink into mere melodrama. They survive, rather, as anecdotes and broken memories in the random movement of family particles down through the many generations. . . .

Beginning in the present, Govier employs the collector of family secrets (there is one in every family), Jennifer Beecham, as a mildly questing spirit visiting her grandparents in California. Their photographs, clippings and memories are used to reconstruct the past, an activity which Jennifer feels necessary if she is to discover her place in the scheme of things. Her marriage has just collapsed, she has aborted a child, her new life is as yet undefined. But the end of her search is a dream of laundry, its markings faded, its meaning unsure. Though she has ranged through five generations and summoned up several families—a confusing operation for the reader even though an interlocking family tree is provided on the inside covers—she reaches no decisive confrontation with the past. The pattern revealed is that of people who come across Canada, settling for a time, then moving on. . . .

This sequence of "spasmodic truths" has the ring of the documentary and the authenticity of the family anecdote, not to mention their limitations, chiefly an absence of dramatic thrust and intensity within the whole pattern. Govier is, after all, depicting the gradual assembling of the great Canadian middle class as it accumulated things, houses and automobiles. Thus the concept of history implicit throughout is that of a series of unconnected individual gestures against a backdrop of forces and circumstances which go largely unanalyzed and unquestioned. At the end of the novel, Govier leaves her Jennifer with the rather disappointing insight that the true secrets reside in oneself here and now, that the past is in her somehow. But Jennifer, alas, is not very interesting and we don't really care about her very much. A visionary grandmother with the extraordinary name of Submitta Bapett appears at the end and points to a parade of ducks holding up traffic on a busy Vancouver boulevard as they head for new water. Is this it? History as little more than the noisy waddle of ducks? It's a good scene, but I think the irony of it is evasive rather than illuminating. One is left questioning the novel's fundamental assumptions despite the skill with which they have been developed.

The whole book has a low-key, disjunctive movement and a prose which is economical, straightforward and declarative. . . . There is a trace of Doctorow's *Ragtime* syncopations in Govier's prose, and some of his tricky business too as when she has a man unknowingly glimpse his future wife from a moving train as she stands at the wayside, or introduces the historical Edouard Beaupré, the eight foot giant from Willow Bunch Saskatchewan as pathetic suitor to one of the women.

On the whole, the prose of **Random Descent** is characterized by a cool professionalism. There are many scenes which are vividly realized, several striking and memorable characterizations, and a judicious and economical use of period detail. She has learned her craft from Rudy Wiebe and Dorothy Livesay and also from her work as a freelance journalist. What has emerged from this apprenticeship is a writer willing, I think, to work steadily for the next miracle.

Phil Lanthier, "Depending on the Red Wheelbarrow," in The Canadian Forum, *Vol. LIX, No. 690, June-July, 1979, p. 47.*

JOHN BEMROSE

Going Through The Motions echoes the tragic novels of the 19th century that illustrate the sometimes perilous extremes of human existence. A young, beautiful girl from an affluent family works her way to the brink of success in that most difficult métier, ballet; by age 30 her luck has changed, and she finds herself taking off her clothes in a Yonge Street strip joint.

Such is the fall of Joan Sincere, the embattled heroine of Toronto writer Katherine Govier's second novel. But since self-realization, not tragedy, is the theme of most serious fiction today, Govier does not leave Sincere in the gutter. Indeed, she starts her tale there—Sincere is charged with assault for having kicked a too eager burlesque fan in the face. This incident brings the desperate tensions of her life to a crisis: she can either sink farther or she can come to grips with the destructive forces that have plagued her youth. Not surprisingly she opts for the latter, and so *Motions* becomes a search for the redeeming truth, as it swings deftly between the past and the traumatic present.

That past began promisingly in the Edmonton ballet studio of an authoritarian spinster. Govier's evocation of the harsh regime of ballet is a tour de force of clear-eyed reportage. . . .

Through almost demonic determination, Sincere survives and is accepted by a prestigious British ballet school. But she becomes pregnant and stubbornly refuses an abortion—only to surrender the baby for adoption. These events, which effectively wreck her career, make for a rather mystifying rebellion. It is not that such events are unlikely but that Govier does not make them credible. At the source of this failure is the rather odd absence of Sincere from much of the novel. She is not *literally* absent, but a great part of what she experiences is seen through strangely neutral eyes; it is as if Govier were more bent on writing objective journalism than on creating a world saturated with the feelings of an individual.

Govier further obscures our view of Sincere by her constant editorializing. Her intrusions rarely work since they are not convincingly backed up by the events of Sincere's life. When Govier tells us that Sincere "had learned to talk, it had taken her life thus far to find the words to come to her own defence," we are baffled: inarticulateness has never seemed Sincere's problem. Only in a few strong, isolated scenes does Sincere really live.

John Bemrose, "A Bump and Grind Toward Redemption," in Maclean's Magazine, *Vol. 95, No. 38, September 20, 1982, p. 63.*

BARBARA NOVAK

Katherine Govier has chosen an apt title for [*Going through the Motions,* a] novel about 30-year-old Joan Sincere, a trained ballet dancer turned stripper who is determined to live life by her own rules. As the narrator points out, however, her rules prove far more rigid than any she has left behind. During the novel's three-month time frame Joan confronts her past (*without* benefit of therapy) and frees herself from the forces that have spiraled her into a self-destructive, life-denying pattern of existence. (p. 17)

Pyschologically, the novel is sound, and the plot is strong and well developed. But structurally the novel has weaknesses. Essentially, it is Joan's story, and as such it concentrates too much on daily events and insights into the life and character of David, her current lover. The novel would have been better served had the point of view remained exclusively with Joan, if we had perceived David through her growing awareness.

The narrator, particularly for a psychological novel, is too knowing, frequently interjecting comments that would be better left unsaid. During an early exchange between Joan and David, the narrator comments on a remark of David's by pointing out, "That's how dumb he was. He couldn't believe she was truly interested in what he'd been saying." Joan could have said that. Joan's friend might have said it. The reader might have thought it, or even David, at some later point, might have thought it. But it's certainly not the type of intrusion readers appreciate from a narrator.

The novel's diction is also problematic, especially in the case of Joan. Granted, she's a complex character—a stripper who listens to classical music, who pops vitamins rather than tranquillizers, who is fascinated by the metaphorical implications of the paramoecium. . . . But still, it is unlikely that her diction, both in dialogue and in thought, should be stylistically so inconsistent. Similarly, the imagery, though moving and powerful, is not always consistent with the character whose feelings it is intended to convey.

Govier has the talent and the vision to be a fine novelist, but she needs to sharpen her technique in order to master control over her material. (pp. 17-18)

Barbara Novak, "Past Imperfect," in Books in Canada, *Vol. 12, No. 2, February, 1983, pp. 17-18.*

DAVID MYERS

[In *Going through the Motions*], Miss Govier understands that the strip joint is not just a sleazy bar where men sit by themselves in the dark and peer at their fantasies, occasionally hooting; it is also, she knows, a workplace where solitary, hardened women grind out a living.

The novel sets its sights on Joan Sincere, a 30-year-old stripper who studied at the Royal Ballet School in London. The other strippers in the book have adopted stage names—Sugar Bush, Unity Drawson, Maxima X, Polly Anna—but Joan sticks with her real name, distinguishing herself even from a caste of women who "held themselves apart to be special." Unlike her sister strippers, Joan strips not to expose but to express herself. . . .

The story is straightforward. Arrested one night for kicking a beer-sodden salesman in the jaw, Joan passes the time before her court date by falling in love with a talk show host from the CBC and deciding to change her career.

Because the story is thin, Miss Govier has trouble coming up with incidents to fill out her book. But she is more interested in character than incident anyway. And what interests her most

is the inner life of a serious-minded woman who must bare herself for a living—someone like a novelist, for that matter.

Miss Govier means for you to pity Joan, and she almost succeeds. Along the way you begin to root for the stripper, to be afraid for her, especially when threats—a hunting knife, a rusty hammer—are left at her apartment door. But Joan's keenest emotions, her fear, her pride, her self-pity, are exaggerated. And you can be forgiven for wondering if this isn't because Miss Govier has identified too closely with her heroine.

David Myers, "Revealing Heroine," in The New York Times Book Review, *April 17, 1983, p. 26.*

JUDY MARGOLIS

These "fables" [in *Fables of Brunswick Avenue*] are no refuge for those who want to snuggle up with a nice fat pillow and read themselves into a smug, sweet sleep. The lessons they point to are invariably dark, welling up out of a seemingly bottomless pool of deep anger, frustration, guilt, jealousy, ambition, and lust; grim reminders of what a sorry emotional state the human condition is in, particularly women's half of it.

And there's definitely something inhospitable, ungracious, about the manner in which the stories are told. Govier obviously prefers to keep her readers at arm's length; she uses the third-person voice for all but one of them, **"Eternal Snow."** As a result, our involvement with the unexamined lives her characters stumble or slip through is only half-felt.

Certainly these often callous creatures (just bare bones, most of them) are all alike: frantic for a toehold, something external, to keep them upright—be it an old friend, a man, a marriage, a mirror, a memory, or some place on the map like the title story's Brunswick Avenue. And all make the same mistake. They lose sight of who they are by fixating on those elements of their lives they think need straightening out.

There are few rewards for the reader moved even momentarily to empathize or commiserate with any of Govier's unregenerate characters. Should we catch the merest glimpse of light flickering uncertainly, down crashes the shade and we're back out on the street again.

Judy Margolis, in a review of "Fables of Brunswick Avenue," in Books in Canada, *Vol. 14, No. 5, June-July, 1985, p. 21.*

MARIANNE MICROS

Katherine Govier's stories [in *Fables of Brunswick Avenue*] . . . do not succeed, for me, in making the everyday and the normal interesting. Written in a style, and sometimes according to a structure, popular a few decades ago, the tone is melancholy and mournful, and the protagonists plagued by alienation because they are too self-obsessed to see clearly beyond themselves. It may have been Govier's intention to show us the inner working of this kind of mind, but the author is usually not distanced enough from her characters to indicate her purpose. Most of the stories are about women who have difficulty choosing between marriage and a writing career, who have failed at one or the other, or, having found some form of happiness, wonder if they have made the right choice. They frequently engage in interior monologues, seeing scenery and people as aspects of themselves, a practice which annoys me here only because it is used too often as a structural device, a rather clichéd way of showing the character's new inner awareness. I was also bothered by Govier's over-use of similes ("behind them, the city looked like an untidy pile of toys," for example), and her lapses into cliché and melodrama. . . .

Nevertheless, there were two stories that impressed me and which I have carried in my mind since reading them: "**The Thief,**" about a woman who, betrayed by her husband, is now betraying another man's wife in the same way; and "**The Night-tender,**" in which a burned-out, alcoholic former poet both offends and guides the young woman who tries to help her revive her failed career. However, if the last paragraph, the introspective one, had been omitted from "**The Night-tender,**" the story would have ended on a stronger note. (p. 99)

Marianne Micros, "The Miracle of Everyday Life,"
in The Fiddlehead, *No. 147, Spring, 1986, pp. 98-101.*

ANNE BOSTON

Katherine Govier's *Fables of Brunswick Avenue* is Greenwich Village, the Left Bank before it became fashionable, Earl's Court, anywhere with bedsits in dilapidated houses occupied by young and upwardly mobile artistes, and those with aspirations bigger than their talent. The stories follow the fortunes of some of these transients, mostly young women, from poverty in a single room to marriage, writing "success" and children. Several deal with failures in female friendship: the erstwhile best friend who fails at suicide, as at everything else she attempts; the companion on a trip to Europe, embittered by her single status, who pronounces Cornwall "twee" and won't eat foreign food. In the first story, "**Brunswick Avenue**", the narrator makes a return trip to the street; meets an old acquaintance, now a single parent for whom it's too late to escape, and realizes that she, not the old landlady, now represents the enemy, her success threatening the rickety lives of those who will never leave.

"There but for the grace of God" is the moral we are presumably intended to draw; but the final effect is less compassionate than patronizing, an uneasy combination of self-righteousness and fear of failure. Govier's undoubted skill is shown to best advantage where there is no axe to grind—in "**The Best Dog**", for instance, in which an East European tourist guide, a professional Lothario, reveals after a routine seduction attempt that his dearest wish is to obtain a pedigree for his adored dog Mike from the American Kennel Club. The stories are sharply observed, written with accuracy and restraint. But you have to work hard to counter the prevailing superiority of tone, and the author's case isn't helped by a strikingly pretentious introduction—an account of the author's and publisher's choice of a cover picture, posing as a parable about how reality is transformed into fiction.

Anne Boston, "Irrational Areas," in The Times Literary Supplement, *No. 4346, July 18, 1986, p. 792.*

MICHAEL HELM

Govier's *Fables of Brunswick Avenue* is an uneven first collection. In her two novels, *Random Descent* and *Going Through the Motions,* Govier skilfully delineated dramatic detail, particularly through imaginative and accurate similes. Her new fiction also includes poetic figures ("The cars darted off the arrivals ramp and into the traffic like drops of water down a window pane"), but in several of these stories Govier takes the very use of such figures as her topic. In "**Responding to Pain,**" the narrative of a moderately successful writer who

saves the life of her less successful and suicidal friend, the characters have different attitudes towards language and what it attempts to represent. Though the two characters "often played simile games" before the attempted suicide, when she awakens from her coma, Jackie says to the protagonist, Sarah. "'The world's gone mad . . . Are you going to do a show about it?'" The story ends with the ambitious Sarah, who once enjoyed having Jackie "as audience," envying the sympathy shown to her recovering friend and feeling isolated by her own relative success and clear-visioned eloquence.

Similarly, differences about the relation of image to reality separate the characters in "**The Independent Woman,**" which ends with the cleverly ambiguous disappearance of the principal character. An even more direct examination of perceptual isolation is offered in "**Tongues,**" told from the point of view of a Canadian woman speculating upon the conversations she hears at a diplomats' party in Washington. The protagonist, Ellen, remembers that as a girl she had believed "only people from Western Canada spoke English without an accent. She had heard this said and had not understood it as a relative statement." The relativity of all communicative acts is now plainly evident to her, but nevertheless, she realizes that she will inevitably go on imposing subjective meanings on her perceptions.

The collection's best story, "**Eternal Snow,**" suggestively interconnects images and events in the first-person narrative of a woman who returns to a ski resort she had visited as a child. She senses her inability to communicate to her husband the significance of this place from her past; she notes the absence of what had once been an "unspoken understanding" between them. An understated irony enforces this motif of difference, and as in other stories, the separation of linguistic figure and factual referent is examined. For example, a beautiful woman (who provides a vague threat to the marriage) is not, as the couple had first imagined, a prostitute, but "an aeronautical engineer"—a fact that lends retrospective significance to the narrator's observation that the skiers look like "spacemen in . . . padded jumpsuits" and to her moment of secluded crisis in a stalled gondola car. As the story ends she warms herself in a hot bath and feels the solitary and ineffable sadness that comes from recognizing that her past is irretrievable: "I remember I hurt more as the warmth invaded each cell than I had when the cold took over."

Characters in "**Brunswick Avenue,**" "**Going to Europe,**" and "**The Best Dog**" reach the same unhappy awareness that past and present cannot always be reconciled. As "**Eternal Snow**" demonstrates, Govier is capable of skilfully handling familiar themes, but too often her stories are made ineffective by mannered structuring and by her tendency to make explicit or too easily evident those narrative aspects that ought to be conveyed indirectly. For this reason, many of the stories do not stand up to successive readings. "**The Best Dog**" suffers from a connect-the-dots symbolism, and in "**The Garden,**" "**The Dragon,**" and "**The Dancer**" the reader is distanced from the narrative by an insistent third-person narrator who provides too much summary and not enough scene, as if Govier had missed the point of her epigraph—Henry David Thoreau's often quoted apology, "Not that the story need be long, but it will take a long while to make it short." (pp. 93-4)

Michael Helm, "Memory & Words," in Canadian Literature, *No. 112, Spring, 1987, pp. 92-5.*

CAROLE GERSON

Govier's *Fables of Brunswick Avenue* is indeed a book of allegories of modern city life, sometimes thin on characterization (as the genre is apt to be), but meaningful in depicting the failures in communication and personal relationships that constitute the urban blight of the generation now reaching middle age. (p. 483)

I found Govier's introduction, recounting her futile hunt for a painting of Brunswick Avenue to serve as a cover illustration, one of the most engaging pieces in the book. . . . [She] presents a [bleak] vision of contemporary human affairs, the despair of her characters expressed in their impulse toward obliteration, particularly of themselves. Her allegorical impulse, strongest in the stories of fractured relationships (their settings not always Toronto), is typified in **"The Independent Woman,"** where the protagonist's suicide takes the characteristically female form of drowning.

Refreshing for the unexpectedness of their contents and particularly admirable for the competence of their execution are several stories far removed from Brunswick Avenue. **"Eternal Snow,"** set in Banff, counterpoints the narrator's uncertainty about the direction of her life with the sensation of being trapped alone in a stopped ski gondola at dusk; the punningly titled **"The Night-tender"** details an Edinburgh evening in the speaking tour of an elderly poet and her younger, frustrated companion; **"The Best Dog"** recounts the rather bizarre connection formed between a young Canadian woman and the enigmatic Russian gentleman (or con artist?) she meets while visiting the Soviet Union. (p. 484)

> Carole Gerson, in a review of "Fables of Brunswick Avenue," in Queen's Quarterly, Vol. 94, No. 2, Summer, 1987, pp. 483-84.

KENNETH McGOOGAN

Several fine writers have set novels in and around Calgary, among them W. O. Mitchell, L. R. Wright, and Aritha van Herk. But until now no novelist has dared to place Calgary at the heart of a full-length fiction, to make it the focus of attention in a work designed to put the city on Canada's literary map.

Katherine Govier, an expatriate Albertan based in Toronto, establishes her controlling metaphor early in *Between Men.* "This matter of getting on the map," one of her narrators writes: "first it was the railway that was going to do it, then the boom, then the fire of 1886. And still it hadn't happened. There was a sense of something owing." Later, he observes: "Calgary will be the first Western town to have streetlights. The power project will put us on the map."

Between Men is a complex, well-crafted novel that intertwines two story-lines. The first of these, the framing tale, is a contemporary love story that focuses on Suzanne Vail, a thirty-fivish history professor recently returned to Calgary after an absence of 10 years. She is torn between two men—her businessman husband Ace, whom she is divorcing, and a jaded, 53-year-old politician named Simon, with whom she has an intense affair.

This contemporary story is rich and detailed. It includes vignettes from Suzanne's past (most of them involving Ace) and an ongoing skirmish in the present, with Suzanne battling an attempt by her departmental chairman to cut the most significant course she teaches (Reinventing the West). It's populated with memorable minor characters, notably Suzanne's oilman father-in-law, Block, and her friend Gemma, a shameless gold-digger who founds a group called SWARM (Single Women After Rich Men), incidentally providing light relief.

Suzanne is researching a historical paper about the brutal and mysterious murder of an Indian woman named Rosalie New Grass. She is obsessed with this real-life event, which happened in 1889 at a down-and-dirty Calgary bar called the Turf Club. Her search for facts becomes a quest for truth, and her imaginings form the story within the story, and eventually reveal the death to have been "something that happened between men."

Suzanne's quest is linked carefully with Govier's larger purpose:

> This murdered Indian woman, that dark club and the men who frequented it, the town's panic: it was one of those occasions where the layers of custom broke open, and one could see straight to the core of the place. But to see that core, Suzanne would need a way in.

To this end, Suzanne creates a newspaperman-narrator named Murphy, who is present at key historical scenes and himself comes vividly to life. Murphy's dark, brooding chapters are among the novel's chief attractions and clearly demonstrate the great power of Govier's imagination.

Dipping her brush now in the dark colours of the past, now in the bright ones of the present, the author creates a multi-hued portrait of the city in which she became a woman. Riding in hot air balloons, canoeing in Bowness Park, camping in the nearby Kananaskis mountains—all of the distinctive local tones are here.

When Suzanne pushes her bicycle up 11A Street towards Riley Park, those who know Calgary will exclaim: "Yes! I see it! I see it happening!" But the author doesn't forget those unfamiliar with the city, for she immediately rounds out the image: "She intended to go to sit by the playground and watch the mothers and children. . . ."

Govier combines an insider's intimate knowledge of Calgary with an outsider's cool detachment. Her depiction of the city is profound. . . . (p. 18)

Between Men can't be considered an allegory. It's far too subtle. Yet, Simon is quintessentially an ugly easterner—older, experienced, smugly superior, he has come to teach the local yokels a thing or two. Ace, on the other hand, is 35 but looks 20. He's a great maker of mistakes—but also vital and alive. And he's identified with Calgary and the West.

Govier's novel is also notable, finally, for its insight into male-female relations. . . .

No ambitious novel is without flaws. In this one, Ace's possessiveness is hard to believe, given his years-long separation from Suzanne. There's also a curious, whimsical scene between Ace and his mother that might have been better omitted. Some will object to certain supernatural effects, others to Govier's habit of sometimes using commas to separate complete clauses.

Still, *Between Men* is a powerful, multi-faceted assertion of identity by a gifted fiction writer. When all of the clever but placeless novels churned out this decade have been forgotten, *Between Men* will still be showing up on Canadian literature courses. It puts Calgary on the map. (p. 19)

Kenneth McGoogan, "Heart of the City," in Books in Canada, *Vol. 16, No. 6, August-September, 1987, pp. 18-19.*

RUBY ANDREW

Part of the silliness that undermines Govier's novel [*Between Men*] is the author's determination to sort out the West and women once and for all. Despite her accomplished voice, Govier's ambitious plans make for an unreasonably complicated plot featuring a large cast of half-baked characters. She has clearly bitten off more than she can chew—a fate she shares with her heroine, Dr. Suzanne Vail.

Back in Calgary after a lengthy, self-imposed period of exile in Toronto, Suzanne falls into some bad habits—one being a series of afternoon trysts with her soon-to-be ex-husband, Ace. As simple as his name, Ace has been left behind in Suzanne's academic dust. Yet despite the brevity of their marriage and the lengthiness of their separation (10 years), Ace spends a good deal of his time begging her to end the divorce proceedings and move back in with him.

Suzanne has also scandalized her friends by falling for the charms of a transplanted Easterner, a sophisticate she can appreciate intellectually as well as physically, and the only male who doesn't shrink into mental midgetry alongside her. Simon, 18 years her senior, has only recently arrived on the Calgary scene from Ottawa, where most of his career was spent writing federal policy for the energy sector. Now that he's flown his coop, he wants to teach western oilmen how to manipulate the laws he's helped create. To Suzanne, however, this would-be consultant "was the satyr she had always been waiting for, not at all handsome, not always charming, ill-mannered and difficult around the house, but still the magical whiskered, hooved, sinewed man of her dreams."

Well, sure—if you're into that. Perhaps it's not so surprising that Suzanne just can't stop hankering after the unwhiskered, unhooved Ace. But there's another who demands her allegiance as well. As a professor at Foothills College, Suzanne teaches "History 301: Reinventing the West". Troubled by the historian's reliance on major events, Suzanne prefers to do her research at the local archives. And that's how she discovers the woeful tale of Rosalie New Grass.

A grislier episode in western history is difficult to imagine. Rosalie New Grass lived in or near Calgary in 1889, when she was brutally raped and murdered by one William Jumbo Fisk. In her acknowledgements, the author states that "Rosalie New Grass lived and died in the manner described" but then adds this caveat: "Some of the major characters named existed; others were created by the author to tell her story."

Like her creator, Govier's heroine begins to toy with fact and fiction—a state of affairs bound to offend "the standards of the likes of *Studies in Western Canadian History* editors." But readers, as much as the aforementioned editors, may take offence at Govier's clumsy attempts to rewrite an episode of western history into a feminist manifesto.

Whether it's the cast-study within a novel or the sexual friskiness of eastern satyrs versus western good ol' boys, Govier always prefers symbols to substance or subtlety. Forced dialogue, wooden characterizations, and a heavy-handed mixture of romance interspersed with blood-curdling historical speculation combine to stop Govier's novel—and her heroine—in their tracks.

Ruby Andrew, "Frontier Women: Two Tales in Search of the Perfect Marriage," in Quill and Quire, *Vol. 53, No. 9, September, 1987, p. 76.*

Rodney Hall
1935-

English-born Australian novelist, poet, editor, critic, biographer, and nonfiction writer.

Hall has received international attention for his novels *Just Relations* (1983) and *Captivity Captive* (1987), which develop mythic significance in their depiction of life in the isolated Australian outback. These works evince Hall's expansive, poetic prose style, through which he evokes several levels of meaning and various implications. *Just Relations* is a comic fantasy featuring aged and eccentric characters whose carefree lifestyles and rapport with nature are threatened when government workers attempt to develop their town for tourism. To highlight the colorful personalities of the residents, Hall vividly details their fantasies and memories and recreates rural idioms. In addition, he introduces extraordinary events into realistic scenarios and imbues various inanimate objects with a humanlike consciousness. Frances Taliaferro commented: "The long-winded charm of *Just Relations* springs from its leisurely playfulness, and from the fact that it is never far from the surprising edges of mild surrealism." In contrast to *Just Relations,* Hall's epical work, *Captivity Captive,* is a fictionalized recreation of the events that culminated in the grisly, unsolved murders of three members of an Australian family in 1898. The novel is narrated in retrospect by eighty-year-old Peter Murphy, who details his family's violent history and their struggle to fashion a self-reliant existence in an extremely harsh environment. Michiko Kakutani called *Captivity Captive* "a richly textured tale that stands at once as an absorbing detective story and as a Faulknerian parable about innocence and guilt, passion and betrayal." Kakutani added: "[As in *Just Relations*], Mr. Hall succeeds in dazzling us with his storytelling powers, planting in our minds images that burn with the fierce power of bad dreams."

Prior to the publication of these novels, Hall established himself in Australia as an important contemporary poet. Along with Les A. Murray, Thomas Shapcott, and David Malouf, all of whom came into prominence during the 1960s, Hall is credited with having helped to expand the styles, forms, and concerns of Australian poetry. Peter Porter commented: "Stick to the local flora and fauna and to the quiddities of the Australian character was for generations the commandment. The paradox of the present-day situation . . . is that, though they are very conscious of being Australian, the new poets feel entirely free to write about any subject under the sun and to adopt or adapt any mode of expression from overseas which attracts them." Hall's neoromantic verse is suffused with witty observations and examines personal and private themes relating to love, death, violence, and the role of the artist. Several of Hall's volumes contain what he has termed "progressions"—accumulations of individual lyrics that develop and explore similar themes and can be read individually or as a collective whole. Early collections structured as progressions include *Forty Beads on a Hangman's Rope: Fragments of Memory* (1962), which develops themes relating to the cycle of life; *The Law of Karma: A Progression of Poems* (1968), which is based upon the Hindu doctrine of transmigratory souls and follows five hundred years of violent betrayal in several different countries before cul-

© Jerry Bauer

minating with the World War II horrors at the Auschwitz death camp; and *The Autobiography of a Gorgon and Other Poems* (1968), in which Hall ruminates on the life of a poet who seeks to participate yet remain detached from human affairs in order to gain command of his craft. *Eyewitness* (1967) and *Heaven, in a Way* (1970) include lyrics on various topics while also examining the art of writing poetry. According to Thomas Shapcott, "[*Heaven, in a Way*] is certainly entirely representative of Hall's range and style, which can move easily from smoothly polished trivia . . . through sharp and piercing observations of people, including himself." The final sequence in *Heaven, in a Way*, "Romulus and Remus," is a study of power and psychological conflict composed in several styles that is generally considered Hall's finest poetic achievement.

Hall has also published several other works. *A Place among People* (1975), his first novel, details the local color of a quiet Australian fishing settlement; *Black Bagatelles* (1978) consists of fifty lyrics focusing on themes relating to death; and *The Most Beautiful World* (1982) blends short prose fragments and sermons to comment on contemporary social ills.

(See also *Contemporary Authors*, Vol. 109.)

H. P. HESELTINE

[David Malouf, Don Maynard, Judith Green, and Rodney Hall] are all represented in a volume entitled simply *Four Poets.* (p. 503)

"Statues and Lovers", Rodney Hall's contribution to *Four Poets*, reproduces some of the material of *Penniless till Doomsday,* a slight collection devoted entirely to his own work. Like Malouf, Hall writes of past childhood and present loves. But he moves more easily into public life than Malouf. **"To a distant statue of King George V"**, **"Aden"** and **"St. Paul's Cathedral"** are the work of a man with his eye on the world. Indeed, of all the younger poets, Hall comes closest (particularly in *Penniless till Doomsday)* to sympathy with the Left. Elsewhere, in **"Madam's Music"** and **"Indoor Perennials"**, he displays a waspish sense of humour. But even Hall cannot avoid the prevailing addiction to an evocative and expansive imagery. **"She"** is an impressively mysterious poem, but it is difficult to establish just what is meant to be at the heart of its mystery. (p. 504)

> *H. P. Heseltine, in a review of "Four Poets," in Meanjin, Vol. XXI, No. 4, December, 1962, pp. 503-04.*

S. E. LEE

[The "beads" in Rodney Hall's *Forty Beads on a Hangman's Rope*], despite the rather ominous dust-jacket blurb—"a member of the Avant Garde of Australian writers of poetry"—are carefully wrought in disciplined verse which shows some flexibility, from the freedom of No. VII

> The holy one
> was a tiny man
> (they'd heard it said)
> soft and round
> with pious hands
> whose imbecile
> commandments ruled
> the flinching mind.

to the jingly No. XIII

> Hump your crosses on your backs
> and bleed through your stigmata—
> a thousand million fellow christs
> adore a fellow martyr.

The forty poems . . . have some value as individual pieces, but for full appreciation and understanding demand sustained sequential reading. Not only does each poem ("a fragment of memory recalled at the moment of death at the hand of society or after") comment, sometimes with ironic bitterness, on its neighbour, but the narrative connexions and development of thought are carefully organized and sustained in six cycles. There are four "life cycles" going from childhood, through religious education and love and marriage to middle-aged cynicism; and two cycles celebrating "death in public" and "death in private" (both already witnessed in the earlier life cycles). Rodney Hall's spiritual exploration of life's meanings for our war-torn, revolution-rife, hate-filled generation is strangely sombre and moving. (pp. 136-37)

> *S. E. Lee, in a review of "Forty Beads on a Hangman's Rope," in Southerly, Vol. 24, No. 2, 1964, pp. 136-37.*

RONALD DUNLOP

The versatility of contemporary Australian poetry is well attested in the work of four poets whose works have been published recently: it's a far cry from the odd blend of foreboding, sensuality, and comedy in the poetry of Eric C. Rolls to the very private world of Joan Mas, or from the disenchantment of Laurence Collinson to the sombre meditations of Rodney Hall. The diversity of these poets' concerns is matched by their diversity of tone and style. It is also matched, less happily, with marked unevenness in the quality of the poems.

The most consistently sustained poetry is in Rodney Hall's recent collection, *Eyewitness.* The title of Mr Hall's book points to a characteristic of the best poems in it: the detachment of the poet from the experience worked out in the poem; or, to put it another way, the poet's ability to stand apart from himself, and synthesize his experience in the artifice of the poem. Despite the occasional awkwardness of over-compressed syntax, and the intrusion here and there of the self-conscious line, Rodney Hall's insistence on the primacy of individual experience, the boldness with which he selects and hammers out the images that give it expression, are eye- and mind-catching. Between **"Viewpoint"** and **"Under Icebergs"**, the first and last poems of the opening section of *Eyewitness,* the poet's experiences are explored with varying degrees of success. In the best poems, the links between the external world of nature and the inner world of the mind are firmly established. This is what happens in **"Rat's Eye"**, **"Matador: A Soliloquy"**, **"Cat in the Garden"**, or **"Kittiwake"**. (p. 293)

Generally, the tone of Rodney Hall's poems is subdued. But their movement is graceful and in some of them, **"Spider on the Clothesline"** for example, he reveals a nice turn of wit:

> He strolls our hempen clothesline
> like a swindler at his trade,
> to rush away when the universe
> vibrates at our touch: afraid
> he's tightrope walking the web
> of some titanic spider?

At times, too, as in **"Wedding Day"**, from the short section "Six Poems from Greece", he brings to the verse a charmingly light touch. Essentially, however, he is a poet of the inner self. For the work of such a poet, the concluding line of the last poem in his book, **"Youth—manhood—middle age"**, could well be the motto:

> Even my heart is old from growing new.
> (pp. 293-94)

> *Ronald Dunlop, "New Poetry: Old Preoccupations," in Southerly, Vol. 27, No. 4, 1967, pp. 293-96.*

ROBERT WARD

[Rodney Hall's *The Law of Karma* is] neat, controlled and tasteful. . . . As the title suggests, the Hindu doctrine of transmigratory souls is featured in what is, as the blurb says,

> really one long poem comprising a "progression" of sixty-six parts through eleven life cycles.

It is a gigantic conceit: the Hindu Saint's distaste for the mob leads his soul in a degenerate spiral that five hundred years and ten lives later reaches Auschwitz as **"Reichs-Kommissar 1915-1944"**.

The five hundred year fall from Hindu grace takes the soul from India to Persia, then to Turkey, Malta, Venice, Trieste,

Austria, Moscow, Guinea, France, and finally Poland. Again quoting the publisher, we are told that

> the basic theme of the poem is that each betrayal of human responsibility opens the way to another more degenerate betrayal.

This is not a very profound thought, in fact it's nonsense, but it does make a good foundation for the poem. What is more interesting is the carefully detailed historical, social and geographical contexts each life cycle is given. These are handled very neatly with cross-referring imagery adding texture and binding the poem together.

To my mind *The Law of Karma* contains the best, the most accomplished and polished poetry Rodney Hall has written. In evoking mood and place he is quite excellent....

> *Robert Ward, in a review of "The Law of Karma,"*
> *in* Australian Book Review, *Vol. 8, Nos. 2 & 3,*
> *December, 1968 & January, 1969, p. 44.*

DON ANDERSON

The title poem of the volume *The Autobiography of a Gorgon* is described as a "progression" of poems. It thus resembles [Hall's] earlier *Forty Beads on a Hangman's Rope* and the later *The Law of Karma.* (p. 74)

The Autobiography of a Gorgon, then, is a sequence or "progression" of thirty-eight poems falling into two sections and having a Foreword and an Afterword.... If I may be rash enough to interpret—*pace* Miss Sontag—Mr Hall's sequence, then his Gorgon becomes for me the Muse of Poetry, if not the poet and the poetic act itself. Appropriately, many of these fine poems are, to use Lowell's telling word (from "91 Revere Street") "rocklike". The speaking tone is one of detachment, is cold as stone....

> The cemetery attests my purpose:
> figures crowding on the hill
> to stand, immutable as marble,
> indifferent to the streaming rain. . . .

This seems to me very fine indeed, of a delicacy and poise that challenge explication and almost forbid interpretation. The choice of the verb "attests", the syllabic quality and alliteration of "immutable as marble", the rightness of "indifferent" all attest a fineness of ear and firmness of control that command great respect.... Though one might point to the climactic nature of the final poem, to its significance in the meaning of the progression, I am totally loath to offer an interpretation of the sequence as a whole. At this early stage of one's relationship with it, it still has much of the aura and properties of mystery. Which is appropriate to its subject matter, the relation of art and life. The poem echoes in the memory, sets off ripples in the lake of one's belief, one's share of the collective unconscious, rather than partaking of the world of knowledge. (pp. 74-5)

> *Don Anderson, in a review of "The Autobiography*
> *of a Gorgon," in* Southerly, *Vol. 29, No. 1, 1969,*
> *pp. 74-5.*

ROBERT WARD

Rodney Hall certainly appears one of the few younger poets steadily developing his craft and expanding his range of poetic concerns in an interesting way. He is a very neat poet, one whose small, polished stanzas, occasional off-rhymes, and carefully selected images, display a definite technical accomplishment and a conscious stylishness. At that point he seems to know where he's going.

His *Autobiography of a Gorgon* contains two sections, **"Poems of Many Places"** and the title sequence. They were probably written before his more recent 'progression' entitled *The Law of Karma,* and are not as good. **"Poems of Many Places"** are simply short lyric comments and statements about countries the poet has visited—from Australia to Vietnam, Europe, Africa and the Pacific—and their achievement is one of mood, carefully set, urbane and somewhat remote.

The third poem in this series, set in Australia, introduces one of the volume's main themes, and it's worth taking it up. The idea is that the artist's preoccupation with his art isolates him from life and even changes the shape and texture of his world. In **"The Lake"** his "companions shout and rush down slopes as steep / as any gamut of emotions" to see the lake, while the poet stands

> . . . back in the scrub we've struggled through,
> needing a frame to recognise perfection,
> needing to fit the world to my constriction,
> needing to curb myself with self-control
> as if my duty were devising whole
> perspective laws for every circumstance.

His stance here is introversive; his craft demands that the lake be invested with a more emotive significance, and at the back of his mind, perhaps, he sees the possibility of the poem. There in his brown study he judges his hedonistic friends and finds them wanting as their faces turn to him "bright with the failure of transparency".

This is taking oneself very seriously. Poetry, I think he suggests, is an isolating activity, and this is an idea that obviously worries him quite a lot. I suppose it's possible that the more exquisite the idea of one's sensibility is, the more real become such feelings of isolation, and like Mr. Hall many artists have from time to time rationalised this in terms of what they feel are the special, intuitive, even inspirational demands of their craft. They feel that they can't help seeing the world in a special way. But all this really means is that they're trying hard, and it is well to remember that dedicated plumbers have a special regard for taps and cannot see them without thinking of washers. If the poet feels that his feeling for life is unique or uniquely poetic, and writes about it, he's simply wearing his art on his sleeve.

That may be a harsh judgment of Mr. Hall's main theme, and it should be said that he writes of other things as well. But it is a thought which is expanded subsequently, and the overall feeling one gets is that while his technical accomplishments and polish increase, he is really now in search of something big to say.

Autobiography of a Gorgon is one of his experiments in a 'progression' of poems in which it is explained

> each poem should be capable of standing alone, but
> all should interact to form a total unity.

The method was used most successfully with *The Law of Karma* in which the story of a transmigratory soul allowed for a variety of situations in which cross-references and echoing imagery played an important part. In the *Gorgon* sequence, much less ambitious, thirty-eight small, hard-edged, coldy elegant poems take up and expand the theme of **"The Lake"**, elevated now and embodied in an elaborate myth which expresses a very sanguine, full blown vision of the poetic act. The Gorgon becomes by extension the poet, uttering

> . . . my instincts my desire my will
> crushed by the art of stone.

It is an interesting allegory on the whole. The Poet/Gorgon turns even the gifts of love into something frightening or unreal and synthetic. . . . But the final vision is an evangelistic one:

> My mission is to save the world from age,
> so the young and beautiful endure forever
> as at their single moment of perfection.

And allied with this is the sad, inescapable fact that the images of his art succeed only by holding their subjects fixed and dead:

> The cemetery attests my purpose:
> figures crowding on the hill
> to stand, immutable as marble,
> indifferent to the streaming rain.

(pp. 70-1)

Robert Ward, in a review of "The Autobiography of a Gorgon," in Australian Book Review, *Vol. 8, No. 4, February, 1969, pp. 70-1.*

THOMAS W. SHAPCOTT

Heaven, in a Way is Rodney Hall's fourth collection in three years, which must be a record, certainly in Australia. Apart from the book-length cycle *The Law of Karma,* the present collection is probably his best; it is certainly entirely representative of Hall's range and style, which can move easily from smoothly polished trivia ("**A Question of Manners**"—Queen Vic. and the saucer, again) through sharp and piercing observations of people, including himself, to the final set-piece sequence "**Romulus and Remus**", an extensive study of power and psychological conflict. "**Romulus and Remus**" is the high point of this collection. In form and style it is a sort of offshoot from *The Law of Karma*—a sequence of short sections ranging from lyric to unabashed theatricality (in the "**Lupercalia**" section, with its modishly visual eccentricity). But the basic tension of twin love/rivalry conflict is a gripping one, and Hall's poetry is spare, vivid, completely assured in tone and pace. At his best, Rodney Hall attains a sort of virtuoso spiritedness, an élan sadly lacking in most of his contemporaries. When his material is suitably malleable (as in "**Romulus and Remus**", the title poem, and "**Mrs Macintosh**", for instance) Hall is breathtakingly memorable. When the material is doggedly weak, so is the poem (e.g. "**Husband and Wife with newspaper**"), and no amount of verbal finesse will save it. Sometimes, indeed, as in "**Drugged**", even this seems more a conjurer's bag of tricks than a technician's error of judgment. Nevertheless, Hall is undoubtedly among the best poets writing in Australia today, and *Heaven, in a Way* is a strong indication of just how far he has travelled since [*Penniless till Doomsday*] was published eight years ago. (pp. 255-56)

Thomas W. Shapcott, "Paperback Poets & Others," in Australian Book Review, *Vol. 9, No. 9, July, 1970, pp. 255-56.*

JAMES TULIP

If Tom Shapcott is the saint at his devotions, Rodney Hall is something of a Devil's Advocate. We recall that together they edited *New Impulses in Australian Poetry* in 1968, and I for one was never quite sure just what the new impulses really were except for the new poets. What principles Shapcott and Hall have in common must remain an open question since now three years later they seem to be moving in such different directions—almost like a Wordsworth and Coleridge after *Lyrical Ballads.* It seems now more a coincidence of energies and talents rather than a new impulse of poetic principles.

Heaven, in a way brings the issue of Hall's distinctiveness as a poet into clear focus. It seems quite fair to call him a Devil's Advocate. He stands off from his poems marshalling his energies for some more public performance, amused it seems at his own involvement in particular experiences and the cause of art, pleading the case of irony in order to allow some larger truth to establish itself finally in essential form, resisting the allurements of easy belief. His poems have a provisional air to them, of being part of a larger whole; they seem instrumental to some end that words of themselves cannot satisfy, only allude to. So it is that we do *not* look to Hall for the *poem as object,* as the totally embodied and imagined form, as has been the case with the prevailing orthodoxy in twentieth-century poetry. We learn, instead, to expect the presence and performance of the artist himself *qua* artist as the subject of Hall's work—that lithe, dry, critical yet immensely sensitive presence that Hall has come to be known by in his several volumes of verse and in the public readings from his poems. As he says in "**personal tour**": . . .

> It took me
> years to cut these steps in rock.
> The bridge across my creek
> is narrow, growing shaky, I'll admit
> But everything belongs. . . .

Hall's disbelief—even at times in himself—is radical.

But what matters poetically here is Hall's conversion of the stance of disbelief into an energy and form of social communication, with the poet standing poised ironically at the centre playing with his reader, with his Muse, with the formal necessities of verse making. And all to allow reader, Muse and poem to get in touch with one another in a way that poetry since the Romantics has precluded by its willingness to believe too easily in the poet's voice as the voice of truth and sincerity. Hall's stance is paradoxical: he says *No* in order to say *Yes.* I can think of no other English poet quite like him. He belongs with Jonson, Pope and Browning in his respect for art as a social medium. Yet he avoids internal pointing to his lines and has a preoccupation with his own experience and personality that make him very much a modern and a child of the Romantics. If we said that Hall has taken up the salient modern aspects of Romanticism as his content and forged out of the English classical tradition in poetry a new form for himself, we might be close to his overall achievement. He is not like the Movement poets of the 1950s and 1960s in England, even though by birth and temperament he is very much English. Robert Graves might once have been his mentor, but it is pleasing to think that Australia may have had an invaluable influence on Hall in forcing him back to the cruder, more prosaic state where men who are not mandarins actually live their lives.

I am trying to define a dramatic role for Hall's poetry as a shaping principle in his work over the past ten years, and he has indeed been persistent in his concerns and themes. Just now this matter of his dramatic quality is a pertinent one since the University of Queensland Press has recently issued a recording of his reading the "**Romulus & Remus**" sequence from

Heaven, in a way. To call the reading a *tour de force* is simple. The poetry, as I have been suggesting, is meant for this kind of performance—whether consciously or unconsciously. We find Hall in the reading right *inside* his lines, punching them out at us, filling with his brisk active tones the strategical outlines of his words. Yet because of the inbuilt quality of negation to his whole position the reading never advances beyond an enactment, it disciplines itself to a role, a communication, a performance that impels us to think and reflect on the issues in the poetry; it does not set out simply to please.

Now in some respects I view this fulfilment of Hall's poetic with misgiving. It may be too complete, too knowing in its ways. That energizing dual identity inside and outside a Hall poem is here resolved into the dual identities of Romulus and Remus within the poem; and all that the reader is left to do is to add empathy. It may be an achievement in dramatization rather than a dramatic achievement. Then I also have in mind the striking title poem to Hall's book, for **"Heaven, in a way"** has made overt this dual stance inside the poem, the "poet" standing over and looking down on the "reader" in a brilliant exchange on the poet's part. This poem crystallizes so much in Hall that one fears for the risk he has taken in letting the personality of the "poet" appear so limited. Doubtless we do not have to identify the speaker's voice and the poet's, nor think of the experience as being necessarily Hall's. The poem works with several possible interpretations. I see it as a sustained, and even bitter, irony at the so-called "achievement and status" of the "arrived" poet, but this feels as soon as I write it an unfortunately narrow reading. The play of wit and learning is too light and elusive for any one point to be made of it: . . .

> If anyone should care to live
> in Gothic or in Romanesque cathedrals
> that's alright too: you spread
> your palliasse upon the altar or in the nave
> and wake to find the morning sun
> shattered to a flower of jewelled glass—
> to find the ghost of a multicoloured
> saint or two in bed beside you

The wit, more generous here than later in the poem, yet belongs way back in the poet's experience; it is not merely verbal. But that it does rise up inside the verse with such suppleness of tone and rhythm and understanding is undoubtedly a real sign of "how far" Hall has come as a poet. (pp. 77-9)

> *James Tulip, in a review of "Heaven, in a Way,"*
> *in* Southerly, *Vol. 31, No. 1, 1971, pp. 77-9.*

PETER PORTER

Rodney Hall has been an important influence, along with Tom Shapcott, in the change which has come over Australian poetry since the 1950s. He has earned the commendation of Robert Graves, which is not surprising, if rather unusual: his earlier poems are highly Gravesian. I like him best when he is inventing stories and creating myths. Like many poets today, he is fond of the extended sequence of brief poems, a device which allows a poet to be short-winded and yet obliges him to outstay his welcome. His best effects [in *Selected Poems*] are cameos or vignettes, often direct pieces of observation, as in **"Tree Children"**:

> the tree was lofty, delicate,
> seemed to have been there longer
> than the house, longer than our lives.

> When we felled the silky oak
> its clustered flowers
> sprayed us with their honey.
>
>   (p. 432)

> *Peter Porter, "Breaking the Tribal Bounds," in* The Times Literary Supplement, *No. 3865, April 9, 1976, pp. 431-32.*

DAVID GILBEY

[*A Place Among People*] is a fairly conventional "imagist" novel which, despite its many fine parts, doesn't quite get itself together. Like a half-assembled jigsaw puzzle, it seems casually constructed, with individual details striking one disproportionately. Although on the whole highly articulate and having some fine scenes and insights, pervading the book is an ostentatious flourish which makes the perceptions, tensions and impact of the book unconvincing.

At the beginning for example, Collocott is a balding, nervous thirty-seven-year-old man who has bought an old wooden house in Battery Spit, a quiet fishing settlement near Brisbane. Having retreated from his family and his teaching profession he is watching a Punch and Judy show from the back row. . . . The pressure to compare Collocott (hypersensitive about his own intelligence and bowed down by unconfidence) with Punch is obvious but Hall pushes the imagery further:

> . . .Then down went Death and up jumped the Devil
> with a switch of his red tail and a wag of his black
> papier-maché face and a voice the same as Punch's.
>
> "I don't need you," said Punch.
>
> "So I'm not afraid of you," said Punch.
>
> "So I'm going to kill you," said Punch.
>
> The triumphant hunchback gloated over his victories,
> ogled at the assembled families, lolled out of his box
> like some sort of malevolent spastic.

The last sentence is luridly excessive, not really dramatizing for us Collocott's sensibilities or subtly suggesting a further dimension to the image but rather showing Hall's own determination to "gloat" over his verbal abilities. The imagery in these scenes is directed at revealing the author's acrobatics, not the dimensions of the character, and the result is often closer to melodrama or farce than, I suspect, Hall intended.

As the show ends and the audience disperses, Collocott watches the "ritual of stowing away each item in the station waggon". Hall elaborates portentously: "Dead: their meanings lived on in himself" then provides an aptly conclusive image: "Tyres crunched across shelly sand", but concludes the paragraph on a wispy, vague note:

> *Something* complete was suddenly endangered by the temptation to go on sitting there too long. (my emphasis)

Hall hints at an experience or an insight or an emotion without clarifying it. The prose isolates this "something" as solid and separable but doesn't quite define it. This kind of coyness is created many times in *A Place Among People* by the overuse of "something". . . . There is in *A Place Among People* a pervasive sense of unreality which, in prose that insists on the undefinability of experiences, quickly becomes unbelievable.

The novel concerns itself with Collocott's awakening from an eight-year cocoon of unconsciousness (symbolically ended by his digging over the soil in spring) to the lives of the characters in Battery Spit and his desire for relationship with them. Several narrative strands cross and recross the stage of Battery Spit as Collocott gradually becomes involved (conversations with the postman; business through Mr Fennel the bank manager; tutor to the boisterous Charlton kids) and eventually, from having feared them he stands up to them over their hasty suspicions that a local aborigine, Daisy Daisy, whom Collocott sheltered in his house, killed old Sissons, "a small tough old man with a stringy neck and hideous blotched skin".

In fact the novel can be seen as Collocott's search for love and acceptance in which his private romantic fantasy for Bobbie Douglas parallels his social aspirations. In terms of both perspectives however, the novel is clumsily handled and often drowned in words. When Collocott first catches sight of Bobbie he retreats into his house, but Hall intrudes:

> the girl was *assertive in her brightness,* moving at the point where the soft dull slope of the hill levelled out to become part or [sic] a wide river bank. (emphasis mine)

What we get is not what Collocott sees but Hall's appraisal of that landscape. Collocott who has lived much of his life to date in his imagination invests Bobbie with the characteristics of a romantic heroine, seeing in her gestures and conversation hints of a love that she sees differently. Collocott accepts her offer of tidying up his house and creates a whole fantasy on the basis of her many small actions. (pp. 464-65)

In a sense Hall's presence in the novel is that of critic/commentator, anxious to ensure the reader doesn't miss all the implications he intends to be there and keen to supply brilliant images, parallels, interpretations and asides. Hall doesn't seem to believe that Collocott as created by him is sufficiently well-drawn to dramatize his own impressions.

Another effect of this approach can be seen in the canvas of Battery Spit. . . . The "characters" are colourful caricatures which conjure up the different attitudes of derision at their foibles and yet affection for their quaintness. . . . Collocott sees the place as "The Battery Spit jigsaw" and with innocent detachment treats Mrs Pascoe's brothel (obvious similarities with Mrs Khalil in *Riders in the Chariot*) as a gallant social gathering, in his attempt to put the pieces together. (p. 466)

Collocott blunders through the fragments, searching for the key that will open the doors to acceptance and break the ties to his family, brother and earlier experiences. He decides he will break his "eight years of mental convalescence" and go to Brisbane to see the former owner of his cottage, an old lady, Mrs O'Shea, now in a geriatric home. . . . The search which "could not end nor could it be avoided" spews Collocott into the presence of the inarticulate oracle ("Will she tell me what I want to know?"). . . . Predictably, Mrs O'Shea fails to reveal the truth ("the flat jellies looked at him, seeing nothing") but Collocott, embarrassed and speechless feels the intensity of their interview and presses into her hand a powder compact he'd bought for Bobbie. . . . The scene hovers between the sublime and the ridiculous. The inflated perceptions seem to be insisting on the former, while the prose reads like a piece of grotesque bathos. Part of the problem, I think is that Hall takes himself so seriously and is clearly heavily influenced by Patrick White, without having yet found his own style. Several kinds of meaning are hinted at for particular images and expressions, but Hall doesn't seem to be able to make up his mind *which* he wants to stress. Thus, in the scene just referred

to, Collocott is presented as an explorer, an adventurer, a knight-errant, a novitiate, a neighbour and a blunderer. These perspectives are jumbled together with the result that no convincing picture of Collocott emerges. Perhaps fittingly the novel ends on a heroically ambiguous note with Collocott selling up:

> He had betrayed his long search for meanings . . .
> At last, he said, when I am fully despicable it seems
> I cannot despise myself.

The apparent open-endedness of this conclusion . . . seems to me to betray the uncertainty in Hall's mind about how he regards Collocott. The hints that Collocott has understood or come to terms with his experience are not supported by the inconclusive and fragmented poetic prose. (pp. 466-67)

> *David Gilbey, "Experiments in Narrative," in* Southerly, *Vol. 37, No. 4, December, 1977, pp. 461-74.*

VERNON YOUNG

Rodney Hall's verse—much of it, at any rate, in the *Selected Poems* (1975)—is so much more interesting than Manifold's that his slavish defence of the elder poet [in *J. S. Manifold: An Introduction to the Man and His Work*] is really quite unbelievable. Since I have reviewed [*Selected Poems*] elsewhere [see excerpt below] I shall deal only with his newest poems here, simply noting that I was previously impressed by Hall's ability to create generic characters from the past, by his tendency to write in sequences (which argued, perhaps, a passion for continuity), and by the intermittent intensity of a late series of poems he had written on the difficulties of love. The new publication *Black Bagatelles* confirms neither the strength of characterization I had praised nor the potency of his engagement with our *zeitgeist,* even though he has worked hard to find new images for old grievances—putting "up a tremendous show of not finding things funny," what? These poems are a disintegration product, imbued with a species of prophetic pessimism not quite novel, the panic moments of an Australian just catching up with the Decline of the West, a latecomer preempted by the dirges of many precedent poets.

> what can language say?
> whose words are not themselves a condemnation?
> —should I have shot my old headmaster?
> —crippled the girl I loved?
> —derailed a train?
> > what is mine I'm free to hate

The reference here is to racial inequality but the last line quoted is a leitmotif: freedom to hate is the conspicuous feature of these looseleaf ruminations and polemics, grouped under coy subtitles: *Little reminders that Death is still around; Intimations that Death is trying to make contact; Death turns nasty: that is, personal;* and the two final ones, most revelatory: *The hopeless hope that wisdom and experience will help us cope* and *The search for identity is a search for Death—as running away from Death is running towards Death,* no clause of which is self-evident; to me, they sound sophomoric, whether Hall's invoking Society or the Self. If you can say that wisdom and experience won't help you cope, you have attained neither. As for running away from Death and finding it, that's a Pardoner's Tale or the fatalism of "appointment in Samarra," a colorful trope but a suspect premise. In what precise way is a search for identity a search for Death? Insofar as Hall is addressing a debauched civilisation, it is surely the *flight* from identity which is a pursuit of death! But the poems to which these superscriptive crepe-hangers are attached are far from philosophic: they are lamentations over the dying of the light. . . . Yes, yes, it's all true. We know too much and our saturation renders us ignorant. Yet, as you read Hall from one stepping-stone to another (this is in effect a single long poem; the separate short statements are not formally self-contained), you suspect that the poet is inspired not so much by sadness at the failing effort of mankind as by detestation of middle-class phenomena in our time. . . . Yes, yes, it's all true and haven't we heard it all before and isn't it more truth than poetry and is there not an unattractive relish to be heard in these lines? Our facile Jeremiahs never seem prepared to acknowledge that the culture by which they are enraged and which they would like to see erased is the same that gave them Gothic cathedrals, Elizabethan English, the paintings of Titian, the music of Bach and Schubert, the quadrant and the discovery of Australasia, the marvels of Tolstoi and Proust and brain surgery and sanitation engineers and mass-market publication that secures the attention of New York reviewers to down-under poets. (pp. 89-91)

> Vernon Young, "Poetry Down Under," in Parnassus: Poetry in Review, *Vol. 7, No. 1, 1978, pp. 76-95.*

VERNON YOUNG

Rodney Hall, an Australian, is as little familiar to most of us, I daresay, as Basil Bunting. . . . His professional honors at home have taken him into international territory and [the pieces in **Selected Poems**] have been gleaned from eight volumes. . . . He appears to favor the *sequence,* unified by a subject which is not imposed, but emerges; which argues a way of seeing things whole, or at least of their having a *connectedness,* the single personality, emotion, place or deed linked with another as the poet's consciousness perceives, develops and shapes a "progression" or a "contrary." He is very damn good and I can best ratify that brisk opinion by directly quoting him, in a necessarily limited attempt to illustrate his range. This characterization, **"The Medieval,"** is part of a progression, **"The Molecule as Mosaic,"** the subject of which I'll risk defining as the revenges of history.

> His two concerns are siege defences
> and the men's obedience—those menforms
> satisfactorily turning totem heads his way
> (the badger, frog, the bear and pig)
> captive, as fear dictates it, in his mind. . . .

I find that as vivid as Bunting, with less striving after syntactical warp. It was written before 1973. *"The Owner of My Face,"* a group of sixty poems not previously published (dated 1973-74), is from another scheme altogether, a soliloquy in the form of an address to someone never specified, an eloquent private narrative that embraces a considerable montage of the "outside" world. . . . (pp. 681-82)

> Vernon Young, "Poetry Chronicle: First, Second and Third Person—Singular," in The Hudson Review, *Vol. XXXI, No. 4, Winter, 1978-79, pp. 677-92.*

S. E. LEE

Rodney Hall's *Forty Beads on a Hangman's Rope* introduced me to new, intelligent and resourceful talent which I welcomed at the time [see excerpt above]. Since then Hall has become an influential figure whose originality and daring have appealed to contemporary and mostly youngish neo-romantics. Yet it

has been a dangerous influence because what seems so easy on the surface is really most difficult, and certainly is not for an undeveloped, undisciplined or opinionated talent to attempt. Three aspects come to mind: the skilful use of free, flexible, cadenced verse forms; the romantic's preoccupation with me, my and mine and ours (all recurring pronouns); and the associative seemingly logically disconnected flow of imagery and thought of the exploratory mind and imagination revealing themselves at work. Euphonious and delicate lines like these avoid easy slackness because of the trained musical ear and practised hand behind their making:

> I blow my flute
> grief against the mountain
> where my heart
> each note whispering to the distance
> falters with height

And a poem that threatens to disintegrate into violent nonsense—the conglomerate of images crowding in on one another and drawn from natural disaster, colour, architecture, flight and war—may be saved by technique, and the supporting line of thought carried from and on to other units in the sequence it comes from. . . . (p. 454)

Further, the romantic pitfall of wilful self-indulgence is avoided in Hall because, as in Sylvia Plath, poet and persona are intermixed. An epigraph from Baudelaire—"The poet enjoys the incomparable privilege that he can, at will, be either himself or another"—warns that the speaker is both actor and observer. The "I"—who by turns is edgy, unpredictable, saturnine, macabre, outrageous, tortured, pre-occupied with death by violence and occasionally himself menacing—is a creation, not just a confessor. . . . (pp. 454-55)

There are lapses: for example factitious figures such as "the weather in attendance like a well trained pet" or "I dry out on the bleached horizon of your sleeping mind"; and occasionally metaphors are pursued just too relentlessly:

> My letters stutter—dispatches from the last ditch—
> cryptic as communiques
>   hint at
> loss of blood in each campaign
> of this Great War loneliness inside me
> where all my hopes are bogged
> and the trenches we call home
> are running drains of piss and blood.
> Is my message getting through?

Yes, indeed; but then the last three lines show how well Hall can write, with the parenthesis on this occasion not intruding as a mannerism:

> The answer (tidy as a bullet in the brain) In
> Italy you warm yourself
> before a fire of olive branches

All these quotations are from the first and previously unpublished sequence (entitled **"The Owner of My Face"**) in *Selected Poems.* With *Black Bagatelles,* published last year, they prove that it is too early by far to try to be definitive about Hall's final achievement. The bagatelles—fifty short musical pieces about Death, some trifling ("black jokes", the poet calls them), should become a collector's piece. As with the **"Owner of My Face",** they are better read in context and in their bizarrely titled groupings such as **"Seeing Death in the murderous look of an unknown black man whom I admire and deducing from this certain proprietorial privileges".** Yet they can be read separately. (pp. 455-56)

S. E. Lee, ''Too Many?: A Review of Recent Australian Poetry,'' in Southerly, *Vol. 39, No. 4, December, 1979, pp. 432-61.*

John Tranter, in a review of ''The Most Beautiful World,'' in Meanjin, *Vol. 41, No. 3, September, 1982, pp. 399-400.*

JOHN TRANTER

The Most Beautiful World is subtitled 'Fictions and Sermons', and consists of five 'Suites', each of which is made up of seven short unpunctuated dream-like prose scenes ('Fictions'), and one unpunctuated peroration in the style of a sermon ('Sermons'). . . . This book is a development in Rodney Hall's work, and he's a poet who has consistently experimented with new forms.

The prose pieces, with their strange characters and surreal episodes, are intriguing at first. . . . But a growing doubt troubled me as I read on through the thirty-five 'Fictions' in the book. What did they add up to? Where was the overall pattern?

Their erratic and apparently unconnected sequences of events, lack of punctuation, choppy syntax and garbled construction prevent them fully claiming the virtues of 'creative prose', either traditional or modern; and they can hardly be called poems.

They read, in fact, exactly like jotted-down descriptions of dreams. Ordinary dreams, I mean, such as anyone might note down on waking in the morning. And most of us get restless, to put it politely, when other people start telling us about the interesting dream they had last night.

Though the pieces are divided into five groups (only Rodney Hall would call them 'Suites'), there seems little reason for a particular piece to be in one group rather than another, and I can find no clear thematic development or narrative shape to the book. For me, the prose pieces remain simply interesting jottings.

The 'Sermons', in the form of loosely-lined prose poems, are more ambitious, and have a Biblical resonance to them, but I wonder how appropriate—or even how useful—such a style can be in an age of multiple vernaculars. Of all the modes of rhetoric available to the poet today, it seems to me that the vaguely Biblical has the least chance of engaging a contemporary audience's interest. (pp. 399-400)

There are flashes of stylishness ('We live our opulent stooge routines behind the mask of etiquette') and many well-intentioned critiques of modern sins, including genocide and bad ecology, but too often the oracular becomes the orotund. . . . The sermon is a difficult form to bring off—you usually need a captive audience, for a start, and the use of 'we' ('We have come into the land bringing fire and murder . . .') hardly prevents these jeremiads sounding like lists of accusations.

The main problem with the book, to me, is its lack of structure and focus, but this is what the author has turned into a minor virtue. Freed from the need to write orthodox prose, with its sequential narrative and formal restraints, and freed from the complex demands of the kind of poetry that asks to be read closely and admired for its texture and control of language and detail, Rodney Hall can—and does—write whatever he likes. The book is full of strange incidents and weird conjunctions that are interesting mainly because they are unexpected and irrational. His pieces may not be verse, but they certainly are free, and in the climate of earnest labour that weighs down much current writing, perhaps that's not a bad thing. (p. 400)

ELIZABETH WARD

Just Relations is a splendid book; original, readable and profound; and, though inimitably Australian in setting and speech and feeling, it achieves the universality which Yeats was convinced was inseparable from loyalty to one's native place, and is thus anything but parochial.

The ''just relations'' of the title are the 49 inhabitants of Whitey's Fall, a ghostly goldmining town set on a mountain of diggers' rubble in coastal New South Wales. Most of them are extremely aged, having been progressively abandoned by the younger generations, and move blithely or bitterly between past and present, altogether isolated from the modern world. Vaguely aware that ''history is not a chain of things done, but a continuance of things been,'' they have cast off conventional religion in favor of their own ritual of ''Remembering,'' practiced in the bar of the local pub. ''You let go and permit yourself to live again, or *still live,* what happened at some other time and place,'' explains Miss Brinsmead, not the least notable in this village of eccentrics, out of whose foibles and squabbles, dreams and nightmares, Hall fashions a hilarious, yet moving, study in geriatrics.

But the modern world in the shape of the Department of Main Roads, in alliance with the Australian Aesthetic and Historical Resources Commission, threatens the ''accumulated meanings'' of Whitey's Fall. It is proposed to put a highway through the town and to restore and preserve its ramshackle buildings as tourist attractions. The aged inhabitants put aside their petty differences and join forces against the bulldozers and earthmovers. . . . (p. 7)

Just Relations addresses in this way one of the century's hardiest themes: the defense of the country against the city, the Garden against the Machine, tradition against progress. The inhabitants of Whitey's Fall are so identified with the natural world—the mountain, the forest, the wind and the light—that Nature almost becomes another character in the novel. The very idea of progress is caricatured unmercifully throughout: giant motors mutilate the land, tourists and parliamentary yesmen swarm upon it, the old rural Australia is cheapened by the rise of ''trinket shops and them car-park things.'' Without doubt, *Just Relations* draws its inspiration from the great antitechnological animus that has fueled so many modern ideologies, both conservative and revolutionary. Yet, surprisingly, the novel avoids ideological conclusions of its own. Though Hall's sympathies clearly lie with the ancient mountain folk who ''represent'' a society uniquely attuned to the past and to nature's ways, the book as a whole remains non-prescriptive, even dispassionate. ''Everything's your business I hope if you're truly alive to the world,'' says Miss Brinsmead. With the eye of a true Romantic, Rodney Hall ''sees into the life of things,'' but passes no judgment and certainly sanctions no political action.

Technically, the novel defies categorization. It is reminiscent in different ways of both Joyce and Garcia Marquez, but to say this is not to impugn its originality, especially in the context of contemporary Australian literature. It is at once comic fantasy (the dead wander among the living; an elderly lady flies above the treetops) and tragedy (a small boy hidden in a secret room blows himself up with gelignite). It is that rare thing, a successful novel of ideas, but also a book abounding with memorable characters, thanks in no small part to Hall's ear for rural Australian speech. (The American edition may even require a glossary.) It spins out one of the most gripping plots I have encountered in a long while, but at the same time it is a lyric performance which reveals on every page Rodney Hall's background as a poet.

The novel's style is in fact its strength. The writing is amazingly strong and inventive, rarely indulging in the poetic for its own sake. At its best, lyrical observation is sharpened by a distinctive intelligence. . . . (pp. 7, 14)

There are faults, of course. The novel is probably too long; a few chapters drag and flounder in pointless evocation of detail; occasionally one wishes for relief from the relentless exuberance of language and over-use of adjectives. Like the lush forest growth on its own symbolic mountain, *Just Relations* could do with some pruning. But these are relatively minor criticisms, not intended to detract from the real magnitude of Rodney Hall's achievement. (p. 14)

> *Elizabeth Ward, "Wheelchairs vs. Bulldozers in Australia," in* Book World—The Washington Post, *February 13, 1983, pp. 7, 14.*

FRANCES TALIAFERRO

Whitey's Fall [the setting of *Just Relations*] is a tiny town in New South Wales. Perched halfway up a mountainside, the little settlement was founded in the last century by the fossickers who prospected the mountain for gold. Now the entire population of the town—forty-nine—fits handily into the barroom at the Mountain Hotel, the "religious centre," where the sacred mysteries of Remembering are observed over pots of beer. Past and present, reality and fantasy, can hardly be distinguished in Whitey's Fall, for here at the edge of the bush, "History is not a chain of things done, but a continuance of things been." . . .

What do people *do* in this place so small and dull and boonified that a cow passing by is an event? Well, they knit, they garden among the mushrooms and passion fruit, they drink their beer in silence at the Mountain Hotel. They age.

Almost everyone in Whitey's Fall is very old. If you don't know them, these "ancient ugly folk" have a frightening look: they are "figures of arthritic gnomes and of huge dislocated ruins," "tough flap-eared hairy-nosed coarse-skinned grannies" who knit and wheeze the days away. But Whitey's Fall is crammed with secrets. If you could hear their thoughts ticking, you'd know that these ancients enjoy all the foolishness and longing of the middle-aged or the adolescent. "Here I am at ninety year," says Uncle Arthur Swan, "and no more sense than I had at twenty."

Miss Bertha McAloon, eighty-one last birthday, goes for a swim in the yellow water of the dam, floats on her back, and dreams of boys. . . .

It takes the coming of strangers to disturb the town's cryptic equilibrium. One of them is an enemy: Senator Halloran, spokesman of the Aesthetic and Historical Resources Commission, the bureaucratic world beyond the Brinsmeads' general store and Mr. McTaggart's garden. In buttery tones, the senator describes the Regional Development Scheme: a lovely highway, delightful petrol stations, a quaint antique Devonshire

tea shop to put Whitey's Fall on the map. Won't it be grand? Progress! Prosperity!

Whitey's Fall is not amused. "Down with the amenities! Down with the government! Walk gently on the land!" the ancients cry, and the battle lines are drawn. For the bulldozers have turned up gold and the road builders know that the little town sits on a mountain of pure gold. If Regional Development arrives, the forces of greedy civilization will be unleashed. Miss Felicia Brinsmead's consultants, Julius Caesar and George Santayana, have plenty of advice on the subject ("Now listen here Miss Felicia, said George Santayana, those who cannot remember the past are condemned to repeat it.") Progress must be stopped at all costs. (p. 74)

Alas, their noble violence ends in negotiation: a Regional Scheme committee meeting from which only Sebastian Brinsmead emerges alive. The rest have died of boredom and "protocolitis." . . . [Uncle Arthur] leads his people in a peaceful exodus, turning round only to curse Gomorrah: "Them bastards back there . . . they'd pull down Westminster Abbey to find the Holy Ghost." Never mind; Uncle's faithful remnant will live and flourish in a New Jerusalem not far away.

Such a brief summary oversimplifies this slow-moving, dreamy, proliferous novel. Imagine a combination of *Under Milk Wood* and Toni Morrison's *Song of Solomon:* a good snoop into the neighbors' cupboards, some pawky fantasies and melodramatic subplots, some scenes of geriatric comedy, some full-scale set pieces, and a few sentimental meditations on the nature of love and time. The long-winded charm of *Just Relations* springs from its leisurely playfulness, and from the fact that it is never far from the surprising edges of mild surrealism.

It is no neat topiary, clipped to preserve form and unity. It is a novel of sprigs and tendrils, bushy excrescences with wild thyme and the gadding vine o'ergrown. Hardly a wink goes unnoticed in this talky book; the reader longs to prune, to toss out a set piece or a subplot here, an interior monologue there. Beneath all the overgrowth, however, is a well-made, poetic novel. *Just Relations* is not for the impatient or the dyspeptic, but any reader who takes it at its own speed will discover its cheerful virtues. (pp. 74-5)

> *Frances Taliaferro, in a review of "Just Relations," in* Harper's, *Vol. 266, No. 1594, March, 1983, pp. 74-5.*

JAMES TULIP

Rodney Hall must have begun his widely acclaimed novel *Just Relations* in the mid-1970s. It was a time for him, arguably, of profound disaffection with Australian society. The sacking of Prime Minister Whitlam carried for Hall some radical message of avarice operating through the guise of politics. It is a message that lies deep inside the almost allegorical structure of *Just Relations*. An old mountain of gold (seemingly worked out by the nineteenth-century rush for riches) is uncovered again by a Canberra-inspired move to push a road through Whitey's Fall, a forgotten township whose few inhabitants are sinking into age and oblivion. Hall sides with the instinctive resistance of the townsfolk to "progress" and views the resulting goldrush as a universal sign of worldwide self-destructive greed.

It is a significant stand for someone of radical and leftish persuasion and expresses the deep feeling of hostility and alienation from society that those who supported Labor in Whitlam's coming to power experienced at their rejection by the Australian people. In many ways it represents a retreat from idealism and from hope for social change through the political process. If politics is only a toy of money, and if when challenged avarice shows its real face and power, then the lot of the people, including the intelligentsia, is the lot of the people of Whitey's Fall, given over to "remembering" and dying and finding what power they have left in their relations with one another and with a world they want to preserve.

But to enlarge on the allegory in this way is to portray *Just Relations* as other than it actually is. For instead of being a *cri de coeur* it is a comedy of massively sustained proportions. The climax comes when the townsfolk block the building of the road. A mock (though seriously written) heroic battle takes place between the road builders and the inhabitants, and at the all-important consultative committee the key man of whom the locals had despaired votes "No". The battle is won even though the war (now gold is re-discovered) is lost.

Hall can hardly avoid patronizing the concerns and the characters which Whitey's Fall offers him. Yet something in his own temperament and self-dramatizing personality permits him to share with the people their eccentricity as if it were something universal. They are all, seemingly, "just relations", and the author becomes a member of the family. Now how this happens is a measure of his achievement as a writer. The book curiously has an absence of authorial irony and omniscience. There is, instead, a process of almost epical dramatization, a kind of endless conversation going on that absorbs the narration into itself. A half-conversing, half-narrating voice builds up in the novel which establishes an artistic order of "just relations".

I dare not begin to comment on the detail of the book. It is the fictional equivalent of a doctoral dissertation in sociology on small-town Australia, and will require many readings (and many dissertations) to unravel it. There is a risk, too, that Hall has run in asking his parochial world to bear so much bulk and weight of analysis. Do the people in themselves matter quite so much? Is there any affective centre of interest?

Perhaps we see it best in the Englishwoman Vivien who inherits an old house in Whitey's Fall and finds herself stumbling into and through a world of caricatures who slowly become for her a world of characters. She has to come to terms with "remembering", the town religion. It is a lesson the novel is painfully teaching itself and us: the importance of the past, the reality of aging, the need for roots, an acceptance of nature, human humility and a suspicion of progress (when it means power given away to others seeking power). Hall follows Vivien through her transformation into love, even when it means love for poverty. It is the price he sees that has to be paid for a lost ideal—or lost idolatry—as an Australian at this time. (pp. 117-18)

James Tulip, "Poets & Their Novels," in Southerly, *Vol. 43, No. 1, March, 1983, pp. 113-18.*

BENJAMIN DE MOTT

Just Relations tells several linked stories, each of which touches fantasy before it's done. The chief story concerns a conflict between the residents of Whitey's Fall, an Australian mining town in decline (population down from 2,000 to 49), and their governors in the nation's capital. Officialdom, full of ambition for Whitey's Fall, is intent on refurbishing the town and putting it on the tourist map. . . .

Another story focuses on the intense rivalry of three males for the hand of an attractive, opera-singing, 34-year-old visitor from England named Vivien; two of the rivals are teen-agers, and the third is a grandfather in his 92d year. We also follow the misadventures of Mercy Ping, owner of Alice, an ailing cow, and wife of an unsympathetic Chinese machinist-welder; Mercy is killed in an auto accident while seeking medical aid for her beast. And the climax of *Just Relations* involves the secret of a seam of gold whose location may be known to a pair of Whitey's Fall elders; a town lad named Billy Swan, who thinks he's learned the secret, undertakes to dynamite the treasure and instead blows up a 12-year-old boy, setting in train a massive gold rush that threatens to destroy the world's systems of finance. . . .

The book's major theme—progress is hateful—is conventional, and the mining town itself fairly easy to imagine. But the author jibes from one literary mode to another—from satire to hard-edged realism to fantasy, from nature lyricism to historical meditation to black comedy—in a fashion that requires agility of the reader. And his fanciful prose tends to obscure key events of the tale in the "difficult" manner made familiar by generations of modernists.

Australian reviewers hailed *Just Relations* for its author's "exuberant flamboyance," "lusty vigorous" writing and "joy of words"—and they too have a point. Rodney Hall's canvas is densely populated, filled with lively, rough-speaking codgers and young uns, whimsical inventions (a religion called Remembering, for instance, the services for which are conducted in a bar), lusty mistresses, shouting parent-child confrontations and old-timey Joycean sentences that occasionally stream on for unpunctuated pages at a stretch. . . . (p. 7)

Although the energy is impressive, as is the determination to break out of the cage of understatement wherein much contemporary prose is locked, there are some problems. The severest of them, to my mind, is the author's overeagerness to direct our attention away from the world of objects and feelings to his own amused omnipotence as a giver and taker of life. One sign of the eagerness is the abrupt doing in of characters according to authorial convenience. Another sign is the compulsion to animate the inanimate: herbs in the garden, trees in the woods, dresses on racks, canned goods on shelves all murmur or gossip in these pages, invariably drawing fresh attention to the Creative Writer. ("Who are you?" grunts a feelingful side of bacon when the attractive operatic Vivien first arrives at the town's general store.)

Still another sign is Mr. Hall's reluctance to allow low-intensity human action any space in his tale. Heads that "shriek with memory" and "breath hissing in a flared nose" are expected during, say, a father-son fistfight, but one also expects a little easing up after the scrap, and that's not permitted in *Just Relations*. The fist-fighting father in bed with his wife broods about killing her, and outdoors "flowers explode . . . into nothing." Speaking of flowers, Mr. Hall's revving-up rage obliges him to deny tranquillity even to harmless old gents watering their gardens. . . .

Something obsessive as well as funny here—and it became counterproductive for me well before the end. Instead of heightening appreciation of the humming, buzzing vitality of the universe, it woke suspicion that the novelist somehow doubted whether, without his hyping power, anything interesting actually breathes out there. The project of *Just Relations*—the attempt to reinvigorate the language of fiction—is, to repeat, admirable, and I respect both the author's virtuosity and his wit. But I'm afraid that in addressing his own rich materials, Mr. Hall makes one extremely serious mistake: He condescends. (p. 17)

Benjamin de Mott, "Hijinks Down Under," in The New York Times Book Review, *March 13, 1983,* pp. 7, 17.

MICHIKO KAKUTANI

On Boxing Day in the year 1898, three children of Daniel and Mary Murphy were found brutally murdered in the Australian countryside . . .

[Using] facts from an actual murder case as a springboard for his imagination, Rodney Hall, an Australian poet and novelist, has constructed a richly textured tale that stands at once as an absorbing detective story and as a Faulknerian parable about innocence and guilt, passion and betrayal. Like *The Sound and the Fury*, Mr. Hall's novel [*Captivity Captive*] cuts back and forth in time to chronicle several decades of familial love and hate, and like *The Sound and the Fury,* it uses the decline and dissolution of a single family to underscore the moral disorder of an entire community—in this case, colonial Australia rather than our own post-Reconstruction South.

On first reading, the Murphy clan in the ill-named *Captivity Captive* may seem overly reminiscent of the Compsons. . . .

What saves *Captivity Captive* from being merely derivative is Mr. Hall's intimate knowledge of the Australian land, which becomes less a simple backdrop for his story than a sort of catalyst for good and evil; and his ability to invest the Murphys with a vitality and felt emotion that ultimately set them apart from their famous predecessors, and give them a life of their own.

At 6 feet 10 inches, Daniel Murphy is a giant of a man, a brutal father, who thinks nothing of beating his children, and even chains one of his sons to his bed when he misbehaves. An immigrant's son, he has wrested his farm (somewhat heavy-handedly named Paradise) from the harsh Australian bush, and he sees the world beyond as "filled with enemies: trees, men, women, kangaroos." . . .

To the Murphys, Paradise is a self-sufficient world, but in its autonomy, its arrogant disdain of the ordinary, there is also danger—and stifled passions that will ultimately lead to the murder of Michael, Norah and Ellen. In his discursive account of the events before and after that event, Pat [another child in the family] gives us carefully shaded portraits of his parents, his siblings, and their neighbors, and in doing so, gives us a selection of murder suspects.

Did Daniel Murphy's willful need to control his children's lives lead him to kill those who posed the greatest threat to his authority?

Did Billy McNeil, the husband of another Murphy daughter, Polly, have a motive for doing away with members of his new family? Why did he volunteer to search for the missing siblings, and how was he able to locate their bodies so quickly?

Did Barney Barnett, Ellen's former fiancé, want to get even with the Murphys for having appropriated some of his own family's land? Is his deathbed confession to be taken as the truth—or merely a last-minute attempt to win fame and notoriety?

Could Willie, the brain-damaged brother, have suddenly turned violent, his bitterness at being crippled by his father turning, unconsciously, to resentment of his healthy siblings?

And what about the narrator, Pat? What role did his secret lust for Norah play in the tragic events that transpired so many years ago?

The actual solution to the murders is far more complicated—and disturbing—than most readers could imagine; and the gradual emergence of the truth is fluently orchestrated by Mr. Hall. Indeed, he uses the process of revelation as a means of exposing the infinitely complex relationships that exist within the Murphy clan; and on a grander scale, of delineating Australia's evolving relationship to the outside world. Some of the larger, mythic parallels seem a bit forced: we are asked, for instance, to see the Murphys' loss of innocence as a metaphor for both the colonists' destruction of aborigine culture and their eventual participation in World War I. Yet as in his previous book, the well-received novel *Just Relations,* Mr. Hall succeeds in dazzling us with his storytelling powers, planting in our minds images that burn with the fierce power of bad dreams.

Michiko Kakutani, in a review of "Captivity Captive," in The New York Times, *January 20, 1988, p. 21.*

RICHARD EDER

A microscope turns our blood corpuscles into tropical ferns, our fingerprints into mountain ranges, our hairs into stalactites. Even a simple magnifying glass tells us that we are giants; under a high-powered electronic instrument, we become galaxies.

Rodney Hall's *Captivity Captive* is just such an instrument. In an outback settlement in Australia's New South Wales, he has taken a family and its passions, and enlarged them. His Murphys are enormous. Daniel Murphy, the patriarch, is 6 feet 10; his wife is only two inches shorter, and they have 10 children.

Everything else about the family is out-sized: its violence, its labors, its picnics, its love and hatred; and above all, the bonding and unbonding and the lurching shifts of power that make the interior of any family a tectonic convulsion.

But Hall's purpose, in a book built around an incident of incest and triple murder, is not really to provide the epic story that all this implies. (It does sound rather like the embossed cover of a bodice-ripper.)

His purpose is to change our lenses. He tells a little story big. He suggests that the passions of any family can only be understood under magnification, and that our domestic aches, voids and horrors are the work of giants inside. . . .

On the day after Christmas, three bodies were discovered in a field near the Murphy land. They were those of three of the children: Norah, 27, Ellen, 18, and Michael, 29. All three were bound; the women had been clubbed to death and appeared to have been raped; Michael had been shot as well as clubbed.

No perpetrator was ever found. The horror, augmented by the mystery, made a national scandal and later a local legend. It also shattered the self-contained world of the Murphys, whose cohesiveness, pride and violent energy had made them something of a buccaneer clan in the region. . . .

Patrick, short and slight among his huge brothers, lettered and reflective amid the family's tumultuous instinctiveness, was signaled out from childhood as the scribe. . . .

Now, with the family dying out, he tells what he knows. His narrative is cryptic and devious. By turns, it is a flood of rhetoric and a suspiciously parched trickle. It is told painfully, skipping about in time, approaching revelation, turning away and returning. It can be hard to make out and sometimes, in its foggy vehemence, hard to put up with. Hall has wedded the obduracy and pain of his story to the style in which it is told. We get no easy ride.

At the end, we learn what happened in the bloody field, or most of it. It is a terrible story, a family story, and finally as much of a mystery as before it was told.

Because the point of the narrative and of the book is not the family's deaths but the family's life. A volcano erupted that night; a volcano that lets us see for a moment the turmoil that churns beneath the countryside.

Patrick—finally, no detached witness but part of the turmoil—wrestles with the mysteries of his family's existence. There is the father's violence, capable of smashing one son's ribs and of chaining another, howling, to his bed. It is a violence indistinguishable from the will to create, to form the inert clay, to subdue the harsh farmland, to make a family different from any other. It is a violence indistinguishable from love.

And love, in the Murphy family, is violence, or a whole array of differing violences. It is the parents' will both to dominate the children and to resist them; it is the children's will to resist their parents—and each other—and to dominate them.

The Murphys are monsters, in a sense, but enlarged only to demonstrate the minute motions of creation and destruction inherent in the very essence of what a family is. Life is made, fought and yielded by monstrous means that we try not to recognize, the author is saying. In a seemingly arbitrary aside, he links the massacre of the Murphy children with the family massacre that would take place throughout Europe a few years later; World War I, that is.

The switch is abrupt, unprepared and apparently hasty. Hall's novel is told in a state of feverishness. The writing is often brilliant; there are descriptions of the bitter and beautiful landscape, and of the shocking burden of physical labor that are unforgettable.

There are also times when the knottiness, the sheer recalcitrance of the narration are excessive. Hall burns to make us see, and we do see; and from time to time, our eyes fill with smoke from his unruly fire.

> *Richard Eder, "Giants Under the Skin," in* Los Angeles Times Book Review, *January 24, 1988, p. 3.*

JOYCE REISER KORNBLATT

The Murphys, all 12 of them, live on a farm called Paradise, a befouled nest in the Australian bush "that Pa's father first broke into, a forest so thick you worked in it by intuition." In *Captivity Captive,* the accomplished Australian novelist Rodney Hall summons us into another kind of labyrinth—into a story that is as grim and harrowing and beautiful as the wilderness it evokes, a raw spiritual landscape that brings to mind Flannery O'Connor and William Faulkner. This is a book that makes demands on the reader's soul.

"We were the tribe of the savage Paradise," the narrator, Patrick Murphy, tells us. One of the surviving siblings, he is 80 now, "beyond that age when a man's mind occasionally tumbles headlong down shafts of memory, glimpsing some small moment among humble objects and feeling his heart contract with grief for a life he once led: I have reached a point where this is my normal condition." That he should feel anything like nostalgia for his youth is one of the perversities on which this narrative insists. "I suppose we loved one another," Patrick decides in the midst of this horrific tale of domestic violence, of 10 children relentlessly abused by their father and by one another. We are speaking here of insults, beatings, crushed bones, a bleeding child chained all night to his parents' bed. We are speaking of a man and a woman who, their son concludes, "must be victims of an unwanted, unnatural fertility, hating us for coming."

Captivity Captive is a brilliant psychological portrait of family pathology in its most extreme form. . . .

But to read this book simply as an eloquently rendered case study is to do both author and reader a disservice. Rodney Hall is making a myth here. He is a visionary, and myth will not be contained in the intellectual categories we invent to shield ourselves from its transforming power. One could argue that Mr. Hall's symbols—a corrupted Eden, innocence butchered, ritual slaughter that precedes actual murder, memory as the only atonement God allows—are, in fact, pressed upon us too overtly by a narrator (and writer) who is more conscious of this dimension of his story than might be wise. But how rich such a consciousness is, how its rare courage stuns us, how hungry we are for the voices that carry its suffered wisdom. For in exploring the myth of his tormented family, the murders of three of his siblings and the terrible meaning of those murders, Patrick Murphy enters the realm of mystery: "The power of what was being played out in this tragedy went so far beyond me," he says, "that I had acted as a mere instrument in the conflict without waking up to the fact that I was never my own master in any sense."

In Patrick the shadow worlds of instinct and history and foretold doom rise up, and he acknowledges their claim on his character. If this novel is a confession, it is a collective one, with the narrator ceding his own significance, his voice striving to become that ancient chorus Sophocles understood, and Shakespeare. Regrettably, there are places in *Captivity Captive* where the mythic energy slackens, the narrative takes on a programmatic quality or struggles too hard to transcend the facts of its plot. But how wonderful it is to witness a contemporary writer taking on the shaman's ambition.

Rodney Hall is most compelling when he trusts his material to yield up its larger meanings on its own. . . .

Captivity Captive is a wise novel, and a frightening one, and a brave one too. Rodney Hall might have lost his nerve as his story's power grew, but he has the strength to confront his own imagination, to enter that wilderness and work in it by intuition. What emerges is that sullied paradise in which we all reside, which resides within. Here only language redeems—and in our capacity to receive the tormented narrator's tale, Rodney Hall offers us too the possibility of grace.

> *Joyce Reiser Kornblatt, "Lost in Each Other Just That Once," in* The New York Times Book Review, *February 14, 1988, p. 15.*

ANNE JANETTE JOHNSON

The true-life murder on which Rodney Hall's new novel [*Captivity Captive*] is based is gruesome even by our jaded modern standards. In 1898, a brother and two sisters—all young adults—were bludgeoned without any sign of struggle as they returned from a dance in rural Australia. The women were bound and raped, the man shot in the head and beaten. Even their horse was killed.

The unsolved case, still Australia's most bizarre murder mystery, has been the subject of several recent non-fiction books in that country.

From such a grisly scenario Hall crafts his novel, a first-person account of the deadly events by a surviving brother.

The tale as it unfolds becomes not only a riveting whodunit with the requisite twist at the end, but also an engrossing portrait of a family as savage as the Australian land they struggle to farm. . . .

Captivity Captive presents the relatively rare effort to elevate a murder mystery into the realm of great literature. Its prose reveals a careful artist with more than a touch of the poet.

For instance, one chapter begins:

The disgraceful scene in the illegal bar at the Brian Boru Hotel erupted out of the bare branches of a dream plum tree suddenly flowering such multitudes of white anger the dangerous bees worked crazily to stuff their trouser pockets full of pollen before it all flew away in a final explosion of deathly perfume.

The reader who likes mystery prose that is as cut-and-dried as the standard bullet-ridden corpse may falter on such overblown eloquence as this. But the literary maverick who sneers at pulp fiction will find *Captivity Captive* a delightfully poetic composition.

Australia, that final earthly frontier, is not a central element of this tale. Patrick's life is painfully insular, his story one of family rather than region. As such, however, *Captivity Captive* excites the senses in the way that fine psychological drama is wont to do.

Hall has jumped the boundary between genre fiction and high literature, admirably satisfying both sets of standards.

The book is a fine piece of work, and a horrible multiple murder may well have found its elusive solution.

Anne Janette Johnson, "Poetic Style Lifts Mystery to Realm of Art," in Detroit Free Press, Sec. J, March 13, 1988, p. 9.

(Anthony Walter) Patrick Hamilton

1904-1962

English dramatist, novelist, and scriptwriter.

Best known during his lifetime for his suspenseful dramas *Rope* and *Gaslight: A Victorian Thriller,* Hamilton was also the author of numerous tragicomic novels in which he sympathetically examined the lives of alcoholics, criminals, prostitutes, and young people in and around London between the two World Wars. Although Hamilton often made use of potentially maudlin situations and sensational subject matter, critics generally agree that his work is superior to that of most popular fiction writers because of his precise settings and characterizations, his intricate use of dialogue, and his wry, satirical approach to human existence. John Russell Taylor praised Hamilton's "way of playing tragedy as though it is farce: hearts are broken and lives wrecked as we roll round, helpless with mirth."

During the early 1920s, Hamilton worked as an actor and assistant stage manager for two touring productions of English playwright Sutton Vane. The financial success of Vane's drama *Outward Bound* allowed him to support Hamilton's early writing career. Although he began his career as a novelist, Hamilton's first notable literary achievement came with his short drama *Rope* (1929), a thriller about two Oxford undergraduate students who murder a fellow pupil for excitement and danger. Several critics praised Hamilton's ability to manipulate situations of dramatic tension and irony, as in one scene in which the youths entertain the murdered boy's father while sitting atop a trunk containing his son's corpse. Although he wrote several popular dramas during the 1930s, including *The Procurator of Judea* (1930) and *John Brown's Body* (1931), Hamilton did not surpass the international acclaim of *Rope* until the 1938 debut of *Gaslight.* In this melodramatic thriller, a man tries to drive his wife insane and have her committed to an institution so that he may search for precious rubies that he believes are hidden in her house. His wife, however, discovers that he murdered the original owner of the house for refusing to disclose the location of the gems. The play, which ran for more than three years on Broadway under the title *Angel Street: A Victorian Thriller* and was also adapted into a popular film, was commended for its suspenseful development of a simple plot and its use of such practical theatrical devices as a single setting, a limited cast of characters, and a gas lamp that illuminates the motions of the murderer. Although Hamilton gained recognition for such radio dramas as *To the Public Danger* (1939) and *Caller Anonymous* (1952), his later plays, including *The Duke in Darkness* (1942), *The Governess* (1946), and *The Man Upstairs* (1953), attained only moderate success.

Hamilton's earliest novels, *Monday Morning* (1925) and *Craven House* (1926), are social comedies set in London boardinghouses. These books were frequently compared to the works of Charles Dickens for their lightly satirical, optimistic portrayals of eccentric characters. A darker, more sardonic style characterizes Hamilton's next novel, *Twopence Coloured* (1928). "[Terse] with a certain dry quality that allows no romanticizing," according to one reviewer, this book reflects Hamilton's experience in London's theatrical community through its depiction of a young girl who attempts to further her acting career by offering sexual favors to stage managers. Although faulted

Raymond Mander & Joe Mitchenson Theatre Collection, London

for its pessimistic conclusion, *Twopence Coloured* elicited positive reviews for Hamilton's accurate rendering of English society and his compassionate yet unsentimentalized approach.

In *The Midnight Bell: A Love Story* (1929), *The Siege of Pleasure* (1932), and *The Plains of Cement* (1934), a triad of tragicomic novels later collected as *Twenty Thousand Streets under the Sky: A London Trilogy* (1935), Hamilton explores the dreams and frustrations of several characters associated with The Midnight Bell, a London pub. *The Midnight Bell* is the story of Bob, a young waiter at the tavern, whose alternately pathetic and farcical efforts to help Jenny Maple, a beguiling young prostitute, lead to disappointment and rejection when he unwittingly falls in love with her. Praised for its blend of pathos and comedy and for its memorable portrayals, *The Midnight Bell* established Hamilton's early literary reputation as a realist who focuses on the working classes. In *The Siege of Pleasure,* Hamilton shifts back in time to depict Jenny's victimization as a youth by exploitative employers. He compassionately yet objectively delineates the period in Jenny's life when, as she says, she "took the wrong turning . . . all through a glass of port." *The Plains of Cement,* the best-regarded installment of the trilogy, features Ella, a barmaid at The Midnight Bell. Ella's unrequited love for Bob, the protagonist of the first novel in the series, is tested when she is approached by a tyrannical but wealthy elderly suitor. Although she maintains her freedom by rejecting his proposal of marriage at the novel's conclusion, Ella's alternative prospects fade, and she is forced to continue in her unsatisfying position as a barmaid. Iris Barry commented: "Even Wodehouse has not unveiled, in his different way, more awful depths of life-like vacuity."

Hamilton's next novel, *Impromptu in Moribundia* (1939), is a fantasy informed by his study of left-wing politics and Marxism. Set on a planet where people converse by means of advertising slogans encapsulated in balloons above their heads, this novel, which was intended as a satire of post-World War I Britain, did not achieve the acclaim of Hamilton's earlier works. Many critics agree that *Hangover Square; or, The Man with Two Minds: A Story of Darkest Earl's Court in the Year 1939* (1941) is Hamilton's most refined and mature treatment of the theme of victim turned victimizer. The protagonist of this novel, possessed by two personalities, one loving and one hateful, falls in love with a beautiful but deceitful young prostitute who drives him to commit murder and then suicide. Although the book initially drew mixed reviews, critics have more recently praised Hamilton's wry, compassionate approach to his potentially sensational subject matter. Several commentators have noted further refinement in Hamilton's next novel, *The Slaves of Solitude* (1947), in which a publisher's reader prompts a domestic war between a group of isolated individuals in a shabby London boardinghouse through her casual acquaintance with an alcoholic American soldier and a hostile German girl. J. B. Priestley praised both *Hangover Square* and *The Slaves of Solitude* as among "the minor masterpieces of English fiction."

During the 1950s, Hamilton wrote three in an intended series of four novels examining the criminal mentality of a character named Ernest Ralph Gorse. These works include *The West Pier* (1951), in which Gorse reveals his immorality as a youth through acts of petty theft and manipulation; *Mr. Stimpson and Mr. Gorse* (1953), in which he ruins a potential love affair more for personal satisfaction than financial gain; and *Unknown Assailant* (1955), in which he resorts to vicious opportunism to cheat a family out of their money. Hamilton died before the fourth Gorse volume was completed. While many reviewers faulted the character's obscure motivations and his inability to elicit reader sympathy, Bill Greenwell deemed Gorse "a masterly creation," and John Russell Taylor declared that he is "the ideal centre-piece for [Hamilton's] darkly hilarious dissection of middle-class England between the wars."

(See also *Contemporary Authors*, Vol. 113 [obituary] and *Dictionary of Literary Biography*, Vol. 10.)

KATHARINE TYNAN

One turns with a sense of refreshment to the jolly rag of *Monday Morning*. It is a book for a light mood. Youth is certainly at the helm in Mr. Hamilton's book, with a hero who is always gay, often amusing and always ridiculous. [The heroine] Diana is all this, only more so. In spite of their absurdity the book is highly exhilarating. They are refreshingly cheerful and optimistic young people to meet with in a pessimistic world. One can forget in their absurd company that there has been a war, that there is unemployment and a deferred coal strike.... Mr. Hamilton has the gift of recalling to his readers their own sensations—sea-sickness for example—and it is impossible not to chuckle over these light-hearted pages. But are the modern maid and youth quite so inept as is Mr. Hamilton's portrayal of them?

> *Katharine Tynan, in a review of "Monday Morning," in* The Bookman, *London, Vol. LXVIII, No. 408, September, 1925, p. 300.*

THE BOOKMAN, LONDON

The author of *Monday Morning* has succeeded in a very difficult task. He has allowed a very humorous, sensitive and vivid imagination to play upon the inmates and fortunes of a London boarding-house, and, in the sequel [*Craven House*], has expressed his vision in a very considerable novel. Fun, character, youth, in a suburban setting with the ample canvas and grotesque touches of a Dickens are the dominant merits of *Craven House*. There is a simple love story, told with fine feeling, which only ends when Craven House itself is no more and long-suffering Elsie Nixon joins Master Wildman at the gate. A perfect study, complete, ironical and hugely diverting, of a modern "vamp," Miss Cotterill, with flesh-coloured stockings, a warm, rosy mouth, a little dog and a polo-playing uncle.... [Elsie's mother], Mrs. Nixon, shakes the foundations of the boarding-house in which she, and others well worth meeting, had lived for three guineas a week for fifteen years. It is a delight to read the book and see how she did it. *Craven House* is one of those rare books one re-reads and remembers.

> *A review of "Craven House," in* The Bookman, *London, Vol. LXXI, No. 423, December, 1926, p. 195.*

NEW YORK HERALD TRIBUNE BOOKS

Shortly before midnight, several years ago, a pretty but unusually foolish girl, for her age (which was nineteen)—"had come to the decision that she intended . . . to Go on the Stage." Of course, "you were not likely to Succeed upon the Stage unless you Carried On with the Manager." This, Mr. Hamilton assures us [in *Twopence Colored*], was only the first of Jackie Mortimer's many subsequent misinterpretations. His story of a young girl who throws herself against the hardened bosom of the theatrical world, is terse with a certain dry quality that allows no romanticizing.

There is a slow dreariness to Jackie's struggle—a valiant, unglamorous battle. Extremely objective is the author, and smiling quietly. He is laughing with his Capitals, tolerant of human foibles, amused and critically aware, with a bubbling sense of the ridiculousness in important and serious things. Yet however he mocks, he is whimsical....

Mr. Hamilton makes us enjoy with him delicious incongruities and imbues with a delicate charm the love of Jackie and Richard. But when he drops his Capitals, he may become very grave. And in the more thoughtful moments, he is somewhat less successful. Eager to emphasize the tedium of rehearsals instead of the excitement of performances, Mr. Hamilton has kept us at them rather too long for the balance of the whole. The excessive similarity of working days casts into shadow both the scintillating personality of the author and the colors of his characters. And when he puts forth Jackie's reflections on the life around her, especially in the latter portion of the book, the reactions are his rather than hers—a trifle too solemn for a girl who is essentially light. But in the vein of light irony and kindly ridicule, Mr. Hamilton is delightful.

A review of "Twopence Colored," in New York
Herald Tribune Books, *October 7, 1928, p. 12.*

THE TIMES LITERARY SUPPLEMENT

[*The Midnight Bell*] is the story, with pathetic, humorous and
sentimental elaborations, of the love of a romantic young barman for a prostitute. Mr. Patrick Hamilton does not make the
mistake of making Jenny, the prostitute, consciously heartless
or insincere. She is not, for instance, as fundamentally callous
as Michael Fane's Lily in *Sinister Street*, but she has all Lily's
apathy and disregard for anything that does not touch her material comfort.... Instead of a young man from Oxford there
is a young man behind a bar, but in both of them is the same
romantic urge, the same passionate belief that the very fact of
loving can bestow on the loved person all those graces of mind,
spirit and body that are demanded by the nature of their own
idealism—and both met the same shattering disillusionment.
Bob, at the beginning of the book, is a cheerful, pleasant young
man with aspirations towards culture.... His first meeting
with Jenny, however, cuts his whole background away from
him on the instant—no longer is he a young barman with a
taste for books and £80 in the bank; he is a lover starting on
a perilous and magnificent enterprise, a sleeper who has awoken
in a land indescribably different from the prosaic one he had
known before. His relationship with Jenny is a tormenting
succession of short jerks forward to the realization of an impossible happiness and long pauses in which all the ground
precariously won is lost. As Jenny adds spiritual failure to
spiritual failure, so does Bob's own character begin to dete-
riorate, and it is lucky for him that a final betrayal is comprehensive enough to shake him out of a degrading slavery.

Mr. Hamilton is indulgently detached from the attitude struck
by the romantic Bob, but his sympathy, if sometimes amused,
is never less than kindly. *The Midnight Bell* is a generous,
warm-hearted book; and, in describing the nightly *clientèle* of
the saloon bar, Mr. Hamilton gives the reader some comic
relief which would almost be strong enough to carry the book
had the story of Bob's sentimental education sunk to the bottom
of that morass of false pathos which is never far away from
novels that deal with the lives and loves of women of the streets,
but which Mr. Hamilton deftly avoids.

A review of "The Midnight Bell," in The Times
Literary Supplement, *No. 1433, July 18, 1929, p.
574.*

LYN LL. IRVINE

Possibly some of the readers of Mr. Hamilton's new novel *The
Midnight Bell* will be ready to swear that they read it merely
for the story. They delude themselves, and if they like *The
Midnight Bell* they are better judges of good prose than they
know.... No traces of admiration for James Joyce or D. H.
Lawrence or Marcel Proust are likely to crop up in this novel.
Nor will the relationships of Bob and Ella or anyone else prove
very complicated.... Business, as it happens, has thrown Bob
and Ella together—Ella being the barmaid and Bob the waiter
at "The Midnight Bell." Bob is the sort of young man whose
hair is always well-brushed, and who merits the slightly caustic
affection of nice barmaids. And until Jenny enters his life he
has £80 in the bank. Jenny is a prostitute, twenty-one and
pretty, ignorant but infinitely cunning, an expert in man-and-
money lore. Her favourite victims are good, decent citizens
who are so moved by her youth and tragedy that they pay to

give her holidays from her prostitution. According to Mr. Hamilton, prostitution, like playing the bagpipes, is as richly rewarded for the breach as for the observance. (And, unlike the
bagpipes, it can simulate a breach.) Bob falls desperately in
love with Jenny, and complete disillusionment descends only
when the last of the £80 has gone. The trouble about Jenny as
a central character is that she has nothing to say—and even so
her vocabulary can scarcely stand the strain. She is in this way
far more convincing than, for instance, Caliban, grunting out
some of the best lines in *The Tempest*. Conviction, however,
is dearly bought. Jenny is what Harriette Wilson would call
"a dead bore"—and so would Caliban have been, had Shakespeare been a realist. (pp. 567-68)

*Lyn Ll. Irvine, in a review of "The Midnight Bell,"
in* The Nation and the Athenaeum, *Vol. XLV, No.
17, July 27, 1929, pp. 567-68.*

THE NEW YORK TIMES BOOK REVIEW

At the age of 26, Patrick Hamilton is already a veteran novelist.
This book, *The Midnight Bell,* is the fourth to be credited to
his pen. The word credit is advisedly used—Mr. Hamilton's
smooth and competent technique might be envied by many an
older literary craftsman. This unpretentious little love story of
a young tavern waiter and a blue-eyed street-walker is in the
naturalistic tradition of Somerset Maugham's *Liza of Lambeth*
and Stephen Crane's *Maggie*. But, unlike its more experimental
elders, Patrick Hamilton's study is entirely unstrained and lacking in apparent self-consciousness. He approaches his characters with no hint of apology or show of defense. The situations which he depicts are simple, and the emotions he evokes
are fresh and genuine.

The background for the novel is provided by the Midnight Bell,
a London public house, and the unheroic young hero, known
simply and exclusively as Bob, is a waiter in the saloon bar....

In the saloon bar he encountered Jenny Maple, rather a pretty
girl whose profession was obvious to him from the start. By
her own confession she was pressed for money to pay her rent,
and Bob lent her 10 shillings and enjoyed the feeling of uncommon virtue which he derived from asking nothing in return.
The next day—his day off—Jenny met him by arrangement
and returned his money, or tried to return it. Again Bob indulged himself in magnanimity and refused the offer. Afterward they went to a theatre and Bob spent rather more than
he could well afford. He made an appointment with Jenny for
the next week.... When Jenny failed to appear, Bob's disappointment was, to himself, surprising and disconcerting. He
discovered with some dismay that he was in love with a common little street-walker.

Jenny's interest in Bob increased perceptibly after he allowed
her to hear of the existence of his bank account. Her difficulties
with her landlady continued, and Bob's small gifts of money
became more frequent. Finally, in desperation—but still thinking rather well of himself for the generosity of his behavior—
Bob offers to marry Jenny. He is dashed by the statement that
she already has a husband. Nevertheless, the affair drags on
and Bob's emotion grows as his bank account dwindles. The
immediate object of his life is a promised holiday with Jenny
at Brighton. He draws out of the bank his last £25 and goes
to meet her at the railway station. Jenny does not come. He
finds, upon frantic inquiry, that she has disappeared from her
lodgings without leaving an address....

If Mr. Hamilton had been content to leave the story there, without further comment, there would be no possible fault to find with it. But he has added, in his last pages, a generalization upon Bob's history which may, it is true, make Bob seem a somewhat more significant individual, but which mars the integrity of a story concerning an essentially insignificant human being.

> *"Love in a Tavern," in* The New York Times Book Review, *January 5, 1930, p. 6.*

NEW YORK HERALD TRIBUNE BOOKS

In pretty Jenny Maple, girl of the West End streets, Patrick Hamilton has created one of those striking figures whose life does not end with the passing of a single publishing season. Jenny and Mr. Hamilton shared a triumph in *The Midnight Bell,* a volume which charmed judicious readers with its brilliant composition and its touching irony, and especially with its pathetic central figure. *The Siege of Pleasure* is no less successful a tragi-comedy of the seamier side of London existence.

This time the author turns to Jenny's earlier days. He tells how she came to take the wrong turning, "all through a glass of port" at a pub with some chance acquaintances. . . . Mr. Hamilton has achieved a rather tremendous feat in his lengthy and never-sentimental description of Jenny's fateful night out with the glaring Violet, Andy and Rex. The story's ending is unusual and impressive.

Portraiture of a high order is not least among Mr. Hamilton's talents. Among the memorable characters in his latest book one cherishes most poor Jenny's too-temporary employers at Chiswick: "the tall parrotlike, red-eyed, fussy, fatuously hatted Miss Chingford," "the small, thin-lipped, anaemic, wrinkled Mrs. Rodgers," and old Dr. Chingford, with his journeys up and down the eternal stairs of the surburban villa. They are the ones who lend the climactic touch of irony to this wholly admirable story.

> *"Wrong Turning," in* New York Herald Tribune Books, *March 27, 1932, p. 12.*

THE TIMES LITERARY SUPPLEMENT

[*The Siege of Pleasure*] is, in length and scope, little more than a long short story, and takes the form of a picture within a frame, an episode staged in the light of its aftermath. Jenny Maple, a London prostitute, who played a considerable part in *The Midnight Bell,* accosts a man in Piccadilly-circus. On their way to a Paddington hotel she tells him that she "took the wrong turning . . . all through a glass of port," and the story turns back to the incident of "that single glass." The succession of events is not unfamiliar. . . . One might even term it all commonplace and not very engaging. But Mr. Hamilton holds his reader by his accomplished writing, his gift for realistic portraiture, his pitiless refusal to cast any befogging glamour over what can only falsely be romanticized, and, not least, by his ability to make the least of his characters—sub-human as some of them are—real personalities, and to make their personalities the motive forces of his story. The girl Jenny's employers, Dr. Chingford, Miss Chingford and Mrs. Rodgers, may seem at first sight mere grotesques created out of sheer love of the bizarre, but, to a degree at least, the story is what it is because they are what they are. And that is true, too, of Tom, Jenny's ineffective lover. Still, readers who have followed Mr. Hamilton's past work with interest, and who regard his future with expectation, may not unjustifiably feel that he is here doing little more than marking time.

> *A review of ''The Siege of Pleasure,'' in* The Times Literary Supplement, *No. 1575, April 7, 1932, p. 252.*

IRIS BARRY

A homely barmaid of twenty-eight years, simple-hearted and inarticulate—such is the intensely likeable heroine of Mr. Hamilton's latest London tale [*The Plains of Cement*]. Of course, a barmaid of any type is, as a rule, by very reason of her calling a remarkable and venerable character. Hers is as special a vocation as that of a stewardess or sister of mercy: a barmaid is a ministering angel. She dispenses cheer out of bottles, while being also "lovely woman" in the abstract and something of an avenging conscience. Particularly, she is the preserver and guardian of that feeling for the niceties which is one characteristic of the respectable urban working class in England. It is the class which provides the country with its policemen and nursemaids, the man who comes to read the meter, its valets and its Tommy Atkins and Jack Tar. They wake and dress and feed and protect and admonish and admire the ruling class from the cradle to the grave; by them "typical" British humor and "typical" British character are preserved. . . .

[The barmaid Ella] was full of natural humility which was considerably increased by the frequent realization that Bob, the waiter in the saloon bar of The Midnight Bell, was committed to comradely affection for her and nothing more. She sincerely loved him, but she knew she was a plain girl.

Her wistful peace of mind was suddenly shattered by an elderly gentleman in a blatantly new hat. For a time she could not decide whether this rather peculiar duffer were making improper advances to her or looming up as a potential husband: there was something disturbing about him even when he proffered trips to the theater and bunches of flowers. . . .

Ella's adventures with Mr. Eccles were various, and Mr. Hamilton relates them miraculously well. The conversation between the two of them, almost as unliterary as the mewing of two cats, are marvelously rendered: every tone and phrase has the rich ring of truth. Indeed, this brief and vivid study of London life is very funny as well as very sad and painfully veracious. . . .

In its unpretentious way, *The Plains of Cement* is a gem. It has wholeness and proportion, no sentimentality and a story with a surprising if pathetic conclusion. The passages about the "healthy yet loathsome little boy" who teases Ella with schoolboy ingenuity are masterly, only surpassed by the unlabored descriptions of that "unfortunate murmuring man," Mr. Eccles. Elderly gentlemen who enjoy female society should consider this portrait and tremble. Even Wodehouse has not unveiled, in his different way, more awful depths of life-like vacuity.

> *Iris Barry, in a review of ''The Plains of Cement,'' in* New York Herald Tribune Books, *January 6, 1935, p. 9.*

JANE SPENCE SOUTHRON

The Plains of Cement, we are told, ends Patrick Hamilton's projected trilogy, but one would not be surprised later to find a fourth volume eventuating. It has followed a course uniquely the author's own. Each individual book, while complete in itself, is referable to one or other of the trilogy, but by no means in strict chronological sequence. Together they make a vivid picture of the London known in its reality only to the poor of that city or at second hand to those who have been sufficiently interested to make the subject a matter of special investigation. . . .

In *The Plains of Cement* Ella, a barmaid at The Midnight Bell—a typical London pub—is the centre of interest, though the most striking character is the girl's elderly suitor, Eccles. This casual visitor to the pub, who becomes a frequenter because he is fascinated by the 28-year-old barmaid, reminds one of Wells's Sir Isaac Harman, but he is more elaborated and he is too individual in his unpleasing idiosyncrasies to be considered derivative. He has the same middle-aged acquisitiveness as Sir Isaac, and the tyranny he tries to establish over Ella is like that Sir Isaac did succeed in establishing over his wife. Outside the realm of sex, however, they are immensely different, Eccles's inferior mentality making it possible for Ella eventually to escape marrying him.

The girl's unrequited love for Bob is the background of [*The Plains of Cement*], though Bob himself hardly enters into the narrative at all except as motivating Ella's actions. Because she realizes that it is hopeless to expect him to be interested in her and because of the consequent bleakness of her outlook she encourages Eccles. This condescending and class-conscious gentleman's courtship . . . is presented with sardonic humorousness; an effect the author has achieved without bestowing even a particle of humor on either the self-centred Eccles or the poverty-driven barmaid.

Subsidiary characters of interest are the Prossers, Ella's mother and stepfather, both of whom are highly original in conception. Prosser, spoken of by his wife and stepdaughter, with bated breath, as "him," is a domestic tyrant with no redeeming feature. . . . [He] is known to have saved some time in the past £500, which the girl and her mother allude to, in the cautious language of the London poor, as a "Little Something Coming." The crisis of the story is bound up with an illness which seems likely to carry Prosser off.

Psychologically, this part of the novel is extremely effective. The oscillation of Ella's purpose is sympathetically portrayed. If Prosser dies there will be a cottage in the country—the Londoner's idea of Paradise—for the two women; and Eccles can be dismissed. . . .

Mr. Hamilton relies neither on extraordinary incident in the narrative nor unusual charm or beauty in his heroine to hold our attention. But he does hold it. Ella, attractive only by reason of her sex to her one acknowledged admirer, is strong as a fictional character because her personality is revealed naturally and thoroughly. Hers is the tragedy of a simple and largely inarticulate soul made manifest.

Prosser obstinately recovers. . . . Ella, faced with a decision, chooses the continuance of her dreary round of barmaiding. Bob, coming temporarily on the scene toward the close of the book, goes off to sea.

Has Mr. Hamilton ended his trilogy purposely in this indeterminate manner as a reflection of life? Both Ella and Bob are comparatively young and are broken neither physically nor mentally. As the story is left we can imagine nothing further for them but a succession of monotonous, gray years. Would

two spirited young people have no less lugubrious futures? If *The Plains of Cement* was a single unrelated story one could regard it as a moment captured and expressed. As it is, one cannot help feeling that an additional instalment is distinctly called for.

> *Jane Spence Southron, "A London Trilogy," in* The New York Times Book Review, *January 13, 1935, p. 7.*

THE LONDON MERCURY

The hero [of *Impromptu in Moribundia*] makes a terrifying journey to another planet. He finds there a world which no satirist before Mr. Hamilton has imagined: a world of popular ideals made actual, . . . of people who converse with each other by means of balloons issuing from their mouths and heads, a world of advertisements and best-sellers come true. It is an excellent idea for a satire, and Mr. Hamilton makes good use of it. He explains the habits of the Moribundians with suave lucidity and writes with an admirable air of scientific curiosity.

> *A review of "Impromptu in Moribundia," in* The London Mercury, *Vol. XXXIX, No. 232, February, 1939, p. 470.*

KATE O'BRIEN

Impromptu In Moribundia is a satirical commentary on our times and customs which many people will find clever, I suppose, but which seemed to me both schoolboyish and *démodé*. It is surely somewhat dowdy now to bring up heavy artillery against Sir Henry Newbolt, and "Play up, play up and play the game"? And nearly all the irony is either as dated as that, or, even when topical, too laboured to be persevered with. The thought and speech balloons floating out of the heads of the Moribundians—you know, about "personal freshness" and "waking up tired," and "Sloshall for delicate fabrics"—is funny enough, perhaps, for a piece of journalism, but is far too superficial and too old a joke to be lashed at as it is here.

Moribundia, I regret to have to tell you, is a hitherto unknown planet on to which the narrator of these impromptu adventures is shot in a contraption called an asteradio. It is "a land in which the ideals and ideas of our world, the striving and subconscious wishes of our time, the fictions and figments of our imagination, are calm, cold actuality." The capital of this planet-country is called *Nwotsemaht*—spell it backwards, *à la* Butler, and see where you have got to. Its streets are called *Drofxo, Tneger*, &c. Really maddening—and to very little purpose. There is some heavy fun about Moribundian writers called *Gnilpik, Wahs*, and *Sllew*, and—believe it or not—Colonel Lovelace's two best-known lines are printed backwards, for the joke of the thing. I hardly smiled once, I think, throughout this book but neither did I wince for us poor moribundian victims. I wonder why on earth Mr. Hamilton has forsaken the grave, good manner of *The Midnight Bell* and *The Siege of Pleasure*.

> *Kate O'Brien, in a review of "Impromptu in Moribundia," in* The Spectator, *Vol. 162, No. 5775, March 3, 1939, p. 364.*

JOSEPH WOOD KRUTCH

I would not, offhand, have been inclined to suppose that a good scare is what theatrical audiences want most just now. . . .

The fact remains, nevertheless, that [Hamilton's] *Angel Street* was a sensational hit in London and that it will almost certainly repeat its success [in New York]. The fact is also that the only purpose of the play is to make each particular hair stand on end like quills upon the fretful porpentine.

Not since [Edward Chodorov's] *Kind Lady*—also an importation from England—has that particular purpose been achieved so completely, and it is obvious that our native purveyors of terror and crime will have to look to their laurels. There was a time when we thought we alone knew how to turn that trick, when we spoke condescendingly of the slow pace and simple plots of the English thrillers. But we were, it now appears, burning our candle at both ends. Our plays got to moving so fast and to pulling so many surprises that nothing seemed surprising any more, and even a temporary suspension of unbelief became impossible. In desperation we increased the farcical element and spoofed our own horrors more and more until we came at last to *Arsenic and Old Lace,* which, for all its success, is a thriller to end thrillers. In that direction it is impossible to go any farther, and anything which goes less far in the same direction is bound to seem feeble. Meanwhile, however, the English continued to work along another line, achieving passable effects in the plays of Emlyn Williams and two masterpieces in *Kind Lady* and *Angel Street.*

For a plot the author of *Angel Street* has chosen a story at once simple and gaudy, rather like some of those which Conan Doyle used to think up for Sherlock Holmes. It is concerned with a murderer who comes with his innocent wife to live in a house where years ago he had failed to find certain fabulous rubies for whose sake he had done the owner to a bloody death, and this story is told, again like those of Conan Doyle, with an air of absolute seriousness. There is no mystery, for one understands fully just what the situation is, and there are no violent twists as the action proceeds. In an American play the detective would probably have turned out to be the murderer, and the terrified wife would probably have revealed herself in the end as a star of the FBI. Here, on the contrary, everything proceeds at an unhurried pace and toward an expected end, but also in such a way that every ounce of theatrical effectiveness is squeezed out of every situation, and one is reminded . . . that the tension produced by waiting for something which one knows is going to happen can be greater than the tension of uncertainty and surprise. Obviously it is on tension of the first kind that the present play depends almost exclusively; yet the audience sits waiting in agony for the things which must happen. Why such agony should be worth paying good money to get I am not quite sure unless, perhaps, it is because one knows that relief is sweet and knows also that the happy end is as inevitable as everything else in the play. (pp. 649-50)

> *Joseph Wood Krutch, "Murder by Gaslight," in* The Nation, *New York, Vol. 153, No. 25, December 20, 1941, pp. 649-50.*

ROSAMOND GILDER

Patrick Hamilton, accustomed to feeding shudders to shudder-loving audiences, attempts [in *Angel Street*] nothing more serious than to continue this amiable avocation. His play deals with such appropriate ingredients as a scared little wife . . . ; a supposedly kindly-but-stern Victorian husband who is deliberately frightening her out of her wits . . . ; lost jewels and old murders. The frightening, all through the first act, is highly effective. . . . [The appearance of] a fatherly ex-sleuth doing a spot of informal detection relieves the situation considerably. . . . If the second act is thin, the third provides a curtain that packs a sufficient wallop to satisfy any reasonable entertainment seeker. *Angel Street* is a pleasant addition to that lengthening list of amusing evenings which Broadway affords, a list which includes such veterans as *Life with Father, My Sister Eileen,* [and] *Arsenic and Old Lace.* . . .

> *Rosamond Gilder, in a review of "Angel Street," in* Theatre Arts, *Vol. XXVI, No. 2, February, 1942, p. 87.*

CLIFTON FADIMAN

Of late years I have noted a tendency among publishers to ring in *An American Tragedy* whenever the hero of a novel comes with sufficient slowness to no good end and to cry *Of Human Bondage* whenever a novel has a bitch for a heroine. This week, Patrick Hamilton's new book, a diverting exercise in the sinister, is launched to the full-orchestra accompaniment of precisely these two comparisons. Says the blurb, "In the case of *Hangover Square* the publishers are willing to fling caution to the winds." In the case of *Hangover Square* any reasonably well-read wind will, I daresay, fling caution straight back at the publishers.

The comparison with [Francis Iles's] *Before the Fact,* also noted on the jacket, is, on the other hand, just. *Hangover Square* is one of those highly intelligent chillers, full of cozy horrors, in the manufacture of which the English are so infuriatingly our superiors. I have not seen Mr. Hamilton's *Angel Street,* but I do remember his hellish little melodrama *Rope's End,* of perhaps fifteen years ago, and I conceive this novel to be pretty much in the vein of his plays. An excellent vein it is, too, but hardly a main artery.

The hero is a large, simple-minded Londoner, George Bone. Mr. Hamilton successfully maneuvers poor George into committing a double murder and then suicide. . . . George is bothered by two things. One of the things is a chilly girl named Netta, as nasty as she is beautiful, who plays George for a sucker. . . . [The second is] schizophrenia, which, as Mr. Hamilton informs us via Black's Medical Dictionary, is "a cleavage of the mental functions, associated with assumption by the affected person of a second personality." When George is himself, he loves nasty Netta to distraction. When he clicks into his alter ego, he is obsessed by the desire to murder her and her lover, Peter. Any sensible reader is apt to rate George's judgment more highly when he has gone out of his mind than when he is in it.

With what seems to this unlearned reader almost academic obedience to the dicta of psychiatry, the narrative shuttles trickily between the two Georges. Mr. Hamilton's horrors are all of the mind, and he manipulates them with extraordinary skill, though perhaps at slightly excessive length. He is no less adept at picturing the murky world Netta and her dipsomaniacal pals infest, though I think his endeavor to identify them with the Fascist viewpoint (the time is just after Munich) is a bit pretentious, as are his chapter-head quotations from Suckling, Milton, Shakespeare, Shelley, and the thesaurian Roget. He weakens his story by this gratuitous intellectualization. *Hangover Square* stands up firmly as a first-class melodrama of abnormal psychology, but as a satire on a decadent society it wavers and hesitates. Gifted as is Mr. Hamilton, he is no Aldous Huxley. (p. 59)

Clifton Fadiman, "Horrors, Homilies, Yarns," in
The New Yorker, *Vol. XVII, No. 53, February 14,
1942, pp. 59-60.*

LOUISE MAUNSELL FIELD

Tense, grim, moving steadily onward to a climax foreshadowed
from the very beginning, *Hangover Square* is the tragic story
of a man destroyed by his own weakness. The novel inevitably
challenges comparison with Somerset Maugham's *Of Human
Bondage;* it too has for dominating theme a man's overmas-
tering desire for an utterly worthless woman.

Netta Longdon has not a single redeeming quality. She is unimaginative, ungenerous, lazy, dishonest, unintelligent,
cruel.... Untidy, a drunkard, a snob, dishonest even in her
snobbishness, without one touch of human kindliness, she was
beneath contempt in every way but one; her physical beauty,
a beauty which seemed significant of all the inner loveliness
she did not have.

In his mind, George Harvey Bone knew her for what she was,
the dirtiest of "a dirty lot"; in his mind, he actually hated her.
But to his heart and his senses she was "violets and primroses
in an April rain." He loved her desperately, abjectly, and she
treated him as only such a woman . . . would treat the mangiest
of curs.

Circumstances had combined against George Bone, a big, humble, simple man, not stupid but slow, pathetically grateful for
kindness, with a charm of his own which made him attractive
to people of brains and character. Only it so happened that his
life seldom brought him into contact with people of brains and
character.... His passion for Netta had made him a mere
hanger-on to her crowd, and her crowd were the "low-downs,"
pub-crawlers, they were called in 1939, the year George Bone,
the normal George Bone, knelt both actually and metaphorically to a woman he knew to be a slut.

The normal George Bone. There was another, and very different, George Bone. Ever since his early boyhood George had
had what he called "dead moods," and of late these had come
more often. Every now and then a shutter would seem to click
down over his brain; then life became "a silent film without
music," and his own sensitive, suffering self a creature devoid
of feeling, dreary, numb, dead.... A victim of schizophrenia,
he had not the faintest idea that this secondary personality of
his was absorbed in a mission, and a plan; the mission, to kill
Netta Longdon, the plan of how to do it and then escape to
the place which for him symbolized all he had ever known of
happiness and peace.

The novel is exceptionally impressive. George Bone is a living,
breathing person whose pitiably inadequate attempts to free
himself, to salvage at least a few fragments of his poor shattered
pride are almost unendurably pathetic. The atmosphere of dread,
of an incessantly threatening horror totally unsuspected by any
one of the book's characters, is admirably done, somber, terrifying, yet clean as compared to the sordid air of Earl's Court,
the "Hangover Square" in which Netta and her associates lived
their mean lives, pretending to despise convention, yet slav-
ishly obedient to their own "convention of being rude and
unpunctual and unconventional and broke." These people and
their sort of existence are sharply etched with an instrument
of steel dipped in acid, a treatment which might be repellent
were it not for the aching tenderness, a tenderness which has
no alloy of sentimentality, but only understanding and a stern

fatalism with which the author draws the weakness and helplessness and unwillingness to hurt any one, of George Bone.
Mr. Hamilton writes with a directness, a simplicity and restraint
which enable him to surmount even such dangers as those of
the white cat episodes. A grim, powerful, sympathetic novel,
sensitive, atmospheric, exceptionally well balanced, *Hangover
Square* need have no fear of any of the comparisons it will
undoubtedly suggest to every experienced reader.

Louise Maunsell Field, "The Second Man," in The
New York Times Book Review, *February 15, 1942,
p. 7.*

FRED T. MARSH

[*Hangover Square*] is an adventure in schizophrenia . . . with
a method in its madness. The schizophrenia, as in *The Strange
Case of Doctor Jekyll and Mr. Hyde,* amounts to partial amnesia; the attraction of the man for the woman amounts to a
physical fixation. The whole Love-Hate, Hyde-Jekyll fusion
of themes has, as in the Stevenson classic, symbolic meaning.
But it remains, despite faults and limitations, a highly effective
and exciting story.

The place is London, specifically Earl's Court, "Hangover
Square"—with excursions ranging from Brighton to Maidenhead. The time is 1939 with England on the eve of war, the
story ending just as war is declared. The people are a small
group of wasters.... [They] are no more true bohemians than
they are really county or actually university—although they
frequently affect one or another of the attitudes.... Their
occupation is principally drinking from noon to dawn, while
keeping a sharp eye out for connections, their contempt for
most of the world, even in their own fields, being matched
only by their sycophancy when a possible connection appears
on the scene.

Into this milieu of pubs and partying has come a big, shy,
uncertain man, one who obviously does not belong in the set,
a man as gentle as they are hard, but an unhappy man in a sick
time as they are unhappy. His name is George Bone and he
has, although without connections (until later), the desidera-
tum, the emollient, of a modest private income. In other words,
he is good for any amount of drink. For this reason and because
in his simplicity (which is not stupidity) he makes an excellent
stooge, doormat and punching bag for their varying moods,
they suffer him. It must be said in their favor that they are not
hypocrites; they make no bones about their attitude toward him.
Everybody knows that he is so smitten with Netta Longdon,
that you couldn't drive him away short of murder, certainly
not by insult. He practically begs for it, and he gets it, and he
takes it, and he knows it. Nobody fools him; he just can't seem
to help himself and get clear of the woman....

And Netta is no frail little mongrel. She has everything, including brains; she's blue ribbon—pointer type, I should say.
Her troubles are chiefly that she can't act, won't work and will
drink. Old George's doglike devotion and knightly chivalry
are a scream, Netta's promiscuity being governed only by her
hopes of a career and an aristocratic fastidiousness even in
(unless too much) liquor. What the gang do not know about
George is just this: Dr. Jekyll is not fooled, and Mr. Hyde is
murderous.

The potentialities here are enormous. But Mr. Hamilton has
not attempted to fill out his brief, brittle and swift story to the
dimensions of a serious realistic novel. Neither his English

Fascist nor his brown-shirt types, few of his minor figures seem to be real people. They are symbols; for this is a symbolical tale of England on the outbreak of war. Wherefore it is rather more clever in invention and serious in aim than profound as a novel. But it is an item; no question about that. I do not think I have ever used the word before—save possibly in a forgotten moment of weakness—but this, just as a story, is gripping.

Fred T. Marsh, "Alcoholic Hedonists," in New York Herald Tribune Books, February 22, 1942, p. 5.

THE COMMONWEAL

[The Duke in Darkness is] a play whose only possible interest, either to the actors or the audience, was its long, long, over-and-over-again parts. It's all a little too pat. The story of a French nobleman imprisoned in a Chateau by a rival faction in sixteenth-century France, the Patrick Hamilton script, although short, elongates itself by repeating every line of dialogue three times, and depends for its effect upon a quality which I can only call buried suspense. In spite of an endless second-act harangue devoted to the virtues of "the people," I found it without significance or excitement. (pp. 420-21)

A review of "The Duke in Darkness," in The Commonweal, Vol. XXXIX, No. 17, February 11, 1944, pp. 420-21.

ROSAMOND GILDER

There are certain plays that remain in memory longer than they have lived on the stage, for some element of unfulfilled promise they contained. Patrick Hamilton's The Duke in Darkness is one of these. The high-arched Renaissance room, the lonely romantic figure of the mysterious Duke, and the situation established by the first act of this tale of a captive leader and his henchman suggested the possibility of a reincarnation of the cloak-and-sword drama that has its own particular niche in the theatre's many-walled gallery. The Jest succeeded in capturing this atmosphere some twenty-five years ago; The Duke in Darkness failed. Patrick Hamilton, whose Angel Street is now in the third year of its run in New York and whose Rope's End can still evoke shuddery memories, is a writer of ability usually able to achieve the effects he desires. Yet in The Duke in Darkness he was not able to follow up the advantage of his first act. He became involved in a labored and not very convincing political thesis and at the same time indulged in an ornate and artificial prose that clogged the whole proceedings.... Though The Duke in Darkness missed fire, the impression remains that a play lay dormant somewhere behind its many shortcomings.

Rosamond Gilder, in a review of "The Duke in Darkness," in Theatre Arts, Vol. XXVIII, No. 4, April, 1944, p. 208.

GEORGE JEAN NATHAN

If Mr. Hamilton were as artful in other directions of playwriting as he sometimes is in the matter of suspense he would be a dramatist of some position. Suspense, however, seems often to be the especial gift of minor playwrights who have little of consequence beyond it. Any number of fabricators of simple melodrama or detective and mystery plays have been pretty smart at the business of making audiences nervously antici-

pative. Mr. Hamilton is one of these, much better than the majority but otherwise still one whose genius inclines immeasurably more toward inducing in his clients a childish wonder as to what will happen next than toward evoking in them emotions somewhat less closely associated with the feverish tearing of eight or nine layers of gaudy paper off a ten-cent Christmas present.

In this critically negligible way Mr. Hamilton, as noted, has indicated himself a relatively superior fellow. The presents which he bestows upon the stage sometimes might cost as much as a quarter or even half dollar. Some persons, indeed, . . . have esteemed his opera as being worth as much as $3.85. It is these who see in his Rope's End and Angel Street not simply much better than ordinary "psychological" thrillers but genuinely profound psychological dramas, damnigh worthy of Strindberg. To this way of looking at them, however, they remain simply the much better than ordinary thrillers. Which should be sufficient praise.

In The Duke In Darkness, Mr. Hamilton has attempted the relatively more costly dramatic form of historical romance wherein certain elements other than mere curiosity over what is coming next are necessarily called for and has discovered himself in such unaccustomed surroundings that even his former knack of suspense deserts him. What he has essayed to write is a "literary" melodrama laid in the sixteenth century and concerned with a ducal follower of Henry of Navarre whose faith is in the people, who has been imprisoned for fifteen years by a rival and dictatorially minded duke, and who by one stratagem and another succeeds eventually in managing his escape. Aside from a gratuitous identification of the subject matter with the current world situation the play is a slack throwback to the stage of a half century ago.... (pp. 218-19)

Mr. Hamilton's writing is of the "Very well, don't stand there gaping; go!" school. It also is the kind in which no character is permitted to say simply, for example, "It can not be," but must needs invariably say it twice over. (p. 219)

George Jean Nathan, in a review of "The Duke in Darkness," in his The Theatre Book of the Year, 1943-1944: A Record and an Interpretation, Alfred A. Knopf, 1944, pp. 218-20.

THE TIMES LITERARY SUPPLEMENT

[In The Slaves of Solitude (published in the United States as Riverside), Mr. Hamilton] has moved out to Henley-on-Thames, to a new boarding-house which shelters as gruesome a collection of the disengaged as one could decently imagine.

The period is the recent past, and it would be fair to describe this as in some sense a war novel. True, none of the characters is actively engaged in the struggle, but their enforced aloofness due to age, disability or fear is a potent factor in their discontent. The old sadist, Mr. Thwaites, who dominates the company and selects for his victim the humble but intelligent Miss Roach, seems himself to be the embodiment of the principle of aggression. He represents the inevitable degradation of the unoccupied heart and mind. The elderly ladies with mysterious complaints who pursue their aimless walks through park and graveyard retain enough human memories to preserve an ineffectual benevolence. But they need the stimulation of Mr. Thwaites's malice to keep them alive. Miss Roach, who is a publisher's reader, is the only link between these derelicts and the outside world and it is through her casual friendships with a boozing American soldier and an unpleasant German girl that the deadly battle of the boarding-house—the war in miniature—develops. Mr. Hamilton does the boarding-house *décor* and the horrors of enforced propinquity very well. The impact upon the victims of the wholly inconsequent and amoral American is brilliantly described. What is to be regretted is the over-emphasized style, the too insistent pity, the scream of personal anguish which Mr. Hamilton permits himself too often.

A review of "The Slaves of Solitude," in The Times Literary Supplement, No. 2366, June 7, 1947, p. 277.

JAMES MacBRIDE

A generation of theatre-goers will bless Patrick Hamilton for his gelid magic in **Angel Street**, addicts of the psycho-thriller will turn back to his **Hangover Square**, no less fondly, for a retrospective chill. The dour little novel [*Riverside*] ... is strictly a minor-league item. *Riverside* details the blackout blues of a dreary Thames-side boarding house and its drearier denizens—the twittery, too healthy old-maid secretary, the bombastic, sadistic tyrant of the dining room, the brooding, retired music-hall comedian, the avid, evil female refugee and the rest. Unfortunately, the blue note is so relentlessly sustained, the agony so grimly suppressed, that even the most ardent Hamilton fan will be bored by the monotone.

Mr. Hamilton lets his story channel through the mind of Miss Roach, the above-mentioned old maid who has not quite given up "hope" as the novel opens. ... [We] see the autumn fires glow in her heart when the bibulous American lieutenant dallies with her beside the river bank ...; finally, we watch her grim surrender as the brassy refugee cuts her out.

There's a climax, of course—a few pages of taut screaming, no more: things are wound up fast thereafter, as though Mr. Hamilton, too, had grown bored with his sleazy material. It goes without saying that his sense of character never falters: each person we meet is brilliantly observed, etched with cameo sharpness. But these are characters with no place to go: the evil that simmers in their souls is sparked by boredom, nothing more; the chill is there, but it does not reach the reader.

James MacBride, "Ghoulies, Ghosties—and Boarding-House Ogres," in The New York Times Book Review, *July 13, 1947, p. 22.*

THE TIMES LITERARY SUPPLEMENT

Mr. Patrick Hamilton has a distinction of his own. No one has an ear so accurate for the recording of the horrors of the vernacular. ... With the sort of zest that animates the collector of landladies' Victoriana, he treasures phrases of conversation and mannerisms, ponderous with inanity. ... He not only suffers bores gladly; he hunts them down, as if they were truffles. For a period he contemplated compiling an Anatomy of Boredom as exhaustive as Burton's of Melancholy. His interest in the significant *cliché* is professional, not perverse. He works in the banal, because the lost and lonely people whose misfortunes and desires have engaged his sympathy have no first-hand words of their own. They communicate with one another in phrases which are as far removed from the precise formulation of their thoughts as they are from the grunts of animals. He is as fascinated by the interpretation of these borrowed phrases as an ornithologist in the identification of birdcalls.

Whereas most of his fellow-novelists operate their characters as unobtrusively as puppet masters, Mr. Hamilton never leaves the scene for long. He is always at hand to explain what his inarticulate creatures really mean or think or feel; and his own gentle smile prevents even his most elephantine creations from becoming as boring in print as they would be in real life. He is as unself-conscious in the advances which he makes towards his readers as his master Dickens, and almost as leisurely in his narrative pace. He is not, however, a facile writer. His first novel, **Craven House,** was published in 1925, since when there have been only nine novels and five plays, three for the theatre and two for radio. His method is intensive. In his trilogy **Twenty Thousand Streets under the Sky** (**The Midnight Bell; The Siege of Pleasure;** and **The Plains of Cement**), he took three characters—Bob, the barman at the Midnight Bell, Jenny, the prostitute, with whom Bob fell in love, and Ella, the barmaid, who loved Bob but was courted by the formidable Mr. Eccles. The combination of their three stories ... produces an impression of the lives of hundreds of thousands of people in the London of that time which justifies the author's choice of title. He is an artist of the typical. His people and places are familiar to us all; (it is to Mr. Hamilton, rather than to Mr. Graham Greene, that the social historian will go for authentic atmosphere); the author does not want to create a mental climate of his own, because his individual effects depend upon naturalism.

Whereas Mr. Greene's apprenticeship to writing was served in journalism and the element of reporting runs through all his novels, Mr. Hamilton's early experience of the theatre leads him instinctively to choose stock characters [and locations]. ... The thought of adultery in Knocke-le-Zoute or Margate would never enter the minds of his characters, for whom exist clichés of behaviour as rigid as those of language. There is no subtlety in Mr. Hamilton's world, because he is dealing with people produced by crude social and economic forces. There is only one exception to this generalization; and that is the Rosamund Tea Rooms in the blacked-out Thames-side town which is the locale of **The Slaves of Solitude.** This dreadful asylum of evacuees appears to be a more original background than the others used by Mr. Hamilton, because it is one with which few of us are familiar. It is, however, built up in exactly the same way, with careful elaboration and repetition of detail so that the reader becomes as familiar with the sights, smells and routine of the place as if he himself was an inmate. ...

Having surveyed the ground anthropologically, Mr. Hamilton chooses for his story the point of strain or weakness. **The Midnight Bell** and **Hangover Square** are variations on the same theme. A good young man forms an obsessional attachment to a beautiful but mercenary girl, who despises him for his love but cultivates him for his money, while giving nothing in return. In each case, the promised trip to Brighton is a ghastly failure. Bob, the barman of the Midnight Bell, recovers his sanity and goes back to sea. George Harvey Bone, the schizophrenic of **Hangover Square,** commits a double murder and makes off, symbolically, for Maidenhead.

The central theme of **The Siege of Pleasure** and the radio play **To the Public Danger** is the real or supposed killing of a cyclist by a carload of drunken people. The description in **The Siege of Pleasure** is the most sustained passage of dramatic writing accomplished by the author. ... In **The Plains of Cement,** the study of cruelty is hidden deeper. Ella, bitterly unhappy at Bob's indifference to her and at the way her mother is bullied by her stepfather, seriously considers getting married to Mr.

Eccles, who clearly would have made her life a hell once he had her for his wife. But she, like Bob, is not made to be a victim and recoils in time to avoid the monstrous old man. Miss Roach, in *The Slaves of Solitude,* older, more sensitive and vulnerable, was born and bred to be a scapegoat.

By the year 1946 Mr. Hamilton had established his claim to certain areas of the urban wilderness sufficiently strongly for it to be remarked that the flagellant murderer George Neville Heath had obviously belonged to the Hangover Square crowd. It was as if a creature of Mr. Hamilton's brain had broken from the lines of type and run amok in the real world, without the constraint which that author laid upon his meanest villains. It is not therefore surprising to find that *The West Pier* is the first of a series of novels to be devoted to different phases in the life of a criminal, Ernest Ralph Gorse....

Gorse is an orphan. He is a lonely youth who passes his idle hours racing white mice in the bath, a great one for the vainglorious pursuit of hobbies, the finest collection of cigarette cards or model battleships. One day a policeman comes to the school to tell that a small girl has been found tied up in a shed on the local cricket ground and robbed of her purse containing sevenpence halfpenny. She accuses a "little man" or perhaps a boy, who had very fair hair and a green cap in his jacket pocket. While the head master protests that such conduct is unthinkable in any of his pupils, he cannot prevent the image of the boy Gorse coming into his mind, even though Gorse's hair is red, not fair. Anyway, Gorse is soon after removed to London by his stepmother and sent first to Colet Court, and then to St. Paul's School.

We next meet Gorse on holiday in Brighton, in company with his two old schoolfellows Ryan and Bell.... The three of them pick up two shop girls on the West Pier, one of whom, Esther Downes, is of remarkable beauty and the other, Gertrude Perks, of remarkable plainness.

A struggle develops between Gorse and Ryan for the conquest of Miss Downes....

The holiday at Brighton is the story of Gorse's prep-school days rewritten in the terms of a vicious and cold-blooded adolescent.... To break the relation he sees developing between the girl and Ryan, he sends Esther a series of poison-pen letters threatening her if she does not cease to meet Ryan. When asked by her what she should do, he gives her avuncular warnings that Ryan is a sexual maniac and not to be trusted. Then, finding a curious satisfaction in the composition of these anonymous letters, he warns Ryan in one that the girl is suffering from some horrible disease. Mr. Hamilton succeeds in creating the feeling that Gorse is in two senses an adventurer. When he discovers that Esther Downes has a sum of £60 or so saved up, he decides immediately that he will lay his hands on it because he needs money and his instincts are predatory. But there is more to it than that, a heightening of consciousness through the courtship of danger. Gorse is an atavistic type, of the sort that achieves distinction in a war, but in peace, for lack of a socially approved enemy, falls on society itself.

The author chooses, probably judiciously, to remain outside his villain's soul (he is an anthropologist, not an advocate for prosecution or defence), and to enter into Gorse's darkness would tax the pity of a Greene or the love of a Dostoevsky. Mr. Hamilton has always shown his caution by doing exactly what is within his power. It seems, however, that in the portrayal of this monster who can only "live" under the shadow of danger Mr. Hamilton himself is frightened. His conjurer's

patter, which has kept the narrative of previous books rattling on, in *The West Pier* is over-emphatic. "You see," he seems to bawl, as if his audience was inept at managing its deaf-aids, "there's nothing up my sleeve. Absolutely Nothing." He is so anxious to clarify the atmosphere around his sombre character that he sums up the story at every stage of its development and repeats the summing-up as if his readers were a jury of good men and dull.

The more a writer relies on factual accuracy to produce psychological conviction, the more severely his mistakes throw him. In *Twenty Thousand Streets under the Sky* it does not seem to matter very much that the glasses are left unwashed at the end of each evening or that the barman and barmaid have the same day out. These are factual inaccuracies excused by the force of the narrative. But in *The West Pier* Mr. Hamilton makes such a song and dance about telling us what happened just as it did happen that when he slips down on page 137 and writes "after his success last night" instead of "the night before last," we feel as swindled as we do when on a naturalistic stage-set a character opens a door and the whole back wall shudders....

Mr. Hamilton has built a wonderful character in Ernest Ralph Gorse; but in *The West Pier* he appears afraid—of what exactly it is difficult to say; his own ability to stand the pace which Gorse will set? or the censorable ways into which this crook will lead him? Hitherto Mr. Hamilton has managed to combine artistic with financial success in the happiest of ways.... Mr. Hamilton, having created Ernest Ralph Gorse, is in danger of being haunted. If he gives this monster his rein he is liable to lose a large part of his loyal public in return for writing a masterpiece.

But with a creature as unreliable as Gorse as collaborator there is always the possibility that he could lose his public without writing a masterpiece. At least half a dozen novelists, fascinated by his theme, are standing by, wishing him with that open mind, characteristic of their profession, a safe voyage and a speedy shipwreck.

> *"Patrick Hamilton's Novels," in* The Times Literary Supplement, *No. 2587, September 7, 1951, p. 564.*

EUDORA WELTY

In *The West Pier* Patrick Hamilton tells of the formative years and early manhood of Ernest Ralph Gorse, born in 1903 in Hove, England, and introduced to us as, practically from that year, a member of "the criminal class." At the novel's conclusion, the young Gorse has successfully sown his seeds of evil in Brighton and is just setting out for London, with a trophy of youthful and petty crimes all undetected or unpunished, presumably to carry on in the future on a grander scale. His ruthless spoliation of a young love affair is his most serious and significant act....

The West Pier, sticking out in the water at Brighton, is seen as "the battleship of sex." On this pier the four chief characters—two young couples—meet by chance in the opening chapters, picking one another up as happens every day, the author points out, on the West Pier. Young Gorse, almost lacking in such human feelings, being wholeheartedly preoccupied with the inhuman, proceeds to make use as he can of the human feelings of others.

Mr. Hamilton has organized his novel with calmness of purpose—that of sober, thorough investigation—and with patience toward what he finds always staring back at him, the character's ultimate inscrutability, and its ubiquity in the world as well. It follows that a certain quality of fatalism pervades the work.

To its credit, *The West Pier* is never sensational. It is unadorned and strict as a lecture, the style plain and in its plainness foreboding. Set down in a laudable attempt at dispassion, it is, however, without passion. It is true that a curious effect of reality does somehow result from sheer accumulation of fact; the drearier the facts, the more accumulation it takes, and sometimes the heavier the going. The novel is warmest, or only warm, in the depiction of the secondary characters. The young lovers are appealing, but helpless as a pair of baby chicks under the shadow of a hawk.

The character of the poisonous young villain is never gone into much below the surface of his behavior—for the reason the author gives that it is opaque. Will this do? Nobody knows, says Mr. Hamilton outright, what makes his Ernest Ralph Gorse the way he is. . . .

There is little humor, except what lies in mordant reporting of schoolroom and seaside repartee, and little sensory feeling in the scene, these not being Mr. Hamilton's tools here. But the reader feels that the use of them at moments, in treating of life however sordid, might not come amiss—and might even bring light to bear on this work, which promises to extend beyond the present volume.

> *Eudora Welty, "The Seeds of Evil," in* The New York Times Book Review, *October 5, 1952, p. 5.*

HUGH McGOVERN

The "hero" of Mr. Hamilton's new novel [*The West Pier*] is an enigma named Ernest Gorse. We first encounter him when he is attending an English public school. . . .

We next meet him when, with two of his companions, he picks up a couple of young women in an amusement park. One of the girls is Esther Downes, a beautiful but "low-class" creature who lives in a semi-slum and is fascinated by these "gentlemen." She is attracted particularly to Ryan, Gorse's friend, and begins dating him. Gorse, actuated apparently by nothing but meanness, sets about in a nasty underhanded campaign to break up Ryan and Esther: he succeeds at that and then discovering that the poor little girl has a private hoard of £68 undertakes to mulct her out of it. . . .

All this is told mostly in a starkly objective manner, with never any attempt to reveal the wellsprings that make Gorse the unmitigated dog that he is. Thus he seems to us a kind of reptilian freak, commanding not a particle of the human identification on the reader's part which is necessary for understanding. Nor is Esther any more credibly human—both she and Gorse seem sexless, her thoughts and actions being those of a wax doll. There is nothing in this novel reminiscent of the very sizable talent for suspenseful drama Mr. Hamilton displayed in *Angel Street* and *Rope*.

> *Hugh McGovern, "Mean, Vicious Character," in* New York Herald Tribune, *November 16, 1952, p. 25.*

ANTHONY POWELL?

[*Mr. Stimpson and Mr. Gorse* is the] second volume of the trilogy dealing with the life of Ernest Ralph Gorse, introduced to us in *The West Pier*. . . . We find Gorse at Reading in 1928, making friends with Mrs. Plumleigh-Bruce, a colonel's widow, courted by Mr. Stimpson, a house agent.

Mr. Patrick Hamilton is one of our best novelists, but he is showing disturbing signs of writing in what is almost in danger of becoming an officially Marxian style, in which "the bourgeoisie" can do nothing right, "the workers" are treated with rich sentimentality, and the failure of the general strike in 1926 is offered as the explanation of everything disagreeable. However, he is never dull; though we sometimes wish he would come to grips more thoroughly with Gorse's inner psychological state. Innate commonness, vanity, and exhibitionism never quite explain Gorse. Mr. Hamilton at present seems to shy away from his central figure in favour of those who surround him; but perhaps we shall get all we need in the final volume.

> *Anthony Powell? in a review of "Mr. Stimpson and Mr. Gorse," in* Punch, *Vol. CCXXIV, No. 5882, July 1, 1953, p. 780.*

J. MACLAREN-ROSS

The abominable Ernest Ralph Gorse, 'expert and resourceful liar', impostor, defrauder of women, and potential 'slayer', with his reddish hair and toothbrush moustache, his rimless monocle, bogus breeziness, and slightly nasal voice, would— so his creator, Mr Patrick Hamilton, assures us—'have served, indeed, as a perfect model for, or archetype of, all the pitiless and not-to-be-pitied criminals who have been discovered and exposed in the last hundred years or so in Great Britain.'

According to a fictitious future biographer of Gorse, John George Haigh and Neville George Heath exhibited, compared with him, 'a certain charm, kindliness, generosity and dash', and that 'in the matter of purely repulsive, sustained, and thoroughgoing evil, Gorse belonged to a sort of upper class'. (p. 58)

These are big claims—the criminological equivalent of declaring a promising young novelist to be the equal of Hardy, Conrad and Henry James—but they will doubtless be justified by the iniquities that Gorse has still to commit: certainly, to readers of the three novels in which he has featured so far [*The West Pier, Mr Stimpson and Mr Gorse,* and *Unknown Assailant*], he has already—on the strength of three cunning swindles, three acts of robbery with violence (including one perpetrated at the age of twelve), and the promise of murder-yet-to-come, acquired the status of a real figure in the calendar of crime; and the aforementioned physical characteristics, though not photographically represented, have become as familiar as the wide toothpaste smile and laughing Irish eyes of Patrick Mahon, the sad Faustian face of Eugen Weidmann, or the single earring and bushy naval beard of Ronald Chesney—one who surely had many psychological traits in common with Mr Hamilton's character.

Mr Hamilton insists several times that Gorse 'had not any sort of good in him', that he 'loved trickery and evil for their own sakes', and that his motives are 'only partially commercial'; we are also told that his ruling passion is social snobbery: he is animated, moreover, by a strong power-complex, which expresses itself in the sending of anonymous letters to his victims (among other methods of spreading stealthy terror), and is symbolized by his 'almost pathological' obsession with militarism and its attendant trappings. . . . (pp. 58-9)

In addition to these already repellent attributes, he knows more about 'car-buying, car-selling and car-trickery' than any other young man 'in England, Europe or the world', has histrionic ambitions, is powerfully attracted to the theatrical world in general, and passes as either a person of aristocratic connections or an ex-army officer of the 1914 war.... [He] has assumed in adult life a manner of facetious gaiety, performing a 'silly-ass act' when in liquor, and modelling his behaviour and speech on Bertie Wooster, with an admixture—especially in his epistolary style—of the late Jeffrey Farnol.

This latter idiosyncracy alone reveals Gorse to be a more Machiavellian and sinister descendant of those pretentious and often malevolent bores whose anatomy Mr Hamilton so ably dissected in *The Plains of Cement* and *The Slaves of Solitude*, combined with the raffish and dangerous ne'er-do-wells of *The Siege of Pleasure, To the Public Danger* and *Hangover Square*: 'Doctor Margrave' in the radio-play *Caller Anonymous*, the blackmailer in *Money with Menaces*, and Brandon in *Rope*— not to mention the Victorian husband in *Gaslight*—also possessed something of the same patient, tortuous, diabolic temperament.

That such figures as this—even apart from the examples already cited—have in reality existed, any student of crime or the sensational Sunday papers will confirm; but to make an *imaginary* incarnation of evil credible is almost as difficult as attempting to portray a saint in print, and most writers of fiction would hesitate to choose so detestable a protagonist for even a single book, let alone a whole series. Mr Hamilton, notwithstanding, avoids all the obvious pitfalls triumphantly, with more than a touch of the astuteness which has enabled Gorse himself to keep out of gaol hitherto. Both as dramatist and novelist, he has long been preoccupied with 'that cruelty and inhumanity in the nature of men' which Fielding, before him, 'contemplated with concern'...; and while in his plays, where such conflicts are expressed in terms of melodrama, the oppressed are finally allowed to humiliate, in their turn, the oppressor, the underdog in the quieter scheme of the early novels is rarely permitted to rebel.... In *Hangover Square* and *The Slaves of Solitude*, the author, however, was evidently working towards a synthesis of the suspense-story and the tragi-comic realism of his London trilogy. The obnoxious Gorse, who belongs to both worlds (his predatory instincts and latent homicidal tendencies supplying the necessary element of tension and menace) provided an answer to this technical problem: by allowing him to develop in the anomalous period between the two world wars, against a rootless urban background of red brick and fumed oak, slot-machines on fluorescent seaside piers, huge ornate hotel-lounges, equivocal metropolitan cocktail-bars and fake-tudor provincial pubs, Mr Hamilton was able to exercise to the full his outstanding talents as social satirist and historian of the uneasy peace.

While refusing resolutely to endow his chief character with any redeeming or romantic qualities, denying even the legend of his Hypnotic Eyes..., and emphasizing constantly Gorse's vulgarity, lack of taste and fundamental caddishness, as well as his more nefarious and lethal potentialities, he succeeds none the less in making the novels consistently diverting and entertaining, in a manner which writers dealing with more likeable characters and pleasanter themes often fail significantly to achieve.

Gorse, though now in his thirtieth year, has not yet murdered; his two previous adventures were solely concerned with the devious machinations employed by him to deprive two women, diametrically opposed in age, character and upbringing, of their savings.... [The] main interest lies in the skill with which

the women themselves, and their respective environments, are presented. Esther Downes, the beautiful, slum-dwelling Brighton shop-girl whom Gorse—returning on holiday to the scenes of his boyhood—picks up, in company with two old schoolmates, Ryan and Bell, on *The West Pier*; and Mrs Plumleigh-Bruce, Colonel's daughter and Colonel's widow, the middle-aged 'drawling, fruity, affectedly-indolent', self-styled Lady of Reading... whom the young trickster separates, not only from her bank-balance, but from a rival suitor, the boorish, 'subterraneously lecherous' local estate-agent who shares the title-rôle in *Mr Stimpson and Mr Gorse*.

The third, and latest, instalment, *Unknown Assailant,* set 'early in the year 1933', follows the previous examples, beginning with a Defoe-like simplicity and directness:

> Ivy Barton, a Chelsea barmaid, was on Sundays able
> to stay in bed an hour later than on weekdays. This
> she relished very much.

Opening her *News of the World*, Ivy ('a decidedly foolish but very good and lovable girl... twenty-nine years of age') reads an account of a working-girl who was tied to a tractor in the country and robbed of £20 by an 'unknown assailant'. The latter is, naturally, Ernest Ralph Gorse, who... now, posing as 'the Honourable Gerald Claridge', frequents the pub where Ivy is employed. Later, when she is herself trussed-up in a wood in Berkshire, he compels her to read the relevant extract aloud to him as a concession to his vanity before disappearing with *her* savings (£50 in cash), plus a cheque for £200 belonging to her 'harsh, vain, grasping and embittered' father: an ex-gamekeeper who imagined that he was investing this sum in a musical comedy backed by Gorse's acquaintance, the theatrical impresario Lord Lyddon.

That is the story in outline: on the face of it not a very edifying one; the delight we take in reading it is due, as usual, to the incidentals: the first interview between Gorse and Ivy's father, when they both address each other as 'Sir' and there seems no way out of the tangle;... and the delectable drunken sequence, in Mr Hamilton's happiest vein, when the ex-gamekeeper, being put to bed by his wife after a meeting with a rich industrialist, babbles lyrically 'about hearts of gold, bricks of gold, bricks with hearts of gold, hearts with bricks of gold, golds with hearts of bricks, and, even, half-bricks with halfs of gold.' (pp. 59-62)

Students of the Gorse saga may notice several technical changes in [*Unknown Assailant*] (apart from its extreme shortness by comparison with the two preceding volumes): the scheme of ironically-titled sections ('Gorse the Tempter', 'Gorse the Revealer', 'Gorse the Absent', etc—and, perhaps most amusing of all, 'Gorse of Assandrava') seems, regrettably, to have been abandoned; secondly, the sense of period which Mr Hamilton, as a rule, so vividly conveys is noticeably lacking: despite the year in which the story takes place, there is no allusion (as the Kaiser's war is mentioned in *The West Pier* or the General Strike in *Mr Stimpson*), to the encroaching Nazi menace or the world-situation generally, to which one would have expected Gorse, with his feeling for incipient evil, to be well attuned; on the other hand, the personal picture is gradually growing darker, and Gorse's unnecessarily vicious treatment of Ivy shows that murder cannot be delayed much longer: the disclosure of his particular sexual 'perversion'—foreshadowed in the first chapter of *The West Pier*—seeming to indicate strangulation as his eventual method of killing.

Of the present trilogy, despite many felicities contained in *Unknown Assailant, Mr Stimpson and Mr Gorse* is probably the most rewarding: the sections dealing with Major Perry's agonized attempts at versification, or Mr Stimpson's struggles with his crossword-puzzles, are among the funniest in contemporary fiction, while the closing chapters, in which motor cars are seen as a sinister coleopterous species that has conquered and enslaved mankind, is an extraordinary piece of *bravura* which might astonish those who have thought of the author as a purely realistic and colloquial writer, with an unrivalled ear for catching the conversational banalities of daily life. (pp. 62-3)

[It is] surely time to second Mr John Betjeman's opinion that Mr Hamilton is one of the best living English novelists. (p. 63)

> *J. Maclaren-Ross, ''Mr. Hamilton and Mr. Gorse,''* in London Magazine, *Vol. 3, No. 1, January, 1956, pp. 58-63.*

JOHN RUSSELL TAYLOR

It was entirely by accident that I came to read *The Slaves of Solitude* a few months ago.... No further than fifty pages in, I realized that without warning I had blundered into one of those marvellous, terrible author-reader relationships which imperatively require the reader to find and gobble down every accessible word the writer has written—which, in the next couple of months, I did.

Not that it was easy. Patrick Hamilton the playwright still has a reputation—everyone has heard at least of *Rope* and *Gaslight*—but Patrick Hamilton the novelist has virtually none, as far as I can discover. Many of Hamilton's books, from a novel-writing career spanning thirty years, 1925-55, are out of print; none of his novels is in paper back, though apparently a paperback version of *Hangover Square* is about to emerge.... (p. 53)

Why? It really is very strange.... Certainly his novels are never experimental in technique—unless cultivation in the 1930s and 1940s of certain narrative techniques which have been regarded somewhat askance since the days of Thackeray may itself be considered experimental. There is nothing in the subject-matter or the way it is organized to mark out Patrick Hamilton as anything but a popular novelist. And yet, the final effect of his books is certainly not popular in any normal sense. His attitude to his characters is too involved and ambiguous. His merciless precision and unsentimentality in dealing with people and situations which seem bound to lead their creator into sentimentality or sensationalism or both must puzzle and alienate the sort of reader who (period image) might have picked up a Hamilton novel at his local Boots library while harmlessly in search of a good read. And his meticulous cultivation of his own particular social garden, the dead middle of the middle classes, is hardly calculated to endear him to any section of the reading public, least of all the middle-middle classes themselves. (pp. 53-4)

[Hamilton's] first novel, *Monday Morning,* was published in 1925, and in the long tradition of first novels is largely autobiographical in its materials: it is about a young man with vague writing aspirations who lives in a private hotel in Earl's Court, drifts into a romantic attachment with a girl who lives there too, and becomes an actor almost by accident. It is light, and charming, and sympathetically funny about its hero to just the right degree; it is also in many ways a sketch for Hamilton's first big success, *Craven House,* which followed the next year. Again the setting is a private hotel, or more strictly, a boarding house, near Turnham Green, and again the hero is a young

man with vague writing ambitions. But this time the hero is only one thread in a complex pattern: we see him in relation with his father, who dies, very movingly, in the course of the book, and with the other inhabitants of the boarding house, a splendid collection of eccentrics who also take off outside young master Wildman's ken, on devious paths of their own.

For the first time we get some clear idea of Hamilton's range, and some hint of the things he is especially good at. There is his remarkable way with children ... and with the elderly; in particular *Craven House* has, in Mr Spicer, the first of his wonderful gallery of aging oddities, flowery of speech and shifty of purpose, whose choice exhibits are Mr Eccles in *The Plains of Cement,* Mr Thwaites in *The Slaves of Solitude* and Mr Stimpson in *Mr Stimpson and Mr Gorse.* There is his brilliance in handling the big scene, like the disgrace of the maid Audrey Custard and the dinner with a Russian guest. There is the passionate romance Hamilton conducted throughout his life with London, its sights, sounds and smells, which have perhaps never found an extoller at once so devoutly poetic and so ironically detached. And above all there is his way of playing tragedy as though it is farce: hearts are broken and lives wrecked as we roll round, helpless with mirth. And yet Hamilton is never heartless: the sadness of his stories is never any the less sad because they are so funny. Quite the reverse, in fact; Mr Eccles's courtship of Ella in *The Plains of Cement* is funny enough to provoke that ultimate solecism for an Englishman, laughing aloud while alone on the Underground, and yet there is no character we feel with more strongly than Ella, and none about whose future we more fervently wonder when the book comes to an end.

This last remark perhaps suggests in what way Hamilton's appeal is 'old-fashioned'. All his books have clear, well-articulated stories and rounded characters in whom it is fully intended that we shall believe as real human beings with lives they have lived before the book begins and usually will continue to live after the book ends. (pp. 54-5)

20,000 Streets Under the Sky is the work with which, after the less notable interlude of his 1928 theatre novel *Twopence Coloured* (despite the interest of the background, it suffers from some diffuseness and a rather vapid heroine), he consolidated his reputation. The first section in particular, *The Midnight Bell,* was enthusiastically praised by J. B. Priestley, and established Hamilton in the rather unlikely niche of a working-class realist. Oddly enough, this and *Hangover Square* (1941), which remain perhaps the best-remembered of Hamilton's novels—in so far, that is, as any are remembered—are, seen in retrospect, among his least appealing. Both concern the hopeless, not entirely blind infatuation of a generally well-disposed, well-meaning man for an utterly no-good girl; the second is complicated somewhat by the fact that the hero also goes mad from time to time and finally manages to kill the girl. *The Midnight Bell,* though, offers no such incidental diversions: it concerns itself exclusively with the not particularly interesting relationship between Bob, barman at the Midnight Bell public house, and Jenny, a prostitute he mistakenly thinks he can reform.

But then, unexpectedly after this not specially promising beginning the sequence finds its form with *The Siege of Pleasure.* Here we go back a few years to discover exactly how Jenny embarked on her way of life. The tale is of classic brevity and directness, taking place almost entirely in the twenty-four hours during which Jenny lapses from being the new-found treasure of a family of doddering septuagenarians to a life of sleazy sluttery all because she has a few drinks too many and just can't be bothered to go and sort things out afterwards. The third section, *The Plains of Cement,* is even better: in time, it starts before *The Midnight Bell* and ends slightly later, and its central figure is one on the margin of *The Midnight Bell,* Ella, the barmaid who nourishes a hopeless passion for Bob. In the main, it is an account of the extraordinary wooing of Ella by an elderly and very peculiar customer who almost but not quite persuades her to drift into marriage by his sheer vagueness, assuming everything and stating nothing. The scene in which his passion reduces him to a state where all he can do is to answer everything Ella says with a maddening 'What? What?' . . . , is one of the funniest in the twentieth-century English novel, and yet the final effect of the whole book is to distil a pervasive bitter-sweet melancholy: Hamilton's world is sad because the good (and Ella is an extraordinary example of a character who is thoroughly good without being cloying or insipid) never really triumph. After the first three books the best they can hope for is some sort of epiphany, a visionary glimpse of another order of life. . . . (pp. 55-7)

The ultimate demonstration of this, and perhaps all things considered Hamilton's best book, is *The Slaves of Solitude.* Here he is back on home ground, the shabby-genteel boarding house occupied by a whole group of unforgettable characters. . . . It is difficult to explain to anyone who has not read Patrick Hamilton exactly what makes a book like *The Slaves of Solitude* so hypnotically gripping. Certainly his mastery of dialogue plays a large part in it: Mr Thwaites's addiction to repeating, twisting and turning inside out the more hair-raising clichés of everyday speech . . . ; Vicki Kugelmann's eager display of 1925ish colloquialisms in a general context of appalling archness and effrontery ('Can I make a cocktail, or can I make a cocktail? Uh-huh! Oh, boy! Wizard!')—all these exert a horrid fascination.

But, contrary to what one might expect of a novelist who was also a spectacularly successful dramatist, the dialogue is not the most important factor in the success of his novels: indeed, many of the best passages come when his characters are quite alone, or are observed unconsciously revealing themselves in action. His eye for detail is impeccable. . . . In *The Slaves of Solitude* there is too a particular virtuosity in juggling with perspective in the narrative: whenever we are becoming too enclosed in the world the three principal characters create for themselves we are neatly shaken out of it by some endistancing device, such as the short chapter in which a piano-tuner friend of the landlady's comes to eat at the Rosamund Tea Rooms and suddenly we see the whole milieu as it appears to an observant outsider. . . . (pp. 57-8)

Perhaps *The Slaves of Solitude* shows Patrick Hamilton's gifts as a novelist at their height, but in practice it would be very difficult to choose between it and the first two Gorse novels [*The West Pier* and *Mr Stimpson and Mr Gorse*]. These really are if anything even more extraordinary as *tours de force.* At the time their reception was mixed: why, some critics started asking, should a writer choose to build a sequence of novels around anyone quite so lacking in redeeming features as Ernest Ralph Gorse, whose most innocent moments are occupied in defrauding naïve young women out of their life savings, and whose end, so hints scattered throughout the three books lead us to believe, would turn out much worse. It is not a question many readers coming to the books now would ask, for whatever his reasons for creating Gorse may have been, Hamilton has found in him the ideal centre-piece for his darkly hilarious dissection of middle-class England between the wars. In *The West Pier* we catch a premonitory glimpse of Gorse the schoolboy, getting away with his first crime by robbing and tying up a little girl, and through his headmaster's practised professional evasiveness, escaping the consequences. . . . In *Mr Stimpson and Mr Gorse* Gorse is at the high point of his career, manoeuvring his victim, the insufferable Mrs Plumleigh-Bruce, and her opportunistic swain Mr Stimpson, with consummate virtuosity towards the desirable end in which Stimpson leaves her flat and Gorse departs with a nice lump sum from her savings. *Unknown Assailant* starts Gorse on the downward path, back defrauding shopgirls and barmaids; it shows signs of tiredness both in the materials, which hark back too closely to *The West Pier,* and in their treatment, which is larded with quotations from two unlikely books alleged to have been written on Gorse afterwards and dealing with all sorts of matters which their authors could not, from what we have already been told, possibly know. The concluding volume was apparently never written; no novel appeared from Hamilton in the remaining seven years of his life, and when he died in 1962 he was, it seems, almost forgotten, despite the enthusiasm of earlier critics who had not hesitated to find him 'one of the best living English novelists' (John Betjeman, apropos of *The Slaves of Solitude*).

How can this situation be remedied; is it, in fact, worth remedying? Patrick Hamilton is not, I suppose, a great novelist; he has neither contributed anything significant to the techniques of the novel, nor presented in his novels a vision of the world so compelling that the readers' perceptions are never quite the same again, nor done any of the other things a great novelist is supposed to do. On the other hand, there are places, and situations, and types of people that one can never encounter again without thinking of Hamilton and seeing them at least partially through his eyes. In particular there are some backwaters of middle-class English life which have never been explored so well as by Hamilton, and sometimes never at all otherwise. . . . He is excellent being funny or sinister about love, not so compelling when he tries to deal with it seriously and straightforwardly. His is, admittedly, a very small, compact world, and when he tries to step right out of it, as in *Impromptu in Moribundia* (1939), a satirical fantasy about a planet where people think and live entirely according to advertising slogans, the results are only intermittently effective.

But then novelists do not have to be universally regarded as great in order to continue to be read. For the addict much of the fascination . . . lies precisely in their limitations and the skill with which they turn them into advantages. Patrick Hamilton is a writer somewhat in this special class: his very quirks and prejudices, carried from book to book, become in themselves endearing. . . . Patrick Hamilton is certainly not one of those writers who will suddenly turn out posthumously to have been, all unsuspected, a key figure in twentieth-century literature. But as a giver of large and lasting pleasure . . . , it is difficult to believe we have heard the last of him. (pp. 58-60)

John Russell Taylor, "Patrick Hamilton," in London Magazine, *n.s. Vol. 6, No. 2, May, 1966, pp. 53-60.*

ABE LAUFE

Popularity on Broadway from 1920 to 1950 was not limited to comedies, farces, or plays which sacrificed serious themes to emphasize humor. Audiences for the most part did prefer amusing plays, but they also supported the more serious dramas.

Angel Street, a melodrama, . . . ran over one thousand performances. (p. 129)

Angel Street is an old-fashioned thriller with no embellishments of farce, novel setting, or new property devices to delude audiences into believing it is anything but pure melodrama. It pits a homicidal man against a virtuous heroine who is rescued at the opportune moment just as the heroines were rescued by the United States Marines in the old ten-twenty-thirty-cent tent-show thrillers at the turn of the century.

Angel Street, however, is neither hackneyed nor poorly written. It has excellent characterization, dramatic structure, and suspense. It presents no strikingly new plot variations as it unfolds the relatively simple and familiar story of a man, Mr. Manningham, who deliberately tries to drive his wife insane. While Mr. Manningham is out of the house, Inspector Rough visits Mrs. Manningham and explains that her husband is suspected of having killed a Mrs. Barlow in the very same room fifteen years earlier and that Manningham's reason for returning to the scene of his crime is to find the famous Barlow rubies. . . . When Mrs. Manningham is convinced that her husband is planning to place her in an institution to get her out of the way, she agrees to help the inspector find the necessary evidence to prove her husband's guilt. The inspector picks the lock on Manningham's desk and finds missing letters and an old brooch. Mrs. Manningham says the brooch originally contained some loose beads she has hidden in a vase, and when she produces the beads, they prove to be the missing rubies. In the third act, Manningham discovers his desk drawer has been rifled, sends for Mrs. Manningham, threatens her, and then starts to choke her just as Inspector Rough appears and accuses Manningham of the murder. Manningham tries to escape but is captured by deputies.

The major difference between *Angel Street* and other Victorian melodramas is the plot development. Unlike the typical mystery melodrama, *Angel Street* does not resort to sliding doors, secret panels, and unidentified characters who slink across a dimly lighted stage. The play does not build up false clues, kill off suspects, or capitalize on the blunders of strange policemen. Instead, *Angel Street* arouses suspense in a slight story singularly free from complexities by combining intellectual and emotional reactions rather than by physical action on the stage. The dramatist's use of the technique of naturalizing the audience also makes the mystery more effective. In the first act, the audience knows as much as Mrs. Manningham and Inspector Rough, and knows more than Mr. Manningham suspects. The dramatist places himself at a disadvantage, for, by not withholding information, he must develop the second and third acts with little more than a search for the evidence. This disadvantage of having the detective take both Mrs. Manningham and the audience into his confidence, however, gives the dramatist the advantage of heightening the suspense, for the audience shares Mrs. Manningham's fears and Inspector Rough's realization that Mr. Manningham may return before any definite clues are uncovered. When Inspector Rough hides off stage and the audience realizes he has left his hat on stage where Mr. Manningham is certain to see it, the situation causes an almost uncontrollable urge to shout a warning just as audiences did in the old-fashioned thrillers. At the last minute, Rough dashes in to retrieve his hat, and the audience sighs in relief; for if Mr. Manningham had discovered the hat, the audience would have lost its naturalized position in watching the evidence being uncovered.

The suspense keeps mounting until the third-act climax. After Manningham has been captured and bound securely, Mrs. Manningham asks to be left alone with her husband. The pace appears retarded as Manningham asks his wife to cut his bonds, and Mrs. Manningham mumbles to herself while she gets a razor, then seems to misplace it, then picks it up again. It is the uncertainty which makes the tempo seem too deliberately casual, for the audience is not sure if Mrs. Manningham has asked to be alone with her husband because she really has gone mad or because she wants to help him escape. Then, at the height of the suspense, Mrs. Manningham's rage finally releases her fears and she violently denounces her husband in a theatrically effective, well-written denouement. The emotional response of the audience is strong because it has shared Mrs. Manningham's terror as well as her desire to expose the villain to the same type of treatment he has given her. When Manningham is taken away and Inspector Rough says he has given Mrs. Manningham the most horrible evening of her life, she says, "Oh, no—the most wonderful," a fitting curtain speech, with which the audience agrees.

The basic characterizations in *Angel Street* may seem to be typically melodramatic. Mr. Manningham personifies an evil menace; Mrs. Manningham, the virtuous and persecuted heroine; Rough, the kindly police inspector; Elizabeth, the heroine's faithful servant; and Nancy, the brazen young servant who encourages Manningham to seduce her. The development of the characterizations, however, is not typical of melodrama. Mr. Manningham's evil is projected without resorting to snarls or sneers. His evil is far more vicious because it is a calculating mental torture which he inflicts upon his wife. Mrs. Manningham's terror is not projected by the conventional screams or shouting of an anguished heroine. In the first act, she does plead for patience and sympathy, but in the second and third acts, she conveys her fears in her bewilderment, her confusion, and her suppressed rages. Rough is neither the extremely clever Sherlock Holmes-type detective nor the dull, plodding policeman. He is shrewd, rather than cunning; efficient; and a bit whimsical. Intelligent dialogue, free from obvious attempts to insert cleverness or humor, which would destroy the mood of mounting suspense, aids the characterizations.

Angel Street proved that a well-written Victorian thriller, if effectively produced, could please audiences and critics in the 1940s. Yet the story circulated about the play just after its opening revealed the skepticism with which Broadway regarded its chance for survival. The play had been a success in London under the title *Gaslight* and then had been tried out on the West Coast with no great success. According to Broadway gossip, when *Angel Street* opened in New York, tickets had been printed to cover only the first performance on Friday night and the subsequent Saturday matinee and evening performances. Instead of being a failure, as the management had feared, the play appealed to reviewers, many of whom felt that *Angel Street* was one of the first plays with genuine entertainment value produced that season. Obviously the producer rushed through a ticket order, for *Angel Street* developed into a hit and ran over three years to establish a record of 1,295 performances. (pp. 131-34)

> Abe Laufe, "*Eight Dramas the Critics Liked and One Maverick,*" *in his* Anatomy of a Hit: Long-Run Plays on Broadway from 1900 to the Present Day, *Hawthorn Books, Inc., 1966, pp. 129-57.*

CAROLE MANSUR

[When Hamilton died in 1962, he] was by then an alcoholic but had produced eleven novels, two of which, **Hangover Square** and *The Slaves of Solitude,* were rated among ''the minor masterpieces of English fiction'' by J. B. Priestley when they were reissued . . . in 1972. Now one of the later novels, *The West Pier,* first published in 1951, has been [republished] . . . , vaunting on its cover an accolade from Graham Greene who pronounces it ''The best novel written about Brighton''. . . .

The West Pier doesn't match the achievement of [Hamilton's] other books. By the time he embarked upon it, the first of a trilogy tracing the career in crime of one Ernest Ralph Gorse—he was canny at choosing names to make you wriggle with discomfort from the start—Patrick Hamilton was in decline, ravaged by the addiction which so often complicated the lives of his condemned characters. Too deliberate and too distant a manner slows down the steady scrutiny of personality and the measured development of the story which were the compelling strengths of his earlier writing.

Gorse's misdemeanours—a series of poison pen letters, very petty theft—are trifling enough, but every detail is introduced as part of a grand design which is the examination of the calculating, really rather sinister, intelligence of this ''rare but identifiable'' type. . . . So adamant is Hamilton to label the distinguishing features of this species that we fail to feel involved with his peculiar history.

What is still haunting, though, is the strange, very personal vision of the world nurtured by Hamilton, a vision manifest in settings not dissimilar from those chosen by Greene: his generous tribute was perhaps made in recognition of that twilight territory shared between them, epitomised by the epithet ''seedy''. The word may seem a little worn and predictable attached to Graham Greene but it should still be respectable to utter it in conjunction with Hamilton's less familiar name. . . .

The evocation of the atmosphere of a place to mirror despair is one of Patrick Hamilton's distinctive traits. Each of these novels, although so relatively unambitious in scope, is profoundly depressing; the protagonists become prisoners of these purgatorial landscapes, and their creator fatalistically resigned to their perpetual wandering. He neither grants nor is granted a glimmer of hope, is incapable of reaching beyond to higher things and a clear blue heaven.

Yet it is precisely this earthbound quality, the sense of insignificance of his characters in a mysterious world, which makes his novels still so sympathetic. And, of course, there is the aggravation of this alienation by alcohol: tragically in *Hangover Square,* simply ludicrously in the farcical amorous overtures of *The Slaves of Solitude,* and most insidiously in *The West Pier* when it is hinted that the innocent cocktails at the awesome Metropole are the beginning of a drinking problem. The weaknesses of these sad, doomed, often inarticulate people, emotionally deprived or deceived, are compassionately probed, with no pat solutions offered, no smart dinner party philosophies, no social programmes or charities.

> *Carole Mansur, ''Brighton Boozy,'' in* Punch, *Vol. 288, No. 7530, April 10, 1985, p. 64.*

BILL GREENWELL

In 1972, writing of Patrick Hamilton, J. B. Priestley felt sure that 'there must be a whole generation of readers who know nothing about him and his fiction'. Certainly this must still be true. I'd never encountered him except—as Priestley also speculated—as the playwright of the unexceptional *Gaslight.* For this reason, the wild hilarity of *The West Pier,* first published

in 1951 and unaccountably never reprinted 'til this year, came as a welcome astonishment. . . .

Priestley accorded [Hamilton] that most damaging accolade: 'a master among minor novelists'. Such epithets are all too liable to blot the reputation of real genius and this republication of *The West Pier* arrived with a more boggling recommendation still: '''The best novel written about Brighton''—Graham Greene'. . . .

Gorse is a masterly creation, an unemotional schemer who practises his reptilian charm upon the petty-minded, the pea-brained, the witless scorers of tiny social points. He is not credited with intelligence, only with sufficient skill to trick his victims out of every last penny. Nor is he presented as supremely deft. He is liable to bungle. He simply battens on those sufficiently credulous to believe him. And his skill is to parody every social inanity going. In effect, Gorse is a nasty shadow of his compassionate creator, since Hamilton is a highly 'astute social botanist', a phrase used in this novel's successor, *Mr Stimpson and Mr Gorse*—which is, if anything, even funnier.

Hamilton is a pastmaster of social rigmarole, of the trite and trifling gambits with which people attempt to elevate their status. He has a brilliant ear for the fibbing banalities of bar-talk, the phoney pleasantries of casual acquaintance, the dreadful airs and disgraces of that class of people for whom there are hundreds of rungs on the social ladder. In *The West Pier,* he excels in his descriptions of schoolboy one-upmanship and the nonsensical banter of Getting Off. Hamilton's best tactic is to comment on every foible with a sublime mock-pedantry, in an explanatory deadpan assisted by his use of quick paragraphs.

Priestley rather disparaged the Gorse books, thinking them shorter on creative energy than the two Hamiltons still in print, *Hangover Square* and *The Slaves of Solitude.* I disagree, with the fervency of instant conversion.

> *Bill Greenwell, ''Snake and Ladder,'' in* New Statesman, *Vol. 110, No. 2839, August 16, 1985, p. 26.*

NICK KIMBERLEY

[It is] strange that the pub novel has never become a genre in the same way as, say, the sports novel or the hospital novel. The absence of the genre makes Patrick Hamilton's trilogy of London novels, *Twenty Thousand Streets Under the Sky,* all the more remarkable. The three novels . . . originally appeared separately: *The Midnight Bell* in 1930, *The Siege of Pleasure* in 1932, *The Plains of Cement* in 1934. . . .

'The Midnight Bell' is a pub near the Euston Road and Warren Street; it's neither opulent nor seedy but pleasantly in-between. Its staff is Bob, the waiter, and Ella, the barmaid. The first part of the trilogy [*The Midnight Bell*] is Bob's Story (there *is* something soapily operatic here), the last [*The Plains of Cement*] is Ella's. In between, the much shorter *The Siege of Pleasure* takes us away from the Fitzrovian pub to show us the life of Jenny, a streetwalker who has already broken Bob's heart in Part One and whose existence needs explaining. In Hamilton's eyes, these are simple and largely unmalicious folk, unable to take control of their lives or their passions. There's something lofty, even patrician about the way he punctures their ambitions, their pretensions: Hamilton was a satirist and didn't hesitate to caricature.

But his cruelty is always tempered by fellow-feeling: he understood the metropolitan loneliness that drives his characters, he knew why most of them sought release in the bottle. His understanding wasn't mere abstract sympathy either. He himself was a serious drinker—he eventually sought help from the same Dr Dent who was later to cure William Burroughs' junk habit. No doubt personal experience gives his accounts of alcoholic oblivion their queasy authenticity.

More to the point, Bob's infatuation for Jenny replays more or less blow by blow Hamilton's own affair with a prostitute, Lily. Bruce Hamilton wrote a biography of his brother, *The Light Went Out,* in which he said, 'His pursuit of Lily often led him into strange company and brought him queer experiences; and it was now that he began to drink heavily . . . *The Midnight Bell* was the story of his enslavement to Lily, tailored to the needs of fiction and form.' No doubt this accounts for the venomous, almost misogynistic glee with which Hamilton sets Jenny on the road to depravity.

But the trilogy isn't all venom and satire; for all his aloofness, Hamilton liked most of his characters. . . . His pessimism went deep, never deeper than in his two best novels, *Hangover Square* and *The Slaves of Solitude.* . . . [*Twenty Thousand Streets Under the Sky*] finds him not quite so harsh, allowing Bob, at least, an escape route from his infatuation—which is in any case never simple blind love.

But the most remarkable and enjoyable thing about *Twenty Thousand Streets Under the Sky* is its London-ness, its sense of a teeming population at odds with each other yet still managing to make a city. That city had a life of its own, almost predatory: *The Siege of Pleasure* ends with one of Jenny's customers 'swallowed up for ever in the great world of London'. Against that predator, the pub provides a sanctuary.

This isn't a flawless masterpiece; during his life, Hamilton was best known as a playwright (*Rope, Gaslight*) and there's a staginess about his trilogy—he explicitly refers to the pub as a 'theatre' and later takes us 'behind the scenes, now the curtain was up'. There's also something heavy handed—like a music-hall monologue—in the way he mockingly underlines his moral. But this is nearly 60 years ago and he was a young writer, only 25 when he wrote *The Midnight Bell.*

In the end, there's a lot to enjoy here, not least an impossible nostalgia for a London full of rattling trams. . . . But Hamilton's London wasn't that different from ours: even then, Warren Street was just round the corner from the Euston Road. Even now, the same plains of cement are made up of the same 20,000 streets, under the same sky.

Nick Kimberley, "One Man in His Time," in New Statesman, *Vol. 114, No. 2938, July 17, 1987, p. 29.*

JOHN BAYLEY

[The uniqueness of Hamilton's *Twenty Thousand Streets Under the Sky*] consists to a very large extent in the *dégustation,* as

the French say, of boredom: excruciating, fascinating, endless banality, interspersed—not varied—with a pathos so homely and total that it brings tears to the eyes. Beckett and Pinter have nothing on Patrick Hamilton at his best: in fact, beside him they seem as mannered and as formulaic as the Jacobean dramatists do after Shakespeare. Patrick Hamilton is not exploiting urban boredom, or making it witty: it just comes up in a great wave out of his commitment to his subject, to the pubs and prostitutes and streets, the flotsam of the great dense city. Nothing is on show, or self-consciously revealed. . . . Almost as if by accident, Hamilton contrived an artistic truth out of Dr Johnson's observation that nothing is too little for so little a creature as man.

It is for these reasons that even the *Times* was moved to comment in its obituary that Hamilton was 'a genuine minor poet of the loneliness, purposelessness and frustration of contemporary urban life'. Handsome as it seems, the tribute is misleading. Urban life is the same everywhere, and always has been, and only during the last century has it become a fashionable cliché to refer to it in these terms. Where Hamilton is concerned, it would be equally true to say he is a connoisseur of the excitement, obsessions and enjoyments of urban life, for his characters are submerged in these, as they are in the pubs, the cinemas and Lyons Corner Houses, and all the rituals and consolations of such places. *The Midnight Bell,* the most directly autobiographical of the trilogy, recounts the obsession of Bob, the young waiter at the pub, with the prostitute Jenny, who happens to come in one day. . . . The barmaid, Ella, loves him hopelessly, and he is always nice to her. What a cliché situation, and yet Hamilton makes the trio astonishingly individualised—seeing, for example, the natural refinement of Bob, and his old fondness for reading history books, through Ella's hopelessly devoted gaze.

There is no sense of 'waste' in all this. . . . The second volume of the trilogy, *The Siege of Pleasure,* is about Jenny, and how she became a prostitute, and here the plot does receive a certain stiffening of dogma which carries it along all the more authoritatively. Her downfall may be due to drink and social pressures, and yet the novel inexorably shows that Jenny is the sort of girl—and not a bad sort either—who is bound for trouble. Today she would be a one-parent family with a permanent entourage of social workers. [*The Plains of Cement,* the] last section of the trilogy, about Ella, is in some ways the most moving. Ella is one of the losers, but is not in the least sentimentalised. Her sober charms always seem to attract the wrong kind of suitor—bores adore her endless patience and good nature—and after Bob's disappearance she ends up in her old job as barmaid at the Midnight Bell. (p. 6)

John Bayley, "Falling in Love with the Traffic Warden," in London Review of Books, *Vol. 9, No. 17, October 1, 1987, pp. 6-8.*

Alice Hoffman

1952-

American novelist, scriptwriter, and short story writer.

In her novels, Hoffman imparts mythic significance to ordinary American life. While delineating the interactions of small groups of characters within vividly evoked settings, Hoffman introduces into her narratives such elements as symbolism, folklore, and stylized, richly descriptive language to express the powerful emotional forces underlying the thoughts and actions of her protagonists. Alexandra Johnson observed that the hallmarks of Hoffman's fiction include "a shimmering prose style, the fusing of fantasy and realism, the preoccupation with the way the mythic weaves itself into the everyday. Hoffman's narrative domain is the domestic, the daily. Yet her vision—and voice—are lyrical." Although some critics regard Hoffman's intense portrayals of birth, desire, love, dreams, and death as occasionally exaggerated, others praise her insight into human psychology and behavior.

With her first novel, *Property Of* (1977), Hoffman impressed reviewers by infusing qualities of epic romance into a realistic story of juvenile delinquency. The unnamed narrator of this work is a seventeen-year-old girl from suburban New York City who falls in love and becomes "property of" the leader of a street gang. After lapsing into a world of violence and drug addiction, the narrator ultimately rejects her lover and his environment. Critics admired Hoffman's depiction of the impassioned and self-destructive lifestyles of her characters. In subsequent works, Hoffman refines and varies the heightened realism of *Property Of. The Drowning Season* (1979) is a fabulistic depiction of intergenerational relationships within a family. This novel concerns a dying Long Island matriarch, known as Esther the White, who endeavors to maintain dominance over her suicidal son and his daughter, Esther the Black, whom the family views as a potential usurper of her grandmother's power. This novel's menacing atmosphere is underscored by recurring images, symbols, and sordid events. In *Angel Landing* (1980), Hoffman contrasts the reactions of both passive and active characters who are confronted by personal problems and the threatened destruction of their environment.

Hoffman's use of folklore, symbolism, and eccentric characters to suggest mythic elements within realistic settings and scenarios is again featured prominently in her novels *White Horses* (1982), *Fortune's Daughter* (1985), and *Illumination Night* (1987). *White Horses* is set in California and centers on the tale of the arias—supernatural men who free women from dull and unfulfilling lives by leading them into romance and adventure. In this novel, a young girl becomes obsessed by this legend, which was related to her by her mother, and develops an incestuous longing for her brother under the delusion that he is one of the arias. *Fortune's Daughter* concerns two abandoned mothers who become friends through their maternal instincts. Using expressionistic effects to illustrate mythic feminine powers, Hoffman evokes metaphorical parallels between childbirth and such natural upheavals as ice storms and earthquakes. *Illumination Night*, which several critics consider Hoffman's finest work, depicts several residents of Martha's Vineyard, Massachusetts, who struggle to come to terms with their desires, anxieties, and loneliness. By developing symbolic

© Jerry Bauer

images and events and shifting points of view among various characters, including a brooding husband, his agoraphobic wife, a promiscuous teenage girl, and an aging woman dying of cancer, Hoffman weaves a richly textured narrative that assumes various implications. Characteristic of Hoffman's works, this novel juxtaposes ordinary people and universal concerns with eccentric characters and fantastical events rendered in a lushly descriptive prose style.

(See also *Contemporary Authors,* Vols. 77-80.)

MICHAEL MEWSHAW

In *Property Of* Alice Hoffman views life as if through the jagged prisms of a broken whisky bottle or a haze of heroin. Although much of her material is familiar—the corner candy store, warring teenage gangs, leather jackets, young love in customized cars, dope and disaster—she brings a fierce personal intensity to it.

When the unnamed 17-year-old narrator first meets McKay, president of the Orphans, she admits, "What I want . . . is for you to fall in love with me." McKay will have none of that, but with his adrenalin high after a street fight, he drives onto the George Washington Bridge and makes love to her in an emergency parking area. Youthful romanticism still intact, she moves in with him, accepting his churlish machismo, his petty criminality and a drag racing code that makes him sound like a Hemingway of the highway.... Addicted to love, she becomes addicted to heroin, because she cannot stand to be outside, alone. In the end when she kicks both habits, the reader is moved, but cannot understand why she took so long.

The problem is mostly with the first-person narrator who is so sensitive, lyrical and perceptive it is difficult to believe she's 17, that she would fall for McKay, or that she would hang around a candy store unless it was close to Barnard....

Furthermore, Alice Hoffman seldom trusts the reader. After each dramatic scene, she offers an explanation. After almost every line of dialogue, she repeats herself or asks a rhetorical question. Sometimes both: "It's only a cousin of Jose's. A friend of the Orphans.... Some cousin of Jose's. What did I know about Jose?"

Alice Hoffman's story is too strong to be destroyed by these annoying stylistic tics, but they do diminish an otherwise impressive debut.

Michael Mewshaw, in a review of "Property Of," in The New York Times Book Review, *July 10, 1977, p. 10.*

RICHARD R. LINGEMAN

Alice Hoffman's world in *Property Of* is as harsh and gritty as the city streets, yet as shadowy and eerily composed as a bad dream. It is the world of "the Avenue," the urban territory roamed by a gang, the Orphans, and as the book opens it is the Night of the Wolf, when the Orphans take to the dark, snow-silvered streets, hunting down their rivals, the Pack, in ritualistic vengeance for the murder of their former president. The novel's unnamed "I," a young girl, is mesmerized by McKay, the new leader of the Orphans, and, like a knight and his lady, they seal a bond of attraction before he goes out into the night to do battle. She waits with the gang's girl friends, known as the "Property," vowing she will not become property too.

But she does—McKay's property, at once independent yet bound up in his life. McKay has his rudimentary code of honor: "There's no winning. There's only defending your honor. You do a good job of it, or you don't." She hates this "honor," this word that falls like a sword between them, but she can't leave. Honor, like McKay's love for her, is a spell; but McKay is sucked into the ultimate spell—heroin—and she is drawn down with him. At one point she sees that being property is to belong and "It is not so very despicable to belong.... The self that does not belong is not owned by itself but by others. By another."

Property Of is a remarkably envisioned novel, almost mythic in its cadences, hypnotic. McKay and the heroine are like tragic lovers in a courtly romance played out in candy stores, clubhouses and mean streets; even heroin is like some enchanted potion of death. Ultimately, though, the fable's clean arc is spent in novelistic plot complications that drag it down, but the imagining is true, the writing lovely....

Alice Hoffman imbues her juvenile delinquents with a romantic intensity that lifts them out of sociology.

Richard R. Lingeman, in a review of "Property Of," in The New York Times, *July 14, 1977, p. 25.*

EDITH MILTON

[In] Alice Hoffman's first novel, *Property Of,* the world is already destroyed and anarchy is its center. There are no families. There is also no recognizable culture, no home, no past, no future. People do not even have real names; the narrator-heroine is nameless, the others are called things like Danny the Sweet, Starry, Viet Nam, and the Dolphin. We are in the urban jungle, and the action Hoffman describes is in the drug-motivated rivalry between street gangs. But they are very odd gangs. First of all, they are not city gangs, but roam the edge of suburbia. Secondly, they have none of the usual gang loyalties to race or religion, kin or culture. They are, of all things, gangs of WASPS, and they speak of war and honor in a street-epic lingo close to parody. The hero behaves with the gutter panache of el Cid caught on the pages of *True Romances.* Nevertheless, Hoffman is not writing a *True Romances* piece; in fact, she comes close to turning the shoddy values, tarnished ideals, and vanishing culture of white, middle-class America into a sort of fairy tale. Her gangs of cutthroats come close to allegory, even in their names, which spell the two antitheses of modern identity: they are called the Pack and the Orphans. Women are simply the Property.

The heroine, a bright middle-class girl, comes from nowhere. She refuses to be Property, although she falls deeply in love with the Orphan leader, McKay, a splendid, doomed character, who lives by a code of honor which he discovers is no more than self-delusion. His name and style suggest MacHeath of *The Beggar's Opera,* and his gleaming, power-giving Chevy is more than a casual parallel to the white horses of erstwhile outlaws. Hoffman, indeed, often echoes the technicolor legends of the past; her candy store proprietor and wise man is not very far from the candy store proprietor of *West Side Story,* for instance. It would be hard to say how conscious these echoes are, or how consciously she keeps her balance between parody and sentiment, cutting her own flights of panting prose with acid self-mockery. Her intention hardly matters: the fact is that she does keep her balance, and that her love story is a remarkably moving one. Her whole gang chronicle, in fact, is a fine description of society gone back to its primitive beginnings without losing the corruptions of its prime. Totem and taboo have once again replaced reason and knowledge; but the real magic, the high magic, is heroin. The street fights, mortal, savage violence for abstract and distant principles, echo the Vietnam war, which is now and again rumored in the novel, and a slightly drunk witch doctor, the candy store owner, is the only adult voice there is. The narrative is engrossing because Hoffman creates characters touched by legend; it is memorable because it evokes such lyrical parallels for a mindless state somewhere between violence and apathy with which we have become drearily familiar.

In a way, *Property Of* is a novel about our sentimental myths and romances as much as it is a novel about street gangs. (pp. 267-68)

Edith Milton, in a review of "Property Of," in The Yale Review, *Vol. LXVII, No. 2, Winter, 1978, pp. 267-68.*

ZACHARY LEADER

[*Property Of*] is a sort of punk or pop-gothic *Jane Eyre*. Its nameless heroine and narrator, a tough-talking seventeen-year-old from a bleak, unspecified suburb of New York, falls desperately in love with McKay, the cobra-cool president of the Orphans and scourge of the Avenue's rival gang, the Pack. McKay's hooded eyes and air of quick-fire violence make him irresistible to women. He's all steel and black leather, and the narrator's attraction to him, like that of the gothic heroines to their equally dangerous dream-lovers, is masochistic; pain being an integral part of desire in fiction of this sort. . . .

McKay and the narrator play out their doomed love affair against a backdrop of dope deals, gang warfare, and bloody intrigue. Their world and its rhythms are those of pop romance; of leaders of the pack, meetings across the river, and couplings under the board-walk. McKay, the love-struck narrator tells us, "didn't look evil, but he sure looked bad"—a line worthy of the Ronettes. As he and the Orphans speed down the Avenue in their customized Chevys and Fords, "the street ice flies through the night air like bullets".

Property Of is at its best in lines like these (only a few of which come quite so close to parody), and in patches of equally supercharged dialogue: in effect, when it takes its stylized characters and settings seriously. It is less good when Miss Hoffman distances herself from her story, either by focusing too closely on its tawdry or violent details (in the manner of a photograph by Diane Arbus), or by "explaining" what she's about, as when she has the narrator distinguishing between "the property of capitalism, the historical sort that is discussed at the cocktail parties of the world" and the property of "the self that does not belong, is not owned by itself but by others".

These lapses, though, are relatively few, and most of them occur in the first half of the novel, before the intricate unfolding of McKay's revenge. Nor are there many moments of obtrusively "fine" writing. Sometimes a character can sound oddly formal or antique, but this is as it should be, given the Avenue's rigid codes and hierarchies. Miss Hoffman, in short, knows her world, and artfully reproduces its super-cool and solemn dignities.

> Zachary Leader, "Cool as a Cobra," in The Times Literary Supplement, *No. 3968, April 21, 1978, p. 432.*

JEROME CHARYN

Esther the White is a beautiful, aging witch. She has a son, Phillip, who is something of a lunatic. Phillip likes to drown. He makes one attempt each year, during the Drowning Season, July and August. Phillip is always rescued by his keeper, a man named Cohen. Cohen loves Esther the White and is loyal to her, but how can he declare his love for the witch, when she has a husband, a dwarf (her brother-in-law), a crazy son, and a granddaughter, Esther the Black, who all whirl around her at the family Compound on Long Island? Such is the material of Alice Hoffman's second novel, *The Drowning Season,* a fierce and wicked fairytale of these "modern times."

Esther the White seems a bit too large for the novel. She's a wondrous creation, spiteful, cunning and mean, who has smothered her own sexual powers to hold on to this Compound, which is "America" for her, but a kind of trap for everyone else: even the frogs on Esther's Compound have become bewitched. . . .

The one flaw in the novel is Esther the Black. She seems like a spook with too little flesh. Her desires are speckled and thin. Perhaps this other Esther is too close to Alice Hoffman herself, and therefore has no real fictional voice of her own. But the novel's energies run on without her.

Alice Hoffman has an extraordinary sense of the fabulous. Esther the White leaps from her brittle childhood in Russia to a grandmother's reign on Long Island in a marvelous "immigrant story." And the witch does warm up by the end of the novel. She becomes reconciled with Esther the Black and falls for her minion, Cohen. "She moved through men, watching their eyes change too, from desire to dust, and now, with Cohen, back again to desire." *The Drowning Season* is a touching and startling novel by a young writer who has a feeling for myth, genuine wickedness and the nagging perversity of love.

> Jerome Charyn, "The Witches' Tale," in The New York Times Book Review, *July 15, 1979, p. 13.*

MARGO JEFFERSON

Folk and fairy tales, tradition has it, are told by an old woman—grandmother or nurse—to a young child, freeing the teller of the burden of unshared experience and the listener of the burden of unexpressed fears and longings. *The Drowning Season* has the quality of these tales: it begins with a young girl, held in thrall by seemingly "wicked" adults dreaming of escape. (p. 34)

The Drowning Season is Alice Hoffman's second novel. In her first, *Property Of,* an audacious, vulnerable 17-year-old told the story of her year as girlfriend and favored possession of a gang leader. Parents and grandparents did not exist in that world of street fights, petty thievery, and drug deals; life went on in a perpetual present, like a 45-rpm record played over and over. The writing had speed, wit, and a mordant lyricism. *The Drowning Season* has extravagance and generosity as well. It moves across generations and continents. And it is filled with stories. Everyone—the melancholy Phillip and the ineffectual Rose, the poaching fishermen, the Compound bodyguard who loves Esther the White, and the aspiring punk rock star enamored of Esther the Black—has a story that is told. Some are amusing, some outrageous, some pathetic. Each plays a role in the reconciliation of the two Esthers: a tale in which the "happily ever after" is not marriage to a king's son but understanding between a grandmother and granddaughter that allows one to make peace with her past and the other to make whatever she will of her future. (p. 37)

> Margo Jefferson, "A Tale of Two Esthers," in Ms., *Vol. VIII, No. 2, August, 1979, pp. 34-5, 37.*

JEAN STROUSE

Just about everybody in *The Drowning Season* wants to escape. In the sweltering August heat, 18-year-old Esther (called "Esther the Black") vows to get away from her wealthy family's Long Island, N.Y., compound and the dominion of her icy grandmother (called "Esther the White"). Rose, young Esther's mother, watches TV and swills gin, dreaming of the Nevada desert. A giant captive sea turtle named Miriam keeps "her gray eyes closed against the odor of the sea which rose around the dock." And Phillip, son of Esther the White and father of Esther the Black, wants only to walk out into the water and drown. . . .

Alice Hoffman's hallucinatory novel skims along just above the surface of the real like a finely wrought nightmare. It traces a legacy of lovelessness from frozen White Russia to modern New York. People talk in epigrams. Emblems float above the page: ice, heat, incest, wolves, a dancing dwarf, a tattooed man and a punk rocker named Pagan Rath. A band of local fishermen, timeless as the harbor's eelgrass, waits to reclaim the compound. But the drama of the two Esthers roots the story in strong emotional truth.

When Esther the White was a young Jewish girl walking out of Russia, she decided the way not to fall into the ice was not to feel anything. She succeeded, and reared a son who wanted not so much to kill himself as to "merge with the water . . . to be a part of that beauty, traveling at a natural speed through the waves, without effort." He named his daughter Esther "with an ancient hostility and a smile," knowing his mother would hate it, wanting to steal from her, to turn her into a ghost. Haunted, and dying of cancer, old Esther with her white hair and ice-blue eyes begins to see what she has lost in giving nothing, in trading emotion for control. Now, even her cells have gone crazy. . . .

Only Cohen and Esther the Black have life in their veins. The old woman reaches toward them at last to effect her own difficult escape, and the ending of Hoffman's stark modern fable is not exactly happy but fitting, haunting and wise.

> Jean Strouse, "Esther the White, Esther the Black," in Newsweek, Vol. XCIV, No. 8, August 20, 1979, p. 72.

SUZANNE FREEMAN

One of those chill November days when the sun has set too soon, a half-built nuclear power plant explodes on Long Island and [*Angel Landing*] begins. But things aren't quite the way they sound. This is no modish disaster story, no sticky thicket of nuclear intrigue. This power plant, called Angel Landing III, billows into a hazy, shifting purple cloud. It fills the sky and then settles, like an enchantment, onto the simple, seaside town of Fishers Cove. Sirens go off. Lives change. Girl meets boy. This is the beginning of a good, old-fashioned love story.

Angel Landing is Alice Hoffman's third novel. The 28-year-old writer unfolds this story with the same sort of perfect, sad-funny scenes that graced her previous books, *Property Of* and *The Drowning Season*. Images from those two works turn up here—rows of orange lilies, seashells shaped like angels' wings, men with scarred faces. But the people of Fishers Cove are different from Hoffman's past characters. They are drawn with finer lines—with a sharp pencil perhaps, instead of spray paint. They are social workers instead of street toughs. They run boarding houses instead of beachfront estates. These are small-town people with big plans, impossible hopes, wishy-washy ideals. These are people we can understand.

When the power plant blows, Natalie Lansky is sitting in the parlor of her Aunt Minnie's boarding house waiting for her boyfriend to call. The house is mostly vacant now, but in years past it overflowed with Lanskys. . . .

Minnie Lansky is 74 now. Her husband (also a Lansky—a distant cousin) is dead. Her relatives have moved on to other, more fashionable, vacation spots. But Minnie is not easily diminished. She still stands almost six feet tall. When she unfurls her knot of hair, it hangs to her waist. She drives a Mustang, writes her congressman, does volunteer work in an old-age home. But, most of all, she tries to bring her niece to her senses.

"Women don't sit around waiting for men to call," she tells Natalie. "Nobody does that anymore. Believe me."

Natalie is in love with Carter Sugarland, an antinuclear activist as fair and sweet as his name suggests—and just as poisonous to Minnie's vegetarian sensibilities. Carter is as pink as peppermint, as rich and flaky as French pastry, and, for five years, Natalie has been unable to resist. For five years, she has sat by the telephone waiting for Carter's calls, waiting to be summoned for their occasional evenings of "lovemaking, marijuana and endless games of hearts." . . .

After the explosion, Fishers Cove is abuzz. Carter leaves town to rally his antinuclear chums. Minnie sips golden seal tea and cries alone in the parlor. Natalie returns to Outreach, the counseling center where she spends her days as an inept therapist. Her clients never seem to improve. The anorectic girl continues to shrivel. The high school truant is hopelessly adrift. Between clients, Natalie studies the blackberry canes outside her office window. She considers writing a letter of resignation.

And then, Michael Finn walks into Outreach and into Natalie's life.

Finn is everybody's bad boy. He smokes, and wears a leather jacket. A thin scar cuts across his cheek. What's more, he has a confession to make: he is the bomber. Michael Finn is responsible for the explosion at Angel Landing III. Almost at once, Natalie is in love. Again. And, this time, Minnie approves.

The small tragedies of Michael Finn's past, as told to Natalie—his lost, drunken father, his reform school days, his broken promises to a child who trusted him—make up the shining scenes of this book. They show Alice Hoffman's writing at its precise and heartbreaking best. . . .

It is difficult to believe that stories . . . could really spill out of Michael Finn in the course of his therapy with Natalie. Finn has never been so articulate. Natalie has never inspired such confidence. Fortunately, Hoffman does not really expect us to believe it. She sets Finn's confessions apart, complete and dreamlike, away from the rest of the narrative. But other parts of this book are harder to swallow. There is, for instance, the coincidence of a second power plant explosion which happens to fall in the nick of time for Michael Finn. There is the sudden blossoming of Finn's mean little father and a rosy moment of reunion between the two men. And then, there is the ending—a final fantasy scene for Natalie and Finn, a scene of stars and sweet night air and the hint of happily ever after.

But, this is a love story after all. It is a story that began with a sprinkling of purple dust from a place called Angel Landing. So maybe anything is possible. Maybe the future will bring starry nights and the scent of jasmine. Maybe bombers make better lovers. Certainly, Alice Hoffman's writing has the magic that makes us want to believe it.

> Suzanne Freeman, "Love at the Crisis Center," in Book World—The Washington Post, December 21, 1980, p. 4.

MIRIAM SAGAN

The heroine of *Angel Landing* [Natalie Lansky], like those of Hoffman's *Property Of* and *The Drowning Season*, is a sensitive and intelligent observer, alienated from her surroundings. . . .

Angel Landing is essentially a novel of character, in which individuals struggle for meaning and control. Aunt Minnie, a bold political activist at 74, serves as a foil for Natalie's inertia. An unusual and charming character, she also adds the dimension of humor missing from Hoffman's previous novels. The bomber, Michael Finn, is trapped by the pain of an unhappy childhood; the bombing is not political sabotage but an act of personal despair. Natalie is able to help heal him and is changed in the process.

Place, both geographic and in terms of social milieu, is essential in *Angel Landing*. . . . Fishers Cove is a natural environment threatened with destruction. This is a novel about politics without being didactic. Both Aunt Minnie and Carter Sugarland, Natalie's first boyfriend, act out of political conviction, while Natalie and Finn react in a more personal manner.

Hoffman's novel is also about the human ability to heal and change. Her descriptions of an eccentric group therapy are vivid and hilarious, as accurate as her accounts of political maneuverings. Hoffman takes a compassionate yet ironic look at the belief systems that keep her characters going in a world menaced by destruction.

> *Miriam Sagan, in a review of "Angel Landing," in Ms., Vol. IX, No. 8, February, 1981, p. 37.*

ANNE TYLER

White Horses combines the concrete and the dreamlike. Its characters are people we think we recognize at first; but then on second thought we're not so sure. There's an almost seamless transition from the real to the unreal, back and forth and back again.

We're introduced to the father, King Connors, as he's heading off to his construction job in his pickup truck. "Other people have cars," his wife tells his daughter. "Other people have cars," she calls after him. It's a hot summer morning in California; you can almost feel the heat rising from the pages. You can plainly see Dina, the mother, and the quiet, compliant daughter, Teresa, and the two sons, Reuben who crates vegetables at the Safeway and lazy Silver who sleeps late. It's an ordinary family, from the looks of things.

But then Bergen shows up—the detective hired by Dina's father 20 years ago, back when Dina eloped with King Connors and vanished. All these years Bergen has pocketed his fee and made no effort to find Dina. But he has reached retirement age, and Dina's father is no longer alive and her mother has taken Bergen off the case. . . . Bergen gazes through the screen door at Dina—who seems less real to him than the young pretty girl in the photograph he's carried for so long—and he announces her father's death, after which he takes his leave.

It's a peculiar event—but possible, of course. Next, though, in a scene that results indirectly from Bergen's announcement, Teresa falls into a comalike sleep while an inexplicable scent of roses hangs over her. Not even the doctors can wake her; nor can they find a reason for her sleep, which will recur at various times in her life, sometimes lasting for whole days, always accompanied by the scent of roses.

These three early scenes—the family's everyday morning activities, Bergen's appearance, Teresa's sleep—typify the different levels of reality that exist side by side in *White Horses*. There is much that is convincingly matter-of-fact here. King Connors deserts his family in a burst of frustration, Dina takes her children on a disorganized and aimless visit to her mother in New Mexico, the favorite son, Silver, embarks on a shabby marriage. Palpable details—Silver's cool, tough way of speaking, the steely dignity of the grandmother—verify all that happens.

There are other events that strike us as strange but still explainable. Dina, for instance, falls ill with a disease that cannot be diagnosed. Dina's garden withers and flourishes according to her mood. Silver exercises an eerily compelling power over everyone he meets, particularly women, and especially his own sister.

And still other events—hints of magic, herbal remedies, Teresa's trancelike behavior through most of her life—make us wonder if we're reading a fairy tale. However, this book avoids a fairy tale's irritating airiness. The secret of Dina's unforgettable coffee, the coffee that becomes a legend after her death, is nothing more than a pinch of cinnamon. The dark and dashing night riders for whom she waits during most of her days are the stuff of a young girl's fantasy, and it's a fantasy that ends up robbing both Dina and her daughter of an appreciation of ordinary life. The elusive shadow invisibly trailing Silver is only an old underworld enemy trying to get on his nerves. And atmospheres—the solidity of scorching mornings, flash floods at night—make firm ballast for the most weightless of miracles. (pp. 11, 38)

At times, particularly toward the end, the book seems to go on just a little too long, burdened by the very musicality that was so appealing in the beginning. Teresa's attachment to her brother Silver puts us off ultimately, not because it's incestuous but because it's so romanticized. But these are quibbles, and very minor quibbles at that. The overall impression is one of abundant life, masterfully orchestrated by the author. *White Horses* is a satisfying novel, at the same time mysterious and believable, and it marks a significant advance for Alice Hoffman. (p. 38)

> *Anne Tyler, "Ordinary Family, with a Difference," in The New York Times Book Review, March 28, 1982, pp. 11, 38.*

PETER S. PRESCOTT

Imagine Emily Brontë alive and writing in California, reworking the *Sleeping Beauty* story because she knows that the Prince's kiss is less likely to redeem a dreaming girl than to condemn her. The world over which Alice Hoffman presides in [*White Horses*] is charged with raging weather and movements by night, with a doomed obsession and a dream corrupted, with hummingbirds, moths, bees, lizards, flowers—and particularly with scents: among them that of roses, lilacs, sage, rosemary and lemon flowers. I found reading this novel to be like eating my way through a pan of fudge: it's probably fattening and certainly not the kind of fare you can live on, but once in a while the sheer sensual delinquency is fun.

The heroine is 13 when the story begins, and already a genuine beauty. Throughout her childhood in Santa Rosa, Teresa had heard her mother tell of the legendary Arias, outlaws who appeared out of nowhere riding their white horses always westward toward the sun. . . . Deserted by her father and subject to a sleeping sickness that may be epilepsy or may just be her way of retreating from the world, Teresa worships her brother Silver, a young man irresistibly attractive to women. Although Silver seems to her an Aria, a nightrider who will always protect her, the only nightriding he does involves his traffic in drugs.

I won't go further into the story except to say that the love Teresa bears for Silver soon surpasses sisterly affection. Incest may be the most difficult theme for a novelist to undertake, yet Hoffman here makes it tolerable by the mythic mold in which she has cast her story. She regards her characters from a distance greater than that employed in realistic fiction and wraps her narrative in clouds of simile. . . . Rich stuff . . . and not to everyone's taste, but Hoffman prevents us from getting stuck in her prose by moving her plot quickly along.

> Peter S. Prescott, "Night Moves," in Newsweek,
> Vol. XCIX, No. 15, April 12, 1982, p. 82.

HERMIONE LEE

[*White Horses* is] a pullulating tale of incest, magic and myth in a Californian landscape. Teresa's mother, who eloped from New Mexico with the wrong man, has brought her up to believe in the legend of the 'Arias,' dark strangers on white horses forever riding towards the sun. This tiresome piece of folklore inspires Teresa's incurable passion for her drug-peddling brother, Silver . . . , which is accompanied by a strange sleeping-sickness. No witches' herbs or new lovers, both of which Teresa takes in large quantities, can cure her. A lot of very careful Creative Writing has to be got through before Teresa escapes her fate: 'There, among the roses and the regrets, she looked back at him.' Any interesting ideas about incestuous love are buried deep beneath the drifts of self-conscious mush and whimsy.

> Hermione Lee, "Frantic Obsessions," in The Ob-
> server, May 29, 1983, p. 30.

PERRI KLASS

There are moments in *Fortune's Daughter* when it is almost a shock to come upon the specific details of everyday life. It seems remarkable that a character should drive an Oldsmobile, apply to the U.C.L.A. business school, take the Long Island Expressway or discuss "Charlie's Angels." The novel is mainly concerned with tremendous events, with childbirth and the loss of children, with earthquakes and ice storms, with enduring love and devastating infatuation. The writing has the quality of folk tale—of amazing events calmly recounted—and the effect of using name brands and mundane particulars is to suggest that the novel has found a kind of mythological reality thriving beneath all the tackiest and most ephemeral trappings of daily life.

In Alice Hoffman's last novel, *White Horses,* a legend of exciting outlaw men was part of the young heroine's upbringing; she had to fight free of its seductive magic, personified by her no-good brother, before she could set out toward her own future. The novel is explicitly concerned with this legend, with its power and importance. In *Fortune's Daughter* there is no such explicit myth. Instead, the sense of magic and elemental force arises from the central mystery of childbirth. This novel's great strength lies in its two heroines, who both find themselves drawn, without plans, hopes or full understanding, into the inevitably mythological process of pregnancy and childbirth.

These are two women who enter each other's lives when one tells the other's fortune. Rae Perry has come out to Hollywood with Jessup, a rather angry, rather lost man picking his way

between the life of a drifter and his own version of a midlife crisis. Rae, who has loved Jessup since she was 14, has run away from her home near Boston to travel with him from place to place, and now finally in California, their relationship is dissolving. "She had been waiting so long for something to go wrong between them that it took a while before she realized that it already had." Jessup moves on, in search of success, and Rae discovers she is pregnant.

Lila Grey tells fortunes by reading tea leaves. But she does not want to tell Rae's fortune, she does not want to be involved in her pregnancy. Buried in Lila's past, a secret from her own husband, is the child she bore when she was 18 and unmarried, a daughter who was immediately taken from her and given away. This phantom child haunts her life, binding her tight with the terror of bearing children, losing children.

This is in some ways a rather terrifying novel. It is much concerned with the loss of children, with a loved baby given up because her mother cannot care for her, with a desperately wanted child who dies, with a once-loved baby lost to the estrangements of adolescence. As in a dark fairy tale, the actual events and the imaginings of the characters manage to echo many of the most basic parental fears—the baby who stops growing, the teen-age daughter who disappears.

The most powerful scene in the book is a flashback to Lila in childbirth—after successfully concealing her entire pregnancy from her parents, Lila goes into labor on a night of apocalyptic cold and ice, with a human storm of parental fury raging around her as the ice storm freezes the city of New York. . . .

This scene, which gives the book its essential power, is echoed by Rae's pregnancy and impending labor, which is also associated with natural cataclysm, in this case with an earthquake that threatens the city of Los Angeles. There is a sense here that the cataclysm of childbirth is the central event of life, and perhaps this is the reason that some of the male characters in the novel are left helplessly watching, frittering away their time far from this basic mystery.

In this, the men are sometimes reminiscent of those in the novels of Anne Tyler, some of whom have this same quality of watching the women around them with bewilderment—occasionally awed, occasionally resentful. *Fortune's Daughter* calls up other comparisons with Miss Tyler, who has at times combined folk tale and contemporary detail in ways that are not so different from Miss Hoffman's; think of the fortuneteller at the beginning of *Searching for Caleb,* going from city to city in search of a long-lost man—and taking Amtrak, and munching Cheez Doodles. Other aspects of *Fortune's Daughter*—the wild dogs in the streets of Hollywood and the impending earthquake—are reminiscent of Nathanael West's *Day of the Locust.* But Miss Hoffman never sinks completely into California grotesque, though she is capable of touches of it. . . .

Still, amidst all the touches of fairy tale and the grotesque, the thrust is toward the normal; the characters aspire to the most everyday kind of happiness. The question is whether Rae's childbirth will end up a repeat of Lila's, a lonely, terrifying ordeal ending in the loss of a child. Rae takes her Lamaze classes, tries to talk Lila into being her childbirth coach. But all the time growing more urgent within her is Lila's own private quest—the desire to find her own lost child, to claim her, to soothe the great pain that has been there since that ice storm. Lila will not get involved with Rae, who is her own daughter's age; she wants the real thing. And she is afraid of what will happen to Rae, afraid of the dark symbol she saw at the bottom of Rae's teacup, a symbol that may be for Rae, and may be for Lila herself.

And so through the novel there are several searches, several struggles. Rae must free herself from Jessup, Lila must resolve her past, find her daughter or let her go. More peripherally there are Rae's mother and the mother who adopted Lila's child, all these lives reflecting the risk and the terror of having a child, loving a child.

The novel is much concerned with the rituals of accepting loss and death, the ways that people find to renew their strength and then go on....

The writing is confident, powerful and essentially laconic, but it is also lush; description is limited but rich, vivid and sharp.... The peculiar offbeat humor keeps the narrative from drifting into melodrama....

It is in its juxtaposition of the mythic, the apocalyptic, with the resolutely ordinary, in its portrait of eccentric characters living in a very familiar world, that this novel finds its unique voice. It is beautifully and matter-of-factly told, and it leaves the reader with an almost bewildered sense that this primal mythological level does exist in everyday reality, and that there is no event, from the standard miracle of childbirth to the most bizarre magic imaginable, that cannot occur in a setting of familiar, everyday details.

> *Perri Klass, "Childbirth, with Fire and Ice," in* The New York Times Book Review, *March 24, 1985, p. 7.*

SUSAN DOOLEY

It is not just love that fills the space between mothers and daughters, but history. The daughter makes a certain gesture which takes the mother into her own forgotten past. Lines begin to pleat the skin around the mother's mouth and the daughter sees her own aging. Sometimes the connection is a comfort, at others it's as irritating as being mocked by a funhouse mirror.

But even if we break the connection, we can't float free, as Alice Hoffman tells us in *Fortune's Daughter.* At 18, Lila, actress, fortune teller, psychic, "whose hair was so thick she had to brush it twice a day with a wire brush made in France" gives birth to an illegitimate baby girl. The baby is wrapped in a towel and taken out into a cold New York night to become someone else's daughter. Over the years, the lost baby fills Lila's mind as completely as it once filled her body....

While the past surrounds Lila, the future reaches for the novel's other female protagonist, Rae. For seven years, Rae has followed her boyfriend Jessup across the country. When they bump to a stop in Los Angeles, Jessup, with no place left to leave, leaves Rae who "had been waiting so long for something to go wrong between them that it took a while before she realized that it already had."

Rae, pregnant, tries to claim Lila's help. But the reality of Rae's baby is a threat. "Lila could almost see inside Rae to the baby she was carrying. Its eyes were closed, but it was moving its fingers, making a fist, then letting go . . . Beside this baby Lila's own child grew more ghostly."

There is a magic, mystical quality to Alice Hoffman's writing. Here the mind retrieves what the body has lost so that the phantom scent of her mother's perfume infuses Rae's apartment until, "she found herself searching through the closets and

kneeling to peer under the bed—and there were times when she actually believed she might find someone hiding." And Lila, making love for the last time with her married lover, conceives his child as she leaves him behind. . . .

Hoffman's magic isn't witches and warlocks, but real people in an intensity of grief. . . .

Hoffman is a marvelous writer with a painter's eye who takes the landscape of ordinary people experiencing ordinary emotions and colors them in unexpected ways. . . .

The people in *Fortune's Daughter* are like neighbors knocking on your door, wearing gaudy, unexpected costumes. They startle you into noticing them anew, so that when, at the end of the book, Lila takes Rae's baby a cake into which she has "baked three gifts: a cool hand to test for fevers, a kiss with the power to chase away nightmares, a heart that can tell when it's time to let go," those familiar sentiments, far from seeming banal, are new.

> *Susan Dooley, "Mothers and Daughters," in* Book World—The Washington Post, *May 19, 1985, p. 11.*

SUSAN LARDNER

Besides human interest and a certain length, a novel ought to offer a certain complication—ingenuity of thought and ripeness of expression that surpasses what the reader has time for or talent. Emotional effectiveness, as a rule, doesn't make up for a shortage of characters and plot and familiar narrative routines. There are no lasting surprises in *Fortune's Daughter,* by Alice Hoffman, a streamlined tale of two women in distress, plumped up with dreams and portents. Unwed motherhood is the plight under consideration, and the theme is the strengths and weaknesses of maternal feeling. Lila, a gloomy woman of forty-six who works as a fortune-teller, has been mourning for more than twenty years, since her baby daughter was born and immediately taken from her to be adopted by strangers. Rae, young enough to be Lila's daughter, has run away from home with a ne'er-do-well and become pregnant, just as he is heading elsewhere to find himself. Although married (to a paragon of patience), Lila lives like a hermit, mainly in her mind, brooding, dreaming, hallucinating, while Rae, abandoned, grows spunky. However, she, too, is prone to significant dreams. "It was earthquake weather," goes the opening line of the book, "and everyone knew it." The earthquake occurs, of course, about two hundred and thirty pages later, heralding the less predictable turns of the plot.

Fortune's Daughter is written well; the stories run smoothly alongside one another, propelled by brisk declarative sentences from ominous beginning to sentimental ending. Adverbial phrases insure that shifts back and forth in time are intelligible; e.g., "At first," "That night," "After that," "Late one night, in the middle of a warm, dry winter," "Eight days later," "In the mornings," "In November," "The following week." And Hoffman is an insouciant narrator, explaining what Lila was certain of, what she began to wonder, that she felt perfectly safe; that Rae woke up after five, that she felt like crying, that she couldn't stop herself from imagining the worst. Dialogue is well done, and in the scenes between Rae and her boyfriend there are touches of humor. Hoffman ably exploits the suspense of Rae's pregnancy and of Lila's deep depression, and, with the aid of traditional symbols—the moon, ice, assorted birds and flowers, including blood-red roses—evokes the intense emotions that seize women at turning points in their lives. In its manipulation of meteorological, floral, and other imagery (red shoes, food) to steer a contemporary story in the direction of folklore, *Fortune's Daughter* is reminiscent of the novels of Toni Morrison, but Hoffman lacks the conviction that enables Morrison to introduce flying men and bloomless marigolds into human affairs; her effects are more decorative than persuasive. The observations of the activity of birds and flowers may enhance the poignancy of the circumstances described, and perhaps their universality, but more social information and less botany would have been welcome.

To a susceptible reader, at least, *Fortune's Daughter* is something of a tearjerker. (It is hard to imagine a man reading it beyond the first few pages.) Like the quickly forgotten pain of childbirth, however, which is referred to in the book, the euphoria of Hoffman's ending wears off, leaving the reader with a gullible feeling and certain questions. As though there were hardship enough in the life of a middle-class unwed mother, the difficulties of relationships between women and men are underplayed, and, in contrast to the demonstrated force of maternal instinct in Rae and Lila, the coldness of *their* mothers is presented with little comment. These omissions and others, like the peculiar passivity of Lila's husband, contribute to a finale that suits the moment but not a residual sense of the indefinite and complicated future implied by the book itself. Unlike the end of *Jane Eyre*, for example, where "Reader, I married him" is uttered by a woman who has shown herself able to handle anything. (p. 83)

Susan Lardner, "Complications," in The New Yorker, *Vol. LXI, No. 21, July 15, 1985, pp. 83-5.*

PATRICIA MEYER SPACKS

A girl bears an illegitimate daughter and, at her parents' insistence, gives it up for adoption; almost thirty years later, menopausal, she seeks her lost child. Another young woman, deserted by a ne'er-do-well lover, finds herself alone and pregnant in Los Angeles. The two women, Lila and Rae, more than twenty years apart in age, discover one another; despite distress for both along the way, matters turn out all right. . . .

Soap-opera sentimentalities of plot and characterization do not, however, altogether define *Fortune's Daughter,* a novel partly redeemed by its attempt to explore seriously the shared life of women. Literal mothers of grown-up daughters get short shrift here, but symbolic mothers nourish their pseudo-offspring. (p. 25)

Psychologists say that women typically fear abandonment more than any other fate. This novel apparently assumes the truth of this pronouncement, its women characters obsessed with relationship, with loss and reparation, with the possibility of their own maternity as a form of closeness. (pp. 25-6)

Fortune's Daughter conveys a rather old-fashioned but not unattractive air of didacticism. Its somewhat shadowy male characters must learn intimacy; its more vivid females must learn to relinquish without losing closeness. To transmit such learning appears to constitute the narrative's purpose. Yet other, vaguer, purposes glimmer.

The novel's last sentence reads, "You could take one look at the sky and know it was the perfect time of night for a miracle." The possibility of miracles never seems far away in this tale, which relies heavily on a kind of symbolism closely related to the magical. Sleeping dreams, portentously symbolic, yield to equally freighted waking ones. A dead baby materializes next to her mother—product, presumably, of that mother's will and imagination, but endowed with increasingly unnerving physicality and apparent independence, crawling off, finally, across a patio. Past and present fuse and exchange; commonplace details assume magical significance. Rae comes to visit Lila, who refuses to acknowledge her presence or to admit her to the house.

> And later, when Lila summoned up the courage to pull back the drapes and look outside, there wasn't one single sign that anyone had come to see her, and no one who wasn't looking carefully would have noticed that there were at least a dozen new buds on the rosebushes at the front door, and that each and every one of them was blood red.

The ambiguous presentation of those rosebuds (natural? supernatural? fraught with meaning? interpretable accidents?) epitomizes the novel's typical mergings and withholdings.

By devices of this sort, *Fortune's Daughter* dramatizes female psychic experience, and experiments with embodying a female aesthetic. It thus almost—but not quite—transcends its sentimentalities and its often arbitrary handling of character and event. An ambitious attempt to examine and to enliven commonplaces about women's nature, the novel does not altogether fulfill its own ambitions, but it compels interest by the integrity of its effort. (p. 26)

Patricia Meyer Spacks, in a review of "Fortune's Daughter," in Boston Review, *Vol. X, No. 4, September, 1985, pp. 25-6.*

CHRISTOPHER LEHMANN-HAUPT

The title of Alice Hoffman's latest novel, *Illumination Night,* refers to an annual August ceremony in Oak Bluffs on Martha's Vineyard. "For more than a hundred years," the novel's omniscient narrator tells us,

> since Oak Bluffs was a Methodist camp with believers' tents set beneath the old, enormous trees, there has been a Grand Illumination once a year. The Victorian cottages that ring Trinity Park are hung with Japanese lanterns, lit by candles, illuminated all at once by a signal from within the Tabernacle in the center of the park.

On the Illumination Night that occurs in Ms. Hoffman's novel, nothing of startling moment happens. Late in the afternoon, Andre, a young year-round resident of Chilmark who tries to eke out a living by renovating motorcycles, drives into town on errands with Jody, a teen-ager who has moved to the Vineyard to look after her grandmother, and who has developed a crush on Andre. They get back late. In their absence, Andre's wife, Vonny, takes their 4-year-old son, Simon, into Oak Bluffs to see the lights and join the sing-along.

No enlightenment occurs for these characters; if anything, a shadow is cast across their lives by this intrusion into Andre's and Vonny's marriage. But for us readers there are illuminations. The characters' fantasies of each other are lighted as if by the stars, which on this night are "as white and sharp as dragon's teeth."

From this point on in the story, the tension grows between Andre, Vonny and Jody. Simon, who is too small for his age, successfully enters kindergarten. Jody, spurned by Andre, starts staying out all night with local boys. Her grandmother, Elizabeth Renny, frets about growing blind. Andre and Vonny run out of money. Vonny, after unsuccessfully asking her rich, divorced father for money, develops agoraphobia and can no longer leave the house. Nelson, an over-empathetic dog, worries about being too doglike.

This may sound like cute soap opera, but Alice Hoffman, whose five previous novels include *The Drowning Season* and *Fortune's Daughter,* has enough power of empathy to make her characters matter to us. Daringly mixing comedy with tragedy, and the quotidian with the fabulous, she has created a narrative that somehow makes myth out of the sticky complexities of contemporary marriage.

Not all of her gambles pay off. There is a giant who begins as a scary bedtime story and later materializes as a reclusive eight-footer who maintains a roadside vegetable stand. Jody and the giant fall in love. This complication verges on the sentimental. There are two lengthy italicized passages that show Vonny in crisis and address her as "you." *"Here you are. The sky is blue and it is October. Your child, who will soon be five, has started school more than a month ago and you have not once driven him there."* You can't help thinking of Jimmy Cannon, the late sportswriter.

But these lapses are forgivable. Ms. Hoffman writes so simply about human passions that her characters are branded onto one's memory. At their most passionate they hurl themselves down staircases, out of windows, in front of speeding cars. One awakens from the dream of this novel with a memory of trying to catch them. In the light of the story's afterglow, one keeps on trying to catch them.

> Christopher Lehmann-Haupt, "Lights of the Vineyard," in The New York Times, *Section 1, July 25, 1987, p. 19.*

JACK SULLIVAN

Hoffman's unglamorous characters [in *Illumination Night*] include Andre, a silent, somewhat depressed motorcycle repairman whose business is failing; Vonny, his wife, who experiences panic attacks that grow into full-blown agoraphobia; Simon, their 4-year-old son, who seems stunted for his age and may have medical problems; Jody, the lonely teen-ager next door who develops a passionate crush on Andre that threatens his already-tenuous marriage; and Elizabeth, Jody's dying grandmother whose "bones feel as if they're already drawing her into the earth." Given the bleakness of these lives, Vonny's agoraphobia seems merely a physical variation on the entrapment all the characters feel. . . .

The most remarkable writing evokes the closing circle of Vonny's panic attacks, which drive her into her house and make the post office and grocery store "as unreachable as distant planets."

But Hoffmann is not just a gritty realist. She also has a penchant for finding a near-gothic strangeness and enchantment on the edges of everyday experience. Here the mystery starts when the younger characters begin seeing an abnormally huge and beautiful young man—referred to throughout the novel simply as the Giant. This myth-like character becomes as convincingly real as anyone else, especially when Jody begins a secret love affair with him that sets in motion a series of frightening, ultimately healing transformations in the other characters' abilities to face anxiety, loneliness and death.

Most contemporary novels give the reader either one point of view or at least one point of view at a time. Hoffmann, however, practices an unusually fluid form of subjectivity that becomes a kind of total omniscience: she glides from one character's consciousness to another—sometimes floating above them all to make a judgment—in a single paragraph or even sentence, without breaking the rhythm of her prose or storyline. From a technical as well as emotional standpoint, this is an impressive, stirring performance. (p. 13)

> Jack Sullivan, "Better to Have Loved," in Book World—The Washington Post, *August 2, 1987, pp. 8, 13.*

GWYNETH CRAVENS

At the beginning of *Illumination Night,* set on Martha's Vineyard, Vonny, a woman in her 20's, takes Simon, her 3-year-old, to an annual celebration called the Grand Illumination. . . .

The novel goes on to illuminate six intersecting—sometimes colliding—lives. Vonny, a potter who never used to worry, even about mixing gin and Valium, becomes preoccupied with Simon's apparent failure to grow normally, with a baffling fear that begins on Illumination Night and with the possible infidelity of her husband, Andre. He's a loner with an old pickup who prefers silence to almost anything; he restores motorcycles to sell and evades Jody, the sultry teen-age neighbor who has been sent to care for her grandmother, Elizabeth Renny. This old woman, after years of not seeing much, suddenly sees everything. "In seventy-three years Elizabeth Renny has made only two decisions of consequence: when she married Jack Renny and left New York for Chilmark, and when she imagined that she could fly" from an upper window of her house. Her attempt at flight, ending in embarrassment and broken bones, is witnessed by Simon, who has never heard the word "death," who refuses to act any older until he is taller and who will find his life changed when he gets a glimpse of the Giant. The Giant is a beautiful freak, somewhat taller than the tallest of basketball players; he keeps himself hidden and paints miniatures, going out at night to garden, tend his chickens and make furtive visits to leave gifts for Jody. A glimpse of him changes her life, too.

Subtle touches here and there make this intelligent novel shine. Ms. Hoffman knows how to tell a story in clear language and how to avoid subordinating the meanderings of temperament to logic or plot. The characters suddenly, and believably, change their behavior toward one another in the presence of the irrational—Vonny and Jody become friends, despite Vonny's suspicions, when Simon tries to ride a bicycle down a stairway. None of the characters have much in the way of the usual family bonds, and perhaps that's why they've wound up on an island, making connections with one another. Although they seldom speak about what matters most to them, they mirror one another. Vonny's and Jody's parents are divorced; the Giant's mother abandoned him when he was 10; Andre's mother was killed when he was 11. (p. 7)

At different times, reacting to trouble, Andre and Jody lose their voices. At different times, Jody and Vonny give way to the impulse to leap in a car and jam down the accelerator and go, without thought of destination. A wordless empathy arises between Simon and the Giant. It's not easy to write convincingly from a child's point of view, but Ms. Hoffman succeeds except for one lapse, when Simon mixes a potion to restore harmony between his parents.

Amid everyday details—the tuna fish sandwiches, the plastic earrings, the Play-Doh, the Tina Turner songs—Ms. Hoffman's observations span a wide range, from the mysteries of childhood and the bone-shaking eroticism of adolescence to the ironies of marriage and the mysteries of old age. . . . (pp. 7, 9)

Ms. Hoffman's last novel, *Fortune's Daughter,* portrayed strong women, maternal attachments and childbirth; the male characters were rather sketchy. In *Illumination Night,* women, with their sexual longings and inexplicable fears, also hold center stage, but the men are more of a presence—the Giant in particular. At moments, *Fortune's Daughter* reached a crazed intensity, with the characters tossed this way and that by mysterious, seemingly external forces. *Illumination Night* is calmer; the impulses—equally mysterious—arise from within. . . . Ms. Hoffman's settings are reliably wonderful; like the Grand Illumination, they are "irradiated with color and heat" and with the spookiness of ordinary things—the nocturnal squeaking of a hamster's wheel, the world viewed through the fabric of a shirt pulled over your head, cigarettes flying off a dashboard "like shrapnel." She seems always to be saying that where you are is just as important as whatever you're thinking and doing. (p. 9)

> *Gwyneth Cravens, "Flying from the Windows, Biking Down the Stairs," in* The New York Times Book Review, *August 9, 1987, pp. 7, 9.*

ALEXANDRA JOHNSON

"You keep your fears secret and when you are certain no one is home you will try to get past the force field." The thought belongs to Vonny, a thirty-four-year-old mother battling agoraphobia, but it could be claimed by any of the other characters in Alice Hoffman's newest novel [*Illumination Night*]. All have secrets. All are caught in the force field of the family where love and loneliness, memory and desire exert a fatal gravity in their daily lives.

Illumination Night, Hoffman's sixth novel, is in many ways her most subtle. In it she honors the promise her talent has shown in such luminous novels as *White Horses* and *Fortune's Daughter.* Here readers will recognize the hallmarks of Hoffman's work: a shimmering prose style, the fusing of fantasy and realism, the preoccupation with the way the mythic weaves itself into the everyday. Hoffman's narrative domain is the domestic, the daily. Yet her vision—and voice—are lyrical. She is a writer whose prose style is often praised as painterly, and, indeed, Hoffman's fictional world is like a Vermeer: a beautifully crafted study of the interior life.

Illumination Night is a powerful if often disturbing look at the interior lives, domestic and emotional, of a young family and the teenage girl set on destroying them all. . . .

In this novel home is where life's toughest lessons are learned. The family as primer. If *Illumination Night* is, ultimately, about love's redemptive power, it is also about the hard-won ways in which both parents and children, husbands and wives claim that power in life. In Alice Hoffman's fictional world the family shapes or stunts. *Illumination Night* abounds with the myriad ways children parent adults, adults confront the child within themselves, and parents are forever haunted by the child that still shivers inside the grown son or daughter.

As its title implies, *Illumination Night* exposes things normally kept in the dark. If the novel holds up to the light the small, chronic infidelities of daily life, it also illuminates its terrors. The terrors lurk everywhere: a spouse's adultery, a teenager bent on seduction out of summer boredom, a child being hit by a car. But just as Vonny learns to brave her agoraphobia by using Andre or Simon as a "safety" anchor, so all the characters here eventually learn to tame the darkness all about them with trust in themselves, in others. Passion, Andre realizes, "has less to do with uncontrollable urges than with hope."

In Alice Hoffman's radiantly sharp novel hope is the beacon that illuminates if not the whole of life's pathway, at least the small reference points along the way.

> *Alexandra Johnson, in a review of "Illumination Night," in* Boston Review, *Vol. XII, No. 5, October, 1987, p. 31.*

A(lec) D(erwent) Hope

1907-

Australian poet, critic, and essayist.

Among the most significant and controversial figures in contemporary Australian poetry, Hope is often considered a Romantic classicist who celebrates the virtues of nature, beauty, love, and sexuality while disdaining twentieth-century cultural disintegration and humanity's capacity for corruptibility. Rejecting the lyricism of such literary movements as imagism, surrealism, and modernism, as well as the diverse varieties of "pure poetry" espoused by T. S. Eliot, Hope makes frequent use of myths from classical literature and the Old Testament to address esoteric concerns. He emphasizes structure and style and employs traditional verse forms, often reflecting the influence of such classicists as Geoffrey Chaucer, Robert Browning, and William Butler Yeats, to reaffirm the value of intellectual and theosophical traditions. David Kalstone asserted: "Many of Hope's poems are triumphantly responsive to literature. They revive the sense of excitement in being a cultivated reader."

A Professor of English at the Australian National University at Canberra from 1951 until his retirement in 1968, Hope began writing poetry for national magazines during the late 1930s, but his work was known only to a small academic circle prior to the publication of his first collection, *The Wandering Islands* (1955). Poems in this volume elicited diverse critical interpretations for their satirical attacks on contemporary values and their formal intellectual treatment of such topics as solitude, anxiety, and guilt. The theme of isolation is delineated in the book's title poem, which, according to G. A. Wilkes, "expresses the impossibility of communion between separate minds, which are like wandering islands in an ocean, islands that are never charted or annexed, meeting sometimes in a violent collision, but then inevitably falling asunder again." In "Imperial Adam," one of the most widely analyzed pieces in *The Wandering Islands,* Hope posits sexuality as the original source of human evil and guilt. Alternating between disgust and desire, the poem describes Eve in the act of childbirth and culminates in the ironic resolution: "And the first murderer lay upon the earth."

Hope's second collection, *Poems* (1960), also inspired diverse interpretations. Pieces in this volume reflect Hope's commitment to the revival of traditional poetic forms, which, he contends, were displaced by the advent of modernism and other experimental styles of contemporary poetry. In "The Discursive Mode," a theoretical essay included in *The Cave and the Spring: Essays on Poetry* (1965), Hope equates the demise of the epic, the ode, the verse satire, and the epistle with the decline of humanity's nobility while defending the capacity of poetry to deal flexibly and effectively with exposition, argument, satire, and narrative. Most critics agree that Hope's *Collected Poems, 1930-1965* (1966), a selection of new verse and early pieces not previously published in book form, exhibits a wider variety of tone than his previous volumes. Reviewers detected further refinement in *New Poems, 1965-1969* (1969), noting a movement away from personal themes toward more universal, communal concerns. This volume helped further Hope's reputation as an intellectual poet and prompted Daniel

Courtesy of A. D. Hope

Hoffman to describe him as "one of the master conservative poets in English in this century."

Hope's poetry of the 1970s maintains his preoccupation with classical, literary, and esoteric concerns. The satire *Dunciad Minor: An Heroick Poem* (1970), parts of which were originally published in *Melbourne University Magazine* in 1950 under the title *Dunciad Minimus,* begins as a defense of Alexander Pope and ends, according to Arthur Pollard, as a "devastating indictment of modern critics and writers." In pieces collected in *A Late Picking: Poems, 1965-1974* (1975), Hope examines humanity's ambivalent response to such dichotomies as carnality and love, reason and intuition. His later collections include *The Drifting Continent and Other Poems* (1979), *Antechinus: Poems, 1975-1980* (1981), and *The Age of Reason* (1985); the latter volume makes use of heroic couplets in eleven narrative poems set in the eighteenth century. Donald Revell maintained that in *The Age of Reason* "Hope looks lovingly though unsentimentally back through time to the Augustan Age from the vantage point of our most un-Augustan, parlous day. What he sees is . . . a different world of persons like ourselves, striving with different means to solve mortal problems identical to our own." Hope has also published several literary studies and collections of essays, including *Henry Kendall: A Dialogue with the Past* (1971), *Native Companions: Essays and Com-*

ments on Australian Literature, 1936-1966 (1974), and *The New Cratylus: Notes on the Craft of Poetry* (1979).

(See also *CLC*, Vol. 3 and *Contemporary Authors*, Vols. 21-24, rev. ed.)

VINCENT BUCKLEY

I am convinced that Hope is one of the three or four best living Australian poets, and our most discriminating living critic. I should like to state this conviction so firmly early in the piece, in order to remove any contrary impression which may be given when I come to deal with certain aspects of his work.

Despite the fact that he is a man of middle-age, his first book, **The Wandering Islands,** has only lately appeared. This fact largely justifies the scanty amount of attention his work has so far received; yet it does not entirely excuse the lack of understanding which has attended the infrequent references to it. For Hope had published quite enough of his best poetry to enable us to see of what spirit and of what stature he is. (p. 142)

Hope is usually called an 'intellectual poet'; and it would be well to discuss what this word can possibly mean in terms of his actual poetry. Certainly, as I shall suggest later, his satire is that of an intellectual rather than of a superficially educated man with a set of personal grievances. But his more 'lyrical' poetry is the more important; and here we find nothing of philosophical argument given a tortuous poetic dress. In this sense, Hope is not a 'philosophical poet'. Really intelligent poets rarely are. One mistakes the nature of Brennan's poetry, for example, if one thinks that it is concerned with working out philosophical arguments. His esoteric symbolism may be a sign of intellectual force and of deep convictions about intellectual values, but it is not in itself argument, it does not work philosophically. FitzGerald and Browning are argufying poets. Brennan is not; nor is Hope. In his poetry, ideas become images and symbols, the sequences of argument become patterns of deed and perception. (p. 144)

This is without doubt a very satisfying poetry, and yet it does not argue a case, it simply creates a pattern of ineluctably solid things and images in which two or more varying conceptions of human permanence are brought together and allied. We feel in poetry of this kind the constant play and impact of a mind revolving the profound issues of its own existence—but objectifying them, spinning them away from the smaller world where 'discussion' takes place. The revolutions of the wheeling mind are finished by the time the poetry begins; all that is left is its vibration, and of that vibration poetry comes, not further argument. (p. 145)

[Hope's best poems presuppose] a philosophical argument which has already taken place, and which . . . has its reverberations— its consolidation and completion—in attitude and phrasing. To my mind, it is a conception much more sophisticated than that of, say, R. D. FitzGerald, whose poetry, at its most 'philosophical', tends to become something of a platform on which to raise the issues of his own necessarily half-formulated conceptions.

I do not want to give a false impression of Hope; and this is always a present danger when one is concerned to dispel a false impression of a different sort. He is, after all, an extremely reflective poet, and his poetry *is,* among other things, a way of clarifying for himself the issues which he finds most important in life. Yet it would be a mistake to see him as a clever, abstruse man whose poetry is (like that of so many modern poets) a substitute for something else, for other disciplines in which he ought, by rights, to engage separately.

There is another fact, too; Hope's intellectual vigour and competence may be seen in his attitude to, and control of, poetic forms as such:

> Here are the weaving branches
> Of that resplendent eye,
> The rivers' wandering trenches
> Left when the rivers dry.
>
> And through the blank of summer
> Their parching channels spread;
> The last pools steam and shimmer;
> The reeds are brown and dead.
>
> For you are both the season
> That brimmed their banks with rain
> And the blind, wasting passion
> That dries them out again.
>
> The eye, whose large horizons
> Were quick with liquid sight,
> Now circles in your prison's
> Impenetrable light.

The approach to form here may be called syllogistic. The natural scene is set, simply and neatly, before its analogy with the human situation is stated; and both things are indicated with a complete sense of and attention to what we ought, I suppose, to call their inner logic. The dried summer river-bed is like an eye, but it is also a river-bed; and it is evoked in terms appropriate to a river-bed before the conceit is taken up once more and extended. In this way, the extension of the conceit is seen to follow logically (and I am sure that Hope himself would add 'naturally') from the description of nature.

Yet the language of logic and syllogistic form may be misleading. It is not simply a question of his working out a thought in his poetry, and presenting the premises before the conclusion to be derived from them. It is rather a question of his having brought image and idea into a relationship of such a kind that the completion of the one can be accomplished only with the proper working out of the other. The terms in which the idea is imaged determine the extent to which it is to be developed as an idea; and in developing it, Hope is intent on developing image and idea *together,* making them complementary and mutually expressive.

The point I am making is one difficult to grasp unless it is fully illustrated. . . . It may help matters, however, if I add that many of Hope's poems are concerned with objective situations, and that he imposes his logical order on them by making them as much like events as possible. We see the use of such a method in **"Imperial Adam"**, a poem which has an ironic twist in the last line, but which pays attention to other human realities besides the paradoxical way in which joy seems to beget horror. In evoking the atmosphere of the garden of Eden, Hope treats the situation of Adam and Eve not as a mere piece of symbolism, but as a set of events; and he uses his poetic form to give those events the kind of logical sequence which events must have if they are to be properly understood. . . . (pp. 146-47)

In its combination of strong formal control, rich sensuous perception, and extremely precise diction, [**"Imperial Adam"**] is remarkable among modern poetry. There is no need to defend my statement about its chief qualities. It has the air of passionate and most pointed utterance avoiding rhetoric by a sheer control of form; and that control is achieved, as I have been insisting, by treating the poem's situation as a sequence of events, and giving them the authority not only of the author's manner but also of their own strong logic.

It is not always so in Hope's poetry. . . . [Some of his earlier verse] lacks precisely those virtues which are so compellingly displayed in [later poems such as **"Imperial Adam"**]. . . . (pp. 147-48)

But we are interested mainly in Hope at his best; and Hope at his· best is a poet as unusual in achievement as he is positive in statement. We find in his work, what is surely an unusual thing for an Australian poet, a highly developed tactile sense, a sense of our actually touching things, or of being touched by them. In most Australian poetry, the tactile tends to give way to the visual sense; there is usually a facile music, a thinning of the sense, a certain evidence that eyes accustomed to long and distant horizons do not readily see things in such an immediate way that they are brought present to the sense of touch as well. With Hope it is different, and he is almost alone among Australian poets in the degree to which his tactile sense dominates the other senses and directs his mind. . . .

There is nothing of chant about [Hope's] work, and little of song. This preference is quite in keeping with his attitude to form, and any other kind of music would probably tend to the dissolution of his form rather than to its firmer establishment. After all, he is not a deliberate self-expressionist; in fact, he avoids expressionist poetry as far as he can. He *does* express his own inner states, and in his earlier poetry he does so in a rather compulsive manner; but he does so mostly by the way, as a necessary part of the attempt to do something else. This is largely the reason for his eschewing a lyrical form and a lyrical manner. (p. 149)

Hope is a classical poet whose material is Romantic; it is not possible to give a glib definition of those terms; I am relying on the probability that their meaning will be instinctively recognized. He absorbs the world in terms of a sensibility which is unusual, individualistic, even at times unbalanced and anarchistic; but, that world once part of him, it is subjected to the judgment, to the formative influence, of a strong, deliberate, rather heavy mind. . . . [In] the poetic event, he gives us a poetry in which the tension between his mind and emotions does not issue, as we might have expected it to issue, in an investigation of his own states of mind, but in an arrangement of deeds and symbols. The 'classical' control of form, its syllogistic bent, is Hope's way of making fully objective, of removing from himself, his own tensions and preoccupations. More than any other Australian poet of the present day, the nature of his preoccupations demands that he put them into perspective. A classical form is his way of doing this; and so we get a poetry which is implicitly dramatic, but never explicitly so, either in its form or in its methods of investigation.

McAuley too is a classical poet in something the same sense. Yet Hope's poetry is much less lyrical, much less supple and subjective, than his. The reason is that Hope's poetry derives more directly than McAuley's from his own preoccupations (I had almost said, his own obsessions), and his more rigid use of form is a creative reaction to that fact. Certainly, it enables him to do things, to achieve effects, which no other Australian poet can do or achieve. One may paraphrase somebody else

in saying: 'If Hope did not exist, it would be necessary to invent him'.

We have, then, a heavy almost brooding mind consciously detaching itself in the act of poetry from what most exercises and torments it. This gives readily enough an impression of complete objectivity which is by no means in accordance with the facts. Certainly, it seems to be the explanation for his writing so much satirical poetry, and satirical poetry of such a kind.

I had better make it clear that I neither like most of Hope's satire nor consider it important. It is true that it does not express either shallow criticisms of unimportant social follies or personal grievances; it is true, too, that it is directed against men who fail, for one reason or another, to achieve their full human stature, or who try to overshoot the bounds of their own nature and possibilities. Yet in their actual working-out, such poems as **"The Return from the Freudian Islands"**, **"The Brides"**, and **"Heldensagen"** themselves overshoot their mark, and express a revulsion disproportionate to the follies which they attack. They are, in general, too much and too flamboyantly coloured by Hope's personal worries. Only in such a work as *Dunciad Minimus,* part of which was published in 1950 in *Melbourne University Magazine,* does the true satirical note fully emerge and claim our sympathy. I suppose it emerges too in **"Easter Hymn"**, which is, in any case, only partly a satire:

> The City of God is built like other cities:
> Judas negotiates the loans you float;
> You will meet Caiaphas upon committees;
> You will be glad of Pilate's casting vote.
>
> Your truest lovers still the foolish virgins,
> Your heart will sicken at the marriage feast
> Knowing they watch you from the darkened gardens
> Being polite to your offical guests.

The anger and its cause are glimpsed through a dissolving haze of good humour, or at least a tinge of playfulness. At its occasional best, this kind of satirical verse manages to effect a balance between condemnation and genuine amusement, between the compulsive and the light-hearted. One gets the impression that Hope uses satire partly as a safety-valve, partly as a means of objective comment, and partly as a game. When the first of these predominates (as it too often does) we get unbalanced satire, a statement of revulsion which itself comes to seem repulsive, the suggestion that a God's eye view is being taken of the human situation. And this we cannot allow; we cannot defer to a criticism of human folly which goes so far as to express disgust with life itself, and to condemn, by defacing it, the human image. Perhaps, with Hope, the process does not often go as far as this; but it approaches it too often. The quality in him which goes to mar some of his other poetry operates in his satire by reaction. And one feels that it is not only inferior as a genre, it is not the most suited to Hope's particular talent. (pp. 149-51)

When we consider Hope's typical attitudes and conceptions we see further evidence of something which I have been stressing throughout, of his savage subjectivism made objective, given a more general application, simply by a control of form. He is teaching us, in his own way, the lesson which Shelley and Coleridge, for example, unhappily failed to learn. At any rate, his love for the eighteenth century helps him to understand it, as they did not.

The subject is inevitably approached by considering Hope's emphasis on sex, which is one of the most controversial features of his work. For the sake of comment his poem **"Chorale"** needs to be quoted in full:

> Often had I found her fair;
> Most when to my bed she came,
> Naked as the moving air,
> Slender, walking like a flame.
> In that grace I sink and drown:
> Opening like the liquid wave
> To my touch she laid her down,
> Drew me to her crystal cave.
>   Love me ever, love me long—
>   Was the burden of her song.
>
> All divisions vanish there;
> Now her eyes grow dark and still;
> Now I feel the living air
> With contending thunder fill;
> Hear the shuddering cry begin,
> Feel the heart leap in her breast,
> And her moving loins within
> Clasp their strong, rejoicing guest.
>   Love me now, O now, O long!
>   Is the burden of her song.
>
> Now the wave recedes and dies;
> Dancing fires descend the hill;
> Blessed spirits from our eyes
> Gaze in wonder and are still.
> Yes our wondering spirits come
> From their timeless anguish freed:
> Yet within they hear the womb
> Sighing for the wasted seed.
>   Love may not delay too long—
>   Is the burden of their song.

This is a forceful and lovely poem; there is no need to stress the fact that it is also a poem hymning sexual union, and doing so with unashamed lyricism. I have taken it for comment in order to anticipate and refute a criticism which will no doubt be made time and time again about Hope's poetry: that it is sexually obsessed, and obsessed in an unpleasant manner. It would be a mistake to regard this poem, for example (and it is perhaps the most explicit of his sexual poems) as *that* and no more. It would be ridiculous to regard it as pornography. It is true that the drama of the poem's development comes to its climax with the climax of the sexual act which provides its theme. But the total effect of the poem itself is to initiate us into a world in which sex is a representative, but by no means the only value, perhaps not even the dominant value. Sexual union is recognizably the theme, but the context of the whole poem is such that the union comes to *represent* more than it *is*. The world into which we are initiated is one in which the most intense quality of living and perception is presented through a pattern of images (of air, water, movement, light, and so on) which focus on and elevate sex itself. This is admittedly only one of Hope's poetic attitudes to sex, but it is the attitude expressed in his best poetry. (pp. 152-53)

The other sexual strain in his writing is less likeable; it is, in fact, extraordinarily unpleasant and disturbing at times. There is a recurrent bitter carnality, even a sort of bestiality (perhaps beastishness is a better word) discernible in Hope's work; and it is nearly always associated with sex. One of his poems is called **"Circe"**, and it is a very interesting piece of work; I mention it here only to say that, from a casual reading of his poems, one might gather the impression that he regards woman as being, of her nature, a Circe. Yet a closer inspection would show not only that Hope does not make any such suggestion but that it is a suggestion actually quite foreign to his most profound attitudes, to his concern with an order at once personal and cosmic.

The point is that his attitude to sex is intimately connected with his attitude to the physical world as such. His advanced tactile sense gives him an unusually, almost an abnormally, acute sense of the physical—of its contours and its relations, even of the feel of its inner biological life. And he is quite as conscious of decomposition and distortion as he is of the positive *being* which it contains. So we see him alternating between a controlled affirmation of the physical and a less firmly controlled revulsion from it. Sometimes his sense of physical corruption emerges so strongly that it goes over the edge of control into an almost Manichæan disgust. In **"Massacre of the Innocents"**, we find horror given its full carnal flavour in a statement which is barely held back from rhetoric by an anguished yet controlling hand:

> This is the classic painter's butcher shop;
> —Choice cuts from the Antique—Triumphant Mars
> Takes his revenge, the whistling falchions swoop
> Round Venus as the type of all mammas.

This will bear comparison with (say) **"Imperial Adam"** because they are both 'objective' poems, both reworkings of well-known events, and both based on previous accounts of those events. This poem, for example, is a comment on a painting by Cornelius van Haarlem. Yet no matter how much Hope may disapprove of van Haarlem's excessive physicality, he is surely showing his own excess in the very act of protest. The bantering tone is quite ineffectual to conceal or laugh away the horror of (or, perhaps, the horrified attraction to) the physical with which the lines are laden.

The truth is that, almost alone among Australian poets since Brennan, Hope has a tragic dimension, which, however, his poetry reveals but imperfectly. When he exalts the passions, including the passion of thought, he does so in a finely controlled, 'eventful' rhetoric and in a beautifully physical way—very unlike McAuley's more graceful, more Irish gift. When he states the case *against* man's dignity, he does so in similar language, but in a poetically far less satisfying way. He is himself so much involved in the physical universe which merits variously his praise and condemnation that he has to make his poetry a means of distancing himself from that world. As I have suggested, it is when physical horror enters his consciousness that he fails most signally to do this.

There is more to it than that, of course. The world as Hope sees and presents it is a world of human beings rather than of natural objects. He is wedded to the idea of the primacy of the human, even while he is most intensely insistent on the final insufficiency of the human. He is not at all a political poet, as so many modern poets are; he sees man in a metaphysical dimension rather than a social one—and in a metaphysical dimension which seems to exclude the social as either irrelevant or unimportant. We could do with a little more of this sort of thing; and I am content to say so even though I do not share Hope's apparent disdain for the social life of man. This is a reaction against what the last two centuries have made of Renaissance humanism. It is, in some sense, a reaction against Renaissance values as such, even though Hope seems to me in many ways a type of Renaissance man. It would probably be truer to say that he is a type of eighteenth-century man, sharing with him an emphasis on the primacy of reason and an intense awareness of the physical universe, but differing from him in his belief that man is perfectible, that the world began with the reign of Queen Elizabeth I, and that society is a pleasant and necessary contract for the mutual protection of man. In other words, despite his emphasis on reason, Hope is not really a poet of the Enlightenment.

It is difficult, of course, to decide the dates of many of his poems; yet I feel little hesitation in saying that his later poetry (that in the section entitled **"Pyramis or The House of Ascent"**) is his best, as it is certainly his most 'classical'. We can see him on the whole gradually writing his way out of satire, out of a largely satirical approach to life, and gradually achieving a hard joy. He is beginning more and more to combine his deeply ironic qualities with a sense of the real value of persons and things, grasped and expressed in all their sensuous compactness. The early poetry, with its somewhat random experimental tendencies, is yielding to a poetry in which a consistent attempt is made to get a form more suited to Hope's 'classical' view of man and his destiny. He is giving mythology a modern twist, while preserving its traditional force and authority. At the same time, he has never ceased to put his own doubts and dilemmas into a comparatively rigid classical context in order at once to disguise them and to give them an added reverberation and a permanent solidity. One of the disturbing things about his total output is that, despite the increasing maturity of his verse, there is no corresponding increase in its fertility. It is an output in many ways too small for comfort. One senses a lack either of energy or of the more obvious kind of dedication to the art itself. And so, if we are to account for the feeling of solidity which we get about his work, we shall have to seek a different and more profound dedication.

I feel that Hope is a recognizably modern poet, in whom lyricism and satire combine and sharpen each other. In his best poems, his control of his material is of a remarkable order. (pp. 153-56)

[Hope] shares with Swift a passionate lucid mind, with Blake a sense of reverence and uncompromising scorn, and is developing, as Yeats did, a speech which may well be called candid and even noble. Despite the puzzling crudities of much of his work, therefore, and despite the irregularity of his inspiration, we must insist that he is a part of the new humanist tradition in Australian poetry, of sophistication and depth working together. (p. 157)

> *Vincent Buckley, "A. D. Hope: The Unknown Poet,"*
> *in his* Essays in Poetry: Mainly Australian, *Melbourne University Press, 1957, pp. 142-57.*

JAMES MCAULEY

The tendency of literature to remain true to a few themes, which are inexhaustible in their possibilities, can be illustrated by the work of three Australian poets, superficially quite unlike one another: Christopher Brennan, Harold Stewart, and A.D. Hope. Yet the prevailing theme in each is one and the same: the search for a principle of personal (and by wider operation social) integration, hence creativity and joy. Such a principle must be transfiguring and salvific. The search involves a journey into the underworld to grapple with nightmares and despairs and to win the gift of grace. It is also envisaged in its erotic aspect: the divinized or paradisal state longed for is identified with nuptial union, which, however, breaks down into disillusion and severance and the vain hope of somehow attaining the longed-for divinization in an authentic form. Brennan wrote of practically nothing else. Stewart traced it out in his *Orpheus*

sequence. Hope, in a relatively early attempt, **"Pygmalion"** (in *The Wandering Islands*) gives a resumé in one poem of the experience which Brennan could not have imagined presenting in such raw painfulness and shocking terseness.

This poem is not reprinted in Hope's recent collection which was published in England (*Poems*) and one can hazard a guess why. It was one of the first of a number of poems in which poetry is used as an instrument of self-knowledge. The most deep-seated and violent tensions and conflicts, the most painful ulcerations of the spirit are probed and exposed. Either in direct confession, or by dramatic images thrown onto a screen in the endeavour to exteriorize the theme, the inner anguish and dread, shame, horror, longing and despair are *avowed*.

Clearly such private and often obscure subjective material, charged with violent emotions rendered explosive by inhibition, threatens the maintenance of artistic control. **"Pygmalion"** does not, like the later poems, have stylistic unity. It falls into three different pieces tacked together, each but precariously in control of its mode of expression.

As one would expect, [Hope's] earlier poems are the most uncertain in their style and tone. They are also in many cases (e.g. **"Observation Car"**) full of a sense of frustration, stopped growth, defeat of psychic energies . . . even a kind of fear of the death of the personality. It is from this state of apparent defeat that the poet begins the search and struggle recorded, directly or indirectly, in the later poems.

One can make a rough sort of classification. Sometimes the poet deals with his material by turning it into satire or invective, or farce or serious-grotesque entertainment. Sometimes he objectifies the experience by casting it into myth or legend or other figurations. Sometimes the presumably 'autobiographical' content is either left on the surface, or stands behind a thinning veil, as in such poems, in the second volume [*Poems*], as the admirable [**"An Epistle: Edward Sackville to Venetia Digby"**], the stark **"Meditation on a Bone"**, or the ballad-like **"The Walker"**. (pp. 61-2)

Hope has, to an almost dangerous degree, a facility in adopting the different modes of expression that have prevailed in poetry from the sixteenth to the twentieth century. The danger is that this facility of literary mimicry will become mere virtuosity. But it does seem to me that, although this element has increased, if anything, in Hope's work, it has also become more organically essential to what he is doing: it has become a resource of expressiveness giving a further resonance to the meaning. I would observe also that this exploitation of various styles within the tradition is wide-ranging and renders misleading any characterization of the poet as a 'classicist' or 'Augustan'. If one had to choose a word, I should think 'romantic' in some of its important meanings a truer label.

The poems have their starting point from a high degree of dissociation and conflict within the personality: reason versus passion, morality versus desire, sociality versus individual feeling. There is the constant endeavour to integrate the personality, to achieve wholeness and consequent joy and spontaneity—to consummate, in Blake's terms, a Marriage of Heaven and Hell. . . . (pp. 62-3)

In order to penetrate these poems and understand that they are not mere literary exercises in the sardonic or the erotic, one must discern the basic structure of assumptions and values which informs the work. Like all serious poetry it has an intrinsic metaphysic, without an understanding of which the true *morphe* of the poems cannot be grasped.

In Western civilization there has been a long struggle, carried on partly within Christianity and partly without, between two rival conceptions of the nature of man and his spiritual destiny. One is the orthodox Christian view, and the other, under various disguises, is the Manichean heresy.

In the orthodox view matter and spirit, body and soul, are both good, since created by God; and though body and soul are in a fallen state both are redeemable and are predestined to a final transfiguration. . . . The materiality of our human existence is not in itself a degradation. This applies not only to the goodness of sexuality and sensual enjoyment but also to all those social institutions with their material thickness and weight in which the person becomes embedded: marriage, organized religion, political and economic affairs. (pp. 63-4)

The Manichean view is opposite. This is explicit in the Catharist heresy of mediaeval times. Matter is the principle and source of evil and is irredeemable. It stands opposite to spirit in an irreconcilable dualism. Man in his actual worldly being is in a state of degradation, a pure spirit imprisoned in the defiling flesh. Redemption consists in liberation from materiality. This involves the condemnation of sexuality and sense-life as such; and also of social institutions with their material structures that oppress the spirit. In mediaeval Catharism the path of perfection consisted of the rejection of marriage and generation as evil; suicide is the highest act of final liberation. (p. 64)

As I read it, the ground-structure of assumptions and valuations in Hope's poetry is the Manichean inheritance, presumably mediated by Calvinism. This is the starting-point, but what actually develops thereafter is quite complicated: it is an attempt to establish a new structure of assumptions and valuations different from either Manicheism or Christian orthodoxy. Let us, however, first observe passages where the Manichean ground-plan shows through unmistakably.

In "Ascent into Hell" the poet goes back through childhood—through fear, nightmare, guilt and punishment—until he passes beyond memory to the moment of birth. Birth into this world is equated with damnation, the mouth of the womb is identified with the gate of hell in Dante's *Inferno*. . . . The institutional aspects of courtship and marriage are throughout fiercely satirized, not merely as suburban vulgarities, but as a betrayal and death of the spirit. This is the meaning of the brilliantly funny "The Brides", in which the suburban brides are likened to motor-cars passing from the assembly line through the salesman's hands to the customer. It is no less the message of "The Explorers", and of "The Lingam and the Yoni" where authentic joy dies of the materiality of suburban circumstances. (pp. 64-5)

The critical instance for my interpretation is the much-admired poem "Imperial Adam", in which the Adam and Eve legend is re-written to give a different account of the Fall. Matter, the flesh, sensual enjoyment and sexuality, are presented in all their glowing delight. Yet they are also presented as the direct and immediate source of the appearance of evil and guilt. The wills of the two are entirely naive and innocent. But the fruit of their fleshly delight is guilt and death: not as the result of disobedience, or misuse of natural appetite, but simply by instinctive and normal use. The birth of the murderer Cain at the end of this glowing rhapsody is not just a gratuitous shock effect: it is the consummation of the poem.

Now, in advancing this poem as evidence, I am in the delicate and temerarious position of contradicting the poet's own reading. The problem is not that the poem celebrates the natural splendour of the material creation. That I can allow for, as we shall see. The difficulty is that, in a letter in reply to my advancing this interpretation (in an admittedly incomplete form), the poet amicably began, 'Probably you are right about "Imperial Adam"', but went on to say: 'But I did not mean it that way. I meant to put a case for the spontaneous generation of evil from things not in themselves evil at all—rather like the occurrence of lethal mutations in biology.' If I nevertheless do not give up my point, it is because I am concerned with the pressure—almost automatic and unconscious—of a mode of interpreting reality which can persist underneath many surface manoeuvres. The assumption that such a pattern exists is necessary if one is to make sense of Hope's poetry. How explain the vehemence of its reasons, unless one knows what it is reacting *against;* how explain its metaphysical torment, which is something more than the record of personal grief and ill-starred love? Finally, in regard to "Imperial Adam" in particular, what is the point of the following description of Eve?—

> This plump gourd severed from his virile root,
> She promised on the turf of Paradise
> Delicious pulp of the forbidden fruit;
> Sly as the snake she loosed her sinuous thighs . . .

By the identification with the forbidden fruit and the serpent, Eve's body becomes the source of evil. Notice too that at this point the shadow of something not naïve and innocent touches the scene in the 'slyness' of the amorous invitation.

What we must now place in its significance is the celebration of sensuality which (in alternation with images of disgust) is a feature of Hope's poetry. . . . Now, in the first place, it is to be observed that the adult Hope is an unbeliever, an atheist Manichee. The whole conception of the 'spiritual' is imperilled, and the spirit has certainly no heaven to go to after liberation. (This is part of the point of the suicide-meditation, "The Sleeper".) Half at least of the Manichean scheme has collapsed. There is earth, and a hell, which is really the psychic underworld of nightmare and dread and slavery to instinct, a dimension of this life. Where, in such a universe, is to be found the principle of grace, of transcendence, of reconciliation and reintegration? This is the point at which the poems come face to face with nihilism and despair. In a Manicheism turned atheist there would seem to be no solution.

But in the second place, the collapse of the original Manichean scheme, with its supernal plane of celestial liberation or pure spirituality, also invalidates the condemnation of the flesh as evil. The poet is in conscious revolt against the condemnation of the flesh: he affirms the beauty of the material world, the legitimacy and innocence of the senses. The tension of "Imperial Adam" is precisely that the poem brings its celebration of the natural order into abrupt collision with the lurking Manichean heritage.

This celebration is the poet's clue to a new path of integration and transcendence—one that can be stated in purely naturalistic, this-worldly terms. Where is the salvific principle to be found? The lines along which a solution is attempted are as follows:—Look again at the instinctual life, the fleshly libido, the passionate eros, round which so many images of guilt, nightmare and disgust accumulate. Is it not, nevertheless, the principle of life? See what paradises of beauty, promises of joy, spring up on its way! Even if they lie under an obscure condemnation these ecstatic moments exist! Within passion there is a daemonic power capable of transcending our everyday selves and transfiguring us. This power is, as it were, an 'infernal' or 'daemonic' grace, which has its own myths and rituals, and confers salvation on those strong enough to give it sway. A precarious 'heaven' can be built by the titanic powers of the underworld. But make no mistake: this transcendence takes us beyond good and evil. The categories of guilt and innocence are transcended by those strong enough. Such persons form an elite, and are a law to themselves, not answerable to 'the frantic devotees of good and ill'. Their union is a divinizing union. . . . (pp. 66-8)

The poems of Hope's 'middle period' are revealing for this stage of the quest. "The Muse" is Hope's 'infernal' or 'daemonic' riposte to my 'celestial' account of poetic creation. In "Pyramis", the achievements of human power and art are due to the infernal energies, to an extremity of passion and pride, not excluding political despotism and cruelty, bordering on madness and criminality. "The Invocation" is the proclamation of the need to ascend beyond good and evil. Everything truly great is ascribed to sheer will and energy, assertion and defiance. . . . (p. 68)

You can recognize the general name for this type of spiritual adventure: it is Nietzscheanism. Nietzsche faced the threat of nihilism and proclaimed the superman. Dionysian excess, enthusiasm, amorality, are affirmed against Apollonian balance and measure.

In many of these poems I am reminded of Wilhelm Schmidt's comment in his *Primitive Revelation* on the effects of the Fall: 'Perhaps the partaking of the fruit produced at first a certain intoxication, momentarily unleashing wonderful powers and conjuring up glittering phantoms of delight, even as it burst the shackles that had restrained the passions.'. . . One may say that the enterprise is doomed to failure: that the daemonic powers will not build Jerusalem, that the higher criminality is still criminality, and heroic mania is still mania. From a literary point of view, I would also observe that a tremendous strain is put upon the language of poetry, which has to do the work of providing rhetorical transfigurations and resolutions which are not properly grounded in reality. It is the same difficulty that one finds in Rilke, whose influence is discernible in some of Hope's poems of this period.

It was not likely that his overstrained Nietzschean posture—however brilliant and moving its literary products—would satisfy Hope, and it seems to me that the direction of Hope's further development has been away from this extreme and untenable romanticism. It is significant, I suppose, that Hope's criticism has increasingly set a course close to 'orthodoxy', against romantic and post-romantic irrationalism—very eloquently indeed in his essay "The Discursive Mode". There he affirms the sense of a 'natural order' and rejects the tendency to equate poetry with excitement, and neglect the discursive forms of literature in favour of incoherent spasma of intoxicated irrationality. One may say generally that wherever the notion of a 'natural order' is reasserted, not as a demand imposed on reality but as a recognition of the possible perfections actually present in reality, one is on the way to reconciling the Dionysian-Apollonian dualism and achieving *centrality,* which need not be *mediocrity.*

In the poetry, I would instance, in the first place, the unpublished satirical work *Dunciad Minimus* as a celebration, which rises to impressive beauty, of 'orthodoxy' in the realm of culture: an affirmation of an intellectual order to which the poet has obligations, and of the need to defend this against the barbarians.

Among other later poems I would instance one which, while it does not seem to me to be without unresolved problems, is of great interest, "An Epistle from Holofernes". The poem deals in part with the difficulty that the daemonic transfigurations proclaimed in the 'middle-period' poems are 'beyond good and evil'. We have seen enough cut-rate Nietzscheanism in the form of beatniks and fascists to make the dish unattractive once it is recognized. The cult has lost its aristocratic air and has been vulgarized. Hope shifts the problem along to the need for some kind of balance between the night-powers and the daytime world. We must live two modes of existence, symbolized . . . by daylight vision and starlight vision. . . . [It] is the Marriage of Heaven and Hell that is somehow required—but not really achieved, save by rhetorical trompe l'oeil. Intellectual vision, wisdom, creativity and love are *not* merely the resultants of extremity of passion, of the surge of organic energies, of heroic guilt or mania.

It is easy enough to say that the drama of Hope's poetry revolves, if I have read it aright, around a false problem. The truth is that man has a certain nature, a certain structure of being, a natural hierarchy of powers, and a natural orientation towards the Good. The way out of the Manichean trap is not by a glorification of body against spirit, passion against reason—that is a mere reversing of the signs—but by holding fast to the body-soul unity of man, to the created goodness of the person thus constituted, and by distinguishing between two possible end-states that this body-soul unity can attain: the kingdom of God, in which all energies are integrated and glorified, and the kingdom of Satan, in which all energies are set in conflict and degraded.

But the fact that the problem is at bottom a false problem does not empty of value the literary record of Hope's wrestling with the problem, nor does it affect the moving quality of many of the poems as records of personal experience. The order of doctrine is one thing; the complexity of human life is another. The dignity and eloquence of two of the most recent poems, the "Soledades" and "An Epistle: Edward Sackville to Venetia Digby", and the humane realism of "A Bidding Grace", make one look forward to what may be yet to come. Also, "A Commination" (though I think it partly fails by adopting too fully the traditionally coarse ranting style of invective) and the relentless satire "The Kings", which take up again the defence of civilization against barbarism and parasitism, point beyond the tormented and ambiguous splendours which first brought Hope into prominence. (pp. 68-70)

James McAuley, "The Pyramid in the Waste: An Introduction to A. D. Hope's Poetry," in Quadrant, *Vol. V, No. 4, September, 1961, pp. 61-70.*

G. A. WILKES

In the last ten years A. D. Hope has become established as one of the leading Australian poets, and also as one of the most difficult to classify. His work has been so unruly in its development, so apt to take fresh directions, that it has successfully resisted the patterns that critics have formulated to account for it. Although Hope's first collection, *The Wandering Islands,* did not appear until 1955, he had won his first reputation as a poet almost fifteen years earlier, from work sporadically published and known to a small circle. If such early pieces as those in the *Australian National Review* for February, 1939, are set aside, then Hope's first characteristic poems were published in 1943 in a brochure written jointly by himself, Harry Hooton and Garry Lyle. Without a title, and without a price, this brochure ran for three issues. . . . [Poems from the brochure that Hope has chosen to reprint] include **"The Lingam and the Yoni", "Observation Car"** and **"Massacre of the Innocents"**. Others of about the same period are **"Pygmalion"** (dated 1941, published in 1944 as **"The Invocation"**), **"The Return from the Freudian Islands"** (1943) and **"Australia"** and **"Standardisation"** (1944).

The climate to which these poems belong is part of an unwritten chapter (or at least a footnote to one) in Australian literary history. In the early 1940's there was a minor cult of parody and satire among a group of poets in Sydney, associated with the University, the Myrtle St. pub, and a coffee-shop or two downtown. (p. 41)

Of the verse of that time, Hope's has best retained its pungency and impact. [His] early poems are forceful and incisive, written from the standpoint of a critical observer, alert to expose fake and sham wherever they are found. **"Observation Car"** (1943), though not one of the most accomplished of the early satires, yet suggests their general mood and temper. The *persona* is an unwilling passenger in a train bound on a purposeless journey: he is disenchanted but still protesting, cynical but determined not to be deceived ("the future is rumour and drivel"), his aggressiveness felt in the imaginary assault on the lollipop blonde, and diffused in the truculent tone of the whole. The attention won by the element of sex in Hope's early poems has helped to obscure the seriousness underlying them. What makes for coherence in the verse published before *The Wandering Islands* is the vision of a world lacking any heroic dimension. If this is something common to all social satire, it is also a theme that Hope deliberately presses. It is best illustrated in **"Conquistador"** (1947), the odyssey of the contemporary hero, Henry Clay. . . . Henry's adventure comes from an encounter with a huge girl in a hotel lounge, and from the invitation to accompany her home. . . . The modern hero is [revealed to be] a pigmy, who, when he stands up to life finds that it rolls over and squashes him flat. (pp. 42-3)

To choose **"Conquistador"** (rather than **"Sportsfield"**, for instance) may be to represent Hope's satire at its least complex, but it does isolate the theme in the early poems that comes to occupy the later ones. From the standpoint of *The Wandering Islands* and some later work, Hope's early verse has come to seem to Professor McAuley [see excerpt above] the product of a personality in conflict with itself, seeking a principle of integration, casting off poems in the throes of the Manichean heresy. From the standpoint of *Poems* (1960), certain of the early pieces have seemed to Judith Wright the work of a junior rhymester whom the mature Hope has left behind, the work of "smart Alec". Neither diagnosis is valid. To grant the vehemence, or the sensuality that vies with disgust, is not to convict the author of these early satires of a dissociated personality: he already possesses an "integrity", though it may be expressed in nothing more than a repudiation of the values of the world about him. At times there is something more. There is in **"Observation Car"** the muffled ambition to be "The Eater of Time, a poet"; or in **"The Lingam and the Yoni"** (referred to by McAuley) the lament for the passing of youth and fertility in a suburban marriage, where the partners are absorbed in calculating time-payments and guaranteeing security. . . . The attack on the false is sometimes by implication an assertion of the true. Hope's later poems will be occupied with evolving a positive standard to set against the values of the unheroic world he has exposed.

If there has been a phase of disturbance and uncertainty in Hope's development, it might be placed later, in the period of *The Wandering Islands* (1955). The title-poem of this collection develops the theme of "the long isolation of the heart". [**"The Wandering Islands"**] expresses the impossibility of communion between separate minds, which are like wandering islands in an ocean, islands that are never charted or annexed, meeting sometimes in a violent collision, but then inevitably falling asunder again:

> You cannot build bridges between the wandering islands;
> The Mind has no neighbours, and the unteachable heart
> Announces its armistice time after time, but spends
> Its love to draw them closer and closer apart.
>
> (pp. 43-4)

"The Wandering Islands" is one of a group of poems, including **"Chorale"** and **"The Death of the Bird"**, that show a more marked lyric quality, and a more assured craftsmanship, than any of Hope's previous work. **"Chorale"** is a treatment of physical love, celebrating it in one of the moments when "the long isolation of the heart" seems about to be overcome. The progression of the poem follows the stages of the sexual act, the union of the flesh described in the second stanza becoming in the third a union of the spirit, even as passion subsides. . . . But then the moment of communion slips away, as fruition is denied. . . . The same resignation, or denial of fulfilment, is felt in **"The Death of the Bird"**. The bird journeys each year across the world to a speck beckoning her in the other hemisphere, as "Love pricks the course in lights across the chart"; in her last response to the summons, the invisible thread of instinct is broken as she flies, abandoning the bird to the waste leagues of air. . . . (pp. 44-5)

Yet it is not possible to characterise *The Wandering Islands* as preoccupied with "the long isolation of the heart", however much **"Chorale"** and **"The Death of the Bird"** show the assertive poetry of observation yielding to a poetry of reflection and enquiry, with a control and sensitivity that had not been encountered before. Equally conspicuous is Hope's attraction to myth, and his effort to dramatise and objectify his material in the terms that legend and fable afford. The immediately arresting feature of these poems is the calculated reversal of the normal interpretation of a myth, as in the switching of sympathies in **"The Return of Persephone"**, or in the exposure in **"Lot and his Daughters"** of the later history of "the one Just Man from Sodom saved alive". The most celebrated poem of this group is **"Imperial Adam"** (1951), which recreates the idyllic state of man in the garden of Eden, awakening to find the companion provided for him:

> Imperial Adam, naked in the dew,
> Felt his brown flanks and found the rib was gone.
> Puzzled he turned and saw where, two and two,
> The mighty spoor of Jahweh marked the lawn.
>
> Then he remembered through mysterious sleep
> The surgeon fingers probing at the bone,
> The voice so far away, so rich and deep:
> 'It is not good for him to live alone.'
>
> Turning once more he found Man's counterpart
> In tender parody breathing at his side.
> He knew her at first sight, he knew by heart
> Her allegory of sense unsatisfied.

The stanzas that follow have been interpreted as one of Hope's celebrations of sex as part of the natural splendour of the world, spontaneous and innocent, . . . but the sardonic tone of the introductory stanzas ("tender parody", the surgeon's voice "so far away, so rich and deep") shows him "distancing" himself from what he describes, preserving an ironic detachment. Adam obeys the command to increase and multiply, and the animals of the garden serve Eve as the first midwives of the human race:

> The proud vicuna nuzzled her as she slept
> Lax on the grass; and Adam watching too
> Saw how her dumb breasts at their ripening wept,
> The great pod of her belly swelled and grew,
>
> And saw its water break, and saw, in fear,
> Its quaking muscles in the act of birth,
> Between her legs a pigmy face appear,
> And the first murderer lay upon the earth.

One feature of the "mythical" poems is this determination to confront certain brutal facts. Their more positive, affirmative quality emerges as Hope touches on the theme of the poet, as in **"Pyramis or The House of Ascent"**. The pyramids, according to one of the theories presented in I.E.S. Edwards' *The Pyramids of Egypt*, were built to provide the Pharaohs with a stairway to heaven, and Hope's poem begins in the contemplation of the kings raising in the desert this "solid, blind, invincible masonry" as a means of deification. . . . Then attention turns to the builders of the pyramids of art, who spent their energies like slaves toiling in the sun. . . . (pp 45-7)

The first heroic personality to emerge in Hope's verse [in **"Pyramis or The House of Ascent"**] is the personality of the poet, seen as one of those who "put aside Consideration, dared and stood alone". The poets named are Blake and Swift, both rebels against the values of their age, and Milton, last exemplar in English of the tradition of the heroic poem. To them might be added Yeats, the student of Blake and Swift, who in Hope's tribute **"On the Death of W. B. Yeats"** (1955) becomes a figure in the myth, a symbol of the poet as hero.

The emergence of this conception carries us from *The Wandering Islands* to *Poems* (1960). The alienation of the satirist from the values of the mass, attested in the early verse, has developed in **"Pyramis"** and **"William Butler Yeats"** into a sense of the antithesis between the godlike poet and the unheroic world—an antagonism to be made even sharper in **"Persons from Porlock"** (1956). Yet within *The Wandering Islands* the poet as hero is presented in an egocentric, almost demonic guise: in **"Pyramis"**, whether or not by ironic intent, he appears as some kind of inspired lunatic. The question then is what Hope is to do with his heroic conception, once it has been formulated: is he to write a series of poems simply asserting it?

The answer is indicated in his prose-writings in the 1950's. In an essay on **"The Discursive Mode"**. . . (1956), Hope resumed a theme of his 1952 inaugural lecture at Canberra University College: the decay, in the last two hundred years or so, of such major poetic forms as the epic, verse tragedy, the ode, the great philosophic poem—and with them other traditional forms like the epistle, the elegy, the pastoral, the verse satire. (p. 47)

[Hope's essay soon] becomes a plea for the revival of "the discursive mode", the middle form of poetry. It is the equable style in which Chaucer wrote his tales, Dryden his *Religio Laici*, Browning his monologues, and Robert Frost his New England poems. Hope sees the discursive mode as the flexible style that is adequate for exposition, argument, narrative, satire, and meditation, depending not on "a profusion of startling images, but on the plain resources of ordinary English used with inimitable aptness and animated by metre and rhyme". The rehabilitation of the poetry of discourse is the first stage in a programme to reclaim the desert to which the poetic landscape has been reduced by the erosion of the last two centuries.

The newer work in *Poems* (1960) seems at first to upset most of the critical generalisations and to confound the prophecies made about Hope from *The Wandering Islands*. Yet it proves to be continuous with the earlier collection, in working out the conception of the poet adumbrated there. The brilliantly sustained **"The Elegy (Variations on a Theme of the Seventeenth Century)"**, the moving **"An Epistle: Edward Sackville to Venetia Digby"**, together with such pieces as **"Man Friday"** and **"Lambkin: A Fable"**, reflect the effort to re-establish the discursive mode. If *The Wandering Islands* had encouraged the view that the early satires were like an attack of measles that Hope was now recovering from—a view that the *Dunciad Minimus* (1950) should have discounted—in *Poems* (1960) the satires are set in perspective in another way, by **"Persons from Porlock"**. Coleridge was fortunate to have suffered but one intrusion, to have had but a single poem ruined: he escaped the contamination of Porlock as a whole—

> Think of his fate had Porlock been less kind;
> The paps of Porlock might have given him suck;
> Teachers from Porlock organised his mind,
> And Porlock's Muse inspired the vapid strain
> Of: 'Porlock, Loveliest Village of the Plain!'. . .

The traveller in **"Observation Car"** had expressed an ambition "to be the Eater of Time, a poet", and the other satires of the period show him (in retrospect) to have been keeping the world of Porlock at bay, sharing Blake's "uncompromising scorn" and like Yeats, breeding "passion against the times".

The rôle of the poet is now coming to exceed the chest-beating stance of **"Pyramis"**, and the achievement of *Poems* (1960) is to take it to a further stage still. The decay of the great poetic forms seemed to Hope a token of the decay of civilisation itself. When the epic died and the novel replaced it, he wrote, "something noble in the mind of man died . . . and something more comfortable and amusing took its place". The present predicament is described in Hope's largest recent venture in the discursive mode, **"Conversation with Calliope"** (1962). In a parable, the muse explains to her balding protégé how the epic is one of the casualties of the Great Society, of the processes by which over-population and mass-production have cheapened and diluted all the arts. With culture "sterilised and tinned and tested", the last vineyard replaced by a coca-cola factory, the last poet tethered on the campus, we reach an epoch when the great forms must for a time disappear. But they are not lost irretrievably, so long as the isolated poet will preserve his values through a barren and hostile age, ready

> through his art to bring to birth
> New modes of being here on earth.

I shall not try to formulate Hope's "mystique" of the poet, in its latest version, as this is something Hope himself has still to do. But this sense of the poet's rôle and mission lends a new complexity and resonance to such poems in the 1960 collection as **"An Epistle from Holofernes"** and **"Soledades of the Sun and Moon"**.

"An Epistle from Holofernes" looks to the myths as a repository of truths that persist down the centuries, transcending the accidentals of time and place to "speak to us the truth of what we are". The poet's rôle in re-awakening the myth is akin to bringing new modes of being to birth. . . . The epistle describes two worlds, the one of daylight vision ("plain sight and common touch"), and the other of "mythic night", and it is the poet who must bring them into adjustment. . . . (pp. 48-50)

The limitation of **"An Epistle from Holofernes"** is that the doctrines about poetry enunciated in it are not made dramatically relevant to the situation with which the poem itself deals. The theorising that concludes **"An Epistle: Edward Sackville to Venetia Digby"** may cause disquiet in the same way, though this second epistle is for other reasons far more compelling. Of the later poems specifically concerned with the mystique of the poet, **"Soledades of the Sun and Moon"** is the most impressive. Owing something to the *Solitudes* of Gongora, it deals (according to the author's note) with "the isolation of poets and the unity of poetry whatever its mode". The world of myth now finds an equivalence in the constellations in the heavens, changeless and immortal, yet isolated one from the other by the very order and harmony of the emotion to which they are bound. It is through the poet that they become articulate . . . , and the poet is moved and entreated by the distant spheres, their rivalries forgotten, so that the cosmic dance itself seems almost to pay homage to the poets of the world, even as it embodies the "enchanted motion" that they celebrate. . . . (p. 50)

The third selection of Hope's verse—this one not made by the author—appeared in 1963 in the *Australian Poets* series. Though it is restricted to "poems mostly written since I was forty", and contains only ten that had not previously appeared in book form, the volume stresses again the restlessness of Hope's development, and shows the range his work has acquired since the first joint venture twenty years before. . . . Whatever the generalisations about it that one may submit, Hope's poetry continues to demand to be evaluated afresh at every stage. (p. 51)

G. A. Wilkes, "The Poetry of A. D. Hope," in The Australian Quarterly, *Vol. XXXVI, No. 1, March, 1964, pp. 41-51.*

KENNETH REXROTH

A. D. Hope is one of Australia's leading poets. His work [as displayed in **Collected Poems, 1930-1965**] is very competent, often witty . . . , often sardonic, and always something that so much poetry is not, the expression of a perfectly mature man. Yet it is conventional indeed, in an old fashioned way that no one in America could possibly manage today. Reviewers have said all sorts of wild things about him. His ease amongst the rhymes and meters seems to demoralize them. He does not resemble Swift or Pope in the least, as one maintains, nor is he deeply rooted in classical antiquity, nor do his poems "bear the mark of eternity" any more conspicuously than lots of others.

He writes like Calverly, or Belloc, or Day Lewis, or the inventors of the more savage limericks, the wit of the more mordant Balliol men of other days. It is provincial verse in the sense that the problems, spiritual, moral, psychological, and technical with which it copes endure in this degree of purity only far out in the world outback, away from the great metropoles with their Baudelaires, Rilkes, Artauds and Alan Ginsbergs. . . . If written by an American or Frenchman, poetry like Hope's would be fatuous and hackneyed. His is not only better than many an avant-gardist's, but much better than the

fag end of his tradition in the homeland—say somebody like Betjeman. (pp. 373-74)

Kenneth Rexroth, in a review of "Collected Poems," in Commonweal, *Vol. LXXXIV, No. 13, June 17, 1966, pp. 373-74.*

THE TIMES LITERARY SUPPLEMENT

Mr. A. D. Hope is Professor of English at Canberra but he is also one of the most distinguished living Australian poets. This latest collection [**Collected Poems, 1930-1965**] not only includes work written since his *Poems* (1960) but also offers a number of early pieces not previously published in book form. A good many of Mr. Hope's critical attitudes might easily be deduced from the deft Augustanism of his verse, but it is interesting none the less to have them argued out in [**The Cave and the Spring,** a collection of] short, provocative and bluntly outspoken essays. The essays are intended, he explains, not as contributions to scholarship but "as a poet's occasional reflections on aspects of his craft". The poet's occasional reflections on his other profession are also pungent. In the terminal essay, **"Literature Versus the Universities"**, Mr. Hope sees our age as an Alexandrian one, in which published commentary on literature (he takes the obvious example of the contrasted bulk of T. S. Eliot's production in poetry and of the many expository works about it) is multiplying alarmingly beyond necessity, and in which, in the United States, creative writing classes and the need for writers to earn their living mainly in universities are beginning to make the creator morally, and financially, dependent on his commentators. Soon, he fears, there will be no more wild writers, only campus poets and novelists.

Mr. Hope is doubtful, also, about approved methods of commentary. He has a disturbing essay in which he examines three commentaries on a fine poem of his own, by three leading Australian critics. [James McAuley (see excerpt above)], obsessed with the idea that a poet must be either Christian or Manichean, read into the poem a Manichean philosophy which Mr. Hope did not intend to express, and which he is not conscious of holding. Another saw that the poem about Adam and Eve, the bliss of the first human sexual rapture, and its ironical sequence in the birth of Cain, was in fact a condensed narrative poem, not a moral allegory, but found in it a tone of gloom where Mr. Hope intended one of tough masculine humour. A third critic blamed the poet for presenting a paradox without resolving it, where the presentation of an unresolvable paradox was perhaps part of the poet's intention.

All three critics looked for the "idea" of the poem as its total poetic "meaning", and none reflected that, for a poet in the throes of composition, "ideas" are merely an element in composition, like rhythms, images and decisions about diction, and that for a poet the "meaning" of a poem is never a detachable "message" but simply how well, or badly, the poem comes off as a total shape. The whole tradition of "practical criticism" may, in fact, in the end have led not to greater suppleness and detachment in response but merely to subtler ways of manipulating "stock responses" and unargued presuppositions about what a poem should be.

Mr. Hope has a gift of powerful, blunt argumentative statement, and also a basic conservatism of taste that makes him in some ways like an Australian equivalent of Professor Yvor Winters. He has an excellent introductory essay ["**The Discursive Mode"**], regretting the decay of the "discursive mode" in poetry, and with it the decay of "the maintenance and modulation of tone, the arts of being at once well bred, elegant, sincere and adept''. He regrets also the passing of the theory of poetic kinds and their hierarchy, and deplores Poe's and the Symbolists' reduction of the truly poetic to the transient moment of "elevating excitement''. . . .

It follows from this position that Mr. Hope's feelings about "modernist'' poetry are cool. He speaks always rather slightingly of T. S. Eliot and in an essay on free verse quotes with approval Mr. Graham Hough's shocking attempt to turn the wonderful passage about the cat-like fog in "Prufrock'' into limping iambics. Mr. Hope himself, by breaking up Eliot's own line arrangement (and also by printing the passage as prose) discredits the rhythmical beauty of one of the finest passages in "Ash Wednesday''. Professor Winter's famous attack on the rationale of free verse seemed . . . to justify good free verse, by showing that there is a cunningly hidden regularity under its apparent arbitrariness. Mr. Hope's attack is, in comparison, coarse and inept, and the answer to it is not argument but simply reopening one's volume of Eliot.

The same sort of vigour, combined with a certain moral coarseness of appeal, is shown in a fine essay on *Tamburlaine,* in which Mr. Hope ingeniously reconciles Tamburlaines's love of the beauty of poetry and of the beauty of Zenocrate with his fiendish ruthlessness as a conqueror. . . .

Some of the best essays [in *The Cave and the Spring*], in spite of Mr. Hope's disclaimer, show the professor rather than the poet at work. An examination of Dryden's ode to the memory of Anne Killigrew sees Dryden not as flattering the young lady but as aggrandizing her, in a way proper to a funereal ode, by associating her with all the grand things that can properly be said about poetry and painting; and as making the extravagance of the baroque mode acceptable by being aware himself of the element of the comic inseparable from the baroque mode. The picture of the Last Day is not merely comic but is made acceptable by Dryden's awareness of its comic potentialities—"The Sacred Poets bounding from their tombs like a set of jack-in-the-boxes''. Another very interesting essay on Dryden, on *All for Love,* defines that play as not a proper tragedy, but a success in a new kind, pathetic comedy. Dryden is obviously one of Mr. Hope's favourite poets, and, however much one may disagree with some of Mr. Hope's judgments, these brisk, informal, sometimes rash and petulant essays have a speed and gaiety that might well remind one of Dryden's prose criticism.

> *"Australian Augustan,"* in The Times Literary Supplement, *No. 3364, August 18, 1966, p. 744.*

BARRY ARGYLE

[*The essay from which this excerpt is taken was originally published in* Journal of Commonwealth Literature, *1967.*]

In traditional metres that chide the incompetence of many practitioners of freer verse, Hope's poetry has appeared in two selections, *The Wandering Islands* and *Poems.* (p. 392)

James McAuley, the Australian Roman Catholic poet and critic, has recently pronounced Hope a heretic, a follower of Mani [see excerpt above]; but as McAuley suggests, Manicheism has been a widely held heresy. . . . Among poets, from Marlowe and Milton to Yeats and Eliot, the heresy has been so common that it has among many non-Catholic writers seemed to be orthodoxy itself. Another name for it is protestantism, the pre-Lutheran kind that Satan upheld when he revolted against the celestial autocracy. Compared with Blake, however, Hope of-

fers little faith and less charity. Whatever the symbolism of Blake's tiger, there is a sense of effulgent wonder surrounding the symbol, the force of wonder increasing until syntax is abandoned or subsumed; the verbs of active and immediate creation are not present. . . . (p. 393)

In Hope's poem called "The Trophy" (in which he refers to Blake's poems "The Tiger" and "London") the wonder, which is the root of faith, is tangled. . . . Wonder is here neither engendered by any natural thing like a tiger, nor seen to have been once enshrined in a blackening church. Hope's sense of damaged wonder in this poem, as in many others, is aroused by the sexual act; yet he is aware that while its appeal is intense, its duration is short and its conclusion ambiguous. . . . Though the discovery may not be new, the uses to which Hope puts it are profoundly modern: for it is in the sexual act that the most omnifarious problem of modernity, alienation, is momentarily and perhaps only seemingly solved. As the Outsider is distant cousin to Milton's Satan, so alienation is the last stage of wilful protestantism; and it is the central concern in Hope's two best-known poems, "Imperial Adam" and "The Wandering Islands".

In ["Imperial Adam"], the title of which refers us back to both the Roman soldier and 'the single force of pride' in "The Trophy", Adam, having 'learned the jolly deed of kind' from the beasts, takes Eve and

> Like the clean beasts, embracing from behind,
> Began in joy to found the breed of men.

More than flippancy is intended here. The position Adam assumes was one which medieval Catholic theologians had pronounced against precisely because it was 'beastly'. Natural man thus appears as a prelapsarian protestant though without the necessity of recognizing himself as such. His love-making is not without its warning of ambiguity:

> Then from the spurt of seed within her broke
> Her terrible and triumphant female cry,
> Split upward by the sexual lightning stroke.
> It was the beasts now who stood watching by.

Original love is compromised, however, by its inevitable fruit. Adam sees

> Between her legs a pigmy face appear
> And the first murderer lay upon the earth.

The tropical Australian Eden, where 'the pawpaw drooped its golden breasts' is created in splendour and with wit. God the 'surgeon' voices the oldest of modern dilemmas which Eve is meant to solve: 'It is not good for him to live alone.'

God's 'voice so far away, so rich and deep', with its associations of the psychiatrist's couch, encourages an urbane response in the reader. He is willing to treat a huge myth lightly, to appreciate those aesthetic qualities of its setting which require a relaxation of moral imperatives. The announcement of Cain's birth in the last line (which the rest of the poem justifies) shocks the sensibilities into a briefly renewed awareness of the timeless quality of the original myth. The poem is an exercise in wit to rejuvenate a myth, though it is important to note that Hope refuses to pursue the theological implication that Abel was the first martyr. Theological interpretation of the original myth attributes so much to divine intention that it accommodates disruptive human force in a comforting symmetry which belies the poet's experience. Thus the need for the myth's rejuvenation. By contrasting the seriousness of the myth with the lightness of its treatment in the poem, Hope creates a total effect of urgency resulting in surprise. But surprise can only work once, and what remains after several readings of the poem is an appreciation of the wit, the final example of which is in the surprise of the last line. One is left admiring the means.

In the later poem **"The Wandering Islands"**, there is the same persistent wit but the ends to which it is employed are more fully realized, despite what at first sight seems a failure in the means. This is all evident in the first stanza:

> You cannot build bridges between wandering islands;
> The Mind has no neighbours, and the unteachable heart
> Announces its armistice time after time, but spends
> Its love to draw them closer and closer apart.

There is here what Johnson called the 'dignity of generality'. The stanza is an assertion (in old-fashioned pre-Freudian terms of heart and mind) for which the rest of the poem continues the discovery of 'objective correlatives'. The poem assumes what Johnson so urgently asserted: 'Life is a state in which much is to be endured and little to be enjoyed.' To prevent what would otherwise be the overwhelming force of chaos, it is essential to extract from life that little which is to be enjoyed in order that endurance should be strengthened. The sexual act is the armistice which allows the 'wandering islands' their brief charismatic view of truth. . . . It is also the occasion of a tense and transitory peace between mind, the furnace of intention, and heart, the distant deeps of oceanic force.

The wit of the last line of the stanza, concerning the heart which spends its love to draw the wandering islands 'closer and closer apart', seems to over-reach itself and, when appraised intellectually, results in meaninglessness. Hope is attempting an enforced union of disparate concepts, and the attempt fails only at the intellectual or logical level. It succeeds within the terms of the poem, which are, that the dichotomy between heart and mind cannot be bridged nor the gulf between one island and another even momentarily disappear unless the islands' 'promontories lock'. . . . Although the poem employs an ordered syntax and conjunctions which encourage the relaxation that prose normally affords, it embodies more than logic and the language of cerebration. A symbol is being explored; and the exploration requires that we should not treat it merely

> with convenient lies
> As part of geography or an institution.

In offering more, love demands more than the correct location of the genitalia or the usual exchange of rings and smiles at a wedding. Hope's wit in **"The Wandering Islands"** is a substantiation of the poem's theme, which is expressed unequivocally in the first line:

> You cannot build bridges between wandering islands.

Hope exploits the generality in all its particulars, as Donne does when he asserts that no man is an island. They share the same useful delight in wit.

If 'metaphysical' today means anything at all, it means what Hope calls a 'passion for a synoptic view'. It is too difficult a passion for more recent poets who are aware only that they live in a fragmenting universe. Despite their use of metaphor, which as Aristotle points out is an assertion of a synoptic view as well as the mark by which men may know a poet, they eschew symbol and myth. Hope does not. Yet perhaps, as he says, a man possessed of such a passion 'cannot write the slightest of poems on the most particular of themes without reflecting this ruling passion'; but to reflect the passion is

different from embodying it in poetry. **"The Wandering Islands"** embodies it, **"Imperial Adam"** only reflects it.

The reflection is visible in too many of Hope's other poems. It would be unfair to say that all are among 'the slightest of poems'; some are, even in the 1960 *Poems*, which is a vigorously pruned collection of *The Wandering Islands* with twenty-two poems added. Poems like **"Circe"**, **"Pasiphae"**, **"Easter Hymn"**, and **"Totentanz"** are five-finger exercises on the theme of monstrous love in its classical, medieval, and modern guises. To say that they are 'literary' poems is not enough, for many of Hope's more successful poems (like **"Soledades of the Sun and Moon"**, **"An Epistle: Edward Sackville to Venetia Digby"**, **"The Tomb of Penthesilea"**, or **"An Epistle from Holofernes"**) are 'literary' in the sense that they exhibit a character, tale, or situation taken from literature and use them so that the poems then grow into something new. The growth itself is 'unliterary'; it is the poet's personal experience, which imposes its conviction on the literary experience and transforms it. But in **"Circe"** and **"Pasiphae"**, for instance, (poems which seem to say that love has its bestial side) Hope's treatment brings nothing new to what the myths were originally created to acknowledge. Such poems appear as Hope's follies, erected in the suburban city of Canberra to the consternation of its susceptible population, but a desire to shock suburban Australia fails on its own to invest such poems with any wider appeal. (pp. 393-97)

Hope produces shock effects by other means. In **"Easter Hymn"**, with its associations of Milton and Dryden, the desire to shock seems to increase. From the first two lines one feels the hot breath of certainty:

> Make no mistake; there will be no forgiveness;
> No voice can harm you and no hand will save.

The ambiguity of the first line is clever. This shrewd young poet, one feels, is privy counsellor to the Holy Ghost, as though he had often interviewed God on television. It is a generality from which dignity has gone. What is being said is identical with what is said in the last line of **"The Wandering Islands"**. 'The rescue will not take place.' **"The Wandering Islands"** retains its dignity because through symbol all the implications of generality are explored; they are given concrete form and thereby impose their own terms. The terms of **"Easter Hymn"** are adapted from Christ's ministry and trial. . . . The poem zealously attempts to impose on the reader's credibility and his experience, in the same way as does the Prayer for all Protestants recently approved by the Roman Curia: 'so that the Protestants may realize that the Catholic Church, under the rule of the Pope and the hierarchy, is the same Church which was born the day of Pentecost'. The reader of both prayer and poem is entitled to say: 'This is not true to my experience; I simply do not believe it.' And the poem, unlike the prayer, offers no other experience. The reader refuses not the generality but the dogma of both.

The ambiguity of the first line of [**"Easter Hymn"**] is similarly weakened. If it is compared even to one of Hope's not entirely successful poems like **"Imperial Adam"**, one recognizes in the second poem an irony of situation: that man's first love should result in the birth of the first murderer; or, to extend the situation, love is ambiguous. But in the **"Easter Hymn"** line, 'Make no mistake; there will be no forgiveness', the paronomasia is only seemingly a pun. The injunction, 'Make no mistake', reflects only a quantitative difference, whereas a pun, like a metaphor or symbol, requires a difference of quality. In other words, the punctuative ingenuity of the line does not serve the synoptic vision which Hope is trying to express. What has happened in **"Easter Hymn"** is that Hope's fine contempt for all that is mistakenly called 'life' has spilled out in a flood of petulance towards even what he calls life. It is perhaps an example of what Gustav Cross has called Hope's almost Elizabethan raillery; but it can also be seen as an example of that too-clever-by-half kind of poetry more common in the 1930s than now. The same social references are present ('loans', 'committees', 'official guests') which disguise a fundamental contempt for any kind of social concourse. There is also the same earnest flippancy and the reader's response is the same too. As his best poems show, Hope has never understood social man.

His fine contempt for those who try to diminish a fine concern for individual man is expressed in his overt satires that form the third part of *Poems*. In illustrating that 'The life of a wit is warfare upon earth', most of these poems (**"A Commination"**, **"The Age of Innocence"**, **"The House of God"**, **"The Return from the Freudian Islands"**, and **"Conquistador"**) wage war in today's impersonal terms. Just as in modern war there is no Hector but only 'the enemy', so in Hope's satire there is no Atticus but only a university professor, or advertising man, or plain Henry Clay. The law of libel, like the Genevan Convention, by making the world a safer place to die in, has resulted in the personification of attitudes. Sometimes, as with Henry Clay, the projection is not complete. The attitude which Clay embodies is not utterly alien to the poet; he becomes a persona only masquerading as a personification, so that the combative nature of satire is muted and assumes some of the defensiveness of irony. The narrative in which Henry Clay takes part becomes too real for wit and metre to contain it and Hope begins to view him synoptically. Henry's bizarre end is commemorated thus:

> He was the Hero of our time. He may
> With any luck, one day, be you or me.

The elaborate fantasy of the poem takes on a wryness that blurs the distinction between friend and enemy; Clay is not only malleable but human.

The other satires are straightforward 'comminations'. Even the fantasy is straightforward, which naturally increases the impact of the poems. In **"The House of God"**, for example, the point of the poem is slight: that love for God is often no more than cupboard-love; but the fantasy which makes the point proliferates into grotesque fun. With God's people turned into cats, the humour persists logically to the last stanza, which, though it adds nothing to the point being made, explodes in a vision of comic genius:

> Looking down He smiles and ponders,
> Thinks of something extra nice:
> From his beard, O Joy, O wonders,
> Falls a shower of little mice.

This is Blake's drawing of The Ancient of Days with one or two doodles added to it, an example of Hope's satire and his iconoclastic glee.

The many-sided appeal of Hope's poetry accounts for the multitudinous labels that have been attached to it. This is surprising when one considers that he has written very little in a long time, even when compared to his Australian contemporaries or near-contemporaries like Robert FitzGerald, Douglas Stewart, or Judith Wright. His subjects are also few, for there are large areas of human experience which Hope does not use, precisely because, one suspects, he has little faith and less

charity. Born in 1907 he is Auden's exact contemporary, but unlike him has never recorded any attempts to come to terms with God or men. Though it can be said of any poet, it can more usefully be said of Hope that his overriding concern has been to come to terms with himself. As he says again and again, 'The rescue will not take place.' When he explores even his own history, he does so very much as an ascent into hell, to use the 'metaphysical' title of one of his finest poems; while the future concludes in a death as inconsequential and unremarked as that of the bird in the poem called **"The Death of the Bird"**. . . . Man's lot is briefly meliorated in sexual union, though that too is often nasty, sometimes brutish, and always short; yet he persists in his faith based on experience that it can be otherwise. As Hope expresses it in **"An Epistle from Holofernes"**:

> And we must learn and live, as yet we may,
> Vision that keeps the night and saves the day.

But, for the present, 'The rescue will not take place.' From this private awareness of terror Hope has created most of his poetry and he has relaxed only in order to heap scorn and contumely on the gods of scientific materialism listed in **"A Commination"**, being sustained otherwise by literature and his poethood. Milton, Swift, Blake, and Yeats are what he calls 'the builders of the pyramid' and they are 'everywhere'. To do as they, or even to be aware of what they have done, is to help build the house of ascent, the title of the poem [**"Pyramis; or, The House of Ascent"**] in which the poet's task is most fiercely defined. They are:

> . . . men who put aside
> Consideration, dared, and stood alone,
> Strengthening those powers that fence the failing heart:
> Intemperate will and incorruptible pride.

Their protestant Satanic qualities offer the only orthodoxy to which the poet can subscribe.

Hope, however, seldom convinces us that he shares more than an ultimate respect for any theurgical manifestation of the poet's vision, and his soul is seldom able to clap its hands and sing for every tatter in its mortal dress. He lacks that seriousness of mind, the willing suspension of relief, which can accommodate without laughter Swedenborg's remark that 'the sexual intercourse of angels is a conflagration of the whole being'. Hope must often doodle on an old man's beard, fortunately. The only thing that keeps his own face straight is terror. He is without a mythology of his own, and in refusing to be enslaved by another's makes poor use of that of the Greeks. To Yeats, Leda's swan seems often a phoenix, but to Hope (to adapt a conceit from his own **"Persons from Porlock"**) the swan is no more than a kind of duck.

It is when he uses poetic forms of an earlier age that Hope can convince the reader of more than a respect for literature's continuity. In his two Epistles, in **"Man Friday"** and **"The Elegy"**, he uses the couplet as though to the manner born. They are not parodies or copies, but re-creations, rejuvenations of the kind that Eliot did for blank verse. In Hope the form encourages the exercise of intelligence, as it did in Dryden and Pope. That the form has been rarely used in English since their time is to comment not on its absence but on the dearth of intelligence. In his best poetry Hope's is a distinctive voice, crying as he admits in a wilderness; but his cry makes sense, even of the wilderness. In his much misunderstood poem **"Australia"**, he expressed exactly the white colonial's ambivalence towards the founding country and towards the place of his inherited exile. . . . It is an honest poem, a mature appraisal of the contemporary white colonial situation, whether Australian, New Zealand, Canadian, or American. Having done it once, Hope has intelligently refused to do it again. Even in this poem he is not an Australian poet, as FitzGerald, Slessor and McAuley so often and so tediously are: there are no more than the one or two decorative rather than obligatory gum trees in his poetry. He does not demand that the reader be a specialist in Australian botany, marsupials, or the dialects of the few remaining members of Australia's decimated aboriginal population. Hope does not buy indulgences from anybody. No one has ever been able to say of his poetry, as has been so unfortunately said of Douglas Stewart's, 'We have no other desert poems as good as these.' Hope is a poet who happens to have been born in Australia and writes in English, for the most part on themes which transcend nationality. To read the best of those poems—no more than a handful—is a rewarding experience because they communicate a defined awareness of modernity. If labels are to be attached, it is enough to say that Hope is a modern poet. (pp. 397-403)

> *Barry Argyle, "The Poetry of A. D. Hope," in* Readings in Commonwealth Literature, *edited by William Walsh, Oxford at the Clarendon Press, 1973, pp. 392-403.*

DAVID KIRBY

A. D. Hope writes for a race that is "Under Sedation". In his poem ["**Under Sedation**"], he alludes to "the drug of custom", the opiate of "putting one foot after another" that keeps us from seeing "what in his passionate age drove Goya wild: / That old, mad god eating his naked child". But if Hope seems to be recommending rather than merely describing the "sedation of habit" in this poem, it is a prescription noticeably absent from most of the rest of *A Late Picking,* [a recent] book of poetry from a writer described in *The Penguin Book of Australian Verse* (1972) as "one of the leading modern Australian poets".

In the same poem, Hope poses this question: were it not for the drug of custom, "how could we possibly bear / Our civilization for a single day?" At this point in history, there is no insufficiency of respondents to that query, and naturally all of them have a superior physic. What Hope does is to bring down from the attic of history an old-fashioned dualism, a dualism that is still bright under the dust that has been allowed to accumulate by a race whose main goal has been to avert its eyes from that cannibal god (after all, he may still be hungry).

This dualism is given its most sophisticated treatment in the eleven-page "**The Countess of Pembroke's Dream**" which takes as its basis John Aubrey's description of the countess with the "pritty sharpe-ovall face" (the quote is from *Brief Lives,* not *A Late Picking*) and the habit of watching, then imitating with her gallants, the sport of the mares and stallions that belonged to her husband....

"**The Countess of Pembroke's Dream**" is not a particularly erotic poem, for the reader is taken beyond mere subliminal musings (only a dream within a dream could go that far) to a prelapsarian time when centaurs lived but prurience was unknown and incest had not been given a name. That is to say, this is a poem about the days when the world was unitary, and eroticism, after all, is assuredly dualistic in nature....

Hope's point is that the frustration, the tension, the sublimated eroticism that leads noble ladies to dream of centaurs and poets to make music of their grief is owed to the dualist's instinctive knowledge of the world's essential oneness, a verity which the dualist must acknowledge, because it is true, yet reject, because oneness is fine as a philosophical or religious concept yet impossible to contemplate rationally and impractical so far as its applicability to daily life is concerned.

This paradox underlies, among other poems in [*A Late Picking*], "**Poor Charley's Dream**", in which C. P. Snow visits Dame Nature's Parliament; there he is taken to task for deploring the separation between the two cultures, because, ". . . Charley, I would have you know / I, Nature, have arranged it so: / That double blessing I designed / For the improvement of mankind." For unless Science and Art, once joined in "the same inspissate mass", are separated and made to think each other hopelessly out of reach, they will never ". . . love and mingle and command / And spread their offspring through the land".

Philosophically and poetically situated between the world's original unity and that which is to come, Hope plays a double flute, like Cheiron in "**The Countess of Pembroke's Dream**", out of which instrument come the poems that I have named and others equally witty, learned, and profound: "**Exercise on a Sphere**", where he receives a lecture from a non-Euclidean alter ego who stares at him from a silvered ball on a Christmas tree; "**Tiger Thoughts**", in which a tiger ogles Hope's scantily clad companion and contemplates the ways of men and women in the cage which, to him, they evidently inhabit; and others too numerous to name.

> *David Kirby, "On a Double Flute," in* The Times Literary Supplement, *No. 3966, April 7, 1978, p. 394.*

LYNDY ABRAHAM

The past in A. D. Hope's poetry is very much a literary past. The poems show that Hope's relationship to the past and present is that of a man of culture. He sees the past mediated through art and literature and his concern is to renew and revivify literary traditions. . . . Instead of creating new myths, Hope's poetry rather commemorates the need to keep alive past myths, forms and traditions. Hope once said of Coleridge and his poem "Kubla Khan" that:

> Nothing that Coleridge ever wrote conveys such a sense of vivid and magical pictures in the mind— such an impression of intense and brilliant vision. Yet note that not one detail comes from direct observation of nature which Wordsworth's theory demands. Every least detail has been traced to its source, and every one came, not from Coleridge's observation, but from his reading.

The same can be said of Hope's own poetry—the literature of the past is one of his main sources of inspiration.

Hope is a writer for whom the past is not only important, but a milieu that is more appealing than the present. His essay, "**The Discursive Mode**" from *The Cave and the Spring,* is a lament for the past. While it is impossible to agree with Hope that all of today's literature is a barren field, his essay is nevertheless an engaging piece of writing. Using an ecological metaphor, he argues that we are eliminating the various forms and genres of poetry, just as we are chopping down forests and killing more and more species of animal every year. . . . According to Hope, the loss of the epic and tragedy from the living forms becomes, too, a loss of 'a certain nobility of mind' and 'real magnanimity'. He also sees this 'loss' of traditional forms as a 'limitation' of consciousness. In the space left by the disappearance of the epic, Hope tells us, the mock epic has flourished in its 'pigmy shape'. . . . [By] calling the new forms 'pigmies', he is viewing the world and its literature as a process of decay and decline.

Hope's longing for the beauty of the past in the face of modern destruction can be seen in one of his most economically written and successful poems, **"Moschus Moschiferus"** (1967), where the voice of the poet laments the extinction of the 'small Kastura, most archaic of deer' which is killed by hunters for the purpose of extracting glands which are a necessary ingredient in a much demanded musk perfume. On one level, this poem is the cry of a conservationist who cannot bear the way that man and civilisation, by indiscriminately plundering nature for marketable products, is steadily wiping out whole species of animals. But there are more subtle protests being made at the same time about poetry itself.

In **"Moschus Moschiferus"**, the instruments of death employed by the deer hunters consist, not only of the bow and arrow, but also a musical instrument—the flute. And within the line, 'Each carries a bow and one a slender flute', the musical implications reflect back upon 'bow', making it a musical pun on the weapon of death. This is possibly an allusion to Auden's 'O cry created as the bow of sin / Is drawn across our trembling violin' in Auden's own version of a hymn to St Cecilia. Hope tells us that the hunter seduces the deer from the thickets by weaving a beautiful melody on the flute so that his 'comrades' can, Cupid-like with 'poisoned shafts', kill the deer and plunder it for the musk. The music of the hunters, however, is not the 'real' music of the spheres or of divine love in literary tradition, but the 'false' music of the Sirens whose nets lure men into death: the hunters' music is a 'tremulous skein' and a 'net of crystalline sound' whose ecstasy and enchantment is a trap that will end in the extinction of the deer. Hope's poetry is full of allusions to the seduction of men by sirens (he specifically takes up this theme in **"The Coasts of Cerigo"**). But in **"Moschus Moschiferus"**, Hope's "Song for St Cecilia", he is confronting the Muse of Music with his horror at the power of music which, though previously praised for its beauty, can paradoxically lead to the death of beauty—the deer itself. He faces the St Cecilia of the Twentieth Century with the problem of the price that can be paid for the production of art. (pp. 167-69)

There is a long tradition of poets who have written about the song of the siren. But Hope is the first to specifically confront St Cecilia herself with the implications of such a song. The closest forerunner to Hope's position is Keats, to whom Hope alludes in **"Moschus Moschiferus"**. In "Ode to a Nightingale", Keats has written an Ode to the 'song' of the Poetic Muse, in which he poses the problem of the siren's song. The Nightingale is identified with the Muse of Poetry, 'the viewless wings of poesy', and its song passes through various modulations ending with the siren's song with its implications of disillusionment. The modulations through which the Nightingale's song passes, are remarkably similar to those of the hunters' melody in Hope's poem—the connection cannot be accidental: Keats' Nightingale modulates from a song of summer, to a song of ecstasy, then a 'requiem' which moves into the song of a captive bird in the Emperor's Cage, the song of homesickness, a 'plaintive anthem', through to the siren's song 'opening on the foam / Of perilous seas in faery lands forlorn'. Hope's hunters' melody moves from dance to 'pensive' tune, to 'a rain / Of pure, bright drops of sound' (possibly an allusion to the deceptive appearance of Zeus as 'golden rain' for the

seduction of Danae, mother of Perseus), then the hunters' melody modulates into a wailing 'lament' and finally a song of ecstasy at the point of death. Just as Keats' vision and song ends 'buried deep', so Hope's vision of music as an instrument of beauty lies buried in the metaphor of the slain deer. In **"Moschus Moschiferus"**, the musician and poet, Orpheus, once able to charm the forest and its animals with his music, is now 'dead'—the musician and poet has become hunter and killer; he no longer scans the poetry of beauty, but now 'scans' the glade for his prey. Hope's awareness of the way that art can be seen as plunder, is made clear by his identification of the hunter and the poet: the poet in this poem, while describing the hunters' melody, employs the same erotic seductiveness of language as the hunters' 'false music' of death. And the lines, 'The search / Employs new means, more exquisite and refined' refer not only to the hunters but also to the poet's search for the beauty of past poetical forms.

"Moschus Moschiferus" also alludes to Marvell's "The Nymph Complaining for the Death of her Faun". Here the nymph is left by her lover, Sylvio, who presents her with a faun but it is then shot by brutal troopers. She mourns that Sylvio, 'Left me his Faun, but took his Heart'. The reader cannot read Hope's description of the hunters leaving the deer's carcass but taking its 'heart' or life essence for the musk scent, without recalling Marvell's poem.

It is clear that Hope, like Keats, has not been able to 'sing' an Ode without its changing into a lament. Neither can the song in the Ode be separated from the song of illusion, the siren's song. In this way, Hope laments not only the extinction of the deer, but also the loss of beauty and the poetic genre of the Ode, where the poet could whole-heartedly praise music or art with a clear conscience. (pp. 169-70)

In **"Persons from Porlock"** (1956), Hope expresses a similar horror for the loss of the poetic vision, though here the tone is rather sardonic and humorous. He chooses a literary anecdote which tells how Coleridge was interrupted in his composition of "Kubla Khan" by a visitor from the neighbouring town of Porlock, and uses it, not only as a departure point for his own poem, but paradoxically, takes up Coleridge's loss of inspiration to create a poem of his own.

Coleridge, says Hope, was in fact very lucky that this only happened to him once in his life, since most poets' visions these days seem to be perpetually interrupted by the mundane realities of wives, neighbours, relatives, teachers, jobs, the obligatory suburban garden, dinner parties, ALL from Porlock. The academic poet will inevitably be subjected to the 'young / Persons from Porlock'—not just his own children, but the students in the Universities of Porlock. Whereas Coleridge was only bothered by a single Person from Porlock, today's poet finds himself surrounded by a multitude of Porlock people, all breeding and multiplying in nightmare proportions. Even the Muse of Porlock inspires 'flat' poetic lines about her city being on 'the Plain'—not on the slopes or heights of Parnassus, but at the bottom of the mountain—an allusion to the 'Moderns' who wallow in the fens and the bogs at the foot of Mount Parnassus in Pope's "Peri Bathous or The Art of Sinking". (p. 170)

For all Hope's playfulness and joking about all the poems that never get written, **"Persons from Porlock"** is also a serious poem—it laments his own inability to escape the ubiquitous mundaneness of the world and soar to poetic heights, it embodies the moment of disillusionment and fall from the vision of Paradise, and it pays a tribute to one of the finest poems in the English language.

If we look at a much earlier poem **"Ascent into Hell"** (1943-44), it is clear that one of Hope's main concerns, even from the beginnings of his writing career, is with the past. He begins his 'ascent' into Hell by alluding to Dante's 'descent' into the Inferno. The poem traces the poet's journey in his imagination back to his own personal origin. He evokes not only Dante's journey but also previous 'mythical' journeys made in the imagination of past poets . . . while simultaneously mapping specific details of remembered nightmare imaginings, events and dreams from his own childhood in the quest for the unattainable moment of birth and perhaps even the original paradise. On the map of his journey he charts the real island Tasmania and also the fact that Tasmania was one of the scenes of early childhood consciousness: 'Tasmania, my receding childish island.' This 'receding island' recalls the shipwrecked sailor on one of the 'wandering' islands who 'senses / His own despair in a retreating face' in **"The Wandering Islands"** (written earlier in the same year as **"Ascent into Hell"**—1943). **"The Wandering Islands"** charts a map of the estrangement of mind and heart by telling what the islands 'are not', and yet clearly telling us what they 'are'—civilisation's misfits. We recognise the plight of the 'castaway' who has never treated 'the sudden ravages of love' 'with convenient lies / As a part of geography or an institution'. This inverted castaway, not from but *in* civilisation, appears later in Hope's poem **"Man Friday"** which reverses the situation in Defoe's *Robinson Crusoe,* and instead depicts Man Friday as a castaway on 'England's Desert Island' and has him 'drowning' in 'civilisation'.

But to return to the map of events in **"Ascent into Hell"**, Hope gives us visual but emotional detail of valley and river, gum trees roaring in the gale, shivering poplars, 'church pines' imitating the ocean and other evocative and disturbing sounds of approaching night. Via this pathway he moves into the nightmare of the ascending 'soul': the fear of World War I, endless and empty labyrinths of a 'well-known' house of the mind, the familiar horrors and 'anguish' of being chased by inescapable wild animals—these images are interwoven with details of his waking life—comfort from his mother, whippings from his father, early sexual sensations brutally 'cut off' like a 'stump'. But from this point on, he can no longer remember or map what has occurred in this mysterious territory from which his consciousness has risen and to which he is trying to return, until:

> . . . through the uncertain gloom, sudden I see
> Beyond remembered time the imagined entry,
> The enormous Birth-gate whispering, ''per me,
> per me si va tra la perduta gente.''

Though he cannot remember this mysterious point of entry into the world, he can enter it again by way of a combination of Dante's myth and his own imagination because he has converted the third inscription of Dante's triple anaphora carved on the Gates of Hell in grand, forbidding capital letters (canto 3), into the whispering, 'per me, per me', of the Gates of *Birth,* thus identifying birth with hell. Similarly, he identifies Dante's 'lost people' or shades, with the living in our world.

At the beginning of the poem, Hope begins, like Dante in the opening of the *Inferno,* 'at the midpoint', but he is situated in a 'well-lit wood' and 'Of second-rate purpose and mediocre success', unlike Dante who is in 'una selva oscura' (a dark wood) and is well on the way to winning the literary laurels. From this midpoint Dante descends into Hell while Hope, an inverted Dante 'ascends' into his Hell. We also notice that the previous 'pilgrims' have been accompanied by guides. . . . What kind of art or memory guides Hope on this particular nightmare journey? He tells us that 'Fear' is his guide into these regions: 'The voice of my fear, the voice of my unseen guide.' He is afraid since there is no guide for him, so 'fear' becomes his only guide, his mode of exploration. In **"Ascent into Hell"** Hope is charting the memory points of fear only in his quest for his origin, but critics who insist that Hope's sole identification of the womb is with Hell must consider his poem **"The Gateway"** to see that he has also celebrated his journey 'home' into the well-known 'country' where they know his name and 'speak it with delight'—a place where the tree and city of his body and heart are able to 'tap' the secret spring of the 'sweet waters' of renewal. By way of these gates of Entry he is able to waken not into the nightmare of Hell but into the resurrection of 'grace' and 'light'. (pp. 172-74)

In one of his most complex poems, **"The Double Looking Glass"**, Hope's allusions are drawn from a wider cultural context. He alludes not only to literary works but also to Renaissance art and its metaphysical concepts as well. This poem reflects upon and remakes images and themes from a number of past myths, but the basic myth upon which the reflections are generated is that of Susannah and the Elders told in the Apocrypha. (p. 174)

One interpretation of the 'double nature' of the looking glass is immediately obvious—we are seeing Susannah through the 'mirror' of the poet's consciousness and he in turn seeing through the 'mirror' of the artist; within the painting itself Susannah is in the presence of two mirrors, that of the pool and the looking glass of her 'toilette'. With this poem, Hope has not only chosen to write in the Renaissance tradition of 'ut pictura poesis', but he has also chosen one of the most popular subjects of Renaissance contemplation in Neoplatonic iconography— the mirror. **"The Double Looking Glass"** also recalls Auden's poem, ''Through the Looking Glass'' in which the woman in the portrait has 'amorous dreams' and a 'would-be lover who has never come', and in which the poet, too, 'sails' to the woman to 'enjoy the untransfigured scene'. In Auden's poem, too, the poet tells us that 'All lust' is 'at once informed on and suppressed'. But to return to the earlier source of Hope's poem— the 'mirrors' of the Renaissance were never the mere physical mirrors of everyday life. They were inevitably a metaphor for metaphysical and philosophical contemplation which was often concerned with the problems of paradox: of imagination and reality, subject and object, the two and the one, earthly and heavenly, time and timelessness, chastity and lust, youth and age, male and female, lover and beloved, naked and clothed, the watcher and the watched, and sacred and profane.

The most obvious paradoxical tension in **"The Double Looking Glass"** is that of the 'dry branch' or old age of the Elders, who as voyeurs into Susannah's private, naked, sexual 'enclosed garden', are taunted by her 'bud' of youth and her sexual 'ripeness'. But there is a much more complex interplay of paradox within this setting, achieved by a continual flow of allusions to various writers and myths. . . . [The] reader can detect at least Marvell, Milton, Donne, Yeats and Poliziano, the Renaissance Italian poet 'par excellence' of enclosed gardens and mirrors, all 'lurking' in the literary 'laurels' on the bank of Susannah's pool. It is through the echo from Yeats' ''Byzantium''—'Shade and substance meet'—that we realise that both Susannah's mind and body, her appearance and reality, are pure and chaste. As we first behold her wading into her bath or pool she is seen as a 'lily'—a symbol of whiteness and innocence. These qualities are wedded as she begins to merge in the pool with her own image, 'Candour with candour'. . . . At this point, Susannah, the lily, has become one with the glory of naked, innocent nature.

The poem also evokes the myth of the chaste huntress Diana at her pool, spied upon by the lustful Acteon. Susannah is endowed with the moon-like attributes of Diana: her armpit and breast are like arrows—they 'splinter their white shafts through our envious green'. . . . And her arms are moon-silver, sharing 'Their pure and slender crescent with the pool'. Susannah, like the moon, is of a watery nature—her tresses are 'cascades' and 'falls' and her breast is 'liquid'.

But within Susannah there is a paradox, for while she appears as the pure lily and the chaste Diana, she also shows signs of partaking in the nature of the very 'serpent' who is about to undo her. In this way she is like Eve in the Garden of Eden—even the 'fig-tree' grows in this garden—and the whole poem is an enactment of the 'original' temptation scene, with the possibility of the Fall always shimmering on the edges of her consciousness. Her tumbling hair is not only *like* water-falls but she can be seen as loosening it in preparation for her own 'fall'. Similarly, her tresses fall, not in ripples or any other word that Hope could have chosen, but in 'coils', evoking the recognisable insignia of Milton's serpent. . . . The 'double' nature of Susannah's looking glass here is good versus evil, innocence versus lust, contemplation versus voyeurism. This double nature is also present in the rhetoric and metaphysics of Hope's poem, for although he states that 'the contemplative intellect' is one of man's 'finest' achievements, the voyeuristic aspect in him is never far away.

In Stanza 17, we enter Susannah's dream garden. The lines, 'My garden holds me like its private dream / A secret pleasure, guarded and apart', echo the solitary and metaphysical garden of 'roses and lilies' belonging to Marvell's "Nymph"—'I have a garden of my own'. But Susannah's pool in Stanza 18 more directly mirrors the happy contemplation of the timeless world in Marvell's "Garden" where:

> The Mind, that ocean where each kind
> Does streight its own resemblance find.

In Susannah's pool, Marvell's metaphor has become a less effective simile:

> In that inverted world a scarlet fish
> Drifts through the trees and swims into the sky,
> So in the contemplative mind a wish
> Drifts through the mirror of eternity.

This eternal mirror soon melts into the flow of time in which the possibility of Susannah's fall is ever present. To highlight the paradox of time and eternity, Hope contrasts the contemplative 'pool' with 'the languid current of the day' into which Susannah flows, alluding to Heraclitus' metaphysical metaphor of the 'river of time'.

In her solitary dream she imagines that both nature and the sun are becoming sexually aroused as she herself is, using nature as an anthropomorphic mirror for herself. And just as the moon is a reflector of the sun's light, Susannah as moon goddess, becomes an 'image of my image' and a 'mirror for man's images of love'. She is a reflection of her reflection like Narcissus, like her imagined male lover who becomes 'possessed by what he can never possess', and caught in the paradox of an infinite regression of mirrors—a favorite preoccupation of the Renaissance.

Again the menace of the Elders interrupts her dream, their lust rising in coordination with her erotic dream. This in turn generates a fantasy of her male lover longing for her as 'the sense / Impels, the hour invites'. She is being lured into the world of time and the physical senses. And why, she asks herself, can she not indulge in and reveal 'Such thoughts as women find to recompense / Their hidden lives when secret and alone?' So she continues to generate her fantasy of being desired and loved until she realises that she herself can also do the loving and the desiring, that 'she' can become 'he', both the lover and the beloved. Like the reflexive verb to bathe (in Romance languages) she can bathe in her pool and become both the object and subject of the verb or action, and so both male and female.

Now, when we read the lines 'he lies / And feeds among the lilies', . . . we recall that Susannah has been endowed with masculine qualities as well as feminine: her whiteness is described as a 'shaft', not only of Diana but of the god of love, Cupid, and her 'lily' is also the lily of the Annunciation, the sexual instrument with which the Holy Ghost chastely impregnates the Virgin Mary. . . . So the imagery of the poem has prepared us for the merging of the male and female in Susannah from the beginning.

Her fantasy now creates yet another dream within itself as 'he' journeys . . . to a garden and pool within her garden and pool, where he sees himself asleep on the bank, now the one 'watched' as 'she' watches him from the bushes and moves to wake him to consummate their desire. The action of the poem reaches its crescendo when suddenly the beautiful erotic dream is shattered by the Elders bursting in on the scene to rape her. Here the imaginary world of her sexuality is in conflict with the reality of the Elders' lust, and yet, paradoxically the arousal in the imaginations of both Susannah and the Elders are sinisterly and inextricably connected—the poem implies that the Satanic part of Susannah has been responsible for her own undoing, that her erotic dream has perhaps conjured up the presences of the Elders in her garden or that she allowed their presences to intrude upon her by indulging in her fantasies. The sexual encounter that is about to happen has already been enacted in the dream.

In the way that Hope has written this poem, Susannah, the watched, is closely associated with the watching Elders. The narration of the poem elusively modulates in and out of presenting Susannah as the narrator and also the object of narration; one moment she, as well as the Elders, is 'objectively' watching herself wade into the pool and lie in the sun, and the next moment she becomes the narrator of the poem, the 'I' not 'she' who is being watched. The active and passive, the 'I' and 'she' merge tantalizingly in and out of each other, while being one and the same.

We notice, too, that with the Elders' rude interruption, Hope's **"Persons from Porlock"** theme again intrudes and shatters the vision of the imagination. The dimension that Hope has added to the myth of Susannah is both her beautiful erotic dream and its seemingly inevitable disillusionment. But it is also clear that while Hope has attempted to remake the story, he has disappointingly converted yet another of his poems into the even earlier myth—that of the 'Fall' of man, his loss of innocence.

The myths and Biblical histories to which Hope refers in the above poems include the myth of the journey, of Diana, Orpheus, Persephone, the Sirens, Eve and the garden of Eden, the myth of the Temptation and the Fall, and Susannah and the Elders. And the poets to whom Hope alludes include Virgil, Dante, Dryden, Milton, Donne, Marvell, Pope, Defoe, Coleridge, Keats, Yeats and Auden. This is clearly a very literary set of allusions which in itself helps to locate Hope's poetic position. The fact that he bases his work so much on Pope, a poet who, following in the tradition of Dryden, is an adept poet of allusion, shows that Hope is consciously writing in the allusive tradition. In addition to this, we might note that the works and authors referred to in his poetry are very much in the acceptable Twentieth Century academic canon. The *Dunciad Minor: [Book V]* (Hope's "Pierre Menard" opus) provides a useful key to Hope's poetry. It quite specifically maps the mainstream of Twentieth Century academic criticism in literature, satirising G. Wilson Knight, F. R. Leavis, Carolyn Spurgeon, Maud Bodkin, David Daiches, William Empson, Northrop Frye, Cleanth Brooks, Allen Tate and Ernest Jones, the critics with whom Hope as an academic was familiar and who wrote about the works to which he alludes. (pp. 174-78)

> *Lyndy Abraham, "A. D. Hope and the Poetry of Allusion," in* Australian Literary Studies, *Vol. 9, No. 2, October, 1979, pp. 167-78.*

DONALD REVELL

The Australian poet A. D. Hope is an anachronism on several counts and so is easy prey to [certain critics]. . . . Hope's style, lucid and calm, exercising the wit and closure of classical rhetoric, resembles not at all the jagged discontinuities and open-ended self-reference characteristic of modernist and contemporary poetics. Hope's subjects are developed through straightforward narratives that take no particular notice of either the labyrinthine strategems of twentieth-century prose narrative or of twentieth-century poetry's abandonment of narrative as a mode of poetic discourse hopelessly inappropriate to its sense of language as an expressive rather than a communicative medium. Hope thus seems a poet out of his time, a voice, if not reactionary, at least superfluous to what matters now.

The word "seems," however, cannot in this context be overstressed. Though I must confess myself to be an ardent advocate of my own abstract, expressive time, one who distrusts on principle rationalism and all of its works and means as masks for either intellectual reaction or for intellectual sloth, I very much hope that my principles do not blind me. . . . I am grateful for beauty and grace in words, whatever their shapes, attitudes, or origins may be.

The Age of Reason contains poetry of genuine eloquence. Hope's eleven narrative poems, set in the eighteenth century and framed in that century's measure of preference (the heroic couplet), are not mere exercises in a difficult, outdated form, nor are they simply vignettes of reactionary nostalgia. Hope looks lovingly though unsentimentally back through time to the Augustan Age from the vantage point of our most un-Augustan, parlous day. What he sees is not some lost Utopia, but a different world of persons like ourselves, striving with different means to solve mortal problems identical to our own. *The Age of Reason* thus serves two muses. The classic loveliness of lines . . . from "**Sir William Herschel's Long Year**" must delight the muse of lyric verse. . . . Similarly, the muse of history must be well pleased by [passages from "**Printer's Pie**"]. . . . One does not have to read very far into *The Age of Reason* to be convinced that Hope is a poet who knows his craft and who has mastered what Chaucer called the "form of speech." Read-

ing on, one begins to realize that craft here is in the service of a fine and humane mind, a mind that looks into history and sees the persistent, complex humanity behind its shifting pageant.

There is great variety here, as well there should be. The eighteenth century delighted in variousness as much as does our own. To prize humanity, one must, of necessity, prize variety as well. The poems look to fiction and fact both, imaginatively entering the lives of Gulliver ("**The Isle of Aves**") and Crusoe ("**Man Friday**") as well as those of mad George III ("**The Kew Stakes**"), John Wesley ("**Tea with the Devil**"), and, in Hope's crowning achievement, "**Botany Bay or The Rights of Women,**" of the powerfully sympathetic Elizabeth Chamberlain and her convict husband as they lived through the twilight of the Age of Reason in London and in the penal colony that was then Australia. In all of the poems, Hope's poetic grace seizes the reader's attention, and his compassionate, lucid wisdom rewards it. Hope's is a sad wisdom (who can know history and not be sad?), but he is not pessimistic. If not perfectible, human nature is at least persistent and capable, by moments, of a provisional splendor. In these poems Hope finds and advocates that splendor and, for all his sadness, manages his share of genuine awe. (pp. 13, 15)

> *Donald Revell, "Humane & Eloquent History," in* The Bloomsbury Review, *Vol. 6, No. 6, June, 1986, pp. 13, 15.*

NEIL CORCORAN

Hope is imperious, disdainful, prejudiced, autocratic, satiric and erotic. His mythologies are the traditional European classical and biblical ones. He never wavers in his allegiance to the conventional metres and verse forms of English poetry: Yeats, Byron, Pope, Donne and Herrick are clearly, sometimes explicitly, exemplars, and he is as scathing as Yeats was about free verse, that "dreary shuffle", as he calls it in an essay. . . . Hope's great effort is to yoke himself—by as much violence as it takes—to "literature". . . .

Hope's obedience, however, is always self-scrutinizing and fully aware of its oblique, "outsider" status. In the early, well-known and controversial "**Australia**" [included in *Selected Poems*], the country is savagely rebuked as an "Arabian desert of the human mind", but Hope nevertheless expects to discover there "some spirit which escapes / The learned doubt, the chatter of cultured apes / Which is called civilization over there". And the splendidly handled fiction of "**Man Friday**" may be regarded, I suppose, as Hope's guilty myth of the European treatment of the Aborigine: Friday, returned to England with Crusoe, must "labour to invent his nakedness" on this new "Cannibal Island" which "ate his past away". In a plangently mysterious conclusion, Friday strips himself naked and drowns himself, suffering extremes of deprivation, homesickness and loss. (The poem makes an interesting companion-piece for Elizabeth Bishop's "Crusoe in England".)

Nevertheless, the old civilization and the old literature remain immensely seductive. Perhaps only a poet intent on defining a difficult relationship could allow himself to be so unembarrassed by the powerful ghosts of the literary past that stalk through Hope's work. The willed confidence veers close to pastiche; and in attempting so frequently to rise to his occasion in his always sonorous iambics, Hope sometimes seems merely to be putting on airs (the hyperbolically inflated "**Soledades of the Sun and Moon**" in the present selection is a notable case in point). And when, in **"A Letter from Rome"**, the relationship between Australia (''those dim regions / Where Dante planted Hell's Back Door'') and the old world (Rome as ''the *fons et origo* of Western Man'') is debated, Hope's intendedly Byronic *ottava rima* takes on a prim, schoolmasterly, over-explanatory earnestness. It is, frankly, difficult to credit his encounter with the *numen* at Nemi in the poem: when Hope pours a libation of wine on the sacred lake, the new world seems not so much to be making an enquiry of the old as genuflecting abjectly before its fetishized image. To counterbalance this portentously strained mystical moment, this selection, made by Ruth Morse, could perhaps have given us a little more of Hope's successful visionary poetry—the very ambitious **"Vivaldi, Bird and Angel"**, for instance.

What [*Selected Poems*] does testify to again is that Hope's greatest theme is the erotic. His imagination works best when it plays, morosely or lubriciously, in the bedroom, and particularly when it is entangled in quasi-Jacobean obsessions about sexuality and death, as it is, for instance, in **"X-Ray Photograph"**:

> These bones are calm and beautiful;
> The flesh, like water, strains and clears
> To show the face my future wears
> Drowned at the bottom of its pool.
>
> Then I am full of rage and bliss,
> For in our naked bed I feel,
> Mate of your panting mouth as well,
> The deathshead lean toward your kiss;

> And I am mad to have you here,
> Now, now, the instant shield of lust,
> Deep in your flesh my flesh to thrust
> Against a more tremendous fear.

That perhaps stays, like a lot of Hope's work, just on the right side of the dangerously belated and derivative (Donne, Webster, Eliot), but it has its genuine *frisson* too, originating in the urgent imperatives of Hope's exacerbated sensitivity, the old Christian dualism heightened to a virtually Manichaean degree. Although Hope has his glancing, momentary tendernesses and levities, and his intimations of transcendence (''Time has an end whose end is not in time''), the almost despairingly violent energy of this seems to me his truest note. Indeed, his poems often convey, alarmingly, an energy of anger or vituperation or boredom or lust being held in check, with difficulty, by elaborate formal artifice.

Like Wallace Stevens, Hope began publishing late in his life—at the age of forty-eight, in 1955; and this is probably the main reason for the lack of the usual sense of ''development'' in this **Selected**. However, the recent nostalgic evocations of his Tasmanian childhood are a surprise and a delight, and such a poem as **"Hay Fever"** has a new mellowness of tone, as it reads an old man's allegory from its pastoral. . . .

Neil Corcoran, "The Invention of Australia," in The Times Literary Supplement, *No. 4351, August 22, 1986, p. 919.*

Charles (Richard) Johnson

1948-

American novelist, short story writer, scriptwriter, and essayist.

Johnson has won critical acclaim for erudite fiction in which he variously incorporates elements of fantasy, the parable, folklore, the slave narrative, nineteenth-century realism, and Eastern and Western philosophies. Critics also praise his imaginative explorations of racism, personal relationships, and the role of the black intellectual in American society. Johnson's overriding concern with moral behavior was prompted by his association with novelist and theoretician John Gardner, his writing instructor at Southern Illinois University. Raymond Olderman described Johnson as an author whose works "can *embody* contact with reality, have the spiritual significance of myth, and have the authority of science."

Johnson's first novel, *Faith and the Good Thing* (1974), is an intricate, often humorous philosophical work in which he combines fantasy, realism, folk wisdom, and satire to depict a Southern black girl's journey to Chicago in search of the "Good Thing," or the true meaning of life. During her odyssey, Faith, the story's Candide-like protagonist, suffers physical degradation but nonetheless attains spiritual resurrection. In his next novel, *Oxherding Tale* (1982), Johnson again employs humor and philosophy to trace the development of his hero from innocence to experience. The plot of this work is modeled on the slave narratives of nineteenth-century author Frederick Douglass. Using a combination of realism and allegory and mixing modern slang with mid-nineteenth-century vernacular, Johnson follows a slave's escape to freedom and his quest for knowledge through the guidance of an eccentric mentor. Critics generally agreed that Johnson's characterizations and philosophical digressions are handled more adeptly in *Oxherding Tale* than in *Faith and the Good Thing*. Stanley Crouch observed: "[The protagonist's] growth is thrilling because Johnson skillfully avoids melodramatic platitudes while creating suspense and comedy, pathos and nostalgia. In the process, he invents a fresh set of variations on questions about race, sex, and freedom."

Johnson's collection of short stories, *The Sorcerer's Apprentice* (1986), also exhibits his interest in moral tales. The pieces in this volume examine the cultural alienation of black Americans through a blend of formal language and street argot. Fred Pfeil commented: "[In *The Sorcerer's Apprentice*], Johnson demonstrates more clearly than ever his Melvillean ambition to use narrative to fuse concept and event, politics, philosophy and drama, and to make ideas dance." In addition to fiction, Johnson has written scripts for several public television series and has worked as a political cartoonist and journalist.

(See also *CLC*, Vol. 7; *Contemporary Authors*, Vol. 116; and *Dictionary of Literary Biography*, Vol. 33.)

Photograph by Wayne Sourbeer. Courtesy of Charles Johnson.

ELIZABETH A. SCHULTZ

Perhaps closest to Ellison's [*Invisible Man*] in overall mythic design is Charles Johnson's *Faith and the Good Thing* (1974). Faith, cautioned by her dying mother to get herself a "Good Thing," begins a Platonic search in the cave of life for Truth, an Arthurian quest for the Grail, or, like the African Kujichagulia, a climb toward the peak of Mount Kilimanjaro and the source of knowledge. Traveling from rural Georgia to urban Chicago, she embraces numerous roles and ideologies—her mother's fundamentalist Christianity, middle-class materialism and opportunism, a street-walker's self-sacrifice, an artist's solipsism. As she passes from one ideology to another—ever hopeful—she also finds herself involved with a variety of people, most of whom exploit her for their own ends, few of whom see her according to her own needs and complexity. Burned by an apocalyptic fire at the novel's conclusion, she becomes a wraith: seen and not seen, a visual symbol of her former existence and an obvious analogy to Ellison's Invisible Man. Faith's invisibility differs, however, from that of Ellison's protagonist, for throughout her travels she has been in touch with the unseen world—not the unseen world of Plato's perfect forms, Kujichagulia's absolute answers, or the nightmares of Ellison's protagonist, which are no alternative to his waking world; she is in touch with memories, or more accurately, the spiritual presences of three human beings who persist in haunt-

228

ing her; they keep alive the faith in her, the faith which gives her her name and identity, the faith that believes that the search itself is its own end. These familiar presences are "the living dead," and only when Faith stops searching, momentarily convinced she has found the "Good Thing" in a materialistic middle-class life, and joins "the dead living," do they cease to appear before her. Following the fire and a hospital internment—events which also force Ellison's protagonist to new perspectives on himself—they are restored to her, however, as she herself becomes one of them.

Indeed, as Faith, the wraith, returns to the swamp from which she had started her journey, she is reincarnated as the Swamp Woman. In his cellar Ellison's hero gains perspective on his personal agonies by reviewing in a dream sequence the ambiguities of his own life and of black Americans from the days of slavery; similarly, Faith's sufferings seem to give her access to the werewitch's esoteric and folk wisdom, her knowledge of Western and African philosophical and cabalistic systems as well as her consciousness of the terrible history of oppression. Like Ellison's protagonist's, Faith's journey has also been cyclical, returning her to her own past—the swamp and the Briar Patch of her own mind—as well as to the historical past, represented by the conflation of her experiences with the Swamp Woman's lore. By Faith's return to the swamp as well as by the old crone's marvelous subsequent assumption of Faith's guise and her return to the world to continue Faith's search, Johnson demonstrates his commitment, however, to myth rather than history, for he seeks to guarantee its truth by suggesting its endless repetition. Finally, Faith, like Ellison's protagonist, contemplates the possibilities of the mind to conceive a pattern for living; she, living in a state of faith rather than of paralysis, imagines both progress and responsibility beyond the control of history:

> When she'd traveled the existing paths, she would create a new, untrodden one. That was progress. If she discovered X number of paths and traveled them all, then she, before she died, would leave X-plus-1. That was responsibility: factoring the possible number of paths to the Good Thing, but not becoming fixed, or held to those paths in her history, or the history of the race.

Finally, then, unlike Ellison's protagonist, she envisions a way to reconcile the many with the one.

In the conclusion of his novel, Johnson informs us that Faith's way will not be a solitary one. Not only do we learn that she is preparing to relate Aristotle's Illusion and "Stagolee's great battle with Lucifer in West Hell" to two children who seek her out in the swamp as she herself had once sought the werewitch, but we are also reminded that we ourselves have been children throughout the novel, listening to Johnson relate Faith's own tale. Ellison, too, somewhat perfunctorily, reminds us in the last sentence of his novel that we have also been an audience for his protagonist's story when he queries, "Who knows but that, on the lower frequencies, I speak for you?" Johnson's repeated imperative reference to his readers as "Children" and Faith's preparations for her young visitors suggest, however, a more than rhetorical involvement with others; the "Good Thing" is not only the search itself but also the fact that the search is everyone's, and that we are on it together. (pp. 106-08)

> *Elizabeth A. Schultz, "The Heirs of Ralph Ellison:
> Patterns of Individualism in the Contemporary Afro-
> American Novel," in CLA Journal, Vol. XXII, No.
> 2, December, 1978, pp. 101-22.*

STANLEY CROUCH

Since most contemporary novels involving race are scandals of contrivance, unwheeled wagons hitched to cardboard horses, it's a particular pleasure to read Charles Johnson's *Oxherding Tale*. This is his second novel and, being a long ball past his first, *Faith and the Good Thing* (1974), it separates him even further from conventional sensibilities. In *Faith,* Johnson told the tall tale of a black girl's search for meaning—What is the good life? What is good?—and soaked it through with skills he had developed as a cartoonist, television writer, journalist, and student of philosophy. This time out, he has written a novel made important by his artful use of the slave narrative's structure to examine the narrator's developing consciousness, a consciousness that must painfully evaluate both the master and slave cultures.

The primary theme is freedom and the responsibility that comes with it. Given the time of the novel, 1838 to 1860, one would expect such a theme, but Johnson makes it clear in the most human—and often hilarious—terms that the question of freedom in a democratic society is essentially moral, and that social revolution pivots on an expanding redefinition of citizenry and its relationship to law. The adventure of escape only partially prepares Andrew Hawkins, the narrator, for the courage and commitment that come with moral comprehension. Andrew's growth is thrilling because Johnson skillfully avoids melodramatic platitudes while creating suspense and comedy, pathos and nostalgia. In the process, he invents a fresh set of variations on questions about race, sex, and freedom.

Though only 176 pages, *Oxherding Tale* is so rich that Johnson's contrapuntal developments of character and theme gain epic resonance. He expands his tale with adventures of style that span the work of Melville and Ellison, Twain and Bradbury, opting for everything from the facetious philosophical treatise to a variation on *The Illustrated Man*. Like a jazz musician's high-handed use of harmony, Johnson's prose pivots between the language of the novel's time and terms from contemporary slang, regional vernacular, folklore, the blues, academia, and Madison Avenue. The technique recalls American film comedians' pushing the talk and attitudes of the day into period situations, lampooning the conventions of the past and the present. But Johnson is essentially a gallows humorist who manipulates microscopic realism to sober and control the reader's response, just as he takes narrative liberties to create an echoing, circular tension in which characters and dangers rhyme and contrast.

Johnson models his book on the work of Frederick Douglass, especially *Narrative of the Life of Frederick Douglass, An American Slave*, published in 1845. Douglass was an epic hero if there ever was one, and his work spans experience that moves from slavery to partial freedom to escape and eventual celebrity. His greatest importance to Johnson, however, is that he took Hawthorne's assault on New England hypocrisy south. In order to assert his humanity, Douglass questioned the Southern social order and everything that upheld it, from force to compliance, superstition to imposed illiteracy. He continually attacked the amoral sexual practices of the slaveholders and the distortions of American ideals caused by their defense of the chattel system. Douglass's native intelligence allowed for insights that only our finest novelists have been able to extend—the often dangerous nature of personal responsibility, the mutual infantilization of master and slave, the roles of religion and folklore, music and humor, risk and victory. In effect, Douglass is the figure who provides the moral passageway between Hawthorne and Melville and supplies the foundation for *Huckleberry Finn.* . . .

By using Douglass's achievement as a model, Johnson perforates the layers of canvas-thick clichés that block our access to the human realities of American slavery. He also creates a successful metaphor for the 1960s, when black militants and intellectuals (students mostly) rejected Christianity, capitalism, and collided head-on with elements of black culture as basic as food (familial conflicts between emulation of Islam's disdain for pork and the hippie concern with health foods are symbolized by Andrew's embracing vegetarianism in imitation of his first white guru). The metaphor's impact comes from Johnson's sense of the play between history, cultural convention, and the assertion of identity in personal and ethnic terms.

Like Douglass, Andrew Hawkins is a mulatto. Unlike Douglass, he can pass for white, a fact that adds complexity to the moral choices he must make when he becomes a runaway. That fact also places him between what seem only two worlds but are actually many, and it adds the texture of an espionage tale in which "passing" is essential to suspense and victory. To thicken the plot, Johnson introduces a transcendentalist who supplies Andrew with a set of Eastern references and a pursuit of "The Whole"—though all systems of thought the hero encounters are satirized mercilessly. These devices allow Johnson to undercut Andrew's theorizing with concrete summonings of the worlds through which he passes—even inserting, as Melville might, a two-page treatise on the nature of slave narratives!

Johnson's ironic humor resounds at the novel's beginning as he pushes the master's wife into the position of slave woman by proxy. . . . As the novel opens, a drinking session is in progress. Jonathan Polkinghorne, master of Cripplegate, and his butler, George Hawkins, who is also his favorite slave, are indulging in a distinctly male camaraderie that seems to transcend their races and stations—each catches hell from his spouse when he comes home drunk. Literally inebriated with power, Jonathan proposes that they exchange wives for the evening in order to avoid static in the bedroom. George follows orders after the master makes it clear that he intends for them to be carried out.

Wobbling from the effects of wine and anticipation, George crosses the territory of *Invisible Man* and *The Odyssey*. In Ellison's novel, the narrator is upbraided and expelled from a Southern Negro college for following orders rather than pretending to, for not knowing he should give white people what they *want*, rather than what they ask for. George makes a parallel mistake and proves himself an even bigger fool by revealing his identity. As he makes love to Anna Polkinghorne in the darkness, she yowls with delight, calling him "Jonathan," but George can't resist telling her who's doing the satisfying, just as Odysseus couldn't resist shouting his name to the Cyclops. Like Odysseus, George is humbled by losing almost everything: as Anna swells, pregnant with George's child, his social position diminishes. He falls to the position of field hand—oxherd—outcast and laughing stock of the slave quarters, given his comeuppance for ever having felt secure and superior to his fellow slaves. Though George's wife, Mattie, accepts Andrew as her own after Anna refuses to see him, she is forever fighting with George, a mad battle in which their mutual needs are persistently camouflaged by complaint and derision. (p. 30)

Jonathan is estranged from Anna because of the immoral nature of the order he gave George, and because he is a victim of a

system in which immoral power choices can also ricochet. George's problems with Mattie stem from something only he knows—that his action could be explained as the result of many things, including cowardice, but when he felt lust for Anna and rationalized his act as an expression of God's will, he was using the order for his own purposes, embracing the slaveholder's self-justifications, and was culpable. Just as Jonathan and George mirror and provide contrast to each other, so do Anna and Mattie. Anna rejects Andrew because he complicates her identity in a way she finds repulsive, while Mattie, however embittered, saves her outrage for the men responsible and loves the child. While Mattie becomes more contentious, Anna becomes a voluntary spinster whose desexualization by slavery will be echoed by Minty, Andrew's first love and the daughter of a womanizing mulatto slave. . . . Minty is seen a few years later, after Andrew has escaped and is passing himself off as a white man at a slave auction.

> . . . I stood trying to recognize something of the girl in Cripplegate, in whom the world once chose to concretize its possibilities in the casement of her skin. . . . If you looked, without sentiment, you could see that her dress was too small and crawled up when she moved, flashing work-scorched stretches of skin and a latticework of whipmarks. Her belly pushed forward. From the cholesterol-high, nutritionless diet of the quarters, or a child, I could not tell. She was unlovely, drudgelike, sexless, the farm tool squeezed . . . for every ounce of surplus value, then put on sale for whatever price she could bring. She was, like my stepmother, perhaps doubly denied—in both caste and gender—and driven to Christ (she wore a cross) as the only decent man who would have her.

The road to that hideous epiphany is a long one, taking Andrew through continual redefinitions of his identity and the nature of his surroundings. When Anna demands that Andrew be sent away because he symbolizes her humiliation, Jonathan refuses and makes provisions for his education. From Ezekiel William Sykes-Withers, Andrew gets a classical education expanded to include the teachings of the Eastern philosophers and mystics. Andrew embraces the idea of the universe as the Great Mother, becomes an intellectual fop, and makes pompous evaluations of the problems of man. Ezekiel, with his head ever in the clouds, and George, with his pushed into the earth, give Andrew antithetical perspectives experience will allow him to synthesize. George's bitterness at his fall from grace shapes an overview that defines anything connected with white people as bad. . . . That homemade ethnic nationalism is the spiritual tragedy of Andrew's father, a man who sustains his hurt and sands down the universe to fit his disappointment: "Grief was the grillwork—the emotional grid—through which George Hawkins sifted and sorted events, simplified a world so overrich in sense it outstripped him . . ." George had no knowledge of the threat that education and imagination posed.

Andrew's schooling will later make it possible for him to read and forge documents, to make language work for him, just as the slaves had made Christianity function as religion, self-expression, style, political editorial, and code of revolt. And because of his learning, Andrew, for all his naiveté, comes to realize he must ask for his freedom:

> Consider the fact: Like a man who had fallen or been rudely flung into the world, I owned nothing. My knowledge, my clothes, my language, even, were shamefully second-hand, made by, and perhaps for, other men. . . . My argument was: Whatever my or-

igin, I would be wholly responsible for the shape I gave myself in the future, for shirting myself handsomely with a new life that called me like a siren to possibilities that were real but forever out of reach.

The oblique references to Caliban and Odysseus are apt: the runaway slave that Andrew will soon become is a man whose knowledge must be used to free him from teachers as he looks for home—except that the home for which slaves felt nostalgia was more the dream of freedom than an actual place. But before Andrew chooses to pursue freedom in concrete geographical terms, he floats along in the philosophical clouds he shares with Ezekiel. Too mystical to trust sensuality, Ezekiel longs for a system that will explain everything and sends Karl Marx the money to visit America. Johnson brilliantly satirizes the relationship between a revolutionary's self-obsession and his theories:

> As of late, political affairs affected Marx physically. When he felt a headcold coming on, a toothache, he looked immediately for its social cause. A new tax law had cost Marx a molar. Nearby at a button factory a strike that failed brought on an attack of asthma. These things were dialectical.

Marx's appearance signals Andrew's first awareness that ideas have human sources or targets. Marx, a jolly family man and sensualist, has as his credo, "Everything I've vritten has been for a voman—is *one* vay to view Socialism, no?" Marx's boredom inspires Andrew to look more closely at the stern Ezekiel:

> Abruptly, I saw my tutor through his eyes: a lonely, unsocial creature unused to visitors, awkward with people as a recluse. Not a Socialist, as he fancied himself. No, his rejection of society, his radicalism, was not, as he thought, due to some rareness of the soul. It was stinginess. Resentment for the richness of things. A smoke screen for his own social shortcomings.

What Andrew had thought the opposite of George's vision was substantially the same—a world view created out of bitterness. Yet Andrew, the pampered mulatto, has still to taste the sourness and terror of slavery, the black world beyond abstraction. His decision to ask for his freedom will bring him cheek to jowl with sexual decadence, drugs, and death.

Andrew's second white mentor is Flo Hatfield, a ruthless voluptuary on whose plantation he expects to earn money that will buy freedom for George, Mattie, and Minty. Middle-aged and beautiful, Flo Hatfield has been infantilized by her power over others, but Johnson makes her as sympathetic as she is repulsive, self-obsessed, and petulant. Good at business and something of a feminist, Hatfield's resentment of male privilege becomes a justification for her appetites. She dresses her lovers, all of whom are slaves, as gigolos; when she tires of them, they're sent to work in her mines, where death is certain. Though she seems sexually free at first, a cosmopolitan upperclass white woman beyond the erotic provincialism of Negro women, she is actually so much a slave to sensation that Andrew's job as sexual servant results in addiction to opium, her favorite aphrodisiac. When Johnson writes that her lovers had "died and gone to Heaven, you might say," he is playing on the black dictum: "A colored man with a white woman is a Negro who has died and gone to heaven," but he is also creating a metaphor for the inevitable fall that follows the spiritual death of decadence.

No more than a tool of Hatfield's narcissism, Andrew falls from her hedonistic heaven when he strikes her in anger after she refuses to allow him to earn his freedom. Andrew is sent to the Yellow Dog Mine, where the landscape echoes Bessie Smith: "Wild country so tough the hootowls all sang bass." With him is Reb, his second father figure. En route, Andrew asserts his white features and they escape, pretending to be master and slave. In the process, they must outwit the Soulcatcher, Horace Bannon, a man who psychologically *becomes* a slave, then goes where slaves would hide. Bannon's technique is close to the one Reb preaches—a slave must learn exactly how masters think so that he can control their relationship as much as possible. Bannon is a psychopath whose "collage of features" suggests mixed ancestry and whose bloodlust is allowed free rein by the constant flight of slaves. Perhaps the greatest condemnation of the chattel system is that it instituted sadistic behavior for the maintenance of injustice. From Reb, Andrew learns what historian Forrest G. Wood meant when he said that what had been endured by the vast majority of Negro slaves exceeded the suffering of even the most oppressed white group. A captured African slave whose name has been changed twice by different masters, Reb is himself a harsh lesson in the stoicism born of tragedy. He no longer dreams of Africa, where Islam was as much an imposition of slavery as Christianity was in America. Reb faces his fate, raising his fists in his own way.

All that Andrew has learned, both intellectual and moral, is put to the test when he decides to marry a white woman—or she decides for him. Once Andrew enters that world, the theme of espionage, of assumed identity that allows for information about the opposition, also allows for a fantastic parody of the liberal wing of the town. . . . From there, Johnson moves to a climax remarkable for its brutality and humbling tenderness; Andrew must dive into the briar patch of his identity and risk destruction in order to express his humanity.

That a work of such courage and compassion, virtuosity and intelligence, has been published by a university press is further proof that commercial houses have a very circumscribed notion of African-American writing. But then, any black writer who chooses human nature over platitudes, opportunism, or trends faces probable rejection. Charles Johnson has enriched contemporary American fiction as few young writers can, and it is difficult to imagine that such a talented artist will forever miss the big time that is equal to his gifts. (pp. 30,32)

Stanley Crouch, "Charles Johnson: Free at Last!" in The Village Voice, *Vol. XXVII, No. 29, July 19, 1983, pp. 30, 32.*

ANGELA McROBBIE

There is something a little too measured about *Oxherding Tale,* by the black American writer Charles Johnson, for it to achieve what it seems to aspire to—to enter, thoroughly and decisively, the canons of Black American Literature. Ironically, it is this self-consciousness which prevents it from gaining the kind of visionary quality towards which it so clearly moves. In structure, it is strongly reminiscent of some of the recent work of J. M. Coetzee. . . . Both writers place the black man (in Coetzee's case, his shadow) at the centre of the murky universe, which they then proceed to reconstruct. And each of them uses this motif as a reference point with which they can make forays, or voyages of exploration, into modern history.

But where Coetzee's voice bursts upon the reader as though from nowhere, wildly, from the vacuum of non-history which is the Afrikaner's Africa, Johnson makes do by at once challenging and paying his respects to the whole white American literary tradition, of which he is obviously a dislocated part. It's as though he cannot escape memories of Hawthorne, Poe, Melville, even Faulkner, and has, as a result, to knit them into his concern with the black experience. In the spirit of all these white shadows, *Oxherding Tale* is a book which charts a male journey. From slavery to freedom, from ignorance to understanding, from degradation to self respect, from being black to passing as a white, and from passing as a white to being made aware again of being black. . . .

Much of the humour and style of the book derives from the tricks that it plays with time and language. Its narrator, solidly ensconced within the Deep South of the mid 19th century, speaks, indeed raps, with all the cultural know-how of a streetwise young American. But even this fails to raise the temperature. It's a tale caught in the circularity of the myths with which it over-identifies. (p. 25)

> Angela McRobbie, "Hand-Me-Downs," in New Statesman, *Vol. 106, No. 2751, December 9, 1983,* pp. 25-6.

STEVEN WEISENBURGER

The title of Charles Johnson's strangely delightful novel [*Oxherding Tale*] refers to the "Ten Oxherding Pictures" of Kuoan Shih-yuan, a twelfth century Zen master. In the paintings a young man pursues a wayward animal, a symbol of the self, and the irony is that he never finds the beast. He finds himself always in between loss and recovery, desire and its resolution. To these oppositions Charles Johnson has added black and white. *Oxherding Tale* translates the Zen enigma of in-betweenness to the antebellum South, and to a beautifully voiced narrator named Andrew Hawkins, a mulatto who becomes a master of the in-between.

The novel opens on an autumn night, in 1837, at a South Carolina plantation called "Cripplegate," a locus that is "ruin now, mere parable." This stands as an apt warning. For despite its many gestures toward picaresque, realistic fiction, *Oxherding Tale* is always riskily half-and-half. From its opening "Long ago," to its concluding "This is my tale," Johnson makes equally as many gestures toward realism as he does to the conventions of parable, or, more specifically, allegorical satire. Many of his characters are therefore drawn as grotesque abstracts. They embody an eccentric side of things, and their one-sidedness sets the boundaries within which Andrew's moral odyssey unfolds. At the same time, Johnson gives his eccentrics a roundedness, a power to speak themselves that is rare in comparable satires by an Ishmael Reed or a Flannery O'Connor. As Andrew Hawkins might put it, the novel therefore takes up all the conventions of allegorical satire even as it commences to "worry" them with the needs of historical, realistic fiction.

One immediate result is a stylistic tension that will initially put many readers off stride. Nodding toward realistic conventions, Johnson fills the story with artifacts of nineteenth century culture: beardboxes, cooling-boards (for the dead), trollopees, phrenology, Mesmer's "Animal Magnetism," even Karl Marx (who makes a weirdly incongruous visit to Cripplegate). At the same time, Andrew's story is skewed by a more familiar diction, with its "Sensuality 101, Section A" and its "sexual politics," each as obviously anachronistic as the "biology text" Andrew reads, circa 1850. To some extent we can put this aside as an elaborate ruse, saying (with Andrew's father-in-law) that novels are "A tissue of ostrobogulous lies . . . with the writer laughing behind each page at the reader's gullibility."

But there is more at stake. With their fullness, Johnson's welter of minor characters cannot simply be read as stick figures in a satirical drama. That temptation is however there from the start, given the low-comedy scene in Chapter One. On an autumn night in 1837 George Hawkins, devoted butler at "the Big House," gets quietly drunk with his master, Jonathan Polkinghorne. When he proposes they swap wives for the night, George, in no position to refuse, gives a reluctant assent. It goes well enough until Anna Polkinghorne groans out her sexual climax in the dark:

> "Oh *gawd,* Jonathan!"
>
> "No ma'am, it ain't Jonathan."
>
> "Geo-*o-o-o*rge?" Her voice pulled at the vowel like taffy. She yanked her sheet to her chin. "Is this *George?*"
>
> "Yo husband's in the quarters." George was on his feet. "He's, uh, with my wife."

Anna screams, then lapses forever into an insane seclusion. Andrew is born a mulatto, banished like the memory of an appendicitis to the quarters, yet raised with the benefit of an extraordinary education—American Transcendentalism, European dialectical philosophy, Eastern mysticism—paid for by his "stepfather," Jonathan. These contrary paternal influences keep pulling at him. George nourishes in Andrew a responsibility for "the world-historical mission of Africa," a sense that everything he does "pushes the Race forward, or pulls us back." His is the philosophy of Inchin' Along. But Andrew objects: "I didn't *want* this obligation." In Part Two of the novel Andrew appears to reject George's advice altogether, when he begins to "pass" in white society. And yet by then the education which was so freely given has begun to weigh on him like an absolute servitude. Ever a bond-servant to the Emersonian ideal of Self-Reliance, Andrew troubles over his isolation, his distance from the family he knew in the quarters.

One answer is to start, however haphazardly, a family of his own. Yet even then Andrew keeps troubling himself over Western definitions of the Self. His Zen training keeps referring the questions back to that wayward, illusory ox. And this is why George, the only actual oxherder in the novel, keeps shadowing Andrew's tale until its end. George is a beautifully drawn comical figure, and something in him arouses a great empathy in us. I think it is the sense that at every fateful moment in his life George, like Andrew, does not act; instead *he is acted.* In between he keeps the fictions going, and this is precisely why he matters.

Other characters have more one-sided roles to fulfill. Ezekiel William Sykes-Withers, Andrew's tutor, is a fine parody of the American Renaissance Intellectual—a cross between Poe the nympholept, the ironist in Melville, and the learnedness of Emerson. When Andrew falls in love with a girl from the quarters, Jonathan Polkinghorne cynically deals his step-son to Flo Hatfield, a cross between Catherine the Great, Mae West, and The White Goddess. After a year of exhausting servility to her sexual appetites at "Leviathan," Andrew is dealt away again, only this time he escapes with a black coffin-maker with the impossible name of "Reb" (remember, this is in 1858). Passing as a white schoolteacher, Reb and Andrew settle in Spartanburg, South Carolina. A doctor railroads Andrew into marrying his spinster daughter, and Reb leaves for Canada. Thus events careen toward certain bleakly unavoidable—that is, realistic—ends. Of course Andrew's black heritage will be discovered; it has been foreshadowed all along.

Yet even as this discovery occurs Johnson brings forward his most allegorical character. Nominally he is Horace Bannon, a murderer who collects bounties on runaway slaves. Allegorically he is "The Soulcatcher," a personification of Death. Andrew listens to his method: "you got to have something dead or static inside you—an image of self—fo' a real slave catcher to latch onto." Give in to that static image of one's self, The Soulcatcher explains, and the hunt is finished: the Slave offers *himself* to the Soulcatcher's knife. This makes for a fine irony with Reb, the master coffin-maker who has "no pockets of death" within him. Reb becomes the only slave ever to elude The Soulcatcher. However, the allegory of Death must also key two of Johnson's biggest risks. It does little to help one through the reappearance of Minty, Andrew's lost love from the quarters who dies a withering death from pellagra, depicted in frighteningly realistic detail. One has somewhat less trouble with the last trick, which is neatly arranged: The Soulcatcher metamorphoses back into Horace Bannon, the simple-minded redneck whose one aim in life is to be happily married. At that moment, the satirical stroke is swift and decisive. But one also has an aftertaste of ashes caused, I think, by the fact that Andrew's marriage to "The White World" of Part 2 is cemented by Minty's death.

The thing I most admire about *Oxherding Tale* is the way Charles Johnson wants to unfold such a moment of equilibrium from his shifting terrain. The writing moves in a middle ground between the cultures of the East and the West, between realism and parable. And Johnson sets himself the task of doing it in the first person, though it is exactly the fixture of a Self that his work calls into doubt. In two short, essayistic chapters Johnson steps out of his fictional persona to discuss this paradox. He points to models for his work in Slave Narratives, Puritan narratives of Redemption, and St. Augustine's *The Confessions*. In these, the Self is equally a fiction, a "proposition" in motion between sin and salvation, ignorance and knowledge, slavery and freedom. As "metafictional" interludes such chapters are informative, but I don't think readers need to be reminded how the great works of fiction have "worried" the conventions, hybridized the forms, occupied the in-between.

If anything, these interludes demonstrate how ambitious Charles Johnson is for his writing. *Oxherding Tale* is his second novel. *Faith and the Good Thing* appeared when he was twenty-six, and it was flawed mainly by short lapses into wooden, academic exposition. The metafictional asides of his latest novel are one way of transforming the teaching into performance, but they're still beside the point. Johnson's real gifts are a beautiful sense of voice and a delight in skewing one's formal expectations. (pp. 153-56)

Steven Weisenburger, "In-Between," in Callaloo, Vol. 7, No. 1, Winter, 1984, pp. 153-56.

MICHAEL KRASNY

In Charles Johnson's *Oxherding Tale* an author named Evelyn Pomeroy writes a letter to the novel's protagonist, Andrew Hawkins, from New York, where she has gone to publish her second novel. She writes her friend Hawkins of how sterile and empty contemporary fiction is, how "a novel *should* be an experiential *feast,* a three-ring circus of humor, suspense, ideas and images, a whole world of people tied together by plot. . . ." She laments the fact that writers have nothing positive to say and appear to write mainly to stay published and in the spotlight, "even if they have to cannibalize their first work, or resort to formulae." Pomeroy's novel, we are told toward the end of *Oxherding Tale,* was only reviewed with five other books in the "bookbin" column of the Press and was overshadowed by the American edition of Trollope's *Framley Parsonage.*

What Evelyn Pomeroy says a novel should be is what Charles Johnson tries to write in this second novel by the author of *Faith and the Good Thing*. Hardly a cannibalization of that promising work, *Oxherding Tale* is essentially a bildungsroman about a young light skinned black who is conceived from the accidental union of a slave and his owner's wife. We follow Hawkins as he wends his way to a white wife and freedom—in that order! The novel is well researched, rich in detail, the product of a not untalented stylist. Why, then, do I feel tepid about it.

First off, reading this novel is at times a bit like reading Josiah Henson or Frederick Douglass after they have gone through briefings in a Kung-fu monastery. I do not mean to sound flip. Johnson wants to write a positive novel. Surely that is commendable and noble when so much serious contemporary writing is inundated by post-wastelanders and entropists. Johnson, on the other hand, is in deadly earnest as a moral voice. No wonder the late John Gardner liked and praised this novel. But Johnson's morality grows more out of primer ontology lessons and readings from *The Gita* and a spate of other books on metaphysics than it does out of an often engaging plot. *Oxherding Tale* is best when it is what William Carlos Williams called "fictionalized recall," the picaresque odyssey of a hero who moves out of both human and metaphysical bondage. It succeeds in creating memorable scenes and characters but Johnson and his editors should have gone lighter on all of the philosophy and stayed with the more exciting entertainment of the plot. (p. 14)

On the other hand, plot is Johnson's strong suit. His story of young Hawkins, though it omits the important racial dilemmas of the hero's early years, is energetic, fluid and well-paced. Karl Marx is cleverly brought in as a visitor. The Ur commie enters the novel on an excursion to the plantation, curiously called Cripplegate. Another impressive creation of Johnson's that makes the plot move well is Horace Bannon, a so-called soulcatcher who hunts slaves down as bounty with an unerring instinct for getting in his prey's skins. Bannon is much more compelling to us when we discover that he gets erections at funerals or finds killing a superior means of satisfaction to masturbation than when he is pictured for us as a sort of Satanic embodiment of the grim reaper. The bane of Johnson's writings is when he toys with such archetypes or uses his philosophical mouthpiece Hawkins to dispense transcendent knowledge.

Though it is refreshing in some novels and certainly not formula, I also found myself uncomfortable with Johnson's excursions outside the narrative as, for example, when he lectures his readers on the form and history of the slave narrative. His characterizations of women are also a problem. Flo Hatfield, a mine owning hedonist and sexual exploiter of Negro bondsmen, is a great idea for a character who never quite makes it beyond that. And Johnson can find himself down a River Styx of mannered prose, as in a line describing the reaction of Andrew's black love object, Minty, when she finds her former lover has purchased her off a slave auction block: "She made the sort of face Jocasta reportedly gave Oedipus after his interview with the Herdsman." (p. 15)

Michael Krasny, "A Black History Tale," in The American Book Review, *Vol. 6, No. 4, May-June, 1984, pp. 14-15.*

MICHIKO KAKUTANI

"Was sorcery a gift given to a few, like poetry?" wonders Allan, the aspiring magician in the title story of Charles Johnson's new collection [*The Sorcerer's Apprentice*]. . . .

In this story, as in the other tales in *The Sorcerer's Apprentice*, Mr. Johnson . . . addresses both the Faustian dilemma of the knowledge-seeker and the more specific condition of the black artist in America, cut off from his cultural roots and suspended between worlds. . . .

It is one of the achievements of these stories that, while concerned at heart with questions of prejudice and cultural assimilation, they are never parochial and only rarely didactic. Rather, Mr. Johnson has used his generous storytelling gifts and his easy familiarity with a variety of literary genres to conjure up eight moral fables that limn the fabulous even as they remain grounded in the language and social idioms of black American communities. The finest ones, in fact, become fables that implicitly mirror the quotation from Herman Melville that Mr. Johnson has chosen as an epigraph for this volume—they "present another world, and yet one to which we feel the tie."

In relating the meeting between a country doctor and the angst-ridden creature from outer space whom he's called upon to treat, **"Popper's Disease"** evolves from a fairly conventional exercise in sci-fi into a Kafkaesque exploration of identity. **"Menagerie, a Child's Fable,"** a parable about racism told from the point of view of a dog, borrows heavily from Orwell's *Animal Farm*—the story tells what happens when the animals in a pet store take over from its absent owner—and **"The Education of Mingo"** invokes Mary Shelley's *Frankenstein* to make its point about the dangers of liberalism and assimilation.

In **"The Education of Mingo,"** a farmer by the name of Moses Green buys a slave named Mingo, whom he attempts to educate. Moses teaches Mingo farming and table etiquette, he teaches him not "to sop cornbread in his coffee; or pick his nose at public market." He teaches him how to think, how to talk and how to behave, and in no time at all, Mingo appears to have become "his own spitting image"—a development that makes Moses feel "now like a father, now like an artist fingering something fine and noble from a rude chump of foreign clay." If Moses' intentions are entirely well-meaning, however, they're also paternalistic and patronizing, and in time they have serious—and violent—consequences that affect both him and Mingo.

With the exception of one direct allusion to *Frankenstein* that feels superfluous and strained, this story attests to Mr. Johnson's narrative finesse—his ability both to rework old legends, and to create a glowing alloy of the colloquial and the mythic, the naturalistic and the surreal. Though its action retains a powerful, symbolic resonance, the tale never gets that sticky, overworked quality that comes from an author trying to force his material into a predetermined mold; in this case, Mr. Johnson simply lets the overall Frankenstein legend gently inform the actions of his characters, without allowing it to dictate their fates or erase their own idiosyncrasies and humor.

Unfortunately, in the weaker stories in this volume, Mr. Johnson's taste for parables—his desire to locate some sort of Aesop-like moral in each tale—tends to overwhelm his delicate conjurations of social detail and vernacular description. **"Exchange Value,"** for instance, entirely robs its characters—two aspiring hoods who end up adopting their would-be victim's peculiar habits—of their individuality, turning them into passive objects doomed to act out their creator's predictable design. And **"Moving Pictures"** moves even further in this unpromising direction—devoid of characters except for a faceless narrator who speaks in the second person, the story is little but a tired one-liner about escapism and the movies. The reader can only conclude that it was included in this otherwise accomplished collection as padding or a silly afterthought.

Michiko Kakutani, in a review of "The Sorcerer's Apprentice," in The New York Times, *February 5, 1986, p. 24.*

JONATHAN PENNER

[The eight stories in *The Sorcerer's Apprentice*], though designed with wit and written with craft, aren't for pleasure cruising. They're stripped models, the vehicles of ideas, built not for acceleration or sweet ride but payload.

Each asserts a philosophical point. Generally, the stories express distrust in ratiocination, free will, "the ooga-booga of Christianity," and Western culture in general. Readers will enjoy the play of Johnson's thought, even while wishing his characters were permitted thoughts, especially dumb ones, of their own.

Most start, like **"China,"** with an appearance of close-grained realism: "Evelyn's problems with her husband, Rudolph, began one evening in early March—a dreary winter evening in Seattle—when he complained after a heavy meal of pig's feet and mashed potatoes of shortness of breath."

But soon the characters' diction grows learned, their acts fanciful. Overfed Rudolph, a 54-year-old postman, becomes a mystical warrior of the martial arts. At the end, he appears to gain spiritual ascendance over his church-going, life-denying wife by leaping 20 feet in the air. . . .

In fiction, the figure of the sorcerer customarily stands for that of another conjurer, the writer. So it is in **"The Sorcerer's Apprentice,"** which investigates the origins of creativity. The story's surface is so attenuated that we apprehend the symbolic level without pausing at the literal. Don't place your faith in study, the story advises apprentice writers, nor in reason, nor in models. Just trust the mysterious springs of talent.

Though most of these stories have black protagonists, the author seems interested in black people no more than he is in people. Rather, he tends to treat blackness—often ingeniously—as a condition, a state of being, which is already halfway to a metaphor.

In **"Popper's Disease,"** a black physician observes the crash of a flying saucer. Entering the craft to provide medical assistance, he meets a lone alien, resembling "what you might expect to find on a seafood platter in a decent restaurant," dying of an incurable disease.

This disease proves to be, simply, "the Self." It arises from the painful relationship between Self—that "lonely Leibnizean monad"—and not-Self.

Dr. Popper suffers from it too, a black (Self) in a white society (not-Self). In this sense, being black is like being an extra-terrestrial—"It seems we are both strangers here," the alien tells Popper. It all goes back to "the ontogenesis of person-ality," for "Personality is the product—no—the historical cre-ation of society."

A similar determinism informs **"The Education of Mingo."** The slave Mingo, fresh from Africa, knows nothing—not even how to laugh—so Moses Green, his master, sets out to teach him. Soon Moses finds himself actually creating Mingo.... The slave learns with frightening speed and spooky complete-ness, mimicking even his master's limp.

"It's like I just shot out another arm," Moses muses, "and that's Mingo." Or, as Mingo puts it, "When Mingo works, it bees Massa Green workin', right? Bees Massa Green work-in', thinkin', doin' through Mingo."

In time, Mingo performs bloody acts that Moses dares not acknowledge as his own desires, though they are. The black man here is not only the white man's creation but also the expression of his darker nature.

Even readers who feel patronized when argument displaces experience, and bored when information drives out feeling, will at the same time be charmed by some of these stories. Often the ideas are nimbly expressed. Sometimes the plots take dramatic turns. Charles Johnson writes so well that one is disposed to patience when he puts down his pen for other tools: his grindstone, his saws.

> *Jonathan Penner, "Magical Mystery Tours," in* Book World—The Washington Post, *February 16, 1986, p. 8.*

J. J. PHILLIPS

The Sorcerer's Apprentice, a collection of short fiction by the author of *Oxherding Tale,* is a slim volume. But it has a depth and range of perspective that more than compensate for its brevity.

The writing of short stories is a delicate task in that the economy of form requires that words be used with precision, and such isn't always easy to come by. In these wild yet darkly elegant stories, which also function as emblematic fables and caution-ary tales, Charles Johnson exhibits such precision as he probes various aspects of the human condition.

His language is an invigorating interweaving of hieratic and demotic English and everything in between. His tales are peopled by characters who, by virture of their all-too-human wit un-witting itself, for good or ill, tumble into surreal existential trick-bags; and whoever they were, their heretofore quotidian lives are never to be the same again.

Though these stories might strike terror in the heart, as in **"The Education of Mingo"** or the title story **"The Sorcerer's Ap-prentice,"** gentleness, warmth and humor are by no means lacking. These elements are inextricably fused with the horror of descent into the yawning void, and the stories linger pro-vocatively in the mind long after one has read them.

In one way or another all of the stories are concerned with language: its use and misuse, the power it has over us, and how that power shapes and defines, indeed conjures up that which we call reality. **"The Education of Mingo"** chronicles an elderly farmer's misguided attempts to acculturate his newly purchased African slave. The plot turns explicitly on the issue of language and identity in a novel way. It is a brooding story of the word literally becoming flesh, and the Frankensteinian consequences which ensue....

In **"Popper's Disease,"** an unassuming black physician, mar-ried to a Swedish woman who teaches piano, finds himself trapped inside a flying saucer with a dying alien creature.... Mildred, his wife, is at home giving a piano lesson when this misadventure happens to him on his way to make a house call. Trapped inside the saucer, he is more curious than fearful. He wants to save the life of the alien being and tries to console it. He also wants to find a way out, but while exploring the flying saucer, thanks to advanced extraterrestrial technology, he learns to his dismay that at that very moment Mildred is providing instruction in carnal, as well as musical, knowledge to her student. It is a very funny story which hearkens back to the refreshingly unsophisticated pre-Spielberg outer space fantasies and constructs of the 1950s.

The title story, **"The Sorcerer's Apprentice"** again directly addresses the power of the word to conjure up and thereby reify itself. This time, though, it is a fatal doubt in such power which leads the protagonist, along with his father, to a har-rowing, Gnostic self-obliteration. However, because the char-acter of the apprentice's father is not sharply drawn, his pres-ence diminishes the force of the story for me.

These minor disappointments aside, the stories collected here are well-told tales, riveting, thought-provoking and well worth reading.

> *J. J. Phillips, in a review of "The Sorcerer's Ap-prentice," in* Los Angeles Times Book Review, *March 30, 1986, p. 11.*

MICHAEL VENTURA

Charles Johnson's brief, highly concentrated *Sorcerer's Ap-prentice* has the feel of a good short novel rather than a col-lection of stories. These tales—or are they fables?—are realistic without strictly adhering to realism, fantastic without getting lost in fantasy. Mr. Johnson, a professor of English at the University of Washington, writes of truths that intersect and sometimes intercept our everyday trajectories.

Each of the eight fictions not only stands on its own but seems to support and invoke its companions. The opening story, **"The Education of Mingo,"** applies the Frankenstein myth to Amer-ican slavery. Mingo is "the youngest son of the reigning king of the Allmuseri, a tribe of wizards," and his mere presence is enough to enslave his American master. In the last tale, **"The Sorcerer's Apprentice,"** the sorcerer is a former slave in South Carolina who was also born an Allmuseri in Africa. He attempts to pass on his knowledge to a boy who was born free and has become, simply and terribly, too American to absorb African magic. The two tales are the opposite poles of a magnetic field within which Mr. Johnson's other stories are held.

They echo one another without straining for effect. As Mingo enslaves his master, so sudden wealth enslaves Mingo's de-scendants. Loftis and Cooter, the thieves in **"Exchange Value,"** provide a chilling lesson in the witchy powers of money. The reader realizes almost by osmosis that each story in *The Sorcerer's Apprentice* reveals the underside of the last or next.

A structure is just a frame that squeaks if you lean on it—unless the author has a vision of how the world works. Mr. Johnson has been somewhere most people have not. As the narrator of **"Alethia"** says, "I am hardly a man to conjure a fabulation so odd in its transfiguration of things, so strange, so terrifying." Transfigurations are at once Mr. Johnson's subject and vision. He knows how a master becomes a slave, how a postal worker becomes a kung fu knight (**"China"**) and how magic can be gained (**"Alethia"**) and lost (**"The Sorcerer's Apprentice"**). And when Mr. Johnson says magic, he means magic. He's not using the word to invoke a mood. Sometimes it's outright voodoo; sometimes it's something more subtle that gives an otherwise powerless individual the power to transfigure both himself and his world.

According to Mr. Johnson, an exaggerated sense of self is what gets in the way of magic. . . .

Magic, then, requires a surrender of self that terrifies most people. Our terror is Mr. Johnson's meat. Confronting it, his characters take sudden turns, like flowers in a time-lapse film, sometimes surprising, sometimes fascinating, sometimes, like certain unfolding petals, almost repulsive, but always growing, succeeding or failing with their own logic and force.

Mr. Johnson's word magic wears thin only once, with **"Moving Pictures,"** a grouchy diatribe about mass culture that uses the same metaphors for Hollywood that writers intimidated by the movies have used for the better part of a century. But there's no risk in predicting that **"The Education of Mingo," "Exchange Value," "China," "Alethia"** and **"The Sorcerer's Apprentice"** will be anthologized for a very long time. Mr. Johnson's spell of a book comes on with the authority of a classic.

Michael Ventura, "Voodoo and Subtler Powers," in The New York Times Book Review, *March 30, 1986, p. 7.*

George (Benson) Johnston

1913-

Canadian poet, translator, and editor.

An admired figure in Canadian literature, Johnston writes serio-comic verse characterized by a light, conversational tone, restrained style, and wry wit. He typically employs conventional poetic structures, including variations on traditional rhyme schemes and stanzaic forms, as well as rhythmic patterns derived from Anglo-Saxon and Norse literature. Emphasizing simplicity, social consciousness, and morality in his work, Johnston evinces concern for humanity's complacency toward life's destructive elements as he satirizes assorted facets of modern existence. By using inventive diction and such techniques as irony, exaggeration, and parody, Johnston offers humor and imagination as alternatives to the artificial elements that he recognizes in contemporary life.

Johnston was born in Hamilton, Ontario, and received his undergraduate education at the University of Toronto. A regular contributor of drama, poetry, and fiction to several university literary journals while a student, Johnston published stories in such magazines as the *London Mercury,* the *Atlantic,* and *Partisan Review* after receiving his degree. Following four years' service in the Royal Canadian Air Force during World War II, Johnston returned to the University of Toronto for his graduate studies. He began teaching at Mount Allison University in 1946 and in 1950 took a position with the English faculty of Carleton University, where he remained until his retirement in 1979.

In his first book of poetry, *The Cruising Auk* (1959), Johnston creates a community of fictional characters whose attitudes and actions reflect and comment upon the absurdity he perceives in much human endeavor. Although primarily whimsical, these poems combine comic and tragic elements to reveal Johnston's underlying concern with such topics as the acceptance of life and the inevitability of death. Northrop Frye observed: "[*The Cruising Auk* is] a beautifully unified book, the apparently casual poems carrying the reader along from the first poem to the last in a voyage of self-discovery." In *Home Free* (1966), Johnston expands upon the bittersweet observations introduced in his first book while offering darker insights into his subject matter. Simultaneously relaxed in tone and dense in structure and theme, these poems often adhere to strict stanzaic guidelines but achieve flexibility through varied metrical patterns and colloquial diction. Comprising mainly short lyrics, *Home Free* also features direct social satire, particularly in the critically acclaimed long poem "Under the Tree," which implies humanity's collective guilt in the matter of capital punishment. Despite such somber thematic material, Hugh MacCallum observed: "[No] matter how bitter the reflection, there is a vitality in [Johnston's] style that is perpetually refreshing." *Happy Enough: Poems, 1935-1972* (1972) reprints in their entirety Johnston's first two volumes and includes a section of previously unpublished verse. In these new pieces, Johnston produces disturbing effects through his use of dislocated forms and syntactic experiments while maintaining his characteristic wit and incisive vision. Featuring autobiographical poems in which Johnston celebrates the joys of family and friends, this collection also introduces his concern for humanity's relationship with nature.

Courtesy of George Johnston

In *Taking a Grip* (1979), Johnston displays an energetically affirmative attitude toward life's vicissitudes. Largely concerned with the process of aging, these poems demonstrate Johnston's acceptance of death as an integral part of life and continue his celebrations of friends and relations. *Ask Again* (1985) further exhibits Johnston's preoccupation with these issues and his observations on nature. The poems in the first two sections of this volume, which honor such formal occasions from Johnston's life as birthdays, retirements, and convocations, exude a sense of playfulness through his use of varied meters, acrostic patterns, and wit. The lyrics in the final section emphasize Johnston's vision of renewal by making use of sensuous imagery, loose poetic forms, and his continuing interest in natural phenomena.

In addition to his verse, Johnston has published translations of several Norse sagas, including *The Saga of Gisli* (1963), *The Faroe Islanders' Saga* (1975), and *The Greenlanders' Saga* (1976), as well as translations of works by Scandanavian poet Knut Ødegård.

(See also *Contemporary Authors,* Vols. 1-4, rev. ed. and *Contemporary Authors New Revision Series,* Vols. 5, 20.)

ERIC NICOL

In a time when comic verse, like the newspaper "funnies", usually proves as comic as a clout in the kidney, it is pleasant to come upon a poet like George Johnston. Mr. Johnston's humour [in *The Cruising Auk*] is, certainly, grained with melancholy, but the substance remains solid fun. It is not inlaid with the shards of fractured wit that often characterise Canadian light verse (and Mr. Johnston is a Canadian). Much of our humorous verse in fact reads as though written as an alternative to kicking the dog, drawing inspiration less from Calliope than from Dyspepsia, but Mr. Johnston amiably celebrates canine ritual in **"Noctambule"**:

> Mr. Murple's got a dog that's long
> And underslung and sort of pointed wrong;
> When daylight fades and evening lights come out
> He takes him round the neighbour lawns about
> The which he does in drops and by degrees
> Leaving his hoarded fluid only where
> Three-legged ceremonious hairy care
> Has been before . . .

This sensitivity to the call of nature is not restricted, in Mr. Johnston's verse, to dogdom. It is human nature, in its setting of the city rather than the country, that he finds evocative. Rain pools in city streets, cats, Mrs. McGonigle's boarders, even fish are citified, humanised. . . . (pp. 83-4)

Mr. Johnston is well aware that he is jesting in the shadow of the nuclear come-uppance, but remains alert to the human comedy that continues to play itself out. That the sober note at times dominates the major of amusement attests to the profounder element in the poet's work. But he has the disposition to be objective about everything, including his own temptation into gravity.

The result is a kind of poetry that the traditional masks of comedy and tragedy no longer suit. A third mask, for the bittersweet, is required to represent coexistence of the smile on the lips and sadness in the eye. Despite the intimations of extinction, however, good temper is not grounded. The auk is cruising:

> The world is a boat and I'm in it
> Going like hell with the breeze . . .

It is to be hoped that Mr. Johnston will be encouraged, by the public response to this first book of his collected verse, to provide more, though he risk general popularity and a fate worse than Betjeman. (p. 84)

> *Eric Nicol, "Bittersweet Mask," in* Canadian Literature, *No. 1, Summer, 1959, pp. 83-4.*

MILTON WILSON

George Johnston's book [*The Cruising Auk*], like its emblem, is a . . . remarkable apparition. Out of his simple quatrains and couplets, Mr. Johnston gets enough variety in rhythm and phrasing to make the reputation of half a dozen writers of free verse. He also introduces enough characters to furnish a saga. They include Mrs. McGonigle (who keeps a family, a boarding house and the reluctant Mr. Smith, and contemplates the intense inane through her kitchen window), Mr. Murple (who pipes pastorals on his flute and skates with an almost Wordsworthian pomp), Edward (that fugitive from a ballad), Mrs. Belaney and her "bad" daughter, and too many aunts to mention (although the author lists most of them with melancholy unction in **"The Roll Call"**). (p. 136)

The Cruising Auk is a very funny book, and the more seriously you take it, the funnier it gets. But any reviewer who takes it seriously is doomed to self-parody. I suppose it's possible to chart the criss-crossing human pattern in the Johnstonian rug and end up with an essay called "The World of George Johnston", but I don't think anyone ought to try. I'm even more doubtful about "The Comic Vision of George Johnston", although no doubt we're all "in it", flappping or floating around, not airborne exactly, but not sunk yet either, hoping to ignite a dry spark or two in the wet dark. At moments things get pretty wet indeed.

> It's rained sort of day after day
> Till the bottom is, as it were, wet;
> My feelings are all washed away
> But something is left of me yet
>
> And whatever the something may be
> I take it to eat and to bed
> Because after all it's still me—
> Come rain, wash the lot. Let's be dead.

But what's really characteristic about a poem like this is less the image than the diction, grammar and rhythm. I can imagine a "Variorum Dunciad" edition of *The Auk,* with learned notes on Johnston's use of the parenthetical phrase or on his idiomatic favorites like "maybe", "no doubt", "sort of", "all right", etc. (pp. 136-37)

What we finally take away from these poems is the turn of the phrase and the inflection of the voice rather than the rich surface of character and image. Their subject matter is important only as it affords the opportunity for achieving a special and valuable kind of human poise in words. It's easy to describe the Johnstonian world, but not the Johnstonian balance. . . . The reader of these poems isn't cut by "the ecstatic edge" of joy or pain; nor, unlike the creatures who listen to Mr. Murple's flutings, is he simply "soothed to a charming diffidence." His feelings are likely to be much more companionable, as he floats in Mr. Johnston's wide, wide pond. This auk has one unmistakable advantage: nobody is likely to shoot it for an albatross. (p. 137)

> *Milton Wilson, "Turning New Leaves (2)," in* The Canadian Forum, *Vol. XXXIX, No. 464, September, 1959, pp. 136-37.*

IAN SOWTON

I gather from other reviews [of *The Cruising Auk*] that Mr. Johnston's verse is light. If so, it's light as Margot Fonteyn's Harlequin would be light. It conveys man's classic and sometimes funny tragedies with deft, sure-footed grace; its rhetorical gestures are wry, spare, and firm. . . . The verse is witty all right but its wit is just: man—tragic, comic, pathetic, and game—is the subject as well as object of his wit. The "I" of the book is firmly pool-bound along with Mr. Murple, Mrs. McGonigle, Aunt Beleek *et al.,* but the eye of Mr. Johnston's witty imagination is firmly on that Auk cruising at tree-level, detached and close at the same time. And light or not, these verses are substantial enough to pry wide open our patched-up gaps between innocence and experience and show how dark and damp it is inside. . . . (p. 281)

In seeking a direction of response one always thumbs the rule of the familiar. In *The Cruising Auk*'s case there is something like the open-eyed, undertone bizarreness of [Roy Daniell's] *Deeper into the Forest* (no value comparisons here), something like the educated zaniness of [James Reaney's] *A Suit of Nettles,* and something like the dexterous precisions of [Jay Macpherson's] *The Boatman*. These books are high-class company and if there's one thing each resists completely it's togetherness. So does the *Auk,* but for class it belongs. I can detect only two or three bits of flab—as for example in the last line of "**A Saint**", which becomes coy and cute with the English language—in all this neat, lean shape, and that's a heavenly bird, not to be shot down.

The universe of these poems is nice, complex, and clear. Its elements are air and water. In them an amphibious, disassociated self gazes half-enviously up at the free unfallen birds ("**The Cruising Auk**", "**In the Pond**", "**Flight**"), half-wistfully down at the uncomplicated fish ("**Life from a Goldfish Bowl**"), and with unafraid, amused compassion at its Dickensian, boardinghouse neighbours and itself. The role of the lyric self is critical in this book. It consciously presides over a fallen community as in the case (say) of poems by Housman, Hardy, and Masters. But where they preside and spectate, this self presides and participates; that is to say, it is truly ironic. Ironic lyricism that merely presides always ascends to ersatz Olympianism; only that lyricism which comprehends the canker within can rest truly ironic, truly humane. The self in *The Cruising Auk* would like to fly but knows it's in the wet; and it spends its skilful speech celebrating the neighbours' attempts to swim, not proving they can't fly.

That sustained flight is impossible is, however, one of the theme-strands of this book. The Auk (a web-footed water bird) cruises in air, the fish in water, while man gets along, but can't really cruise, in either. Mrs. McGonigle is briefly and artificially airborne in a plane ("**A Mystic of the Air Age**"); and when the chosen hear the "apocalyptic squawk" in "**The Dufluflu Bird**"

> Our hearts respond, our souls respond,
>   The very we of us
> Takes off, as one might say, beyond,
>   But then comes back, alas!

Flight is a metaphorical pun: flight in neither sense is possible. Or, if you like, to take flight in one sense would be to take flight in the other. Another theme-strand, disassociation of the self, is imaged in the fractured link between man and boy, man and bird, man and his reflection in the water. The book begins with a man-boy image and ends with the self's central riddle accepted rather than solved. What I like is that there's no complaining, or very little of it. The poetry is in the knowing acceptance and the shrewd compassion. The style and temper haven't much to do with promethean disillusions, rages against the dying of light, or loud declarations of independence of unkind destiny. In a world which by and large only looks and listens, to really see and really hear, as Mr. Johnston does, is to be rebel enough. (pp. 281, 283)

> *Ian Sowton, in a review of "The Cruising Auk," in*
> The Dalhousie Review, *Vol. 40, No. 2, Summer,*
> *1960, pp. 281, 283.*

NORTHROP FRYE

George Johnston's *The Cruising Auk* should appeal to a wider audience than most books of poems surveyed in these reviews. Even the envious reader should be disarmed by the simplicity, which may make him feel that he could do as well if he set his mind to it, or that here at last is a "light" verse which "doesn't take itself too seriously," the favourite *cliché* of the culturally submerged. The critic, however, has to explain that the substance of Mr. Johnston's poetry is not at all the image of the ordinary reader that is reflected from its polished surface. He must explain that seriousness is not the opposite of lightness, but of portentousness, and that genuine simplicity is always a technical *tour de force*. In short, he must insist that Mr. Johnston's most pellucid lyrics have to be read as carefully as the most baffling paper chase of E. E. Cummings.

The difference between the simple and the insipid, in poetry, is that while simplicity uses much the same words, it puts them together in a way that keeps them echoing and reverberating with infinite associations, rippling away into the furthest reaches of imaginative thought. It is difficult for a critic to demonstrate the contrast between the simplicity that keeps him awake at night and the mediocrity that puts him to sleep in the day. In *The Cruising Auk*, however, there is one major clue to the simplicity. Like Mr. Reaney and Miss Macpherson before him, Mr. Johnston has produced a beautifully unified book, the apparently casual poems carrying the reader along from the first poem to the last in a voyage of self-discovery. We begin with a Narcissus image, a boy gazing into a pool and feeling an identity with "the abyss he gazes on," and we end with "O Earth, Turn!" (the echo of Miss Macpherson can hardly be an accident) where the abyss opens up again inside the adult. . . . (pp. 440-41)

Between these two points, a state of innocence and a state in which all paradise is lost except a residual intuition, Mr. Johnston surveys the ages of man. He first explores the "pool" or pond, life or the objective side of existence, which remains the controlling image of the book. In "**In the Pond**" the poet lies beneath it; in "**In It**" he sails over it in a boat; in "**The Queen of Lop**" it enters a girl's dreams as a death symbol; in "**Poor Edward**" it forms the basis for a beautifully cadenced death-by-water poem of suicide; in "**Wet**" the death symbol modulates into rain. Human life is thus looked at as symbolically under water, hence the watching fish in "**Rapture**" and "**Life from a Goldfish Bowl**," and the fine "**Eating Fish**," where the fish disappears into the man, a quizzical analogue to Miss Macpherson's fisherman. The poet first discovers that the innocence of childhood is not self-contained but rebellious, a battle with invisible gods revealed in the noise of a small boy. . . . As one gets older one comes to terms with experience, and the age of anxiety settles more or less contentedly into

> . . . this excellent street-scattered city
> This home, this network, this great roof of pity.

The cosiness of domestic life among family and friends occupies much of Mr. Johnston's foreground: he depicts it without rancour and without insisting, like so many more obsessed intellectuals, that only a damned soul can remain absorbed in it. . . . For if one can be deeply moved (in "**Cathleen Sweeping**") by a three-year-old daughter struggling with a broom, one can appreciate that a small suburban life, even as lived by adults, may have something equally pathetic and dauntless about it. Thus Mr. Murple's mother, who gets a bottle of gin from her son on Mother's Day but defiantly buys her own flower. . . . In fact Mr. Johnston has a Dickensian sense of the violence of the life force in drab or even squalid surroundings, a sense not many modern poets show, apart from Thomas's *Under Milk Wood*. He admires his gigantic aunts and the vast pregnancy of Bridget, and wonders why Eternity should be too stuffy for the "bugs and bottles and hairpins" of Mrs. McWhirter's highly unsanitary existence and should reduce her instead to a more impersonal dust.

Yet it is still the age of anxiety: the clock, a recurring image, keeps placidly ticking away the moments of life; the "spider's small eye'' is watching and waiting, and all around is a sinister and conspiratorial darkness, of a kind that scares Edward reading ''Light Literature'' and eventually pulls him into it, and that forms the background of the very lovely **''A Little Light.''** Actual ghosts appear in **''A Happy Ghost''** and the demure parody of Yeats's ''All Souls' Night.'' Part of this world is a cheerfully murderous nature: a cat stalking a squirrel reminds us that

> Life is exquisite when it's just
> Out of reach by a bound
> Of filigree jaws and delicate paws

and Miss Beleek is visited by ''Moments almost too bright to bear'' when she thinks of shooting the children who trample over her garden. A darker ferocity appears on the horizon in **''War on the Periphery,''** in the marching of

> The violent, obedient ones
> Guarding my family with guns.

Part of it again is the sense of a submerged communion in nature, like the dogs reconnoitering at posts in **''Noctambule,''** or the ''ecstatic edge of pain'' in **''After Thunder.''** Part of it is the hidden private world that everyone retires into in sleep, the world so prominent in sexual love, with its hard narcist core of self-absorption represented by **''Elaine in a Bikini,''** by the Lorelei figure in **''Music on the Water,''** and by the woman in **''Home Again''** who returns from a night on the tiles with this inner core almost, but not quite, violated.... Even altruism may be expressed by the same kind of ego, like the contracting heart of Boom the ''saint,'' or the pity that the poet feels for his other friend Goom.

And as we go on we feel less reassured by ''the savoir faire of doom'' and by the poet's insistence, sailing his crowded boat on the sea of life, that ''Important people are in it as well.'' Life is not going anywhere except into death, and its minor pleasures of beer and love and sleep are all rehearsals for death. In **''Smilers''** something of the bewilderment of Willy Loman appears in the successful extroverts surrounded by what he is beginning to realize are fixed and glassy grins.... And eventually one begins to see that the ''pond'' has a bottom, familiarly known as death and hell, and that perhaps the ''airborne'' career of the cruising auk, an absurd and extinct bird that nevertheless manages somehow to get above himself, may have something to be said for it. At any rate it, or something like it, inspires Mrs. McGonigle into the stratosphere, frightens Mr. Smith, her protégé, into a coffin-like telephone booth, and sends Mr. Murple into a tree, where, in the curious Orpheus poem at the end of the second part, he sits charming the local frogs and bugs (in contrast to the crow at the end of the first part, who can only choose ''Empty tree for empty tree''). Even a much rarer event, the ''apocalyptic squawk'' of the great dufluflu bird, does not pass wholly unheeded.

If I have not demonstrated how simplicity reverberates, at any rate I have shown that Mr. Johnston is an irresistibly readable and quotable poet. His finest technical achievement, I think, apart from his faultless sense of timing, is his ability to incorporate the language of the suburbs into his own diction. He does not write in the actual vulgate, but he manages to suggest with great subtlety the emotional confusions behind the pretentious diction and vague syntax of ordinary speech:

> Mrs. Belaney has a son
> —Had, I should say, perhaps—
> Who deeds of gallantry has done,
> Him and some other chaps.

Or the exclusiveness of large ideas as their shadows pass over an inarticulate mind:

> And as it happened we agreed
> On many things, but on the need
> Especially of mental strife
> And of a whole new source of life.

It is this controlled portrayal of the ineffectual that gives Mr. Johnston his unique bittersweet flavour, and a ''disconsolate'' tone, to use one of his favourite words, that would be merely coy if it were less detached, or merely brittle if it were more so. (pp. 441-44)

Northrop Frye, in a review of ''The Cruising Auk,'' in University of Toronto Quarterly, *Vol. XXIX, No. 4, July, 1960, pp. 440-44.*

DOROTHY LIVESAY

[George Johnston's] talent, as seen in his successful first book, *The Cruising Auk,* was one of brevity, lightness, and wit. The thrusts and parries were couched in lively quatrains. While these characteristics still reveal themselves in *Home Free,* the effect is much less intense, the impact of wit with word less happily fused. In the shorter poems of 'light verse' the effect is only faintly amusing:

> Plenty to drink and plenty to eat
> is how the country is run
> Hungry and sober is merely confusion and defeat
> besides not being much fun

and so on: seven stanzas of it. A longer satire is **''Bicultural''**, with its pastiche of Eliot:

> Ottawa,
> N'as-tu pas tes grandes saisons,
> Tes longues soirées d'été!
> Puis tes orages, tonneres, terminent tes paresses.
> The lamps tremble all night long in your waters
> After the rain, for the pullulation of your daughters.

This passage is lively and memorable, but not breath-taking. It ends rather lamely on the note:

> Ottawattawattawa
> Busieas place you ever saw
> Busy busy busy busy,
> Life is earnest, life's a tizzy:
> If you are looking for a cure
> Protocol is safe and sure.

Not really very funny! But when the poet is more intensely personal in his wit, the result is more pleasing, as in **''French Kissing''**. And then there are a series of 'mood' poems where the poet, in the manner of Auden or Macneice, ironically considers his role in the flux of modern living: as in **''Old-Fashioned Chords''**, **''Pied à Terre''**.

It should be noted that George Johnston is one of the few Canadian poets who are interested in trying their hand at a longer poem; and perhaps this is because he remains close to the English tradition of Auden, Macneice, and latterly, Philip Larkin. The two long poems in *Home Free,* **''Under the Tree''** and **''Love in High Places''**, are serious poems critical of our political *moeurs* but couched in an engagingly offhand and colloquial language.... But this has been done, often and often before. Where Mr. Johnston is more completely himself is in his tone: the ironic resignation, for instance, with which he handles the theme of capital punishment in **''Under the Tree''**. Thus the poem is not one of propaganda, but of sorrowful comment. As with Leacock's best essays, the poem includes the author in its sallies. He is as responsible as his reader. (pp. 67-9)

There is a similar commitment in **"Love in High Places"**, the story of Sadie and her unexpectedly successful son, Sam, the Ottawa politician. . . .

Such poetry relates George Johnston to the stream of F. R. Scott, Layton in his lighter moods, Alfred Purdy in his; and it is a refreshing contrast to the high seriousness of our lyric poets. Perhaps what Johnston lacks is an intensity of sensuous perception. . . . The result is a certain flabbiness and lack of tension; the pace lags, the rhythm suffers. But in [this book] . . . there is meat to be found; each reader to his taste. (p. 69)

> *Dorothy Livesay, in a review of "Home Free," in The Fiddlehead, No. 70, Winter, 1967, pp. 67-9.*

HUGH MacCALLUM

George Johnston's most recent collection of poetry, **Home Free,** has a considerable range of mood and subject. Several poems continue to expand the enchanting and gossipy world of the poet's private mythology. Mrs. McGonigle (that eternal landlady) and Mr. Murple are back, and so, too, is "poor Edward," whose suffering and defeat remain the source of mingled sadness and humour. ("Edward's asleep where brown stalks fuss and wave / And a squirrel has planted oaks beside his grave.") The girls are back, too, to disturb us with perfume, grace, and pity. There are some splendidly weightless poems, deft and humorous meditations on such subjects as home-made sloe whisky and French kissing. There are also several more substantial comic poems, including one about a cat (**"Lopey"**) which is wholly absorbing in the ease and precision of its description. But there are in addition a number of poems in which the relaxed surface only partially disguises undercurrents of strong feeling. **"Under the Tree,"** for example, is one of the fullest statements Johnston has yet made about the complexities of guilt, and although a bit diffuse, it is a moving celebration of the mingled pain and glory of man's lot.

Johnston writes with such engaging urbanity that one only gradually becomes aware of the vein of melancholy that touches all but the frothiest of his poems. Veterans of loving, we are told, "are wary-eyed and scarred / And they see into everything they see." That suggests both the value of illusion and the value of disillusion, and on the whole the poems do convey a vision of experience that is poignant and bittersweet. There are black moods here, but even the darkest poems contain some comfort—their wry, civilized view of our intransigent ways somehow makes things more bearable. And no matter how bitter the reflection, there is a vitality in the style that is perpetually refreshing. Johnston is an unusually resourceful poet, and he has a versatility reminiscent of W. H. Auden. The reader is kept on his toes by the flexibility of the style: the norm is plain and conversational, but there is a dexterous use of slang and *cliché*, and effects of grandeur are always within easy reach. Rhythm never becomes mechanical, and the poet can flirt with strong sound patterns suggestive of doggerel and nursery rhyme without being trapped by them. There are many small graces for the observant, and rhyme is a continuous source of pleasure. Such vitality lends an air of delight to the most sober reflections. . . . (pp. 359-60)

> *Hugh MacCallum, in a review of "Home Free," in University of Toronto Quarterly, Vol. XXXVI, No. 4, July, 1967, pp. 359-60.*

ALAN PEARSON

Johnston is called a *light poet* (a suspiciously evasive term). Frankly, I didn't like the poems [in **Home Free**]: they were not funny, and clearly many of them were intended to be. Then there was the irritating undertone of petulance; one got the feeling that these poems were safety valves allowing a steam pressure of about a quarter pound per square inch to escape. Before long one begins to sense through the type, the spectral image of a downtrodden fellow, full of peeves, trudging the streets in damp shoes and an old mac.

Why, for instance, should the poet be fretful that a girl (presumably his daughter) should have the audacity to dab perfume on her knees and bosom—yet this is the idea behind **"Musk."** Don't poets love exciting women anymore? Small wonder then I can't take the poet seriously when, in **"No Way Out"** he complains he is "wearied by sin". Actually this poem (by itself) might have succeeded if it hadn't been for the last lines, "But what / I glimpse of unspoiled things brings me to my knees." Ye Gods, in this age of LSD, mini-skirts and hipsterdom, can people still (so romantically) be brought to their knees? I wouldn't have thought so.

In **"The Lily Pond"** twelve lines take a flat-footed walk into Bathos. The poem starts, "Down at the bottom of Third Avenue / Ottawa has a lily pond on view, / " Not a thrilling beginning. It ends "And on the benches round it and beyond / Old men sit, and pregnant mothers sit / Taking their time, and making the most of it."

"Bliss" starts out, "The less said about Edward's slut the better." SLUT—what Victorian melodrama is this? I begin to wonder if the next poem will be a reproach to someone for winking at a chorus-girl. The poem ends:

> Bliss is nice, but a little bit will do;
> Edward has had too much, and his slut has too:
> Only to see the hoof marks in their eyes
> And hear them wheeze would make a fellow wise.

Well, well, well, I may be going out on a limb, but I'm pretty sure Edward knew what he was doing.

There are false alarms here too. **"French Kissing"** is one. I really expected, at least SOMETHING—but what I got was an empty box. No, no luscious description follows, he merely refers to it and uses it to make the observation that it leads to ". . . diapers, runny noses, parent-teachers associations . . ." I don't CARE.—this isn't the stuff of poetry.

Johnston senses this. Somewhere he says, "I know / That life is earnest, time is tough, / But me, I'm not, I'm soft and slow / Look I'm not asking half enough." Amen. **"Veterans"** is the best poem in the book, but that's a poor percentage out of a total of 57. Light poetry, if it attempts to be funny should have "bite"; if the poet is trying to write real poetry, it should gain the reader's sympathy by the soundness of the poet's response. Within this frame of reference **Home Free** fails, for me. (pp. 185-86)

> *Alan Pearson, in a review of "Home Free," in The Canadian Forum, Vol. XLVII, No. 562, November, 1967, pp. 185-86.*

GEORGE WHALLEY

In **The Cruising Auk** a universe of desire and muted wonder is fleshed out with swift but dreamy strokes. No narrative can be inferred to bind Edward to Sadie, or to his death by drowning; we could not prophesy the amorous fate of Sadie, or of Elaine's disruptive femininity (in or out of a bikini); we have no way of formulating the philosophy of Mr Murple or his dog. A girl, singing to herself from a boat, makes crooked music on the waters, a little Pentecostal, certainly out of tune; she has betrayed and forgotten her many lovers, is untouched and unchanged by the "nights of splendour" she has brought them. Edward's hat, "moving on the water's face", makes towards the sea, and the boats pass up and down the river and through the bridge.... Mr Murple, hitherto earthbound, is suddenly Orpheus—and we are not surprised.... So disposed in psychic space the figures imply a dream, a world, a garden entered under a guest's privilege.... The unifying principle is the activity of an ironic intelligence, a clear glance, an embracing compassion. My memory of the book is of something allusively single. Turning back to the text, some of the poems one by one may seem occasional, or "light", and a few don't put their feet exactly right. Yet out of materials whimsically diverse and light-heartedly random, materials of a strange and vulnerable fragility, a substantial world has been constructed. There is no escaping the moral fervour; yet the poet, responsive and watchful, always withdrawn, does not hector with earnest counsels or utter superior judgments through the mask of satire. We respond instantly, beguiled by the simplicity of a candid host who—a little eccentric and absent-minded—refrains even from afflicting us with geniality.

Home Free is a different matter and I don't see how it could have been otherwise. The world of *The Cruising Auk* is not only single but complete: to have designed extensions, gazebos, and outworks would have placed too great a burden upon a structure so delicately poised. If *Home Free* is less consistent than the first book, it gives clear signs of exploring deliberately a new manner and a wider ambience. About half the poems in this book are written in clear-cut stanzaic forms that give edge to irony. A new metric provides colloquial fluency and pace in other poems; and both manners cross-fertilize each other, the flexibility sometimes relaxing the stanzaic sharpness, the echoes of definite metre and rhyme giving unobtrusive rigour to fluency. Two poems are of much greater length than anything in *The Cruising Auk,* and in these George Johnston addresses himself—as he had not done before—to public themes of present concern. The short stanzaic poems are at once more relaxed and more dense in texture, and only occasionally—usually when couplets are used—do they take refuge in the emotional and verbal approximateness that the tradition of light verse permits. (Avowedly satiric pieces—"**Bicultural**" and "**The Royal Commission**"—lose points through some rather permissive marksmanship.) Generally the shorter poems are more personal than before, and less playful. And almost all the figures from the dreamscape have departed. Mr Murple and Mrs McGonigle appear only once, together; they have become emblems, like the Mrs Porter to whom the sounds of horns and motors bring Sweeney in the spring. Edward in three poems returns in his old self—bemused, sinning, self-destroying; but when he is linked to Sadie in marriage he moves out of the world of myth and their son is to be seen under the harsh unallusive light of journalistic biography.

Of the two long poems, I much prefer "**Under the Tree**". "**Love in High Places**" can be seen as an extension in space and time of "**Music on the Water**" (*The Cruising Auk*). A freely evolved parody of a conceivable ballad-stanza gives Audenish sharpness to the fall of words and encourages reflective comment; it offers plenty of scope, for irony, sorrowful lyricism, satiric sharpness, narrative, moody comment. But the

story and moral place too heavy demands on the poetic resources, as though an epigram were asked to carry the weight of a novel. For the poem covers two generations and there is some doubt whether it intends an incisive vision of a little group of persons or the framework for a more generalized social and satiric comment. As the poem grows it seems to lose its initial direction and fineness of sensitivity and, though the emphasis shifts more to inclusive comment and reflection, the deep compassion that shapes and colours just about everything George Johnston's pen touches slips away into a mood of weary disgust. Stan is son enough of his father that he "Reminded Sadie of Edward and the dead years—" and "Made her choke"; but his stature is much smaller, his allusiveness reduced. Through his own neuter passivity and the incubus machinations of his mother, he springs fullblown into the stock figure of the blind self-seeking man—rudderless, subservient, cowardly, deceitful, abortive. Edward could at least see his own habit of betrayal.... Stan seems incapable of anything as positive as sentimentality. His central position in the poem would be easier to understand and accept if he were firmly related to the poignant opening section. Sadie, exhausted by the emptiness of her life with Edward, tries to kill herself; and the episode and its lyrical aftermath is drawn with harrowing precision. Then by abrupt transition, Edward has vanished and Sadie assumes the pitiless and parasitic role of the possessive mother, her womanhood obliterated by her terrible ambition to manage and organize her son into a worldly but hollow success—a success which he neither deserves nor savours and which by definition she has made herself incapable of making her own fulfilment. To say that George Johnston has not successfully solved the formal and dramatic problems that the theme poses is perhaps to say that he is not capable of the savage contempt and passionate disgust that would shape such a theme to self-declarative form. The strength at the beginning is clear, where compassion rules; later, when brutality is demanded, structure and precision falter.

"**Love in High Places**" is the last poem but one in the book; "**Under the Tree**" is the first. If "**Love in High Places**" is a modern parable with a moral too near the surface, "**Under the Tree**"—on capital punishment—is a meditation of such sustained ardour that it never lapses into propaganda. The poem is in six movements, each with its own tone and form. The opening states that our implication in a guilt for which we are not technically responsible binds us together in a disgraceful fellowship we have not deliberately chosen.... Then the tree itself—as wood, skilfully hewed out, beautiful—and the limestone of the prison: and the judge.... (But I could wish that the judge were not also a parody of the successful unrooted man whose life, arrested years ago, is no more than an expedient compromise.) A lyrical movement follows for the child's world of wonder where "so long as childhood lasts" there is safety—as, in default of innocence, there is not for us—in the way that "every watched road has a secret way out." Then the hanging is considered from the fundamentalist position as "a prayerful thing", but a recollection of the furtive and senseless squalor of the murder undermines facile rationalization. In an interior scene the murderer's aunt and young friends, unable to commend either the crime or the sentence, are powerless to mitigate the punishment even if they knew how—there is no time. The sixth movement picks from the opening lines of the poem the key-word *waiting:* everything waits, numbed and aimless, for the final constellation of objects and people that will comprise the event of execution, the execution of the event; they are waiting, time suspended, for the last and conclusive item in the pattern, the condemned man. The poem closes in a prayer that the earth in its huge compassion will take to itself even our guilt; and the verse broadens to a noble and afflicting cadence. . . . The overt theme is hanging; but the poem meditates upon the even larger reality of our complicity in society and in law that protects society, and the impotence of the individual in that necessary implication; for neither the plea of impotence, nor even the prospect of social or political action, will ever resolve our personal responsibility.

The shorter poems can to some extent be seen in thematic groups though they are not so definitely arranged. Poems about places and creatures have a rich and elegiac sweetness, a little Georgian perhaps, affectionate and intent without affectation—**"Fields"**, **"Honey"**, **"The Siberian Olive Tree"**, **"Windy Streets"**, **"The Huntress"**, **"Spring Moon"**, **"The Lily Pond"**, and sharpest of all **"Sloe Whisky"**. These are all acutely perceived, happily turned, imagist at times in their concentration, envigorated by unexpected turns of grave wit. (**"Beside the Sea"**, however, seems not to establish its angle of vision crisply enough or its way of going; and if the cat-poem **"Lopey"** moves too exuberantly from the peculiar individual to the *genus* cat, it reminds us what a stern master Hilaire Belloc is in fitting nervous octosyllabic couplets to the world of animals and children.) Three poems on love are among the best—**"Veterans"** (on the "seventy times seven kinds of loving"), **"Musk"**, and **"Us Together"**—the last two of an enchanting half-playful delicacy. Certain poems of a meditative kind are more personal than anything in *The Cruising Auk*—**"The Bargain Sale"**, **"The Creature's Claim"**, **"No Way Out"**, **"The Old Man"**: these are important in establishing a presence that elsewhere seems deliberately withheld. **"Pied à Terre"** reminds me of **"Love of the City"**—one of the most distinctive poems in *The Cruising Auk*—and provides a counter-image to Stan's "place among the Pre-Cambrian rocks" in **"Love in High Places"**.

The book closes with a series of poems that bring Edward and Sadie back, at least in name, from their earlier poetic existence; but three diverse poems, two of them bitter, intervene—**"Daisy"**, **"A Night-Piece to Mrs Treed"**, and **"Ballad of Jarvis Street"**—to destroy any impression of an Edward cycle. **"Bliss"**, a comment on Edward and "Edward's slut", is an unforgiving poem, though incisive. The title poem **"Home Free"** restores Edward to that mystery of damnation he had reserved for himself in *The Cruising Auk*. . . . **"Multitude"**, in praise of Sadie and her polyerotic verminous kindness, joins with **"Bliss"** to prepare the ground for **"Love in High Places"**: there is no fantasy here and pity has been stretched beyond breaking point by embodiments of aimless and deliquescent mortality. But the last poem in the book, **"Bed-Time"**, recovers the characteristic manner in which restraint is the mark of seriousness and the lightness of touch encompasses in a gesture of ironic regret and simple pity the gift of life, the fact of death. (pp. 85-90)

This is probably a transitional book, but it is in no sense tentative: in modes not attempted before by George Johnston, the achievement is substantial, skilful, and emotionally exact. The extended technical resources broaden and establish more solidly his own tunes and his own vision—distinctive, quaint, witty, serious, recognizable, unashamedly idiosyncratic. I shall turn to his two books of poems with pleasure and admiration, delighting in all that most amazes me for its subtle and effortless precision, its unobtrusive technical skill, the absence of rhetoric, the grave unpretentious wisdom, the compassionate gaiety. (p. 90)

> *George Whalley, "George Johnston," in* Canadian Literature, *No. 35, Winter, 1968, pp. 85-90.*

LAWRENCE W. JONES

George Johnston is surely an anomaly among the present generation of Canadian poets. His work defies classification, refuses to fit any of the dominant patterns such as that of metaphysical exploration (as exemplified by Margaret Avison) or that of verbal and intellectual subtlety (as exemplified by Stanley Cooperman), yet in its own curious way it is every bit as effective. It is also, for the most part, a more truly "Canadian" poetry than that of his contemporaries in the images it evokes and the way of life it describes (a fact which must please Mr. Johnston's militantly pro-Canadian colleagues at Carleton University).

Although much of *The Cruising Auk* (1959) and *Home Free* (1966) is about the city of Ottawa and its people, George Johnston consistently finds elements in our country's capital (as does Raymond Souster in Ontario's capital) which are symptomatic of some confusing, often sickening tendencies in urban life. It is this which places his work outside the pale of the merely "regional". Evidence of this is perhaps the very popularity of *The Cruising Auk,* which, for a collection of poetry, has sold rather widely across Canada and is presently going into its seventh printing.

However, for those of us who know George Johnston it is perhaps difficult to square away his incisive poetic comments, his function as a cultural seismograph, with the man himself. For he is both a scholar of some repute (his translation of the Old Norse *Saga of Gísli* was published in 1963) and a Quaker whose views on pacifism are both well-known and well-exemplified by his life. The scholarship would seem inimical to the folksy charm exuded by his lyrics (although not to the starched black humour which underlies them); the pacifism, although it appears in many of his poems (**"Under the Tree"** in *Home Free* is the best example, **"War on the Periphery"** and **"The Hero's Kitchen"** in *The Cruising Auk* being others), would seem out of keeping with his unrelenting attack upon certain types of people. But Johnston manages to avoid either unsophistication or blatant indictment by a technique most often used in fiction—that of the microcosm.

The world he portrays, taken *in toto,* is a self-enclosed one. The people who populate it and the actions which take place in it are *reflections* of the real world, as though the poet were making his observations from the surface of a pool, which means that things are often grossly distorted, grotesque, absurd. Like the goldfish in **"Life from a Goldfish Bowl"**, the poet himself "notes the goings-on with goggle face / Of all the world around about in air", and draws for us a serio-comic picture of its insanities. I would like to look briefly at this microcosmic world Johnston details, at the almost Swiftian satire which arises from his portrayal (which has its undercurrent of serious commentary) and finally at the peculiar style the poet employs in order to frame his lyrical pictures.

The first striking thing I notice about Johnston's world is the presence in it of a great number of weird people. Their names are chosen with Dickensian care: Mr. Goom, Mr. Boom, Mrs. McGonigle, Mr. Murple, Miss Descharmes, Mr. Byer, Dr. Gay, Joad—the list seems endless. And most of them seem to be less individuals than personifications of traits which belong to identifiable groups in our society: middle-class businessmen, spinsters in their second childhood, giggling young things, bachelors who seem to be eternally out "on the town". In **"Escape"**, for example, we hear of a belated affair between the conscience-stricken Mr. Smith and the vulture-like widow Mrs. McGonigle:

> Fleeing from Mrs. McGonigle, Mr. Smith
> Took refuge in a public telephone booth
> Whence he rang, as he always did, forthwith,
> The gospel tabernacle, home of Truth.
>
> Mrs. McGonigle meanwhile searched the streets
> Asking herself as she did so why she did.
> His life with her she knew was a nest of sweets
> From which he beat it, now and again, and hid.

The poet, tongue-in-cheek, sums up the situation neatly:

> Truly a man is never lonely here
> And least of all at the moment of wild escape
> In the telephone booth, a moment of bliss and fear
> Between this world and the next, between fire and rape.

The last line of this poem is evidence of a technique George Johnston constantly uses in evoking his microcosmic world—the inflation or elevation of the inconsequential and seemingly ordinary. The denizens of his world become mock heroes and heroines. In **"Fun"** we clearly see a parallel with the story of Snow White; Elaine "sleeps in her maiden bed" while across the street the seven boarders dream about her. (pp. 28-30)

Some of the poems' titles even reflect this mock-heroic dimension. In **"Queens and Duchesses"** the subject is the promiscuous life of one Miss Belaney who "doesn't remember who kissed her last / But he did it good, all right" but around whose head shines a "haze of gold".... In these cases and so many others we are confronted with recognizable character-types whose attitudes toward life are satirized, never directly condemned.

The activities in which these delightful people engage, although utterly human, even mundane, are also blown out of proportion. In **"Art and Life"** the poet describes the artistic ablutions of Sadie McGonigle who has

> spent the afternoon with suds and water
> And creams and mud; her lines and points are put
> And every inch is tender to the view—
> Elegant work of art and artist too.

but who has dressed up only to be undressed:

> Sweet love, that takes a master piece like this
> And rumples it and tumbles it about,
> Why can he not be happy with a kiss?
> He turns the shimmering object inside out
> And all for life, that's enemy to art.
> Now where's your treasure, little scented heart? ...

The same kind of satire can be seen in **"Mrs. McGonigle on Decorum," "Home Again"** and **"Dust,"** and it brings to mind the sardonic humor with which James Thurber always viewed domestic life.

Significantly, much of the activity so satirized throughout Johnston's poetry is city-related. For, as I mentioned earlier, the city is really the cosmic entity which the poetry reflects. Occasionally this is obvious, as in **"The Alderman's Day in the City"** and **"Love of the City"**. In the former the fairy-tale pattern of the poem almost, but not quite, covers up the fact that this lazy city official is lining his pockets at the city's expense.... In the latter the poet makes a more general comment about the artificiality and the suffocating nature of urban life. (pp. 30-2)

Clearly, there is a serious side to all of this Thurber-like light-hearted satire. There is always a meaningful comment made

by effective satire or parody, and it seems to me that George Johnston is very concerned about the passivity of people in the urban *milieu,* about the non-commital nature of people's lives in the city. There is a general feeling of helplessness conveyed in Johnston's descriptions of his McGonigles and Murples, a feeling which comes across openly only infrequently, as it does in **"Flight,"** where the poet watches a crow taking off from one barren tree in search of another.... Much the same feeling is articulated in the final stanza of **"In It"**, where the poet declares:

> The world is a pond and I'm in it,
> In it up to my neck;
> Important people are in it too,
> It's deeper than this, if we only knew;
> Under we go, any minute—
> A swirl, some bubbles, a fleck....

The submission to the "destructive element" which is implied here may come in the form of routine drudgery which holds us captive in the city's grasp. This is the problem with **"The Queen of Lop"** who

> works all day at a big machine that lops and lops and
> lops;
> At five o'clock she does her face and the big machine it stops;
> Home again on a public bus she goes to her little flat,
> Cooks a chop and forgets the lop and the wash-up and all that.

Even in her dreams, as the poet tells us later in the poem, when she tries to find some vicarious excitement in "a boat on the ocean dark and queer" she finds that "the big machine is aboard the boat"—there is no escape. Not only is there this routine of the work-a-day world, but there is the smug complacency of the settled routine of marriage, as we see in **"Domestic"**:

> A man should build himself a house and put himself inside
> And fill it full of furniture, and get himself a bride
> To fill it full of cooking smells and pickle smells and wit
> And all in pleasure breed it full and make a nest of it.

The repetition of "full" here only serves to emphasize the emptiness of the way of life being described. Likewise, the mock-heroic nature of Johnston's people serves to point up the unheroic, unchallenging nature of their lives, which is perhaps the whole point of the satire.

In any case, if this reading of much of *The Cruising Auk* is correct, we might ask whether the poet suggests any alternative to the frothy existence he portrays. While it is not the poet's function to offer solutions to society's problems (indeed, poets are notoriously bad at that), I think George Johnston suggests at least one possibility: that we need to consciously seek our *own* freedom from slavish routine, perhaps by the use of our imagination. In **"This Way Down"** the poet admits that "my roof is wide to Heaven" and asks the vital question: "Why am I not then airborne?" This is where the cruising auk of the title poem comes in. The bird is simply a symbol of the imagination which has freed itself; his virtue is that he *is* airborne, and this is why we must "rejoice in him, cruising there". We must strive to extricate ourselves from the life which the bird sees as he looks down upon us.... To change this life, the poet seems to be saying (as does Raymond Souster in "Good Fortune" in *The Colour of the Times*) we must take charge of our own lives rather than waiting passively for something to happen. (pp. 32-4)

Ways in which we may exercise our whys and hows are suggested in some of the more serious lyrics in **Home Free** (a book which has unaccountably not lived up to the promise or popularity of its predecessor). In the stylistically-superb **"Under the Tree,"** for example, we are exhorted to recognize our complicity with the judge and the rest of society when a man is condemned to hang. "We hardly know each other," says the poet, "But here we meet, under the hanging tree." In subsequent sections of the poem various individuals and groups are described—the judge himself, religious people, the condemned man's relatives and friends—and we can see how each of them avoids having to *think* about capital punishment. The religious folk justify the hanging by soliciting the will of God, by placing their emphasis upon the "mean and casual" murder itself and not upon what led up to it; the man's aunt and his erstwhile cronies drown any serious considerations in small talk, in "notions soaked in beer." Finally, the poet says, we must consider the paradox that although the Earth is the "pit whence we were dug" it is also by necessity "the garden in which we grope / For love."

In the book's title poem, **"Home Free,"** Edward is given a chance to break the bonds of a deadening life, but refuses to take the chance. . . . What Edward cannot understand is that the world is a garden only if you make it so in spite of the ugliness. . . . Edward does not feel himself part of what the poet calls elsewhere (in **"The Creature's Claim"**) the "creatureliness of Earth", and so in the final poem in *Home Free* we find him "asleep where brown stalks fuss and wave / And a squirrel has planted oaks beside his grave."

Although the poetry of *Home Free* is not generally as effective as that of *The Cruising Auk*—Johnston seems much more at home when dealing with his little microcosmic world of Murples—all of the poetry is consistent in style. Unlike other Canadian poets, Johnston eschews experimentation with rhyme and phraseology. But the very presence of rhyme and regular metre gives emphasis to the routine he often describes. Occasionally he resorts to couplets, as in **"A Little Light"** in *The Cruising Auk;* but most common is the rhyme a-b-a-b and its variations, which is apt for what Johnston has to convey. Where the poet is most inventive (and here his vast knowledge of the history of the language is useful) is in the matter of diction. He is fond of creating words to match sounds—as seen in the "kechunk" of anchored boats in **"Poor Edward"** or the "kaplink" of falling hairpins in **"Dust"**, and of simply creating words to fill his lyrical needs: "gogglesful" in **"Elaine in a Bikini"** and "emplaned" in **"Dust"**. Often, slang is used to give a clearer idea of the level of life being described: "neither I suppose I ain't" (**"A Saint"**), "no dice" (**"Domestic"**) and "shot down" (**"On the Porch"**) are examples.

I began by saying that George Johnston is an anomaly among Canadian poets. But as I have tried to point out, his is a unique kind of poetry with its own values, with its own valid statement to make. Taken together, the poems of *The Cruising Auk* remind us of the urban dilemma we are faced with and with which we must cope. The symbolic people and events in George Johnston's little world shed light on their counterparts in our real world. And we are forced to ask ourselves, as we watch the auk cruising overhead: "Why am *I* not then airborne?" (pp. 34-6)

Lawrence W. Jones, "The Cruising Auk and the World Below," in Canadian Literature, No. 48, Spring, 1971, pp. 28-36.

STEPHEN SCOBIE

Many of the poems [in *Happy Enough: Poems, 1935-1972*] deal with public subject matter, and comparatively few of them are

concerned with the poet's private personality; yet Johnston's wit speaks of the public world in a uniquely private way. His satire is informed by a whimsical humour which extends affectionately towards all the characters he creates; it is a genial satire, without malice. It achieves a poised and balanced tone, which can embrace both humorous and serious subject-matter, preserving each quality intact.

The values of such a poetry are not, perhaps, immediately striking; and read in bulk, Johnston's poetry might threaten to become dull. But taken slowly, each poem measured and relished at leisure, he provides a refreshing alternative to much contemporary Canadian poetry. Certainly, he deserves recognition as a fully serious poetic artist, rather than as the odd, old-fashioned creator of a few good jokes.

Most readers of Johnston's early poetry will have their own favourites among the humorous verse of that period: the **"Noctambule"** of Mr. Murple's dog, **"The Bulge"** unknowably growing in Bridget, the biculturalism of **"French Kissing"** in Ottawa. The present collection reprints in their entirety the now unavailable volumes *The Cruising Auk* (1959) and *Home Free* (1966), and it is very welcome and useful to have these poems so cheaply and attractively available. . . . But most critical interest now will centre on the section of newer poems at the beginning of the book.

Wit is still very much in evidence, as in the conclusion of the delightful address to a stewardess on a **"Nonstop Jetflight to Halifax"**: "Never mind, I say. Sit down / beside me. Perhaps on me." But most of the poems are less openly comic, and the darker concerns visible in *Home Free* are here to the fore, as in the remarkable poem about death, **"Then Oblique Stroke Now."** . . . (pp. 310-11)

Many of the poems also use much shorter lines and less regular stanzaic forms; they concentrate on the precise registering of physical impressions in an almost Imagist manner. . . . The movement of these poems is slow, measured, intense: but still with a sense of quiet assurance, of working out of the centre of a total cultural experience rather than from the edges. The dust jacket describes the tone as "mellow," but I doubt if that is really the right word. It is assured, certainly, but its very restraint hints at times of the depth and disturbingness of the experiences described. This is very evident in the title poem, [**"Happy Enough"**]: the words "Happy enough" are actually grimly ironical, for the poem (bravely challenging, and I think surviving, the inevitable comparison to Layton's "Bull Calf") describes the slaughter of a heifer. Here the dislocations of regular verse form, however restrained they might appear by the standards of more experimental poets, produce a deeply disturbing effect. . . .

These poems are best at short length: the **"Convocation Address"** is too long for the verse form, and too loosely organized in its wit. But most of the new poems display a sharp, tight precision of language which extends the range of Johnston's accomplishment. He is still a "witty" poet, still recognizably the creator of Mr. Murple's dog; but *Happy Enough* displays in new ways the incisiveness of his vision, and the seriousness of his wit. (p. 311)

Stephen Scobie, in a review of "Happy Enough: Poems, 1935-1972," in Queen's Quarterly, Vol. LXXX, No. 2, Summer, 1973, pp. 310-11.

JONATHAN GALASSI

The Canadian poet George Johnston's *Happy Enough* includes the contents of two earlier volumes, *The Cruising Auk* (1959) and *Home Free* (1966), as well as thirty-two new poems by a master of colloquial style. Johnston's earlier compositions were pure, unassuming rhymes, simple-seeming musings of a sympathetic intelligence. His latest poems are syntactically freer, more impressionistic, and exhibit the serenity of high maturity. All of them bear Johnston's unmistakable mark in their display of whimsy, good-humored self-disparagement and a Protestant sense of the pains that necessarily accompany joy. In a placid world subliminally "whining its unimaginable threat" this middle-class man "of the town" makes the lives of his everyday characters—the Murples, Sadie, Edward, the poet's "aunts"—breathe through the unexpected illuminating perfect word. Johnston has spent a quiet lifetime teaching English and "knowing my dark"; with the approach of age, "my time now transcendental", he has made a "pretend peace, / peaceful almost as peace" with his gods and demons. It's a poetry of limits and depths, of the profound ordinary. When Johnston widens his scope, he's less acute; his longish poems don't quite attain that remarkable intensity and cleanness of detail which grace the brief ones. But when he's dead on, as he is time after time, his poems are small masterpieces, worthy of being memorized and recited to one's children. (p. 118)

> *Jonathan Galassi, "Dealing with Tradition," in Poetry, Vol. CXXIII, No. 2, November, 1973, pp. 113-19.*

D. G. JONES

Trying to get a quick line on George Johnston's poetry, I once said it lies somewhere between John Betjeman and John Berryman. One could also mention Auden and Eliot and Edgar Lear. The title poem of the collected volume *Happy Enough: Poems 1935-1972* sounds a bit like Robert Creeley. But this kind of bench mark is not very helpful. It makes most sense to look at Johnston's work within a Canadian context.

One thing that Johnston shares with most of the poets mentioned is his ironic stance, toward the world around him and toward himself.

Once, when my voice gave out at an academic conference, George Johnston was kind enough to read my paper for me. The paper was partly about Souster's pedestrian muse, his deliberate adoption of a figure more like Snow's Walking Woman than like Milton's Urania, and his chosen persona or role as an *eiron*. Johnston is an *eiron* too.

The self-effacing eiron can be irritating, indeed insufferable. He has a tendency never to stick his neck out so he can be hit, never to climb high enough to fall, to be forever superior because he can say, we honest worms will be around long after you blow-hards are dead and gone. Like Socrates, he only knows that you know nothing. Like Souster, he knows nothing, except what is normal, natural, good and right.

This strikes me as a typical Canadian posture, all the more irritating if you recognize yourself in it. And it occurs to me that Canadians typically play the *eiron* to the American *alazon*, the loud-mouth know-it-all or big shot. As Frye suggests, they are basic roles in the structure of much comedy.

Irving Layton makes a dramatic entry on the Canadian scene as an *alazon*. (His friend Neitzsche had no use for Christian meekness or for Socratic irony.) Layton is always sticking out his neck, and other things, and daring you to do something about it. He adopts heroic and melodramatic postures. Irving Layton's "The Bull Calf" and George Johnston's **"Happy Enough"** centre on roughly the same event, the killing of a

bull or heifer. Where Layton ends melodramatically, identifying with the calf, weeping and thinking of Richard II, Johnston ends identifying with the farmer and his toothache, saying:

> Get it fixed Fred it
> hurts just knowing how it hurts.

Both Johnston and Souster eschew the heroic pose, adopt the persona of the ordinary man, modest, domestic and suburban, with memories and occasional glimpses of the rural countryside. This is especially true of Johnston for whom the great events of life, like war, are said to lie on the periphery. . . . The people in Souster's world also lead small, ordinary lives, but they are by contrast often more violent.

Johnston's sense of the eiron's role is quite different from Souster's, in style as well as in substance. A Souster reading is less than a performance, more like a man deciphering an item in the newspaper for the benefit of his wife. There is something there on the page in black and white, a fact that is presumably not to be disturbed by style. Johnston is a man who reads poems through glasses with no glass in them from a book with blank pages. He insists that it is a performance, poetry not reporting, a game with formal conventions. Like Sadie McGonigle's daughter, a poem is "in a state of art from head to foot." Souster likes to give the illusion that his poems are in a state of nature. He avoids obviously poetic diction, syntactical inversions, certain kinds of wit, and rhyme. Johnston indulges them freely. (pp. 81-2)

Beside Souster, he may appear academic or simply frivolous. Certainly he is often having more fun, and is often funnier. But this is deliberate and serious. We may hear echoes of the seventeenth century, of Herrick or Cowley or of a later mode of mock-heroic poetry that adjusts the epic and the mythical to the banal and domestic. But says Johnston, let us recognize the fact that that is just what happens in life, which is no less conventional than literature. So we have Mrs. Belaney, unfastened and happy and slightly drunk. (p. 82)

Win a little, lose a little. Mrs. Belaney is not heroic; neither is her fate tragic. But for that very reason she is caught and defined in terms of everyday morality. She is happy, and bad. (The discrimination might escape Layton.) Littleness diminishes both the horror and the glory, as Mrs. McGonigle suggests to the young woman who might find marriage demeaning, frustrating, quite disillusioning. . . . Johnston is something of a humorist for whom the little is his chosen field, but for whom a right sense of decorum allows you to see the big in the little, and more striking, perhaps, the ironic shifts in value or in the conventions that apply when you shift from the relatively big to the relatively small, or vice versa—a kind of quantum theory of morality.

In his best poems, Johnston anchors his perspective firmly and precisely in the quotidian, but gradually makes us aware of the whole range of the imagination, of life itself, shading off from that precise centre. For example, **"Eating Fish"** begins neatly in the home or in the Travellers' Hotel. . . . But the "ancient fishy smell permeating man" leads to a much broader perspective. (pp. 82-3)

The ironic distancing is achieved through a nice play of ambiguity, the slightly mannered use of everyday words and images, the sudden shift in meaning of the language or imagery that reveals at least two perspectives at work. **"Elaine in a Bikini"** begins very close to the vulgar.

> Mrs. McGonigle's boys enjoy the sun
> By gogglesful, and stare along the beach
> Whose innocence is almost all Elaine,
> Almost but not quite, all.

Felicitously she comes in every eye
Bending her knees and tender finger nails
While the incalculable strings gather in
　　What's hers to gather in.

There is the fun of "gogglesful" with its suggestion of "ogle" and its echo of "McGonigle." There is the surprise bending of "tender fingernails" which suggests affectation, a calculated grace, or art. There is a whole series of ambiguous suggestions in "innocence", the innocent natural world, the not so innocent flesh, the beach innocent of all but Elaine, innocent of all but her bikini, the incalculable strings.

Elaine's world is closer to Hollywood than Olympus. The narrator is no Paris, any more than Mrs. McGonigle's boys are the elders on the wall of Troy; yet in her effect on them, and more especially on the old sea that "fumbles about the naked afternoon as though in paradise", Elaine may take on just the faintest trace of Helen. And the larger aura grows in the last verse, as the incalculable strings multiply and become the various strings of morality and desire, youth and age, Eros and Thanatos.

I am felicitous too on the bright shore
Waiting for darkness with the roving boys
And all but gathered in myself with strings,
　　What's mine to gather in.

All these poems except the first come from *The Cruising Auk,* which makes up the third and last section of the collected *Happy Enough: Poems 1935-1972.* Now *The Cruising Auk* was published in 1959, but if we look at the poems from the point of view of 1935, when Canadian poetry was still dominated by Roberts, Carman, Lampman and Scott, we may be struck by one thing: they are poems about the city and the people who live in the city. More particularly, we might suggest, it is Lampman's city of Ottawa. With the exception of the quite different poet, Klein, no one has cultivated such a particular urban world to such an extent as have Johnston and Souster. Unlike Souster, and again with the possible exception of Klein, unlike any other poet of that generation, to say nothing of Lampman, Johnston cultivates the city with affection. In this perspective, the very title of one of the first poems in *The Cruising Auk* is startling, "Love of the City." . . . It is not, as for Lampman, a beautiful facade, within which you find frustration and violence; nor, as for Souster, a cage or trap. Johnston's city appears humane, despite the irony that it is regarded from the point of view of death, and perhaps because it is so viewed. (pp. 83-4)

Johnston is almost alone in providing us with an image of the city as a humane community. He has managed to do so by virtue of his own humane acceptance of the ordinary, in himself and in the world around him, by virtue of his ironic view of life as a rather poignant comedy, his nice sense of the working of convention, and his capacity to invent an almost Dickensian cast of characters who reflect a very Canadian middle class world, a world of English, Irish, Scotch and very occasionally French origin: Mr. Murple, Mrs. Belaney, Mrs. McGonigle, Mrs. McWhirter and Mrs. Beleek, Miss Descharmes, Sadie and Edward and Andrew and Elaine. As becomes especially evident in the longer "Love in High Places" from *Home Free,* dealing with Sadie McGonigle's son Stan, his care in public life and his discovery of his girl friend Gert, these characters reflect particularly the world of Ottawa—Lampman's Ottawa. They do for Ottawa what poems like Klein's "Monsieur Gaston" do for Montreal, and even more thoroughly. They fill a very real lacuna in the imaginative landscape of Canadian po-

etry. Johnston articulates something that existed. It was not a big world nor a strong world. And when we move into the second generation and explore that world in detail in "Love in High Places", its confusion and drabness, its mediocrity and sham—its lack of any real vision or necessity—makes it simply sad. (pp. 84-5)

As we move into *Home Free* and *Happy Enough,* the ironic brilliance fades, the characters become more marginal or fragmentary, their stylized world begins to disintegrate. It gives way before direct satirical comments on Ottawa or a Royal Commission or Remembrance Day; before more straightforward occasional, descriptive and elegiac poems about actual friends and acquaintances. It dissolves in the dark that was an ever present element in the first volume but that grows deeper and, perhaps, more intimate, as in the very first poem of *Happy Enough.* Here this is no sharp irony, but an attractive simplicity.

Everyone gone away
feasting but Nora, Mark
and me. Neither do we
stay put. It is getting dark . . .

There is an orange moon and bits of fields somewhere in the haze; the children race ahead. . . . (pp. 85-6)

As the urban world fades it is Lampman's world that emerges more and more strongly, that of Fred's farm, Fred's apple wine or Farmer Elliott's bees, that of the rocky coast or islands in the sea. Once again, it is in the natural world that the writer finds some kind of enduring reality, the "ongoing," the elemental. It is in life's commerce with the earth, as in the case of Elliot's bees. . . . It is the natural and not the conventional world that Johnston is drawn to, that increasingly claims him, as in "The Creature's Claim":

I brood over the creatureliness of Earth
This gibbous night, fifty years from my birth,
And feel her claim, not on my yielded life
But on my heart, cut out with a stone knife.

The bird in *The Cruising Auk* was a rather far-fetched or bizarre symbol of a freer, larger, more imaginative life, that both mocks and consoles the earth-bound Mr. Murple and the speaker. In the parallel poem from the second volume, "Music in the Air," the auk gives way to the more familiar duck, whose quack in the night is more direct and more disturbing in its impact. (p. 86)

Finally, Johnston does not want the city, its friendly rooms, its great roof of pity, its modest life drowned in conventions. Finally, like Lampman or Scott, it is wilderness he wants; like Layton or Newlove he would lie down with earth. . . . In "Pied à Terre" he rejects the great urban hotel, the company of men, the fastidiousness and sweetness of women, its comfort, its security, its delight and its art. He has another address:

An island with a cave, burnt-out fires and bones;
　No-one can get at me there, it is my own,
　No-one lets it to me, I just own it,
And I can be cruel as nature there, and alone.

Johnston's later poems do not, I think, constitute as striking or as original an achievement as those in *The Cruising Auk.* But their direction is reassuring, both to the reader of Canadian poetry and, I think, to Johnston himself, in that they bring us back to a kind of true north in Canadian poetry and Canadian experience, to something that doesn't have to be maintained by a delicate ironic balancing act, to something elemental and indeed fierce.

In their diction, rhythm and overall tone, I find such relatively simple poems as **"Outdoors"** and **"Happy Enough"** as satisfying as any George Johnston has produced. And a brief poem like **"October"** may not be of any great note, but it connects with the world of Lampman and I suspect with something authentic and ultimate in Canadian life. (pp. 86-7)

D. G. Jones, "George Johnston," in Canadian Literature, *No. 59, Winter, 1974, pp. 81-7.*

PETER SANGER

Ask Again contains . . . gentle, deceptively casual poems ranging in form from clipped syllabics, which slip into free verse when conversational tone requires, to intricate constructions of eye rhyme and off-rhyme, wittily stopped at each strophe's end by spondees. . . . Part of the delight taken in any Johnston poem (as in the poetry of Stevie Smith) has always arisen from seeing this kind of match between what is said and how it is said, leaving room for castaway sallies.

The book is divided into three sections. The first and second celebrate private and public occasions. They contain verse letters and gift poems from marriages, birthdays, retirements (among them, Johnston's own). The second also offers three elegies. . . . (pp. 27-8)

The third section of *Ask Again,* perhaps the one to which readers will return most frequently, contains 15 nature lyrics, influenced by Johnston's translation of Norse poetry. . . .

[Several of these poems] have implications as interesting as those in Johnston's translations of the poems in *The Saga of Gisli* (1963). They offer some alternative to the rhythmic vacuity and obtuseness, the tiresome diffuseness of much recent Canadian verse.

In *Ask Again,* Johnston may (to use Lyly the Euphuist's words) govern an island of only small compass, but his great civility, his wit, his willingness to experiment with possibilities of sound and form make that island one which many should visit. (p. 28)

Peter Sanger, in a review of "Ask Again," in Books in Canada, *Vol. 14, No. 9, December, 1985, pp. 27-8.*

P. K. PAGE

How Johnstonian the title—*Ask Again. Home Free, Happy Enough, Taking a Grip, Ask Again*—in that order, almost the story of a life.

Equally Johnstonian the thirty-seven poems in this beautifully designed volume: poems for named people—Johnston honors his friendships and kinships; quirky, idiosyncratic poems; acrostics; poems knit from the strict pattern of scaldic verse; poems with cadences that teeter and tilt as delicately as mobiles.

Of the three sections in the book, two—**"Friends and Occasions"** and **"Marriages, Births, Deaths"**—contain lamentations for life passing, life concluded and celebrations for life begun. Personal but not private, this is loving, often colloquial, unsentimental poetry. The diction does not permit sentimen-

tality, nor, I think, do the rhythms. But, of course, projections of the man, himself, who knows

> Márried life is whát
> one mákes of it; there's lúck,
>   blíssful tímes—and nót,
>   thín ánd thíck,
>   júst sítting it óut
>   áll párt of the lífe.
> Máy you máke the lót. . . .
>   (**"A Marriage Poem for Peg and John"**)

I have marked the stresses as I hear them—in this case, three to a line. They are always worth paying attention to—for one thing, they tell you how to read the poem. But I have marked them for the purpose of showing that where they fall controls the gait of a poem and how, here, combined as they are with whole and half-rhymes, they create an uneven gait, perfectly suited to the subject matter. (p. 50)

One might be tempted to surmise, on the basis of the poems from which I have quoted, that his sense of structure and its attendant graces are the result of Johnston's work of translating the intricate verse of the scalds—the court poets of the Viking age; that these skills are a gift, as it were, in return for submitting to so exacting a discipline. But in his poems in *The Cruising Auk,* written before the real work of translation began, we find similar structures and graces. More probable, then, that like called to like, that the conjunction arose from affinity.

Let me quote briefly from **"What Do the Scalds Tell Us?"**— an article by Johnston which appeared in the *University of Toronto Quarterly* in 1982. It will give us a glimpse of his attitude to translation and to his own work.

> What I had done was place first importance on the form. The sense had to realize itself in the form. What I have learned since, gradually—or rather, *learned over again,* (italics mine) is that this is the most fruitful approach to the composing of my own poetry. I unlearned the dictum that the poem should find its own form. The poem finds its form more surely within a convention than not.

In Johnston's hand, the form invariably draws attention to the language itself. Variations on rhyme and half-rhyme—a requirement of scaldic verse—expose the very skeleton of word sounds; while alliteration—another requirement—sets up a pattern of reverberations. This is aural poetry, indeed, and must be read as such.

For all the poetic pleasures to be found in the first two sections of *Ask Again,* it is the third section that pleases me most. Here we see the fine eye Johnston has for nature, here we are treated to the most astonishing of his syntactical singularities, to his most serious play. What to say about a poem like **"Onset"**?

> A between time; what's to come
> looms. Let it not loom.
> It has loomed enough.
> Let it, whatever it is, loom off . . .

Funny, yes. Darkly funny. The half rhymes, the short sentences and all those "looms"—that conjure and re-conjure the never-written, rhyming "doom"—lead the reader on from autumn towards a metaphorical and literal winter.

"Onset," "White," "Spring Chorus," "Swept Sky" are the poems I found most moving. It is as if the very constraints he imposes upon himself force something to break loose. There is no compass too small for the big winds and thunder. In even his sunniest poems one can hear thunder in the distance, in even the briefest, "close / stars crowd".

Johnston is one of the most finely-tuned poets we have—a master watch-maker who can also build Big Ben. (pp. 51-2)

P. K. Page, in a review of "Ask Again," in Journal of Canadian Poetry: The Poetry Review, *n.s. Vol. 1, 1986, pp. 50-2.*

[ALLAN BROWN]

The first section of [*Ask Again*], **"Friends and Occasions,"** exhibits the mid-range of Johnston's work. It is conservative in outlook, somewhat abstracted and coloured throughout by a light, slightly teasing irony. The individual poems, especially those designed for some public occasion, are deft and often ingenious in form, with consistent use of slant rhymes and intricate stanza play, e.g., **"A Celebration for Northrop Frye"** and **"Ode for James Downey."** There is a considerable degree of sameness to this material, maintaining the practical virtue of being "orderly in form and pace; / reasonable, as it should be" (**"A Return"**), while at the same time tending to soften and disperse the concern for particular people and events.

Most of the pieces in the following section, **"Marriages, Births, Deaths,"** have little more than their formal ingenuity to commend them. Even this is badly strained at times, as with the "Acrostics" for Seamus and Maggie, or the mere Hudibrastic silliness of **"Love and Marriage."** Yet this section also includes the two richest and most finely finished poems in the book: **"Laura's Funeral,"** a small triumph of the power of simple statement, and the moving **"Elegy"** for George Whalley.

The "Meters" in the third section of *Ask Again* are experiments in the use of alliterative half-lines and some semi-archaic diction that appear to be original poems rather than translations. They are more mysterious than effective.... The remaining nature poems, "Seasons," are the most varied in the collection, ranging from the near haiku effect of **"Frost"** to the Gustafson-like rhetoric of the concluding **"Majestic."** Somewhere between these poles in its effect rests the subtly evocative poem, **"White,"** a haunting personification of winter snows.

It is the gentle, restrained, yet sensitively tuned **"Elegy"** for George Whalley (first published in *Quarry,* Winter 1984) that probably best shows Johnston's strengths as a poet, his formal and tonal control and ability for apt characterization:

> Fingers of the disease wrought
> artistry out of your deep
> resources, made you ghostly,
> exquisite, still the same hid
> wistfulness always in your
> eyes.

[*Allan Brown*], *in a review of "Ask Again," in* Queen's Quarterly, *Vol. 93, No. 3, Autumn, 1986, p. 719.*

HARVEY DE ROO

[*Portions of the essay from which this excerpt is taken were originally published in* The West Coast Review of Books, *October, 1985.*]

My first encounter with George Johnston's work was his translation of *The Saga of Gisli* (1963), where I remember noting the beautiful cadences—tough, masculine, supple—of the prose.

Later, when I learned Old Norse myself, I realized what an achievement it was. For behind the flawless English the Old Norse constructions remained discernible, constructions splendidly colloquial and idiomatic and therefore maddeningly difficult for the student and translator. And there was Johnston, square on that supposedly impossible ground of fidelity to both languages at once. This was true also of his renderings of the verse utterance of the characters, arguably the most esoteric and complicated kind of verse in Western literature. How delighted (but hardly surprised) I was to learn that he was a poet.

All his poetry shows this mastery of language, and is marked by a degree of elegance not often found, or sought after, these days. His is an art that conceals its art, apparently simple and effortless, but full of resonance and subtlety. It is almost always an accessible poetry, straightforward rather than oblique or refractory. The language has a colloquial flavour, an uncanny sense of idiom. It is written by a man who loves and understands the Englishness of English. And a man who knows cadence, that if the rhythm is right, the rest is too. But we can generalize only so far, since the poetry has not stood still; it has had a real career, shifting radically in attitude and opening progressively in form.

In his first two books, *The Cruising Auk* (1959) and *Home Free* (1966), Johnston's vision is darkly comic. The voice in the poems speaks with the knowledge that we must accept the facts of life, operate within their bounds, in order to survive. But survival is all that is offered. The mood is most often one of dissatisfied acceptance. It is nonetheless conveyed with a tone that is overall light, amusing, classical in restraint. The poems are traditional in form, with some signs of loosening in the second book.

The Cruising Auk is the most complex and idiosyncratic of Johnston's work. It is his most controlled book of poems, carefully orchestrated in three parts, each distinct from the other in stance and mode of representation, yet forming a coherent whole. The nature of that whole can best be described by calling it Johnston's *Songs of Innocence and Experience*.

Each part is named for the initial poem of its sequence. Part 1, **"The Pool,"** focuses on children as figures of innocence, but from the perspective of the observing or contrasted adult, who knows that experience—the diminished life of repression and compromise—is their inevitable heritage. These poems depict a recognizable, everyday world. Part 2, **"The Cruising Auk,"** introduces us to a myriad of delightfully named but sadly entrapped characters—Mr Murple, Mrs McGonigle, Miss Descharmes, Mr Goom, and so on upwards of thirty. They are Johnston's mythic representation of the world of Experience: here are people caught in a fallen world, struggling through the mundane burdened with a sense of incompleteness, yearning for something freer, catching occasional glimpses of it. Part 3, **"In It,"** leaves the world of these colourful characters for one completely unspecified, in which Experience temporarily overcomes. The voice for a time despairs, but rallies in the last few poems with hope for going on, a belief that, as long as there is any light in the dark, and one expects no explanations, the earth is a place one can love.

The opening poem, **"The Pool,"** establishes both the perspective which operates throughout Part 1, and one of the recurrent symbols of the book.... The poem is perfect in its simplicity, based on the contrast between the boy and the man, the one who *is* innocence, the other looking for it. The second and third stanzas answer the first. The boy simply gazes, no effort made, almost unvolitional, whereas the man "searches," a deliberate and teleological act. Whereas he fails, the boy, not trying anything, simply is. The boy's eyes are "cool" in a sublime detachment; the man's are warm with human commitment and knowledge. Whereas the boy seems not yet to have entered time and its inexorabilities, "Time makes a measure of [the man's] breath." Whereas the boy is profound, in the last stanza the world is. The boy has "gone"—has the power of transcending the self, but the man is delimited by "there and here," territory of pride, insecurity, mortality. The boy is what he gazes on; the man stands outside it. Like all of us, he is aware of a lost state he would like to regain.

The initial thematic contrast established, the next few poems present the diminished life of the adult. Always, perhaps from awareness of this fall, even the best of times are a source of pain. . . . This sense of pain that comes from beauty is a feeling that Johnston's poetry is long in escaping. (pp. 106-08)

"**Kind Offices**" shows the appalling anger of the little girl, Cathleen, despite and because of her elder brother Andrew's "kind offices" of picking up her toys for her and even of helping her to sit up. . . . The poem shows an amusing and common enough event: an elder child's attempts to help a younger only lead to the latter's frustration and anger. But the poem points past amusement. An attempt to be kind has been met with fury. Cathleen's implacability is perhaps a response to what she feels as the imposition of another's will. And who can say for sure that the offices are as kind as the boy lets on? Perhaps he is playing cruelly with her through a mask of kindness. This is a common phenomenon in sibling play, and would explain the persistence, despite the rage, of his attempts to help. However we interpret the motivations of these children, they are disharmony in microcosm. While both may be in the age of innocence, emotional violence and perhaps cruelty are not absent from their children's world.

"**War on the Periphery**," like "**The Pool**," places adult and children within an adult's perspective, this time the parent's. It seems to elaborate "**Kind Offices**," and thus introduces to us the fact of alteration of the order of poems in *The Cruising Auk* in that book's subsequent appearance in *Happy Enough*. The first occurrence of such alteration places "**War on the Periphery**" in the following sequence: "**The Public Ward**," "**Kind Offices**," "**Rain**," "**War on the Periphery**," "**Rest Hour**." In the original the sequence was as follows: "**The Public Ward**," "**War on the Periphery**," "**Kind Offices**," "**Rain**," "**Rest Hour**." We might infer that in the original edition Johnston wanted "**War on the Periphery**" at the end of the sequence of poems on adult experience in order to form a bridge between it and that on children, but that he subsequently realized the possibilities for the poem in the adult's concern for his children and decided therefore to place it *after* "**Kind Offices**" (a poem on children at their own—as yet innocent—kind of war) and "**Rain**" (presenting his depression, perhaps caused by the implications of Cathleen's behaviour). Perhaps Johnston placed the poems in this order to convey his sense that another kind of war protects his children from external violence, but not, by implication from the earlier poem, that violence they are heir to, that inevitable decline from innocence to experience through their own frailty as human beings.

Certainly, the third stanza could lend support to this possibility.

> My little children eat my heart;
> At seven o'clock we kiss and part,
> At seven o'clock we meet again;
> They eat my heart and grow to men.

The image of cannibalism suggests more than parental worry and sacrifice; it suggests aggression of some kind on the children's part. Every child, as part of growing up, must to some degree turn on the parent in order to become an independent being. If this is what Johnston is referring to, it is certainly the loss of innocence, for it involves the exercise of power over another for the sake of self. But, for the moment, at this age, they are still tender, still children, not yet men. . . . The poem may therefore go beyond a simple contrast between innocence at home and violence abroad. One seems implicated in the other; the innocence at home has an element of violence to it which will increase as the children grow to adults. The father's fear may be addressed as much to this possibility as to any other.

The next two poems in the sequence, "**Rest Hour**" and "**Cathleen Sweeping**," make the concerns of Part 1 unequivocal. Rest hour is specifically identified as a state of diminishment, and it is Andrew—this time the one filled with violent but as yet innocent energy—who refuses to submit, who "Fight[s] the gods with heave and punch." His energy and opposition are innocent because elemental. . . . Against his giant force the gods seem small, but that diminishment will claim Andrew at last. . . . The poem is wonderful for its doubleness. It is an amusing and hyperbolic treatment of a little boy's refusal to take his nap, but it tells also, through its images and the consonance of its hyperbole with the surrounding poems, a much darker story.

"**Cathleen Sweeping**" again uses the voice of the parent speaking of his child and drawing the inevitable contrast. It is a beautiful sonnet, both for its poignant depiction of the child's fragility against the enormity of the world, and, as in "**After Thunder**," for the speaker's inability to deal with beauty. The beauty here is that of innocence in the face of a world as yet uncomprehended. The octave presents the contrast between the child's innocent determination and the father's distance from such confidence. First the child:

> The wind blows, and with a little broom
> She sweeps against the cold clumsy sky.
> She's three years old. What an enormous room
> The world is that she sweeps, making fly
> A little busy dust!

How lovely the contrast of the "little broom" and the whole sky itself, inimical but unrecognized. Then comes the bald half-line statement of realization: she's only three, and, by implication, what chance does she have! But, by direct statement, the contrast varied, how splendidly oblivious she is to the impossibility of her undertaking.

The father sees himself watching her from the perspective of a quite different response to the same weather. . . . It is "**The Pool**" all over again, but with the adult himself aware of the discrepancies. And he questions his ability to believe in such confidence in the face of his knowledge of the adult's diminished condition. . . . Not so the child, however, who thinks nothing through in her instinctive sense that she is the same size as the world. Finally, the parent gives up his own awareness, surrenders himself to his delight in the child's innocence: "I give it up. Why should I doubt delight?"

Part 2 is marked by a transformation of the imitated world. Whereas the one we enter in Part 1 is the ordinary and domestic, that we enter in Part 2 is mythic. The first poem, "**The Cruising Auk**," brings this home: here the impossible happens and occasions no astonishment. The characters throughout this part, through the homely outlandishness of their names and their shared condition, partake of the mythic quality. That shared condition is, without exception, the diminished life, the life of Experience. In their exploration of this state the poems fall under three heads: most present some aspect of a life entrapped in an unsatisfactory world; others focus on the state of longing to be free of it, and others still, the third group, give moments—tantalizing glimpses—of freedom.

As in Part 1, the sequence of the poems forms part of their experience. In fact, the last poem of Part 1, "**Flight,**" has already established for this sequence the notion of flight as a symbol for escape, though here presented in the very utterance as futile. (pp. 108-12)

"**The Cruising Auk,**" like "**The Pool,**" acts as the organizing focus for its section. It introduces us to the three aspects of the life of Experience—entrapment, longing, snatches of glory. Upon questioning Mr Murple and others, the speaker finds that they all agree: "It was a splendid auk / Flying across the sky." The auk is a superior being, whose "eye belittles our despair." Turning this scrutiny on us, it sees our diminishment from past or imagined glory—"Our heroic mornings, afternoons / Disconsolate in the echo-laden air— / Echoes of trumpet noises, horses hooves." More than that, however, he is free, in a higher element. . . . We mere mortals bound to the earth can enjoy vicariously the splendour of the auk, feel the connection of the relationship to him. The essential fact, highlighted by the syntactical delay to the last line, is that he is, as we all wish to be, airborne. The auk represents a freedom unattainable by us except in rare moments. But this hope of escape through identification is absurd, as the sight of a cruising auk would be absurd. . . . The poem is perfectly charming, witty, amusing, but at the same time fraught with the shadow of our own unrealizable longings.

The next poem, "**In the Pond,**" modulates imagery previously employed, in order to explore the nature of our entrapment. First, it uses the water imagery introduced in "**The Pool,**" transforming it from the state of innocence to death through desire for it. The speaker, impelled to submerge himself in Mr Murple's pond, asks how much wiser he will be for it. Suddenly he is lying at the bottom, with a little bird watching him. . . . Again the bird appears as representative of elemental wisdom, as in "**After Thunder,**" and, by virtue of its comparative physical situation, of transcendence, like the auk. But here we see the inadequacy of the auk elaborated in the poem immediately following its ambiguous celebration. The point of this poem is that the bird may represent as much as we like, may even know "the way to Paradise," but cannot understand or partake of the despair and frustrated desire of humankind, just as humankind cannot rise through flight.

The next two poems give us our glimpse of escape through free movement associated with the sky. In "**A Mystic of the Air Age**" it is Mrs McGonigle who experiences freedom in flight, while the rest of us remain earthbound: "And while our mortal clay is here / Mrs McGonigle is there." And in the unrimed sonnet, "**Ice at Last,**" it is Mr Murple who achieves liberating connection with the sky, through skating, while coffee drinkers in the hut are satisfied just to warm themselves. . . . The doubleness so common to these poems is delightfully apparent here: the ordinariness of the event—skating, and of the name—Mr Murple, stands against the extraordinary freedom conveyed in the metaphor and the freed syntax. (pp. 112-14)

From these heights, comic though they be, we descend into the life of Edward, whose connections, far from liberating, are rather with a second-hand life that cripples him in living his own. In "**Light Fiction,**" we see *Edward's* response to winter: indoors, artificial light, someone else's life in a detective book, which so frightens him that his own becomes one of anxious withdrawal. (p. 114)

And so Part 2 progresses in its mood of comic sadness, through its unhappy and trivial characters, living their small and meaningless lives, with only occasional glimpses of the possibility of innocence.

The three parts of the book are, as I said earlier, distinguished by the stance of the speaker as much as by the mode of representation. In Part 1 the represented world is domestic, and thereby gives the impression of deriving from the speaker's personal experience. Here the "I" appears in six out of the fifteen poems, and in five out of six appears as the voice of the adult contrasting himself with his children. This lends an air of intimacy to this section. In Part 2, however, the represented world is mythic, and the "I," in eleven of its thirteen appearances out of thirty-four poems, is used to contrast the self with the self's or another's wish for escape to a different reality. Here the "I" becomes representative of a condition within a more impersonal frame. This use of the "I" was anticipated in "**Flight,**" the last poem in Part 1, and the sixth of those poems in that section to use the first person perspective. In Part 3, "**In It,**" the world represented is no longer either domestic or mythic, but simply unspecified. The voice of the "I," in five of its six occurrences out of nine poems, carries on the same perspective as it had in Part 2, except that its mood now is one of despair almost to the last poem.

"**In It**" begins its sequence with yet another occurrence of the pond as symbol. We are all "in it," the world as a pond, and we all drown, no matter how confidently we set out upon it. . . . This mood of despair carries through up to the last two poems. In the penultimate, we are made aware that light exists, despite the overwhelming presence of darkness. And in the last, "**O Earth, Turn!**", while the "I" is once again speaking from his sense of discrepancy between ourselves and the world we occupy, it is no longer cause for alarm, or even explanation. The fact is simply that the world is our place, not our identity, and the gap between the two will always be there. But it is more positive than that. Despite our sense of lost innocence, of alienation from our surroundings, the life of Experience is worth living because, when all is said and done, we can still find the world beautiful. With this recognition the voice achieves finally the tone of love. (pp. 114-15)

The Cruising Auk is a significant poetic achievement. Its vision is dark certainly, but the comedy is deft, its tone amusing, and amazingly, out of keeping with its mood. But tone wins. After all, the book is comic, our sad state cause for amusement. This tone is enhanced by the gracefulness apparent in the whole book, the classical form and restraint of its poems. Traditional, almost all of them rime, syllables meticulously counted. Every line begins with the upper case, and is discrete, enjambment almost always kept to major junctures only. The syntax throughout is that of full predication.

Home Free, while it holds the same view of the world as imperfect, our place in it poignantly out of kilter, is a very different book from *The Cruising Auk.* Nor is the difference simply technical. It is true that the poems show signs of loosening—not as many are so strict metrically, and a significant number show no rime—but they generally exhibit the same classical sense of form and restraint as those of the earlier book. Nor do they really differ in mood or tone. The tone is still amused, the resonance dark. The difference, rather, is one of *mimesis.*

The Cruising Auk is dominated by the middle section—thirty-four poems as opposed to fifteen in Part 1 and nine in Part 3. Its world of fictional characters lend to the whole book—all of it lacking a sense of specific time and place—its mythic quality. It has to it a strong sense of *imagined* space, and this gives it its special flavour and attractiveness. In *Home Free,* on the other hand, Johnston has largely removed his Mr Murples and Mrs McGonigles, who appear in only eight out of the thirty-six poems. He has also let real places enter: seven of the poems feature his domicile, Ottawa, one, Toronto. With *Home Free,* and from this book on, he enters more and more the "real" world. And in this way too he becomes more contemporary, joining the ranks of poets to whom local place is important. Perhaps in this way he is making deliberate contribution to that movement which puts paramount importance on the Canadianization of Canadian poetry.

Home Free also shows greater formal breadth than its predecessor. The poems in *The Cruising Auk* were all short lyrics, whereas in *Home Free* Johnston includes poems of social satire, one long narrative poem, and one long lyric poem, among shorter lyrics. The satiric poems, **"Bicultural," "Remembrance Day,"** and **"The Royal Commission,"** are topical, all set in Ottawa. Johnston makes them "funny," but I do not find them effective. I feel that his special gift is not realized in funny verse, but in comedy—witty yet poignant revelation of the discrepancies between hope and reality. (pp. 116-17)

In the shorter lyrics, the voice is much what it was in *The Cruising Auk,* estranged from the surrounding world. In **"The Creature's Claim,"** for example, the speaker feels a sense of connection with the moon, but sees it as one of violent coercion. . . . Or the beautiful **"Siberian Olive Tree,"** where we hear an echo of **"After Thunder"** or **"Cathleen Sweeping"** in the voice of one unable to cope with beauty or its demands. . . . Or, finally, **"No Way Out,"** where the speaker acknowledges that he is entrapped in a fallen world, yet longs for innocence. (p. 117)

This brings us to the title poem [**"Home Free"**], the central figure of which is our old friend Edward, from the mythical section of *The Cruising Auk,* and thereby universalized. Edward has been offered a pass to that Paradise never seen by the speaker of **"No Way Out,"** a chance to get "home free," but, a sinner like all of us, he is terrified to take advantage of it. . . . This is the state of us all, and of the voices in this book. The world we occupy is not our home, and though we long for such a place we would be afraid to make the try for it even if given the chance. The irony lies not just in our distance from true "home," but in our lack of claim to it, and our consequent mistrust of the free offer. In Johnston's poetry the gap between us and Paradise is sadly critical.

The poems in *Home Free* also continue to show the expertise of those in the earlier volume. In them, like many in *The Cruising Auk,* Johnston employs a favourite strategy: he ends on a shift. Much is bright and clear, innocuous even, until the last stanza or line. Like Farmer Elliott's bees, these poems go out gathering honey, but return with a sting. (pp. 117-18)

In this book, as I've said, Johnston tries his hand for the first time at the longer poem. The narrative poem, **"Love in High Places,"** I don't care for, but the lyrical, **"Under the Tree,"** a poem on hanging, which opens the book, is a marvellous

work. It also demonstrates that he is capable of the high style, though he rarely uses it. My favourite stanza is the concluding one, magnificently eloquent.

> God's good kind Earth, God's manybosomed Earth,
> God's suffering ugly cunning beautiful
>   Wounded creature of Earth,
> The pit whence we were dug,
> The garden in which we grope
>   For love;
> Kind Earth, our gorgeousness of blood,
> Our fleeting pain of birdsong,
> Our poised in air, our footsore, delicate,
> Our lifted up in grief, our loosed in death,
>   Carrion;
> Darktongued Earth, tell our deeds to the dark.

What poetry could be better? How beautiful the holding back of the verb until the last line, and the preparation for it by the long buildup of the syntax, through the repetition of "Earth" and "our" within the audacious massing of adjectives and adjective phrases. How compelling *their* advance from larger, looser units into structures of incantation. How powerful the experience, after moving through the last such sequence, of arriving at the word "Carrion." The adjectives are perfect in themselves, poignant in their juxtapositions, surprising and inevitable. The rhythm augments and impels the flow of specificity like waves toward a beach, enormous and heart-breaking.

Happy Enough is the transitional work. It shows a real move away from the first two in representation, attitude, and style. In these poems Johnston is centred at last in the "real" world. Gone are Murple and Co. As Ottawa began to appear as place in *Home Free,* now Johnston's other world—his country home in Athelstan, Québec—show through.

The book starts difficult. For the first time poems appear whose tone and mood are hard to decipher, whose surfaces are opaque. In them, lucidity, Johnston's trademark, is absent. But, as we move through the book, we discover that it is moving with us, its pattern progressive. It starts dark and thorny, but ends light and clear, and, with that clarity, the darkness has gone from Johnston's poems for good. In its place stands an attitude best described as deliberated content. The poems become autobiographical, presenting the concerns and relations of the private man. There are poems of family relationships and, especially, of friendships—of working with friends, visiting friends, partaking of food with friends. These acts are seen as sacramental, as conferring grace. Friends are talked to who are present, absent, dead. Many poems operate in memory. This book is that of an older man, aware of his aging (he was fifty-eight at the time of publication) which reveals deep ambivalence toward that condition. In this way also the book is transitional: it seems that Johnston was using it to work his way through the trauma of awareness of aging, and those attendant, crucial, problems of attitude to the world and one's place in it.

"Outdoors," the first poem of the book, sets the stage for the conflict the whole reveals. The situation is homely, undramatic, everyone away feasting except Nora, Mark, and the "I," who instead go for a walk in twilight. . . . The verse is noncommittal. Is it simply descriptive of this minor event (it may well be), or is its point the discrepancy between age—slow and weak of eye, and youth—energetic and full of joy? Certainly the distinction is there, and gains strength, I think, by being followed by three snow poems all suggesting a death-wish (in much the same oblique way as in Frost's "Stopping by Woods on a Snowy Evening"). . . . The other winter poems convey the same wish. The speaker of this sequence of poems is so traumatized by aging that his initial response is to give up, to wish simply to die.

The next dozen poems portray a conflict of ambivalence, poems of death-wish alternating with those of a pull toward life. This sequence culminates in the title poem, **"Happy Enough,"** and it is here that the shift in the book, and in Johnston's poetry, occurs. He effects this turn by playing cunningly with perspective. He begins "Happy enough up the / empty headed / to the little field corner / building. . . ." "Happy enough" is not thinking, not focusing on one's condition. But the poem's main incident, the killing of the heifer, *is* occasion for thought. Johnston deflects it, however, by contrasting the heifer's plight with Fred's abscessed tooth, and choosing to concentrate on the latter instead. Fred, with lopsided face,

> takes her and gently
> brings her head down to the
> gun she
> drops he
> opens her throat.
>
> Get it fixed Fred it
> hurts just knowing how it hurts.

What provocative ambiguity in "Get it fixed . . . it hurts"! Of course it refers to the tooth, but, coming as it does just after the slaughter of the calf, it refers to the open throat as well, to death—the concern of the book up to now. By means of this double reference Johnston deliberately slides away from the larger issue to the lesser. And that is one of concerned friendship. This is the connection with the book's title. This is Johnston's way round the fact of death: don't brood, don't make yourself unhappy obsessing on things you can't change; enjoy the fact of your connection to others. The farmer Fred, here and in later poems in this book and beyond, is the comrade in work which keeps one sane, the friend one shares constructive, unreflecting labour with. From this point on Johnston's poetry abandons dissatisfaction for a cautious optimism: if you stop focusing on the dark questions and learn to live within the limitations, and real rewards, of human community, you can be happy. Not as happy as you dream of being, but happy enough. You can achieve content through stoic acceptance.

The next two poems, **"Eugene Thornton"** and **"F. H. Un-derhill, 1889-1971,"** acknowledge the fact of death—both are memorial testimonies to dead men—but stress the relation Johnston enjoyed with them and the values inherent in that connection. It is "our comfort," he says, "to remember / a man." And so the poems progress into celebration of relationship and a reasonable happiness.

Johnston's happiness consists of the old virtues: marriage, domesticity, loyalty, friendship, work. His attitude has turned around from the uneasy irony in **"War on the Periphery"** ("My pleasures, how discreet they are! / A little booze, a little car, / Two little children and a wife / Living a small suburban life"). But happiness does not come of itself; it is a *choice* one makes, but with no illusions, no belief that we can live care free. Johnston is never complacent. In fact, while happiness may be a matter of choice, it is nonetheless touched by fate. The word *luck* becomes a key one in Johnston's poems from this point on. . . . The world has not ceased to be the threat it was in the earlier books, and the friends are not unaware of it; but they have chosen to make the darkness small with their lamp of light, domestic ritual, talk, and love. And it is cause for contentment; they are "happy enough."

The deliberateness is underscored by the penultimate poem of the book, **"Convocation Address:** *Queen's University, 29/5/ 71."*

> . . . some of us
> recognize
> what it is when it comes
> in disguise;
> we name its name
> happy
> and coax it.

His anguish resolved, Johnston now allows himself to speak with the assurance of a public voice. This is his first poem in such a voice, but not his last.

And, finally, age is not the enemy it seemed; it is a time for unillusioned satisfaction. . . . Compromise is acknowledged, but no longer tinged with disconsolateness. Gone are the deeper shadows and dark endings of the poems.

These poems are less traditional than previously. The lines are less regular, and often begin in lower case. Mid-phrase, even mid-word, enjambment appears. The syntax is freer, often abandoning predication. At times this makes for an impressionistic representation, which is strengthened by a style which allows image more than statement to carry the experience. The last stanza of **"The Commonwealth Air Training Plan"**: "war weather gods, toy / thunders / hardly more airborne / than grasshoppers." Or image and statement in perfect harmony, as in the last stanza from **"October Snow"**: "My blood / keeps a strict / beat in the multitudinous / calm earthward of white."

Taking a Grip is a fine collection, much like *Happy Enough,* only more positive. The resemblances are uncanny. Not only are both autobiographical in a similar way, but they follow the same pattern: both begin with "problem" lyrics, and shift through poems on animal deaths to celebration of human relations. But, whereas in the earlier book the move from a concern with death to one with relations in life involved a sleight of mind, in the more recent there is a squarer facing of death as a necessary and integral part of life. The very titles tell the difference. *Happy Enough* is an affirmation, but tinged with qualification. *Taking a Grip* implies a less cautious, more energetic stance toward life's vicissitudes.

Both books open with a poem showing the felt discrepancy between age and youth (father and child)—**"Outdoors"** and **"On the Ferry from Suduroy to Torshavn"**; but, whereas *Happy Enough* follows with winter poems of death-wish, *Taking a Grip* follows with spring poems of more complex attitudes. Take, for example, the second poem of the latter book, the richly suggestive **"Between."** On Easter Saturday, the speaker and several others undertake a walk in rural Québec, the walk one of the symbols, in this book, of human community. Such community is established early: "We are all three / witty. The walk is going well." As they examine the tree that was their destination, they are aware of being in suspension from quotidian reality.

> At this standstill
> harmlessness becomes imaginable;
> yet who can believe himself harmless, or herself
> even for a moment?

This is a characteristic worry with Johnston: we are all looking to be harmless, but are always potentially or actually dangerous. The answer to this dangerousness, as to all the dark aspects of life, lies in the defusing activity, the civilizing ritual of domestic life. At this moment of awareness, Johnston acknowledges that they have this safety to head back into. . . . But something special in this moment causes him to look beyond safety to a state of innocence (no longer much of an overt concern with him in his later poetry, but the ghost of it is sometimes there, hovering beyond articulation):

> But in this warm early dusk we are
> spellbound, as though shut away from all that, no
> mutability any more, no ties,
> no crucified yesterday, no risen tomorrow.

How powerful a stanza, beautifully cadenced, the repeated ''no''-phrases, beginning in enjambment, the metonymy in the last line joining cosmic and mundane realities, the Easter season brilliantly brought to bear on this country walk in Québec. And thus the symbolism of the tree itself is released. But there is none of the pain of regret of the earlier books, only a moment revealing the illusion of grace, of freedom, followed by a more reflective continuation of the walk toward happiness.

> Mark runs, he dwindles
> before our pace from which hurry
> has been put by.

These last lines are wonderfully suggestive. Youth and age again, enthusiasm and wisdom, innocence and experience. Hurry has been put by our pace, not just because we are pondering the ''between'' moment in the dusk, but because we have learned to walk contentedly ''between,'' toward and within our measured world.

These spring poems portray a range of attitude and experience, with age never far, and with a general sense that spring is a cruel season: ''Cold air warm sun uncover old / hurts over again'' (**''The B-flat Sonata''**). But it is a season of life and engagement, not withdrawal and death-wish. Nonetheless its cruelty reopens the possibilities of our harmfulness, of our own contribution to the fact of death. In two poems as transitional in their context as **''Happy Enough''** in its, Johnston again finds himself in death's presence in the killing of animals. In **''The Marauder''** the speaker, waking early, remembers his trap, takes his gun, and heads to the barn hoping the marauder won't be there, hoping he won't have to kill. . . . Here Johnston acknowledges that violent death is sometimes regrettably necessary, and squarely faces his own responsibility.

The next poem, **''Ribs, Roasts, Chops, Bacon,''** effects the shift from death to human communion. Here the relation is causal. The poem moves from the slaughter of two pigs to their parcelling out into packages of meat, to the convivial meals they provide. The poem is responsible, not ironic: the animals are respected, their feelings recorded, their deaths experienced, not distanced by abattoirs and supermarkets. . . . No backing off or sliding away here. The death is true, the second-person address unflinching. But the law that both killer and killed are subject to is the law of survival, and the pigs will later provide occasion for human connection. . . . The control of language is perfect, of tone, masterly. We have not been made comfortable, but we nonetheless know he is speaking without irony of a mystery of death and life.

We move almost immediately into poems celebrating human relations and occasions: a memoir to school friends, a letter to a friend on his retirement, to one on his ordination, remembered visits and feasts, invitations, work shared. (pp. 119-27)

So the poems of this book go, elegantly written, with a love of idiom and colloquialism, somewhat folksy at times, always giving the impression of sanity and decency. Like *Happy Enough*, *Taking a Grip* feels written by an older man, not always comfortable with age and its closeness to death, but who has gone through enough to have gained equanimity, who has learned a gracious way to live in it.

Ask Again provides interesting continuity and contrast with *Happy Enough* and *Taking a Grip*. It carries on with the same kinds of poem—social poems, several in the public voice, and lyrics concerned with age and death. The titles of its sections make this clear: **''Friends and Occasions,'' ''Marriages, Births, Deaths,'' ''Seasons and Meters.''** Two sections out of three are, therefore, in some way occasional. This is only fitting, for Johnston was, at the time of publication, seventy-three years old, and the book is of a man who is old and knows it, who is putting his life in order before he exits. The attitude is the same as in the previous two books: Johnston feels lucky in the choices he has made. He is content. This is true of his public as well as his private life, for he has been poet, translator, teacher, as well as husband, father, friend.

But the organization of this book is different. It reverses the order we have come to expect. It begins with the poems on human community and ends on the lyric note. This too is fitting. The primacy of Johnston's life of human connection is proclaimed, but the last consideration, the last word, is individual. But even the season poems are hopeful, despite the nearness of death. Unlike those of the earlier books, these do not focus on a single season, but move from summer to fall to winter to spring, and renewal.

The poems of the first two sections are good, but I must confess that I find it hard to sustain interest in poems with public occasions as subject. More than one, but particularly the tribute to Northrop Frye, have too much of the laureate ring to them. But these poems are a necessary part of the curve of Johnston's development from the beginning. We have seen him win his way to an attitude appropriate to the big events and questions of life, including the public, and these poems provide them: retirement, convocation, presidential instalment, accomplishment, friendship, aging, birthday, marriage, birth, death. We see a man who has deliberately pared his world to fit the professional and domestic identities. His is a world made stable and decent through loyalty—to institutions, colleagues, friends, family. These are the poems of a good man who has feared for his goodness all his life, and has not deceived himself. But he has admirably learned at last ''enough / to get on with.''

As always, the skill, the well-turned line, is apparent. There is also a sense of play in these poems, perhaps to relieve them of the formality of their occasions. The metres vary, some strict, some open. Several are acrostics, playing with the names of those honoured or addressed. Some play with scaldic measures, derived from Johnston's interests as translator. All seem to present him with a formal problem to work through and solve. (pp. 127-28)

The lyrics of the last section are of a high order, finely crafted, some freer in form than ever before. Several continue to employ the scaldic measure to good effect. The ending of **''Ecstatic,''** about bees in summertime:

> A massive murmer   moves through the basswood
> and breathes blissful   the bosom kiss.
> Caressed queen   she crowns the season
> her senses swarming   in shared ferment.

The rich sensuousness of the lines is heightened by the ancient sound system (I leave to the reader the delight of finding the *hendings* and alliterations). We share the positive feeling of this summer lyric, and of all these final season lyrics. Even the connection between winter and intimations of death is gentle, almost reassuring, in the beautiful **"Let Go."** . . . And, in the delightfully cummings-like **"Spring Chorus,"** spring brings the renewal of energy, the love of life: "be glad," the speaker begs at the onset of spring, "squeeze me / o be gladder / o squeeze squeeze / o squeeze." Everything in nature says "no," but the speaker, the aged persona of all these poems, persists. . . . (pp. 129-30)

Following this moving plea for the continuance of life come the final two poems, both with birds as subjects, symbolic, it may be, of some kind of resurrection. If so, we have come full circle to the bird as a figure of transcendence. (p. 130)

I wish to close with the piece that begins this last section, the lovely poem on beekeeping (and much else) called **"Lesson One,"** which ends like this:

> Lesson one, a hard one:
> go gently; likewise get
> proper gloves; likewise let
> not your hand be hurried
> by numbers in the world.

Lesson hard won. Do it right, take your time, don't succumb to pressure. Fitting lines to end this paper on, apt for a poet of so high a calibre that his sense of doing it right, including living it right, has, ironically, relegated him to the rank of minor poet. But his life has simply been more important to him finally than his art. In his own words: "I am not so much a poet as a family man who has been lucky enough to have written some acceptable poems." (pp. 130-31)

> *Harvey De Roo, "'Happy Enough': The Poetry of George Johnston," in* The Malahat Review, *No. 78, March, 1987, pp. 106-31.*

Romulus Linney

1930-

American dramatist, novelist, scriptwriter, and editor.

A respected yet largely unknown dramatist whose plays are frequently produced off-Broadway and in regional theater, Linney often employs what Mel Gussow termed a "Faulknerian sense of humor" to examine the eccentricities of small-town life in the American South. He is also noted for his dramas which focus upon such historical figures as Frederick the Great, Lord Byron, and Jesus Christ. Among Linney's predominant concerns are death, religion, individual responsibility, and the conflict between social and personal values. While Linney has been faulted for creating underdeveloped characters and implausible, melodramatic plots, critics generally praise his humorous perceptions into the human condition and his accurate rendering of southern life.

Linney's first play set in a southern milieu, *Holy Ghosts* (1974), involves a married woman who joins a Pentecostal sect in which members are required to handle poisonous snakes as a test of faith. After the woman's husband arrives at the mission intent upon abducting her, he gradually becomes a convert, while she forsakes her beliefs. Critics applauded Linney's skill at capturing the bizarre yet believable conduct of the congregation. John Simon noted of the play's 1987 revival: "What makes *Holy Ghosts* valuable is Linney's steering clear of both condescension to and idealization of his characters. . . . The author comes from this sort of background . . . and though he himself had to escape from it . . . , he is full of sympathy for the one that doesn't." *The Captivity of Pixie Shedman* (1981) portrays a southern novelist and dramatist whose struggle to come to terms with his heritage compels him to write a book based on his late grandmother's diary. During the play, the writer's deceased ancestors return to life to recreate events from the diary. *Laughing Stock* (1984) is composed of three one-act dramas set in different regions of the South: *Goodbye, Howard* takes place in a North Carolina hospital where three quarrelsome elderly sisters await the death of their brother; *Tennessee* dramatizes a North Carolina woman's return to her rural childhood home; and *F.M.* depicts a gifted young author who enrolls in a writing course taught by an unsuccessful novelist at a college in Alabama. Mel Gussow observed: "While sharing a lyrical, homespun language, [these dramas] also demonstrate the breadth of the author's comic vision."

Linney's historical dramas include his first dramatic work, *The Sorrows of Frederick* (1967), a psychological study of Frederick William II, king of Prussia from 1786 to 1797. In a series of sketches chronicling the ruler's accession to the throne and his ensuing reign, Linney reveals Frederick's lifelong anguish and subsequent mental deterioration, which resulted from abandoning his youthful idealism. Alvin Klein remarked that *The Sorrows of Frederick* is "a powerful play of panoramic sweep, political intrigue, historical interest and contemporary resonance—a work of psychological insight and universal pertinence." In *The Love Suicide at Schofield Barracks* (1972), a military investigation into the double suicide of an Army general and his wife determines that the couple acted in protest against American involvement in the Vietnam War. Linney reinterprets the life of Jesus Christ in *Old Man Joseph and His*

Marilynn K. Yee/NYT Pictures

Family (1977). In this play, Joseph refuses to accept his son's birth as an act of divine grace, while Jesus is portrayed as a disillusioned youth who rebels against authority. *Childe Byron* (1977) details the final hours in the life of Lord Byron's young, cancer-stricken daughter, who summons her father's ghost so he can relate the more infamous events of his life. Clive Barnes commented: "It is not exactly the official picture, this portrait of the artist as a young tramp, with all his sexual and alcoholic excesses, yet it is persuasive and, yes, perversely attractive."

Linney's recent plays are lighthearted in tone and subject matter. *Pops* (1986), for instance, contains six sketches concerned with the agelessness of love. One of these pieces, *Tonight We Love,* revolves around two elderly residents of a nursing home who rediscover their need for companionship and romance. *April Snow* (1987) focuses upon the offbeat personalities of several New York intellectuals. Mimi Kramer observed: "The play is a screwball comedy, but more interesting than, say, *You Can't Take It with You,* because it's concerned with the moral condition of its characters."

Linney's fiction shares many of the concerns of his dramas. His first novel, *Heathen Valley* (1962), is set in the mountains of North Carolina during the nineteenth century and centers on the efforts of an Episcopalian bishop to erect a mission in an irreligious valley community. Linney contrasts the conversion of an indigent drifter with the bishop's eventual renunciation of his faith. In his second novel, *Slowly by Thy Hand Unfurled* (1965), he adopts the diary form to tell of a nineteenth-century woman whose possessive love has destroyed the lives of her children. David Galloway commented: "[The] progress of this pitiable woman, her tormented journey toward the outer reaches of her own suffering and understanding, is something which Romulus Linney has etched with a vividness that sheds a weirdly engrossing light on the ambiguities of love and human responsibility." In *Jesus Tales* (1980), as in his drama *Old Man Joseph and His Family,* Linney infuses the legend of Jesus with humor and personal insight.

(See also *Contemporary Authors,* Vols. 1-4, rev. ed.)

HENRY CAVENDISH

[Linney's *Heathen Valley*] is an absorbing picturization of life in the high mountains of western North Carolina during the middle of the last century. . . .

In a certain sense, the story is difficult to assess, because it is fashioned of gossamer and tends to fall apart at the slightest probing touch. At one point, the author is telling a tale; at another, a character is reciting the thoughts passing thru his mind. Yet there seems almost no jar in the transition from one to the other.

The content is equally difficult to apprehend. Among the people dealt with here, murder seems neither morally nor legally wrong; it's merely a simple method of settling a point, gaining an end, squaring an account. Similarly, incest is not a sin—merely something that happens when there aren't enough women to go around. . . .

The book, perhaps, is best described as a gallery of mountain primitives, rather than as a novel measurable by technical standards. The plot, such as it is, deals with the efforts of Bishop Nahum Immanuel Ames to establish an Episcopal mission in a remote valley high in the mountains west of Raleigh. He is assisted by a native of the region, William Starns, a drunken drifter he takes on and converts because the latter reminds him of his own drunken father, long since deceased.

The narrative is thickened considerably by involvements with the difference between essential goodness and essential evil, but it comes clear, eventually, in a tale that contains the elements of a thought provoker, an icon smasher, and a tearjerker.

> Henry Cavendish, *"Gallery of North Carolina Mountain Primitives,"* in Chicago Sunday Tribune Magazine of Books, *June 17, 1962, p. 4.*

JOSEPH BLOTNER

[Linney has filled *Heathen Valley*] with historical and botanical lore as well as psychological insight; throughout, the book shows a deep concern with the spiritual natures of men, with the qualities which reveal them at their best and their worst.

These extremes are embodied not only in the atavistic mountaineers of Heathen Valley but also in the novel's protagonist, mountain-born William Starns, and in Episcopal Bishop Nahum Ames, who lifts him from bestial degradation and gives him his vocation and his mission. . . . Starns' fifteen years in

the Valley end with his death in 1865; his last years are darkened by the Bishop's ruinous conversion of the mission brotherhood into a heterodox order of Essenes based on a pre-Christian Jewish society of healers. Ames' dark destiny leads to apostasy and madness, but a faithful disciple memorializes the lives of both men with a lifelong devotion to the mission. . . .

Linney focuses also on the interior dramas of these lives. He concentrates on the motive power behind these spiritual reclamations. Seeing his own self-destructive father in Starns, the Bishop helps him to transfigure his life. Perceiving his former debasement enacted by the Valley's heathens, Starns helps them rejoin the human—and Christian—community. A whole series of such perceptions links disparate characters.

Characterization is one of this novel's strengths. Writing as omniscient narrator, the author endows his people and their milieu with life through vivid and sometimes poetic detail. When he writes in their voices, as an old reflective woman or a young hallucinated man, the idiom they use is as convincing as the thoughts and emotions it embodies. As the events are viewed from time perspectives fifty years apart, the valedictory meditations of Ames' and Starns' now moribund disciple produce a psychological continuity.

Though the Bishop's tragedy seems overly catastrophic (despite the predisposing factors) and though the nymphomania of a villainous clergyman's wife is implausible (despite the precipitating bacchanal) the novel's deficiencies are few. Mr. Linney has composed it with power and skill. If he can retain these attributes and move to wider human and geographical vistas, he should fulfill the promise of *Heathen Valley.*

> Joseph Blotner, *"Religious Zeal Was Rampant,"* in The New York Times Book Review, *June 17, 1962, p. 5.*

MARTIN PRICE

[In *Heathen Valley*], Linney tends to impose too simple an order on his extraordinary material. As a result, the characters tend to polarize. . . . But not quite. The book comes off to a surprising extent. If the author's imagination doesn't stretch beyond certain stereotypes, his mind is admirably open to real issues and to their full difficulty. He gives us a striking sense of the precariousness of the mission and the constant threat, with each maladroit gesture or tactless word of the pastors, of a relapse into savagery and superstition. But he does not take morose and finally simple-minded pleasure in Facing Up to Original Sin. He is as much aware of the difficult task of teaching men to find the image of their God that dwells in their own unhappy and frightening selves. He conveys this in part by superimposing the painful career of Bishop Ames on the story of the mission. The torments of a theologian are made a telling commentary on the inarticulate confusion of others, and the book achieves depth for all its limitations. (p. 263)

> Martin Price, *"The Complexity of Awareness and the Awareness of Complexity: Some Recent Novels,"* in The Yale Review, *Vol. LII, No. 2, December, 1963, pp. 258-67.*

MILLICENT BELL

The outer shape of [Romulus Linney's] short second novel [*Slowly by Thy Hand Unfurled*] is so unassuming, even artless, that one is likely to fall back upon clichés concerning its "quality of life'' in order to describe its truly remarkable strength and freshness. ''Unforgettable,'' I will also not be the last to say, registering how deeply the author has impressed upon my mind his image of a nameless 19th century American housewife who tells her own story in the entries of a diary.

The diary device is an awkward one, for its very principle is the notation of days as a steady beat of equal and disconnected happenings, a denial of the modulations of plot. And the diarist, in this case, can't give much conscious form to what she sets down. She is a plain woman out of a plain time and place, and though her nature is really quite complex, she has no literary or philosophic sophistication, she has none of the formulas of analysis—psychological or whatever—which obviously define her conflicts, frustrations, errors and recoveries to the modern watcher. She does possess, of course, since she is religious, a powerful instrument of self-definition by whose means she reaches some understanding of herself, stumblingly and painfully.

This, the traditional Christian description of the soul's realization of sin and penitence, the passage from pride to redemption and humility, does, in a rough way, give the novel a certain outline. But it is we and not the diarist who perceive other significance embedded in the narrative. As we listen in fascinated pity and terror to the narrator's ruminations we realize that she is no other than our terrible American Mom—lovingly destructive, who ''kills'' (though not literally) her children lest they leave her, and maims the sex in her men, who is herself an engine of perverted sexual energy venting itself in household cleanliness and temperence zeal. (pp. 4 5)

[The] eye of the diarist, sharply seeing as a bird's yet blind to the meaning of much she sees, discloses portraits and scenes. Most brilliantly revealed is her own husband, the untidy, easygoing male whose drinking and fishing jaunts arouse her secret rage. There are remarkable scenes, set down with that same mixture of perceptiveness and incomprehension—a Fourth of July picnic at which an old half-breed trapper spits a significant mouthful of contemptuous phlegm upon a prissy girl's frilled skirt, or the burying of a ''pillar of society'' beneath a great phallic obelisk on which has been engraved, with unintended humor, the name of the deceased, ''Mabee.''

In these scenes alone, Mr. Linney's instinct for the grotesquerie of our culture is superlatively evident. But it is, above all, in his central figure whose half-articulate and self-deceiving vision is his central focus, that he shows a first-rate talent for defining not only a representative but a personal reality. (p. 5)

Millicent Bell, ''A Sweet Mouth, Smiling in Unconscious Cruelty,'' in The New York Times Book Review, *August 15, 1965, pp. 4-5.*

STANLEY KAUFFMANN

[*Slowly by Thy Hand Unfurled*] is in an old American literary tradition. It is a tradition of rural dissection (usually New England) that first shows the tree-lined streets with the white picket fences and the neat houses and churches, then strips the skins off the inhabitants to reveal the moral cesspools under the (usually) Congregational hides. It is a tradition that runs from Hawthorne through Eugene O'Neill to Grace Metalious. . . .

The diary method is neither immediately attractive nor fully satisfactory. Initially, it seems too egregiously a device, especially since in this case every word has to come through a

not-quite-literate character. Moreover, in order to preserve the journal form and the pace of the woman's perceptions and imperceptions, much trivia have to be included for verisimilitude. Yet the book holds and grows. We see that the method has been used so that we will get all the events at first entirely from her point of view; later, we get the truth of them, or additional truths, from what she tells us of the reactions of others. This interplay among the facets of truth underscores the grimness in the story. A foreboding of doom is established early, and without strain; and the narrator is eventually disclosed as an angel of horror, unwittingly spreading death and some destruction, always sustained by religious belief. She seems at first—and also at last—a highly devout, dedicated, old-fashioned wife and mother. But we know her at the end as an unconscious lesbian and the probable cause of the deaths of her three children. (p. 32)

The existence of monstrosity under whited sepulchre is no longer news, and its disclosure is no longer artistic novelty. Linney's achievement here proves yet again how little art needs to depend on either. . . . Sometimes he lapses from invigoration of the familiar into mere novelistic cliché: for example, the son is a painter of anachronistic and schocking genius whose work, after his death, is burned by his scandalized mother. But Linney has written a good piece of what may be called glandular Gothic. It is more than a successful period-work, its horror is relevant. Self-disguises are eternal. Our self-rationalizations may now be Freudian rather than pious righteousness, but the darkness has not stopped unfurling. (p. 33)

Stanley Kauffmann, ''Queer Lives,'' in The New York Review of Books, *Vol. V, No. 7, November 11, 1965, pp. 31-3.*

DAVID GALLOWAY

In his review of Romulus Linney's *Slowly, By Thy Hand Unfurled*, Stanley Kauffmann referred to the novel as ''glandular Gothic'' [see excerpt above], and the phrase perhaps does as well as any to describe the bizarre manner in which Linney lays bare the heart and the disturbed mind of a nameless woman who might, indeed, have stepped not merely out of the past, but out of a canvas by Grant Wood; but the phrase can hardly do justice to the quite unique tour de force which Linney has brought off here. . . . [The journal form] encourages introspection, and among the trivial detailing of a chauvinistic Fourth of July celebration or a contentious Temperance Society meeting, the narrator begins to find ways of expressing wonder and bewilderment as she weighs the catastrophes and the occasional happiness of her own life; language more nearly approaches the real nature of her reflections when she avails herself of her husband's Christmas gifts—the Standard Dictionary and Colbert Morehead's *Correct English Usage*. Self-indulgent, bigoted and deceitful, she nonetheless imagines herself to have been a good wife and mother, and perhaps—in light of her limited comprehension—she has been; obviously, too, self-deceit has been in some measure necessary in order to protect her against the tragedies of her life—and in particular against the deaths of three children. . . . Her surviving son accuses her of murder, and she may, in fact, have forced her first child to undergo the fatal abortion; but Charlie's ultimate charge is both more vague and more terrifying: ''He pointed his poor shaking hand at me Her love he said yes she has loved us all thats right she has loved us all to death.'' That she loved her children is clear, but it is equally clear that her love was possessive, ignorant, intolerant, and perhaps in its own way destructive.

In her realization of this paradox the novel reaches its supreme lyrical moment—one in which the long-awaited triumph of language and the triumph of feeling (if not comprehension) dramatically coincide. The narrator describes a church service during which the minister is seized by a fit of asthma in the middle of his sermon. . . . In this "torment of death" she is able to forgive the doctor who performed the operation on her pregnant daughter, and gradually she recovers the control insanely lost in grief and self-doubt. She sees a child baptized and remembers the old village blacksmith pounding a piece of white-hot metal and then thrusting it into a rainbarrel: that, he had said, was "annealment," and she too is annealed, made whole once more after her anguish. The exact measure of her guilt we can never gauge, but the progress of his pitiable woman, her tormented journey toward the outer reaches of her own suffering and understanding, is something which Romulus Linney has etched with a vividness that sheds a weirdly engrossing light on the ambiguities of love and human responsibility. (pp. 857-59)

> *David Galloway, "Visions of Life in Recent Fiction," in* The Southern Review, *Louisiana State University, Vol. IV, No. 3, Summer, 1968, pp. 850-63.*

CLIVE BARNES

I only wished I liked [*The Love Suicide at Schofield Barracks*] as much as I liked its sentiments. But the play takes a long time to say very little, carries unlikelihood to even more unlikely lengths and leaves it there, and makes unduly portentous that normally viable dramatic vehicle, the military inquiry.

An American general and his wife kill themselves during the enactment of a Japanese style play at a Halloween party. The general shoots his wife through the neck with a bow and arrow and then blows his brains out. It breaks up the party.

Early on in the play we hear that the general thought "he was going to Heaven to stop the war." This is Hawaii in 1970, and that, it seems, is precisely what he was going to do. Tired of bloodshed—they have lost a son in Vietnam—they plan to kill an infant of American-Eurasian parenthood in front of President Nixon and then commit suicide, a sequence of events that would undoubtedly get into the newspapers. Only the very naive would believe that it "would stop the war," and it is naiveté not so much of the general as of the playwright, Romulus Linney, who created him.

The military tribunal is one of the greatest forensic devices known to theater, and plots can be guaranteed to thicken in this dramatic grab-bag of parade ground and courtroom, where law and order often make such strange bedfellows. But the essence of such plays must surely be the accumulation of surprise. In *The Love Suicide at Schofield Barracks* the only real surprise is right there at the beginning. We have to accept that a four-star general would not only be prepared to do such a thing in front of his President, but that he would have a wife crazy enough to join him, and that they would continue with their plans even after the President fails to make the trip, the child is rescued and the proceedings have descended into farce. Then we have to believe that the general would have left an order to his second in command to hold an informal, unstructured tribunal and that the Army would permit such an inquiry to proceed. Generals and armies are not like that—not even in movies.

Well, Shakespeare was not always rational, and if Mr. Linney had dazzled with his writing or his pacific perceptions, all, I have no doubt, could still have been well. But the construction of the play was clumsy, and the writing only rarely rose above sincerity to any point of eloquence.

The only justification for the play could have been in making the general and his wife—who for obvious reasons do not appear—into real, understandably motivated individuals, and this the play fails to do.

> *Clive Barnes, in a review of "The Love Suicide at Schofield Barracks," in* The New York Times, *February 10, 1972, p. 60.*

B. H. FUSSELL

[In *Democracy and Esther* Linney] has skilfully turned into drama two novels of Henry Adams, set in the 1870's in Washington D.C., in order to dramatize the persistent "conflicts of American idealism versus American pragmatism," so painfully evident in the 1970's. But his best achievement is to have put on the American stage that embraces Stanley Kowalski but not Isabel Archer, witty and cultivated people whose intelligent discourse both masks and reveals undercurrents of a Jamesian subtlety. *The Love Suicide at Schofield Barracks* is an equally intelligent play, but there is an emotional flaccidity and a diffusion of energy that we cannot ignore because the playwright has set himself an impossible task: to show by reverse chronology how a General became a Man. What might work in fiction cannot work here, for the crucial event of the General's suicide, which it is the play's task to explain through witnesses, takes place before the play begins, so that the General can exist for us only as an abstraction. (p. 756)

> *B. H. Fussell, "On the Trail of the Lonesome Dramaturge," in* The Hudson Review, *Vol. XXVI, No. 4, Winter, 1973-74, pp. 753-62.*

LAWRENCE VAN GELDER

Essential as a mainspring is to a watch is the triangle established by Romulus Linney as the foundation of *Holy Ghosts,* his play set among a Pentecostal sect of snake handlers. . . .

For, on the literary strength of three characters—Nancy Shedman, a runaway wife; Coleman, said to be her drinking, unfaithful, abusive and sexually disappointing husband; and Obediah Buckhorn, the preacher's son whom Nancy has run off with—rests the dramatic plausibility of Mr. Linney's creation.

Accompanied by Rogers Canfield, a gentle, septuagenarian lawyer bored with retirement, Coleman, preceded by a burst of gunfire, has swooped down on the abandoned nightclub where Nancy and Obie are living. His purpose, divorce. As events unfold, he finds himself in the midst of a meeting of the members of the Amalgamation Church With Signs Following.

One by one they arrive, and one by one, despite the hostile disbelief of Coleman, they reveal themselves by their testimony—the boy with the boxes of snakes; the stalwart preacher; the man with the phantom bird dog; the ousted Sunday school pianist; the woman with an accomodating past; the young wife and husband with the new baby he doesn't want; the man afflicted with cancer; the two brawny friends, and the frail little woman who has spent all her life being told what to do.

With these characters, *Holy Ghosts* is at its best; they are closely observed and sharply sketched. . . .

But the underlying triangle remains unsatisfactory. Nancy seems far too capable and strong-willed to have accepted a year of abuse. She appears not so much revivified either by religion or Obie as liberated by having put an end to her ordeal. It is a theory that finds support in the character of Obie, who, for all his virtues, emerges as a simpleton rather than a savior. As for Coleman, his flaws are too commonplace, his anguish too shallow for his ultimate behavior to constitute more than shamed recognition of rudeness rather than a religious experience.

Holy Ghosts is good documentary, flawed drama.

> Lawrence Van Gelder, in a review of "Holy Ghosts," in The New York Times, *November 18, 1974, p. 47.*

MEL GUSSOW

As Mr. Linney indicates in a program note, his sources [for *Old Man Joseph and His Family*] are gospels and folk stories about familiar biblical figures.

Old Man Joseph is about Joseph, an aged carpenter; Mary, his teenage bride, and their miraculous son, Jesus. The play poses and answers two questions: How did Joseph feel about being the father of the son of God, and what was Jesus like as a boy?

In keeping with folkloric tradition, the story is told as if it were a peasant's yarn spun around a campfire and passed orally from generation to generation. The work has a childlike innocence, and, cut to one hour it might have an appeal as a holiday entertainment for children. But as a full-length evening of theater, it is of limited interest.

Mr. Linney keeps the most dramatic stories—Jesus's birth, the Three Wise Men—off stage and focuses on the hominess of the situation. This is an attempt to humanize the Holy Family. Joseph is suspicious of his wife's tale of immaculate conception—he assumes that he has been cuckolded—and stubbornly convinced that their son is no different from anyone else. On the other hand, Mary is a total believer. Jesus, as he grows up, is rebellious and confused—a troublemaker in the neighborhood. The characters are plainspoken. . . .

[As] the pageant plods from scene to scene, from miracle to miracle, we realize that . . . [the play lacks] lightness and imagination. Perhaps this material could be choreographed or completely scored . . . or transformed by magical performers. . . .

Old Man Joseph is a harmless primitive. Disappointment arises chiefly because Mr. Linney has demonstrated in the past that he is a playwright capable of ambitious and explorative work, such as his enlightening historical drama, *The Sorrows of Frederick* of the more adventurous sources of theater.

> Mel Gussow, in a review of "Old Man Joseph and His Family," in The New York Times, *January 20, 1978, p. C3.*

MEL GUSSOW

[The one-act play *Tennessee*] is a folk tale about mountain people in Appalachia—provincials who are inseparable from their rustic environment. Shifting back and forth in time, Mr. Linney shows the immutability of the home and of homesteaders.

In 1870 a family stakes out an existence in a cabin in the wilderness. Daily chores are interrupted by the unannounced arrival of an apparently dotty old woman, carrying a cowbell and chattering to herself. She sits on the porch, eats spoonbread, and begins to reminisce about her youth—same cabin, same wilderness, and similar characters. The family members step in and out of roles in the woman's personal history. . . .

In flashback, courtship is precise and unromantic. A young man sets his cap for the lady, interprets no as yes, and is willing to make promises in pursuit of opportunity. He even agrees to move to distant Tennessee. . . .

The play itself is an amiable ramble through the thicket of folk wisdom, unified by that garrulous old woman, and climaxed by a clever plot twist.

> Mel Gussow, "Schisgal and Linney," in The New York Times, *November 22, 1979, p. C21.*

MEL GUSSOW

El Hermano is a short play with resonance.

It is a period piece, taking place in the 1950's in a seedy bar in San Francisco, the kind of place inhabited by servicemen trying to pick up women. Two soldiers, one a leathery veteran, the other an eager draftee, encounter two young Latin American women, recent immigrants to the United States. Later, "el hermano," the brother of one of them, arrives. He is either their protector or their pimp.

Mr. Linney sketches this group portrait with gentle, understated strokes, never overplaying his hand. Each of the characters is in studied contrast. The veteran is a personification of male bravado, the youngster tentatively attempting to communicate with his spare, schoolboy Spanish.

The entrance of the brother does not spin the play into melodrama, as might be the case with a lesser writer, but offers the drama a bittersweet coating.

> Mel Gussow, in a review of "El Hermano," in The New York Times, *February 1, 1981, p. 47.*

PETER S. PRESCOTT

The late Marc Connelly once wrote that his play *The Green Pastures* was "an attempt to present certain aspects of a living religion in the terms of its believers." His was a burden that playwrights and storytellers have felt obliged to shoulder ever since the first four biographers of Jesus left so much out of the story. If Jesus was God, he was also a man, and a man is generally possessed of a childhood, strong feelings, perhaps even a sense of humor that leads him into mischief. In the silence of the evangelists, an apocrypha has developed, some of it as old as the Gospels themselves. From these distinctly uncanonical texts, and from folk tales that have sprung up in every Christian country, Romulus Linney has created a sequence of enchanting stories [in *Jesus Tales*]. (pp. 69-70)

In structure and diction, these stories are strictly contemporary, but in spirit and content they are noticeably medieval: mid-fifteenth century, I should say, about the time of the Wakefield mystery plays. The Jesus that emerges is a plain man's Lord—not a teacher of self-denying ethics or a prophet of a world to come, but a magus who enjoys breaking the rules, swapping stories and taking a light wine at lunch. . . .

The solemn-minded (and atheists, who are always the first to be offended by Christian levity) may find these stories sacrilegious. They are not; far from it. They are witty, inventive tales steeped in an old tradition which is not, like the Gospels, intended to create faith but to make life for the faithful more tolerable. Like his predecessors, Linney casts his stories in the vernacular, departing from Scripture in search of a little coarse humanity. Unlike them—for the tellers of folk tales were fond of pointing a moral—he stresses the mystery of Christ's mission. Nothing is explained. Jesus *is*, and Peter is left to scratch his head, uncomprehending. (p. 70)

> *Peter S. Prescott, "Unholy Jesus," in* Newsweek, *Vol. XCVII, No. 5, February 2, 1981, pp. 69-70.*

FRANK RICH

At one point in Romulus Linney's *The Captivity of Pixie Shedman,* the hero announces, "Bad writing is bad enough; bad Southern writing is the worst." The audience giggles—very nervously. If Mr. Linney recognizes bad Southern writing when he sees it, why has he included so much of it in his new play? Surely this veteran dramatist [and novelist] . . . knows better, but on this occasion he seems unable to control himself. *Pixie Shedman* . . . is a tortuous autobiographical exorcism that belongs in a drawer, not a theater.

The evening's hero is Bertram Shedman, a struggling young novelist and playwright who lives in seclusion in a New York studio apartment. Bertram has decided to write a book based on a diary left behind by Pixie, his late grandmother from North Carolina. The diary seems senile: Pixie claims, falsely, to have been held captive by Indians in her youth. But the grandmother soon pops out of the shadows and explains that her hyperbolic rantings are merely metaphors for her actual life story. As she tells Bertram, "The truth is in the poetry, dumbbell!"

Pixie is just the first of many dead people who return to life to act out the events of the diary. The playwright interweaves past and present throughout the evening, hoping to illuminate not only the nature of literary truth but also his hero's predicament as a contemporary Southern writer. Bertram is overburdened by his family heritage in both his work and his miserable personal life. To succeed as a writer and a man, he must come to terms with his legacy.

Fair enough, but Mr. Linney's intentions are far different from what he actually achieves. His flashback anecdotes never amount to more than a windy yet sketchy Southern Gothic melodrama about a conventionally strong-willed belle and the stereotypically craven beaux in her life. There's the usual run of illegitimate births, attempted shootings, sordid affairs and untimely deaths. The links between this overheated family saga and Bertram's current marital distress are stated rather than dramatized; the contrasts between Pixie's high-flown diary entries and her actual biography are academic. The play's ultimate payoff, an incredibly sentimental, deus ex machina reunion between Bertram and his young daughter, seems to have more to do with *Kramer vs. Kramer* than anything in *Pixie Shedman.*

> *Frank Rich, "Southern Gothic," in* The New York Times, *February 3, 1981, p. C5.*

JOHN SIMON

Romulus Linney has in the past engaged my interest, but his current offering, *The Captivity of Pixie Shedman,* is enough to undo all pleasant memories past and forestall all hope and future suavity. It would seem that every southern writer has some dreadful family chronicle bursting out of his closet and hell-bent on turning some innocent theater into a mausoleum. In this case, we must suppose that what Linney presents as a conceit—the ghost of the playwright-protagonist's grandmother foisting her memoirs upon him—is not to be taken merely as a theatrical metaphor but also as the awful truth. (pp. 64-5)

In Pirandellian fashion, Bertram, his dad, granddad, and great-granddad (who may actually be Bertram's grandfather, Pixie having gone precipitately from father to son) proceed, along with Pixie, to act out a family chronicle that even some of the lesser Snopeses might have considered déclassé. Only one scene, in which Pixie's disgruntled husband tears apart—figuratively and literally—one of her poems, rises to a measure of genuine, hate-filled exasperation . . . ; the rest is all simulacra flapping scarecrow arms. Even the language couldn't chase away a gnat. (p. 65)

> *John Simon, "Fallen Sparrow," in* New York Magazine, *Vol. 14, No. 7, February 16, 1981, pp. 64-5.*

FRANK RICH

[*Childe Byron* is] a comic-book version of the life of Lord Byron. . . .

Mr. Linney may scatter his evening with readings from Byron's works and some of the poet's wittier lines (there are 10 published volumes of letters and journals to plunder), but his attempt at biographical theater recalls television's "This Is Your Life."

Here again, as in last month's calamitous *The Captivity of Pixie Shedman,* Mr. Linney has written a ghost play. This man had better visit an exorcist soon, for this fixation is wrecking his work. In *Childe Byron,* the ghost is the hero, who comes back from the dead to visit his one legitimate child, Ada, on the last day of her life in 1852. Mr. Linney is wondering why Ada, who never saw Byron after infancy, ended her life revering him. This isn't a bad subject for dramatic speculation, but, after setting up his premise, Mr. Linney leaves it dangling until the end of Act II—at which point he gives father and daughter a singularly pat, unenlightening and anticlimactic reconciliation.

The evening is otherwise devoted to a sporadically amusing but mostly ludicrous retelling of the rest of Byron's history. There are many composite characters; some major Byron loves and cronies are omitted entirely; the poet's noncarnal passions (literary and political) are short-changed. While Mr. Linney is entitled to take a selective, rather than encyclopedic, approach to his real-life subject, his choices are all aimed in the direction of melodrama and sentimentality.

Byron's many homosexual liaisons are telescoped into one mawkish one, and the most enduring heterosexual romance of his life, with his half-sister Augusta, is reduced to a tabloid scandal. So much time is spent on Byron's brief and relatively unimportant marriage to Annabella Milbanke that his later adventures in exile, notably in Greece, must finally be rushed through in the form of slide shows and news bulletins.

> *Frank Rich, "The Ghost as Hero," in* The New York Times, *February 27, 1981, p. C3.*

EDITH OLIVER

[*Childe Byron*] is an odd one, all right. The time is November, 1852; the place is the bedroom of Augusta Ada, only surviving daughter of Lord Byron. A countess, and a mathematician who has built a machine that appears to be a forerunner of the computer, thirty-six and bankrupt, she is now dying of cancer. She summons up the ghost of her father (another father's ghost!), who left her when she was a baby, and demands that he play out his life story for her. She is a very bossy type, and he, obviously delighted with her, obeys. And so, scene by scene, we see his life played out—perhaps the best documented life in English literature, what with letters of, journals of, and multivolume biographies of. . . . The action is dotted with familiar and unfamiliar quotations from the collected poems, and with a kind of chorus of sarcastic snippets from reviews, then of adulation, and then of gossip, gossip, gossip—all contributed by the supporting cast. There is a stormy reconciliation scene of father and daughter, and at the end Ada reads aloud her will, in which she asks to be buried with him. (She sounds throughout, by the way, more an imperious young woman of 1981 than of 1852.)

Except for some passages of foolishness and some highfalutin writing on Mr. Linney's part, the play does work. . . . I have not much to offer in the way of opinion, except to say that I was never bored and was occasionally amused; one's attention, I suspect, is held more by the performance than by the script, which is no worse than silly and not much better than serviceable. (p. 74)

> Edith Oliver, in a review of ''Childe Byron,'' in The New Yorker, *Vol. LVII, No. 3, March 9, 1981, pp. 74, 76.*

MEL GUSSOW

Romulus Linney is a playwright with a rich, Faulknerian sense of humor. In the best tradition, he is a local colorist, taking regional characters and showing us how their lives are inextricably bound up with land, family and ancestral roots.

The Manhattan Punch Line is fulfilling a valuable purpose by presenting three of Mr. Linney's one-act plays, grouped under the title *Laughing Stock.* . . . All three [plays, *Goodbye, Howard, Tennessee,* and *F.M.*], are vintage proof of the playwright's mastery of the short theatrical form.

Each deals with favorite Linney themes—death and departure, and the tricks that trip those who are unprepared for the inevitable. While sharing a lyrical, homespun language, they also demonstrate the breadth of the author's comic vision. . . .

In *Goodbye, Howard,* three elderly sisters are in a North Carolina hospital ''practicing repose'' while keeping a death watch over their celebrated brother, Howard. The relationship is filled with sibling friction. . . .

Howard is approaching 85, and his sisters are mostly worried how their absent mother will react to his imminent demise. One hesitates to think how old the old lady is. With a forward young man acting as buffer, Mr. Linney sends his three sisters spinning on eccentric byways of rambunctious comedy.

F.M. moves to an Alabama college for an adult course in writing fiction, led by a novelist forced to teach for a living. Two of her students are dilettantes. The third is a scurvy outsider in club-lady company.

Passionately reading aloud from his thick, whisky-stained manuscript, [the outsider] is clearly an offense to his classmates' decorum. He is also an artist on the hoof, in his own writing akin to Faulkner himself. This is not parody, but serious comedy, with a heartwarming conclusion. As in the other plays, the predictability of the plot does not detract from the vividness of the dialogue and characters. . . .

[*Tennessee* is] a bucolic tale about the indomitability of the land and of the pioneer spirit. . . .

In flashback, the [play's] heroine succumbs to the wooing of an undiscourageable swain, who then takes her on a roundabout journey to marital bliss. The path is strewn with folk wisdom, sights and aromas, as characters travel through forests of sourwood to return to ''places of powerful remembrance.'' That phrase sums up the locus of Mr. Linney's plangent provincial comedies.

> Mel Gussow, in a review of ''Laughing Stock,'' in The New York Times, *April 14, 1984, p. 18.*

RICHARD SCHICKEL

In *F.M.*, the masterly miniature that is the centerpiece in this evening of one-acters [entitled *Laughing Stock*, Linney] places at one end of the seminar table a prim-looking teacher whose lack of success as a novelist has not yet sapped her idealism. At the other end sits Bufford Bullough. Bufford looks like Thomas Wolfe, writes like William Faulkner and carries around with him in a cardboard box the burden of his dreams: a thousand-page manuscript and a bottle of booze. It is hard to say whether the other students are more appalled by the erotic spew of language in Bufford's work or by the way their teacher reaches across the barriers of age, sex and class to acknowledge the right of great gifts to wrap themselves in socially unappetizing forms. What one can say is that the act of commitment to another committed writer turns rich comic turmoil into touching drama.

At 53 still one of the American theater's most mysteriously buried treasures, Linney, who also teaches writing, is obviously speaking from the heart here. *Laughing Stock*'s other short plays are slighter: an anecdote about death and telephones and a shaggy-dog story about an old woman's discovery that her 70-year marriage was founded on a sly joke. But they too are marked by Linney's singular talent for stating wild ideas with high, simplifying intelligence and for drawing deft portraits of the half mad in which not a line is misplaced or wasted.

> Richard Schickel, in a review of ''Laughing Stock,'' in Time, *New York, Vol. 123, No. 18, April 30, 1984, p. 72.*

ALVIN KLEIN

Romulus Linney's first play, *The Sorrows of Frederick,* traveled a tenuous, rocky road from its world premiere in Los Angeles in 1967 to Off Broadway, where it wound up in 1976 after side trips to Canada, West Germany, Austria and England. . . .

Plans to bring it to Broadway . . . never panned out.

Pity. One who expected an idle curiosity or conversation piece . . . was unprepared for what turned out to be a real event.

The Sorrows of Frederick is an evening of high theater, a powerful play of panoramic sweep, political intrigue, historical interest and contemporary resonance—a work of psychological insight and universal pertinence.

The play concerns the 18th-century Prussian king Frederick William II, who in today's jargon might be said to have had a "split personality" but whose quirks of temperament, flashes of civility and bursts of belligerence had earthshaking repercussions.

Even when Frederick is first seen, he is wasted: an opium-addicted wreck succumbing to an array of ailments both physical (hemorrhoids and gout) and psychological (the whining aftereffects of being the "bullied child" of a father who was a "drunken fool.")

The play's constant time shifts span more than a half-century and its free-flowing structure mixes memory and momentary crises, the ostensibly bisexual (but actually asexual) Frederick becoming progressively unhinged and degeneratively venereal disease-ridden.

> *Alvin Klein, "'Frederick' Reigns," in* The New York Times, *March 3, 1985, p. 7.*

ALVIN KLEIN

Romulus Linney's *Pops* is six short plays all about love. The 90-minute evening . . . is an event.

It was not Mr. Linney's intention to connect the plays thematically. Five were written for one occasion or another over a period of a few years, as the playwright explains in a program note. It then dawned on Mr. Linney that these ostensibly different pieces were linked by love. To make a full evening of them, he wrote a sixth play.

Since the plays are also all about music, Mr. Linney thought up an overall title that stands for the popularization of the classics, as in a "pops concert." (p. 22)

If love and music are Mr. Linney's concerns, then words, he proves, are their equivalent. In the theater, where the purity of language is at a premium, *Pops* is a restorative. In it—all of it—the words dance and sing and play and delight.

For a time, things don't look promising. In the first piece, *Can-Can,* four characters, on stools, take turns taking parts in two overlapping love stories. One involves a soldier and a young French woman, the other, two women.

The style here is more in the manner of a recitation than a play. Throughout *Can-Can* one has the uneasy feeling that an evening of preciosity—pretty, but self-conscious and untheatrical—lies ahead.

Wrong.

What awaits one is varied and theatrical indeed. Mr. Linney travels through time—from the 10th century to 1877 to the present—and through memory.

His love notions take in Jesse Grant, Ulysses S. Grant's fiercely independent 19-year-old son, and the nun Hrosvitha of Gandersheim, the only female playwright of the Middle Ages.

In the context of a newly written play within a play, *Ave Maria,* Mr. Linney implies, amusingly, that the Mother Superior was the period's only female director. (pp. 22-3)

Most appealing is Mr. Linney's love for how elderly people love. In a variation of the "What did we do wrong?" syndrome,

one retired couple muses about shared happiness, wondering why their children are so messed up.

And in *Tonight We Love,* the last play, two people in their 80's experience "sexual recrudescence" in a nursing home.

The nurse's eloquent ode to those who have reached "the edge of existence"—she calls them "the most gallant people I know"—caps an evening of tenderness, tears, grace and cheer. . . .

Pops is fresh, life enhancing and quite wonderful. Everyone should love Romulus Linney. (p. 23)

> *Alvin Klein, "Love Is the Theme on Montclair Stage," in* The New York Times, *October 12, 1986, pp. 22-3.*

MEL GUSSOW

Romulus Linney's *Pops* is an evening of curtain raisers, six very short plays dealing with the subject of romantic love. The effect is like a buffet of tempting appetizers; taken together, the appetizers substitute for a main course. The title of the anthology . . . refers to familiar classical music as played by the Boston Pops Orchestra. In each play we know the tune, but Mr. Linney, as an imaginative dramatist, adds his special variations. . . .

By the end of the 90-minute anthology, Mr. Linney has moved all the way from young love to octogenarian love and a tale of "sexual recrudescence." . . .

For four of the six plays, one would raise a positive sign. The other two earn a mixed (*Claire de Lune,* about a retired couple in a trailer camp) and a negative (*Yankee Doodle,* which deals with Ulysses S. Grant and Queen Victoria). On the affirmative side, in addition to *Can-Can* and *Tonight We Love* is a historical drama entitled *Ave Maria,* which dramatizes an incident in the life of Hrosvitha of Gandersheim, the 10th-century nun who was the only female playwright of her time.

In Mr. Linney's version of a play by Hrosvitha, love is both spiritual and sensual. The intensity of the nun's story is contrasted to the outrage of a visiting monk who is mortally offended by the idea of nuns expressing thoughts other than those officially sanctioned.

Gold and Silver Waltz—raise a positive sign—is a brief reminiscence about boyhood and the passage of time, delivered by a character named Romulus Linney, and in it we glimpse the autobiographical roots of the playwright's art.

> *Mel Gussow, "'Pops,' by Romulus Linney," in* The New York Times, *October 14, 1986, p. C14.*

MIMI KRAMER

No one can eat anything at the beginning of Romulus Linney's *April Snow.* Gordon Tate can't seem to taste his fine wines anymore and never finds time to be hungry; Millicent Beck has learned to do without food almost entirely; and Grady Gunn is too much in love to be hungry. But everyone is blissfully happy. Grady is happy because her lover, Mona, is back, and Gordon, too, has at last found love—with Millicent, a girl forty years his junior. There's snow falling outside, and Christmas carols are playing on the radio.

It's nice that Gordon and Grady and Milly are so happy: they've all known a certain amount of sorrow. At sixty-one, Gordon has been married four times, once to Grady, and (as Grady puts it) has lived too long "alone in empty rooms with crushed ice and his throbbing heart." As for Grady, her Mona is always leaving her for the husband and child she initially left for Grady, while Millicent, at twenty, has seen the inside of a mental institution. "I once was mad but now am sane," she tells Gordon in the love note she leaves speared on a statue of Don Quixote. In fact, all the habitués of Gordon's loft are a little mad. They're intellectuals: Gordon, a medievalist, is the sort of academic who acts as a consultant on bad-sounding historical movies; Millicent is an expert on obscure German literature and Grady on the life and writings of Mme. de Staël ("the only woman Napoleon was afraid of"). They're kooks, but unusually interesting and articulate kooks—the kind New Yorkers love to watch and listen to. (p. 69)

April Snow is probably the best play I've seen in New York all year. . . . The play is a screwball comedy, but more interesting than, say, *You Can't Take It with You*, because it's concerned with the moral condition of its characters, which is to say with their mental health and happiness. It's less hypocritical, too: where the Kaufman and Hart play pretends to bring the audience around to a celebration of nonconformity, it really banks on the fact that we all come into the theatre loving nonconformity anyway. *April Snow* does just the opposite. It relies on the cosmopolitan tact with which we have all learned not to judge people's actions or behavior and then asks us to do so. (pp. 69-70)

Mimi Kramer, " . . .And a Peach," in The New Yorker, *Vol. LXIII, No. 18, June 22, 1987, pp. 69-70.*

JOHN SIMON

Let me say it outright: There is hardly a boring moment in Linney's sweet sixteen-year-old play [*Holy Ghosts*], but not many an affecting one, either. These rambunctious rustics provide the kind of exotic side-show that on this grass-roots level is far more stimulating than on prime-time TV with the Bakkers, in academia with Oral Roberts, or in politics with Jerry Falwell. And it would be a mistake for us city slickers not to recognize in the flailings and thrashings of these rubes our own manias writ large—or at any rate in tumbledown block capitals. But still, still. . . .

What makes *Holy Ghosts* valuable is Linney's steering clear of both condescension to and idealization of his characters. This is probably a matter not so much of rigorous fairness as of profound ambivalence toward his roots. The author comes from this sort of background—in fact, the name Shedman in one of his plays always stands for a Linney—and though he himself had to escape from it, as one of he play's Shedmans does, he is full of sympathy for the one that doesn't.

The main problem with the play is that, as it contains many characters each of whom Linney grants a good scene or two, no one has time to become a fully rounded person and certain plot developments seem rushed if not downright forced. Yet this flaw is mitigated by Linney's acute eye and ear for the all too believable absurdities of these folks, by the unjudgmental veracity with which he chronicles their odd, desperate, gallant behavior. And also by his ability to make us laugh without affording us the easy out of laughing merely at them and not, just possibly, at ourselves as well.

John Simon, "Handle with Care," in New York Magazine, *Vol. 20, No. 33, August 24, 1987, p. 119.*

MICHAEL FEINGOLD

Romulus Linney's sensibility, like Caesar's Gaul, is divided into three parts: One is an intellectual, highly educated, questioning spirit that delights in history and searches everywhere for material: Frederick the Great, the novels of Henry Adams, the life of Lord Byron's daughter, and the Kabuki plays of Chikamatsu have fueled him dramatically. Like all knights-errant, though, this questing soul has an earthy peasant companion: Linney's North Carolina upbringing, which gives him an abiding, almost sentimentally dogmatic, love for ordinary folk, their feelings, beliefs and superstitions—a love that, inevitably, is often in open conflict with his rational, educated, urban side. ("A Southern childhood," he told a *Times* interviewer, "is a very primal thing.")

The battle between Linney's thinking and instinctual components is fought out in all his plays, but both are often stalemated by a third element, nowhere more frustratingly than in *Holy Ghosts*. . . . (p. 87)

At a time when religious extremism, and all the attendant corruptions that feed on it, have practically taken over American life and politics, a dramatic collision between such a congregation and a skeptic with a full panoply of rational arguments could be both thrilling and informative. Linney's skeptics, however, don't speak from a rational standpoint. Instead, they're the products of the third component that so often truncates and shortchanges the spirit of his writing—his commitment, however uneasy, to the old-style Broadway manipulativeness so often mistaken in New York for craftsmanship.

Wanting to give his snake-handlers their due, Linney sorts them into types like a Grand-Hotel parade of characters: one deranged man, one dying of cancer, one guiltily promiscuous woman, one uncertainly homosexual couple, one pair of shotgun newlyweds dogged by doubts. Needing a story line to justify antagonistic presences at the service, he carpenters up an unlikely one, about a maltreated young wife who has found love with the aging Reverend Buckhorn, and her irate, cussin'-'n'-drinkin' godless husband, who wants her back. As the split between them has everything to do with the way human beings treat each other on earth, and very little to do with ecstasies or the perfection of one's faith in the other world, Nancy and Coleman Shedman are badly equipped by the playwright to argue his dramatic case, and their marital squabble fits into the evening about as comfortably as an episode of "Divorce Court" spliced at random into a documentary about Pentecostalism.

In particular, Coleman, the husband, who ought to be the audience's voice of skepticism in the play, is made into such an odd case (sexual dysfunction triggered by his unhappy relationship with his father and abetted by alcohol) that the playwright can scarcely find room for rationality in his blinded vision, and so has to parcel it out willy-nilly among the other characters—first Coleman's elderly-gent lawyer, then a shy newcomer to the church, and finally (most improbably) Nancy, who leaves the group just as Coleman, predictably, is transfixed by the service into joining it (anyone remember Chayefsky's *The Tenth Man*?).

An earlier version of [*Holy Ghosts*], published by Harcourt Brace in 1977, gave a tenuous justification for Nancy's exit: Looking to find herself, she has been accepted by a business school in a nearby town. Linney presumably realized that this said nothing about either the church or her marriage, but his cutting it has left the play with an unexplained, arbitrarily symmetrical about-face in lieu of an ending. . . . (pp. 87, 90)

This production may not, however, say anything about Linney's tastes or his feelings in the matter. Even in the most schematically rigged of his plays, he fights against schematism, as he does in many speeches here. His folksier plays tend to be followed by scripts that swing sharply into the literary and the analytic. New York has never seen, and should, ***Democracy and Esther,*** his ingenious stage conflation of two Henry Adams novels; and we ought to get a second look at ***The Love-Suicide at Schofield Barracks,*** which lasted barely a week on Broadway in the early '70s, and is probably the most serious nondocumentary play provoked by the Vietnam War. In the meantime, Linney's writing will undoubtedly keep reflecting the strange, three-handed war of his spirit, with his intelligence, even if it doesn't always win, at least striving to make sure the other two sides fight honorably. (p. 90)

Michael Feingold, "Snaky Arguments," in The Village Voice, *Vol. XXXII, No. 34, August 25, 1987, pp. 87, 90.*

Earl Lovelace

1935-

Trinidadian novelist, dramatist, short story writer, and poet.

Lovelace's novels portray the lives of native Trinidadians and examine conflicts arising from the encroachment of modern civilization upon the traditional culture of his homeland. Although some critics contend that Lovelace's preoccupation with his country's social and political problems narrows the appeal of his books, many praise his lucid, lyrical prose and precise rendering of West Indian dialect and culture. Julius Lester observed: "Mr. Lovelace writes about his homeland from the inside, creating characters with whom the reader quickly identifies despite differences of race, place and time."

Lovelace's first novel, *While Gods Are Falling* (1965), is set in the slums of Port of Spain, the capital of Trinidad, where protagonist Walter Castle struggles in a low-paying position to support a wife and child. Like many of Lovelace's characters, Castle attempts to retain his personal and cultural identity despite the urbanization of his homeland and the influx of modern customs and values. When he fails to receive a promotion, Castle considers moving his family to a rural farming community, but he later resolves to stay in the city and help organize the occupants of his tenement in an effort to improve living conditions. In *The Schoolmaster* (1968), Lovelace's next novel, the establishment of a school and the construction of a road to the outer world threaten the purity and serenity of an isolated Trinidadian village. Martin Levin commented: "*The Schoolmaster* is a folk fable with the clean, elemental structure of Steinbeck's *The Pearl*. But unlike *The Pearl,* Mr. Lovelace tells his story from the inside looking out, using the unsophisticated accents of everyday speech to lead to a Homeric conclusion."

In *The Dragon Can't Dance* (1979), Lovelace depicts a group of displaced Trinidadians who attempt to reestablish their cultural identity by participating in the revelries of Carnival, an annual celebration commemorating the crucifixion and resurrection of Jesus Christ. Several of the characters recognize the shallow and sacrilegious aspects of this event, however, and come to realize their responsibility toward one another to achieve a meaningful existence. *The Wine of Astonishment* (1982) chronicles from the perspective of a peasant woman an actual historical incident in which members of the Spiritual Baptist Church were denied the right to worship by government authorities. Although a staged revolt restores their religious freedom, the villagers are stripped of their cultural spirit and must hope for renewal of their faith through the ardency of the younger generation. Razia Iqbal remarked: "[The] very textures of Trinidad can be tasted in [Lovelace's] language. It is the enormous power of his story, however . . . , that impresses. His ability to discuss the complex issues of a dispossessed West Indian community . . . displays a writing force to be reckoned with."

Lovelace has written several dramas which share many of the concerns of his novels. These pieces are collected in *Jestina's Calypso and Other Plays* (1984).

(See also *Contemporary Authors,* Vols. 77-80.)

Courtesy of Longman Group (U.K.) Ltd.

THE TIMES LITERARY SUPPLEMENT

Chosen by Mr. J. B. Priestley for a $5,000 prize which the BP companies offered for a Trinidadian novel, [*While Gods Are Falling,* the] story of a young "Tess" despairing of any kind of future in the rough, swarming slums of Port of Spain does not at first sound like the triumphant cry of optimism we might expect from a nation newly celebrating its independence. Walter, embittered because his background still thwarts him from promotion, worried at the thought of supporting a second child in the noisy tenement where fights end most often in murder, is too sick at heart to stay in the city another day. . . . [Only] when a neighbour, her son unjustly accused of violence, shows him that neither government nor gods can better things does he face a struggle on behalf of his fellows, knowing that every man must try to lend hope to another if he is not to be guilty of precisely the indifference which creates poverty, failure, and violence.

Mr. Lovelace is a little heavy-handed in his zeal to get at the roots of social discontent, but his young couple and the world they must hate enough to improve are sharply observed and excitingly alive; the purpose and the imagination are there, and experience will surely create the skill to organize material more economically.

"Men Only," in The Times Literary Supplement, No. 3302, June 10, 1965, p. 469.

MORRIS GILBERT

A notable minor school of fiction recently emerged in the British Caribbean. Presumably, it is based on the improved educational facilities which have given a lift to people of all races down there....

The best of this special group of stories have come from Jamaica, and from the Hindu colony in Trinidad, whose forebears had succumbed to the blandishments of the canegrowers: e.g., V.S. Naipaul's *A House for Mr. Biswas,* a witty, graceful, accomplished novel. Now we have *While Gods Are Falling*....

In a series of flashbacks, a brooding, hardworking young Negro, who has been passed over for promotion on his job, recalls his pathetic past, the recurring antagonisms and frustrations he has suffered. A typical picture of a slightly earlier day in Trinidad comes sharply forth. Coupled with that is a picture of recent developments in Port of Spain, youthful hooliganism in the slum area where the protagonist lives and which is seldom or never seen by tourists. For part of the action, Walter Castle indulges the urge to flee the city and try his luck as a farmer on his own land. In the end, he decides to stick it out, to do what he can to work with existing agencies to bring help to his neighborhood....

[Mr. Lovelace] has an intimate knowledge of the hard life he describes. He has produced a creditable novel. Inevitably, its subject-matter will be more gripping to his fellow-countrymen than to outsiders. Perhaps it is time for this pleasing school of young writers to move beyond their present themes of oppression, ignorance and superstition and branch into more general fields. Once again, it seems clear they have the capacity.

Morris Gilbert, "Walter Castle Sticks It Out," in The New York Times Book Review, October 30, 1966, p. 76.

A. S. BYATT

Earl Lovelace's *The Schoolmaster* is set in Trinidad and is a real story-teller's novel, moving with grace from a gentle sentimental beginning to a tragic climax. It is about the building of a school in a village in the inaccessible interior, and when a rather stereotyped and simple-minded priest began worrying about the dangers of progress and the eroding of traditional values by new ones I felt I wasn't going to like it. But the story is better than that and sharply gripping. The shadowy nonentity of a pompous and do-gooding schoolmaster rapes his assistant, who is promised to a youth she loves. She becomes pregnant and drowns herself and suddenly the old values which seemed to be a kind of golden hedonistic innocence turn out, in the entirely satisfactory and delicately ambivalent climax, to include honour and revenge as well, and to be both more dangerous and more worthy of respect than one had supposed.

A. S. Byatt, "Life-Lies," in New Statesman, Vol. 75, No. 1921, January 5, 1968, p. 15.

THE TIMES LITERARY SUPPLEMENT

The sacrifice of innocence on the altar of knowledge is hardly an original subject. However, Earl Lovelace, in his new novel *The Schoolmaster,* manages to avoid the tempting error of making the innocent too ingenuous and the knowledgeable too dastardly.

A remote village in the Trinidadian interior acquires a school; and it is with the arrival of the schoolmaster that the trouble begins.... The villagers are no strangers ... to cupidity, pride and (demonstrably) a propensity towards summary justice; but it is the schoolmaster's more sophisticated approach to sin—especially the obligatory lust and his gift for exploitation—which eventually leads to a rather foreseeable tragedy.

Events move towards this end with an inevitability which is reflected in the fatalism of the people themselves, their grave pessimism and their solemn yet colourful speech which seems, at times, to fall into unintentional self-parody. Mr. Lovelace tells his story in a curious and sometimes irritating mixture of the villagers' pidgin English and a vivid, staccato prose, which merge occasionally to produce passages as florid as the scenery they describe.

"School for Scandal," in The Times Literary Supplement, No. 3437, January 11, 1968, p. 29.

MARTIN LEVIN

The Schoolmaster is a folk fable with the clean, elemental structure of Steinbeck's *The Pearl.* But unlike *The Pearl,* Mr. Lovelace tells his story from the inside looking out, using the unsophisticated accents of everyday speech to lead to a Homeric conclusion.

The village of Kumaca, inaccessible to the fleshpots except by a mountain road traversible only by donkeys, decides to establish an elementary school. Father Vincent, the parish priest, has unspoken intimations of corruption. But the village elders prevail, Kumaca is exposed to literacy, and there now ensues a delicate counterpoint between progress and paradise. Mr. Lovelace is a writer of elegant skills, with an infectious sensitivity to the heady Caribbean atmosphere. (pp. 68-9)

Martin Levin, in a review of "The Schoolmaster," in The New York Times Book Review, November 24, 1968, pp. 68-9.

PETER NAZARETH

The Dragon Can't Dance, first published in 1979, is concerned with a small community on the appropriately named Calvary Hill. Their poverty is resistance to slavery over hundreds of years. And Aldrick Prospect, who does the dragon dance at the annual carnival, is heir to this tradition, making his costume afresh every year. Through the dragon Aldrick carries on a dance with religious significance all the way from Africa, which he remembers in his blood, not in his brain. When he makes the costume, he stitches into each patch something of each member of his family, of his family history.

However, at the crossroads, it is not enough to remember things in the blood, for then one will continue an action in static externals instead of inner meaning. This is the challenge placed before Aldrick Prospect. He gets caught up in a last-ditch rebellion by Fish-eye (the "warrior") and the remaining warrior-band: they capture a police jeep and call on the people to rise up against their oppression. Of course, without a plan (which Aldrick had called for), they fail. All that is left is the memory of a powerful speech Aldrick made to the people: "Make no peace with slavery. . . . We have to live as people, people. We have to rise. Rise up, up. But how do you rise up when your brothers are making peace for a few dollars?" . . . He ends, "I don't know." In prison he gets a chance to know, to read, to think, to plan, to use time. And when he comes out, he is in a position to take up the challenge consciously. . . . (pp. 394-95)

There are several characters in the novel who state, "All o' we is one." This is an ideal to be achieved. The question is of defining oneself as a scout for the group: hence the protagonist is named "Prospect." It is not material things as such that are important. Instead, it is the question of self-understanding, of the conversion of images from the imprisoningly static to the liberatingly dynamic, of moving the lessons of history from the blood to the mind so that people can do things out of conscious self-knowledge, for static images can be manipulated. Pariag has been making the mistake of trying to define himself by what people think of him instead of looking within. Within Lovelace's rich, sensuous prose, it is Aldrick who holds the key: when the dragon stops dancing, Prospect is able to emerge into his own dance. (p. 395)

> *Peter Nazareth, in a review of "The Dragon Can't Dance," in* World Literature Today, *Vol. 56, No. 2, Spring, 1982, pp. 394-95.*

HAROLD BARRATT

Calvary Hill, the setting of Earl Lovelace's **The Dragon Can't Dance,** is a Port of Spain slum of appalling squalor. . . . The landscape is familiar; Lovelace had already described it in **While Gods Are Falling,** his first novel. Walter Castle, the harried hero of this novel, is convinced that God has abandoned the slums of Port of Spain, and, moreover, "there is nothing to look up to, no shrine to worship at, and man is left only bare flesh and naked passions." The residents of Calvary Hill also feel abandoned by both God and man, but they are—all of them—preoccupied with their own identities in this dunghill, where a nihilistic attitude towards existence can be alleviated only by the sensual excesses of Carnival and furtive sex.

Aldrick Prospect, Lovelace's central intelligence, embodies the relentless search for personhood. This search is of a piece with two events, both of which are full of symbolic resonances: the abortive rebellion, which some of the residents stage, and the annual rite of Carnival. Taking Calvary and the Christian celebration of the Eucharist (which is itself regarded as a symbolic re-enactment of the Crucifixion) as his dominant symbols, Lovelace combines these with the Carnival ritual which, together with the rebellion, is conceived of in terms of a sacred liturgy. Lovelace captures the essence of this particular society by dramatizing it as a parody of the Crucifixion and Redemption—a sort of black mass at which the celebrants and congregation are "wrongsided" saints and "the mother superiors of whoredom."

The Carnival and the rebellion are at once a quest and a form of escapism. "Once upon a time," Lovelace writes, "the entire Carnival was expressions [*sic*] of rebellion. Once there were stickfighters who assembled each year to keep alive in battles between themselves the practice of a warriorhood born in them; and there were devils, black men who blackened themselves further with black grease to make of their very blackness a

menace, a threat." Now, however, only the dragon is left to carry the message. Aldrick, Lovelace's metaphorical dragon, seeks to reaffirm this rebellion which he believes is a statement of his identity. . . . The rebellion, led by Fisheye, the Hill's hooligan in residence, is also a quest for personhood. It is described as an attempt to "affirm a personhood for themselves, to proclaim a personhood for people deprived and illegitimized as they." But the rebellion and Carnival are also crucial elements in the residents' fantasy life. Lovelace, we notice, describes the rebellion in Carnival terms: "As the jeep cruised slowly down the street . . . he had a feeling of being imprisoned in a dragon costume on Carnival Tuesday. This feeling pierced him more as he saw their route lined with people. . . . It was as if they had been given a holiday and the keys to the city. . . ." Aldrick's attitude towards the crowds is that of "the masquerader who parades before the judges, filled with the sense of the character he portrays"; and Fisheye, with Monday morning hindsight, sees the rebellion as nothing more than the playing of a mas'. The escapist undertones of the rebellion are especially noticeable in Fisheye's behaviour. Like Philo, the Hill's resident calypsonian, who wants "to make a space for himself in the world," Fisheye, frustrated by a sense of inadequacy, wishes to make "some dent in the real world"; but since he cannot escape the moribund reality of Calvary Hill, he seeks release in violence, intimidation and an aping of the heroes of B-grade American movies. . . . When Fisheye, displaying this new persona in his black pants, black silk jersey and black hat, commandeers a police jeep at gunpoint and stages an ill-conceived revolt, it is actually less a desire to rebel against the nihilism of the slums than an acting out of his most cherished fantasies. . . . (pp. 405-06)

Since neither God nor man is willing to notice them, let alone alleviate their problems, the residents of Calvary Hill seek salvation through the rite of Carnival, a rite which Lovelace more than once connects with the rebellious days of their African past and the quest for identity. . . . Now, however, the rite of Carnival—commonly referred to as "playing mas'"—is depicted in terms of the Catholic mass, embodying the entire Christian myth of sin, redemption and salvation. This myth is written deeply into the novel's idiom. The Indian Pariag, feeling cabined, cribbed and confined by the narrowness of a country sugar estate and dependence on an overbearing uncle, comes to Port of Spain, "where people could see him, and he could be somebody in their eyes." From the very beginning, however, Pariag, who occupies a shack on the Hill, has been a man rejected and despised. . . . When on Christmas Day the residents perform the traditional act of visiting each neighbour's house, but deliberately bypass Pariag's, the Indian rationalizes the rejection by convincing himself that *he* ought to have invited them in. Moreover, he attributes this rejection to ignorance of "the kinda man I really is." It is not enough to be known as "channa boy"; they "had to know that he was somebody, a person." Pariag tries to achieve this by buying a new carrier-bicycle, which he uses to sell his sweetmeats. (p. 407)

But the acquisition of the bicycle, which he hopes will bring him recognition and acceptance, increases rather than diminishes Pariag's alienation. When some curious, pesky children begin to examine the bike with too much enthusiasm, Pariag panics and Miss Olive, acting on behalf of the people, violently removes them. . . . Christ-like, Pariag stands defenceless against those who have accused and condemned him. . . . The residents, believing that he is the "only one who could rescue [them] from the catastrophe which had overtaken them," choose Aldrick as Pariag's judge; but even though Pariag has violated the principle of "non-possession as a way of life," which Aldrick has always upheld, the dragon, Pilate-like, is not "so sure that to buy a bicycle was such a sacrilege, [such a] treason," and eventually he neither condemns nor exonerates Pariag, thereby allowing the people to take matters into their own hands.

The fourteen stations of the cross are telescoped, rather farcically, in the experiences of Aldrick, Philo and Pariag. Aldrick, awakening on Ash Wednesday morning to the searing pain "of carrying around his dragon costume for the two full days of the festival," experiences Christ's sense of condemnation and abandonment; and Philo's final, tawdry victory—the bedding of Cleothilda, sometime beauty queen, but now a dried up "old prune"—is not only achieved at Carnival time, but is described in terms of Christ's agony:

> And even that fool Philo . . . running like a dog up her steps when Carnival come and she invite him in for a drink. He blind. In all these years the farthest she allow him is on her verandah. Three steps a year is the quota she give him, and he climbing them steps as if they is the fourteen stations of the cross; so that . . . at that rate it will take him . . . twenty more years to get in the room she have her bed in, which is where he think he heading. Twenty more years before he reach to glory.

Pariag undergoes his own symbolic crucifixion when the people, convinced that his purchase of the new bicycle is his way of trying to rise above "the equalness of everybody," and is, moreover, a sign of his dangerous nature, deliberately smash the bicycle to pieces. The farcical crucifixion of a religious crackpot in the opening pages of the novel, which Lovelace works rather early into the novel's parodic structure, points to the symbolic nails hammered into Pariag's flesh. . . . (pp. 408-09)

Pariag's symbolic death is also adumbrated in the imagery of Ash Wednesday and the Lenten period. His bicycle settles upon the Yard "like a death"; Miss Cleothilda, wearing a "black scarf" upon her head and a "blackened cross of ashes" upon her forehead, is depicted as if she were the embodiment of bereavement; a sombre, antiseptic Mr. Guy, wearing a "grey jacket and black polka-dot bow tie" and a clean-shaven face, assumes the posture of "an insulted, if not grievously injured party." . . . When Pariag, finally surrendering himself to the Hill's cruelty, laments "with the gentleness of a hurt that [goes] beyond the green Humber bicycle: It mash up. It mash up," there are echoes of Christ's cry: "It is finished." But Lovelace turns Pariag's symbolic death into a victory and rebirth, for his stoic acceptance of his victimization finally makes him "alive and a person to them." It is said to be a "sacred" moment "for it joined people together to a sense of their humanness and beauty. . . ."

This striving for humanness reaches a climax in the Carnival-Eucharist celebration. Aldrick is the high priest, and as he makes and puts on the dragon costume, assisted by a boy-acolyte, Lovelace emphasizes the sacredness of the preparatory ritual: the acolyte, acting with "ceremonial solemnity . . . as if he were in the presence of holiness," matches the priest's solemn, ritualistic actions. The making of the costume is said to be "a new miracle," a test "not only of his skill but of his faith"; and when he puts on the costume Aldrick enters a "sacred mask." This act is at once a symbolic link with his African past and what he believes is an assertion of his identity. . . . This searching for identity, which is clearly linked with Aldrick's sense of giving birth to something sacred, is

again noticeable in the almost mystical experiences of the steel-bandsmen. They, too, are priests performing amid the incense of dog excrement in the cathedral of the steelband tent. . . . The steelbandsmen, moreover, are taking part in a "sacred" and "holy" mystery which Lovelace describes as "the celebration and consecration of a greater brotherhood." Meanwhile, the Carnival dance is itself "a chant that cuts off the power from the devil," and this is matched by the dance of the Hill's priestesses which is said to herald "a new spring." The priestesses, we notice, are also said to catch "the spirit"; thus Lovelace invites us to see an important parallel between their sense of identity and rebirth and the Baptist religion which was outlawed in Trinidad in 1919 because, as Lovelace himself points out, "the authorities wanted them to conform—give up that side of their character which involved religion, and join the status quo."

Ostensibly, the rebellion is an attempt to turn the rival warring bands into a single army. But it is more than this: it is the very core of the Eucharistic celebration. Its connection with the escapism of the Carnival has already been noticed; now, as the rebels pass the revolver from hand to hand, treating it, we notice, with the awe and respect one would give to a sacred object, Lovelace describes the gun as "the Chalice with the Body and Blood of Christ at Holy Communion." The consummation takes place in the Cathedral where they "drink the wine and eat the communion bread."

But for the rebels—and especially Aldrick, whose restlessness is too implacable to be quelled by forces stronger than he—the rite of Carnival cannot bring salvation. Nor does it bring self-fulfillment. In other words, the dragon cannot dance. This realization comes to Aldrick in two stages. First, he understands that just as the dragon is only a mock creature, so too he and the residents have no real power: they can only make "a threatening gesture." . . . Aldrick, secondly, turns to his own inner resources for identity. This is not a sudden change. Doubts about the efficacy of the dragon have always nagged him, and, haunted by a sense of undefined failure, he has always been a man of brooding anxiety and restlessness. For too long he has been living in the make-believe world of the dragon, "avoiding and denying the full touch of the Hill." Meanwhile, "he had been cheating himself of the pain, of the love, of his living." Now Aldrick wants to come home to himself. . . . To find this deeply buried self Aldrick sets himself free from the prison of the dragon, thereby exposing the self which has remained disguised behind the Carnival mask. . . . As Aldrick himself realizes, sooner or later the Carnival costumes must be taken off; sooner or later the reign of kings and princesses must end, and the self beneath the tinsel must be faced. . . . Just as Fisheye, sobered to the point of intelligence by seven years in jail, comes to reject the Bad Johnism of the early years of the steelband ("Now a man have to learn how to live"), so too does Aldrick reject the escapism and impotence of the dragon. Like Sylvia, the virgin-whore whom he tries to save from the emptiness of the Hill and the wastefulness of becoming Guy's wife, Aldrick understands that he does not have to hide "underneath no polish." He, too must act upon the very advice he gave her: "You want to be a self that is free, girl . . . to be yourself, girl." He acknowledges, moreover, that he knew "nothing about life before," or, as he puts it: "Now I know I ain't a dragon. . . . Now I know I is more than just to play a masquerade once a year for two days." . . . And there is more: he realizes that he is responsible for the world around him, and that his most important responsibility is "to grow and to grow and to grow." . . . The rebirth we have been noticing in Aldrick is matched by Sylvia's growing awareness that she can find fulfilment only with Aldrick and not with Guy, who has given, and can only give her, material comforts. Her last-minute rejection of Guy and her acceptance of Aldrick and his new, enthusiastic faith in the efficacy of their own inner strength is a hard and, we may say, heroic decision for Sylvia, who has known nothing but the physical and spiritual squalor of the Hill.

The significance of Aldrick's (and Sylvia's) transformation is brought home to us when Lovelace counterpoints it with Miss Cleothilda's stagnation. She has, of course, opened her bedroom door to Philo; but, we notice, she is still desperately holding on to the past when she was Queen of the Band. "Whatever prop that had been propping up the muscles of her face had collapsed now," Lovelace writes; "and neither the powder nor the rouge would be able to hold them." Nonetheless Miss Cleothilda cannot accept the reality that her beauty, once compelling enough to force Philo to pursue her "like a dog," is rapidly fading. Indeed, "she had contrived to go through life, even towards her grave, as a schoolgirl." As she invites Philo to her bed for one last fling, a bed he does not seem particularly enthusiastic about sharing with her, a note of pathos is sounded:

> "Come," she said, stretching out a hand for him to hold. "You doing like if you don't know where my bedroom is. But with the way the world going, even that wouldn't surprise me," she said in a voice as if the world was truly coming to an end.

For Aldrick and Sylvia, however, the world is just beginning. (pp. 409-13)

> Harold Barratt, "Metaphor and Symbol in 'The Dragon Can't Dance'," in World Literature Written in English, *Vol. 23, No. 2, Spring, 1984, pp. 405-13.*

ROBERT P. SMITH, JR.

Though the quest is an ageless theme in literature, rarely has the search for identity and freedom been connected with the prohibition of religious practices of members of a Spiritual Baptist church in a village in Trinidad, who only wanted to "gather to sing hymns and ring the bell and shout hallelujah and speak in tongues when the Spirit come . . . touch black people soul." With this his fourth novel, Earl Lovelace continues to maintain a prominent position among Caribbean authors, in spite of the limited appeal that *The Wine of Astonishment* may have for the general public.

On one level the salient thematic element is the struggle throughout the novel between the Bonasse Spiritual Baptists and the established authorities, a symbolic conflict between African and European cultural traditions. . . . On another level familiar motifs occur: customs, beliefs and superstitions among blacks in the Caribbean; the Christ-figure hero (Bee); local black boy makes good and forgets his black heritage (Morton); colonial oppression; disrupting U.S. military presence; stick-fighting; and the problematic black hero caught between conflicting cultures (Bolo). . . .

Lovelace's true-to-life portrayal of the characters is commendable. Witticism, joking and storytelling add a certain humor to the narrative and provoke a laughter of which the characters themselves are often the victims. There are moments of catching descriptive passages (e.g., the thrill of stickfighting), even if for the most part the book's idiom is the natural, un-

structured speech of a peasant woman (Eva), the first-person narrator. The author breaks away from the conventionalities of literature to create authentic Trinidadian speech patterns.

> Robert P. Smith, Jr., in a review of "The Wine of Astonishment," in World Literature Today, *Vol. 58, No. 4, Autumn, 1984, p. 651.*

JULIUS LESTER

The American publication of Earl Lovelace's [*The Wine of Astonishment*] introduces a writer of consummate skill. A native of Trinidad, Mr. Lovelace writes about his homeland from the inside, creating characters with whom the reader quickly identifies despite differences of race, place and time. In *The Wine of Astonishment*—written entirely in the soft sibilance of Trinidadian speech—Mr. Lovelace sensitively and perceptively explores ancient conflicts, both personal and political.

The novel's basic theme is the clash between the traditional and the modern, between cultural integrity and assimilation, in the village of Bonasse. Tradition is represented by Bolo, the champion stick warrior, and Bee, the leader of a small religious group, the Spiritual Baptists, whose worship is rooted in African tradition. Modernity is brought by the United States Army during World War II and those indigenous blacks for whom America and England symbolize the desirable future and Africa the unwanted past. . . .

During the war, stick fighting (a ritual encounter in which the prowess of participants, their status as tribal warriors, is demonstrated) and the Spiritual Baptist Church are banned as detrimental to the war effort and racial "progress." The Spiritual Baptists are forced to give up their spontaneous, ecstatic form of worship for decorum and Anglican hymns. Bolo advocates physical rebellion. Bee argues successfully for patience. The novel's climax comes when Bolo forces the village into action to redeem its African spirit.

Many years after the war, when the Spiritual Baptists are legally reinstated, they return eagerly to worship in the old way. Although the old rituals are followed, the spontaneity and enthusiasm are missing; all they know now are the Anglican hymns. But as Bee and his wife, Eva, the novel's narrator, are returning to the village after church, they discover the old ways have found a new expression in a younger generation.

The book is much more than its plot suggests. As in most truly worthy novels, the narrative style cannot be separated from the tale. Mr. Lovelace writes with such fidelity to emotional truths that we know these people as ourselves. . . .

The Wine of Astonishment is a poetic wonder. Mr. Lovelace has written a sustained prose poem molded from the lyricism of everyday speech and life; it is a powerful, moving tale.

> Julius Lester, "Bee and Bolo vs. the Modern World," in The New York Times Book Review, *January 6, 1985, p. 9.*

RAZIA IQBAL

[Earl Lovelace] uses creole language throughout his novel *Wine of Astonishment,* and his ability to string the words together in itself lifts the heart in reading; the very textures of Trinidad can be tasted in his language. It is the enormous power of his story, however, with its historical back-drop of the ban of the Southern Baptist Church in Trinidad from 1917 to 1951 and the personal plight of a people's wish to pray to God freely, that impresses. His ability to discuss the complex issues of a dispossessed West Indian community, refusing outright confrontation and equally refusing submission, displays a writing force to be reckoned with. Young Bolo, an angry, frustrated individual, suggests ways of fighting not only the law but the black men the community has pinned its hopes on. He is isolated in a passive black community which seems to stand still waiting for change. Their stillness is amplified by their fear; fear of Bolo, fear of being caught surreptitiously praying, fear of never being full of their past joys. Although a set of bizarre circumstances re-creates the Church for the community their sheer will seems to have pulled them through; I am reminded of the simplicity of this will and faith in Eva's description of the same: 'We have this church in the village. We have this church . . . Black people own it . . . and we touch black people soul'. Lovelace's talents are rightfully recognized in this reissue as a classic.

Razia Iqbal, "Black People Soul," in British Book News, *November, 1986, p. 621.*

DARYL CUMBER DANCE

The major theme in Earl Lovelace's work is the quest for personhood, a term which he prefers to *manhood* or *identity* and which he describes as "man's view of himself, the search as it were for his integrity." . . . Frequently, however, this quest is threatened as his characters encounter the impersonal, dehumanizing urban world.

Lovelace begins the development of this theme in his first novel, *While Gods Are Falling,* where we witness Walter Castle's doomed efforts to assert his manhood in the Port of Spain slum where he lives, which Lovelace describes as "dark, poisonous and stinking, something like a sore in this city." When he moved into the city following the disintegration of his rural family, Castle (whose sense of manhood is thwarted both by his physical shortcomings [he is small and bandy-legged] and his inability to support his wife and children adequately) joined other similarly poor and frustrated remnants of broken families. In poignantly moving and realistic scenes, Lovelace powerfully evokes the many problems that afflict the urban poor and destroy their families, especially their youths; he moves less surely and convincingly to conclude his novel on a positive note with all factions of the community joined together as one family concerned about and assuming responsibility for each other and for the youths in their midst. Walter Castle's role in bringing his community together confirms his sense of personhood.

Such a reinforcing unity naturally characterizes Kumaca, the rural community of *The Schoolmaster,* which, despite its poverty, is unified, orderly, honorable, and secure, bound together by strong traditions and stable family units: "In a place like Kumaca, . . . everybody is one." The dominant tranquility of this pastoral paradise (into which *some* influences of the outside world have already begun to creep at the time of our novel) is fatefully disrupted when a schoolmaster is sent in to establish a school and rumors are heard that a road is to be built to tie the village to the outside world. Both endeavors, designed to benefit the village, serve only to bring the evil and destruction that inevitably accompany the encroachment of urban society into secure rural Edens. The schoolmaster, like many of Lovelace's educated characters, has been educated *away* from self, rejects the basic traditional values of his culture, and embraces

the worst elements of the exploiters. . . . Many of the tragic problems that result in this novel are shown to be the result of the more sophisticated and educated outsiders' failure to respect the individuality and personhood of the simple country folk whom they encounter. The theme of the quest for personhood here is most effectively emphasized by a minor character, the drunken philosopher Benn, whose reflections on his own life and the drama he witnesses provide an important commentary on the meaning of the events going on around him and reinforce the need of the individual to seek meaning, significance, and dignity in his life.

Though *The Wine of Astonishment* was not published until 1982, it was written before *The Dragon Can't Dance.* . . . The disappointment and despair of the community is somewhat assuaged by the warrior Bolo, the stickfighter whose dance not only expressed his own beauty but also served to express the beauty and humanity of his people. His fight and his dance were not for himself; "what he really want was for people to see in him a beauty that wasn't his alone, was theirs, ours, to let us know that we in this wilderness country was people too, with drums and song and warriors." Bolo, angry that his people will not join him in his fights against their oppressors, becomes a Bad John, terrorizing his community. His outrageous acts finally provoke his neighbors to determine to kill him, but even as they reach that decision, Bea recognizes the deliberateness and the import of Bolo's actions: "He choose out himself . . . to be the sacrifice. To be the one terrible enough and strong enough and close enough to our heart to drive us to take up our manhood challenge that we turn away from for too long. He push us and push us until we have to stand up against him." That the possibility of retaining and asserting their personhood remains is reinforced at the close of the novel. The despair the villagers feel when they discover that, though they have regained their freedom to worship, the spirit is gone from their church, is ameliorated when they hear the youngsters playing in their steelband: "I listening to the music; for the music that those boys playing on the steelband have in it that same Spirit that we miss in our church: the same Spirit; and listening to them, my heart swell and it is like resurrection morning." (pp. 277-79)

[Lovelace's drama *Jestina's Calypso*] treats the poignant efforts of an ugly Black woman to be loved for what she is rather than for her appearance. The play focuses on her preparations to go to the airport and meet a penpal, a Trinidadian immigrant to the United States with whom she has been corresponding. They have fallen in love and plan to marry, but the only problem is that she has sent him a photograph of her attractive, light-complexioned friend rather than of herself. Lamenting, "I should have write and say I is a ugly woman," she still prays that "you'd come and discover me yourself, that you would see me and care . . . that you would be able to look at me and say: This is my woman. This is my island with the bruises and sagging breasts, with the teeth marks of soucouyants on her thighs, still standing after the rapes." Unfortunately, her fiancé is unable to see her for what she really is and to accept her— or by extension, to recognize the realities and the true essence of the Trinidad to which he is returning. Like many others in previous Lovelace works who through their blindness reject some of the basic values of their culture, their past, their source, he compromises something of his own personhood in his inability to appreciate the personhood of Jestina.

Lovelace's most successful treatment of the quest for personhood comes in *The Dragon Can't Dance.* . . . As in earlier

novels, the inhabitants of Calvary Hill have also been repressed, brutalized, dehumanized. Here as elsewhere we see
them refusing to accept the condition that society has dictated
for them and striving through whatever means are available to
force recognition of their personhood. The inhabitants of the
Hill have for the most part migrated to the city from a more
stable rural family and community. They have left the protective custody of that organized society, which offered them a
secure sense of self and a clearly defined role within its confines, to seek their destiny, place, and identity in the larger
world. In a world that places its values on wealth, material
possessions, political clout, family, etc., these outcasts on Calvary Hill have precious little with which to proclaim their
importance. (p. 279)

Lovelace traces the efforts of a number of characters to assert
their personhood through the limited means available to them,
including violence, music, rebellion, masquerade, and the attainment of material possessions. The efforts of several of the
main characters to achieve such recognition are directly or
indirectly related to Carnival, which serves on one hand to link
the people with their past and to unite and revitalize them in
a symbolic revolution, but which appears, on the other hand,
to be a hoax, encouraging the people to dissipate their energies
in Carnival revelries rather than to direct them toward any
meaningful kind of revolt. Most of the major characters are
involved in some pose to effect recognition: Aldrick plays the
dragon each year at Carnival, threatening and terrorizing; Cleothilda masquerades as a queen, for these few days showering
her "subjects" with unwonted friendship and attention; Philo
sings his calypsos, calling attention to a persona antithetical to
his true self; Fisheye becomes a warrior in the steelband, provoking confrontations with other bands; other young men troop
to the steelband tents to produce that "tune that will sing their
person and their pose."

Those characters who achieve awareness in this novel come to
recognize the emptiness of efforts at achieving personhood that
are based upon temporary poses, or that rely upon approval
from an outside world. . . . The enlightened characters recognize that true self-understanding and personhood rest upon
an awareness of their responsibility toward those around them,
with whom they must join in a loving, caring community. Thus
when they acknowledge their obligations to others, they move
closer toward the attainment of their own personhood. (p. 280)

Lovelace may not give us in this novel any satisfying political
or sociological solution to the problems of the inhabitants of
Calvary Hill (as he attempted to do in *While Gods Are Falling*),
he may not propose any kind of practical rebellion that can
effect recognizable change, but he has powerfully revealed the
folk of Calvary Hill and involved us in their lives in such a
meaningful and moving manner that we appreciate their traditions, applaud their victories, suffer their defeats, rejoice in
their growth, and acknowledge their personhood. Here too, as
in all of his previous works, he has successfully captured the
sights and sounds and rhythms of Trinidad in a captivating tale,
often tragic, but also often relieved by the comic tone, style,
language, and interludes that are vintage Lovelace. (pp. 280-81)

Daryl Cumber Dance, "Earl Lovelace," in Fifty
Caribbean Writers: A Bio-Bibliographical Critical
Sourcebook, *edited by Daryl Cumber Dance, Green-
wood Press, 1986, pp. 276-83.*

Jill (Collins) McCorkle

1958-

American novelist and short story writer.

McCorkle has emerged during the 1980s as a prominent chronicler of the New South. Her novels are set in the small towns of North Carolina and explore such topics as teenagers coping with impending adulthood, the inescapable effects of the past on the present, and the ways in which families and individuals are bound together by common experiences and concerns. Comparing McCorkle to such prominent female Southern authors as Eudora Welty and Flannery O'Connor, Fred Chappell noted that she uses such characteristic elements of their work as "the pungent and faintly repugnant detail, the belligerent vulgarity, [and] the relentless concern with minutiae" to delineate the values and personalities of her characters.

McCorkle gained widespread critical attention when her first two novels, *The Cheer Leader* and *July 7th,* were published simultaneously in 1984. *The Cheer Leader* is narrated by Jo Spencer, a popular student while in high school who suffers a nervous breakdown when faced with the complexities of growing up during her college years. Sam Swett, the similarly troubled protagonist of *July 7th,* is fearful of becoming like everyone else and goes to extremes to be different. Both Jo and Sam regain their emotional equilibrium after returning to their hometowns for brief visits. Deborah G. Robertson observed: "These novels examine innocence and experience through a young adult at the crossroads, yet they don't tell the same story; each book is complete, thoughtful, affecting, and finds a separate and distinct course to the same conclusion."

In McCorkle's recent novel, *Tending to Virginia* (1987), Ginny Sue Turner is eight months pregnant and faced with doubts about her marriage. When Ginny retreats to her grandmother's home and becomes confined with toxemia, four generations of her family's females come together to take care of her. This novel revolves around the women's conversations, through which they reveal past secrets, desires, and experiences that ultimately foster optimism for their present circumstances. Alice McDermott, among others, praised the distinct characterizations and voices of the women, concluding: "It is [their] talking—the perfect dialogue, the vivid recollections, the memories and emotions . . .—that make *Tending to Virginia* so rewarding."

(See also *Contemporary Authors,* Vol. 121 and *Dictionary of Literary Biography Yearbook: 1987.*)

Courtesy of Algonquin Books of Chapel Hill

Published simultaneously, *July 7th* is McCorkle's longer, more accomplished second novel. An absorbing cast of meticulously developed characters includes Sam Swett, only just visible as the central, linking character, who exhibits angst similar to Jo Spencer. Like Jo, Sam experiences first love, and he, too, ultimately goes home to his family for refuge while at the same time coming to a reckoning with adulthood.

These novels examine innocence and experience through a young adult at the crossroads, yet they don't tell the same story; each book is complete, thoughtful, affecting, and finds a separate and distinct course to the same conclusion. McCorkle shows considerable skill in both works and a marked growth even with her second.

> *Deborah G. Robertson, in a review of "The Cheer Leader" and "July 7th," in* Booklist, *Vol. 81, No. 2, September 15, 1984, p. 109.*

DEBORAH G. ROBERTSON

Jill McCorkle's first novel, *The Cheer Leader,* concerns Jo Spencer, a young woman who grows up bright, happy, pretty, and popular in a small town in North Carolina. When she goes away to college, Jo descends into depression and self-imposed isolation reminiscent of the fate of Esther Greenwood in *The Bell Jar.* A visit home eventually restores the balance of this precocious, disoriented, but not humorless cheerleader.

ANNIE GOTTLIEB

It is common, and probably unfair, to assume that a young writer's first novel is thinly veiled autobiography. If the writer is any good and is really a novelist by calling, considerably more will have happened even in the first book than a hasty disguising of fact. . . . A good novelist matures in much the way the human psyche does ideally, growing out of adolescent myopia toward a farsighted capacity for empathy with people different from oneself.

Jill McCorkle is a real novelist, and we have an unusual opportunity to watch her mature, because her publisher is issuing her first and second novels simultaneously. And mature she does, in one big stride. The leap from *The Cheer Leader,* a good but familiar first novel showing glimmers of wicked talent, to *July 7th,* a book highearted enough to embrace a whole small town, is startling. That the writer herself is aware of the significance of this leap and exhilarated by it is apparent from the presence in *July 7th*—among a cast of full-bodied characters, old and young, black and white, male and female, rich and poor—of one character who is like the shed skin of the author's earlier self. He is a bewildered young writer, a figure of tender fun who is rescued from his adolescent angst through one day's encounter with the people of Marshboro, N.C.

Adolescent angst is what *The Cheer Leader* is all about. Its heroine and sometime narrator, Jo Spencer, is a "good girl" and achiever whose brittle identity doesn't survive the end of high school—the abrupt shift from childhood into adult sexuality that 1970's America foisted on its young. Jo's first love affair, with a "wild" older boy whom she naïvely believes loves her, leads to a horrified sense of betrayal, an anorexic breakdown in her first year of college and finally a tentative recovery. This plot seems familiar, and not only because many of us know a young person to whom something similar has happened; it recalls, of course, Sylvia Plath's *The Bell Jar.* . . . What is original is the skill and irony, the dual eye for the private and the social, with which this potentially solipsistic tale is told.

The high point of Miss McCorkle's first novel is a party scene in which Jo, manic and emaciated, makes a fool of herself and everyone around her while believing she is a smashing success. Miss McCorkle instinctively stepped out of the first person during this part of the story. The shift to the third person enables her to portray the most interior of experiences, madness, from a dual perspective and at the same time suggest Jo's estrangement from herself. While remaining faithful to Jo's perceptions, she also indirectly suggests how Jo must have appeared to others. The result is both black comedy and a chilling anatomy of isolation.

The Cheer Leader ends with an ambiguous first-person epilogue in which Jo, three years older, is in limbo, no longer in deep trouble but still far from firmly rooted in life. It's an unsatisfying ending. After an account of disintegration, one somehow wants a reborn sense of the precious tangibility of things. This is what Sam Swett, the young writer of *July 7th,* finds in Marshboro, the little town two hours from his own North Carolina home where he staggers out of a trucker's cab after hitching drunkenly down from New York.

Middle-class Sam has ardently courted madness and alcoholism in New York but has still failed "to find out what it is I want to do with my life." He has shaved his head, thrown away most of this clothes and half-starved himself to make sure he won't "become like everybody else." Jo Spencer swung between a terror of exposure and a craving for control. Sam's dread is that everything in America is becoming "the same," and his antidote is a vague romantic notion of being "different." One day in Marshboro will show him and us that holding aloof from humanity doesn't makes one unique; rather, it's the

most common passions and needs that can be trusted to give each life its particularity.

Arriving in Marshboro, Sam stumbles onto the scene of a murder seemingly as random and meaningless as anything in New York. Yet the dead man and the man who finds his body are part of a meaningful web of relations that binds the people of the town together through family and fantasy, business and gossip, envy and grief. Departing from feckless Sam, Miss McCorkle allows us to discover these people and their connections to one another as slowly and engrossingly as a magician drawing knotted many-colored scarves out of his wand. There is comedy and poignancy, romance, suspense and surprise in the process. . . .

Encountering [the people of Marshboro], being slowly drawn into their warmth and stubbornness, Sam wonders what it's like to be each of them. "He doesn't know anything; he can only imagine how it all must feel, and he can't help but wonder how he can possibly write it all down as he has planned to do without really knowing and understanding." In *July 7th* Jill McCorkle triumphantly shows that it all *can* be written down. Even if her characters' identifying tics are repeated a little too often, the reader's chief reaction remains astonishment. How did she do it? How did she capture the exact tone of an aging black woman's sympathy for and disapproval of her employer or a *nouveau riche* businessman's sweaty guilt over his first affair? One suspects the author of *The Cheer Leader* might be a born novelist; with *July 7th* she is also a full-grown one.

Annie Gottlieb, "Manic Jo and Romantic Sam," in The New York Times Book Review, *October 7, 1984, p. 9.*

URSULA HEGI

The Cheer Leader tears down old stereotypes—pretty, peppy, popular—while at the same time reinforcing them.

Jo Spencer pretends to participate, trying to keep up with changes expected from her although she isn't emotionally ready for them. In conflict over what she feels and believes she should feel, she needs to convince herself of her reality by drawing black circles around her image in family photos, even circling her mother's abdomen in a photo taken before Jo was born.

Belonging. Being accepted. Part of a group. Part of a family. Playing by the rules of others. To hide her feelings of inadequacy, Jo plays her part better than the others, emerging head cheerleader, most popular senior girl, even May queen. Though her success puzzles her, she believes she has what she wants. But gradually the rules stop working for her; layer by layer, the borrowed sense of security is peeled away and she feels alienated from friends, family, self.

McCorkle takes a startling—and unsentimental look at popularity and its price, at the rituals that hold people together. She moves from the past into the present tense, holding a moment against the light, exploring its fragility, its sharpness. Her prose changes, reflecting Jo's disorientation and panic.

Although the ending is an attempt to summarize, to make sense of experiences that stood for themselves, *The Cheer Leader* is a strong and subtle novel about a young woman's struggle to reveal her own reality.

While *The Cheer Leader* is written entirely from Jo Spencer's point of view, *July 7th* has a multitude of voices. The time span is 24 hours, the setting a small North Carolina town where a night clerk in a convenience store is murdered. McCorkle's attempt at multiple point of view is ambitious but lends a fragmented quality to the first part of the novel. The plot dominates; too much happens and is not experienced deeply enough by any one of the characters.

Gradually they emerge and become more complex, their voices more distinctive. The most interesting character is 18-year-old Corky Revels—timid and wise, strong and childlike—who sees the world with stunning clarity and compassion. Her mother left years ago, and her father shot himself, yet Corky is able to instill her sense of survival in others, even in Sam Swett, a hitchhiker who is running from his family and from himself.

July 7th is a novel about continuity, about people bonded by greed, shame and hypocrisy—connections as strong as the hope, caring and forgiveness that persist in their relationships despite the ugliness.

> Ursula Hegi, "A Couple of Novels from the Same Southern Milieu," in Los Angeles Times, *November 15, 1984, p. 34.*

FRED CHAPPELL

The Cheer Leader and *July 7th* well deserve their success and celebrity, and surely nothing will detract from these if we observe that both novels fit comfortably into the newest tradition in Southern fiction, a tradition that might be described as being fetched out of Leota's purse.

Leota, of course, is the garrulous beautician in Eudora Welty's short story "Petrified Man." That story opens with Leota asking her customer, Mrs. Fletcher, to get a cigarette out of Leota's purse.

> Mrs. Fletcher gladly reached over to the lavender shelf under the lavender-framed mirror, shook a hair net loose from the clasp of the patent-leather bag, and slapped her hand down quickly on a powder puff which burst out when the purse was opened.
>
> "Why, look at the peanuts, Leota!" said Mrs. Fletcher in her marveling voice.
>
> "Honey, them goobers has been in my purse a week if they's been in it a day. Mrs. Pike bought them peanuts."

It's all there, the pungent and faintly repugnant detail, the belligerent vulgarity, the relentless concern with minutiae, the extremely close focus, the sincerely ugly tackiness. It is all expressive, gives us a world of information about lower-middle-class values as well as about individual personalities, and sets a raucous and slightly irritating comic tone.

Miss Welty didn't exactly invent this kind of writing, but she has done it so well that we find its influence widespread in the current generation of female Southern writers. Flannery O'Connor could do this sort of thing to perfection, and so can Bobbie Ann Mason, Anne Tyler, Joan Williams, Lee Zacharias, Lee Smith, Candace Flynt, and—Jill McCorkle. (p. 6)

But there is a singular and important difference between the way Eudora Welty and Flannery O'Connor employ such accurately tedious detail and the way our later novelists use it. In Welty and O'Connor the intention is clearly satiric; the reader is expected to judge the taste, intelligence, and ethical values of the characters by the inescapable trashiness of their daily lives and to find them lacking. Tacky detail depicted moral morons or moral innocents.

But when we come to Smith and Zacharias, and especially to Jill McCorkle, the purpose has changed from satire to what we might regard as a sort of photorealism. These K-Mart details are no longer comically indicative; they are the ultimate terms in which these petty lives are lived. Cellophaned sandwiches, Conway Twitty songs, "beaver books," women's day-glo slacks do not now distinguish even economic classes; the poor and the wealthy alike inhabit a cultural penury as bleak as any Siberia. Satiric tone diminishes when such objects are depicted as ends in themselves because they become impervious to judgment, unless the authors clearly mean to condescend—as the new writers carefully do not.

It is possible that the newest Southern fiction is the first truly classless literature in America? Traditional Southern literature, represented in modern times by writers like Faulkner, Warren, Ellen Glasgow, and Peter Taylor, was finely class conscious. Class consciousness was one of its main strengths, and one which allied it with traditional European literature, with the classical novel of manners. And quite apart from economics, the existence of a spiritual aristocracy was acknowledged; there is nobility in some of Faulkner's poor Blacks as well as in some of his wealthy planters.

The new books describe no spiritual nobility whatsoever. Certainly Jill McCorkle describes none. The closest she comes—and it is a long way off—is in the drawing of a simple "nice guy" like Pat Reeves in *The Cheer Leader.* But even the "nice" people in McCorkle's work share in the schlock cultural values of all the other not-so-nice people, and it is difficult to see how they manage to come by their minor but basic decencies.

This depiction depends upon a relentless cynicism, as if the author approves, or has at least accepted, the morality of her characters. The teenaged murderers in *July 7th* get off scot-free not because they belong to prominent families, but because nobody gives a damn who lives or dies. Jo Spencer, the one literate character in either novel, we are supposed to see as crazy. Lee Smith says that "Jill McCorkle has left the old stereotypes dead under the magnolias," but *The Cheer Leader*—which is dangerously close in conception and treatment to Smith's own *Black Mountain Breakdown*—comes near, with its new but immediately recognizable characterizations, to an easy use of current stereotypes. Our present generation of novelists is building condominiums on *Tobacco Road.*

But as long as the approach is new, it's pretty fresh, and McCorkle is enormously skillful with it. Her first books are already expert, and if she can learn to treat her characters in their spiritual and intellectual aspects, she has an important future. But we will have to see if she believes these aspects exist. (p. 7)

> Fred Chappell, "Powder Puffs & Loose Peanuts," *in Chronicles of Culture, Vol. 9, No. 7, July, 1985, pp. 6-7.*

ALICE McDERMOTT

In *Tending to Virginia,* Jill McCorkle's exuberant third novel, three generations of Southern women are talking. They are talking to one another and talking to themselves, talking about their pasts as wives and mothers and children and about their lives now, in nursing homes and wheelchairs, in new retirements and young marriages. They are talking about the ties that bind them and the secrets that set them apart; about letting go and getting on. It is this talking—the perfect dialogue, the vivid recollections, the memories and emotions that in the end will not fit neatly into the shape of its plot—that make *Tending to Virginia* so rewarding. And it is Jill McCorkle's skillful use of voice, both here and in her earlier novels, *The Cheer Leader* and *July 7th,* . . . that distinguishes the work of this bright young chronicler of the new South.

Virginia Suzanne Turner Ballard (Ginny Sue to her North Carolina relatives) provides the occasion for much of the novel's talk. Twenty-eight years old and miserably pregnant, she is about to move to Richmond with her lawyer husband, as far away from her family as she has ever been, when he reveals that his first marriage ended not by mutual agreement as he had said but because his wife aborted the baby he so much wanted to have. Confused and angry, already homesick for the familiar, "the quiet coolness of her grandmother's old house, Lena's laughter, the rhythmic whirr of her mother's sewing machine," Ginny Sue flees to Saxapaw, her hometown and the seat of what her husband has called the secret club: Grandmother Emily; Great Aunt Lena; Ginny Sue's mother, Hannah; Hannah's cousin Madge; and Madge's daughter Cindy. "All the women," her husband has said. "When a man comes in it gets quiet."

Arriving at her grandmother's cramped duplex (the old house was torn down and replaced by a Piggly Wiggly), Ginny Sue is stricken with toxemia and confined to bed. The women come and go, tending to her. As Ginny Sue drifts in and out of sleep, histories are recalled, familiar family stories are made new again, the past is applied like a balm to the present. When tornadoes touch down in the countryside around them, trapping the women together for one long afternoon, things never before spoken of finally get said.

But while Ginny Sue provides the occasion within the novel for much discussion and revelation, she is hardly the catalyst for the talk itself. The women in *Tending to Virginia,* Southern to the core, are bursting from the start with their stories and recollections and wise counsel. They hit the page talking. (pp. 1, 26)

Grandmother Emily, Ginny Sue's favorite relative, is . . . senile, but Ms. McCorkle moves her between the vivid past and the confused present with such skill that her voice too is strong and vital, a constant fascinating monologue. It is she who finally speaks the words Ginny Sue so much needs to hear. "Mama said you gotta know when to let go a little, let go and just leave it there behind you and then go make yourself a plate of biscuits and bleach them shirts of your husband's just as white as they can get and then just let go a little."

The advice comes at the end of the long afternoon of the storm, an afternoon in which Madge finally describes the part she had in her husband's suicide, in which Cindy is forced to face her beloved father's madness and Ginny Sue to reveal what she always knew of it; when Hannah, placid and strong and selfless, finally makes claim to her own griefs and Ginny Sue tells of her fears for her marriage. If the words seem a little too pointed, if Ginny Sue's reaction to them seems a little too pat, it is not so much due to lack of inventiveness on Jill McCorkle's part as to the tremendous exuberance of her characters.

The women in *Tending to Virginia* are so full of life, so full of stories to tell, that the small stage the plot of the novel finally brings them to—the single afternoon in the cramped duplex, Ginny Sue's reconciliation with her future—simply cannot contain them: they outweigh it, they overflow it. The clearest evidence of this is in the book's final section. Here

Aunt Tessy—Madge's mother, Emily and Lena's sister-in-law—is described from her own point of view. Tessy died years ago and so has had no part in the ostensible events of the narrative, the tending to Virginia, indeed her voice, unlike all the others, has no basis within the present narrative at all. And yet her story, which describes one of her three miscarriages, her love for an itinerant fiddle player who is not her husband and her dawning love for her husband as well, is one of the most touching sections in the novel.

It is as if Ms. McCorkle, finding herself with this cast of marvelously rich, garrulous, complex women whose lives span a century, sought to contain them in a conventional tale of a young woman's coming of age. When they would not be contained, she simply threw up her hands and let them keep talking. It was a wise decision. (p. 26)

> *Alice McDermott, in a review of "Tending to Virginia," in* The New York Times Book Review, *October 11, 1987, pp. 1, 26.*

LINDA BRINSON

Jill McCorkle's fine third novel [*Tending to Virginia*] should become a model for what publicists and reviewers call "a woman's book." That term is bandied about a lot, sometimes in an attempt to promote a novel that is more feminist diatribe than literary art, other times in an effort to denigrate a book that, because of its limited subject matter or its inferior quality, is considered to be "only" for women readers of a certain type.

But what if "woman's book" could be made an honorific, a term praising a work of fiction that does a particularly good job of portraying women characters and their concerns—such a fine job that any reader, of either sex, should relish the story and benefit from its insights? That's the kind of "woman's book" *Tending to Virginia* is. . . .

Tending to Virginia is an engaging story with a small-town North Carolina setting. This new novel has much of the psychological and emotional insight, the interior drama, of *The Cheer Leader,* and echoes of the humor and exterior action of *July 7th.* By blending elements of those two quite different earlier works, Ms. McCorkle has achieved a story that is more mature, more rounded than either.

This is the story of Virginia . . . , a young woman who grew up in Saxapaw, North Carolina. Virginia is heavily pregnant during an oppressively hot and prolonged drought. Her physical discomforts are compounded by her emotional distress. . . . [Her husband] Mark has just told her that the reason he split with his first wife was the she had had an abortion, and Virginia finds herself haunted by the specter of Sheila and the baby that would have been Mark's first-born.

Suddenly, she feels that she has no relationship with the man she has married, the man who is the father of her child. Instead, she feels the strong ties of her family, particularly her beloved grandmother. One hot, hot day, Virginia drives home to Saxapaw and takes refuge in Gram's house. . . .

There is very little immediate action. Virginia ponders and finally makes a decision about whether she should leave Mark. The weather finally breaks, with a tornado and much-needed rain. Almost nothing else goes on in the present, except for the antics of Cousin Cindy, who also provides much of the humor. . . .

There is, however, a great deal of action, and dramatic tension, in the conversations and memories of Virginia and the women who are gathered to tend to her. The fascinating narrative gives us first hints and then information, bit by bit, so that we gradually come to know these women and the important things in their lives—the public details that all the relatives think they know, and the secrets that have been kept private.

Unlike many of the highly touted "woman's books," *Tending to Virginia* does not paint all women characters favorably and all men negatively. We see how women oppress one another and repress themselves, as well as how they can provide important support.

While we do not get to know the men characters nearly as intimately as we do the women, they are present as real people, good and bad.

In the end, we, like Virginia, come to realize the importance and the complexity of family history, and of each person's particular vision of its truth.

> *Linda Brinson, "Jill McCorkle's Latest Novel Is What a 'Woman's Book' Ought to Be," in* The Winston-Salem Journal, *October 11, 1987, p. H4.*

FRANK LEVERING

On its surface, 29-year-old Jill McCorkle's third novel is as static as a hot Sunday afternoon in rural North Carolina. Set in the author's native Tar Heel state, the plot of *Tending to Virginia* moves at the pace of a sullen mule in a tobacco field. We wait for more than 300 pages to discover whether pregnant, self-pitying, 28-year-old Virginia Turner will leave her insufferable husband, law student Mark Ballard. She does not.

The book is, nonetheless, the work of a prodigious young talent. Not trendy, not clever, not ostentatious with her prose, McCorkle has a flawless ear for small-town dialogue and a ravenous appetite for the quirks and yearnings of the New South, for the favored brand names, for shopping at K Mart. Her observations crackle with witty authenticity. . . .

Seldom, if ever, have working-class Southern women been so realistically portrayed. Taking bits and pieces from the lives of four generations in Virginia's family, McCorkle stitches a rare and intricate quilt, a pattern of women supporting women that bridges new South and old, feminism and old female remedies for heartsickness. McCorkle's needlework is not flawless—as with many young novelists, the characters dwarf the narrative; and their thoughts, as she reveals them, often impart information rather than spring organically from dramatic context. But this is a writer to watch—a talent already to behold.

> *Frank Levering, "New South Humor," in* Los Angeles Times Book Review, *November 29, 1987, p. 15.*

SUZANNE BERNE

Tending to Virginia is one of those intricate Southern family sagas that requires you to memorize the genealogy provided on the opening page. Otherwise you will never remember who is whose sister's husband, which children belong to whom, and how they all managed to be related in the first place.

The family here are the Pearson sisters, Emily and Lena, their dead sister-in-law Tessy, their dead husbands, their children, and their children's children. Virginia is Emily's granddaughter, who has left home to live with her law student husband, Mark, in North Carolina. "Barefoot and pregnant," she mopes in their rented house, homesick for her family, disgusted with her physical condition and alienated from Mark because she has discovered that his first wife left him. "You told me your divorce was mutual, a joint mistake," she accuses him. Whether she is more tormented by being married to someone else's "mistake" or by the fact that Mark might still love this other woman is never made clear.

One afternoon, after painting a nursery mural with vultures, snakes, and parasites instead of the cheerful cartoon characters she had planned, Virginia gives up, gets in the car, and drives home. "Home" is Saxapaw, one of those somnolent small towns perched on a river bank where entire families can still be discovered living within a five-mile radius. Desperate to return to the security she knew as a child in "Gram's house," Virginia arrives at Gram's duplex . . . , collapses, and thus provides the catalyst for a convention of her female relatives.

The women tending to Virginia are Gram and Lena, both suffering from Alzheimer's disease and no longer able to care for themselves; Tessy's daughter Madge, a widowed dental hygienist; her daughter Cindy, a wise-cracking, brassy medical secretary who lives for her weekly romantic assignations in the local Ramada Inn parking lot; and Virginia's mother Hannah. . . . The memories, distortions, and reveries of these women provide the dramatic heart of the novel. Virginia, in fact, slips out of importance soon after her arrival. Instead the story is taken over by a rather aggressively presented family mythology, pieced together by her relatives like something at a quilting bee.

As Gram and Lena weave in and out of reality, portraits of the men in the family begin to emerge. Both women are still intensely preoccupied with their lost husbands, whom they remember as perfect mates: "'Fireworks,' Lena said. 'I met Roy Carter and it was fireworks.'" These husbands end up rather more like icons than men, however. Madge's husband Raymond, who committed suicide, is the only male character to come truly alive. Literally worshiped by Cindy, mythologized by himself into a reincarnation of King Tut . . . , Raymond comes forth as pathetically human when Madge finally tells Cindy the truth about him and their relationship. "He was a very sick man," she says anti-climactically.

Cindy is the one character who resists revisiting the past. "Every time I come over here, ya'll start on those depressing stories," she tells the assemblage. "This family is full of death." She has a point. There is something slightly ghoulish about this family's determination to invoke the past. . . .

McCorkle tries hard to create a living mythology as a way to show how the past informs the present in our lives. Yet this intention becomes so obvious that it becomes unwieldy. The characters seem to know each other's stories already; the retelling feels staged. . . . We get the feeling that we have heard a lot of these stories before, too.

Tending to Virginia winds up very neatly, with everyone's life aired out. Indeed, the end effect is of having sorted through a trunk of old clothes, salvaging a few interesting items to be dry cleaned and packing the rest tidily away again in the attic. Virginia goes happily back to Mark, dismissing all of her former confusion and resentment as "something psychological." Cindy and Madge are reconciled. Gram and Lena return to their rocking chairs. Life in Saxapaw goes on.

McCorkle is an interesting writer. This novel has considerable lyrical power at times; the scenes where Gram remembers herself as a young bride and then as a new widow are particularly moving. Yet there are so many main characters that we never have time to get truly attached to any particular one. And for all its memories and reflections, the pace of the book as a whole is curiously inert—not unlike Virginia lying on Gram's sofa in a semi-daze. What you find yourself waiting for, by the end of 300 pages, is to be genuinely startled.

Suzanne Berne, "Not That Story Again," in Belles Lettres: A Review of Books by Women, *Vol. 3, No. 3, January-February, 1988, p. 12.*

DANIEL MAX

[*July 7th*] narrated a day in the life of Marshboro, North Carolina, land of tobacco farms and Quik Piks, porch swings and I-95 developments, as seen through the colliding perspectives of a disparate set of locals. Most memorable of Marshboro's inhabitants was sexy Juanita, paradigm of the New South and the "owner and fully-trained electrologist" of Hair Today, Gone Tomorrow.

July 7th is nearly flawless, true to life and constructed with a feather-light touch. *Tending to Virginia* sounds a note of greater complexity. And if, contrasted with *July 7th,* the novel is less perfectly graceful, it is also far meatier. The Virginia of the title—Ginny Sue before she went to college and put on airs—is pregnant, self-absorbed, and mildly neurotic. Uncertain of her love for her husband (who mostly remains off-stage) and of her willingness to bring new life into the world, she is propped up—both physically and psychically—by four generations of family, the Pearson women. The eldest is long deceased and lives only in the family's memory. Still around are a pair of elderly, nearly senile sisters, Lena and Emily, the middle-aged mothers, Madge and Hannah, and their children, Ginny Sue and her feisty, catty cousin Cindy. The Pearson women, protozoa-like, constantly bubble, shift, engulf, and digest their own history. . . .

McCorkle simply has a gift for rendering voices. No amount of practice could explain her ability to convey Lena's and Emily's slightly different mixtures of senility and nostalgia,

for instance. The tour de force of the novel is the final set piece, in which the three living generations gather under one roof—Emily's garden apartment—in the midst of a storm. There, portrayed only in dialogue, the Pearson women work through—comically, movingly, and ultimately cathartically—their discordant memories of what their family has been and now is. Lena and Emily, the older generation, whose fading minds have been reeling, confusing past and present, fact and wish, finally come to rest on the bedrock of family identity. Made comfortable by their memories, they prepare to become, in turn, remembered. The middle generation of Madge and Hannah more conventionally reveals a skeleton in the closet. Cindy, acknowledging the affection she always insisted her family denied her, drops the wisecracking, tough Southern girl routine and makes up her mind to go into the world looking for love instead of put downs and battles. Virginia comes simply to the certainty that she loves her husband and can bring a new Pearson into the crazy family.

All this revelation is handled in a single scene of remarkable subtlety, a small masterpiece of oblique pacing and accidental revelations. It is much easier to draw a character than to show him changing, and ordinarily the more convincingly he is initially drawn, the less we believe in his subsequent alteration; but McCorkle has pulled it off.

Most fun of all McCorkle's types—those characters in any good author's gallery recognizable from novel to novel—is the New South bitch. In *July 7th* she is Juanita, who thinks she has the goods on the other women of Marshboro because she knows their shameful hair-laden secrets, who works out on the Nautilus, and who reads *Cosmopolitan* for the trends. In *Tending to Virginia* Cindy plays the role, fond of Friday nights at the Ramada Inn bar and convinced all other women are either shrews or "slutbuckets."

One looks forward to this funny, telling character appearing in many McCorkle novels to come. . . . Nobody has written of such women better—just one of McCorkle's many and fast-growing talents.

Daniel Max, in a review of "Tending to Virginia," in Boston Review, *Vol. XIII, No. 1, February, 1988. p. 27.*

Lisel Mueller

1924-

German-born American poet and critic.

In her poems, Mueller combines vivid imagery with a minimalistic style to affirm the importance of personal concerns and to examine the implications underlying private and public perception. She explained: "I write about experiences that come along to disturb or excite me, experiences that I believe to be natural landmarks in the course of living for everyone." Critics frequently praise Mueller for precise, balanced imagery and her ability to evoke emotion without resorting to sentimentality.

In her first collection of poetry, *Dependencies* (1965), Mueller explores such traditional topics as death, doubt, spiritual anguish, and love. Eileen Sanzo praised this work as "intellectually strong and cerebral, yet filled with emotion, exquisitely sensitive and finely wrought." In *The Private Life* (1976), Mueller reflects on the importance of seemingly insignificant concerns and highlights the need to maintain a well-balanced inner self. Louis Martz observed: "These are honest, open poems, a kind of verse that one is glad to have, because it runs so close to our own better responses." The chapbook *Voices from the Forest* (1977) contains Mueller's acclaimed poem "The Triumph of Life: Mary Shelley," which contrasts contemporary notions of feminism with nineteenth-century author Mary Shelley's assertion that personal freedom can be effectively achieved within existing social structures.

In her next major collection of verse, *The Need to Hold Still* (1980), Mueller addresses such subjects as her childhood and early adult life in Germany and her gradual awareness and acceptance of middle age. Stephen Corey maintained that in this volume "Mueller perfects a voice that has learned to react personally to all people, things, times, and places." In *Second Language* (1986), she again renders profound insights from ordinary experience while exploring memory as an instrument of self-knowledge and suggesting ways in which language shapes and defines existence. Praising Mueller's "skillful absorption and depiction of images," Peter Stitt noted: "She works almost photographically, recording impressions, scenes, and events in flawless and beautiful form." Mueller has also contributed poems and critical essays to numerous literary periodicals.

(See also *CLC*, Vol. 13 and *Contemporary Authors*, Vols. 93-96.)

EILEEN SANZO

Lisel Mueller sees life "as a Process—a matter of gain and loss, current and counter-current, which refuses to hold still and be sorted out, the 'old dependency of day and night' which confronts me at every turn." Her themes [in *Dependencies*] are abstract, frequently about death, as in "**Woman with Chrysanthemum,**" spiritual darkness, as in "**The Blind Leading the Blind,**" doubt and wonder. But the poems do not remain only abstract. They are written in terms of an experience—the experience of one person fraught with illumination of the inner

Photograph by Alan Plog. Courtesy of Lisel Mueller.

lives of others. She writes "I write about experiences that come along to disturb or excite me, experiences that I believe to be natural landmarks in the course of living for everyone." Because Miss Mueller writes about an important inner experience, her poetry is profound with emotion.

Second to the theme of death, in such poems as "**The Ancient Woman,**" and "**In Memory of Anton Webern,**" is the theme of love. . . . Miss Mueller writes of new love, of forgotten love, of true love and false love and the difference. There is a fine balance of ideas in the volume. In one of the finest poems of the book, "**In the Thriving Season: In Memory of My Mother,**" her love of her young first born daughter meets the pain of the death of her mother. In the poem, "**The Blind Leading the Blind,**" the touch of the other person in life's cave of spiritual blackness is a consolation. In such poems as "**The Power of Music to Disturb,**" and "**On Finding a Bird's Bones in the Woods,**" mystery is met with patience. Trying to plumb the nature of life, Miss Mueller writes of the mystery of life—change and death and their attendant shock, doubt and anguish, and an answer in the form of wonder and love.

A lesser number of the poems contain social satire, such as "**The People at the Party,**" and fantasy, such as "**The Mermaid,**" and "**Moon Fishing.**" Much of the imagery describes nature. It is appropriate and fitted to the subject. Miss Mueller writes with ease and clarity. The touch is delicate. It seems that the mind of the poet is skipping, then turning back on itself in a happy, brilliant choice of imagery, then running on again. [*Dependencies*] is intellectually strong and cerebral, yet filled with emotion, exquisitely sensitive and finely wrought. (pp. 165-66)

Eileen Sanzo, "Inner Experience," in Spirit, *Vol. XXXII, No. 6, January, 1966, pp. 165-66.*

MARK McCLOSKEY

Lisel Mueller's verse [in *Dependencies*] often considers love in its quotidian aspects. The birth of the speaker's first child heals the memory of her mother's death (**"In the Thriving Season"**); the woman at first grieved by the absence of her lover yields to the pleasure of a romantic setting and finally, it seems, to the man who creates it by his music (**"The Siege"**). **"The Fall"** concerns primeval sin as the distance between lovers; **"Nine Months Making,"** love as a physical rather than intellectual truth; **"The Mermaid,"** the illusory ideal woman; **"The Lonesome Dream,"** Eden where love is exquisite and death charming; and **"A Prayer for Rain,"** love paralyzed by silence and alienation.

The virtue of personal involvement in her themes inclines Miss Mueller to the vice of over-statement and ambiguous imagery. The last two stanzas of **"Nine Months Making,"** for example, are unnecessary, for the first two stanzas embody the theme and the intention. . . .

But where intelligence and feeling merge, and where the traditional rhetorical capacities of English are used to manage this fusion, excellent poems result, such as **"For Lucy," "In the Thriving Season," "The Siege," "The Fall," "The Mermaid," "A Plain Sonnet," "Apology," "A Prayer for Rain,"** and **"The Expense of Spirit in a Waste of Shame."**

Mark McCloskey, in a review of "Dependencies," in Poetry, *Vol. CVIII, No. 4, July, 1966, p. 275.*

JOHN N. MORRIS

Lisel Mueller's **"The Triumph of Life: Mary Shelley"** is to my mind the most striking piece in [*Voices from the Forest*]. The easiest thing to say about the poem is that in it Mary Shelley, speaking across the years, admonishes as self-dramatizing certain of her modern sisters. *"An idea whose time has come* / you say about your freedom / but you forget the reason"*—the reason the time has come. That reason is history, which has transformed what was a matter of biological chance into an object of choice: "Almost two hundred years / of medical science divide us." But such a view of the poem is reductive. Mary Shelley reproaches all simple modern rational optimism, as prefigured in her father, the optimism that, forgetful of certain of the hard terms on which we hold title to our lives, supposes the Good to be a matter of arranging things properly. . . . It is not that there is anything wrong with the ends desired. "I wanted what you want, / what you have." But the poem at last is not about these desires, these ends. Mueller's subject is heroism, the exercise of freedom in the face of limitation and contingency, and in point of heroism we moderns, male and female, for whom history has done so much, are infinitely Mary Shelley's inferiors. In the mechanical exercise of our historically given liberty and in our rage against the restraints upon it that yet (perhaps necessarily) remain, we are, in comparison with her, morally trivial. This is truly a

poem of the triumph of life, the triumph of the persistence of life which faces down what it knows must at last defeat it, limit and circumstance, those emblems of mortality that give meaning to freedom.

Such language may suggest that I have mistaken Lisel Mueller for Homer. If so, I apologize. The poem's eight quiet pages do not suppose that they make up an *Iliad*. Still, the poem is, as Mary Shelley finely says of her *Frankenstein*, "a tale to tremble by." And, oddly, it is, as she also says of that work of hers, "what is oddly called a romance." (pp. 109-110)

John N. Morris, "Eight Poets from the Small Presses," in The Ohio Review, *Vol. XIX, No. 1, Winter, 1978, pp. 98-112.*

STEPHEN COREY

Lisel Mueller's third book, *The Need to Hold Still,* shows her to be a minimalist of words and forms. . . . [In her opening poem, she] offers her 13-year-old daughter a copy of *Sister Carrie* as a birthday gift:

> And so I give you Dreiser,
> his measure of certainty:
> a table that's oak all the way through,
> real and fragrant flowers,
> skirts from sheep and silkworms,
> no unknown fibers.

Mueller will offer us this same hard and pure world in her poems, but not because we should be finally content with such a world:

> I give you names like nails,
> walls that withstand your pounding,
> doors that are hard to open,
> but once they are open, admit you
> into rooms that breathe pure sun.

A quantum leap from plain experience to some complex revelation about or through that experience—such is Mueller's goal, a goal she announces . . . with the following quote from [William] Stafford as epigraph to her volume:

> So, the world happens twice—
> once what we see it as;
> second it legends itself
> deep, the way it is.

Stafford believes that the natural world can speak its own legends, but for Mueller all legends have human sources. Among the legends she explores are those of ancient religions, historical figures, folk and fairy tales, and childhood dreams and fantasies.

In *The Need to Hold Still* Mueller perfects a voice that has learned to react personally to all people, things, times, and places. [**"The Need to Hold Still"**], speaking of an aging woman who gathers bouquets of skeletal winter weeds, renders in human terms what Mueller's voice has learned in poetic terms: living is caring, simplicity can be wisdom. If we care, we can sometimes see ourselves in the world just by speaking its names, without any intervention from any applied forms or notions. . . . To become that world, to be governed by its winter, can be immeasurably sad:

> A woman
> coming in from a walk
> notices how drab

her hair has become
that gray and brown
are colors
she disappears into
that her body
has stopped asking
for anything but calm.

But the sadness carries wisdom unavailable to blossoming weeds and young women, "the dignity of form / after seduction / and betrayal / by color." We look beneath the surface to a beauty born of, and surviving, experience: "dullness of straw, / which underlies / the rose / the grape / the kiss / the narrow leaf blades, / shape of the body."

This is the world legending itself deep, and time after time Mueller's language helps us break through to such depths. In the historical monologue, **"The Triumph of Life: Mary Shelley,"** the dead poet's wife derides all who would be offended by Byron's rescuing of Shelley's heart from the funeral pyre:

> You don't trust the heart
> though you define death
> as the absence of heartbeat
>
> You would have taken a ring,
> a strand of hair, a shoelace
> —a symbol, a souvenir
>
> not the center, the real thing

Brazenly and imaginatively touching the real to get beyond the real—this is Mueller's tactic. Sometimes she applies herself to a subject as apparently simple as children's drawings of themselves, with the result that we see innocence and experience—those tired poetic troopers—become meaningful one more time. . . . Other times, Mueller goes after realities and legends as large as the poetic process itself. In **"The End of Science Fiction,"** she argues that our chaotic space-age life has outstripped our forward-looking imaginings, and that therefore we must look backward and inward for meaningful subjects: "invent a child that will save the world, / a man who carries his father out of a burning city."

Nothing about such a task, such legend-making, is easy. Nothing about vigorous and sincere working toward minimal subjects, words, and forms is easy. (pp. 739-43)

Stephen Corey, "Lives on Leaves," in The Virginia Quarterly Review, *Vol. 57, No. 4, Autumn, 1981, pp. 732-43.*

ANN LOUISE HENTZ

The dialectic suggested by such opposites as affirmation and negation, violence and forgiveness, darkness and light, is an integral part of Lisel Mueller's poetry. So although her poetry is filled with music and musicians, one is not surprised to find that it is also concerned with an examination of tangible silence. Aware of life's violences, its cruelties, its despairs, she is also aware of and evokes the silent life around us: a flower coming into bloom after months of denial, a sense of birth and growth, a mysteriousness in life of which we are only partly aware.

Although the most direct statement of this theme can be found in the title poem of the collection *The Private Life,* one finds that it also pervades Mueller's earlier poetry, providing us with an introduction to her use of the theme. In her first book, *Dependencies,* she explores the quality of silence, a silence that is paradoxically sound. In **"Cicadas,"** for example, the "high, sustained note" of the insects is "the rapt voice of silence,"

a voice so single that one cannot tell the quality of the sound or whether indeed it is sound. This palpable stillness is gone in "scrubbed autumn," gone in "the second skin, / hot and close, of silence." Here we find the poet evoking the indescribable, making us feel on a sensory level that which is so subtle that we can know it in some sense only when it is gone. (p. 24)

Mueller's silence has many faces, but always it is insistent and important in the poem. The quiet, gentle evening of **"The Annunciation"** in which "Dusk was the angel" is the setting and vehicle of the Virgin's growing receptivity to the "hovering mystery." At the moment of conception, however, the silence is broken by the rush of wings, her cry, and her divine knowledge of everything. Although the moment of conception is one of sound, the landscape of silence is the ground on which such illumination can take place. (p. 25)

The most direct statement of the importance of silence in our lives is found in **"The Private Life,"** the title poem of the collection, a poem so central to a discussion of this theme that it warrants a thorough explication. The statement of this three-part poem opens the first section and is repeated in the last: "What happens, happens in silence." The silent happenings of the first section are particularities of hope and despair across the nation and the world which universalize the opening statement. The man who feels himself going insane is located specifically in a large, cosmopolitan center, New York City, and the country he flies to in order to rest is also particularized, Brazil. The piano student (music again) is located only in the midwest state of Indiana, but his dreams and hero-worship are epitomized by his lovingly gathering the prune-pits left over from [his hero] Horowitz's breakfast. As the named locations fade in the poem, the incidents become more particularized, so we move from the broad expanse of the flight of the New York man trying to escape insanity to the concrete incident of the gathering of prune pits. The implied daydreams of the student look forward to the next particular, "My daughter daydreams of marriage" as she has suddenly grown three inches taller than her mother. As the poem moves from the international in the first lines to the immediate life of the speaker it is also particularized in time. . . . Within the first section, then, Mueller gives us the broken things of the world as well as the hopes and dreams of the young of marriage and careers.

The second section depicts a fruit market, telescoping human life, "our violent history," into the description of the speechless fruit. Since the reader becomes adjusted to the analogies of human life with the "age-spotted avocados" and the "lemons with goose flesh," as the descriptions build to the hostile "pineapples like stockades" and culminate in the instructions for the coconut heads, one sees these instructions in terms of the human. We have been led into these analogies in such a mild way that we are shocked to realize where the poet has been leading us:

> Pierce the eyes with an awl,
> allowing the milk to run out,
> then tap hard with a hammer
> until the outer covering cracks—

In the third section of the poem the noise of the assault on our lives by the news media increases in volume and speed until the voice in the poem interposes "Stop it." Opening with the statement "We are being eaten by words," this section begins to build with the intrusion on the speaker's private life of headlines, TV, and printer's ink. The physical self is violated, the face is "smeared," the lungs, like TV's "blue tubes, are always on,'' even the husband comes home ''smelling'' of print. This assault of words that has the power to ''smear'' and smell up our lives becomes the ''dragon's mouth'' of the teletype, unconquerable, irresistible, as the images become more violent with ''ripped out,'' and the speed of the poem becomes faster as the tongue of the ''dragon's mouth'' ''grows back / at the speed of sound.'' The headlines which follow, tumbling over each other, are a hilarious combination of disaster and trivia, ''The terrorist wore a business suit,'' the absurdity underlined by the witty insertion of Felicia Hemans' line, ''The boy stood on the burning deck.'' To such banality have we been led. The speed and volume of the headlines culminate in the capitalized shout, ''YOUR HOUSE IS ON FIRE, YOUR CHILDREN ARE GONE,'' only to be cut short by the quiet, firm ''Stop it'' and the reassertion, ''What happens, happens in silence.''

The poem concludes with images that show that the truly important things happen in silence, an argument with which the whole of John Donne's ''A Valediction Forbidding Mourning'' is concerned. Unlike Donne, Lisel Mueller draws her images from the individual, beginning with the unseen physiology of the body, the red blood cell, the ''curl in the brain,'' the ovum, the ''switched-on nerves,'' and moving to the consciousness of the individual with the ''eyes before the scream,'' memory, conscience, and ''the smile that says, *Come to bed.*''

As in the first section, the poem ends by being particularized in a wintry time and focused on the speaker's personal life using a plant as the image: ''Today—my snow-capped birthday.'' The image of the red hibiscus provides the color of blood and life to the ''snow-capped birthday'' and closes the poem with the hard-won, quiet affirmation found in so many of Mueller's poems:

> Months of refusal; now
> one sudden silent flower
> one inscrutable life.
>
> (pp. 27-9)

Lisel Mueller's poetry reaches beyond the surfaces of noise and sound to lead us to an awareness of the silence that is the essence of things, the silence of growth and decay, as well as that ''shimmer of silence'' at the end of the fearful journey. To evoke these qualities below the surfaces of our lives, to make us feel on the sensory level the palpable silence, the sounds ''above the shut-off level / of our simple ears,'' one must be a poet of acute perceptions; Lisel Mueller is indeed a poet who is, in Yeats's words, ''gifted with so fine an ear.'' (p. 30)

> *Ann Louise Hentz, ''The Sounds and Silences of Lisel Mueller's 'Private Life','' in* Contemporary Poetry, *Vol. IV, No. 3, 1982, pp. 24-32.*

TOM HANSEN

A key to Lisel Mueller's *The Need to Hold Still* can be found in the headnote to the book:

> So, the world happens twice—
> once what we see it as;
> second it legends itself
> deep, the way it is. . .
>
> William Stafford

The key is the word ''legends,'' used here as a verb, as if it were a process. In order to get beyond ''what we see it as,'' in order to go deeper, Mueller looks at the unexpected patterns lurking just below the surface of our lives. Her motifs are not the recurrent myths that have given us so many weighty archetypes and names for Freudian complexes, but the airy legends of childhood—the ones we adults have stopped believing in, almost, and have begun living behind our backs. The deep forest whose greatest danger is lurking always just out of sight (**''Voices from the Forest''**). The wicked witch who, so they say, devours children (**''Found in the Cabbage Patch''**). The hateful Doppelgänger whose life is one's own, a ghostly contrary who bodies forth underground energies (**''The False Bride's Story''** from *Voices from the Forest*). The deep forest, the wicked witch, and the dark other are real. We are children lost on our dangerous journey. And no one seems to be living happily ever after.

This is not a book about fairy tales or the psychology of fairy tales. It is about the way the world legends itself in each person's life. The voice we hear in many of these poems is that of a woman who sees herself entering middle age—more than halfway home. Most of her choices have by now been made, either by her or for her. She lives what sounds like an ordinary middle-class life: family, home, financial security, and all that these things usually imply. But inwardly she burns with a restless energy. As she goes about the day-to-day business of her life, some of this energy breaks free and the world recovers some of its original strangeness. . . . (pp. 124-25)

Many of the poems in *The Need to Hold Still* are about childhood, innocence, and other beginnings: Mueller's parents-to-be meeting in World War I Germany and her own growing up in Germany before World War II; Helen Keller's miraculous discovery of language; the beginnings of abstraction in modern painting; a strong, sustained poem in which Mary Shelley examines the meaning of her life and declares that she was not a precursor of modern feminist thought; and, in several poems, a woman's growing realization and acceptance of her passage into middle age. In these latter poems, especially, we hear the voice of one who is haunted by the legendary world of childhood. **''Drawings by Children,''** for example, begins by describing typical features of drawings by children. It lists childish absolutes we are all forced to surrender:

> . . . the sky is always blue
> if it is day. . . .
> it is clearly day or night,
> it is bright or totally dark,
> it is here and never there.

In time, we come to discover that it is neither day nor night, that we are neither here nor there. We become different from what we used to be, different from all the rest of creation. But when we were children, we lived closer to our instincts. We were so caught up by the great current bearing us forward every moment into a new world that we had no consciousness of time. We lived in an endless, lost Now. . . . (pp. 125-26)

[However, we] fell headlong into rational adult consciousness. And then more and more we began to see through things, all the way through to the hidden nothing just out of sight but always there:

> But the house has only two dimensions,
> like a mask without its face;
> the people who live there stand outside
> as though time were always summer—
> there is nothing behind the wall
> except a space where the wind whistles,
> but you cannot see that.

Poems like this rehearse the fall of man. But this is more than another version of "The soul longs to return from whence it came." The soul does long to return, but not because of any sentimental attachment to its lost and irrecoverable state of presumed innocence. Like Eliot, Mueller believes that "the river is within us, the sea is all about us." The voices of our forgotten past will not entirely quit echoing in our ears, because they are our voices. At unpredictable times they rise up from subterranean vaults below everyday consciousness: our personal childhoods, the childhood of the race, the wordless memories of prehuman existence. . . . (p. 126)

Here is the brotherhood—"beinghood" is a better word; it includes all living things—of all instinctive life, a state man has largely outgrown. Here is the loss of various physical gifts. And here, too, is self-reflective consciousness—both the greatest gift and the greatest loss. Consciousness cuts through everything. Suddenly the world is no longer given. Suddenly we are responsible for our lives. . . .

Many people never hear [the voices] at all. Others, perhaps only a few, hear the voices often, urging them to take the fearful journey into the forest. In **"Voices from the Forest,"** we hear the dark energies speak: the protean manshape who warns virgins that one or another of his disguises will lead to their undoing; the ex-beauty, now aging into haghood, who warns young wives that she is what they will become; and the shadowy other, whose warning is equally terrifying. . . . (p. 127)

These voices still frighten us, because we intuitively recognize that they are real, even as we consciously dismiss them as being nothing more than the shadows cast by a childlike imagination. They are shadows. This is why they still retain at least some of their power over us—because the child is still there entombed within the adult, sleeping in a deep trance, waiting. It is an elemental part of the human psyche, a part which instinctively senses that our spiritual as well as our physical survival is intimately intertwined with the life of nature. This is the dark forest from which those voices arise. This is the world that legends itself deep. Mueller evokes this world, which is almost lost to the adult imagination, sometimes using fairy tale motifs, sometimes taking the long evolutionary view. But evolution in these poems is just as compelling and disturbing as the mythic approach is. . . . (p. 128)

[In her poem **"Why We Tell Stories,"** Mueller seems] to say that we tell stories in order to invent ourselves back into the great forgotten journey. It is not that we are the end of the journey, or even that we are the present moment. But the journey itself—the whole endless, beginningless mystery of it—is our life. All of it is written in each of us.

In various stages of embryonic development, the human fetus re-enacts major stages in the evolution of animal life—from that first pulse of life in the primordial ocean, through later stages in which the gill slit is clearly visible; from stages in which the reptilian forebrain is overlaid by the old mammalian limbic cortex and later by the new mammalian neocortex and the webbing between the fingers disappears, to those final stages in which the fetus is uniquely human in its morphology. Just as each human body, in the nine months following conception, knows how to grow itself, because it in some way remembers the story of its long journey, so, somewhere below consciousness, we carry the memory of our long psychic journey. This memory is what we meet and intuitively recognize and feel so unaccountably moved by in the presence of certain dreams, fairy tales, and myths. And this is why we tell stories—

to articulate, in the only way we know how, the lost meaning of our lives. . . . (pp. 128-29)

Tom Hansen, in a review of "The Need to Hold Still," in The Ohio Review, *No. 28, 1982, pp. 124-29.*

FRED MURATORI

Mueller's [*Second Language*] exhibits her continued interests in the imagination's tendency to extrapolate the extraordinary from the mundane. Her tools are the traditional, but lately discredited, techniques of simile, metaphor ("Hope is a fat seed pod"), apostrophe, and personification. She speaks to objects and invents lives for abstractions . . . , unable to resist investing the world with her own generous sensibility. But so many poems are first-person meditations (even the frequent "you" is an "I" in disguise) that one feels one's attention repeatedly called to the poet's sensitivity rather than to the poem. In the strongest pieces, like **"Necessities,"** the poet steps aside, allowing the most admirable facets of her talent to speak for themselves.

Fred Muratori, in a review of "Second Language," in Library Journal, *Vol. 111, No. 15, September 15, 1986, p. 90.*

JOSEPH PARISI

Mueller's many fans have good reason to rejoice in [*Second Language*]. Her evocative title takes on ever greater meaning as the poet . . . examines the multiple meanings of experience—past and present, image and reality, sensory perception and symbolism. Many of the first poems here poignantly recall her father and mother, a childhood and way of life lost but for memory. In **"Your Tired, Your Poor,"** she brings fresh insight into the nature of exile, while exploring how in learning a new language even the shapes of the letters become emblems of transformation. Time and again, the poet surprises with aperçus: about what it must be like to have a face-lift, to be a "southpaw" or an abused child. . . . But Mueller's gift for synesthesia is matched by her human sympathy: we not only come to know what she has identified, but also to share her uncommon empathy. Poem for poem, this is one of the strongest volumes of this or many another year.

Joseph Parisi, in a review of "Second Language: Poems," in Booklist, *Vol. 83, No. 9, January 1, 1987, p. 679.*

PETER STITT

[Lisel Mueller's] conceptual predeliction for a poetry that achieves its ends through the use of imagery is indicated both directly and indirectly at many points in [*Second Language*]—which offers, as a kind of prefatory piece, a poem called **"Necessities."** At first glance, the five sections of this poem seem to correspond to the five sections of the book itself, but this turns out not to be the case. Instead, Mueller is here indicating both her general methodology and her central thematic concerns. The fifth section functions almost as a theoretical explanation of how she intends to employ imagery:

> Even now, *the old things first things,*
> which taught us language. Things of day and of night.
> Irrational lightning, fickle clouds, the incorruptible moon.

Fire as revolution, grass as the heir
to all revolutions. Snow
as the alphabet of the dead, subtle, undeciphered.
The river as what we wish it to be.
Trees in their humanness, animals in their otherness.
Summits. Chasms. Clearings.
And stars, which gave us the word distance,
so we could name our deepest sadness.

Human concerns and interpretations are an inseparable part of each of the things mentioned in these lines. It is the objects around her, the objects she welcomes into her poems, that give meaning to the world for Mueller. The passage also illustrates some of the major strengths of her writing as art—the precision of the descriptions, the balance inherent in the phrasing, and the wonderful way in which the lines build to their moving closure. The elegiac strain delineated here is the most prominent feature of the human landscape in the rest of the book, and it is in presenting this that **"Necessities"** best serves its introductory function.

Another theoretical passage (but one that moves in a different direction) occurs in **"English as a Second Language,"** the second section of **"Your Tired, Your Poor."** . . . For the teacher in this passage, the meaning of the word creates an image; for the students, the letters of the word are seen as images in their own right at the same time that they suggest additional images. The teacher (tired, overworked, and underpaid) visualizes a bower of bliss, while the students (apparently refugees, like Mueller, from prewar Europe) see primarily implements of torture. Meanwhile, the hopeful poet, who presumably traveled through this whole process many years ago, is able at the end to envision a future in which the word *tree* will grow into a real tree, even for the students. What is most significant in these lines, however, is not this variety of interpretations but the fact that all the characters think in terms of images.

Though *Second Language* contains poems that illustrate more directly the way in which Lisel Mueller extracts meanings from images, it does not contain any poems better written and more moving than one she calls **"Widow."** . . . The poem has its minor imagistic triumphs . . . but is good primarily because of the way Mueller presents the psychology of grief through imagery related to food. Mortality is a constant preoccupation in these pages generally and is one of the reasons this volume is so powerful. Another reason is Mueller's skillful absorption and depiction of images. She works almost photographically, recording impressions, scenes, and events in flawless and beautiful form. The negative side to such a method is that the poems in this book tend to remain images separate from one another, leaving us with a series of discrete dazzlements rather than a unified whole. This is a minor problem, however, when the individual poems are as good as they are in *Second Language*. (pp. 193-95)

Peter Stitt, "The Whirlpool of Image and Narrative Flow," in The Georgia Review, *Vol. XLI, No. 1, Spring, 1987, pp. 192-208.*

ALICE FULTON

Reading Lisel Mueller's fourth book, *Second Language,* is a bit like gazing at a lake or a tree. At first you think nothing new here: another wave, another leaf. But if you bring your full attention to bear, you're amazed at the implication and activity of an apparently simple surface. Like so many plain-style poems, these equate invisibility of craft with authenticity. The important difference here is that one does not feel manip-

ulated by a disingenuous sincerity. There is no see-how-sensitive-I-am posing, no subtext of self-congratulation. Instead, the sensibility couples kindness with intelligence.

Mueller favors short, imagistic free verse lyrics or longer meditations in numbered sections. The sense of closure is one of the keenest pleasures of the poems. Even if the previous lines didn't make me want to jump and shout, I was usually won over by the aptness of the ending. Although the book's five sections share overriding concerns, the first part focuses upon an autobiographical past. In a moving elegy to her father (**"Voyager"**), the poet holds a negative up to the light and contemplates its ghoulish reversal. The poem's reticent closure is typical of her delicacy:

How can you see, your glasses
are whitewashed and there are holes
where your teeth used to be

Nevertheless you smile at me
across an enormous distance
as you have so many times
to let me know you have arrived.

This poem, like others in the book, establishes values without succumbing to didacticism: engagement is prized and distance mourned as the ultimate hardship. In Mueller's view, memory is the great moral necessity, begetting self-knowledge and culpability. It is also an ungovernable force that "raises landmarks, / unbidden, out of place / and time." . . . In its guise of garden "where . . . / nothing ever changes," remembrance affords the only immortality we will ever know. However, other poems imply that the Eden of recollection is neither permanent nor infinitely expandable. When one becomes comfortable in a new language, for example, the old tongue, old home, takes on a quality of strangeness akin to forgetfulness. Memories, moreover, are generative: broadcast like seed, they may fall on someone who in turn recalls "a forgotten childhood scene." In its obsessive aspect, reminiscence can be a prison. But it also allows us to crack the code of absence: a widow listens until familiar sounds "turn into messages in the new language" her husband "has been forced to learn," and "All night she works on the code, / almost happy,. . . / . . . while the food in its china caskets / dries out on the kitchen table."

The tongue we learn after death is but one of many second languages in this book. Nature has a script, although we are poor translators: blackbirds compose themselves "in the ancient penstrokes," the "unreadable signature." Looking at milkwood pods, Mueller thinks this is "what we would say to each other / if we could find the heart. . . ." **"Letter to California,"** an argument for landscape's effect on semantics, reveals the multiplicity of English. To one speaker it's "strictureless," to another it's "a low-keyed continuous struggle." Music and sex are dialects, as is confabulation, the language we invent, like Scheherazade, to save our lives.

Several poems explore the aberrant: identical twins who point to the double within us all; the Cassandra figure of a psychic; a disco queen turned gospel preacher; the otherworldly daughters mothers worry about; the abused child who "will not betray her keeper". Far from being a random assemblage of freaks, these lives reveal the discrepancy between facade and inner life. Mueller is especially attentive to the masks women forge to get by in our culture. **"Southpaw"** celebrates difference, the self as "a mermaid with two left arms," while **"Face-Lift"** asks facetiously if the operation also removed memories "like the soiled / part of a roller towel." A poem about a suicide observes "her mind was not like her house / with its open door, its yard full of flowers. . . .'' Home, for Mueller, is more state of mind than geographical locale. In answer to the question ''How can one teach 'Spring and Fall: To a Young Child' in the Hawaiian Islands?'' Mueller argues that the mind's climate supersedes the actual weather: for the bereaved a tropical paradise can become *''bare ruin'd choirs.''* Several poems seek intention in nature, even as they recognize ''childish superstition'' in the impulse of the search. . . . Mueller finds the will to believe a self-protective hoax: it saves us from having to admit to ''the broken connection, / that the world resists meaning / not to tease us, but because / there is no meaning / except the one we invent.''

The last poems examine self-definition and free will: to what degree are we formed by others' expectations of us? **''What Is Left to Say''** describes maturity as a ''new frugality,'' a time when the self ''stops trying to please / by learning everyone's dialect. . . .'' In *Second Language* Mueller attains such a calm majority. (pp. 368-70)

Alice Fulton, ''Main Things,'' in Poetry, *Vol. CLI, No. 4, January, 1988, pp. 360-77.*

(Jean) Iris Murdoch

1919-

Irish-born English novelist, nonfiction writer, dramatist, poet, essayist, and scriptwriter.

A scholar of philosophy specializing in Platonic and existential theory, Murdoch is also a distinguished and prolific novelist who makes use of intricately developed plots and witty observations to examine emotional, spiritual, and intellectual pursuits of well-educated, upper middle-class British characters. Nicholas Spice stated: "Like Henry James's, Iris Murdoch's style is high, in the sense that she writes about lofty matters—the nature of morality, the reasons for existence, how we should live and love, how we should die." The complexities of her plots and the interrelationships she develops among characters have led critics to compare Murdoch's novels with those of such nineteenth-century writers as Fedor Dostoevski and Charles Dickens. While Murdoch writes primarily in the realist mode, many of her works describe supernatural events that lend allegorical and symbolic implications to her themes. Murdoch explained: "In real life the fantastic and the ordinary, the plain and the symbolic, are often indissolubly joined together, and I think the best novels explore and exhibit life without disjoining them."

Between 1954 and 1987, Murdoch published twenty-three novels that explore various types of love, the relationship between imagination and reality, the role of art, and moral issues and dilemmas pertaining to questions of good and evil. By developing diverse scenarios and characters, employing such literary devices as twists of plot and symbolic overtones, and presenting fantasies and supernatural events, Murdoch examines abstract ideas within the context of human drama. Michael Levenson commented: "Murdoch, a philosophic novelist, spurns the idea of the philosophic novel. This is because she believes that fiction should shiver like the quicksilver of life. She wants a fiction that can engage with urgencies and accidents. She wants to respect the stuffy dust of the universe, the hard rubber, the concrete pieces, the loose chips, the tiny animals; wants to be able to write a novel (such as [*The Book and the Brotherhood*]) that not only can engage with '80s Marxism but can also have a parrot and a snail as two of its most important figures."

Several of Murdoch's works revolve around a manipulative character who achieves power and control over the lives of others. For example, her first novel, *Under the Net* (1954), focuses upon Jake Donoghue, who attempts to establish a pattern for his life in order to insulate himself from the impact of "contingencies," or random happenings that are not part of his design. During the course of the novel, Jake comes to accept contingency as a part of life while acknowledging the influence of others, thus freeing him to love. The lives of most of the characters in *The Flight from the Enchanter* (1956) are determined by how they respond to a charismatic and domineering "enchanter" who preys upon their personal obsessions. Murdoch introduces supernatural elements into this work that illuminate her examination of myth and reality. *The Black Prince* (1973) blends a murder mystery with ruminations on creativity by centering on an aged writer who attempts to impose his fantasies on others. Several critics noted parallels between this work and such Shakespeare plays as *Hamlet* and *The Tempest;*

Photograph by Mark Gerson

many of Murdoch's works involve characters whose relationships resemble that of the domineering Prospero and the servile Caliban in *The Tempest*. *The Black Prince* won the James Tait Black Memorial Prize in fiction.

Murdoch explores various forms of love throughout her fiction, particularly in *A Severed Head* (1961) and *The Sea, the Sea* (1978). *A Severed Head* addresses such topics as promiscuity, self-deception, and the unpredictable actions of individuals in love by detailing the interactions of three groups of characters who share progressive attitudes toward sex and male-female relationships. *The Sea, the Sea* depicts a man who sustains an obsessive love for a girl he knew during childhood. When they meet again years later, the man uses his expertise as a magician and theater director to interfere in her happy marriage. *The Sea, the Sea* was awarded the Booker McConnell Prize. In addition to her exploration of themes relating to love, Murdoch frequently examines spiritual issues. *The Bell* (1958), for example, is set in a religious community and involves conflicts among characters with diverse personalities, and a central character in *Henry and Cato* (1976) is a Catholic priest who gradually loses his faith. *Nuns and Soldiers* (1980), which concerns a wealthy and attractive widow who chooses from among her many suitors a feckless artist to be her husband, is replete with themes relating to love, art, and religion. One critic commented: ''Naturally, this being a Murdoch novel, nothing is so simple as it might appear to be. While *Nuns and Soldiers* works wonderfully as an archetypal tale of love triumphant, it presents dozens of other possibilities. . . . This is an exceptionally full book, packed with ideas, symbols, references, questionings, and with characters who, more than usually in Murdoch's novels, seem caught in the real web of life.''

Murdoch's novels of the 1980s contain features familiar to her earlier work. In *The Philosopher's Pupil* (1983), a respected scholar and stern moralist affects the lives of a large and diverse group of characters. Among the topics explored in this work are romantic and erotic infatuation, intellectual presumptions, and spiritual issues. *The Good Apprentice* (1985), which relates a man's search for redemption after he inadvertently contributes to the death of his friend, features allusions to the biblical tale of the Prodigal Son, a network of symbols centering on an elaborate house in the wilderness designed by a strange artist, and various subplots involving a group of characters in emotional, spiritual, sexual, and intellectual entanglements. *The Book and the Brotherhood* (1987) revolves around an insular circle of complacent intellectuals who offer financial support to David Crimond, an energetic peer, to write works of political philosophy. The revolutionary Marxist ideals espoused by Crimond clash with the conservative values of his colleagues, however, resulting in a series of arguments concerning social, political, and personal issues that force each of the characters to examine their own beliefs and actions.

Murdoch's complementary interests in philosophy and art are also evidenced in her nonfiction writings. For example, her first book, *Sartre: Romantic Rationalist* (1953), examines the existentialism of Jean-Paul Sartre by focusing on his use of the novel as a means of developing and exploring philosophical ideas, a recurring trait in Murdoch's novels as well. Among her other theoretical works, *The Fire and the Sun: Why Plato Banished the Artists* (1977) expounds upon Plato's views of art, while *Acastos: Two Platonic Dialogues* (1986) involves several characters who discuss the role of art in human life.

(See also *CLC*, Vols. 1, 2, 3, 4, 6, 8, 11, 15, 22, 31; *Contemporary Authors*, Vols. 13-16, rev. ed.; *Contemporary Authors New Revision Series*, Vol. 8; and *Dictionary of Literary Biography*, Vol. 14.)

A. N. WILSON

Iris Murdoch's readers divide between those who think that her characters are fantastic, unbelievable, weird, improbable; and those who say that 'there really are people like that.' One hears similar discussions from time to time about Dickens. . . . Novelists are 'only' fantasists, illusionists, magicians. It is the alchemy of great novelists which transforms these illusions into reality. What begins with the most extreme frivolity—the enlistment of our interest in unreal people in an unreal setting—becomes thereby morally serious. Many of us who are older than the heroine of *Northanger Abbey* (old enough, perhaps, to know better) feel that our greatest moments of moral discovery have come, not when reading philosophers or theologians, nor when having 'real' experiences, but when sitting in a chair with a novel open in our hands.

Consciousness of such matters is woven into the texture of everything Iris Murdoch writes, and this, to my mind, makes

her books all the more remarkable. As the Murdoch *oeuvre* expands, becoming ever more generous, ever more serious, it gets no less entertaining. She falls neither into the Tolstoyan pitfall of wishing to discard art in favour of preaching; nor into the Leavisite mistake (a mistake of taste, chiefly) of making art a substitute for religion.

There must be many explanations for the phenomenon, but the simplest is that she obviously loves writing novels; the sheer enjoyment of the exercise is communicated time and again. In recent books, too, one has felt how closely linked are the pleasures of writing and those of reading. Her favourite authors hover in the background as 'the Masters' are supposed to do at a seance. They do not inspire her to parody. Her style, her world, the whole feel of her books, are completely her own. But the Masters act as kindly midwives to her own purely distinctive art. Her last book, *The Philosopher's Pupil* was brought to birth, I felt, by Dostoevski. Not only is it the only modern novel I know to use with creative effect the narrative manner of *The Devils*, but in its presentations of spiritual evil and human vulnerability it was highly Dostoevskian. Similarly, though no one but Iris Murdoch could have written it, *The Sea, the Sea* is the story of a man reliving his entire past; it is the story of an obsessive love, a love which wants to make its object a prisoner. There is not much in common between Hartley and Albertine, but we feel Proust lending a helping hand to bring her to being. The most conscious example of the Master midwifing the Murdoch novel is *The Black Prince*, which is not only a love story and a murder story but also a celebration of two sides of Shakespeare's genius: the obsessive, inner author of the sonnets and *Hamlet* and the fecund, over-productive, cynical Shakespeare who could churn out the plays with seeming effortlessness.

The Good Apprentice is, once more, Shakespearian, but we feel here not the tormented Shakespeare of the sonnets who guided the pen of Bradley Pearson so much as the benign old all-forgiving magician of the last romances. This is a novel in which a young man gives his friend a drug sandwich, and by this act of silly thoughtlessness, is responsible for his death. His easy good looks and casual hedonism quickly land him in a ghastly mess. His half-brother Stuart, on the other hand, is a virtuous young man who keeps himself unspotted from the world. His idea in life is simply to be good; he is dedicating himself to it. His self-righteousness is awful. It is the best justification I have ever read for Bertrand Russell's peculiar statement that he could not imagine a more repulsive or dangerous ambition than the desire to be good. It is not Russell's wisdom, however, which informs this book so much as the warm Christianity of Shakespeare; Christianity, of course, with a highly Murdochian flavour. Not a single character in this huge book believes in God. And yet they nearly all seem to believe in some kind of moral absolute, they are all preoccupied with the question of how forgiveness is to be found. (p. 25)

Apart from anything else, one ought to stress that, although it is very long, this book is exciting in a way that the early Murdoch novels were exciting. It has all their verve and pace, their alarming sense that anything might happen, that strange reversals await the characters in every chapter. It is compulsive reading. I found myself reading it late into the night, and woken early by the excitement of it, I continued to read at dawn. It is the sort of book which takes hold of you completely, and which makes the 'real life' going on around you momentarily unvivid. Any attempt to summarise the story of Iris Murdoch's novels conveys nothing of the way they feel when you are inside them. It is a familiar trick of reviewers, who are often unkind to her, to rehearse the rapid emotional all-change among the distinctively named and usually enormous *dramatis personae* of her books. Yet the mystery of it is something one of the characters here discerns in Proust: "What a lot of pain there was all the way through. So how was it that the whole thing could vibrate with such a pure joy?" There are passages of raw, terrible emotion in this book which are so painful that you wish you had not read them. They are strung together in a fantastic plot of almost gothic unseriousness. There are unforgettably weird scenes: a seance; the shriek of a poltergeist; a secret grave where, barefooted a beautiful girl pirouettes in the dew, watched furtively by her unseen brother who is partly in love with her; a large house with forbidden rooms and a secret tower; a marsh where mists descend and where footing is unsure, on whose edges lurk sinister figures called the tree men; water, beneath which lies a dead old man with a ring on his finger, a ring which his son stoops to remove. These could be scenes from Malory or Spenser, and they co-exist beside wholly realistic, and frequently very funny depictions of London dinner parties and modern adultery. . . .

I would say that this is the best of Iris Murdoch's novels. She does here things which she has done before, but she does them more stylishly than ever, with even more bigness of heart, and with passages of magnificent celebration of the beauties of the natural world. (p. 26)

> *A. N. Wilson, "A Prodigal Novelist," in* The Spectator, *Vol. 255, No. 8203, September 28, 1985, pp. 25-6.*

HAROLD BLOOM

At the end of her first book, [*Sartre: Romantic Rationalist*], an enduring study of Jean-Paul Sartre published in 1953, Iris Murdoch prophetically lamented that Sartre's "inability to write a great novel is a tragic symptom of a situation which afflicts us all." Her own inability has extended now through 22 novels, of which the best seem to me *Bruno's Dream* (1969), *The Black Prince* (1973), *A Word Child* (1975) and her latest, *The Good Apprentice.* So fecund and exuberant is Miss Murdoch's talent that many more novels may be expected from her. If *The Good Apprentice* marks the start of her strongest phase, and it may, then a great novel could yet come, rather surprisingly in the incongruous form of the 19th century realistic novel. The age of Samuel Beckett and Thomas Pynchon, post-Joycean and post-Faulknerian, is set aside by Miss Murdoch's novelistic procedures, almost as though she thus chose to assert her own direct continuity with the major 19-century Russian and British masters of fiction.

Miss Murdoch's conventional style and traditional narrative devices are not, in my experience of reading her, the principal flaws in her work. Like Gabriel García Márquez, she favors a realism that can be more phantasmagoric than naturalistic, but she tends not to be able to sustain this mixed mode, whereas he can. Consistency of stance is one of Miss Murdoch's problems. She is both fantasist and realist, each on principle, but her abrupt modulations between the two visions sometimes seem less than fully controlled. Her novels rush by us, each a successful entertainment but none perhaps fully distinct from the others in our memories.

Yet her fictions fuse into a social cosmos, one that is reasonably recognizable as contemporary British upper-middle-class. Of all her talents, the gift of plotting is the most formidable,

including a near-Shakespearean faculty for intricate double plots. Again, her strength seems sometimes uncontrolled, and even the most responsible reader can feel harried and at last indifferent as labyrinthine developments are worked through. Yet that is how Miss Murdoch tends to manifest her considerable exuberance as a writer, rather than in the creation of endless diversity in her characters, which nevertheless (and rather sadly) seems to constitute her largest ambition. She does not excel at fresh invention of personalities. We learn to expect certain basic types to repeat themselves in her novels. Fierce, very young women, compulsive and cunning, violent in their pursuit of much older men, are omnipresent. Their quarry, those older men, are narcissistic charmers but weak, self-indulgent, hesitant skeptics, fearful of reality yet, in defiance of their fears, frequently brash in engaging it. Then there are the power figures whom Miss Murdoch once called "alien gods." These are frequently male Middle European Jewish charismatics, who may perhaps have some allegorical or ironic link to the Nobel laureate novelist and philosopher Elias Canetti, a friend of Miss Murdoch in her youth. Unfulfilled older women abound also; they are marked by resentment, anxieties about identity and a tendency to fall in love drastically, absurdly and abruptly.

Miss Murdoch's particular mastery is in representing the maelstrom of falling in love, which is the characteristic activity of nearly all her men and women, who somehow have time for busy professional careers in London while obsessively suffering convulsive yet enlivening love relationships. Somewhere in one of her early novels, Miss Murdoch cannily observes that falling out of love is one of the great human experiences, a kind of rebirth in which we see the world with freshly awakened eyes. Though an academic philosopher earlier in her career, Miss Murdoch's actual philosophical achievement is located where she clearly wishes it to be: in her novels, which demonstrate her to be a major student of Eros, not of the stature of Freud or Proust but still an original and endlessly provocative theorist of the tragi-comedy of sexual love, with its peculiar hell of jealousy and self-hatred. Her nearest American equivalent in this dark area is Saul Bellow, a novelist whom otherwise she does not much resemble.

Indeed, she resembles no other contemporary novelist, in part because she is essentially a religious fabulist, of an original and unorthodox sort, and therefore very unlike Graham Greene or John Updike or Walker Percy or Cynthia Ozick, whose varied religious outlooks are located in more definite spiritual traditions. Miss Murdoch thinks for herself theologically as well as philosophically, and her conceptual originality is difficult for readers to apprehend, particularly when it is veiled by her conventional forms of storytelling and her rather mixed success in the representation of original characters. There is a perpetual incongruity between Miss Murdoch's formulaic procedures and her spiritual insights, an incongruity that continues in *The Good Apprentice.*

The good apprentice is 20-year-old Edward Baltram, a university student who begins the novel by slyly feeding a drug-laden sandwich to his best friend and fellow student, Mark Wilsden. While Edward goes off to visit a girl in the neighborhood, Mark wakes up and falls or jumps out of the window to his death. Edward's grief and guilt dominate the book, which is his quest for a secular absolution at the hands of his actual father, Jesse Baltram, an insane vitalist and reclusive painter who begat Edward upon one of his models and has not seen him apart from a childhood meeting or two. Miss Murdoch's ironic opening sentence is the novel's spiritual signature: "I will arise and go to my father, and will say unto him, Father I have sinned against heaven and before thee, and am no more worthy to be called thy son.''

In a narrative that chronicles Edward's journey from hell to purgatory, we might expect that he would encounter at least one figure who unequivocally embodies love, wisdom or at least power. But that underestimates Miss Murdoch's authentic spiritual originality, which has now matured to the point that all such figures are negated. Though Edward regards himself as a dead soul, he is nevertheless the book's only legitimate representative of the good, in however apprentice a guise. His elders all fail him and themselves are exposed as souls deader than he is. (pp. 1, 30)

With her alien gods and charismatics so discredited, Miss Murdoch boldly steps into their place herself, editorializing directly about her characters' psychological and spiritual miseries. . . .

Admirers of Miss Murdoch are fond of defending such authorial interpolations by citing their prevalence in the 19th-century novel. It is certainly true that George Eliot is never more impressive than in such interventions, and Miss Murdoch is recognizably in Eliot's explicitly moral tradition. Unfortunately, what worked sublimely for Eliot cannot work so well for Miss Murdoch, despite her engaging refusal to be self-conscious about her belatedness. . . . Her gifts for dramatic action are considerable, but her own narrative voice lacks George Eliot's authority, being too qualified and fussy when a rugged simplicity is required. She is no less acute a moral analyst than Eliot, but she does not persuade us that her judgments are a necessary part of the story she has made for us.

Yet I do not wish to slight her conceptual strength as a religious writer, which is her particular excellence, since she has taught herself how subtly story and magic, narrative art and the questing spirit, can fuse in a novel, even if the fusion is incomplete so far in her work. Starting as an existentialist writer in *Under the Net* in 1954, she has evolved into that curious oxymoron, a Platonist novelist, perpetually in pursuit of the Good, a quest that she herself parodies in the hilarious and painful couplings of her romantic questers. Her obsessive symbol for this sadomasochistic pattern is the myth of Apollo and Marsyas, which I recall as being exploited in *The Black Prince* and several other novels and which is repeated in *The Good Apprentice.* Marsyas the flutist, having challenged Apollo to a music contest, loses and suffers the penalty of being flayed alive. Miss Murdoch reads the myth so that the agony of Marsyas is our agony now in seeking to know God in an age when God is dead. (p. 30)

Whatever Socrates meant by saying we should study dying, Miss Murdoch harshly means that death is the truth, since it destroys every image and every story. Her savage Platonism in the novels is consistent with her stance in *The Fire and the Sun: Why Plato Banished the Artists:*

> Plato feared the consolations of art. He did not offer a consoling theology. His psychological realism depicted God as subjecting mankind to a judgment as relentless as that of the old Zeus, although more just. . . . To present the idea of God at all, even as myth, is a consolation, since it is impossible to defend this image against the prettifying attentions of art. Art will mediate and adorn, and develop magical structures to conceal the absence of God or his distance. . . .

Miss Murdoch exploits magic while endlessly disowning it. *The Good Apprentice* seems to me an advance upon all of Miss Murdoch's previous novels, even *The Black Prince,* because the ferocious moralist finally has allowed herself a wholly sympathetic protagonist in the self-purging Edward. His progress out of an inner hell has no false consolations or illusory images haunting it. In some sense, Edward's achievement and torment is wholly Freudian in its spirit, resembling as it does the later Freud of *Beyond the Pleasure Principle* through *Civilization and Its Discontents.* Freud's only spirituality was his worship of reality testing, or the reality principle, which was his way of naming the conditions imposed upon us by mortality. Miss Murdoch's only consistent spirituality is grimly parallel to Freud's, since her novels insist that religious consciousness, in our postreligious era, must begin with the conviction that only death centers life, that death is the only valid representation of a life better than the life-in-death we all suffer daily.

This is the impressive, if rather stark, structure that Miss Murdoch imposes on *The Good Apprentice,* where the first section is called ''The Prodigal Son'' and depicts Edward's descent into a private hell and the second, ''Seegard,'' recounts his purgatorial search for his enigmatic magician of a father. The third and last part Miss Murdoch names ''Life After Death,'' implying that the still anguished Edward has begun an ascent into the upper reaches of his personal purgatory.

Like nearly all of her 22 novels, Miss Murdoch's *Good Apprentice* has a surface that constitutes a brilliant entertainment, a social comedy of and for the highly literate. Beneath that surface an astringent post-Christian Platonism has evolved into a negative theology that pragmatically offers only the dialectical alternations of either total libertinism or total puritanism in the moral life. The esthetic puzzle is whether the comic story and the spiritual kernel can be held together by Miss Murdoch's archaic stance as an authorial will. And yet no other contemporary British novelist seems to me of her eminence. Her formidable combination of intellectual drive and storytelling exuberance may never fuse into a great novel, but she has earned now the tribute she made to Sartre more than 30 years ago. She too has the style of the age. (p. 31)

> Harold Bloom, ''A Comedy of Worldly Salvation,'' in The New York Times Book Review, *January 12, 1986, pp. 1, 30-1.*

SHARON THOMPSON

When Harold Bloom saw fit to test Iris Murdoch's work against the standard of The Great Novel recently [see excerpt above], I was taken aback. It had never occurred to me to look to Murdoch for greatness. I thought her novels absorbing, mildly addictive, but not in the running. My own habituation seemed idiosyncratic. In late adolescence, I abruptly concluded that Catholic doctrine was itself a fiction on the order of a Borges— one of logic as well as plot. It was a nervy conclusion, given my surround, but as context hissed out of my mind like helium, confusion succeeded the thrill of apostasy. I was struck dumb by the loss of faith. Recuperating, I read Murdoch. At the time I thought I was diddling my hours away, but in her preoccupation with the moral consequences of the death of God, she was an ideal read, I now see, for someone shifting from a religious to a secular point of view.

Gradually I found reasons other than ''God cares'' for taking daily life seriously, learned a political approach to weighing ideas, and got used to the absence of ceremony and prayer, those interludes of intense desire. Finally the problem of a life without religion ceased to interest me altogether. It has never ceased to interest Murdoch.

Another serious woman writer who can turn out a novel almost every other year, Murdoch writes patterned novels that—like Muriel Spark's—pivot on mortality and mix the comic and the deadly serious. But her novels aren't pared clean to the bone the way Spark's are. While Spark shaves, Murdoch expatiates. This proclivity has earned her a reputation—half praise, half condemnation—as the last of the 19th century realists, an atavism. She is not, however, chiefly a realist. Her novels are one part Dostoevsky, one part James, one Lewis (Monk), several parts Augustine. They consist of three distinguishing elements: her turns on mythic or biblical texts are often brilliantly rendered, and were her perspective more generally shared, she could rest on them, without explication. As it is, she has to spell her assumptions out. Her primary means for accomplishing this is a subspecies of the stream of consciousness—the postpsychoanalytic examination of conscience—by which she shows the soul in motion, rationalizing and tallying its spiritual victories and losses. Conscience is a cliffhanger in Murdoch, and these are amazing passages, intricate and revelatory. She is some grand inquisitor. Last and in a sense least important are the Chinese boxes that enclose her work: the realistic and gothic plots.

All in all, it's a workable formula for a difficult narrative problem, and she deploys it with extraordinary finesse. Most of these fairly long novels are close-knit, although occasionally Murdoch writes a looser novel in which she seems to be biding her time. *The Good Apprentice* is loose. It has all the elements of a late Murdoch, and it's brilliantly conceived, but there's a flaw that she never manages to overcome or mask (doesn't try very hard, I think, perhaps because her formula and her material unexpectedly proved an imperfect fit). (p. 8)

I have two major complaints, the lesser with this novel, the greater—since Bloom has called the question—with Murdoch's work as a whole. The novel's clever premise requires splitting the good and bad son, an unfortunate move. What makes her moralism palatable—even fascinating—is not her hedging, her philosophical facility, but her genius at depicting frail human vessels. Tempted, her characters hold off for a while, but sooner or later they bite on the lure. They fall obsessively, abruptly in love. They drink. They are cowardly. They fabricate injurious diaries and leave them behind to bedevil their loved ones. They acknowledge the desire to dominate, to submit. Murdoch charts these falls with a generosity and perspicacity, not to mention patience, unusual in a moralist. Often her examinations of conscience are riveting, but in this novel, because Stuart is all-good, he is totally unbelievable. Luke knew what he was doing when he made the faithful son pissed off—as in human. Edward could save the novel, but he's too dumb. Result: tedium. If Murdoch were Dostoevsky, she might get away with it, but as it is, back to the drawing board. . . .

[Why] hasn't Murdoch given up grieving for God and gone on to other dedications? Why peddle death? I think it is because the issues at the top of her postreligious agenda are not answered by social commitments other than marriage, parenting, and the cloister. She mourns not God so much as a culture of contemplation, endurance, and responsibility, a way of prayer and fasting instead of—as she apparently sees the tradeoff—sex and amnesia. This is an eccentric agenda in the late 20th century, but is it, as Bloom says, an instance of "conceptual originality"?

In the early work, Murdoch's Shakespearean device of ending each book at the beginning of another—with a few characters on the brink of essay and temptation—left open the possibility of novels that would reverse earlier themes, bringing home a point of relativity instead of dogmatism. This gave her fusion of Irish Catholicism, existentialism, and Buddhism a narrative promise that now seems misleading. With over 20 novels in the till, by now we know pretty well who will fall and under what circumstances and what a fall is: what rules and ways she wants to keep going, God or no God; toward what interest she invokes our terror of mortality, that whip of guilt and superstitious obedience. Give or take a little room for the disseminating text (and Murdoch earns this leeway), these are: the doctrine of irrevocability; the opposition of flesh and spirit; the culture of temptation, resistance, and reform; and finally spiritual experience itself—ecstasy, pure concentration. As phrased more colloquially by the women in the Irish Catholic half of my family, these ideas are all too familiar to me: (1) you make your bed, you lie in it; (2) you can't have your cake and eat it too (i.e., forget about fusing body and mind); (3) temptation's not a sin—fantasy and actions are (i.e., it's okay for a man to be tempted by men, as long as he doesn't touch them or elaborate erotic dreams). Spiritual experience they didn't have much truck with.

It's less astounding that Murdoch has dressed these ideas up grand and taken them out in high critical society—we Irish have a traditionally dialectical relationship to airs and blarney—than that she has succeeded stupendously at the shenanigan, hoodwinking some of the most illustrious critics of our time. So what if Professor Bloom doesn't think she has written a great novel? He *has* taken her seriously, as few scholars would take such a program in any respectable forum outside the bastions of fundamentalism. And he is not alone. It's a lark. My Irish pride rises at the victory.

But it won't do. Murdoch's parochial agenda overwhelms her Buddhism and existentialism, making them seem more smoke screen than substance. Because we must die, her work argues, we must not only pay attention, as the Buddhists teach, we must also live by traditional rules. If this makes sense, I am so much in the devil's power that I just can't see it. How do you get to a principle of celibacy from mortality? If her moral principles were connected to the compassionate life, or to justice, she might have a case. But human justice is not at issue in these novels. Class, for example, never comes up. Virtually all her male characters went to Oxford, and live either on inherited wealth or fees for their services as those modern priests, psychoanalysts.

While her work suffers from her judgment, it is also made hilarious by it. As a satirist of modern life and sexuality, Murdoch is often marvelously on point and funny. If she sees lust and obsessive desire as sins and temptations, still, like so many Irish writers, she has a developed narrative taste for them. She is, for example, the great narrator of the cheap feel—the sudden plunge of hand inside blouse, the lunge for a forbidden kiss, the heady brief moment of an inspired sexual invitation, the brazen seduction that is a text in itself.

But aren't these achievements too small for a novelist of seriousness, one who clearly had a chance at writing a novel that would have stopped readers as disparate as Bloom and me in our critical tracks? Aren't they less than she intended, at the outset, to accomplish? Of course, Murdoch still has a chance at the Great Novel sweepstakes, but it's slim. To take it, she would have to challenge her circular view of the world: write a novel that either reverses her moral position (unimaginable, I think) or reaches for uncharacteristic material—money, politics, the world. In this sense, a novel like *The Red and the Green* represents, at least, an opening in the thick hedge of her work, a possible exit from her maze. But why presume that the Great Novel is her goal at all? On the basis of the work itself, and her evident savvy and capability, it seems as credible that her intentions and accomplishment are parallel; that her novels are meant as salutary doses against what she sees as the chronic disease of postreligious immorality—a problem requiring periodic treatment, the equivalent of Easter duty.

If so, I'd say she's effective in her lesser task, little as I approve of it. But then, these ideas were mother's milk to me. They go down so easily coated with the gothic, the erotic—there is still nothing so sexy as taboo in my experience—and unlike my female kin, I have always had a weakness for alpha-wave states and wishful thinking. Even irrevocability has a cozy, secure look sometimes. I finish one volume and wonder: can I pick and choose? Reject her on homosexuality, accept her on contemplation? Can't actions be irrevocable and yet undone? (If I promise to remember I got married, can I go to Reno?) And how about death as an argument for freedom? As I open another volume, I get a sneaky, illicit feeling, as if I am considering naughty pranks under the covers.

I figure as long as I don't act, I'm safe. (p. 9)

> *Sharon Thompson, "Iris Murdoch's Moral Orders,"*
> *in VLS, No. 43, March, 1986, pp. 8-9.*

MARTHA NUSSBAUM

It is easy to see why Iris Murdoch might be drawn to the idea of writing philosophy as Platonic dialogue. Throughout her work she has insisted that our besetting vice is our obsession with the personal, which mires us in fantasy, preventing our ascent to an objective, loving vision of good. "Egoistic fantasy", the delusions of love, these need to be cut through by a dialectical practice that will free the soul from constraint and lead it to impersonal love. We would expect a Murdochian dialogue to preserve concern for particular people and things, and not to follow Plato when he insists that we ought to see particulars simply as participants in universal forms. But vision of particularity need not be personalized vision; and since for Murdoch all true vision is free of subjective interest, she is just as ready as Plato to urge us towards impersonality.

It is, then, with eagerness that we turn to *Acastos*. We expect to find here the working out of Platonic ideas about the relation between philosophy and its literary form; and to find embodied in this form some rich and challenging Platonist arguments. We look, too, for an acknowledgement, by a writer who has persistently denied that her literary and philosophical activities have any important common link, that there is, after all, a fruitful relationship between them. On almost every level, our expectations are disappointed.

The slim volume contains no introduction and two brief dialogues. The first, **"Art and Eros"**, depicts a conversation between Socrates and several friends about the definition of art. . . .

The dialogue on religion, **"Above the Gods"**, depicts an argument among a rationalist who holds that religion is simply a primitive, though socially useful, form of morality; a proto-Marxist who attacks religion as a drug that makes people resist social change; Acastos, who urges us to see religion as a perpetual effort to take up a humble, unselfish vision of the world

as a whole; an embarrassingly caricatured slave, who loves his God and asks no questions; and Socrates and Plato, who have the same views as before. Alcibiades puts in a brief appearance, speaking rather like a decadent Christ Church undergraduate, imagined by the *Daily Mirror*. He addresses Socrates as "Pusskins". Plato threatens to kill him. Socrates objects: "You can't kill ideas; you must learn to *think*."

These dialogues, sadly, have not learned. They do not know what Murdoch knows about the power of thought contained in the literary imagination; and they do not go far as argument. The trouble begins with their Greekness. Plato's characters were his near contemporaries; their speech, their political concerns, their ideas, all would have had a lively immediacy for his audience. And because the semi-fictional world he creates is realized with marvellous consistency and thoroughness of vision, they can, in a different way, be near to us as well. Murdoch's Greek world is imagined half-heartedly. It is neither Greek nor contemporary, nor any interesting combination of the two. Many aspects of this world can be understood only as ancient. Indeed, to follow the dialogues one needs a reasonable knowledge of Greek history—and of Plato, since there are many casual, cryptic allusions to his arguments. But a reader who had thought about the Theory of Forms, or the image of the cave, or the other less famous material Murdoch mines, will feel that little has been done to illuminate the ideas. On the other hand, there is much here that can have no connection with Greece or Plato: for example, casual reference to prescriptivism; to current controversies over pornography; to arguments about the aesthetic status of *objets trouvés*. All this convinces us that we are, after all, in a twentieth-century world. Yet little is done to explore these contemporary issues either. We come away feeling that the intellectual fun of these pieces is bought cheaply, as a series of in-jokes. How cute that a Greek boy should know G. E. Moore's reply to scepticism. How amusing that Socrates should invent (as R. M. Hare, after all, once said he did) Hare's prescriptive analysis of evaluative discourse.

The trouble is graver still when we consider that the central notions in these two pieces were understood by the Greeks in a way very different from ours. Murdoch's characters, like us but unlike the Greeks, speak of "art" and "the arts"; they puzzle over the definition of art. Yet at the same time they cite Greek examples and seem to believe that dramatic performance is a part of civic religion—an idea foreign to us. Whose concept is being investigated here? Again, religion is discussed using Greek examples and some Greek concepts. But the characters assume that religion is a matter of believing in something and of having certain sorts of inner personal experiences, involving, perhaps, a "personal god". They easily refer to the entirely non-Greek virtue of humility. (They even debate the modernization of the language of traditional liturgy—here cuteness overwhelms us.) Murdoch's sensibility is so resolutely Christian, albeit agnostic, that she has no curiosity and no love for the Greeks themselves. Her own personal vision, ironically prevents her from seeing them.

None of this would be fatal if the arguments were powerful enough. They are not. There are too many characters, conversing too half-heartedly. The ideas that emerge have been better argued in *The Sovereignty of Good*, and even in the lesser *The Fire and the Sun*. What is more, they have been better worked out, in a truly Platonic spirit, in the best of Murdoch's novels, such as *The Bell* and *The Black Prince*. In those fully imagined works we do see her philosophical ideas about religion, art, morality and desire unfolding through the lives and conversations of men and women for whom these ideas have the importance of life itself. When we read *The Bell*'s contrasting speeches about morality, we know out of what troubled histories these thoughts emerge, and how they inform, in turn, those histories. And in working through the thoughts we are ourselves made intellectually and emotionally attentive. Our concern for the characters and their world makes us attempt a clearer vision of our own.

That is how a literary work can be a Platonic dialogue. **"Art and Eros"** and **"Above the Gods"**, despite the philosophical value of their basic conceptions, are not Platonic dialogues. Their failure of thought is a failure of imagination.

> Martha Nussbaum, *"Miscast in Dialogue Form,"* in The Times Literary Supplement, *No. 4350, August 15, 1986, p. 881.*

JOHN UPDIKE

Acastos binds together two Platonic dialogues, one of which has actually been produced in London as a short play. . . .

[Murdoch's] own Platonism informs the intellectual and erotic seethe of her tireless novels, whose characters reside half in a solidly realized England and half in a translucent realm of immaterial passions and ideas. "Yes," she and her favorite characters seem to keep saying, "the Good and the True and the Beautiful *do* exist, compellingly, bafflingly, absolutely." Plato himself, as a somewhat minor character in these two dialogues, asserts, "People know that good is real and absolute, not optional and relative, all their life proves it," and, when challenged by Alcibiades, gets quite sputtery about it. . . . Plato, here a callow youth of only twenty, has already developed a lot of bullying mental maneuvers. God, too, *must* exist: "Religion isn't just a feeling, it isn't just a hypothesis, it's not like something we happen not to know, a God who might perhaps be there isn't a God, it's got to be necessary, it's got to be certain, it's got to be proved by the whole of life, it's got to be the magnetic centre of everything—" Miss Murdoch is the philosopher, and knows better than I how true to Plato's mature thought is this rather Kantian or Kierkegaardian sense of God's stern obligation to exist. Socrates gently says, "Then your 'ground of things,' your 'it must be so,' is really 'I want it to be so,' it's a cry of fear?" Plato begs off, and even Socrates seems to concede more than a strictly materialist and relativist standpoint would warrant: "The most important thing in life is virtue, and virtue isn't a mystery, it's truthfulness and justice and kindness and courage, things we understand. Anybody can *try* to be good, it's not obscure!"

Yet, of course, goodness is obscure, to an age that has heard it preached that the state is organized violence, that humility and submission help perpetuate the powerful in their crimes, that altruism is a kind of neuroticism, that a repressed "drive" (Freud) becomes self-destructive, and that "slave morality" (Nietzsche) should be despised and supplanted. Miss Murdoch has the aesthetic problem, in contriving these new Platonic dialogues, of how much of modern thought's dark, chaotic winds to admit to the forum: to stay entirely within the intellectual frame of Periclean Athens would be a pointless tour de force, and yet her exercises would be hopelessly campy did they feel any more up-to-date than they do. "Public morality . . . *is* breaking down" is no doubt a timeless complaint, but "Love is energy" seems a contemporary formulation put into Plato's mouth. . . . A distinctly modern view of the evan-

gelized lower classes and a certain West Indian accent creep into a servant's refreshing testimony on these great matters: "Like little fish in sea am I in God's love! All I eat, sleep, work, do, inside his love. . . . I am not good man, I have many sin, many fault, many, many. I need my God. I am all bad, he is all good, I have bad thoughts—"

But religion and its conundrums are enduring enough to straddle epochs, and the dialogue on religion is much the livelier one. The dialogue on art, which was the one to see performance (in the National Theatre, in 1980), seems relatively insipid, in part because its argumentation is confined to examples of art no later than the fifth century B. C. Even as a provisional definition, Miss Murdoch's Callistos could never, had he seen a single Rauschenberg construct or Pollock painting (or read a Pinget novel), have described art as "copying into a world where everything looks different and clearer, and there's no muddle and no horrid accidental things like in life." After Céline and Kafka, can we still, as Socrates urges, "thank the gods for great artists who draw away the veil of anxiety and selfishness"? Plato is made to say, "Art softens the demand of the gods. It puts an attractive veil over that *final* awful demand, that final transformation into goodness, the almost impossible *last step* which is what human life is really all about." This is thrillingly put, and in tune with the relevant chapters of *The Republic*—but are the demands of, say, *Finnegans Wake* really so soft, and is, say, a fur-lined teacup or a latrine displayed on a museum wall such an attractive veil? The phrase hardly seems true even of *Oedipus Rex*, or of the satyrical activities painted on Greek vases.

When we turn to *The Republic* or to any of the authentic Platonic dialogues, we realize how much a novelist and sentimental *Neo*platonist Miss Murdoch is in her adroit and charming imitations. The original atmosphere was much more Spartan: In *The Republic,* Socrates proposed to ban poets because human emotion, which poetry indulges, is "irrational, useless, and cowardly." Poetry "feeds and waters the passions instead of drying them up; she lets them rule, although they ought to be controlled, if mankind are ever to increase in happiness and virtue." Dry reason and manly endurance should rule "the sympathetic element." Callistos' babbling suggestion that art is "exciting and sexy" would have fallen on stony ground in the fifth century. The element of homoerotic byplay . . . pervades Murdoch's dialogues and verges on making them farcical playlets. As if in one of her irrepressible novels, each character strains to rattle off in his own direction; Socrates is a kindly presiding tutor but nothing of the remorseless logical engine who bulldozes his way through Plato's dialogues, reducing all others to yes-men. Plato composed in a time when truth was thought to be attainable, when permanent conclusions could be achieved and built upon; this live possibility, so near the beginnings of reasoned thought, throws a white light upon the stylized figures of his debates. Miss Murdoch writes in a time of multiplying shadows, of built-in indeterminacy and ambiguity, when Eros is the only apprehensible god. Socrates concludes the animated but highly inconclusive dialogue on art by claiming, "In truly loving each other we learn more perhaps than in all our other studies." The excitable young Plato tells his teacher, "I'm so happy. I don't know why. I love you so much," and "*Socrates puts his arm round him and leads him off.*" This note of affectionate fellowship among high-minded men and boys also ended Miss Murdoch's last novel, *The Good Apprentice,* and appears strangely satisfying to her. She and Pinget are almost exactly the same age and, in their different way, show a high tolerance for ambiguity. Models of creative integrity in a slack age, they sing oddly rapturous hymns to muddle. (pp. 113-15)

John Updike, "Back to the Classics," in The New Yorker, *Vol. LXIII, No. 13, May 18, 1987, pp. 110, 113-15.*

STEPHEN R. L. CLARK

Iris Murdoch's latest novel [*The Book and the Brotherhood*] concerns the circle of friends and family managed or mismanaged by Gerard Hernshaw, once-upon-a-time scholar and prematurely retired civil servant. The action takes place in Oxford (an appallingly realistic Commem Ball), London and Boyars, the Curtlands' ancestral home. Locked in undergraduate promises and hopes, incapable of starting any novel enterprise, or children, by the memories of the young Sinclair Curtland, thirty years dead, the circle has, as its sole quixotic gesture, offered financial support (in memory of Sinclair) to David Crimond, sometime Marxist intellectual, to write political philosophy. His character, and the likely content of his book, are increasingly distasteful to them all, except Jean Cambus (née Kowitz) whose life and marriage he seems set to ruin. No one but Crimond, and Jenkin Riderhood, a budding saint, has a job that he or she takes seriously. Gerard's aim, in retirement, is to write a book himself—on Plato, Plotinus, Augustine or magic versus philosophy—though till the novel's end he has no idea what he needs to say. They have all learnt to admire scholarship—chiefly in the person of Professor Levquist—and the good, but have no serious intention of working hard at either.

This is a long book, rich in allusion and contrivance. Murdoch-fanciers may play the usual games. How many names are hymn-tunes? Where else have we met the Filthy Kitchen, Strangers in the House, the Demon Figure, the Woman in Debt, the Virgin (perhaps) Priestess, the Agonizingly Remembered Animal? There is a fine collection of significant stones, a dying father-figure, a suicide pact, a saint, and many detailed accounts of Gulliver Ashe's dress-sense. Marriages are made or mended; young persons take, or fail to take, some necessary steps away. The things that men expect to happen do not happen; the unexpected God makes possible.

The novel, despite appearances, is not too long. It is not just a comedy (or tragedy) of manners. Philosophical argument is pervasive, though curiously foggy and over-allusive. Plato and Plotinus figure largely here, as labels for an ideal of goodness never to be realized in the ordinary world. . . .

The central question that the novel explores is this: how can we live in a world divorced from good? Is it enough—as Gerard feebly supposes—that we should have ideals of friendship, mutual help, which are never in fact realized? Gerard believes himself helpful to his friends, merely because he thinks of helping them. Or must obedience to that distant ideal involve a real agony? Should we hide our eyes from what is going on and make a little sensual refuge out of minor pleasures of food, drink and comfortable memory? Or hope only for "a decent (not a perfectly good) society that depends on freedom and order and circumstances and an endless tinkering that can't be programmed from a distance"? Or hope to force the world into the shape it should be by magical self-sacrifice, and the sacrifice of others? . . .

The most moving passages in the book, and maybe those that offer an inarticulate, unarticulable promise, concern one of Murdoch's Remembered Animals: the parrot, Grey, whom Gerard loved in childhood and who was wrenched from him forty years ago in an act of betrayal that has never been talked out or forgiven. He has lived with the image of that parrot, somewhere, still alive, and given nothing of himself to any creature since. In the sudden realization that Grey may after all have been starved or battered to death Gerard experiences an identification with the sufferings of sentient creation that culminates in a dream-vision of an angel's descent "in the form of a great grey parrot with loving clever eyes and the parrot perched upon the book [that Gerard held] and the parrot was the book".

Because this is not, despite appearances, a realistic novel, nor yet a systematic treatise of philosophy, we can be content with the magical resolution of conflict offered in that vision, in Jenkin's expectation of a change of life, a great white light. Maybe the truth that Murdoch would have us see lies in some unimaginable synthesis of philosophy and magic, "a moment when Plato's Good [can be remarried] to the God of the psalms". As Gerard, for once accurately, muses: "We haven't got a genius to teach us a new way to think about goodness and the soul". Iris Murdoch has written neither Crimond's book, nor Gerard's promised antidote. What she has created is an absorbing image of our present confusions.

Stephen R. L. Clark, "Squaring the Circle," in The Times Literary Supplement, *No. 4405, September 4, 1987, p. 947.*

NICHOLAS SPICE

Like Henry James's, Iris Murdoch's style is high, in the sense that she writes about lofty matters—the nature of morality, the reasons for existence, how we should live and love, how we should die—as they arise in stories about the upper middle classes, stories about people who have the leisure, education, civilisation, plausibly to think and speak about these lofty matters in a suitably lofty way, stories about people who live at a level of society supposed, for the sake of the convention, to be above the distracting contingencies of everyday life. A high style will purge itself of references to vulgar reality. Racine wrote within a vocabulary of two thousand words. Iris Murdoch cannot write about supermarket trolleys, traffic wardens or blocked drains. (p. 8)

When the high style deals with politics it does so at a distance, in formal conflicts between idea and personality or public and private loyalties, as in the plays of Corneille or in *Coriolanus,* Shakespeare's most Classical play. *The Book and the Brotherhood* is roughly in this tradition. Its political material is kept remote from the world of contemporary politics and confined to the realm of intellectual debate and psychological speculation. We hear about 'scandalous and violent and sickening goings-on' in the public sphere, but that is all, and it is like the echo of distant gunfire.

The political debate in *The Book and the Brotherhood* is conducted between David Crimond, writer of a book of left-wing political theory, and the brotherhood, a sort of trust set up by a group of friends to provide Crimond with a regular income while he writes the book. The brotherhood, otherwise humorously known as the *Crimondgesellschaft,* consists of Gerard Hernshaw, Jenkin Riderhood and Duncan Cambus, three of Crimond's contemporaries at Oxford (same college, studying Greats), Rose Curtland, sister of Sinclair Curtland who also studied at Oxford with Crimond but died tragically young in a glider accident, and Gulliver Ashe, a younger later addition to the Rose-Gerard-Jenkin-Duncan set. The novel opens when relations between Crimond and his support committee have broken down. The split is manifold and complex. Since the early days of the *Crimondgesellschaft,* David Crimond has moved further and further to the left, putting himself outside the pale of conventional party politics by advocating violent revolutionary solutions to society's problems. The brotherhood meanwhile has drifted in the other direction, coming to rest somewhere on the liberal wing of the Tory Party. Crimond is a Scotsman, and though the book does not say so, he seems to conform to the type of the lower middle-class or working-class boy made good by intellect and ambition. He's a puritan ascetic who thinks his uncompromising thoughts in the basement of a shabby, underheated house in South London. The brotherhood, on the other hand, are born to the Establishment. They live in the smart parts of London and meet three times a year for reading-parties at Rose Curtland's modest country house 'Boyars', where they are looked after splendidly by the housekeeper Annushka (though the days of kidneys and kedgeree for breakfast are sadly over). (pp. 8-9)

David Crimond is this novel's obsession. In creating him, Murdoch seems to have seen him with unusual clarity, to have been fixated, frightened, repelled, fascinated by him, to have been in love with him—like her characters, and like her characters she has not in the end been able to be conclusive about him. His function in *The Book and the Brotherhood* is richly paradoxical. We are certainly meant to see him as half-crazy and unstable, a havoc-raiser in the lives of other people. His humourlessness, his affinity with cold dead things, with Greek clarity rather than Shakespearean mess, his inability to dither or to take a break, his rigid habit of telling the truth, his games of death—are all things the book comes down against. Seen close to, Crimond is shown up as a mean, petulant, restless, pathetic figure. His grand passion for Jean Cambus is disclosed as a necrophiliac delusion. The two great tragedies in the novel—Tamar Hernshaw's abortion (Tamar is the daughter of Gerard's cousin), and the accidental death of Jenkin Riderhood—are both in large measure Crimond's responsibility. Moreover, the most loving passages of the book are devoted to those aspects of the world that Rose Curtland and Jenkin Riderhood hold dear: to the world of 'Boyars' and the countryside in winter, to the settled comforts of Rose's flat, the excitement and fun of a firework party, the exhilaration of an afternoon out skating.

On the other hand, the novel benefits hugely from Crimond's clarity. His decisiveness activates the plot. His madness draws out the confusion in those around him, exposing their rottenness to each other and to themselves. While Crimond is either a god or a devil, all black or brilliant white, they are shabbily mortal and every shade of grey. Having no inside, he is an antidote to their obsessive, swarming subjectivity. And while they have achieved little in their lives, he has written a book that Gerard says is wonderful, likely to change the world.

Aside from Crimond, the novel does not spare Duncan, Rose, Gerard, Jean and the others (there are several characters I've not even mentioned) its complex critical scrutiny. Under that scrutiny only Jenkin really passes muster, and it is in Jenkin's consciousness that the book's point of moral and intellectual balance is to be located. 'Perhaps it is not only our fate but our truth to be weak and uncertain,' muses Jenkin in one of the novel's many stretches of worried dialectic. As *The Book and the Brotherhood* develops, weakness and uncertainty take over. An unease creeps into the minds of Gerard, Rose, Jenkin and Duncan, the characters who bear the largest share of the

novel's great burden of troubled consciousness—a weariness with life, a sense of depleted resources and hopes disappointed, a fear at the approaching dark. A dim awareness that their world and its values are exhausted and at an end, that, as Gerard puts it, 'the Oxford Colleges and Big Ben can't buy us off now.'

This self-doubt is the novel's own, and it is its most remarkable and moving quality. Somehow *The Book and the Brotherhood* manages to signal that it understands its own anachronism, its having appeared now to rehearse a political argument which has no vital bearing upon what is actually happening to us all. It is as though the contemporary situation which the novel cannot deal with is exerting an unseen pressure on Murdoch's imaginative and stylistic equilibrium, knocking her into a state of turbulent ambiguity. With Rose Curtland, the book wants to believe that the *Times* is as fixed a phenomenon as half a pound of butter. Yet it can't sustain this illusion, seeming to know that the times and the *Times* have changed, that what they once were has gone the way of the kidneys and the kedgeree, swept into oblivion not by the forces of the fanatical Left but by rampant entrepreneurial capitalism with its productivity targets, performance indicators and the like. *The Book and the Brotherhood* cannot mention the existence of such things, yet manages to acknowledge that they have made the writing of high fiction a thing of the past.

'The best lack all conviction, while the worst are full of passionate intensity.' If they were not so famous, Yeats's famous lines could have been the motto for *The Book and the Brotherhood.* Like 'The Second Coming' but without its portentous bluster, Murdoch's novel ends on a note of foreboding, a dark and open question about what may be coming to term in the womb of time. (p. 9)

Nicholas Spice, "Thatcherschaft," in London Review of Books, *Vol. 9, No. 17, October 1, 1987, pp. 8-9.*

CHARLES NEWMAN

[*The Book and the Brotherhood*] is that rarest of fictions these days: a social and political novel that is not journalistic, a novel of ideas that is not ideological, and a deep exploration of national character that is not parochial. While it details unsparingly the fragility of modern human relationships, the book is finally a triumphal celebration of literacy as a social bond—a theme that no doubt will come as a shock to a modern audience.

The book is set in contemporary England, one of the most depressing and pathetic places on the face of the earth. Nevertheless, we deeply sympathize with all of the characters and even come to admire most of them.

The Book and the Brotherhood (in which women feature most prominently) traces a group of intelligent if confused and lazy contemporaries, known as the Brotherhood, from their halcyon days at Oxford through middle age; the group is united in its fascination with the charismatic David Crimond. Crimond is writing a book, a revolutionary utopian tract of political philosophy, and his engagement is inversely proportionate to his acolytes' lapsed political faith. Nevertheless, they band together to support him financially in his lonely endeavor.

A sociologist would find a lot of cheap thrills here: the baleful bond of Oxford days, vaguely bisexual men and de-eroticized women stumbling through a series of affairs into wizened bachelor/spinsterhoods, the process of how we come to fall in love with old friends, and above all, the strange fascination of the English upper middle classes with Communists of their own social credentials—the remnants of inherited wealth subsidizing the remnants of revolutionary ideology. It is the very stuff of satire—and yet, never once does Miss Murdoch stoop to easy ridicule or fall back on the easy clichés of black humor. In fact, there is a kind of modern heroism embedded in her book.

David Crimond is one of the most interesting characters in recent literature, embodying that peculiar combination of puritanism and passion of the old-fashioned British intelligentsia, a man of the left who expends all his energy attacking the left, an intellectual loner without a constituency save the Brotherhood, which regards him, alternately, as a fanatic and a demigod. (p. 1)

It is worth remarking that this delineation of a man of iron discipline, in a culture with none, is accomplished without quoting a single phrase from his book, and while all the other characters are amplified through long interior monologues, we never once enter Crimond's own mind. Indeed, that is the secret of his power—like all mythic characters he exists through others' paraphrase—we are aware of his power primarily through his affair with Jean Kowitz Cambus. . . .

It is a testament to Miss Murdoch's subtlety that she can attribute a style of thought as devoid of reality as Oxbridge Marxism to a character, and then bring him off as a serious utopian thinker and activist. Undoubtedly, she will be criticized first for invoking a romantic anachronistic oppositionism, and then for not spelling it out in a program. This is, of course, the Brotherhood's objection to Crimond; they believe they have become more conservative, but in fact they have simply quit thinking in political terms at all. If anything would hurt their feelings, it would be Marx's basic insight that all acts have political consequences, the truth of which is certified every day within their own circle, but never has broader application except as a recognition that their culture has lost control over its destiny. But there are two very good reasons for Miss Murdoch's strategy here—and they ought not to be lost on an American reader—effected by the strange mix of ideology and political passivity of the 80's, as well as the concomitant loss of both wealth and self-respect.

The first lesson is artistic: it is death to turn a novel into an argument, no matter how much its characters and readers may desire it. Serious fiction must engage philosophy without sounding like it. The second is a profoundly accurate psychology. In the real world, ideas are transmitted not as abstract entities, but by the force of personality, delineated as lines of allegiances and betrayals between human beings, and it takes a mind as comfortable with ideas as Miss Murdoch's to know just how much intellect to put on display in a novel. At any rate, while we begin with the suspicion that Crimond is something of a charlatan and a sponger, by the time he confronts the liberal platitudes of Gerard, on behalf of the Brotherhood, we want to stand up and cheer him. . . .

Watching Crimond in his terrifying industry, we're also reminded, as we need to be, just how strenuous, rare and exhausting real writing is, and in fact what an elaborate support system it requires—though it is a rare author who will ever acknowledge it.

Unlike most writers portrayed in contemporary fiction, Crimond not only finishes his book, but we are persuaded that it is wonderful, original and even accessible to a wide audience, despite the fact that it is published by Oxford University Press. The Brotherhood, by this time having been put through quite a lot by Crimond, is legitimately ambivalent about its unreserved bleakness and its authoritarian solutions. . . .

[In] a stunning section, Gerard is moved to reply. Poor lazy, unfocused, vain, spoilt Gerard, whose main intellectual effort to date has been pondering a monograph on Plotinus, is moved to address the right and wrong of Crimond's book with a rejoinder of equal density and effort. (p. 26)

And so the Brotherhood, so pathetic as solitary, worried individuals, has in fact created a red thread of continuity, perhaps the only one possible in the present time. Just as we come to believe in Crimond's exceptionality, wrongheaded or not, so we come to believe that Gerard will respond to him, despite the fact that the book constitutes a kind of "life sentence," in every sense of that phrase.

And at this moment, the real meaning of this corrupted Oxford dream is opened like a flower. For the dream of the Brotherhood is not nostalgia for lost youth or first loves, not regret for lost community, lessened status or class mystique—it is the recreation of those few moments, getting rarer all the time by all accounts, when one is first exposed to impossibly high standards, to books that are our judges and not the other way around, that excitement of learning not yet canceled out by careerist fears—that brief time in youth when you read in a pure state, not because you are innocent, but because you're watching yourself get smarter.

But when Crimond's project is finished, the relationships that have made it possible are finished as well. Proposing an elaborate suicide pact to Jean, a kind of Russian roulette with speeding cars, he makes it certain that she will fail him, and is thus cast out, returning to her husband. Eventually Crimond, fastidious and focused to the end, gives the husband an opportunity to kill him, but this only results in the accidental death of an old friend who tries to intercede. It is the quintessential Murdochian plot, a lurching contingency that keeps you wondering whether it is hopelessly contrived or genuinely random. (pp. 26-7)

She has an impatience not only with plot but with characters who take themselves too seriously, and to whom she often gives a long speech quite out of character, a kind of impromptu spontaneous meditation that surprises the character quite as much as the reader. It is an endearing trait, and it reminds us that a good writer can break every rule in the book without the slightest avant-garde pretense or self-consciousness. Indeed, no review can do justice to the wealth of characters who revolve about Crimond, and their more muted lives put his obsessional behavior in perspective. For what he acts out, almost criminally, is seen as the basic human drive—to make a pact with another person, a pact of mutual presence which in itself generates a larger social purpose, "an ecstasy to which happiness was irrelevant." "Poor human beings . . . always wanting security, but unwilling to provide it!"

By the end, almost everyone in the book has tried to make a pact with a most unlikely other and been frustrated, and then made another wiser if more rueful choice, so that the final bond is conditioned by the broken one, a captive love that never quite dies forever energizing the accommodations of the new love. Forgiveness is based on the fact that there is no adequate form of revenge. But in this there is also the recognition (which the contrivances of the plot enforce) that human life is "a chain of coincidences," which offer some latitude of choice, and which confound Crimond's brutally deterministic and inexorable history. "It's the accidentalness we have to live with," one character says, but, as another elaborates, accidents must be explained as a story. And life is like fiction in that respect, that is, the constant tension between fortuity and predetermination, not expressed as "ideas," but as the constant interchange between the human guises of assuming power and honoring defenselessness. "It's all accidental, but the values are absolute. That's the simple point about human life"; and the presumption is that any person (or culture) that cannot hold those two opposed ideas simultaneously is doomed.

Well, maybe it's not perfect. There's a certain lapidary style, the old pro warming up in her own good time, which can become tedious, particularly in the opening pages. The ending seems a gratuitous bow to Dickens, and there are rather too many emblems skittering through the carnage. But the human process by which ideas are transformed into feelings, feelings into gestures, and gestures into always unforeseen consequences—no other living writer has it down so well. We're like "happy Kafka," Jean exclaims. That's it exactly. (p. 27)

> Charles Newman, "Leftists in Love," in The New York Times Book Review, *January 31, 1988, pp. 1, 26-7.*

MARK CALDWELL

The new Iris Murdoch is in stock. Its title, ***The Book and the Brotherhood,*** is in a sense beside the point. Murdoch, for all her sophistication and seriousness, is an industry like Barbara Cartland or Laura Lee Hope; we fans, for all our respect, think of her books as, well, merchandise. We need it, we run out of it, we go for more. The new shipment is in, and it's middle-quality Murdoch, palatable but not vintage.

Here, as nearly always, the cast is neither large nor small and consists of dithering middle-aged British intellectuals. In this case, it's an informal yet tightly linked brotherhood of Oxford men and women, lovers and admirers of the long-dead Sinclair, a Rupert Brooke figure, an *homme fatal*—but, we are given to understand, brilliant and awash in promise. . . .

The story proceeds in the regulation Murdoch manner, like a tank over a field of boulders. The characters bumble into one another in twos and threes until every possible permutation has been tried. A (Crimond) loves B (Jean), who loves C (Duncan), who seduces D (Tamar), who trusts E (Jenkin), who is loved by F (Gerard). But D (Tamar) foolishly turns to G (Lily), who, rebuffed in a desperate appeal to A (Crimond), little knowing that he prefers H (Rose), turns her attentions to the hitherto ignored I (Gulliver). These lurchings entertain and instruct, but Murdoch has dished up similar fare with more panache in other novels. Here, the crises, underdramatized by the novelist and overanalyzed by the characters, seem halfhearted. There's a pregnancy (Tamar), a suicide pact (Jean and Crimond), a murder (Jenkin), all rather listless and predictable.

But the biggest problem is Crimond's book, the great synthesis, which in Murdoch's conceit either brilliantly does or catastrophically doesn't solve the moral muddles of the brotherhood, and incidentally of the plot. Gerard and Rose, probably but not decisively the main characters, are obsessed, Gerard hungering for it, Rose dreading it. But when the book actually appears, after the requisite sensations, it's vacuous. We never

learn what the damned thing *says,* and Gerard's gushing doesn't help.

> It's brilliant, it's all that we thought it might be when we decided it was worth financing it. It's all we hoped—it's also all we feared, later on that is. It will be immensely read, immensely discussed, and I believe, very influential. . . . Of course, it isn't at all what we expected then, it's more than that, and it's not what we want to hear now, though we *have* to hear it.

Now there's an honorable reason for this resounding absence: Murdoch's approach to absolutes, like goodness, perfection, and God. She believes in them, but not as presences, only as admittedly impossible and in a sense nonexistent goals toward which humans fumble, each in his own hapless way. So her books always strive to express something that, by her own conviction, can't be expressed. A sympathetic idea, at least in theory, which explains why Crimond's book can't ever take a final shape, either as beatitude or bust. If it did, it would belie Murdoch's belief that final causes are necessary yet unrealizable.

In other books, Murdoch has solved the problem of the inevitably missing center, or at least obviated it, by introducing the supernatural—Murdoch Gothic, like the haunted East Anglia farmstead in ***The Good Apprentice,*** the sea serpent and Tibetan demons in ***The Sea, The Sea.*** Here she's largely avoided such devices (save for a casual pair of telepathic snails), and that saps her narrative, while perhaps making it truer to her theories. ***The Book and the Brotherhood*** has all Murdoch's intelligence, all her charity and tolerance (no other living writer I know of writes, for example, so unaffectedly well about homosexuality), some of her taste for bourgeois absurdities, but not much of her verve.

> Mark Caldwell, "Old Wine, Old Bottles," in The Village Voice, *Vol. XXXIII, No. 8, February 23, 1988, p. 51.*

MICHAEL LEVENSON

"I'm tired of this century," said a character in [***The Good Apprentice***], "I want to start living in the next one." This, for Murdoch, is the lazy sentimentality that we need to contest. Here is where, now is when, we tired creatures live; the two seductions of our epoch are a cozy return to the old certainties, especially religious certainty, and a thrilling leap into the unknown. To live, really to live, unconsoled by the past and unintoxicated by the future is our hard charge.

Murdoch has said that Marxism is the subject of [***The Book and the Brotherhood***]. This is false. Marxism is not her subject, but her pretext. Does she know this? It's not easy to say. But nothing could be further from her sensibility than a genuine interest in class struggle. Far better to see the subject of ***The Book and the Brotherhood*** as the fate of liberalism when its center no longer holds, and when liberals themselves are no longer sure why they wear the name. . . .

Over the years Murdoch has developed a powerful critique of liberalism from within its ramshackle house, based on her rejection of the liberal confidence in the view that "happiness equals freedom equals personality." As this new novel aggressively demonstrates, when a brotherhood merely pursues happiness, cherishes freedom, and cultivates personality, it will cease to be a community. Much of Murdoch's fiction has been devoted to projecting possible lives for her solitary worried individuals, who must live after both an Age of Faith and an Age of Reason, keeping up their liberal habits without any liberal foundations. (p. 40)

[The] Existentialist has been the characteristic hero of the modern novel; and for some time, one of her leading aims has been to change the terms of modern heroism. Instead of the brave, lonely self-creator, she has been struggling to imagine these other figures, especially the Mystics, who don't wear the familiar aspects of heroism, and who are apt to be neglected or misunderstood by readers (and characters) craving the usual ceremonies of personal triumph. Humility is not a sexy virtue, but Murdoch has been at pains to teach us its grandeur, guided by the thought that "the humble man, because he sees himself as nothing, can see other things as they are."

Murdoch, a philosophic novelist, spurns the idea of the philosophic novel. This is because she believes that fiction should shiver like the quicksilver of life. She wants a fiction that can engage with urgencies and accidents. She wants to respect the stuffy dust of the universe, the hard rubber, the concrete pieces, the loose chips, the tiny animals; wants to be able to write a novel (such as this one) that not only can engage with '80s Marxism but can also have a parrot and a snail as two of its most important figures. (In [*The Good Apprentice*] it was psychoanalysis and a mouse.) For Murdoch, it is one high aesthetic principle, not her only one, to let her fiction get close to the ground and to feed her imagination with the *topics* of our lives—abortion, rock music, recreational drugs. These contemporaneities have always been her great temptation and her great weakness: they work against the grain of her conceptual clarity, and they lead her to some embarrassing portraits of those she takes to be hipsters. On the other hand, her one unembarrassing, non-contemporary topic is Love, love unrestrained or unrequited, love vulgar, love cruel, love profane, love sacred, love as Plato has taught her to think of it, as fullness of being, as a form of knowledge, as the energy of the soul.

As a philosopher, Murdoch is herself a confessed Platonist who believes in the purity of the Idea, but as a novelist she is the Mystic who refuses to let ideas remain pure, who rubs them in the greasy world. The result in *The Book and the Brotherhood* is that she surrenders her own tidy moral allegory of late liberalism, refuses to bring it to conclusion, and lets it dissolve in the miasma of common life and love.

The politics in *The Book and the Brotherhood* is finally a feint and a tease; to speak of the plot of the novel is to speak of the many strange paths of Eros. It is also, and revealingly, to speak in the terms of melodrama. (p. 41)

Murdoch can stoop to these banalities, because her Love is finally indifferent to the clothes it wears. Let there be melodrama, let there be implausibility. None of that matters. The situations of her plots—infidelity, abortion, abstinence, promiscuity, masochism—are just so many sources of friction to bring the real issue to combustion: the raw recognition "that other people exist." That other people exist, she has said, is incomparably the most important thing that the novel can reveal.

Being as we are, fantasizing as we do, we easily lose the sense of the quick, untranslatable, incalculable being of persons not ourselves. On the foundation of this thought, Murdoch has erected a theory of the novel alongside a theory of the moral life. From the start, her position was willfully anti-modern, at least as "modern" had come to mean. She looked back to Austen, Tolstoy, George Eliot; she made a loving study of Shakespeare. What kept this from becoming merely a nostalgia for lost greatness was its part in a stern positive program, a program for reviving a moribund literature and reanimating a languid moral sense.

Moral Philosophy, Murdoch argued, has bequeathed us an impoverished picture of the human being. We see the self as simply a "brave naked will"; we fail to place the individual against a rich background transcending the self; we have surrendered the notion of truth for the comfortable notion of sincerity; we no longer have a language rich enough to describe the particularity, the variety, the density of our experience. The task of modern literature is to recover that density, specifically "the difficulty and complexity of the moral life and the opacity of persons." The poverty of our ideas of the self can be countered, she believes, by the wealth of the novel. For most of life our imaginations run dry. Fantasy is our besetting vice. We console ourselves with soothing images, and we drift in daydream; and most art encourages us to do just that. But the great tradition of the novel, the tradition of Scott, Austen, Eliot, and above all Tolstoy, broke the grip of fantasy, and let us see, made us see, the world beyond the haze of self.

And the failure of the modern novel—Murdoch has been nervelessly sweeping in her view—is that it tends to reduce to the mind of a single character, who reduces in turn to the mind of the creator: "We feel the ruthless subjection of the characters to the will of the author. The characters are no longer free." The glory of the 19th-century novel was precisely that its fictional figures were "free and separate beings," liberated from the personality of the writer. In a view that anticipated the attitudes of Milan Kundera, Murdoch wrote that "a society which can produce great novelists and which can appreciate great novelists is a society in which tolerance and respect for the existence of other persons is likely to flourish." The high task of the novelist is to release independent characters into the world of the book, and then to respect and love these free beings. Murdoch herself has done it.

But having done it, what has she done? *The Book and the Brotherhood* lets its characters wander freely, wander into a variety of personal romantic crises, wander until they have shattered the idea of collective destiny. Having asked Gerard the pointed question "Who's we?" Rose follows it with the equally pointed "Who's they?" After all the portentous negotiations between Platonist, Mystic, and Existentialist, the book sends its characters into the endless diversity of private fate. Self alone with Other: the politics of the novel collapses into this relation, which for Murdoch is mirrored in the relation of novelist alone with character. She has contended that the novelist can stand as an image of the "good man," because the humble devotion to a character is a model for the humble attention we should pay to one another. It would be consoling to believe this, but here is where Murdoch, the enemy of fantasy, indulges in her own daydream.

Jenkin at one point looks at Gerard, and "a telepathic message passed between them to the effect that neither was cross with the other." It is a small detail, but it epitomizes Murdoch's loftiest intentions. To think oneself into the current of another life, to escape the tight ring of the ego, to achieve a perfect transparency between two selves, to know and to be known—here is the moral image guiding her pen. It is a stirring moment. But can there be such a moment outside the universe of fiction? Only within the pages of a novel, and only with the connivance of an author, can we know that telepathy has occurred, that two beings are as one. Only for a writer, or a reader, of fiction can another soul be thrown so open to knowing eyes.

When Hernshaw's father dies, the novel records his last un-uttered thought. This is Murdoch's way of reminding us that there is a world outside our narrow comprehension. It is a salutary reminder; but with a real death, the final silence is just a silence. Wanting so much to show life beyond the self, Murdoch takes great pleasure in arranging bumps and bruises for the ego as it knocks against an independent objective reality. She likes to tell us what a character thinks, and then, semi-savagely, to tell us what's true. Would that the distinction were so easy in life.

"I should hate to be alive and not writing a novel"—this title to an interview in the *Women's Journal* says more than it knows. For all Murdoch's commitment to realism inside fiction is where she really dwells. Her stated position is that the novel should be like life, but her underground desire is that life should be like her novels: intellectually adventurous and morally severe. This is not at all to demean the accomplishment; life could do worse than resemble Murdoch's fiction. We are left with the distinctive feeling of satisfaction-in-dissatisfaction that her novels consistently produce. All agree, no one more cheerfully or bravely than Murdoch herself, that the novels are imperfect, but what they aim at is so high and large and good that it's impossible to kill the wish that we too should live inside a fiction where we would be known and loved and tended by the novelist who dreamed us into being. (pp. 41-2, 44)

Michael Levenson, "Liberals in Love," in The New Republic, *Vol. 198, No. 23, June 6, 1988, pp. 40-2, 44.*

Thomas (Bernard) Murphy

1935-

Irish dramatist and scriptwriter.

Murphy's plays examine familial, social, cultural, and religious pressures that influence the lives of Irish citizens in their homeland and as emigrés in England. He often focuses upon characters who are frustrated by oppressive and alienating forces in Irish life as they attempt to establish individual identities. For example, in his best-known work, *A Whistle in the Dark*, Murphy depicts the violent tragedy that arises among brothers who have inherited their father's brutal code of masculinity. D. E. S. Maxwell commented on Murphy's dramas: "From *A Whistle in the Dark*'s deployment of an essentially realist stage, [Murphy] has explored various theatrical shapes to express the collisions between savage actualities of failure and despair and the solace or defence offered by human faiths, rituals, fantasies—most often their incapacities. . . . Usually but not invariably Irish in setting, Murphy's plays, without sacrificing their local identity, carry their scenes and characters into the emotional landscape, universally recognisable, of the twentieth century."

Murphy began his career in the theater by collaborating with Noel O'Donoghue on the one-act play *On the Outside* (1961). This piece underscores the hopelessness of two impoverished Irish youths who are refused entrance to a dance hall. Like most of Murphy's work, *On the Outside* is set in a constricting milieu in which characters experience and respond to alienation. Murphy later wrote a companion piece, *On the Inside* (1974), which is set within the dance hall and focuses upon the concerns of privileged members of Irish society. Similarly, *A Whistle in the Dark* (1961) examines themes relating to provincial Ireland as well as problems confronting an Irish emigré in England. In this play, the urbane life of Michael Carney and his wife is destroyed by a visit from his crude father and violent brothers. Through the conflict between Michael and his relatives, Murphy contrasts personal integrity and intelligence with brutality, ignorance, and denial of individualism. As in several of Murphy's works, *A Whistle in the Dark* climaxes with somber, melodramatic events. Following this play, Murphy wrote four works in which he experimented with dramatic forms and modified his thematic scope. *Famine* (1966) is a naturalistic drama depicting the suffering and heroism of Irish peasants during the potato famine of the mid-nineteenth century; *The Orphans* (1968) and *The Fooleen: A Crucial Week in the Life of a Grocer's Assistant* (1969) comment upon social issues of the 1960s while addressing representative problems confronting emigrés; and *The Morning after Optimism* (1971) is an allegory of sacred and profane love set in a supernatural forest.

Murphy's next work, *The White House* (1972; later produced as *Conversations on a Homecoming*), symbolically portrays the blighted hopes of the Irish populace. The first act of this play depicts a group of disillusioned, middle-aged friends gathered in an Irish pub called The White House; the second act, set ten years earlier, reveals the same characters as idealistic youths admiring a publican who emulates Irish Catholic American President John F. Kennedy. According to critics, the pub represents the fading hopes of contemporary Ireland, and the

Photograph by Peter Reynolds. Courtesy of Thomas Murphy.

assassination of President Kennedy serves to stifle the illusory aspirations of the characters. Murphy's other plays that comment upon historical and contemporary failures undermining Irish national consciousness include *The Gigli Concert* (1983) and *Bailegangaire* (1986). *The Gigli Concert* centers on two characters who represent extremes of Irish culture and, by extension, humanity in general. One is a rational and prosperous Englishman interested in promoting his progressive ideas in Ireland, while the other is a disaffected Irishman who invents a fantasy world to offset the constraints and troubles of his daily existence. In *Bailegangaire*, a young woman caring for her demanding, ill-tempered grandmother serves as a metaphor for the ambivalent relationship between contemporary Ireland and its ancient traditions. Murphy's other works for the theater include *The Sanctuary Lamp* (1975), which focuses on disenchanted Irish Catholics, and *The Blue Macushla* (1980), a satire of the Irish Nationalist Movement. He has also written numerous plays for television, among them several adaptations of his own dramas.

(See also *Contemporary Authors,* Vol. 101.)

THE TIMES, LONDON

Out of six brutes, one coward and one bewildered girl Mr. Thomas Murphy makes [*A Whistle in the Dark*] a quite terrifying play. While he is in control of his story he comes near to convincing us that the whole world consists of stupid fighting animals. His third act lapse into commonplace melodrama is almost welcome. At least it relieves us of the necessity of believing in his people.

An Irish father . . . has brought up four of his sons to believe that their whole object of life is to make the Fighting Carneys feared. . . . When they are not matching themselves with rival gangs they are fighting each other. . . . [The sons] are far too stupid to perceive that [their father] is nothing but a brandy-swilling braggart with a resourceful talent for getting his own way.

The "cad" of the litter is too intelligent to take their simple view of life, and they descend on his home in Coventry and succeed in wrecking his marriage. The father takes the strap to the young husband and orders him, as in boyhood, to go to bed. He finds no way of standing up for himself, and when his brothers go off to fight the Mulryans his wife desperately bids him go out and fight with them, hoping that his display of courage will gain their respect.

The story up to this point holds the stage impressively. It loses its balance in the last act largely because the author, who has led us to expect that the old Carney will be unmasked by the fighting Carneys, so arranges things that the old man is left triumphant in his wickedness.

> *"A Terrifying Play," in* The Times, *London, September 12, 1961, p. 14.*

WILLIAM A. ARMSTRONG

One of the most interesting plays to be staged in London in 1961 was Thomas Murphy's *A Whistle in the Dark*. Here we have yet another variation on the themes of Irish emigration to England, the violence lurking in the background of Irish life, and the conflict between Irish youth and its inherited traditions. . . . *A Whistle in the Dark* is about an Irish family—the Carneys—who have been feuding with another Irish family from time immemorial. Michael, a peace-loving member of the Carney family, emigrates to Coventry, but his violent father and brothers descend upon him and his English wife, take possession of their house, and engage in a savage combat with members of the enemy family who have also come to Coventry. Intoxicated by this combat, the youngest brother provokes Michael into fighting with him and the long-suffering Michael kills him with a bottle. *A Whistle in the Dark* is yet another instance of the current preoccupation of Irish dramatists with life- and death-forces. Michael, the industrious and well-conducted emigrant, is in effect, caught in the trammels of the primitive code of violence which he has tried to transcend. From this point of view, his predicament has something in common with that of Behan's [title character in *The Hostage*] and O'Casey's Senator Chatastray [in *Behind the Green Curtains*]. (pp. 99-100)

Beginning with *Look Back in Anger* in 1956, some of the most important English plays have been directed against what has come to be known as 'The Establishment', a word connoting what is wrong with the powers-that-be, such as their endorsement of prudery, puritanism, and the shibboleths of public school education, their endorsement of the violence of capital punishment and the potential violence of the stock-piles of atomic weapons, their endorsement of class distinctions, racial discrimination, and big business. Collectively, O'Casey, Behan, and Murphy have been concerned with similar defects in the Irish Establishment, with the prudery of censorship, with the puritanical regulation of private life, with the dead hand of tradition in the workings of the I.R.A., with the violence perpetuated by religious superstition and tribal codes of conduct. Their point of view is Irish, and their technique differs from that of their fellow-dramatists in England, but they share with them a faith in youth and a new humanism. (p. 101)

> *William A. Armstrong, "The Irish Point of View: The Plays of Sean O'Casey, Brendan Behan, and Thomas Murphy," in* Experimental Drama, *edited by William A. Armstrong, G. Bell and Sons, Ltd., 1963, pp. 79-102.*

IRVING WARDLE

[Exiles from Ireland are represented in the 1968 Dublin Theatre Festival] by Thomas Murphy's *The Orphans,* a piece which makes the circumstance of Irish birth seem like an incurable disease. Some 10 years ago Mr. Murphy produced a terrifyingly authentic melodrama about Irish immigrants called *A Whistle in the Dark*. Now he has done all he can to abandon national stereotypes—setting the play in an English country house whose occupants (the briefly reunited members of a well-to-do immigrant family) apply themselves strenuously to the task of noncommunication. Calculated flatness replaces melodramatic climaxes; there is much talk about happenings and LSD, and when anyone drops into brogue it is only for purposes of contemptuous mimickry.

The effect of this reversal, however, is more Irish than ever: a piece still saturated in the old themes of physical disgust and religious sentimentality, including the obligatory confession of an ex-whore to an ex-priest. (p. 23)

> *Irving Wardle, "Irish Residents and Exiles," in* The Times, *London, October 12, 1968, pp. 21, 23.*

CLIVE BARNES

[*A Whistle in the Dark*] is a strange, ugly, impressive play. . . .

I was . . . struck by the unusual vigor and directness of a play that interweaves themes of violence, loyalty and cowardice in a study of one of the most unpleasant families in stage history. My colleague, George Oppenheimer, has recently written most attractively about stage characters he would not care to invite home to dinner. Mr. Murphy's family here—"The Fighting Carneys"—are hardly the kind of people you even invite home for a coffee. They are thugs.

Yet there is a great deal more to Mr. Murphy's story than a loving, at times rather melodramatic description of the face of violence. There is in this play something of the horror, complexity and final catharsis of a Greek tragedy. Mr. Murphy is not quite taut enough in the construction of his play. He occasionally skids perilously close to the belly laughs of bathos, and, if anything, he tends to overwrite. But he has the stuff of drama in him and *A Whistle in the Dark* is a good, rousing and gripping play. . . .

It is the kind of play that requires very careful staging and acting. Its rambustiousness is frankly old fashioned—compare the stagey violence here, for example, with the stealthy convincing violence of the movie *Easy Rider* and the point is instantly made. But Mr. Murphy's dramatics can carry conviction. . . .

Clive Barnes, "Study of a Most Unpleasant Family," in The New York Times, *October 9, 1969.*

MARTIN GOTTFRIED

Whether or not Thomas Murphy saw Pinter's *The Homecoming* before writing *A Whistle in the Dark,* the resemblance between the plays is uncanny. Both were written (or at least produced) about the same time, so there's no way of really telling and in any case playwrights as capable as Mr. Murphy are not likely to steal stories, especially from writers as famous as Pinter, and playwrights as talented as Pinter don't need to borrow from anyone. Nevertheless, it is quite impossible to talk about *A Whistle in the Dark* without mentioning the Pinter play. . . .

The Homecoming was about a man who brings his wife home to meet his father and brothers. They promptly assume possession of the woman, humiliate her husband and are ultimately subjugated by her. The play was essentially a study in family relationships and female power, defining a man by his weakness for women. *A Whistle in the Dark* is about a man and his wife who are more or less invaded by his father and brothers. It is a study of masculinity as defined by brutality, as opposed to the masculinity of the mind, and shows a woman as torn between these two male quotients. Ultimately, in this play, the woman chooses decency over brute strength, but the man has no choice. He accepts the brute idea of man because it is made part of pride.

The basic similarities between the plays are obvious—they deal with the idea of masculinity and how it is frightfully instilled in men by stupid, cruel fathers. The differences are just as obvious. Pinter's play is frigidly written, distrustful of words, austere and steel-like. Murphy's play is so densely worded that for most of the time you can't hear any language simply because there is so much of it. And yet, as it heads toward act-endings, the air clears, the language simplifies, and so clarifies. Murphy is a great act-ending playwright. The trouble is that his acts also have beginnings and middles and that his third act is so entirely an act-ending that it is 45 minutes' worth of climax. No climax can be indefinitely sustained without losing potency.

Still, Murphy is without doubt a strong playwright and *A Whistle in the Dark* is without doubt a strong play when it is having its moments. As a story, it is heavily padded with conversation, redundant and often uninteresting. The basic facts hardly demand the three hours the play runs. . . .

It is pretty strong business, and not very far from what real and fake masculinity are all about. I'm sorry it is grossly overwritten and sorry that Murphy's writing isn't graceful.

Martin Gottfried, in a review of "A Whistle in the Dark," in Women's Wear Daily, *October 9, 1969.*

WALTER KERR

Thomas Murphy's *A Whistle in the Dark* is a fine, furious play about men trained to anger. Because its author is Irish, and because he has packed a shabby suburban house in England with a raging assortment of brogues just off the boat, there were those . . . who wanted to wonder if the mood and perhaps the meaning of the evening weren't a bit like *The Playboy of the Western World.* They are not. If anything, they're a great deal more like that last nightmarish piece in *America Hurrah,* the one in which two mammoth automatons, returned relics of an earlier stage in the evolutionary process, moved mindlessly to destroy a motel.

The effect is not at all dissimilar. Though Mr. Murphy's play is on the surface a plausibly naturalistic one, and though his thousands of overwrought words spin torrentially from mouths that have become bottle-shaped from swigging so much actual ale, the oppressive environment that is created is either pre- or post-civilized, the universe is a universe invaded by stone men.

There they sit, broad granite shapes with heads pressed upon necks that might have come from petrified forests, eye-blind, impenetrable, irresistible when they rise and move. They are only ordinary Irishmen who have been taught by their father how to fight, indeed how to make fighting a life work and an identity, and they are terrifying because they are self-winding, timed to explode by an unfathomable mechanism, beyond human reach. They are the original anarchists, and they hint at a new breed of anarchists to come.

Strictly speaking, Mr. Murphy's edgy spellbinder isn't all that naturalistic. What family today is reared to use its fists on the street as evidence of character, charm and authority? Forty years ago, maybe. I can remember walking, when I was a kid and a coward, two blocks around to avoid just such a clan. It's a literal anachronism now, though, and a playgoer might well be puzzled—trying to take the situation straight as to how the poor sods expect to survive, or make beer money, in this mechanized world. Nor is it any more likely that one of five brothers, the eldest, would allow every last male in his family to intrude upon his own Coventry home and remain there endlessly and outrageously, wife or no wife.

But such things do not matter because the sense of subterranean power, of naked unreason scarcely waiting to be unleashed, is simply present on the stage for all to feel. Mr. Murphy has compressed it into his boiling language, guaranteed a temperature to back up his words. . . .

The vision isn't pretty or likeable. But it is powerful because it is secretly familiar, it is with us, it is as ordinary as it is grotesque. Something more than a story about "iron men" gets at us. Foreheads made of marble stalk the stage like so many battering rams, we see an energy born of inner emptiness, and we intuit its readiness to strike. The play is strong and fiercely sustained, and should be seen.

Walter Kerr, in a review of "A Whistle in the Dark," in The New York Times, *Section II, November 9, 1969, p. 3.*

PETER ROBERTS

I found [*The Morning After Optimism*] very interesting indeed—especially as it comes from an author whose *Whistle in the Dark* has accustomed us to expect, years later, more in the way of social realism. In fact *The Morning After Optimism* could not conceivably have strayed further in an opposite direction—being set, as it is, in a forest and having, as it does, four abstract characters—a ponce, a whore, a poet and an orphan.

There is a whimsical air about such a dramatic set-up for which the times are very much out of joint. There is also an engaging downbeat comedy in the writing that prevents the play from actually being quite as earnest and pretentious as a first glance at its programme suggests. The area that Murphy is exploring seems—at evening's end—to be the difficulty of reconciling the idealised romantic conception of adult love as presented in nursery book reading with the way such things actually work out in real life. The idealised figures are embodied by the Poet and the Orphan who inhabit a sort of balletic, fairystory world where they fall in love, marry and are united like *Sleeping Beauty* but come into a spot of trouble when they actually have to face the physical details of actually sleeping together. This is no problem to the Ponce and the Whore, who have obviously both slept around more than a little before coming to picnic in the author's forest setting. . . . *Their* problem is to try, after the sordid encounters of the real world, to recapture the childish conception of 'romance' as gleaned from their childhood reading and entertainment and as epitomised by the Poet and the Orphan. Both Whore and Ponce flirt, respectively, with Poet and Orphan, but end up by destroying once and for all what I take to be beautiful but ineffectual wish-fulfilments of themselves.

It's not a wholly successful work. But I found it an increasingly fascinating one. . . . (p. 54)

> *Peter Roberts, "Dublin 2," in* Plays and Players, *Vol. 18, No. 8, May, 1971, pp. 53-5.*

CHARLES LEWSEN

It is worth saying at once that Thomas Murphy's play [*The White House*] is not parochial in any limiting sense; indeed, as I shall try to indicate, there are respects in which it fails to be properly specific. It concerns an exile's homecoming and his discovery of the barriers dividing him from his past friends; it centres on the day that John F. Kennedy was shot.

Like Kennedy on his visit to Ireland in June, 1963, the actor Michael, protagonist of Mr Murphy's first act, is playing the role of an Irish boy who has made good abroad. Brendan Behan's metaphor for his country in *Richard's Cork Leg* is a graveyard; in **The White House** it is a small town pub where Michael and his past friends erect barriers of trivia and evasion, moving from uneasy camaraderie to open hostility. There is constant reference to the past and mention of the owner JJ, who has slunk off for the evening.

In the second act we have moved back nine years. The boys have lost weight and grain. The partition wall between the two bars has been demolished, decoration is in process, friendly scruffiness is giving way to cool good taste. The pub is becoming the White House, the name by which it has been coyly referred to in the first act. At the centre of the decorating operations, in silk suit, suede shoes and with the hunched shoulders and floppy hair of JFK stands JJ. He is turning his pub into a cultural centre, hanging pictures that he has commissioned from a local artist and, with female advice, setting out display cases of antiques. And incessantly he encourages his helpers with rhetoric from Kennedy's speeches. Two or three times it looks as if someone is trying to tell him that Kennedy has been shot, but JJ is not listening. As he places a piece of Wedgwood on a ledge it falls and smashes.

The youngsters' wholehearted participation in this idealistic game takes poignancy from the disillusioned future which we have already witnessed. . . . It is poignant that Tom, who drafts JJ's address to the Chamber of Commerce, should become the embittered schoolmaster; it is poignant that Tom and Michael, "the twins", as JJ likes to call them, should become divided. Poignancy might give way to tragedy if we experienced JJ's charisma through the specific hopes and illusions of the different youngsters. However, the boys and girls really are blank pages for JJ to write on—which is consistent with Mr Murphy's design but robs it of some texture.

JJ, too, is under-characterized. We understand that he is a driving force in the community, but his social role is expressed only in a dispute with a priest about whether a nude picture should be hung on the wall of the pub. More specifics are needed to define his emptiness. Because they lack definition as people and as pieces in the design (not everyone is carried over from the present to the past) one does not easily focus on the characters at first sight. This probably accounts for my feeling that the first act is too long. Certainly the second-act passage leading up to the inevitable announcement of Kennedy's death needs savage cutting. The kids' departure from JJ and his realization that he hates his hero lacked power simply because they had been delayed.

Nevertheless, this is a resonant work by a writer of passion.

> *Charles Lewsen, "An Exile's Return to the Past,"*
> *in* The Times, *London, March 22, 1972, p. 9.*

MEL GUSSOW

The Morning After Optimism leads to an evening of Irish whimsy. In this play by Thomas Murphy . . . , a pimp and his only prostitute, a handsome prince and an eager maiden meet in an enchanted forest. . . .

The Irish Times in Dublin called it "the most original and one of the most moving and impressive plays to have been presented by the Abbey theater in the past quarter century." This says more about the imagination of drama critics than about the imagination of the playwright.

This is a fanciful yarn that is intended to beguile. Because of its setting, characters and general air of wishfulness, it begs to be compared with, among other works, *Green Mansions, The Enchanted* and *A Midsummer Night's Dream* and . . . it ends as something of a pauper.

The prince and the pimp are long-lost brothers, parted by time and profession and, in the course of the play, by their common attraction for the maiden, "an orphan longing to be found." The prince is supposed to be a poet, but his inflated pronouncements (such as "Our paths have been converging since the exordium") make him less than charming.

The orphan is aery, a sprightly wood nymph. Pimp and prostitute are much more down to earth. He is a loser-prankster, his own worst victim, and she is wryly philosophical about her calling.

The play revolves around the pimp, James, a compulsive talker. "Would you like to hear the story of my life—and I'll erase it as I go along," he says to the maiden in one of the play's better lines. She politely refuses all offers from this pitchman, preferring to save herself for the prince.

By the end of two extremely long acts, one's tolerance for adult fairy tales is stretched.

Mel Gussow, " 'Morning After' Set in Irish Whimsy,"
in The New York Times, June 28, 1974, p. 24.

CLIVE BARNES

If atmosphere constituted plays there would be a play in every Dublin barroom and probably in every Irish dance hall. Unfortunately plays are more than atmosphere—they need to be a translation of life, a view of life, not simply an evocative recording of life.

These simple thoughts have been prompted by [a] new double bill of plays. . . .

The two one-acters are called *On the Outside,* written by Thomas Murphy and Noel O'Donoghue, and *On the Inside,* written by Mr. Murphy by himself. Mr. Murphy, and his collaborator, are skilled writers with an ear open for the life and times of their Irish contemporaries.

Mr. Murphy is best known for his fine verismo drama, *A Whistle in the Dark.* . . . This was a startling family drama— a cross between Harold Pinter and Sean O'Casey—but while the verbal felicity of the earlier play is evident enough in this double bill, the impact is far less. It is as though Mr. Murphy, not quite having the subject matter for a play, let us in on his dramatic musings.

Both plays are about love and money. They have other things in common as well. The scene is a rural Irish dance hall on a Sunday night in the 1950's. It is perhaps the same night, perhaps the same dance hall. We never really know because the characters in the first play (where Mr. Murphy had the collaboration of Mr. O'Donoghue) are not repeated in the second. Yet this probably does not matter, although the dramatic proposition would have been more interesting with a certain judicious overlapping.

On the Outside is precisely what the title suggests. A man has made a date with a young woman. The woman turns up with a friend. She goes into the dance hall. The man turns up, also with a friend. Unfortunately he doesn't have the money to get into the hall. And really that is it. Not quite it. The authors are full of comments about the manipulative powers of money and, of course, about rural Ireland, with all its sex, sin and repression.

The play rings horribly true, but the ring is not quite interesting enough, or, more importantly, perhaps interpretative enough. We do not go to the theater to listen to a tape recorder, however intelligently that tape recorder may have been positioned.

[*On the Inside*] is even less conclusive. A sad and rural pair of lovers, with intimations of happiness, discover they are pregnant. It is the kind of society where the man always gets pregnant alongside the woman. They decide to face the consequences, and even decide they are glad about them. It would have been a more interesting play if they hadn't been. Playwrights should use happy endings as painfully as the guillotine.

Yes, a great deal of Ireland is in this double bill—it is a view certainly with insight but without the structure of interpretation. Atmosphere is really never enough. Yet there is a charm and life to the plays, a realistic approach to the way people lived. . . .

Clive Barnes, in a review of "On the Outside" and "On the Inside," in The New York Times, March 9, 1976, p. 27.

JOHN COLEBY

Literally, *On the Outside* refers to the street outside a dance hall in a small Irish town in the late 1950s; and *On the Inside* is set inside the same dance hall on another occasion in the same period but involves different people. The companion one-act plays are contrasting studies of the havenots and the haves, in any society. . . . [In *On the Outside,* two] boys, Frank and Joe, cannot muster the six bob each to get into the dance. They make several attempts to beg or borrow the three-and-six they are short of, or to cajole the box office lady or the bouncer to let them in for less. They fail. End of story. But the telling of it encapsulates the fate then, and now, of all who find themselves short of a bob or two in our mercenary world. *On the Inside* is a more subtly orchestrated piece about the 'repressed sex market' and the ploys and gambits of people who have got six bob but not much more, and with it all the worry and burden of playing the game by the rules—in a small town. Mr. Murphy spins his stories in a masterly fashion, making no concessions and striking not one false note.

John Coleby, in a review of "On the Outside" and "On the Inside," in Drama, London, No. 128, Spring, 1978, p. 81.

RICHARD KEARNEY

Tom Murphy's *The Gigli Concert,* premiered at the 1983 Dublin Theatre Festival, confirms his reputation as one of the most important and pioneering dramatists writing in Ireland today. While Brian Friel's 'Field Day' company has come to represent a particularly 'northern' movement of response to the fundamental problems of tradition, history, language and identity confronting our contemporary culture, Murphy has now established himself as the most powerful 'southern' counterpart to such a movement.

The 'Field Day' company has tended, in general, to concentrate on the more *historical* dimension of our cultural displacement and dispossession (epitomized in [Friel's play] *Translations* and in its first pamphlet series on the Irish-British conflict which still remains unresolved in the northern province from which the 'Field Day' directors hail). Murphy's work, by contrast, has focused on the *existential* malady of inner displacement and division to which, he believes, the inhabitants of our southern, supposedly more 'settled' provinces are perhaps singularly prone.

In previous plays, Murphy has explored the darker frontiers of the modern Irish experience with magnificent obsessiveness. In a Murphy drama, the border that truncates and polarizes is *within;* it marks a metaphysical rupture between self and self rather than a geographical/historical partition between one community and another (northern/southern, Irish/British etc.). The metaphor of the 'wall' which recurs throughout Murphy's works invariably signals a confinement to our solitary, divided selves. As Malachy puts it in *On the Inside* (1976): 'Self-contempt is the metaphysical key. How can you, I ask myself, love someone, if first, you do not love yourself?' 'My spirit is unwell too', declares Harry in the *Sanctuary Lamp* (1976), as he wrestles with the angel of his own 'holy loneliness', keeping demonic vigil over his deceased loved one (Teresa) and his deceased God (the play takes place within a church: Nietzsche's 'madman' was also carrying a 'sanctuary lamp' when he announced the 'death of God').

In all of his plays, Murphy seems to be saying that we are still, always, *on the outside* (the title of his first play, 1959) even, and most agonizingly, when we are *on the inside:* that is, even when we contrive to escape the alienating circumstances of modern existence by seeking asylum in the sanctuary of our own inner selves. But it is perhaps Michael in *A Whistle in the Dark* [1961], who most poignantly sums up this condition of existential dis-ease when he utters his cry of self-contradiction: 'I want to get out of this kind of life. I want . . . I want us all to be—I don't want to be what I am . . . But I can't get out of all lthis . . . What's wrong with me?'

This metaphysical experience of the dark abyss of self-division—most of Murphy's plays take place at night—confessionally registered yet comically resolved, is the abiding motif of Murphy's *oeuvre* (thirteen plays so far and several adaptations). It suggests that his work shares less with the native 'folk' concerns of Synge, O'Casey or Molloy, than with the 'existentialist' explorations of such continental authors as Dostoevsky, Kierkegaard, Nietzsche, Sartre or Beckett. [In the Abbey Theatre Programme to *The Gigli Concert,* Christopher Murray stated]: 'All of Tom Murphy's work is a "whistle in the dark", an exultant cry of triumph over the facts of death and history. The subject matter can be serious, but the struggle to establish a self, a personality free from the subtle determinants of society, is presented with comic vigour, with what Nietzsche . . . called metaphysical delight'.

Moreover, it is precisely because Murphy has departed from the indigenous tradition of the well-made folk-drama and embraced the modernist idioms of contemporary spiritual crisis and struggle, that he has at times bemused his critics and audiences. While Murphy's plays ostensibly conform to the Irish norm of 'verbal' theatre, they substantially modify this norm in emphasizing the *mood* or *tone* of feeling created by language rather than the narrative plot or storyline as such. Murphy's characters tend to tell stories about themselves rather than simply play out a role in a story told about them (by the author). The action takes place in the actors rather than the actors developing the action. Brian Friel has described Murphy as the 'most distinctive, restless and obsessive imagination working in the Irish theatre today'. There is little doubt that Murphy's many experiments with form and dialogue (ranging from the naturalism of the early plays to the more surreal and stylized later plays) testify to a sense of dramatic *navigatio,* of endlessly attempting to articulate the inarticulate, to sound the unconscious, or as Beckett's Watt put it, to 'eff the ineffable'.

The Gigli Concert is not so much a play within a play as a psychodrama within a psychodrama. It stages a turbulent exchange between two central characters: one from the 'outside', J.P.W. King, a middle-aged Englishman masquerading as a 'resident' psychotherapist (he claims he had a Tipperary grandmother) with messianic pretentions to realize men's secret dreams; the other from the 'inside', an 'Irishman' (as the script describes him) with no name, address or telephone number, posturing as a musically gifted cobbler's son from the Italian town of Recaniti who wants to sing like the great opera singer, Beniamino Gigli. The drama unfolds as a sort of life and death struggle between these *frères enemies,* whose intimate complicity of mutual misunderstanding, deceit and empathy suggests at times that they are perhaps more similar than they pretend, perhaps even alter-egos of each other (as James and Edmund in Murphy's previous play, *The Morning after Optimism,* 1973): psychic doubles of a divided self seeking the completion of a possible unity.

The two protagonists hail from opposite poles. J.P.W. represents the intellectually 'progressive' future-oriented ethos of English and European Enlightenment; he claims to be a 'dynamatologist' sent over to Ireland by the movement's founding-father in order to propagate a new method for helping people to realize their 'potential' (Greek, *Dunamis*). By contrast, the 'Irishman' or Beniamino as J.P.W. insists on calling him, epitomizes the native West-of-Ireland ethos of cunning instinct, memory and tradition (what Frank O'Connor termed the 'backward look'); he has experienced this ethos as fundamentally repressive and refractory to his own dreams and has sought to escape from it first by becoming a *nouveau-riche* 'operator' in the building trade and finally by seeking a form of perfection beyond the materialist idols of power and wealth—the sublimity of music. Though he prides himself on being a no-nonsense 'self made man' who knows far more about life than any psychologist or philosopher, Beniamino feels compelled nonetheless to procure the therapeutic 'self-realizing' services of an 'intellectual' pioneer such as J.P.W.

Beniamino is an Irish man thoroughly disabused with the cult of bourgeois opportunism and careerism (brought about, in part, by the transition from De Valera's idyllic ideology of pastoral piety to Lemass's hardnosed ideology of commercial 'rising tides' and Taca development schemes). Thus while he may invoke the authority of facts and figures, Beniamino ultimately wishes to escape from the determining constraints of such empirical necessities into the 'possible and possibilizing' world of pure art. He wants to trade in fact for fiction, his self-made-man success story having degenerated into a nightmare of despair and violence. Delinquent itinerants, he complains, have overrun his 'territory'; and instead of communicating with his wife and nine year old son, he can now only utter a 'roar of obscenity'. The centre can no longer hold. And so Beniamino wants to transmute the dark energies of that roar within him into music. He wants, quite simply, to sing like Gigli.

As the play unfolds we gradually learn that the differences between the two characters are more apparent than real. If the Italianate 'Beniamino' is no more than a pseudonym for the nameless 'Irishman', the messianic-sounding term 'dynamatologist' is itself no more than a pseudonym for the hapless, narcotic-and-vodka crazed mess of broken dreams that J.P.W. really is. (Both characters admit at different times that they 'do not know how (they) will get through the day'). Far from being able to 'make all things possible' as his title and philosophy profess, J.P.W. King is no *salvator mundi;* and while he chides Beniamino for believing that the 'Romantic Kingdom is of this world', it transpires that he himself is neither king of this world nor of any other. In short, the analyst is just as screwed up as his analysand. (pp. 327-30)

One of the most conspicuous features of Murphy's work is its ability to transcend its local or national setting and to assume a stature of epic, international proportions. Murphy's *The Gigli Concert* will travel well. One can imagine J.P.W. or Beniamino making as powerful an impact on New York, London or Paris audiences as on the Dublin audience of its festival premier (who gave it a standing ovation). For while at one level the dramatic exchanges (in every sense) between J.P.W. and Beniamino can be interpreted as emblems, for example, of the age-old conflict between England and Ireland—with the Northern accented Mona as a sort of neglected go-between: the woman victimized by the male-dominated struggle for power—they also and more immediately represent the problematic opposition between two universal kinds of value system: the future-oriented, Enlightenment versus past-oriented traditionalism; humanist intellect versus native instinct; Utopian idealism versus pragmatic materialism; Herculean authenticity versus Antaean sincerity and so on.

Murphy's capacity to enlarge the parochial into the universal, to go beyond the established conventions of folk-poetic Irishry is shared by few contemporary Irish dramatists (perhaps only by Friel and Kilroy to any significant degree). In *The Gigli Concert* we witness an author grappling with native concerns fully cognizant of the profound fascination which modern European culture—from Gigli to the existentialists—exerts upon our minds and hearts. To take just one comparative example, it is interesting to observe the parallels between Beniamino's desire to sing like Gigli in order to escape the contingent mess of everyday existence and Roquentin's desire, in Sartre's *Nausea*, to reach the condition of pure Being symbolized by the song of a negress. . . . Sartre contends that the greatest power of the song is that it projects an aesthetic world of pure possibility 'cleansed of the sin of existing'. Murphy's view of existence is in this respect strangely akin to that of Sartre and the existentialists. Life, for both, is absurd, chaotic, insane and can only be redeemed, if at all, by a stoical belief in the transforming power of imagination. All truth is an artefact, taught Nietszche, but one which we could not survive without. The only way to combat the absurdity of existence is, therefore, to keep on believing in meaning in spite of everything, like Sisyphus rolling his rock to the top of the hill in the belief that he will eventually reach the summit; and that even if he doesn't the struggle itself—the act of faith in the possible—justifies the effort. Or as Beckett's 'unnamable' narrator put it, if 'I can't go on, I'll go on'. Indeed, Murphy's mis-fits bear a striking resemblance to Beckett's in that both succeed in representing 'existentialist man' in localized, recognizable settings.

Perhaps Beckett's move to Paris and Murphy's ten year sojourn in London (where he worked at The Royal Court and Old Vic, and wrote and staged his first plays) helped both to bring universal 'outside' perspectives to bear on their formative, 'native' experience.

If one examines the implications of this universalist existentialism in the Irish contexts of most of Murphy's plays a slightly unsettling assumption emerges. For the common message that Murphy's repertoire of angst-ridden characters seem to convey is that the mainstream codes and traditions of Irish society are irrevocably alienating and corrupt. In *On the Outside*, set at the doorway of an Irish rural dancehall, it is the small-town provincialism of moral *resentment*, violence and begrudgery which the author exposes. In *Whistle in the Dark*, it is the psychic paralysis produced by introverted family competitiveness and spite. In *On the Inside* and *Sanctuary Lamp*, Murphy turns his satirical attention to the life-denying oppressiveness of our jansenistic pietism: 'Holy medals and genitalia in mortal combat with each other', as Malachy remarks in the former, 'is not sex at all'. Murphy berates this jansenistic God of self-mortificatory devotionalism in *Sanctuary Lamp* as a necrophilic 'metaphysical monster' whose supposed 'real presence' (symbolized by the lamp) of consolation and compassion is little more than a mask for the 'violence-mongering furies' of a moribund deity. Abandoned to their own self-destructive solitude Murphy's godless but god-obsessed 'orphans' resort to the last possible refuge—the sanctuary of insanity: 'Do you think madness must at least be warm', muses Harry, 'I don't mind admitting I keep it as a standby in case all else fails'.

In the *Famine* and *The Blue Macushla*, Murphy indicts the chauvinistic thuggery and pseudo-patriotic hypocrisy which has so contaminated political life in Ireland. The latter play is in fact a hilarious if trenchant send-up of how the coercive expressions of narrow Irish nationalism, from the highest of government ministers to the lowest of paramilitary fanatics (the *Erin go Brágh* splinter group of a splinter group!), conspire to rob one Eddie O'Hara of his 'person' (his sense of self as biographically detailed in the opening soliloquy of the play) and ultimately of his life. 'Wearing patriotism on your sleeve like gold cufflinks', Murphy suggests, is more conducive to the spread of a contagious national disease than to one's sense of personal integrity.

Lastly, in *The Gigli Concert* Murphy unleashes his iconoclastic ire on the consumerist Irish bourgeoisie who resent any deviant flight of imaginative creativity, force many of their artists and intellectuals into exile, or, as Beniamino admonishes (and he should know as he is one of them) will try to destroy those who remain.

This angry, at times even apocalyptic, attitude to contemporary Irish society has made, in Murphy's case at any rate, for exciting drama. The exuberance of dramatic form and language—sometimes straining at the seams—which Murphy's uncompromising *non serviam* has produced cannot be gainsaid. And yet one is tempted to ask if his global repudiation of our social, religious and political institutions does not, at times, run the risk of excessive caricature, even falling back into the romantic cliché of the *poète maudit*: the solitary, wounded, alienated godlike artist guarding the last flame of inspired vision within his breast against the benighted hostility of the community at large. Kierkegaard dismissed the anonymous masses that threatened the creative individual as the 'Crowd' (*The Crowd is Untruth*, ran his celebrated maxim), Nietzsche as the 'Herd', and Sartre as '*les salauds*'. It would seem that Murphy's heroes—or anti-heroes—do not have to identify this social collectivity as such; it has contaminated the very air they breathe; it is witnessed in the visible scars of their pain and failure; it is quite simply that faceless, omnipresent 'they' invoked by Beniamino when he warns J.P.W. that there's kindness in the world but '*they'll* kill you if you stay over here'. Murphy's response to this threat of the collective is invariably one of fierce individualism bordering, at times, on savage Swiftean indignation at the 'yahoo' mentality.

In Murphy's world, the individual is the agent of liberation, the collectivity—and its related idioms of history, tradition, authority, politics, nationalism etc.—the agency of coercion. Nearly all of his plays are centred around an isolated individual's struggle for self-realization over against the oppressive constraints of his/her environmental and socio-political conditioning. Whether it be Eddie O'Hara in *The Blue Macushla*, John Connor in *Famine* or J.P.W. in *The Gigli Concert*, in each case the line of demarcation between the salvation of personal vision and the insanity of personal violence is dangerously nebulous and shifting. Yet despite all that, one cannot help feeling that Ireland remains Murphy's only love, where genius and lunacy go hand in glove.

Perhaps even Murphy's spirited defence of the three-hour duration of *The Gigli Concert* against those 'condescending, begrudging' critics (his terms) who recommended it be cut by an hour, itself revealed the author's conviction that the artist is, almost by his/her very nature, condemned to challenge the conformist conventions and orthodox expectancies of 'public opinion'. Murphy particularly resented the expectancy that plays be written according to a standardized two-hour formula with time 'for a quick dinner beforehand and a drink afterwards'. The work of art has its own laws of time and space. Of course, Murphy's turbulent relation with his native critics is incidental to the nature of his work. But since everything Murphy writes—and *The Gigli Concert* is certainly no exception—is written, after the manner of O'Neill or O'Casey, from the 'blood, sweat and tears' of the author's own personally felt experience, it is perhaps not altogether irrelevant an analogy for the defiant Murphy anti-hero courageously at odds with society.

These remarks on Murphy's individualistic repudiation of the collectivity are in no way intended to diminish Murphy's fidelity to the theatrical community itself. Directors, actors and audiences have all borne witness to his extraordinary sense of commitment to the communal act of collaboration which is a hallmark of all genuine drama. (pp. 331-34)

Moreover, Murphy's recent decision to take up the offer made by the Druid Theatre Group in Galway to work with them as writer in association is yet further testimony to this author's devotion to the 'communal' dimensions of theatre. It is to be hoped that the Druid/Murphy combination will continue to challenge and expose the paralysing forces in our society, compelling us to sound out our most hidden reaches of frustration and fear and encouraging us, where possible, to transcend them in humour and faith. For these above all are the characteristic virtues of Murphy's dramatic enterprise—the laughter that emancipates and the leap of faith towards new *possibilities* of experience, more perfect, more creative, more human. Murphy will not stop writing until we are all singing like Gigli. (p. 334)

> Richard Kearney, "Tom Murphy's Long Night's Journey into Night," in Studies, Vol. LXXII, No. 288, Winter, 1983, pp. 327-35.

D. E. S. MAXWELL

Murphy is a dramatist of sustained and considerable power. From *A Whistle in the Dark*'s deployment of an essentially realist stage, he has explored various theatrical shapes to express the collisions between savage actualities of failure and despair and the solace or defence offered by human faiths, rituals, fantasies—most often their incapacities. The very title of his first play suggests—as Murphy's titles commonly do—the respective fragility and strength of the opposites, the 'whistle' inaudible and ineffective in the oppressive 'dark'. Usually but not invariably Irish in setting, Murphy's plays, without sacrificing their local identity, carry their scenes and characters into the emotional landscape, universally recognisable, of the twentieth century.

A Whistle is set in the living room of a council house in Coventry occupied by Michael Carney and his English wife, Betty. His brothers, Hugo, Iggy, and Harry, are unwelcome lodgers. 'Dada' Carney and Des, the father and youngest brother, are arriving on a visit from Ireland. The emotional action of the play pivots on the swirls of antagonism and an urge for love between Dada and Michael, slightly better educated than his brothers. He is revolted by the brutal violence which for Dada and his other sons is an ennobling manliness, and is bent on preserving Des from it. Almost all the physical violence is off stage, in a brawl, much encouraged by Dada and waged with fists and feet, clubs and chains, between the Carneys and the Mulryans. Dada evades it, and at the drunken victory celebration tells a mendacious Falstaff-like tale of his own prowess when set upon on his way to join his sons.

Violence is in the air throughout. It is in the choreography of the opening preparations to meet Dada and Des, confused, abrupt, abusive, and in a mock cowboy gunfight where one of the party 'dies'. It is electric in the dialogue and the flickering tension between Michael and the rest:

> HARRY: Naw-naw. A bottle is better than a fist. A broken bottle is better than two fists. See the fear of God into them when they start backin' away from you.
>
> IGGY: I seen fellas fightin' better because of the fear of God.
>
> HARRY: Naw, not with the spikey glass in front of their eyes. They don't know what to do they're so frightened. And he tries to save himself with his hands, and they get bleeding first—
>
> MICHAEL: (*Entering with some tea things*) Take it easy, Harry.

The brutality of words and feeling inevitably brings viciousness to its embodiment on stage. Family alliances fluctuate in the spacing of groups. Betty—'which comes first . . . me or your brothers?'—walks out on Michael. Des, now belligerently confident, taunts and punches him. Michael, also drunk, strikes him dead with a bottle, his own self-betrayal. The curtain drops on the maundering self-justifications of Dada, isolated in a corner of the stage.

Failures all, and on an edge of society; Harry a ponce, Iggy bribed to hire men on a building site. Dada is a failed policeman, failed salesman, failed husband, vulnerable in supports which at times he cannot keep from crumbling: his bravery, the respect he is held in, his important friends, his pedantically incorrect grammar—'And whom should judge that?'—and cultural pretensions—'I bet you never read "Ulysses"? Hah? Wha'? Did you? No. A Dublin lad an all wrote "Ulysses". Great book. Famous book. All about how . . . how . . . Yeah . . . Can't be got at all now. All classic books like them I have.'

Yet the play is not judging a simple conflict between brutishness reproved and higher aspirations applauded. Michael's and Dada's overtures to each other are tentative and come to nothing, but both grope towards companionship. Even of Iggy's violence, 'an innate part of his character', we are told that 'it is not without nobility in his case': 'They wasn't expecting the chain. It's not the same winning that way.' Most important, the play very delicately pushes the characters' linguistic boundaries to a tightly strung vernacular poetry, articulating feelings in them of want and deprivation for which their lives have no consolation nor they any normal utterance but aggression. . . . Harry's is a world of first and last things. Murphy observes it in a way that lets us see Harry both as he appears to the outside, drunken, menacingly venomous, and as the man inside too, wounded, anguished, despairing.

Another doubleness is at work in *The Fooleen,* between the waking life of John Joe Moran, the grocer's assistant, and passages from his nightly dreams. The unreality of the latter is suggested by 'unreal' lighting and a stylised speech, complemented by stylised delivery and movement. Though 'unreal', the interior life of the dreams, as we shall see, isolates and sharpens the bewilderments of John Joe's waking hours. A brother in America is doing badly. A friend has gone to England, where he makes good money, but as John Joe asks him, 'if it's that good, what are you so bitter about?' The emigrants did not want to emigrate. They are victims of Ireland's population haemorrhage—ironically, the salvation of its stagnant economy—driven abroad by unemployment and poverty, against the strong Irish sense of local *pietas*. The *pietas*, however, is not idolatrous. It may be for a place clearly seen to have betrayed an ideal of community. Thus the actual circumstances of John Joe's life are a travesty of such a community. In this failed or failing home he moons about late and idle at the shop; to abandon the home or, somehow, to create it?

The town's inhabitants are either doing well for themselves or like John Joe's parents just making do—'feeding on this corpse of a street'. Private affairs are public and maliciously judged. John Joe's courtship of Mona—it is more hers of him—scandalises the sanctimonious. His splendidly sardonic proclamation of rumour and gossip, shouted at the sleeping houses, cauterises their wound in him and brings him to a decision. He will stay. Quite brutally rejecting Mona—her world is not his—he says, 'It's not just a case of staying or going. It's something to do with Frank. And Pakey. And others like me who left. And others like Miko and Mullins and me who stayed. It's something to do with that.' Having transformed his quiet into vocal rebellion John Joe may by staying discover the 'something to do with that', which has certainly to do with the ties of place and history. Murphy says of John Joe's mother— 'a product of Irish history—poverty and ignorance; but something great about her'—that she might be called heroic 'if it were the nineteenth century we were dealing with'. So too might John Joe's hard-won settlement.

His dreams are all of escape, embarked on and thwarted: to start the play, a dream-elopement with Mona; later, a dream-soliloquy on a weird *mélange* of America, England, and his native countryside. The last dream is of Mona's imploring him to ask her father, played by John Joe's employer, for her hand. Its tight, surrealistic structure, full of Joycean word-games and Swiftian lists, makes quotation difficult. (pp. 162-66)

The like of John Joe's town we have encountered in earlier plays. Murphy's version of it is of his own time, seen along the fractured lines of twentieth-century vision. The social issues, obliquely there, are an emblem of a spiritual crisis, beckoning to exile or renewal. Among Murphy's plays, *The Fooleen* has the most gently cadenced resolution.

In *The Sanctuary Lamp,* derelicts again people the stage: Harry, ex-strong man; Francisco, a juggler, his partner in a defunct circus act; and Maudie, a sixteen-year-old child of the streets. Behind these living characters are the dead: Olga, Harry's wife, a contortionist, Francisco's lover; Harry's daughter, Teresa; Maudie's illegitimate son. The scene is a church in a city which might be Dublin. The action stretches from dawn one day until after 3 a.m. the next. The events, the conversational reconstruction of the characters' pasts and speculation on their future, constitute a kind of Passion. Indeed, the duration of the main block of the play, chimes marking the hours, recalls that of the Crucifixion, in a parody conflation with the Last Supper, as Francisco drinks the altar wine, and Harry and Maudie share fish and chips. The furnishings of the church where they doss down are desecrated: the pulpit when Harry lifts it as the sacrilegious Francisco is delivering a mock sermon; a confessional, placed horizontally, in which the trio lie together. (p. 167)

The characters are groping not just within the web of purely human relationships. They 'are obsessed with Innocence and Forgiveness and Guilt and Perfectibility', with a divine solace or illumination, not the torments of the church's God. 'What a poxy con!' says Francisco. 'All Christianity!' (pp. 167-68)

The world of Murphy's plays is a Limbo of frustrated search. It is the work of an imagination 'antic, bleak, agitated, bewildered, capable of great cruelty and great compassion', realised in a language whose complexity remains true to its theatrical function. (p. 168)

D. E. S. Maxwell, "Explorations 1956-1982," in his A Critical History of Modern Irish Drama: 1891-1980, *Cambridge University Press, 1984, pp. 158-87.*

BENEDICT NIGHTINGALE

Bailegangaire takes us into [a] . . . private past of the Irish psyche, the one uneasily cohabited by strong parents and put-upon progeny, the one chronicled by Padraic Colum, Brian Friel and Sam Beckett among others. . . . [This play concerns a] bedridden crone, obsessively drooling out the same endless anecdote from beneath stringy red hair; . . . her hapless granddaughters, seemingly unable to deal with her senility, each other or their own lives; and what we're watching is the night when reminiscence at last reaches a denouement that's painful and ugly in itself but brings catharsis and reconciliation. Not the most theatrically pulsating of pieces, this, but one written with unerring grace and wit. . . .

Benedict Nightingale, "Shaw Line," in New Statesman, *Vol. 111, No. 2866, February 28, 1986, p. 31.*

JOHN SIMON

[In *Conversations on a Homecoming*] Murphy has written a play that differs in no way from the lusher effusions of an Edward Martyn or a Lady Gregory, and can hold its own even against the peak achievements of William Boyle and Rutherford Mayne. You could, except for a few four-letter words, lift any passage from *Conversations* and stick it into a comedy by Lennox Robinson—say, *The White-Headed Boy* (1916) or *Crabbed Youth and Age* (1922)—or vice versa, and no one the wiser for it. Except that Robinson, forgotten as he is today outside Ireland, was a far better craftsman than Thomas (or Tom) Murphy.

In *Conversations,* Michael, a former gay blade who went off to New York to become an actor, has come back (it seems) on a visit to the pub in East Galway where he and his friend Tom, the most promising boys in that part of the bog, hatched high hopes under the beneficent gaze of J. J. Kilkenny, the publican who looked like J.F.K., with whom he identified himself and to whose greatness he aspired. Indeed, this humble East Galway pub was thought of as Camelot, to which it had, I daresay, just as good claims as Washington, D.C., ever did. Michael's eagerness to see J. J., Tom, and the rest of the gang is not exactly reciprocated, although at first Tom (who has become an embittered, cynical schoolmaster), Liam, a successful functionary, and Junior, an apparently carefree fellow of uncertain trade, appear cordial enough as all buy pints for one another. Serving these phoenix-like pints are the Missus, J. J.'s browbeaten spouse, the gleam in whose eye is for Liam, who is expected to marry her daughter, Anne, just out of school and alternating with her mother in dishing out the pints.

As good as wine in bringing forth *veritas*, the pints—supplemented by the odd double whisky—duly reveal unpleasant truths about everyone, especially the offstage J. J., now nothing but a drunken bum and apparently not much more in his heyday, if truth be told. Tom, the likeliest to leave Galway for a glorious literary career, has stayed to teach and rot, write radical pamphlets, use his aged parents as an excuse, and bully his wretched fiancée, Peggy, whom he'll clearly never marry. Even worse things surface about Liam and Junior, as well as about another offstage character, Josephine, the bank clerk and town whore. As for Michael, he was a flop in the U.S.A. and is now back permanently, sponging on his poor mother. His one ray of hope is irresponsibly seducing the innocent Anne, though why that would be a worse fate for her than marrying the repulsive Irish Catholic chauvinist Liam, known as Cowboy for his renditions of country-western songs, is hard to say.

For most of the play's hundred intermissionless and remissionless minutes nothing much happens, except that the pints keep coming, tempers get shorter, accusations and counter-accusations fly, and all are beastly to all. Then the obligatory beery-teary reconciliations, followed by warnings to Michael should he seduce the willing Anne, and, finally, Michael's grand—and improbable—renunciation. There are poor jokes . . . [and] lots of boozy singing. . . . Though *Conversations on a Homecoming* is a dreadful play, I must admit it has its pints.

John Simon, *"Sodden Old Sod,"* in New York *Magazine, Vol. 19, No. 31, August 11, 1986, p. 56.*

KATHY McARDLE

Murphy's drama often makes its most vital explorations of the human spirit in traditional locations. In *A Whistle in the Dark,* the action moves from the local pub to Betty's kitchen and living area. For Murphy, both are theatrical spaces in which the realities of our national consciousness can be recognized and confronted. *Bailegangaire* is set in a kitchen, but Murphy takes care to point out that "the set should be stylised to avoid cliche and to achieve best effect." This is not the naturalistic kitchen of the 1950's but a theatrical space in which the relationships between the three women of the play (Mommo, Mary and Dolly) are explored. It is an entirely female space. *Conversations on a Homecoming* is set in a pub. It is a theatrical space dominated entirely by the men in the play. In one play, an old woman tells and retells her story; in another, there is an old man whom we never see, who once thought of himself as President Kennedy. Both plays are about homecomings. In *Conversations on a Homecoming,* set in the 1970's, Michael returns from America to the pub which he and his friends called "The White House" in the 1960's, "our refuge, the wellspring of our hope and aspiration," and is confronted by Tom, once his best friend, with the fact of his own failure. In *Bailegangaire,* set in the 1980's, Mary, who has been living at home looking after Mommo, her grandmother, finally really comes home. Both are plays about the starvation of the Irish spirit, the "famine" of small-town Ireland, which in these plays, has its roots in the way we as a nation tend to adopt images of ourselves increasingly from other societies. Tom talks about how "we're in such a ridiculous race that even our choice of assumed images is quite arbitrary." The anomaly of transpos-

ing the figure of John F. Kennedy into a small Irish town wrapped up in the country-and-western system illustrates clearly the failure of our society.

The failure of selfhood, of identity of the people in both plays is thus also at a deeper level the failure of their society to sustain them. It is connected with the legacy of guilt which is the heritage of Ireland.

The need to confront this legacy and our history is another of the themes of *Bailegangaire*. Dolly says of Mommo, "She's guilty . . . An' that's why she goes on like a gramaphone. Guilty." Mommo is on one level the personification of Mother Ireland, an old crone blathering an old story to herself over and over again. What the people in both these plays want is to establish a self free from the constraints of society and history, both national and personal. In *Conversations on a Homecoming,* this involves what Tom calls "a true and honest account of the situation first. What? A bit of clarity and sanity. Definitions. Facts." At the end of the play, there is a sense that this has been achieved through the truth in Anne, "smiling her gentle hope out at the night." In *Bailegangaire,* more is achieved. The story of the laughing competition, "how the town of Bailegangaire came to its appelation," is in another sense the story of Mommo's personal history and that of her daughters. When the story is finished, due to the efforts of Mary to get her to "live out the story—finish it," one experiences a moment of true clarity and luminosity, almost of revelation, because Mary, Mommo and Dolly are now free, free to say "My soul is now my own." In both plays, there is a feeling at the end that "properly pruned of all the dead wood, you could almost be anything . . . you could almost be yourself . . . and get on with the business of living." In *Bailegangaire,* this hope is embodied in the symbol of the new baby. Both plays give home for what Mommo might call the "ridiculosity" of our nation.

Patrick Mason has said that for him a play is like a map. It is a guide, the only guide a person has to a previously uncharted landscape or territory of human experience. . . . A Murphy map is a particularly difficult one because it seems unfinished, fragmented. And with it, if you miss by an inch on the map you miss by a mile. The publication of both of these plays simultaneously makes these maps available to those who wish to explore this undiscovered country. . . .

Over the last five years, some of the greatest performances in Irish theatre have been in Murphy's plays. Actors and directors respond to the challenge of his plays and will continue to do so. The destination will always be the same, to arrive at the truth of the plays, but the means of travel with these maps are multiple.

Kathy McArdle, *"Two Murphy Plays About Homecoming,"* in Irish Literary Supplement, *Vol. 6, No. 1, Spring, 1987, p. 28.*

(Philip) Michael Ondaatje

1943-

Ceylonese-born Canadian poet, novelist, dramatist, editor, critic, and filmmaker.

Ondaatje emerged during the 1960s as one of Canada's most respected young poets. In his verse, Ondaatje examines the dichotomy between rational intellect and disorderly reality and suggests that the poet's efforts to render personal experience must necessarily result in distortion. Ondaatje's style is characterized by humor, flamboyant imagery, extravagant metaphors, and sudden shifts in tone. Sam Solecki observed that in Ondaatje's poetry, "the fundamental or essential nature of experience is consistently being described and examined. The entire thrust of his vision is directed at compelling the reader to reperceive reality, to assume an unusual angle of vision from which reality appears surreal, absurd, inchoate, dynamic, and, most importantly, ambiguous."

Ondaatje's early collections of poetry, *The Dainty Monsters* (1967) and *The Man with Seven Toes* (1969), display a preoccupation with domestic and personal conflicts, mythical and historical figures, the often violent relationship between humans and animals, and destructive impulses among artists. Critics noted that his verse is consistently presented in musical, sound-conscious language. *The Collected Works of Billy the Kid: Left Handed Poems* (1970), which won a Governor General's Award, is considered Ondaatje's most important volume of poetry. Combining prose, verse, photographs, and drawings, Ondaatje presents a fictionalized biography that probes the psyche of notorious American outlaw William Bonney. According to Stephen Scobie, "[*The Collected Works of Billy the Kid*] is an attempt to comprehend the legend of Billy the Kid, to see him as one of the exemplary figures of modern consciousness, outlaw as artist, artist as outlaw." *There's a Trick with a Knife I'm Learning to Do: Poems, 1963-1978* (1979), which also won a Governor General's Award, contains selections from *The Dainty Monsters* and *Rat Jelly* (1973) as well as nineteen new poems centering on such topics as friendship and family history. *Secular Love* (1984) comprises four unified sequences of confessional lyrics exploring paternal love, Ondaatje's traumatic divorce, and the redemptive qualities of love. In these poems, Ondaatje is both a character and a creative observer molding his experiences into art. John Cook stated: "Throughout [*Secular Love*] the poetry finds energy in the dynamic interplay between the cunning duplicity of the artist and the heartfelt truth of a suffering man."

Ondaatje has also received critical acclaim as a novelist. *Coming through Slaughter* (1976), his first novel, again reflects his fascination with extraordinary personality types. In this work, Ondaatje employs what William Logan has termed "creative mythologizing" to depict the tormented life of legendary jazz pioneer Buddy Bolden. While *Coming through Slaughter* resembles *The Collected Works of Billy the Kid* in its blend of poetry and various prose forms, Ondaatje also makes use of such quasi-factual journalistic material as interviews and documented reports. *Running in the Family* (1982) is set in Ondaatje's birthplace of Ceylon and integrates a travelogue with memoirs of his youth. In this novel, Ondaatje attempts an imaginative reconstruction of his family history, with particular

© 1988 Thomas Victor

emphasis on the eccentric personalities of his maternal grandmother and his father. While some critics considered the prose of *Running in the Family* overly poetic and occasionally obscure, others praised the novel's innovative structure and Ondaatje's descriptive power. *In the Skin of a Lion* (1987) chronicles the oppressed lives of immigrant workers who helped expand and modernize the city of Toronto, Ontario, early in the twentieth century. Employing a nonlinear plot and a surreal, collage-like narrative, Ondaatje traces the growing social awareness of his protagonist, artist Patrick Lewis. Michael Hulse commented that *In the Skin of a Lion* "does for Toronto what Joyce did for Dublin or Döblin for Berlin." Ondaatje has also written a well-regarded critical study, *Leonard Cohen* (1970). In addition, he has adapted three of his works for the stage and has directed several films.

(See also *CLC*, Vols. 14, 29; *Contemporary Authors*, Vols. 77-80; and *Dictionary of Literary Biography*, Vol. 60.)

SAM SOLECKI

[*The essay excerpted below was originally published in* Studies in Canadian Literature, *Winter, 1977.*]

Michael Ondaatje is a poet of reality. In applying this phrase to Ondaatje, I wish to call attention to the fact that in his poetry the fundamental or essential nature of experience is consistently being described and examined. The entire thrust of his vision is directed at compelling the reader to reperceive reality, to assume an unusual angle of vision from which reality appears surreal, absurd, inchoate, dynamic, and, most importantly, ambiguous. His poetic world is filled with mad or suicidal herons, one-eyed mythic dogs, tortured people, oneiric scenes, gorillas, dragons, creative spiders, and imploding stars. These extraordinary images function as a kind of metaphoric short-hand to disorient the reader, to make him enter a psychological or material reality which has been revealed as almost over-whelmingly anarchic or chaotic. What is at issue in Ondaatje's poetry is the existence not of an alternate reality but of different perceptions of one which the reader has always assumed to be clear, patterned, and meaningful. To use Wallace Stevens' apt phrase, Ondaatje is often a "connoisseur of chaos"; and whether his poems depict an unconscious mode of being similar to Freud's primary process (**"Biography," "King Kong," "King Kong meets Wallace Stevens"**) or simply the ordinary phe-nomenal flux of life (**"Loop," "We're at the graveyard"**), the central formal and thematic concern in his work has been the description of internal and external reality as dynamic, chaotic, and ambiguous.

But his major poems not only redefine our sense of reality; they also create an awareness of the extent to which the mind distorts reality in any act of perception and description. In the period between *The Dainty Monsters* (1967) and *Rat Jelly* (1973), Ondaatje has shown an increasing awareness of the episte-mological difficulties involved in the relationship between the "nets" of the perceiving and recreating mind and the "chaos" of life. Not content to raise just the usual issue about the limitations of language as a representational medium, Ondaatje has shown more concern for the possibility that poetry might not be able to do justice to the existential complexity of reality because of the inevitable tendency of the mind to see pattern and clarity where life offers only flux and ambiguity. This tension between mind and chaos is at the centre of Ondaatje's poetry; and its implications can be seen in the dualistic nature of his imagery, in the deliberate thematic irresolution of his major lyrics, and in the complex structuring of his two longer poems, *the man with seven toes* and *The Collected Works of Billy the Kid.* (pp. 93-4)

In his first collection, *The Dainty Monsters,* most of the poems simply reflect the assumption that a lyric can recreate any aspect of reality or re-enact any experience which the poet chooses. Only in the poems about poetry—**"Four Eyes," "The Mar-tinique,"** and **"Eventually the Poem for Keewaydin"**—is the question raised—but only implicitly—to what extent is such an assumption valid, and if it is valid, what are the problems involved in transfiguring life into poetry? Many poems describe life dualistically in terms of a suggestive dialectic between a dark oneiric or surreal world and a daylight one. The former is shown as co-existent with the latter (**"The Republic"**), vaguely threatening to it (**"Gorillas"**), or in danger of being extirpated by it (**"Dragon"**). As is usual in his work, Ondaatje is primarily concerned with the relationship between kinds of reality or modes of being. (p. 94)

While **"The Republic"** is primarily concerned with the de-scription of a scene or an event, **"Four Eyes"** is more con-cerned with an examination of the actual process by which a poet transforms a lived, dynamic moment into poetry. The

speaker, choosing to see only what is within his companion's field of vision, breaks from the moment in order to record it. . . . In its focus on the act of creation, the poem anticipates that group of difficult and ambitious lyrics in *Rat Jelly* which deal explicitly with this theme. **"Four Eyes"** does not examine the problems as perceptively as those more mature poems do, but it is nevertheless exploring a similar area of creative ex-perience. Ondaatje is concerned here with what happens when a poet tries to "reconstruct" a lived moment into art. In **"Four Eyes"** the first consequence of such an attempt is the poet's necessary separation from the experience itself. In order to write about it, he must leave it: "This moment I broke to record." With its double meaning of separating and breaking, "broke" questions the quality of the writer's departure and suggests that ultimately he values art over life. Instead of being a participant, he becomes a detached observer who prefers searching for a verbal equivalent of a lived moment to life itself. While "record" indicates the probability of a point by point imitation, the final stanza reveals that the reconstruction will be metaphoric. The writer will use "pianos / and craggy black horses on a beach," images not present in the original scene. The poem ends by suggesting that the essential qualities of a scene "still being unfurled" can only be captured in metaphor. But Ondaatje's final lines simultaneously point to the possibility that even this reconstruction may misrepresent the original moment. . . . If my reading is correct, then **"Four Eyes"** offers both a solution to the problem it poses and a searching critique of that solution. It is not the best poem in Ondaatje's first volume—**"Dragon"** and **"The Time Around Scars"** are better—but, together with **"The Martinique"** and **"Eventually the Poem for Keewaydin,"** is the one in which he most profoundly questions the possibilities of the kind of poetry he is writing.

In his second book, the long narrative poem *the man with seven toes* (1969), the very form and texture of the poem attempt to recreate for the reader the sense of an unpredictable and often chaotic experience "being unfurled" in the actual body of the poem. Without resorting to formlessness, Ondaatje neverthe-less conveys the sense of a descent into a psychological and material chaos. The book is concerned with the response of an anonymous civilized woman to a landscape and culture com-pletely different from her own. Like Margaret Atwood's Su-sanna Moodie, she is placed in a world whose reality is os-tensibly unrelated to her own. The poem is the account of the confrontation with and gradual acceptance of the darker and more chaotic aspects of life which, by the end of the book, are recognized as not only outside the self but within it as well.

Each of the brief self-contained lyrics vividly re-enacts a stage in her development. . . . The syntax, imagery, and rhythm, the very texture of the verse, re-enact her complex response to an experience which, prior to becoming lost, she had not even imagined. The violent rape evokes a curiously ambivalent re-sponse; some of the similes—"like birds," "white leaping like fountains"—have quite positive connotations, but their hint of beauty suddenly disappears in an image—"a scar"—which begins the comparison of the rape and the cutting up of a fox. Her confusion and terror are brilliantly caught in a simile which, because of the deliberate absence of punctuation, has a double reference: "open and blood spraying out like dyna-mite / caught in the children's mouths on the ground." Because of the syntactical ambiguity, both the blood and the dynamite are "caught in the children's mouths"; this occasion of vio-lence, sexuality, and innocence stunningly registers the wom-an's own shocked response. But the similes in this lyric also fulfill another function: they indicate her attempt to appropriate, in terms of analogous or more familiar images, certain experiences which she finds almost indescribable. In describing the tearing apart of a fox in terms of a rape, for example, she is able to articulate her reaction to what has happened to herself as well.

Yet, despite her suffering throughout the journey . . . she is described at the end of the book as lying on a bed and

> sensing herself like a map, then
> lowering her hands into her body.

This suggests than an increased awareness of herself has been gained from her experiences. (pp. 95-9)

A similar but even more developed and complex reperception of reality takes place in *The Collected Works of Billy the Kid* (1970), the events of which are consistently ambiguous in their significance and in which the two central characters are both paradoxes. Billy the Kid is a murderer and "the pink of politeness / and as courteous a little gentleman / as I ever met." Pat Garrett, the ostensible representative of law and order, is a "sane assassin sane assassin sane assassin sane assassin sane assassin sane" with the final stress falling on "—in sane." In the world of *The Collected Works of Billy the Kid,* peace and violence, sanity and insanity, order and chaos, and darkness and light are almost inextricably confused. It is as if the key characters have all made "the one altered move" to remove themselves from the normal expectations and moral judgments taken for granted by the reader.

Ondaatje's handling of the story subjects the reader to a process of defamiliarization in which the standard western made familiar by Burns, Penn, and Peckinpah is deliberately "made new." Every aspect of Ondaatje's version emphasizes both the difficulties inherent and the artistic problems involved in recreating that reality in art. As in *the man with seven toes,* Ondaatje achieves this by making the reader experience many of the episodes as if he were a direct witness to them, a temporary insider in the events themselves. But then in his normal position as an objective reader, inevitably outside the text, he must also stand back, organize and evaluate these "collected" but still, so to speak, disorganized "works" which are told from a variety of viewpoints and which lack a summarizing judgment by an omniscient narrator. The effect is similar to that achieved in Robbe-Grillet's fiction where the reader also enters a confusing fictive world knowing that there will be no ostensible authorial guidance. Both authors compel the reader to become both a surrogate character and a surrogate author in order to make him implicitly aware of the difficulties involved in the perceiving and describing of reality. The initial disorientation leads ultimately to a new awareness. (pp. 99-100)

While Ondaatje was writing his two longer works, he was also working on those poems in *Rat Jelly* which as a group constitute his most explicit exploration of the relationship between poetry and reality: **"King Kong meets Wallace Stevens," "Spider Blues," "Taking," "The gate in his head," "Burning Hills,"** and **"White Dwarfs."** In its concern with the creative mind's "fencing" of chaos, [**"King Kong meets Wallace Stevens"**] is representative of the group:

> Take two photographs—
> Wallace Stevens and King Kong
> (Is it significant that I eat bananas as I write this?)

Stevens is portly, benign, a white brush cut
striped tie. Businessman but
for the dark thick hands, the naked brain
the thought in him.

Kong is staggering
lost in New York streets again
a spawn of annoyed cars at his toes.
The mind is nowhere.
Fingers are plastic, electric under the skin.
He's at the call of Metro-Goldwyn-Mayer.

Meanwhile W.S. in his suit
is thinking chaos is thinking fences.
In his head the seeds of fresh pain
his exorcising,
the bellow of locked blood.

The hands drain from his jacket,
pose in the murderer's shadow.

The poem is structured upon a series of antitheses; the primary contrast is between Stevens, the businessman whose "thought is in him," and Kong, whose "mind is nowhere." But, as so often in Ondaatje's poetry, the opposed terms are ultimately related. Kong, after all, is more than just a suggestive photographer's image of directable energy; he is also, as the poem's structure and imagery suggest, an aspect of Stevens himself, and the meeting between them occurs not only in the juxtaposing of their photographs but also within Stevens' mind. This is established by the presentation of analogous situations in the third and fourth stanzas: MGM directs Kong; Stevens fences the chaos and blood within himself. No comma or conjunction appears between the two clauses of "is thinking chaos is thinking fences" because the poem is suggesting the problematic simultaneity of both the "chaos" and the "fences" in the "thinking" of Stevens. If, as I have suggested, Kong and "chaos" or "blood" are synonymous, then the entire fourth stanza points to Kong's presence within Stevens himself: both the containing form and the contained energy are within the mind of the businessman who is also a poet. This connection between the two is also present in the image of Stevens' "dark thick hands" which, at the poem's end, "drain from his jacket, / pose in the murderer's shadow." The poem closes on the alarming association between Stevens and "the murderer's shadow" which can only be his own. He is a murderer because he has subdued his "chaos" or "blood," his unconscious self.

But the poem also suggests, almost too casually, that Stevens is not the only poet with a shadow self. After all, the writer-speaker of the poem asks humorously in the opening stanza, "Is it significant that I eat bananas as I write this?" In view of the almost symbiotic relationship between Stevens and Kong, there can only be one answer. Despite the parenthetical nature of the question, the image of the "bananas" functions as a comic allusion to the speaker's Kong-like aspect. Thus the poem indicates that both of the poets within it are in creative contact with everything that the ostensibly antithetical Kong represents; but they are able to transform, control, and shape this "chaos" within the self into an aesthetic construct, into **"King Kong meets Wallace Stevens."** There is also a lingering suggestion, however, that some of the "chaos" will resist and even escape the poet's act of transformation. Both "the *bellow* of locked blood" and "hands *drain* from his jacket" (my italics) raise this possibility.

The notion that the poet pays a price for creating a poem— "In his head the seeds of fresh pain / his exorcising"—reappears in **"Spider Blues"** in which the poet is seen as an admirable, because dexterous, spider. . . . The spider as creative artist is a cartographer of the unknown, and . . . he brings back a message about some essential or primal reality. But, like the speaker in **"Four Eyes,"** he can only do this by separating himself from that reality. The spider may be more talented than the fly; yet, in terms of the allegory of the poem, the fly, because it is closer to life, is the necessary subject matter of art. . . . Mind distinguishes Wallace Stevens from King Kong, and "intelligence" the spider from the fly; but the cost of the distinction is registered by the title of the poem, "Spider Blues": it is sung by Ray Charles, not Anne Murray. But the poem is also a blues song because in the relationship between the spider and the fly, the former creates "beauty" by "crucifying" the latter. It is not clear what alternative modes of creation are possible, but the suggestion is nevertheless felt that this is not an ideal relationship between art and life.

If a poem is a mediation between mind and experience, then the ultimate poem for Ondaatje is the one which transforms reality into poetry without "crucifying" it. **"The gate in his head"** is not that poem, but it is Ondaatje's most emphatic statement about what poetry should be:

> My mind is pouring chaos
> in nets onto the page.
> A blind lover, dont know
> what I love till I write it out.
> And then from Gibson's your letter
> with a blurred photograph of a gull.
> Caught vision. The stunning white bird
> an unclear stir.
>
> And that is all this writing should be then.
> The beautiful formed things caught at the wrong moment
> so they are shapeless, awkward
> moving to the clear.

The "chaos" here is synonymous with whatever reality the poet has chosen to describe. It is the basic life stuff or substance out of which he shapes a poem. The central tension of the poem is between this "chaos" and the mental "nets" of language within which the poet represents it. The "nets" recall the "fences" in **"King Kong meets Wallace Stevens"** and the "webs" in **"Spider Blues"** and *The Collected Works of Billy the Kid:* they are the actual medium—film or words—in which the vision is recreated or caught. Although "caught" is Ondaatje's word, it does not really do justice to either his essentially heuristic assumption about poetic creativity—"A blind lover, dont know / what I love till I write it out"—or his concern with registering as sensitively as possible the dynamic quality of a moment or of an image. His concern is that the poem describe "the unclear stir" made by "a beautiful formed thing" perceived "at the wrong moment." This last detail is particularly important if the poetic perception is to yield a new, unexpected awareness of the image and, consequently, of reality. Yet, as I pointed out earlier, the poem must deal with motion, flux and formlessness within the confines of poetic form. Ondaatje's poem achieves this by hinting at forms—the page, the photograph—and then subtly, through oxymoron, syntax, and an inter-weaving of sounds—n's and r's—recreating the reality, the image of the bird.

The photograph is by Victor Coleman and the entire poem is an *homage* to a writer whose extremely difficult poems reveal

> . . . the faint scars
> coloured strata of the brain,
> not clarity but *the sense of shift.* (my emphasis)

The "faint scars" are metaphors for Coleman's poems . . . which, in a mode much more radical than Ondaatje's, attempt

to give the reader a sense of life as pure process, as "shift" and "chaos." But the "scars" are also literally scars. Here, as elsewhere in Ondaatje's work, a physical scar represents caught motion, just as a mental scar or an emotional scar is caught memory. In other words, the scar literally incorporates and memorializes an emotion, an act, or an experience. In terms of the imagery of **"The Time Around Scars,"** a scar is a "medallion" or "watch" which records a violent and revealing event. One could even say that a scar is finally analogous to an ideal, because nonverbal, poem in which the distinction between word and thing or state of being has finally disappeared. (pp. 101-05)

The very fact that in comparing his work to Coleman's Ondaatje writes "that is all this writing *should be* then" (my emphasis) is a reminder of an ideal which he feels he has not yet achieved. I would suggest that it is a mark of Ondaatje's integrity as a poet that his most successful poems raise this kind of question. He has said in an interview that "in writing you have to get all the truth down—the qualifications, the lies, the uncertainties—." And if **"The gate in his head"** voices his doubts about the possibility—or impossibility—of an adequate linguistic representation—"all the truth"—of external or objective reality, **"Burning Hills,"** one of his finest personal poems, indicates an awareness that any attempt to come to terms with an emotionally charged complex of memories carries with it its own difficulties:

> Since he began burning hills
> the Shell strip has taken effect.
> A wasp is crawling on the floor
> tumbling over, its motor fanatic.
> He has smoked five cigarettes.
> He has written slowly and carefully
> with great love and great coldness.
> When he finishes he will go back
> hunting for the lies that are obvious.

Unlike most of Ondaatje's personal poems, this one is written, almost over-insistently ("He has. . . / He has"), in the third person. The repetition of the pronoun suggests the attempted, but not completely realized, distancing of his personal memories. The "burning hills," the wasp, and the five cigarettes are not random details; their cumulative significance is to point to how difficult it is for him to achieve an attitude of "great love and great coldness." Yet this is how he must write in order to achieve a successful, because objective, recreation of his personal experiences. In this poem his "coldness," both emotional and tonal, is evident in the ending's unsentimental and deliberately monotoned voice "hunting for the lies that are obvious." In what sounds like a line from Cohen's *The Energy of Slaves* (but isn't), Ondaatje is indicating that, despite his attempts at objectivity, his poem may be a misrepresentation or lie. And if the lies to be sought out are the "obvious" ones, there is the disturbing implication that the "unobvious" lies will remain. In either case, the reader has been warned about the poem and the poet's limitations in getting "all the truth down."

Ondaatje's most radical gesture in the direction of indicating that there are times when "all the truth" cannot be stated, described, or reenacted is the final poem in *Rat Jelly,* **"White Dwarfs."** Here the poet confronts not just the unconscious, or process or chaos, but events that in their total human significance seem to demand a response of awed silence. A variation on T.W. Adorno's "No poetry after Auschwitz," the poem is a profound mediation on both life and art. It is a tribute to those who have gone beyond "social fuel" and language. . . .

The key word [in this poem] is "moral," which, although slightly ambiguous, does seem to be synonymous with life-meaning or mode of being. Those who "shave their moral . . . raw" live in a condition in which their character or self exists without a social persona, "where there is no social fuel"; consequently, they come in touch with the very ground of their being, which is here quite subtly associated with heaven. . . . Like Ondaatje's outlaws (Billy), alienated loners (Pat Garrett and Charlie Wilson), and sufferers (Philoctetes, his father), they are the ones who can provide a glimpse of what the terrifyingly brilliant poem about his father calls the "other worlds" lying beyond either consciousness or social forms.

In "White Dwarfs" the speaker admires those people whose achievement or experience in patience or suffering is beyond him. . . . Himself afraid of "no words of / falling without words," he loves those whose language is an expressive and deafening silence: for them the experience and their expression of it are one. Silence is here a final poetry—like the earlier image of a scar—which cannot be improved upon by the poet's facility with words. This is a supreme fiction in which the dualities of nets and chaos, Wallace Stevens and King Kong, art and life, words and objects have been finally dissolved—but only at a price which the traditional poet cannot pay. Even as he suggests that poetry in such a context would be superfluous and perhaps blasphemous, he is nevertheless writing a poem. Like other poets who interrogate the validity of language—Rózewicz and Celan, for example—Ondaatje inevitably uses language to conduct that interrogation. This dialectic of language and silence leads finally not to despair about poetry but to an affirmation. The confrontation with a reality which at first seemed resistant to the "nets" of verbal representation has not silenced the poet; rather it has provoked him into an even more ambitious poetry. In the final movement of the poem, he attempts to describe the unknown. . . . The poem ends by pointing hauntingly to a beauty ("an egg") and a human profundity (the personified "star") which are beyond more explicit description and discussion. The tentative metaphoric gestures of the poem are all that can be expected of poetry in such a situation. Yet Ondaatje's willingness to risk these inevitably anti-climactic lines. . . , to explore "the perfect white between the words" and "the colours we cannot see," is a paradoxical attestation of his belief in poetry.

Ondaatje's work as a whole can be described as an attempt to make us aware of aspects of reality—surreal, oneiric, dynamic, chaotic—which we normally "cannot see" or perhaps do not want to see. Sheila Watson has written that Ondaatje "is as intelligent as Auden but less afraid of what living means." To be unafraid of life involves a willingness to confront and, if one is an artist, to describe reality in its full tragic complexity. Ondaatje has done this, and his poems, among the most impressive of his generation, are the re-enactments of such confrontations with life and art. (pp. 105-09)

Sam Solecki, "Nets and Chaos: The Poetry of Michael Ondaatje," in Spider Blues: Essays on Michael Ondaatje, *edited by Sam Solecki, Véhicule Press, 1985, pp. 93-110.*

LUCILLE KING-EDWARDS

[The expectancy of a new book by Michael Ondaatje] is qualified by the memory of one's first encounter with *The Collected Works of Billy the Kid,* a book that swept one through it on an ever-cresting wave. Until *Running in the Family* and now *Sec-*

ular Love, the passion that Ondaatje has put into his poems and novels has been projected onto characters from the myths of his imagination: Billy of the Wild West and Buddy Bolden of Storyville. This imagination produced powerful books, but they were books that allowed their author a certain privacy removed from the scene of passion. (pp. 16-17)

Running in the Family certainly opens the door for this book of poetry, for it takes Ondaatje back to his roots and the passions of his family, particularly of his father, a drunk and drowning man as he is portrayed in the book. It is almost as if *Secular Love* was written in order to get closer to the psyche of this father. The title comes from **"Women Like You,"** a poem set in the heart of Sri Lanka:

> Seeing you
> I want no other life
> and turn around
> to the sky
> and everywhere below
> jungle, waves of heat
> secular love.

I find this passage enigmatic, but would suggest that it opens the possibilities of the passionate journey that is the book.

Secular Love opens with **"Claude Glass,"** and the poem does embody the "luscious chiaroscuro" of the concentrated night imagery, but the focus is on the man flowing drunkenly through it. This man appears in the first person. He is called to the river; a river flows through his house, and finally the people of the poem exist for him underwater. It is also the stream of the unconscious that functions here; in that river he embraces nature as he would a woman, kissing both arm and branch with equal love. **"Claude Glass"** is a romantic poem, a poem of night and darkness, and one immediately recognizes its precursors in Lowry, in John Berryman, who pops up a couple of times later in the volume, and in the romantic strain from Keats on down.

Away from reason and control seems to be the main thrust of this book. . . . If the opening poem depends on drunkenness to achieve this letting-go of emotions, in **"Tin Roof"** it is the exposure of a man on the edge of the sea. He is facing whatever is in the blue beyond the volcanic shore. Alone he contemplates the loss of self:

> How to arrive at this
> drowning
> on the edge of sea

The structure of **"Tin Roof"** is of individual poems that make up a long poem; the writing appropriately becomes spare. Dense long lines disappear. The writing has an acerbic quality, and bamboo as a talisman seems to be correct for this stripping away. Sparse as furnishings in the cabin in which he lives, the poet's pretensions are jettisoned. It is the poem of a man functioning on the brink who sees the plunge into the sea as a compelling magic. . . .

The third section of the book, **"Rock Bottom,"** is divided into two sections. The first is a series of poems that plays with the idea of exposure and the confessional mode. They are primarily a prelude to the second section, a testing of the poet's willingness to, as he puts it, go "whole hog the pigs testament / what I know of passion." It has its ironic as well as its romantic moments, neatly described as

> near the delicate
> heart
> of Billie Holiday

The second part of **"Rock Bottom"** is more of a mixture of styles and types of poems than the previous parts of the book. There is the passion of a love affair as theme for part of it, but we bump into the domestic Ondaatje of children, suburbs, and friends as well. The dominant theme is that of a man painfully removing himself from a known domestic environment out onto the edge of the desert with Billy the Kid.

The early part of the book has led one into expectations of continuity of tone and timbre. It is jarring now in this last section to go from the confessional poems of anguished, passionate love to the more mundane ones of friendship and fatherly love, even a clever dog poem. This is not to say that these latter poems are not well-made, but that they appear gratuitous here. In real life one does linger on friends and children when life is in upheaval, but the whole hog of passion diminishes these poems, which would thrive better in a different book. (p.17)

Lucille King-Edwards, *"On the Brink," in* Books in Canada, *Vol. 13, No. 10, December, 1984, pp. 16-17.*

SAM SOLECKI

[*Secular Love*] is made up of four chronologically arranged sequences telling the story of the break-up of a marriage and a way of life, the poet's own near breakdown and finally, after what one section calls **"Rock Bottom,"** his recovery and return through the love of another woman. The book should be read as a seamless poetic journal rather than as a collection of discrete lyrics. Some of the poems, like the lovingly nuanced and mutedly elegiac **"To a Sad Daughter,"** can be read by themselves, yet the volume is so closely organized with so much of the overall emotional and artistic effect depending on repetitions and echoes of sound, image, situation and emotion that the poems often seem more like the chapters of a novel than parts of a collection of poems (another equally significant context is provided by Ondaatje's earlier work, and sections of *Secular Love* often seem like rewritings of earlier texts).

The opening epigraph from Peter Handke's *The Left-Handed Woman* simultaneously warns us about the unexpected stylistic and experiential openness, even rawness of *Secular Love,* and offers an implied judgment on Ondaatje's earlier work:

> Your trouble, I believe, is that you always hold back something of yourself. In my opinion you should learn how to run properly and scream properly, with your mouth wide open. I've noticed that even when you yawn you're afraid to open your mouth all the way.

In poetry, as in any art, holding back or opening up is obviously a matter of degree as well as of technique; by holding back the clutter of irrelevant detail and by compressing events and characters the writer can often create a greater impression of self-exposure and openness. *Secular Love* shows a writer who has found a style and a form that allows openness without sacrificing the economy and selectivity necessary for art.

A crucial aspect of that style is Ondaatje's delicate management of what I call the book's two voices or points of view: the first is that of Ondaatje the character in the story; the second of Ondaatje the poet and creative voyeur who watches his own life, reflecting and recreating it as art. This is the slightly guilty voice of the man who observes life even as he lives it always in the hope of turning "these giant scratches / of pain" into art; who when he writes that "I fear / how anything can grow

from this" knows that in addition to the growing suffering and pain there is also the potential poem. (pp. 32-3)

The opening section is pervaded by images of merging, drowning, darkness, disappearance and drunkenness. This is the book's dark night of the soul, the son's rewriting in personal terms of the father's breakdown in **"Letters and Other Worlds"** and *Running in the Family*. At once, it's an apology, an hommage and the beginning of another story in which the central character—described here only as "he"—is shown at a party on a farm, surrounded by family and friends, and inexplicably but inexorably drinking himself into oblivion. A disturbing point of departure for the love story to follow, it sketches in a suggestive emotional landscape of unfocussed discontent and undefined anxiety and pain leaving the reader wondering why the central figure feels like an intruder, drinks so heavily and longs for the darkness of the surrounding fields. The answers can be inferred from some of the details available later in the book: a marriage and a family are breaking up.

> In the midst of love for you
> my wife's suffering
> anger in every direction
> and the children wise
> as tough shrubs
> but they are not tough
> —so I fear
> how anything can grow from this

Without self-pity, simplification of sentimentality, *Secular Love* follows the course of the one story of our time. It's a sign of Ondaatje's integrity as an artist (and as a human being) that he registers the impact of the break-up on everyone. The transitional lyric just quoted places the love affair within the full and necessary context, reminding us of a suffering other than the speaker's. And even in the final affirmative, celebratory section, **"Skin Boat,"** images and words repeated from earlier poems recall what has been lived through. The gentle, genial **"Pacific Letter"** celebrates friendship—and by the way shows Ondaatje's ability to deal with the domestic emotions of the middle range—but recalls that "After separation had come to its worst / we met and travelled the Mazinaw with my sons / through all the thirty-six folds of that creature river / into the valley of bright lichen." The beautifully poignant **"To a Sad Daughter"** (which will bring to tears all fathers of all teenage daughters) offers advice about getting through while letting the images of swimming and drowning and "cuts and wounds" recall the earlier darker experiences against which the poem must be read. Telling his daughter that "If you break / break going out not in" Ondaatje takes us back not only to the earlier lyrics but also to **"White Dwarfs,"** a poem of the early 1970s about "imploding," as well as to *Coming Through Slaughter,* whose hero "broke into" silence and madness. The book closes, although one aspect of the story is just beginning, with a tender prose piece in which a man and woman walk in and along a shallow creek in a scene recalled by him at night as he lies next to her. Walking he loses his balance, falls in, recovers and surfaces looking for her:

> He stands very still and cold in the shadow of long trees. He has gone far enough to look for a bridge and has not found it. Turns upriver. He holds onto the cedar root the way he holds her forearm.

The entire section has a quiet inevitability after the perfervid panic of much of the book, a panic recalled in the slip into the cold water. Similarly the merging of "the cedar root" and "her forearm" reminds us why in his day-to-day life he no longer feels that he is drowning, why, in D.H. Lawrence's words, he has come through. Begun in darkness, drowning and panic, the unfinished story ends with light, surfacing and tenderness. (p. 33)

Secular Love [is] a book rich in human experience, carefully structured and beautifully crafted. Almost every page shows evidence of Ondaatje's brilliant visual imagination and his auditory sensitivity to the musical possibilities of free verse. (p. 34)

> *Sam Solecki, "Coming Through," in* The Canadian Forum, *Vol. LXIV, No. 745, January, 1985, pp. 32-4.*

STEPHEN SCOBIE

Ondaatje has always been good with epigraphs. In *Secular Love,* the section **"Tin Roof"** begins by quoting the American thriller-writer Elmore Leonord, one of whose characters says "I'm trying to tell you how I feel without exposing myself." It's an attitude typical of Ondaatje's poems: remember the balance of "great love" and "great coldness" described in **"Burning Hills."** There is deep emotion in this book—much of it sitting open, raw, and jagged on the page—yet there is also that reticence, wariness, control, "coldness," deviousness, with which Ondaatje protects himself from total "exposure." In previous books, Ondaatje has been able to deflect much of his pain through a series of shields or baffles—Billy the Kid, Buddy Bolden, his own family—but here it is all closer to home. *Secular Love* contains some of the most painful, and hurtfully honest, poems Ondaatje has ever written; yet, though there is clearly a strong autobiographical element, it would be unworthy (both to the reader and to the poems) to screen it through a voyeuristic curiosity in the details of his marriage. The poems demand much more than that, as all Ondaatje's gifts of phrasing, of rhythm, of imagery, direct us towards a more collective vision of personal hell and redemption—such as that achieved, in a stunning tour-de-force, by **"Bessie Smith at Roy Thomson Hall."**

> *Stephen Scobie, in a review of "Secular Love," in* The Malahat Review, *No. 70, March, 1985, p. 163.*

LIZ ROSENBERG

Michael Ondaatje's new book, *Secular Love,* is persistently and often intelligently obsessed with art. He cares more about the relationship between art and nature than any other poet since the Romantics, and more than most contemporary poets care about any ideas at all. Mr. Ondaatje is an oddity—a passionate intellect—and his book is alternatingly exasperating and beautiful. Most of the poems in it are about a fragmentary-seeming world, written from a fragmentary self. The result is that in too many cases there is a lack of ambition or accomplishment in the work. A few of the shorter poems, particularly, feel like ditties. Others have a raw, unfinished, lurching quality, skittering in fits and starts from place to place. In some of the longer poems, this scattered effect can be powerful, like the cumulative charge of fireworks. But even the longer poems, with a few happy exceptions, are seldom entirely satisfying or evenly gifted, and Mr. Ondaatje tends to indulge in posturing and nonsense. . . .

His reliance on whimsy is even more unfortunate: "Schools of Chinese-Spanish Linguistics! / Rivers of the world meet!" or "I will never let a chicken / into my life." There are times, of course, when what seems nonsense is another way of ap-

proaching sense, through surrealism and dream images of great beauty. . . .

His fascination with the relation between the artist and the world, observer and creator, keeps him alive to the slightest breath in each. . . .

Part of what I love in Mr. Ondaatje is [his] remarkable honesty, which emerges in deep seriousness and sly humor and comes out most winningly when he is writing beyond purely internal musings—as in the last prose poem of the book, **"Escarpment,"** or the long, beautiful poem **"The Concessions,"** which is about poetry and community, the ways in which art brings the world to life, as it does here, at once, with a wash of sound.

Mr. Ondaatje's poetry is like glass, or old, fragile bone china, like the gecko's "almost transparent body." Its power is intellectual and above all visual: "If I could paint this I would." In his best poems, the transparency of vision works in both directions, so that the mirror becomes a window opening out, the window a mirror. . . . (p. 22)

> *Liz Rosenberg, "Geckos, Porch Lights and Sighing Gardens," in* The New York Times Book Review, *December 22, 1985, pp. 22-3.*

GEORGE BOWERING

The development of Ondaatje's poetry, from his early years in [Canada] to the present, resembles the development of the main currents of Canadian verse over a period perhaps twice as long. Unlike the Vancouver poets with their advocation of open-ended, process form, Ondaatje emerged from the school that believes the poem to be an artifact, something well-made and thus rescued from the chaos of contemporary world and mind. If the Vancouver poets might loosely be said to descend from Duncan, and Victor Coleman from Zukofsky, Ondaatje might be said to descend from Yeats and Stevens.

But over the course of his first fifteen years as a Canadian poet, Ondaatje has come to seck a less British and more American poetic. Having come by way of England from colonial Ceylon, and once here through UEL universities to the Coach House Press, he had many skins to rub off. In his fourth book, *Rat Jelly* (1973), he arrived at a poem called **"'The gate in his head,'"** and dedicated to Victor Coleman. It finished with a passage that may not open that gate but at least points to its location, that signals the way out and in:

> My mind is pouring chaos
> in nets onto the page.
> A blind lover, dont know
> what I love till I write it out.
> And then from Gibson's your letter
> with a blurred photograph of a gull.
> Caught vision. The stunning white bird
> an unclear stir.
>
> And that is all this writing should be then.
> The beautiful formed things caught at the wrong moment
> so they are shapeless, awkward
> moving to the clear.

It is a departure, if not in form at least in intention, from his earlier predilection for preserving his objects in the amber of his directed emotions. In his poetry since 1973, and more so in his non-lyric works, we have seen him seeking the unrested form he requires, and the realization that it is in form that we present what we deem the real. All content is, as William

Carlos Williams pointed out, dream; and while dream is interesting, it is interesting only when it is not volitional.

In his earlier poems Ondaatje had a habit, that is, of intensifying the world, of fashioning artifice, as I have said. In them we found steady images of brutality, especially of the suffering of beasts, as in the verse of Pat Lane. I was slow to respond favourably to the poems in *The Dainty Monsters* (1967), attractive as they might have seemed with all their violence, because they were, by the time I the reader got to them, over with; there was no mystery left, no labour for the reader, just puzzle or rue. No mystery for writer *or* reader, that is. (pp. 61-2)

On reading the first two books of lyrical poetry [*The Dainty Monsters* and *The Man with Seven Toes*] (though on reading the selected poems at the end of the decade I was to change my view to my gain) I saw the poems as anecdotal, really Canadian, and considered them to be exercises written between sessions of work on Ondaatje's more serious and larger concerns, such as [Billy the Kid] and Buddy Bolden. The shorter pieces were poems for enjoyment, and I enjoyed them. They were, in my view, well cut and shaped, but not risky.

An exception was his famous poem about his father, **"Letters & Other Worlds."** It does take risks, and for most of its three pages it is a world rather than a picture of one. But at the last, in getting out, Ondaatje the son trips over a Figure of Speech which contains "blood screaming." That sort of thing the reader can only accept or reject as a *mot* performed by the author; he cannot experience it. (p. 63)

Rat Jelly was an improvement on *The Dainty Monsters,* rather than an advance, for the most part. But it was and is that rare kind of collection nowadays, a book of poems to enjoy, not to be dislocated or awed by. The poems are, I suspect, among the last id-haunted remnants from an ex-English boyhood. The aforementioned poem addressed to Victor Coleman probably satisfies the essentially neo-Georgian literary people who make up the Eastern establishment, but the aim it announces, when totally realized, will turn them right off and thus conserve energy, and we will use the reserve to warm the house for the invited not the commanded muse.

On the cover of Michael Ondaatje's selected shorter poems, *There's a Trick with a Knife I'm Learning to Do* (1979), there is a photograph of a seated man using his *left* foot to throw knives around the body of a woman who looks like Dorothy Livesay. Whether or not that says anything about the course of Canadian poetry, it does suggest the nature of Ondaatje's wit: among other things (especially while we notice that the title of the book is nowhere to be found among the poems), the poet's "trick" is to use an edge that seems to miss its target, barely.

When Ondaatje, while learning, comes closest to his boundary, there is a great deal to admire in his performance of these left-footed poems. The newest ones, in a section of the book called **"Pig Glass: 1973-1978,"** are intent upon not quite that dislocation I looked for earlier, but a dislocating settlement, a resolute oddity. The last line of each poem sounds like your most adept friend's final smack of his hammer on his fifteen-story birdhouse, or the last knife thudding into the board above your own pate. (pp. 63-4)

Subtitled "Poems 1963-1978," [*There's a Trick with a Knife I'm Learning to Do*] is made up of Ondaatje's selections from *The Dainty Monsters* and *Rat Jelly,* plus thirty-five pages of **"Pig Glass."** We see just over a hundred pages of work of the

lyric poet from the age of twenty to the age of thirty-five, a bracket that always seems interesting in the careers of Canadian poets.

That Ondaatje has always been interested in animals as figures is apparent from the three titles just mentioned (as well as his anthology, *The Broken Ark,* published originally in 1971 and reprinted in 1979 as *A Book of Beasts*). In his twenties he explored and exploited the violence implied in the confrontation between people and animals, but as I now read it, with a spectral uneasiness rather than the advantageous exposition of Pat Lane's lyrics. Lane tells us that man is naturally murderous toward his fellow beasts, but Ondaatje is interested in the experiential philosophy developing from a paradox pronounced early in his verse:

> Deep in the fields
> behind stiff dirt fern
> nature breeds the unnatural.

So did Ondaatje, especially in his first poems. Here is a typical example of his early predilection for the wry metamorphosing of the Anglo-American academic poets in the post-Eliot age, the sort of exterior design then found in the Donald Hall anthologies:

> I have been seeing dragons again.
> Last night, hunched on a beaver dam,
> one clutched a body like a badly held cocktail;
> his tail, keeping the beat of a waltz,
> sent a morse of ripples to my canoe.

("Dragon")

That figuring was carved while Ondaatje was still a British immigrant student, at the Waspy English departments of Sherbrooke and Queen's. His poetic during that time might be characterized by a stanza from another poem:

> I would freeze this moment
> and in supreme patience
> place pianos
> and craggy black horses on a beach
> and in immobilized time
> attempt to reconstruct.

("Four Eyes")

But then came the association with the poets at the Coach House Press, and a poetics that espoused a non-Euclidian order. One need only compare the above passage with the later poem addressed to Victor Coleman, with its "blind lover" and "caught vision." There is a concomitant change in the music, from deliberate manipulation to more subtle and patient rime. (pp. 65-6)

So the younger Ondaatje's poems deliver a diction that is formalized, literary, or British; at least it signifies an elevation into printed language. But from the beginning the poet shows us a sure comprehension of what a line is, not just a length, not only a syntactic unit, but a necessary step in knowing and surprise. It is telling that when he comes to contemplating a painter's work, it is the work of Henri Rousseau, with his sharply defined wonderment. Thus, even while the subject is eerie or terrible, the words suggesting the man's observations of them are "exact," "exactness," "order" and "freeze."

In *Rat Jelly* there appear some family poems, with constructed metaphors; *i.e.,* what is this (thing, experience, feeling) like? It's like a _____. It is still a geocentric world, in which the poet's invention is the earth, albeit an unusually interesting one. But **"Billboards,"** the opening poem of the selection from *Rat Jelly* in *Trick With a Knife* seems deliberately to exhibit a promising progression of the poet's means, from fancy to phe-nomenological imagination. (pp. 66-7)

Other poems, such as the oft-remembered "**Notes for the leg-end of Salad Woman,**" enact wonderful images without any academic super-structure, though perhaps Laytonic exaggera-tion, and lots of robust humour. The last is a feature of On-daatje's writing that deserves an extended study. There are, in *Rat Jelly,* still some laconic poems about men's mistreatment of wild animals, as well as the poet's amused admiration for his dogs. But Ondaatje is still there looking for a magically charged world, a world with Margaret Atwood's immanent peril and Gwendolyn MacEwen's legerdemainous nature. "**Burning Hills,**" an important piece, suggests on the other hand the self-reflexive narrative put to such good use in On-daatje's most important books, *The Collected Works of Billy the Kid* and *Coming Through Slaughter.* (p. 67)

"**Pig Glass**" is a collection of lyrics that benefit from the practice of *Billy* and *Slaughter,* partaking of their concern with the ironies inherent in the act of composition, the acknowl-edgement that a writer who participates in motion cannot "freeze" a scene for the universal literary museum. In "**Coun-try Night**" the poet notes the liveliness of the unseen creatures of the farmhouse while people are abed. He finishes by saying, "All night the truth happens." A pretty clear statement of poetic. But when is he composing this? During the continuous present of the poem's night-time verbs, or out of bed in the daytime? Is this poem truth, that is, and is that last line from it?

The poems in "**Pig Glass**" are as the pervious lyrics are, usually one page filled, a regularity suggesting that the author is work-ing on a contract, as both entertainers (see title, *There's a Trick With a Knife I'm Learning to Do*) and bridegrooms (see cover photograph) do. The last section sports some travel-to-roots poems, some family poems, but most important, some depar-tures from the regular observing occasional poem, in the di-rection of his peculiar pamphlet from Nairn Press, *Elimination Dance* (1977). There is, for example, "**Sweet like a Crow,**" two pages of outrageous similes, in which the addressed one's voice is "Like a crow swimming in milk, / like a nose being hit by a mango" etc. And there is "**Pure Memory,**" the non-sequential meditations on Chris Dewdney, and there is the poem of Sally Chisum's recollections of Billy the Kid thirty-seven years later, the heartening evidence that Ondaatje does not consider *Billy* to be a polished artifact, over and closed. These are all good signs that Ondaatje is bringing to his shorter verse the engaging fabrication of his longer works: that the nature of invention has met and bested the culture of mastery.

In his career to this date, Michael Ondaatje has been a poet who makes art that is like the best of Canadian poetry. As a novelist he writes stuff most of our respected novelists do not begin to dream of. As a fiction writer he is superior; as a poet he is one of our most proficient. (pp. 68-9)

> George Bowering, "Ondaatje Learning to Do," in
> Spider Blues: Essays on Michael Ondaatje, edited by
> Sam Solecki, Véhicule Press, 1985, pp. 61-9.

JOHN COOK

Secular Love is Ondaatje's first volume of new poems since *There's a Trick With a Knife I'm Learning to Do,* and what a fine collection it is. Ondaatje moves us again with the sen-suousness of his language, the controlled lushness of his im-agery, and with the remarkable sensitivity, even tenderness, of his response to his subjects. But more than this, the volume is again suffused with Ondaatje's perception of the patterns of thought and feeling that shape our imagination, our culture, and our sense of place. One ought to note, in this respect, the heady allusiveness of his poetry. In this collection we journey through a landscape that has been both shaped and named by poets. Leonard Cohen's wounded nature is here. So are his "midnight choirs." The rocks and trees and the shaping human hand evoke Purdy's "Country North of Belleville." There are, as well, echoes of the hot-house images of Theodore Roethke.

In earlier works Ondaatje has shown himself to be a poet intensely aware of the way language and experience interpen-etrate. At the heart of *The Collected Works of Billy the Kid* are the gun and the word, the shot and the call, the murders and the myth, and it is out of these cohering elements that Ondaatje weaves a vision of a very complex proportion. This new col-lection seems, at first glance, to take Ondaatje down a new trail. It begins with a quotation from Peter Handke in which an actor is advised to "open your mouth all the way." "You always hold back something of yourself. You're not shameless enough for an actor," says the critic in the epigraph leading us, I suspect, to believe that in the poems to follow the poet will reveal all, "open [his] mouth all the way," and tell us in terms at once both private and revealing of the crises of a family in dissolution.

Although the subject of *Secular Love* is indeed this intensely personal one, I am convinced that we need to be on guard. For the poet has learned a trick or two about revelation and the collection is larded with evidence of his craftiness. I don't mean to question in any way the depth and intensity of the feelings expressed, but a reader ought to note that elsewhere in the book the poet quotes Elmore Leonard: "I'm trying to tell you how I feel without exposing myself. You know what I mean?" Throughout the collection the poetry finds energy in the dynamic interplay between the cunning duplicity of the artist and the heartfelt truth of a suffering man.

Secular Love is a charting of a "voyage/out to the heart," "a map of the dreadful night" of a marriage's collapse. To read the collection as a personal, private confession or revelation alone is to miss the extent to which the new work is very much in the tradition of the mythopoeic Billy the Kid poems. In this case, however, the myth is woven around the private sacrament of skin and blood for in this work the poet is the subject of his own imagination. As such, there are two voices here—the voice of the poet as participant, as husband, father, son, lover, and the voice of the poet as somewhat distanced observer and maker of fine poems. Part of the power of these poems is to be found in the ironic interplay of these two voices. At times the poet as songmaker realizes that his talent can be both se-ductive and destructive. The maker of poetry can glorify life in art, but he can also make "fiction of your arm" and write about others as though he "owns" them.

In a collection which is at once both highly moving and daz-zling, the drama of withdrawal and touch, of closings and reopenings, of loss and discovery finds its apogee in two poems. "**To a Sad Daughter**" is, as we might expect, a particularly wrenching but poetically powerful statement:

> If you break
> break going out not in.
> How you live your life I don't care
> but I'll sell my arms for you,
> hold your secrets forever.

The penultimate poem of the book, **"Birch Bark,"** dedicated to the late George Whalley, is not only one of the best in this collection, but it is also perhaps one of the finest poems Ondaatje has written. Its images of separation and union eloquently celebrate a friendship and give voice to the sense of emotional and spiritual recovery with which the "voyage out to the heart" ends. (pp. 415-16)

John Cook, in a review of "Secular Love," in Queen's Quarterly, Vol. 93, No. 2, Summer, 1986, pp. 415-16.

TOM MARSHALL

There are at least two different ways of regarding [*In the Skin of a Lion*]: as a commendable and ambitious attempt at a social novel (one that might bear comparison in some respects to a Matt Cohen or a Timothy Findley work) or as another somewhat disjointed compilation of those disparate magical moments, spectacular or bizarre "special effects," and vividly compelling sex 'n' blood 'n' rock 'n' roll (correction: jazz) rhythms that have made Michael Ondaatje something of a cult writer. . . .

The novel introduces a number of potentially interesting characters but is slow to develop them or to trace connections between and among them. Ondaatje's men are, as always, "legendary" in their habits, appetites, and capacities; his two principal women are strong and sexy and (as fictional presences) more or less interchangeable. These people eventually undergo numerous physical adventures in various combinations and this often makes for good reading. But one reads (at least, *I* had to read) for a good hundred and more pages before discovering what connects these remarkable people whose lives are much more vivid than most lives. It is a little like watching a long and intermittently lively experimental film.

The connecting link that emerges is the growth of revolutionary consciousness in Patrick, Ondaatje's chief hero. From childhood on he identifies more and more with the exploited immigrant workers, especially after he lives with Alice, an actress who has become involved with Toronto's Macedonian community. The book takes on a new coherence and purpose at this point, and the author even attempts quite explicitly, if belatedly, to justify his meandering narrative method. . . .

But the emotional and imaginative energies of the book have, finally, no necessary connection with class warfare or the march of history. For there is more of fairy tale and heroic romance than of serious social comment in the best sections of this dreamlike book. The social message seems, finally, somewhat willed and perfunctory.

I suspect this is because the author is far more drawn, imaginatively and dramatically, to the emotional complex of fathers and sons and to Leonard Cohen-esque variations on the Oedipal romantic triangle than he is to the struggle of workers and bosses. Or shall I say that he can see the latter only in terms of the former. . . .

But probably Ondaatje knows all this. His Patrick is a curiously passive character, as he himself observes, who ultimately fails as a revolutionary. He fails for the best of reasons: he is a decent human being who does not really believe in violence. He is dominated by his two women, one of whom tells him, "You were born to be a younger brother." He is by temperament one of life's observers, and thus a potential artist like Ondaatje's earlier protagonists.

The author's new expansiveness is an interesting development. He is attempting some sort of social-historical panorama—one thinks of E. L. Doctorow's *Ragtime,* which was, however, much more tightly constructed, as was *Coming Through Slaughter,* Ondaatje's previous novel. I think this one will be read for its best passages, some of which are as marvellous as anything he has written: a nun falling off a bridge but caught by a daredevil construction worker; a gang of Finnish labourers skating on a river at night with torches; a fabulous puppet show in a waterworks, and many more such scenes. Indeed, reading this novel *is* rather like watching some over-ambitious and over-long Stanley Kubrick film that has, however, absolutely wonderful moments.

Tom Marshall, "Missed Connections," in Books in Canada, Vol. 16, No. 5, July, 1987, p. 16.

MICHAEL HULSE

In the Skin of a Lion follows the daylight and darkness of a number of men and women, granting the definition that redeems them from nowhere. In his previous fiction, *The Collected Works of Billy the Kid* and *Coming through Slaughter,* as in his (auto-)biographical *Running in the Family,* Ondaatje devised a distinctive technique for presenting such definition and redemption. Combining psychological sensitivity and physical sensuality with a meticulous fidelity to factual detail, the method employs juxtaposition and cinematic intercutting to create continuity of depth out of an apparent discontinuity of surface. *In the Skin of a Lion,* his most ambitious work to date, is a triumph for this technique and for Ondaatje's unique sensibility.

At the heart of the novel is Patrick Lewis, who grows up in Canadian logging country and in 1923, at the age of twenty-one, arrives in Toronto "as if it were land after years at sea." He becomes one of an army of searchers for Ambrose Small, millionaire personification of "bare-knuckle capitalism," who has vanished. Lewis's success in the search brings him into contact with Small's lover Clara Dickens and then into a deepening relationship with Clara's intimate friend Alice Gull, an actress and political activist. . . .

In the Skin of a Lion maps high society and the sub culture of the underprivileged in Toronto in the 1920s and 1930s, and in the process does for Toronto what Joyce did for Dublin or Döblin for Berlin. But it is also a novel about communication, about men "utterly alone" who are waiting (in Ondaatje's terms) to break through a chrysalis. The breakthrough may come, for immigrants, in the hilarious grotesquerie of learning English. . . . For those like Lewis or [Macedonian immigrant Nicholas Temelcoff] who inhabit a complex of actions or objects, a sense of the sublime may be granted by a visionary epiphany (as when Lewis, as a boy, watches Finnish loggers skating at night by the light of burning rushes). Above all, the breakthrough into communication is found instinctually in sexual harmony. From Buddy Bolden and Robin Brewitt, to his poem **"The Cinnamon Peeler,"** this has been Ondaatje's constant theme, and in the love story of Patrick Lewis and Alice Gull he establishes tenderness and harmony with an unsentimental control of scene and tone.

But in Ondaatje's fiction, horror is always closest when happiness seems most assured: Alice is accidentally killed by a bomb, and Lewis turns arsonist and later saboteur, trying to blow up a water-filtration plant. The plant is the brainchild of the Commissioner of Public Works, who wears a coat "that cost more than the combined weeks' salaries of five bridge workers'' and who has visions of a new Toronto. Through the confrontation of the two men the novel implies that civilization is built as much upon struggles and griefs, exhaustion and despair, as on hope and harmony. For Ondaatje, history must be grasped as individual lives. A striking image tells of a whim of the Moghul prince Akbar, whose court "remained frozen at whatever they were doing" when a gong sounded, on pain of death. Ondaatje is Akbar's opposite: monarch-as-author, he moves among his people "to study their dress and activity," and their hearts, and then releases them once more into that movement which is life. And the novel that results is a powerful and relevatory accomplishment.

Michael Hulse, "Worlds in Collision," in The Times Literary Supplement, *No. 4405, September 4, 1987, p. 948.*

CAROLYN KIZER

Like most normal readers when handed a novel by a poet, or a work described as written in "poetic prose," I usually drop it like a live coal. However, that would be an error in the case of *In the Skin of a Lion,* whose author, Michael Ondaatje, is a brilliantly gifted poet and memoirist. Central to his story is the life and character of Patrick Lewis, who as a lad learns from his logger father how to clear logjams with dynamite, and who grows up to use high explosives to express his hatred of the wretched conditions of working men and women in the Toronto of the 1920's.

An orderly and linear account of Patrick's youth this is not. So that the reader isn't put off by the frequent and sometimes lengthy divagations into the lives of seemingly unconnected characters, he or she should ponder well an epigraph by John Berger, the British Marxist art critic and novelist, at the opening of this tale: "Never again will a single story be told as though it were the only one." Mr. Ondaatje manages to pick up most of the loose threads in his complex tapestry by the time the book winds down. Not all of them. Crucial events go unexplained; characters who seem important at the time disappear without a trace. Other characters are scantily identified, if at all. . . . It's like life itself.

The novel is a story—or more accurately stories—told to a young girl by Patrick as he drives north to rendezvous with an old mistress, one of the two great passions of his life. People who are fussy about academic niceties such as "point of view" are not going to be entirely happy with this book. They will take irritable note of the number of times scenes take place or emotions are expressed about which the protagonist could have no knowledge. I have a feeling Mr. Ondaatje knows all this perfectly well and doesn't care. Born in Sri Lanka when it was Ceylon, he was educated and grew up in England and Canada. This book more closely resembles the writing that is being done on the Continent these days: episodic, fragmentary, structurally loose and shifty. And he's a beautiful writer.

What he writes about most beautifully is *work*. Mr. Ondaatje is passionate about process, the way work, particularly construction of all kinds, is done and how it feels to do it. This is, of course, a rarity in fiction at any time, and one can only be grateful for a man who is not focused on the classroom, the bedroom and the bar. (p. 12)

After he comes to Toronto, Patrick gets a job as a "searcher." Men are paid $4 a week, in 1921, to look for a missing mil-

lionaire named Ambrose Small. We are told that "gradually [Patrick] came into contact with Small's two sisters," without a word of explanation of how a young workman from the woods pulls off this feat. They tell him to look up Clara Dickens, Small's mistress, in Paris, Ontario. Patrick and Clara become lovers almost immediately. "He was drawing out her history with Small, a splinter from a lady's palm." In the course of this we come to my favorite line of dialogue: "'Would it be forgivable to say I stayed with him because he gave me a piano?'"

But there seems to be a good deal more to the relationship than this: Clara knows where Small is, and goes to him, abandoning her obsessed young lover. She does leave him a souvenir, however: a live iguana. (I had thought iguanas required a hot climate definitely not like Toronto, but so what? I guess he is an emblem of the ugly Small.) In the most preposterous episode in the book, Patrick figures out where Clara and Small are and pursues Clara. Small answers the door and tells Patrick he will go get Clara. Instead, this millionaire, who presumably commands the services of numberless minions, pours kerosene on Patrick from the roof and drops a match on him. Patrick runs for his life and jumps in a pool, whereupon Small throws something like a Molotov cocktail at him and nearly blinds him. The next day Clara visits Patrick at the hotel and finds him bruised, blood-covered, one-eyed and cut up. And we have my second-favorite bit of dialogue, also by Clara: "It would be terrible if we met under perfect conditions. Don't you think?" And despite these imperfect conditions, they of course make love.

Many more astounding adventures and surreal episodes lie ahead. I trust that the author doesn't mind a little gentle teasing on the part of the reviewer. I am keeping in mind what Mr. Ondaatje says in rebuttal: "All his life Patrick Lewis has lived beside novels and their clear stories. Authors accompanying their heroes clarified motives. World events raised characters from destitution. The books would conclude with all wills rectified and all romances solvent." And who, these days, wants to write, or read, another neat novel like that? (pp. 12-13)

Carolyn Kizer, "Mr. Small Isn't Here. Have an Iguana!" in The New York Times Book Review, *September 27, 1987, pp. 12-13.*

GEORGE PACKER

The Collected Works of Billy the Kid tracked the consciousness of the young outlaw through acts of brutal violence and equally astonishing tenderness; *Coming Through Slaughter* descended into New Orleans and the madness of the early jazz cornetist Buddy Bolden. Both books use interpolated verse, journalism, photographs and deliberate disjunctions of plot. Their language consists of explosions saved by precision; they come off as a series of sensual images, which in their totality create a state of mind and evoke the moral tone of an era. They care less than most fictional histories about getting across the facts of a life. And indeed Ondaatje's new novel [*In the Skin of a Lion*] passes over from fictional history into historical fiction, accent on the latter, for the characters—as far as one can tell—are made up, and the historical background figures not much more prominently than in ordinary novels. But *In the Skin of a Lion* is not at all ordinary.

The book begins with a prologue: a man telling a girl a story on a long night drive. The story—this novel—is his, though that only becomes clear toward the end, so the reader is like a back-seat passenger who got on a few miles late and has to strain to follow. For a while the going is rough, as the story jumps between plots in resolutely nonlinear fashion: a boy in the Canadian woods works alongside his father, who dynamites logjams; a nun is windblown off a Toronto bridge and snatched to safety by a Macedonian workman; the boy—now a man, Patrick Lewis—comes to Toronto in the 1920s. Like the Macedonian, Patrick "was an immigrant to the city," and in his ignorance and passion fantastic things happen to him. He finds work as a "searcher" for a disappeared millionaire, and falls in love with the millionaire's mistress, Clara; she seduces him, before returning to the other man. The story leaps to 1930: Patrick, still obsessed, having "reduced himself almost to nothing," is now a tunneler digging under Lake Ontario for a new waterworks, the brainchild of a powerful commissioner. Reluctantly Patrick becomes involved with workers and immigrants, and then with Clara's friend Alice, an actress and political firebrand. He is "a chameleon among the minds of women," and when Alice is accidentally killed by an anarchist's bomb, Patrick in his mad grief puts his boyhood training to use by burning down a lakefront hotel and blowing up the dock.

The third part of the novel brings earlier stories together and wanders into new ones. In prison Patrick meets Caravaggio, a house painter and thief who appeared briefly in the Toronto bridge interlude; later he tracks down the Macedonian from the bridge, who has been taking care of Alice's orphaned daughter Hana. Caravaggio and Patrick, newly politicized by work and prison, concoct a scheme to dynamite the waterworks and cut off Toronto's water supply in the midst of labor strife. The attempt ends with an inconclusive, oddly benign encounter between Patrick and the water commissioner in his wired office. Finally Patrick and Hana set off on the drive that begins the book: they are going in search of Clara, and the man is telling the girl this very convoluted story.

More convoluted, in fact, than any summary, for Ondaatje always jumpcuts, moves ahead, circles back, criss-crosses. A plot as twisted and fabulous as this is not in itself a bad idea. Where Ondaatje goes wrong is in not inventing madly enough. Patrick is the nexus of all the stories, "a prism that refracted their lives." Though forever setting off after a woman or trying to blow something up, he is basically a passive figure, alive for sensation rather than connection and action. The Macedonian, the thief, Clara and Alice all do things in the world, whereas "he feels removed from any context of the world, wanting to sleep at this moment, wanting to swim back into the current he has just escaped." Too much of the book is wrapped in the skin of a kitten, Patrick's sensibility. Billy the Kid with his rifle and Buddy Bolden with his horn (and both, to a lesser extent, with their penises) drive their stories by more and more intemperate action. But with Patrick, observation usually melts into feeling before it can harden into motive.

In a poem from his latest collection, *Secular Love,* Ondaatje gives a self-critique, perhaps unintended:

> —and sometimes
> I think
> women in novels are too
> controlled by the adverb.
> As they depart
> a perfume of description
>
> "She rose from the table
> and left her shoe
> behind, *casually*"

> "Let's keep our minds
> clear, she said drunkenly,"
> the print hardly dry
> on words like that.

This applies to some men in novels too. The same tendency can be found in *In the Skin of a Lion.* . . . This "perfume of description" clings to Patrick till very near the end. As a result the already fragmented plot is broken up more, into separate moments of illumination, which "clarify not the information but his state" and don't convincingly propel what happens next. The problem, then, is not that the plot is convoluted but that Ondaatje yokes it to Patrick's aesthetic consciousness.

This is not a minor problem, and it has already led at least one reviewer to dismiss the novel. But I don't think *In the Skin of a Lion* ought to be dismissed. One reason is that the language is generally great enough to make every episode interesting. . . . The image of light helps bind the unruly plot, as do other leitmotifs: explosions, the colors of dyes and paints, human and animal skins, labor. Ondaatje describes manual work as well as any writer I have read, not the psychological effects but its physical sensations: he describes it from the inside, as if he knows it. Work brutalizes, but it is one's connection to the world, and when Patrick begins to work—as a tunneler, a tanner and later, a saboteur—he finally enters the lives he has brought together, sheds one skin for another. Far from merely ornamental, the book's motifs are the symbolic pieces of its central theme, which seems to me to be the making of an artist into a man.

"How can she who had torn his heart open at the waterworks with her art lie now like a human in his arms?" Patrick wonders about the actress Alice, in the middle of a long passage at the end of the second part. In these pages he emerges as a writer-figure. Beyond realizing that "his own life was no longer a single story but part of a mural," he enables others to see their own lives as well. The worker who snatched the nun out of the air tells Patrick that story; and now

> Nicholas is aware of himself standing there within the pleasure of recall. It is something new to him. This is what history means. He came to this country like a torch on fire and he swallowed air as he walked forward and he gave out light. Energy poured through him . . . Patrick's gift, that arrow into the past, shows [Nicholas] the wealth in himself, how he has been sewn into history. Now he will begin to tell stories.

And from this point, Nicholas's and the others' gift is to move Patrick the story-teller from consciousness to life. By the end he has become a commando of labor.

If the last-ditch politics seem rather facile, it may be because rhetoric and style are still at odds. The words say, "Nothing to lose but our chains," but the voice is the voice of Patrick, and the final transformation is not completely convincing. Yet the potent suggestion that the writer must be a human being and citizen remains. . . . Michael Ondaatje is not the easiest writer around, but he is one of the more interesting. *In the Skin of a Lion* is worth reading and sticking with; it might even win Ondaatje the wider audience he has earned. (pp. 421-22)

George Packer, "Refractions," in The Nation, *New York, Vol. 245, No. 12, October 17, 1987, pp. 421-22.*

WHITNEY BALLIETT

Ondaatje has already shown us, in his novel *Coming Through Slaughter* and in his eloquent memoir *Running in the Family,* that he likes to write in curves, in time lapses, in underwater gestures. He has also shown us that his narratives never falter. At the center of each meander is a precise, stark, lyrical episode that gathers in the slack and shoots the book forward.

Consider the first two episodes in his new novel [*In the Skin of a Lion*]. Patrick grows up on a farm in the wilds northwest of Toronto. His father, a six-foot-six-inch giant who hires out as a handyman to neighboring farmers, allows a cow to get loose, and it falls through the ice.... Father and son slither across the ice and, plunging into the water, work two ropes under the cow and, with the help of a couple of horses, pull it to safety. The second episode takes place in Toronto a few years later—in 1917, during the building of the Bloor Street Viaduct. Nicholas Temelcoff, a Balkan immigrant, is the bridge's gadfly: he swings out into the air and falls, held only by a harness and a rope, to check plates and beams and joints and scaffolds.... One windy night, a group of nuns wander onto the unfinished bridge, and one is blown over the edge. Temelcoff, suspended just below, catches her with one arm. His other arm, locked around a pipe, is pulled out of its socket. Temelcoff and the nun, stunned by pain and shock, swing themselves onto a catwalk, and make their way unseen off the bridge to a restaurant Temelcoff frequents. It is closed, but the owner, a friend of Temelcoff's, lets them in. Temelcoff kills his pain with brandy and falls asleep, and the nun, without her veil and with her habit altered, waits for help and then disappears. The nun's body is never found, of course, and she becomes, by way of the novelist's license, an actress (and anarchist) named Alice Gull.

We learn that Patrick Lewis is a decent man—hardworking, kind, loving. He is also difficult to handle, as most virtuous characters in fiction are. Lewis is a cipher, an axle around which the book turns. We are told that he was "born to be a younger brother," that he had "always been alien, the third person in the picture," that he was "a watcher, a corrector." It is the women in the book—Alice Gull and her friend Clara Dickens, a radio actress—who offer the strongest images. Patrick reflects them: they head him this way and that. They love him, and bamboozle him, and nearly destroy him. Near the end of the book, fired by the left-wing dreams of Alice Gull, he comes to life—but in a disastrous, foolish way. He burns down a resort hotel and goes to jail (another galvanizing episode). Then he decides to blow up the palatial Toronto waterworks. He had been a sandhog in its feeder tunnel under Lake Ontario, and he swims through the tunnel and breaks into the waterworks. There he confronts its builder, Commissioner Harris, also the builder of the Bloor Street Viaduct. Harris, a far more effective dreamer than Patrick, calms him, and Patrick, badly hurt while breaking in, and exhausted, falls sleep in Harris's office, his blasting box at his side. (The scene sounds absurd, but Ondaatje, who is fearless, carries it off.)

It is not always clear what Ondaatje is saying in *In the Skin of a Lion*. The book is, to a point, a political novel about the mistreatment of the immigrants who settled in Canada early in this century. Like all of Ondaatje's recent books, it is about the past, but it never seems to be *in* the past. Either Ondaatje is so skilled he makes the past present or, despite his efforts at sliding backward in time, he is unable to make his way out of the present. And I'm not sure that the ancient and honorable practice of a fictional narrator telling a tale to a reader works here. There are no gas stops or coffee breaks in Lewis and Hana's trip—indeed, no sense of a trip at all. But we read Ondaatje for his technical daring and for his prose. (pp. 109-10)

Whitney Balliett, "Growing Up," in The New Yorker, *Vol. LXIII, No. 49, January 25, 1988, pp. 109-10.*

Octavio Paz

1914-

Mexican poet, essayist, critic, nonfiction writer, dramatist, editor, journalist, and translator.

A renowned poet, essayist, and translator who has also founded and edited several periodicals that provide forums for literature and debate on political issues, Paz has earned an international reputation for works in which he seeks to reconcile divisive and opposing forces in human life. He stresses that language and love can provide means for attaining unity and wholeness, and his works accommodate such antithetical topics as culture and nature, the meditative and the sensuous, and the linear and circular nature of time. Paz's works reflect his knowledge of the history, myths, and landscape of Mexico as well as his interest in surrealism, existentialism, romanticism, Oriental thought, and diverse political ideologies. In his verse, Paz experiments with form to achieve clarity and directness while expressing a sense of vitality and vivacity. He stated: "Wouldn't it be better to turn life into poetry rather than to make poetry from life? And cannot poetry have as its primary objective, rather than the creation of poems, the creation of poetic moments?" Paz's essays are praised for their lyrical prose, witty epigrams, and insightful explorations of art, literature, culture, language, and political ideologies. Carlos Fuentes declared: "Literature in Paz becomes a synonym of civilization: both are a network of communicating vessels, and only the totality of communication can reveal the true face of humankind. . . . I know of no other living writer who has so powerfully expressed the existence of a plurality of times, a plurality of possibilities for harmony and truth, outside the limited range of our inherited dogmas."

Paz began his literary career while in his late teens when he founded *Barrandal,* an avant-garde literary journal, and published his first volume of poems, *Luna silvestre* (1933). In 1937, Paz traveled to Spain, where he became involved in antifascist activities, and then to France, where he met several proponents of surrealism. After returning to Mexico in 1938, Paz founded and edited several literary and political periodicals and wrote newspaper columns on international affairs. During the mid-1940s, he traveled extensively in the United States, where he was influenced by the formal experiments of such modernist poets as William Carlos Williams and Wallace Stevens, and in France, where he became reacquainted with the aesthetics of surrealism and the philosophy of existentialism while serving as a Mexican diplomat. Paz eventually favored the "vital attitude" of surrealism over the philosophical tenets of existentialism. He identified surrealism as a "negation of the contemporary world and at the same time an attempt to substitute other values for those of democratic bourgeois society: eroticism, poetry, imagination, liberty, spiritual adventure, vision." Paz solidified his international reputation as a major literary figure during the 1950s with the publication of three of his most acclaimed works: *El laberinto de la soledad* (1950; *The Labyrinth of Solitude*), a sociocultural analysis of Mexico; *El arco y la lira: El poema, la revelación poetica, poesia, e historia* (1956; *The Bow and the Lyre: The Poem, the Poetic Revelation, Poetry, and History*), an exploration of the process of composition and a defense of poetry as a force

© Lutfi Özkök

for social change; and *Piedra de sol* (1957; *Sun Stone*), a long poem generally considered his finest achievement in verse. Paz was named ambassador to India in 1962 and served in this position until 1968, when he resigned in protest following the killings of student demonstrators in Mexico City by government forces. *Posdata* (1970; *The Other Mexico: Critique of the Pyramid*) details the reasons for his resignation and examines the failure of communication between students and the Mexican government. Since relinquishing his ambassadorship, Paz has traveled extensively while continuing his prolific literary career.

In his early poetry, Paz experimented with such diverse forms as the sonnet and vers libre, reflecting his desire to renew and clarify Spanish language in order to lyrically evoke images and impressions. In many of these pieces, Paz employed the surrealist technique of developing a series of related or unrelated images to emphasize sudden moments of perception, a particular state of mind, or a fusion of such opposites as dream and reality, life and death. Topics of Paz's formative verse include political and social issues, the brutality of war, and eroticism and love. *Aguila o sol?* (1951; *Eagle or Sun?*), one of his most important early volumes, is a sequence of visionary prose poems concerning the past, present, and future of Mexico. *Selected Poems* (1963) and *Early Poems, 1935-1955* (1973) contain representative compositions rendered both in their original Spanish and in English translation.

Critics frequently note that *Sun Stone*, which adheres to the format of the Aztec calendar, initiates a more radical phase of experimentation in Paz's career. Comprising 584 eleven-syllable lines that form a circular sentence, this poem blends myth, cosmology, social commentary, and personal and historical references in a phantasmagoric presentation of images and allusions to project the psychological processes of an individual attempting to make sense of existence. Sven Birkerts noted: "*Sun Stone* is, like so many of Paz's longer poems, a lyrically discursive exploration of time and memory, of erotic love, of art and writing, of myth and mysticism."

The variety of forms and topics in Paz's later verse reflects his diverse interests. *Blanco* (1967), widely considered his most complex work, consists of three columns of verse in a chapbook format that folds out into a long single page; each column develops four main themes relating to language, nature, and the ways in which an individual makes sense and order of life. In *Ladera este, 1962-1968* (1969), Paz blends simple diction and complicated syntax to create poems that investigate Oriental philosophy, religion, and art. In the long poem *Pasado en claro* (1975; *A Draft of Shadows*), Paz examines selfhood and memory by focusing on poignant moments in his life in the manner of William Wordsworth's autobiographical poem *The Prelude*. *Vuelta* (1976) collects topical verse that Paz wrote after resigning from his ambassadorship. *The Collected Poems of Octavio Paz, 1957-1987* (1988) reprints poems in Spanish and in English translation from the latter phase of his career. Paz's verse is also represented in *Poemas, 1935-1975* (1979) and *Selected Poems* (1984).

The Labyrinth of Solitude, a prose volume in which Paz explores Mexican history, mythology, and social behavior, is perhaps his most famous work. According to Paz, modern Mexico and its people suffer a collective identity crisis resulting from their mixed Indian and Spanish heritage, marginal association with Western cultural traditions, the influence of the United States, and recurring experiences with war and isolation. While critics debated the appropriateness of Paz's portrayal of the Mexican psyche as emblematic of the modern human condition, *The Labyrinth of Solitude* received widespread praise. Irving Howe commented: "This book roams through the phases of Mexican past and present seeking to define the outrages, violation and defeats that have left the Mexican personality fixed into a social mask of passive hauteur. . . . At once brilliant and sad, *The Labyrinth of Solitude* constitutes an elegy for a people martyred, perhaps destroyed by history. It is a central text of our time."

Paz's numerous essays on culture, art, politics, and language are collected in several volumes. *Corriente alterna* (1967; *Alternating Current*) contains pieces on aesthetics, literary theory, and contemporary social issues. *El mono gramático (The Monkey Grammarian)*, which was first published in France in 1972 under the title *Le singe grammairien*, discusses the structural and referential qualities of language. *Los hijos del limo: Del romanticismo a la vanguardia* (1974; *Children of the Mire: Modern Poetry from Romanticism to the Avant-Garde*) traces the evolution of verse and examines how poets can be agents for social change through experiments with language. *Tiempo nublado* (1984; *One Earth, Four or Five Worlds: Reflections on Contemporary History*) examines communism, American involvement in Latin America, and the Islamic revolution in Iran. Many of Paz's best-regarded essays are collected in En-

glish translation in *On Poets and Others* (1986) and *Convergences: Essays on Art and Literature* (1987).

(See also *CLC*, Vols. 3, 4, 6, 10, 19 and *Contemporary Authors*, Vols. 73-76.)

KEITH BOTSFORD

This exceedingly curious book [*The Monkey Grammarian*] by the chaste and fiery Mexican metaphysical poet Octavio Paz is an extended meditation on the nature of language. Its title refers to Hanuman, the Indian monkey God, uprooter of mountains, conqueror of space and mythic author of systematic language, the divine simian hero of the Sanskrit epic *Ramayana*.

The very concept of grammar—a system in which language can be fixed, structured and therefore transformed—is one of the great achievements of Indian culture. In the past 50 years philosophers and linguists have devoted enormous intellectual energies to the investigation of how the concept was developed among the thinkers of ancient India, for whom the idea became a central problem in their philosophical tradition. Was language, our faculty for naming objects, given by God or did man invent it, either on his own or with powers borrowed from the divine realm?. . .

Mr. Paz's meditation is illustrated with a rich iconography of Hanuman—photographs of the ancient decaying temple of Galta, of people and animals there, of the exploits of Hanuman and others depicted on manuscripts and in paintings and tapestries. Taken together, they are striking manifestations of change, luxuriant decay. He ponders the paradox by which words cancel out words, images destroy images, sex creates and annihilates, and the very variety of nature defeats its own identification. Nature, love, art all interwine and turn into language. . . .

In one central passage, the poet considers Hanuman contemplating the tangled calligraphy of plants:

> He compares its rhetoric to a page of indecipherable calligraphy and thinks: the difference between human writing and divine consists in the fact that the number of signs in the former is limited, whereas that of the latter is infinite; hence the universe is a meaningless text, one which even the gods find illegible.

It is a theme that indeed might appeal to a writer from Latin America where in imagination plethora seems to rule: the pullulation of life, the death worship of the Mexicans, sun and shade, the flow of time defeating any attempt to get a firm grasp on events. The world as seen by Octavio Paz in this book is not very remote from that seen by Gabriel García Márquez—an incoherence from which we grasp such meaning as we can. The style of the book reflects its subject: Much of **The Monkey Grammarian** is made up of elaborated paradox, perfervid prose and seemingly self-defeating questioning of the phrase just gone by. Written in the evening of a long and brilliant poetic career, it is an old man's book. It looks back to the erotic; it contemplates the death of forms and language; it offers the wisdom of one about to drop out of time. It is telling that the only poem cited in it is T. S. Eliot's "Gerontion."

This is a book that wants a hard-nosed and skeptical reading. But as there is no denying the richness of the mythology on which it is based, there is also no way in which a diligent excavation of this slightly precious text (the translation by Helen R. Lane is admirable) will not twist the reader's mind into new ways of seeing and a new awareness of the profound mystery of language.

Keith Botsford, "A God Who Made Words," in The New York Times Book Review, *December 27, 1981, p. 8.*

JAIME ALAZRAKI

There is a strong parallel between the problems that occupied Wittgenstein and those that absorb Paz, and this intersection of concerns will be a good point of departure for dealing with Paz's own perception of language as presented in one of his most complex works: *El mono gramático (The Monkey Grammarian).*

Wittgenstein believed that there should be a philosophy to end philosophy, and he apparently thought he had achieved this in his *Tractatus.* The structure of reality is contained in the basic structure of all languages; language is a sort of mirror of the world, and what that mirror fails to reflect belongs to the realm of silence: "What we cannot speak about we must pass over in silence." But he later abandoned this theory and postulated its very opposite: the structure of language is not determined by the structure of reality but the other way around; our language determines our view of reality because we see things through it.

Paz begins his discussion on language in *The Bow and the Lyre* with a similar train of thought. . . .

> The distance between the word and the object . . . is the result of another distance: as soon as man acquired consciousness of himself, he broke away from the natural world and made himself another world inside himself. The word is not identical to the reality it names because between man and things—and, more deeply, between man and his being—consciousness of himself intervenes. . . . If the primordial unity between the world and man were reconquered, would not words be superfluous? The end of alienation would also be the end of language. Utopia, like mysticism, would terminate in silence.

A good segment of Wittgenstein's *Philosophical Investigations* is devoted to the elucidation of this gap separating the name from the object or the subject:

> How does the word *refer* to sensations?—There doesn't seem to be any problem here; don't we talk about sensations every day, and give them names? But how is the connexion between the name and the thing named set up? This question is the same as: how does a human being learn the meaning of the names of sensations?—of the word 'pain' for example.

Wittgenstein's answer—"The verbal expression 'pain' replaces pain and does not describe it"—is similar to that given by Paz.

> The essence of language is symbolic because it consists in the representation of one element of reality by another, as occurs with metaphors. . . . Each word or group of words is a metaphor. . . . Man is man because of language, because of the original metaphor that caused him to be another and separated him from the natural world. Man is a being who has created himself in creating a language. By means of the word, man is a metaphor of himself.

There is an obvious difference here: Wittgenstein is concerned with the correlation between names and things; Paz gives up that correlation and assumes the metaphorical nature of language. The philosopher sought to establish the limits of language by ascertaining the chasm between names and things; the poet, on the other hand, transforms the word—the very cause of his alienation from the world—into a bridge with the world. . . . How does language, which has separated man from the world, become a bridge between man and the world? The answer is of course through poetry, and *The Bow and the Lyre* is a meditation on the powers of poetry in the pursuit of that magic reunion.

In *The Monkey Grammarian* Paz again takes up that long reflection initiated in *The Bow,* but between the two books almost twenty years elapsed, during which time he wrote two of his most important collections of poems—*Salamandra* (1962) and *Ladera este* (1969)—and several new books of short essays. It is only natural that Paz's contemplations in *The Bow* should have evolved considerably by the time he wrote *The Monkey Grammarian.* Very little has been written on this most beautiful book which, like an inverted prism, reintegrates all the hues of his poetic vision scattered throughout his poems and essays. Yet it is here that Paz has given his most poignant answer to the enigma of poetry as a bridge reuniting man with himself and the world.

The Monkey Grammarian is a description of a stroll to Galta, an abandoned city in India, following—as Paz explains—the metaphor that gives the name to the collection ("Les sentiers de la création") in which the work was first published in 1972 in French. Paz turns from the metaphorical side of *path* to its more literal use by giving a physical account of his visit to the decayed city: its dusty road, aged vegetation, ruined buildings, outcast inhabitants. But the book is neither a guide nor a travel book. The text and some photographs give enough information about the visit, but its core is rather a reflection on Galta which becomes a reflection on the poetic act, which in turn broadens into a reflection on language.

What brought Paz to Galta? Chapter twenty-seven gives the most direct answer: "On the third and uppermost story of that massive structure, at the top of the stairway and below one of the arches crowning the building, the altar of Hanumān had been erected". And who is Hanumān? "A celebrated monkey chief. He was able to fly and is a conspicuous figure in the *Rāmāyana.* . . . Hanumān leaped from India to Ceylon in one bound; tore up trees, carried away the Himalayas, seized the clouds and performed many other wonderful exploits. . . . Among his other accomplishments, Hanumān was a grammarian". But in addition, Hanumān is *the* poet: "Son of the wind, Hanumān is the divine messenger, the Holy Spirit of India. He is a monkey that is a bird that is a vital and spiritual breath". And isn't this protean nature of the Indian divinity a definition of the language chosen by poetry? In *The Bow and the Lyre* Paz presents poetic language at large in its inception as a sort of Proteus reminiscent of Hanumān:

> Language is poetry in a natural state. Each word or group of words is a metaphor. And it is also a magic instrument, that is, a thing susceptible to being changed into something else and transmuting what it touches: the word *bread,* touched by the word *sun,* actually becomes a star; and the sun, in turn, becomes a luminous food. The word is a symbol that gives off symbols.

Hanumān is therefore a metaphor of language, but then language is also a metaphor of Hanumān. The visit to Galta is thus a journey to the Indian divinity which in turn becomes a meditation on language and poetry and woman. What makes *The Monkey Grammarian* a unique prose piece is the fact that its references are not different from its referents: the latter perform what the former describe. The metaphor is explained by means of another metaphor that mirrors the first that mirrors the second and a third. This is art, and "in the realm of art only form possesses meaning."

The story of Hanumān is also the story of poetry:

> Hanumān wrote on the rocky cliffs of a mountain the *Mahanātaka*, based on the same subject as the *Rāmāyana*; on reading it Vālmīki feared that it would overshadow his poem and begged Hanumān to keep his drama a secret. The Monkey yielded to the poet's entreaty, uprooted the mountain and threw the rocks into the sea. Vālmīki's ink and pen on the paper are a metaphor for the lightning and the rain with which Hanumān wrote his drama on the rocky mountainside.

Hanumān destroyed his "text" so that Vālmīki would be able to write his. Language too is a kind of emulation of the original Word.... Language and poetry were born when the bond uniting the world and the word tore, when their primordial unity broke and an abysmal gap between things and names opened. Language accepts this gap; poetry is an effort to bridge it. (pp. 608-10)

[Paz] is a poet who reasons about poetry with the same transparency found in a poem. His discussion on the limits and reaches of poetry is not articulated in terms of logic, although his arguments are logically impeccable. His is the "logic" of poetry, and it is through this "poetic reasoning" that he provides an answer as to how poetry, being language—that is, exile—becomes also a route of return, a bridge, a leap back. His premise is the acknowledgment of that same gap between things and words which Wittgenstein saw as the true subject of philosophy. The only reality we know, says Paz in *The Monkey Grammarian,* is that of names: "The tree that I say is not the tree that I see, tree does not say tree, the tree is beyond its name, a leafy woody reality". Confronted with this inaccessible reality, language invents its own reality: "My eyes, on reading what I am writing, invent the reality of the person who is writing this long phrase; they are not inventing me, however, but rather a figure of speech". Between the real tree and the tree invented by language mediates "the single tree of sensation" as a sheer perception which inevitably vanishes when the mediator ceases to act. We face again the same gap separating objects and names:

> We come and go: the reality beyond names is not habitable and the reality of names is a perpetual falling to pieces, there is nothing solid in the universe, in the entire dictionary there is not a single word on which to rest our heads, everything is a continual coming and going from things to names to things.

But is this a blind quest? Are we forever condemned to this perpetual wandering between things and their names? Is this coming and going as senseless as the task of Sisyphus? Is there no possible reconciliation? In *The Monkey Grammarian* Paz offers some of his ruminations on these questions. Poetry, he reasons, is neither the name nor the object. Names are the realm of language, and since language cannot reach the world, "the world becomes language." But "the critique of language is called poetry: names grow thinner and thinner to the point of transparency, of evaporation.... Thanks to the poet, the world is left without names. Then, for the space of an instant,

we can see it precisely as it is". What happened? If the poem is the answer as experience, *The Monkey Grammarian* is an attempt to explain that experience. The description of the road to Galta is also the description of the poetic act. Galta is the road to Hanumān; Hanumān is the road to Vālmīki; Vālmīki wants to be the road to poetry but to no avail, since poetry is that territory where all frontiers end and all roads disappear: "There is no end and no beginning; everything is center. Neither before nor after, neither in front of nor behind, neither inside nor outside: everything is in everything". The vision of poetry is one in which all points converge, the end of the road; it is the vision of Hanumān.

How does poetry perform this feat? In the same way Vālmīki re-created Hanumān's play. The *Rāmāyana* is and is not Hanumān's *Mahanātaka:* "Human writing reflects that of the universe, it is its translation, but also its metaphor: it says something totally different and it says the same thing". By means of metaphor, poetry brings together the scattered fragments of the original Word: a vision of unity and reconciliation. It no longer accepts or even respects the rigid identity of signs: poetry depends on language, and at the same time it becomes a subversive act against language. "Modern poetry," says Paz, "is an attempt to do away with all conventional meanings because poetry itself becomes the ultimate meaning of life and mankind; therefore, it is at once the destruction and the creation of language—the destruction of words and meanings, the realm of silence, but at the same time, words in search of the Word". Language, as we know it in daily life, disappears to yield to a second language: the signs remain, the words are those of the dictionary; but they now say something never heard before, they see what our language cannot see: "Crystallizations of the universal play of analogy, transparent objects which ... are waterspouts of new analogies."

While all this is being explained in *The Monkey Grammarian,* the text itself becomes at once the theorem and its demonstration: the road to Galta is also the road to poetry; to follow the road is to write; text and road overlap. The road to Galta leads to Hanumān—that is, to poetry before poetry, to the Word before words. But the road to Galta leads also to poetry after the break of the Word—not only because Vālmīki was able to write his poem after Hanumān destroyed his own text, but because the road is inscribed in the text as poetry. The road is the text, which becomes the body of a woman, Splendor, which is in turn "the other path to Galta." Metaphors elicit new metaphors, paths open to new paths, words lose their tracks to find themselves in a space where the roads have vanished. The visit to Galta is also the encounter with Hanumān; the poet who tells the origins of the *Rāmāyana* touches Vālmīki; the road to Galta is also the text that tells the story; the text is also the body of a woman. (pp. 610-11)

It is apparent that *The Monkey Grammarian* is not an essay. It is also apparent that it is not a poem, at least not in the conventional sense. It is both an essay and a poem, or perhaps neither. The text has been woven in a way that shares the same interplay of similarities and differences which the book seeks to elucidate as the mark of poetry. Poetry in the end is an act of reconciliation: with the world, with man, with a lost wholeness. If language differentiates, separates and isolates—the tree from the table, the table from the chair—then poetry reunites and reconciles: the world of pariahs, prostitutes and beggars of today's Galta merges with the mountain, the ocean and the lightning which Hanumān used to write his play; the *Rāmāyana* merges with the world; the act of telling the story merges with the actual story; the body of Splendor merges with poetry, with the text of the book, with the path to Galta and with the experience of Hanumān. [According to Paz]:

> The poet is not one who names things, but one who dissolves their names, one who discovers that things do not have a name and that the names that we call them are not theirs. . . . Through writing we abolish things, we turn them into meaning; through reading we abolish signs, we extract the meaning from them, and almost immediately thereafter, we dissipate it; the meaning returns to the primordial stuff.

What is left? Almost nothing. A sense that as the road to Galta fades away, so does the text that records the journey. . . . And yet, perhaps because poetry *is* an allegory of mortality, it leaves us with a feeling of reconciliation: the text we are reading has touched upon or hinted at that other untranscribable text, the one Hanumān once wrote on stone with rain and lightning—Creation. It is a text from which we have been banished and long forgotten, one which language strives to remember to no avail. But if language has separated us from the same text it seeks to read, poetry has managed to establish a fleeting contact with that text. By reconciling words with each other, poetry has opened a slit in the opacity of language, and through that opening—the transparency created by the poem—intimations of that Word "immense . . . like a sun" flicker through the text during its reading. The illumination kindled by the poem cannot be fixed. It is not in the text, but rather in its interstices and silences ("bridge between the lines"). The poem acts as a catalyst, and only by reading it is its poetry summoned. The effect of this catalysis is simply a sense of reconciliation: between names and things, between words and the Word, between man and the world or, as Paz has masterfully put it:

> Reconciliation was a womb and a vulva, but also blinks of an eye, provinces of sand. It was night. Islands, universal gravitation, elective affinities, the hesitations of light that at six o'clock in the late afternoon does not know whether to go or to stay. Reconciliation was not I. It was not all of you, nor a house, nor a past or a future. It was there over yonder. It was not a homecoming, a return to the kingdom of closed eyes. It was going out into the air and saying: *good morning.*

And isn't this definition of reconciliation the closest name for poetry? Without losing its condition of sign devoid of all reality, language becomes the embodiment of that face of reality absent in daily life. When, through the lines of a poem, the dusky hour of the afternoon is transfigured into the rusty color and the liquid silence of a cup of tea, something of the harmony and reflective quality of the sunset time has been recovered. This metaphorical twist is to poetry what *incantatio* was to sorcery, and the poetic act depends on the same faith required by magic. Words are still empty symbols, but in the act of reconciling culture and nature, signs and things, the poems has turned those same words into epiphanies of the Word. (p. 611)

> *Jaime Alazraki, "'The Monkey Grammarian' or Poetry as Reconciliation," in* World Literature Today, *Vol. 56, No. 4, Autumn, 1982, pp. 607-12.*

CALVIN BEDIENT

Literary modernism has been divided between romanticism, or the desire to grasp the infinite, and nihilism, the impulse to trash—to punish—that desire (this last having become the "postmodernist" specialty). The modernist question, as Octavio Paz's brilliant manifesto of 1956, *The Bow and the Lyre,* provided the terms for seeing—is whether man, who "wants to be another," has the wherewithal "to go beyond himself." Man is "temporality and change," but is he merely the changed or can he change himself—even, magically, back to "the original man [who] is every man"? . . .

On balance, the modernist moment has been one of suspension, or irony—what Mr. Paz calls "disillusionment with the consciousness, which is unable to annul the distance that separates it from the world outside." Despite his worldly success—both as a Mexican diplomat and as a distinguished man of letters—Mr. Paz himself feels "expelled from the sphere of reality." Like Yeats, he is a Gnostic, part of a "secret society of [modern] poets, a participant in a "nocturnal mystery." He notes that "the situation of exile"—an exile enforced by bourgeois contempt—"leads the poet to intuit that condemnation will cease only if he touches the furthest point of the solitary condition . . . [where] appears the *other,* we *all* appear."

But how to get around language (which is "consciousness of the fall") by means of language itself? One of the first poems in the new *Selected Poems* . . . reads in its entirety:

> The hand of day opens
> Three clouds
> And these few words.

The phrase "these few words" trembles with the possibility of sufficiency. Is "few" a triumph or a poverty? Mr. Paz is "postmodern" only when putting language—in the deconstructionist phrase—into question. The epigraph of his best long poem, *A Draft of Shadows* (1974), consists of Wordsworth's famous and spacious lines, "Fair seed-time had my soul, and I grew up / Foster'd alike by beauty and by fear." But soon we read:

> Like drizzle on embers,
> footsteps within me step
> toward places that turn to air.

and

> the sun
> razes the places as they dawn,
> hesitantly, on this page.

The poem . . . is already in crisis. From Wordsworth's solid-earth romanticism we slide at once into postmodernism. The title, *A Draft of Shadows,* means that language is darkened air, and more fear than beauty.

But even the nihilist, who spits out the bitter pill of nostalgia for cosmic oneness, is already—in terms from *The Bow and the Lyre*—"beyond himself" as he uses language, since man is an "entity of words" and words are "one of the means he possesses to make himself another." Both the nihilist and the romantic step excitedly onto the same suspension "bridge slung from one letter to the next." . . .

Mr. Paz's phrases flash with the "decision to be": "Flames in the snow of the clouds. / The afternoon turns to burnt honey"—Mr. Paz does not hold back anything from language. In this he shares in the glory of Latin American poetry in general (this Mexican poet and the Chilean Pablo Neruda and the Peruvian César Vallejo form an incandescent trio). How unlike our own hesitant, flickering poets are these Latin Americans with their continual heroics of imagination, their "dazzling progression from the limits to the Limits" (Vallejo). Mr. Paz's "green exclamations" and "draft of shadows" are drawn from a cultural palette older and more pristine than ours, the rude Aztec pigments still damp within it. Even as he claims that "language recants," his own proves a red sun. His imagination in *A Draft of Shadows* is all attack, indefatigably vivid. (p. 13)

Poetry, Mr. Paz argues, is necessarily double, belonging to both history and inspiration, fragmentation and universal discourse. But he protests this doubleness—resents history. "To be," he says in *A Draft of Shadows,* "is the desire to be more, / to always be more than more," and this seems unjust, "the injustice of being." This is the unreason of history; then there is all the surrounding evidence of the unreason, the unliftable world of fact. For the most part, Mr. Paz furiously spurns what we unprepossessingly name "mimesis" or "realism," preferring the *"madness of discourse."* Compared to Neruda or even Vallejo, he affords scant attention to the historical or local, scant variation. Back come the sun, shadow, the city (any city), the stones, time, the word (any word), man, water, wind, woman; back come the worn counters of history and, in reprisal, eyes rubbed till "the sky walks the land."

A Draft of Shadows is not least remarkable for containing a rare autobiographical passage from a poet who usually writes as if he had sprung fully formed into the Mexican landscape, where "Rage is mineral," a "sunflower / charred light," and woman the only sinuous fountain. . . . For Mr. Paz, the alternative to being "trash" has been the decision to be—a mad decision, since history is "the well where, / from the beginning, a boy is falling." But then poets and madmen are near allied. Shakespeare grouped not only madmen but lovers with poets, and so does Mr. Paz. (He notes that in both romanticism and its activist offshoot, surrealism, "love and woman occupy a central place . . . Woman opens the doors of night and of truth.") Here again he differs from most American poets, his sexuality as ardent as his need for "voices that think me as I think them"—in fact, one and the same hunger for "Being." Perhaps it takes two to overleap time? If, as he writes in **"Two Bodies,"**

> Two bodies face to face
> are at times two stones
> and night a desert

they can also be "two roots / laced into night." The modern poet, Mr. Paz notes in *The Bow and the Lyre,* has "cut the umbilical cord," killed "the Mother . . . The young poet must discover Woman." "Touch my grass breasts," says a voice in **"Obsidian Butterfly,"** one of his prose poems. "Kiss my belly, sacrificial stone. In my navel the whirlwind grows calm: I am the fixed center that moves the dance. . . . Take my necklace of tears. I wait for you on this side of time where light has inaugurated a joyous reign."

Still, the poet, as such, tries to appease through language alone "the god of time, the god that is time." "To find the way out: the poem" is every poet's shibboleth. The "joyous reign" of greatest note in *Selected Poems* is that of Mr. Paz's own imperious imagination: his belief (whatever the twinges of doubt) that "to name is to create, and to imagine, to be born."

The purity—the unashamedness, the intensity—of his imagination is most accessible in his small poems (those "classical" reactions from his disjointed repetitious stormings of recalcitrant language). An imagination not afraid to be extravagant—to throw everything upon a figure that must *consume*—is Mr. Paz's appeal, his provocation. (What can be too extravagant, he might be asking, in a universe that is itself a mad discourse?) One North American poet does, after all, come to mind: the extravagant Hart Crane, whose Pocahontas (*"a forest shudders*

in your hair!") is recalled by Mr. Paz's lines, "Your hair lost in the forest, / your feet touching mine."

Having grown up outside Mexico City, where "the wind" is "centuries of wind," Mr. Paz trusts instinctively in the prodigiousness of inspiration. But this is not to be confused (aside from his dubious experiment, the long poem *Blanco*) with the imagination's throwing itself about. Nor does Mr. Paz see only "with eyes closed . . . and through the wall." His observation can be exquisitely precise, as in **"Exclamation"** . . . :

> Stillness
> 　　　not on the branch
> in the air
> 　　　not in the air
> in the moment
> 　　　hummingbird

In this verbal mobile, this series of negations and recommencements, Mr. Paz would achieve exemption from meaning (that "wound of meaning" through which "the poem bleeds and becomes prose") simply by exclaiming over an event that is itself all exclamation. He would sculpt a moment as if time itself were Being (in fact a real possibility that forms its most maddening characteristic).

Extraordinary, this masterful sensibility which (like Emily Dickinson's) encompasses both "three clouds" and the transparency of time, both "And I named that half-hour: / Perfection of the Finite" and the Gnostic "dark forgotten marvel of being alive." (pp. 13-14)

> *Calvin Bedient, "Heroics of Imagination," in* The New York Times Book Review, *August 19, 1984, pp. 13-14.*

LARRY D. NACHMAN

The Mexican poet and thinker Octavio Paz has distinguished himself for decades not only by his intelligence and eloquence but by the breadth of his interests. In addition to his poetic works, he has brought out two volumes of philosophical and sociological reflections on Mexico; he has written regularly on contemporary philosophical and literary themes; and he has been a frequent commentator on politics. In this volume of political essays [*One Earth, Four or Five Worlds: Reflections on Contemporary History*], he examines the current state of global affairs, particularly as it pertains to Latin America.

Two positions separate Paz from the general run of Latin American intellectuals. He is hostile to the Soviet Union and to those who ally themselves with it; and, though often a critic of the United States, he is a friendly and generous critic.

Paz's opposition to the Soviet Union is deep and substantial. It has none of that incantatory quality one so frequently observes among those who criticize the Soviet Union and then go on to other matters as if its presence in global affairs were without consequence. Paz sees the Soviet Union as totalitarian and expansionist. Although he hopes and believes that war with it can be averted, he does not think that the Soviet Union will ever accept a definitive international settlement. . . .

Nor does Paz believe that Communism improves with travel. Unlike those apologists who discover a moral and political distance between the Communist party of the Soviet Union and Communist parties throughout the world, Paz argues that all Communist parties share a political vision that is hostile to democracy and to freedom. European Communists, he contends, will not have broken with their past until they cease to regard the Soviet Union as a socialist nation and begin to practice internal democracy in their own parties. (p. 70)

If this uncompromising anti-Communism is not often evident among Latin American intellectuals—it is, after all, not that common among our own intellectuals—Paz's willingness to defend Western democracies, including the United States, has to be viewed as a singular act of courage. That is why his criticisms of American policies, which are clearly made in good faith and are not generated by reflexive anti-Americanism, deserve to be weighed carefully.

One curious quality of Paz's brief against American foreign policy is that it seems to lack a coherent foundation. Often, his criticisms seem to issue from what would in the United States be a clearly conservative position. Thus, he finds American policy to be wavering, inconsistent, and subject to the ever-changing currents of domestic politics. In other words, our conduct of foreign affairs is inhibited by our democratic institutions. Although he is constant in his support for democracy, Paz, like Henry Kissinger, believes that a central issue for the government of the United States is "to find, within the plurality and diversity of wills and interests, a unity of purpose and a unity of action."

Another "conservative" aspect of Paz's thought can be seen in his condemnation of liberal and left-wing intellectuals for their failure to appreciate the awful nature of Communist regimes. He speaks of the "naiveté bordering on complicity of liberals." Although he has a certain moral sympathy for the critics of the Vietnamese war, he nevertheless savages them for their failure to understand the political and human consequences of a Communist victory. (pp. 70-1)

But if statements like these would seem to assign Paz to the political Right, with equal frequency he voices criticisms which flow from a social-democratic position. The United States, Paz charges, has acted wrongly and destructively in Latin America. It has pursued its interests short-sightedly. It has obstructed modernization, favored dictatorships, and corrupted political institutions. In short, the United States has been an enemy of democracy and equality.

These are familiar arguments, the points upon which, for decades, the debate over the ends and means of American foreign policy has turned. What makes Paz's presentation fascinating is that he offers in support of his position an intriguing analysis that is as useful to the case he is attacking as it is to his own.

Since their independence, Paz observes, Latin American nations have universally recognized democracy as the only legitimate form of government. Even dictators at the head of stable, long-standing regimes have presented themselves as transient interruptions of a legitimate democratic tradition. Nor does Paz take such protestations as evidence of hypocrisy or cynicism. Dictatorship in Latin America can never present itself as anything other than an expedient, for it cannot evoke the citizens' deepest loyalties.

Here, in Paz's judgment, is where Fidel Castro has accomplished his greatest transformation in Latin American politics. It was Castro, Paz believes, who not only brought totalitarianism to the Americas, not only introduced Soviet arms and Soviet policies into the area, and not only serves as a vehicle for Communist expansion, but who for the first time has convinced large numbers of Latin Americans of the possibility of

a legitimate government *other* than democracy. Castro substituted a revolutionary for a democratic legitimacy.

Thus, Paz contends, there are now two political systems, democracy and Communism, competing for the loyalties of the peoples of Latin America. Dictatorships are simply not in the running. For this reason, he asserts, the United States is deluding itself whenever it perceives in a dictatorship a bulwark against Communism. In fact, dictatorships actually increase the opportunities for Communism by replacing the only kind of government, democracy, that can effectively contend with the Communists. . . . (pp. 71-2)

There is . . . an unrealistic air to Paz's discussion, with its implicit suggestion that if only the United States stopped supporting dictatorships, we would be surrounded by democracies. The facts often are other than we would like them to be. The question usually posed to our government is what kind of relations we will have with governments that are *not* to our liking. The alternative, for us, is isolation. If we cannot help friendly governments to become democratic, we can at least help them to preserve their independence in the hope of better days for them and for us.

The irony is that following Paz's advice would require us to intervene in the internal affairs of other countries on a scale that would confirm the demonic visions of America's most bitter critics. Moreover, once one gets down to real cases, it turns out that it is not democracies that we are asked to support. Paz, for instance, charges that our hostile policies toward Castro drove him into the arms of the Soviet Union. Let us assume for argument's sake that this is true (although solid historical evidence disproves it). Whatever Castro was at the beginning of his reign, he was not a democrat. And so, in effect what Paz suggests is that we should have supported a dictatorial regime in order to prevent the spread of Soviet power. That is to say, we should have pursued precisely the kind of policy for which we are regularly attacked when the dictatorships in question are of the right-wing variety. One can compile a fairly interesting list of instances in the last thirty years in which liberal opinion castigated the United States for supporting dictators and offered as alternatives such figures as Castro, Khomeini, Ortega. . . .

Paz, at least, does not claim that Communism does better. He points out that before Castro, Cuba was criticized for its dependence on the sugar crops and on the United States. Now Cuba depends on sugar and the Soviet Union. As Paz rightly concludes "'socialism' has not enabled Cuba to change its economy: what has changed is its dependence." He might have added that the depth of its present dependence would have been unimaginable to anyone in pre-Castro Cuba.

But all in all one does not wish to carp. In economics as in politics, Paz's intellectual honesty generally leads him away from the formulas which have been adopted so blithely in North and South America. His very criticisms reveal the narrow range of alternatives in which our foreign policy must operate. His testimony confirms the gravity of the issues that occupy us in Central America and the Caribbean. One can only guess at the depths of isolation he must experience, and one only wishes that all our critics had his integrity. (p. 72)

Larry D. Nachman, "Democrat," in Commentary,
Vol. 80, No. 3, September, 1985, pp. 70-2.

NAOMI BLIVEN

One Earth, Four or Five Worlds: Reflections on Contemporary History, by Octavio Paz, collects recent essays by the Mexican poet on modern politics and their roots in the past. Paz treats these mundane topics in a style that, for all its prosaic sequential coherence, retains qualities of poetic expression. His language never splays; it invariably suggests more than it states; and it makes his truths memorable. (The translator [Helen R. Lane], obviously, deserves credit.) I like Paz's description of the new assertiveness of small ethnic, linguistic, or religious groups as "the rebellion of exceptions" to modern universalisms. And his observation that "literature is an answer to the questions that society asks itself about itself, but this answer is almost always unexpected." And "Ideology converts ideas into masks: they hide the person who wears them, and at the same time they keep him from seeing reality." His quotability also demonstrates his grasp of diverse cultures—not only what is foreign to him but what is specific to, say, China or India—and his ability to convey what he sees. The most fascinating passages—to me, at any rate—show his insight into another foreign culture: our own.

Despite its multiplicity of themes, the book has a unity—a unity of concern. Paz cares deeply for the development of democracy in Latin America, which he feels is threatened intellectually by the popularity of Marxism, physically by the invasion of Soviet power, and practically by the United States' ineptitude in foreign policy. I do not know how Americans will read his apt and eloquent criticisms of Marxism and Russian policy. Marxism is not very influential here, nor is the Soviet Union widely esteemed. For North American readers, he is preaching, though brilliantly, to the converted. (p. 134)

Reading Paz's views of the United States, I found myself reflecting on the relation between one's sense of oneself and one's sense of national identity. If I had been born and raised in Wilhelmine Germany, would I have grown up to feel myself encircled? I find references to the United States as big, strong, and rich somewhat unsettling, because I think I am none of these. Paz's vision of us as a northern giant—sometimes cruel, sometimes foolish, and invariably clumsy in dealing with his southern neighbors—is shocking. Do *I* look like that? Perhaps because I have always loved comedy, I have believed that we Americans were, first, last, and always, funny—creators of comedy, consumers of comedy, and subjects of comedy—and have tended to suspect the testimony of those who find us imposing, let alone scary. I still do. But I accept much of what Paz says, because so much of it agrees with our own self-descriptions. And then, too, many of his accounts of the way we are strike me as exactly the way things should be—for example, our separation of state and church and our large number of believers. I think there is a causal connection: when people choose the church they support, they care for it. The text is "Where your treasure is, there will your heart be also" (Matthew 6:21). When Paz comments on the historical novelty of the United States' allocating "ultimate ends"—"questions and answers as to life and its meaning"—to "the private domain," I cannot imagine any other arrangement: certainly not a government functionary probing the state of my soul. He remarks, however, that the absence of a single dominant belief and of a sense of national historical purpose makes it difficult to say what all our activity is for—what we are about collectively. I am not sure there is any advantage in a culture that is easy to sum up. I think we have another way of being American. My school memories suggest that being an American was a matter not of belonging to a collectivity with a shared faith or mission but of becoming a certain kind of person—for example, one who was not snobbish. This early indoctrination in egalitarianism, which Paz believes has limited

the political influence of intellectuals, has, of course, had many other political effects. Paz is disturbed that justified protest movements against genuine inequities in Latin America often become tools of the Communists. He suggests that young rebels are attracted by the Communists' "organization and discipline." This seems a difference in national or cultural personalities. Americans do not like élites or insiders, and when we discover a disciplined cell within a group we have joined we try to break it up or vote it down. I daresay our desire to scatter power does make us hard to read.

Yet I think Paz is reading me all too well when he writes, "If they could, Americans would lock themselves up inside their country and turn their backs on the whole world, except to trade with it and visit it." He forces me to recognize my own irrational irritation at our need to have a foreign policy, and my profound and unrealistic feeling that for the United States foreign affairs are a distraction from our real business, which is to make our own country better. When he comments on our virtues and remarks on the likelihood of our becoming "the first multiracial democracy in history," I find myself excited at the prospect of an achievement worth working for, but it is hard for me to think of a foreign-policy purpose with equal enthusiasm. Paz accuses us of every kind of insensitivity in our foreign relations, and mentions not only the extensive list of our sins in Latin America but the fact that in domestic arguments about foreign policy Americans seem not to care if they help the Russians. I suppose this is true, and I wonder whether being citizens of a great power affects our personalities with what looks like arrogance, in the sense that we do not feel as nervous about being overheard as citizens of small powers do. It is very hard to imagine being somebody else, and Paz made me think back to the nineteen-thirties, when people in the small nations of Europe worried what impression their public statements made on the Germans. We remain touchy about any limitation on our freedom of speech, and find it difficult to imagine both what it would be like to be forced to whisper and what it is like for foreigners who listen to us shout at each other.

It is undeniable that, as Paz alleges, our foreign policy zigzags; that it has usually been responsive to domestic interests; and—as Paz does not remark—that many of our foreign-policy debates have been fights for party advantage. These phenomena may be inescapable drawbacks of democracy—a system that Paz, in agreement with Tocqueville, regards as inherently ineffective in foreign policy. Yet cultures that have produced men whom historians regard as great diplomats—Talleyrand and Metternich, for two examples—are societies in which none of us would wish to live. Here is a puzzler. I am not sure I thank Paz for posing it. Being ourselves seems irresponsible because we are a great power, but it also seems that we are permitted to be ourselves—noisy, disorganized, indifferent to outsiders, and, I insist, comic—because we are a great power.

Another reason our foreign policy has been poor, Paz argues, is that Americans have always been so strongly oriented toward the future that we lack a sense of history. I doubt this. The foreign-policy uses of history have been national self-glorification, the promotion of a mission, and the cultivation of grievances and grudges. Along with not being snobbish, being American means not staying mad. (We can scarcely remember that the British burned Washington, while the Russians are never allowed to forget that the French burned Moscow. I do not think that the Slavs have a superior sense of history: they use the fact of having been invaded to justify invading others, and never mention that their own diplomatic blundering brought on 1812, 1914, and 1941.) Paz, however, goes further in indicting the United States. He thinks that our very foundation was an attempt to abolish history, and to place our country outside it. I think, however, that the American effort was something else: it reflected that element of the Enlightenment which wanted to do away with all the prehistory that is entwined with history. Modernization—the abolition of prehistory, with its baggage of sacred monarchy and castes and shamans—is a difficult process, because prehistory keeps reasserting itself in new guises. When we consider prehistory, we are astonished by the ingenuity of its inhabitants but bemused by their preference for ideas or theories over reality (which inclines them to magic) and horrified by their lack of respect for human rights. The work of modernization did not begin with us and has not been a uniquely American project. Here is an example from *The Men Who Ruled India,* by Philip Mason (1985). He tells of a Captain Campbell who in the nineteenth century persuaded the Khonds of Orissa to cease their system of human sacrifice by asking if their crops grew better or their men were stronger than those of the tribes who did not sacrifice human beings. It seems to me that, allowing for differences in time, place, and national and personal style, Paz's essays attempt to bring that sort of rational question before the peoples of all the Americas. (pp. 137-38)

Naomi Bliven, "As Others See Us," in The New Yorker, *Vol. LXI, No. 33, October 7, 1985, pp. 134, 137-38.*

COLIN WELCH

'A book that pleases me is like a woman whose charms seduce me into an affair with her. I couldn't care less about her family, her birthplace, her class, her relatives, her education, her childhood, her friends. . . .' No, it is not Senor Paz talking, but some raving Frenchman into whose company he unluckily falls on page 190 [of *One Earth, Four or Five Worlds: Reflections on Contemporary History*]. Sr Paz does himself a great injustice by quoting such twaddle with approval; admittedly I do him another by giving it prominence. His book greatly pleased me. As an inevitable result I have become greatly interested in his family, birthplace and the rest. . . .

Sr Paz's book is in no sense an autobiography, unless all books are; but it has told me something about his birthplace, assuming that to be Mexico, about his education, obviously superb, and his friends, or at least about the excellent company he keeps in his reading.

All I had heard about him before was that he was a Mexican poet and intellectual who had won a peace prize. These will seem to many grave charges indeed. Yet after reading his book I must pronounce him innocent or almost innocent of them all. From the national, professional and mental deformations perhaps unjustly associated with the state of being Mexican or poet or intellectual or recipient of peace prizes he is free, or almost free. (p. 39)

To be a Mexican or Latin American intellectual is to have been unconsciously shaped by a Spanish past you have rejected. You were born with the Counter-Reformation and neo-Scholasticism—that is, according to Sr Paz, 'against the modern world'. Your mother was prodigiously fertile in the arts and literature, but theology closed her eyes to new thought: she produced no Descartes, Spinoza, Leibniz, Galileo or Newton. The modern age began by criticising first principles; Spanish

Neo-Thomism defended them as necessary, eternal and inviolable, regarding reason as valuable only for that purpose. It sought not to explore the unknown but to guard the known. This philosophy disappeared from Latin America in the 18th century; yet the attitudes it engendered still survive. Latin American intellectuals have successively embraced liberalism, positivism and now Marxism. Their ideas are always today's (if Marxism be today's), their attitudes yesterday's. Their forefathers swore by St Thomas, they by St Karl. Still for these radicalised Jesuits and crusaders is reason the armed servant of a revealed Truth. Ideas are for them a mask, preventing them from seeing reality or being seen. Still they swallow and regurgitate lies about communism which cannot be repeated elsewhere (really, Sr Paz?). Self-blindfolded, they refuse to see what is happening in, say, Nicaragua before their very eyes.

Of course, this picture can't be wholly true. Sr Paz, a Latin American intellectual himself, proves that as he paints it. But he must be very lonely. And what does he see in Nicaragua?

The fall (to him welcome) of Somoza at once awakened in him fears of a Cuban-style dictatorship, the beginning of terrible conflicts in Central America, contagious phenomena, impossible to isolate, bound to spread to Mexico, Venezuela and Colombia. Since then he has seen in Nicaragua regimentation and militarisation, attacks on the one free newspaper, thought control, internal espionage, leaders who speak and act in an increasingly dictatorial way, all signs of another revolution that will end in totalitarian petrification. He sees that Mexico's traditional policy of non-intervention is now 'inadequate'; she has principles and interests to defend. 'We want democratic and peaceful regimes in our continent. We want friends, not armed agents of an imperial power.'

And what does Sr Paz see in Cuba? Nothing to his taste. . . . (pp. 39-40)

If Castro is a totalitarian dictator of a sort entirely new to Latin America, which has known so many dictators, and totally subservient to and dependent on Moscow, Sr Paz is to my mind over-inclined to blame Washington for all that. A virulent anti-Americanism is epidemic among Latin American intellectuals. Sr Paz notes with distaste many examples, including the 'liberation theologians' for whom American imperialism is 'the prefiguration of the Anti-Christ'. From this deformation too Sr Paz is in general quite free. His picture of the United States is understanding, thoughtful, loving, even envious in a quite innocent way. In particular he denounces as itself 'monstrous' any attempt to equate the United States and the Soviet Union as twin monsters. Yet incongruous carpings at America do stain his pages, as if inserted by some 'liberation theologian', though an unusually polite and intelligible one. Was it perhaps this theologian who speaks ritually of the 'victims of European imperialism', in a world in which, for instance, the average income of the people of Zaire has declined ten-fold since the Belgians left?

Sr Paz chides Washington for its 'insensitivity and obtuseness' during the first phase of the Cuban revolution, 'before it was taken over by the communist bureaucracy': now when was that? 'Washington's disdainful and hostile policy', he continues, 'threw Castro into Russia's arms.' Is this not historically untrue? Was not Castro always in Russia's arms? If so, Sr Paz sees clearly now in Nicaragua what he failed to see in Cuba, and still fails to see: 'a regime transforming itself day by day . . . into a communist dictatorship.' Why? Perhaps because he is now a sadder and wiser man, yet cannot yet bring himself to part with every cherished illusion.

Moreover, by chiding Washington for not having been more forthcoming with the young Castro, Sr Paz contradicts himself. More in sorrow than in anger, he charges United States imperialism not with inventing Latin American dictatorships, indeed, but of exploiting them for profit, to further its interests and to dominate. Washington, he declares, has been in Latin America 'the protector of tyrants'. Yet Castro was always a tyrant, first *in posse,* then *in esse.* Should Washington have embraced and protected him to further its interests? Well?

Is it the theologian who causes Sr Paz to declare that plutocracy (presumably in the United States) 'provokes and accentuates inequality; inequality in turn makes political freedoms and individual rights nothing more than illusions. Here Marx's criticisms went straight to the heart of the matter'? Did they? If so, what value can Sr Paz set on the freedoms and rights extinguished by Castro and to a lesser extent by Batista? They were only illusions! American plutocracy, Sr Paz concedes, 'creates abundance'. It is thus able to lighten 'the burden of unjust differences between individuals and classes. But it has done so by shifting the most scandalous inequalities from the national scene to the international.' Doesn't this suggest that America's abundance is in some way derived from the poverty of others? Were there no poor before America became rich? Is there not less poverty wherever America is free to trade and aid? As Sr Paz, a student of Hobbes, should know well, the world in which America has prospered has always been full of poverty, as of tyrants. She did not create them. They are for her unwelcome *data.* (pp. 40-1)

*Colin Welch, "A Mexican Poet and Intellectual?"
in* The Spectator, *Vol. 255, No. 8213, December 7,
1985, pp. 39-41.*

PAUL WEST

The Mexican philosopher-poet Octavio Paz writes with winning informality, honoring the externals of life [in *On Poets and Others*], its tone, its casual encounters, mocking the pomp with which many intellectuals handle ideas. . . . His anecdotal mood is hard to resist, and I don't think he works it just for variety's sake; it is more that he sees ideas in a narrative context and finds himself—as walker, caller, observer, friend, opponent—an interesting piece of the universe on the move.

Sometimes, however, this relaxed mood gets him into less engaging postures. One essay begins: "The death of Jean Paul Sartre, after the initial shock this kind of news produces, aroused in me a feeling of resigned melancholy." Of course: it hardly needs saying, whereas sometimes what he says doesn't need saying at all. He ends the first of his two essays on Solzhenitsyn thus: "I say this with sadness, and humility." Anyone finishing *The Gulag Archipelago* will feel the same, at the very least. . . .

Still, Paz has much to say that is worth hearing, although I felt let down by his heavily political pair of essays on Solzhenitsyn. I wish he had heeded *The Gulag's* subtitle: "An Experiment in Literary Investigation," or the literary quality, the involutedly elliptical strategies, of Solzhenitsyn's rhetoric. Paz rightly tells us that the Russian's voice is "not modern but ancient" and that *The Gulag* is "a witnessing," but then gets off into villainous names—the Cheka, Mao, Fidel, Lenin, Marx—until Solzhenitsyn gets lost in a prison camp of a new kind: of abstract politicism, however rightminded.

The best of this book is concise, visionary stuff such as we find in the essay on Whitman ("One ought rather to speak of the invention of America than of its discovery") and that on the poet Charles Tomlinson: "The world turns to air, temperature, sensation, thought; and we become stone, window, orange peel, turf, oil stain, helix." This is his way of fleshing out his point that in Tomlinson's poems "outer reality . . . is a climate which involves us," and the same is true too of Paz's best essays. . . .

Paz is at his most refreshing and stimulating when he gets allusive and complex, when he takes a chance or two, as in "The great invention of man is men" (though you could make a case for the reverse too). On a point, he tends to harp; off it, he lets his mind and memory unfurl, making lively fusions of the trivial with the grand. As he himself says, the essayist "must be diverse, penetrating, acute, fresh, and he must master the difficult art of using three dots." I wonder about those dots. Sometimes the essayist must elide, of course, but must also expose ideas to the wind, to the noise of buses, the sound of children coughing, even if only to evince thereby the big buzzing blooming confusion that the chastest, severest essays ignore in order to achieve inductive purity. Sometimes, the essayist must use irrelevance.

Some of these essays have appeared in another book (*Alternating Current*), most notably the brilliant, ground-breaking one on Henri Michaux and mescaline. . . .

There is a lovely essay here on William Carlos Williams, whom Paz understands in the profoundest way, rightly drawing attention to Williams' doctrine that "art does not imitate nature: it imitates its creative processes." This is Paz's view too, and it is instructive, as well as somewhat amusing, to find him applying it to the Spanish poets Jorge Guillén and Luis Cernuda, to Baudelaire and André Breton. Paz is hardly ever Procrustean, relishing instead the fluidity and mercuriality of the human mind. "Man does not speak," he writes, "because he thinks but thinks because he speaks." I find his emphasis on the helplessness of human brilliance both moving and timely, most of all when he says, a propos of André Breton, "The I does not save itself because it does not exist." Identity for him, whoever he is, is a process, not a fixity.

All the more praise to him, then, for achieving so consistent a tone in these essays; you would never mistake him for anyone else, oddly enough. It is one of the predictable oddities of minds as open as his that they sometimes, like Paz when he shuffles around a bit before starting, behave as their own gatekeepers, nervous at being responsible for so vast a terrain. For him the Territory is cosmic, the Frontier is mental, while Art is "a bridge" alluding to something it never names, a something "which is identical with nothing." No wonder he seems like a thought with a thousand arms.

Paul West, "Paz, Poetry and People," in Book
World—The Washington Post, *January 25, 1987, p.
10.*

ALFRED CORN

Octavio Paz is among those poet-critics whose prose counts as much as his poetry in any consideration of his achievement. A series of definitive books like *The Labyrinth of Solitude, The Bow and the Lyre, Alternating Current, Conjunctions and Disjunctions,* and others, shows him to be a cultural critic with skills that resemble, at one extreme, Tocqueville's, and, at the other, Valéry's. He can comment with great cogency on the national character of Mexico or Spain as well as on the paradoxes of poetic composition. His career has included long sojourns in Europe, the United States, and India, occasions for the beginner's customary contact and acquaintance with influential artists and cultural figures of his time—in Paz's case, Pablo Neruda, André Breton, Luis Buñuel, José Ortega y Gasset, Jean-Paul Sartre, Antonio Machado, Jorge Guillén, and, among North Americans, Robert Frost, William Carlos Williams, and Elizabeth Bishop. His knowledge of European and South and North American literature is profound, to which he adds an anthropological and cultural familiarity with the pre-Columbian culture of his homeland, plus a devotee's understanding of the religion and literature of Asia. Among Latin American writers, he is the most universal. . . . (p. 45)

[*On Poets and Others*] is a collection of disparate essays drawn from the forties right up to the eighties. (p. 46)

One very powerful current in the book as it stands is a political critique of communism, occasioned by considerations of the work and public pronouncements of Sartre and of Solzhenitsyn. Octavio Paz's first enthusiasm for communism began to fade when he encountered the Popular Front in Spain at the time of the Civil War. With the Nazi-Soviet pact, he saw clearly that the god had failed, and he was ever after an opponent of Stalinism. In 1951 he published an article in the Argentinean journal *Sur* about Soviet concentration camps, an article which put him out of favor with most Latin American intellectuals. Paz sees that the dominance of the United States in Latin America and much of the Third World is unacceptable, but he does not propose Soviet-style communism as an alternative. His essay on Solzhenitsyn, fiercely reasonable and convincing, makes important distinctions. Solzhenitsyn merits admiration for his courage, his artistry, and for his refusal to accept secular American culture as a replacement for more vivifying values. Paz parts company with Solzhenitsyn over his proposal of Orthodox Christianity and Pan-Slavism as the antidote to Soviet repression and the spiritual vacancy of the United States. Understanding Solzhenitsyn's effort is part of Paz's own task of contributing ideas toward a South American solution to South American problems:

> Our failure to adapt democratic institutions, in their two modern versions—the Anglo-Saxon and the French—ought to compel us to think on our own account, without looking through the spectacles of modish ideology. . . . We need to *name* our past, to find political and juridical forms to integrate it and transform it into a creative force. Only thus will we be free.

The emphasis of this book is not mainly political. There is an appealing memoir about a meeting with Robert Frost in the early forties; an account of his association with Breton, and with Buñuel; an essay on Baudelaire's art criticism; reflections on Henri Michaux's experiments with mescaline and artistic expression; exploratory essays on the poetry of Guillén, Luis Cernuda, and William Carlos Williams. Paz's grasp of our literary tradition is not superficial, to judge by this comment taken from the article on Williams:

> *Paterson* belongs to the poetic genre invented by modern American poetry which oscillates between the *Aeneid* and a treatise on political economy, the *Divine Comedy* and journalism: huge collections of fragments, the most imposing example of which is Pound's *Cantos*. All these poems, obsessed as much by a desire to *speak* the American reality as to *make*

it, are the contemporary descendants of Whitman, and all of them, one way or another, set out to fulfill the prophecy of *Leaves of Grass*.

I have copied many excerpts from these essays into my commonplace book but, unwilling to consign them to that relative oblivion, include them here as well: "Just as criticism becomes a creation by analogy, so creation is also criticism because it is historical. In constant battle with the past, modern art is in conflict with itself. The art of our time lives and dies of modernity" ("**Baudelaire as Art Critic**"). . . . And from [**"José Ortega y Gasset"**]:

> We are living an Ending, but ending is no less fascinating and worthy than beginning. Endings and beginnings resemble each other: at the outset, poetry and thought were united; then an act of rational violence divided them; today they tend, almost at random, to come together again.

(pp. 46-8)

Alfred Corn, "The Poet's Criteria," in The Yale Review, *Vol. 77, No. 1, Autumn, 1987, pp. 41-51.*

SVEN BIRKERTS

Paz is at once dialectical and poetical. His conceptual oppositions vie at every turn with the imperatives of metaphoric formulation. The mind is always pushing its way forward by way of assertion and negation, plying among theses and antitheses in order to reach some still-point of synthesis. Any arrival, however, is but a preparation for the next departure. An inspection of Paz's poetry, or his myriad writings on literature, art, tantrism, or Mexican culture will convince anyone that the man whose name means "peace" never has any.

Born in a suburb of Mexico City in 1914, Paz has been his country's busiest thinker and man of letters for the better part of our century. If Mexico is, as is often asserted, the land that the European Enlightenment bypassed (it experienced the reaction of the Counter-Reformation instead), then Paz can be seen as one of the bearers of lost light. He has grappled with the historical and artistic legacies of both hemispheres; he has directed the concentrated rays of international modernism upon the dark mythic strata of pre- and post-colonial Mexico; and he has successfully combined the implicitly political role of the public intellectual with the solitary gestations required by the poetic muse—no small task.

Assembling between covers the poetic output of this dynamo is a bit like trying to hang a stationary frame around a Catherine wheel. Poem by poem, of course, the centrifugal bursts of his talent are arrested within lines and stanzas. But the cumulative effect of any larger sequence is of a motion very much at odds with the customarily tranquil development of a poet's career.

Readers, then, should be alerted. The beautifully designed, classic-looking *The Collected Poems of Octavio Paz, 1957-1987* is not a memorial slab—Paz in his mid-70s is creating valorously. But neither is the book's enormous heft a token of uncontested greatness. The contents manifest a profusion that becomes at times unruly: poems of great distinction are set out side by side with less engaging exploratory exercises. Only on the plane of translation is the uniformity of excellence certain. Paul Blackburn, Elizabeth Bishop, Charles Tomlinson, Mark Strand, Lysander Kemp, Denise Levertov, John Frederick Nims, and Eliot Weinberger, who has rendered the bulk of the poetry, are as fine a team of translators as any writer could dream of having. This is not to say that there will not be quibbles. . . .

The assertion implicit in Weinberger's editing—which will not be contested here—is that Paz first came into his own with the publication of his tour-de-force long poem *Sunstone* (1957), which is the opening selection. He had been writing poems for decades already (an *Early Poems, 1935-1955* was published [in 1973]), but with this performance he is ready to start making his mark on international literature. Indeed, in its ambitiously synthetic momentum, *Sunstone* can be viewed as an important precursor of the innovative work of Carlos Fuentes, Gabriel García-Márquez, Julio Cortazar, and other writers of the celebrated "boom" of the 1960s.

Sunstone is written as a single circular sentence—its end joining its beginning—of 584 11-syllable lines. Its structural basis is the circular Aztec calendar, which measures the synodic period of the planet Venus. (I take this from the helpful "Author's Notes" at the back.) But the reader need not be alarmed by this esoteric correlative design. While it organizes the work, it does not circumscribe its subject. *Sunstone* is, like so many of Paz's longer poems, a lyrically discursive exploration of time and memory, of erotic love, of art and writing, of myth and mysticism. The axis is the urgently ruminating "I"; the links between one flight and the next, often between one line and the next, are forged by the relentless alchemical transformations of metaphor. . . . (p. 36)

Paz's procedure allows him to create a vast and fluid-feeling panorama of the psyche in intensified motion, with all of its dilations and shifts. The hazard is one that threatens all such inclusive (and, yes, baroque) undertakings: that the pressure of necessity will be vitiated by the too-bountiful imaginings, that the progress on the page will at times resemble a free-for-all of competing ideas and images. Stunning as Paz's cadenzas can be, the reader may long at times for a clearer sense of directional development. (Paz's polymorphous tendency is encouraged, I suspect, by the vowel-rich sonorities of the Spanish language; it would be difficult to generate so hypnotic a flow of sounds in our Anglo-Saxon-based tongue).

Though Paz's reigning structural conceit in *Sunstone* harks back to the indigenous Aztecs, his poetic art strongly reflects the influence of André Breton and the French surrealists, as well as the deep Symbolist heritage running back through Eliot to Rimbaud. . . . Paz is clearly less interested in subject matter than he is in recreating the momentum of psychic—and spiritual—processes. *Sunstone* is as much about the porosity of boundaries and the frailty of the ego as it is about the solar mythologies of the Aztecs.

One does not have to read far to discover a rather striking artistic split at the core of Paz's endeavor. Throughout the compendium, long, all-embracing poems of the *Sunstone* variety alternate with short, stripped-down lyrics. The latter are often lyrically superior—cleaner, more mysterious, less didactic—but they bear no freight of ideas. It is almost as if these were the two warring sides of the poet's nature—a will to proliferation and a will to asceticism. (pp. 36-7)

In 1962, when he was 48, Paz was appointed to the post of Mexican ambassador to India. Out of the 6-year period that he served—the key years of poetic maturity—came the collection *Ladera Este*, or *Eastern Slope*. The impact of Indian religious creeds on a sensibility avid for spiritual syntheses was, predictably, immense. Paz already suspected the fortified boundaries of the ego. Now, for a time, he would seek to tear asunder the veil of Maya (or "illusion"). Here, for instance, are some lines from **"Reading John Cage,"** a remarkable fusion of Paz's avant-garde inclinations and his more mystical probings:

> It is not the same,
> hearing the footsteps of the afternoon
> 　　among the trees and houses,
> 　　　　　　　　　　　and
> 　　seeing this same afternoon
> 　　among the same trees and
> 　　houses now
> 　　　　　　after reading
> *Silence:*
> 　　Nirvana is Samsara,
> 　　　silence is music.

Even more ethereally pitched is Paz's long fugal poem *Blanco,* which reads in places like some Eastern holy text. . . . (p. 37)

Paz is not the first Occidental poet to have embraced Oriental ways. The great Swedish poet Gunnar Ekelöf put himself through a similar sea-change; and both Gary Snyder and Allen Ginsberg have, for periods, brought their aesthetics in line with the practice of Eastern religious disciplines. The marriage of strains has often resulted, as it did in some of Paz's poetry of the time, in a haunting, if peculiar, music.

But the Indian period was not to last. The 1968 massacre of student demonstrators by government troops at the Mexico City Olympiad stunned Paz. He resigned his post in protest and returned home. Though he had long since broken with the leftist orthodoxy of the Latin American intelligentsia, he had no tolerance for the repressions of the state's pretend democracy, either. His gesture marked him as a radical without an ideological portfolio—a status that continues to irk many of his countrymen.

The poetry from this turbulent epoch (1969-1975) was collected in *Vuelta,* or *Return.* (*Vuelta* is also the name of the cultural journal that Paz began to edit at this time.) The poet appeared to be turning away from the quietistic meditations of his India years. A poem like the title-piece, **"Return,"** reveals a preoccupation with the crises of the day, and sequences of sharply surrealistic imagery expose a distinctly non-transcendental point of vantage:

> We have dug up Rage
> The amphitheater of the genital sun is a dungheap
> The fountain of lunar water is a dungheap
> The lovers' park is a dungheap
> The library is a nest of killer rats
> The university is a muck full of frogs
> The altar is Chanfalla's swindle
> The eggheads are stained with ink
> The doctors dispute in a den of thieves

Once again, Ginsberg comes to mind, this time the Ginsberg of "Howl" (1956). We see the same effort in both writers to find a declamatory idiom adequate to the outrageous character of contemporary events.

Rage is not the only thing that Paz disinterred upon his return. He also became fascinated with the myth of the self and of the past (a fascination that might have signalled the return of the repressed ego). In 1974 Paz published his long poem *A Draft of Shadows.* The epigraph is drawn from Wordsworth's *Prelude:* "A Fair seed-time had my soul, and I grew up / Fostered alike by beauty and by fear." Throughout the poem, Paz attempts through repeated elisions of memory to come to terms with his family history, his own emotional and spiritual experience, and his poetic vocation. He begins with an Eliotic evocation of the mysteries of memory . . . carries on through hundreds of lines figuring phrases in his autobiography . . . and finally concludes with these enigmatically Symbolist lines:

I am where I was:
I walk behind the murmur,
footsteps within me, heard with my eyes,
the murmur is in the mind, I am my footsteps,
I hear the voices that I think,
the voices that think me as I think them.
I am the shadow my words cast.

If Paz had earlier, in *Blanco*, opposed the reality of the world to that of the word, he appears here to have cast his lot with the latter. He is hardly the first poet to have looked to language as the seat of the real—Rimbaud, Mallarmé, Eliot, and Stevens all did—but few poets have subjected their readers at such length to the to-and-fro of the preliminary meditations. Indeed, this might well be the main complaint against this grand *oeuvre*: that it asks us to track what are often just the reflex actions of a soul bent on transcending the here and now. When Paz is at his best, we can feel the struggle pressurizing the verse. But there are too many instances of the mind milling abstract nouns, and too many patches of "sublime" musing that come across more as a conjuring with verbal counters than as a pitched battle with necessity. This unevenness keeps Paz from being a poet of the very first order—the ore keeps disappearing inside the bedrock. (pp. 37-8)

[*The Collected Poems of Octavio Paz, 1957-1987*] concludes with the hitherto uncollected poems of *Arbol Adentro* (*A Tree Within, 1976-1987*). Paz's spiritual battles continue unabated. It may be tempting to read the more recent poems as episodes in an elderly poet's confrontation with mortality. And the evidence can be found for such a tack. In the long poem "**Preparatory Exercise (Diptych with votive tablet),**" for instance, the speaker laments: "The Buddha did not teach me how to die." But an open-eyed assessment shows a contrary development as well. Many of these poems give us Paz at his most celebratory—and most youthful. He sounded older at 40 when he was tormenting himself with metaphysics. Now, in places, we heed a sprightlier voice, a vision that looks to the earthly as well as to the ineffable. . . . Paz's career may yet have room for a poetry of earth. (p. 39)

Sven Birkerts, "Rage and Return," in The New Republic, *Vol. 198, No. 11, March 14, 1988, pp. 36-9.*

HELEN VENDLER

Nothing in the visible estrangement of poetry from prose is more astonishing than their estrangement in one person. Octavio Paz—Mexico's famous poet, born in 1914—is a torrential writer, whose successive books of prose and verse have enriched our century; while his prose is often circumstantial, historical, and evidential, his poetry is not. It is something else. Someone reading the verse as one reads prose might say, "Abstract, generalizing, unreal." But someone reading the verse as one reads verse would say, "Musical, sensual, real." When a single historical writer slips into two such different gears, some explanation is required. For Paz, the political real (present in all his essays) is not the desired real (aspired to in all his poems). In his divided self Paz replicates what he has said of the history of his country:

The history of Mexico is the history of a man seeking his parentage, his origins. He has been influenced at one time or another by France, Spain, the United States and the militant indigenists of his own country,

and he crosses history like a jade comet, now and then giving off flashes of lightning. What is he pursuing in his eccentric course? He wants to go back beyond the catastrophe he suffered: he wants to be a sun again.

The return to origins is for Paz a social ideal; it will throw off the alien mentalities of the Conquistadores, the Jesuits, and Enlightenment rationalist positivism, thereby allowing Mexico a non-European, non-North American existence. Paz's Shelleyan hopes refuse the larger, Yeatsian view that all change—even imposed change, like that of conquest—is proof of human creativity. Yeats' Chinese sages stare on the tragic scene with gaiety, seeing only the enlivening spectacle of temporal change. Paz, though he appreciates and meditates on the Buddhist equation of the phenomenal world with the void, finally falls into the ranks of reformist humanists. He is called to utterance, especially in his prose, by the immense social, intellectual, and aesthetic needs of Mexico—a state still in the process of active formation. (p. 97)

Paz has vowed to recover radical innocence—whatever in Mexico (or in himself) survives from a pre-Conquest, non-Christian past.

Paz's own part-Indian descent, strongly marked in his features, may account in part for his mission, but it is also true that his youthful Marxism and modernism repudiated the religious and political status quo into which he was born. . . . Paz's quest may have been determined at birth: coming into the world with the surname Peace is, for a poet, itself a destiny.

The sumptuous *Collected Poems of Octavio Paz, 1957-1987* . . . [contains poems written after the span of Paz's early career (1935-1955) covered in *Selected Poems* (1963)]. "To be a sun again"—this ambition means that in poetry Paz must speak as the sun would speak. It would speak from its own turbulent and radiant center, the voice of action, not reaction; origin, not consequence; morality, not acculturation; innocence, not conviction of guilt. In short, Paz's poetic voice aims to be not that of the historical man but in the strictest sense an assumed voice—prophetic, solar, essential, erotic.

For Paz, imagined unity is historically recoverable, chiefly in a sensuality motivated by love. (Sexual intercourse without love does not interest Paz, nor does a sexless, platonic love.) The importance of eroticism for Paz—as an engagement in which the shell of the self is broken, depression is vanquished by joy, the other is perceived to be a part of, and consequently as real as, the self, and only the present is actual—guarantees the persistence of the erotic theme through Paz's fifty years of writing. For him, eroticism answers not only solipsism but also historical determinism, geographical difference, and even the mortality of the body. It is, says the poem "**Axis,**" the spindle on which the world turns. This poem uses interpenetration of natural essences to mime the physical reconfigurations made by two interlaced bodies. (pp. 97-8)

It is tempting, in the light of such poems, to describe Paz as a writer confined to archetypal symbols; and critics who do not examine the Spanish original are likely to yield to the temptation. But symbols alone—even the powerful, elemental ones (water, fire, forest, etc.) on which Paz relies—never made a poem. A poem is a system of relations composed of subsystems of relations—musical, rhythmic, structural, semantic, tonal. In "**Axis,**" for example, an intricate pattern of repetitions moving left to right, right to left, governs one phrase and its variations in time:

> Through the conduits of blood . . .
> Through the conduits of bone . . .
> Through the conduits of night . . .
> Through the conduits of sun . . .
> Through the conduits of the body.

Another system of relations governs the several words ("blood," "body," "fountain," "night," "wheat," "forest") that in the ritual dance of **"Axis"** change places between the man and the woman. After calling himself "red wheat," "night," and "water," the male speaker attributes these nouns to the woman, calling her "you, nighttime of wheat," "you, water waiting." And, lest it be thought that she only borrows embodiment from him, the poem makes her a "fountain of night" and "forest" before he, in turn, becomes night or forest, and before their bodies become joint fountains. As he remakes her, she remakes him. In Paz's reworking of Petrarchan love, the erotic exchange is to be an equal one, and this ideal is represented in formal terms when the symbols of love are seen to be deliberately balanced and exchanged between male and female.

"Axis" is a good example of the generalizing and symbolist Paz. When Paz does become particular, even confessional, he does so after a gradual, meditative progress from the whole to the part. (pp. 98-9)

Between . . . autobiographical poems and the incantatory ones we read Paz's panoramic descriptions of contemporary Mexican reality, from the savagely disappointed denunciations of **"Return"** (written after Paz resigned the Ambassadorship to India, in 1968, when the Mexican government massacred unarmed students) to the more recent, cinematic **"I Speak of the City"**. . . . The expansiveness visible in the catalogues of **"I Speak of the City"** is a trait found also in Rubén Darío and Pablo Neruda, Paz's great predecessors (both of them influenced by Whitman). Like Whitman, Paz never forgets musicality, even in his most socially panoramic poems. "Form has meaning," he reminds us, "and, what is more, in the realm of art only form possesses meaning." His fidelity to form has kept Paz from subordinating poetry to social commentary, even in his long descriptive poems.

Besides Paz the incantatory and social poet, there is another Paz—an epigrammatic poet. Some of his best poems suggest Emily Dickinson (see **"The Hummingbird"**). **"Epitaph for an Old Woman"** superimposes, with perfect concision, a couple's embrace in death on their embrace in life:

> They buried her in the family grave
> and deep down the dust
> that was once her husband
> > shuddered:
> what was delight in life
> > is grief in death.

A more recent epigrammatic poem offers a definition of poetry, mediating with both wit and profundity between poem as dream and silence and poem as deed and voice. Poetry exists, as the title suggests, **"Between What I See and What I Say"**:

> > it speaks
> what I hush.
> > hushes
> what I speak,
> > dreams
> what I forget.
> > It's not speech:
> it's a deed.
> > It's a deed
> of speech.

(p. 99)

In such poems Paz is the disciple of poets like Bashō, of whose haiku he writes, "The whole world fits inside seventeen syllables."

Fitting the world into syllables in a new way resembles for Paz nothing so much as the radical uniqueness of each sexual act: even with the same partner, there is never identity of mood, moment, sensation. The leap of imaginative energy into embodiment in words and the dispersion of erotic energy in sexual activity seem to Paz virtually identical processes, both in excitation and in dissipation. Each is a proving of the self-in-act upon the pulses of the moment. As the basis of a poetics, this conviction has some dubious results: because words are desperately inadequate (though they are all we have) as representations of sexual sensations and erotic passion, Paz's love poems sometimes seem, even in Spanish, to resemble each other overmuch.

A still riskier poetic enterprise is the representation of nothingness, when Paz's interest in Buddhism leads to attempts to pass beyond the phenomenal to Nirvana. Beyond time passing and time staying, says Paz (somewhat in the manner of Eliot in the "Quartets"), there is a third state, a way of being of a third sort:

> being without being, empty plenitude,
> hour without hours. . . .
> > It is god:
> it inhabits the names that deny it.

This *via negativa* leads in writing to "air that sculpts itself and dissolves, / a fleeting allegory of the true names" of reality.

Perhaps more congenial to Paz's love of imagery is his representation of the work of art as "Veronica's veil / with that faceless Christ that is time." The many European paintings of Veronica's veil intend it often as an allegory of painting itself—the miraculous impression on linen of a divine yet representable image. If, as Paz has said, the true poetic imagination is always a creator of myths, it is also an activity that "feeds upon history, that is to say, upon the language, impulses, myths, and images of its own time." The veil of Veronica exhibits myth and history at once.

Paz worries about his placement, as a poet, between myth and history:

> I am not a historian. My passion is poetry and my
> occupation literature; neither gives me the authority
> to pass judgment on the agitations and upheavals of
> our era.

Nonetheless, he has written persistently on the contemporary scene. He argues that his writing is non-ideological, that he has never written "from a perspective firmly rooted in the certainties of an ideology with encyclopedic pretensions such as Marxism, or in the immutable truths of religions such as Christianity or Islam." Yet to one who does not share it Paz's myth of recoverable permanence—of an essential mythical principle—reads like an ideology. "Modern poets," he has remarked, "looked for the principle of change; poets of the dawning age look for the unalterable principle that is the root of change." To original sin, Paz says, he prefers "the *other* central theme of the West, that of Rousseau and Blake: original innocence." Paz's investigation of Tantric Buddhism, his interest in Tantric art and erotic temple sculpture in India are attempts to understand an undivided consciousness that can dwell in a pure present, a consciousness recoverable for us, he firmly asserts, through "sex, passions, dreams"—especially through sex, where "lovers descend toward always more ancient and naked states: they recover the animal and even the plant that live in each of us.'' All this—radical innocence, changelessness, undivided unity of being, sex as spiritual discipline—has a long history in Western poetry. (See the work of Yeats for another modern instance.) It is a symbolic system, if not an ideology, that is identifiable with Romanticism (as Paz himself asserts). It counters the skeptical, classical, and intellectual emphasis of the Enlightenment. It is not in these beliefs that Paz is original; it is in finding for them an embodiment in contemporary Spanish that he makes a claim upon us, retooling the "arthritic Spanish" of the past into a Mexican present.

This collection offers enormous pleasure to anyone who can read Spanish with the help of an *en face* translation. It is a pity that the translation is not always accurate. (pp. 99-101)

Nonetheless, the *en face* presentation provides, for those of us with only amateur Spanish, a welcome entry into Paz's opulent lyric conceptions and haunting music. We leave with images of Aztec ruins, sunlit odalisques, Indian jungles, and modern cities, having heard hymns, prophecies, denunciations, dirges, and limpid songs. Of these, the most beautiful is the very recent **"Wind and Water and Stone;"** its hypnotic permutations are a permanent addition to the literature of the four elements, even though, as an earthly poem, it must leave out the element of Heaven—fire. I give only the opening stanza, with the translation first:

> The water hollows the stone,
> the wind disperses the water,
> the stone stops the wind.
> Water and wind and stone.
>
> *El agua horada la piedra,*
> *el viento dispersa el agua,*
> *la piedra detiene al viento.*
> *Agua, viento, piedra.*

The three other stanzas are worth looking up, and learning by heart as a charm for living. (p. 101)

> Helen Vendler, "To Be a Sun Again," *in* The New Yorker, *Vol. LXIV, No. 7, April 4, 1988, pp. 97-101.*

ROBERTO GONZÁLEZ ECHEVARRÍA

Octavio Paz is such a masterly presence in the dialogue of Latin American culture that it is easy to forget he is first and foremost a poet. His essays on poetry and poetics—especially in his books *The Bow and the Lyre* (originally published in 1956) and *Children of the Mire* (1974)—and his volumes on Mexican culture, modern art, anthropology and other subjects have been enormously influential. As an essayist Mr. Paz has taken the role José Ortega y Gasset played earlier: he has been a translator in the broadest and profoundest sense. He has made the leading artistic and ideological trends in the world intelligible and relevant to Hispanic culture. And he has fashioned a Spanish capable of speaking the discourse of modernity; even when those of us who write in Spanish disagree with Mr. Paz, we still must do it in the language he has given us. . . .

Mr. Paz is a vestige, an *homme de lettres* alive to all that is happening around him, willing to incorporate everything into his meditation, convinced that his perspective as a literate, nonspecialized observer is one worthy to be taken into account not only by intellectuals but by the public at large. The poet, however, is the founder of the vision. Flashes of Mr. Paz's poetic vision appear in all of his other activities. Latin Amer-

ican politics, cultural or otherwise, have claimed the poetic lives of many, but a reading of *The Collected Poems of Octavio Paz: 1957-1987* reveals that this has not been the case with him; in the polyphony of his voices, the poetic one still rings loudest and clearest. . . .

From this volume a reader could get the impression that, as a poet, Mr. Paz was born fully grown in *Sunstone,* a superb poem that bears traces of the French Surrealist André Breton and scorns the abstractions of metaphysics. In fact, hints of the poet's metaphysical origins remain in it. But *Sunstone* transcends all origins; I can think of nothing the Surrealists wrote that can even come close to this powerful poem. One can understand why Mr. Paz wanted to open *The Collected Poems* with it.

In *Sunstone* a nameless voice appears to be falling through space and time. Falling is a major trope in the poem—an echo of "Altazor," a 1919 work by the Chilean poet Vicente Huidobro, but also, because of the cosmic resonances of the poem, a Dantesque tumbling through the heavens. The anxious voice seeks connectedness. The cosmic debris of historical catastrophes floats by. Love looms as the only salvation; desire must become incarnate in the present, a present in which physical love will provide a momentary sense of order. . . . (p. 24)

But violence and sacrifice appear as offerings to hungry and demanding gods. Christian and Aztec mythology furnishes the background here, but the mythology is given historical embodiment in the figures of Lincoln, Montezuma, Trotsky and the slain President of Mexico, Francisco Madero—leaders assassinated in the pursuit of good. Eros and good are held in precarious balance. At the end of the poem the opening lines are repeated. Unable to reach the plenitude it seeks, the voice falls into repetition, a physical, erotic repetition that joins together disparate echoes in the reader's mind and provides a momentary bliss, a recognition. The repetition also signals the cosmological structure of *Sunstone.* The poem's 584 lines reflect the Aztec calendar's period, as well as the synodical period of the planet Venus (the time between two successive conjunctions of the planet with the sun). Goddess of love in Western mythology, Venus is the guiding star; the voice's fall through time was always measured by eros.

Sunstone provides the master plot of Mr. Paz's poetry and his vision of history. Denuded of its verbal finery, the plot appears reductive. But it is far from it in the poetic texts, in the drama of poetic self-creation. This poet lives in and through the desire, the nostalgia sometimes, for sacredness, a sacredness briefly revealed in the ruins of ancient religions or in quivering bodies moved by always-present love. That master plot continues to furnish the subtext of poems written in the 1960's and 70's, poems in which there is an increasing appearance of the city as the site of historical catastrophe and of the East as a landscape strewn with ruins left by colonialism but also as a place in which a sense of the sacred abides. Utopia remains an erotic feast. The copulating figures in Indian architecture defy the shattering effect of history and return to an origin in which the poet can reinvest the ruins with sacredness.

In his 1960 book, *Homage and Desecrations,* Mr. Paz rewrote "Constant Love Beyond Death," a famous sonnet by the 17th-century poet Francisco Quevedo, thereby claiming as his poetic antecedents the baroque poets, whose echoes were audible in his poetry much earlier. His return to the baroque is emblematic. Realizing that the language inherited from the Spanish-language Romantics was derivative and hollow, modern Spanish poets reached back to Quevedo, his contemporary Luis de Góngora and their disciples as the only worthy models, poets who had achieved an original poetic revolution. Mr. Paz is torn between the glittering, imagistic world of Góngora and the wit, paradox and sober vision of Quevedo, but he seems to settle finally on the latter as a mentor, and on the 17th-century Mexican nun and poet Sor Juana Inés de la Cruz. Quevedo's language, oscillating between excrement and the most purified love, repulsion and desire, is particularly appropriate for Mr. Paz's sense of the failure of history.

His homage to Quevedo and Sor Juana continues in his poetry after 1960, especially in **"Clear Night,"** a stupendous poem that rivals *Sunstone* and reveals much about Mr. Paz's mature poetry. A punk in the subway has written the letters "l," "o," "v" and "e" on the fingers of one of his hands, which caresses his girlfriend. During an infernal night in Paris, this inscription establishes cosmic connections with an erotic force that again appears as a salvation:

> oh hand collar around the eager neck of life
> thirsty horse and falcon's quarry
> hand full of eyes in the night of the body
> tiny sun and cool river
> hand that brings resurrection and dreams.

It is important to understand the original title of the poem. Mr. Weinberger's translation, **"Clear Night,"** is a bit tangential. **"Noche en Claro"** means a sleepless night. That is a key to understanding Mr. Paz, who revels in the lucidity of insomnia, in the half light of a city left to lovers, fugitives and other marginals. These ironically visionary poems, such as *A Draft of Shadows* and **"Clear Night,"** are Mr. Paz's best.

A significant change appears in poems written between 1969 and 1975, contained in a book titled **Return.** An unassuaged bitterness and pessimism predominate. What returns are spent utopian dreams that have become nightmares. In the remarkable **"San Ildefonso Nocturne"** Mr. Paz laments the emergence of a political clergy of the left who, like the Jesuits of another age, are willing to overlook or even justify the most horrendous atrocities. The poem contains satire of the bitterest kind, directed against all the bureaucracies the utopias of the West have turned into. What has happened to him and others like him, the poet asks, who in their youth wanted to "set the world right"? "Some / became secretaries to the secretary / to the General Secretary of the Inferno." The bitter apprenticeship of the young poet, at odds with his family, comes back also, as part of a larger disillusionment. The way back is littered with the debris of a personal history. The images become more introspective, an inner panorama with no correspondence in the world outside. This is particularly true of *A Draft of Shadows*—a sequel or response to **"Clear Night."** In it Mr. Paz returns to an astounding image of the globe as a gourd filled with dried seeds. The world is a giant rattle, shaken by God, to make meaningless sounds with seeds that can no longer germinate. The rattle cannot produce a harmonious music of the spheres. (pp. 24-5)

Roberto González Echevarría, "Cosmic Connections and Erotic Salvation," in The New York Times Book Review, *May 15, 1988, pp. 24-5.*

Sylvia Plath

1932-1963

(Also wrote under pseudonym of Victoria Lucas) American poet, novelist, short story writer, essayist, memoirist, and scriptwriter.

Considered one of the most powerful poets of the post-World War II era, Plath became a cult figure following her suicide in 1963 and the posthumous publication of *Ariel,* a collection which contains her most startling and acclaimed verse. Plath is best known for her vivid, intense poems that explore such topics as personal and feminine identity, individual suffering and oppression, and the inevitability of death. Through bold metaphors and stark, often violent and unsettling imagery, her works evoke mythic qualities in nature and humanity. In addition to citing her command of poetic craft, critics often identify two other reasons for widespread interest in Plath's work: the autobiographical elements in her writings poignantly reflect her struggle with despair and mental illness, and her efforts to assert a strong female identity and to balance familial, marital, and career aspirations have established her as a representative voice for feminist concerns. While Plath is frequently linked with confessional poets Robert Lowell, Anne Sexton, and John Berryman, all of whom directly express personal torments and anguish in their work, critics have noted that many of her poems are dramatic monologues voiced by a character who is not necessarily autobiographical. Although sometimes faulted as indulgent and preoccupied with death and psychological suffering, Plath's work continues to be read widely and has generated numerous scholarly exegeses.

Born in Jamaica Plain, Massachusetts, Plath enjoyed an idyllic early childhood near the sea. Her father, a German immigrant, was a professor of entomology who maintained a special interest in the study of bees. His sudden death from diabetes mellitus in 1940 devastated the eight-year-old Plath, and many critics note the significance of this traumatic experience in interpreting her poetry, which frequently contains both brutal and reverential images of her father as well as sea imagery and allusions to bees. Plath began publishing poetry at an early age in such periodicals as *Seventeen* and the *Christian Science Monitor,* and in 1950 she earned a scholarship to Smith College. After spending a month during the summer of her junior year in New York City as a guest editor for *Mademoiselle* magazine, Plath suffered a mental collapse which resulted in a suicide attempt and her subsequent institutionalization. Plath later chronicled the circumstances and consequences of this breakdown in her best-selling novel, *The Bell Jar.* Following her recovery, Plath returned to Smith and graduated summa cum laude. After winning a Fulbright fellowship to study at Cambridge University, Plath met and soon married Ted Hughes, an English poet. The eventual failure of their marriage during the early 1960s and the ensuing struggles with severe depression that led to her suicide are considered crucial elements of Plath's most critically acclaimed poetry.

Plath's verse is represented in several volumes. *The Colossus* (1960), the only compilation of poems published during her lifetime, collects pieces dating from the mid- to late 1950s; *Ariel* (1965) contains poems selected by Hughes from among the many works Plath composed during the months before her

UPI/Bettmann Newsphotos

death and had intended to publish as a unified volume; *Winter Trees* (1971) collects several more of the *Ariel* poems and reflects Hughes's plan to publish Plath's later works in intervals; *Crossing the Water: Transitional Poems* (1971) reprints most of her post-*Colossus* and pre-*Ariel* verse; and *The Collected Poems* (1981), which won a Pulitzer Prize, features all of her verse, including several previously unpublished pieces, in order of composition. Critics often maintain that during her brief career, Plath's verse evolved from a somewhat derivative early style to that of a unique and accomplished poetic voice. Katha Pollitt commented: "Plath's was one of those rare poetic careers—Keats's was another—that moved consistently and with gathering rapidity and assurance to an ever greater daring and individuality."

Plath's early verse reflects various poetic influences, evoking the mythic qualities of the works of William Butler Yeats and Ted Hughes, the diverse experiments with form and language of Gerard Manley Hopkins and W. H. Auden, and the focus on personal concerns which dominate the verse of Robert Lowell and Theodore Roethke. Most of her early poems are formal, meticulously crafted, and feature elaborate syntax and well-developed metaphors, as Plath employed such forms as the ode, the villanelle, and the pastoral lyric to examine art, love, nature, and personal themes. These pieces are more subdued than the later work for which she would become renowned. Critics generally believe that some of the later poems in *The Colossus* herald a new phase in Plath's career. Marjorie Perloff commented: "[When], in the last two years of her life, [Plath] finally came into her own, the adopted voices merely evaporated, and a new harsh, demonic, devastating self, only partially prefigured in such poems as 'The Thin People' (1957) and 'The Stones' (1959), came into being."

Plath's later work evidences the increasing frustration of her desires. Her ambitions of finding happiness through work, marriage, and family were thwarted by such events as hospital stays for a miscarriage and an appendectomy, the breakup of her marriage, and fluctuating moods in which she felt vulnerable to male domination and threatening natural forces, particularly death. Jon Rosenblatt noted: "Life and death operate in Plath's poetic world as tangible powers: they appear as dramatic agents embodied in people, trees, houses, colors, and animals. And they proceed to control the self's actions and desires, its present and its future." Following the dissolution of her marriage, Plath moved with her two children from the Devon countryside to a London apartment and wrote feverishly from the summer of 1962 until her death in February of the following year. Many of her best-known poems, including "Daddy," "Lady Lazarus," "Lesbos," "Purdah," and "Edge," were composed during this period and form the nucleus of the *Ariel* poems. These pieces, which reflect her increasing anger, bitterness, and despair toward life, feature intense, rhythmic language that blends terse statements, sing-song passages, repetitive phrasing, and sudden violent images, metaphors, and declarations. For example, in "Daddy," perhaps her most frequently discussed work, Plath denounces her father's dominance over her life and, among other allusions, associates him with nazism and herself with Jewish victims of the Holocaust. Plath explained: "The poem is spoken by a girl with an Electra complex. Her father died while she thought he was God." Response to this poem reflects the general opinion of much of her later work. Some critics contend that Plath's jarring effects are extravagant, and many object to her equation of personal sufferings with such horrors as those experienced by victims of Nazi genocide. Others, however, praise the passion and formal structure of her later poems, through which she confronts her tensions and conflicts. Robert Lowell observed that in the *Ariel* poems, "Sylvia Plath becomes herself, becomes something imaginary, newly, wildly, and subtly created—hardly a person at all, or a woman, certainly not a 'poetess,' but one of those super-real, hypnotic, great classical heroines."

Plath published *The Bell Jar* (1963), which appeared shortly before her death, under the pseudonym of Victoria Lucas. She was unsure of the quality of the work and feared that it might offend those people, particularly her mother, on whom the characters are based. This novel details a college student's disappointing adventures during a summer month in New York City as a guest editor for a fashion magazine, her despair upon returning home, her attempted suicide, and the electroshock treatments and institutionalization she undergoes to "cure" her of depression and lethargy. The narrator of *The Bell Jar* encounters many of the pressures and problems Plath examined in her verse: her attempts to establish her identity are consistently undermined, she projects an ambivalent attitude toward men, society remains indifferent to her sensitivity, vulnerability, and artistic ambitions, and she is haunted by events from her past, particularly the death of her father. Although critical reception to *The Bell Jar* was mixed, reviewers praised the

novel's satiric portrait of American society and its poignant study of the growing disillusionment of a talented young woman.

The posthumous publication of Plath's writings in other genres, many of which were edited by Ted Hughes, reflects the continuing interest in her work. *Three Women: A Monologue for Three Voices* (1968) is a verse play originally presented on British radio in 1962 in which three women discuss pregnancy. *Letters Home: Correspondence, 1950-1963* (1975) reveals Plath's reactions to pivotal events in her adult life through the publication of letters she exchanged with her mother. *Johnny Panic and the Bible of Dreams and Other Prose Writings* (1977) collects short stories and excerpts from her diaries in which Plath reworked the personal experiences, themes, and topics she frequently explored in her verse. *The Journals of Sylvia Plath* (1982), which includes most of the extensive diary entries Plath compiled during her lifetime, received substantial critical attention. Katha Pollitt described this collection as "a storehouse of ideas for stories, novels, and poems; of stray phrases and incidents that would turn up, sometimes years later, in her finished work. They are the place, too, where she chronicled an almost unbroken parade of depressions, blocks, and visits of the 'Panic Bird,' and where she urged herself, over and over, year after dragging year, to throw herself into writing."

(See also *CLC*, Vols. 1, 2, 3, 5, 9, 11, 14, 17, 50; *Contemporary Authors*, Vols. 19-20; *Contemporary Authors Permanent Series*, Vol. 2; *Dictionary of Literary Biography*, Vols. 5, 6; and *Concise Dictionary of American Literary Biography, 1941-1968*.)

MARJORIE PERLOFF

At last, almost twenty years after her death on February 11, 1963, here are the *Collected Poems* of Sylvia Plath. It is a book that should have appeared much sooner. By 1982, its publication seems somehow anti-climactic: witness the rather cool response it has received from newspaper reviewers. To reread Sylvia Plath today is to realize, somewhat ruefully, how different the early 1980s are from the early 1960s. Schizophrenia, of consuming interest to a generation brought up on R. D. Laing's *The Divided Self*, is now regarded either as a disease to be controlled biochemically or as part of a larger cultural phenomenon: Lacanian criticism, for instance, is more interested in unmasking the verbal strategies of "sane" discourse than in dealing with individual psychosis. Again, the feminist revolution—the only *real* revolution of our time—has put the "marriage plus career" problem at the center of Plath's writing in a rather different perspective; it is not that the problem has been solved, but Plath's stated desire to have "millions of babies" and her scorn for the "spinster bluestockings" of Cambridge and Smith is not likely to strike a sympathetic chord in women undergraduates today. Most important: Plath's rhetoric, at least the rhetoric of the poems she wrote prior to *Ariel*, now seems anything but revolutionary. Her controlled stanzas, heavy with assonance and consonance, her elaborate syntax with its inversions and subordinate clauses, her ingenious metaphors—all these now look almost genteel, almost Victorian.

Nevertheless, Plath remains an extraordinary poet and *The Collected Poems* reveals a side of her we have not really seen before. In his brief introduction, Ted Hughes remarks: "Some time around Christmas 1962, she gathered most of what are now known as the 'Ariel' poems in a black spring binder, and arranged them in a careful sequence. (At the time, she pointed out that it began with the word 'Love' and ended with the word 'Spring'. The exact order of her text is given in the Notes)." The list contains the following poems not included in *Ariel* (1965): **"The Rabbit Catcher," "Thalidomide," "Barren Woman," "A Secret," "The Jailer," "The Detective," "The Other," "Magi," "Stopped Dead," "The Courage of Shutting-Up," "Purdah,"** and **"Amnesiac."** Why did Hughes omit twelve of the forty-one poems that Plath had so carefully chosen for inclusion just a month before her suicide? Here is his explanation:

> The *Ariel* eventually published in 1965 was a somewhat different volume from the one she had planned. It incorporated most of the dozen or so poems she had gone on to write in 1963, though she herself, recognizing the different inspiration of these new pieces, regarded them as the beginnings of a third book. It omitted some of the more personally aggressive poems from 1962, and might have omitted one or two more if she had not already published them herself in magazines—so that by 1965 they were widely known. The collection that appeared was my eventual compromise between publishing a large bulk of her work—including much of the post-*Colossus* and pre-*Ariel* verse—and introducing her late work more cautiously, printing perhaps only twenty poems to begin with.

What Ted Hughes doesn't say is that the "more personally aggressive poems from 1962" he chose to omit were those that expressed, most directly and brutally, Plath's anger, bitterness, and despair over his desertion of her for another woman. Five of the poems on Plath's list (**"The Rabbit Catcher," "Thalidomide," "The Other," "The Courage of Shutting-Up,"** and **"Purdah"**) eventually made their way into the collection *Winter Trees* (1971), but the rest are published here for the first time along with a number of other previously unpublished poems of 1962. As a group, these "Terrible Lyrics," as we might call them by analogy to Hopkins' "Terrible Sonnets," are powerful works in which Plath the passive sufferer of **"I Am Vertical"** or **"Last Words"** (both 1961) becomes Plath the avenger—Medea as well as Dido. (pp. 304-05)

Faced with so many poems (more than half the volume covers the poetry written prior to 1960, the year *The Colossus* was published in Britain), many reviewers of *The Collected Poems* have declared that too much attention has been paid to the *Ariel* poems, that the early work is just as important and as accomplished. I find this now-fashionable judgment wholly frivolous, for, as I have argued elsewhere [see *CLC*, Vol. 17], Plath's carefully constructed persona, the mask she presented to her adoring mother as well as to editors, professors, and friends, governed not only her domestic life but her poetry as well: until the summer of 1962, when Aurelia Plath [Sylvia Plath's mother] became an inadvertent witness to the dissolution of the Plath-Hughes marriage, Syliva Plath—or "Sivvy" as she called herself in her letters home, never quite abandoned the carefully constructed voice that won her prizes and awards in all the right quarters, a voice her mother could and did approve of. Indeed, the early poems display a bewildering hodge-podge of influences: Hopkins and Yeats, Auden and Wilbur, Stevens and Thomas, and, a little later, first Lowell and then Roethke and Hughes himself. Influence is not quite the word here, for most of the early poems are merely imitative. . . . (pp. 307-08)

It is curious how impervious Plath was to what Harold Bloom has called the anxiety of influence. Hers was not the struggle with the great precursor so as to clear a space for herself.

Rather, when, in the last two years of her life, she finally came into her own, the adopted voices merely evaporated, and a new harsh, demonic, devastating self, only partially prefigured in such poems as **"The Thin People"** (1957) and **"The Stones"** (1959), came into being.

The transformation of the "Sivvy" who wrote **"The Ghost's Leavetaking"** and **"A Winter's Tale"** into the Sylvia of **"Tulips"** or **'Cut'** or **"Medusa"** has been discussed often enough, and I won't dwell on it here. Rather, I want to take a closer look at the poems of anger and outrage written in 1962 when Plath discovered that Hughes was having an affair with someone else. The first of these poems, **"The Rabbit Catcher,"** is dated May 21, 1962, and evidently refers to the brief interval when Plath and Hughes were still living together despite her discovery of his infidelity. **"The Rabbit Catcher"** oddly inverts the imagery of Lawrence's "Love on the Farm": in both poems, the woman who speaks identifies with the rabbit her husband has killed, but whereas in Lawrence, the caress of "his fingers that still smell grim / Of the rabbit's fur" produces instant sexual arousal, in Plath, the same incident, as viewed by a female poet, not just a female speaker, spells only death. . . . (pp. 309-10)

In the next poem, **"Event,"** the woman who cannot sleep in the hours before dawn perceives the marriage bed as a kind of tomb: "The moonlight, that chalk cliff / In whose rift we lie / Back to back." In this landscape, everything is frozen, petrified: "the stars—ineradicable, hard," the "apple bloom [that] ices the night"—even "The child in the white crib" who "Opens its mouth now, demanding," has a "little face . . . carved in pained, red wood." The loved baby is an intolerable reminder of its unloving father:

> Love cannot come here.
> A black gap discloses itself
> On the opposite lip.
>
> A small white soul is waving, a small white maggot.
> My limbs, also, have left me.
> Who has dismembered us?
>
> The dark is melting. We touch like cripples.

The poem avoids self-pity by focusing so sharply on effect rather than cause; there is no circumstantial detail here, no rehashing of the events and bitter words that precipitated the current crisis. The poem's very reticence, coupled with its explosive anger, has a painful effect on the reader: Hughes becomes a kind of shadow ("Who has dismembered us?") and since one can't fight shadows there is only a "black gap," a gap measured by Plath's new staccato lines and straightforward syntax.

"Burning the Letters," dated August 13, 1962, takes us to a further stage of anger and despair. It might have been an embarrassing poem: what, on the face of it, is more maudlin than the image of a woman burning the love letters of the man who no longer wants her? But Plath renews this tired theme by treating the letters as if they had a life of their own even as their author and recipient are transformed into objects. Thus the letters have "white fists" (they can strike and hurt); they rattle in the wastebasket; inside their "cardboard cartons the color of cement" they become "a dog pack / Holding in its hate / Dully." The dog pack, moreover, brings to mind the image of hunters ("a pack of men in red jackets"), and the very postmarks have "eyes," eyes that burn like wounds inflicted by the hunters.

As the letters "melt and sag" in the fire, the poet remarks: "here is an end to the writing, / The spry hooks that bend and cringe, and the smiles, the smiles." But she knows very well that there is really no end to it. As she "flake[s] up papers that breathe like people . . . fan[ning] them out / Between the yellow lettuces and the German cabbage" of her garden, they appallingly come back to life: "a name with black edges / Wilts at my foot." A condolence card of sorts—condolence for her loss, for her lover's "death," but also the name of the other woman, the "Sinuous orchis / In a nest of roothairs and boredom— / Pale Eyes, patent-leather gutturals!" (Assia, the other woman was part German, part Russian). When the rain begins to fall, it brings no relief; on the contrary, it "greases my hair, extinguishes nothing." There cannot, in fact, be any relief for the pain:

> My veins glow like trees.
> The dogs are tearing a fox. This is what it is like—
> A red burst and a cry
> That splits from its ripped bag and does not stop
> With the dead eye
> And the stuffed expression, but goes on
> Dyeing the air,
> Telling the particles of the clouds, the leaves, the water
> What immortality is. That it is immortal.

The weary, self-correcting repetition in the last line tells us that burning the letters has changed nothing. The eyes of the postmarks, like the dead eye of the fox, cannot be erased from consciousness. (pp. 310-12)

In "**The Fearful,**" the surrender to death that becomes prominent in slightly later poems like "**Paralytic,**" "**Sheep in a Fog,**" and "**Contusion**" is still held in abeyance. For the speaker of this poem still cares; she is still a fighter, protecting her own from the "Stealer of cells." She is the avenger of "**Purdah**" (October 29, 1962), who declares:

> And at his next step
> I shall unloose
> From the small jeweled
> Doll he guards like a heart—
>
> The lioness,
> The shriek in the bath,
> The cloak of holes.

As a group, these "Terrible Lyrics" of 1962 thus extend Sylvia Plath's range and heighten the pathos of her work. We see her as more than the schizophrenic whose earlier suicide attempts prefigure her final successful one, the Lady Lazarus who has "done it again" ("Dying / Is an art, like everything else. / I do it exceptionally well"). Rather, she becomes the outraged wife, a modern Medea who gave everything and was nevertheless betrayed. What an irony that the publication of these poems has depended precisely on the man who is their subject. What an irony that in "burning the letters," Sylvia Plath really could not destroy them or their legacy. Even as carbon, scattered around the cabbage patch of the poetry world, they continue to punish the dead poet. (pp. 312-13)

Marjorie Perloff, "Sylvia Plath's 'Collected Poems': A Review-Essay," in Resources for American Literary Study, *Vol. XI, No. 2, Autumn, 1981, pp. 304-13.*

JOHN BAYLEY

Being somebody always eluded Sylvia Plath, and to her as a poet it seems to have mattered. To achieve poetic being in this way may be a matter of talent, or come of itself, but it must not be seen to be attempted. Now, at this distance in time and after the ballyhoo has died down, we can see [in *The Collected Poems*] with what determination, what saving absence of tact, she tried to achieve it. Indeed it seems part of her skill and intention to invite the reader to cast a cold eye, to involve her or him with the same displays that a patient makes up for an analyst. Patients make them as effective as possible not because they are malingering but for the opposite reason: their efficiency in creating the story of themselves both conceals and reveals the desperation of nothingness, the sense of not being anyone. . . . As Lady Lazarus she achieves her individuality by the power to die and revive. The reader, the doctor, can see that the vocation to neurosis is wholly genuine, but also that its tales and acts are made up in order that the vocation, and the personality that goes with it, can be seen to exist.

Another way of putting it would be to say that Sylvia Plath's poems are verbal games of attention and observation, beautifully controlled, and not—as Lowell's and Berryman's are— the history and projection of a self. Her poetic gifts are more like those of Marianne Moore, or even Elizabeth Bishop, for although one can say that Marianne Moore's patterns and animals are really perceptive acts of vengeance on the way she has to live and the people she has to meet, it is none the less true that the game of close attention is what counts. This sort of talent has an increasingly weightless role in Sylvia Plath's poetry, because its powers are seeking to establish a situation which would give them a true natural history, an interior both personal and inevitable. The new woman's cliché of discovering 'who I really am', exploited today in a hundred mostly bad novels, gives a pervasive anxiety to her poems and yet seems irrelevant to their true qualities.

How much do they need it? In one sense the only subject of her poetry is its own anxiety to become poetry. Paradoxically it would have been much easier for her if she had been a neurotic of the comfortably self-absorbed, self-communing kind, like Stevie Smith. As pretty girl, bright student and teacher, wife and mother, and then as poet, professional author and trauma-maker as well, she had an impossible task in adding herself up to an incontestable personality. The poetry is in the gallantry of the process, and its failure. A greater talent would not have needed either, or not have had to make so much of them. (p. 19)

Two points may strike us particularly, already foreshadowed in what I have been saying. First the posthumous Ariel poems no longer seem the 'revelation' they seemed to many after the poet's death, when they were at once assimilated into the mushrooming legend about her. Second, and relatedly, her 'development' is really a sort of hallucination, produced by our sense of the ending. Hughes, in an appropriate metaphor, puts the matter in a significantly negative way. She went 'through successive moults of style . . . at each move we made, she seemed to shed a style'.

What then was new grown? Sentences become shorter, more elliptic—here she has influenced a new generation of poets today—and their isolate meanings more rigorously workmanlike. This is especially notable in "**Berck-Plage,**" of which every couplet is a succulent and separate pleasure. But it is not, except in striving and intention, an integrated poem. Hughes's note is again of interest, if only theoretically. We learn that there was a hospital for war veterans at this coast resort in Normandy, and that the patients took their exercise on the beach; also that the funeral in the poem is that of the poet's friend Peter Key, an old countryman 'who died in June 1962, exactly a year after her visit to Berck-Plage'.

The poem's virtues are really much the same as those of the neat and composed **"Cut"**, which almost uncannily anticipates the small 'metaphysical'' domestic poems fashionable to-day.... **"Cut"** has a rather disturbing air of being exactly fitted to Sylvia Plath's practice and techniques as is the equally successful **"Balloons"**, the penultimate poem she ever wrote, date 5 February 1963 (she died on the 11th).

> Since Christmas they have lived with us,
> Guileless and clear,
> Oval soul-animals. . . .

The balloons and her children's reaction to them provide just the right set-up for her intentness, and as in **"Cut"** the subject lends itself naturally to something unstable and sinister just outside the focus of the poem but a vital part of its total effect. Hughes observes that 'her attitude to her verse was artisan-like: if she couldn't get a table out of the material, she was quite happy to get a chair, or even a toy . . . something that temporarily exhausted her ingenuity'. Certainly the image that fits these poems . . . is of a delicate carver using a keen tool that may suddenly enter her own body. It is this that gives an impression of dangerous games with words, what Hughes calls 'her unique excitement', an excitement symbolised in the very striking early poem **"Aerialist"**, printed in the appendix of juvenilia. 'This adroit young lady' 'serenely plummets down' from the most hazardous trapeze act, but 'as penalty for her skill' must walk in dread of the day, the traffic, the normality of things.

> Lest, out of spite, the whole
> Elaborate scaffold of sky overhead
> Fall racketing finale on the luck.

"Aerialist" recalls the later **"Ariel"**, which, we learn, was also the name of a horse which the poet used to ride in Devon.

It is in such poems that Sylvia Plath spoke with what has to be called her most natural voice. But she must also do 'the big bow-wow', and the poems that helped to launch her cult—**"Lesbos"**, **"Lady Lazarus"**, and particularly **"Daddy"**—make embarrassing reading today. The willed violence, the sturm and drang of Auschwitz lampshade skins and 'the man in black with a Meinkampf look', now seem merely factitious. Strange that Robert Lowell, in almost equally frenetic terms, praised this farrago as if it triumphantly equated and surmounted the sufferings of death camps and of personal madness. Sylvia Plath herself, one feels, would have come to dislike it and would have made no claims for it. Indeed there is something slightly embarrassed about the glosses on the poems she prepared for BBC radio. **"Daddy"** is a poem

> spoken by a girl with an Electra complex. Her father died while she thought he was God. Her case is complicated by the fact that her father was also a Nazi and her mother very possibly part Jewish . . . the two strains marry and she has to act out the awful little allegory before she is free of it.

Certainly it is an awful little allegory, but one must remember that the poet needed the publicity that went with such things. Her ambition was fighting indifference and publishers who turned her down. The same reasons must be behind the almost equally disastrous 'public' poem set in a maternity ward, *Three Women*.

These poems sink under a weight of willed significance, and her explications both are outside them and occlude them. The exception is **"Death and Co."**, a poem about death as a quiet man, as a smiling insinuating man, in which the true Plath humour appears in the poem if not in the explication ('the poem is about the double or schizophrenic nature of death—the marmoreal coldness of Blake's death mask, say, hand in glove with the fearful softness of worms, water, and other katabolists . . .'). (pp. 19-20)

Sylvia Plath wrote that 'The blood jet is poetry / There is no stopping it', but that is not the impression that her poetry as a whole gives. Rather it seems a particular triumph of hard work and artifice, attempting more than it can do in the same spirit in which the poet attempts more than she can be, a natural and involuntary spirit instead of 'the voice of nothing, that was your madness'.... But the lack of identity is also a strength, as is the rare sense of a poetry succeeding by doing more than it can. Schizophrenia brings its own rewards; death, like the horse Ariel, must somehow be caught up with. 'The only trouble is', as Sylvia Plath wrote of Lady Lazarus, 'she has to die first. She is the Phoenix, the libertarian spirit, what you will. She is also just a good, plain, very resourceful woman'. (p. 20)

John Bayley, "Games with Death and Co.," in New Statesman, *Vol. 102, No. 2637, October 2, 1981, pp. 19-20.*

MICHAEL HULSE

'I am writing the best poems of my life,' wrote Sylvia Plath on 16 October, 1962, four months before her death. She knew what her standards were and knew when she had reached what she was aiming at, and only in that October do her letters betray so full a satisfaction with the poems she was writing. In *The Collected Poems* that month's astonishing achievement becomes apparent: 25 poems, nearly half the year's output, were written in that October alone, including nearly all the now classic Plath—**"Daddy"**, **"Lesbos'**, **'Lady Lazarus,'** **'Fever 103°'**, **'The Arrival of the Bee Box'** and the other bee poems. 'Daddy, daddy, you bastard, I'm through': the anguished Plath clinch that strangles her most finely crafted poems at their conclusions clips tightly on all of these poems.

In such statements the authority that is in pain found an expression at once simple and complex. It is simple because Plath had by then gone far beyond those early influences (Marianne Moore, the Wilbur generation of the Forties and Fifties) that had introduced the baroque tone into her voice; but it is also complex because other influences—the abiding presence of Emily Dickinson and the more recent revelation of Lowell's *Life Studies*—had come together with the personal experiences of marriage and childbirth to produce a rich texture in Plath's perception of inner being. Simplicity of language wedded to complexity of emotional perception: it is this that constitutes the origin of everything that is typical of Plath, from the shredded syntax to the startling, beautiful images.

Her distinctive authority derives from her stern, almost harsh insistence on submitting the responses of the emotions to the scrutiny of the intellect, on wedding the result of this scrutiny to images and ideas distilled by acts of indefatigable will and active curiosity from the life around her. Robert Lowell, who also knew the strength that is in a poem which unites inner experience and public fact, praised those October poems highly; John Bayley [see excerpt above], recently dismissing them as 'factitious' and 'embarrassing reading', fails to understand that power.

Those who see Plath as a daemonically-inspired explorer of anguish will see more clearly now that in any of the individual volumes how earnestly and passionately she grappled with the technical problems of the stanza—how, for example, late tercet poems like **"Lady Lazarus"**, **"Purdah"** or **"Ariel"** come at the end of a long development which begins with *terza rima* variants like **"Sow"** or **"Lorelei"**, written in 1957 and included in *The Colossus,* the only one of her collections to appear in her lifetime.

Those who see Plath as obsessed with the landscape of the self can now see more clearly than before how high a proportion of her poems are quite literally topographical—her sense of place was keen. *Collected Poems* is not only the most important collected volume of the last 20 years, it is also a corrective to many myths and misunderstandings.

Michael Hulse, "Formal Bleeding," in The Spectator, *Vol. 247, No. 8001, November 14, 1981, p. 20.*

DENIS DONOGHUE

It is not an insult to Plath to say that her death was widely used to serve a wretched rhetorical purpose. It was already volubly assumed that the only valid experience was an experience of the abyss: Risk was suffused with an aura entirely heroic. The ideal death was supposed to fulfill the appalling logic of being forced to live in such a world at such a time. Suicide was the sign of authenticity. Sanity was supposed to feel ashamed of itself. R. D. Laing and other writers made this sentiment popular and encouraged people to believe, or at least to assert, that divinest sense is indeed constituted by much madness. The jargon of authenticity, heightened with the vocabulary of sacrifice, provided the context in which Plath's poems were first widely read. . . . (p. 1)

Plath's early poems, many of them, offered themselves for sacrifice, transmuting agony, "heart's waste," into gestures and styles. In a short and often commonplace life, Plath's experience was not extensive. The fact that it was extraordinarily intense does not mean that it was in other respects remarkable. Self-absorbed, she showed what self-absorption makes possible in art, and the price that must be paid for it, in the art as clearly as in the death. Even in her famous poems she resented experience for not being enough or for not suiting her well enough or disposing itself warmly enough in her favor. The truth is that there was much in life, even in those bad years, which she prematurely rejected, despised even when it was not despicable. Probably the world is never worthy of us, but this is a conclusion we should reach later rather than sooner and never as a matter of theory or principle. The intensity of Plath's poems is beyond dispute, but not the justice of their complaint. Famous poems, including **"Tulips"** and **"Lady Lazarus,"** now seem petulant to me, their self-regard understandable but still, when all is said, a pity. . . . You could also say, I guess, that self-absorption has turned into self-satisfaction and that the reader is unjustly taken for one of the "peanut-crunching crowd" pushing forward to see the big striptease, Lady doing her number and singing the blues.

The moral claims enforced by these poems now seem exorbitant. It requires an indecently grandiose rhetoric to make a cut finger, in the poem **"Cut,"** bleed such global agony. The same rhetoric, in such poems as **"The Tour"** and **"Eavesdropper"** sends the poet's rage over the edge into spleen. Reading *The Bell Jar* again, I find blatant rather than just

Plath's comparison between the electric shock treatment administered to the heroine and the execution of the Rosenbergs. Even in Plath's most admired poem, **"Daddy,"** the poet's conceit of herself as an imaginary Jew, "a Jew to Dachau, Auschwitz, Belsen," is far less convincing, by which I mean far less earned and imagined, than Berryman's in his story "The Imaginary Jew." The thrill we get from such poems is something we have no good cause to admire in ourselves. It is true, as T. S. Eliot wrote in "The Dry Salvages," that moments of agony are permanent, "with such permanence as time has," and that the torment of others remains an experience "unqualified, unworn by subsequent attrition." That is what we resent in the torment of others, that we cannot see it, as we see our own, wearing away. I recognize that this is a factor in my recent experience of going through Plath's poems again.

But there is something else. I can't recall feeling, in 1963, that Plath's death proved her life authentic or indeed that proof was required. As a Christian, I acknowledge one sacrificial hero, and one is enough. But I recall that *Ariel* was received as if it were a bracelet of bright hair about the bone, a relic more than a book. Even if I wanted to have that feeling today, reading *The Collected Poems,* I would find it impossible. For one thing, the times have changed. The elaborate mixture of rage, guilt, frustration and hysteria does not seem a mark of the present years. About death, evidently, there is much to be said; ignorance of the experience is not a constraint. Many of Plath's poems say on that subject as much as can decently be said, and more. In one of William Empson's coolest poems, "Ignorance of Death," the poet says that death, though an important subject, is one most people "should be prepared to be blank upon." I agree with him. . . . (pp. 1, 30)

I am not saying that our first reading of Plath was wrong, or even naïve, but that it seized upon an element in her poetry which spoke the hectic, uncontrolled things our conscience needed, or thought it needed. By being real, the poems made us real, certain that we existed. We accepted their violence as the true form of our own and were grateful. But in some respects we were naïve. I don't recall thinking, for instance, how derivative so many of Plath's poems are. . . . Debts don't matter, but the limiting factor in Plath's debts is that they begin and end by miming their originals, their relation to their masters is never more than adhesion.

What we should have noticed, though, in our first reading of Plath's poems was the distrust she turned upon communication. Not that her poetry is obscure. Part of its appeal is its directness. But her sense of language and her sense of other people were equally untrusting. Like many modern poets, she felt herself short changed by words:

> The word, defining, muzzles; the drawn line
> Ousts mistier peers and thrives, murderous,
> In establishments which imagined lines
> Can only haunt.

"Establishments" is a wonderful perception, especially as Plath wanted nothing established but a free range, open to ambrosial revelations. She never trusted words or trusted to luck with them or believed that words sometimes give, by grace and favor and courtship, more than they are importuned to give. She often took to language as if to revenge.

But I have to be more specific. Many of Plath's poems speak of words as if they were hooks, twisted with malice, letters twisted into smiles, hooks on which she, poor fish, is hung up to wriggle to her death. (pp. 30-1)

In **"The Courage of Shutting Up,"** '' . . . there is that antique billhook, the tongue, / Indefatigable, purple.'' And in one of the heartbreaking hospital poems, **"Tulips"**:

> My husband and child smiling out of the family photo;
> Their smiles catch onto my skin, little smiling hooks.

Every inviting gesture falls under the shadow of suspicion; nothing is innocent.

It is my recollection that in our first reading of Plath we thought her best work was that which expressed her talent, which we called her genius, most extremely. The poems were good in proportion to the outrage that provoked them. I read them differently now. In poems like **"Wreath for a Bridal,"** there is a serious disproportion between what is being said and the moral claim enforced by the saying. The best poems now emerge as those that live without fuss, poems in her middle style which eschew willed sublimities, often poems of pure observation, the way something looks, the music it makes by looking so. I'm thinking of **"Black Rook in Rainy Weather"** or poems that discover something in the world other than Sylvia Plath worth attending to, like **"All the Dead Dears"** or poems about landscapes ''unaltered by eyes'' or felt to be so unaltered. . . . As for **"Daddy"** and **"Lady Lazarus,"** I am unrepentant; they are too pleased with themselves. The last stanza of **"The Disquieting Muses"** is unforgettable, but what leads to that place is rather slack. . . .

What [*The Collected Poems*] shows is that Plath's work makes not so much a development but unpredictable explosions. The poems she wrote in October 1962 are the work of a poet possessed by a demon if not by herself, and from then to Feb. 5, 1963, every day, virtually, is torrent and a torment till the end. (p. 31)

> Denis Donoghue, *"You Could Say She Had a Calling for Death,"* in The New York Times Book Review, *November 22, 1981, pp. 1, 30-1.*

KATHA POLLITT

Complete collections often have an unintended effect: instead of displaying a poet's accomplishment, they subtly diminish it. Swamped by their pale, sluggish brothers and sisters, the special poems seem less and less unusual. We put the book away with the thought that the poet was, after all, quite right to have left half his work in the drawer.

That is not what happens [in *The Collected Poems*]. One reason is that Plath was a superb craftsman who never, Hughes tells us, abandoned a poem until it had ''exhausted her ingenuity.'' She wrote recalcitrant poems and failed poems, but none that were idle or blathering or tentative. With very few exceptions, every poem has a shape of its own. Another reason is that she was dazzlingly inventive. Even poems that fail to come off frequently contain lines of extraordinary loveliness. **"Ouija"** may bog down in Stevensish rhetoric, but it opens with eerie splendor: ''It is a chilly god, a god of shades, / Rises to the glass from his black fathoms.'' The dreadful **"Leaving Early,"** a savage account of a visit to an elderly woman who has somehow incurred the poet's hatred, offers the startling image of the poet ''bored as a leopard'' in her hostess's fuggy living room.

But the most important source of the pleasure to be found in these pages is the fact that Plath's was one of those rare poetic careers—Keats's was another—that moved consistently and with gathering rapidity and assurance to an ever greater daring and individuality. She was always becoming more distinctly herself, and by the time she came to write her last seventy or eighty poems, there was no other voice like hers on earth. Her end may have been tragic, her character not what we would choose in our friends, but her work records a triumph. Chronologically arranged, her 224 adult poems make a kind of diary of artistic self-discovery that is exhilarating to contemplate.

It was not an easy process. *The Collected Poems* shows just how hard Plath worked to transform herself from a subdued, well-mannered student of Auden, Eliot, Ransom and Lowell into the effortlessly associative poet of the late work. Discards vastly outnumber ''book poems'' in the entries for 1956-59, the years Plath was working on *The Colossus,* and it's hard to disagree with her verdicts. For all their skill, the rejects strike me as devitalized, strangled by the very technical proficiency that was later to be so liberating. . . . (pp. 52-3)

The Colossus is a book of considerable interest quite apart from the fact that it was written by the author of *Ariel*. **"Black Rook in Rainy Weather,"** The Disquieting Muses,'' **"Full Fathom Five,"** **"All the Dead Dears"** and many others have a controlled, melancholy beauty and a redeeming wit. Yet all but a handful—the musical, dreamlike **"Lorelei,"** the playful **"Mushrooms,"** and **"The Thin People"**—have about them a quality of having been willed into existence, of having fought for breath against an anxiety or depression that threatened to engulf them. . . . ''A fury of frustration,'' she wrote after completing the elegant pastoral **"Watercolor of Grantchester Meadows."** ''Some inhibition keeping me from writing what I really feel.''

It is certainly cause for wonder that this same poet should a mere three years later be turning out poems like **"Daddy,"** **"Lady Lazarus"** and **"Elm"** with the speed, in Hughes's phrase, of urgent letters. Nonetheless, critics who deny a continuity between the early and late Plaths—usually to dismiss one in favor of the other—will want to rethink their positions in light of the wealth of evidence provided here for a broadly continuous development. As the chronological arrangement makes clear, Plath found and lost her voice many times. **"The Stones,"** the first poem that hints at the new manner, was followed by a raft of poems in the old. The old bobs up long after the new has established itself: the Lowellian exercise **"The Babysitters"** postdates **"The Rival"** and **"Tulips."**

On the deeper level of themes and images, there was not so much a rift as a reformulation. Throughout her career, Plath worked with a tightly connected cluster of concerns—metamorphosis, rebirth, the self as threatened by death, the otherness of the natural world, fertility and sterility—and applied them all to what she was as the central situation of her life, the death of her worshipped father when she was 9 years old and the complex emotions of loss, guilt and resentment it aroused in her even as an adult. But where the early Plath is autobiographical, Freudian (**"Electra on Azalea Path,"** **"The Colossus"**), the later Plath is working in another mode entirely—of fixed symbols, drama and myth.

Jon Rosenblatt has argued [see *CLC,* Vol. 17] that the late poems are governed by a vision of ''negative vitalism,'' a conviction that all life is at the mercy of a cosmic, merciless principle of death, of which the dead father—along with God, male-dominated marriage, fascism, war and mass society—is only an aspect. Judith Kroll, who has traced the profound influence on Plath of Robert Graves's *The White Goddess,* makes a similar point, and shows how Plath cast her life in the form of a ritual drama of death and rebirth which the poems enact. "Tulips," "Ariel," "Daddy" and "A Birthday Present" are thus not confessional poems in which the poet displays her wounds but dramatic monologues in which the speaker moves from a state of psychological bondage to freedom, from spiritual death to life, with suicide, paradoxically, standing as a metaphor for this transformation. In the late poems, Plath enters the world of death—the hospital room in "Tulips," the death train in "Getting There," the fever-induced fantasy of Hades in "Fever 103°"—suffers a ritual death and emerges reborn. (pp. 53-4)

The impact of "Ariel" has been so great that other late poems, as well as the "transitional" ones of the early 1960s, have been overshadowed. One of the accomplishments of *The Collected Poems* will be, I hope, to remind us of the strength of much of this work. Any poet less rapidly evolving than Plath would have been tempted to rest on such laurels as "I am Vertical," "Wuthering Heights" and "Parliament Hill Fields." It is a great thing, too, to see late poems like "Stopped Dead," "Purdah" and "The Jailer" placed, finally, at the culmination of Plath's career, where they belong.

All these poems, but especially the late ones, fill out and qualify our sense of Plath's vision. To give but one instance: The critics who see her work as a rejection of life, and the feminists, too, will have to come to terms with the tenderness and purity of Plath's maternal feelings, as displayed in "Brasilia," "Child," "For a Fatherless Son" and her radio verse play *Three Women.*

If Sylvia Plath were alive now, she would be 49 years old—younger than Adrienne Rich, John Ashbery, Philip Levine and W. S. Merwin, younger, incredibly, than Allen Ginsberg. It is often said that when she died, she had gone as far as poetry could take her, and indeed, the very last poems do seem to leave no way out. I cannot believe, though, that a poet as fertile and energetic and fearless as Plath here shows herself to be could ever have been reduced to silence by her own imagination. Had she lived, like Lady Lazarus she would surely have transformed herself yet again, as she had done before. "The loss to poetry has been inestimable," wrote A. Alvarez after her death. Surveying the current state of poetry, one can see how sadly right he was. (pp. 54-5)

Katha Pollitt, "A Note of Triumph," in The Nation, *New York, Vol. 234, No. 2, January 16, 1982, pp. 52-5.*

IRVIN EHRENPREIS

The habit of reading Sylvia Plath's poems biographically is so common that one forgets how many of them are dramatic monologues, how many are spoken by imaginary characters who have no obvious connection with the poet. The new, long-awaited edition of *The Collected Poems* brings together many such pieces, balancing the unmediated lyrics.

The most elaborate of the monologues is the highly effective *Three Women,* in which Plath interweaves the speeches of a mother, a secretary, and a university student all responding to the experience of pregnancy. Here the poet discloses the separate dispositions of the introspective women by steadily shifting images which convey their veering moods through subtle parallels and contrasts. What fascinates the author is the way each speaker wholly redefines herself according to the experience. With no external narrative, Plath manages to give haunt-

ing embodiment to three lives at the same, supreme turning point.

Reading and rereading the many monologues, one must be struck by the poet's genius for using physical bodies as emblems of inner character. Not through Balzacian physiognomy but through the manipulation of the body as an object, she expresses her preoccupation with selfhood and personality. In the monologues Plath regularly brings the speaker's thoughts to a focus on this theme....

At what seems to me the deepest level of her best poems, Sylvia Plath dramatizes the willed effort of the human identity to establish itself, to find a stable base, to grow and unfold. For there is a ferociously ambiguous environment standing against the hesitant first movements of the primitive personality. Things that look kind to it become cruel. Things that look dangerous become nourishing. Bewildered by the duplicity of people, clothes, food, domestic furniture, the infant self wavers between expansion and shrinkage.

At the same time, the tentative personality suffers the pressure of its inner, overwhelming moods and instincts. Hurting what it loves, grasping what it detests, the self learns anxious diffidence. Its multiple, conflicting desires threaten to frustrate the yearning for coherence. In America, where homogeneous cultural patterns are rare, and the individual must forge the conscience of his race along with his own, the problem is aggravated. Plath carried further the experiments of Eliot and Lowell in handling the theme.

In fact, she created a vocabulary of images and gestures to convey the primal condition. For instance, she uses hooks, again and again, to suggest the mixture of seduction and menace offered by apparently neutral stimuli....

Nets are another form of the image. They are hidden traps that work with deceptively pleasing sensations. In "Purdah," a betrayed wife thinks of herself as wearing veils because she hides her true feelings from her husband. Moonlight is dangerous, for it encourages her to reveal emotion. So the moon rises with "cancerous pallors," illuminating trees which in turn act like "little nets," since the poet must evade the softening of landscape and not expose her "visibilities."

The word "glitter" also belongs to this pattern of moral ambiguity, because, like the Latinate equivalent, "specious," it suggests allurement and falsehood at once. In "Death & Co." the poet combines the word with another, "plausive," a rare adjective that can mean approving or specious. She implies that the person described is concealing real hostility and pretending to like somebody whom he wishes to make use of for his own purposes. Wearing hair that is "long and plausive," he is "masturbating a glitter."...

Syntax, figures of speech, and modes of expression enrich Plath's double vision of moral reality. Often she frames questions to bring out the doubtfulness of the signals from the environment, or the anxiety of the self trying to get a secure footing. So the brilliant colors of poppies in July trouble the poet. "Do you no harm?" she asks ("Poppies in July"); for if she lets down her guard and warms to the blossoms, she will be hurt. In "Getting There" the misery of holding the fragmented self together until the final release into death is conveyed by the allegory of a hideous journey in wartime, punctuated by the frantic question, "How far is it?"

To combine the various effects is not difficult for her. In "Mystic" the poet faces the irrational spasm of hopefulness which often strikes one during a season of well-earned despair. "The air is a mill of hooks," she says as she considers the many, confusing stimuli that make life seem not only endurable but (perhaps!) promising. The hooks, however, turn at once into questions, partly because question marks look like hooks. Then the movement from ambiguous hope to uncertainty slips over into images of menace as the air-filling questions become flies, which kiss and sting at once. After a central section on religious experience, the poet closes with the world regaining significance. The sun blooms like a geranium, and she can say, "The heart has not stopped." . . .

Certain themes recur in the poems, to enlarge the meaning of the images and technical devices. Dismemberment suggests the difficulty of putting or keeping together the personality. The self can disintegrate, fly apart, or merely flake off. (p. 22)

[In "**Event**"], a husband and his embittered wife are in bed, back to back. Disillusionment has changed her view of him and of herself. As she lies there, she senses her angry feelings emanating from the creatures and things of the house and neighborhood. The moonlight is a "chalk cliff / In whose rift we lie. . . ." Coldness and whiteness loom against the heat of private emotions. The wife imagines herself walking around like a needle in the groove of a record, as she goes over and over the suppressed recriminations. She has been transformed by the "event"—i.e., his treachery. Even more—in her eyes—has his nature been changed. "Who has dismembered us?" she asks, referring both to their falling out and to the disintegration of their separate characters.

During such crises the role of the will grows important. The person fears that any relaxation of control will leave the components of the self without cement. To hold them in place, when forces within and without are tearing them apart, requires constant effort. Even death must be arranged ahead of time. In a faultless monologue, "**Last Words**," the speaker is an ancient Egyptian planning her own burial. Through the instructions she indicates the self she means to become in death; and the poem ends,

> They will roll me up in bandages, they will store my heart
> Under my feet in a neat parcel.
> I shall hardly know myself. It will be dark,
> And the shine of these small things sweeter than the face of
>   Ishtar.

"Things" here refers to the domestic objects that will accompany the body: cooking vessels, rouge pots, etc.—more reliable than the spirit. Plath's poetry abounds in such articles. She sets her tremendous agons in humble locations, often indoors—kitchens, bedrooms, offices.

It is a short step for her imagination to replace parts of the self by equivalents or by things. In "**The Applicant**," one of Plath's masterpieces, prosthesis, the substitution of artificial parts of the body for real ones, suggests a lack of authenticity—false, incomplete, corrupt character—along with dependence. It suggests the interchangeability of the meaningless parts of abortive personalities. (p. 23)

In "**The Stones**"—a controlled triumph of nightmare vision—doctors make prosthesis their occupation. The hospital or factory (a mental institution) is a "city of spare parts," and health here means a surrender of intrinsic personality. Almost like Frankenstein's monster, the individual is reassembled, new-born into the fake harmlessness of compliant normality: "My swaddled legs and arms smell sweet as rubber." The theme emerges more lightly in "**Tulips**," as the speaker, drugged in

a hospital bed, loses her hostility along with her character: "I am nobody; I have nothing to do with explosions." There is a hint here of the ruthlessness of authentic responses. The tulips trouble her because they induce her to respond as a person, and she is afraid of the destructiveness that may be released if she gives way.

At this stage the principle of the double, or total prosthesis, moves into the foreground of Sylvia Plath's imagination. Instead of letting the split between dangerous and benign impulses remain an internal affair, the poet sometimes represents it as opening between herself and a shadowy figure, created to receive blame. There is a communal aspect to the concept. Socially and politically, the victim of oppression is linked to a tyrannical community or government just as a mistreated wife is bound to an unfeeling husband. Yet sufferers may teach cruelty to their masters. The victim can be a prosecutor, too, once she embodies the regime or the spouse in Another.

The speaker of "**In Plaster**" first accepts the humble ministrations of her new, white companion, who seems a benignly blank version of herself. But since the replica is only a projection, she has the underlying defects of her original; and these soon appear. For the white figure tires of good works, turns censorious, and at last reveals malice. The speaker then complains, "She wanted to leave me, she thought she was superior." However, instead of being tolerant and good-natured, the speaker reacts with a plan to collect her own strength and abandon the Other first. "And she'll perish with emptiness then," says the poet vindictively.

Drawing out the implications, one may say that the martyr invents a torturer in her own image. Neither could exist without the other. . . . Eventually, therefore, the parts of oppressor and oppressed become reversible, like Lucky and Pozzo in *Waiting for Godot*.

Such a confusion of roles between victim and persecutor is barely intimated in "**Death & Co.**" Here the poet is visited and feels threatened by two evil men. One has the "scald scar of water" and reminds her of a condor. The scar suggests a victim, and recalls the scars of Lady Lazarus. But the condor is certainly a bird of prey. The second man "wants to be loved," and is a helper in the mysterious, criminal enterprise. But the poet refuses to be taken in; she will not "stir." Yet she ends with the words, "Somebody's done for." Is it the poet, or one of the dangerous but vulnerable men, who is done for? Is she destroying them, or are they destroying her?

Possibly, then, the tormentor was correct all along? It is a masterstroke of irony for the poet to join the opposed characters of victim and avenger in one. That is the accomplishment of "**The Applicant**." Again, in "**Lady Lazarus**," deservedly the best known of Sylvia Plath's poems, the two roles are united. Here the victimized speaker shows her rage at first only by her tone. But at last she drops the disguise of passive sufferer and turns into nemesis. The doctors who have revived her are persecutors, Nazis, even Lucifer. Now, therefore, the tyrant, the social order, the male state that tortured the victims of the Holocaust, are themselves savagely threatened.

The poet becomes her own prosthesis. Instead of imagining an Other on whom to smear the hostilities and inadequacies of her inner nature, she will die as the outer, beguiling social person and be reborn as the vengeful "true" self. The role of martyr gives way to that of assassin. Like a phoenix, the speaker will come back:

> Out of the ash
> I rise with my red hair
> And I eat men like air.

Irvin Ehrenpreis, "The Other Sylvia Plath," in The New York Review of Books, *Vol. XXIX, No. 1, February 4, 1982, pp. 22-4.*

TED HUGHES

The motive in publishing [*The Journals of Sylvia Plath*] will be questioned. The argument against is still strong. A decisive factor has been certain evident confusions, provoked in the minds of many of her readers by her later poetry. *Ariel* is dramatic speech of a kind. But to what persona and to what drama is it to be fitted? The poems don't seem to supply enough evidence of the definitive sort. This might have been no bad thing, if a riddle fertile in hypotheses is a good one. But the circumstances of her death, it seems, multiplied every one of her statements by a wild, unknown quantity. The results, among her interpreters, have hardly been steadied by the account she gave of herself in her letters to her mother, or by the errant versions supplied by her biographers. So the question grows: how do we find our way through this accompaniment, which has now become almost a part of the opus? Would we be helped if we had more firsthand testimony, a more intimately assured image, of what she was really like? In answer to this, these papers, which contain the nearest thing to a living portrait of her, are offered in the hope of providing some ballast for our idea of the reality behind the poems. Maybe they will do more. (p. 86)

If we read [these surviving diaries] with understanding, they can give us the key to the most intriguing mystery about her, the key to our biggest difficulty in our approach to her poetry.

That difficulty is the extreme peculiarity in kind of her poetic gift. And the difficulty is not lessened by the fact that she left behind two completely different kinds of poetry.

Few poets have disclosed in any way the birth circumstances of their poetic gift, or the necessary purpose these serve in their psychic economy. . . . Sylvia Plath's poetry, like a species on its own, exists in little else but the revelation of that birth and purpose. Though her whole considerable ambition was fixed on becoming the normal flowering and fruiting kind of writer, her work was roots only. Almost as if her entire oeuvre were enclosed within those processes and transformations that happen in other poets before they can even begin, before the muse can hold out a leaf. Or as if all poetry were made up of the feats and shows performed by the poetic spirit Ariel. Whereas her poetry is the biology of Ariel, the ontology of Ariel—the story of Ariel's imprisonment in the pine, before Prospero opened it. And it continued to be so even after the end of *The Colossus,* which fell, as it happens, in the last entries of this surviving bulk of her journal, where the opening of the pine took place and was recorded. (p. 87)

The root system of her talent was a deep and inclusive inner crisis which seems to have been quite distinctly formulated in its chief symbols (presumably going back at least as far as the death of her father, when she was ten) by the time of her first attempted suicide, in 1953, when she was twenty-one.

After 1953, it became a much more serious business, a continuous hermetically sealed process that changed only very slowly, so that for years it looked like deadlock. Though its preoccupation dominated her life, it remained largely outside her ordinary consciousness, but in her poems we see the inner working of it. It seems to have been scarcely disturbed at all by the outer upheavals she passed through, by her energetic involvement in her studies, in her love affairs and her marriage, and in her jobs, though she used details from them as a matter of course for images to develop her X-rays.

The importance of these diaries lies in the rich account they give of her attempts to understand this obscure process, to follow it, and (in vain) to hasten it. As time went on, she interpreted what was happening to her inwardly, more and more consciously, as a "drama" of some sort. After its introductory overture (everything up to 1953), the drama proper began with a "death," which was followed by a long "gestation" or "regeneration," which in turn would ultimately require a "birth" or a "rebirth," as in Dostoevsky and Lawrence and those other prophets of rebirth whose works were her sacred books.

The "death," so important in all that she wrote after it, was that almost successful suicide attempt in the summer of 1953. The mythical dimensions of the experience seem to have been deepened, and made absolute, and illuminated, by two accidents: she lay undiscovered, in darkness, only intermittently half-conscious, for "three days"; and the electric shock treatment which followed went wrong, and she was all but electrocuted—at least so she always claimed. Whether it did and she was, or not, there seems little doubt that her "three day" death, and that thunderbolt awakening, fused her dangerous inheritance into a matrix from which everything later seemed to develop—as from a radical change in the structure of her brain.

She would describe her suicide attempt as a bid to get back to her father, and one can imagine that in her case this was a routine reconstruction, from a psychoanalytical point of view. But she made much of it, and it played an increasingly dominant role in her recovery and in what her poetry was able to become. (pp. 89-9)

The strange limbo of "gestation/regeneration," which followed her "death," lasted throughout the period of this journal, and she drew from the latter part of it all the poems of *The Colossus,* her first collection. We have spoken of this process as a "nursing" of the "nucleus of the self," as a hermetically sealed, slow transformation of her inner crisis; and the evidence surely supports these descriptions of it as a deeply secluded mythic and symbolic inner theater (sometimes a hospital theater), accessible to her only in her poetry. One would like to emphasize even more strongly the weird autonomy of what was going on in there. It gave the impression of being a secret crucible, or rather a womb, an almost biological process—and just as much beyond her manipulative interference. And like a pregnancy, selfish with her resources.

We can hardly make too much of this special condition, both in our understanding of her journal and in our reading of the poems of her first book. A reader of the journal might wonder why she did not make more of day-to-day events. She had several outlandish adventures during these years, and interesting things were always happening to her. But her diary entries habitually ignore them. When she came to talk to herself in these pages, that magnetic inner process seemed to engross all her attention, one way or another. And in her poems and stories, throughout this period, she felt her creative dependence on that same process as subjection to a tyrant. It commandeered every proposal. Many passages in this present book show the deliberate—almost frantic—effort with which she tried to extend her writing to turn it toward the world and other people, to stretch it over more of outer reality, to forget herself in some exploration of outer reality—in which she took, after all, such constant, intense delight. But the hidden workshop, the tangle of roots, the crucible, controlled everything. Everything became another image of itself, another lens into itself. And whatever it could not use in this way, to objectify some disclosure of itself, did not get onto the page at all.

Unless we take account of this we shall almost certainly misread the moods of her journal—her nightmare sense of claustrophobia and suspended life, her sense of being only the flimsy, brittle husk of what was going heavily and fierily on, somewhere out of reach inside her. And we shall probably find ourselves looking into her poems for things and qualities which could only be there if that process had been less fiercely concentrated on its own purposeful chemistry. We shall misconstrue the tone and content of the poetry that did manage to transmit from the center, and the psychological exactness and immediacy of its mournful, stressful confinement. (pp. 89-90)

The significant thing . . . in the progress she made, was surely the way she applied herself to the task. Her battered and so-often-exhausted determination, the relentless way she renewed the assault without ever really knowing what she was up against. The seriousness, finally, of her will to face what was wrong in herself, and to drag it out into examination, and to remake it—that is what is so impressive. Her refusal to rest in any halfway consolation or evasive delusion. And it produced some exemplary pieces of writing, here and there, in her diaries. It would not be so impressive if she were not so manifestly terrified of doing what she nevertheless did. At times, she seems almost invalid in her lack of inner protections. Her writing here (as in her poems) simplifies itself in baring itself to what hurts her. It is unusually devoid of intellectual superstructures—of provisional ideas, theorizings, developed fantasies, which are all protective clothing as well as tools. What she did have, clearly, was character—and passionate character at that. (p. 91)

Late in 1959 (toward the end of the surviving diaries) she had a dream, which at the time made a visionary impact on her, in which she was trying to reassemble a giant, shattered, stone Colossus. In the light of her private mythology, we can see this dream was momentous, and she versified it, addressing the ruins as **"Father,"** in a poem which she regarded, at the time, as a breakthrough. But the real significance of the dream emerges, perhaps, a few days later, when the quarry of anthropomorphic ruins reappears, in a poem titled **"The Stones."** In this second poem, the ruins are no other than the hospital city, the factory where men are remade, and where, among the fragments, a new self has been put together. Or rather an old shattered self, reduced by violence to its essential core, has been repaired and renovated and born again, and—most significant of all—speaks with a new voice.

This "birth" is the culmination of her prolonged six-year "drama." It is doubtful whether we would be reading this journal at all if the "birth" recorded in that poem, **"The Stones,"** had not happened in a very real sense, in November 1959. (pp. 91-2)

["**The Stones**"] is unlike anything that had gone before in her work. The system of association, from image to image and within the images, is quite new, and—as we can now see—it

is that of *Ariel*. And throughout the poem what we hear coming clear is the now-familiar voice of *Ariel*.

In its double focus, **"The Stones"** is both a "birth" and a "rebirth." It is the birth of her real poetic voice, but it is the rebirth of herself. That poem encapsulates, with literal details, her "death," her treatment, and her slow, buried recovery. And this is where we can see the peculiarity of her imagination at work, where we can see how the substance of her poetry and the very substance of her survival are the same. In another poet, **"The Stones"** might have been an artistic assemblage of fantasy images. But she was incapable of free fantasy, in the ordinary sense. If an image of hers had its source in sleeping or waking "dream," it was inevitably the image of some meaning she had paid for or would have to pay for, in some way—that she had lived or would have to live. It had the *necessity* of a physical symptom. This is the objectivity of her subjective mode. Her internal crystal ball was helplessly truthful, in this sense. (And truthfulness of that sort has inescapable inner consequences.) It determined her lack of freedom, sure enough, as we have already seen. But it secured her loyalty to what was, for her, the most important duty of all. And for this reason the succession of images in **"The Stones,"** in which we see her raising a new self out of the ruins of her mythical father, has to be given the status of fact. The "drama," in which she redeemed and balanced the earlier "death" with this "birth/rebirth," and from which she drew so much confidence later on, was a great simplification, but we cannot easily doubt that it epitomizes, in ritual form, the main inner labor of her life up to the age of twenty-seven.

And this is the story her diaries have to tell: how a poetic talent was forced into full expressive being, by internal need, for a purpose vital to the whole organism. (pp. 92-3)

After the promise of **"The Stones,"** we look at [her new poems] with fresh attention. And they *are* different from what had gone before. But superficially not very different. For one thing, there is little sign of *Ariel*. And she herself seemed to feel that these pieces were an interlude. She published them in magazines, but otherwise let them lie—not exactly rejected by her, but certainly not coaxed anxiously toward a next collection, as this journal shows her worrying over her earlier poems. The demands of her baby occupied her time, but this does not entirely explain the lull in her poetry. The poems themselves, as before, reveal what was going on.

Everything about her writing at this time suggests that after 1959, after she had brought her "death-rebirth" drama to a successful issue, she found herself confronted, on that inner stage, by a whole new dramatic situation—one that made her first drama seem no more than the preliminaries, before the lifting of the curtain.

And in fact that birth, which had seemed so complete in **"The Stones,"** was dragging on. And it went on dragging on. We can follow the problematic accouchement in the poems. They swing from the apprehensions of a woman or women of sterility and death at one extreme, to joyful maternal celebration of the living and almost-born fetus at the other—with one or two encouraging pronouncements from the oracular fetus itself in between. . . . It is not until we come to the poems of September, October, and November of 1961—a full two years after **"The Stones"**—that the newborn seems to feel the draft of the outer world. And even now the voice of *Ariel*, still swaddled in the old mannerisms, is hardly more than a whimper. But at least we can see what the new situation is. We see her new self confronting—to begin with—the sea, not just the sea off Finisterre and off Hartland, but the Bay of the Dead, and "nothing, nothing but a great space"—which becomes the surgeon's 2 A.M. ward of mutilations (reminiscent of the hospital city in **"The Stones"**). She confronts her own moon-faced sarcophagus, her mirror clouding over, the moon in its most sinister aspect, and the yews—"blackness and silence." In this group of poems—the most chilling pieces she had written up to this time—what she confronts is all that she had freed herself from. (pp. 95-6)

But now that she was resurrected, as a self that she could think of as an Eve (as she tried so hard to do in her radio play *Three Women*), a lover of life and of her children, she still had to deal with everything in her that remained otherwise, everything that had held her in the grave for "three days," The Other. And, it was only now, for the first time, at her first step into independent life, that she could see it clearly for what it was—confronting her, separated from her at last, to be contemplated and, if possible, overcome. (p. 96)

From her new position of strength, she came to grips quite quickly. After *Three Women* (which has to be heard, as naïve speech, rather than read as a literary artifact) quite suddenly the ghost of her father reappears, for the first time in two and a half years, and meets a daunting, point-blank, demythologized assessment. This is followed by the most precise description she ever gave of The Other—the deathly woman at the heart of everything she now closed in on. After this, her poems arrived at a marvelous brief poise. Three of them together, titled **"Crossing the Water," "Among the Narcissi"** and **"Pheasant,"** all written within three or four days of one another in early April 1962, are unique in her work. And maybe it was this achievement, inwardly, this cool, light, very beautiful moment of mastery, that enabled her to take the next step.

Within a day or two of writing **"Pheasant,"** she started a poem about a giant wych elm that overshadowed the yard of her home. The manuscript of this piece reveals how she began it in her usual fashion, as another poem of the interlude, maybe a successor to **"Pheasant"** (the actual pheasant of the poem had flown up into the actual elm) and the customary features began to assemble. But then we see a struggle break out, which continues over several pages, as the lines try to take the law into their own hands. She forced the poem back into order, and even got a stranglehold on it, and seemed to have won, when suddenly it burst all her restraints and she let it go.

And at once the *Ariel* voice emerged in full. From that day on, it never really faltered again. During the next five months she produced ten more poems. The subject matter didn't alarm her. Why should it, when Ariel was doing the very thing it had been created and liberated to do? In each poem, the terror is encountered head on, and the angel is mastered and brought to terms. The energy released by these victories was noticeable. According to the appointed coincidence of such things, after July her outer circumstances intensified her inner battle to the limits. In October, when she and her husband began to live apart, every detail of the antagonist seemed to come into focus, and she started writing at top speed. . . . (pp. 96-7)

[She] had overcome, by a stunning display of power, the bogies of her life. Yet her attitude to the poems was detached. "They saved me," she said, and spoke of them as an episode that was past. And indeed it was blazingly clear that she had come through, in Lawrence's sense, and that she was triumphant.

The impression of growth and a new large strength in her personality was striking. (pp. 97-8)

All her poems are in a sense by-products. Her real creation was that inner gestation and eventual birth of a new self-conquering self, to which her journal bears witness, and which proved itself so overwhelmingly in the *Ariel* poems of 1962. If this is the most important task a human being can undertake (and it must surely be one of the most difficult), then this is the importance of her poems, that they provide such an intimate, accurate embodiment of the whole process from beginning to end—or almost to the end.

That her new self, who could do so much, could not ultimately save her, is perhaps only to say what has often been learned on this particular field of conflict—that the moment of turning one's back on an enemy who seems safely defeated, and is defeated, is the most dangerous moment of all. And that there can be no guarantees. (pp. 98-9)

Ted Hughes, "Sylvia Plath and Her Journals," in Grand Street, *Vol. 1, No. 3, Spring, 1982, pp. 86-99.*

PETER DAVISON

Robert Frost used to advise young aspirants not to go into the arts unless they had "a snout for punishment." Sylvia Plath suffered, God knows, her share of punishment—some of it self-administered—but all the memoirs agree, and [*The Journals of Sylvia Plath*] bear it out, that she didn't have much of a snout. You could make a good case for a view of Plath's work as a poetry of incompleteness, of self-surgery, even, as Irvin Ehrenpreis [see excerpt above] has recently suggested, a poetry of the self as prosthesis, as a willful assemblage of ticktock inventory. . . .

To have known Sylvia Plath in her lifetime hardly helps this reviewer reconcile the selves looming out of her claustrophobic, self-lacerating journals. These are as different as they could be from the gee-whiz braggadocio of *Letters Home:* these are the notes of a worker, busy as the bumblebees her father had been so expert on. . . .

It may be that the quest in all of Plath's poetry was to discover two things: whether she herself was real; whether other people were. The journals give little evidence that she understood others. Plath's friends, even those closest to her, hardly ever receive a kind word in the journals, except when being useful or admiring. Sylvia's mother is praised for her maternal devotion—but then, in psychotherapy, poor Mrs. Plath is as deeply excoriated as the rest: I hate my mother in order to live free. The journal keeper could hardly be more self-centered, mean-spirited, narrowly ambitious, envious of reputations like May Swenson's or (especially) Adrienne Rich's. Sometimes she speaks warmly of men, teachers and lovers, who enter her life as mentor and protectors. Ted Hughes himself is described as titan, genius, emperor. She washes his feet, types his poems, irons his shirts, and does all that a girl can do to feel greater happiness for his successes than her own. But women? Women are competitors.

The real subject here (no headlines, no public events, no leakage from the real world) is writing, writing and success. Success was her true worship, a bitchier goddess than William James had imagined. To make herself a poet (which meant making herself complete) was one thing; but to make herself *successful* was the conscious aim. (p. 3)

[Mostly] the journals are crammed with plans, plans for work, plans for prizes, plans for success, plans to be professional. The true vitality was reserved for her poems, but the *Journals* are full of what Jane Davison, one of Sylvia Plath's Smith classmates, described as "the dangerous illusion we shared, a belief in unlimited possibilities that was, I fear, closer to greed than to innocence."

Without dwelling on the checkered posthumous publishing history of Sylvia Plath's works, I think the *Journals* can hardly be counted among the important items in the Plath catalogue. Their biographical significance, given their vacuous self-absorption, consists mainly in the light they throw on Plath's suspect ambitions for herself. Their writing style inadvertently repeats some of the major metaphor-chains in her poetry. But by any reasonable comparison with Plath's finished work, this is a depressing bore.... We value artists for the work they finish, for their insistence on perfection, on truthfulness. How can we content ourselves, then, with a book so riddled with editorial expurgations, with omissions that stud the text like angry scars, with allusions to destroyed and "disappeared" parts of the journals?

It reminds us of all the "authorized" Plath biographies that never got written, and of the one awful unauthorized one that did, and of the nearly 20 years that passed after Plath's death before her *Collected Poems* were published in 1981. Couldn't there be some malign witchcraft here, something working as hard to cover up the poet's true accomplishment as Sylvia Plath did to dig her true self out of the sand? Does anyone imagine that Sylvia Plath herself, had she lived, would have permitted these journals to be set in type? (p. 11)

> Peter Davison, "*Sylvia Plath: Consumed by the Anxieties of Ambition*," *in* Book World—The Washington Post, *April 18, 1982, pp. 3, 11.*

KATHA POLLITT

[*The Journals of Sylvia Plath*] cannot tell us what Plath was reading, thinking, or living through when she wrote the *Ariel* poems, or whether she really thought *The Bell Jar* was a potboiler, as she wrote to her mother, or by what steps she dredged to the surface her final, excoriating fury. They give us, in other words, not the Sylvia Plath we think of as Sylvia Plath but her spiritual younger sister, a kind of Sylvia Plath in training.

The first thing that strikes one about Plath's journals is what they leave out.... There is little of the leisurely speculation on the characters or doings of others that makes the diaries of Virginia Woolf so much fun to read, and little in the way of gossip, anecdote, and reported conversation. Out of all those afternoons in the Ritz bar with Anne Sexton and George Starbuck, for example, not one remark struck her as clever or true or even annoying enough to write down. She mentioned no movies, few plays, and only a handful of books.

What the journals are, as Plath said, is "a litany of dreams, directives and imperatives." They are a storehouse of ideas for stories, novels, and poems; of stray phrases and incidents that would turn up, sometimes years later, in her finished work. They are the place, too, where she chronicled an almost unbroken parade of depressions, blocks, and visits of the "Panic Bird," and where she urged herself, over and over, year after dragging year, to throw herself into writing. (pp. 103-04)

All serious writers are ambitious, no matter how disarmingly modest they appear in interviews or memoirs. I think it is safe to say, though, that no writer has ever been more driven by a need for bankable, quantifiable, publicly rewarded success than the young Plath, or more obsessed with measuring herself against the competition.... Except for Ted Hughes, and him only sometimes, there seem to have been no living writers whose work she could enjoy without falling into a fit of envy. Distorted by jealousy and a worship of fame on any terms, her literary judgments were remarkably superficial, especially in view of her gifts and education: Elizabeth Bishop was "lesbian and fanciful," "easily surpassed"; on the other hand, "the weight of Irwin Shaw and Peter De Vries . . . oppresses me."

It's hard not to frown at Plath's lack of generosity, a quality that extended far beyond the bounds of literature. She does not seem to have been a warm person, or to have had the gift of friendship. Her life, even after marriage, was a narrow one, grimly governed by her struggles to write, and she often complained of feeling housebound and lonely. "My life is a discipline, a prison," she wrote. Typically, though, her isolation distressed her mostly as a literary problem: how could she write fiction when she had so few connections with others, so little "material"?

One is struck by her obliviousness of the difficulties and sorrows of others, even those few she genuinely liked. Afraid at one point that she was infertile, she noted bitterly that "Esther [Baskin, a good friend] has multiple sclerosis, but she has children." It is as though other people did not seem real to her except as they served as yardsticks for comparison.

But, then, Plath did not seem real to herself, either. She wrote that she was loathsome, not human, full of "rot"; or else she felt nothing at all, and lived trapped in a "glass caul" of affectlessness. This sense of unreality was one source of her infatuation with the more sugary aspects of American domesticity as preached in the commercial magazines she was always trying to write for. Real people, even "stupid housewives and people with polio," sold stories to *The Saturday Evening Post,* so why couldn't she? There must be something wrong with her.

Certainly, one of the things that was wrong with Plath was the era in which she lived, and the cramped, stultifying images it held out for women. There is something infinitely sad and moving in the way she veered in and out of understanding the implications of femininity as the Age of Eisenhower defined it; again and again she teetered on the edge of rage and defiance, and then drew back into acquiescence. Thus, in the earliest entries, she furiously denounced the double standard that allowed her boyfriends to sleep around but not her. At the same time, she recognized the value of a carefully maintained virginity.... "Being born a woman is my awful tragedy," she observed sadly; on the other hand, she was almost nineteen, with "at best three years in which to meet eligible people." Years later, she wrote, "I have hated men because I felt them physically necessary: hated them because they would degrade me, by their attitude: women shouldn't think, shouldn't be unfaithful (but their husbands may be), must stay home, cook, wash," and we hold our breath: she was so close to putting her finger on one source of all those depressions, of all those poems she herself described as "crystal-brittle and sugar-faceted." As her mature poems would testify, that truer, deeper self from which she felt cut off and which she strived energetically to uncover in these journals was seething with rage at belonging to the dependent, hedged-in sex—the sex that could not write about wars and adventures and do as it liked, but could only "cry and freeze, cry and freeze." In the diaries, as soon as she has her moments of awareness, she suppresses them: "Get bathrobe and slippers and nightgown & work on femininity." How utterly revealing that verb *work* is!

The eligible person came along, although not within the three-year time limit: Ted Hughes, "the man the unsatisfied ladies scan the stories in *The Ladies' Home Journal* for," as Plath noted with her usual rivalrousness. Here at last was a man strong enough and brilliant enough for Plath to accept as her superior, and that was what marriage was all about. . . . Ted was so far ahead of her that there was no point in being jealous, and so she could act as his secretary with no sense of servitude. His triumphs were her triumphs, too: "It's rather as if neither of us—or especially myself—had any skin, or one skin between us. . . ."

It sounds like an ideal solution for a woman as competitive as Plath, but as we know, it wasn't. Soon there were quarrels, and resentments brooded over in secret: she *wouldn't* sew on his buttons, and wouldn't show him her poems, either—he'd only criticize them to death; he was vain and pompous and pretended he couldn't tell her old classmates apart; he ran around with girlfriends the way all husbands do, while the wives try to look sweet and virtuous. . . . What else could they do, after all: "He is a genius. [omission] I his wife."

One wonders about that omission, and others, too; the text is littered with them. One sympathizes with Hughes's difficult editorial job—this is his life, too—and honors him for offering us as much as he does. All the same, one can't help speculating that the original manuscript might make clear some of the points left vague by the editors. (pp. 104-05)

The journals do contain some splendid writing—although, unlike the editors, I still think her best prose work is *The Bell Jar*, potboiler or no. If the book does not answer all our questions, it answers a good many. And until Plath's biography is written, we shall have to be content with that. (p. 105)

Katha Pollitt, "Poet in Training," in The Atlantic Monthly, *Vol. 249, No. 5, May, 1982, pp. 102-05.*

NANCY MILFORD

[*The Journals of Sylvia Plath* begins] in the summer of 1950, just before she enters Smith College, when she is 17. (Although we are told by her editor, Frances McCullough, that she began keeping a diary when she was a child, no portions of it are printed here.) They are marked by an immense will to succeed, and she is as relentless in her dedication to her craft as she is in her search for a self from which to shape it.

Why has it taken nearly 20 years for these "curtailed" journals to be published, let alone *The Collected Poems?* Is it because these journals are dominated from the first by the twin thrusts of sex and vocation, which are, unfortunately for her, linked to idealized domesticity and female dependence? (p. 1)

There are extraordinary things to notice [in the passages which record Plath's first meeting Ted Hughes (February 26, 1956)]: the fierce passion of their meeting, as if they were in combat, and that it is he who kisses and she who draws blood; the stunning urgency with which she records wanting him, without equivocation. And, finally, of course, the omissions. For who can tell from this docked text what provoked her bite? Surely it serves to confirm:

> Out of the ash
> I rise with my red hair
> And I eat men like air.
> ("**Lady Lazarus,**" 23-29 October 1962)

But does it? Here is what was cut between the galleys and the published book:

> . . . and I was stamping and he was stamping on the floor, and then he kissed me bang smash on the mouth and ripped my hairband off, my lovely red hairband scarf which has weathered the sun and much love, and whose like I shall never find again, and my favorite silver earrings: hah, I shall keep, he barked. And when he kissed my neck I bit him long and hard on the cheek, and when we came out of the room, blood was running down his face. His poem 'I did it, I.' Such violence, and I see how women lie down for artists. The one man in the room who was as big as his poems, huge, with hulk and dynamic chunks of words; his poems are strong and blasting like a high wind in steel girders. And I screamed in myself, thinking: oh, to give myself crashing, fighting, to you.

What has been deleted in his action: he kisses and he rips, he takes and he keeps. Those are not small details. What we are left with instead is a text pared to her reaction. This seems to me a disservice to both of them.

She had been waiting for him for years. . . .

After she has met Hughes, but less than two weeks have passed, he is again in Cambridge.

> Please let him come; let me have him for this British spring. Please, please. . . .Oh, he is here; my black marauder; oh hungry hungry. I am so hungry for a big smashing creative burgeoning burdened love: I am here; I wait; and he plays on the banks of the river Cam like a casual faun.

By June she will have married him in a ceremony secret from everyone but her mother, who is there to bear witness.

There is an awful convention at work here, but can it truly be called commonplace? Who knew in the heart of the 50's the cost not only of domesticity, but of the violence to the self involved in loving that "black marauder"—that fierce and equally talented romantic hero who would father us into our fullest selves and art. It was a devastating bargain and not a woman I can think of has not paid her dues, in her own voice, which if she is a writer is her only coin. One becomes increasingly cautious these days about throwing stones, for the breakage comes dear, and close to home.

After she has married, her mood is for a while celebratory. . . .

She finishes out her year at Cambridge and accepts a teaching position at Smith for the following fall. Her mother treats them to a summer on Cape Cod. Plath frets about her work, her "bright glittery" adolescent success is behind her and she fights "to make the experience of my early maturity available to my typewriter." She casts a green eye at the competition, Donald Hall and Adrienne Rich, "and only 16 poems published in the last year." And she's tough on herself. (p. 30)

[What] she wished and worked for was to be "The Poetess of America (as Ted will be The Poet of England and her dominions). Who rivals? Well, in history Sappho, Elizabeth Barrett

Browning, Christina Rossetti, Amy Lowell, Emily Dickinson, Edna St. Vincent Millay—all dead.'' Marianne Moore and Edith Sitwell are her ''aging giantesses,'' and among the living she lists only the female poets: May Swenson, Isabella Gardner, ''and most close, Adrienne Cecile Rich,'' toward whom she felt both rivalrous and admiring. Adrienne Rich was a scant three years older and when they met at Radcliffe that spring Plath eyed her closely: ''little, round and stumpy, all vibrant short black hair, great sparkling black eyes and a tulip-red umbrella: honest, frank, forthright and even opiniated.''

She was careful to scrutinize the work and the lives of other women who wrote, and she paid particular attention to those whose sexual choices were at odds with hers. (pp. 30-1)

It is worth noting that these reflections about other women's lives are made when Plath is pregnant for the first time. Before that she fears being barren, and is rhapsodic about what she's missing. . . .

When she knows she is going to have a child she is considerably cooler, even funny.

> Children might humanize me. But I must rely on them for nothing. Fable of children changing existence and character as absurd as fable of marriage doing it. Here I am, the same old sourdough.

Isn't this precisely why we read a writer's journals? Not as a key to the poetry, but to know about the life from which the poems sprang. Poetry is never simply autobiography; even if its heat and urgency is stoked by the dilemmas of ordinary life, it is an act of transformation. For even among the so called ''Confessional'' poets, whether Lowell, Berryman or Plath, their revelations are not to be confused with fact. Hidden, shaped, toyed with and mercilessly reworked, fabricated even, the facts of their lives become the instruments of their art. Even journals tell only a kind of truth—taken on the run, or when the mood is foul, when one is feeling too dim, or pressed to make the real work, which is the poetry. Still, a journal must be a record clear of the filtering hands and mind of a biographer, and clear, too, of anyone as deeply implicated in her life, and her work, as Mr. Hughes is. Finally, it seems to me disingenuous to suggest that these Journals can be used as a gloss to Sylvia Plath's poetry when they do not cover the period, 1959-1963, when her major work got written.

Mr. Hughes has something quite extraordinary to say about all this in an essay titled ''Sylvia Plath and Her Journals'' [see excerpt above]. . . .

The Journals should be crucial. They are. They are also a peculiarly broken record; Mr. Hughes calls them ''curtailed.'' But by whom, if not by him, and why? Notice the pronouns [in Hughes's essay], for they are chilling

> Two other notebooks survived for a while after her death. They continued from where the surviving record breaks off in late 1959 and covered the last three years of her life. The second of these two books her husband destroyed, because he did not want her children to have to read it (in those days he regarded forgetfulness as an essential part of survival). The earlier one disappeared more recently (and may, presumably, still turn up).

In the Foreword published [in *The Journals of Sylvia Plath*], his wording is different enough to be striking.

> Two more notebooks survived for a while, maroon-backed ledgers like the '57-'59 volume, and continued the record from late '59 to within three days of

her death. The last of these contained entries for several months, and I destroyed it because I did not want her children to have to read it (in those days I regarded forgetfulness as an essential part of survival). The other disappeared.

To within three days of her death? I'm a betting woman: the earlier notebook will surface. Mr. Hughes is hardly unaware of what he's done; again he writes in [the essay],

> we cannot help wondering whether the lost entries for her last three years were not the more important section of it. Those years, after all, produced the work that made her name.

(p. 31)

The question about these Journals is always the same: who is doing the cutting? And why? There is almost no rage expressed in these Journals, no sex described, but everywhere suggested. Why, for instance, in an entry that describes two teenagers dancing, is the boy's erection omitted while Plath's breasts are allowed ''aching firm against his chest.'' Gracious sakes. And can we believe that this woman would have recorded no response to childbirth in her Journals? No woman living would have made such cuts without the pressure of a male hand. It is not enough for Mr. Hughes to tell us that ''This is her autobiography, far from complete, but complex and accurate.'' Not in the face of such crucial missing material: the two years after her first suicide attempt in 1953: the entire period of her courtship with Hughes between April 1956 when she returns to him in England and their marriage in June: the entire last three years of her life, with the exception of certain character sketches which Mrs. McCullough tells us ''were separate from her regular journals, and are all that survive in prose from this period, though she was also at work on a second novel.'' This too, 130 manuscript pages of a novel called *Double Exposure*, is lost. (pp. 31-2)

Against the immense seriousness of Sylvia Plath's quest for herself, and the perhaps monstrous and unrelenting self-observation that could not in the end sustain her, we will usefully place her poetry, her letters, and these Journals. She would be 50 this October. Instead she is forever caught in her 30th year, the fever heroine. (p. 32)

> *Nancy Milford, in a review of ''The Journals of Sylvia Plath,'' in* The New York Times Book Review, *May 2, 1982, pp. 1, 30-2.*

PHOEBE PETTINGELL

Outlining a novel she never finished about a young American woman living in England in the mid-1950s, Sylvia Plath wrote a note to herself in her diary concerning the autobiographical heroine: ''Make her enigmatic: who is that blond girl: she is a bitch: she is the white goddess. Make her a statement of the generation. Which is you.'' One encounters this sketchy protagonist in *The Journals of Sylvia Plath* with a shock of recognition, for she is the surprising voice that controls the poems of *Ariel*. Plath certainly set out to be an archetype. . . .

In late 1981 her husband, Ted Hughes, finally published her *Collected Poems*—the work from her four books of verse, plus all the mature uncollected poems and 50 examples of juvenilia. Now, to round out the portrait of this still elusive woman, he has edited *The Journals*. Plath kept diaries from childhood until her death in 1963. The selections culled by Hughes (roughly one third of the material extant, according to co-editor Frances McCullough) have been chosen mostly for the light they cast on her poetic apprenticeship. Hughes believes that throughout her life Plath was consumed by "a craving to strip away everything from some ultimate intensity, some communion with spirit, or with reality, or simply with intensity itself."

Her journals, in common with her poems, testify to a progression of startling transformations. As with the nymph stages of some insect who breaks through the dried up husk into a shining metamorphosis, so Plath cast aside one style for another that suddenly seemed more authentic—sometimes with violence to herself and others. (p. 10)

Plath's goals tended to be the conventional ones: She sought fulfilment in devotion to her man and children; she longed to become a successful writer published in all the right places, from the *New Yorker* to the high-paying women's magazines; she dreamed of a satisfying career in some prestigious field. The unconventional part was her refusal to compromise: She wanted everything at once, no matter how incompatible her desires.

The Journals cover the years 1951-62, from the time Plath entered college to just after the Hugheses decided to leave their jobs in America and resettle permanently in England. The earliest entries, though full of schoolgirl philosophizing, are obsessed with Plath's perennial concern—the relationship between life and art. (pp. 10-11)

After her first suicide attempt, a recovered Plath threw herself even more voraciously at life. She dyed her hair platinum, devoured boyfriends like chocolates, played the American coed abroad to the hilt in England, and continued to write prize-winning verse. Yet all this merely raised her old nemesis.

> So I am not worth the really good boys. . . . If my poems were really good, there might be some chance, but until I make something tight and riding over the limits of sweet sestinas and sonnets, away from the reflection of myself in [a boyfriend's] eyes, and the inevitable narrow bed, too small for a smashing act of love, until then they can ignore me and make up pretty jokes.

A skeptic might wonder how often poems actually win strong men. But the very night after this entry was made she met Ted Hughes for the first time at a wild literary party. They admired each other's work, and he inspired her first mature poems. They were married four months later.

Plath despised her juvenilia; nonetheless, it was technically superior to most college efforts and concerned pretty much the same themes as her subsequent poetry. *The Journals* confirm that her subjects picked her long before she had the experience to choose them. The main flaw of the early work is the absence of a firm voice; high polish stifles emotional immediacy.

No doubt this is why during her marriage to Hughes, when she was still groping painfully toward a true self, many of her best poems were landscape word-paintings. Quite a few of these were taken from preliminary observations in the journals. . . . The minutely described external world often allowed her to summon a feeling—usually of panic and emptiness—

through the back door as it were. **"Blackberrying,"** for example, twists down an enclosed lane where nature is both beautiful and repulsive, to an unexpected hill above the sea "That looks out on nothing, nothing but a great space / Of white and pewter lights, and a din like silversmiths / Beating and beating at an intractable metal." **"The Moon and the Yew Tree,"** after serenely invoking the clouds "flowering blue and mystical over the face of the stars," concludes bleakly, "The moon sees nothing of this. She is bald and wild. / And the message of the yew tree is blackness—blackness and silence."

Although these are strong, somber poems, they still represent an inhibition of Plath's true gift. In 1959, near the end of *The Journals,* and just before another one of her poetic metamorphoses, she prayed "To be true to my own weirdness." For someone who spent much of her time trying to satisfy the expectations of others, this was a daring request, terrifyingly answered in the last few months of her life.

Unfortunately, we do not have the last two diaries Plath kept. Hughes destroyed one, and the other disappeared. We can only guess, therefore, at the means of the ultimate transformation that allowed Plath to write the poems of *Ariel* and *Winter Trees.* The existing journals confirm our impression, however, that anger liberated her writing. So it is reasonable to suggest that the collapse of her marriage released the voice of the abused daughter of **"Daddy,"** the vengeful harpy of **"Lady Lazarus,"** the abandoned mother of **"By Candlelight."** . . .

The publication of diaries is a dubious business—they can be boring, inchoate, too intimate, or cruel (Plath, for instance, frequently caricatured her friends, made catty remarks, or recorded her private grievances against family members). But I think Hughes was fully justified in giving us "the daily struggle of her warring selves . . . the making and remaking of herself." He has not always received the credit he deserves for his work as Plath's editor (that it must have been a painful task is evident from the length of time it has taken *The Collected Poems* and *The Journals* to appear). Some reviewers have criticized the number of omissions and ellipses in the text, yet rarely have I seen such a sensitive or tasteful presentation of diaries that were, after all, the most secret thoughts of their author.

Now that Plath's poetry has been around for nearly two decades, she may be assessed more fairly than heretofore. Critics need no longer be put off by Saint Sylvia/Bitch Goddess, a figure first mockingly created by her, then seized upon with deadly earnestness by her worshippers. Seen objectively, she was a gifted lyricist at every stage of her career, who wrote a handful of unforgettable poems right before the end. Her outlook was limited to one not always mature perspective at a time. Still, at her best she conveyed feelings of chaos with a sense of absolute mastery and control few can equal. She may remain for us an enigmatic person, an archetype of the doomed poet, but her voice will continue to be heard. (p. 11)

Phoebe Pettingell, "The Voices of Sylvia Plath," in The New Leader, *Vol. LXV, No. 10, May 17, 1982, pp. 10-11.*

Jean Rhys

1890-1979

(Born Ella Gwendolen Rees Williams) West Indian-born English novelist, short story writer, autobiographer, and translator.

Rhys's works combine personal experience with emotional and psychological insight to examine the nature of relationships between the sexes. She typically focused upon complex, intelligent, sensitive women who are dominated and victimized by men and society. Alone and alienated, these women are unable or unwilling to learn from past mistakes, achieve emotional and financial independence, or gain control of their lives. Rhys is frequently praised as a master stylist whose narrative forms reflect and modulate the content of her fiction. Her spare, understated prose, realistic characterizations, dreamlike imagery, and ironic, often embittered tone dramatize the plights of her characters while evoking sympathy for their situations.

The daughter of a Welsh father and a Creole mother, Rhys was born in Roseau, Dominica, an island in the Lesser Antilles. After receiving religious training in a convent as a young girl, Rhys relocated to England and lived with an aunt while attending school. In 1919, amid the aftermath of World War I, Rhys married Jean Lenglet, moved to Paris, and bore a son who died shortly after birth. Because of her husband's position with the Allied Commission, which was responsible for the administration of postwar Vienna, Rhys lived throughout continental Europe, returning to Paris during the early 1920s with Lenglet and their newborn daughter. While in Paris, Rhys worked at various jobs, pursued occasional writing opportunities, and in 1924, through a literary connection, met author and editor Ford Madox Ford. After Lenglet was jailed in 1925 for dubious business practices, Rhys turned to Ford for comfort and support. Responsible for launching her literary career, Ford encouraged Rhys by printing several of her early works in his *Transatlantic Review* and sponsoring the publication of her first book, *The Left Bank and Other Stories* (1927). A collection of fragments, sketches, and impressions that are deeply informed by events in Rhys's life, *The Left Bank* examines bohemian existence in Paris during the 1920s from feminine perspectives. In his preface to this volume, praising Rhys's "singular instinct for form," Ford stated: "Miss Rhys' work seems to me to be so very good, so vivid, so extraordinarily distinguished by the rendering of passion, and so true, that I wish to be connected with it."

In her first novel, *Postures* (1928), which was republished as *Quartet,* Rhys fictionalizes her increasingly complicated relationship with Ford and his common-law wife. The story of Marya Zelli, who is left emotionally and financially desolate after her husband is imprisoned, *Quartet* focuses upon the psychological forces and moral consequences of the association that develops between the protagonist and the Heidlers, an older couple on whom Marya becomes dependent. Using sparse, ironic prose, interrelated images, and extended metaphors, Rhys probes Marya's victimization and subsequent mental collapse. Following her husband's release from prison in the late 1920s, both Rhys's affair with Ford and her marriage to Jean Lenglet ended while her literary career displayed promise. Her second novel, *After Leaving Mr. Mackenzie* (1931), chronicles the

Fay Godwin's Photo Files

failure of a forty-year-old divorcée to rediscover the value of human engagement. Living an enclosed and restricted existence, the protagonist simultaneously fears and desires companionship, and her reckless behavior functions as a response to male-dominated interaction between the sexes. In this novel, Rhys maintains authorial distance by utilizing shifting points of view to offer detailed analyses of modern sexual attitudes while exploring the lies and self-deceptions upon which many relationships are based.

Voyage in the Dark (1934) is based on Rhys's experiences as a young actress in an itinerant English musical troupe. This novel depicts the life of Anna Morgan, with particular emphasis upon her first love affair and subsequent abortion, as well as recollections of her childhood in the Caribbean islands. Typical of many of Rhys's heroines, Anna seeks comfort and security in relationships with men despite repeated rejections. Sustained by a will to survive and by memories of her youth, Anna resolves at the story's end to change her behavior and begin her life anew. Rhys emphasizes the irony of her protagonist's situation by establishing a parallel narrative structure that reflects the oppositional nature of Caribbean and English culture, past and present, and dream and reality while revealing Anna's failure to reconcile her affinities for each of these elements. In her fourth novel, *Good Morning, Midnight* (1939), Rhys advances her major themes and extends her portrayal of female consciousness. Set in Paris shortly before the onset of World War II, this book explores a middle-aged woman's attempts to discover meaning in her life by confronting her past. Deserted by husbands and lovers, she becomes involved with a gigolo who mistakes her for a wealthy woman. Fearful of her own desire for love and affection, the protagonist withdraws from the relationship while maintaining hope that the man will return. Nevertheless, a bizarre and variously interpreted final scene reveals the woman engaged in a sexual encounter with a salesman for whom she simultaneously feels compassion and repulsion. Considered more than merely a study of a lonely, aging woman, this novel was described by one critic as "the tragedy of a distinguished mind and generous nature that have gone unappreciated in a conventional, unimaginative world."

Rhys remarried during the 1930s. Her second husband died in 1945, and she married again two years later. During this time, Rhys's literary career remained dormant, and many of her followers thought that she had died. In 1949, however, Rhys answered a classified advertisement placed by a woman wanting to produce a dramatic adaptation of *Good Morning, Midnight,* thereby disproving the rumors of her death and initiating the revival of her career. Encouraged by the knowledge that her work had not been forgotten, Rhys began her fifth and most highly acclaimed novel, *Wide Sargasso Sea* (1966). Set within the lush terrain of the West Indies following the abolition of slavery, a period characterized by the volatile sentiments of many islanders, this work reinterprets events in Charlotte Brontë's novel *Jane Eyre,* centering on the relationship between Brontë's character Edward Rochester and his first wife, Antoinette. Portrayed in *Jane Eyre* as a mad Creole woman living in the attic of Rochester's house, Antoinette is transformed in *Wide Sargasso Sea* into an exotic, passionate, and complex woman whose attraction to native culture conflicts sharply with her colonial upbringing and with Rochester's English background. Rochester, who is considered Rhys's most fully realized male character, allows his fear of sexual passion to dominate his desire for Antoinette, and in attempting to protect his pride and sense of honor, he restricts his wife's natural yearnings and contributes to her demise. Concentrating on the psychological, emotional, and cultural elements of her story, Rhys explores such thematic concerns as the effects of historical events on individuals, the functions of myth and religion, and the connection between the physical and metaphysical realms.

Prior to her death, Rhys also published the short story collections *Tigers Are Better-Looking* (1968) and *Sleep It Off Lady* (1976), as well as *My Day: Three Pieces* (1975), a privately printed autobiographical work. *Smile Please: An Unfinished Autobiography* (1979) was issued posthumously, as were several other books, including *The Letters of Jean Rhys* (1984), *Jean Rhys: The Complete Novels* (1985), and *Jean Rhys: The Collected Short Stories* (1987).

(See also *CLC,* Vols. 2, 4, 6, 14, 19; *Contemporary Authors,* Vols. 25-28, rev. ed., Vols. 85-88 [obituary]; and *Dictionary of Literary Biography,* Vol. 36.)

THE TIMES LITERARY SUPPLEMENT

Miss Rhys's sketches and short character studies [in *The Left Bank and Other Stories*] seem almost tentative. Miss Rhys has an intimate knowledge of the Rive Gauche, but she is inclined to disturb the necessary content of her work by a rather self-conscious antagonism towards the Anglo-Amerian invaders of Paris and her championship of the outcast, unhappy, and fallen. She attains joy in her quick objective sketches of mannequins, models, and artists, and her glimpses of those English spinsters who are to be found, lonely and forgotten, in tiny niches of the Latin Quarter have pathos and insight. Her subjective studies, written in the French manner in the first-person, are less effective: this sensitized style always seems to produce a contrary, amateurish effect in English. **"La Grosse Fifi,"** a story of a good-hearted though mercenary woman on the Riviera, is the most sustained piece of writing in the book and it is the best; the rather sordid theme is lightened by complete humanity and humorous charity. This fine study proves that Miss Rhys requires space and a certain amount of plot-action to give free play to her original talent.

A review of "The Left Bank and Other Stories," in The Times Literary Supplement, *No. 1318, May 5, 1927, p. 320.*

THE SATURDAY REVIEW OF LITERATURE

The "Left Bank" of Miss Rhys's [*The Left Bank*] is meant to indicate more than the far side of the Seine. It is the far side of life to which she most often carries the people of her stories, the side of poverty, Bohemianism, unhappiness mixed with reckless freedom. Her little segments of this life, brief, effective, and tinged with a slightly hysterical sentiment, deal with a mixed lot, artists of every nationality. Ford Madox Ford has pointed out in a generous introduction the excellencies of her work, the technical skill, the vividness with which she renders passion. He does not add that these anecdotes and sketches are often so slight, so flashing, that their impression on the mind scarcely survives the reading. The final series of impressions, connected by a narrative thread, of Vienna just after the war, is more considerable, but the book as a whole indicates that Miss Rhys's vision of things has not yet clarified, though the tricks of her trade are already mastered.

A review of "The Left Bank," in The Saturday Review of Literature, *Vol. IV, No. 15, November 5, 1927, p. 287.*

THE NEW REPUBLIC

The Left Bank is a collection of brief and very brief sketches which Miss Rhys will probably look back on some day as her apprenticeship. They deal chiefly with the precarious fringes of life in Europe: women who are on their uppers, men who are lying in French jails, embezzlers, prostitutes, mannequins, artists. When she does write about those who have found soft seats in this world, Miss Rhys is merciless in putting her finger on their fatuousness or lust or timidity. Her sympathy goes to the down-and-outers, who are crippled by fear of starvation and the law. And while this identification with one class limits her understanding, it sharpens her eyes. Most of her stories are not more than half a dozen pages in length, and each of them has been filed down to such a careful concision that the reader is sometimes uncomfortably aware of the rub of the file. But what is left is sharp. We are shown, for example, a woman who is starving being set up to dinner by a "lady" who had evidently been her friend in more prosperous days. We are told merely what the lady says and, in alternate paragraphs, what she thinks. That is all: we never learn the story behind the incident. But we do see the triviality and complacency of all stupid people who have been lucky toward those who have been unlucky.

L.S.M., in a review of "The Left Bank and Other Stories," in The New Republic, *Vol. LII, No. 676, November 16, 1927, p. 345.*

THE NEW YORK TIMES BOOK REVIEW

One cannot escape the feeling that [**The Left Bank**] takes its title from Ford Madox Ford's preface rather than from the book itself, for, unless that preface is to be considered a story, there is no story in the book called "The Left Bank." . . . Yet the title, actually a misnomer, is not so misleading as it might be, for it symbolizes the material with which Miss Rhys has worked, the people, the situations, the life in general—as Mr. Ford suggests. The Montmartre and Montparnasse of recent fiction have very little place in it. One of the stories takes place in a jail, another along the Riviera, and the longest and best in Vienna. But the spirit these stories show of undisciplined and unconventional youth, of hardship, of disillusion, of loose and nervous and artificial existences, is expressively brought out by the term "left bank."

For the most part Miss Rhys's stories and sketches are very brief. Her method is to reject the descriptive and the expository, to reject for the most part structural plot, and even to reject fullness of characterization as we understand it. Casually and conversationally she leads one into a situation, presents one to a character and gives one glimpses of both. For the most part, that is all. She gains her effects as much by what she omits as by what she includes; and she omits a great deal. Yet one is sometimes able, so strong is Miss Rhys's gift of connotation, to grasp in a moment all that is behind the situation and inherent in the character. This is true, for example, of **"Tea With an Artist."** Sometimes we are not given enough to make the picture significant, as was sometimes true of Katherine Mansfield, whom Miss Rhys resembles more than she does any one else.

To this reviewer's mind, Miss Rhys is at her best when she appears to be autobiographical. There is something more than clever about **"Hunger"**—in which, with great brevity, she manages to express the ever-changing thoughts and emotions of a person who does not eat for five days. And there is something fascinatingly real about **"Vienne"**—a record of contacts and experiences with an assortment of unusual people encountered in Vienna. The best part of this series of episodes is the last, when the finances of the narrator's husband go to smash, and the two of them flee from Vienna, distraught in mind, by automobile. In **"Vienne"** Miss Rhys carries her promise very close to fulfillment, and writes with unusual penetration and individuality.

For all its frequent fumbling, its frequent sketchiness, its occasional fiascoes of experimentalism, **The Left Bank** is the work of one who has something to say and who is finding her own way to say it. Katherine Mansfield, Martin Armstrong, any number of people, might have written **"Illusion"**; but **"Hunger"** and **"Tea With an Artist"** and **"Vienne"** are proofs of a fresh and personal talent. Miss Rhys is worth keeping an eye on. (pp. 28, 30)

"Miss Rhys's Short Stories," in The New York Times Book Review, *December 11, 1927, pp. 28, 30.*

HERBERT GORMAN

So few novels really get to the bottom of the twisted lives of expatriates living in the Quartier Montparnasse that when one with the unmistakable accents of truth appears the pleasantly surprised commentator is liable to err on the side of enthusiastic acceptance. Such an effort is Miss Jean Rhys's **Quartet.** Here, for the first time since Ernest Hemingway's *The Sun Also Rises,* is an unsentimentalized development of an impossible situation in that curious corner of Paris where the spurious constantly rubs shoulders with the real. It is not as good as Mr. Hemingway's novel, but it is quite as ruthless. With an almost malicious objectivity, Miss Rhys sets before her readers four characters who, when all the veils of self-disguise are unwrapped from them, represent what futility and weakness may make of the human soul. The types are sharply distinguished. There is Marya Zelli, the sole personage upon whom Miss Rhys expends any particular sympathy, who is caught beneath the nether mill-stone of a dishonest husband and the upper mill-stone of a selfish and cowardly lover. Marya, because of her helplessness, is victimized outrageously, so outrageously, in fact, that more than her helplessness would seem to be the cause of it. The husband, Stephen, is a vicious-minded weakling who passes most of his time in a French prison. It is because of the detention of Stephen and her penniless condition that Marya is forced into the milieu of the Heidlers, that revolting couple who make up the quartet of the book. Heidler himself is a surprisingly complete characterization of a coward who has self-hypnotized himself into a semblance of strength because of the lecherous urge in him. He is both physically and spiritually dishonest. Mrs. Heidler, who is drawn with such maliciousness by Miss Rhys that the suspicion persists that she hated and, sometimes, feared this character, is a strange mixture of jealousy, hardness and supineness.

With four such personalities reacting upon one another the result of the book is never in doubt. All of them will destroy each other through themselves and each other. Marya, flung into the household of Heidler, is seduced by him. Mrs. Heidler, listening at doors and alternately sympathetic and jealously hysterical, becomes both pander and accuser of her husband. Stephen, fresh from prison, is lost in the pettiness of his own soul. There is no hope for any one of these unlovely people (in spite of Miss Rhys's determined attempt to construct Marya into a long-suffering sympathetic character the commentator can feel no pity for her) who wander about the Quartier Montparnasse, dine at Lefranc's and sip their *aperitifs* at little *bistros.* They are part of that "lost generation" that Gertrude Stein described. They are all cases of nerves and studies in selfishness. Their puerility is manifest in our last remembrances of them when the book is finished. Heidler, large, portentous, hook-nosed, cowardly eyed, pressing his fat knee against Marya when Mrs. Heidler isn't looking; Mrs. Heidler listening at the keyhole and running up to her bedroom to weep; Marya disgustingly supine in her acquiescence to the heavy demands of Heidler and deluding herself by putting it all on emotionally psychological grounds; Stephen so rat-like in his demeanor and riding off with the nearest *grue* when the situation passes beyond his powers.

There is no doubt about the power of Miss Rhys's characterizations. She knows these characters with that peculiar intimacy that always suggests prototypes, and, because of this surprising verisimilitude, the painful reality of the situation is raised to a higher plane than that of mere story telling. Her prose is staccato and purposeful and calculated to bring out clearly the essential note of her theme. It would be futile to go into a discussion as to whether or not **Quartet** is an artistic libel on the Quartier Montparnasse, for there is too much to be said on both sides. But it is safe to assume that characters very much like the four unfortunate personalities in Miss Rhys's book may be encountered drifting up and down the boulevard, dining at Lavenue's, and dancing till long after midnight in the high studios of the district. The same semi-truth that strengthened the effect of *The Sun Also Rises* is to be found in **Quartet**. That portion of the denizens of the Quartier, who live upon nerves and lose themselves in a disastrous gluttony for sensations are the "lost generation." And, of course, there is that other portion from whose lives might be fashioned an equally striking novel.

Herbert Gorman, "The Unholy Four," in New York Herald Tribune Books, *February 10, 1929, p. 7.*

THE NEW YORK TIMES BOOK REVIEW

Beginning with what promises to be merely one more record of the blatant disillusionment of Left Bank bohemianism, [*Quartet*] soon takes on an import which separates it at once from the general class suggested by its background and from all but the most potent and conscientious of recent fiction. The unstable and highly factitious world of cafés, studios, taxicabs is one which we should be amply familiar with by this time; the shifting value of conduct and thought, the temper of the life transcribed, are no longer curious or inexplicable enough to command our interest in themselves. As her book progresses it becomes clear that Miss Rhys has either ignored or takes for granted whatever superficies of romantic sentiment may still be inherent in her setting. Throughout, the setting is distinctly subordinated to character; although the tragedy of Marya Zelli is to a large extent shaped and determined by her environment, the essence of her tragedy, residing in the profound conflict of life and character, is universalized beyond any particular time or place. The theme of the book, in universal terms, is that one cannot survive in human relationships without some more reliable means of control than the emotions. The tragedy of its protagonist is that she was too unrelenting in her emotional loyalties to protect her self against circumstance. To achieve this, Miss Rhys shows her hedged around by circumstances which permit no escape, which entrap her in a situation from which she cannot free herself except through compromise or death.

For several years Marya Zelli has enjoyed the placid contentment of living with a husband as indifferent to the purposeful ordering of life as herself. His sudden arrest and imprisonment for theft forces her to some adjustment to the world. The world comes to mean to her the Heidlers, whose assistance she allows herself to accept, and the first problem of her new life appears when Heidler admits he is in love with her. The Heidlers are sophisticated, prosperous, highly enterprising in their relationships. Lois Heidler is sensible enough not to be disturbed by what she realizes from the beginning is no more than a temporary challenge to her marital security. But Marya is not sensible enough to withstand Heidler's robust personality; she moves from his home only to become his mistress in a cheap Montparnasse hotel. Not until Stephan Zelli is released from prison does the hopelessness of her predicament become apparent to her. The "quartet" is brought together only once, around a café table on the Boul' Miche, and the meeting is packed with the tight, inarticulate and half submerged drama which has accumulated during the year of Stephan's imprisonment. In this scene Lois Heidler alone is omniscient and

contained. Thereafter the dissolution of the quartet is inevitable. Heidler first indicates his desire to close the episode by sending Marya to Cannes for her health; upon her sudden return to Paris to say good-bye to Stephan, who is preparing to leave for the Argentine, the break is complete. Penniless, abandoned by Heidler, soon to be abandoned also by Stephan, Marya is at the end of her rope. She confesses to Stephan her long infidelity to him and her own betrayal; but when Stephan announces his intention to seek out Heidler and shoot him, Marya refuses to let him pass through the doorway, screaming aloud that she still loves Heidler. At the end we leave her, struck down by Stephan's blow, lying lifeless on the floor.

If difficulty of subject is to be considered in judging the merit of a novel, Miss Rhys must be accredited with high achievement. Not only does she deal with the most complex personalities, exploring the most intimate recesses of their psychology, but she does so with the directness and certitude of the fine artist. The style, especially of the dialogue, belongs to the new tradition in prose, which shuns elaboration for sharpness and intensity of effect. Whatever extension of range in character or setting that Miss Rhys may bring to her future work, it seems scarcely possible that she will be able to surpass the strength and poignancy of **Quartet**.

"Poignant Tragedy," in The New York Times Book Review, *February 10, 1929, p. 8.*

THE SATURDAY REVIEW OF LITERATURE

No one reading **Quartet** will escape a sudden sharp remembrance of that other novel of drunken dawns in Paris that Ernest Hemingway sent home to America some seasons ago. The likenesses in the two books are extraneous, however, and in no way reflect upon Miss Rhys's beautifully articulated anatomy of disintegration. Anglo-Saxons gone Dome are prevalent enough to furnish material for as many writers as may be able to find new significance in their spiritual nomadery. Jean Rhys has done this.

The four characters of **Quartet** walk the same boulevards, climb the same stairs, drink the same aperitifs as do the lost legions of *The Sun Also Rises*, but they think different thoughts, sin different sins, and will die different deaths. **Quartet** is a close-knit study of mordant personality. Its people carry their destinies within their veins. The quartet move to their fates with inevitability beating time as relentlessly as in any Greek drama, but here is no accompaniment of rushing winds and wings above, only the thin voice of a mechanical piano inspired by a nickel in its gullet.

The author has gone deep to fish this murex up, and it is bitter blue indeed. The brittle objectivity of the very modern style which Miss Rhys employs scrupulously throughout only adds by its impersonality to her indictment of emotional egotism. There are no concessions made for the characters, there are none for the reader.

A review of "Quartet," in The Saturday Review of Literature, *Vol. V, No. 39, April 20, 1929, p. 936.*

THE NEW YORK TIMES BOOK REVIEW

After leaving Mr. Mackenzie, Julia Martin [in Jean Rhys' novel ***After Leaving Mr. Mackenzie***] goes to live in a cheap hotel on a mean Paris street. She lives there alone in a benumbed state, subsisting on the 300 francs a week that Mr. Mackenzie sends her, spending her daytimes reading, her evenings in solitary drinking. The callousness of Mr. Mackenzie's dismissal of her, her poverty, the growing realization that she is older, shabbier, and less attractive than she once was—all these factors combine to undermine a spirit never very strong. One week the note from Mr. Mackenzie's lawyer contains 1,500 francs and the information that no more will be forthcoming. Now Julia must rouse herself from her stupor and set about the business of getting back upon her own feet. The pitiful story of her weak attempts to do so, her rapid disintegration in the face of harsh necessity, cruel treatment from others, and her own sapped courage, is the story which this brief novel tells. In the beginning we see her, a woman in her early thirties, suffering from a recent humiliation—a woman who had had her first love affair at 19, who had married and been deserted by her husband, who, through inertia and the force of circumstances, had allowed herself to drift from man to man. At the end—a few months later—we find Julia little better than an ordinary Parisian street walker.

Miss Rhys tells her story sparely. She attempts by small devices to make you see and feel with Julia—to make you understand her. But she never intrudes on the narrative or touches it up with sentimentality or bitterness. Julia is Julia, an individual who, in a broad sense, may also stand for a type. No moral judgment is intended either on Julia, on men in their relations with women, on society or on humanity. The reader may or may not pass moral judgment on any of these phenomena. He may or may not like Julia. The author has no interest in achieving anything except a portrait of a certain woman. The other figures—the three men, the sister who has devoted her life to the paralyzed mother, the fleeting figures encountered in small London and Paris hotels—stay in the background.

Julia is a girl and woman of keen sensibility with little practical sense. Put to the test she has considerable bravery, but she has no real courage. She has not the egotism that would give her the hardness to stand up against the buffets of a free, adventurous life. Neither has she the reserve strength to do anything for herself in quiet solitude. She is weak, unstable, easily crushed—but never bad.

Miss Rhys's novel is the latest addition to the vast body of fiction which hails Flaubert as master. It offers no new note in treatment. Because no human particle is deemed unworthy to be celebrated, the school, as its master claimed for it, takes on a significance as large as life. If one, wearied of the method and tempted by the allusion, were inclined to add "and twice as natural," that the technique of *Madame Bovary* and *Pierre et Jean* made for over-simplification to the point of naïveté when used by more ordinary mortals, the fact remains that out of this method have come masterpieces and much excellent secondary work. Miss Rhys's study, slight and certainly over-simplified as it is, contains many of the merits of its species. It succeeds in bringing to the reader a small fragment of a life which is in turn an infinitesimal fragment of all life.

"*Twice-as-Naturalism,*" *in* The New York Times Book Review, *June 28, 1931, p. 6.*

GLADYS GRAHAM

If [*After Leaving Mr. Mackenzie*] were written with a shade less artistry it would be unbearable. It is a tale of horror as truly as any that deals with the more obvious and objective machinations of the evil spirit. Miss Rhys's novel is a terrible portrait of a woman done to death by life but denied the final *coup de grace* that would free her from the daily and nightly gestures of living. There have been enough bad women, weak women, and victimized women in novels since novels began, yet where will one turn to find so bedraggled and impotent a creature as this Julia Martin of Miss Rhys?

Julia Martin is a woman, no longer quite young, with whom "going from man to man had become a habit," a habit so well established and mechanical when the story opens that whatever emotional beginnings it may have had are buried deep and unguessable under ennui. Julia is the quintessentially supine, but she has the devastating stubbornness of the will-less. Fundamentally there is no help for her because she cannot care about anything long enough even to hope for change. She knows fear, she knows humiliation, and yet almost at the moment of their intensity they begin to slip a little and merge into the general feeling of depression that is to be dulled only with that bottle which the French landlady disapproved of Julia's taking to her room at night ("A man, yes; a bottle, no.")

Julia has become an expert at dulling the edge of life. Feeling darkly, without ever letting herself quite face it, that she is no match for reality, she lies in her room and dreams of places— "of dark shadows of houses in a street white with sunshine; or of trees with slender black branches and young green leaves. . . . She hardly ever thought of men, or of love. . . ." Then on a day, an hour, she will determine on action. Mr. Mackenzie must be made to pay. She whips herself into frenetic activity. She dresses, she goes out, nothing can stop her. But meanwhile she will sit a moment at the café, will take a drink. A pleasant state of relaxation begins to creep over her. Another drink, and memories becloud the present. And so back to the safe isolation of her room, her bed; another day will do for deeds, now for dreams. Never able to get a foothold in the conventionally notched ways of life that ordinary people take for granted, Julia slips little by little down the shabby incline that leads to no kindly specific hell but to that much hollower one—nowhere.

The book is written with something of the balance and beauty of verse. The shifting of a phrase would be a threat against the whole. Words are used like little weights, placed with an almost fractional delicacy. Phrases and words that are lovely and beguiling in their form but ruthless and explicit in their content march the pages undeterred. Slight in scope, minor in key, it perfects itself within its spherical intent. it is a book that does not invite comparisons. It does not appeal as being as-good-as or better-than. Its excellence is individual, intrinsic; it measures itself against itself.

Gladys Graham, "*A Bedraggled Career,*" *in* The Saturday Review of Literature, *Vol. 8, No. 1, July 25, 1931, p. 5.*

GEOFFREY STONE

[*After Leaving Mr. Mackenzie*] is a sordid story, with that especial brand of sordidness lack of money brings; yet one wonders if Julia Martin had had money whether she would have done anything but drift from lover to lover with the same dull throbbing weariness—a weariness that is always described in physical terms. It seems that under any conditions Julia's life would have been sordid; that quality was inevitable in anything occurring to her: she walked into everything "hands down". Life, surely, had used her cruelly, but in that there was only pathos, no tragedy, for it was not her passions that had placed her where she was but her very lack of them. If Mr. Mackenzie's dismissal of his mistress was the thing that ''smashed'' her up and made her ''want to go away and hide'', it cannot be regarded so much a result of Mr. Mackenzie's obtuseness and selfishness as the result of a life that, because it was held together by nothing intense, could only eventually disintegrate. Perhaps disintegrate is not the exact word, for Julia's life became the final reduction of what it had been before, only the begging became more obvious, the irresolution was crystallized into doubts what to do the next hour, where to spend the evening.

Miss Rhys has written this novel brilliantly, with an economy that is not the outcome of a monotonous formula nor a reflection of the minds of moronic characters. To say that she has left out the irrelevant would be untrue; her effects are largely gained by a judicious use of the irrelevant—the expression on a waiter's face, people in a cinema, paper blown along a street. The use of the word irrelevant is, of course, paradoxical, because Julia's existence and the existence of those with whom she came in contact are somehow made meaningful by these very meaningless odds and ends of observation. As one follows the hopeless course of Julia, lying in bed occupied by thoughts hardly worthy of the name, supplanting the act of judgement by the tooting of taxi horns, one is surprised to find that the meaning of the book as a whole appears just as clearly, and is much the same, as in any tale with a moral. It is no defect in the work. (pp. 84-5)

> *Geoffrey Stone, in a review of "After Leaving Mr. Mackenzie," in* The Bookman, *New York, Vol. LXXIV, No. 1, September, 1931, pp. 84-5.*

FLORENCE HAXTON BRITTEN

Miss Jean Rhys in *Voyage in the Dark* tells the simple story of a little girl lost, or virgin into prostitute. And she tells it with such sympathetic, lovely precision that the brief story of Anna Morgan's little year in London stands for perfection of accomplishment and sustained mood, like a first-rate lyric poem.

Voyage in the Dark is a study of inertia. No, not that. It is not a study at all; but a telling. The bewildered girl of eighteen, young for her years, uprooted from a tiny British West Indian island—she adored the hot tropical sun there and the warm-hearted blacks—arrives in London and show business without momentum of any sort. Her stepmother, on the death of her father, has brought her here, and that's that. She makes friends easily—too easily, perhaps—because she is such a baby, and seems to need looking after. She is dimly aware of the drive every one else in her world seems to have to scheme and get on. ''Everybody says, 'Get on.' Of course, some people do get on. But how many? What about what's-her-name? She got on, didn't she? 'Chorus-Girl Marries Peer's Son.' Well, what about Her? Get on or get out, they say. Get on or get out.'' But little Anna Morgan is helpless to make any move to join the vast procession. There's nothing she wants intensely or greatly enjoys—until she meets ''Walter.''

Walter is a nearly anonymous gentleman twenty years older than she who takes her on for a bit and teaches her what pure joy is. But she knew, from the beginning, that she had no facilities for holding him. So she was happy and sad together.

> When it was sad was when you woke up at night and thought about being alone and that everybody says the man's bound to get tired. (You make up letters that you never send or even write. 'My darling Walter.' . . .) Everybody says the man's bound to get

tired and you read it in all books. But I never read now, so they can't get at me like that, anyway. ('My darling Walter.' . . .)

Voyage in the Dark follows Anna out of the chorus and cheerless theatrical rooming houses into idleness and a little flat provided by Walter but never visited by him, through dinners at restaurants and nights of ecstasy cut short by the necessity to get up and get out, and on into that desolate time when, driven by no urge of any sort, she moves through feckless days and nights establishing her place, unwittingly, in the ''profession.''

The utter simplicity of Miss Rhys's method—deceptive in its apparent ease, of course—is of itself thrilling. *Voyage in the Dark* is written in the first person, but the ''I'' is never sufficiently self-conscious to make this a straight-ahead narrative. It is rather a beautifully organized brooding; a stream-of-consciousness account of the futile effort of a bewildered child to orient herself in a confusing world. The story of Anna Morgan is no social document, however; it is too utterly, intensely individual for that. But it floods one nevertheless with an awed sense of responsibility for the weak. ''Inasmuch as ye have done it unto the least of these'' . . .

My guess is that Miss Rhys and *Voyage in the Dark* will have a fairly limited, but extremely enthusiastic audience.

> *Florence Haxton Britten, in a review of "Voyage in the Dark," in* New York Herald Tribune Books, *March 17, 1935, p. 10.*

JANE SPENCE SOUTHRON

Between 1927 and the present time Jean Rhys has produced three volumes of fiction, all of which may be regarded as preparation for *Voyage in the Dark. The Left Bank,* a collection of tales and sketches dealing for the most part with the Parisian underworld, was less definitely anticipatory than *Quartet,* the story of an English girl left penniless by the adventurer she had married. *After Leaving Mr. Mackenzie* came still closer in subject; but in treatment and feeling it is far beneath the more recent work. The central figure was a prostitute. Anna Morgan, who tells her own story in *Voyage in the Dark* falls, technically, into the same class. The girls and women with whom she is thrown are prostitutes, confessed or camouflaged. The men who meet her in the company of these women regard her—and, eventually, treat her—as deserving of no better consideration. In reality she is a bewildered child, infinitely pitiable, made for love and human happiness; the sport of circumstances and the victim of hypocrites. Without ever resorting to pathos Miss Rhys has created a figure and a history intensely pathetic, and she has done it by indirect satire and by showing us the workings of this young girl's mind.

Miss Rhys has made use of modern methods where it suited her. Anna's early life and upbringing in the West Indies; her selfish, backboneless father; her callous, shifty and hypocritical stepmother; the easy happiness of her earlier years; her passion for the tropical loveliness of her home and her fondness for Francine, the colored maid who tended her, are brought before us in a series of mental back-flashes. Some of these are written without punctuation, but with spaces to represent quick changes of thought. Others, that more closely resemble deliberate soliloquy, are in ordinary narrative style. By means of these brilliant, exotic pictures, evoked ever and again in the midst of the sordid grayness of the scenes through which the girl is moving, the pattern of the past is woven bit by bit into the tapestry of the present, accounting for much in the given moment that would otherwise be inexplicable and heightening the drama by vivid contrast.

It should be a perfect subject for the screen, especially if color were used in the West Indian flash-backs. But you could not get, as you actually do in the novel, the smell of the tropics, the sensation of warmth and pleasant languor, the million and one delicacies of tropical sound. These Miss Rhys scatters throughout her book by virtue of her ability to render the sensuous in subtly glowing prose.

It is the story of a girl brought to England on her father's death by a mercenary stepmother anxious only to be rid of an encumbrance, and thrown into the theatrical world, with neither preparation nor special talent, to find her feet as best she might. The succession of horrible lodgings in different parts of England that forms the background of this young actress's peregrinations is depicted in language that is as starkly realistic as it is mordantly terse.

Most of the satire is directed against hypocrisy. ''I'm in a nice, clean English room, with all the dirt swept under the bed,'' says Anna when she is coming down with flu and has just been ordered to vacate her miserable London shelter by a virtuous landlady. . . .

The stages of brooding wretchedness through which she falls to her final, unspeakable catastrophe are personal to herself, not typical of a class. She attempts to become hard-boiled in action no less than in speech, but with only superficial success. . . .

When she finds she has a child coming she is persuaded to get rid of it. Cynically the doctor who is hurriedly called in declares: ''She'll be all right . . . Ready to start all over again in no time, I've no doubt.''

''I lay,'' she says—this smirched and unhappy child—''and thought about starting all over again . . . And about mornings, and misty days, when anything might happen.'' Still the dreamer, voyaging in the dark!

Aside altogether from its undeniable artistic excellence the book displays unusually broad sympathy and quite exceptional insight.

Jane Spence Southron, ''A Girl's Ordeal,'' in The New York Times Book Review, *March 17, 1935, p. 7.*

THE TIMES LITERARY SUPPLEMENT

[*Good Morning, Midnight*] is about a woman in the forties who longed to feel young and desirable again and was terrified of making a fool of herself. Whether Miss Rhys would approve this description of her new novel is doubtful, since for all her economy of words she evidently distrusts plain statements and prefers the coloured and the allusive. Still, the facts are that Sasha, as the no longer youthful woman chose to call herself, lamented the triumph of time, dyed her hair, was kissed by a young man of the gigolo type and funked the dawning sensation of life and happiness. Around these facts Miss Rhys has built a story, doggedly tough in a feminine way, that is always clever and is sometimes poignant. There is not a lot of it, but what there is goes a little in advance of, say, Mr. Hemingway, the father of all such as wear a hard-boiled heart on their sleeve.

It is Sasha who tells her own story. She speaks her mind in a staccato, rather fevered, highly self-conscious fashion, but at the same time hers is an accent of genuine and acute emotional distress. You feel that she is not merely an unhappy woman but a woman capable of suffering because she is unhappy. After some years spent abroad she lives in a back room off the Gray's Inn Road and hates English gentility and English humbug; she is very poor, very mocking, very misanthropical; she avoids people and resolutely gets tipsy from time to time. A friend of the sort that kills by kindness lends her enough money to spend a fortnight in Paris. To Paris Sasha goes. It has memories for her of love and poverty, of spring mornings and the bread of bitterness, of the Lapin Agile, of life that went a-maying with Nature, Hope and Poesy when she was young. Now she is dead in spirit and all doors are shut to her: in this visitation of the past a couple of drinks make her tearful and she feels she has come to the end of her tether. All this Miss Rhys conveys at the start through oblique little touches of reminiscence or sharp spells of introspection in an hotel bedroom in the Quarter. What, you ask, has crushed Sasha? Life? The weight of her own romantic expectations? Too many Pernods, too many *fines?* All these, it appears; but it is a weakness of the tale that Miss Rhys does not clearly distinguish between them. Wandering the streets or sitting alone at a Montparnasse café, Sasha too often seems to confuse a fatal excess of temperament with the experience life has dealt her.

It is, in its fretted and intense way, a revealing piece of work, in which time and again honesty comes to the rescue and enables Miss Rhys to escape sentimentality by the skin of her teeth. There is, indeed, an air of almost desperate urgency about the whole thing that claims and rewards sympathy. It is apparent even in the studied licence of the gigolo episode, whose closing sensationalism flickers with a protesting innocence. Yet the last impression, like the first, is of cleverness vainly held in leash, cleverness that continually gets the better of Miss Rhys. Since earlier work by her has won tribute in the shape of standard exclamations of genius, work of art, originality, perfection and the rest, something may be said of the limitations of the present novel. Its subjective manner, a variant of the stream of consciousness, is anything but fresh nowadays and is more than commonly monotonous where the subject is forever stretched on a bed of live coals. More, it necessarily evades three parts of the problem of presenting life in the round. Perhaps most important, self-consciousness as unrelenting and as oracular as Sasha's needs more than sincerity to recommend it. One can be sincerely sorry for oneself, sincerely maudlin in drink and yet communicate nothing that is not obvious or that matters twopence to the sober.

The book is piquantly readable, however, and there are shrewd and penetrating things in it. The shadow of Enno, whom Sasha had doubtfully married, falls with ominous effect across her memories, and the gigolo René, who begins by telling her cock-and-bull-stories about himself and ends by challenging her to share his own joy in life, is an adroit and knowledgeable study. The difficulty is Sasha. Becky Sharp's trouble was that she believed she could be a good woman if she had five thousand a year. Was it, after all, Sasha's trouble that she believed she could be a happy woman on the same terms?

''Lost Years,'' in The Times Literary Supplement, *No. 1942, April 22, 1939, p. 231.*

THOMAS F. STALEY

Wide Sargasso Sea is both easy and difficult to place in Jean Rhys's canon. It is at once, as one critic asserts, 'a logical outgrowth of the developments in the previous four novels', and quite different in treatment and subject matter, if not theme, from the four earlier novels. Rhys, of course, first used her West Indian background for material in *Voyage in the Dark,* and even in her first volume of stories explicit West Indian backgrounds are used in two of them. But the themes in *Wide Sargasso Sea* are more than an outgrowth of the earlier novels; they do . . . embody many of these same themes, but there are many subtle variations and real differences, especially in the treatment of the male personality. Her characterisation of Edward Rochester, for example, is by far the most complex and fully drawn male she has ever accomplished. *Wide Sargasso Sea* is very much a part of the Rhys canon, dealing as it does with those aspects of personality and human relationships which have always engaged her. In spite of the limitations in the character of Antoinette, the novel simultaneously deepens and, in several important ways, reexamines the nature of male and female understanding, suggesting an attitude different from her earlier novels and one especially more understanding and comprehensive of male behaviour and feeling.

Playing as it does against the background of *Jane Eyre*, *Wide Sargasso Sea* initially directs our attention to Charlotte Brontë's novel. Certainly this aspect of the novel has been the one upon which most critical discussion has fallen. Several articles have treated the novel exclusively in relation to *Jane Eyre* and the Gothic mode generally; those that have not concentrate on the West Indian background [see excerpt by Louis James in *CLC*, Vol. 14]. Since *Wide Sargasso Sea* deals mainly with the early life of Rochester and his mad Creole wife who lives in the attic of Thornfield Hall and finally burns it down in *Jane Eyre,* this is perhaps one reason for the novel's initial, general popularity. The exploration of the novel through its treatment of the early lives of Brontë's characters is a fruitful avenue in which to explore it, as Michael Thorpe's excellent essay makes clear, but it can also lead to a serious misunderstanding of the novel if it is not well handled. (pp. 100-01)

The achievement of this novel is that it engages our moral and intellectual awareness more thoroughly than do the earlier works. It does so because of its more fully balanced and amplified treatment of the male-female relationship. We recognise in this novel, as Lionel Trilling has written of *Mansfield Park,* 'an analogue with the malice of the experienced universe, with the irony of circumstance, which is always disclosing more than we bargained for'. Although culture, race, nationality, all of the large categories which divide us, are thematically central to *Wide Sargasso Sea,* Rhys makes abundantly clear that it is in the exposure of our individual 'doubts' and 'hesitations', our private needs and motivations, our exposure to each other, that we discover the malice of the universe. It is out of this mutual relationship of Antoinette and Edward, of the male and the female, that Rhys's view of the self is fully expressed. The horrible vision in *Good Morning, Midnight* is somewhat released by the sympathy for and understanding of the heroine and our anger at the forces which nearly destroy her, but the anger is really without individual human focus. However, in *Wide Sargasso Sea* our release must come from our understanding of those nearly inexpressible truths which lie at the heart of all of our relationships.

The design of *Wide Sargasso Sea,* like that of all of Rhys's novels, clearly reflects her major thematic concerns; the scenes owe their symbolic quality to the thematic patterns which are crucial to the structure of the novel. We learn of the child Antoinette from the novel's opening section, and also gain a view of the insular world which emerged from childhood's impact on the interior self. Part I, besides establishing a childhood basis and pattern of experience for Antoinette's later behaviour, develops through carefully elaborated events and her reactions to them our understanding of the formation of her consciousness. By drawing attention to the cultural and historical forces and events which surround her, we are made aware of the violence, disruption, and tragedy which mark her for life. The radical social and emotional upheaval in the West Indies contained in this section provide a kind of psycho-historical background for Antoinette's life. (pp. 101-02)

Much attention could be given to the historical turmoil which so drastically affects Antoinette's early life, for it is of considerable importance to the entire social and domestic fabric of her existence; but Rhys's concentration is on the psychological, the personal traumas which historical events produce rather than on the events themselves. Of major significance is her treatment of the formation of the fears and deeply rooted feelings resulting from the slave and master, black and white relationships. The attitudes resulting from these are central to the novel's tensions. The attraction and repulsion, the sympathy and hatred, that Antoinette feels for the blacks is so basically different from Edward's comprehension of them that it epitomises the young couple's vast cultural separation. This fact is stressed again and again, and as they act out of these widely different attitudes, we are constantly made aware of the unbridgeable gulf of understanding which separates them. It is most dramatically revealed in sexual terms, as we shall see.

For all her estrangement from the native and black population, Antoinette is a part of the Islands; her attraction to the wild and the exotic confirms her affinity; it ties her irrevocably to this land, in spite of her hostility to it and it to her.

But it is a grim and dying world. In both myth and reality the whites of the Island feel as though they are in the heart of Eden after the fall. . . . With the fall, of course, come desperation and violence. It is a land of deserted estates, burned houses, scorched land, overgrown roads, as though nature and man collaborated in erasing a past. (pp. 103-04)

And in Rhys's novel as the lush growth of nature settles over the marks of the white civilisation so, too, do the power of superstition—obeah—and other mysterious practices surface through the remnants of Christianity. When a group of blacks burn down the Coulibri Estate that Mr. Mason, her mother's new husband, had restored, the family escapes only because the blacks grow fearful when the family's pet parrot is engulfed by fire and falls to the earth in a flaming mass. Antoinette recalls, 'I heard someone say something about bad luck and remembered that it was very unlucky to kill a parrot, or even to see a parrot die.'

As she and her family escape to a carriage, Antoinette sees her friend, Tia, and the whole black rebellion becomes a personal betrayal as Tia hits her in the head with a stone. But in this dramatic conflict, Antoinette feels an affinity for the blacks that even the violence cannot erase: 'I looked at her and I saw her face crumble up as she began to cry. We stared at each other, blood on my face, tears on hers. It was as if I saw myself. Like in a looking-glass.' In spite of the violent rupture, Antoinette remains constant in her identification with the blacks. Tia's act, however, confirms Antoinette's ultimate separation from the black culture; but she is a victim, not an agent. She will vacillate between the separate worlds of blacks and whites because in her childhood she needed both, but with the rebellion she can no longer be comfortable with both identities, a disjunction ultimately a source of her doom. She grows dependent upon both worlds but is accepted in neither. In each she will become identified with the other and be looked upon with suspicion. Furthermore, her brother's death and her mother's madness after the fire not only mark Antoinette's final separation from her childhood, they confirm her complete isolation and seal her own fate in a private schizophrenic world between two times, races, and cultures. Her mother's submission and sexual subjugation at the hands of her black caretaker is also of major significance, for its dramatises and reinforces the strong current of sexuality between the races that moves through the novel. Her mother's experiences in an admittedly different way foreshadow her own and the psycho-sexual elements are, on one level, expressive of the complicated relationships between the two races that years of slavery developed, relationships which surface in Antoinette's relationship with Edward.

The latter sections of Antoinette's narrative record the life of ritual, prayers, and order within the convent school, which becomes for her a 'refuge, a place of sunshine'. She feels safe inside its walls, but her childhood illusions have apparently disappeared ('I soon forgot about happiness.'). And the convent, although a place of sunshine, is also one 'of death'. (pp. 104-05)

Part II, which takes up nearly two-thirds of the novel, is largely Edward's account of the events following his marriage to Antoinette, and it forms the narrative and thematic centre of the book. Told largely from his point of view, it records the financial arrangements prior to their wedding, the journey and arrival at Granbois, the early days of sexual passion at the doom-laden but idyllic honeymoon house, and the eventual mistrust, conflict and sundering. There is also a short but enormously important scene between Antoinette and Christophine, the wise old native, narrated by Antoinette. Although certain elements of the Gothic mode have been earlier introduced, it is in this section that Rhys makes it an active element and combines the Gothic with pathetic fallacy to reflect Edward's rapidly changing states of being. . . . The Gothic mode—besides its obvious relation to *Jane Eyre*—functions as a narrative idiom where the descriptions themselves, with their frequently elaborate portents, achieve a metaphysical relationship to the characters, not unlike the early descriptions in Conrad's *Heart of Darkness,* when the terrors of the natural world are precursive and reflective of the horror and fear of the interior self.

Although Part II is centered within Edward's intelligence, the dialogue between Antoinette and Edward is extensive and this not only expands the focus beyond Edward, who is at once cold and naïve, it dramatises the interplay of forces which work on both of them. (pp. 105-06)

For both Edward and Antoinette their honeymoon is a journey, metaphorical as well as real. Edward, smug that he has captured a beautiful if strange and exotic woman with a substantial dowry, feels little emotion and far less love for his bride—a condition not unusual among second sons in Victorian families who must get along on their own—but from the beginning he is aware that he must depend upon her, for this enclosed and intoxicating world where she is leading him is 'not only wild but menacing'. The journey, of course, ends in failure for a number of reasons, not the least of which is Edward's inability to accept any dependence which gradually becomes apparent. His motives for marrying Antoinette, callous from the beginning, are not, however, the source of the failure of the marriage; it is finally his inability and refusal to give of himself. His

sense of responsibility for her proceeds from his code of honour, not from love. Antoinette's own disengagement, her enclosed world, contribute to the impossibility of their marriage. She desires closeness, but closeness circumscribed by her own narrow universe, which is strange and threatening to Edward.

For Antoinette their trip is not only a return but an escape—a chance to recapture some lost tranquility of childhood and avoid, for a short time at least, the responsibilities and further displacement of her marriage. The complex of emotions which compel Antoinette to return to her past elude Edward completely from the beginning. He does, however, begin to realise how fundamentally disparate he and his wife are, and the significance of his realisation becomes increasingly apparent to him.

As he is led deeper into the natural landscape, however, he is forced to see Antoinette as more than a testament to his enterprise. He sees her as a human being, and in so doing he partially sees for the first time the wide cultural and emotional gulf which separates them. . . . And as he begins to know more of his wife and she appears increasingly alien and strange to him, he gradually begins to identify her with the blacks. . . . (pp. 106-08)

For both of them, however, it is this lush, mysterious jungle that works on them, in opposite ways, and lays bare their passions and fears. For Edward, 'everything is too much', and this feeling extends to the entire natural scene: 'Too much blue, too much purple, too much green. The flowers too red, the mountains too high, the hills too near.' Yet his instincts are also awakened by these same surroundings and the startlingly attractive girl he has married; he is ambivalent; Antoinette is 'beautiful. And yet. . . .' (ellipsis in text). The primitive beauty of the country has about it a pristine quality, 'an intoxicating freshness as if all this had never been breathed before'. For Edward it had not, and this is part of its seductive quality.

The whole exotic experience of the first few days at Granbois is a kind of initiation for Edward. There is a dominant sensual element to nearly everything, and it is as though he were entering upon some erotic rite where every scene and act has a meaning beyond itself. Like all initiates to an alien experience, 'the feeling of security had left him'.

It is important to observe carefully Edward's initial emotions, because they explain if not condone his later behaviour toward Antoinette. From the beginning he finds himself in a world at once seductive and hostile, so far distant from his English roots that there is little in his past which has prepared him to understand much of what he observes: 'As for my confused impressions they will never be written. There are blanks in my mind that cannot be filled up.' His confusion only increases as the days in this remote place with Antoinette pass.

His reactions of puzzlement and mistrust slowly begin to transfer themselves to Antoinette, and his changing perceptions of her only deepen his apprehensions. At one point she asks him if he thinks, '"that I have slept too long in the moonlight?"'. For Edward there is about Antoinette a kind of lunar association, and for him the moon becomes a kind of 'objective correlative' of Antoinette. It is an association through which his insecurity and suspicions are apparent. Like Rhys's heroines before her, Antoinette senses some fatal flaw within herself, some curious turn of mind that will eventually collapse the will, a sense at once as indefinite and ominous as Edward's association of her with the moon. (p. 108)

For a few short days and nights after [the first of their passionate unions] . . . , both of them are locked in an oblivion of sensual gluttony, the intensity of which obscures the borders of a darker meaning and fear. The passion itself is induced more by the lushness and sensuousness of their environment than by mutual response. Antoinette is drawn to Edward by a desperate urgency to bring him into her private world, to live naturally and passionately within the rhythms of the natural environment she knows. But it is a world which Edward can neither accept nor understand. Edward recognises that this inordinate expression of passion without the deeper resonance of love, at least on his part, releases too much. . . . Furthermore, it is clear that this unstable idyll will break with the same intensity and passion that gave it shape; the atmosphere itself is as deep with foreboding as it is with sensuality. The desperate quality of Antoinette's passion and the callousness with which Edward accepts it is seemingly typical of the male-female relationship which Rhys created in her earlier work, except that in this case the female is more a participant than an object. This difference, however, does not diminish the desperate quality, it only heightens the sense of inevitable tragic outcome. The exclusive quality of Antoinette's desire for Edward represents a withdrawal from all other outward connections into isolation which is an escape into her own private world, and, as we have seen, isolation is the condition of despair for Rhys's heroines.

The letter Edward receives from the mulatto, Daniel Cosway, who claims to be Antoinette's half-brother, the son of her father by a black woman, is the first overt intrusion of the outside world. It tells Edward of the madness of Antoinette's mother. It can be argued that the appearance of the letter is the thread of evidence that Edward has been looking for—an excuse to put into effect a plan that will allow him to return to England and no longer have to act as a husband, but only as a caretaker to Antoinette. But such conniving is, it seems to me, beyond Edward's capability. He is a dogged Englishman whose thought and values have crystalised; he is the egocentric male figure so convinced of his 'higher level of feeling' and intelligence that he can see no other point of view. He is blind rather than deliberately malicious.

The psychological movement of the novel, however, is governed as much by what Edward does not explain as by what he does. Cosway's letter provides the dramatic turning point, and Edward's reaction to the revelation of its contents reveals his inauthentic feelings for Antoinette and his own false pride rather than the first intimations of some sinister plan that has lain hidden only to be set in motion by some external event. Rhys's characterisation has been far too subtle for such clarity of purpose to emerge suddenly from Edward. The tone of Edward's narrative suggests self-pity rather than self-justification and the dominant mood is one of sadness not revenge.

More than anything else, Cosway's letter releases the unexpressed and implied emotions which remained in abeyance during the first days at Granbois; the abridged feelings begin to emerge with rapid and horrible force. When Edward finally meets with Cosway, Cosway tells him of Antoinette's relationship with Sandi, a young black. . . . Edward's response to Cosway's revelation is self-righteous—even fearful. It reminds me somewhat of Gabriel Conroy's reaction to his wife's, Gretta's, recollection of her dead lover Michael Fury in Joyce's "The Dead", not in the mode of revelation, but rather in the way in which the two men's egos operate. Lacking the generosity of spirit which would enable him to accept or at least understand this very human desire for contact and leap from

loneliness, Edward is wounded and outraged. Like Gabriel, Edward's inflated pride and imperious personality entrap his feelings exclusively in the self. The implications of Edward's reactions also reveal not only a central moral question in the novel, but the deeply rooted conflict in the natures of both himself and Antoinette. Violating as it does what is for Edward a gigantic taboo, Antoinette's relationship with Sandi confirms the impossibility of union on Edward's part. Throughout the narrative Edward presents his values as the normative ones, and from this point on he sees Antoinette as forever savage and given to self-abandonment in lust. In failing to love her he also fails to comprehend her. Also, like Gabriel Conroy, locked in his own ego, he can at best feel pity, an emotion far less costly than love. And his pity justifies his sense of honour. His male hubris not only limits the quality of his responsibility, it enfeebles his reason.   .

The latent antagonisms of both Edward and Antoinette are set loose by Cosway's revelation and the actions which follow—desperate on the part of Antoinette and self-assertive yet confused on the part of Edward—bring the violent forces within the novel to their climax. The deeper racial prejudices, and the compelling but ominous environment begin to recede from prominence as Antoinette and Edward confront the mystery of each other and inevitably fail to understand the sources of their opposition. Two scenes, both explicitly sexual, reveal not only their widely opposed natures, but the deeper psychological forces which motivate them.

Antoinette, desperate to keep Edward, visits Christophine, the wise old native woman who practices obeah. Christophine's involvement in the novel from this point on becomes increasingly prominent. Her position is ambiguous, and yet she has the clearest head of all. Besides her suspected powers in the black arts, she sees clearly through Edward's motives and recognises the futility of Antoinette's desperate struggle to capture Edward's love. Christophine at first advises her to flee, but Antoinette explains to her the 'white laws' which subjugate her; nevertheless, Antoinette entertains the notion of escape, and in a moving passage imagines what England would be like fore her. . . . Her image of England is gradually dominated by cold and snow, all of its features set in careful contrast to the warmth of her native land. England holds no hope for her; it is cold, menacing, isolated, dead.

Against Christophine's advice, Antoinette pleads with her to practice obeah in order to bring Edward back to her: "'But Christophine, if he, my husband, could come to me one night. Once more. I would make him love me.'" Christophine knows that the primitive gods of the Islands are, in the end, helpless against the coldness of the Englishman, but she is moved to help Antoinette. Antoinette, of course, longs to return to what she imagined to be that idyllic state during those early days after she and Edward's arrival at Granbois. In spite of the violence in her life, she is still innocent, unable to accept the fact that their union was for Edward a business transaction, and he is incapable of accepting anything more, and certainly not love, which was never a part of the deal he made with her step-brother. And, ironically enough, those very qualities in Antoinette which attract him are the ones which he fears the most: the fundamental flaw in Antoinette's plan lies in her assumption that sexual passion can evoke and redeem love. It is a terrible irony that leaves the couple at cross-purposes. There is no unifying element where the two of them can meet; there is no context to join them. Edward can never allow himself to lose control, to abandon the self, and for Antoinette to attempt to bring them together through obeah will leave him to despise her forever.

While Antoinette visits Christophine, Edward and the villainous Daniel Cosway finally meet. This scene is carefully placed in ironic juxtaposition with the previous one. Here we have another older figure of the Islands giving advice to the young. The obvious clue to his reliability as opposed to Christophine's is that in the end he demands £500 silence money from Edward, whereas Christophine insists that Antoinette pay her nothing. Cosway not only reiterates to Edward the story of Antoinette's mother's madness, but tells him of Antoinette's relationship with the black boy, Sandi, with no intention of doing either Antoinette or Edward any good. The revelation enrages Edward, but by the time he confronts Antoinette his mood has changed. . . . Antoinette tells him for the first time about her family and includes her account of her last visit to her mother: 'Then she seemed to grow tired and sat down in the rocking-chair. I saw the man lift her up out of the chair and kiss her. I saw his mouth fasten on hers and she went all soft and limp in his arms and he laughed.'

The explicit sexual domination which Antoinette describes deepens his fears of Antoinette's own possible madness and strengthens his sense of the sinister powers which surround him. He, nevertheless, remains physically susceptible to his 'moon-drenched' wife; she is momentarily transformed by his own sexual desires into an erotic temptress. . . . But his aroused sexual feelings will give him all the more reason to feel repelled by her later. . . . This is the real source of his fear—his own violent passions which Antoinette released and which he saw as leaving him exposed and vulnerable to another person. In other words, he fears the closeness of relationship—he fears love. Obeah's powers can raise the passions in man, but they cannot create love where it does not exist. (pp. 109-14)

The next morning, when the effects of the drug wear off, he recalls dreaming that he had been 'buried alive'. He is confused; he looks around the room and focuses on the objects surrounding the orgy of the night before. His thoughts are those of '. . . a child spelling out the letters of a word which he cannot read, and which if he could, have no meaning or context'. He is disoriented as he tries to remember his abandonment. Finally he fixes his gaze on the sleeping, spent figure of Antoinette, who is still a sensual and erotic figure, but seeing her as the source of his having been brought over the edge of passion and control, hate wells up in him. His entire being rebels.

It is still in this state that he takes the black servant girl Amelie to bed, just 'behind the thin partition which divided us from my wife's bedroom'. It is a deliberate act of revenge—an act which dramatises his hostility and need to dominate, which symbolises his essential attitude toward life. He affronts Antoinette and, equally important, the marriage itself. When it is over he feels no remorse; he is 'satisfied and peaceful'. He has demonstrated to himself the power of his maleness—an ego far stronger than little Antoinette or her gods can oppose—but in so doing he has shown us his ability to destroy Antoinette. The powers of love which Antoinette called upon have been transformed by Edward's ego into hatred.

Near the close of Part II Christophine points out to Edward his real sin, 'nobody is to have any pride but you'. He is not in the end a scoundrel intent upon destroying Antoinette; rather he wants a relationship which guarantees both his protection and Antoinette's. We feel by the end of the novel that he would have been quite willing to assume a marriage at a distance, but Antoinette's passionate and naïve being would never accept this. Edward comes from another world and cannot fathom the life of the passions; everything in the natural surroundings which epitomises sensuous beauty tells him that this is Antoinette's world, and this is why he fears it from the beginning. (pp. 114-15)

Part III of the novel is a code which confirms Antoinette's wretched destiny. The novel's denouement occurs at the end of Part II as Edward and Antoinette leave Granbois on horseback and we recall her exuberance, happiness, and promise as she leads Edward up to the mountain retreat. The full tragedy lies in the fact that Edward could see a glimmer of that promise but could not realise it, and in his misplaced hatred: 'Above all I hated her. For she belonged to the magic and the loveliness. She had left me thirsty and all my life would be thirst and longing for what I had lost before I found it.' Edward could not find it amid all the loveliness and magic because he could not allow himself to look, and Antoinette, who offered it, could not understand his fear.

But there is something uneasy and vaguely unsatisfying about these closing implications as well as in the entire thematic movement of *Wide Sargasso Sea*. In spite of its insights into the male-female relationship, it is a disturbing text, because underneath the brilliant surface qualities and revealing delineation of character, there is a lingering doubt that the dominant emotion, always subtly rendered, is somehow wide of the mark. At the heart of this reservation is the characterisation of Antoinette. Somewhere Elizabeth Bowen writes that it is not our fate but our business to lose innocence, and once we have lost it it is futile to attempt a picnic in Eden. However much blame the reader places upon Edward for Antoinette's tragic demise—admittedly my own reading of the novel does not view Edward as malicious in spite of his cold self-interest—there is something hollow in Antoinette's character which is covered over by the exotic and mysterious qualities Rhys gives to her. The nature of her passion and the sincerity of her feeling are not enough to establish that quality of empathy which attention to the themes of the novel demands.

The heroines in Rhys's four earlier novels, in spite of their frequent lassitude and indirection, have in varying degrees not only an instinct for survival but an understanding of human nature and the world that is completely lacking in Antoinette. This does not make the earlier heroines appear less vulnerable, but it does make them more fully realised characters. For example, the young Anna Morgan in *Voyage in the Dark,* for all of her naïveté, is engaged in both the world outside and the private world of the self; whereas Antoinette never gropes beyond the world of her childhood, and this fact alone reduces the quality of her relationship from the beginning. It is in the limitations in the characterisation of Antoinette, it seems to me, that the demands Rhys imposed upon her novel by using *Jane Eyre* reveal themselves as too confining. On the whole, her autobiographical background enriches the entire fabric of *Wide Sargasso Sea*, but in the end, in revealing brilliantly the internal source of Antoinette's ultimate pathological condition, she must diminish the full impact of the tragedy of Antoinette's and Edward's marriage. The conclusion of the novel implies a lost meeting ground for love, where there was never one to be found. My point is not that this subtle conflict violates the informing principle of the novel, but rather that the reader is left with a conceptual problem in his final judgment of Edward. If it were simply a question of his taking advantage of a young innocent, there would be no problem, but the denouement of the novel implies in its description of Edward's loss that somehow he and Antoinette could have formed a vital union had only he been more open and generous. But if I understand Antoinette, a mature union would have been impossible because of her own limited capacity for understanding. Perhaps the argument of the novel is embodied in this very subtlety with which I have trouble, but it seems that Antoinette's innocence is not only the major source of her own failure, it also reduces the quality of her entire relationship with Edward and in so doing lessens our sense of his incapacity to love which the novel, conversely, implies.

Wide Sargasso Sea, even with its exotic setting, its links with *Jane Eyre,* its more explicit qualities of narration, is not all that far distant from Rhys's novels of the 1930s. If not a fulfillment, it is certainly an extension of her most basic themes, and the same quality of feeling pervades *Wide Sargasso Sea* as the earlier novels. In spite of the limitations which I see in the characterisation of Antoinette, the novel's achievement is considerable, especially in the way it captures with a lyrical intensity the rhythm between the physical and metaphysical world. (pp. 115-16)

The effects of Rhys's expansion of character, subject matter and treatment of the material from *Jane Eyre* present interesting challenges for the reader of both texts. Critical studies of *Wide Sargasso Sea* have accounted for the way in which Rhys incorporated the basic elements and themes of the Brontë novel and used her own knowledge of the West Indies with skill to amplify and in effect, create new characterisations. In short, the way in which Rhys used *Jane Eyre* as the basis for her novel is fairly clear to us, but there are two other observations which need to be made. The first is fairly obvious; most novels which emerge from other novels are usually sequels—treatments of the fictional world after the conclusion of the first work. Sequels allow for much more latitude but are invariably inferior, imitative, and sterile. Rhys undertook a much more demanding task; the outcome of the plot, the direction of the narration, the fate of the characters, all, in a way were formed. But this predetermined outcome offered a number of advantages of which Rhys was clearly aware: although what lay at the end of the road was settled, it permitted her to concentrate on the road itself—the tale of the telling rather than the telling of the tale—an emphasis which had always been in her work from the beginning.

The reader's built-in curiosity about the shadowy Bertha from *Jane Eyre,* preserves plot interest and allows Rhys to concentrate on those aspects of her novel which most concerned her anyway—the cultural, racial and psychological forces which played on Antoinette, and, more importantly, the devastating effects she and Edward had on each other, for, as I have tried to indicate, their relationship lies at the heart of *Wide Sargasso Sea,* even though many other aspects of the novel challenge our interest. In fact, the limitations imposed by developing her novel out of *Jane Eyre* and the way in which Rhys dealt with them, even with the difficulty of Antoinette, in the development, design, and narrative control of her own novel became the sources of her considerable achievement.

A second point to be considered is the effect of this relationship on the reader. Readers have quite naturally accounted for the way in which Rhys incorporated the Brontë material and how the reader's knowledge of *Jane Eyre* is fundamental to an appreciation of *Wide Sargasso Sea;* but equally important, I believe, is the way in which the latter novel enriches and even

transforms our understanding of the former. To re-read *Jane Eyre* after reading *Wide Sargasso Sea* is a startling experience. It is a feeling different from that which Eliot discusses in his essay "Tradition and the Individual Talent" when he speaks of the way literature transforms our understanding of previous literature, or of the way in which reading Joyce's *Ulysses* enriches our experience and understanding of the *Odyssey.* *Wide Sargasso Sea* focuses the reader both within and before the spatio-temporal frame of *Jane Eyre;* it amplifies our considerations of character formation within *Jane Eyre* and even tests our sense of enclosure of a narrative text. Obviously this point raises a number of theoretical issues that are far too broad for our consideration here. My point, however, is that there is a more complex process going on for the reader of *Wide Sargasso Sea* involving more than simple recognition of the use of *Jane Eyre* in Rhys's text. The text of *Jane Eyre* is expanded by the reader's participation in *Wide Sargasso Sea,* and the aesthetic awareness is widened. Surely when we re-read *Jane Eyre* after reading *Wide Sargasso Sea* our participation in that experience is transformed; our considerations of Rochester and certainly of Bertha are more deeply engaged.

Although *Jane Eyre* ends in matrimonial fulfillment, an achievement of balance between the elements of nature and personality, and a discovery of mature love, a recognition of an essential unity among all of these potentially warring elements, the affirming emphasis of the novel is on human passion. *Wide Sargasso Sea* poses the same affirmation of passion but without the measures of control achieved through reconciliation of these elements in the natural order which externalise our internal conflicts. Rhys's novel is a study in unfulfillment, in unreconciled oppositions and contrasts—between cultures, races, temperaments, the sexes, and, above all, the way in which human beings perceive the world, each other and themselves in such widely opposing ways. The novel is not a one-sided treatment of any of these oppositions; on the contrary, it achieves its unity and renders its theme by a thorough recognition and exploration of all of them. And therein lies the great source of its final achievement. (pp. 118-20)

> *Thomas F. Staley, "Wide Sargasso Sea," in his* Jean Rhys: A Critical Study, *The Macmillan Press Ltd., 1979, pp. 100-20.*

PHYLLIS ROSE

Anyone who likes Jean Rhys's novels (as I do) will love [*The Letters of Jean Rhys*]. The "heroine" of the letters is passive, fragile, helpless, depressed, angry, more than slightly paranoid, and alcoholic—very much like the heroine of the four elegant novels that Rhys published from 1928 to 1939 in the first phase of her eccentric literary career.... In the letters as in the novels the Rhys heroine, convinced that the world is against her, battles loneliness and despair, and loses. Like the novels, the letters are lyrical riffs on dark themes, with occasional flashes of gallantry and wit. The difference? The victimized woman of Rhys's novels is just that and no more; in the letters she is also an artist.

The young Jean Rhys was a chorus girl in London and a demimondaine in the Paris of the 1920s. She was involved in a complex intrigue with Ford Madox Ford and his wife, fictionalized in *Quartet.* Her life in her twenties and thirties, as revealed in the autobiographical novels, bears a remote resemblance to Colette's. The locales were similar. Rhys, too, lived marginally, and she struggled, less successfully than Colette, for independence from men. But the story of Rhys's fifties and sixties, as revealed for the first time in these letters, resembles the life of no other woman writer I know. Most writers build on a success such as Rhys had in the 1930s; Rhys disappeared. She lived obscurely in the country with her second husband, Leslie Tilden-Smith, a publisher's reader, until he died, in 1945. Thereafter she married his cousin, Max Hamer, a solicitor, and lived obscurely with him. She allowed herself to be swallowed up in English tackiness. She was poor. She was too numb and hopeless to write. Her "fierce boiling hatred of this dirty mob" (English middle-class Philistines) could not be contained. An upstairs neighbor was rude to her, she slapped him, he charged her with assault, and she spent five days in Holloway Prison. You have to admit that this is a long way from Virginia Woolf.

In 1949 an ad in the *New Statesman and Nation* asked for information about Jean Rhys. It was placed by Selma Vaz Dias, an actress who had adapted **Good Morning, Midnight** for radio. She needed permission from Rhys or her estate to broadcast it; she assumed that Rhys was dead. Rhys answered the ad herself, reestablishing a kind of contact with the literary world, but people continued, eerily, to think her dead. Her next-door neighbor spread the word that she was a fraud "impersonating a dead writer called Jean Rhys." In 1956 a Miss Smith inquired about copyrights, again assuming Rhys was dead. "I don't know why Miss Smith & Co. thought I was dead," Rhys responded. "It does seem more fitting I know, but life is never neat and tidy. I feel a bit like poor old Rasputin, who was poisoned, stabbed in the front and shot in the back but was still alive kicking and crowing when flung out into the snow."

Nothing went right for Jean Rhys. When her work was finally read on the BBC, there was a power failure in her village and she couldn't hear it. More serious, in 1949 Max Hamer was caught embezzling. He was tried and sent to Maidstone Prison. Jean Rhys had watched him head toward his downfall but had not known what to do about it. Max looked like a sensible man of business; she looked like a madwoman. If she had said something was wrong, no one would have believed her. So she went "all of a doodah" and started to drink. While Max was in prison, she stayed near him in Kent. Their life after that was a succession of moves from one uncomfortable and dreary residence in the country to another. One cottage was so damp that toadstools grew on the kitchen walls. (pp. 109,111)

All this reads like a Rhys novel. It is not the only one embedded in **The Letters of Jean Rhys.** Another one focuses on the writing of **Wide Sargasso Sea,** which took almost a decade. Max was sick. Rhys took care of him by day and worked by night—powered by speed and booze. The neighbors thought her a witch. She struggled with self-doubt, yet was fiercely determined to get the book written: "I think I have some reserves of strength. It is only outwardly that I'm a lightweight person." When Max went into the hospital, things got no easier. She was oppressed by loneliness and self-pity. She hated Cheriton Fitz Paine, the village that fate had brought her to. It was isolated, graceless, intolerant, and without typists. The lack of typists was a real problem in producing her novel. She wrote drunk, revised sober. The manuscript was messy. She could not pull it all together, could not pull herself together. She received £25 from the publisher André Deutsch in exchange for an option on the novel, and this meager sum provoked terrible guilt. She apologized continually for not getting on with it more quickly. But this story, unlike most Jean Rhys narratives, had a happy ending. For she did finish **Wide Sar-**

gasso Sea, and it was worth the trouble. It is a lush historical novel about a West Indian beauty married off to an Englishman who, fearing her mystery and sensuality, locks her up as mad; it is a retelling of *Jane Eyre* from the point of view of Rochester's wife. It is also Rhys's spiritual autobiography: born on Dominica, in the West Indies, she was transplanted to England at the age of sixteen. She suffered for the rest of her life from the actual and metaphorical cold and from the sense that most English people thought her mad.

These letters establish once and for all Jean Rhys's seriousness as a writer. Even her most devoted readers may sometimes have wondered whether the novels—so close to her life—were written or merely exuded. The letters prove that the novels were written, shaped, crafted, and did not just ooze from her experience. They also show her to have possessed a moving belief in the importance of the literary enterprise and the insignificance of any one practitioner of it: "I don't believe in the individual Writer so much as in Writing. It uses you and throws you away when you are not useful any longer.... Meanwhile there is nothing to do but plod along line by line. Then there's a drink of course which is awfully handy." The most characteristic and endearing of her statements about the dignity of art are followed by some such reference to the glories of whiskey, or they execute a Rhysian pirouette into whine—more than a hint that the world should have treated her better. ("The writer doesn't matter at all—he is only the instrument. But.... he must not be smashed.... No music if you smash the violin.") Her life seems at times so ghastly, so lacking in minimal comfort and joy, that one wonders what kept her going. The answer is Art. "For I know that to write as well as I can is my truth and why I was born. Though the Lord knows I wish I hadn't been!"

Rhys's letters have something of the immediacy and fluidity of Virginia Woolf's, although they are less gorgeous. She moves, for example, from a complaint about confusing street signs in Penge to a description of the trees there, which "have all been lopped so that they look like badly done poodles. A bit ashamed. It is *terrible* what they do to trees. Why? Can you tell me? I've an idea (another of my ideas) that some men are jealous of trees and love making them look ridiculous." There's an off-balance, scat-singing rhythm to her epistolary prose. Her fear and hatred of the English, her sufferings from the cold, form a bass line underlying happier strains, such as her enjoyment of beauty in many odd forms. Occasionally she can even muster some humor. (pp. 111-12)

Some of the best and bravest letters are to her daughter (by her first husband), Maryvonne Moerman. With her husband and young daughter, Maryvonne lived for a while in Indonesia, and Jean Rhys wrote consoling her on her sufferings from heat and complaining about her own sufferings from cold. She advised Maryvonne on how to kill cockroaches, by mixing sugar with boracic powder. (They can't resist the sugar, and the boracic powder gets them.) Always changing addresses and unable to send nice presents, Rhys felt she made a "not very satisfactory granny" and mother. Still, she was a granny; she was a mother. Her daughter evidently cared for her. So did her husbands. And she for them. We can relax. Life was not quite so grim for Jean Rhys as it was for Sasha and Anna and Julia, of her early novels.

Rhys's autobiography, **Smile, Please,** unfinished at the time of her death, in 1979, and published a year later, told us none of that—nothing about her husbands or her daughter or her dedication to her writing. It was a poor book, produced when Rhys was in her eighties and often drunk. It disappointed anyone who hoped to learn from it the story of the mysterious lost years between the publication of *Good Morning, Midnight* and that of *Wide Sargasso Sea*. Happily, her letters serve to tell that story, and, in a manner characteristic of Jean Rhys's art, the story is both depressing in content and exhilarating in its effect. (p. 112)

Phyllis Rose, "An Obscure Life," in The Atlantic Monthly, Vol. 254, No. 2, August, 1984, pp. 109, 111-12.

ANNE TYLER

Jean Rhys was a perfectly wonderful writer, with a spare and glittering style, whose subject matter is said to have been shaped by a single episode in her life. As a young woman in England, fresh from the island of Dominica, she was taken up by an older man and then, a year or so later, "pensioned off." The experience evidently shattered her. The fiction she published in the 1920s and 1930s had a bitter, plaintive note, with an emphasis upon women who were in some way victimized by men.

She married and had a child, divorced, married again and was widowed, and married yet again—this time choosing a man who eventually served a stretch in prison for a white-collar crime. For twenty-seven years—from midway through her second marriage till just after her third husband died—she published nothing, although she did work fitfully at writing. She lived in poverty, sometimes even in squalor, and she drank far too much.

Around the time she was rediscovered, in the late 1950s, she was wrestling with the beginnings of *Wide Sargasso Sea*. It is arguably her best book, a haunting novel about a Dominican girl who would become Mr. Rochester's mad wife in *Jane Eyre*. That and everything published afterward met with immediate critical approval, and she finally achieved the recognition she deserved. But by the end of her life, as mercilessly recorded in David Plante's *Difficult Women*, the squalor seemed to have gained the upper hand. She died in 1979.

Her literary executor, Francis Wyndham, had her instructions prohibiting a biography. His decision was to publish part of her correspondence instead; for as he says in his introduction [to *The Letters of Jean Rhys*], he felt that her concern was "not so much a desire for secrecy as a dread of inaccuracy." But the person revealed in her letters is a woman who intensely dislikes herself, who continually apologizes for herself, who makes dismal mistakes in her life and knows it and winces for herself. Accuracy? God forbid! She would probably have permitted a biography only if she'd been guaranteed the opposite of accuracy.

Whining, raging, rationalizing, self-deprecating, she emerges from these pages as a charter member of the "Of course it rained" school. That is, not only does she bemoan her misfortunes interminably, but she believes she has been singled out for these misfortunes by some personally vindictive and ironic fate. (pp. 29-30)

But as often happens with this type, there were times when her view of life seemed justified. When she tried to listen to a BBC broadcast of her work, the electricity promptly failed; on another occasion the clock was wrong and she missed most of the program. She appears to have attracted the craziest of neighbors; one accused her of being a witch, while another

insisted that the real author was dead and Jean Rhys an imposter.

She alienated her friends, Francis Wyndham says, with "the air of helpless passivity with which she made her exigent demands." He suggests two reasons for this passivity: a lost, dependent feeling that dated from the breakup of that first love affair, and a "congenital physical fatigue." One wonders whether the dependent feeling might have pre-existed the love affair; it seems unusual for an educated, self-supporting young woman to have been set up (and then "pensioned off"—What a phrase!) by a lover. As for the fatigue, it forms the very fabric of these letters, for her most common plea is, "A quiet place, a quiet room where they'll let me have some tea and bread and butter in the morning. . . . And a bed that isn't hard where I can sleep and sleep and sleep." She writes, "My dear this is such an idiotic epistle but I can't write another. I'm so tired—" and (excusing a drinking bout), "But remember that I was also deadly deadly tired—cannot explain how tired." At times she seems barely able to haul her pen across the page.

She begs forgiveness for her drunken outbursts but reminds her correspondents that the parties insulted deserved it; she apologizes for the tone of her letters but never goes so far as to revise them; she wails about her inability to type but never thinks to pick up a manual and learn. Oh, good grief, we say in exasperation; and yet . . .

And yet, there are moments when she comes through as so sad and anxious and fluttery, so desperate to be liked that it breaks your heart. . . . This is the value of the letters, finally: they form a magnificent character study. It's as if the author—an inspired characterizer in her fiction—could not resist exercising her talent upon herself as well, even if at her own expense. So a hopeless, helpless, infuriating but oddly appealing woman comes alive on these pages, and fairly elbows the reader in the ribs.

It's not all that important that the woman happens to have been a famous writer; as is the case with most writers, her day-to-day life sheds little light upon her fiction (though it's true that literary scholars will be interested in her extended discussions of *Wide Sargasso Sea*). You'll get more out of *The Letters of Jean Rhys* if you view it as a novel. A one-character novel, granted. But oh, what a character. (p. 30)

Anne Tyler, "Poor Me," in The New Republic, Vol. 191, No. 11, September 10, 1984, pp. 29-30.

GLORIA G. FROMM

Jean Rhys's five novels are available for the first time in a one-volume edition [*Jean Rhys: The Complete Novels*] handsomely produced, with period photographs of French scenes. . . . Since Jean Rhys's death in 1979, an unfinished autobiography (*Smile Please*) and a selection of her letters have also appeared, plus David Plante's memoir in *Difficult Women*, based upon his brief but intense association with Jean Rhys in the mid-Seventies. She was then over eighty, no matter which of the two recorded birthdates—1890 or 1894—you accept, ill and exhausted, yet sporadically engaged in composing an account of her life, her ostensible aim being to correct all the misstatements made about her, to "get the facts down," as one of her editors put it. The trouble was, facts, dates, chronology bored and exasperated her, as David Plante learned when he tried to help her organize her material. But the descriptive details, he also learned, had to be right, for in them lay the truth about everything. Indeed, she was convinced that if you used the wrong word or image, nothing you said could be believed.

That old woman in Plante's disturbing memoir is not to be brushed away. Far too vivid in her rages as well as her helplessness, she sticks in the mind—a physical wreck sporting a broad-brimmed hat and a raffish look, the all-too-familiar drink in her shaky hand. With the same hand, she has made up her face, a thick patch of powder here, another there, lipstick as much around as on the lips. But her eyes, despite the criss-crossed penciling on the lids, are "clear and blue and strong." She knew, then, what—at eighty-five or so—she looked like? A good question, perhaps crucial. For to read the luncheon menu, she puts on glasses with such smeared lenses that Plante wonders how she can see through them.

When you know what you want to see, as well as what you want, glasses are superfluous. So, too, for the current practice of reading Jean Rhys herself through the smeared lenses of her fiction, through novels in which her own experience may have been applied cosmetically but which, at their complex heart, had little to do with the real events in her life. Put another way, as the novelty of her reappearance in old age wears off, and her characters find their places in literature's huge portrait gallery, one is more and more convinced that the woman being made up—or drawn—in the Sixties and Seventies was actually the product of her novels: ontogeny out of phylogeny.

The story of Jean Rhys's "comeback," her emergence from an obscurity that had seemed permanent, has been told many times: how, in 1949, she answered an ad in the *New Statesman* for information about her; how behind the ad lay the BBC project to dramatize *Good Morning, Midnight,* her last novel, published in 1939 and swallowed up by the war; how the news that Jean Rhys was still alive caught the attention of Francis Wyndham, then with the publishing firm of André Deutsch; and how for the next fifteen years Wyndham and his fellow editor, Diana Athill, coaxed out of Jean Rhys the novel that brought her fame, *Wide Sargasso Sea.* Her one and only "romance," it was set where she was born, in the West Indies, but in the middle of the nineteenth century, in order to fill in the background—missing from Charlotte Brontë's *Jane Eyre*—for Rochester's first marriage to his mysterious Creole wife. Rhys's novel, however, was to have its own evasive ellipses.

When *Wide Sargasso Sea* finally appeared in 1966 and won two literary prizes, the creation of Jean Rhys by her new audience was already underway. During the years of struggle to finish a book not only different from any other she had ever written but also much more difficult than anticipated, she was the object of a form of attention both new to her and problematic. The actress who had orchestrated the BBC dramatization expected gratitude and made requests that verged on demands, throwing Jean Rhys into fits of panic and anger. The editors waiting for her novel provided invaluable encouragement but also filled her with anxiety and guilt. Against her principles, in order to justify the lengthening delay, she tried to explain what she was trying to do, attempts—given her acknowledged "lack of method"—that only succeeded in making her miserable. And not least, chronically tight-lipped about her personal life and past, she had to make known a sick husband in trouble with the law. The ingredients were all there for the preferred portrait of her—the perfectionist, the heroine, the martyr, the victim, the outsider, the underdog. So that with the re-publication in the late Sixties of her earlier novels—fictions not only strongly autobiographical in their settings and flavor but also seeming to tell a continuous story, which surely

led up to the "mad-woman in the attic"?—the die was cast and the critics could produce the Jean Rhys they liked best.

The order of the novels in the current edition bears out this scenario. *Voyage in the Dark* comes first, even though it was published third. Its position here is not so much—as the editor argues—because Jean Rhys had drafted it in rough form early on and then revised it after *Quartet* and *After Leaving Mr. Mackenzie,* but mainly because it allows for a narrative sequence. Until Antoinette in *Wide Sargasso Sea,* Anna Morgan in *Voyage in the Dark* is the youngest heroine, her situation corresponding to the plight Jean Rhys found herself in when she first went to London from Dominica, a teen-aged "loner," and met the older man who introduced her to sex and English gentility and then grew tired of the burden she had become. *Quartet,* published as *Postures* in 1928, follows naturally, picking up the young woman (named Marya Zelli this time) in Paris in the early Twenties, her husband a shadowy art dealer who lands in prison, thus forcing her into the hands of a *woman-dealer* named Heidler, who is reminiscent of Ford Madox Ford but hardly a portrait of him. (The notion that Heidler was Ford and that she, like Marya, had fallen in love with him shook Jean Rhys to the core.) With *After Leaving Mr. Mackenzie* (1930), the "tale" continues to unfold, the already shopworn woman (now Julia Martin) down and out in Paris and London—before Orwell—but pretending, without great success, that she has a future consisting of more than just one farewell after another. In *Good Morning, Midnight* (1939), the middle-aged and desperate Sasha Jansen concludes the saga of the luckless Rhys character adrift in a hostile world, a world of cheap hotels and "cafés where they like [her] and cafés where they don't," above all, a world in which the present is infected by memories of the past. It all works so well: how could this not add up to the history of Jean Rhys's emotional life, especially when you cap it with the story of a young Creole woman driven mad by an uncomprehending Englishman?

Tempting as it is not to take Jean Rhys's protests seriously and to disregard the contradictory evidence, the novels make their own plea for an impersonal judgment upon them, divorced from autobiography. *Quartet* and *After Leaving Mr. Mackenzie* are flawed fictions, the work of a writer who had not yet learned how to control point of view or to dramatize sensibility. They rely heavily on direct statements of feeling instead of drama, even on uncharacteristic chapter titles in *Mackenzie,* and on all-too-obvious symbolism imported from the Nineties. The result of Rhys's awkwardness as well as her disconcerting shifts of focus is that the consciousness at the center of these early novels becomes diluted and unconvincing. But by the time she was ready to revise her earliest manuscript—the record that may well have been a faithful account of her first unhappy love affair in England—she had mastered the art of the internal monologue and discovered how to alternate it with dramatic narrative. *Voyage in the Dark,* published in 1934, was Jean Rhys's first genuinely accomplished novel—and she knew it. That was why she bitterly resented and resisted her publisher's request for a different, less harsh final paragraph, one that would allow the reader to think Anna Morgan might survive the bungled abortion (which had, by the way, no factual basis in the author's life). In the end, Rhys made the change—and years later condemned herself for it.

The development she cared about—from the clumsy *Quartet* (that had followed close upon the Left Bank stories praised by Ford) to the near-perfect *Voyage in the Dark*—is only obscured and trivialized by the placement of her third novel first in this edition. Moreover, the extraordinary achievement that followed with *Good Morning, Midnight* loses some of its force when the continuum emphasized is the dubiously autobiographical one. For this remarkable novel is Jean Rhys's finished form of the experimental fiction she grew up with in Paris, fiction that began in the late Eighties with Dujardin's *Les Lauriers sont coupés*. Hailed years later by Joyce for its *monologue intérieur*, *Les Lauriers* is echoed in *Quartet* and subtly parodied in *Good Morning, Midnight*. Daniel Prince, Dujardin's philosopher-dandy, primed and perfumed in an equally redolent Paris, anticipating a night at last with the actress he feels he has earned, seems an absurdly self-conscious forerunner of the existentialist Sasha, for whom everything touched turns to dust. Prince's quest, whatever its outcome, is the time-honored serious one of the male for the female; Sasha's self-lacerating odyssey from hotel room to café and back again has the comically astringent flavor of a woman with "such a cafard!" trying to hold nothing together. In *Good Morning, Midnight*, Rhys proved herself the equal of any of the modernists, creating musical fragments, whole in themselves, out of her own special brand of shame and failure. Yet Rhys's art has been valued less than its raw materials.

What makes her life story sad is the neglect at the heart of the attention she has gotten since *Wide Sargasso Sea*. There is tribute paid, of course, to her temperament and her style, but the harrowing of the woman counts for more than anything else. No one has thought to connect the ordeals of her fictional characters with the element *missing* in all of them: none has the soul of an artist, despite the uncommon sensibility of an Anna Morgan, a Sasha Jansen, or the Creole Antoinette. In other words, if writing was indeed "therapy" for Jean Rhys, perhaps it consisted of imagining what would have happened to her without the saving grace of her gift. The dreadful possibilities must have haunted and obsessed her. They probably explain her fondness for George Moore's *Esther Waters*, a novel she read and re-read, in which the religion imbibed in childhood finally provides a lifeline after years of sexual misfortune; and they surely lie behind her most brilliant character creation, Sasha Jansen, who, more than any of the others, has the "je ne sais quoi" of the true original—but without the slightest drive or ambition. *She* is beaten, too, of course, for Rhys's allegory cannot have it otherwise. What, after all, does the return—in *Wide Sargasso Sea*—to the West Indies of Rhys's birth signify, if not one more demonstration of what might have happened to the girl who stayed at home in Dominica just a little too long, who had her life—like Antoinette's—arranged for her, and who then found herself with neither defenses nor allies? Jean Rhys thanked God that she had managed to go her own way and do her own bungling, finding out in the process where her own sanity lay—not in West Indies Obeah but in the magic of craft.

It is all very well for her supporters to point out the ways in which Jean Rhys's characters and situations (monochromatic as they are) touch upon the social and political issues that dominated the Sixties and Seventies: class, race, gender, colonialism. Her fiction—like most—does have content, but it lacks ideas, and its themes are sound patterns of feeling rather than intellectual formulations. Jean Rhys knew this about her novels. She knew, too, what people wanted from them—verification, corroboration, weapons for war against the "other"—and she tried not to give in. But once a novel was published, she no longer felt attached or responsible, unless it were made the basis for an inaccuracy about *her*. Perhaps she hated most the labeling that went along with such narrow views of literature

and life—the penny-in-the-slot syndrome. As she put it in a letter of 1963, "There is *no* penny for the slots. Not for writing or the black versus white question—the *lies* that are told—or for anything that matters. Only for lies. Yet everybody believes in the nonexistent penny and the invisible slot. So what to do?"

She certainly had her priorities, and no one understood better than she that they were tied up with self-expression and self-gratification, sought almost exclusively through the act of writing, no matter what some of her partisan readers claim. (pp. 47-50)

Gloria G. Fromm, "Making Up Jean Rhys," in The New Criterion, *Vol. IV, No. 4, December, 1985, pp. 47-50.*

TERESA F. O'CONNOR

In her early twenties, Jean Rhys, living alone in England and far from her West Indian home, began a journal in which she wrote of a recent and devastating love affair. She wrote obsessively until she completed her account and then packed her notebooks away for almost two decades. That journal eventually became the basis for her third published novel, *Voyage in the Dark* (1934).

Between 1924 and 1939, Rhys wrote and published three other novels, the genesis of each bearing a relation to that of *Voyage in the Dark*—the necessary outpouring of autobiographical pain relieved only by the act of writing. That Rhys was also a painstaking editor and reworked her compositions endlessly is a well-known fact. But the impulse for her writing, she always claimed to be the exorcism of unhappiness. In a private and unpublished exercise book Rhys, recalling her childhood and the intense moments of feeling she experienced, writes:

> It was so intolerable this longing this sadness I got from the shapes of the mountains, the sound of the rain the moment just after sunset that one day I spoke of it to my mother and she at once gave me a large dose of castor oil.

> One day I discovered however that I could work off the worst of it by writing poems and was happier.

This brief entry indicates Rhys's literary preoccupations: the very direct connection of place to feeling, the impossibility of expressing that feeling otherwise than in writing and the mixture of sadness and pain caused by the perception and experience even of beauty. That original impulse toward expression for Rhys, even in her last novel, remained rooted in the West Indies in which she was born and spent her youth, specifically the island of Dominica. That the West Indies always posed a problem in understanding for Rhys, that they remained an enigmatic and tainted paradise, is also clear in the conclusion to her journal entry. She says: "There is an atmosphere of pain and violence about the West Indies. Perhaps it wasn't astonishing that I was tuned in to it." While England later became the embodiment of hell for Rhys, unlike Dante's Paolo, who says there is no greater pain than to recall a happy time in the midst of misery, her memories of the past in the West Indies and her compulsive summoning up of them, both in her private and published writing, provided a mixed blessing: the pain that Paolo alludes to, mixed with the pleasure of escaping the present time and place.

Place is what informs Rhys's novels and what distinguishes them each from the other. In her writing, place is most concretely represented by three countries: Dominica, England and

France—the first representing an Eden-like state of grace, at least on first recollection, the second a cold and neurasthenic hell, and the third a limbo capable of at least providing distraction from the self. (pp. 1-2)

In writing *Wide Sargasso Sea,* almost half a century after the initial composition of *Voyage in the Dark,* Jean Rhys returned again to the themes and concerns of her first writing: the relationship between colonial and colonizer, black and white, child and parent, woman and man and, weaving them together, the very intricate connections they have in her work to sex and to money. Underlying all of Rhys's fiction, sustained in its tone and its atmosphere, is a pervasive note of loss and of death coupled to a paralysis of the spirit that makes action impossible. In *Voyage in the Dark* and *Wide Sargasso Sea,* Rhys explores the sources and causes of that dread and of that inertia.

While *Voyage in the Dark* was Rhys's fourth novel published, its position in terms of her development as a writer—the establishment of major themes and concerns, the "recording" of her own life and its transmutation into literature, even the decision to consider herself a writer at all—is closer to that of a first novel.

The novels that lie between the composition of *Voyage in the Dark* and *Wide Sargasso Sea,* what I term her Continental novels, are most concerned with the peripatetic life of heroines who seem variants of the same woman as she ages. Her personality, her obsessions and frailties, even much of her history remain constant. Rhys's first published novel, *Quartet* (1928), about the young Marya Zelli, is virtually a roman à clef: already living in France, Rhys wrote of the breakup of her first marriage following her affair with Ford Madox Ford after her husband was imprisoned by the French authorities. Rhys's second novel, *After Leaving Mr. Mackenzie* (1930) follows Julia Martin as she moves, bereft of family, friends and lovers, between Paris and London. Her fourth novel, *Good Morning, Midnight* (1939)— like its predecessor *Voyage in the Dark,* a first-person narration—examines the life of Sasha Jansen, a woman similar to Marya Zelli and Julia Martin who, now older, attempts to hold on to her sanity and a sense of worth and power as she haunts the places of Paris she knew in her youth.

Rhys's Continental novels have much in common with the West Indian ones: the passive and masochistic heroine without home, mother or apparent center, the sparseness of the prose, and the bleakness of the emotional landscape. The themes and concerns treated in the West Indian novels are present too, though at times submerged and subterranean. But in her first and last compositions, Rhys seeks a center for her heroines, a center that is clearly attached to Rhys's own literal home in the West Indies, the island of Dominica.

Jean Rhys is an intensely personal writer. More directly than most, she has used her own emotional and biographical history as the source and stuff of her writing. She has said: "There's very little invention in my books," and "I don't know other people. I never have known other people. I have only ever written about myself." She wrote about what she knew best, her own life. That Rhys apparently had little curiosity about others, including the lives and histories of her three husbands, is a fact she often acknowledged. The lives both of Rhys and her self-reflecting heroines turn forever inward, revolving about a center and source that is connected to her being a woman and a colonial; in Rhys, the two ultimately become synonymous.

That Rhys used her self as the model for all her heroines, and her own experiences as the basis of the material for their lives, many critics have noted. None, however, has examined in detail the very intricate relationship between her life and her work and the way in which her private and unpublished journals became a constant source for her fiction. Indeed, parts of *Voyage in the Dark, Good Morning, Midnight* and *Wide Sargasso Sea,* as well as her more public autobiography, *Smile Please,* and several short stories ("**Goodbye Marcus, Goodbye Rose;**" "**The Day They Burned the Books**") appear verbatim in an exercise book of hers, henceforth referred to as the Black Exercise Book, in the Jean Rhys Collection of the McFarlin Library at the University of Tulsa.

In the Black Exercise Book, Rhys writes at length about her early life in Dominica and describes episodes between her and her mother, father and other members of the household, most notably her despised nurse Meta. Rhys also describes in detail, though the handwriting degenerates enough to act as a mask to the material, a highly disturbing psycho-sexual involvement with an elderly British gentleman, Mr. Howard, who visited Dominica with his wife. The need to write about this episode, an episode which she believed was essential in the formation of her character, is one of the reasons she wrote in the book at all. The episode is scarcely fictionalized in the short story "**Goodbye Marcus, Goodbye Rose.**"

The Black Exercise Book was sold to Tulsa by Rhys in 1976, along with what remaining papers and manuscripts she still possessed. The book is most difficult to follow. For the most part Rhys kept the journal in pencil and apparently often wrote in it while she was drunk. Most of the inclusions are fragmentary, almost incoherent and with virtually no punctuation; it is not quite clear at times whether certain inclusions are notes for fiction or whether Rhys was writing about fact—in some cases probably a combination of the two.

Although Jean Rhys was an autobiographical writer, she was strongly aware of the process by which she turned autobiography into fiction, a problem she struggled with in reverse in her old age as she tried to write her autobiography. In the interview in the *Paris Review* in 1979, she discussed the relationship between life and literature: "The things you remember have no form. When you write about them, you have to give them a beginning, a middle, and an end. To give life shape—that is what a writer does. That is what is so difficult." In that same interview, Rhys tried to explain the problems in writing her autobiography, in trying *not* to write fiction. She said:

> Reality is what I remember. You can push onto reality what you feel. Just as I felt that I disliked England so much. It was my feeling which made me dislike it. Now I make a lot of the nice part of the Indies, and I've sort of more or less forgotten the other part, like going to the dentist who only came to the island every now and again. I'm trying to write the beauty of it and how I saw it. And how I did see it as a child. That's what I've been toiling at. It's such a battle.

Certainly there is an overlap in the process of writing fiction and autobiography. The dilemma Rhys describes in writing nonfiction suggests that overlap and the problems involved in writing the kind of fiction that she did.

Rhys's initial impulse for writing apparently took the form of a need to write out events and feelings as if all were accidental. Writing meant ordering her experience and rendering it meaningful. In writing, as in nothing else, the past could be retrieved and redeemed. Even when Rhys recognized herself as "a writer," she perceived herself at once as an "instrument" and as an artist pursuing her craft. Both aspects of herself as writer could be triggered by "returning" to the West Indies. (pp. 2-5)

In the Black Exercise Book Rhys laments that she has ruined herself with alcohol, that she "will never succeed in England" and that she shall never be able to "make a little money for" her daughter. But then, recalling her relationship to her art, she says: "Then I think that after all I've done it. I've given myself up to something which is greater than I am. I have tried to be a good instrument. Then I'm not unhappy—I am even rather happy perhaps."

Although Jean Rhys left Dominica in 1907 at the age of 17, the island and its inhabitants figure strongly in her first and last compositions, marking that in Rhys's work culture, character and place are inseparable. The past constantly intrudes on the present. In *Voyage in the Dark,* a personal history shaped by a childhood in the West Indies continually recurs for Anna Morgan. In *Wide Sargasso Sea,* a cultural history is mutated by the individual personalities of the characters. But in both works the formation of what we might term a colonial sensibility and psychology is a deep and early experience crystallized perhaps by change, by time passing, and by exile. One should note that Rhys's family's intention for her, and her own intentions, had not been immigration. But even though her father died shortly after her leaving Dominica, her sojourn away from "home" became permanent, interrupted only by a brief and apparently disappointing return visit in 1936. All of Rhys's siblings, in fact, left the island, a migration that David Plante, Rhys's friend and sometime amanuensis, attributes to the colonial mentality of the family, their sense that the entire empire was at their disposal.

It might also be true that Rhys's lifelong obsession with her first and perhaps only home was due, in part, to the early and difficult age at which she left Dominica. Neither child nor woman, she left with many conflicts yet unresolved. If we look at the particulars of Rhys's youth in Dominica we see even there early elements that engendered her own sense of being an "outsider" and outcast—a feeling that permeates all of her work and which continued in her peripatetic life in England and the Continent. Her alienation in her childhood and adolescence was a result of a combination of factors which include the nature of the island of Dominica, the West Indian colonial experience, her relationship to her family, especially her mother, and the already mentioned sexual trauma of the episode with Mr. Howard.

Rhys's entire oeuvre is an attempt to create or locate a wholeness, to fit the pieces together, the problem with which the young Anna Morgan struggles in *Voyage in the Dark;* to separate myth from reality, while paradoxically regenerating and recreating myth; and to synthesize what was essentially an alienated and outcast position—perhaps an impossible task in life and a difficult one in literature.

Rhys often claimed that *Voyage in the Dark* was her favorite novel. Certainly it is her most clearly autobiographical in that it explores, in terms that mirror her own life, the facts of Anna Morgan's youth, spent on an island which is clearly Dominica. That Rhys continued to identify with Anna Morgan seems apparent even in her lying about her own age—her alteration of the date from 1890 to 1894, making her the same age as Anna Morgan.

Most sources still give Jean Rhys's year of birth as 1894. However, Diana Athill, in her foreword to *Smile Please,* suggests an 1890 date. She writes that the confusion about Rhys's age was because Jean Rhys "disliked revealing it." (pp. 6-8)

While Athill is correct that Rhys disliked telling her age, I think that the fallacy goes deeper than that. Rhys not only gave her own life to her heroines, she also took her heroines to be herself. For example, in interviews Rhys often interchanged references to her heroines with "she" and "I," It is this very confounding that perhaps gives truth to her heroines' voices, especially the first-person narrations of Anna Morgan, Sasha Jansen, and Antoinette Cosway. Rhys, herself caught between places and cultures, classes and races, never able to identify clearly with one or another, gives the same marginality to her heroines, so that they reflect the unique experience of dislocation of the white Creole woman, even when not identified as such.

While Jean Rhys later became peripherally involved with American and British expatriates in France during the 1920s and 1930s, none was perhaps so lost as she. She remained an outsider even to that band of outsiders. It is this dislocation that Rhys explores in her fiction and the source of which she locates in her two West Indian novels, a source which is identified with the distinct experience of her own life.

The critical reputation of Jean Rhys is substantial, although the biographical sources of her work have not been fully probed. Francis Wyndham, who was among those who had read and admired Rhys's earlier works and who later was instrumental in bringing her to public attention, attributes her long literary absence before *Wide Sargasso Sea,* in the years that her books were out of print, to the fact that "they were ahead of their age, both in spirit and in style." Later, in a widely heralded article in the *New York Times Book Review,* after Rhys had begun to win public attention, A. Alvarez referred to her as "the greatest living British novelist" [see *CLC*, Vol. 4]. In her last years, Rhys figured in many interviews and short articles, many of them unnervingly repetitive. The first book on Jean Rhys, by Louis James, appeared in 1978; it is a short, impressionistic work in which he unqualifiedly reads Rhys's work as simple autobiography. It is at times unreliable and confusing, in part because when detailing her biography he quotes from her fiction, without noting that it is fiction. James, for the most part, ignores the subtle ways in which Rhys both used her own history and transmuted it.

In 1979, shortly after Rhys's death, Thomas Staley published a critical study of Jean Rhys. [see excerpt above]. It remains the most comprehensive treatment of Rhys and her work, though Staley is prone to oversimplifying the relationship of her work to her biography. That is, he tends to hypothesize the colonial experience Rhys *might* have had and deduce generalizations about what should have been true, minimizing her specific experiences, the personal influences on her, and her idiosyncratic examination of the colonial theme.

Thus far, no published work has dealt in depth with Rhys's *need,* to reinvoke the myth of her own beginnings: her colonial upbringing in a land that is for her at once female- and black-identified, a place for which she yearns and which is at best indifferent to her. Nor has any critic discussed the "negative motherliness" Rhys attaches to the island: the unsatisfying mothering she received as a child and her own identification, often unconscious, of the island and her mother. This identification of the island with her mother is both mythical and literal, since Rhys's father, born in Wales, was not Creole. It is primarily because of this unresolved relationship with her mother that I think Rhys returned again and again, in her youth and in her old age, to the myth of Dominica. That this maternal indifference and failure coincided with the failure of colonialism in developing a clearly defined and centered people, that the mother country too failed to give sustenance and definition to its child colonies, is an identification Rhys makes. It is inherent in her own life and in her work and is an insight that unites the experiences of the child, the woman and the colonial in one voice. (pp. 8-10)

Teresa F. O'Connor, in an introduction to her Jean Rhys: The West Indian Novels, *New York University Press, 1986, pp. 1-10.*

MISSY DEHN KUBITSCHEK

The idea of woman as alien in a patriarchal culture has now become widely accepted within the women's movement. In her 1966 novel *Wide Sargasso Sea,* Jean Rhys addresses this alienation by representing patriarchy as women's Sargasso Sea: like the apparently navigable but in fact treacherous ocean, patriarchy's surface offers inviting opportunities, but its real substance chokes all progress. The women's movement at present charts two courses through this sea: one travels the mainstream of economic and social realities; the other maintains secret, marginal routes from which it subverts those realities via guerrilla attack. *Wide Sargasso Sea* shows both of these strategies, assimilating and remaining marginal, in action; it indicates that assimilating is not only disastrous as a personal strategy, but invalid or at least incomplete as a means of interpreting any experience, including that of reading a novel.

Wide Sargasso Sea revises Charlotte Brontë's *Jane Eyre* by presenting the life of Rochester's first wife, called Bertha in *Jane Eyre* and Antoinette in this work. Antoinette's narration, which constitutes a considerable portion of the novel, gives her own version of her courtship and marriage to Edward Fairfax Rochester, desirable Byronic hero in *Jane Eyre* and villain extraordinaire in *Wide Sargasso Sea.* Thus, in Antoinette, Rhys chooses a previously peripheral character to narrate most of the novel. Antoinette's initial social and psychological position could hardly be more marginal: a West Indian Creole from a slave-owning family, she is a child when emancipation frees the slaves and for practical purposes abolishes plantation culture. Antoinette naturally belongs neither to the English fortunne hunters who buy up the plantations nor to the "native" population of ex-slaves. Antoinette's mother, Annette, offers her no support, and the lonely child lives in fear of the ex-slave population, most of whom refer to her as a white cockroach. Antoinette receives emotional sustenance only from Christophine, originally a slave who was a wedding present to Annette and is now the only functioning adult in the household. Realizing Antoinette's needs, Christophine introduces her to Tia, a black child with whom she becomes friends. Even with these two emotional contacts, Antoinette's position remains precarious, marginal.

Although Annette marries the rich Englishman, Mason, Antoinette's situation does not improve—not understanding the cultural system with which he perforce deals, Mason unwittingly provokes already resentful laborers into burning his estate, Coulibri. In the ensuing chaos, when Antoinette sees Tia and approaches her for comfort, Tia literally and figuratively wounds her by throwing a sharp stone. Following the burning

of Coulibri, and as a direct result of it, Annette goes mad, Antoinette's brother Pierre dies, and Antoinette is sent to a convent for schooling, isolated from nearly all her earlier contacts.

When Mason dies and his son arranges for Antoinette's marriage to a young, impoverished Englishman, Edward Rochester, Antoinette loses control over her inheritance, which under English law becomes Rochester's if not specially settled on her. Rochester fiercely resents his younger-son status, which has necessitated this financially profitable marriage, and he is intensely frightened of Antoinette's sexuality. For these reasons, he seizes on gossip about Antoinette to distance himself from her. Soon he decides to break up her identity—he rechristens her "Bertha," for example, and refuses to call her Antoinette; successful in the initial stages, he removes her to England for the final obliteration. There she becomes the character familiar from *Jane Eyre,* the madwoman who sets fire to Rochester's ancestral home, Thornfield. And yet, by this point, she cannot be quite that same character, for the reader is now familiar with her history, a context that revises the meaning of her actions.

Described in this way, Antoinette's story seems exactly that depressing, familiar archetype, woman-as-victim. But Rhys accents point of view—both Rochester and Grace Poole ("Bertha's" caretaker at Thornfield) narrate sections of *Wide Sargasso Sea,* for example. In this way Rhys draws attention to the selectivity of all of the characters' perceptions as they choose and define essential details according to their operative conceptual frameworks. And the definition of Antoinette as helpless victim belongs to a destructive framework that Barbara Hill Rigney alludes to in the last sections of *Madness and Sexual Politics in the Feminist Novel,* one that encourages both men and women to see women as passive, helpless beings. Because Rhys gives us sufficient material to revise this summary of a fated victim's life, the reader can see that Antoinette participates in her own destruction: her choices matter, and she chooses badly. Although it remains sympathetic to Antoinette, the novel does not offer merely another helpless victim of a patriarchal, imperialist system. Instead, *Wide Sargasso Sea* contrasts Antoinette's self-destructive attempts to assimilate with Christophine's successful preservation of her marginal status.

This challenge to traditional interpretation of marginal experience demands a new understanding of both the theme and the structure of *Wide Sargasso Sea:* Antoinette Mason is not simply a pathetic victim, nor is she the heroine. The critical assumption that Antoinette is the heroine, the focus, never becomes explicit, of course; from the mainstream perspective that defines the book narrowly as a rebuttal of *Jane Eyre,* the premise is too obvious to require expression. As a direct result, Christophine, Antoinette's surrogate mother, becomes a minor character and her successful marginal strategy receives no recognition, while Antoinette's victimization receives substantial critical commentary.

Antoinette remains, of course, a major character; Rhys wished to combat what she considered Brontë's slander of West Indian Creoles. In an interview, Rhys recalled: "I was convinced that Charlotte Brontë must have had something against the West Indies, and I was angry about it. Otherwise, why did she take a West Indian for that horrible lunatic, that really dreadful creature? I hadn't really formulated the idea of vindicating the mad woman in a novel but when I was rediscovered I was encouraged to do so." Clearly, Rhys felt the marginalist's resentment of the mainstream's power to characterize and define her.

This choice of the margin has not been the subject of critical commentary, which tends to focus on Antoinette as a creature "stripped of her name, her money, and her property . . . a prisoner in a small attic, denied the fresh air and sunlight enjoyed by other living creatures." Then, perhaps because victims are in and of themselves often rather dull, criticism has examined the pressure of social and political conditions embodied in characters who influence her. These examinations generally seek to explain the origin of Antoinette's madness, by, for example, showing the failure of Antoinette's mother to nurture her or by assessing the degree of Rochester's guilt [see excerpt above by Thomas F. Staley]. These approaches, however diverse their focuses, concentrate on who does (or does not) do what to Antoinette.

Here and there the critical commentary suggests this perception without really developing it. Peter Wolfe notes of Antoinette, for instance, that "[h]er womanly tendency to reflect her male surroundings makes his [Rochester's] obsessiveness the iron bars of her cage." The only interpretation of the novel that concentrates on the issue, Helen Nebeker's archetypal analysis, concludes that "Rhys reveals without hypocrisy or glossing, that woman is ultimately the victim, not of man, but of herself." But while Nebeker accurately perceives Antoinette's responsibility, she locates the cause of her destruction in an overly romantic approach to love complicated by loss of financial independence. Antoinette's version of romantic love, I would argue, is a comfortably vague rationalization to disguise a more fundamental and even less attainable desire for safety through assimilation.

Antoinette very much wants peace and safety, certainly understandable goals. In order to achieve these goals, however, she abandons her own feelings and experiences, or more accurately, redefines them from a point of view not her own. Her shifting attitudes toward two other characters, Tia and Christophine, demonstrate this process. When Antoinette's mother is unwilling or unable to support her daughter, the ex-slave Christophine becomes a kind of surrogate mother. Christophine attempts to find companioship for the friendless child and later advises the adult Antoinette. Antoinette cannot, of course, enter Rochester's society with a black mother and friend. The cultural mainstream defines both Tia and Christophine as inferior, and Antoinette half-consciously comes to accept these definitions, not realizing that the system will also define her as a subhuman.

Antoinette demonstrates this capacity to accept and act on destructive definitions very early. Tia's attack during the burning of Coulibri is motivated by the girls' childish quarrel over three pennies belonging to Antoinette, who calls Tia a "cheating nigger." Clearly both the quarrel's subject and its outcome are a microcosm of the island's colonial problems. And by allying herself with the wealthy English and plantation owners against the natives, Antoinette relinquishes any claim to Tia's affection. Rhys's description of the girls after Tia has thrown the stone clarifies the reader's understanding of Antoinette's earlier choice: "We stared at each other, blood on my face, tears on hers. It was as if I saw myself. Like in a looking-glass." In defining Tia as a "cheating nigger," Antoinette has denied a part of herself, has in effect thrown the first stone.

Before her marriage to Rochester, Antoinette shows at least a limited ability to judge from her own experience rather than conforming to cultural norms. Initially, Antoinette values Christophine's tenderness and understanding. When she hears from gossip that Christophine practices obeah—more commonly known as voodoo—Antoinette becomes afraid to enter Christophine's room. Upon actually seeing Christophine again, however, she regains her faith in her friend. Temporarily, Antoinette relies on her own experience and rejects the native cultural definition of Christophine as a threatening figure. (pp. 23-5)

Not only social pressures but also her own emotional needs, however, predispose Antoinette to exchange her experiential standards for cultural norms. In at least one instance, she is able to maintain a marginal position long enough to feel its very mixed emotional consequences. Abandoning Catholicism's alien judgments of her experience, she feels "bolder, happier, more free. But not so safe." Although the tolerant convent does not insist on conformity, Antoinette ominously learns "to gabble without thinking as the others did."

With her marriage to Rochester, both the external pressure to conform and her desire for safety intensify. Antoinette actively wants to enter the dominant culture and is at least subconsciously willing to forfeit her own to secure the anticipated safety of belonging. Antoinette's exchange of her own values for those of the dominant culture centers on redefining Christophine. Rochester's culture, of course, sees Christophine's voodoo as ignorant superstition rather than fearsome power, and Antoinette adopts this viewpoint: "I stared at her thinking, 'but how can she know the best thing for me to do, this ignorant, obstinate old negro woman, who is not certain if there is such a place as England?'." Despite Christophine's extremely sensible advice—she says, for instance, that Antoinette can use potions to seduce Rochester but not to command his love—and her demonstrated ability to analyze people, Antoinette distances herself from her friend and protectress.

This redefinition of Christophine and Tia is part of Antoinette's growing conformity to a culture that will rename her "Bertha," will rob her of her inheritance, and will finally confine her to an attic prison. This culture denies Antoinette any settled identity even while it wars on her original identity. Rochester complains that Antoinette is maddeningly unsure of even basic facts—for example, whether the snakes on the island are poisonous. In fact, Antoinette's confusion generally amounts to an uncertainty over which culture she will accept as her defining conceptual system. For example, when she is ill after Tia's attack, her hair is cut off, and when she later sees the braid lying in a drawer, she thinks at first that it is a snake. This scene has vastly different resonances depending upon one's conceptual scheme. The Euro-American tradition, present in Antoinette's description of Coulibri as Eden-gone-wild, defines the snake as evil. The voodoo tradition, however, considers snakes not only sacred to Damballah, the mightiest of gods, but manifestations of him. Antoinette's discovery of the snake made by her shorn braid can therefore be seen either as the discovery of evil through the experience of Tia's attack or as the sign of a deep connection with a powerful spirit. Throughout the novel, because she adopts mainstream rather than marginal definitions, Antoinette interprets her own experience and her resultant identity as passive, subordinate, and finally untenable.

Antoinette thus participates in her own destruction, and though Rhys does not morally condemn her or judge her harshly, the novel contains in Christophine a corrective example, a woman as marginal as Antoinette who nevertheless survives intact. . . .

A slave, isolated from all family and familiar terrain when probably still a child, Christophine has preserved the integrity that Antoinette surrenders.

The dominant critical perception of Antoinette as the heroine of *Wide Sargasso Sea* has obscured Christophine's importance. This focus probably results from the unconscious assumption that as both a main character and a point-of-view character Antoinette must be, for better or worse, the heroine, the focus of theme as well as plot. Antoinette fits the conventional definition of a hero, one who participates in large actions or great intensities. Yet Rhys's choice of subject matter, her concentration on a minor character from *Jane Eyre,* indicates a marginal focus. In other words, *Wide Sargasso Sea* does something different from and something more important than merely substituting the heroine Antoinette for the anti-heroine Bertha. Instead, it demands that the reader interpret the plot from a marginalist perspective that nowhere directs the narration (not Antoinette's, Rochester's, or Grace Poole's account) but that nevertheless informs it.

Most revisions of a myth retain the plot structure of the original but alter the motivations sufficiently to recreate the meaning of the action. Thus, *Jane Eyre* determines the fate of Antoinette Bertha Mason Rochester in *Wide Sargasso Sea;* the reader knows from the beginning that she will die in a fire at Rochester's home. That event is in *Jane Eyre* presented through Rochester's account to Jane; in *Wide Sargasso Sea* the reader experiences it through Antoinette's dream vision preceding her waking actions, and the meaning thus changes radically. The relationships of Antoinette to Tia and Christophine, touchstones for the larger issue of assimilation versus marginality, displace *Jane Eyre*'s preoccupation with Rochester and Bertha's relationship. As Bertha/Antoinette recalls her third dream of a fire at Thornfield, she remembers that she "called help me Christophine help me and looking behind me I saw that I had been helped;" standing on Thornfield's battlements, she

> turned round and saw the sky. It was red and all my life was in it. . . . I heard the parrot call as he did when he saw a stranger, *Qui est là? Qui est là?* and the man who hated me was calling too, Bertha! Bertha! . . . The wind caught my hair and it streamed out like wings. It might bear me up, I thought, if I jumped to those hard stones. But when I looked over the edge I saw the pool at Coulibri. Tia was there. She beckoned to me and when I hesitated, she laughed. . . . I called "Tia!" and jumped and woke.

Rochester's presence in the dream picture explains the parrot's lack of recognition: Antoinette has obliterated her original identity in attempting to conform to Rochester's and England's modes. But after her last cry to Tia, Antoinette awakens with a new certainty about herself and purpose: "Now at last I know why I was brought here and what I have to do. There must have been a draught for the flame flickered and I thought it was out. But I shielded it with my hand and it burned up again to light me along the dark passage." After setting fire to Thornfield, Antoinette will jump to the dream pool and Tia, her vengeful suicide the only means of rediscovering and affirming her earlier self in England and English culture. This redefinition of the meaning of the plot cannot occur in a traditional context, which would deny the reality or the validity of the vision; it can exist only in a context that allows for the continuity of the present with what is physically dead or absent, a continuity central to the voodoo with which Christophine is associated.

Christophine is never assimilated by Jamaican culture; instead she preserves her Martinican dress and practices as a voodoo priestess, a *mambo*. Her only friend Maillotte is not Jamaican, and the native Jamaicans are frightened of her. Christophine exploits her marginal status in order to secure the space she needs to live. Rhys never exaggerates the power of the marginal position vis-à-vis the imperialist, patriarchal system. When, for example, Rochester discovers that Christophine has been jailed once for her activities, and threatens to jail her again, she must leave Antoinette.

By that time, however, Antoinette's fate is really already sealed. Besides, Christophine succeeds in prying concessions from Rochester, as no one else does, by sheer affirmation of her definitions and rejection of his satirical attempts to make her doubt them. Taunted about her belief in spirits, Christophine "steadily" says, "In your Bible it say God is a spirit—it don't say no others." Rochester cannot shake her confidence, much less her identity. Christophine need not deny his truths; her own can subsume them. She compels even from this quintessential representative of English culture a grudging respect: "She was a fighter, I had to admit. Against my will I repeated, 'Do you wish to say good-bye to Antoinette?'." Just after this conversation, when Rochester stupidly or maliciously invites her to write to Antoinette, she says merely, "Read and write I don't know. Other things I know." Here Christophine acknowledges her ignorance in Rochester's system, an ignorance that she admits to without shame because her own values center on "other things," other kinds of knowledge and other definitions of what is valuable. Though Christophine cannot save Antoinette, she saves herself and offers Antoinette aid and comfort that might be sufficient if Antoinette were not deluded by the vision of joining the dominant culture.

The practice of obeah or voodoo offers Christophine direct spiritual experience and power that Rochester's culture would deny her, and it further serves both to express her marginality and to protect it. Voodoo represents an accommodation of African thought to the conditions of Caribbean slavery; it combines aspects of many different tribal religions and Roman Catholicism. Unlike most European and Asian religions, it allows women to be not only acolytes, but priestesses. (Incidentally, the critical response to obeah often either dismisses it as superstition or indignantly denies that Christophine practices it; this mixture of condescension and fear can also be seen in Rochester.)

Christophine perceives the incompatibility of the dominant cultural systems and her own with a clarity that Antoinette never develops. To maintain the system that defends her integrity, Christophine refuses to participate in other systems. She never marries, for instance, noting that "All women, all colours, nothing but fools. Three children I have. One living in this world, each one a different father, but no husband, I thank my God. I keep my money. I don't give it to no worthless man." Having escaped one kind of legal slavery, Christophine has no desire to enter into another. Antoinette, on the other hand, hopes for an impossible compromise that will allow her to assimilate without wholly giving up her personality. She thus takes as genuine Rochester's definite interest in and implied acceptance of important parts of her self, for example her sexuality. He reneges on what he implies, of course, rejecting her as coarse and even depraved. His attraction to Antoinette's "otherness" as expressed in her sexuality is an emblem of patriarchy's awareness of, fascination with, and finally revulsion from what Elaine Showalter and other feminist writers have called "the wild zone," that area of female experience that is not and cannot be inscribed in patriarchal language. As he leaves for England, Rochester laments that "she belonged to the magic and the loveliness. She had left me thirsty and all my life would be thirst and longing for what I had lost before I found it." His plaint testifies to the truth of James Baldwin's assertion that racist oppressors as well as the oppressed bear huge psychic and emotional costs. The reader must not sentimentalize Rochester's response, however. The self-pitying tone, his absolute unwillingness to risk any part of his financial or emotional patrimony to quench his thirst, and his cruelty—all these reveal the shallowness of his desire and his essential solipsism.

Most critical commentary, by privileging Antoinette, ignores the novel's wider context: critics have interpreted *Wide Sargasso Sea* as though its form were the same as that of *Jane Eyre,* with their divergence consisting of a disagreement about judgment and emphasis rather than a difference in premise and perspective. In this framework Christophine remains a part of the island's lush foliage, undifferentiated from other secondary characters and places that make up the background for Antoinette's destruction. Foregrounding Christophine revises substantially the meaning of Antoinette's life and death; it juxtaposes the traditional narrative of tragedy or pathos with a narrative of persistence. The center of value, Christophine, is thus not central at all but marginal to the traditional perception of the form of the novel. As the true heroine, Christophine performs no dramatic actions—except, that is, maintaining her personal integrity against the very forces that defeat Antoinette.

Rhys herself would undoubtedly be surprised at this interpretation. Because she is known to have drawn on her own life for her fiction, critics tend to view her heroines, built from parts of herself, as she viewed her own experience. And because she frequently saw herself as a helpless victim, they often perceive Antoinette as an innocent unable to cope with the breakdown of her family and of her wider society.

Self-dramatizing fatalism evidently typified Rhys's approach to her own experience. David Plante's memories of the elderly Rhys in *Difficult Women* reveal her self-pity, her suspicions that others were victimizing her, and her listless approach to both her present and her past life. In her autobiography Rhys sounds almost entirely fatalistic. Speaking of herself in childhood, for instance, she says, "So as soon as I could I lost myself in the immense world of books and tried to blot out the real world which was so puzzling to me. Even then I had a vague, persistent feeling that I'd always be lost in it, defeated." Or, when she is sixteen and her dog dies, she responds with, "After that I decided that the Devil was undoubtedly stronger than God, so what was the use?"

And what, after all, is the use? What can a poor woman do? Poor Jean Rhys. Poor Antoinette. As Wolfe says, "Jean Rhys stresses betrayal in her religious symbolism. The crowing cock, the yellow-eyed Judas figure of Daniel, and the banished savior, Christophine, all limn in a world in which prayers are ignored and where obeah outpaces Christianity." It is a tribute to the force of Jean Rhys's personality that critics have by and large defined the avenging angel of the ends of both *Jane Eyre* and *Wide Sargasso Sea* as a helpless victim.

Rhys's earlier works accentuate the critical inclination, of course. Looking for discontinuities has only recently become fashionable; until fairly lately, academic critics have tended to view a writer's works as a continuous, flowing whole. In regard to Rhys's oeuvre, Thomas Staley states this propensity directly: "*Wide Sargasso Sea,* even with its exotic setting, its links with

Jane Eyre, its more explicit qualities of narration, is not all that far distant from Rhys's novels of the 1930s. If not a fulfillment, it is certainly an extension of her most basic themes, and the same quality of feeling pervades *Wide Sargasso Sea* as the earlier novels" [see excerpt above]. One need not share deconstructionist premises to question this assumption, which, even when unexpressed, underlies a good deal of criticism on this novel. The assumption works best when a writer produces many works in a short period or produces almost continuously over a long period; either way, the gaps from work to work are likely to be small. Rhys's oeuvre, however, does not fit either paradigm.

The publication in 1966 of *Wide Sargasso Sea* broke an almost total silence of twenty-seven years: only a few short stories intervene between *Good Morning, Midnight* (1939) and *Wide Sargasso Sea.* Between 1934 and 1966 Jean Rhys's world experienced the Second World War, the Holocaust, and the advent of the nuclear age; between 1934 and 1966 Ella Gwendolen Rees Williams ("Jean Rhys" is a pen name) experienced the death of a lover, marriage to Max Hamer, Hamer's imprisonment for misappropriating funds, Hamer's death, and the utter eclipse of her literary reputation. It would not be remarkable if these events had affected Rhys's subsequent work. Of those intervening short stories written during and immediately after the war, **"Till September Petronella"** (1960) does have a feckless, victimized heroine, but two others indicate Rhys's consideration of other possibilities that became central to *Wide Sargasso Sea.* The narrator of **"Let Them Call It Jazz"** (1962) may be confused and victimized, but she can accept the dominant culture's misperception and mislabeling of a song that she heard in prison without losing her essential feeling for the song. **"The Day They Burned the Books"** (1960) takes its title from the action of a woman who, after the death of her abusive and racist husband, burns the library that she associates with his oppression of her. Her young son Eddie questions the narrator's equation of "home" with "England" and challenges the racism that attacks his mother. These sketches of marginal characters' self-definition and resistance to oppression suggest crucial, if perhaps unconscious, changes in Rhys's world view.

Both the action of *Wide Sargasso Sea* and Rhys's action in writing the novel speak for remaining marginal rather than attempting to assimilate. Rhys utilizes her empowering heritage as successor to powerful women writers, Charlotte Brontë among them, to create her novel; simultaneously she rejects the part of Brontë that supports mainstream literary tradition. Thus, Rhys revises the canon of "accepted literature" by making visible and audible a minority element previously ignored. Remaining marginal in her choice of subject (a minor character from another woman's novel) and her theme (the necessity of avoiding assimilation), she nonetheless re-routes mainstream traffic. (pp. 25-7)

Missy Dehn Kubitschek, "Charting the Empty Spaces of Jean Rhys's 'Wide Sargasso Sea'," in Frontiers: A Journal of Women Studies, *Vol. IX, No. 2, 1987, pp. 23-8.*

PEARL K. BELL

With [*The Collected Short Stories*] the resurrection of Jean Rhys is now complete. It is heartening to realize how much she managed to write in the years when she was believed dead, but the stories, ranging from the 1920s to the 1970s, are on the whole disappointing. Still, even in the hurried early sketches of Paris in *The Left Bank,* we can immediately recognize Rhys's distinct and unmistakable literary turf: a floating, inconstant world of gigolos, artist's models, con men, and rejected women sinking into "the bitter and dangerous voluptuousness of misery." The Paris she made so vividly her own was a maze of narrow streets jammed with noisy cafés and "horrible men who walked softly behind one for several steps before they spoke," a menacing quarter of cheap hotels perfect for suicide, with their dripping taps, their naked light bulbs, their smell of fear. But these early stories don't burrow into the mind the way the novels do. Most of the Paris vignettes now seem as dated as Katherine Mansfield's artfully breathless snippets of the "real life" of Paris in the 1920s.

Like the Australian Christina Stead, that other colonial writer, Rhys needed the scope of a novel to define her singular and frightening vision of life. In the brief span of a short story she couldn't do justice to her mercilessly observant eye. In most of the pieces in this volume she sounds impatient to get it over with, and tends to settle, uncharacteristically, for neat, trite endings very much against her grain. But in one remarkable story, **"I Spy a Stranger,"** which she probably wrote during the Second World War, she did make powerful use of her lifelong alienation from England, and gave that estrangement an idiosyncratic shape entirely her own.

An elderly woman, Laura, who has lived on the Continent for many years, is forced to return to England during the war, and is assaulted by the mindless xenophobic bigots in a country village. When she tries to fight back with a "foreign" weapon, irony, the villagers decide she is a German spy, and eventually she is driven into the madhouse. We get to know her mainly through a sad and witty notebook she keeps, in a futile attempt to hang on to her sanity. She cheers herself up with sardonically imagined titles of books about women, such as *Misogyny and British Humor,* which, she dryly adds, "will write itself." In these notes Rhys lets fly at the crabbed narrowness of the English with a directness she rarely indulged so nakedly in her work:

> There is something strange about the [English] attitude to women as women. Not the dislike (or fear). That isn't strange of course. But it's all so completely taken for granted. . . . It has settled down and become an atmosphere . . . a climate, and no one questions it, least of all the women themselves. There is *no* opposition. . . . Most of the women seem to be carefully trained to revenge any unhappiness they feel on each other, or on children. . . . In dealing with men as a whole, a streak of subservience, of servility, usually appears, something cold, calculating, lacking in imagination.

Shrewd and angry words, from which we might be tempted to think that Rhys shared the feminists' concern about the oppression of women in a society dominated by men. But her mind did not work in such categorical ways, and the nervous despair that runs so wide and deep through her books attests to a more unsettling view of woman's fate. She had been mistreated by men such as Ford Madox Ford, but her idea of herself was not solely that of a victim. She felt no vengeful defiance. When an interviewer once suggested that she hated men, she was shocked, and firmly denied it. For Rhys the final reality was an irreducible sense of herself as an individual. Even in the bleakest circumstances she insisted on both the intuitive and the aesthetic power of her femininity, a sensibility at once vulnerable and seductively charming. But femininity is not feminism, and feminism is not the whole of the literary imagination, which transcends conventional distinctions between male and female attitudes and judgments. If she assigned blame anywhere, it was to "the whole system" that could be so "rotten," the demeaning, ignoble humiliations of disappointment, cruelty, and failed expectations. Writing was the only defense she had against the darkness.

Yet Jean Rhys was more than a martyr to poverty and neglect, and the place to see her whole is in her letters, which were published a few years ago. They were written to the very few who read and admired her novels during the years when they were hard to find; to her daughter, who married a Dutch businessman and lived in Indonesia for many years; to the editors who encouraged her so patiently when she was writing *Wide Sargasso Sea.* These marvelous letters make one feel especially incensed about the portrait of Rhys in her last years—a silly, feeble, maudlin old drunk—that her friend David Plante drew in a tasteless and ungenerous memoir called *Difficult Women.* The letters that streamed from her fingers with such unflagging vitality and wit during the drought-ridden decades are a record of gallantry triumphing over bitterness, of a warm, very feminine, feisty spirit determined to outwit the worst of times and relish the best. They prove that, unlike her heroic heroines, she did know how to live. (pp. 33-4)

Pearl K. Bell, "The Voyage Out," in The New Republic, *Vol. 196, No. 21, May 25, 1987, pp. 30-4.*

(James) Radcliffe Squires

1917-

American poet, critic, biographer, and editor.

In his verse, Squires draws from his extensive knowledge of Greek mythology to delineate problems and concerns of modern existence. The mythical figures on whom he centers his early pieces, including the god Hermes and the artisan Daedalus, are considered by many critics to exemplify concepts of creativity, enlightenment, and destruction in Squires's poetry. For example, in *Daedalus* (1968), an extended poem recounting the legend of the title character, Squires comments on the loss of individual freedom in a technocratic society. This work features a first-person narrator whose voice, according to Stuart Curran, is "that of a monstrous artist, a Dr. Frankenstein who has forgotten the limits of humanity." Squires has also been commended for his proficiency with blank verse, rhyme, alliteration, and narrative form.

Squires's subsequent volumes feature more personal and meditative verse. In *Waiting in the Bone and Other Poems* (1973), he contemplates such topics as love, loss of innocence, and humanity's relationship with nature. *Gardens of the World* (1981) features poetry first published in the collections *Cornar* (1940), *Where the Compass Spins* (1951), and *Fingers of Hermes* (1965) as well as new works that evoke the landscapes of the American West and the Mediterranean coast. Reviewers particularly noted a sequence on gardens named after Greek deities and supernatural creatures in which Squires revises the myths of such characters as Aphrodite, Eros, and Medusa to demonstrate their contemporary relevance. Theodore Haddin commented: "In a world fast spending itself to nothingness, [*Gardens of the World*] is a refreshing spring to the human in need of being human, in need of having complete experiences, indeed, of realizing sanity in an environment often cruel and destructive."

Squires is well known for his poetry criticism, having published studies of Robinson Jeffers, Robert Frost, and Frederick Prokosch. In addition, he has edited an anthology of essays devoted to Allen Tate.

(See also *Contemporary Authors*, Vols. 1-4, rev. ed. and *Contemporary Authors New Revision Series*, Vols. 6, 21.)

Courtesy of Radcliffe Squires

THOMAS LASK

Quiet and subdued in manner and tone, Radcliffe Squires is at his best in [*Fingers of Hermes*] when he captures a moment in time that combines the permanency of landscape or artifact with the impermanence of man. Though each element stands distinct and clear, the poem is greater than all: the white marble of the magnolia leaf is less real than the poem that celebrates it.

Among the finest poems are "The Visible Moments," a delicate and restrained love lyric; "A Letter to Pausanias," which treats of the quick and the dead but emphasizes the primacy of the living; and "Poem Without Theme," in which the ambiguity that hovers over an elusive experience is exceedingly well rendered. On more formal occasions. . . . Mr. Squires is less successful; in a few poems, language and symbol are overly elaborate. But these are small faults among much that is very good.

Thomas Lask, "End Papers," in The New York Times, *June 25, 1965, p. 31.*

JAMES DICKEY

Radcliffe Squires' new book [*Fingers of Hermes*] is so superior to his first—which was very good—that it is as though Mr. Squires had simply turned a corner in his mind and come upon an entirely new, more beautiful and more profound field of interest than he had suspected. All these poems are worth reading, but the best of them are those about Greece. Europe has provided so many timid American poets with material for timid, sightseeing poems, that one almost expects to miss in them the feeling that travel can and does give: that of being reborn.

This becoming—say, at the first sight of Greek islands—at once another being, more perceptive, more eager, more vulnerable, more innocent and also more immoral, more beyond-good-and-evil, Squires has captured in a series of remarkable poems.

> To gaze from an island toward
>   Asia
> Is to feel the disguises of God
>   drop
> Slowly over life again.

he says, and one realizes that the whole ancient mythological world can open up and reflower in the modern mind, when one stands among olive trees "where the skin/Stares through clothes." (p. 75)

> *James Dickey, "Of Human Concern," in* The New York Times Book Review, *November 21, 1965, pp. 74-5.*

STUART CURRAN

In May of 1967, three weeks after the coup that suddenly resolved years of petty squabbles into an order imposed by upstart and petty colonels, Greece signed an agreement with Litton Industries for a massive, long-range development program. Jumping aboard the bandwagon of the new imperialism barely four generations after throwing off the old, a fallen land, overshadowed by its awesome past, mired in political and economic destitution, with a somnolescence constantly troubled by flickerings of innate nobility, bowed to the twentieth century. (p. 214)

All this is by way of introducing Radcliffe Squires's new poem, *Daedalus,* a long, serene, and ultimately terrifying narrative whose central figure, in Professor Squires's conception, is the prototype of all technocrats. Joyce's Stephen Dedalus called his namesake the "fabulous artificer" and emulated him as the perfect artist, committed to no ends but those of his art. Squires probes the implications of that emulation, for his artificer is a man without a country, employed as a mere servant of the private and public lusts of rulers and at last betraying them into death. Daedalus assumes the role of Judas not for a few paltry pieces of silver—the technological engineer is highly paid in all cultures—but to assert his freedom from human ties. (p. 215)

Two mythologies converge to brilliant effect in *Daedalus*: that of Greece, which has preoccupied Squires in his last two volumes and which he is the only distinguished poet writing in English today to revive in a modern context; and that of Blake, who separated his universe into the antitheses of Urizen and Los, the forces of order and energy, forever at odds since forever battling for supremacy. The substance of Squires's poem is this elemental conflict, the implied solution to which is also Blakean: an uneasy and complex synthesis within the identity of the unified personality—and on a larger plane, the unified culture. The setting is thus doubly appropriate to Squires's stern vision. Man looks to the ancient Greeks for that simultaneous affirmation of law and Bacchic mystery, for the worship of Apollo and Dionysus as dual divinities over the nature of man. The "fabulous artificer" serves neither: only Athena, the cold and cynical voice of the intellect who drives her apostles into amoral isolation, the destruction of their progeny, the worship of death.

The public relevance of Squires's poem is obvious; yet it would be simplistic to view this controlled and moving narrative as merely another public statement for our time. In his last volume, *The Light Under Islands,* Squires moved farther into the public realm than he had attempted earlier, but even in such poems as his elegy on the death of President Kennedy one felt that the verse rose from intensely personal concerns to questions of cultural identity. The merging of the private and public worlds is a natural development in the work of any maturing poet, secure in his own powers. The questions broached in *Daedalus* are directed to the man as well as his society. The "fabulous artificer" is, after all, a kind of artist, one too secure in his powers, whose art drives him at last to despair of life, to refine himself out of existence. *Daedalus* is written entirely in the first person, its voice that of a monstrous artist, a Dr. Frankenstein who has forgotten the limits of humanity. In the last lines of the artificer's narrative Squires conceals a pun on Daedalus's name that suggests his intimate relation to all creators.

> This was only
> The daedal earth of the poets. *My* earth I saw
> As from a distance, spinning like a great metal
> Plaything, the perfect ball, toward my clever hand.
>   (pp. 215-16)

> *Stuart Curran, in a review of "Daedalus," in* Michigan Quarterly Review, *Vol. VIII, No. 3, Summer, 1969, pp. 214-16.*

BREWSTER GHISELIN

The strength of a poetry of such disciplined vitality as that of Radcliffe Squires, poetry of organic power so completely devoted to being simply what it is that it advertises nothing and is devoid of insignia, will escape notice unless the poetry is read with more than casual attention. It reveals itself in action—upon us, within us. How it moves, not with whom or with what fanfare or under what ready signs, of school or phalanx, will tell us what it is. . . . It is unobtrusive, like Donatello's David. The reader, then, must look to the poetry itself, as moved by living breath it rises alive from the page and goes quietly to work. The reviewer can offer little but indications of an approach he has tested and some evidence of its validity.

Waiting in the Bone and Other Poems—more precisely a sequence than a collection—moves from beginning to end with one intent, revealed in insights and attitudes made evident mainly through concrete design of the experience afforded in each poem, often in imagery simultaneously visionary and natural. These means and their effects are apparent in the opening poem, **"Christmas at the End of a Decade,"** which announces the dominant theme and displays the argument—in skeletal bareness—of the whole book. We look from a window into snowstorm, a "forsaken bay of snow gone blind. . . . world's ghost sieved through world's ghost," upon a cold absence we shall encounter again in [**"Waiting in the Bone"**], penultimate in the book, which is so far reciprocal in purport and complementary in substance as to seem antiphony and development of the earlier one. Out of the blank cold of life in extreme subsidence, out of the winter (that as we are reminded in the course of this book drives the very blood back toward the bone within which the red of its stream has its source) emerges a stir "of shadow no darker than the churn of petals / In the heart of white peonies," to take shape as a bird "in a sudden garden, a great white swan / Among snow and trees." . . . (p. 721)

The wintry void of unhope is thus revealed as a matrix, of salvation manifest in the swan of passage. Barren in appearance, it is like that actual and figurative snow and sky "pallor, as quiet as mother of pearl'' which in **"Winter Solstice,"** fifth poem in the book, adumbrates through suggestion of nacre and pearl a relation between formless ground and emergent or finished forms that holds true of the objective and subjective worlds simultaneously. Is this a real swan that has flown here out of the vast of snow, inexplicably, as life has arisen out of the vast of the inanimate universe, and as a matter itself appears to our blind speculation to have issued from featureless mystery? Or is it an apparition shaped in the need of the mind for a vital image of its own saving power and intent? I take it to be both. It is a token of promise, existent in the external universe and in the subjectivity of man.

All will recognize the truth that when the swan goes north it flies toward spring. The sense of this fact in its rich implications comes immediately to us in moving concreteness, as we read, before any concept of it arises from the focus of thought. Those readers who cannot stop with that image, instinct with meaning though it is, will add to it as they may—joining the poet in a larger communion of understanding, wholly consonant, however, with the vision of the visitant swan that points the way to the goal of life's desire. For of course far more is available, for enrichment and enlargement of perspective, much of it almost inevitably implied: the garden, benignly fostering enclosure of natural abundance, as temenos tended by man—or at his peril neglected; the bird as image of the soul, in flight and ascent; the white swan (bird of Venus and Apollo, of love, and of art, healing, and light,) as image of beauty—of vital form, order concretely realized for the whole sensibility. Thus deathly deprivation is seen to be transcended in resurrection of essential warmth and urgency, out of the snow-white depletion that purifies of all but the motive of life.

The next poem, entitled significantly **"New Year's Day at the End of a Decade,"** is likewise a celebration of vital transcendence. . . . This poem recounts the protagonist's displacement of pretty, falsifying pictures, decorating the calendar of the concluded year, by other imagined ones of the horror and truth of our time, and finally by one emblematic of hope: a ludicrous and touching depiction of a boy's hatching a sparrow's egg taped in the nest of his navel, in an act of abandonment "giving up his sex," overtly perhaps for curiosity's sake, yet for something further. Here again is represented a bird given life through an action of a human being, but new-hatched in helpless and hideous nakedness, propped on featherless wings and lifting the bony skull of the ancestral lizard, yet jaunty in readiness and, like the swan, one of Venus's birds: the sparrow of the gutter and the temple and of the yoked chariot of her journeys. (pp. 722-23)

That impression of union in aspects of the universe that we tend upon too meager assurance to separate is clarified and augmented in **"Ramifications,"** another poem of the opening series, in which the theme of transcendence is prominent among many others. Our inveterately compartmental thinking is rebuked as the poem elaborates new insight: that the landscape of Wyoming, once thought by the protagonist to be "the least human of lands," is really "the most human . . . , made like my hand" and "like a leaf" and "like thought whose / Streams long to intersect / In a valley." In the ending of the poem all falls into unity, is seen as one of substance and of one mode of being, as one light—both phenomenon and spirit, married, made one flesh and one life, in a landscape of vision. . . . (p. 723)

Dealing with movement beyond deprivative constrictions, toward ampler and more tolerable circumstances, in enlargement

and enhancement of life, the first eleven poems introduce a book-long development. Deliberately or not, overtly or obliquely, they exhibit the nature and consequences of flexibility and scope in those modes of action requisite for the sanity of human life, for its integrity and completeness, in being, in vision, and in behavior. But in the next six poems such movements and attainments are for the most part merely intimated, though emphatically, by their absence, in display of what counters or destroys them. The theme of transcendence has its negative aspects. There is a kind of transcendence, in violation, more precisely specifiable as transgression.

In these latter poems, and thereafter throughout the book, the transgressions of mankind are considered in various manifestations, including a great deal that characterizes what passes for civilization in our time. The first of this series, **"Skull Valley, Utah,"** representing the speaking ghosts of sheep killed there years ago by a spill of nerve gas, focuses on man as butcher—of men and flocks—and wholly by implication shows how we may yet be delivered from our own evil: though quite accidentally poured from our "butcher's hands" the nerve gas that opens no wound fell like a cleaver.

The rest of this sequence, five poems, turns attention to areas where human energy concentrates in promotion of the projects of our kind: the cities, centers of civilization. Two of them are identifiable only as of the old world and of the new, two as the capitals of the most exemplary powers in the modern and the ancient worlds, Washington and Rome. The last is that once lofty center of learning and of spiritual cultivation Salamanca, at whose great university Christopher Columbus lectured, and where St. John of the Cross was ordained priest.

In the first of these poems of the cities, which contrasts with the mode of the world's action that has laid down "history's rubble" the way of a woman whose deviant innocence of vision causes her to be called "quite mad," the real madness is shown to be that of the spiritually slack yet rigidly coercive world. The poems that follow compel reflection upon the truth of that characterization. Squires's depiction of the behavior of Heliogabalus in Rome suggests more than one of the popular roles of our day—most directly that of the statesman serving the people and that of the many who will not serve, including the superficially innocent stereotype of those who declare their dissociation from our whole way of life. **"Heliogabalus"** begins in representing the profligate emperor dancing "blind as a flower," before the people, the dance that like the flower's is of consent and accord, offered by life to the sun. Yet the blitheness of the dance is deceptive; in the end the implication is clear that human beings living heedless as flowers may be careless of life. For the emperor's shocking act in the "play of castration," climax of his dance, is an image of mankind's self-undoing. (pp. 723-24)

It is not my purpose to name every theme, but to show how as each is declared and developed their overlapping and intermingling creates a texture and tide of meaning moving in continually greater abundance and more massive power. **"A Day in Salamanca,"** last poem of the sequence of cities and dramatic culmination of what may be called the first movement of the book, shows this effect in full force. At its climax the protagonist, who has been sitting alone at a table in a great sunlit square of the city, is approached by a gangling boy, slowly—as if in some macabre ceremony—coming to thrust forward a captive sparrow that unless it is ransomed is to become a "blood-sacrifice." . . . (p. 725)

Freed, but soon back in its cage, the bird seems merely the ludicrously unconscious instrument of the boy's disreputable designs. Yet the comedy of its ransoming, repeated day after day, becomes like a ritual, charged with realization of something neglected in our lives, a sorry enactment—not quite a travesty—of love.

Is this bird—the familiar sparrow of the gutters and eaves—symbolic, is it to be seen perhaps as the old universal emblem of the soul? It is a little caged creature, "freed" in a city square, for a bit of money that compassion yields skeptically to cupidity. It rises from the ashen focus of an occasion created by the market. Its wings, absolutely subservient to human will, carry it only to the nearest house-front; returning at the call of its masters, it creeps into its little cage as if into the ultimate luxury: "like a spoiled princess." No: it is certainly not a symbol to which attention is diverted—by a shift in which the vast context of objective reality is lost; the bird is no symbol put forward for contemplation. Yet it exists and moves in modes more than a little suggestive of those the submissive psyche of each of us now endures and in some ways even enjoys ("the century being the century it is"). The analogy, complete and compelling, must be inescapable for the imagination that in reaching the core of insight determined by the realistic presentation must embrace the inner life of the actors in the little drama and place them in the theater of the world we know. (p. 726)

If we would read a poem, we must read into it all that is really there. "The bird spurts away like breath." Breath too is a natural, immemorial metaphor of inmost life, of spirit. In the long poem **"Daedalus,"** which constitutes the second of the three parts distinguishable in *Waiting in the Bone,* the idea of the bird as soul becomes explicit.

That powerfully apocalyptic poem merges the themes of the book and without distorting the myth makes it the story of mankind's sacrifice of grace and scope through preoccupation with the external objects of the self. Single-mindedly the artificer Daedalus devotes his skill to production of toys, armor, labyrinth, and other devices that entertain and empower those who think to dominate the world. In Talos, the boy inventor of the potter's wheel that through forming beautiful objects of daily use supplies both physical and spiritual needs simultaneously, Daedalus recognizes his enemy, and topples him from the Acropolis to his death. Thus the towering rock of the city lifting its temple to Athena, goddess of the genius and creative power of the Greeks, is usurped by the loveless and cunning manipulator of material substance and force.

Yet before his fall Talos has foretold consequences of that violence done to the body and the inner life: "I see you, or I see your kind, / In towers of glass and metal, with nothing / To do but watch wheels measuring space." And with the instinct of all true scientists and artists he has divined the deathliness of Daedalus's way and argued against it, opposing to it metaphoric images of the kiln and of its shards "strewn like flower petals." . . . (pp. 726-27)

Quick to know the enemies of his metallic mode, Daedalus feels himself threatened by the living, by evidence even of enthusiastic inclinations toward poetry in his son Icarus, and is reassured by their deaths. At the end of the poem, walking securely alone over ground that is "only / The daedal earth of the poets," he envisages the bloodless future, imaged in reduction to one form mechanically exact: "*My* earth . . . spin-

ning like a great metal / Plaything, the perfect ball, toward my clever hand."

The remainder of *Waiting in the Bone* meditates the clay and the fire. In the poem immediately following **"Daedalus"** lovers entering an art gallery are seen as the life of the works displayed; when they leave it "the light fails. / . . . The vase sinks back into the potter's wheel." In the next poems it is not cunning or cleverness but love that moves the hands of human communion and constructive power and directs flesh and formative intelligence in that shaping of matter which overcomes nonentity and gathers the scattered dust of the universe into the order of life. Gradually there emerges a vision of physical substance and stress of spirit interdeterminant, as in **"Chasms,"** in which untrodden hollows of varied conformation, beyond "where footpaths suddenly end," have the aspect simultaneously of landscape and of meaning adumbrated. Seeing in far-strewn stone the chance images of forms like those that men make, but fragmentary and loosely determined, as if they embodied merely tentative intimations of idea, we seem to be looking into the depths of possibility. . . . (pp. 727-28)

Even more fundamental in motivation of Radcliffe Squires's poetry than concern for the shaping of substance and the ordering of action in the objective world is a passion for truth: desire to accord insight and being with the ground of life, overlooking nothing, yielding to no distorting preference, capitulating to no preconception, scanting no aspect of appalling immensity. All the poems in this book look to that end. In the perspectives of light, much becomes tolerable, even the ephemerality of the earth and ourselves. So in **"Storm in the Desert,"** as movement of storm and stone, of all existence, toward nonentity becomes apparent, one man's participation in the action of the objective scene, a drama of matter more ancient than that of Thebes, brings recognition of its meaning and liberation from conceit, the universal conceit of blind being that fights against the ways of reality till in discovering they are really its own, it can savor the repose of acceptance.

Recognitions more difficult are faced in succeeding poems. The murdered children of Medea, the stillborn manhood of **"The Castrato Singer,"** who cannot fall from his abstraction into sin because like the wolves and the angels he cannot deviate into the wholeness of human flesh, are aspects of an enormity that must not be dismissed in contemplation of the sun. (pp. 728-29)

In the final poem, **"Self as an Eye,"** the self given wholly to vision—recognizing all, the gnawing snail and the night—embraces all in grief and in homage to the sun in its fullest meaning: "My eye, like a shore, narrows on its yes. / A squint of tears can hold the sun."

A great and extraordinary strength of Radcliffe Squires's poetry is the force and cogency of its design, concretely realized, poem by poem, from the beginning to the end of this highly unitary book. In its full perspective, the disorder and disaster of sheer circumstance made enormous by the inveterate indifference and compulsive machinations of self-serving mankind is gathered with energy and brilliant perception into comprehensive light, at the heart of which is a focus of fire, a kiln. (p. 729)

Brewster Ghiselin, "In the Garden of Talos: The Poetry of Radcliffe Squires," in The Sewanee Review, *Vol. LXXXIII, No. 4, Fall, 1975, pp. 720-29.*

JOHN R. REED

Radcliffe Squires' Greece evokes common existence.... In the poems of *Fingers of Hermes* (1965), for example, it was children playing ("**The Aegean**"), or a shepherd boy catching a ride home at night ("**Thasos**") that caught his attention. "**The Statues of Athens**" contrasted ideal figures preserved in museums with the gritty life captured in a workman's note scratched on an ancient shard.

> Ankesimos, you were shy and cruel. Goat's hair
> Sprouted in the impure marble of your
> Thigh. There is no statue of *you*.
> Your ordinary stink, your clumsy misery
> Did not survive, but they endure
> As I hasten to you twenty-five centuries late.

But that ordinariness is no salvation, as the poems of *Gardens of the World* show. In "**The Sons of Medea**" we are all sons of one Mother—life, experience, the tragedy of human fate. "We are impaled, mother, on your roundness / And we cry out in the knowledge of / A certain ecstasy: that life has no violence, / No crime, no triumphant revenge. Only incest." "**The First Day out from Troy**" tells Aeneas' story, except that the heroic Aeneas also represents the common destiny of man, the relentlessness of history.... Departure from Troy implies the founding of Rome and all of its subsequent history—the barbarians massing to break its gates and then "moaning for the gates to open and let them go." (pp. 682-83)

[These] are poems of resignation, but an uncomfortable resignation, as though momentous events impend and mysteries await disclosure. This seems to be the significance of the poems on the gardens of Medusa, Eros, Aphrodite, Ariadne, Maia, the World, and Prometheus, each of which captures some central feature of man's condition. In the Garden of Medusa you may learn to deal with the horror of life one way or another; in the Garden of Eros with desire, though you will not enter this garden, "The garden will enter you." Each garden has its lesson of praise or sorrow; one offers a knowledge that is almost miraculous. In the Garden of Niobe you may learn, if you are lucky, "That all music is a lost self, / And the lost self returns to you only when / Your grief for him makes you kind."

Squires constantly invokes the lost self of youth and adolescence, whether actual ("**First Day of School**"), metaphorical ("**Old Leaves**"), or both ("**New Year's Day at the End of a Decade**"), but he is haunted as well by the need to survive the relentless movement of existence by learning to command daily experience.... Squires does not entirely embrace dailiness. Consequential events intrude.

The Audenesque "**A March on Washington**" describes the possible consequences of political attempts to alter history. The speaker watches a poet, probably Lowell, on t.v. addressing a youthful crowd and telling History to be good. She doesn't hear, but a small boy does and puts away his toys and childishness "Or any of the fantasies usual and small / Which in the long run make people slightly bearable. / His followers, even now bored with mechano sets, / Are calmly waiting for him to say, 'What / We must do to our brothers is wrong except it is good.'"

Squires' poems are uncertain of their power to redeem dailiness from disaster, and his language is accordingly edgier and more complicated.... "**A March on Washington**" toys with near rhymes: Washington / brimstone, muses / chooses, brother / mother / father. "**Christmas at the End of a Decade**" rhymes more closely and uses alliteration, repetition, and unusual dic-

tion ('squinnied,' 'ripple-riddle') freely to construct its mood. Squires chooses whatever mode seems appropriate to his purpose, and generally he chooses well.

My favorite poem in *Gardens of the World* sums up Squires' position, his embattled defense of the ordinary in the face of a stupefying and unending need to choose between freedom and cruelty. In "**A Day in Salamanca**," the poet sits at a table in the square near sundown. A priest and some students are nearby, the latter talking "erotically of revolution." A boy crosses the square to the poet's table and threatens to kill a bird he holds in his hand, asking: "Which shall it be, freedom / Or blood sacrifice?" The poet drops a coin on the table and the boy releases the bird, but it does not fly far. When the boy whistles, it returns to enter a little cage like a "spoiled princess."

> The priest and the students, bored now, turn away.
> But the boy and I smile at each other,
> Not decently nor gratefully, but with a certain love.
> Each day now for a week, I have bought
> This same bird's life from this same boy
> At this same table.
>
>   Why not?
> The century being the century it is,
> The role is a role worth perfecting.

(pp. 683-84)

John R. Reed, "Redeeming Dailiness: Three New Books of Poetry," in Michigan Quarterly Review, *Vol. XXI, No. 4, Fall, 1982, pp. 680-87.*

THEODORE HADDIN

Readers of Radcliffe Squires's seventh book of poems [*Gardens of the World*] will discover here some of the most interesting, original, and provocative poems of his career, which spans over forty years. Much of the best that appeared in *Where the Compass Spins, Fingers of Hermes,* and *Waiting in the Bone* culminates now in a book we shall be long in appreciating. It is poetry that speaks immediately to our age, and for the ages; for Squires is far from an ordinary poet, and these poems in their quiet persistence possess such remarkable originality and imaginative brilliance as to draw the reader into a new world—a world that the twentieth-century mind craves, perhaps, without knowing.

Gardens of the World addresses itself to legacies of history and time, art and beauty, in a way that few contemporary books of poetry seem capable. In a world fast spending itself to nothingness, *Gardens* is a refreshing spring to the human in need of being human, in need of having complete experiences, indeed, of realizing sanity in an environment often cruel and destructive.

The title of this book is more apt than would at first appear. While some of the thirty-nine poems range from the purely personal ("**First Day of School**"), to the political ("**March on Washington**"), and the salutary ("**Winchester**"), it steals upon the reader that the poems dealing with deserts and mountains of the first two sections complement the amazing imaginative power of the nine garden poems of the third section. These latter poems, which constitute the self's existential journey of the imagination, thus have their counterpart in the self's encounter with the real deserts and mountains, valleys and chasms of the world. There is no mistaking that for Squires, both encounters are of immense significance. Together they enlarge the scope of imaginative enquiry to include both geological time and the history of the poetic self that has always been an important part of all of Squires's poetry. Add to these the original development of myth and mythology that runs through so many of the earlier poems and especially the garden poems, and we have poetry that begins to compare with Eliot's *Four Quartets* or Stevens's "Notes Toward a Supreme Fiction."

For evidence of this we must look to poems like **"Chasms"** or **"Storm in the Desert,"** that makes a philosophical question of absence and ends with a "love of a vast absence." The voice that questions here confronts the reader with reality, deliberately forcing us to look at the underside, or the other side, of everything we take for granted in the natural world. This looking of Squires's, his capacity to go past the seemingly trivial to the matter of great moment, makes him a true poet and historian of modern consciousness. He has not written as much as those who seem to have more to say, but his vision is unerring, and his thought is concentrated on man's hopes in a world he yet loves.

Nowhere is this more evident in the book than in the imaginative journeys of the nine garden poems, all of which involve some version or interpretation of the self's encounters in a mythical garden. And since the meaning of each encounter depends upon a dramatic use of the personal pronoun "you," the encounter is both the reader's and the poet's, not to be refused even if not desired. These are the poems of Squires's deepest reasonings that begin frankly in **"The Garden of Medusa"** with the statement, "You have the choice whether to go or not," and end nobly in **"The Garden of Prometheus,"** with the salutation, "There is the garden from which you cannot fall." Between these lie the risk and uncertainty in journeys we seem to have made before, but did not know until the poem came into being, and even then may not understand. The way in these journeys is redolent with possibilities of life and death, appearance and reality, betrayal, love, lust, hope, and illusion, everything we would expect of life intensely lived. The transformation of the journeys into art is the reward of the reader's involvement, from the Catullus-like encounter with Aphrodite to the surrealistic celebration of the dead in **"The Garden of Medusa"** and the surrealistic experience of love in **"The Garden of Niobe."**

The latter poem, one of the most powerful in the book, recounts the journey of the self from and towards a rival, perhaps a lost sibling or twin, in which the journeying self is blessed by children, one of whom may "take the fireflies from an eye and put / Them in your hand" as a guide for the return by night. And the return is overwhelming. . . . (pp. 110-11)

One reading of this book will hardly exhaust all that can be written about these rich and penetrating poems. Their power lives long after. They will certainly make us go back to his earlier books. Critics have linked Squires with Robinson Jeffers and Robert Frost, about whom he has written excellent books, but none has mentioned the long-time friend about whom he has also written, Allen Tate, nor Squires's deceased wife, Eileen, both of whom were brilliant classicists in their ways and share the world of his poems. Squires and his wife grew exquisite gardens in Utah and Michigan. He writes all of these poems as if the garden in which he labored for so many years is at last the garden he has always wanted. There can be no greater testimonial to poetry, that the garden can now also be ours. (p. 112)

Theodore Haddin, in a review of "Gardens of the World," in South Atlantic Review, *Vol. 48, No. 2, May, 1983, pp. 110-12.*

SANDRA M. GILBERT

[Radcliffe Squires's poetry is often threatened by] an illness of the imagination expressed not through an awareness of the compromises required by, say, the claims of housekeeping but through a consciousness of the concessions demanded by the tedious repetitions of history and by what Matthew Arnold called "this strange disease of modern life." **"A Day in Salamanca,"** the first piece in *Gardens of the World*, his latest collection, announces his sense of his own dilemma. Though the poem's setting (**"Salamanca"**) and its characters—"a beautiful priest," students who "talk erotically of revolution," a sinister-looking boy who threatens to sacrifice a sparrow unless the speaker pays him off—appear more exotic than most of the places and people we encounter in [other poetry]. . . . (p. 156)

"The century being the century it is": like twentieth-century precursors from Yeats, Eliot and Stevens to Auden and Lowell, Squires is trapped by his own feeling of belatedness as well as by a characteristically contemporary fear of the millenium that seems (in **"New Year's Day at the End of a Decade"**) to loom out of "all history's bottomless calendar." But where the major modernists' attempts to extricate themselves from such almost apocalyptic exhaustion issued in **"Supreme Fictions,"** visionary self-dramatizations, religious renewals, or meditations on the salvation of "the individual talent" by the cathedral of "tradition," Squires finds that all he has to set against the enervation of the ordinary is refreshment by the ordinary—refreshment, for instance, by the serenity of "brown hands / Searching blind in brown / Leaves for delicate lavender heads" (in **"Spring"**) or by (in **"New Year's Day at the End of a Decade"**) the casual

> . . . story told
> Me of a boy who found a not quite cold
> Sparrow's egg on the black sill
> Outside his window and taped it in his navel till
> It hatched.

At his most visionary, in fact, what Squires both dreads and desires appears to be the fragmentation of that history which, say, Eliot so famously shored against his ruin, and its replacement by the bare "light of common day" in which we can find the simple instrumentality of animals and plants "more truly and more strange." In **"In the Gallery,"** walking through a symbolic salon in which a "ninth century Attic vase . . . smiles" across at a Warhol painting of a "face / Repeated until it is meaningless," he imagines himself saying

> . . . "This is all.
> We have endured much history, but this is all.
> History has come back on itself. There is no more
> To endure."

And as "the light fails," in a moment of "horror" which is also a consummation devoutly wished, "The frames stand empty along the wall. / The vase sinks back into the potter's wheel." All we are left with, all we can be left with, this poet assures us, is the minimal "beginning of all things . . . Light flowing like rivers / Down mountains of light" (**"Ramifications"**).

As both **"In the Gallery"** and **"Ramifications"** suggest, Squires is at times driven to making . . . grandiose statements . . . , no doubt because he experiences . . . an "anxiety of influence" that forces him to compare his own solutions to the more extreme fictions proposed by his poetic fathers. In **"Waiting in the Bone,"** which was (not insignificantly) a publicly delivered Phi Beta Kappa poem at the University of Michigan in

1972, he uses the stripped language that Eliot essayed in *Four Quartets* but attempts (as Eliot also did) to turn this lean rhetoric to larger purposes.... [However], where Eliot's deployment of such language often succccds—perhaps, indeed, because he sets prosaic understatement contrapuntally against more intricately musical passages—Squires's does not.... Squires comes across as a leader-writer for the local paper or a self-consciously passionate speaker at a Fourth of July picnic ("we burned our cities . . . we killed our fathers"), and his tentative solution, a vision of a "red bird" rising "from the dazed ash of the winter plain" like "tears / Falling upward / On the sky" therefore fails to ring true. (pp. 157-58)

[Because] he is a scholar/critic as well as a poet, and—judging from his *oeuvre* as a whole—a classicist of sorts, Squires often tries to escape from the confinement of the commonplace into the more emphatic drama of literary allusions. His **"Winchester,"** for instance, paraphrases Wordsworth's "Milton! Thou shouldst be living at this hour" to conclude "Jane Austen, John Keats, how much you need / Each other. How much I need you both." And his **"Lines for the English"** postulates "a thousand gentle / Clerks, snubnosed like so many William Blakes" who "ascend / The sky of a land more green / And pleasant than any New Jerusalem." Yet significantly, this green and pleasant land that is better than a "New Jerusalem" is one about which he has already observed, in a crucial annihilation of the traditional melodrama of political history, that

> In an hour empires fall
> But in a century nothing at all
> Of importance happens,

and his prayer to Austen and Keats praises "the sundries of drawing rooms and tea, / Which comprise the bliss of [Austen's] originality," even while the poem's conclusion reduces Wordsworth's grandly prophetic "England hath need of thee" to a sadly bathetic, late-twentieth-century "How much I need you both."

Similarly, the sequence of garden poems from which Squires's new collection [*Gardens of the World*] takes its title depends on classical allusions (**"The Garden of Medusa," "The Garden of Hecate," "The Garden of Eros,"** etc.), but the strongest poems in the series are not those in which the author revitalizes ancient myths to show their extraordinary power; rather they are those in which he revises such legends to show their ordinary relevance. The **"Garden of Medusa,"** for instance, is a place where you may look into "the dark mirror you will find / Has grown in the palm of your hand" and "make a notorious marriage," or you may observe the statues in the garden, noting "How beautifully they / Have weathered," or "You may, after all, choose to forget the mirror and / See what the face really looks like," with the poet adding ironically that "These are the choices, and none of them easy." No Perseus triumphs here; instead, the garden's malady, with all its Jamesian complications, is precisely the ill ease of quotidian reality. As for a Delphic solution, moreover, the one that grows in Squires's gardens is equally calm and "ordinary," for, as if echoing the "delicate lavender heads" of **"In Spring,"** it

is most elegantly offered in the early **"Garden of Maia,"** whose proprietress urges her visitors to

> . . . Go now and forget
> Me. Or, if you think of me at all, think
> Of me as the white violet crushed beneath
> Your instep. Its will gathers to lift you.

Ultimately, in fact, it is this apparently minor but guardedly majestic "will" that Squires invokes to combat the exhaustion of history, whose extremities he sometimes seems determined not to explore in any detail. Thus, in **"Some Marvelous Quarry"** and **"First Day of School,"** he examines small private records, personal memories, far more effectively than in **"Waiting in the Bone"** he had explored public chronicles. **"Some Marvelous Quarry,"** interestingly, describes a child's vision of a dead porcupine and, swerving from Richard Eberhart's classic "The Groundhog," defines the experience of encountering the dead animal as obdurately individual. Refusing to widen the poem from gazing subject and decaying body to "St. Teresa and her wild lament," this perhaps overly modest contemporary insists, rather, on the haunting and haunted consciousness of one child.... Similarly, **"First Day of School"** focuses on the almost surrealistically real experience of a single kindergartener who discovers that "the crone" who has come to fetch him from a traumatic day

> . . . is my sister, bloodying her handkerchief
> On my knee, saying they were worried when
> I was late, and she had come
> To find me and bring me home.
>
> Oh home!

Mild and ironic as it is, that last wistful exclamation embodies perhaps the greatest intensity some poets can allow themselves in this era when a "lilting house" sounds all too much like a stilted house. "Oh home!" the poet—certainly the poet like . . . Squires—murmurs nervously, nostalgically, and in the end he . . . has little else to say, except what Squires writes to conclude **"Animal Crossing,"** a self-deprecatingly visionary account of a highway sign which is perhaps the most moving of the works in this collection:

> Then let me, animals, let me, who motionless
> Lie athwart the road, let me be the path you cross.
> Let my stasis feel the raccoon's skeptical claws
> Move across me toward lost groves.
> Let the sharp-footed deer pierce my stayed flesh.
> Let the little three-toed horse discover
> Footing between my ribs, and so cross over.

Here human history, both public and private, becomes simply a bridge or conduit by which the unselfconscious stubbornness of animal life can pass from one moment of being to another. And though the Eohippus whom Squires marvelously resurrects in his last lines may be as exotic as "baboons and periwinkles," it is really the sharp feet of the common deer and the "skeptical claws" of the ordinary raccoon that he imagines puncturing whatever grand pretensions he may have. Their history qualifies and clarifies his, finally subduing him to silence. (pp. 158-61)

Sandra M. Gilbert, "The Melody of the Quotidian," in Parnassus: Poetry in Review, *Vol. 11, No. 1, 1983, pp. 147-67.*

Peter (Ulrich) Weiss

1916-1982

German-born Swedish dramatist, autobiographer, novelist, scriptwriter, nonfiction writer, filmmaker, translator, journalist, and illustrator.

Best known for his play *Die Verfolgung und Ermordung Jean Paul Marats, dargestellt durch die Schauspielgruppe des Hospizes zu Charenton unter Anleitung des Hernn de Sade* (1964; *The Persecution and Assassination of Jean-Paul Marat as Performed by the Inmates of the Asylum of Charenton under the Direction of the Marquis de Sade*), commonly known as *Marat/Sade*, Weiss is widely considered among the most important and controversial dramatists to emerge in post-World War II Europe. Throughout his career, Weiss viewed his work as an instrument for self-discovery and political debate. His dramas, autobiographies, films, and other artistic endeavors are informed by his lifelong commitment to Marxism, his sense of displacement from society, and the guilt he harbored for having escaped the horrors of nazism and the Holocaust. Weiss's most significant topics include alienation, the mechanisms of history, and the conflicts between individualism and collectivism, reality and illusion. Drawing from such dramatic movements as the Theater of Cruelty and the Theater of the Absurd, as well as the writings of Franz Kafka, André Gide, and Bertolt Brecht, Weiss created highly unorthodox plays that are imbued with vivid sensory perceptions intended to shock and assault the sensibilities of his audience. Because the majority of his dramas revolve primarily around his Marxist beliefs and his nihilistic vision of postwar society, Weiss's works have been faulted for lack of artistic merit. Roger Ellis, however, contended that "Weiss always sought something contemporary in his studies of the past: an understanding of the roots of social violence, of the extent of human influence upon historical development, of the restrictive conditions which bear upon modern artists and how to overcome them, and, most especially, an understanding of the roots of the seemingly paradoxical faith of certain individuals who struggle unsuccessfully to improve apparently hopeless situations."

Weiss was born into a prominent family in Nowawes, an industrial province near Berlin. His father was a textile manufacturer of Jewish descent who had converted to Christianity long before the rise to power of Adolf Hitler's regime and raised his son in the Lutheran church. In 1934, Weiss emigrated with his family to London, where he lived for three years before enrolling in the Art Academy in Prague. He fled Czechoslovakia in 1938 before the Nazi invasion and moved to Sweden, where his parents had permanently settled. Disillusioned by his family's adherence to bourgeois values while most of Europe was under siege, Weiss joined a commune of German-speaking artists and refugees in Stockholm. He later became a citizen of Sweden and resided there until his death.

Weiss's first published work, *Från ö till ö* (1946), was written in Swedish and consists of prose poems on ordinary topics; a companion volume, *De besegrade*, was published in 1948. In 1947, on assignment for a Stockholm newspaper, Weiss visited Germany for the first time since the end of World War II. Upon his return to Sweden, he began writing dramatic scripts for radio as well as several one-act theater pieces in German.

© Isolde Ohlbaum

The radio play *Der Turm* (1948; *The Tower*) foreshadows his artistic and political direction in its surreal tale of captivity and freedom. Weiss was also involved in filmmaking during this period and over the next decade wrote and produced several documentary and feature-length films. These heavily symbolic cinematic works helped to establish Weiss's reputation among avant-garde artistic circles in Europe and the United States.

In his early fiction, Weiss employed imaginative techniques similar to those in his films. In *Der Schatten des Körpers des Kutschers* (1960; *The Shadow of the Coachman's Body*), his first major work written in German, Weiss employs a deliberate, disjointed prose style to record the observations of an alienated narrator who is unable to relate to the objects and people around him at the isolated country boarding house where he lives. *Das Gespräch der drei Gehenden* (1963; *Conversation of the Three Wayfarers*) consists of a series of dialogues between three anonymous travelers that are rich in biblical, mythical, and philosophical allusions. These books were republished together in 1969 as *Bodies and Shadows: Two Short Novels*. Hans-Bernhard Moeller commented that both works "recall Weiss's own description of Strindberg's concept of man: a collage in flux rather than a unified character." In his autobiographical novels *Abschied von den Eltern: Erzählung* (1961; *The Leavetaking*) and *Fluchtpunkt* (1962; *Vanishing Point*),

Weiss recounts the alienation and guilt he experienced during his adolescence and his eventual triumph of self-realization, juxtaposing his maturation with the rise of nazism, World War II, and his family's flight from Germany. *The Leavetaking* and *Vanishing Point* were reprinted in a single volume, *Exile* (1968), which Stanley Kauffmann praised as "a unique antinomic addition to the European literature of the war years: the old, old search of a youth for selfhood, seen here in the reflected light of our century's huge fires."

Marat/Sade accelerated Weiss's international reputation and has generated extensive critical discussion and interpretation since its 1964 premiere in West Berlin. The first of his "documentary dramas," *Marat/Sade* illuminates Weiss's pessimistic view of human existence since World War II. The protagonists, the Marquis de Sade and French revolutionary Jean-Paul Marat, embody for Weiss the dualism of humanity. Marat is the ideological, pre-Marxist intellectual who commits violent acts for the good of society, while Sade symbolizes self-indulgence and mindless anarchy. The play is set in 1808 in the bath house of Charenton, a French asylum, where Sade directs a company of inmates in a play enacting events leading to Marat's assassination in 1793. The "actor" portraying Marat becomes involved in a sequence of dialectical debates with Sade in order to convince the inmates that his ideological beliefs are best suited for restructuring the existing social order. Weiss employed elements from the Theater of the Absurd and the Theater of Cruelty and utilized surrealist devices and cinematic techniques to create what he termed "total theater," through which he hoped to evoke intense emotional reactions from the audience. Allowing for disparate interpretations, *Marat/Sade* ends ambiguously; either Sade or Marat may triumph. Weiss said that he preferred productions which favored Marat's pre-Marxist stance: "[My] point is that even if the world is a madhouse like Charenton and nobody wants to belong in it, this is still where we are and the least we can do is to take a stand for or against madness." While many critics contended that the play's meaning is ambivalent or equivocal, Susan Sontag responded: "That the ideas taken up in *Marat/Sade* are not resolved, in an intellectual sense, is far less important than the extent to which they do work together in the sensory arena." *Marat/Sade* won a Tony Award and the New York Drama Critics Circle Award for best foreign play.

Weiss's next major drama, *Die Ermittlung: Oratorium in Elf Gesängen* (1965; *The Investigation*), consists of transcribed testimony taken from the Auschwitz War Crimes trial held in Frankfurt in 1964 and 1965. The characters in this play deliver their testimony in a monotone and display no physical expression. By deliberately omitting the words "Jew," "Nazi," and "Germany" from the text, Weiss implies that the atrocities committed at Auschwitz were universal in nature and that all of humanity should share in their responsibility and guilt. Originally five hours in length but edited to two hours upon its American premiere on Broadway in 1966, *The Investigation* garnered wide acclaim. Lothar Kahn asserted: "The phrase 'Jewish question' to [Weiss] is not real. It should be supplanted by 'human question,' with the Jews being merely the prototypes of the weak everywhere and their tormentors the representatives of the strong." *The Investigation* was adapted for American television in 1967. Weiss's next documentary drama, *Gesang vom lusitanischen Popanz* (1968; *Song of the Lusitanian Bogey*), is a "political musical." While focusing specifically on the exploitation of Angola and Mozambique by Portugal, this play also indicts imperialism and colonialism throughout history. This piece garnered largely negative reviews. Theophilus

Lewis charged: "The play is ineffectual as protest drama, since it is merely a repetitive recital of cruelties. Although its atrocities may be well documented, the work is too consistently one-sided to make impressive documentary drama." In *Diskurs über die Vorgeschichte und den Verlauf des lang andauernden Befreiungskrieges in Viet Nam als Beispiel für die Notwendigkeit des bewaffneten Kampfes der Unterdrückten gegen ihre Unterdrücker, sowie über die Versuche der Vereinigten Staaten von Amerika die Grundlagen der Revolution zu vernichten* (1968; *Discourse on the Progress of the Prolonged War of Liberation in Viet Nam . . .*), commonly referred to as *Vietnam Discourse,* Weiss combines music, poetry, dance, and photography to present the history of Vietnam from antiquity to President Lyndon B. Johnson's decision to escalate American involvement in the country's civil war. Although not a critical success, this play fared better among audiences than *Song of the Lusitanian Bogey.* Richard Aspen observed: "For an age peculiarly marked by economic and political thinking, Weiss' theater of fact can function as a needed reminder of our 'civilized' stupidities and cruelties."

Weiss's final dramas focus more on individuals than on historical incidents. Like his previous plays, these pieces are informed by Marxist doctrine. In *Trotzki im Exil* (1970; *Trotsky in Exile*), Weiss employs flashbacks to chronicle the life of Leon Trotsky, documenting his role as a leader of the 1917 Russian Revolution, his ideological differences with Joseph Stalin during the early years of the Soviet Republic followed by his expulsion from Russia, and his murder in Mexico City in 1940. *Hölderlin* (1971) details the tragic life and death of German poet Friedrich Hölderlin, whose personal and artistic failures drove him to insanity. Roger Ellis said of these plays: "Weiss accurately traced the reasons behind the political failure of these two men, but he also showed how both had perceived the germs of the future. Most importantly, Weiss showed both men acting in accordance with those futurizing ideals despite the contradictions which inhibited and ultimately destroyed them."

Weiss also published three installments of *Die Ästhetik des Widerstands,* a series of novels centering on the artistic and ideological maturation of a young German intellectual. In these works, Weiss draws upon his own experiences while depicting historical incidents and personages to chronicle Europe's turbulent political climate preceding World War II. Volume one of the trilogy, issued in 1975, begins at the end of the Spanish Civil War, in which the protagonist fought with the Loyalists against the regime of Generalissimo Francisco Franco and details the genesis of the Nazi and Soviet subjugation of eastern Europe. The second installment, published in 1978, dramatizes the hero's flight to Sweden to escape the Nazis and recounts his meeting with exiled dramatist Bertolt Brecht. The final volume, which appeared in 1981, focuses upon the protagonist's settlement in Stockholm and his underground political activities, ending with Germany's surrender to the Allied Forces in 1945. While praised for its authenticity and historical scope, *Die Ästhetik des Widerstands* was considered demanding by many commentators because of Weiss's omission of individual paragraphs, chapter headings, and quotation marks designating dialogue. Some reviewers also contended that the political discussions in these novels are one-sided and dated. Wes Blomster summarized critical opinion: "[Enthusiasm] for Weiss's trilogy will depend to a large degree upon the sympathy in the reader for the author's commitment to the Left. For many the work will be nothing more than a political pamphlet. . . . Those who respond positively to Weiss's work might well ask whether monumental writing is possible in the present day without this precise definition of position.''

In addition to his dramas and autobiographical fiction, Weiss produced several nonfiction books, including *Avantgardefilm* (1956) and *Notizen zum kulturellen Leben in der Demokratischen Republik Viet Nam* (1968; *Notes on the Cultural Life of the Democratic Republic of Vietnam*), the latter a companion piece to his play *Vietnam Discourse*. In 1982, Weiss was posthumously awarded the Georg Büchner Prize for outstanding achievement in German letters.

(See also *CLC*, Vols, 3, 15; *Contemporary Authors*, Vols. 45-48, Vol. 106 [obituary]; and *Contemporary Authors New Revision Series*, Vol. 3.)

THE TIMES LITERARY SUPPLEMENT

Peter Weiss's two most recent plays were both initially responses to centenary celebrations of one kind or another. *Trotsky in Exile* was described by its author as his ''contribution to the Lenin Year'' of 1970, for it was intended to honour Lenin by furthering the kind of open debate about history which he favoured, by counteracting the combination of outright taboo and official vilification of Trotsky which took place in many of the countries which paid homage to Lenin. . . .

Hölderlin was begun during the bicentenary year of the Swabian poet's birth, although the main impetus for this interpretation came from two books on the political background of the times: Werner Kirchner's *Der Hochverratsprozess gegen Sinclair* and Pierre Bertaux's *Hölderlin und die Französische Revolution*, both of which appeared in 1969. Instead of the clash of diametrically opposed personalities which dominated the *Marat/Sade* or Weiss's rather impersonal, didactic documentaries of the 1960s, we are here offered two biographical plays, centering on familiar but ambiguous figures in history. . . .

It helps to see both plays as historical collages rather than realistic documentaries. The way in which *Trotsky* begins in 1928 with one of the saddest moments of the hero's life—his expulsion from the Soviet Union which he has helped to create—and then moves without further ado back thirty years to his first exile at Verkholensk, so that we feel the 1899 imprisonment is a result of the 1928 arrest, is the first of a well-conceived complex of flashbacks which end up making the champion of permanent revolution seem a permanent exile. The whole play may well be re-enacted in the mind of the dying Trotsky, just as the original version of the *Marat/Sade* was to have been Marat's projection.

By making the time-transitions highly subjective and by portraying the period as if it were one man's reminiscences, Weiss can facilitate certain liberties with history: such as allowing Trotsky to seem to speak in his own defence at the Moscow show trials, or to conduct what might otherwise have been an embarrassingly prophetic discussion with students from Paris, Vietnam, South America and other pertinent settings, about the revolutionary potential of their homelands. The prophetic tone is not always well maintained—it is, as one sees from some of Brecht's plays, a difficult register to work in—but this is to some extent intentional. We are deliberately given a Trotsky, warts and all; there is no wilful hagiography to counteract the dogmatic image, nor any Trotskyist's Trotsky. Like Weiss's

Hölderlin, Trotsky is a figure who raises questions rather than simply corrects misconceptions.

''Of Hölderlin's three great experiences'', Pierre Bertaux has argued, ''the nature and essence of the Greeks, his love for Susette Gontard and the Revolution, the latter is the most decisive.'' Weiss's *Hölderlin* sets out to explore this idea. The play begins with Hölderlin's sojourn as a pupil at the Tübinger Stift, a useful dramatic juncture, for it brings out the poet's youthfully idealistic relationship with such fellow-pupils as Hegel, Schelling and Sinclair, and also contrasts the sense of oppression in the Stift (in many ways another Charenton) with what is happening in France at the same time. For Hölderlin entered this famous seminary in 1788 and his stay there spanned the rise and fall of Fance's revolutionary fervour.

With various allusions to Charlotte Corday, Weiss underlies. Bertaux's suggestion that Hölderlin could best be considered a disappointed Girondiste. But Weiss does not go so far as Bertaux in emphasizing the importance of March 1799, and the role of General Jourdain's proclamation in putting an end to revolutionary hopes for Swabia, as the turning-point in Hölderlin's life. Instead, the play concentrates on a more general picture: having depicted the oppressive Swabian background, it moves or to Hölderlin's relationship with Susette Gontard, his unfortunate meeting with Goethe, and his reunion with Hegel and Schelling in later life. The poet's madness is by no means a source of sensationalism.

We witness Hölderlin's visions of a better future becoming encoded in mythology, we see him gradually being driven inward into a solipsistic world. His friend Sinclair, denounced for a planned attempt on the life of the Duke of Württemberg, and referred to cryptically in the poem ''An Eduard'' (which becomes something of a leitmotif at one point in the play) is the activist contrast to the visionary poet. For all the myths of a better world, the apotheosis of which comes in a dramatic phantasmagoria on *Empedokles*, there seems to be an element of guilty conscience in this depiction of Hölderlin. And this uncertainty about the validity of Hölderlin's kind of cryptic pro-revolutionary stance is made only more pronounced by a bravura apologetic ending which has a young journalist, a certain Karl Marx, visiting the poet to explain [that Hölderlin did not describe the attempted revolution as a scientifically grounded necessity but as mythological intimation is not his fault].

It would have been a good thing for Germany, Thomas Mann once suggested, if Karl Marx had read Hölderlin. Weiss, going one step farther—or to the left—proposes that it would be a good thing for Marx to interpret Hölderlin for us.

''Puppets of History,'' in The Times Literary Supplement, *No. 3659, April 14, 1972, p. 408.*

FRANZ P. HABERL

When an artist is in the midst of his creative career, the task of assessing his work is difficult, perhaps so difficult that it should not even be attempted. To state as Otto F. Best does in his preface [to his book, *Peter Weiss*], that ''the oeuvre of Peter Weiss, founded on self-portrayal and self-analysis, constitutes a unity'' is audacious, to say the least. Reading this sentence on the first page of what purports to be a critical study, one wonders what the author will say about Weiss's **''Princeton Speech''** . . . in which he vowed to leave his ''untouchable sanctuary of art'' and devote himself to political action, or at least to *art engagé*. In this speech Weiss renounced such esthetic endeavors as his highly successful experimental prose works, his painting and film-making. This renunciation marks a definite caesura in his work, but Best does not discuss it at all. Instead, he tries to make his study fit the procrustean bed of his original premise. Again and again Weiss's plays are subjected to the same psychological-biographical interpretation. Proceeding from factors outside the particular drama (e.g., Weiss's unhappy relationship with his father, somewhat à la Kafka), Best interprets the drama itself and then goes on to generalize about later works. At the end of his discussion of *The Tower,* Best links the concept of oppression, "the basic theme of Peter Weiss's work," with the father-son conflict, specifically with the idea of the prodigal son, except that his prodigal son returns as an *homme révolté* who demands justice, rather than asking for forgiveness.... At the end of his discussion of the *Viet Nam Diskurs* Best says: "The distant country [North Vietnam] symbolizes justice, democracy, progress, freedom; it signifies negation of all which overshadowed his [Weiss's] childhood, youth and early manhood." Obviously, this kind of criticism misses the point of Weiss's documentary theater. Even without his immoderate language (e.g. "intellectual no-man's-land" as a collective label applied to Weiss's documentary theater) and his insinuations regarding the authenticity of Weiss's material, Best's arguments would not be convincing. Weiss's documentary dramas (*The Investigation, Song of the Lusitanian Bogey,* and *Viet Nam Diskurs*) are based on mature thought and careful research. On the whole they did have the desired effects of either supplying the audience with basic information concerning vital matters or of increasing their awareness of these matters while at the same time producing the cathartic effect which is the hallmark of all drama. By now there is sample evidence to support this conclusion. (pp. 396-97)

With *Trotzki im Exil* Weiss reached a crucial point in his career as a dramatist and political thinker. The play was generally considered a failure in dramatic terms, and Weiss himself conceded that he suffered a "defeat." The more important aspect of the debacle, however, is the complete rejection of *Trotzki im Exil* by the literary and political establishment of the socialist countries. The play was not performed in East Germany, and Lev Ginsberg, the editor of *Literaturnaja gazeta* in Moscow, accused Weiss of falsifications, of insults to the Soviet Union and of playing into the hands of the enemies of socialism. In his reply Weiss quoted Marx to the effect that revelation and analysis of weaknesses as well as unsparing criticism are healthy for socialism. He further stated that Trotsky in his play does not criticize the socialist state as such, but only its bureaucratic perversions. But to no avail: Weiss has reached the proverbial position between the two chairs which was so aptly described by Friedrich Dürrenmatt in a recent lecture: "Just as for Allah and for the Devil the enemy is neither the Devil nor Allah, but the atheist who believes neither in Allah nor in the Devil, so the intellectuals have become the enemies of the two Games [the capitalist and the communist system]." (pp. 397-98)

Weiss seems to have had this difficult position of the intellectual in mind when he wrote *Hölderlin*. This highly effective epic drama portrays the life of the German poet Friedrich Hölderlin (1770-1843), particularly his relationship to the French Revolution.... This historical framework affords Weiss the opportunity of presenting three different solutions to the problem which faces the intellectual who believes that "everything must be overthrown so that something new can come into being," but who also realizes that the revolution is impossible to achieve. One possibility is to reach some accommodation with the establishment, to infiltrate it with the aim of trans-

forming it from within. The obvious moral dangers lurking on this route are co-option and corruption by the establishment. This is what happens to Hegel in Weiss's play. The second possibility is direct and illegal action, such as Sinclair's attempt at political assassination. This kind of act is often suicidal for the perpetrator and almost always entails even greater oppression for the people whom it was designed to liberate. The third possibility is exemplified by Hölderlin himself: He realizes that a fundamental renewal of society is urgently needed, and at the same time he sees that it is impossible to effect such a revolution. This dichotomy between his conviction that the revolution is necessary and his utter inability to bring it about drives Hölderlin to insanity. Weiss deliberately avoids specifying whether Hölderlin's insanity is real or completely or partly feigned. Apparently the director of each production has some leeway in this respect. Obviously the more lucid Hölderlin appears during the last forty years of his life, i.e., during the oppressive period of the European Restoration, the more he suffers and the more poignant a character he becomes. (p. 398)

"Imagination and action" do "exist in the same space" in *Hölderlin*. In this play he abandoned the practice of clinging to factual truth which he had used in his documentary theater. Instead, he took a historical figure and used imagination and consistency to mold him into a dramatic character. The resulting drama is imbued with that elusive quality known as poetic truth. Somehow, poetic truth has more intensity than factual truth; it illuminates the issues better and it produces a stronger cathartic effect. Consequently this type of imaginative drama is more likely than the documentary theater to help achieve the social changes Peter Weiss advocates. He is on the right track, and never mind the two chairs. (p. 399)

> *Franz P. Haberl, "Peter Weiss: A Progress Report," in* Books Abroad, *Vol. 46, No. 3, Summer, 1972, pp. 396-99.*

ANDREAS HUYSSEN

[In his *Die Ästhetik des Widerstands, Vol. 1*] Peter Weiss sends his hero-narrator, son of a German worker and member of the organized resistance in Nazi Berlin, to the Iberian peninsula. There he fights with the International Brigade and witnesses the defeat of the Popular Front in the Spanish Civil War....

[This] nostalgic and yet tormented look backward into one of the darkest periods of socialism is part of an autobiographical experiment. How would he have developed, had he, the narrator's contemporary, also grown up in a proletarian milieu rather than in a bourgeois family? Of course, most of Weiss's prose writing has been autobiographical. But *Die Ästhetik des Widerstands* should not be regarded merely as a return to an earlier stage of writing. It is the result of more than ten years of political development, and it attempts to construct a belated solidarity with those of the author's generation who, because of their class background, were already active in political struggles when young Peter Weiss was just an emigrant rather than a political refugee.

Thus this book is neither a novel nor a treatise on esthetics. Rather it is a huge quarry with layers of fiction, biography, historical and political analyses, esthetic thought and descriptions of art works. As Weiss indicated in an interview, the point of the book is the necessity of fighting fascism while simultaneously appropriating the cultural heritage of Western Europe from a proletarian point of view.

Against the historical background of the bolshevization of West European communism, the antifascist struggles of the 1930s and the Stalinist purges, Weiss tries to write a fictional intellectual autobiography symptomatic of a whole period. And it is precisely this intellectual tour de force, this mixture of fiction and reality, which makes the book a failure, though a very interesting one. Characters in the book remain intellectual abstractions, the plot is practically nonexistent, many of the historical analyses are schematic and shed no new light on events. The strength of the book lies in its many interpretive descriptions of art works, from the famous Pergamon altar to Picasso's *Guernica*. But while the book tries to integrate politics and esthetics, these often brilliant descriptions could very well do without the concrete historical background in which they are placed. This does not prove anything against Weiss's goal; it rather points to the difficulties inherent in his project.

> *Andreas Huyssen, in a review of "Die Ästhetik des Widerstands," in* Books Abroad, *Vol. 50, No. 4, Autumn, 1976, p. 869.*

WES BLOMSTER

[In Volume 1 of his *Die Ästhetik des Widerstands*] Weiss's narrator-hero involved himself in the Spanish Civil War; [in Volume 2] he now moves north. The Munich appeasement of 1938 is viewed from Paris, where true opposition to German fascism is all too meager; from there the setting changes to Stockholm, where a circle of real and fictive leaders collects around Brecht, who has just arrived at this station of his exile.

The idea is sound; its execution falls short of success. Brecht was indeed an enigma, but here he remains behind an almost surrealistic veil from which he never emerges as a vital person. The best-drawn and most humane figure is Ossietzky's daughter Rosalinde, who fails to come to terms with her father's death at Nazi hands.

At the outset, Géricault's "The Raft of Medusa" replaces the Berlin Pergamum Altar of the earlier volume as the object of esthetic contemplation. The fourteenth-century Swedish Engelbrecht Uprising is narrated in extreme detail as a parallel of modern history through the remainder of the book. (Weiss has Brecht stimulate interest in these events as the basis for a dramatic work in which he, in turn, loses interest.) An extensive account of leftist political development in Sweden results in unneeded filler.

Half [of *Die Ästhetik des Widerstands, Vol. 2*] is highly exciting; it is, above all, Weiss's perfection of a narrative idiom which in tenor corresponds uniquely to the subject matter at hand. By midpoint, however, the narrative impulse is lost and the reader finds himself indifferently adrift upon a sea of prose in which the absence of division into paragraphs bespeaks a loss of position and direction. The volume ends with Brecht's departure for Finland. A third—and shorter—volume is forecast as the conclusion to the work. (p. 282)

> *Wes Blomster, in a review of "Die Ästhetik des Widerstands, Vol. 2," in* World Literature Today, *Vol. 53, No. 2, Spring, 1979, pp. 281-82.*

WES BLOMSTER

Even among the finest products in the genre, there are few postwar German novels entitled to a position beside the profound accomplishments of Mann, Musil and Broch. The trilogy which Peter Weiss has concluded with this new book [*Die Ästhetik des Widerstands, Vol. 3*] might well be celebrated as the rebirth of the German intellectual novel.

Volume three of *Ästhetik des Widerstands* (Esthetics of Resistance) begins with the arrival of Weiss's parents in Sweden in May 1940 and concludes with the final weeks of war in 1945. In this closing installment of his portrayal of social democracy and communism in Europe between 1917 and 1945 Weiss departs from the approach taken in the first two volumes. . . . They were anchored in major works of art; the new book centers rather upon the narrator, who is here less an observer and more an active participant in the story told. The centrality of the young man's family gives this book a poignant strength which makes it a still greater accomplishment than the two which preceded it. The description of the slow demise of the mother belongs to Weiss's finest writing. In the earlier volumes the darkness of tyranny was always illuminated by hope; through the sad irony of history, this hope for a new and better world out of the ruins of the old crumbles as the fissures in the Popular Front—the wartime alliance of social democrats and communists—become visible. The clouds of cold war darken the horizon upon which true peace was never to dawn.

In contrast to the works of the earlier German novelists of the century, enthusiasm for Weiss's trilogy will depend to a large degree upon the sympathy in the reader for the author's commitment to the Left. For many the work will be nothing more than a political pamphlet. . . . Those who respond positively to Weiss's work might well ask whether monumental writing is possible in the present day without this precise definition of position. (p. 328)

> *Wes Blomster, in a review of "Die Ästhetik des Widerstands, Vol. 3," in* World Literature Today, *Vol. 56, No. 2, Spring, 1982, pp. 328-29.*

ANDREAS HUYSSEN

Ever since his first major international success with the *Marat/Sade* of 1964, Peter Weiss has persisted in trying to rescue the radical moment of the historical avantgarde for an age which by and large had comfortably regressed to a domesticated modernism and to an apolitical avantgardism of formal experiment. Plays like the *Marat/Sade* or *The Investigation,* the play about the Frankfurt Auschwitz trial, effectively challenged the complacencies of the institutionalized ideology of modernism of the 1950s and its dogmatic uncoupling of art from politics. In West Germany, the art/politics dichotomy served not only to obliterate the original radical impetus of modernism itself, but also to repress any memory of that cultural catastrophe that was German fascism. By focusing on Germany's contributions to international modernism one could quickly forget the disastrous miscarriage of the national culture. Peter Weiss's plays of the mid-1960s thus represented something like the return of the repressed. Of course, Weiss's voice was that of a permanently displaced exile writer, but the impact of his plays connected him inseparably with the rise of the student movement in West Germany and with the cultural politics of the 1960s which have left us with a remarkable body of works in the writings of Weiss, Enzensberger, Kluge, Kroetz, and Martin Walser among others; the films of, again, Kluge, Straub-Huillet, and Fassbinder; the visual experiments of the Gruppe Zero, the Vienna action and performance artists, Gerhard Richter, and Joseph Beuys.

Weiss's theater has often been described as an uneasy, but fascinating blend of Artaud and Brecht, of the theater of cruelty and the theater of the epic *Lehrstück,* a project that could be compared to that of the East German "successor" of Bertolt Brecht, Heiner Müller. Both authors realized that the classical avantgardism of Brecht had become precisely that: classical. And they tried to rework and revitalize it through a fusion with that other, more submerged, radical tradition of the historical avantgarde, i.e., surrealism. Of course, Brecht's hostility to surrealism is well known, and the very attempt by Weiss and Müller to somehow dissolve the boundary between the two major trends within the historical avantgarde places them in a clearly post-Brechtian *and* postsurrealist situation. In terms of Weiss's development as a writer, however, we should remember that contrary to Heiner Müller he did not start out with Brecht, but rather with surrealism. Weiss's and Müller's project to go beyond Brecht and beyond surrealism was of course never only an aesthetic choice. It was as much, if not more, determined by the historical experiences of fascism, Stalinism, and post-war capitalism which made the Brechtian and Artaudian solutions alone increasingly unsatisfactory. At the same time it was precisely the attempt to rewrite the parameters of avantgardism which makes their work representative for an age which has since then come to be called postmodern.

A few comments on Weiss's development as an artist may be in order. He actually began his artistic career in the 1930s in Swedish exile as a painter of magical realist canvases which were very much indebted to German expressionism and to the Neue Sachlichkeit of the later 1920s. It was only after the war that he switched entirely to writing, at first without any real public success at all. At the same time he underwent analysis and became increasingly fascinated with Jarry, Rimbaud, Buñuel, and the French surrealists. His first major prose texts to be published in West Germany—*Im Schatten des Körpers des Kutschers* (1960) and the two autobiographical texts *Abschied von den Eltern* (1961) and *Fluchtpunkt* (1962)—are unthinkable without the impact of surrealism, but again, they were not much of a success, probably because of their radical experimental subjectivity which baffled German readers used to Böll and Frisch. In the English-speaking world to this day, Peter Weiss is only known as the author of a few major plays who later lapsed into a merely propagandistic play-writing with his didactic dramatic ballads about the Vietnam war and Portuguese colonialism in Angola. The pretense of a revived avantgardist unity of aesthetics and politics seemed to have exhausted itself aesthetically and politically after Weiss's "conversion" to Marxism in 1965. Or so the mainstream critics thought.

But then Weiss wrote *Die Ästhetik des Widerstands.* . . . The novel is doubtlessly one of the major literary events of the 1970s. It can be read not only as the *summa artistica et politica* of the writer Peter Weiss, but also as a sustained narrative reflection, from the viewpoint of the 1970s, on the vicissitudes of avantgardism in relation to political vanguardism in the 20th century. It is this latter aspect, which, I would suggest, pulls Peter Weiss's *opus magnum* into the orbit of the postmodern. Even though he himself did not live to witness the increasingly heated polemics about postmodernism in Europe, it is possible to map the space his novel occupies in the current aesthetic debate. Thus *Die Ästhetik des Widerstands* acknowledges the per se problematic nature of the historical avantgarde's attempt to merge art and life, aesthetics and politics, but at the same time Weiss clearly privileges avantgardist writing strategies such as montage and collage, the documentation of dreams and the blurring of the rigid boundary between fact and fiction. In its writing strategies and overall composition the novel rejects the oeuvre-oriented presuppositions of classical modernism, its focus on individual consciousness and its categorical separation of art and life, literature and politics. Significantly, the novel was published in three large workbooks bound in gray paper, with relatively large print and broad margins for the reader to write on, all of it modeled after Brecht's famous *Versuche* of the Early 1930s. But what we have before us is a massive block of unchangeable text, not a script for a play which would be rewritten in the course of each and every production. Thus Weiss does hold on to a notion of the work of art, cleansed, however, of its pretense to autonomy, self-sufficiency, unity, and wholeness.

Somehow, then, Weiss's aesthetic position seems to be located somewhere on the fault lines between high modernism and the historical avantgarde, both of which have been called in question aesthetically and politically since the 1960s. He operates in a field of tension which has come to be called postmodern, and nowhere more so then where he turns against the modernist dogma of the death of the subject and the concomitant death of the author. Just imagine how the classics of the modernism debate of the 1930s might react to Weiss's novel. Neither Brecht, nor Adorno, not to speak of Lukács, would have an easy time reconciling *Die Ästhetik des Widerstands* with their conceptualizations of a modern aesthetic or, for that matter, with their differing notions of resistance. Where Brecht would probably see a sellout to surrealism, to irrationality and melancholy, and would miss a concept of a *eingreifende Kunst,* Adorno would presumably suspect yet another kind of forced reconciliation, this time between a still too orthodox Marxism and a regressive aesthetic mixture of documentary realism with a fetishistic surrender to the unconscious. This incompatibility of the novel with any of the prominent positions of those earlier theorists of modernity seems all the more surprising since the emphatic link between resistance and the aesthetic was a shared ground of all those writers, and in this sense Weiss does indeed carry on their project. How, then, is Weiss's writing different from that modern tradition as theorized earlier by Adorno or Brecht? And is that difference enough to pull his work into the orbit of the postmodernism problematic?

To come it may seem repugnant even to associate Weiss with post-modernism. Champions of the postmodern, of subtle ironies and of writerly pleasure, will not be able to swallow either Weiss's politics or his tortured and tormented view of human history. Opponents of postmodernism, especially on the left, will have a hard time digesting Weiss's writing strategies, his melancholy world view, and, in the case of "real existing socialists," his presentation of Stalinist horrors as well; but they will still want to salvage Weiss from the taint of the postmodern which they see as only aestheticist and apolitical. As the reception of the novel in the two Germanies shows, Weiss has written a book totally against the grain of the "Zeitgeist," against the grain especially—and this must be emphasized—of what Hal Foster has called an affirmative postmodernism. The question then becomes to what extent we may read Weiss's novel in light of what critics such as Foster have recently posited as a postmodernism of resistance.

But whether we include Peter Weiss's novel in the emerging body of postmodernist works or not is a question of secondary importance. It is more important to show how the novel participates in problematic that distinguishes contemporary culture from high modernism and the avantgarde, a problematic, in other words, that is rooted in the experiences and constellations of the 1960s and 1970s. And, secondly, how within the problematic of the postmodern in Germany Weiss's novel marks a position which cannot easily be recuperated by the culture apparatus, let alone turned into a literary fashion to keep the presses rolling. . . . Some feel that Weiss has written the classical (if not classicist) German novel of the post-1960s era. Others claim that *Die Ästhetik des Widerstands* is the only truly radical and avantgardist work of literature in a desiccated literary landscape from which the creative imagination has increasingly migrated toward the cinema. I would suggest that it is neither, or, put differently, that perhaps it is both.

What, then, is the story of this novel which, more than any other literary work of the 1970s in Germany, resists easy recuperation? The story is deceptively simple and can be told *as if* we were dealing with a conventional historical novel. Weiss develops a "collective fiction" of the tragic history of the working-class movement after World War I and of the antifascist resistance in the late 1930s and during Hitler's war. The novel's trajectory takes us from the illegal work of the socialist resistance in Berlin to the battlefields of the Spanish Civil War, the haunted, persistently threatened life of the German exiles in Paris and Sweden (Peter Weiss's own final space of exile) and back into the belly of the beast, Berlin, Plötzensee, the meat-hooks, the ropes, the serial executions of trapped resistance fighters after the failed plot on Hitler's life in July 1944.

But then the story can be told in another deceptively simple way, *as if* we were dealing with a conventional novel of development, a *Bildungsroman* even, though with an added political dimension. The first-person narrator, born in the year of the October revolution (one year after Peter Weiss himself), is a literarily ambitious, class-conscious young worker in search of his artistic and political identity. This "I," nameless throughout the narration which starts off in 1937, reports his experiences in the years from 1933 to 1945. Hitler's rise to power abruptly cut short his and his friend Coppi's education while their friend Heilmann continued to attend the Gymnasium. The motor of their friendship is a real need for literature and art as a means to become conscious of the world, "to escape that speechlessness" against which Weiss himself struggled all his life. Thus the first volume begins with a powerful description of the Pergamon altar frieze in Berlin's museum which the three friends experience aesthetically and emotionally, relating it to their social position and political consciousness. Ancient art and modern history are thus woven together in an act of cultural reception which provides the basis for Weiss's notion of an aesthetics of resistance. Kafka's *The Castle* and Dante's *Inferno*, Géricault's *Raft of the Medusa* and Picasso's *Guernica* are other art works actively appropriated at crucial junctions of the narrative web.

From his father, always a Social Democrat, the narrator hears the story of the German working-class movement after 1918, its internecine battles and deadly splits which later facilitated Hitler's rise to power. With the help of the Prague Committee on Spain, the narrator joins the Spanish Civil War where he works as a hospital attendant on the side of the defenders of the Republic. Here he meets the physician and psychoanalyst Max Hodann, who had been one of the leading figures of the sexual reform movement of the Weimar Republic and now becomes the narrator's mentor. While taking care of the wounded, he continues his studies of history and politics, art and literature, in the shadow of the Moscow Trials, Stalin's betrayal of the Spanish left, and the irresistible advance of Franco's armies. When the Republic goes down, the narrator is washed, on the raft of the Medusa, as it were, into Paris and later to Stockholm where he finds asylum and work among other exiles. In Sweden he meets Bertolt Brecht and plunges himself into a literary project. Simultaneously, he works as a messenger for the illegal and persecuted exile organization of German communists and their newspaper. In the third and last volume, the personal voice of the male narrator fades almost completely into the background and a variety of women's voices emerge, voices into which speechlessness, loss of self, insanity, and death are even more powerfully inscribed than in the primarily male voices of the earlier volumes: the fall into muteness of the narrator's mother after she witnesses the horrors of Nazi domination in Eastern Europe; the despair of Rosalinde Ossietzky, daughter of the Nobel peace prize winner killed in a Nazi concentration camp; the suicide of Karin Boye, the Swedish poet and writer; and, finally, the return of Lotte Bischoff, member of the Rote Kapelle resistance group, in 1944 into the smouldering ruins of Berlin, that ultimate monument to what the novel calls "die Raserei der Männer" (the rage of the men). Coppi, Heilmann, and the other friends are executed. Lotte Bischoff survives. But the final pages of the novel, written in the future subjunctive I which anticipates the post-war era, give little comfort. The aesthetics of resistance has not been able to prevent the death of the resistance, nor would it succeed in preventing the emergence of that other deadly confrontation of the nuclear age; and yet, the novel suggests, such an aesthetics will remain essential to any future attempts to resist forms of domination which Weiss and, in the novel, Hodann see as rooted not just in the contradiction of labor and capital which communism was meant to overcome, but even more fundamentally in the libidinal economy of the modern patriarchy which capitalism and communism have in common.

And then, finally, there is a third way of reading the story, again conditionally, as Peter Weiss's *Wunschautobiographie* (Would-be-autobiography), a term Weiss himself introduced into the debate and which was turned viciously and sarcastically against him by his critics. Here the narrator would become the fictional embodiment of a life on the left and in the antifascist resistance which Peter Weiss, the self-absorbed artist of bourgeois upbringing who came to socialism only in his late forties, would have desired for himself. Indeed there are those considerable parallels between narrator and author, almost the same year of birth, the same friends, the same encounters, similar experiences. But Weiss is far from simply identifying himself with his proletarian narrator or, for that matter, from simply rewriting the history of the bourgeois subject as that of an imaginary proletarian subject. Such *Tendenzwende* criticism, which jumps on Weiss's politics with intent to denounce, presupposes the literal meaning of *Wunschautobiographie* and thus reintroduces and insists on the categorical boundary between fact and fiction which the novel, like so many other modernist and postmodernist texts, works to erase. Given this political hostility to Weiss, one is almost not surprised to hear established literary critics complain that Weiss's characters are not believable, that the novel is remiss in its representation of feelings, that reflections smother action, that, in one word, the novel is too damned difficult. As so often, the political allergies Weiss has given the West German critical establishment make for lousy aesthetics, but in the critics, not in Weiss. Nevertheless it is precisely this suggested reading of the novel as a *Wunschautobiographie*, as an ambitious attempt to link the problematics of history and subjectivity without erasing the tensions between document, history, and fiction, which may serve to highlight the distance that separates Weiss from the ways in which modernists such as Kafka, Musil, and Thomas Mann treated the relationship between autobiography and fiction in their writing. Thus the narrator's search for identity, in its never-reconciled oscillation between extreme subjectivity and almost total self-effacement, is and is not Peter Weiss's own search for himself and reflects the author's difficulty of saying "I."

Three stories, then—one documenting the historical events shaping the work of the German resistance group Rote Kapelle of which Coppi, Heilmann, and Bischoff were members; the second, in close relation with the first, constructing the aesthetic and literary struggles of the fictional narrator; and the third inscribing Peter Weiss's real/fictional identity as a political artist into the novel.... So let us enter this maze of histories and fictions by focusing of a specific, to my mind crucial, layer of the narration: Weiss's reconstruction of the avantgarde problematic in the earlier 20th century which, like the narrative account of the work of the Rote Kapelle, is undertaken in the name of Mnemosyne, the goddess of memory and mother of the nine muses. The historical avantgarde serves to raise the issue of cultural resistance in the twofold sense which the novel suggests: the resistance to fascism constructs its own aesthetics, vital to its political functioning, *and* aesthetics itself, in the most general way, is inherently able to mobilize resistance to domination of whatever kind. As a historical novel, *Die Ästhetik des Widerstands* incorporates the debates of the 1930s on modernism and avantgardism with great force and discrimination. As a historical novel written in the 1970s, it offers much more than only a retrospective, academic account. In an age of growing cynicism and postmodern burnout, Weiss has given us a political aesthetic in the form of a novel which both rescues and sheds the historical avantgarde for the present. (pp. 115-22)

> Andreas Huyssen, "Memory, Myth, and the Dream of Reason: Peter Weiss's 'Die Ästhetik des Widerstands'," in his After the Great Divide: Modernism, Mass Culture, Postmodernism, *Indiana University Press, 1986, pp. 115-40.*

ROGER ELLIS

In looking back over Peter Weiss's career as a painter, filmmaker, novelist, essayist, and playwright, it is fascinating to note how consistently certain themes have been taken up and worked over again and again in his writings. (p. 119)

Weiss's examination of the relationship between writers and society in his work led him into three major avenues of thought: an exploration of the problem of absurdity, particularly in regard to the limitations experienced by ordinary individuals and by political writers and activists; a consideration of writers and of radical literature as a force for social change; and an assessment of the relationship between artistic independence and the political choices afforded writers in the modern world.

The most important of these themes derives from Weiss's firm belief in the writer as a sort of political prophet, as an artist who often perceives the proper direction for historical development but whose influence upon change is only indirect. Weiss stresses the importance of understanding the restrictive conditions under which politically inspired writers must function, and he dwells on the impact of leftist thought in understanding the present and in planning for the future. We find such themes not only in dramas like *Trotsky* and *Hölderlin* which investigate the problems and solutions which leftist intellectuals have cho-

sen in different historical periods; but also in Weiss's documentary plays and in his own stated objectives as a writer seeking to influence changes in his own society.

These three themes troubled Weiss from his earliest years as an artist; he continually explored new terminologies, new opportunities, and new challenges for testing himself and for refreshing his thoughts upon these issues. Late in 1971, in fact, he himself stressed the importance of this "evolutionary" quality to his total work. Shortly following the premiere of *Hölderlin* he wrote, "Just as history is a continuum, so too are all these plays part of an evolutionary process. Motives are taken up, then worked over and changed."

A study of his writings over the years reveals clear patterns of self-evaluation. For example, Weiss's political difficulties as an artist "caught between the two stools" of East and West was the question which inspired his first major play in 1963, *Marat/Sade,* and which underlay his political work in the decade which followed. At the end of his career we also find this same note of self-examination occupying his thoughts as he describes the role of the first-person narrator in his novel *Äesthetik des Widerstands:* "The central figure of this novel, the narrator, is perhaps an abstraction for many readers, but not for me, the author. For the author it is self-discipline. I narrate the story as myself in order to pose these problems as clearly as possible to myself by identifying with this narrator."

Weiss's trilogy of plays on the careers of revolutionary intellectuals—*Marat/Sade, Trotsky in Exile, Hölderlin*—are especially important because they are the most obvious reflection of his lifelong concern for politically inspired writing. In these dramas Weiss focused attention upon historical figures who struggled to bring about the same kinds of progressive social change that Weiss did. Thus in his plays he not only analyzed historical conditions which paralleled post-World War II political situations, but he also stressed the importance of literature in relation to social activism. Weiss always made it clear that he regarded his profession as an activity directed towards understanding himself and influencing society. His choice and his manner of presenting the dramatic heroes of his plays, therefore, reveals much about his feelings towards the value and the potential of politically inspired writing.

The attention Weiss devoted in these three plays to the literary work of important revolutionary figures is counterbalanced by his concern for the issue of political oppression and resistance in his other four plays, *The Investigation, Song of the Lusitanian Bogeyman, Vietnam Discourse,* and *Mockinpott.* The figure of Weiss's writer-hero has an opposite in the figure of the little man—the Angolan native without travel papers trying to visit his family, the credulous German Jew bewildered by the callous treatment he receives at the train depot, Mockinpott puzzled by his employer's indifference to his plight—although such portraits are never drawn as convincingly as are the heroes of his major plays. In all his documentary dramas, with the exception of *The Investigation,* Weiss optimistically celebrated the struggle for political freedom and the achievement of political consciousness through movements of the masses. Thus, while his search for identity as a leftist author is reflected in *Marat/Sade, Trotsky,* and *Hölderlin,* his search for direct political influence through his art is mainly reflected in his documentary plays on current events.

In creating the characters of the documentary plays, Weiss did not concern himself with the dividedness of human nature as he did in his dramas on leftist intellectuals. This is an important point of distinction between the mass heroes of the minor dramas and the writer-heroes in the other plays. The natives and peasants in **Bogeyman** and *Vietnam Discourse,* for example, must concern themselves with problems of an immediate, practical nature. They must form a rudimentary political consciousness in order to become aware of their oppressed condition and take action to improve it. Unlike the great historical personalities of Marat, Sade, and Trotsky, who must combat restrictive forces both outside of and within themselves, the mass heroes must single out and combat only the external forms of their oppression: colonial domination, exploitative economic relationships, military invasions, and foreign influence. They are not concerned with analyzing mistakes made in the past nor with the future development of socialist thought; they are forging new socialist programs in the immediate present. Although it must stand to Weiss's credit that he was astute enough to recognize and celebrate this quality of "history in the making" which he perceived in the underdeveloped nations, nonetheless the absence of critical analysis in the documentary plays helps to explain their commercial failure. Additionally, these dramas lack depth of characterization, a clear theoretical understanding of the issues, and a broad perspective on problems which are both geographically and culturally remote from Western spectators.

Weiss's major dramas, on the other hand, link more overtly with his understanding of himself. Not only do they celebrate historical figures who became socially committed in their literary work, they also helped Weiss to define a proper social role for himself. Each of the writer-heroes was a model for Peter Weiss's own situation, even though only Hölderlin and Sade were historically prominent as artists. Of course Weiss modified the ideas of these men and delimited their careers by stressing this literary aspect of their work in order to express his own beliefs on the subject of the writer *engagé.* But this is only to be expected and is part of what we customarily understand as poetic license. Weiss always sought something contemporary in his studies of the past: an understanding of the roots of social violence, of the extent of human influence upon historical development, of the restrictive conditions which bear upon modern artists and how to overcome them, and, most especially, an understanding of the roots of the seemingly paradoxical faith of certain individuals who struggle unsuccessfully to improve apparently hopeless situations. (pp. 119-21)

Peter Weiss's dramatic heroes are rebellious intellectuals committed to the struggles of their times. They are men of action and extreme if not ruthless in their political choices. Weiss presents them dynamically and rarely allows them moments of quiet reflection during which they can share their less urgent feelings with audiences. . . . The arguments in which Weiss's heroes are engaged are brutal and relentless. When they analyze their own motives one rarely hears from them overt sentimentality. They struggle against self-deception and despise those who are motivated by self-interest: the Parisian *sans-culottes,* the political powerseekers such as Hegel who place themselves at the service of financiers and politicians. Marat and Sade are vivid examples of such dynamic, rebellious heroes locked in a struggle for ultimate goals. They grapple with discovering the layers of implications in all their decisions.

The "most extreme actions" of which Sade speaks, though, are not limited to strictly political activities. All Weiss's heroes are political extremists, but they are more concerned with the worth of their ideas then they are with the efficacy of their acts. These men are rational political leaders even in periods

of crisis and tragic defeat. They crave upheavals and insurgent causes in order to test their theories. Hölderlin is consumed by the fervid goals of the French Jacobins, but in the absence of any clearly defined German revolutionary movement at the time, he must therefore work out his own theories by urging civil protests wherever and whenever he can. His struggle resembles Marat's in this regard because both men must hammer out theory in light of the political struggles in which they are engaged, and which they have largely provoked. At times, such as in Trotsky's case, Weiss shows the writer in a state of indecision over which of the two modes of action—theory or practice—is more appropriate. (pp. 121-22)

Despite their involvement in political movements, however, these are all men who work alone, often by choice. Trotsky distances himself from contact with the proletariat and refuses to participate in Party struggles. During his later years, even though Weiss shows him in a close relationship with his wife and a few friends, he is forced to flee from one temporary asylum to another, rootless and constantly watchful. Sade is alone, surrounded by madmen. Marat is alone in his bath forming his "ideas about the world / which no longer fit the world outside." And Hölderlin's pathetic sexual encounters and the falling away of his friends leave him with a profound sense of alienation in a world which refuses to understand or accept him. This solitary condition of the writer is reflected in his political status as an exile, pursued by enemies and forced to work conspiratorially. Even Marat "at the head of the movement" is psychologically exiled and paranoid.

Isolation and solitude do have worth. All of Weiss's heroes are men of international outlook precisely because of their experiences of life as exiles. The conditions of exile account for their independence and their courage. Bound to no country, they are permitted to observe events from an intellectual distance. Even Marat, the most "patriotic" and politically powerful of Weiss's heroes, finally defines the revolution's ultimate goal in existential rather than in ideological or nationalistic terms: "The important thing / is to pull yourself up by your own hair / to turn yourself inside out / And see the whole world with fresh eyes." Their international and humanistic outlook allows Weiss's heroes to rise above regional objectives in order to promote universal goals, and this is a strong point of appeal for audiences. Because of this they become men whose concerns are shared by many writers, whatever their political persuasion, who attempt to influence historical change.

The artistic and political independence of Weiss's dramatic heroes is important because it allowed Weiss to analyze their struggles and to understand the context of their achievements and failures in more than just political terms. Specific political programs were less important to Weiss than the impact of his heroes' actions on the development of humanitarian principles of government. For example, some of the obstacles which obstruct his heroes' efforts—the French clergy, Coulmier's censorship, Tsarist nobles, literary conservatives such as Goethe—are the product of socioeconomic class determinations. Other forces, though, which contribute to the writer's oppressed condition, stem from causes which are only partly political in nature: parental upbringing, personal biases, or intellectual limitations. Weiss always portrayed the common people as limited by narrow concerns, by violent and often self-destructive tendencies, and by ignorance. Such influences, which are not dealt with in the documentary plays on Angola and Vietnam, arose from Weiss's concern for humanity's existential dilemma and in many cases they posed more formidable obstacles to the hero's self-development and the realization of his goals than his political circumstances.

It is difficult to connect the rebellious and independent outlooks of Weiss's heroes to any specific political movement in the modern world. These men seem to be generally inspired by socialist principles; certainly they laid the groundwork for ideas which Weiss regarded as central to modern socialist thought: fair distribution of wealth and resources among all social classes, national self-determination without pressure from foreign entanglements, democratic broadening of the political base which would prevent special interest groups from exercising control. Thus Weiss seemed to identify them as socialist planners, but the term "radical intellectuals" is more appropriate for describing their political acumen. His heroes are supranational in their outlook as well as in their struggles against forms of socioeconomic oppression, particularly capitalist systems of government. Jacques Roux praises Marat for destroying the blindness of class outlooks; Trotsky assails the ruthlessness of strongmen like Stalin who manipulate political parties and control world superpowers; and Hölderlin disapproves of the industrial-political system of mutually supportive alliances which defies his attempts at social reform. (pp. 122-24)

The intellectual independence of these heroes stems from their solitary condition as rebellious exiles, and their common weakness of self-doubt also arises from the same source. These writers and intellectuals are continually threatened by the knowledge of their partial successes, their political failures, their ultimate inability to influence history in a controlled, predictable fashion. Marat is forced by Sade to witness the betrayal of his cause by Napoleon's dictatorship; Trotsky must watch helplessly as Stalin ruthlessly eliminates political opponents and bends the course of Marxism to his own will. The control of history is something which continually troubles and eludes the hero in Weiss's plays, just as it eludes leftist writers in today's world. Sometimes, as with Marat and Trotsky, a visionary leader may initiate action and temporarily direct events. At other times, as with Hölderlin, political power remains out of the hero's reach precisely because he criticizes society. In every case, though, these men are brought to a recognition of their failure, and they continue to work with that realization in mind.

This lack of political success is a curse upon all Weiss's heroes. It forms a strong bond between their historical situations and Weiss's personal objectives as a leftist writer. Peter Weiss, like his heroes, could not debase his political ideals by placing them at the service of any particular party or national program. It is noteworthy that Weiss never chose to celebrate the achievements of revolutionary leaders like Castro or Mao Tse Tung. For Mao or for Castro, the goal of their initial efforts was the consolidation of a particular nation-state. In Weiss's analysis, though, what made Trotsky greater and more appealing than such men is the fact that his concerns were more than patriotic; he sought universal permanent revolution through a combination of theory and practice. (p. 124)

Weiss also emphasized that despite political failures, his heroes' radical outlooks on social change deserve serious consideration today. Weiss presented all these men as individuals who relied on their imaginative grasp of universal socialist principles to guide them in their progressive approaches to historical change. And Weiss assigned his heroes a prophetic understanding of historical trends. Trotsky's inner certainty about the important role which the underdeveloped nations would play in the emergence of socialism, and Hölderlin's

recognition of the disastrous implications of a militaristic, industrialized Germany—these were ideas much too radical to be accepted by their societies. Such concepts reflected an historical understanding out of step with their times or far in advance of them. Weiss shows, however, that his heroes' views would have been more valuable for achieving socialist progress than pragmatic social or political planning. Had Trotsky's ideas been adopted by the Bolsheviks, the face of the contemporary Soviet Union would have been profoundly altered. One of the most important conclusions Weiss drew from this point is that avant-garde ideas on culture and politics must find free expression in any society which regards itself as progressive and revolutionary.

Despite their failures, all Weiss's heroes act within the political arena as though success were attainable. His plays celebrate heroes caught in the paradoxical situation of acting politically in order to dispel the fear of meaninglessness. The conclusion to the first act of *Marat/Sade* shows Marat struggling to continue his revolutionary work while trapped in a nightmare. He desperately calls for Simonne to bring his manuscripts, and it is only the need to write a patriotic speech for the fourteenth of July which breaks the spell that holds him trapped in dreams, fears, and hallucinations. The madmen mock his desire to write by plunging him into human feces, but Marat screams for his secretary and emerges from the nightmare to take up the pen again. This moment in performance is particularly dramatic. We see Weiss's Marat driven by an inner compulsion which he cannot deny, and which stems from his deepest fears of failure and pointlessness. Provoked by the vast indifference and confusion of experience surrounding him, Marat struggles angrily and heroically to "invent a meaning." (pp. 125-26)

In *Trotsky* Weiss restated this need for prophets—political or cultural—to invent meaning by introducing the scene between the dadaists and the Bolshevik leaders. Unlike *Marat/Sade,* however, the issue was not stated in terms of radicalism versus skepticism, but instead between political versus aesthetic contributions to revolutionary work. In *Trotsky* the avant-garde artists directly opposed the pragmatic and culturally repressive programs of Lenin and Trotsky. Both groups were inventing meaning for the twentieth century, one of them artistically and the other politically. In this scene Weiss voiced the necessity for an alliance between visionary understanding and reason, between the artist and the revolutionary, in remaking the world. A synthesis of the two approaches to revolutionary reform (which Weiss believed Trotsky dimly perceived) was finally set forth in *Hölderlin.* Karl Marx, Weiss maintained, *did* conceive of the possibility of two approaches towards historical change: "the analysis of concrete / historical situations" as well as "a visionary conception / of the deepest personal significance." The artist's concern for social reform is thus critical, both for his own development as well as for that of society.

Skepticism towards the efficacy of political action can either force the writer into a withdrawal from political affairs (as Sade retreated into an aesthetic experience of life), or else skepticism can spur the writer to develop a sound theoretical understanding of his social purpose and of the laws of historical change. In both cases the writer must work in isolation, exposed to the dangers of madness, paranoia, and despair. His solitary condition, however, places him in familiar contact with the irrational side of his nature, a fact which can produce valuable visionary insights into experience. (p. 126)

Peter Weiss, like his Hölderlin, wrote "visionary" dramas; he refused to celebrate any particular political system in his plays.

Instead he recommended ideal possibilities, ideal choices for socially concerned artists. Weiss could neither accept the world as he found it nor could he identify himself with nationalistic or ideological causes. He created through his plays a complex of ideas which reassured him in his role as an independent writer hoping to guide others. This, then, was the major function of Weiss's dramatic heroes: to provide socialist models whose values could stand in sharp contrast to the destructive political tendencies of our time, both East and West, and whose choices can contribute insight to problems shared by countless other artists and intellectuals. (pp. 126-27)

Weiss usually defined the writer's sociopolitical environment in terms of particular institutions such as law, medicine, religion, and, of course, government and business which are commonly presented as riddled with political bias and in desperate need of reform. In his criticism of social institutions Weiss often tried to explain the reasons why institutional reform is dependent upon changes in man's psychological and philosophical outlook. As Jacques Roux points out in the conclusion to the first act of *Marat/Sade,* revolutionary planners must seek to change fundamental outlooks in human experience if social reforms are to succeed. . . . Weiss's optimistic attitude towards the possibility of reforming social institutions was tempered by his awareness of the likelihood of failure, and especially by his conviction that only partial successes were immediately attainable. At times he attacked a political target in his plays directly, such as the Fascist mentality and the nationalistic fervor which inspired the death camps of Nazi Germany. At the same time, though, Weiss recognized that those targets were only a reflection in miniature of more complex problems. In *The Investigation* Weiss presented Fascism as only one manifestation of harmful nationalistic trends which were very much alive in the post-World War II period. This, of course, led to difficulties with his audiences. Though the villains seemed to be on trial, Weiss argued that their guilt was also to be shared by the judges, the victims, and ultimately by the audience. Considered in these terms, the war crimes trials could produce only superficial results, which almost amounted to a political coverup. Weiss implied that the judicial process might deal effectively with a few notorious criminals, but it was powerless to address itself to correcting the underlying frame of mind and the xenophobia which always produces totalitarianism.

Other plays also express doubts about the possibility of reforming social institutions. In extolling Marat as the precursor of modern socialist revolutionaries, Weiss also pointed out that the order which Marat created led directly to the disastrous emergence of Napoleon. In *Trotsky* we find the interesting suggestion of Weiss's own self-doubt as to the efficacy of literary work. Weiss may have called the play an attempt to celebrate the creation of the greatest social revolution of our century, but his choice of hero sharply contradicted this professed intention. Trotsky was the one man who had let the movement slip through his fingers when he could have led it. Instead of tracing the fulfillment of revolutionary principles in the play, Weiss demonstrated the betrayal of these same principles and the emergence of dictatorship.

Despite the fact, then, that these plays reveal the difficulty of constructing viable social institutions, Weiss did affirm the value of the writer who works to improve the social circumstances of his time. The writer's compulsion to work for progressive social change is an important—if tragic—feature in all his major dramas. Here we encounter Weiss's admiration for the heroic rebellion of certain men who refused to give in to nihilism, who continued to work and to create despite the all too obvious sense of absurdity which crowded their efforts. The intricate and imbecilic web of sociopolitical interrelationships of which Hölderlin gradually becomes aware stimulates the hero to create meaning through his literary work. In the garden scene the hero watches the alliances being formed between Hegelian philosophy, laissez-faire capitalism, and scientific experimentation. He realizes that his political position is untenable; but he continues to work in isolation in the second act, remaining "true to the end" in voicing socialist ideals through his visionary poetry.

It is noteworthy that despite Weiss's socialist outlook on contemporary political affairs, he cautioned writers against the dangers of committing themselves to any particular cause. In his plays he revealed how philosophical goals and ideals are invariably compromised by the writer's abandonment of his independent stance, by his identification with political parties. The betrayal of justice, of progressive educational systems, of a fair distribution of wealth, of free speech and a sharing of political power is certainly common to both capitalist and socialist societies. Despite the immediate vigor and challenge which political activism affords, there is no advantage to be gained from identifying oneself with a system. Weiss himself chose to live in Sweden, thus remaining neutral in his political allegiance. His heroes also avoid identification with political systems and parties, and even with political action in the form of "praxis." Sade confines himself in the asylum, Marat continually finds new factions to be attacked, Trotsky flees and works in isolation, and Hölderlin retires into social obscurity. Society in all Peter Weiss's plays seems eternally corrupt and in need, therefore, of constant reform. (pp. 129-31)

Weiss's attitude towards human nature is overwhelmingly negative, whether he expresses it in terms of the individual or especially in terms of national groups or "the masses." While his heroes might succeed to some extent in bearing with parental and familial oppression, or while they might achieve partial victories in overthrowing the tyranny caused by social institutions, these men never escape their feelings of failure, guilt, selfishness, or ignorance. Nor can they ever optimistically regard their fellow man as capable of shedding destructive psychological tendencies which betray social progress.

This grim view of human potential receives its tersest expression at the conclusion of *Marat/Sade.* Immediately before the murder is committed, Sade insists to Marat that political reforms can only follow upon the reformation of each individual within society. . . . Sade's prison of human nature recurs in all Weiss's writings: in the confinement of Pablo's tower, in the tunnel vision literary perspectives of the early novels, or in the universal guilt implied in *The Investigation.* Social change is always hampered by the unpredictability and inherent destructiveness of human nature, and all Weiss's heroes feel the need to shun society at some point in their careers in order to work in freedom. (p. 131)

The imperfectibility of man's social relationships is almost always demonstrated in grotesque terms. Weiss's plays are replete with descriptions or enactments of brutal violence. Sade's catalogue of the excesses provoked by the revolution overwhelms the arguments of Marat, and it is reinforced by the dismal existence in the asylum of Charenton. The kicking and beating of pregnant women in scenes from *Bogeyman,* and the interminable and gruesome descriptions in *The Investigation* indicate how frequently Weiss returned to dwell upon the theme of imperfectibility in all his plays.

The unpredictable behavior and inconsistent ideals of Weiss's characters are a strong indication of the violent tendencies which influence social reformers who lead them. Weiss's characters often vacillate between cruelty and kindness, loyalty and betrayal, and thus suggest that self-contradiction and ethical ambivalence are staples of human relationships. In *Hölderlin* Weiss established a strong contrast between the behavior of certain characters as idealistic young men and their actions as older, established public figures. Hölderlin's fellow student, Schmid, is a pacifist at the university, but years later he is killed while fighting patriotically in the Napoleonic campaign. Hegel is portrayed exchanging his youthful egalitarian principles for financial rewards later in life: German industrialists of the nineteenth century enjoyed his theory of the *Zeitgeist* as a justification for their rapacious colonial practices. In *Marat/Sade* the four singers vacillate between the expression of humanitarian sentiments and the encouragement of bloodthirsty acts. Violent tendencies can unpredictably burst forth from ordinary German citizens assigned to guard duty at Auschwitz, or from Sade's mild-mannered tailor. The humanitarian tendencies in individuals, no matter what their station in life, are shown to be just as unpredictable as their violent cravings. (pp. 131-32)

It may seem inappropriate for a dark view of human nature to run through the work of a "socialist" writer, but Weiss's use of dramatic tableaux, just as his use of ritual, also asserts the presence of violence and cruelty in the writer's milieu—as a condition against which the hero must always be watchful. This is a point often overlooked by critics who regard Weiss's plays as optimistic statements of socialist doctrine. On the contrary, his dramas often suggest that injustice and cruelty are the staples of life. He shows Marat stabbed while writing manifestoes, and Trotsky is revising manuscripts while the assassin's hatchet is poised. Weiss includes huge, often grisly documentary photographs for the background behind the *Discourse on Vietnam;* and he depicts Hölderlin trussed up in a crucifixion pose raving behind his leather mask. These are powerful statements which undercut any optimistic expectation of the writer's ability to prevail for very long over the destructive tendencies in his society.

Weiss is only slightly less pessimistic in his attitude towards the writer's own self-limitations. The most notable image of entrapment which Weiss employs in this regard is that of madness: the inner world of confused subjectivity and individual pathology encased by a sociopolitical madness. Weiss presents two of his heroes actually living in a madhouse, Sade and Hölderlin, and the ideas of Marat are sharply criticized by the fact that a lunatic plays the role. Though lunacy is not a key feature of Trotsky's situation, Weiss's dream vision production concept suggested that the hero was trapped within the prison of his own mind. In *Marat/Sade* madness is the means whereby Sade can illustrate the senselessness according to which historical events take place, while in *Hölderlin* the hero's insanity is not only historically based, but also stresses his condition as an exile. Weiss uses it in his play to demonstrate the rootlessness of the thoughts of the writer who is detached from social efficacy.

In Weiss's plays the condition of madness is always analogous to sociopolitical conditions. Sade, for example, enjoys having madmen enact revolutionary events because that situation accurately reflects his view of historical experience. Hölderlin seems more inspired than insane in his confinement because lunacy provides insight into the French betrayal of Jacobin ideals or the role of Buonarotti in the history of the socialist movement. Trotsky's prison of the imagination also becomes a positive feature of his condition because it continually provides him with hallucinatory visions and radical perspectives upon past events.

Through the image of madness in his plays Weiss often directs his discussion at subjects which lie beneath the surface of sociopolitical events. Though his heroes are invariably bound up with political causes, Weiss does not attempt to explain the worth of these men solely in terms of their political choices. With the possible exception of the lunatic playing Marat, Weiss's heroes are everywhere conscious that historical reality is a phenomenon quite different from the world of their imagination. In Weiss's prose novels he dwells upon the limitations of human consciousness in grasping phenomena in the outside world. In *Shadow of the Coachman's Body* the image of the flickering shadows thrown by the bodies of the cook and the coachman in violent copulation presage Weiss's view of human consciousness in all its confusing limitations. And as late as 1975 in the first volume of *Ästhetik des Widerstands,* Weiss is still preoccupied with the problem that one critic described as "the continuities and discontinuities of his experience of himself and the world about him."

This confusing inner world of the mind is a powerful force against which Weiss's heroes must struggle; the effectiveness of their political activities is often directly measured against their sense of doubt, failure, and partial knowledge. Thus at the conclusion of *Marat/Sade,* Weiss gives his martyr-hero revealing statements about the nature of political activism:

> Why is everything so confused now
> Everything I wrote or spoke
> was considered and true
> each argument was sound
> And now
> doubt.

Self-doubt is not the only limitation which Weiss's heroes suffer, although it is certainly the most unsettling. There are other weaknesses such as Marat's paranoid hatred of all who oppose his viewpoint, or the criminal tendencies in Sade's own personality which disgust Sade, or the self-degradation of the Jewish prisoners who unprotestingly accept their fate. Only in the Angolan and Vietnamese dramas (and in *Mockinpott*) where Weiss focused upon heroic popular struggles did he ignore the equation between private pathology and political freedom-fighting.

This situation of entrapment within parental, familial, societal, political, and psychological restrictions confirms the heroic stature of the writer because Weiss's dramas make clear how difficult it is to remain true to one's inner convictions within an oppressive society. The violent death of the hero and the betrayal of his goals are crucial features of Weiss's view of history, and this agonistic aspect of heroism is a recurring feature in the major plays. In the minor dramas, Weiss does not deal with entrapment in a personal sense; he is solely concerned with the external, political forms of oppression. In his trilogy of major plays, though, Weiss demonstrates that political activism is necessary and valuable for the writer's self-fulfillment, and therefore his heroes' values cannot be measured simply on the basis of their political successes or failures. (pp. 133-34)

If, then, Weiss's dramatic heroes reflect his own search for meaning as a writer *engagé*, we need also to ask what answers Weiss was able to uncover for himself and for others. Just what was the relationship Weiss was able to recommend between the writer's aesthetic and political choices?

In the documentary plays, and in **Mockinpott,** Weiss adopted a socialist stance in order to criticize the policies of Western nations and to sharpen his own leftist sympathies. In his major historical dramas Weiss dealt with the influence of socialist ideas upon three different political systems in the Western world. To describe Weiss as a socialist, though, is somewhat misleading because one cannot identify him with any specific party. As one interviewer observed in 1966, Weiss continually used the terms "socialism" and "communism" interchangeably. He insisted that his literary work "is for the salvation of all humankind, and indeed he termed the key to it 'Socialist humanism' or 'humanistic Socialism.'" It is probably most accurate to regard Weiss as a member of what Sartre calls "the Left in Western Europe," whose general task is "to answer the fundamental question of our time: how to unite all the exploited to overthrow the old ossified structures of our own society, how to produce new structures which will ensure that the next revolution does not give birth to *that sort of socialism.*"

Sartre's broad definition of the mission of the leftist intellectual offers helpful insight into Weiss's work. Sartre suggests two courses of action for the modern writer: criticism of the political status quo, and theoretical planning for the future. Weiss's analysis of the writer's existential condition is a reflection of Sartre's call for critical understanding; and all Weiss's portraits of writer-heroes stress the importance of Sartre's second demand for a sound understanding of Marxist thought in influencing social change.

Sartre's comment also suggests that the writer must exert influence on society in an indirect manner, primarily planning rather than directly molding political struggles. Weiss echoed this suggestion in his plays because political possibilities for effecting social change are not always available to his heroes. The political failure of these men, the universal guilt implied by *The Investigation,* the betrayal of revolutionary causes which forms the background of his trilogy—such things demonstrate the limitations of political freedom-fighting and stress the importance of the writer's own self-integrity and his indirect contribution to social reform. Because Weiss's heroes evaluate their programs in light of the *horizons* of socialist development, and because they speak for universal, broadly humanitarian goals, they provide what Sartre calls "the experience of being in a world which crushes us . . . and an appeal for freedom addressed to all other men."

The writer who is seriously concerned with the social impact of his work must first of all accept and learn to live with the paradoxical nature of his activity. According to Weiss, he occupies an uncomfortable position in the modern world. He exists as an island in an uncertain sea of political crosscurrents and historical backwaters, struggling to sustain his artistic integrity while responding to the need for assisting progressive social change. All of Weiss's heroes are men compelled to work under lonely, chaotic, and dangerous conditions while maintaining their faith in the importance of their work.

This paradoxical combination of skepticism and historical optimism which inspires the writer's work must be affirmed simply because it is suicidal to deny either side of the paradox.

Although his attempts to improve life may fail, the writer nevertheless must pursue his work not despite but because of his consciousness of human limitations. As one critic has remarked concerning this feature of the writer's situation as expressed in **Marat/Sade:** "No one wins! The aristocrat, the bourgeoisie, the proletariat, the romantic idealist, the social worker, the hedonist, or the socialist theoretician, the existential theoretician, or the anarchist . . . *all of them* live out the failure that is the human condition. Their ideas perish as certainly as they themselves." Such never-ending fratricidal combat between social reformers and political skeptics will be repeated in all historical periods and with many different protagonists. Weiss himself points this out: "It's usually the same conflict—the dualism of Utopia, wishes, dreams, poetry, humanism against outer reality, dogma, the status quo, power, compromise, repression."

In this situation the writer's primary task is to refine revolutionary theory in light of past examples, present problems, and future possibilities. Weiss's documentary plays suggest that the modern writer may occasionally adopt a journalistic stance by commenting upon or by celebrating freedom struggles. In this case, though, Weiss recommended that the writer be cautious about aligning himself with a political party since the results of such upheavals are not likely to duplicate the goals of the initial struggle. The modern writer, he suggested, must function as a focal point of information—historical and contemporary—and must synthesize that information in order to extrapolate the important issues for his public.

Weiss also suggested that the committed writer must learn to accept the fact that he stands in solidarity with many others, despite the remote or indirect influence he is exerting. Trotsky has no real hope of reversing the course of Stalinism, nor have Marat, Sade, or Hölderlin any expectations of immediately or profoundly influencing the course of history by their literary work. Each discovers that writing is only a partial substitute for political action and they all find this knowledge painful. But Weiss recommended that the writer take pleasure in celebrating others' achievements and in speaking on behalf of long-range goals. Trotsky, for example, writes of the future of the underdeveloped nations; Hölderlin expresses his faith in poetry as a vision of future possibilities, and he celebrates the work of early pioneers like Empedocles.

The writer-hero in Weiss's plays thus performs an ancillary function with regard to his society. He may inspire or criticize popular movements, he may add some leverage to them by publicizing their importance, or he may point up their implications for the benefit of other leftist freedom-fighters. Through all such activity the writer increases his self-understanding and reaches an awareness of his social role. Though he cannot directly influence change, he can discover how change must eventually come about, and often with the help of his efforts. This long-range focus to his work helps him distance himself from the dangers of political involvement. (pp. 135-37)

Despite the need for commitment to leftist causes which Weiss's plays demonstrate, he also stressed that the committed writer has an aesthetic responsibility to himself. He must be certain that his choice and treatment of subjects are not governed by topical or strictly propagandistic factors. These are usually hallmarks of the second-rate artist. Instead he must rely upon artistic intuition. His work must stem from serious personal engagement with the issues. The writer must sustain a delicate balance between personal and public concerns in his art.

Weiss's most successful plays, *Marat/Sade* and *Hölderlin,* are cases in point. Weiss's long fascination with the subjects of these dramas and his desire to make those subjects relevant to modern concerns accounted for the inspiration of those plays. As he remarked about the tragic features of Hölderlin's career: "Certainly this is pitiful . . . but the conflict is just as authentic today as yesterday. The author of the play himself struggled hard against such suffering. Naturally the choice of this theme indicates that the author has been puzzled by it . . . but I don't want it to be regarded as entirely personal."

The work of the committed writer, therefore, must be personal as well as political. The writer must ensure that his theme has contemporary applications. . . . At the same time, the writer must constantly challenge himself as he writes. He must experience self-growth in exploring his subject. "I value this play more as something from my former work," Weiss remarked about *Hölderlin,* "as the foundation for my own explorations, a rebellion; something to push away the contradictions and obstacles in my field of view." (pp. 137-38)

The writer's most significant contribution to the socialist cause is his ability to think prophetically, to perceive how political objectives might be realized in the future. Weiss's documentary plays as well as his three portraits of revolutionary writers are all written from a standpoint which places the material within a broad historical perspective. This is most apparent in Weiss's treatments of Trotsky and Hölderlin, which suggest the eventual vindication of the hero's (and author's) beliefs in a later historical period. Weiss accurately traced the reasons behind the political failure of these two men, but he also showed how both had perceived the germs of the future. Most importantly, Weiss showed both men acting in accordance with those futurizing ideals despite the contradictions which inhibited and ultimately destroyed them. Their words and deeds had been, in Artaud's phrase, "the hand signalling through the flames." Weiss presented them as such, "standing alone with revolutionary consciousness, awaiting a kind of restorative period." (pp. 138-39)

The "revolutionary consciousness" of Peter Weiss's heroes is something which is also shared by the audiences of his plays. We must regard the situations of Marat, Sade, Trotsky, and Hölderlin with the same hope that a restorative period will emerge, coupled with our realistic skepticism about the possibilities of our immediate present situation. The failures of Weiss's political martyrs do not discredit the value or the need for rational planning in the political arena. . . . Despite the frustration and the failure of Weiss's historical protagonists, we know that certain men have noticeably altered (if not advanced) human progress by a few degrees. New ages have been "ushered in," even if at first they did resemble the blood-spattered whores of whom Brecht's Galileo spoke.

In the final analysis it is this affirmation of meaning and value in Weiss's dramas, this expression of the Brechtian thesis that "the world is changeable," which makes his plays most dis-

tinctive. Weiss's qualified optimism separates his plays from the all-too-partisan statements of playwrights like Peter Hacks, from the overly negative criticism expressed in such plays as Arthur Kopit's *Indians* and in Peter Brook's famous production of *Marat/Sade*. It is this political impact of Weiss's plays which distinguishes them from the popular heroical excursions into history which we frequently see in films and in such plays as John Osborne's *Luther;* from the stylistic emphasis which often strives for mere theatrical surprise like Peter Shaffer's *Royal Hunt of the Sun;* and from recent avant-garde and absurdist works depicting historical subjects from highly personal, subjective, and fragmented standpoints, like Robert Wilson's *Life and Times of Joseph Stalin* or Wolfgang Hildesheimer's *Maria Stuart.*

The inspiration for Peter Weiss's dramas is best described by Erwin Piscator who commented upon the "atrocious anti-Schopenhauer optimism" which he found in the finest work of modern historical playwrights. Though Weiss's plays include modern absurdist perspectives in their treatments, the plays stress the importance of *searching for and inventing meaning* when undertaking political reform. As in Brecht's plays, truth may be concrete in Weiss's dramas, but it is also elusive, and it is the hero's struggle to uncover the truth which Weiss's plays celebrate. His plays demonstrate a consistent faith in the possibility of historical change through historical understanding. Such dramas, Piscator observed, "will be a force for change. . . . From objective recognition a passionate avowal of values can develop."

More then any other historical playwright, Weiss has been able to summarize in his work the major concerns of other writers who have dealt with the subject of historical change, and in *Hölderlin* Weiss offered a partial—if personal—solution to his problem of playing a meaningful role in society. At the close of his career, therefore, Peter Weiss seemed to remain personally satisfied with a dualistic attitude towards change: revolutionary art and limited revolutionary action. (pp. 139-40)

For Peter Weiss, writing was a form of action. It was, no matter how slow, a force for change and it could, in Artaud's words, "influence the aspect of formation in things." For Weiss, the playwright who recreated historical periods and who celebrated the future possibilities of socialist planning, the immediate present was a nightmare of oppression, a world in need of change. He had to exist within it when he could not dwell within the complex web of his own ideas and imagination. "I never count on anything that lies in the future," he remarked to an observer in 1966. "I have been disillusioned too often since boyhood in Berlin. But my point is that even if the world is a madhouse like Charenton and nobody wants to belong in it, this is still where we are and the least we can do is to take a stand for or against madness. I want my plays, my new kind of theater, to force the inmates to declare themselves." (p. 140)

Roger Ellis, in his Peter Weiss in Exile: A Critical Study of His Works, *UMI Research Press, 1987, 179 p.*

Calder (Baynard) Willingham (Jr.)

1922-

American novelist, short story writer, scriptwriter, dramatist, and essayist.

A controversial novelist whose early literary reputation as an enfant terrible derived from his explicit treatment of violence and sex, Willingham combines realistic narration and dialogue, exaggerated description, and dark humor to satirize various aspects of modern existence. Often parodying Southern Gothic fiction, Willingham focuses upon such topics as the processes of maturation, the nature of sex and love, and humanity's propensity for cruelty and perversion while portraying characters who are frustrated in their search for truth and meaning in their lives. Despite critical disputes concerning allegedly pornographic elements in his works and subsequent accusations of pandering to popular tastes, Willingham has elicited praise for authentic dialogue and a fluid narrative style.

Born in Atlanta, Georgia, the son of a hotel manager and his wife, Willingham was educated at the Citadel, a South Carolina military academy, and later at the University of Virginia. In 1943, he relocated to New York City and embarked upon a literary career. In his fiction, Willingham often draws upon his childhood and adolescent experiences. His first novel, *End as a Man* (1947), is a bluntly realistic portrayal of life in a Southern military institution that centers upon the sadistic initiation of its cadets. In this work, which was twice acquitted of obscenity charges, Willingham explores the relationship between fear and respect and its effects upon individuals. While the culminating events, involving the expulsion of several senior cadets as a result of their illicit activities, prompted some critics to note discrepancies between Willingham's satiric portrait of the armed forces and his ensuing avowal of military authority, others concurred with James T. Farrell, who hailed this novel as "a permanent contribution to American literature."

Willingham originally conceived his next two novels, *Geraldine Bradshaw* (1950) and *Reach to the Stars* (1951), as installments of a trilogy, but he later abandoned the effort. These books center upon the misadventures of Dick Davenport, a college-educated bellboy in pursuit of self-realization and excitement. *Geraldine Bradshaw*, set in Chicago during World War II, follows Davenport's two-day courtship of an elusive elevator operator whose pathological lies deflect his advances and thwart his attempts to understand her. Commenting upon this novel's abundant and detailed descriptions of decadence and sex, Kelsey Guilfoil stated: "[*Geraldine Bradshaw*] will have no serious competitors for the title of the filthiest book of the year." In *Reach to the Stars,* Davenport takes a position in an elegant California hotel in hopes of experiencing a world of glamor, wealth, and power. At the novel's end, disillusioned by the banality and vulnerability of many of the hotel's celebrated guests, the protagonist leaves Los Angeles for New York City. Episodic and virtually without plot, this work emphasizes the aimless nature of Davenport's quest.

Willingham's fourth novel, *Natural Child* (1952), is a cynical coming-of-age story about four young people living among the pseudointellectual fringe of New York City. Imbued with con-

Photograph by Alex Gotfryd; reprinted by permission of Vanguard Press, Inc.

tradictory impulses of youthful longing and despair, these characters attempt to achieve maturity and find fulfillment within the pretentious and depraved atmosphere of modern urban society. Another tale of adolescent development, *To Eat a Peach* (1955), depicts the final weeks at a Southern boys' summer retreat, with particular emphasis upon the sexual involvement of the camp newspaper's editor and its sole female counselor. In *Eternal Fire* (1963), Willingham creates a satiric epic saga of innocence and corruption revolving around the unscrupulous efforts of a sinister judge to prevent his ward from marrying a local schoolteacher and discovering how he has squandered the young man's inheritance. Melodramatically overwritten in prose intended to exaggerate the moral significance of each character's actions, this novel caricatures many stereotypes of Southern Gothic fiction while attesting to the legacy of racism in the United States. *Providence Island* (1969) depicts the erotic exploits of a middle-aged television executive, a lesbian novelist, and a sexually repressed married woman who are shipwrecked together on an uninhabited Caribbean island. *Rambling Rose* (1972) is set in the deep South during the Great Depression and focuses upon the disruption caused when a farming family hires a beautiful, sexually uninhibited young woman as a live-in servant. In *The Big Nickel* (1975), Willingham continues the story of Dick Davenport, the protagonist of *Geraldine Bradshaw* and *Reach to the Stars,* concentrating on his adventures as a novelist in New York.

In addition to his novels, Willingham has published *The Gates of Hell* (1951), a collection of experimental short stories, single-page sketches, essays, and fragments that is considered to have influenced the direction of much subsequent short fiction. An accomplished adapter of novels for film, Willingham's most notable screenplays include *The Strange One* (1957), which he reworked from his 1953 dramatization of *End as a Man*, *Paths of Glory* (1957), *One-Eyed Jacks* (1961), *The Graduate* (1967), and *Little Big Man* (1970).

(See also *CLC*, Vol. 5; *Contemporary Authors*, Vols. 5-8, rev. ed.; *Contemporary Authors New Revision Series*, Vol. 3; and *Dictionary of Literary Biography*, Vols. 2, 44.)

STEPHEN STEPANCHEV

In his first novel, *End as a Man*, Calder Willingham draws a nightmarish picture of life in a Southern military academy. His cadets are as foul-mouthed, sadistic and vicious a lot of adolescents as one is likely to find anywhere. In the name of class discipline they subject one another to sickening tortures. They gamble, cheat and lie without scruple. They connive to get their less aggressive classmates into trouble with the authorities. A number of them even band into an organization called the Hair-of-the-Hound Club, which operates a secret hangout in town. There they drink and take part in other forbidden extra-curricular pastimes. The principal event of the book is the destruction of this club and the expulsion of its members from the academy. . . .

The only admirable character is General A. L. Draughton, commandant of the academy, who finally gets rid of some of the more viperish of his charges.

Mr. Willingham's point is that man carries evil forces inside him whose aim is chaos and that only rigorous discipline can save him from these forces and give him full title to humanity. This thesis contrasts markedly with the widely prevalent notion that release from inhibition and absence of constraint are needed for the healthy development of the individual. The point is defensible, of course, but unfortunately Mr. Willingham fails to integrate it with his story. For three quarters of the novel academic discipline and authority are caricatured and satirized, and the reader naturally expects a resolution in other than military terms. Then suddenly, General Draughton emerges as a sort of deus ex machine who resolves all the author's moral problems by throwing his worst characters out of school. In accepting the general's help Mr. Willingham inevitably takes over his philosophy, and the novel ends by avowing a principle that is not intrinsic to its material. Mr. Willingham finds himself in the awkward position of advocating more of the discipline that he has shown failing to contain man's evil impulses.

The story is told in a straightforward, naturalistic style that omits no detail as to the physiological functioning of the principal characters, many of whom have queasy stomachs and vomit at crucial points throughout the narrative. The dialogue is good when ordinary cadets talk, but insufferably stilted when a person of above-average intelligence makes his appearance on the scene. The best, the most interesting portion of the novel, is a fantastic, feverish chapter at the climax which describes Marquales' visit to the home of a sick [fellow] cadet.

Here one can recognize a vigor and originality that speak well for Mr. Willingham's future as a writer.

Stephen Stepanchev, "In a Military Academy," in New York Herald Tribune Weekly Book Review, February 16, 1947, p. 14.

JAMES T. FARRELL

[*End As a Man*] is the work of an artist, written with power, honesty and courage; it carries its own conviction on every page. Its complete realism may shock the tender-minded; yet few of those who read *End As a Man* are ever likely to forget it. The book is all the more remarkable because it was written by a man of 23. I consider it a permanent contribution to American literature.

End As a Man deals with the life of a group of youths in a Southern military academy. Most of these boys come from the Southern upper class. Their social and scholastic life constitutes, on a small scale, a merciless if petty personal war of each against all. They are without loyalties. Toward those who are their classmates and comrades, they are sadistic. In their pleasures they cheat at cards. The upper-classmen haze and impose discipline on the freshmen for personal emotional ends, for the purpose of enjoying cruel fun, and with a pitilessness that is terrifying to read about. This sadism is bound up with their sectional and class antecedents; and, in some instances, it is also related to homosexuality.

The theme of this book can be described as follows: *End As a Man* states and reveals features of the way in which the disposition of youth is forged in our time. The protagonist of the story becomes the Academy itself. It is conducted in terms of a rigid conception of military discipline. Old General Draughton, who is in charge of this Academy, is seriously convinced that he is making a contribution to the national life. He wants his boys to be gentlemen, to be officers without "the psychology of the enlisted man," and to be leaders in the war that is soon to come. But the conduct of the boys is incompatible with the aims of the general. The Academy really encourages their sadism, and an inevitable scandal breaks out.

The General is shocked to discover what has been going on right under his nose: even some of his best upper-classmen have been involved. He investigates and expels a number of boys. Then he faces the assembled student body, and speaks of the ideals of the Academy. "I will not hesitate to say that I do not know of any other institution in America that can give a more solid basis upon which to construct your life. . . . No youth can pass through four years of the Academy and not end as a man."

Calder Willingham, a native of Georgia, has an unusually sharp and sure ear for speech. Written almost entirely in dialogue, the novel has no interior monologues, no auctorial intrusions. The characters reveal themselves in speech and action. The author shifts his focus from one character to another, so that each in turn becomes the central figure in a scene or an episode. In this way he sharply delineates these characters so that they all exist in their own right and in a setting of the most painful reality. The boys are so real that they almost pop out of the pages: the reader is carried forward with a rush. And bound up in the small world of the Academy, we can discover implications, which cut down toward the very heart of the national life of present-day America.

James T. Farrell, "Sadists in Uniform," in The New York Times Book Review, *February 16, 1947, p. 3.*

J. M. LALLEY

Mr. Calder Willingham's first novel, **End as a Man,** is a remarkable work in almost every respect except style and narrative ingenuity. As the title and first few pages make clear, Mr. Willingham's intention is satire; that is, satire in its earlier sense—a literary exposure of vice by one whose observation of it has sated him to the point of angry revulsion. The author's story has to do with the customs and moral climate of a Spartan military school somewhere in the Deep South, and with their effect upon the psychology of the inmates. The effect is, to put it moderately, horrible. If there is a single variety of evil unknown to the young gentlemen of Mr. Willingham's military school, it is certainly unknown to me; indeed, there are some sins in Mr. Willingham's book that seem altogether implausible.

In his effort to present the conduct and conversation of his cadets with complete fidelity, Mr. Willingham spares his readers no obscene imagery or scatological detail. Quantitatively, this book must set a record, even for contemporary literature, in its employment of short and startling English words. I have no doubt, however, of Mr. Willingham's moral purpose or of his passionate and even fanatical sincerity; from one point of view, I suppose, it could be said that his vocabulary was prescribed by the necessity of reproducing that incessant and monotonous stream of blasphemy and obscenity which seems to be only one of many unfortunate concomitants of the chivalric life. But I am of the persuasion which holds that a perfected narrative art could produce the effect while avoiding the affront. (p. 96)

The real objects of Mr. Willingham's satire, I take it, are the fallacious premises of military discipline, and especially the notion that boys are made brave, truthful, loyal, and generous through moral intimidation and physical fear. What the regimen of systematic bullying and meticulous and unremitting supervision at The Academy really produces are—if we can trust Mr. Willingham—sadists, liars, lechers, cheats, toadies, blackmailers, and sodomists. Thus, intentionally or not, this novel, like most novels nowadays, has political implications; it seems to offer a warning of what we may expect in a militarized society, ruled by the alumni of The Academy and others like them. Fear is the leitmotiv in the lives of these spruce and smart cadets, in their tall hats and glistening visors, their pipe-clayed cross-belts, their furbished buttons and spotless gloves; they respect only what makes them afraid, find pleasure only in what fears they can inspire.

Perhaps it would be fairer to say that, in making them what they are, The Academy merely completes a job begun by nature or by the rural Southern ethos. Most of Mr. Willingham's recruits were apparently nasty young cads before they ever put on a uniform, and some of them seem to have spent an earlier incarnation in one of Mr. Erskine Caldwell's novels. One, however, a young neurotic of Midwestern origins called Sowbelly Simmons, has a morbid religiosity and wants to become a chaplain. He cries and is sick at his stomach when he is tormented, which is, naturally, quite often—and he is also subjected to some rather monstrous indignities. But despite all this, the half-mad Simmons is the least corruptible of the lot. The story is concerned principally with the experiences of another recruit, Robert Marquales. Marquales, it would seem, is

better equipped for life in a military academy, for he has a glib tongue and a sharp instinct for the main chance. He comes under the patronage and influence of an intelligent, ruthless, and completely depraved upperclassman, Sergeant Jocko de Paris. After no great internal struggle, Marquales allows himself to be drawn into some clandestine social activities forbidden by regulations, including a poker game that he knows to be dishonest and by which he is willing to profit. When the scandal is discovered, as the consequence of a drunken brawl, Marquales readily turns informer and saves himself from dishonorable expulsion by betraying his patron.

Mr. Willingham's narrative method, in the prevalently fashionable manner, relies wherever possible upon dialogue. There are pages upon pages of it in the idiom I have already described, much of it unnecessary, some of it preposterous—as in a macabre scene involving two overt and two latent homosexual cadets, an elderly nymphomaniac, an imbecile Negress, a madman, and a doctor. When it is necessary to describe action, Mr. Willingham's prose has something of the sharp, metallic rigidity of his cadets, who are forever sucking in their guts, hauling back their chins, and cutting their corners square. Yet with all its technical crudities and philosophic immaturity, this is a novel capable of evoking, even in a seasoned reader, something like cathartic terror. This is partly because of Mr. Willingham's success in calling his characters to life, but mainly, I think, it is the strange, satanic atmosphere with which he manages to invest his book. "Power," said Burckhardt, "is of its nature evil," and **End as a Man** is testimony in support. Almost all the people in Mr. Willingham's story are idolaters of power—even the commandant, General Draughton, with his narrow nobility, exalted priggishness, and willful blindness to the moral consequences of his system. **End as a Man,** then, is the earnest [work] of an unusual but as yet wholly undisciplined talent. It will be interesting to see what Mr. Willingham will do when he is in less of a rage. (pp. 96-7)

J. M. Lalley, "Single Men in Barracks," in The New Yorker, *Vol. XXIII, No. 3, March 8, 1947, pp. 96-7.*

JOHN FARRELLY

[**End as a Man**] is a caustic study of the American scene as represented by a Southern military academy. The effect is largely achieved by an exact transcription of the cadets' talk, which reads with the imbecile monotony of the scrawl on lavatory walls. It is ironically inevitable that the strict military organization and the decayed society of the "Old South" should combine to promote and shelter an extensive corruption based on idleness, hypocrisy and a fake chivalric privilege. It is also inevitable that these make-believe adult worlds should produce a viciousness which is peculiar to children and morons: sadism and perfervid sexuality. Willingham makes his point, but the shock effect is weakened by repetition and verbosity. The book could have been incalculably improved, like so many current novels, by the simplest editorial deletion.

John Farrelly, in a review of "End as a Man," in The New Republic, *Vol. 116, No. 12, March 24, 1947, p. 35.*

JOHN WOODBURN

[**End as a Man**] is a fearful book, a hard and angry book, filled with a contempt that is close to loathing; but the contempt is made valid and mature because it is balanced with understanding and pity, and the restless, ranging imagination, creative and often brilliant, is laid like a *montage* upon the flat surface of the setting. *End as a Man* is not anything like *The Heart Is a Lonely Hunter*, but I was somehow reminded of it, and although Willingham and Carson McCullers are not trying to say the same thing, sometimes they achieve similar effects.

The novel opens deceptively in the year 1940, with the arrival at the Academy, a military man-factory in the South, of Maurice Simmons, a bumbling, eccentric clod, a sort of Good Soldier Schweik, who almost immediately becomes the cringing victim of the compulsive cruelty of his fellow cadets. But it is Marquales, briefly Simmons's roommate, who, with what may be a tinge of autobiography, becomes both the protagonist of the novel and the window through which the reader observes the Academy. During one year, which is the book's course, Marquales at one time or another reflects in his reaction and behavior the much that is bad and the little, the very, very little that is good in the school. If there is anything of manhood in mere survival, of retaining stubbornly some particles of one's personality, of resisting the thick stain of viciousness and cynicism and fear, then Marquales has made progress toward ending as a man.

Mr. Willingham has obtained many of his best effects by writing of evil in a brusque, matter-of-fact style, rejecting richness, handling scenes which might easily have been weakened by overwriting in a peremptory, parade-ground tempo, and in this way strongly highlighting by starvation the viciousness and hypocrisy which were the real, but tacit curriculum of the Academy. Some of the writing is harsh and brutal, as it should be in writing of a way of life that was harsh and brutal; but this kind of writing many writers can do and have done, and as well as Willingham has done it. What he has done in this searing book, however, and done extremely well and in his own way, is to create characters, completely, brilliantly realized, such as the faun-like Jocko de Paris, the lost, over-intellectualized homosexual Perrin McKee, the ineffable Colton, and the mindless, muscular Gatt. And, most of all, the composite, *multus in unum* character, the Academy.

Calder Willingham is a good and sharply arresting writer, and any young man who can conceive, execute, and sustain such a scene as Marquales's visit to the home of Perrin McKee, to say nothing of the rest of this vivid, brilliant, exasperated book, is someone to watch steadily.

John Woodburn, "Military Man-Factory," in The Saturday Review of Literature, *Vol. XXX, No. 14, April 5, 1947, p. 18.*

ORVILLE PRESCOTT

One of the most shocking, unpleasant, and offensive books in a long time, [*End as a Man*] is still so powerful and obviously sincere that it merits respectful praise rather than the mealy-mouthed abuse it has received in some quarters. Told largely in expert colloquial dialogue, it recounts the experiences of a young cadet among the sadistic, lecherous, perverted upper classmen who ruled the roost at "The Academy." The militarism of the institution fostered and encouraged cruelty and corruption, instead of exerting a healthy influence, charges young Mr. Willingham. Whether he is right or wrong outsiders cannot judge, but that . . . he is a gifted pupil in the naturalist literary school is plain.

Orville Prescott, in a review of "End as a Man," in The Yale Review, *Vol. XXXVI, No. 4, Summer, 1947, p. 766.*

JOHN BARKHAM

Basically, Calder Willingham's second novel [*Geraldine Bradshaw*] is no more than an account of a man's two-day pursuit of a woman. But it is told in such emotional and anatomical detail that it will probably create as great a critical stir as did its exposé predecessor, *End as a Man.*

The author's Chicago hotel is a typical skyscraper operation—frequented by transients, buffeted by conventions. It takes almost a third of the novel to bare its concrete and foam-rubber soul. By that time the reader not only knows what makes it tick, but also how much (or how little) the guest counts for. Fascinating as this milieu is, the author uses it merely to make his bellboy meet girl, whereupon he promptly drops the hotel for the sleazier sections of Chicago, where the prolonged seduction is attempted. The bedroom battle takes up the rest of this oversized book.

That this novelist has real power and talent cannot be denied. At his best he writes with a force, pace and aloofness reminiscent of Dos Passos. It is this drive, plus a passion for significant minutiae, that holds the reader's attention through pages of interminable wise-cracking and what Bernard Shaw would call suspense of the lower centers. Indeed, Mr. Willingham's eloquence on the subject of venery approaches that of Edmund Wilson.

None of the characters in the story is in the least likable, yet even the most subsidiary of them is pinpointed with clarity and economy. The girl herself is a mass of Freudian complexes, whose sex-life is a web of mendacity. Scalpel in hand, the author dissects her without mercy, and in detail. Then, when he has raced on for some 400 pages, Mr. Willingham abruptly brings his clinical history to a simultaneous dénouement and conclusion. In three perfunctory paragraphs he rounds off his story as though he had tired of it.

In its way the book is a dazzling performance. This reviewer prefers to regard it as a technical study, remarkable enough to establish Mr. Willingham among the foremost of our realistic novelists. Having spectacularly flexed his muscles, let him now use them on a theme worthy of his talent.

John Barkham, "Bellboy Meets Girl," in The New York Times Book Review, *February 26, 1950, p. 4.*

TIME

The naturalistic or sweaty-shirt school of novelists is hard up for scholars these days. But old Professor James T. Farrell (*Studs Lonigan, The Road Between*) has one young fellow in his composition class who, Farrell thinks, is making "a permanent contribution to American literature" [see excerpt above]. Calder Willingham is his name.

Willingham's first novel, *End as a Man,* published in 1947 when he was only 24, was a keyhole report on life in a Southern military college; righteously indignant in one breath and droolingly prurient the next, it read like the notes of a small-town peeper on the broom closet of hell. Some critics went part way with Farrell's estimate of Willingham, but others rebuked the book as a discharge of childish hostility by a very young man. But when the book was twice taken to court for obscenity (and twice acquitted), readers caught the scent. *End as a Man* sold some 35,000 copies.

Author Willingham went on to have an adolescent's daydream. *Geraldine Bradshaw,* his second novel, is a 415-page, grab-by-grab description of how a smart bellhop tries to seduce a dumb-Dora elevator girl. It takes time: boy gets girl in bed on page 141; but girl is still standing off boy on page 414. The Willingham method is, of course, one way to keep a reader's attention. Nonetheless, the author sometimes seems hard put to fill space. . . . (pp. 106-07)

When the inspiration for . . . dialogue fails, Willingham fills in with obscenity. By page 318, even the hero is overcome: "The verbal diarrhea. It's getting me down. I'm sinking."

Under that kind of verbal assault, so is the naturalistic novel. Fifteen years ago, with such figures as Theodore Dreiser, John Dos Passos and the early Farrell in the crew, young novelists rushed to sign on the happy ship. But in the hands of those who seem to think of life as just another four-letter word, it becomes a drifting derelict. (p. 107)

"Adolescent's Daydream," in Time, *New York, Vol. LV, No. 11, March 13, 1950, pp. 106-07.*

THE NEW YORKER

It's hard to say what the author is up to in [*Geraldine Bradshaw,* a] long and unremittingly sordid novel. He begins by telling us something of the workings of a big Chicago hotel in wartime, but his interest in Chicago, the hotel, and the war is soon replaced by what must be the most tedious pursuit of love in modern letters—if you want to call it a pursuit and if you want to call it love. Richard Davenport, a young bellhop in the hotel, has it in mind to seduce an elevator operator named Geraldine Bradshaw. The contestants are about evenly matched, for Geraldine is a pathological liar and Richard is a university graduate with a numbing familiarity with Freud and other undergraduate literary favorites. Maybe this novel marks the latest stage in the long-drawn-out bankruptcy of naturalism, or maybe it's a book that the author thought was going to be funny, and isn't. Mr. Willingham, who wrote *End as a Man,* was born only a few years ago, and knows and uses lots of naughty words. (pp. 105-06)

A review of "Geraldine Bradshaw," in The New Yorker, *Vol. XXVI, No. 4, March 18, 1950, pp. 105-06.*

NELSON ALGREN

The Chicago elevator girl with the scar on her chin [in *Geraldine Bradshaw*] didn't care to have dinner her first day on the job with the big-hotel bellhop named Dick Davenport. Yet she did. When he urged her to come to his room she grew indignant. Yet she went. When he elbowed her toward the bed she really thought she meant it when she said, "NO." Yet she got there all the same.

Though when she pleaded virginity he spared her. Only to have her confess, in tears, that she had lied to him: some dirty old hobo had raped her when she was thirteen. Yet that, too, turned out to be a lie; it had really been her brother-in-law during her sister's pregnancy and now she was tied down to a terrible lush-o named Ralph. The bellhop, in such a sweat he doesn't know whether to lie down or change his shirt, naturally despairs of everything.

Unhappily, this chronicle of a woman who can't make up her mind because she doesn't know what she wants, isn't certain who she is, and doesn't mean a thing she says, is reported so humorlessly that by the time half the novel is exhausted in the effort to resolve Geraldine's status the reader has ceased to care. The whole business is so padded with contrived dialogue that the most avid seeker of the four-letter word is likely either to turn back to Henry Miller or, even better, to give up and go on the nod. (pp. 29-30)

Nelson Algren, in a review of "Geraldine Bradshaw," in The Saturday Review of Literature, *Vol. XXXIII, No. 11, March 18, 1950, pp. 29-30.*

KELSEY GUILFOIL

[*Geraldine Bradshaw*] is realism gone mad; realism carried to such a pitch that it conveys a sense of unreality, of life in a strange world where everything is seen with clarity and precision, where every scene is familiar yet unrecognizable, and all is like a madman's dream.

It contains two of the most improbable characters yet to haunt the pages of fiction. One has the name of Beau St. John and the other Dick Davenport, and we are given to understand that they are young men of good Southern families with at least a partial college education.

But tho these two oddities are reported with exceptional detail of speech and action, they remain incredible. Dodging the draft in war time, they have drifted to Chicago, where they find employment, Dick as a bellboy in a big hotel, and Beau as a copy boy on the *Chicago Post.* And what a copy boy! In my newspaper experience, I have never known a copy boy like him, able to spend apparently unlimited cash on drink, taxi rides, and women. Especially women, for these two maggot-like creatures exist, it seems, solely for the pleasures of the chase, or rather the ultimate object of the chase.

Geraldine Bradshaw, who happens to be the unfortunate object of Dick's desire, is a pathological liar who resists, yet in resisting wants to yield, and offers one lie after another as a reason for resisting. The reader comes to know her as tho he had seen her, clad and unclad, lovely and disgusting, appealing and repulsive.

As for the two boys who participate in a two-day inferno of sexual pursuit and drinking, in which Geraldine escapes Dick and is hunted down with the help of the elegantly named Beau, they appear as a pair of sex maniacs, spouting endless streams of obscenities from the depths of their curdled minds. Surely this novel will have no serious competitors for the title of the filthiest book of the year.

One could let it go at that if it were not for the magnitude of Calder Willingham's talent. Few writers have such a sure eye for things seen, such a sure ear for things heard, and such a marvelous insight into the tortured inner workings of the mind. Yet his realistic technique defeats itself by its sheer hardness, and its lack of humor and compassion, to say nothing of being considerably overburdened with details of speech and action which, in their repetitive nastiness, are nauseating and repelling.

Kelsey Guilfoil, "Good Writer Takes Couple of Days Off," in Chicago Sunday Tribune Magazine of Books, *March 19, 1950, p. 5.*

GENE BARO

For the most part, the twenty-five stories in *The Gates of Hell* are unconventional in technique or in subject matter, sometimes both. It may be objected that many of these pieces are not stories at all: some run only a page or two; some are essentially without plot or characters or development. There are humorous sketches, satires, fables, mere incidents of life or character, dreams and fantasies, as well as forceful, realistic narratives. Even such categories are insufficient to explain adequately the nature of these pieces. Calder Willingham has employed a variety and mixture of literary forms and devices, indeed, a profusion of them to hold his thought; his success with them has likewise been varied and mixed.

Perhaps Mr. Willingham has grown dissatisfied with the realistic method of his novels. The present volume gives somewhat the feeling of being a writer's notebook, a series of drafts and experiments looking forward to larger and more serious work. There is a curious quality of incompleteness and even of obviousness in many of these stories, as if they were jottings for the author's records alone.

Even some of the realistic stories suffer from an atmosphere of casualness. For example, **"A Drop of Pure Liquid,"** which takes a little over a page of print, is concerned with an attempted seduction; there are two or three bare introductory sentences and a conversation, mildly uninteresting, rendered apparently with little more art than a stenographic transcript. **"Secret Journal"** and **"The Record of a Man"** deal with a lunatic writer, a "crank," and with his attempts to sell the work or the style of another crank to *The Saturday Evening Post*. There is no exposure of motivation, not much development either in the crank or in his situation. All the more interesting factors of his predicament, its motive force, integral meaning, consequences, are withheld.

Similar objections may be made, in whole or in part, to other stories. However, despite their idiosyncrasies, many of these pieces come through with real and urgent power. **"The Eternal Rectangle"** reveals a thoroughly despicable woman. **"Rupee"** yields the social structure of a Southern town and the character of some of its people with fine economy. **"Afternoon Sun"** and **"Excitement in Ergo"** are excellent treatments of accident and violence. Some of the more purely imaginative stories, such as **"Jane, Steve and Sarah"** and **"Cyril,"** have the haunting quality of legend. And there is much humor in *The Gates of Hell,* sometimes lugubrious, as in **"The Pursuit of Gloom,"** sometimes grim, as in **"The Universe Is Not Really Expanding,"** but sometimes also charming and pointed, as in **"Little Dreams of Mr. Morgan."**

It cannot be denied that Calder Willingham is a writer of considerable accomplishment. At his best, he is master of dialogue and description. He can invoke the mood of reality with what appears to be surprising ease. That he is increasing the range of his interests and exploring his gifts is obvious from this volume. *The Gates of Hell* is not his best book, but it carries the stamp of his genuine talent.

Gene Baro, "A Writer's Expanding Talent," in New
York Herald Tribune Book Review, *June 17, 1951,
p. 8.*

JAMES KELLY

For his novels *End as a Man* and *Geraldine Bradshaw,* Calder Willingham was hailed by some critics as a promising addition to our younger "naturalistic" writers. Yet realism out of context, as it is in the twenty-five short subjects of *The Gates of Hell,* seems to be only a padded version of prose usually found on a washroom wall.

The author demonstrates again that uninhibited imagination, no matter how fertile, can never take the place of something to write about. There are incidents of violence and wild symbolism, glimpses inside the mind of a prostitute, a condemned Negro, a Southern Sheriff, a paranoiac writer, an old actress, a Lesbian. There are satirical fantasies of encounters both inside and outside Hell, and diary notes written in nearly impenetrable dialects.

The best story in the collection appears to be **"Excitement in Ergo,"** a variation on a Faulknerian theme which develops real power. **"Bird Life"** lampoons a bored painter who is all set to raise hell in his wife's absence, instead gets involved in whimsical conversation with a couple of Village types and ends up in a movie. And there is a curious fragment called **"The Pursuit of Gloom"** in which the author shows happy people how to become unhappy.

James Kelly, "Violence and Symbols," in The New
York Times Book Review, *July 22, 1951, p. 15.*

JOHN COURNOS

Of the twenty-five stories in [*The Gates of Hell*] . . . several are not short stories at all but read rather like random jottings from a gifted novelist's notebook. A few of them are frankly essays, with reflections on our age and without the least attempt at creating character or situation. This is true of the short piece **"What Is Rape?,"** which denounces the extent of this phenomenon in intimate and international life and which, we are told, will destroy our civilization. **"The Universe Is Not Really Expanding"** is another rather abstruse piece which scarcely deserves the name of fiction.

On the other hand, there are creative sketches here which reveal a highly gifted hand in intensive realism. An eloquent example is **"Love on Toast,"** which records a rather violent conversation over the phone between husband and wife. What is astonishing about this tiff as well as about the scarcely less violent **"Guardian Angel"** is the brutal frankness of the dialogue, expressing the thoughts of people commonly retained unspoken in the recesses of the mind; yet here it sounds wholly convincing and plausible. Mr. Willingham is adept in this sort of thing; it is inherent in his strength. There is a mordant humor, too, in some of the pieces, notably in **"The Pursuit of Gloom,"** which delves, not without whimsicality, into the mysteries of masochism. There is no question of the uncanny power of this author, though it is a pity that he has not used his material as the warp and woof of a work larger in design.

*John Cournos, in a review of "The Gates of Hell,"
in* The Saturday Review of Literature, *Vol. XXXIV,
No. 30, July 28, 1951, p. 15.*

GENE BARO

Reach to the Stars goes beyond *Geraldine Bradshaw,* this time to a plush West Coast hotel that does occasional double-duty as a sanatorium. The hero, Richard Davenport, bellhops for a variety of unsavory guests whom he discusses at length with his fellow employees, a rather unappetizing group in its own right. Typical crises are reached when an invalid guest screams in the lobby, when a famous comedian has a nervous break-down in the hotel, when a glamorous guest is bitten by the pampered dog of a rich old lady who is one of the hotel's mainstays, when Dick is questioned by the dull-witted house detective in connection with some minor thefts.

Davenport's essentially aimless existence gives rise to his al-most unbearable lethargy, to his conviction that his life and the life of the hotel are built upon corruption and chaos, that life itself is corrupt. A boy with vague ambitions and with an unassimilated sensitivity, he eventually leaves the hotel for New York and, presumably, for the next installment of his story.

Calder Willingham's view of the world is a grim one, and it does not appear to be controlled adequately to the purpose of art. *Reach to the Stars* fails in impact because its individual scenes and characters, though largely static, have more validity than its total design. The scenes, situations, and characters are more or less right, but they do not give the feeling of inevi-tableness. This is the more unfortunate in that Mr. Willingham is a talented writer. His dialogue is usually vivacious. He is able to bring drama to ordinary scenes, and to do this with economy. His characterizations are often deeply convincing. But he does not seem able to command the integration of his capabilities.

> *Gene Baro, "West Coast," in* New York Herald Tribune Book Review, *December 2, 1951, p. 40.*

JOHN BARKHAM

Willingham is a talented young novelist who is steadily frit-tering away the forceful impression he made with his first book, *End as a Man.* That novel, which must have cost him blood and agony of spirit, was a book no one could read without feeling he had been socked with a literary uppercut. It was followed by a strange narrative called *Geraldine Bradshaw,* a clever cliff hanger in seduction, in which a smart-alecky bell-hop tried all through the book to get his girl. Now comes Willingham with [*Reach to the Stars*] which continues the bell-hop's biography as though it were worth telling in the first place. *Geraldine Bradshaw* at least had the merit of freshness and suspense. *Reach to the Stars* has neither. Dick Davenport is overfamiliar (in more senses than one), and, what's more, he acts so bored and languid throughout that neither he nor the reader cares much what happens.

This time Davenport functions in a plush California hostelry frequented by passé movie stars, aged eccentrics and monied homosexuals. (If there are normal people at the Goncourt the author fails to mention them.) Beau St. John, the blasé bellhop who acted as Davenport's sidekick in *Geraldine Bradshaw,* does not appear in this novel, but the two write each other long, saturnine letters that are easy to read but do nothing for the story.

Like everything Willingham has written so far, *Reach for the Stars* is intensely readable. Indeed, he writes a kind of lubri-cated prose that reminds one of the early Dos Passos. But the book is full of verbal muscle flexing which his own blue pencil should have eliminated. The novel, as such, has no plot. The author goes on picturing the hotel and its screwball residents for the requisite period, then abruptly ends the book as though he had tired of it.

> *John Barkham, "Bellhop's Biography: Part Two," in* The New York Times Book Review, *December 16, 1951, p. 16.*

GERTRUDE BUCKMAN

This young man of 30, whose fifth book [*Natural Child*] is, is another of our wonder children, a Southerner for whom the writing of novels seems to be a process of doing what comes naturally. The air of ease strikes us especially in this book, which has no such overlay of stylistic art as other Southern writers offer us. The device of making the narrator a young girl, of singular openness of mind, permits an effect of spon-taneity not otherwise possible—a tone of colloquial innocence at times engaging and disarming as well.

The story concerns the relationships of two young New York "intellectuals" and their girls, fresh from the provinces. Sue has had more worldly experience than Bobbie but Bobbie is the more sensitive and imaginative. She is seen here as "deep," womanly, and complex, and she is indeed a touching figure. The rather unattractive life these four lead in their Fifty-eighth Street rooming house is a kind of sieved Greenwich Village life. On the surface, George and Phil are rough, but they are anything but tough. Their air of Bohemian depravity, their bristling animosities and brutalities, are surface manifestations which cannot conceal the essential youthfulness of their de-spair, their self-contradiction.

These are babes lost in those terrible woods in the heart of modern society. They eat in the Automat, argue furiously at parties, observe the ways of effete artists, talk endlessly of profundities and inanities. But Bobbie, in the moment of losing her virginity to George, also conceives his child, and the gen-uine emotions that arise from this situation, though they seem to set the pair into yet another blind alley, actually put them on a path to maturity.

Since the tone Mr. Willingham has chosen is limiting, he has not scrupled to break through it, derange it, falsify it and ignore it, as necessity requires. When the discipline of the framework loses its authenticity it loses force as well and at times becomes a somewhat tedious and irritating device. But the author pe-riodically recovers the reader to himself by his more amiable talents.

> *Gertrude Buckman, "Automat Bohemia," in* The New York Times Book Review, *November 2, 1952, p. 22.*

EDWARD J. FITZGERALD

There is probably nothing wrong with Calder Willingham that a good editor couldn't correct merely by declining to publish him. His latest effusion is called *Natural Child* and it evidences all the lack of discipline, pretentious volubility, and sopho-moric posturing that have been his hallmark since his first promising novel. Its story has to do with the love life of Bobbie, a girl from the South, and George, a wolf on the fringes of Manhattan's literary bohemia. It is told in selfconsciously il-literate fashion that is supposed to be amusing, now in the first person, now in the third person. There are the customary ref-erences to sex, normal and perverse. There are pages of bom-bastic dialogue by unpleasant characters. And there is a final attempt to explain the whole thing away as an elaborate joke on the reader. That it is.

Edward J. Fitzgerald, "Enfant Terrible," in The
Saturday Review, *New York, Vol. XXXV, No. 48,*
November 29, 1952, p. 38.

ROSE FELD

To the reader of conventional novels, Calder Willingham's
Natural Child may seem like the first experience of listening
to a program of jazz. It seems dischordant, repetitious, raucous,
untrammeled but beneath the unconventional pattern there is
direction, form and melody that show skillful composition. It
may be difficult to get into the mood and swing of this completely individualistic work but once there, once tuned in on
the beam, as it were, it is equally difficult to put the book
down.

To say Mr. Willingham tells a story of four young persons
living in the pseudo-intellectual, pseudo-Bohemian fringe of
New York is putting it too simply. He doesn't tell a story; he
rambles, but the rambling is exceedingly good. The narrator
is a girl called Sue, mouthpiece, commentator and sounding
board for the events that casually emerge. She is naive, she is
dopily articulate; she has a clear eye about human relationships.
From experience she knows that men are wolves, that there is
only one thing they want of women and she is willing to settle
for that.

The three others with whom her life is tangled are Bobbie, a
gentle, idealistic girl from the South; Phil, the intellectual wolf
with whom she lives, and George, the other intellectual wolf
who becomes Bobbie's problem. Love, with its threat of marriage, is a word they all shy from, deliberately and grimly on
the part of the men, self-consciously and realistically on the
part of the girls.

It is the talk, the point of view, the atmosphere of a segment
of youth expressing itself in the action and idiom of the present
that give the book its vitality and color. Living for today only,
rejecting responsibility as a mark of intellectual liberation, the
two young men spend their hours talking, arguing, wise-cracking, breaking down conventions and traditions. Against the
background of an Automat restaurant, Coney Island, a mad
party at a dancer's apartment, in their own rooms, the flood
of words, spiced with references to Santayana, Freud, Adler,
poets, artists, politics rains against the ears of the girls. To
Sue it is mostly noise without meaning; to Bobbie, who has
fallen in love with George, it carries the threat of personal
disintegration.

The denouement, in which four young persons come of age,
has a wry poignancy that stems from an unsuspected challenge
to stop playing at life.

Rose Feld, "New York's Quasi-Bohemia," in New
York Herald Tribune Book Review, *November 30,*
1952, p. 15.

ELIZABETH POLLET

Calder Willingham's new novel [*Natural Child*] is an aborted
comedy by a talented author. It shows none of the emotional
labor-pains of some of his earlier books such as *End as a Man*
or *Geraldine Bradshaw*, in which the individual was pitted
against the world. In *Natural Child* four amateurs in a 58th
Street rooming house attempt to engage in sexual activity and
find it about as amusing and rewarding as a crossword puzzle.
While the boys talk, the girls preen, and if one of the latter

had not been so inane as to get herself pregnant, the four might
have gone on showing off for each other indefinitely. Faced
with a possible heir, one young couple marry and the other
two move into a cold water flat together. All four egos are
now so disrupted that there is nothing to do but write a book
about what has happened. Which character wrote the book?
asks the author, Mr. X, in a note at the end. Unfortunately,
any one of them might have.

Mr. Willingham has a sharp pen when he wants to use it, and
if he had maintained a comic distance from his characters,
perhaps by the use of the third person instead of the first, he
might have been more successful. As it is, the tone is one of
tendentious self-contempt, and the narrator repeats himself or
herself too often. The author seems to be afraid to give the
reader an opening for any remark such as: Look! Your emotions
are showing! (pp. 345-46)

*Elizabeth Pollet, "Fiction Chronicle: The Names of
Love," in* Partisan Review, *Vol. XX, No. 3, Summer,*
1953, pp. 343-48.

HAROLD CLURMAN

End as a Man is a picture of a military academy in the South.
Some people will complain that it goes to pieces in the second
act, even though it seems to pull itself together in the third.
This is only true if you expect or desire that everything produced in the theater conform to certain conventional dramatic
patterns. The first act introduces the central figure, the academy's chief bully, together with his victims and sundry other
fauna of the school. The second presents them in the detail of
their behavior. The third act discloses the punishment that is
meted out to the most culpable and states what may be the
moral of the piece.

But the play can hardly be said to have a moral; it is chiefly
characterization and a feeling. The feeling is probably one of
resentment; it is undeniably bitter. This is both the virtue and
the defect of the play. Its best scene is the one in which the
sharp-witted school demon guys and baits an oafish companion—a scene which leads to an episode of cheating, torment,
and beating. All this has a violence that is not easy to take—
but the essence of the play is here. It is not psychological, for
we are never clear—nor does the author attempt to suggest—
why his perverse protagonist is what he is; the scene is descriptive. It is fact. It happens, has happened. It is significant
as a recognizable ingredient of our life.

I do not believe the play is an indictment of the military mind
or of military schools. One cannot generalize from the given
data. One can only say that the data are convincing though
depressing. It is the ending that is perfunctory as story and
morally disturbing. When the head of the school, a general of
the United States army, tells the student council that for all its
faults the academy does provide a training that makes the recruit
"end as a man," we are not at all certain whether the author
is clearing his play of any subversive implications or is being
ironic and hopes subtly to suggest that the training ends the
recruit as a man.

There is something sadistic in the essence as well as in the
material of this play. It is not wilfully so: one gets sadism in
writing when unmotivated evil is presented, divorced from
other more universally congenial attributes. The fine writer
makes even the most villainous action arise from facets of social
and personal psychology in which all of us share. The male-

factor and the hero in art are equally part of every member of the audience. Yet there is truth in this play: a certain savage humor and, most welcome, a response to experience. (p. 278)

*Harold Clurman, in a review of "End as a Man,"
in* The Nation, *New York, Vol. 177, No. 14, October
3, 1953, pp. 277-78.*

HENRY HEWES

End as a Man began as a novel in 1947 [and] became a play in 1951. . . .

The story, as written by the new thirty-one-year-old Calder Willingham, appears at first to be merely a realistic picture of life at a military academy. But very early in the play we are introduced to a sadistic character named Jocko de Paris, who is so fascinatingly psychopathic that we watch him with the intentness that we would give to a caged panther.

Jocko begins by picking the weakest specimen of freshman he can find, and illegally hazing him without mercy. This, it is implied, is a true function of military training—to put pressure on the most sensitive and thus to weed out those not hardy enough for leadership. Then, because of an anonymous letter protesting against his behavior, Jocko is threatened with expulsion and forced to grovel in order to prevent it. The remainder of the play is concerned with his violent and unreasonable efforts to gain revenge for his humiliation. At the end, however, the school's commandant tells us that the play is really about American methods of military training, which— imperfect as they may be—are in his opinion the best in the world.

Now, any one of these three themes faithfully pursued could make an excellent play, particularly when the author has, as Mr. Willingham does, a good ear for dialogue, a natural feeling for dramatic conflict, and a finely tuned sense of ironic humor. Instead, Mr. Willingham refuses to stay in one focus and goes on to present us with an additional overtone, whose implication is that—like the psychiatric ward in Joseph Kramm's *The Shrike*—the military academy is a milieu representative of our whole society. . . .

But where Mr. Kramm's play starts and ends with the same man, Mr. Willingham's makes the same mistake as did the adapters of "Billy Budd." It starts with one man and ends with another. It would seem an axiom of playwriting that the character within a play who attempts to comprehend its events, and who undergoes some kind of change because of their impact, should be present steadily enough for that change and comprehension to be seen as it occurs.

In *End as a Man* none of the cadets change, and the commandant (who does change to the extent of coming to doubt his own omniscience) appears only twice. . . . And even though he tells us in his second and final appearance that he had no intention of carrying out his threat to expel Jocko, it fails to ring true. But this is almost the only thing that doesn't ring true in *End as a Man.*

Henry Hewes, "Begin as a Novelist," in The Saturday Review, *New York, Vol. XXXVI, No. 40, October 3, 1953, p. 42.*

WOLCOTT GIBBS

I found *End As a Man* rather impressive. It has its seriously crippling faults, which I'll get to in a minute, but on the whole it is honest, moving, and written with a rigid economy and savage, unmistakably authentic humor that mark the author as—potentially, at least—one of the few who can bring a recognizable image of life to the stage. . . .

Altogether, I think that *End As a Man* is a more than ordinarily interesting and worth-while offering. The reason it isn't a wholly satisfactory one lies mainly, I should say, in the fact that the necessary condensation from the novel—also by Mr. Willingham—on which it is based has emphasized the sensational aspects of the cadets' behavior at the expense of an orderly and credible development of character. The young men, that is, often have the air of a gaudy procession of case histories, too violent and various to be the inmates of any college in the world, military or otherwise (the normal ones are present only as a sort of background choral effect), and the action frequently descends to the level of a murky and incomprehensible rigadoon in a lunatic asylum. The author's intention is, I suppose, to demonstrate the brutalizing effect on receptive youth of a system dedicated to the production of efficient mass killers, but as it has come out, the protagonists, with the doubtful exception of the hero, are so cruel, vicious, and moronic that there seems no escaping the conclusion that they were born that way. There is no valid indictment of a specific method or environment; the play simply deals with an arbitrary gathering of a group of unbelievably weak, corrupt, and stupid people at the same place and the same time. There is almost no sense of external and evil forces working on good character; there is just the sense of the further deterioration of bad character in surroundings that happen to be particularly well suited to that end.

While this central mistake of selection and emphasis not only lays the play open to a more or less legitimate charge of sensationalism for its own sake but also largely defeats its purpose as a document of protest, it cannot disguise its very considerable merits as a piece of vivid writing and, in its bitter and occasionally gratuitously shocking fashion, as a remarkably funny report on the speech and customs of a special community. It is certainly an imperfect work, containing almost every conceivable error of theatrical inexperience, but it is very seldom dull, and I, for one, look forward to Mr. Willingham's further contributions with great interest and hope. (p. 68)

Wolcott Gibbs, "Beauty & Some Beasts," in The New Yorker, *Vol. XXIX, No. 36, October 24, 1953, pp. 66, 68-9.*

RICHARD HAYES

The dramatic abstract which Mr. Calder Willingham has fashioned out of his corrosive novel of academic life [*End as a Man*] raises again the question of adaptations in our theater. Adaptation is, as Mr. Eric Bentley remarked on another occasion, a racket; an act indulged in by people unable to make intelligent distinctions, "sometimes defensible in itself, but in the context of a wicked world . . . [leading] to abuses."

Of abuse, Mr. Willingham has certainly not been guilty, yet I am unable to regard his work here with the equanimity and respect it quite probably should evoke. This luckless unease would seem to spring largely from my inability—indeed, disinclination—to rinse from my memory the mordant recollection of Mr. Willingham's novel and replace it with [this] violent, abbreviated sketch. . . . This is no doubt a critical failure, for there is much to admire in *End as a Man:* a smarting perception of character, and the brilliant *éclat* with which the playwright and his company consistently bring off a series of intelligent theatrical strokes. Yet with the greatest degree of good will, I cannot but view the effort as a species of exercise, studded with interest, but dramatically incapable of engaging the attention on the level of moral indignation which Mr. Willingham, as novelist, so boldly inhabited.

The distance of fiction from the drama is one of kind, not degree: the novel permits an amplitude, a slow accretion of detail, exactly designed to support the weight of social portraiture in which a writer of Mr. Willingham's preoccupation excels. And a muscular intellectual structure is proper to fiction as it never is to the drama: indeed, the novel is the primary imaginative form in which we may investigate ideas in their social consequences.

It was this solid grounding in a powerful, assertive impulse of the mind which absolved the fictional *End as a Man* of sensationalism. Without that root, the stage version is more vulnerable. It succumbs too often to a gratuitous sadistic excess; the savagery of its malevolent cadets seems as antic as it does horrifying. And a hasty, final condemnation of the ethics of Mr. Willingham's grisly academy does not bring into any impressive perspective the parade of barbarisms of which the evening has consisted.

> *Richard Hayes, in a review of "End as a Man," in*
> The Commonweal, *Vol. LIX, No. 5, November 6,*
> *1953, p. 119.*

HARRY T. MOORE

The title of this novel, [*To Eat a Peach*], a phrase from Eliot's "Prufrock," emphasizes the way in which members of the staff at Daddy Tom's summer camp in the Tennessee mountains fall shyly or slyly in love with their colleagues. The only one of them to eat his peach is the sardonic young editor of the camp newspaper—who on the last day there finally yields to another typical Willingham character, a girl with an infinite capacity for tantalization. Indeed, the erotic content of the seduction episodes is as high as in similar scenes in *Geraldine Bradshaw,* Mr. Willingham's earlier novel about a bellhop and an elevator girl—to take one of many similar examples from this author's output.

As in that book, the setting is accidental. Jimmy and Madeleine would behave elsewhere pretty much as they do at this boys' camp; all they really need is an accessible room or cabin for their fatal interviews, which have no relation to Daddy Tom and his corn-pone bombast. As to the possible special meaning of Daddy Tom and his dilapidated camp, the reader will probably be happier if he takes them as given instead of worrying about larger implications. But even those who (for its own sake) accept the book's wide range of surface entertainment may be disturbed by the lack of connection between story and background.

The bitter force of Mr. Willingham's military-school novel, *End as a Man,* was intensified by the 'students' experience of the school's essential humbuggery. At Daddy Tom's camp, the boys are only a background chorus of nicknames. Various members of the staff appear in zestful, if often cynical and ignoble caricature. . . .

Mr. Willingham, as before, uses an easy colloquialism mined with ironies. The dialogue, occasionally thickened with Southern oratory, is skillfully done Americanese, somewhere between Hollywood-screenplay slickness and Hemingway-ceremonial repetition. Readers not painfully concerned with the

notion that a promising writer should after five novels give some indications of growth in vision may find much to enjoy in this scattered story. It is almost always fun to read while you are reading it.

> *Harry T. Moore, "Love in a Summer Camp," in*
> The New York Times Book Review, *February 27,*
> *1955, p. 30.*

HARRISON SMITH

Calder Willingham's first novel, *End As a Man,* was a harsh, relentless, and yet brilliant study of a military school, written in a terse style which exactly suited a way of life that was vicious and cynical. Eight years and five novels later Mr. Willingham reveals again his talent for dialogue and narration in the story of the final weeks in a ramshackle boys' camp in the South. But in almost every other way *To Eat a Peach* is the very opposite of *End As a Man:* it is humorous, kindly, at times too verbose, and if Mr. Willingham despised the military academy, it is also apparent that he has a deep affection for this particular summer camp. It had been an unusually trying summer at Camp Walden, and even the orations of Daddy Tom, the loquacious old director, could not bring "the Walden Spirit" to life. Neither could Jimmy McClain, who was hoping to earn enough money at Walden to get an education. Jimmy was a philosophic young man, and aside from keeping the boys out of trouble, he served as the editor of *Walden Ways,* a sheet devoted to the camp's activities. When he spoke after supper to the wretched boys he had to drag in "the Walden Spirit," and it made him sweat because they never acted as if it meant anything to them. He also had other troubles, for during this particular wartime summer Camp Walden was forced to accept a woman as its riding instructor. Toward the end of the summer Jimmy discovered that he could no longer ignore Madeleine. So he visited her and, of course, Nature had its way. The lovers parted forever the next morning in confusion and tears. *To Eat a Peach* is one of the oddest love stories of recent times. But it is a gay and amusing book, faintly satirical, and always entertaining if the reader can stand all of Daddy Tom's longwinded orations.

> *Harrison Smith, "Camp Story," in* The Saturday
> Review, *New York, Vol. XXXVIII, No. 18, April 30,*
> *1955, p. 30.*

MALCOLM BRADBURY

Subtlety and delicacy are the last words one would want to associate with *Eternal Fire*. This very large novel is a ceremonial of innocence and corruption in the American South. Nor is it only the theme that the reader will find rather familiar—some of the characters, too, have readily observable ancestry. The Judge whose corrupt handling of the estate with which he is entrusted brings about all the action seems right out of Robert Penn Warren. His ward, the innocent Southern gentleman, and the ward's fiancée, the pure, angelic but none the less highly-sexed southern girl whose forthcoming marriage the judge must prevent are by no means new in Southern fiction. The heartless, mechanical sexual adventurer who is the instrument of the Judge's purpose is an up-dated version of Faulkner's Popeye, while Grandma, the girl's guardian, seems right out of Lil Abner. Mr. Willingham is clearly mixing an old recipe, and the fact that he has a masterful way with the windings of a complex plot and carries off some set-piece passages—notably the obligatory trial-scene—with the greatest skill and wit doesn't really conceal the fact that the novel itself, like the sexual adventurer, is mechanical and without full integrity, is conceived at the level of caricature. Its most cleverly handled passages are indeed the passages of sexual athletics that are all too clearly primary in the invention of this efficient, violent and finally corrupt book.

Malcolm Bradbury, in a review of "Eternal Fire,"
in Punch, *Vol. CCXLV, No. 6419, September 18,*
1963, p. 434.

JACK KROLL

Providence Island is a calculated tour de force by a writer whose every natural effort has always been a tour de force. Willingham's fable of a semi-hot-shot TV media man shipwrecked on an uninhabited island with two uptight women is a paradoxical book—it is a sex novel that is clean as a whistle, it is a long novel that has not truly earned its length, it is a "big" novel whose bigness has the perilously attenuated translucence of a puffed-up balloon.

Here and there golden jolts of the true Willingham occur—his portrayal of the big brains of television is cutting and funny if a bit behindhand, and his unique ability to see modern character as a sadly hilarious interplay of hypocrisies is as strong as ever, if much too intermittent. But for the first time in his career this brilliant original sounds old-fashioned—it is as if he were really writing, disguised as the kind of big book that is making it these days, a tract against that kind of book and all the moral and esthetic implications of the culture that produces it. Calder Willingham, to whom with only one or two others of his generation can be ascribed genius, will now, one hopes, go back to the natural child in him. It is exactly his rare gift that can restore order and a humane power to our increasingly heartless and metallic literature.

Jack Kroll, "Shipwrecked," in Newsweek, *Vol.*
LXXIII, No. 10, March 10, 1969, p. 106.

JAMES R. FRAKES

[*Providence Island*] is the kind of novel that used to be called a "blockbuster" or "a major breakthrough in outspoken, candid treatment of the new revolution in relations between the sexes." After all, what better way to describe a 559-page novel about an aggressively virile 42-year-old Madison Avenue television executive stranded on an uninhabited Caribbean island with two women—one a voluptuous, repressed, Puritanic wife of a medical missionary, the other a freckled, buck-toothed virgin novelist with Lesbian leanings?

Well, there simply must be some other way, since otherwise Calder Willingham's seventh novel (can you believe that *End as a Man* appeared as long ago as 1947?) is bound to suffer from the same superficial reading and consequent critical downgrading as Philip Roth's *When She Was Good*. . . .

What I suspect is happening here is that the author knows exactly what he's doing at all times: grinding out an extensive survey of contemporary sexual mores (every variety except male homosexuality) with a very knowing eye on the book-buying public and the no-holds-barred Hollywood market. At the same time—and Willingham has pulled such tricks before in *Geraldine Bradshaw* and *Eternal Fire*—he perversely rescues his integrity by undercutting every potentially prurient scene with one or more detumescent techniques: fortuitous French-farce interruptions; outrageous cliff-hanger situations ("We're going to die, darling—don't deny us the only thing we have left? . . . This ship is going to *sink* Melody, I promise you it will, I guarantee it!"); mock-Freudian analyses; and always the awareness of the male's intricate planning and experienced calculation. . . .

To these devices add a reader-be-damned habit of drawing out every scene to absolutely interminable length, complete with the flattest sort of repetitions, naturalistic dialogue and gluey clots of the most abysmal clichés of True Story romanticism: "Her small hand fit into his own as if it belonged there and a strange current not unakin to electricity flowed from it to his own." . . .

I am not usually given to such charitable criticism, but, despite the overwhelming evidence to the contrary, I prefer to believe that the tongue is firmly embedded in Mr. Willingham's cheek and his thumb permanently affixed to his nose. Exhibits A and B (and I have dozens in reserve) for my reading are the choice of setting for the final moment of truth (the fiction section of Brentano's paperbound department)—and the 39 pages devoted to the therapeutic deflowering of the *Lesbian manqué* (more like a defoliation).

The whole sense of waggish overkill, sure to irritate as many readers as it titillates, sprouts organically from the characterization of the inexhaustible hero, Jim Kittering. He thinks the Beatles are great and envies their youthful fearlessness (the novel's epigraph is from Lennon and McCartney's "Hey Jude"). His most recent brainstorm was for a TV series dealing with the wife-swapping proclivities of Greenland Eskimos: "it has charm and innocence, tranquility, a light-heartedness with just a *soupcon* of *post coitum triste* to wet it up a little and make it glisten."

It's especially Jim's encyclopedic though often befuddled knowledge of women that seems to be the sputtering mechanism that propels the whole novel. Are women human beings or grasshoppers? Are they pure and perfect engineers perpetually constructing emotional Rube Goldberg machines? Simone de Beauvoir and Betty Friedan would not like his answers. For myself, I wish Mr. Willingham joy of the jackpot.

James R. Frakes, "Don Juan in the Caribbean," in
The New York Times Book Review, *March 30, 1969,*
p. 40.

PETER ROWLEY

The first 209 pages [of *Providence Island*] are very clever and funny. A *"Lucky Jim"*-type character, Jim Kittering, works as a TV vice president for a human "monster" nicknamed "The Goblin." He insults his boss and his rich bitchy wife and is ordered to spend three weeks on a tramp steamer, concocting a ridiculous TV series, in the company of a supposedly Lesbian writer. Though his life has been a mixture of sleeping and pep pills, alcohol, and marital and extra-marital upsets, he still thinks of himself at the age of 43 as follows: "For all the martinis he had drunk and the strain he had endured, he looked ten years younger than his age." Willingham brilliantly catches the fantasy of his hero's mind while giving him the opportunity to demolish many of the hypocrisies of upper-income suburbia and high-powered New York City communications media.

But the remainder of the book is tedious. When the cargo boat is shipwrecked by a hurricane, Jim, the writer and the third passenger, a heterosexual young married woman, are stranded on a Caribbean island. There is much soggy pornography and amateur psychology. The author, who perfectly balanced absurdity and reality into a believable situation before the accident, seems to have wandered from a world he knows into a new situation without really understanding how his characters would react. The amorous liaisons are tiresomely predictable and the sheer length of this section is painful. (p. 413)

Peter Rowley, in a review of "Providence Island," in The Nation, *New York, Vol. 208, No. 13, March 31, 1969, pp. 412-13.*

JAMES R. FRAKES

Shooting, as he often does, from the Hip, Norman Mailer once called Calder Willingham "a clown with the bite of a ferret," but faulted him for lacking ideas and being too indulgent to his shortcomings. . . . [*Rambling Rose*] is Willingham's eighth novel, and the clowning is still as waggishly pervasive as in *Geraldine Bradshaw* or *Providence Island*. Fish are jumpin' and the cotton is high. Idea-mongering is not even attempted. Shortcomings—prolixity, playful digressions, over-insistence on minor points, attention-numbing redundancy, "cuteness"—are admittedly indulged. But where is the ferret-bite?

For *Rambling Rose* is a love-offering, a valentine composed by a 49-year-old author in tribute to a towhaired country girl with cornflower eyes who came to the Hillyers' Alabama home in 1935 as live-in servant, "companion to Mother, and a friend to us all." A genuine "human girl person," Rose falls in love with Daddy Hillyer, evokes deep affection in Mother and the three children, drives the town boys out of their tomcat minds, and (in a 70-page sequence of ecstatically total recall) spends a September night in bed with the narrator (then a precocious 13 and more avid for education than Henry Adams). In her mindless, good-hearted ramblings, Rose indeed creates, as Daddy put it, "One hell of a damnable commotion." The commotion is all here, as are the innocence, frustration, nostalgia, bawdiness and general exasperation familiar to Willingham fans.

Rose is almost instinctively out of touch with the cruel world. Despite a rather harrowing past for a 19-year-old—incest with a drunken father at 11, gonorrhea and tuberculosis at 14, near-prostitution in Birmingham and several other childhood delights—she endures and perseveres by following one simple-minded but effective rule: "Turn your back, and look away." This refusal to see cruelty and brutality, this principle of survival, which runs like a refrain throughout the book, is shared by Mother Hillyer and binds the two women together.

Mother, you see, is "a cuckoo lady" who often whizzes off into "the fourth dimension," where she contemplates the "creative power of life" and sneers at Freud as a "total learned idiot." ("Imagine, sex determining the human spirit instead of vice versa!") While Mother understands and condones Rose's every misstep, Daddy wears no blinders, seethes with distrust and suspicion, bellows outrage and incredulity. . . . But Daddy, too, loves Rose—perhaps even more fully than does anyone else.

Anyone else, that is, except the narrator, Buddy, who writes this book under the name of Calder Willingham and offers it as eulogy and celebration of Rose, as Faulkner offered a similar nosegay to Miss Emily Grierson. The tricky retrospective point of view produces some uneasy shifts in voice, tone and balance; but for the most part it works remarkably well, carrying you

along like the slickest of con-men. This particular con-man is so sure of his power over the reader that he even calls attention to his legerdemain. The book is full of notes to the reader, warnings to the horny, Fielding-like asides, self-defenses, coy confessions . . . , angry opinions, diatribes against feminine sprays ("What a crass appeal to fear, what an abominable lie! . . . the way you smell is *great*") and television ("the Pukey").

As always, Mr. Willingham derives a great deal of fun from his treatment of sex—clinical without being antiseptic, graphic but never prurient, at once naturalistic and tender. And the earned laughter is never cruel or nasty. Buddy's night with Rose, for instance, is recounted at such great length not to titillate but to allow adequate room for the narrator to defend Rose's conduct and character, explain the boy's fear and bravado and to dramatize fully the life-changing awareness he achieves from the experience. . . . (pp. 56-7)

A book, then, about the South, the Depression, eavesdropping, salty dogs, a beautiful enigma named Rose and, most emphatically, about authentic family love. (p. 57)

James R. Frakes, "Fish Are Jumpin' and the Cotton Is High," in The New York Times Book Review, *October 29, 1972, pp. 56-7.*

THE TIMES LITERARY SUPPLEMENT

[*Rambling Rose* is] rather an old-fashioned kind of book; it bears resemblances to *Life with Father* and *My Life and Hard Times*, but has more in common with the latter. The background is realistic but the events are fictional, and the author tells us that although the "family" characters are based on real people, the eponymous heroine is imaginary.

The narrator, at the time of which he writes, is a boy of twelve and three-quarters, living with his father and mother and two younger children in the Deep South in 1935, in the days of the Great Depression. They run an hotel, but Mother is an academic and is studying for a degree. They employ Rose, a big blonde buxom girl of nineteen, beautiful daughter of a poor tenant farmer, very highly sexed and instinctive in all her behaviour. The local boys at once begin to follow her, as dogs follow a bitch on heat. If Rose "rambles" (and she does), the narrator rambles too; into speculations about Rose's true character and motivation, the nature of human and sexual love, the writing of books, and so on.

Both parents, for that time and place, are liberal in their views. Daddy is characterized partly by the fact that he usually appears with a rolled-up Glenville *News-Tribune* and always asks for "a half-a-cup of coffee." These, in show business terms, are two running gags. Most of the time, because of her outrageous activities, he wants to fire Rose. Mother is religious, a good deal self-deceiving about the remarkable qualities of her children. When she comes across "nasty things", she just turns her back on them and looks away. She may, too, just possibly be a saint.

Rose's goings-on do produce some comic action and good dialogue.

"Out of the Fog," in The Times Literary Supplement, *No. 3722, July 6, 1973, p. 783.*

CHOICE

[*The Big Nickel*] tries to do what Vonnegut usually does better: reduce the trials of the modern American spirit to low farce. It is all here: race, sex, violence and, most centrally, Success, which is, inevitably, portrayed as a woman no better than she should be. The agonies of novelists like Tom Heggeh and Ross Lockridge, the insights of Faulkner and Baldwin, the history of modern American fiction in fact, all become the raw materials of the novelist-as-smart-aleck. Yet, there is occasionally some genuine humor here, and the novel ends with an affirmation of simple human values that Willingham has almost earned.

A review of "The Big Nickel," in Choice, *Vol. 12, No. 4, June, 1975, p. 538.*

JEFFREY A. FRANK

Touting Calder Willingham is like calling attention to a secret vice. His novels are often intricately plotted, filled with outrageous misfortune and baroque language, and, worst of all, you are not always certain he is being serious. I first read Willingham when I was very young, and if my enthusiasm hasn't waned while reading him again, I worry, guiltily, about the sheer enjoyment his work gives me.

His name often baffles when one includes it in those lists of Americans who leaped to literary fame in the late 1940s: Mailer, Capote, Vidal, Bourjaily. Willingham himself has become somewhat invisible. His nine novels and one volume of short stories (*The Gates of Hell,* 1951) have slowly drifted out of print. He hasn't published a book since 1975 and, like other of his contemporaries, he's gone off to do other things. Even Hollywood got him for a time: his screenplays include *The Graduate, Little Big Man* and *Paths of Glory.*

But if scarcity on antiquarian bookshelves is a measure of popularity, a kind of Willinghamania has been building, and in the past year, two of his best books—*End As a Man* and *Eternal Fire*—have returned to print. New readers will discover there is no one like him.

Willingham, Atlanta-born but living in the North since the early '40s, has never had a real "place" in postwar American literature. His sheer Southern-ness sets him apart and, in an era of minimalism, his fiction seems to swarm with exaggeration and exaggerated types. *Eternal Fire*'s plot incorporates incest, blackmail, rape, murder, skulduggery, sadism and suicide; its chief movers include a sexual sociopath, a frenzied radio preacher and a tree-climbing dwarf with superhuman strength. It may be a satire of all 20th-century southern fiction, but it is also a grand epic about good and evil, held together by a roaring narrative.

In *End As a Man,* Willingham's first novel, published in 1947 when the author was 25, such misshapen, misbegotten beings are already alive and well. The book stunned its readers, who, 40 years ago, saw it as an exposé of military schools like The Citadel or VMI.

End As a Man was brilliant in the way it captured the special cruelty of male adolescents. The Academy, like the schools of Kipling's *Stalky & Co.* and John Knowles' *A Separate Peace,* is a universe where the strong terrorize the weak and the establishment preys upon the outsider. . . .

Willingham, though, was not out to avenge himself on a school at which he may have suffered. The Academy's chief officer,

Gen. A. L. Draughton, U.S. Army retired, is a decent fellow, dealing as fairly as he is able with the worst mischief-makers, unbowing to not-so-subtle threats about losing donations from Jocko's wealthy father. And one believes that Cadet Robert Marquales, the not-always-staunch hero, will in fact "end as a man"—no thanks to the rites of The Academy.

But *End As a Man,* with its riveting dialogue, its sometimes scary recreation of the details of life in and around a military college, was Willingham's first examination of what he saw as the ogres inhabiting the world he was born into. Jocko de Paris is not only cruel and vindictive, he is sadistic and utterly without scruple. In fact he is the ancestor of Harry Diadem, the man with the "silvery eyes" who brings so many problems to the innocent victims of *Eternal Fire.* And Roger B. Gatt, the cretinous athlete who becomes a victim, too, is not unlike Hawley, the brain-damaged dwarf of *Eternal Fire,* who is obsessed with protecting the passionate, virginal Laurie Mae.

Eternal Fire, Willingham's sixth novel, published in 1963 and just reissued, is a masterpiece of sorts. His longest and most complicated work, *Eternal Fire* really shows Willingham's gifts as a storyteller. You also read it with a sense that he is having enormous fun throwing almost everything into it. The title itself may mean any number of things: the sun, hell, lust, and even a specific anatomical part of a woman. Sometimes it is mixed together, as when the Reverend Jerry Battle tells Hawley, "Don't you know that the price of looking at that girl's naked body is eternal fire?"

The plot is quickly in motion: Randolph Sudderland Shepherdson III, heir to a fortune, longs to marry Laurie Mae, the beautiful schoolteacher from the wrong side of the Glenville tracks. But Randolph's guardian, the sinister Judge Ball, has not managed the Sudderland fortune honestly and dreads being found out. At the very least, he must stop the impending marriage, and for that he recruits Harry Diadem, the irresistible womanizer who loathes women. Harry enters the novel aboard a bus, engaged in seducing a young lady on her way to a Young Folks Faith-in-Prayer Convention.

Sometimes, you know that Willingham is kidding, as when the judge, recruiting Whit Gallady for evil purposes, brushes aside Whit's assertion that he could not be reinstated as a policeman:

> "Handled right, I don't see why not. After all," smiled the Judge, "you didn't rape that girl, all you did was scare her, burn her with a cigarette, and knock out three of her teeth." The Judge tilted his cigar in Whit's direction and lifted an eyebrow. "We *need* men like you on our Glenville police force."

The novel, though, burns with a fiery energy. Souls are redeemed briefly, then lost; chapters begin, "Night, when deep sleep falleth on men." Evil triumphs, then recedes. In a violent moment, the power of good overcomes the power of bullets in the chest. It is giant, stem-winding fiction; it is also morbidly funny, erotic, bemused and an unsettling reminder of the callous racism that once was a way of American life.

If these novels create a demand for more, a clever publisher ought to begin with *Rambling Rose,* published in 1972, which must be read partly as a novel and partly as a memoir of a 13-year-old's sexual awakening. Willingham is not always to be trusted, but it is certainly his voice when the narrator writes: ". . . this is a book unlike the others I have written, and I cannot claim an icy objectivity toward the characters portrayed in it, however desirable such aloofness might be as a general rule. And I must confess that includes the girl I call Rose, who cannot strictly be said to be a wisp of my imagination . . .''. . . .

It is, a critic I know once remarked, one of the most erotic novels of the century, and that without a naughty word. Sex is a Willingham obsession; he dwells on it philosophically and often with great physical detail, and the subject reached something of a thematic peak in *Providence Island* (1969), which could be seen as the ultimate stranded-on-a-desert-island novel. *Providence Island* enjoyed some book club success, and that it is no longer in stores is a puzzlement.

Willingham, in any case, remains a dangerous sort of writer, mucking about with all sorts of taboos, his dark humor not always covering his tracks. An essay/sketch about rape in *The Gates of Hell* would probably get him stoned were it reprinted

today (and, for that matter, few of the other stories in the collection hold up). But his voice, his wit and his assurance are always present in works such as *Geraldine Bradshaw* (1950) and *Natural Child* (1952), that seem a bit dated now, and, most recently, in *The Big Nickel* (1975).

He is a writer who has written beyond his time and place— soaring beyond them, speaking in a voice that is wise and funny and altogether comfortable in an age frequently dubbed postmodern. Jocko de Paris and Harry Diadem live just down the street, and Willingham has always known them, and their neighbors, exceedingly well.

Jeffrey A. Frank, "Song of the Southern Gothic,"
in Book World—The Washington Post, *May 24, 1987,*
p. 10.

Tom Wolfe
1931-

(Born Thomas Kennerly Wolfe, Jr.) American essayist, journalist, editor, critic, novelist, and short story writer.

Considered among the most original prose stylists in contemporary American literature, Wolfe is credited with developing New Journalism, a form of expository writing that unites traditional newspaper reportage with such techniques of fiction as stream-of-consciousness, shifting points of view, extended dialogue, character description, and detailed scene-setting. According to Wolfe, the intention of New Journalism is "to achieve a nonfiction form that combines the emotional impact usually found only in novels and short stories, the analytical insights of the best essays and scholarly writing, and the deep factual foundation of 'hard reporting.'" Wolfe's witty and informative books and essays, for which he has earned a reputation as an influential social commentator, reflect his critical yet tolerant approach toward icons and trends of popular American culture. His subject matter, eccentric literary technique, and bold opinions have aroused much controversy concerning the significance of both New Journalism and his own work. While some critics contend that Wolfe's exuberant prose style and his use of fictional devices distort or overwhelm the events he reports, many agree with Joe David Bellamy's assessment of Wolfe as "the most astute and popular social observer and cultural chronicler of his generation. . . . No other writer of our time has aspired to capture the fabled Spirit of the Age so fully and has succeeded so well."

After receiving his doctorate in American Studies from Yale University in 1957, Wolfe worked as a reporter for the *Springfield Union* and the *Washington Post*, later becoming a feature writer for the Sunday supplement of the *New York Herald Tribune*. He quickly garnered acclaim for his stories on such disparate phenomena as New York socialites, crime figures, and fashion trends. In 1963, after several weeks of researching a California customized car and hot rod show for *Esquire* magazine, Wolfe was unable to meet his deadline because he found traditional journalistic techniques inadequate to evoke the frenzied, garish subject of his article. Although Wolfe sent his notes to *Esquire* editor Byron Dobell so that another writer could complete the piece, Dobell published the notes unedited, and the resulting essay, "There Goes (Varoom! Varoom!) That Kandy Kolored Tangerine-Flake Baby," focused national attention on Wolfe's style, which came to be known as New Journalism. Later republished as "The Kandy-Kolored Tangerine-Flake Streamline Baby," this piece incorporates street slang, obscure terminology, and eccentric punctuation to convey Wolfe's sensory perceptions and random thoughts and impressions. Although such writers as Norman Mailer and Hunter S. Thompson are recognized for using these techniques in their nonfiction works, Wolfe is largely credited with introducing New Journalism to the general public.

Wolfe based much of his early work on the sector of working-class Americans who became affluent after World War II, contending that many of these individuals were developing alternative subcultures in response to the conformism and hostility of the social, literary, and intellectual establishment. In his first collection of essays, *The Kandy-Kolored Tangerine-*

© Thomas Victor

Flake Streamline Baby (1965), Wolfe examines the lifestyles of unconventional groups and public figures in contemporary culture. Although some critics objected to Wolfe's unorthodox prose style, most argued that this work contained innovative studies of popular trends. Wolfe's next collection, *The Pump House Gang* (1968), continues his discussion of the prominent subcultures of southern California, London, and New York City. Critical reaction to this book was predominantly positive; several reviewers praised Wolfe's portrayal of *Playboy* magazine founder Hugh Hefner as among his most trenchant studies of class structure and America's obsession with status.

Wolfe's next work, *The Electric Kool-Aid Acid Test* (1968), is generally regarded as a definitive portrait of the drug culture of the 1960s. This book relates the experiences of author Ken Kesey and the Merry Pranksters, a group of young people who attempted to introduce American society to hallucinogenic drugs through which, they believed, people could become liberated from the limitations of objective and subjective reality. Drawing from extensive interviews and personal observations recorded while traveling with the Merry Pranksters, Wolfe makes use of an elliptical, surreal style to convey the experience and compares the group's fanatic loyalty to Kesey to similar occurrences in ancient religious cults. Describing the work as "a celebration of psychedelia, of all its sounds and costumes, colors and fantasies,'' C. D. B. Bryan called *The Electric Kool-Aid Acid Test* ''an astonishing, enlightening, at times baffling, and explosively funny book.''

Radical Chic and Mau-Mauing the Flak Catchers (1970) consists of two essays in which Wolfe examines extremist politics and liberal philosophy. The first piece, ''Those Radical Chic Evenings,'' is a satirical sketch of a fund-raising party hosted by composer Leonard Bernstein for the Black Panthers, a militant black liberation organization, which was in need of finances to free twenty-one of its members who had been indicted in New York on charges of conspiracy. Commenting on the incongruity of the scene, Wolfe characterizes the Black Panthers as posturing comics while ridiculing affluent white liberals for ''nibbling caviar while signing checks for the revolution with their free hand.'' In the second essay, ''Mau-Mauing the Flak Catchers,'' Wolfe describes how some urban blacks feign militancy to intimidate the bureaucrats of government and social programs. While several reviewers considered this book degrading to the integrity of the black power movement and accused Wolfe of biased reporting, others lauded *Radical Chic and Mau-Mauing the Flak Catchers* as a vigorous critique of liberal naiveté.

The Painted Word (1975) is a mordant attack upon the modern art world in which Wolfe impugns such experimental painters as Andy Warhol and Jackson Pollock as well as prominent New York art critics, including Clement Greenberg and Leo Steinberg. Response to this book ranged from harsh criticism by those who regarded Wolfe's knowledge of art history as negligible to praise by others who agreed with his thesis that, in the words of Ruth Berenson, ''modern art . . . is a put-on, a gigantic hoax perpetrated on a gullible public by a mysterious cabal of artists, critics, dealers, and collectors.'' In *From Bauhaus to Our House* (1981), Wolfe assails modernist architecture, particularly the Bauhaus school associated with Walter Gropius, Mies van der Rohe, and Marcel Breuer, which he believed represented a lamentable departure from American architecture in its emphasis on function over form. Like *The Painted Word*, this book received sharply mixed reviews.

Wolfe's most widely respected book, *The Right Stuff* (1979), examines the rhetoric surrounding the early years of the American space program. This work, for which he received both an American Book Award and a National Book Critics Circle Award, garnered Wolfe critical plaudits for his meticulous research and his ability to delve beneath the public images of the astronauts to present a realistic picture of their organizational disputes, marital and personal crises, hardships, and triumphs. One reviewer remarked: ''That Wolfe can weave together [the] ragged strands of the astronaut story without minimizing the extraordinary courage, the sometimes incredible technical virtuosity, of these hand-picked space explorers . . . , is a tribute to his skill as a journalist and his sensibility as a student of humanistic values.''

Wolfe's first novel, *The Bonfire of the Vanities*, was originally serialized in *Rolling Stone* magazine during 1984 and 1985 and later rewritten and expanded for book publication in 1987. Described by Wolfe as ''a *Vanity Fair* book about New York, à la Thackeray,'' this work focuses on the downfall of Sherman McCoy, a wealthy bond salesman whose mistress strikes a black youth with his car while the two are on a date. Blamed for the accident, McCoy is publicly scorned and ridiculed as he becomes embroiled in the bureaucracy of New York City's legal system. Although some reviewers considered Wolfe's characterizations superficial, many praised as incisive his examination of New York's criminal justice program and the city's turbulent social and ethnic divisions. Jonathan Yardley commented: ''*The Bonfire of the Vanities* is a superb human comedy and the first novel ever to get contemporary New York, in all its arrogance and shame and heterogeneity and insularity, exactly right.''

(See also *CLC*, Vols. 1, 2, 9, 15, 35; *Contemporary Authors*, Vols. 13-16, rev. ed.; and *Contemporary Authors New Revision Series*, Vol. 9.)

CHRISTOPHER LEHMANN-HAUPT

The incident at the heart of Tom Wolfe's hilarious first novel [*The Bonfire of the Vanities*] is no laughing matter. Sherman McCoy, a well-married $1 million-a-year high-WASP Wall Street bond salesman with a 14-room apartment on Park Avenue, takes a wrong turn while driving his mistress home from Kennedy International Airport, and finds himself lost in the jungle of the east Bronx.

Forced to stop his $48,000 Mercedes-Benz and remove what appears to be some sort of road barrier, he panics when approached by two young black men—starts a fight, and leaps into the passenger seat of his car, his mistress having slid over to the wheel. As she races away, the rear end fishtails and ''*thok!* . . . The skinny boy was no longer standing.'' By the next day the boy is in a coma and black agitators are up in arms.

But what Mr. Wolfe does with this material is very funny indeed—funny and bitterly satirical. Everybody gets into the act, from the Bronx District Attorney who is running for re-election, to Peter Fallow, an alcoholic English reporter who is trying to save his sagging career on a daily tabloid. As Fallow's tipster says about the story:

> And the great thing, Pete, is that this isn't just one
> of those passing sensations. This thing gets down to
> the very structure of the city itself, the class structure,
> the racial structure, the way the system is put to-
> gether.

Indeed it does, and in doing so it gives Mr. Wolfe an opening to have delicious fun with the system. And everyone is mocked. . . . And it all gets so wickedly and perversely funny that at one point we find ourselves laughing helplessly even at a scene in which a man dies of a heart attack in a fancy East Side restaurant. Well of course you had to be there. But Mr. Wolfe lets no prisoners of his comedy escape.

So *The Bonfire of the Vanities* is just vintage Wolfe, you might argue—the author up to his old tricks. . . .

[This] may be true, but the additions are hardly to be scoffed at. The plot of *Bonfire* is an astonishingly intricate machine that manages to mesh at every turn despite its size and complexity. The characters, while being objects of satire, remain sympathetic enough when it matters to hold our interest and keep us rooting, an amazing feat considering how contemptible most of them can be.

It is only what the novel adds up to that may prove troubling to some readers. The closest thing to a hero we get in the story is Sherman McCoy, the Park Avenue bond salesman who becomes "the Great White Defendant" in the Bronx District Attorney's political machinations. . . .

Still, he's the raft we have to cling to in the storm of the novel's plot. By the end, we get rather attached to him, and Mr. Wolfe has to slap an awkward epilogue onto his story to remind us not to gloat over his survival.

The title of the novel helps—*The Bonfire of the Vanities.* Think of New York City today as 15th-century Florence, and consider Reverend Bacon of Harlem, who agitates against Sherman McCoy, as Fra Girolamo Savonarola, the celebrated monk whose sermons and exhortations engulfed Florence in a tidal wave of piety, assisted the ouster of the Medici family and led to the famous burning of the vanities. In such a context, it is easy to curse all rabble-rousers, and feel that people like Savonarola—and by metaphorical extension, Reverend Bacon—deserve to be burned at the stake.

But viewed in a contemporary context, Mr. Wolfe's novel seems to be playing with another kind of fire. It may well be true, as he seems to be suggesting, that the history of New York is, much as we may be reluctant to admit it, the history of predominant ethnic coalitions. And he is doubtless justified in exploiting the comedy arising from that fact.

But a nervousness creeps into one's laugh when he makes sport of current black sensitivity to the attitudes of New York City's whites. And that nervousness is increased by certain signs that the author himself may be a little nervous.

Still, *The Bonfire of the Vanities* is an impressive performance. In some respects, it's what Mr. Wolfe has been doing all along. But in other important ways his embrace of fiction has liberated him. All things considered, it allows him to outperform himself.

Christopher Lehmann-Haupt, in a review of "The Bonfire of the Vanities," in The New York Times, *October 22, 1987, p. C25.*

JONATHAN YARDLEY

It's an odd and eerie coincidence, but coincidence pure and simple, that the same literary publishing house that last summer produced Scott Turow's immensely successful *Presumed Innocent* has now brought out a strikingly similar novel that is likely to enjoy strikingly similar popularity. *The Bonfire of the Vanities,* the first work of fiction by the journalist Tom Wolfe, bears little stylistic resemblance to Turow's novel, but its texture and themes border on the identical: each book is set in the underside of metropolitan life, each is centrally concerned with the imperfect workings of justice, and each is about a man who, in Wolfe's phrase, is "heading for a collision with the real world." Each, moreover, is an unusually accomplished and richly entertaining book—popular fiction that manages, because of its essential seriousness, to attain a higher level.

The Bonfire of the Vanities has its origins in a serial that Wolfe wrote some years ago for *Rolling Stone* magazine, but readers who remember it should be advised that Wolfe has greatly altered, expanded and improved upon the first version; the *Rolling Stone* pieces were intended as something of a tour de force—a 20th-century bow to the Victorian serial novel—but *The Bonfire of the Vanities* is a polished, cohesive, expansive book that stands entirely on its own. There is, to be sure, a certain amount of preening in it, both stylistic and reportorial—Wolfe cannot resist his new-journalistic ruffles and flourishes,

and at times his immersion in the low life looks for all the world like slumming—but weighed against the book's many virtues these excesses are entirely forgivable.

It's a populous book, with a half-dozen characters who take turns occupying the limelight and a supporting cast of dozens, but at its center is Sherman McCoy. . . .

"The guy hit the wrong kind of kid in the wrong part of town driving the wrong brand of car with the wrong woman, not his wife, in the bucket seat next to him": that is how . . . one character succinctly summarizes [Sherman's] case. Sherman McCoy did not go out looking for trouble, but trouble managed to find him. Now, through no fault of anyone except fate, Sherman is where he had never expected to be: the wrong side of the law. More than that, he is in the center of a media circus, "wired into the vast, incalculable circuit of radio and television and newspapers," because he is a prosecutor's dream, "the Great White Defendant," a spectacular alternative to the "eternal prosecution of the blacks and Latins" that is the unhappy lot of the Bronx District Attorney's Office. . . .

[Yet *The Bonfire of the Vanities*] has much less to do with the private agony of Sherman McCoy than with the workings of that infinitely complex piece of human machinery called New York City. It is a tale that moves from the dining salons of the gold coast to the detention cells of the Bronx, from the paneled offices of Wall Street to the tense streets of Harlem, and that does so with remarkable ease and confidence. Unblinkingly, Wolfe examines the economic and racial divisions that set the city against itself, and he spares no one in exploring the causes and manifestations of those divisions; *The Bonfire of the Vanities* is a tough book, and just about anyone who cares to will find reason to take offense at it.

But the particular targets of Wolfe's scorn are the pampered and endlessly self-indulgent rich, insulated by their money from "those people," the ordinary citizens of the city. There are many brilliant and hilarious set-pieces in *The Bonfire of the Vanities,* but none is more brilliant or more hilarious than an elaborate dinner party at a lavish town house, a party at which those in attendance are interested in nothing except putting themselves on display and figuring out what profitable use they can make of their companions. It is toward the vanity of these people that the most intense heat of Wolfe's bonfire is directed, and he torches them to the quick.

The Bonfire of the Vanities is many things: a satire of privileged Manhattan and its ill-gotten riches, a mordant examination of criminal justice and the extraneous influences that pervert it, a sardonic contemplation of ambition and avarice and their unanticipated consequences, a sympathetic portrait of the "decent people" into whose lives the powerful can unexpectedly intrude. Not merely does the novel treat all these themes, but it does so through characters who are unfailingly convincing, interesting and uncaricatured. Though the novel's ending is rather strained and inconclusive—the same, oddly enough, can be said of *Presumed Innocent*—that is of little consequence. What matters most is that *The Bonfire of the Vanities* is a superb human comedy and the first novel ever to get contemporary New York, in all its arrogance and shame and heterogeneity and insularity, exactly right.

Jonathan Yardley, "Tom Wolfe's New York Confidential," in Book World—The Washington Post, *October 25, 1987, p. 3.*

FRANK CONROY

Now comes Tom Wolfe, aging *enfant terrible*, with his first novel, (his first novel!), six hundred and fifty-nine pages of raw energy about New York City and various of its inhabitants—a big, bitter, funny, craftily plotted book that grabs you by the lapels and won't let go. As in much of his other work, such as *The Right Stuff*, Mr. Wolfe's strategy [in *The Bonfire of the Vanities*] is to somehow batter the reader into submission, using an incantatory repetition of certain emblematic phrases, (HIS FIRST NOVEL!), detailed description of people's clothing, hyperbole, interior monologue whenever he feels like it, and various other New Journalism devices he is apparently too fond of to give up. What is amazing is that he gets away with it. I read *The Bonfire of the Vanities* straight through, in two sessions on two consecutive days, and enjoyed it enormously. It swept me right up. When he writes about process he knows what he is writing about, whether it's the Wall Street bond market, the Bronx District Attorney's Office, print and television journalism, or the working habits of sleazy lawyers—the man knows how to prepare and he knows how to tell a story, and how to make us laugh, qualities not always present in the work of some of the more polished, more literary or ultimately more ambitious novelists of his generation. (p. 1)

Mr. Wolfe writes in such a way as to make us read him quickly. Very quickly. (Indeed, if one lingers over the pages the sensation is something like hearing a 78 r.p.m. record played at 33⅓. One perceives the structure, but misses the essence.) Fast as it is—like falling downstairs, sometimes—the pace is superb, and the action, twists of plot, comic setups and jumps from track to track always occur at just the right times.

The plot is simple. Sherman screws up and the dark forces of the city close in on his rich white butt—but the presentation, or the attenuated revelation of the plot, is admirably complex, and allows for the weaving in of much interesting ancillary material. Mr. Wolfe never cheats the reader. He works hard to get every last bit of juice from every scene, every situation.

And yet, when the author has let go of your lapels and the book is over, there is an odd aftertaste, not entirely pleasant. Maybe he doesn't entirely get away with it.

Homophonic attempts to recreate regional or class accents are only irritating. "''N thin mibby nuthun'' seems clumsy rather than Southern. ''Muh uhms uh shakin'' seems strained. Nor is the urban black speech, Long Island WASP or New Yorkese any better. Mr. Wolfe misses, it seems to me, because of a tendency to embrace the grotesque. It is the fact of an accent, rather than the quality or nature of it, that interests him. Elmore Leonard, for instance, goes after the sound and rhythm of certain accents, and does it very well without any tortured spelling. (So does James Baldwin, for that matter.) Mr. Wolfe writes with another agenda, with a kind of malicious glee, and exaggerates in order to make fun of his characters, with whom, truth be told, he has not much sympathy. What they say is fine—the dialogue is fine—but I wish he'd just let them say it, and let my own ear do the work.

The relentless writing about clothing becomes tiresome. As new characters enter the narrative we are immediately told, at length and in elaborate detail, what they are wearing, as if the key to an understanding of their souls might emerge from that information. . . . Mr. Wolfe seems unable to imagine a character who gets dressed simply to avoid being naked. The clothes are always understood to be a choice, a statement, expressing some folly or character flaw or some lie. There is so much about clothes, about appearances, that the author runs the risk of being understood to say that's all there is. (pp. 1, 46)

In an epilogue, written as a *New York Times* story printed a year after the action of the novel, Mr. Wolfe tries to make the point that Sherman is a changed man, now the hounded creature of the criminal justice system. ''Mr. McCoy, 39, was dressed in an open-necked sport shirt, khaki pants, and hiking shoes . . . in sharp contrast to the $2,000 custom-tailored English suits he was famous for.''

Novelists often try to show us how people have changed by describing what they do or say. Mr. Wolfe makes gestures in that direction, but he always falls back on appearances, on descriptions of surfaces. As it turns out, it doesn't matter if we believe Sherman has changed (which is lucky, because we don't). It is enough that we believe he went through the fire.

The odd aftertaste may be in part because there aren't any people in the book who seem to exist independent of the author's will, no one with enough depth to surpass his or her accent, clothing, class or situation, no one for whom believable change is possible. They are all victims of fashion or other surface forces. The fun of the book, and much of its energy, comes from watching Mr. Wolfe eviscerate one pathetic character after another. And he is good at it, really brilliant sometimes—whether it be a society matron or a Jewish business tycoon making money running charter jets to Mecca for Arabs—but after a while, when it turns out that *everyone* is pathetic (except for me and thee, of course), the fun can turn sour. Malice is a powerful spice. Too much can ruin the stew, and Mr. Wolfe comes close.

But in the end everyone is going to read the book, and no one is going to ask for any money back. It positively hums with energy. There are dozens of fine scenes, set pieces, a strong story line, lots of laughs and a solid, psychologically penetrating piece of imaginative writing about Sherman going into the slammer. *The Bonfire of the Vanities* (an earlier version of which ran in serial form in *Rolling Stone* magazine) may be closer to R. Crumb than to Theodore Dreiser, but it satisfies. It definitely does it to you, and isn't that what it's all about? (p. 46)

Frank Conroy, ''Urban Rats in Fashion's Maze,'' in The New York Times Book Review, *November 1, 1987, pp. 1, 46.*

NICHOLAS LEMANN

The news that Tom Wolfe was writing a novel made me feel like the teary-eyed boy of legend who said ''Say it ain't so'' to Shoeless Joe Jackson after he had confessed to a part in the Black Sox scandal. For years Wolfe has been writing that journalists, having learned how to use the traditional techniques of narrative realism, have replaced novelists (who abandoned these techniques just as journalists were adopting them) as the cynosures of American literature. I don't know of any leading critic who agrees with him, but the idiosyncrasy of the argument is part of its appeal. Wolfe's last full-length book, *The Right Stuff*, which belongs on the short shelf of really successful nonfiction novels, seemed to be an attempt to prove his theory through his own work. Now he's gone over to the other side.

To be fair, the novel Wolfe has chosen to write [*The Bonfire of the Vanities*] is exactly the kind he has criticized contemporary novelists for not writing—in his words, ''the so-called 'big novel' of manners and society,'' as invented by nineteenth-century writers like Dickens, Balzac, Thackeray, and Trollope. Over the past fifteen years Wolfe has made it clear that he prefers the nineteenth century's tastes to today's in all the arts. He attacked abstract painting in *The Painted Word,* and modern architecture in *From Bauhaus to Our House.* What little writing and speaking he has done on politics makes it clear that he is no friend of modernism there either. In the fiction of bygone days what he most admires is the novelists' ambition to create a sweeping, accurate portrait of their whole society, which led them to do extensive firsthand reporting before they wrote and to fill their work with what Wolfe calls ''status details'' about food, dress, decoration, speech, and money. He wrote in 1973, ''I think there is a tremendous future for a sort of novel that will be called the journalistic novel or perhaps the documentary novel, novels of intense social realism based on the same painstaking reporting that goes into the New Journalism.''

The Bonfire of the Vanities (which Wolfe at one point said, making his intentions crystal clear, that he was going to call *Vanity Fair*) is a throwback to the point of having been written in serial form, the way Dickens used to write, for *Rolling Stone.* It is about Sherman McCoy, a WASPy Wall Street bond salesman with a palatial apartment on Park Avenue, who is involved in a hit-and-run accident in the South Bronx that leaves a black high school boy fatally injured. Not wanting it known that his mistress, Maria Ruskin, the sexy young wife of an extremely rich old man, was in the car with him, Sherman leaves the scene of the crime. But the case becomes a cause for the press and the black leadership, and Sherman winds up getting found out and, after an agonizing decline, losing everything. The plot gives Wolfe a chance to present a half dozen of New York's demimondes: the Bronx criminal courthouse and a Wall Street trading room (he obviously did a great deal of firsthand research on these two), the British-owned tabloid press, the local-politics left, and the West Side Jewish liberal middle class, to which Sherman's prosecutor belongs.

The story has strong echoes of real events, in particular the case of Edmund Perry, the Exeter graduate who died in a scuffle with a plainclothes cop in 1985, and the sensational insider-trading arrests of last year, which publicly ruined several young Wall Street hotshots and thereby brought enormous pleasure to the rest of New York. In a way this is another form of homage to the good old days of the novel: realistic novels from *Anna Karenina* to *Native Son* have had story lines ripped out of the day's headlines. In further accordance with his views on fiction, Wolfe has packed *The Bonfire of the Vanities* with information: menus, brand names, household budgets, the architectural histories of buildings. He goes into long disquisitions on the differences among the leading white ethnic groups of New York. Every now and then he'll drop in a minor character who's clearly recognizable—to name the three most obvious, the society realtor Alice Mason, the gossip columnist Suzy, and the journalist Alexander Cockburn (''Nick Stopping, the Marxist Journalist—Stalinist was more like it—who lived chiefly on articles flattering the rich in *House & Garden, Art & Antiques,* and *Connoisseur''*). Some scenes exist mainly to show readers what a Fifth Avenue dinner party, or the inside of a jail cell, is really like, or to enter into the record observations about changing social conventions—for instance, that riding in yellow taxis is no longer socially acceptable among New York big shots.

Very occasionally the procession of details becomes ungainly (''Sherman had often seen Hasidic Jews in the Diamond Dis-

trict, which was on Forty-sixth and Forty-seventh Streets between Fifth and Sixth Avenues. . . .''), but for the most part Wolfe has proved his point: the use of reporting, subplots, and interlocking sets of characters need not be the exclusive province of novelists like Judith Krantz and Arthur Hailey. It isn't inimical to literary quality. On the other hand, it isn't a guarantee of literary quality either. A novel, or anyway an old-fashioned ''big novel'' of stature, is supposed to contain a profound vision as well as facts. Here Wolfe doesn't do so well—not because he doesn't have a vision, but because he has two and they're incompatible.

The Bonfire of the Vanities begins as a rollicking but dark satire, closer to Waugh than to Dickens. Wolfe's New York is pretty much the hellish place imagined by people who don't live there. Everyone is obsessed with success, which seems to come mostly from stepping on somebody else. With the exception of the love of parent for child, genuine human relationships, as opposed to temporary alliances based on power-status-ego calculations, don't exist. Everyone feels a constant, gnawing financial panic—even Sherman, with his million-dollar-a-year income. The political system is helplessly in the thrall of the gutter press and black demagogues. Everyone is afraid of street crime, and among whites it's a short step from this fear to a primal urge to get away from blacks. ''If you want to live in New York, you've got to insulate, insulate, insulate,'' a friend of Sherman's tells him. Mississippi in the fifties couldn't have been any more preoccupied with race than Wolfe's New York; the book begins and ends with scenes of panicky white public officials confronting riotous black mobs.

New Yorkers' many vanities seem perfectly understandable, even pleasant, against such a bleak backdrop—a calm, happy, unpretentious life is an impossibility in Wolfe's version of New York. As an authorial voice, high-comic cynicism is appropriate too, and Wolfe can be very funny. The best leitmotif in *The Bonfire of the Vanities* is life in the freeloading, sneering, drunken community of British expatriates in New York. Wolfe skewers these people with dead-on affectionate malice. He's also very good on fancy restaurants, celebrity funerals, and activist ministers.

When Wolfe's humor doesn't work, it is usually because he is writing about people who are earnest, as opposed to faux-earnest. Although he certainly has got the number of his many cheerful hustlers and posturers, he doesn't at all dislike them, because he sees their game as the best revenge against the coldness at the city's heart. In New York, to Wolfe, social pretense is not an overlay masking the true self, it *is* the true self. People who pretend to have no pretensions—mainly, middle class liberals—offend Wolfe, and because he can't summon any love for them he satirizes them ineptly, even cruelly. A scene in which a *Village Voice* writer hosts a brunch in SoHo, which you'd think would be red meat for Wolfe, falls completely flat; he expresses his disapproval by giving the man a receding chin and putting him in a T-shirt bearing the logo of a rock band called Pus Casserole.

Also—oddly, considering that he is trying to create a vast social panorama—Wolfe doesn't even much try to write about women. Every one of his leading characters is a man—in fact, a man in his thirties, the age of maximum unfulfilled ambition and financial strain. The demimondes of Wall Street and the Bronx courts are both particularly macho ones, and thus unrepresentative of the city as a whole, which doesn't have any of the man's-world feeling of London or Chicago. Wolfe's female characters are all sketchy figures who exist mainly as foils for mail preening. The men are absolute slaves to their rampaging sex drives, which don't apply to their wives—but their extra-marital affairs bring them only doom. In the sixties Wolfe often wrote magazine stories with fully realized female protagonists, and because feminism has since then acquired a quarter century's worth of curlicues, by Wolfe's lights the material is even better now. It's too bad he didn't use it.

These are quibbles about what could have been a successful purely satirical novel. Wolfe has, however, an additional ambition for *The Bonfire of the Vanities* which is more substantially unrealized.

The main action of the book is the downfall of Sherman after the accident—his apprehension and indictment. It takes up so much space (more than 500 pages, counting many digressions), and is so elaborately agonizing, that it's clear Wolfe must be up to something more portentous than getting a few chuckles out of showing a winner squirming. There are echoes throughout of the classic American twentieth-century novels about the snatching away of worldly success, such as *An American Tragedy* and *Appointment in Samarra*, both of which are about the disintegration of young businessmen; and the allusion to the towering classic of this genre, *The Great Gatsby*, is direct and unmistakable. For all his feinting toward the literature of Paris and London, Wolfe, who has a Ph.D. in American studies, appears to be trying for a place in the pantheon of chroniclers of the American dream.

Gatsby's downfall, like Sherman's, came as the result of a hit-and-run accident (though in a different outer borough, Queens). In both books the hero takes the blame, although his beautiful, rich, married partner in adultery (in Gatsby's case Daisy, in Sherman's Maria) was really the one driving. Wolfe seems to be using the comparison not just to put himself into a certain league but to make a point about how New York has changed between the twenties and the eighties. In *The Great Gatsby* the unprincipled arriviste, Gatsby, is destroyed, while the established socialites, Tom and Daisy, escape unscathed from the consequences of the accident. What saves them is that they have a ruthlessness of a higher order than Gatsby's: Tom eliminates Gatsby and saves Daisy through the single stroke of telling the husband of the accident victim that it was Gatsby who killed his wife; this sends the man out to Gatsby's estate with a gun. In *The Bonfire of the Vanities* the aristocrat, Sherman, is ruined and the self-invented rich person, Maria, spared, because she is more ruthless by far than he is.

Each step on Sherman's downward path is marked by his irrepressible adherence to the outmoded, gentlemanly moral code of his father, a distinguished lawyer. Sherman doesn't actually believe in the code the way the old man did—he knows New York is shark-town—but he can't quite shake it either. In the final scenes he undergoes a transformation, as a result of which he is able to lie in furtherance of his interests, to punch someone out, and to talk to the tough patois of the Bronx courthouse. His triumphal last line is "It don't matter!" By this time it's too late for Sherman to save himself, but Wolfe's implication is that if he had changed a little earlier he would still be the king of bonds. More broadly, the message is that the vulgarians now run New York (as well they should, since it's either them or the unruly mob), in part because the WASPs have lost some kind of fundamental belief in their right to power.

The trouble is that Wolfe's narrative voice doesn't allow for the deep, almost lovely sadness of *The Great Gatsby*. Nick Carraway, the narrator of *The Great Gatsby*, was a midwestern naif who was both awed and horrified by the rich people with whom he mingled; the invisible narrator of *The Bonfire of the Vanities* is much too knowing to be capable of either awe or horror. So while it is easy to feel sorry for Gatsby, who's a crook, it's hard to feel sorry for Sherman, who's a good man; as a character, Sherman works best in the early going, when he is a lovable cad. The social message of Sherman's story—that is, Wolfe's editorial position on New York, as opposed to his reporting—is difficult to discern through the dense fog of joyful lampooning. Everything about the way Wolfe writes works against his achieving a resonant "bigness" of character and theme, and maybe he shouldn't have tried.

The Bonfire of the Vanities is on the whole such a pleasure to read that the prospect of Wolfe's continued absence from journalism is actually bearable. But since his first novel is at heart an attempt at tragedy, it seems fair to hope that in the second one he'll try farce. (pp. 104, 106-07)

> *Nicholas Lemann, "New York in the Eighties," in*
> The Atlantic Monthly, *Vol. 260, No. 6, December,*
> *1987, pp. 104, 106-07.*

RICHARD VIGILANTE

In 1984 the prophet of the New Journalism announced he was writing a novel. Serialized in *Rolling Stone* over the course of a year, [*The Bonfire of the Vanities*] has just now been released in hardback, after a heavy and not always well advised rewrite. A defeat? An admission that novels are still where the action is?

No and yes. It is a good novel, but it is also of a piece with his earlier work—his earlier *campaign*—and it further secures Wolfe's place as the most important writer of his generation. He is still saving American literature, and largely for that reason he has written a novel whose flaws are even more fascinating than its successes. (pp. 46, 48)

[The characters in *The Bonfire of the Vanities*] are mostly terrific; and the plot is compelling. No one has portrayed New York Society this accurately and devastatingly since Edith Wharton. In short, Wolfe's first novel has all the virtues you would expect.

As for those interesting defects, true to Wolfe's 1973 manifesto ["New Journalism"], this really is an experiment in radically journalistic fiction. Wolfe's authorship itself implies a claim that all this has been observed rather than created. The narrator powerfully, and I assume deliberately, reinforces that impression, through constant digressions on the New York scene, from the protocols of Wall Street power, to the etiquette of the furious status competitions of Park Avenue, to the locker-room ethics of the criminal-justice system. All this stuff is entertaining, splendidly written, and acutely observed. Unfortunately, against the background of this constant, if enormously entertaining, sociology lecture the characters sometimes seem a bit like audio-visual aids—trotted out to verify the thesis. A tad less sociology and a bit more dialogue would have made the same characters much more real.

There is a more fundamental problem. In that 1973 essay, Wolfe made the crucial claim that the New Journalism might become more emotionally powerful than the realistic novel, not because of its claim to be true—the novel makes the same claim—but because of its claim to be factual. "It enjoys an advantage so obvious, so built in, one almost forgets what a power it has: the simple fact that the reader knows all this actually happened.'' In Wolfe at his non-fiction best, this power, always just beneath the surface, bursts forth in a few dazzling epiphanies in the course of a piece. Though the epiphanies function as symbols, their power relies on the claim that they are facts. Start a *novel* with an insane gambler chanting ''hernia hernia hernia'' at a roulette table [as Wolfe did one essay] and you are, Wolfe would say, a ''fabulist'' who has abandoned realism for cheap absurdist thrills.

Wolfe doesn't fall into that trap; instead he mostly drops the epiphanies while maintaining an essentially reportorial approach to his descriptions of scene and society. The net result— by Wolfe's usual standards, anyway—is a bit flat, like old journalism.

So is the experiment a success? Well, let us say that Wolfe is a success, if we are to grade him by his deep, dark, secret do-gooder agenda. With *Bonfire,* Wolfe the literary politician has made an enormous contribution toward breaking the literary Buddhists' death-grip on the serious novel. He has demonstrated that the tedium of three decades' worth of serious fiction derives not from its seriousness but from its solipsism. And he has done this with a best-seller, which is to say he has recruited lots of potential defectors.

He has been recruiting for 25 years. The downtown lit crowd— McInerney, Janowitz, Ellis, for example—are all direct literary descendants of the New Journalism, and of Wolfe in particular. The style footprints, of course, are obvious. More importantly, they are social realists all, with a real interest in the world around them; their work is entertaining, with occasional genuine emotional insights. In short, they are all pretty good writers, and it is upon pretty good writers that great literary eras are founded.

Largely because of Wolfe's efforts, it is finally safe to predict that the social-realist novel will soon re-emerge as an accepted and perhaps dominant force on the serious-fiction scene. Not that he has been alone; American fiction has been so bad for so long we tend to forget how much good work has been done. But Wolfe is the most contagious force the good guys have. Things are looking up. (pp. 48-9)

Richard Vigilante, ''The Truth about Tom Wolfe,'' in National Review, *New York, Vol. XXXIX, December 18, 1987, pp. 46, 48-9.*

CHRIS ANDERSON

[In his essay **''New Journalism''**], Wolfe seems quite confident in the power of language to make experience present on the page. Using the devices of the realistic novel, he claims, a writer can not only render the full details of a scene or event but also describe ''the subjective, emotional life of the characters.'' Freed from the stodgy conventions of traditional journalism, Wolfe seems to be saying, language can penetrate to the heart of things. The rhetorical virtuosity of his own prose seems to embody this confidence. His genius for scene-by-scene reconstruction, his ear for dialogue and mimicry, his ability to manipulate sentence structure apparently at will, all give the impression that Wolfe is completely at home in language, able to do exactly what he wants to do when he wants to do it. He seems to delight in wringing out the rhetorical possibilities of words.

The test pilots in *The Right Stuff* use an interesting metaphor to describe what they do: ''pushing the outside of the envelope.'' The ''envelope'' is a flight test term for ''the limits of a particular aircraft's performance, how tight a turn it could make at such-and-such a speed, and so on.'' To ''push the outside of the envelope'' is to ''probe the outer limits'' of an aircraft's speed and maneuverability, to discover its capabilities and power, to see how far and fast it can go. Wolfe's project is to push the outside of the envelope of language. Like the fighter jocks he celebrates, he probes the limits of his machinery with a kind of cocky enthusiasm, a great confidence in the quickness of his reflexes and the sureness of his instincts.

But underneath Wolfe's energy and abandon is an awareness that language is finally incapable of encompassing reality. The subject of his writing is always the language of the experience he is addressing as much as the experience itself. He is fascinated with the insider's slang, the power words of the privileged groups and underground cultures he seeks out. He loves to mimic private jargons, and he repeatedly comments on the cultural, political, and psychological dimensions of particular phrases and conjuring words. Despite his claims for the purely mimetic function of the New Journalism, his own writing is metadiscursive. While he is not ''sailing off to Lonesome Island on a Tarot boat'' (**''New Journalism''**), writing about writing as an escape from the intensity of experience, his work is in a very important sense *about* language and the possibilities of form. And what seems to concern him most is the inability of language to describe certain central experiences which he regards as private, intuitive, and on several levels both sublime and religious. He continually calls our attention to the ineffable, either explicitly, in narrative exposition, or implicitly, in the dramatized rhetorical situations of his characters.

In **''Las Vegas (What?) Las Vegas (Can't hear you! Too noisy) Las Vegas!!!''** the first essay in his first book, *The Kandy-Kolored Tangerine-Flake Streamline Baby,* Wolfe is concerned with the complex, bizarre and mind-numbing sublimity of Las Vegas and all it represents. I mean sublimity here in its classical sense. The kind of sensory overload Wolfe describes in this essay is sublime: intense, powerful, overwhelming; in the end, beyond words. The title itself suggests the way in which the sheer volume of the experience overwhelms language. (pp. 8-9)

It is arguable whether this kind of experience is lofty or grand or elevated enough to be sublime in Longinus' sense. Wolfe is rejecting conventional notions of sublimity and beauty and celebrating the low-rent and the tacky—perhaps we should call this the ironic sublime. Yet it is clear that he sees in the underside of American culture something powerful and vast. Despite his partly ironic tone, he is caught up in the ''magnitude of the achievement'' of Las Vegas, impressed by the way it ''magnifies,'' ''foliates,'' ''embellishes'' sensory stimulus. . . . What compels Wolfe about Las Vegas is its size and scope. He is drawn to it because it exceeds the normal and everyday, exceeds even spectacle.

In **''The Kandy-Kolored Tangerine-Flake Streamline Baby,''** the title essay on the custom car culture in California, Wolfe shifts terms slightly. He is still interested in the tremendous, the bizarre, the chaotic. . . . But as the description proceeds Wolfe seems more and more fascinated by the specifically religious dimensions of the customizers. In their pursuit of a new ''baroque'' style of design for the automobile, the customizers become a true ''cult,'' devoted like true artists to a private vision. And they strike Wolfe as mysterious and alien, inexplicable. They are ''buried in the alien and suspect underworld of California youth.'' They're like ''Easter Islanders,'' he says. ''Suddenly you come upon the astonishing objects, and then you have to figure out how they got there and why they're there.''

This is the dynamic of Wolfe's reporting throughout *Streamline Baby*. He is the explorer suddenly coming upon astonishing objects, and his essays are attempts to figure out how these objects got there and why. The religious allusions and imagery here are important. Wolfe's strategy is to portray his subject as in some way removed and beyond. He creates a distance between the subject and his attempts to describe it. "We're out on old Easter Island," he says again of the customizers, "in the buried netherworld of teen-age Californians, and those objects, those cars, they have to do with the gods and the spirit and a lot of mystic stuff in the community."

The rhetorical implications of this kind of allusion become clear in *The Electric Kool-Aid Acid Test*. Wolfe is again attracted by the intense and the bizarre. The drug culture of Kesey's pranksters is lavish and spectacular, its style psychedelic, jumbled, nonlinear. Wolfe is again caught up in spectacle—in a broad sense, the sublime. And because these experiences are sublime—at the edges of experience, unusual, bold and over-whelming—they strain and exceed language. In any sublime experience, by definition, language breaks down after a certain point. The failure of language is an index to the grandeur or magnitude of the event or object. Kesey's "considerable new message," his "current fantasy," must somehow be told, Wolfe says. Kesey is not just a prankster but a prophet intent on converting others to his vision. "But how to tell it" [the fantasy]? "It has never been possible, has it, truly, just to come out and *announce* the fantasy?" (pp. 10-11)

"How to tell them?" "How to tell it?" becomes a refrain in *Acid Test*. Wolfe's concern is not only with the special quality of the prankster's experience but with the rhetorical problem of trying to communicate that experience. (pp. 11-12)

In a crucial chapter, Wolfe explains the problem in explicitly religious terms. The center of the prankster's shared vision is the "Unspoken Thing," an inexplicable mental ecstasy. "They made a point of not putting it into words," because "to put it into so many words, to define it, was to limit it." Language would translate the nonlinear into the linear, the simultaneous into the sequential, the infinite into the finite. Thus Kesey's language is "cryptic," metaphorical, consisting of parables and aphorisms. He practices the rhetoric of silence, refusing to explain or teach explicitly.

But more than that, the Unspoken Thing *can't* be described. Like Christianity and Buddhism and all the major world religions, the religion of the pranksters is founded on an "over-whelming *new experience*," an experience of the "holy," of "possession by the deity." Wolfe grants that the pranksters have no theology, no philosophy that can be reduced to an ism, that they don't in fact believe in a hereafter or in any kind of salvation. What makes them religious is that they have shared a flash of private and intuitive insight. They have all lived a moment of transcendence. (p. 12)

Kesey's actions as leader of the pranksters parallel the actions and style of any prophet or leader of a religious group; the pranksters themselves behave exactly like any cult or religious following, performing rituals and adopting special languages much like the early Christians. But the important point for Wolfe is that the pranksters, like all religious groups, are faced with the problem of trying to communicate experiences that are by definition incommunicable. "You're either on the bus or off the bus." You either know, or you don't. Only insiders, only those who have experienced the kairos, the moment, for themselves can understand what the pranksters are trying to achieve.

The Right Stuff is an investigation of language on many levels. Wolfe's interest is in the rhetoric of the space program: the rhetoric of politicians warning the country of Soviet domination in space, the rhetoric of the press idealizing the character and accomplishments of the Mercury astronauts, the rhetoric of the astronauts themselves as they fight to call their "capsule" a "spacecraft." But here too the underlying issue is the inexplicability of the experience Wolfe is trying to describe. The adventures of the fighter jocks and the astronauts are unparalleled. The job of the test pilot is to push the outside of the envelope, take his plane beyond the edge of known experience. What he perceives in the cockpit is privileged: no one else has ever had the opportunity to know what he knows. It is also intense, violent, spectacular, often overwhelming—planes tumbling end over end at the upper reaches of the atmosphere, the air thinning to blackness at the edge of space. "My God!" Wolfe explains, "it was impossible to explain to an outsider." The joys of the right stuff are "ineffable," true "mysteries."

As in *Acid Test*, Wolfe devotes a central chapter of *The Right Stuff* to an explicit discussion of this rhetorical problem. The distinction, in part, is between the actual experience of the right stuff—of being a fighter pilot and experiencing, for example, night landings on an aircraft carrier—and any prior effort to describe that experience in language. "To say that an F-4 was coming back onto this heaving barbecue from out of the sky at a speed of 135 knots," Wolfe observes, "might have been the truth in the training lecture, but it did not begin to get across the idea of what the newcomer saw from the deck itself." During an actual landing, "one experienced a neural alarm that no lecture could have prepared him for." Nor could the pilot himself begin to explain why he would give up the chance for a safe career in business and continue risking his life in high performance military aircraft. "He couldn't explain it . . . the very words for it had been amputated." The young pilot was "like the preacher in *Moby Dick* who climbs up into the pulpit on a rope ladder and then pulls the ladder up behind him; except the pilot could not use the words necessary to express the vital lesson." The sensations of flight, then, are difficult if not impossible to describe; and the quality of the fighter jock himself, his underlying motivations, his sense of himself, is also "ineffable."

At stake in the right stuff is a quality of *"manliness, manhood, manly courage,"* something "ancient, primordial, irresistible." The fighter jock was drawn to flying by a sense of its manly challenge. It tested him in a special way, giving him the opportunity to demonstrate courage and control in what Wolfe later calls "single warrior combat." Furthermore, having such courage was a matter of "election." Those with the right stuff were set apart as gifted and unique. "A man either had it or he didn't! There was no such thing as having most of it." Flight school was designed not to train a pilot but to find out which candidates had the right stuff and which didn't: "All the hot young fighter jocks began trying to test the limits themselves in a superstitious way. They were like believing Presbyterians of a century before who used to probe their own experience to see if they were truly among *the elect*." In *Acid Test* the religious parallel is with mysticism; here it is with Calvinism. But the suggestion is that both the pranksters and the fighter jocks are insiders with a privileged insight or special talent not accessible to others. The fighter jocks make up a "true fraternity" of pilots blessed with that "indefinable, unutterable, integral stuff."

It's not just that the right stuff is inexplicable. It's that discussing the right stuff, even if it were possible, is unmanly. The unwritten code of the fighter pilots is that feelings—joy, courage, fear—are not to be talked about. (pp. 13-15)

While the press inflates and idealizes the story of the Mercury astronauts, indulging in sentimental hyperbole, the true pilot always underplays the danger he might be in, drawling in his Chuck Yeager, West Virginia accent about the "little ol' red light up here on the control panel" even when the plane is close to plunging into the ocean. Understatement demonstrates, through a kind of negative logic, the true bravery of the pilot. (p. 15)

All this obviously has consequences for Wolfe himself. In dramatizing the rhetorical situation of his characters, in repeatedly calling attention to religious parallels and their implications for language, Wolfe is alerting us to the tension underlying his own efforts as a reporter. First, Wolfe ultimately cannot describe the subjects he takes up, for all the reasons that his characters cannot describe their experience. If the experience is truly ineffable, it ultimately resists even Wolfe's attempts to describe it. Second, even if he did succeed in describing these subjects, that success would in itself label him as an outsider: since the experience of the pranksters and the astronauts is fundamentally nonverbal and even antiverbal, the journalist is by definition—by virtue of the fact that he is writing a book, in whatever form, at whatever level of sympathy and engagement—an outsider, someone who is not on the bus, someone who does not have the right stuff. . . . In *The Right Stuff* reporters are outside "all the unspoken things": "The real problem was that reporters violated the invisible walls of the fraternity. They blurted out questions and spoke boorish words about . . . all the unspoken things!—about fear and bravery (they would say the words!) and how you *felt* at such-and-such a moment! It was obscene! They presumed a knowledge and an intimacy they did not have and had no right to." Wolfe is commenting here on his own enterprise. He too is speaking the unspoken words and violating the invisible walls. His effort is to achieve an intimacy with his subject that might enable him to recreate it for his readers, and this effort, he is saying, is intrinsically suspect.

In an author's note at the end of *Acid Test* Wolfe says that he has "tried not only to tell what the pranksters did but to recreate the mental atmosphere or subjective reality of it." What I'm suggesting is that throughout *Acid Test,* and throughout *Streamline Baby* and *The Right Stuff,* Wolfe persistently argues that this enterprise is impossible. He sets out to be an insider having established almost from the beginning that the particular kinds of experiences he is trying to enter into defy words. (pp. 15-16)

> Chris Anderson, "Pushing the Outside of the Envelope," in his Style as Argument: Contemporary American Nonfiction, *Southern Illinois University Press, 1987, pp. 8-47.*

TERRENCE RAFFERTY

Tom Wolfe's *The Bonfire of the Vanities* is a first novel of almost unseemly size and boldness. Sure, Wolfe is a famous journalist—the author of several best-sellers, and a certified Major Influence on the art of magazine feature writing—but,

seeking entry into the loftier reaches of literary art, the penthouse of fiction, shouldn't a mere reporter know enough to show a little deference to his hosts, a touch of quiet awe at his new surroundings, some uncertainty about whether he *belongs*? That really wouldn't be Tom Wolfe's style: he's not about to come on all insecure and timid and terrified of committing a gaffe, as if he were just another eager arriviste. Bearing this gigantic book, he crashes the novelists' party, and it's as if a professional wrestler in full signature regalia had suddenly appeared, waving his arms and declaiming and hurling people to the floor: he makes a big impression. It's quite a performance, full of right-stuff bravado and ferocious self-assertion. Turning himself into a novelist, Wolfe is as fearless and jaunty and authoritative-sounding as he was when he turned himself into a critic of modern art (*The Painted Word*) and modern architecture (*From Bauhaus to Our House*) a few years ago. No matter what subject he's addressing, what form of writing he's adopting, he has the kind of arrogance that great journalists need: the feeling both that the "experts" in any field are basically full of it and that with a little concentrated research—the usual deadline-driven cramming—he, the reporter, can master anything, and give us the real story, the angle the experts are too blind to see or too deceitful to reveal. And on top of the brazen self-confidence of the reporter there's the iron ego of a *stylist,* one who has developed a voice so strong and so distinctive that it allows him to carry anything off. So why should Tom Wolfe be afraid to tackle the novel? With his wised-up attitude and his maniacally overbearing style, he can do to this form exactly what the wild automotive artists he celebrated in **"The Kandy-Kolored Tangerine-Flake Streamline Baby"** do to the standardized products of Detroit's expertise: he can customize it.

It's exhilarating to watch *The Bonfire of the Vanities* come barrelling down the road. Streamlined it's not (six hundred and fifty-nine pages), but it certainly zips along, and the fins and crazy decals and baroque grillwork of Wolfe's style make for a colorful blur. Tom Wolfe is no more a fan of austerity in fiction than in painting or architecture. This book, which has dozens of vivid characters and an elaborate plot covering every inch of the novel's conventional, realistic frame like some fantastic Day-Glo design, seems intended as a reproach to literary modernism: a counter-example, rather than a sermon in the manner of *Painted Word* and *Bauhaus.* In interviews Wolfe has been talking a lot about Thackeray and Balzac, and it's clear that the book derives a good part of its energy from the polemic implied by its grand-manner storytelling and by its huge ambition—to be a full anatomy of contemporary New York society, top to bottom. This, he means to show us, is what a novel is supposed to do: a fat style is our style. His demonstration is a lot more effective than the shrill argumentation of the art and architecture books. *The Bonfire of the Vanities* allows Wolfe to show off his talents as a listener and an observer: he knows how to cram scenes full of visual and verbal details without slowing the momentum of the narrative, so the novel seems rich and generous while we're reading it. But why does it feel so thin when we're done with it? Dazzled by the flamboyant performance, we may still wonder, when the wrestler has finally left the room, what the hell *that* was all about.

What *The Bonfire of the Vanities* is about—Wolfe has said as much—is New York, and that's part of the problem: we can describe the novel as "about New York" without reducing it in any way. We couldn't say that *Ulysses* was "about Dublin" or that *Lost Illusions* was "about Paris" without feeling that we'd simplified it beyond recognition. "New York" is a historian's subject, or a sociologist's—or a journalist's. For a novelist (yes, even for the nineteenth-century novelists who are Wolfe's models), a great abstract entity like a city is only a setting, a backdrop against which to explore the mysteries of human behavior. Judging by the characters in *The Bonfire of the Vanities*, we'd have to conclude that human nature holds few mysteries for Tom Wolfe. There isn't a person in Wolfe's New York who can't be nailed down and labelled within a page or two of his first appearance; the author makes each as immediately recognizable as a character actor in a forties comedy—Eugene Pallette or William Demarest—and not one of them surprises us thereafter. The hero, Sherman McCoy, is a Park Avenue Wasp, an ace bond trader who considers himself one of the Masters of the Universe, and there's nothing Wolfe doesn't know about the surfaces of this man's life: what schools he went to (St. Paul's and Yale); what his wife does (goes to dinner parties and remains thin); how high the ceilings in his co-op are (twelve feet); what he wears to work every day ("a blue-gray nailhead worsted suit, custom-tailored in England for $1,800, two-button, single-breasted, with ordinary notched lapels"). Get the picture? How could you not? Wolfe's precision is impressive, and funny, but a character defined wholly by his class isn't, finally, very satisfying. (pp. 88-9)

All the many, many characters in *The Bonfire of the Vanities* have been conceived in just this way: each a perfectly matched composite of social function, race or ethnicity, accent, and footwear, and each, from word one, entirely predictable.... When Sherman gets lost in the South Bronx, having taken a wrong turn off the Triborough Bridge on his way from the airport, and his car (driven by his mistress) hits a young black man on a deserted highway ramp, he sets in motion a plot whose function is to make all these people, from their radically different social worlds, suddenly collide. The intent is, of course, satiric. The central joke is that Sherman, who has lived his whole life in ignorance of the Universe he thinks he's Master of, now finds himself, thanks to this messy accident, at the mercy of the very system that has been propping him up. His subjects—the underclass, the courts, the media—turn against him, and even the people his crisis forces him to rely on, like his Irish lawyer, don't treat him with the respect he's used to: they're all playing by the arcane rules of sub-universes barely known to Wall Street and Park Avenue, and Sherman is as powerless as a pinball. This satiric scheme allows Wolfe tremendous freedom to stereotype.... Wolfe has custom-designed his first novel so that he can do what he has always done best—size people up swiftly and memorably, and reveal the hidden social imperatives that drive them. In this sense, *The Bonfire of the Vanities* is a flawless machine.

A novel that's a machine is a limited pleasure, though. As much as we may admire the skill of its intricate assembly, and genuinely enjoy the finished product, there's something about the process that makes us a little uncomfortable.... [The] tone of *The Bonfire of the Vanities* sounds far too knowing for a novel. Wolfe has often given us exactly what we wanted in a magazine article: loads of information, a fistful of striking phrases, a quick, sure *take* on people at home in their subcultures. In a more complex form—the takes multiplied, the subcultures intersecting—that's what he gives us here, too, and it's not enough.

The novel form just doesn't customize so easily—not in this way, at least. This is not a matter of reverence, of believing that fiction is inherently superior to journalism, or anything

like that. But, reading a novel like this one, which is composed entirely of meticulous observation and perfectly worked-out illustrations of theories of the relationships among classes, we're bound to wonder: Why are we getting this particular take in the form of fiction? Even while we're laughing and greedily turning the pages of *The Bonfire of the Vanities*, we're never quite convinced that it *needs* to be a novel. It has everything that intelligent research, precision tooling, and strong, unambiguous opinions can give to a narrative, and almost nothing that the imagination, the urge to take oneself into unexplored areas, can.

The Bonfire of the Vanities is a best-seller, deservedly. You couldn't ask for a smarter work of popular fiction: it's a sensational display of craftsmanship. Since the novel has real virtues and its reception has been so euphoric, it's hard to criticize it without feeling that one has done something inappropriate, made a bit of a faux pas—without feeling, that is, a little like the dying English poet in *Bonfire* who stands up in the middle of a posh dinner party and lets rip a long speech about "The Masque of the Red Death," implying that the glittering functions of *this* society are no more effective in cheating death than Prince Prospero's masked ball was. (pp. 89-91)

Tom Wolfe is an absolute master of the world of appearances: he's onto every nuance of how people see themselves, and each other, in society. He's so good at picking up on modes of social perception that he often gives the impression that nothing else matters. It's as if the world really were a party, a masked ball: Wolfe's function, as he sees it, is simply to put the right names to the disguised guests. He guides us through the colorful crowd, keeps up a steady knowing whisper in our ears ("That's *x*, and over there, in the harlequin suit, is *y*, who went to St. Paul's and Yale. His ceilings are twelve feet high..."). When it's all over, we still haven't seen any faces: we're left with names and costumes. Forced to imagine what *x* or *y* might actually look like, we have nothing to go on but our guide's swift sketches and the things we already know—that is to say, our prejudices. At the novelists' party, Wolfe comes on like the avenging intruder from the nineteenth century. But in his more accustomed world—the world that he's got sized up, in a journalist's sense—he seems smug and insinuating, a genius of gossip. He's a novelist in appearance only; for all its strenuous displays of style, *The Bonfire of the Vanities* leaves the author's and the reader's perceptions of the world exactly as they were. In *The Right Stuff* Tom Wolfe wrote admiringly of test pilots (like Chuck Yeager) who "push the outside of the envelope"—those who fly so high and so fast that they seem to be straining against the limitations of their machines, their bodies, the laws of physics. As a novelist, Wolfe never shows that sort of obsessiveness, that urge to transgress. He hasn't dared to push the outside of the envelope, and his invitation to join the company of genuine imaginative artists is still inside, unanswered. (p. 92)

Terrence Rafferty, "The Man Who Knew Too Much," in The New Yorker, *Vol. LXIII, No. 50, February 1, 1988, pp. 88-92.*

THOMAS R. EDWARDS

Authors are not responsible for what even their friendliest critics say about them, and Tom Wolfe shouldn't be blamed for George Will's statement that Wolfe's first novel, *The Bonfire of the Vanities*, is "Victorian, even Dickensian" in its scope and its "capacity to convey and provoke indignation." Both Dickens and Wolfe, to be sure, write social comedy of a broad, even outrageous, theatricality, enlarging social observation into drama, or melodrama, in which conflicting human desires suggest pathological disturbances within the body politic. But Dickens also had the artist's saving interest in mystery. He understood how to hold his reader by concealing the connections between characters and events just as long as possible, and he knew that in serious fiction even caricatures should be hard to see all the way around, that they can suggest more than their assigned parts require.

Tom Wolfe has no discernible interest in mystery. Since his characters must mean what he wants them to mean, they can exist only on the outside—in their clothes, their accents, their living arrangements or colleges or cars, the places where they work and play—and the fun for the author is to read us their IDs and spot them right away for what they are. . . .

Wolfe feels free to mock characters whose souls seem to be subsumed in such surface details, yet without their surfaces he would be at a loss to tell us who they are. When in *Great Expectations* the newly gentrified Pip entertains Joe Gargery in London, the awkwardness of the occasion is pointed up by the way Joe's hat insists on falling off the mantelpiece, but while we may be sure that Joe has worn the wrong kind of hat, the meaning is not in the hat or in its style but in how both men use it—Joe by endlessly fumbling with it, Pip by watching it so impatiently—as a way of withholding some vulnerable part of themselves from a reunion that embarrasses them both, at the time, and deeply shames the wiser Pip, who describes the event long after it has taken place. There is nothing like this in Wolfe's book.

The Bonfire of the Vanities is the story of Sherman McCoy (Buckley, St. Paul's, Yale), who at thirty-eight is *"going broke on a million dollars a year!"* McCoy is the star bond trader for a leading New York investment banking firm (probably he would be making a good deal more than a million, but never mind), but his incompetence at personal finance has put him deeply in the red. . . .

[Sherman] misses the Manhattan turnoff from the Triborough Bridge and gets himself and his frisky passenger (his mistress, Maria Ruskin) thoroughly lost in the South Bronx. Encountering two black youths whose intentions seem dubious, they flee, with Maria at the wheel, while sensing that the car may have struck one of the kids. Fearing discovery of their affair by their spouses, they decide not to report what they're not sure was an injury. But in fact they have seriously hurt a respectable teen-ager, and from that event issues Sherman's nightmare introduction to the world ordinary people inhabit. . . .

Sherman is arrested and booked, indicted, reviled in the press and in various mass demonstrations, and finally brought to trial for reckless endangerment and leaving the scene of an accident, losing along the way his wife, his job, the big deal that was to pay off his debts, and, worst of all, his illusions of mastery.

All of this allows Wolfe, *in propria persona* or through the mind of Sherman McCoy, to say a lot of unpleasant things about most of the residents of New York—WASPs, blacks, Hispanics, Jews (especially rich ones and Hasidim), gays and lesbians, liberals, Brits, social activists, urban (but not national) politicians, social climbers, journalists, smokers and drinkers, faddists about food and clothes, the fat and the thin, exercisers, people with New York accents, and so on. He tends to like the police, criminal lawyers (especially ones who are sharp dressers and went to Yale Law School), Art Deco, and judges, but the world pictured is mainly a theater of malice, and it seems tempting to ask why the book has sold so many copies. No doubt many of its buyers are metropolitan people ready to laugh at the pretentious follies of, if not exactly themselves, then people like the ones they know. But elsewhere in the Republic some may be reading *The Bonfire of the Vanities* more innocently, as the morality play its title suggests it to be. Do such readers, not knowing people like those Wolfe describes (and glad of it), imagine that the book, like a glossy magazine or a TV show, gives believable glimpses of the rich and famous, along with some of the poor and dangerous who are equally stimulating to the powers of moral censure?

Sherman McCoy's career traces an interesting curve. He begins as a weak, cosseted fool, a man without talent or conviction who (like many others) is blessed by living in a time when one can do quite well without having either. He's not guilty, or not very guilty, of anything but hubris, yet a society in which the worst have usurped the power that once belonged to Sherman's class makes sure that he will pay dearly for being white and privileged. His shame and fear in the luridly described holding pens at Bronx Criminal Court seem to him at first a kind of death, but what really begins to die is his assumption that he can live as he wants to without effort.

As the book nears its end he starts to fight back, telling off those of his own circle who have ignored or exploited his disaster, betraying the mistress who has already betrayed him by taping her self-incriminating conversation, and finally, in an exciting but preposterous climax, when a rabid courtroom mob of blacks and do-gooders attack both him and the courageous judge who has dismissed the charges against him, claiming his manhood through redemptive physical violence. . . . (p. 8)

Whatever this ugly moment means—the true machismo of the paramilitary racist groups? the hopeless dream of glory that every little person knows but very seldom tries to enact?—it seems clear that for once Wolfe has imagined another mind very well. He knows that the significant detail isn't striking the blow but relishing it afterward. Whatever the author intends, I'd be surprised if there weren't readers out there for whom the moment represents a welcome stirring of counter-revolution, wiping out the space in which stand law, sympathy, generosity, patience, between a resentful "us" and a "them" who have taken away what we once had. Another Sherman McCoy emerges here, the real McCoy, perhaps, a feral fellow who won't be pushed around anymore, as is confirmed at the end of the book, when McCoy appears for his second arraignment, for manslaughter, wearing not a $2,000 suit but "an open-necked sport shirt, khaki pants, and hiking shoes." The outfit might signal a call to arms to those who want to hear one.

Power has always been Wolfe's subject. When, as in his earlier journalism, power took the form of populist cultural power subverting established taste from below—in the rock music industry, for example, car customizers, surfers, or druggies—he could write from his strongest position, laughing at his readers for fearing "vulgar" vitality even while knowing himself that it *was* vulgar, and ludicrous too. When the material becomes more overtly political, however, as in *Radical Chic,* and now in *The Bonfire of the Vanities*, the case is somewhat altered and the laughter grows nasty and the message obvious. (pp. 8-9)

Wolfe manages to have class hostility both ways. The old power of the WASP "establishment" is, he says, now dispossessed without its quite knowing it; New York and places like it are in the hands of the sans-culottes, ethnic whites and (now) nonwhites who have learned how to manipulate and profit from the system. It's a good joke on any WASP who didn't already know this, but the "indignation" George Will praises Wolfe for provoking may not be as healthily self-critical as Will supposes. He reads the book as saying that "flocking to Wall Street . . . is . . . unworthy of 'the sons of the great universities, those legatees of Jefferson, Emerson, Thoreau, William James, . . . inheritors of the lux and the veritas.'" It is true that Wolfe says this—though there may not be nearly so many Sherman McCoys in present-day Wall Street trading rooms as he suggests—but his book seems to me in touch with other kinds of indignation, too, and far less pious ones.

Yet *The Bonfire of the Vanities* probably isn't the "'conservative' novel" Will has been hoping for, or indeed a political novel at all. The depth and acuity of Wolfe's politics are suggested by his quoting the old joke that "a liberal is a conservative who has been arrested," which of course reads as well the other way around. His main interest seems better represented by something Sherman McCoy tells his young daughter when he tries to prepare her for the news that he has been arrested: "There are bad people who want to believe bad things about other people." Tom Wolfe thrives on saying bad things about other people to people he suspects are pretty bad themselves. This game can be entertaining. *The Bonfire of the Vanities* is at least somewhat wittier than the novels of Sidney Sheldon and less sentimental than those of Jimmy Breslin. But it should not be taken seriously, and it has nothing to do with Dickens. (p. 9)

Thomas R. Edwards, "Low Expectations," in The New York Review of Books, *Vol. XXXV, No. 1, February 4, 1988, pp. 8-9.*

Yevgeny (Alexandrovich) Yevtushenko
1933-

(Also transliterated as Evgeni, Evgenii, or Evgeny Evtushenko) Russian poet, novelist, short story writer, dramatist, essayist, scriptwriter, and filmmaker.

The Soviet Union's most publicized contemporary poet, Yevtushenko is probably best known for dramatic readings of his autobiographical verse, in which he incorporates nationalistic and critical views on political, civic, and personal themes. Favoring the primacy of emotion over principles long prescribed by scholars of Russian poetry, Yevtushenko makes use of a lyrical style that many critics have compared to that of early twentieth-century poet Vladimir Mayakovsky for its outraged declamatory tone and condemnation of hyprocrisy and passivity. While Eastern bloc and Western critics often vacillate in their opinions of Yevtushenko's work, in part because of his tendencies to embrace opposing ideologies and to alternately celebrate and censure elements of both civilizations, his poems are often commended for their political significance, optimism, and explosive linguistic characteristics.

Born in Zima, Siberia, Yevtushenko published his first volume of poetry, *Razvedchiki gryadushchego* (1952), while attending Gorky Literary Institute in Moscow. Following the Twentieth Party Congress of 1956, during which Soviet premier Nikita Khrushchev publicly enumerated the crimes of Communist leader Joseph Stalin, Yevtushenko emerged as a prominent spokesman for Russian youth and for the new regime's commitment to more liberal policies. *Stantsiya Zima* (1956; *Winter Station*), a highly acclaimed poem first published in the Soviet journal *Oktiabr* in 1956, is considered among Yevtushenko's most effective early works for its lyrical and colloquial description of his return to Zima, a small junction on the Trans-Siberian railway near Irkutsk. In this work, he attempts to resolve personal doubts as well as moral and political questions raised by Stalin's regime. Yevtushenko's other poetry collections published in Russia during the 1950s include *Tretii sneg: Kniga liriki* (1955), *Shosse entusiastov* (1956), *Obeshchanie* (1957), and *Luk i lira: Stikhi o Gruzii* (1959).

During the late 1950s, Yevtushenko emerged as a leading nationalist proponent of the cold war "thaw" between the Soviet Union and the United States. Granted permission by government authorities to deliver poetry readings in both countries in 1960, Yevtushenko soon became Russia's best-known living poet. While new volumes of his verse, including *Yabloko* (1960), *Nezhnost: Novyii Stikhi* (1962), *Zamlung* (1962), and *Vzmakh ruki* (1962), appeared in the Soviet Union, Yevtushenko's early verse was introduced to English readers through such collections as *Selected Poems* (1962) and *Selected Poetry* (1963). In one of his most controversial poems of this period, "Stalin's Heirs," Yevtushenko describes the reawakening of Stalin following his brief interment in the tomb of Communist leader Vladimir Lenin, implying that Russians should beware the reemergence of Stalinism. Another work to garner international attention at this time was "Babi Yar." The title of this long poem refers to a ravine near Kiev, where historians estimate that between 34,000 and 100,000 Jews were massacred by the Nazis during World War II. Originally published in the periodical *Literaturnaya gazeta,* "Babi Yar" was alternately pro-

© Thomas Victor 1988

claimed and ridiculed by Soviet critics for its accusation that many Russian people harbor anti-Semitic sentiments, a claim which, Yevtushenko asserted, was corroborated by public indifference to erecting a memorial on the site.

The publication in France of *A Precocious Autobiography* (1963), a volume combining Yevtushenko's political views with memoirs of his early youth, was arranged without Soviet permission while he was on a lecture tour. Yevtushenko was reprimanded for his personalized interpretation of Russian history but was permitted to continue publishing, and he again attracted international recognition for his next volume, *Bratskaya GÉS* (1965; *New Works: The Bratsk Station*; also published as *Bratsk Station and Other New Poems*). In this book's title piece, Yevtushenko contrasts the use of slaves to construct the Egyptian pyramids with the willingness of Russian workers to build a hydroelectric complex in Siberia. According to Andrei Sinyavsky, Yevtushenko seeks in this work "to communicate the experience of the modern age and to connect this with the experience of the past, with Russian history." Other collections of Yevtushenko's translated verse from the mid-1960s include *The Poetry of Yevgeny Yevtushenko, 1953-1965* (1965; revised and expanded, 1967, 1969); *Poems* (1966), *The City of Yes and the City of No and Other Poems* (1966), and *Poems Chosen by the Author* (1966).

Yevtushenko's poetry of the early 1970s was collected in several books, including *Flowers and Bullets and Freedom to Kill* (1970) and *Stolen Apples* (1971). The latter volume, a bilingual compilation of Yevtushenko's verse translated by eight acclaimed American poets, contains five sections that form a cycle and comment on such topics as love, travel, and history. In his drama *Pod kozhey Statui Svobody* (1972; *Under the Skin of the Statue of Liberty*), a series of revue sketches set in the United States, Yevtushenko condemns American violence while praising the idealism of the nation's youth. Originally produced by Yuri Lyubimov, a leader in the Soviet avant-garde theater, this play achieved popular success in Russia but was faulted for Yevtushenko's inability to impart his concerns to Western audiences. Alan Brownjohn maintained that the primary interest of Yevtushenko's next collection, *The Face behind the Face* (1979), "lies in the corners illuminated by shafts of self-doubt; and in the poet's zeal to prove that poets and poetry still retain some status, in his world and ours." In *Ivan the Terrible and Ivan the Fool* (1979), Yevtushenko returns to nationalistic concerns to contrast Ivan the Fool, the ill-used but unstoppable working-class folk hero, with Czar Ivan the Terrible, the autocrat who oversaw extensive changes in Russian culture and society during the sixteenth century.

In his later publications, Yevtushenko has gradually moved away from poetry to experiment with various prose forms. *A Dove in Santiago: A Novella in Verse* (1982), which Martin Booth called "a major literary document of life and death," combines blank and free verse to describe the tragic experience of a young art student living in Chile during the presidency of Salvador Allende. Yevtushenko's first novel, *Wild Berries* (1984), ostensibly celebrates Russian philosophy and existence but is similar to an American thriller in its emphasis on action, sex, and exotic locales. Originally published in 1981 in the Soviet periodical *Moskva*, this work features numerous plot shifts, one involving a Soviet search for cassiterite, a tin ore necessary to the advancement of Russian technology and civilization. While faulted by Soviet critics for its emphasis on the miseries of war rather than past military triumphs and for its treatment of Stalin's deportation of the Khulaks in the 1930s, *Wild Berries* was praised by many Western reviewers for Yevtushenko's sincerity of purpose. Susan Jacoby commented: "In American terms, [Yevtushenko] might best be imagined as a hybrid of Walt Whitman and Norman Mailer—with all the extravagant enthusiasms, risk-taking, self-promotion, blundering and talent that might be expected from such a creature."

Yevtushenko's next novel, *Ardabiola* (1984), consists of chapters written in diverse styles, each combining elements from several genres. In this book, Ardabiev, a humanistic Soviet scientist, crosses an insect with a plant to create "Ardabiola," a confection that cures cancer. Ardabiev temporarily sets his work aside to attend his father's funeral, allowing Yevtushenko to satirize Soviet culture and government and to address the influence of American materialism on Russian youth, two of whom attack Ardabiev for his blue jeans, which they believe to be of American manufacture. Although Ardabiev forgets his discovery following the mugging, Ardabiola finally uproots itself, demonstrating, according to John Mellors, "a hard truth: new creations, in art or science, will not go away all that easily—even if their inventors neglect them." *Almost at the End* (1987), a collection of Yevtushenko's recent prose and poetry, established him as a prominent spokesman for premier Mikhail Gorbachev's *glasnost* liberalization campaign. The centerpiece of this collection is "Fuku," a long work first published in the prestigious Soviet magazine *New World* in 1985 in which Yevtushenko uses a cinematic style and combines traditional poetry, free verse, and prose to comment on such characteristic concerns as history, tyranny, and justice.

(See also *CLC*, Vols. 1, 3, 13, 26 and *Contemporary Authors*, Vols. 81-84.)

ANATOLE BROYARD

Wild Berries, Yevgeny Yevtushenko's first novel, is the Soviet equivalent of a potboiler. It consists of action, sex, landscape and elementary discussions of Russian life and literature. The descriptions of landscape are the best part; Mr. Yevtushenko is, after all, a well-known poet. Here and there, he manages a nice vignette or two, but generally the writing and the plotting are slapdash. In fact, it's remarkable that such an experienced poet should be so clumsy even in his first novel.

It's hard to say whether he's careless or disorganized or whether he's attempting to borrow the loose, associational structure of modern Western fiction. Whatever the case may be, it doesn't work. In one chapter, the book leaps from Siberia to Chile to show President Salvador Allende Gossens having his portrait painted. The sole link here seems to be that there are politics everywhere. . . .

Yet there are good moments too. When a young woman gives up her virginity in a playground, the pain she feels derives from the fact that she is lying on a metal toy left behind by the children. The implication that she is leaving behind her own childhood and that this pains her is both eloquently and economically expressed. . . .

Not so persuasive, however, is a beautiful and imperious beekeeper, who sweeps into a camp of young geologists on horseback and takes one of them to her mysterious apiary, where she teaches him how to sing. While her teaching is well described and suggests a poet finding his voice, the episode is so cavalierly and inexplicably introduced that the effect is spoiled.

Wild Berries is good-natured and irresponsible. It begins with the astronaut Yuri Gagarin, who has nothing to do with the plot, simply because he is part of the "atmosphere." There is a mad scientist who mutters in science-fiction jargon about space and immortality. The main thrust of the plot is a search, in Siberia, for cassiterite, a tin ore, and this provides the occasion for shooting rapids in a raft, which we feel we have read before.

Using what he knows, Mr. Yevtushenko allows his young people to bicker about poetry. Maintaining his posture as a nondangerous dissident, he has them complain about the consumerism of the professional classes and discrimination against the proletariat. Perhaps his worst error is a cloying and unconvincing portrait of a saintly hunchback, who asks "When did the earth begin?" and "Where does time go?"

Perhaps the poet in Mr. Yevtushenko lacks the patience that a novel requires—all the ordering of details, development of character and coordination of movement. There's something happy-go-lucky about *Wild Berries,* as if the author were saying, "Here, take this for what it's worth." In the Soviet Union, the publisher tells us, the book sold two and a half million copies when it came out in 1981. Perhaps this is the most significant statement that can be made about it.

Anatole Broyard, in a review of "Wild Berries," in
The New York Times, *June 22, 1984, p. C25.*

Susan Jacoby, "Don't Mention Stalin by Name," in
The New York Times Book Review, *July 15, 1984,*
p. 11.

SUSAN JACOBY

Wild Berries, Mr. Yevtushenko's first novel, has already stirred up the furor in the Soviet Union that invariably accompanies the publication of politically sensitive works. It was originally published in the Soviet journal *Moskva* at the end of 1981, and this American edition is a faithful, deft translation of the Russian text. In a purely literary sense, Mr. Yevtushenko has proven only that he is a much better poet than he is a novelist.

The narrative, which makes room for Chile's former president Salvador Allende, an omniscient Soviet cosmonaut and an assortment of Russian types brought together by a geological expedition in Siberia reads like a cross between the least plausible apparitions in E. L. Doctorow's *Ragtime* and the everything-but-the-kitchen-sink formula of a disaster movie. In a political sense, **Wild Berries** affords a fascinating glimpse of what is and is not possible within the limits of Soviet censorship. When the novel was first published in Moscow—a decision that insured it would be published abroad in translations from the Soviet edition instead of in embarrassing "unofficial" versions—it was received with considerable enthusiasm in the Soviet press. . . .

Wild Berries is, of course, much more elliptical than the poems Mr. Yevtushenko wrote during the relatively relaxed Khrushchev era, but it probably would not be published if it were submitted to Soviet censors today instead of in 1981. In recent months—although the novel's first and only edition has long since been sold out—Mr. Yevtushenko has been sharply attacked in a number of Soviet journals. In the view of Mr. Yevtushenko's critics, his sins include loyalty to the idea of détente, emphasis on the everyday misery of war rather than the glory of Soviet military feats in World War II and, worst of all, a stubborn fixation on the "mistakes" of the Stalin era. . . .

Although *Wild Berries* (which refers to a specific area of Siberia and should have been translated as "Berry Country") does not offer a coherent narrative, it must be said in fairness to Mr. Yevtushenko that he produces some humorous, sparkling and deeply moving passages when he stops trying to be a novelist and reverts to the more condensed, poetic language that is his natural métier. . . .

The most affecting, beautifully written chapter in the book is only seven pages long, and it illustrates the difficulties of a writer trying to speak in his own voice while looking back over his shoulder at the censor. It describes the life of Nikanor Sergeyevich, an old man whose aptitude for painting brought him years in Stalin's camps. "In the thirties, when times took a turn for the worse, an important visitor suddenly noticed a secret mockery painted by the artist in a portrait of Nikanor's that hung at the railroad club." The word "Stalin" is never used, but any Russian reader knows whose portrait would have been responsible for a man's arrest. . . .

In spite of its literary faults, **Wild Berries** amply demonstrates that Mr. Yevtushenko is no hack. In American terms, he might best be imagined as a hybrid of Walt Whitman and Norman Mailer—with all the extravagant enthusiasms, risk-taking, self-promotion, blundering and talent that might be expected from such a creature.

ANTHONY OLCOTT

Loosely centered in a geological expedition to the heart of the *taiga*, **Wild Berries** is Yevgeny Yevtushenko's evocation of modern Siberia. What to American ears implies snow and prison to Russian ones means nature, freedom, and a better life. John Updike has written that Russia is the only country in the world whose people are homesick for it while they're still in it; Yevtushenko's Siberia is what they yearn for, a paradise of fresh berries, pure water, and country maids with bursting blouses who will tup in stacks of new-mown hay (in a thunderstorm, no less), a place where the men are stronger, the women pinker, and life is lived on a grander and more intensely Russian scale.

For the most part *Wild Berries* affects a pleasant artlessness, following the tales of members of the expedition or of people whom they meet, to build up a portrait of a society which enjoys an intrinsic decency. Most of the characters Yevtushenko introduces have faults—too much ambition, an illegitimate child, excessive pride in a poetic talent—but all subscribe to a system of values which Yevtushenko portrays as natural, almost Platonic, as though always capitalized, Womanliness, Work, and Peace. Even the few villains are either a product of poorly balanced virtues . . . or are such vermin as to be beneath contempt. . . .

However, as might be expected of a book which begins with an epilogue and ends with a prologue, this artlessness is far more apparent than real. *Wild Berries* may be his first novel, but Yevtushenko is a 30-year veteran of Soviet publishing who has built a comfortable career by being the slightly dissident exception who proves, approves of, and praises the rule. It is not simply that Yevtushenko is cautious, but that he is sophisticated, adept at improving the look of the Soviet Union by appearing to attack it.

A striking example comes in his account of an aging bureaucrat who through a combination of youth, fear, and ideology once denounced the family of his beloved as kulaks, forcing their deportation. Yevtushenko portrays the man's lifelong remorse convincingly, even giving him an 18th-century moralist's punishment (he is catheterized by a woman doctor who proves to be his daughter, fruit of that love), but vitiates the deed. When millions of such people died in relocation and collectivization, Yevtushenko reduces that act to bureaucratic farce; the displaced family is made merely to trade homes with another, similar family from a nearby village. What in life would have been an act of murderous treachery seems in *Wild Berries* no more than a youthful foible.

More obviously political are the chapters which have no clear connection to *Wild Berries*. . . . In each of these Yevtushenko is on the offensive, showing the West not simply as evil or wrong politically, but as unnatural, as an aberration of nature.

The most political part of Yevtushenko's novel, though, is the part which least appears in it, the prologue with which *Wild Berries* concludes. Here Yevtushenko writes of rocketry pioneer Tsiolkovsky and two "radiant atoms" from the "Galaxy of Immortality"; sent to see whether man will achieve immortality, the atoms see the natural goodness of Tsiolkovsky and Gagarin and conclude that man shall.

What to American readers will seem an innocuous ending must to Soviets have been clearly polemical, for here **Wild Berries** takes issue with a famous Soviet novel of the year before, [Chingiz] Aitmatov's *The Day Lasts Longer Than an Age*. That book too juggled the life stories (and hence Soviet histories) of a small group of people (Kazakhs, in Aitmatov's case) with a didactic science fantasy. . . . [The primary difference] is in the space fantasy; Yevtushenko has men destined inevitably for the stars, if only they cultivate his "natural" values, while in Aitmatov's book Earth is offered advanced civilization, no strings attached, and refuses it, because the leaders of both Washington and Moscow fear the loss of their power.

Aitmatov is no dissident; in fact he is widely praised as the very model of the Soviet writer, in part because he, like Yevtushenko, affirms Soviet society as the best. However, Aitmatov does so on political grounds, after an honest presentation of both the good and bad in that society. Yevtushenko in **Wild Berries** attempts the same assertion subliminally, on sentimental and spuriously natural grounds.

In short, Yevtushenko's book is well-named, for like the half-kilo cones of hand-picked berries old women hawk in the Russian streets in summer, **Wild Berries** is a sweet, slightly sticky bunch of stories which taste so rich and exotic individually that one is tempted to gulp them down by the fistful. Better though to consider each berry by itself, for mixed in among the fruits are lots of little green worms, which can leave quite a nasty taste in the mouth.

> *Anthony Olcott, "Song of a Siberian Homeland," in* Book World—The Washington Post, *July 22, 1984, p. 9.*

ROGER LEWIS

What happens when we enter the house of fiction? *Ardabiola* confronts us with a miscellany of moods. To tell the story of a miracle-plant, Yevtushenko ushers us through chapters decorated in slightly different stylistic shades. Looking back over the plan of the book, we see how we have been strolling through comedy, tragedy, sensationalism, sentiment, fantasy, farce. The deployment of tone is virtuosic. Instead of establishing the level of irony at the outset, the narrator tinkers with the light in which his characters are cast each time they make an entrance. Yevtushenko's house of fiction is a department store of available attitudes.

We are in modern Russia. A mad scientist, his truck full of food and cheap champagne, prowls to find a companion. Ardabiev wants to unveil Ardabiola, a botanic confection which cures cancer. It has been developed by combining the chromosomes of the tse-tse fly with the genes of the fedyunnik (a Russian berry). The inventor hopes his brain-child will make him the person of most use to mankind.

A drug to obliterate carcinomas would certainly be messianic. Ardabiola is first tested out on a rat (an induced tumour recedes) and next on Ardabiev's father. He is cleared of terminal symptoms, too. Just as a celebratory party begins, however, a telegram is received. 'Father dead. Funeral Wednesday. Mama.'

The journey to Khairiuzovsk depicts the slapstick cruelty of life in a Soviet state. Queues, crazed bureaucracy, organised muddle, grey drizzle: the country contains no redeeming gaiety. 'The shortages? Rubbish! A shortage of feeling—that's what it is.' At the airport, Ardabiev is accosted by weary parents who beg him to take their child, Vitya, on an early flight. The

slumbering babe, when awake, is a violent troll. His tantrums prompt the comatose Russians to bestir themselves for he urinates on legs, pulls off wigs, eats soap and breaks other children's toys. . . .

The funeral is performed with industrial honours. The catafalque is erected on the railway tracks at the train-depot and a photographer records the event. The widow poses next to the open coffin ('his hair stirred in the wind as if alive, while he himself was dead') and the parodic wedding-group moves off on a lorry to a parodic wedding-breakfast. Yevtushenko turns his gaze upon the cameraman and makes some points about the mordancy of his craft. Photography is itself funereal: images are frozen, life is stilled. The lens captures a fragment of the soul of those it winks at, and the camera can become an extension of its owner. 'For I'll die too one day, and with me my negatives,' says the melancholy shutter-bug.

It is a relief for Ardabiev to learn that his father died not of cancer but of a trachea blocked by a drinking bout. But relief is short-lived because the hero, returning from a visit to the photographer's dark-room, is knuckledusted and brain-damaged. He starts writing books about the effect of music on the growth of plants and ignores his greatest find. Ardabiola, aggrieved and enlivened by Britten's *Requiem*, uproots and defenestrates itself in protest.

> *Roger Lewis, "Many Mansions," in* New Statesman, *Vol. 108, No. 2785, August 3, 1984, p. 27.*

JOHN MELLORS

Ardabiola is by no means a straightforwardly realistic novel. A young biologist has crossed an insect with a plant. . . . The result is a fruit which appears to cure cancer. Ardabiev calls his discovery 'Ardabiola'. He knows that if a chemical equivalent can be found the world will have a new wonder drug. But Yevtushenko has a cautionary tale to tell. Even in the benevolently ordered society of the Soviet Union there are hooligans, bored teenagers who will stop at nothing to acquire a pair of flared jeans. Ardabiev is mugged and left with a head wound that destroys his memory. Ardabiola is forgotten.

Ardabiev prospers, and is rewarded with a claret-coloured Volga for his dissertation on 'The use of Music in Growing Vegetables'. His wife is uneasy. She says it's a good thing Pushkin's memory had not been knocked out of him, adding that 'you can beat the Pushkin-like qualities out of people . . . with education, lying words, indifference'. The book, then, is an allegory, a fable with a moral. Yevtushenko does not preach. His story is good entertainment, with flashes of humour and a fascinating poet's-eye view of life in the USSR. The dénouement is unashamed fantasy wrapped round a hard truth: new creations, in art or science, will not go away all that easily—even if their inventors neglect them.

> *John Mellors, "Wonder Drug," in* The Listener, *Vol. 112, No. 2872, August 23, 1984, p. 27.*

JOHN BAYLEY

In his latest novel, *The Unbearable Lightness of Being*, Milan Kundera engages in a lively and instructive analysis of the concept of kitsch, and its influence today in literature and in social and political conditioning. He concludes that "the Brotherhood of Man is only possible on a basis of kitsch." Robespierre and Lenin would have dismissed this with impatience and incomprehension, and indeed it is true that kitsch only becomes an insidious force in the public consciousness through the medium of propaganda or advertising, which by definition works with secondhand materials. The first call, the authentic sentiment, whether in art or in revolution, has nothing to do with kitsch, however much it may later be exploited by it. . . .

Kitsch is associated with the weight and responsibilities in our lives, and compulsory socialism has made these false, both in life and in art. So the novelist takes to "lightness of being," to systematic frivolity. Kundera's novel is moving and impressive in its contrast of "lightness" with the weight still surviving in the human heart, the weight of love and fidelity, pity, the awareness of death. Those things are of course part of the official kitsch of Soviet morality, and Kundera's achievement is to release them from that bondage and put them back in the world of privacy and true art. It is highly illuminating to compare his novel with recent examples of Russian fiction, from both inside and outside the Soviet Union, particularly with **Wild Berries,** a first novel by the poet Yevgeny Yevtushenko, which sold more than two and a half million copies in the Soviet Union since its publication in 1981, yet this year came under attack in Soviet literary journals, particularly for its reference to the elimination of the kulaks during the 1930s.

The first thing to be said is that though Yevtushenko has often been cited as the archetypal Soviet literary operator he is probably a decent man, his heart in the right place and all the rest of it. He is a competent poet with a gift of popular appeal—even today the Russians are discriminating about their poets. In **"Zima Junction,"** and still more in **"Babi Yar,"** he has produced poems that are memorable and true, in the soundest Russian tradition. They are not great poems, but in language and feeling they are authentic, as Nekrasov's were in the last century, with an authenticity that comes over even in translation. But his prose is a different matter. The medium he works in here seems so saturated with kitsch, or *poshlost,* with the standard clichés and received ideas and situations from *Soviet Monthly* and other fiction periodicals, that his own personal intelligence and perception can hardly trickle through.

Socialist realism, like the Brotherhood of Man, is only possible on a basis of kitsch. There is no such thing as personal kitsch. True art is always unique and individual. Kitsch is always communal. And in every situation it takes the easy way out, which is also the "caring" way, the compassionate way. It loves the good and rejects evil, but it cannot manage to do this spontaneously, as art inexorably requires. Like many other Soviet authors, Yevtushenko writes from a dangerously naive assumption: if Tolstoy and Dostoevsky can do it, why can't I? If Tolstoy can make a good man utter good words, if Dostoevsky's Ivan Karamazov can still rejoice in the sticky buds of spring, then all we have to do is agree fervently and repeat them in our own way. We rejoice in our pleasure at the sight of happy Soviet kids in the sunshine. Yevtushenko's characters speak of one of their number as "a pure soul," and yes, he does indeed seem to be one, but where does that get us? The most disquieting thing about **Wild Berries** is that each page makes one seriously wonder if honor, kindness, and decency are repulsive in themselves, or only when they are affirmed in this kind of book. Are we so corrupted in the West that we cannot admit and recognize simple virtue when we see it?

No, but the practice of virtue in our society may be disabled by our difficulties and inhibitions about representing it in art. One should not be afraid of kitsch, and it is paralyzing to be too conscious of it. Successful Soviet writers do not suffer from that disability. Or are they, as Kundera takes for granted, two-faced: supporters of the brotherhood of man who really care for nothing but the perks and the roubles? Such a view would seem to be simplistic. But virtue must be paid for in art, and the best currency is humor. Social and political kitsch cannot abide its presence, and yet humor itself suffers from the exclusion and becomes a subversive and anarchic force, a drunken spirit from underground instead of an Ariel moving—as in Sterne and Shakespeare—impartially among vice and virtue, sentiment and cynicism. There is no trace of humor in **Wild Berries,** though there is a quota of joky situations, and a few cautious frivolities about war and sex which might offend the Soviet fathers. But the humor that has been "liberated" in Edward Limonov's "fictional memoir," *It's Me, Eddie,* in Vassily Aksyonov's *The Burn* and *The Island of Crimea,* and in Serge Dovlatov's *The Compromise,* which were published outside the Soviet Union, seems on the other hand excessively conscious of its liberated status. (p. 28)

> *John Bayley, "Kitsch and the Novel," in* The New York Review of Books, *Vol. XXXI, No. 18, November 22, 1984, pp. 28-31.*

JOHN SUTHERLAND

Yevtushenko's face, more cadaverous by the year, stares morosely from the flap of **Wild Berries.** The camera has evidently caught him thinking of his native Taiga, the Siberian tundra which forms the idyllic background to the novel. In fact, the background of **Wild Berries,** which is not the best ordered of narratives, rather usurps the foreground, and for much of its length the novel reads like over-the-top Intourist travel literature, aimed at rehabilitating a region associated in the foreign mind (at least) with exile, sub-zero temperatures and days in the life of Soviet dissidents. A Siberian snow job, one might call it.

The pastoral tones of Yevtushenko's novel, pitched between the buffoonery of peasant comedy and full-blooded romantic lyricism, have not always translated well. Early in the narrative, there is a riverside meeting between a Siberian maiden and a geologist tapping away on the bank. On comes a convenient thunderstorm, and a convenient haystack is nearby. Prior to giving herself to the stranger, the girl dances naked in the downpour and the effects Yevtushenko intends have some difficulty in crossing the linguistic border: 'The storm embraced Ksiuta with its wet, warm arms, showering her with thousands of greedy, rough kisses, blinding her with the white zigzag explosions of uncountable lightning bolts, deafening her with ear-splitting rolls of thunder.' . . . And so, a virgin from a virgin land, she gives herself to the Muscovite, whose child she bears. One can see what's meant here—technology embracing the new frontier, and so on. But as it comes off the page, the rhapsody, like other flights in the novel, is both flat and overwritten. Presumably it rolls with fine mimetic thunder in the original Russian. More successful is the pastoral's Perdita episode, handled with earthy comedy and unflinching sentimentality, in which the horny-handed Commissioner of Berries (Soviet bureaucracy apparently provides for such a post) discovers his long-lost (bastard) daughter, in the person of the macho, surgical-alcohol-swigging doctor who treats him for a kidney stone.

As one of his many book titles proclaims, Yevtushenko is 'of Siberian stock'. But he is also the Soviet Union's most internationally famous writer. **Wild Berries'** meandering narrative allows him a few (immodest) reflections on the making of his own brilliant career, and the cosmopolitan maturity which has sprung from his deep provincial roots. . . . [One] excursion swings to a rock concert by 'the Tails' in Hawaii. As he walks by the shore, after the show, the lead guitarist forgets all the tinsel around him, and remembers 'that white night in Leningrad, when . . . a Russian boy read his poetry, chopping the air with his hand'. The Russian boy is transparently Yevtushenko, whose public readings put him, he thinks, in the same league as the West's pop superstars. . . .

Wild Berries tells how a team of scientists have come into the Taiga, to prospect for 'cassiterite'—a mineral which, one understands, is required for the advancement of Soviet science and civilisation. Under the leadership of Viktor (he of the haystack) an epic battle develops between the men of science and nature, embodied in the Taiga. Viktor is hard and unyielding, but confrontation with the harder forces of Siberia eventually mellows him. . . . The team discover the precious cassiterite only at the peril of their own lives.

Yevtushenko appears to be a novice in fiction. But, as in his poetry, he is masterful at judging how close to the precipice he can go in his social criticism. A novel about post-Revolutionary Siberia has to confront, or timorously evade, the anti-Kulak programme. Yevtushenko gives it three or four pages early in his narrative, implying that the Kulaks mainly died of homesickness when they were transplanted with all humanity into new villages. No mention is made of Stalin. Other digressions criticise contemporary Soviet society. There is routine denunciation of the corrupting effects of jeans, stereos and Marlboros on Russian youth, some satire on the sterility of Moscow literary life, and moderate anger vented at the unfairness of hard-currency shops which tantalisingly display what the native Russian may not buy. The sum total of Yevtushenko's 'criticism', however, is that the Soviet Union hasn't quite got its act together yet. (p. 20)

> *John Sutherland, "Red Stars," in* London Review of Books, *Vol. 6, Nos. 22-23, December 6 to December 19, 1984, pp. 20-1.*

D. KEITH MANO

[*Wild Berries*] sold way over 2.5 million copies *in Russia*. Stuff your nose cone with that payload and puzzle it out. True, Yevtushenko—poet/cultural ambassador/media flash from the JFK era—has always been given more running room than most Russian literati. But this would still seem like an awful lot of tokenism. Maybe it's because Yevtushenko, Siberian born, can't be intimidated. Might as well throw Brer Rabbit back into his briar patch.

No more Western-sounding novel, I reckon, has ever hot-footed it out of Russia. Not just in subject matter, but in prose style—which teeters often between James Dickey at his best and Irving Wallace at his normal worst. Strange, vexed, wondrous thing: less secure about its true environment than lungfish once were: weirder than a "Women of Gulag" pictorial in *Playboy*. There is swivel-gun cinematic plotting . . . , plus cursory, cheap pop-fiction interior monologue. Against this unfortunate aspect of exported capitalism, you have the *taiga*—Siberian evergreen forest. Here Yevtushenko's diction (and people) can be split-rail hard or sweet-dense as fir carpeting. . . . There are, moreover, some inner hints that Yevtushenko adjusted his engine timing for the fast-track American edition. What we've got here, in fact, is stylistic détente.

Yevtushenko does strain too hard: probably because, as a rare peasant-cosmopolitan, he has known too much—left lobe in Zima, right in New York. After all, given the constraint of censorship, his one permissible attitude is a wide, good-hearted, apolitical humanism. Anti-war, pro-life and -love and -*taiga*. The last refuge of oppressed people is sentimentality and vodka. By a Dostoyevskyan standard this plot couldn't be thought either over-complex or over-manipulated—yet coincidence, unlikely parallel event and pat retribution, hyperextend your imagination. Humanism, right and wrong, are lent a managerial power that even God was careful not to assume on earth.

So Kolomeitsev, Yevtushenko's Nietzschean superman, gets humbled. . . . Nothing new here: the string section will play loudly on occasion. It isn't in extremes that Yevtushenko has disc harrow bite. It is in the middle, where his people don't wear their moral designation as if it were some sort of HELLO, I'M GOOD BUT SIMPLE-MINDED lapel sticker. School jive. Fireside conversation. Bureaucratic fishiness. Here Yevtushenko has slid back into a Russian-novel mode: storytelling within the story, poem and song and proverb. Russian fiction is less naturalistic (or expressionistic) than Biblical. It will use parable not, as Jesus did, to instruct, but rather to conceal and diffuse and exaggerate—for even a samovar may overhear.

Chuck all that literary criticism, though. *Wild Berries* is more surprising than an Op-Ed page in *Pravda* would be. Take, for one, the apparently widespread Westernized snob student societies. They read Garcia Márquez and Mark Twain. They speak only English. . . . Yevtushenko will mock this style as elitist and false, yet his own chapter about the Tails (an American rock group in Hawaii) is neither unsympathetic nor ideological. That social observation of this sort, so conversant with America, should get published under official sanction (or shrug) hits me like incoming mail from Peenemünde. (p. 47)

I can get *Novy Mir*, young Krivtsov said, "but there are no subscriptions to the past." Yevtushenko has situated his humanism in memory: personal memory and cultural memory. In Russia, where they chop down, then repaint historical truth like maybe it was a stolen Corvette, this premise alone might be enough to subvert the state. And literature is memory. Throughout *Wild Berries* that Russian passion for book and poem is radiant as arc lighting. You begin to realize—by the flicker of yet one more MTV video—just how Promethean an intellectual force Russia, freed, might be. These people think. They *read*. I understand now why Solzhenitsyn has found our civilization callow. We simply bore him. It's enough to make an American novelist consider living in the USSR. If you would *live* there. (pp. 47-8)

> *D. Keith Mano, "Fairest Socialism," in* National Review, *New York, Vol. XXXVI, December 14, 1984, pp. 47-8.*

JOHN UPDIKE

At a student party in [Yuri Trifonov's] *The House on the Embankment,* one guest is

> a poet who had been deafening people at student parties with his crashingly metallic verses—in those days, for some reason, they were regarded as highly musical. . . . Nowadays, thirty years later, the poet is still grinding out his brassy verse, but no one any longer thinks it musical—just tinny.

It is a compliment, of sorts, to Yevgeny Yevtushenko's fame and durability that a Westerner, without presuming to judge what verse sounds brassy in Russian, thinks first of him in relation to this unkind allusion. Born in 1933 and still going strong, Yevtushenko has managed to steer a daredevil course amid the perils of being a poet, a crowd-pleaser, a sometime protester, a traveling emblem of Russian culture, and lately a movie director and actor—all this within the Soviet system. Too much within it for some former Western admirers, impatient of the intricacies of survival under a government that has insisted since Lenin on supervising the arts. . . . The government has continued to allow Yevtushenko access to print and audiences because, my guess is, for all his rakish and rebellious tendencies, he is a sincere patriot and genuinely at home in the poster-bright, semi-abstract realm of global aspiration wherein the slogans of the Revolution make some sense. Gone are the days, in Russia and the West alike, when he and Andrei Voznesensky were glamour boys, bringing to stadiums and auditoriums on both sides of the Iron Curtain word of the new possibilities stirring in "the thaw." But neither poet has been silenced in the airless decades since. . . . [Yevtushenko's *Wild Berries*] is now published here, in a typeface that looks muddy and a sexy pastel dust jacket showing two haystacks.

Yevtushenko, as a fiction writer, woefully lacks Trifonov's quality of patient truth—of calmly accruing detail, of psychologies permitted to find their own definition in inconsequential and contradictory movements. In *Wild Berries,* the author is ostentatiously in charge, putting an epilogue first and a prologue last and, in between, pouring on importance from an unctuous overview, staging symposia and meaty dialogues in the Siberian taiga, importing significance-laden scenes from as far away as Hawaii and Chile. As a poet, Yevtushenko has developed an irritating trick of self-echo, as if repeating things rendered them profound. *Wild Berries* begins, for example, with a hail of berries, as symbols of succulence, Siberian freedom, and female charms. A seduced and spurned woman ponders, "He's picked all my berries, and now he's looking for new berry patches;" another, also seduced and spurned woman sports "red bilberry nipples" and "dark, berrylike birthmarks" "sprinkled" on her "soft but blinding white" skin; and still another, while being seduced preliminary to being abandoned, has a full basket of berries spilled over her (of course) "naked breasts." Nor are berries the only foodstuff subject to over-utilization; mushrooms, too, come in for a workout. A proposal of marriage is stimulated by the discovery of a "solid white mushroom" that the lady cuts off neatly, "leaving the root in the ground;" a few pages later, the children of this union are seen as "sturdy as white mushrooms;" a few chapters on, an old mushroomer extolls the earthy virtue of his speciality and, when his extolling day is done, dreams of "some extraordinary forest, where giant mushrooms grew taller than a man." His dreamwork leaving no symbol unturned, he cuts a gigantic one down so he can take it "to Hiroshima and show all mankind, to make them ashamed of that other, terrifying mushroom, invented by man." (p. 115)

[Since] Yevtushenko was born and bred in Siberia, and his father was a geologist, some authenticity leaches through his nobly glowing intention to write a panoramic novel of ideas. The stylized characters (hard-driving, out-of-touch-with-himself Kolomeitsev, the leader of the expedition; young, impressionable Seryozha; humpbacked, tenderhearted, highly mechanical Kesha; all-wise, often silent Burshtein; fawning, villainous Sitechkin; and many others, not to mention the in-

terchangeably delicious, berry-breasted young females who pop up in the forest like, well, mushrooms) and the stilted conversations . . . do not totally smother the author's joy in the space and sweet wildness of Siberia. His willingness to entertain basic questions is awkwardly allied with his coarsely imagined tale of adventure and seduction. . . . In the absence of a restraining verisimilitude, the tale branches into such unusual familial scenes as that of a onetime seducer, now grown obese and decrepit, being given a prostate examination by a forty-three-year-old doctor who is, her "malachite eyes" tell him, his long-lost illegitimate daughter. . . . The scenes involving Americans, though they show the superficial knowingness of a world traveller, have a patent falsity, a benign corniness, that serves as an index to the falsity of *Wild Berries* throughout: the book is a pastiche, an assemblage of outsides and signifiers with no real insides or unwilled significance. Yevtushenko's inner self, glimpsable in *A Precocious Autobiography* and such early poems as **"Zima Junction,"** figures here only in the brash naïveté of the novel's ambition.

In Trifonov's novellas, the numerous characters fall into a consistent pattern. There is the generation of the aged, who were exposed to the heat and excitement of the Revolution and still feel it. There is that of the young, the punks and softies, who have felt only the heat of the West and its corrupting consumerism. And there is the middle generation, which fought and endured the Second World War; its members lack their parents' political zeal yet are nagged, unlike their children, by a collective conscience, by the suspicion that the blessings of peace and relative prosperity . . . are not enough, and fall short of some ideal. . . . Yevtushenko is now over fifty and, however young at heart, belongs to the middle generation. A sophisticated and restive spirit, frequently at odds with the Soviet establishment and a staunch protester against the anti-Semitism that is one of Russian ethnocentricity's uglier aspects, he is no Party-liner; but in his role as bard, and now as novelist, he comes up with Socialism's blandest pieties. . . . *Wild Berries,* set in the scarcely tamed spaces of the Soviet hinterland, should be a comfortable, rollicking book; but instead it is a book with a bad conscience, by a writer who wants to feel more than he does, and one that, whenever it might develop some natural momentum out of its own low impulses, is slowed to a halt by another injection of anxious highmindedness. (pp. 116-18)

John Updike, "Back in the U.S.S.R.," in The New Yorker, *Vol. LXI, No. 8, April 15, 1985, pp. 110-26.*

RONALD HINGLEY

[*Ardabiola* is] a short, entertaining novel. It is set in the Soviet Union, has excellent local color and may well appeal to American readers wishing to sample modern Muscovy from a safe distance. The delights of traveling in a packed Moscow tram, the thrills of a Siberian wake and even the joys of changing a naughty Soviet infant's diaper in midair halfway between the two—such topics are adroitly handled. Themes include research into the effect of music on plant growth, muggings by Soviet skinheads with bicycle chains, orgies of vodka swilling, and ecological lamentations. It follows that no one is likely, after reading this book, to feel that the Soviet Union has been entirely left behind by 20th-century progress. . . .

[*Ardabiola*] reminds one that in a few brief eras there has been room for literature that does not always "say yes to the future," though Soviet governments have ordinarily demanded that affirmation. The early 60's were such a time, when Vassily

Aksyonov and other modish authors were developing their feeble echoes of such writers as Jack Kerouac. *Ardabiola*'s science-fiction flavor is also in an older Soviet tradition of fantasy, which flourished in the 1920's with Mikhail Bulgakov's *Fatal Eggs* and other feats of imaginative acrobatics. But the world evoked in *Ardabiola* is very downbeat, squalid and dispirited. The book comes translated from the Russian . . . , but the publisher nowhere indicates in what form it might have appeared in the Soviet Union. This reticence is tediously characteristic of translations of contemporary Russian work; it makes it impossible to judge the worth of the English version.

Cancer Ward, Aleksandr Solzhenitsyn's long novel on a similar subject, has been interpreted as a satire depicting the figurative carcinogens that have infected Soviet society as a whole. Mr. Solzhenitsyn suggested—as, indeed, Boris Pasternak did—that the dreaded scourge flourishes with special exuberance in the demoralized atmosphere that many believe is the most striking feature of Soviet life. But such interpretations bounce straight off Mr. Yevtushenko's tale, even though he does allow his hero to suggest that fatigue and melancholy may be factors predisposing "a body with weak psychological defences" to develop cancer.

These considerations remind us of Mr. Yevtushenko's special, almost unique status as a writer long privileged to commute between the Soviet Union and the West and even to bring out works here, including his autobiography, that have not been issued there. He has skillfully maintained this hemisphere-straddling posture for many years.

On the one hand, his publications and many poetry recitals in the West have been spicy enough to titillate the jaded capitalist palate, especially as he is a talented showman whose spirited performances on the campus of Loyola University in New Orleans and at Oxford happen to be vivid in my own memory. On the other hand, there is a point beyond which Mr. Yevtushenko probably does not wish to go in flouting Soviet convention—beyond which, indeed, he presumably could not expect to go without losing his license to flit to and fro.

In contrast with profounder probers of the Soviet psyche, Mr. Yevtushenko presents a story pure and simple, apart from one or two points where I did seem to detect a minor political innuendo. His book certainly can be read as an indictment of the dreariness of Soviet life. But equally certainly, it wasn't written with that in mind as a major theme.

Ardabiola is curiously humorless for so sprightly a piece of fantasy, but it will pass an hour or two pleasantly enough. No way will it set the Hudson on fire.

> Ronald Hingley, "Music, Muggings and a Cure for Cancer," in The New York Times Book Review, June 23, 1985, p. 13.

R. Z. SHEPPARD

How does Yevgeny Yevtushenko spell relief? G-L-A-S-N-O-S-T. Soviet Leader Mikhail Gorbachev's campaign of "openness" has given him another opportunity to star in his most celebrated role. Since he first packed them in at Mayakovsky Square during the early days of Khrushchev, the dramatic Siberian has been known internationally as the thaw poet. Less privileged Soviet writers know him for his adaptability on thin ice.

Almost at the End demonstrates why. A collection of prose and poetry, the book is nicely timed with the reappearance of Yev-

tushenko, 53, as a prominent spokesman for Gorbachev's liberalization campaign. The new work is theatrical but tame. The targets are either old monsters or the class of unreconstructed bureaucrats whom the new regime has pledged to replace. The daring urgency of earlier poems, such as **"The Heirs of Stalin"** and **"Babi Yar,"** has given way to all-purpose indictments of totalitarianism and effusions of universality. "I would like to be born in every country, / have a passport for them all" is how he begins.

The sentiment is generously larded throughout the collection, although, in fairness, Yevtushenko's verse is more effective in recital. At his best, he is a performance artist whose readings enchant audiences who may not understand what he is saying. He seduces them not with the message but with the medium, the Russian language, with its soft buzzings and throaty sighs.

The centerpiece of the volume is **"Fuku,"** an 87-page autobiographical oddyssey that combines verse and narrative. The title is attributed to an African word used by Latin-American peasants to describe con men and exploiters. Yevtushenko has a little list, starting with Christopher Columbus, whom he evokes as a gold-hungry conquistador and an impatient actor on the set of a television mini-series ("'When will this all end?!' grumbled Columbus, feeling his face to see if his gray beard had come unglued. 'Somebody, bring me a gin and tonic . . .'"). . . .

Almost at the End has a way of passing smoothly through the ideological looking glass. What seems to be the cult of personality on one side appears as celebrity on the other. Perhaps even legend:

> I was not on the stage,
> I was the stage in the blood of my epoch,
> in the vomit of this age,
> and everything in my life
> which seemed to you not my blood,
> but just the thirst for fame,
> I do not doubt
> someday you'll call heroic deeds.

This sort of grandstanding must surely offend writers who have suffered physical and mental pain under the Soviet system while Yevtushenko flourished. But that is an old, sad story of envies, misunderstandings and compromises that the author does not confront. Rather he defends his style on the justifiable grounds that poetry springs from rude experience and common speech. . . .

Unfortunately, a good deal of it is overcooked.

> R. Z. Sheppard, "Hot 'Barracko' from Zima Junction," in Time, New York, Vol. 129, No. 21, May 25, 1987, p. 65.

S. FREDERICK STARR

Years ago Alexander Tvardovsky, editor of the prestigious Moscow journal *Novyi Mir,* told a young Yevgeny Yevtushenko "You are able to seize enemy territory but you can't consolidate your position there." It was a stunning insight, true both for the poet and for Yevtushenko's generation as a whole.

The post-Stalin "thaw" was a youth movement. Seeking to renew a sense of freshness in life, it idolized its chief poets, Yevtushenko and his gifted contemporary, Andrei Voznesensky. . . . As the poets thundered against decades of Stalinist cant many young Soviets thought their country had changed forever. But it had not. True, the rising generation had gained a beachhead, but Stalinists still ruled the land. By the mid-1980s it was clear that the new people were stranded in alien territory. They resigned themselves to waiting. (p. 3)

The late English critic Max Hayward characterized both [Yevtushenko and Voznesensky] as "civic" poets. In their willingness to confront the great issues of the day they stand in the great tradition that links such apparent opposites as the populist Nekrasov and the futurist Mayakovsky. Like Nekrasov, they have often stood in opposition to official policies, but like Mayakovsky they rebelled not so much in the name of some new ideology as of the free personality as such. With great *élan* they reclaimed an authentic "I" from the grips of a leaden and brutal "we." Yevtushenko's poetic tools include a rich, even facile, gift for improvisation. Voznesensky relies on a virtuoso's sense of sound, alliteration, and metaphor. By sharply different means, they both put forward the subversive notion that the solo individual could be the measure of all things Soviet. In the process, they achieved a degree of visibility and notoriety known in the West only to rock stars.

This offended many Western writers and more than a few Russians.... The banal nationalism of several Yevtushenko poems of the 1970s diminished his stature in the eyes of his earlier admirers. What had once seemed revolutionary in Moscow now appeared as mere opportunism and narcissism.... Both poets were accused of being social lion hunters in the West (a charge to which their list of influential friends lent credence) and of abandoning their own muse. (pp. 3-4)

[In *Almost at the End,* Yevtushenko is tough] on himself, characterizing his former *persona* as a "gigantic stage prop." "I grew too proud, too cocky for my own good," he writes in his recent **"Fuku,"** "I became ... impossibly vain." True, even this confession has some of the old narcissism that Yevtushenko borrowed so easily from his charismatic predecessor, Mayakovsky. But when he speaks of "coming late to my own self," when he prays in **"My Universities"** to "help me to be my real self," it seems genuine. "I know you'll say—where's the wholeness?" he tells his readers. In the best of these new poems the wholeness is there.

The fact is, now these singers of youth are no longer young, and know it....

[Yevtushenko] is consumed by thoughts of death. At times, as in his vain and lugubrious **"Come to My Merry Grave,"** this concern seems to be yet another grab for attention, a pose. But when, in his moving lyric **"When the Clover Field Stirs,"** he speaks of "no feeling of life without a feeling of death" one senses a Yevtushenko made more wise by a sense of his own limits....

Everyone has his critics, and neither Voznesensky nor Yevtushenko is an exception.... [The] cosmopolitan and specifically Western aura that both exude is a direct challenge to the Great Russian chauvinism that teems just under the surface of Soviet life. We forget that along with the reform-minded "dissidents" of the 1970s were others who longed for the good old days of Stalinism. Today, a milder Russophilia is evident in the elevation to national prominence of the Siberian novelist Valentin Rasputin and the literary scholar Dmitri Likhachev.... [When] Yevtushenko writes of "The Iron Curtain, unhappily squeaking her rusty brains," it can only provoke Moscow's neoisolationists.

However tempting, it is pointless to prowl about in the works of poets for keys to the evolution of their society as a whole. The U.S.S.R. is far too complex for such simplistic tricks. What is worth noting, however, is that these two Soviet poets, whose early works were narrowly proscribed by time, place, and circumstances, are now preoccupied with universal themes. Granting the vast differences between the art and temperament of this pair of gifted sojourners, their common evolution is cause for hope.... Whenever a young Russian journeys the world and his own national past by reading Yevtushenko's rambling but hard-hitting soliloquy **"Fuku,"** we are all reminded that these large-scale Russian artists have bridged gulfs that even our best negotiators still scan with trepidation. (p. 4)

S. Frederick Starr, "Voznesensky and Yevtushenko: Older, Bolder and Wiser," in Book World—The Washington Post, *June 14, 1987, pp. 3-4.*

MARIA CARLSON

Miss [Irina] Ratushinskaya, a native of Odessa, was sentenced on March 5, 1983, to seven years' hard labor plus five years in internal exile for anti-Soviet "agitation and propaganda." Her crime consisted of being involved in the Soviet human rights movement and writing and disseminating her poetry in carbon copies, called *samizdat*. On the very eve of the Reykjavik summit between President Reagan and the Soviet leader, Mikhail Gorbachev, after serving three years of her sentence, she was unexpectedly released from prison....

The poems in *Beyond the Limit* are proof of Miss Ratushinskaya's blood tie to the lyrical tradition of Russian poetry. She is heir to the line that stems from Pushkin and is represented in the 20th century by Anna Akhmatova, Osip Mandelstam, Boris Pasternak and Marina Tsvetayeva.... Using the potent imagery of cold, earth and execution, Miss Ratushinskaya finds beauty in frost on the prison window and transforms the "violence of prism-ice" into a "holiday" and a "gift." ...

While Miss Ratushinskaya belongs to the Russian lyrical tradition, Mr. Yevtushenko stands in the expansive tradition of Russian declamatory verse; his poems are obviously kin to the exuberant, socially engaged poems of Vladimir Mayakovsky. In his occasional lyrical moments, Mr. Yevtushenko more closely resembles Sergei Esenin. Conservative in technique and language, straightforward, accessible, his poems address topical matters; they tend toward editorializing, polemics and publicity.

Almost at the End includes Mr. Yevtushenko's last major work, **"Fuku,"** first published in the prestigious Soviet literary journal *New World* in September 1985. This innovative work mixes styles and genres and juxtaposes traditional poetry, free verse and prose. **"Fuku"** reflects Mr. Yevtushenko's recent foray into film making. It is fast-paced and cinematographic, and its frequent changes of scene and genre are well suited to the short attention span of the modern reader. The new volume also includes several shorter pieces. It begins with **"I Would Like,"** a bold, vital poem that expresses Mr. Yevtushenko's identification with all mankind, and closes with a series of shorter poems devoted to his usual themes: the poet's vocation, poetry as communication of truth, love. Some of the poems (for example, **"Momma and the Neutron Bomb"**) address official Soviet themes: peace, friendship of peoples, solidarity with the oppressed third world. In such poems Mr. Yevtushenko unfortunately borders on the tendentious and maudlin ("He who takes up the atomic sword will perish by the same!").

Russian poetry, particularly lyrical poetry, is difficult to translate well into English. Pushkin's friend, the poet Vasily Zhukovsky, once observed that the translator should be not an enemy, but a rival whose goal is to equal or surpass the quality of the original. The highly inflected, compact, yet flexible Russian language, however, challenges the translator to make it sound natural and uncontrived. . . .

The very straightforwardness of Mr. Yevtushenko's style makes his brash, steely poetry easier to translate than Miss Ratushinskaya's deceptively simple constructs of "prism-ice." His striking metaphors and startling comparisons, with their unexpected flashes of humor, are just as effective in the bold bluntness of English as in Russian. This translation [of *Almost at the End*] . . . is very readable. Mr. Yevtushenko's cosmopolitanism and universalism, his wider experience, his opportunity to travel—all the advantages the Soviet Writers' Union can confer—make his poetry more accessible to American readers.

He deals with many of the same themes as Miss Ratushinskaya, but from the other side of the prison fence, so to speak. He speaks boldly, even arrogantly, of victims, history, memory, tyranny and justice: "If you forget the victims of yesterday's sorrow / you could become a victim of tomorrow," he writes in **"Fuku."** He speaks in generalities; his editorializing tone reveals him to be a committed observer, but not a participant. He has arrived "almost at the end," but has not gone "beyond the limit." He lacks the spirituality, subtlety of vision and clear inner focus that Miss Ratushinskaya has developed by overcoming the obstacles on her life's path. She sifts the pieces of the Russian experience, while he looks outward to the universe at large. She is an intimate poet, a person-to-person, friend-to-friend, wife-to-husband poet; he speaks of the fates of peoples and nations.

Between them Mr. Yevtushenko and Miss Ratushinskaya offer Americans insights into the Russian mind, official and dissident, arrogant and pious, public and private. They force us to make value judgments about relationships among nations and about the torments and victories of the human soul. The poems of these two very different poets represent the enormous range and richness of the Russian creative spirit, which we are invited to experience and share.

> *Maria Carlson, "Victims of Yesterday and Tomorrow," in* The New York Times Book Review, *June 28, 1987, p. 12.*

CAROL RUMENS

The centre-piece of Yevtushenko's new collection [*Almost at the End*] is a poetry-and-prose extravaganza entitled **"Fuku."** Beginning with **"Winter Station"** in 1956, Yevtushenko has often dared to criticise Stalinism, but here the attack is more full-frontal, as when he writes of Beria '. . . there are names on which history itself puts a *fuku* after their death so they cease to be names.'

Declamatory as Mayakovsky, and similarly constructing his verse-line in steps, Yevtushenko seems more than ever to be trying to embrace the world in a shaggy, shapeless, poetic bear-hug. When he says 'I would like to be born / in every country / have a passport for them all,' one feels that this is not merely a poetic stance. His love-hate affair with America is a constant theme. . . .

Beneath the noisy oratory, the black jokes and the expletives, a sadder mood than usual seems to lurk ('Life gets broken / into hundreds of lifelets / that exhaust / and execute me') and finally one can't help feeling that the slum-boy from Siberia turned jet-setting famous poet is rather a tragic figure, forced by circumstances to carry burdens of ideological responsibility.

> *Carol Rumens, "All-Embracing Bear Hug," in* The Observer, *August 16, 1987, p. 22.*

Appendix

The following is a listing of all sources used in Volume 51 of *Contemporary Literary Criticism*. Included in this list are all copyright and reprint rights and acknowledgments for those essays for which permission was obtained. Every effort has been made to trace copyright, but if ommisions have been made, please let us know.

THE EXCERPTS IN CLC, VOLUME 51, WERE REPRINTED FROM THE FOLLOWING PERIODICALS:

America, v. 143, August 23, 1980 for a review of "Real Presence" by Thomas M. Gannon; v. 154, May 10, 1986 for "Two Fables" by Richard A Blake. © 1980, 1986. All rights reserved. Both reprinted with permission of the respective authors.

The American Book Review, v. 3, September-October, 1981; v. 4, September-October, 1982; v. 6, May-June, 1984. © 1981, 1982, 1984 by *The American Book Review.* All reprinted by permission of the publisher.

American Notes & Queries, v. XIII, June, 1975. Reprinted by permission of the University Press of Kentucky.

The American Poetry Review, v. 6, July-August, 1977 for a review of "Open Doorways" by Stanley Plumly. Copyright © 1977 by World Poetry, Inc. Reprinted by permission of the author.

The Antioch Review, v. XVII, March, 1957. Copyright © 1957, renewed 1985, by the Antioch Review Inc. Reprinted by permission of the Editors.

The Armchair Detective, v. 16, Winter, 1983. Copyright © 1983 by *The Armchair Detective.* Reprinted by permission of the publisher.

The Atlantic Bookshelf, a section of *The Atlantic Monthly,* v. 188, August, 1951 for a review of "Loneliest Girl in the World" by Harvey Breit. Copyright 1951, renewed 1979, by the Atlantic Monthly Company, Boston MA. Reprinted by permission of the Literary Estate of Harvey Breit.

The Atlantic Monthly, v. 222, November, 1968 for "On Misunderstanding Student Rebels" by Martin Duberman; v. 249, May, 1982 for "Poet in Training" by Katha Pollitt; v. 260, December, 1987 for "New York in the Eighties" by Nicholas Lemann. Copyright 1968, 1982, 1987 by The Atlantic Monthly Company, Boston, MA. All reprinted by permission of the respective authors./ v. 254, August, 1984 for "An Obscure Life" by Phyllis Rose. Copyright © 1984 by Phyllis Rose. Reprinted by permission of Georges Borchardt, Inc. and the author.

Australian Book Review, v. 8, December, 1968 & January, 1969; v. 8, February, 1969; v. 9, July, 1970.

Australian Literary Studies, v. 9, October, 1979 for "A. D. Hope and the Poetry of Allusion" by Lyndy Abraham. Reprinted by permission of the publisher and the author.

The Australian Quarterly, v. XXXVI, March, 1964 for "The Poetry of A. D. Hope" by G. A. Wilkes. Copyright by the author. Reprinted by permission of the author.

Belles Lettres: A Review of Books by Women, v. 3, January- February, 1988. Reprinted by permission of the publisher.

Best Sellers, v. 44, February, 1985. Copyright © 1985 Helen Dwight Reid Educational Foundation. Reprinted by permission of the publisher.

The Bloomsbury Review, v. 6, June, 1986. Copyright © by Owaissa Communications Company, Inc. 1986. Reprinted by permission of the publisher.

Book Week—The Sunday Herald Tribune, September 19, 1965. © 1965, *The Washington Post.* Reprinted by permission of the publisher.

Book World—Chicago Tribune, October 24, 1971 for "Just Like a Perfect Martini" by J. R. Frakes. © 1971 Postrib Corp. Reprinted by courtesy of the *The Washington Post* and the author.

Book World—The Washington Post, June 15, 1980; December 21, 1980; May 3, 1981; April 18, 1982; February 13, 1983; July 22, 1984; August 5, 1984; November 18, 1984; April 14, 1985; May 19, 1985; September 15, 1985; February 16, 1986; January 25, 1987; May 24, 1987; June 7, 1987; June 14, 1987; June 28, 1987; July 12, 1987; August 2, 1987; October 25, 1987. © 1980, 1981, 1982, 1983, 1984, 1985, 1986, 1987, *The Washington Post.* All reprinted by permission of the publisher.

Booklist, v. 81, September 15, 1984; v. 83, January 1, 1987. Copyright © 1984, 1987 by the American Library Association. Both reprinted by permission of the publisher.

The Bookman, London, v. LXVIII, September, 1925; v. LXXI, December, 1926.

The Bookman, New York, v. LXXIV, September, 1931.

Books, England, n. 5, August, 1987. © Gradegate Ltd. 1987. Reprinted by permission of the publisher.

Books, New York, July 30, 1961. © 1961 I.H.T. Corporation. Reprinted by permission of the publisher.

Books Abroad, v. 46, Summer, 1972; v. 50, Autumn, 1976. Copyright 1972, 1976 by the University of Oklahoma Press. Both reprinted by permission of the publisher.

Books and Bookmen, n. 359, September, 1985 for "The Freedom of the Spirit" by Jane Gardam. © copyright the author 1985. Reprinted by permission of the author.

Books in Canada, v. 12, February, 1983 for "Past Imperfect" by Barbara Novak; v. 13, December, 1984 for "On the Brink" by Lucille King-Edwards; v. 14, June-July, 1985 for a review of "Fables of Brunswick Avenue" by Judy Margolis; v. 14, December, 1985 for a review of "Ask Again" by Peter Sanger; v. 16, July, 1987 for "Missed Connections" by Tom Marshall; v. 16, August- September, 1987 for "Heart of the City" by Kenneth McGoogan. All reprinted by permission of the respective authors.

Boston Review, v. X, September, 1985 for a review of "Fortune's Daughter" by Patricia Meyer Spacks; v. XII, October, 1987 for a review of "Illumination Night" by Alexandra Johnson; v. XIII, February, 1988 for a review of "Tending to Virginia" by Daniel Max. Copyright © 1985, 1987, 1988 by the Boston Critic, Inc. All reprinted by permission of the respective authors.

British Book News, August, 1985; November, 1986. © *British Book News,* 1985, 1986. Both courtesy of *British Book News.*

Callaloo, v. 7, Winter, 1984 for "In-Between" by Steven Weisenburger. Copyright © 1984 by Charles H. Rowell. All rights reserved. Reprinted by permission of the author.

The Canadian Forum, v. XXXIX, September, 1959; v. XLVII, November, 1967; v. LIX, June-July, 1979; v. LXIV, January, 1985.

Canadian Literature, n. 1, Summer, 1959./ n. 59, Winter, 1974 for "George Johnston" by D. G. Jones; n. 112, Spring, 1987 for "Memory & Words" by Michael Helm. Both reprinted by permission of the respective authors./ n. 35, Winter, 1968; n. 48, Spring, 1971. Both reprinted by courtesy of the publisher.

Chicago Sunday Tribune Magazine of Books, April 11, 1954 for "Fearing's New Delight for the Hardened Thriller Fan" by Milton Crane. Copyright 1954, renewed 1982 by *Chicago Tribune.* Reprinted by permission of the Literary Estate of Milton Crane./ June 17, 1962. Used with permission of the publisher./ March 19, 1950. Copyright 1950, renewed 1978 by *Chicago Tribune.* Used with permission of the publisher.

Choice, v. 12, June, 1975; v. 19, October, 1981; v. 21, October, 1983; v. 22, March, 1985. Copyright © 1975, 1981, 1983, 1985 by American Library Association. All reprinted by permission of the publisher.

The Chowder Review, n. 9, 1977. Copyright 1977. Reprinted by permission of the publisher.

The Christian Century, v. LXIV, January 1, 1947.

Chronicles of Culture, v. 9, July, 1985. Copyright © 1985 by The Rockford Institute. All rights reserved. Reprinted by permission of the publisher.

CLA Journal, v. XXII, December, 1978. Copyright, 1978 by The College Language Association. Used by permission of The College Language Association.

Commentary, v. 80, September, 1985 for "Democrat" by Larry D. Nachman. Copyright © 1985 by the American Jewish Committee. All rights reserved. Reprinted by permission of the publisher and the author.

Commonweal, v. XXXIX, February 11, 1944; v. LIX, November 6, 1953. Copyright 1944, 1953 Commonweal Publishing Co., Inc. Both reprinted by permission of Commonweal Foundation./ v. LXIII, March 16, 1956; v. LXXXIV, June 17, 1966; v. CIII, December 13, 1976. Copyright © 1956, 1966, 1976 Commonweal Publishing Co., Inc. All reprinted by permission of Commonweal Foundation./ v. CXIV, October 9, 1987. Copyright © 1987 Commonweal Foundation. Reprinted by permission of Commonweal Foundation.

Contemporary Poetry, v. IV, 1982 for "The Sounds and Silences of Lisel Mueller's 'Private Life' " by Ann Louise Hentz. © Contemporary Poetry, Inc., 1982. Reprinted by permission of the author.

Contemporary Review, v. 216, January, 1970. © 1970 Contemporary Review Co. Ltd. Reprinted by permission of the publisher.

The Critic, Chicago, v. 39, September, 1980. © *The Critic* 1980. Reprinted with the permission of the Thomas More Association, Chicago, IL.

Daily News, New York, July 16, 1982; June 21, 1984. © 1982, 1984 New York News Inc. Both reprinted with permission.

Dalhousie Review, v. 40, Summer, 1960 for a review of "The Cruising Auk" by Ian Sowton. Reprinted by permission of the publisher and the author.

Delta, France, n. 20, February, 1985. Reprinted by permission of the publisher.

Detroit Free Press, March 13, 1988. Reprinted by permission of the publisher.

Drama, London, n. 128, Spring, 1978. Reprinted by permission of the British Theatre Association.

Encounter, v. LVIII & v. LIX, June-July, 1982. © 1982 by Encounter Ltd. Reprinted by permission of the publisher.

Essays in Arts and Sciences, v. XII, May, 1983 for "Chinua Achebe: Voice of Africa" by Eugene P. A. Schleh. Copyright © 1983 by the University of New Haven. Reprinted by permission of the publisher and the author.

fiction international, n. 2, 1984. Copyright © 1984 by the Editors. Reprinted by permission of the publisher.

The Fiddlehead, n. 70, Winter, 1967 for a review of "Home Free" by Dorothy Livesay; n. 147, Spring, 1986 for "The Miracle of Everyday Life" by Marianne Micros. Copyright by the respective authors. Both reprinted by permission of the respective authors.

Frontiers: A Journal of Women Studies, v. IX, 1987. © copyright 1987, by the Frontiers Editorial Collective. Reprinted by permission of the publisher.

The Georgia Review, v. XLI, Spring, 1987 for "The Whirlpool of Image and Narrative Flow" by Peter Stitt. Copyright, 1987, by the University of Georgia. Reprinted by permission of the publisher and the author.

Grand Street, v. 1, Spring, 1982 for "Sylvia Plath and Her Journals" by Ted Hughes. Copyright © 1982 by Grand Street Publications, Inc. All rights reserved. Reprinted by permission of the publisher and Olywn Hughes.

Harper's, v. 266, March, 1983. Copyright © 1983 by *Harper's Magazine.* All rights reserved. Reprinted by special permission.

The Hollins Critic, v. XIX, June, 1982. Copyright 1982 by Hollins College. Reprinted by permission of the publisher.

The Hudson Review, v. XVII, Autumn, 1964; v. XXVI, Winter, 1973-74; v. XXXI, Winter, 1978-79; v. XXXIV, Autumn, 1981. Copyright © 1964, 1973, 1978, 1981 by The Hudson Review, Inc. All reprinted by permission of the publisher.

The Humanist, v. 45, March-April, 1985. Copyright 1985 by the American Humanist Association. Reprinted by permission of the publisher.

The International Fiction Review, v. 11, Summer, 1984. © copyright International Fiction Association. Reprinted by permission of the publisher.

Irish Literary Supplement, v. 6, Spring, 1987. Copyright © 1987, *Irish Literary Supplement.* Reprinted by permission of the publisher.

The Journal of Aesthetics and Art Criticism, v. XXXIII, Winter, 1974. Copyright © 1974 by The American Society for Aesthetics. Reprinted by permission of the publisher.

Journal of Canadian Poetry: The Poetry Review, n.s. v. 1, 1986 for a review of "Ask Again" by P. K. Page. Copyright © by the author and Borealis Press Limited 1987. Reprinted by permission of the author.

Journal of Commonwealth Literature, n. 3, 1967 for "The Poetry of A. D. Hope" by Barry Argyle. Copyright by the author. Reprinted by permission of Hans Zell Publishers, an imprint of Butterworths.

The Journal of General Education, v. XXVI, Winter, 1975. Copyright 1975 by The Pennsylvania State University Press. Reprinted by permission of the publisher.

Journal of Modern Literature, v. 11, July, 1984. © Temple University 1984. Reprinted by permission of the publisher.

Library Journal, v. 108, January 15, 1983 for a review of "Gerard Manley Hopkins Meets Walt Whitman in Heaven and Other Poems" by Joseph A. Lipari; v. 111, September 15, 1986 for a review of "Second Language" by Fred Muratori. Copyright © 1983, 1986 by Reed Publishing, USA, Division of Reed Holdings, Inc. Both reprinted from *Library Journal,* published by R. R. Bowker, Co., Division of Reed Publishing, USA, by permission of the publisher and the respective authors.

The Listener, v. 107, April 8, 1982 for "Children in Trouble" by Judy Astor; v. 112, August 23, 1984 for "Wonder Drug" by John Mellors; v. 114, September 5, 1985 for "Still Life with Elders" by Derwent May; v. 118, August 20, 1987 for "The Shock of Truth" by Heather Neill; v. 118, October 15, 1987 for " 'Story- tellers Are a Threat' " by Eileen Battersby. © British Broadcasting Corp. 1982, 1984, 1985, 1987. All reprinted by permission of the respective authors.

Lively Arts and Book Review, May 21, 1961. © 1961 I.H.T. Corporation. Reprinted by permission of the publisher.

London Magazine, v. 3, January, 1956./ n.s. v. 6, May, 1966. © *London Magazine* 1966. Reprinted by permission of the publisher.

The London Mercury, v. XXXIX, February, 1939.

London Review of Books, v. 6, December 6 to December 19, 1984 for "Red Stars" by John Sutherland; v. 8, September 4, 1986 for "Ladies" by John Bayley; v. 8, October 9, 1986 for "Chiara Ridolfi" by C. K. Stead; v. 9, October 1, 1987 for "Falling in Love with the Traffic Warden" by John Bayley; v. 9, October 1, 1987 for "Thatcherschaft" by Nicholas Spice. All appear here by permission of the *London Review of Books* and the respective authors.

Los Angeles Times, November 15, 1984. Copyright, 1984, *Los Angeles Times.* Reprinted by permission of the publisher.

Los Angeles Times Book Review, November 18, 1984; March 30, 1986; April 19, 1987; June 28, 1987; July 12, 1987; November 29, 1987; January 24, 1988. Copyright, 1984, 1986, 1987, 1988, *Los Angeles Times.* All reprinted by permission of the publisher.

Maclean's Magazine, v. 92, April 30, 1979; v. 95, September 20, 1982. © 1979, 1982 by *Maclean's Magazine.* Both reprinted by permission of the publisher.

The Malahat Review, n. 70, March, 1985 for a review of "Secular Love" by Stephen Scobie; n. 78, March, 1987 for " 'Happy Enough': The Poetry of George Johnston" by Harvey De Roo. © *The Malahat Review* 1985, 1987. Both reprinted by permission of the respective authors.

Meanjin, v. 41, September, 1982./ v. XXI, December, 1962 for a review of "Four Poets" by H. P. Heseltine. Reprinted by permission of the author.

Michigan Quarterly Review, v. VIII, Summer, 1969. Copyright © The University of Michigan, 1969. Reprinted by permission of the publisher./ v. XXI, Fall, 1982 for "Redeeming Dailiness: Three New Books of Poetry" by John R. Reed; v. XXIII, Summer, 1984 for "A Sense of the Past: Three Historical Novels" by Linda W. Wagner. Copyright © The University of Michigan, 1982, 1984. Both reprinted by permission of the publisher and the respective authors.

Ms., v. VIII, August, 1979 for "A Tale of Two Esthers" by Margo Jefferson; v. IX, February, 1981 for a review of "Angel Landing" by Miriam Sagan. © 1979, 1981 Ms. Magazine. Both reprinted by permission of the respective authors.

The Nation, New York, v. CXXIX, July 3, 1929; v. CXLI, July 31, 1935; v. 149, August 19, 1939; v. 152, May 24, 1941; v. 153, December 20, 1941; v. 163, October 26, 1946; v. 177, October 3, 1953./ v. 208, March 31, 1969; v. 220, March 22, 1975; v. 231, September 20, 1980; v. 234, January 16, 1982; v. 240, June 1, 1985; v. 245, October 17, 1987. Copyright 1969, 1975, 1980, 1982, 1985, 1987 *The Nation* magazine, The Nation Company, Inc. All reprinted by permission of the publisher./ v. 184, January 19, 1957. Copyright 1957 *The Nation* magazine, The Nation Company, Inc. Renewed 1985 the Nation Associates, Inc. Reprinted by permission of the publisher.

The Nation and the Athenaeum, v. XLV, July 27, 1929.

National Review, New York, v. XXXVI, December 14, 1984; v. XXXVII, June 14, 1985; v. XXXVIII, June 6, 1986; v. XXXIX, December 18, 1987. © 1984, 1985, 1986, 1987 by National Review, Inc., 150 East 35th Street, New York, NY 10016. All reprinted with permission of the publisher.

The New Criterion, v. IV, December, 1985 for "Making Up Jean Rhys" by Gloria G. Fromm. Copyright © 1985 by The Foundation for Cultural Review. Reprinted by permission of the author.

The New England Quarterly, v. LVII, March, 1984 for a review of "A Stroll with William James" by John J. McDermott. Copyright 1984 by *The New England Quarterly.* Reprinted by permission of the publisher and the author.

The New Leader, v. LXV, May 17, 1982. © 1982 by The American Labor Conference on International Affairs, Inc. Reprinted by permission of the publisher.

New Mexico Quarterly, v. XXIX, Autumn, 1959 for a review of "The Finished Man" by Edward Abbey. Copyright, 1959 by The University of New Mexico. Reprinted by permission of the author.

The New Republic, v. LII, November 16, 1927; v. LXXXIII, June 26, 1935; v. C, September 20, 1939; v. 103, October 28, 1940; v. 109, November 1, 1943; v. 116, March 24, 1947./ v. 194, March 31, 1986 for "A Carpenter, An Architect" by Stanley Kauffmann. © 1986 by Stanley Kauffmann. Reprinted by permission of Brandt & Brandt Literary Agents, Inc./ v. 145, December 18, 1961; v. 182, June 28, 1980; v. 191, September 10, 1984; v. 196, May 18, 1987; v. 196, May 25, 1987; v. 197, August 10 & 17, 1987; v. 198, March 14, 1988; v. 198, June 6, 1988. © 1961, 1980, 1984, 1987, 1988 The New Republic, Inc. All reprinted by permission of *The New Republic.*

New Statesman, v. LXIV, August 31, 1962; v. 75, January 5, 1968; v. 102, October 2, 1981; v. 106, December 9, 1983; v. 108, August 3, 1984; v. 110, August 16, 1985; v. 111, February 28, 1986; v. 112, August 22, 1986; v. 114, July 17, 1987; v. 114, September 25, 1987. © 1962, 1968, 1981, 1983, 1984, 1985, 1986, 1987 The Statesman & Nation Publishing Co. Ltd. All reprinted by permission of the publisher.

The New Statesman & Nation, v. XV, February 19, 1938.

New York Herald Tribune, November 16, 1952.

New York Herald Tribune Book Review, June 17, 1951; December 2, 1951; November 30, 1952; April 6, 1958; August 3, 1958./ September 4, 1960. © 1960 I.H.T. Corporation. Reprinted by permission of the publisher.

New York Herald Tribune Books, February 10, 1929; March 17, 1935; April 2, 1939; October 15, 1939; February 2, 1941; February 22, 1942; July 5, 1942./ October 7, 1928; March 27, 1932; January 6, 1935; July 7, 1935. Copyright 1928, renewed 1956; copyright 1932, renewed 1960; copyright 1935, renewed 1962; copyright 1935, renewed 1963 I.H.T. Corporation. All reprinted by permission of the publisher.

New York Herald Tribune Weekly Book Review, October 10, 1943; February 16, 1947; March 13, 1949.

New York Magazine, v. 14, February 16, 1981 for "Fallen Sparrow" by John Simon; v. 19, May 26, 1986 for "Marginalia" by John Simon; v. 19, August 11, 1986 for "Sodden Old Sod" by John Simon; v. 20, January 5, 1987 for "Milking Honey" by John Simon; v. 20, August 24, 1987 for "Handle with Care" by John Simon. Copyright © 1981, 1986, 1987 by John Simon. All reprinted with the permission of *New York* Magazine and the Wallace Literary Agency, Inc./ v. 20, April 6, 1987 for "Places in the Heart" by John Leonard. Copyright © 1988 by News America Publishing, Inc. All rights reserved. Reprinted with the permission of *New York* Magazine and Curtis Brown, Ltd. for John Leonard./ v. 20, October 12, 1987. Copyright © 1988 by News America Publishing, Inc. All rights reserved. Reprinted with the permission of *New York* Magazine.

New York Post, July 16, 1982; June 21, 1984; December 13, 1985; April 1, 1987. © 1982, 1984, 1985, 1987, News America Publishing, Incorporated. All reprinted from the *New York Post* by permission.

The New York Review of Books, v. V, November 11, 1965 for "Queer Lives" by Stanley Kauffmann. Copyright © 1965 by Stanley Kauffmann. Reprinted by permission of Brandt & Brandt Literary Agents, Inc./ v. XXIX, February 4, 1982; v. XXXI, November 22, 1984; v. XXXIV, July 16, 1987; v. XXXV, February 4, 1988; v. XXXV, March 3, 1988. Copyright © 1982, 1984, 1987, 1988 Nyrev, Inc. All reprinted with permission from *The New York Review of Books.*

The New York Times, April 30, 1941; January 8, 1942; December 7, 1942; April 5, 1944; April 16, 1952; November 4, 1953; October 28, 1954. Copyright 1941, 1942, 1944, 1952, 1953, 1954 by The New York Times Company. All reprinted by permission of the publisher./ June 25, 1965; October 9, 1969; November 9, 1969; November 30, 1970; February 10, 1972; June 28, 1974; November 18, 1974; March 9, 1976; July 14, 1977; January 20, 1978; November 2, 1979; February 1, 1981; February 3, 1981; February 27, 1981; April 14, 1981; June 21, 1984; June 22, 1984; March 3, 1985; March 18, 1985; April 26, 1985; April 28, 1985; May 27, 1985; October 12, 1985; December 13, 1985; February 5, 1986; October 12, 1986; October 14, 1986; November 21, 1986; March 25, 1987; April 28, 1987; July 25, 1987; October 22, 1987; October 29, 1987; January 20, 1988. Copyright © 1965, 1969, 1970, 1972, 1974, 1976, 1977, 1978, 1979, 1981, 1984, 1985, 1986, 1987, 1988 by The New York Times Company. All reprinted by permission of the publisher.

The New York Times Book Review, December 11, 1927; February 10, 1929; January 5, 1930; June 28, 1931; January 13, 1935; March 17, 1935; September 3, 1939; September 17, 1939; February 15, 1942; June 28, 1942; November 7, 1943; September 22, 1946; February 16, 1947; July 13, 1947; October 19, 1947; October 24, 1948; February 26, 1950; July 22, 1951; July 29, 1951; December 16, 1951; October 5, 1952; November 2, 1952; April 11, 1954. Copyright 1927, 1929, 1930, 1931, 1935, 1939, 1942, 1943, 1946, 1947, 1948, 1950, 1951, 1952, 1954 by The New York Times Company. All reprinted by permission of the publisher./ February 27, 1955; February 17, 1957; March 2, 1958; September 28, 1958; April 26, 1959; October 11, 1959; June 25, 1961; June 17, 1962; June 14, 1964; August 15, 1965; November 21, 1965; October 30, 1966; November 24, 1968; March 30, 1969; October 29, 1972; December 16, 1973; June 23, 1974; October 20, 1974; July 10, 1977; July 15, 1979; September 7, 1980; April 26, 1981; August 9, 1981; November 22, 1981; December 27, 1981; March 28, 1982; May 2, 1982; March 13, 1983; April 17, 1983; May 29, 1983; December 25, 1983; July 15, 1984; August 19, 1984; October 7, 1984; November 18, 1984; December 23, 1984; January 6, 1985; March 24, 1985; June 23, 1985; September 8, 1985; October 6, 1985; December 22, 1985; January 12, 1986; March 30, 1986; May 18, 1986; October 5, 1986; March 29, 1987; May 3, 1987; June 14, 1987; June 28, 1987; August 9, 1987; September 27, 1987; October 11, 1987; November 1, 1987; November 8, 1987; January 31, 1988; February 14, 1988; February 21, 1988; May 15, 1988. Copyright © 1955, 1957, 1958, 1959, 1961, 1962, 1964, 1965, 1966, 1968, 1969, 1972, 1973, 1974, 1977, 1979, 1980, 1981, 1982, 1983, 1984, 1985, 1986, 1987, 1988 by The New York Times Company. All reprinted by permission of the publisher.

The New Yorker, v. LVII, March 9, 1981 for a review of "Childe Byron" by Edith Oliver; v. LXI, April 15, 1985 for "Back in the U.S.S.R." by John Updike; v. LXI, July 15, 1985 for "Complications" by Susan Lardner; v. LXI, October 7, 1985 for "As Others See Us" by Naomi Bliven; v. LXII, December 29, 1986 for "Thwarted Love" by Edith Oliver; v. LXIII, May 18, 1987 for "Back to the Classics" by John Updike; v. LXIII, June 22, 1987 for "...And a Peach" by Mimi Kramer; v. LXIII, January 25, 1988 for "Growing Up" by Whitney Balliett; v. LXIII, February 1,

1988 for "The Man Who Knew Too Much" by Terrence Rafferty; v. LXIV, April 4, 1988 for "To Be a Sun Again" by Helen Vendler. © 1981, 1985, 1986, 1987, 1988 by the respective authors. All reprinted by permission of the publisher./ v. XVII, February 14, 1942 for "Horrors, Homilies, Yarns" by Clifton Fadiman. Copyright 1942, renewed 1969, by The New Yorker Magazine, Inc. Reprinted by permission of the author./ v. XXIII, March 8, 1947; v. XXVI, March 18, 1950; v. XXIX, October 24, 1953. Copyright 1947, renewed 1974; copyright 1950, renewed 1977; copyright 1953, renewed 1981 by The New Yorker Magazine, Inc. All reprinted by permission of the publisher.

Newsday, November 21, 1986. © Newsday, Inc. 1986. Reprinted by permission.

Newsweek, v. LXXIII, March 10, 1969; v. XCIV, August 20, 1979; v. XCVII, February 2, 1981; v. XCIX, April 12, 1982; v. CVI, December 23, 1985; v. CIX, April 13, 1987. Copyright 1969, 1979, 1981, 1982, 1985, 1987, by Newsweek, Inc. All rights reserved. All reprinted by permission of the publisher.

The Observer, May 29, 1983; May 18, 1986; August 16, 1987; September 20, 1987. All reprinted by permission of The Observer Limited.

The Ohio Review, v. XIX, Winter, 1978; v. XIX, Spring-Summer, 1978; n. 28, 1982. Copyright © 1978, 1982 by the Editors of *The Ohio Review.* All reprinted by permission of the publisher.

Parnassus: Poetry in Review, v. 7, no. 1, 1978; v. 9, no. 2, 1981; v. 11, no. 1, 1983. Copyright © 1979, 1982, 1984 Poetry in Review Foundation, NY. All reprinted by permission of the publisher.

Partisan Review, v. XLIX, 1982 for "John Barth Reconsidered" by Jerome Klinkowitz. Copyright © 1982 by *Partisan Review.* Reprinted by permission of the author./ v. XX, Summer, 1953. Copyright 1953, renewed 1981 by *Partisan Review.* Reprinted by permission of the publisher.

Plays and Players, v. 18, May, 1971. © 1971 Brevet Limited. Reprinted with permission of the publisher.

Poetry, v. LIV, April, 1939; v. LVII, January, 1941; v. LXIII, December, 1943./ v. XCIX, November, 1961 for "Revelations and Homilies" by William Dickey; v. CVIII, July, 1966 for a review of "Dependencies" by Mark McCloskey; v. CXII, August, 1968 for a review of "For a Bitter Season" by Laurence Lieberman; v. CXXIII, November, 1973 for "Dealing with Tradition" by Jonathan Galassi; v. CXXX, August, 1977 for "The Small Valleys of Our Living" by Jay Parini; v. CLI, January, 1988 for "Main Things" by Alice Fulton. © 1961, 1966, 1968, 1973, 1977, 1988 by the Modern Poetry Association. All reprinted by permission of the Editor of *Poetry* and the respective authors./ v. LXXIV, May, 1949 for "Program of Entertainment" by William Abrahams; v. XC, August, 1957 for a review of "New and Selected Poems" by Leonard Nathan. Copyright 1949, renewed 1977; © 1957, renewed 1985, by the Modern Poetry Association. Both reprinted by permission of the Editor of *Poetry* and the respective authors.

The Princeton University Library Chronicle, v. XXV, Autumn, 1963. Copyright © 1963 by Princeton University Library. Reprinted by permission of the publisher.

Punch, v. CCXXIV, July 1, 1953./ v. CCXLV, September 18, 1963; v. 288, April 10, 1985. © 1963, 1985 by Punch Publications Ltd. All rights reserved. Both may not be reprinted without permission.

Quadrant, v. V, September, 1961 for "The Pyramid in the Waste: An Introduction to A. D. Hope's Poetry" by James McAuley. Reprinted by permission of *Quadrant,* Sydney, Australia and the author.

Queen's Quarterly, v. LXXX, Summer, 1973 for a review of "Happy Enough: Poems, 1935-1972" by Stephen Scobie; v. 93, Summer, 1986 for a review of "Secular Love" by John Cook; v. 93, Autumn, 1986 for a review of "Ask Again" by Allan Brown; v. 94, Summer, 1987 for a review of "Fables of Brunswick Avenue" by Carole Gerson. Copyright © 1973, 1986, 1987 by the respective authors. All reprinted by permission of the respective authors.

Quill and Quire, v. 45, February, 1979 for a review of "Random Descent" by Anne Gilmore; v. 53, February, 1987 for a review of "Innocence" by Paul Stuewe; v. 53, September, 1987 for "Frontier Women: Two Tales in Search of the Perfect Marriage" by Ruby Andrew. All reprinted by permission of *Quill and Quire* and the respective authors.

Resources for American Literary Study, v. XI, Autumn, 1981. Copyright © 1981, by Resources for American Literary Study, Inc. Reprinted by permission of the publisher.

Salmagundi, n. 68 & 69, Fall, 1985 & Winter, 1986. Copyright © 1986 by Skidmore College. Reprinted by permission of the publisher.

The Saturday Evening Post, v. 255, October, 1983. © 1983. Reprinted with permission from The Saturday Evening Post Company.

The Saturday Review, New York, v. XL, June 29, 1957. © 1957, renewed 1985 *Saturday Review* magazine.

The Saturday Review of Literature, v. IV, November 5, 1927; v. V, April 20, 1929; v. 8, July 25, 1931; v. XXXIV, July 28, 1951; v. XXXV, November 29, 1952; v. XXXVI, October 3, 1953; v. XXXVIII, April 30, 1955./ v. XXIX, October 12, 1946; v. XXX, April 5, 1947; v. 31, November 20, 1948; v. XXXIII, March 18, 1950. Copyright 1946, renewed 1974; copyright 1947, renewed 1975; copyright 1948, renewed 1976; copyright 1950, renewed 1978 *Saturday Review* magazine.

The Sewanee Review, v. LXXI, Winter, 1963; v. LXXXIII, Fall, 1975. © 1963, 1975 by The University of the South. Both reprinted by permission of the editor of *The Sewanee Review.*

Shenandoah, v. XXII, Winter, 1971 for "Awaking to Find It True" by Dabney Stuart. Copyright 1971 by Washington and Lee University. Reprinted from *Shenandoah* with the permission of the Editor and the author.

The Small Press Review, v. 18, April, 1986. © 1986 by Dustbooks. Reprinted by permission of the publisher.

South Atlantic Review, v. 48, May, 1983. Copyright © 1983 by the South Atlantic Modern Language Association. Reprinted by permission of the publisher.

The South Carolina Review, v. 9, November, 1976. Copyright © 1976 by Clemson University. Reprinted by permission of the publisher.

Southerly, v. 27, 1967 for "New Poetry: Old Preoccupations" by Ronald Dunlop. Copyright 1967 by the author./ v. 29, 1969 for a review of "The Autobiography of a Gorgon" by Don Anderson; v. 31, 1971 for a review of "Heaven, in a Way" by James Tulip; v. 37, December, 1977 for "Experiments in Narrative" by David Gilbey; v. 43, March, 1983 for "Poets & Their Novels" by James Tulip. Copyright 1969, 1971, 1977, 1983 by the respective authors. All reprinted by permission of the publisher and the respective authors./ v. 24, 1964 for a review of "Forty Beads on a Hangman's Rope" by S. E. Lee; v. 39, December, 1979 for "Too Many: A Review of Recent Australian Poetry" by S. E. Lee. Copyright 1964, 1979 by the author. Both reprinted by permission of the publisher.

The Southern Review, Louisiana State University, v. IV, Summer, 1968 for "Visions of Life in Recent Fiction" by David Galloway. Copyright, 1968, by the author. Reprinted by permission of the author.

The Spectator, v. 160, February 18, 1938; v. 162, March 3, 1939; v. 203, September 4, 1959./ v. 247, November 14, 1981; v. 255, September 28, 1985; v. 255, December 7, 1985; v. 259, August 22, 1987. © 1981, 1985, 1987 by *The Spectator.* All reprinted by permission of *The Spectator.*

Spirit, v. XXXII, January, 1966. Copyright, Seton Hall University, 1966. Reprinted by permission of the publisher.

Studies, v. LXXII, Winter, 1983. © copyright 1983. Reprinted by permission of the publisher.

Studies in Short Fiction, v. 21, Fall, 1984. Copyright 1984 by Newberry College. Reprinted by permission of the publisher.

The Sunday Times, London, September 20, 1987. © Times Newspapers Limited 1987. Reproduced from *The Sunday Times,* London by permission.

Tar River Poetry, v. 26, Spring, 1987 for "Sex and Violence" by Dabney Stuart. Copyright © 1987 by East Carolina University. Reprinted by permission of the author.

Theatre Arts, v. XXVI, February, 1942 for a review of "Angel Street" by Rosamond Gilder; v. XXVIII, April, 1944 for a review of "The Duke in Darkness" by Rosamond Gilder. Copyright 1942, 1944 by Theatre Arts, Inc. Renewed 1969, 1971 by Jovanna Ceccarelli. Both reprinted by permission of the Literary Estate of Rosamond Gilder.

Time, New York, v. 116, September 22, 1980; v. 123, April 30, 1984; v. 127, April 14, 1986; v. 129, April 6, 1987; v. 129, May 25, 1987. Copyright 1980, 1984, 1986, 1987 Time Inc. All rights reserved. All reprinted by permission from *Time.*/ v. LV, March 13, 1950. Copyright 1950, renewed 1977 Time Inc. All rights reserved. Reprinted by permission from *Time.*

The Times, London, September 12, 1961; October 12, 1968; March 22, 1972. © Times Newspapers Limited 1961, 1968, 1972. All reproduced from *The Times,* London by permission.

The Times Literary Supplement, n. 1318, May 5, 1927; n. 1433, July 18, 1929; n. 1575, April 7, 1932; n. 1942, April 22, 1939; n. 2366, June 7, 1947; n. 2587, September 7, 1951; n. 3000, August 28, 1959./ n. 3302, June 10, 1965; n. 3364, August 18, 1966; n. 3437, January 11, 1968; n. 3659, April 14, 1972; n. 3722, July 6, 1973; n. 3865, April 9, 1976; n. 3966, April 7, 1978; n. 3968, April 21, 1978; n. 4122, April 2, 1982; n. 4336, May 9, 1986; n. 4346, July 18, 1986; n. 4350, August 15, 1986; n. 4351, August 22, 1986; n. 4385, April 17, 1987; n. 4405, September 4, 1987. © Times Newspapers Ltd. (London) 1965, 1966, 1968, 1972, 1973, 1976, 1978, 1982, 1986, 1987. All reproduced from *The Times Literary Supplement* by permission.

University of Toronto Quarterly, v. XXIX, July, 1960; v. XXXVI, July, 1967. Both reprinted by permission of University of Toronto Press.

TV Guide®, v. 35, April 4, 1987. Copyright © 1987 by Triangle Publications, Inc., Radnor, PA. Reprinted with permission from TV Guide® Magazine.

The Village Voice, v. XXVII, July 19, 1983 for "Charles Johnson: Free at Last!" by Stanley Crouch; v. XXXI, July 29, 1986 for "Mail Chauvinism" by Madison Bell; v. XXXII, August 25, 1987 for "Snaky Arguments" by Michael Feingold; v. XXXIII, February 23, 1988 for "Old Wine, Old Bottles" by Mark Caldwell. Copyright © News Group Publications, Inc., 1983, 1986, 1987, 1988. All reprinted by permission of *The Village Voice* and the respective authors.

The Virginia Quarterly Review, v. 42, Winter, 1966; v. 44, Summer, 1968; v. 45, Summer, 1969; v. 48, Spring, 1972; v. 57, Autumn, 1981; v. 59, Summer, 1983; v. 60, Summer, 1984. Copyright, 1966, 1968, 1969, 1972, 1981, 1983, 1984, by *The Virginia Quarterly Review,* The University of Virginia. All reprinted by permission of the publisher.

VLS, n. 43, March, 1986 for "Iris Murdoch's Moral Orders" by Sharon Thompson; n. 53, March, 1987 for a review of "Collected Poems of

Kenneth Fearing" and "The Hospital" by David Rosenthal; n. 64, April, 1988 for "A Gloom of One's Own" by Carol Anshaw. Copyright ©
1986, 1987, 1988 News Group Publications, Inc. All reprinted by permission of *The Village Voice* and the respective authors.

The Wall Street Journal, June 26, 1984; April 12, 1985. © Dow Jones & Company, Inc. 1984, 1985. All rights reserved. Both reprinted by
permission of *The Wall Street Journal.*

Western Humanities Review, v. XXXII, Summer, 1978; v. XXXIX, Summer, 1985. Copyright, 1978, 1985, University of Utah. Both reprinted
by permission of the publisher.

The Western Review, v. 23, Autumn, 1958.

The Winston-Salem Journal, October 11, 1987. Reprinted by permission of the publisher.

Women's Wear Daily, October 9, 1969; December 16, 1985. Copyright 1969, 1985, Fairchild Publications. Both reprinted by permission of the
publisher.

World Literature Today, v. 53, Spring, 1979; v. 56, Spring, 1982; v. 56, Autumn, 1982; v. 58, Autumn, 1984. Copyright 1979, 1982, 1984 by the
University of Oklahoma Press. All reprinted by permission of the publisher.

World Literature Written in English, v. 23, Spring, 1984 for "Metaphor and Symbol in 'The Dragon Can't Dance'" by Harold Barratt. ©
copyright 1984 *WLWE-World Literature Written in English.* Reprinted by permission of the publisher and the author.

The Yale Review, v. 77, Autumn, 1987 for "The Poet's Criteria" by Alfred Corn. Copyright 1987 by Yale University. Reprinted by permission of
the author./ v. LII, December, 1963; v. LXVII, Winter, 1977. Copyright 1962, 1976, by Yale University. Both reprinted by permission of the
editors./ n.s. v. XXX, December, 1940; v. XXXVI, Summer, 1947; v. XLIX, Autumn, 1959. Copyright 1939, renewed 1968; copyright 1947,
renewed 1975; copyright 1959, renewed 1987, by Yale University. All reprinted by permission of the editors.

THE EXCERPTS IN CLC, VOLUME 51, WERE REPRINTED FROM THE FOLLOWING BOOKS:

Anderson, Chris. From *Style as Argument: Contemporary American Nonfiction.* Southern Illinois University Press, 1987. Copyright © 1987 by the Board of Trustees, Southern Illinois University. All rights reserved. Reprinted by permission of the publisher.

Armstrong, William A. From "The Irish Point of View: The Plays of Sean O'Casey, Brendan Behan, and Thomas Murphy," in *Experimental Drama.* Edited by William A. Armstrong. Bell, 1963. Copyright © 1963 by G. Bell and Sons, Ltd. Reprinted by permission of Unwin Hyman Ltd.

Bowering, George. From "Ondaatje Learning to Do," in *Spider Blues: Essays on Michael Ondaatje.* Edited by Sam Solecki. Véhicule Press, 1985. Copyright © The Authors, 1985. Reprinted by permission of the editor.

Bradbury, Malcolm. From *The Modern American Novel.* Oxford University Press, Oxford, 1983. © Malcolm Bradbury, 1983. All rights reserved. Reprinted by permission of Oxford University Press.

Buckley, Vincent. From *Essays in Poetry: Mainly Australian.* Melbourne University Press, 1957.

Charney, Maurice. From "Stanley Elkin and Jewish Black Humor" in *Jewish Wry: Essays on Jewish Humor.* Edited by Sarah Blacher Cohen. Indiana University Press, 1987. © 1987 by Indiana University Press. All rights reserved. Reprinted by permission of the publisher.

Dahlberg, Edward. From an introduction to *Poems.* By Kenneth Fearing. Dynamo, 1935.

Dance, Daryl Cumber. From "Earl Lovelace," in *Fifty Caribbean Writers: A Bio-Bibliographical Critical Sourcebook.* Edited by Daryl Cumber Dance. Greenwood Press, 1986. Copyright © 1986 by Daryl Cumber Dance. All rights reserved. Reprinted by permission of Greenwood Press, Inc., Westport, CT.

Ellis, Roger. From *Peter Weiss in Exile: A Critical Study of His Works.* UMI Research Press, 1987. Copyright © 1987 Roger Ellis. All rights reserved. Reprinted by permission of the publisher.

Huyssen, Andreas. From *After the Great Divide: Modernism, Mass Culture, Postmodernism.* Indiana University Press, 1986. © 1986 by Andreas Huyssen. All rights reserved. Reprinted by permission of Indiana University Press. In Canada by Macmillan, London and Basingstoke.

Kar, Prafulla C. From "The Image of the Vanishing African in Chinua Achebe's Novels," in *The Colonial and the Neo-Colonial Encounters in Commonwealth Literature.* Edited by H. H. Anniah Gowda. Prasaranga, University of Mysore, 1983. Copyright Editor. Reprinted by permission of the editor.

Kiernan, Robert F. From *Noel Coward.* Ungar, 1986. Copyright © 1986 by The Ungar Publishing Company. All rights reserved. Reprinted by permission of the publisher.

Klinkowitz, Jerome. From *Literary Subversions: New American Fiction and the Practice of Criticism.* Southern Illinois University Press, 1985. Copyright © 1985 by the Board of Trustees, Southern Illinois University. All rights reserved. Reprinted by permission of the publisher.

Lahr, John. From *Coward the Playwright.* Methuen, 1982. Copyright © 1982 by John Lahr. Reprinted by permission of Methuen, London.

Laufe, Abe. From *Anatomy of a Hit: Long-Run Plays on Broadway from 1900 to the Present Day.* Hawthorn Books, 1966. Copyright © 1966 by Hawthorn Books, Inc. All rights reserved. Reprinted by permission of The Julian Bach Literary Agency, Inc.

Maxwell, D. E. S. From *A Critical History of Modern Irish Drama: 1891-1980.* Cambridge University Press, 1984. © Cambridge University Press 1984. Reprinted with the permission of the publisher and the author.

Nathan, George Jean. From *The Theatre Book of the Year, 1943-1944: A Record and an Interpretation.* Alfred A. Knopf, Inc., 1944. Copyright 1944 by George Jean Nathan. Renewed 1971 by Mrs. George Jean Nathan. All rights reserved. Reprinted by permission of Associated University Presses, Inc., for the estate of George Jean Nathan.

O'Connor, Teresa F. From *Jean Rhys: The West Indian Novels.* New York University Press, 1986. Copyright © 1986 by Teresa F. O'Connor. All rights reserved. Reprinted by permission of the publisher.

Solecki, Sam. From "Net and Chaos: The Poetry of Michael Ondaatje," in *Spider Blues: Essays on Michael Ondaatje.* Edited by Sam Solecki. Véhicule Press, 1985. Copyright © The Authors, 1985. Reprinted by permission of the author.

Staley, Thomas F. From *Jean Rhys: A Critical Study.* The Macmillan Press Ltd., 1979. © Thomas F. Staley 1979. All rights reserved. Reprinted by permission of Macmillan, London and Basingstoke.

Tharpe, Jac. From *John Barth: The Comic Sublimity of Paradox.* Southern Illinois University Press, 1974. Copyright © 1974 by Southern Illinois University Press. All rights reserved. Reprinted by permission of the publisher.

White, Morton. From *Pragmatism and the American Mind: Essays and Reviews in Philosophy and Intellectual History.* Oxford University Press, 1973. Copyright © 1973 by Morton White. Reprinted by permission of Oxford University Press, Inc.

☐ Contemporary Literary Criticism

Indexes

Literary Criticism Series
　Cumulative Author Index
Cumulative Nationality Index
Title Index, Volume 51

This Index Includes References to Entries in These Gale Series

Contemporary Literary Criticism

Presents excerpts of criticism on the works of novelists, poets, dramatists, short story writers, scriptwriters, and other creative writers who are now living or who have died since 1960. Cumulative indexes to authors and nationalities are included, as well as an index to titles discussed in the individual volume. Volumes 1-51 are in print.

Twentieth-Century Literary Criticism

Contains critical excerpts by the most significant commentators on poets, novelists, short story writers, dramatists, and philosophers who died between 1900 and 1960. Cumulative indexes to authors, nationalities, and titles discussed are included in each new volume. Volumes 1-31 are in print.

Nineteenth-Century Literature Criticism

Offers significant passages from criticism on authors who died between 1800 and 1899. Cumulative indexes to authors, nationalities, and titles discussed are included in each new volume. Volumes 1-20 are in print.

Literature Criticism from 1400 to 1800

Compiles significant passages from the most noteworthy criticism on authors of the fifteenth through eighteenth centuries. Cumulative indexes to authors, nationalities, and titles discussed are included in each new volume. Volumes 1-9 are in print.

Classical and Medieval Literature Criticism

Offers excerpts of criticism on the works of world authors from classical antiquity through the fourteenth century. Cumulative indexes to authors, titles, and critics are included in each volume. Volumes 1-2 are in print.

Short Story Criticism

Compiles excerpts of criticism on short fiction by writers of all eras and nationalities. Cumulative indexes to authors, nationalities, and titles discussed are included in each new volume. Volumes 1-2 are in print.

Children's Literature Review

Includes excerpts from reviews, criticism, and commentary on works of authors and illustrators who create books for children. Cumulative indexes to authors, nationalities, and titles discussed are included in each new volume. Volumes 1-16 are in print.

Contemporary Authors Series

Encompasses five related series. *Contemporary Authors* provides biographical and bibliographical information on more than 90,000 writers of fiction, nonfiction, poetry, journalism, drama, motion pictures, and other fields. Each new volume contains sketches on authors not previously covered in the series. Volumes 1-124 are in print. *Contemporary Authors New Revision Series* provides completely updated information on active authors covered in previously published volumes of *CA*. Only entries requiring significant change are revised for *CA New Revision Series*. Volumes 1-24 are in print. *Contemporary Authors Permanent Series* consists of updated listings for deceased and inactive authors removed from the original volumes 9-36 when these volumes were revised. Volumes 1-2 are in print. *Contemporary Authors Autobiography Series* presents specially commissioned autobiographies by leading contemporary writers. Volumes 1-7 are in print. *Contemporary Authors Bibliographical Series* contains primary and secondary bibliographies as well as analytical bibliographical essays by authorities on major modern authors. Volumes 1-2 are in print.

Dictionary of Literary Biography

Encompasses three related series. *Dictionary of Literary Biography* furnishes illustrated overviews of authors' lives and works and places them in the larger perspective of literary history. Volumes 1-72 are in print. *Dictionary of Literary Biography Documentary Series* illuminates the careers of major figures through a selection of literary documents, including letters, notebook and diary entries, interviews, book reviews, and photographs. Volumes 1-5 are in print. *Dictionary of Literary Biography Yearbook* summarizes the past year's literary activity with articles on genres, major prizes, conferences, and other timely subjects and includes updated and new entries on individual authors. Yearbooks for 1980-1987 are in print. A cumulative index to authors and articles is included in each new volume.

Concise Dictionary of American Literary Biography

A six-volume series that collects revised and updated sketches on major American authors that were originally presented in *Dictionary of Literary Biography*. Volumes 1-3 are in print.

Something about the Author Series

Encompasses two related series. *Something about the Author* contains heavily illustrated biographical sketches on juvenile and young adult authors and illustrators from all eras. Volumes 1-53 are in print. *Something about the Author Autobiography Series* presents specially commissioned autobiographies by prominent authors and illustrators of books for children and young adults. Volumes 1-6 are in print.

Yesterday's Authors of Books for Children

Contains heavily illustrated entries on children's writers who died before 1961. Complete in two volumes. Volumes 1-2 are in print.

Literary Criticism Series
Cumulative Author Index

This index lists all author entries in the Gale Literary Criticism Series and includes cross-references to other Gale sources. For the convenience of the reader, references to the *Yearbook* in the *Contemporary Literary Criticism* series include the page number (in parentheses) after the volume number. References in the index are identified as follows:

AITN:	*Authors in the News*, Volumes 1-2
CAAS:	*Contemporary Authors Autobiography Series*, Volumes 1-7
CA:	*Contemporary Authors* (original series), Volumes 1-124
CABS:	*Contemporary Authors Bibliographical Series*, Volumes 1-2
CANR:	*Contemporary Authors New Revision Series*, Volumes 1-24
CAP:	*Contemporary Authors Permanent Series*, Volumes 1-2
CA-R:	*Contemporary Authors* (revised editions), Volumes 1-44
CDALB:	*Concise Dictionary of American Literary Biography*, Volumes 1-3
CLC:	*Contemporary Literary Criticism*, Volumes 1-51
CLR:	*Children's Literature Review*, Volumes 1-16
CMLC:	*Classical and Medieval Literature Criticism*, Volumes 1-2
DLB:	*Dictionary of Literary Biography*, Volumes 1-72
DLB-DS:	*Dictionary of Literary Biography Documentary Series*, Volumes 1-5
DLB-Y:	*Dictionary of Literary Biography Yearbook*, Volumes 1980-1987
LC:	*Literature Criticism from 1400 to 1800*, Volumes 1-9
NCLC:	*Nineteenth-Century Literature Criticism*, Volumes 1-20
SAAS:	*Something about the Author Autobiography Series*, Volumes 1-6
SATA:	*Something about the Author*, Volumes 1-53
SSC:	*Short Story Criticism*, Volumes 1-2
TCLC:	*Twentieth-Century Literary Criticism*, Volumes 1-31
YABC:	*Yesterday's Authors of Books for Children*, Volumes 1-2

Author Index

Author Index

Author Index

Author Index

Author Index

Author Index

Author Index

Author Index

Author Index

Author Index

Author Index

Author Index

CLC Cumulative Nationality Index

Nationality Index

CLC-51 Title Index

Title Index

Title Index